Y0-BTI-815

The Interpretation of
St. John's Gospel

By
R. C. H. LENSKI

AUGSBURG PUBLISHING HOUSE
Minneapolis, Minnesota

Manufactured in the United States of America

ABBREVIATIONS

R. = A Grammar of the Greek New Testament in the Light of Historical Research, by A. T. Robertson, fourth edition.

B.-D. = Friedrich Blass' Grammatik des neutestamentlichen Griechisch, vierte, voellig neugearbeitete Auflage besorgt von Albert Debrunner.

C.-K. = Biblisch-theologisches Woerterbuch der Neutestamentlichen Graezitaet von D. D. Hermann Cremer, zehnte, etc., Auflage, herausgegeben von D. Dr. Julius Koegel.

B.-P. = Griechisch-Deutsches Woerterbuch zu den Schriften des Neuen Testaments, etc., von D. Walter Bauer, zweite, etc., Auflage zu Erwin Preuschens Vollstaendigem Griechisch-Deutschen Handwoerterbuch, etc.

M.-M. = The Vocabulary of the Greek Testament, by James Hope Moulton and George Milligan.

NOTE.— The translation is intended only as an aid in understanding the Greek.

INTRODUCTION

A complete presentation of the introductory material to the Gospel of St. John would require an entire volume. For more than a hundred years there has been controversy regarding the author of this Gospel, the place and the time, the origin and the purpose of its composition, the early testimonies of the fathers, to say nothing about many of the important details contained in the Gospel itself and their proper interpretation. Even the works which devote themselves to the presentation of this material find it necessary to sift and to sort, and thus omit much that now seems of little value to the student. For the purpose of a commentary, whose one aim is to penetrate the Gospel itself as fully as possible, we need only the assured introductory facts that stand out as the net result of all this effort at investigation.

One may well ask why so much learned investigation does not end in agreement concerning the vital pertinent facts. Happily, we are able to reply that the disagreement is not caused by the nature of these facts but by the character of the investigators. For some of them the results are predetermined in their own minds. John's Gospel, while in perfect harmony with its three predecessors, has marked features of its own. Instead of accepting these features and seeking to understand them, some skeptically inclined minds insert their doubts and thus nullify for themselves the evidence imbedded in the Gospel itself, as well as the testimonies of the early fathers which speak so clearly to this very day. Once started in the wrong direction, some of these men go to extravagant lengths and accept conclusions which are unwarranted when compared with the data from which they are drawn. In addition, minds that do not read the other three Gospels aright also misunderstand John's Gospel and then find only unsubstantiated hypotheses for its explanation. But hypotheses are a rather uncertain foundation on which to build a critical structure.

The observation is correct that, while John himself does not call his writing a "Gospel," the early church did not err when it considered John's composition an εὐαγγέλιον and added it to the three gospel accounts it already possessed. The word "gospel" was originally used to designate the oral message of the apostles in which they told of Jesus' words and works, and then quite naturally the same word was applied to the records which fixed this message in written form for future generations. But when it was so applied, the term meant more than a diary or chronicle, more than a history of certified events intended only to inform. While the substance of what was understood by "gospel" consisted of these assured facts and events, their presentation always included the purpose of enkindling saving faith in the hearts of the hearers or the readers and of strengthening this faith where it already existed. This is true of all four Gospels and is directly stated by John himself in the fourth. A subjective touch with this intent appears already in the prolog, in v. 12: "But as many as received him, to them gave he the right to become children of God, even to them that believe on his name." In two other places John even interrupts his objective narrative and addresses his readers directly. When he records his testimony regarding Christ's death in 19:35 he adds the significant purpose clause, "that ye also may believe," even as he who witnessed this death believes. Then, again, when John brings his personal account to a close he writes in 20:31: "But these (signs) are written, that ye may believe that Jesus is the Christ, the Son of God; and that believing ye may have life in his name." The purpose here expressed applies to the entire document and verifies the fact that it is John's intention to compose a "Gospel" in the sense indicated. In both passages the accredited reading is ἵνα πιστεύσητε, the aorist subjunctive, and not the present πιστεύητε, which is a less accredited variant. Yet John is not thinking of his readers as still being unbelievers, so that we should translate, "in order that you may come to believe," an ingressive aorist. He writes his Gospel for believers, for people who have and who believe the other three Gospels, who thus receive this new testimony as a confirmation of what they already hold in their hearts. We must thus translate these punctiliar aorists, "in order that you may definitely believe." The present subjunctive would be simpler, "in order that you may go on believing," but the assured aorist is, after all, more positive and effective.

The fact that John writes for believers should be considered together with the obvious relation of his Gospel to the other three. John not only knew the other Gospels, he wrote his own in such a manner that entire sections of it cannot be understood by the reader unless he, too, knows the other three Gospels. The effect of this remarkable feature is that all four Gospels are a grand unit, and it is chiefly John who produces this effect. This linking of his own account with the accounts of his predecessors does not prevent John from adding much material that the other evangelists passed by. Both where he takes the other writings for granted and where he brings in matter entirely new, he writes as an independent eyewitness, one who chooses what he records according to his own principle and plan. He has most abundant resources, and he himself remarks on this fact. When John recounts events mentioned in the other Gospels he adds further information and many incidental touches of his own. This is exactly what we should expect on the part of one who knew so much at firsthand; and we ought to be thankful for every added word. Mark also has many items which indicate that he very closely follows Peter's way of telling certain events.

All that John thus adds beyond what the other evangelists offer makes many think that John intends to supplement what the others had already recorded. In a sense this is true. Yet the fact is never apparent that John treats the other accounts as imperfect or even as faulty. The brevity of all the evangelists naturally leaves much that could be added, especially by one who was himself a witness to what transpired. And this is the nature of John's additions. They supplement as the evidence of one witness supplements that of another. They also supplement as one writer's plan of selecting material amplifies what others select according to their plans.

The view is often advanced that John also "corrects" what the other evangelists wrote. But this is certainly not true. In the accounts of the other three evangelists no errors are found that another writer could correct. Every word and every statement is true. The right reading of all four Gospels reveals not a single contradiction. We are never confronted with the alternative: Shall we believe what John writes, or shall we believe what one or more of the other evangelists write? Where contradictions are thought to exist, and where corrections on the part of John are thus assumed, it is the reader who misreads John or the others, or both. These statements are made on the evidence of the four Gospel records as they stand and wholly apart from the doctrine of Inspiration. Yet all that we know about the fact of Inspiration, in particular about the promises given to the apostles by Jesus regarding the infallible guidance of the Holy Spirit, tallies with the results that appear when John is compared with the other evangelists. In the testimonies of the ancient church fathers mistakes have been discovered which we are able to correct, but none of the sacred writers made a single mistake.

John omits quite a number of features, prominent among which are the institutions of the two sacraments, which he, too, might have embodied in his record. All these omissions serve only to corroborate the accounts that had already been given to the church. They mean that John has not even one word to add on these subjects that are so vital to the church. The supposition that John's account about Nicodemus is a substitute for the institution of Baptism, and the discourse on the Bread of Life a substitute for the institution of the Lord's Supper, arises from the assumption that John should have written regarding sacraments. Both this assumption and the supposition drawn from it are ill-advised. We have no call to prescribe to John what he ought or ought not to include in his Gospel. He had far higher guidance than we at this late date can offer him.

John reports many conversations, altercations, and discourses of Jesus. The question constantly arises: Does John report these words exactly as Jesus spoke them, or does he modify them, and, if so, to what extent? This question is far-reaching. It at once involves another: To what extent is John's report of these words trustworthy? From the discourses the question branches out and takes in also the narrative sections. For if the words of Jesus may be modified, why not also the events in which they lie imbedded? We must be on our guard against the tendency to open the door to modern criticism with its subjective principles, permitting the critic eventually to rewrite

John's Gospel according to the critic's own conception.

In seeking to answer this question an appeal to the natural powers of the apostle's memory only is manifestly insufficient. He was twenty to twenty-three years old when he heard what Jesus spoke, and he was somewhere between eighty and ninety when he set these words down in writing. We know about the remarkable tenacity and the astounding exactitude of the memory of the ancients. From the day of Pentecost to his labors in Ephesus, John was associated with other apostles, and their one business was to proclaim the deeds and the words that constitute the Gospel. Constant repetition thus stereotyped much of its form. Yet if John had written immediately after Pentecost while the other apostles were still about him, if he had then depended on his memory alone, he could never have produced the reliable records that we need. To instance only one point, many of the things that Jesus said were not even properly understood by the apostles at the time they were spoken. Now, after so many years intervened, uncertainties, serious variations, and actual contradictions must certainly have crept in, considering both the extent and the profundity of all that had to be remembered, and even one unfortunate word or expression might ruin the true sense. Human memory could certainly not achieve the task of adequate and true reproduction.

We also dare not forget the change of language. Though Jesus may have used some Greek, the bulk of his words was uttered in Aramaic, and the apostles had to translate this into Greek for much of their oral preaching. John wrote his record in Greek. Now translation is a difficult task when it comes to verbal exactitude. Here, too, is where the personal factor counts heavily, for a translator has only his own fund of words and ways of expression on which to draw when it comes to a transfer of thought into another language. John was no exception — Greek was not his native tongue. We see, for instance, that he writes in his Gospel very much as he does in his Epistles. A reference to Revelation we may omit at this point.

Combining all these considerations, the conclusion can only be that, if memory alone was John's dependence, his reproduction of the words of Jesus must to an unknown extent be modified from the original utterances. Our only question would be as to what extent, and the field would be wide open to personal opinion and speculation.

Fortunately, we are not left with the possibilities of mere human memory in answering this question about the discourses of Jesus in John's Gospel. The apostles, including John, had supernatural aid in their proclamation of the deeds and the words of Jesus. The Lord himself gave them the unconditional promise· "Howbeit when he, the Spirit of truth, is come, he shall guide you into all the truth: for he shall not speak from himself; but what things soever he shall hear, these shall he speak: and he shall declare unto you the things that are to come," John 16:13. Compare Paul's testimony in I Cor. 3:13, (translation of the American Committee); the Pentecost miracle; and the promises Matt. 10:18-20; Mark 13:11; Luke 12:11, 12; 21:14, 15. This supernatural guidance and control we call Inspiration. And this is our reliance for the fact that when John wrote the words of Jesus, they are, indeed, trustworthy in every respect. We have no valid reasons for making a subtraction from this assurance. The Holy Spirit enabled John to reproduce the words of Jesus (and also all else connected with them) exactly as this Spirit desired to have them reproduced for the church of all time in the language he had chosen for this purpose. With this forever settled, it concerns us scarcely at all whether in some instances John was led to abbreviate or to condense, to rearrange or recombine, or in other ways to recast the Savior's words. The varying forms in which the other evangelists record, for instance, the Lord's Prayer, the institution of the Lord's Supper, etc., are highly instructive in this respect. We see that the Holy Spirit did not employ a stenographic, merely mechanical exactness in reproducing Christ's spoken words, but he did employ a far more vital and valuable exactness, that of inerrancy in substance and in expression. As we read John's record today, the Lord himself speaks to us through John by the Spirit of truth. Every word in its connection is able to bear the fullest stress that we today can bring to bear upon it, and not a single expression will ever fail in performing this supreme duty.

Textual criticism has done much also for John's Gospel. We have a thoroughly reliable text and are able to judge fairly the variants that remain. Two eliminations from the text must be noted, namely 5:4 and 7:53-8:11, both of which will be discussed in their proper place. John's Gospel today stands as a unit. The so-called interpolation hypotheses of the higher critics, which make of John's Gospel a coat of many colors, merit no serious attention. The source hypotheses, which reduce the Gospel to a relative unity, a compilation of a variety of material and what John himself was able to contribute, have also had their day. Among the latest efforts of this general type are those that make a distinction between the discourses and the narrative sections, stating that in certain places these are joined in "an awkward and disturbing way." On the basis of this judgment we are to conclude that the discourses existed as an earlier and separate collection or document, which eventually was worked into the Gospel as we have it today. The improbability of his hypothesis is apparent. The facts, undoubtedly, are these: John preached and taught all that is contained in his Gospel for many years and then finally put all this material into written form as one magnificent whole.

The fourth Gospel differs markedly from the other three in the fact that it indicates its author. The inner evidence for John's authorship is so convincing that it has been likened to solid granite. Every assault upon this evidence has ended in failure. The exposition of the Gospel itself is the best place for presenting the details of this inner evidence. Here we content ourselves with the following: John never names himself nor any member of his family. But this refined modesty does not prevent him from indicating his own person and making it entirely plain that he is the writer of this Gospel. In this final chapter, which was added as a supplement to the Gospel proper, the disciples of John in Ephesus add their own personal attestation to John's authority like a special seal, 21:24.

The direct indications are strongly supported by many others that are less direct. The fact constantly obtrudes itself that we are reading nothing less than the account of an eyewitness, who either saw and heard in person what we now read, or was in the most excellent position to learn at firsthand and promptly what transpired where he himself was not actually present. We are struck with the fact that, when events already recorded by the other evangelists are retold in whole or in part, new intimate and most valuable details are added, such as only an independent eyewitness could supply. We see very plainly that the writer of this Gospel was a native of Palestine and a former Jew. His perfect acquaintance with things Palestinian and Jewish is beyond question. The type of Greek which he employs is further weighty evidence. The closest examination of the Gospel reveals not a single indication that conflicts with John's authorship. Everything is clear if this apostle is the writer; very much is out of gear if his authorship is denied.

The fact that John spent the latter part of his long life in Ephesus of Asia Minor is fully established by Revelation, 1:4 and 9-11; 2:1, etc. (the seven letters to the "angels" of the seven churches). This testimony is entirely sufficient.

Probably next in importance is the testimony of Irenaeus (about 185). He was a disciple of Polycarp, the bishop of Smyrna, a disciple of the Apostle John together with Papias and others. Polycarp was baptized in the year 69 and died as a martyr in the year 155, 86 years after his baptism. The testimony of Irenaeus thus goes directly back to John through Polycarp, Papias, and others of John's disciples. In his book on *Heresies*, III, 1, 1 he reports that John, the disciple of the Lord who lay upon his breast, published the fourth Gospel while he was in Ephesus of Asia Minor. In III, 4, 4 he adds that the Ephesian church was, indeed, founded by Paul, but that John lived there until the time of the emperor Trajan (98-117). This reference to Trajan is repeated in II, 22, 25. Irenaeus seems to presuppose that John died a natural death, which accords with Tertullian, *De anima*, 50. He also regards John as the writer of the Epistles and of Revelation. Among the other evidence that corroborates that given by Irenaeus is that of Polycrates of Ephesus (about 190) in his letter to bishop Victor, and that of Apollonius (about 197), see Eusebius, *Church History*, III, 31, 2 and V, 18, 14. Some matters that Irenaeus reports regarding the teaching of the elders that were associated with John are manifestly incorrect, but the fact that these elders were in John's company and that some of them had seen Jesus we have no reason to doubt.

Contemporary with Irenaeus is Clement of Alexandria, from whose account Eusebius reports, VI, 14, 7, the fact that John as the last perceived that the other evangelists had recounted the more external parts of the story of Christ (τὰ σωματικά, his birth, travels, miracles, etc.), and that at the solicitation of his pupils, moved by the Spirit, he wrote a spiritual Gospel.

For the fact that John's Gospel soon came to be used in the writings of the early fathers we have abundant evidence, extending back to Papias, who about 130 refers to the aloes mentioned only by John in 19:39 and explains that they were used as incense. The statement that John's Gospel was published during his lifetime, is also attributed to Papias.

The testimony of Irenaeus cannot be nullified by the report of Philip of Side in the sixth century and by the note in the Syrian calendar in the fifth century that in the year 44 John was killed as a martyr together with his brother James (Acts 12:2). This calendar contains other wrong statements. We have Gal. 2:9 to prove that in the year 48 Paul met John in Jerusalem.

A good deal of controversy has arisen because of the surmise that two Johns existed. This began somewhat late, with Dionysius, of Alexandria, in the second half of the third century. He could not bring himself to believe that the Apostle John wrote Revelation and therefore sought some other author for this book. Dionysius heard that two graves were shown in Ephesus, both as graves of John. He thus concluded that there had been two Johns, one of them *not* the Apostle, and this second John, he surmised, might have written Revelation. Here is where the second John first appears — a surmise of Dionysius. Next comes Eusebius (270-340) in his *Church History*, III, 39, who quotes a statement from Papias and interprets this as indicating that there were two Johns, one the Apostle John, and the other "the presbyter John." Like Dionysius, Eusebius seeks an author for Revelation other than the Apostle John. Yet neither Dionysius nor Eusebius entertains the idea that the second John, whom they have discovered, wrote the fourth Gospel, for this Gospel was fully established in their day as having been written by the Apostle John. This cue concerning a supposed second John was taken up by modern critics, who advanced the claim that "the presbyter John" was the author of the fourth Gospel. The new hypothesis ran this course: first, this "presbyter John" was supposed to be an eyewitness of the gospel events and the actual author of the Gospel; next, he was only in a modified sense an eyewitness though still the author of the Gospel; finally, he was neither an eyewitness nor the author but only a kind of prototype of both.

Thus far, starting with Papias, at least the name "John" is retained as the author of the Gospel, which has the great advantage of coinciding, at least in sound, with that of the great Apostle John. When the fading-out process advanced, this name disappeared, and only the title by which this "John" had been distinguished remained. He was no longer "John," but he was still "the elder" — the Great Unknown, called "Elder Theologos." This title "Theologos" is affixed to him, it seems, because the caption of Revelation calls the Apostle John "the theologian." He is pictured as an Alexandrine Jew, a man conversant with Hellenic philosophy, of the type of Apollos. In drawing his picture Apollos is mentioned so often that one is led to wonder whether Apollos will not be next in having John's Gospel attributed to him. Strange to say, however, this mysterious "Elder Theologos" is said to carry forward the distinctive Pauline teaching, and

Paul's theology is made to center on the Logos — a name which Paul never employs.

The exegesis which eliminates the Apostle John from his own writings finds no difficulty in removing the external testimony for John's authorship. Although Papias designates no less than seven Apostles (John among them) as "elders," and then, when he names John a second time, again carefully calls him "elder" in distinction from Aristion, exactly as John terms himself "the elder" in his Second and Third Epistles, all this care on the part of Papias in making it plain that he knows only one John, namely the Apostle, seems to be wasted effort. We are offered a second John who is entitled "the elder John," or "the presbyter John." Though Papias uses a historical aorist ($\epsilon\tilde{\iota}\pi\epsilon\nu$) when he mentions the coming of some pupil of the Apostles into his neighborhood and then, in marked contrast, a present tense ($\lambda\acute{\epsilon}\gamma o\nu\sigma\iota\nu$) when he mentions John a second time, now combined with Aristion, since these two were then still alive, this is ignored by the critics, to the support of whose hypotheses Papias is quoted. We are assured that the fourth Gospel is a pseudo-composition, and yet the church accepted it without question and without hesitation included it in the canon with the other three Gospels whose authors were fully known. The writer of this Gospel, we are told, is *not* the Apostle though he poses as the Apostle; and yet the church accepts the impersonation, it thinks that it has the Gospel, and that the Apostle wrote it. The fourth Gospel is a document so great and wonderful that in all these ages the church has awarded it the palm among the Gospels, and yet the critics assure us that all trace of this master writer's name and person has been lost — was lost from the very start. Other, minor, silences are used with deadly effect against clear testimonies, but this silence is accepted without even an explanatory remark. Sober sense will reply that it is easier to believe the testimony which it finds in the Gospel itself and the testimonies of the ancients that are to the same effect than the changing hypotheses of the critics.

Throughout the second century, even in the far borders of the church, in Italy, in Gaul, in Africa, etc., the orthodox, the heretics, and even an occasional pagan, in their literary remains show conversance with John's Gospel. Clement of Alexandria, about 190, calls it a spiritual Gospel and distinguishes it from the spurious Gospel of the Egyptians. Tertullian, born about 150, quotes a Latin translation of our Gospel from Carthage, Africa, and knows a still earlier translation which in his time had already fallen into disuse. John's Gospel, as the record left by the Apostle, was thus fully established as an unquestioned part of the New Testament canon. Irenaeus, born in Asia Minor about 130, a pupil of Polycarp, writes his *Heresies* in distant Gaul and quotes John's Gospel more than 60 times. Some of his testimonies have already been noted. Theophilus, bishop of Antioch, quotes John's Gospel in the year 180; he also composes a harmony of the four Gospels. He is the first who actually names John, which fact the critics turn to account for their purpose, but in vain, for he, too, is the first who names Paul as the author of Romans. Apollinaris in Hieropolis, about 170, quotes John's Gospel and appeals to it in the controversies of that time. Athenagoras, about 176, addresses the emperor in Rome in an apology and quotes John's Gospel. Tatian composes his *Diatesseron,* a harmony of the four Gospels, which begins with John's prolog and shows how fully the fourth Gospel was accepted at this time. Whether Tatian wrote in Greek or in Syriac is not yet known. The earliest Syriac translations of John's Gospel extend back to this time.

The heretical Valentinians "used in full the Gospel of John" (Irenaeus), and one of them, Heracleon, about 160-170, wrote an entire commentary on this Gospel. The Clementine Homilies, a Judaizing work opposing Paul and his doctrines, about 160, operate with passages from John. The pagan Celsus, about 178, uses passages from John in order "to slay the Christians with their own sword." The canon of Muratori (160-170) expressly lists John's Gospel. Justin, born in Samaria, founded a Christian school in Rome and about 150 in his writings refers seventeen times to the "Memoirs of the Apostles" (ἀπο μνημονεύματα τῶν ἀποστόλων), "which are composed by the apostles and by those who accompanied them." He is a great teacher of the Logos and borrows a number of expressions from the fourth Gospel. The eons of the gnostic system in 140 are certainly drawn from John's Gospel. The gnostic Marcion, who came to Rome in 138, knew John's Gospel and rejected it because it was apostolic; yet he used a section from this Gospel, possibly even two.

The battle regarding the letters of Ignatius will probably continue for many a year. The critics deny that Ignatius wrote these letters, or date them later than about 110, in order to maintain their claim that John did not write his Gospel, and that this Gospel dates from the second century. Ignatius, bishop of Antioch, when sent to his martyrdom in Rome, wrote seven letters, which have been proved genuine in the briefer of the two forms in which they have come down to us. Ignatius writes in his *Romans*: "The living water speaking within me says to me, Come to the Father. I take no pleasure either in corruptible food or in the joys of this life; I want the bread of God, which is in the flesh of Jesus Christ. I want for drink his blood, which is incorruptible love." In his *Phila-*

delphians: "The Spirit does not deceive, he who comes
from God; for he knows whence he comes, and whither
he goes, and he condemns secret things." Again: "He
who is the door of the Father, by which Abraham,
Isaac, Jacob, the prophets, the apostles, the church,
enter in." In his *Ephesians* he calls Jesus "God come
in the flesh." Only one who had and who knew John's
Gospel could write in this fashion.

In Clement of Rome, about 96, in the *Shepherd of
Hermas*, about 100, in the *Didache*, about 110, in the
so-called *Second Epistle of Clement*, about 120, in the
Epistle of Barnabas, about 130, and in a few other
early writings passages occur which clearly evidence
the use of John's Gospel. The critics maintain that
these passages only reflect ideas and expressions current at that time that were afterward incorporated
into what is now called the fourth Gospel.

Before the destruction of Jerusalem, between the
years 66 and 69, the Apostle John, together with other
Apostles and disciples of Jesus, moved to Asia Minor,
and these made their headquarters in Ephesus, where
Paul had established the most important church of this
territory. Here the Apostle John wrote his Gospel
in his old age at the solicitation of the Asiatic elders.
The date of writing lies between the years 75 and 100,
probably somewhere near 80 or 85. The three Epistles
of John were most likely written after the Gospel, and
Revelation last of all. Irenaeus says positively that
the vision of Revelation was seen shortly before he
was born near the close of the reign of Domitian who
died in September of the year 96. This fixes the
approximate date of the writing of Revelation between
the years 93 and 96 on the island of Patmos, whither
the Apostle had been banished. John died a natural
death at the beginning of the reign of Trajan near
the year 100 and was buried in Ephesus. "On a Sunday after the religious services, John went outside the

gates of the city, accompanied by a few trusted disciples, had a deep grave dug, laid aside his outer garments which were to serve him as a bed, prayed once more, stepped down into the grave, greeted the brethren who were present, and gave up the ghost," Zahn, *Introduction*, 3, 193, etc.

Irenaeus, according to Eusebius, reports from Polycarp, his teacher and a disciple of John: "That John, the disciple of the Lord, having gone in Ephesus to take a bath and having seen Cerinthus inside, left the baths, refusing to bathe, and said, Let us flee, lest also the baths fall in, since Cerinthus is inside, the enemy of the truth."

Clement of Alexandria reports that John commended a noble looking youth in a city near Ephesus to the bishop, who then taught and baptized him. Returning some time after, John said to the bishop, "Restore the pledge which I and the Savior entrusted to you before the congregation." The bishop with tears replied, "He is dead, dead to God, a robber!" John replied, "To what a keeper have I entrusted my brother's soul!" John hastened to the robber's stronghold; the sentinel brought him before their captain. The latter fled from him. John cried: "Why do you flee from me, your father, an unarmed old man? You have yet a hope of life. I will yet give an account of you to Christ. If need be I will gladly die for you." John did not leave him until he had rescued him from sin and restored him to Christ.

Jerome reports: When too feeble, through age, to walk to the Christian assemblies, John was carried thither by young men. His only address was, Little children, love one another, (*filioli, diligite alterutrum*). When asked why he repeated these words so much, he replied, Because this is the Lord's command, and enough is done when this is done. — It has well been said that these anecdotes concerning John could hardly

have been invented; they are quite unlike the later
legends that betray their fanciful origin, in particular
those connected with John's grave.

It has taken a surprisingly long time to determine
the theme of John's Gospel together with its division
or structure. Progress in this matter was slow, and
such progress as was made has not always been generally accepted. Some of the best scholars who have
recently interpreted John's Gospel disappoint us in
this regard. The unity of the Gospel is, of course, unquestioned. Any denial of this unity ruins at the out-
set the work of discovering the real structure of this
Gospel. Yet the full recognition of this unity has not
prevented a number of serious mistakes. Thus minor
parts have often been conceived as major parts. John
is supposed to develop an idea, somewhat like a theoretical thesis, instead of writing a record of historical
facts. Three grand facts loom up in John's Gospel.
The one is that Jesus, true man, is the Son of God;
the other two are the rise and the full development
of faith, and the rise and the full development of unbelief. But the relation of these three has not always
been clearly and adequately apprehended in the presentation which John has made. The symbolical notion of
the sacred number three has been imposed on the
Gospel, blurring the entire structure in the interest
of a mere fancy. Even when the two grand parts of
the Gospel are recognized as such, the formulation of
these parts, including the perception and the formulation of the subparts, has often been inadequate and
unsatisfactory.

The following outline will serve our purpose:

    Prolog: The Word became flesh, 1:1-18.

    Theme: **Jesus Christ Attested as the Son of
              God.**

I. *The Attestation of Jesus Christ as the Son of God in his Public Ministry, 1:19-12:50.*

1) The opening attestation as his ministry begins, 1:19-2:11.
2) The public attestation throughout the Holy Land, 2:12-4:54.
3) The attestation arousing unbelief, chapters 5 and 6.
4) The attestation in open conflict with unbelief, chapters 7 to 10.
5) The final attestation before the people, chapters 11 and 12.

II. *The Attestation of Jesus as the Son of God in his Passion and his Resurrection.*

1) The attestation in Jesus' preparation of the Apostles for the end, chapters 13 to 17.
2) The attestation in his death, chapters 18 and 19.
3) The attestation in his resurrection, chapters 20 and 21.

The purpose of John's Gospel is clearly stated in 20:31. It agrees with the general purpose of the other Gospel writers. They differ as follows: Matthew writes with the Jews in mind and shows that Jesus is the promised Messiah. Mark and Luke have the Gentiles in mind and show that Jesus is the Redeemer for whom the nations longed. John wrote when the difference between Jews and Gentiles had disappeared, after the destruction of Jerusalem and of the Temple, in Asia Minor, when the beginnings of gnostic and other heresies appeared, and thus showed that Jesus is the Son of God, and that salvation is found by faith in him alone.

CHAPTER I

THE PROLOG

The Word Became Flesh, 1-18

John's Gospel begins without a title of any kind and thus differs from Revelation, which carries a distinct title from John's own hand, and from the Gospels of Matthew and of Mark, both of which begin with titles. Luke has an introduction and an address and is peculiar in this respect. While John's prolog may be called an introduction, it is one of an entirely different type. This prolog sums up the contents of the entire Gospel. It does this by brief, succinct historical statements. Each of these is wonderfully simple and clear and yet so weighty and profound that the human mind is unable to fathom them. Amid all that has been written by the instruments of Inspiration this prolog stands out as the one paragraph that is most profound, most lofty, and incomparable in every way.

Later hands have added a caption to John's Gospel; it is like those that have been placed at the head of the other Gospels and the other New Testament writings. The oldest is simply: "According to John"; then: "Gospel according to John" and other modifications of this simple title. This was done when the Gospels and the other writings were collected and when the New Testament canon was being formed. The preposition κατά, "according to," designates the Apostle John as the writer of this Gospel. We have no linguistic or other evidence that the preposition is meant in any other sense. The contention that κατά

here means: "according to the type of preaching" done
by John is put forward in order to make room for the
unknown author of this Gospel who is thought to have
used material derived from John and who wrote at
a later date. If this contention holds good, the title
for Mark's Gospel would have to be: "The Gospel
according to Peter," and that of Luke: "The Gospel
according to Paul," for both Mark and Luke are
dependent on these apostles.

John's is the paragon among the Gospels, "the one,
tender, real crown-Gospel of them all" (Luther), and
the prolog is the central jewel set in pure gold. The
very first words show that John writes for Christian
believers, for every sentence presupposes conversance
with the faith. John writes as though he stands in
the midst of the congregation, all eyes and ears being
fixed upon him to hear the blessed Gospel words from
his lips. The prolog has been divided in various ways,
as one or the other of its statements has been stressed.
The most natural division seems to be: 1) The eternal
Word, the Creator of all, is the light and life shining
into the sinful world, v. 1-5; 2) The Word came into
the sinful world, awakening faith and arousing unbelief, v. 6-12; 3) The Word became flesh in the world
and brought us grace and truth from the Father,
v. 13-18. These three parts, however, are not coordinate blocks, laid in a row one beside the other;
they are built up like a pyramid, the one rising above
the other. It is all a most wonderful story, this about
the Word: He shines — he comes — he appears incarnate. It is a mistake to read even the prolog, not to
speak of the entire Gospel, as if John intends to show
us only the eternal godhead of the Son. John attests
the humanity of the Son as fully and as completely
as the divinity and godhead. The miracle of the ages
is that the Word became flesh and dwelt among men.
Some of the most intimate human touches regarding

the Savior are recorded for us by John, and yet the person to whom these human features belong is God's own Son.

1) **In the beginning was the Word, and the Word was with God, and the Word was God. This One was in the beginning with God.** Even the first readers of John's Gospel must have noted the resemblance between the first phrase ἐν ἀρχῇ, "in the beginning," and that with which Moses begins Genesis. This parallel with Moses was, no doubt, intentional on John's part. The phrase points to the instant when time first began and the first creative act of God occurred. But instead of coming down from that first instant into the course of time, John faces in the opposite direction and gazes back into the eternity before time was. We may compare John 17:5; 8:58, and possibly Rev. 3:14, but scarcely ἀπ' ἀρχῆς in Prov. 8:23, for in this passage "from the beginning" refers to Wisdom, a personification, of which v. 25 reports: "I was brought forth," something that is altogether excluded as regards the divine person of the Logos.

In the Greek many phrases lack the article, which is not considered necessary, R. 791; so John writes ἐ ἀρχῇ. But in John's first sentence the emphasis is on this phrase "in the, beginning" and not on the subject "the Word." This means that John is not answering the question, *"Who* was in the beginning?" to which the answer would naturally be, "God"; but the question, *"Since when* was the Logos?" the answer to which is, "Since all eternity." This is why John has the verb ἦν, "was," the durative imperfect, which reaches back indefinitely beyond the instant of the beginning. What R. 833 says about a number of doubtful imperfects, some of which, though they are imperfect in form are yet used as aorists in sense, can hardly be applied in this case. We, of course, must say that the idea of eternity excludes all notions of tense, present, past, and future; for eternity is not time, even vast time, in any sense but the absolute opposite of time — timelessness. Thus, strictly speaking, there is nothing prior to "the beginning," and no duration or durative tense in eternity. In other words, human language has no forms of expression that fit the conditions of the eternal world. Our minds are chained to the concepts of time. Of necessity, then, when anything in eternity is presented to us, it must be by such imperfect means as our minds and our language afford. That is why the durative idea in the imperfect tense ἦν is superior to the punctiliar aoristic idea: In the beginning the Logos "was," *ein ruhendes und waehrendes Sein* (Zahn) — "was" in eternal existence. All else had a beginning, "became," ἐγένετο, was created; not the Logos. This — may we call it — timeless ἦν in John's first sentence utterly refutes the doctrine of Arius, which he summed up in the formula: ἦν ὅτε οὐκ ἦν, "there was (a time) when he (the Son) was not." The eternity of the Logos is co-equal with that of the Father.

Without a modifier, none being necessary for John's readers and hearers, he writes ὁ λόγος, "the Word." This is "the only-begotten Son which is in the bosom of the Father," v. 18. "The Logos" is a title for Christ that is peculiar to John and is used by him alone. In general this title resembles many others, some of them being used also by Christ himself, such as Light, Life, Way, Truth, etc. To imagine that the Logos-title involves a peculiar, profound, and speculative Logos-doctrine on the part of John is to start on that road which in ancient times led to Gnosticism and in modern times to strange views of the doctrine concerning Christ. We must shake off, first of all, the old idea that the title "Logos" is in a class apart from the other titles which the Scriptures bestow upon Christ, which are of a special profundity, and that we must attempt to penetrate into these mysterious depths. This already will release us from the hypothesis that John borrowed this title from extraneous sources, either with it to grace his own doctrine concerning Christ or to correct the misuse of this title among the churches of his day. Not one particle of evidence exists to the effect that in John's day the Logos-title was used for Christ in the Christian churches in any false way whatever. And not one particle of evidence exists to the effect that John employed this title in order to make corrections in its use in the church. The heretical perversions of the title appear after the publication of John's Gospel.

Philo's and the Jewish-Alexandrian doctrine of a *logos* near the time of Christ has nothing to do with the Logos of John. Philo's *logos* is in no sense a person but the impersonal reason or "idea" of God, a sort of link between the transcendent God and the world, like a mental model which an artist forms in his thought and then proceeds to work out in some kind of material. This *logos*, formed in God's mind, is wholly subordinate to him, and though it is personified at times when speaking of it, it is never a person as is the Son of God and could not possibly become flesh and be born a man. Whether John knew of this philosophy it is impossible for us to say; he himself betrays no such knowledge.

As far as legitimate evidence goes, it is John who originated this title for Christ and who made it current and well understood in the church of his day. The observation is also correct that what this title expressed in one weighty word was known in the church from the very start. John's Logos is he that is called "Faithful and True" in Rev. 19:11; see v. 13: "and his name is called The Word of God." He is identical with the "Amen, the faithful and true witness," in Rev. 3:14; and the absolute "Yea," without a single

contradictory "nay" in the promises of God in II Cor.
1:19, 20, to whom the church answers with "Amen."
This Logos is the revealed "mystery" of God, of which
Paul writes Col. 1:27; 2:2; I Tim. 3:16; which he
designates explicitly as "Christ." These designations
go back to the Savior's own words in Matt. 11:27;
16:17. Here already we may define the Logos-title:
the Logos is the final and absolute revelation of God,
embodied in God's own Son, Jesus Christ. Christ is
the Logos because in him all the purposes, plans, and
promises of God are brought to a final focus and an
absolute realization.

But the thesis cannot be maintained that the Logos-
title with its origin and meaning is restricted to the
New Testament alone, in particular to the Son incarnate, and belongs to him only as he became flesh.
When John writes that the Logos became flesh, he
evidently means that he was the Logos long before he
became flesh. How long before we have already seen
— before the beginning of time, in all eternity. The
denial of the Son's activity as the Logos during the
Old Testament era must, therefore, be denied. When
John calls the Son the Logos in eternity, it is in vain
to urge that v. 17 knows only about Moses for the Old
Testament and Christ as the Logos only for the New.
Creation takes place through the Logos, v. 3; and this
eternal Logos is the life and light of men, v. 4, without the least restriction as to time (New as opposed
to Old Testament time). The argument that this Logos
or Word "is spoken" and does not itself "speak" is
specious. This would require that the Son should be
called ὁ λεγόμενος instead of ὁ λόγος. The Logos is,
indeed, spoken, but he also speaks. As being sent,
given, brought to us we may stress the passive idea;
as coming, as revealing himself, as filling us with
light and life, the active idea is just as true and just
as strong.

This opens up the wealth of the Old Testament references to the Logos. "And God *said*, Let there be light," Gen. 1:4. "And God *said*, Let *us* make man in *our* image, after *our* likeness," Gen. 1:26. "Through faith we understand that the worlds were framed by *the word of God*," Heb. 11:3. *"By the word of the Lord* were the heavens made. . . . For he *spake*, and it was done; he *commanded*, and it stood fast," Ps. 33:6 and 9. "He sent his word," Ps. 107:20; 147:15. These are not mere sounds that Jehovah uttered as when a man utters a command, and we hear the sound of his words. In these words and commands the Son stands revealed in his omnipotent and creative power, even as John says in v. 3: "All things were made by him." This active, omnipotent revelation "in the beginning" reveals him as the Logos from all eternity, one with the Father and the Spirit and yet another, namely the Son.

He is the Angel of the Lord, who meets us throughout the Old Testament from Genesis to Malachi, even "the Angel of the Presence," Isa. 63:9. He is "the image of the invisible God, the firstborn of every creature: for by him were all things created, that are in heaven, and that are in earth, visible and invisible, whether they be thrones, or dominions, or principalities, or powers: all things were created by him, and for him: and he was before all things, and by him all things consist. And he is the head of the body, the church: who is the beginning, the firstborn from the dead; that in all things he might have the preeminence. For it pleased the Father, that in him should all fulness dwell," Col. 1:15-19. This is the revelation of the Logos in grace. The idea that by the Logos is meant only the gospel, or the gospel whose content is Christ, falls short of the truth. "Logos" is a *personal* name, the name of him "whose goings forth have been from of old, from everlasting," Micah 5:2. And so we define once more, in the words of Besser, "The Word is the living God as he reveals himself, Isa. 8:25; Heb. 1:1, 2." Using a weak human analogy, we may say: as the spoken word of a man is the reflection of his inmost soul, so the Son is "the brightness of his (the Father's) glory, and the express image of his person," Heb. 1:3. Only of Jesus as the Logos is the word true, "He that hath seen me hath seen the Father," John 16:9; and that other word, "I and my Father are one," John 10:30.

And the Word was with God, πρὸς τὸν θεόν. Here we note the first Hebrew trait in John's Greek, a simple coordination with καί, "and," followed in a moment by a second. The three coordinate statements in v. 1 stand side by side, and each of the three repeats the mighty subject, "the Word." Three times, too, John writes the identical verb ἦν, its sense being as constant as that of the subject: the Logos "was" in all eternity, "was" in an unchanging, timeless existence. In the first statement the phrase "in the beginning" is placed forward for emphasis; in the second statement the phrase "with God" is placed at the end for emphasis.

In the Greek Θεός may or may not have the article, for the word is much like a proper noun, and in the Greek this may be articulated, a usage which the English does not have. Cases in which the presence or the absence of the article bears a significance we shall note as we proceed. The preposition πρός, as distinct from ἐν, παρά, and σύν, is of the greatest importance. R. 623 attempts to render its literal force by translating: "face to face with God." He adds 625 that πρός is employed "for living relationship, intimate converse," which well describes its use in this case. The idea is that of presence and communion with a strong note of reciprocity. The Logos, then, is not an attribute inhering in God, or a power emanating from him, but a person in the presence of God and turned in loving, inseparable communion toward God, and God turned equally toward him. He was another and yet not other than God. This preposition πρός sheds light on Gen. 1:26, "Let *us* make man in *our* image, after *our* likeness."

Now comes the third statement: **And the Word was God.** In English we place the predicate last, while in the Greek it is placed first in order to receive the fullest emphasis. Here Θεός must omit the article thus making sure that we read it as the predicate and not as the subject, R. 791. " 'The Word was with God.' This sounds, speaking according to our reason, as though the Word was something different from God. So he turns about, closes the circle, and says, 'And God was the Word.' " Luther. *God* is the Word, God himself, fully, completely, without diminution, in very essence. What the first statement necessarily involves when it declares that already in the beginning the Word was; what the second statement clearly involves when it declares the eternal reciprocal relation between the Word and God — that is declared with simple directness in the third statement when the Word is pronounced God with no modifier making a subtraction or limitation. And now all is clear; we now see how this Word who is God "was in the beginning," and how this Word who is God was in eternal reciprocal relation with God. This clarity is made perfect when the three ἦν are seen to be eternal, shutting out absolutely a past that in any way is limited. The Logos is one of the three divine persons of the eternal Godhead.

2) And now the three foregoing sentences are joined into one: **This One was in the beginning with God.** Just as we read "the Word," "the Word," "the Word," three times, like the peals of a heavenly bell, like a golden chord on an organ not of earth sounding again and again, so the three rays of heaven-

ly light in the three separate sentences fuse into one — a sun of such brightness that human eyes cannot take in all its effulgence. "It is as if John, i. e., the Spirit of God who reveals all this to him, meant to bar from the beginning all the attempts at denial which in the course of dogmatical and historical development would arise; as though he meant to say: I solemnly repeat, The eternal Godhead of Christ is the foundation of the church, of faith, of true Christology!" G. Mayer.

The Greek has the handy demonstrative οὗτος with which it sums up emphatically all that has just been said concerning a subject. In English we must use a very emphatic "he" or some equivalent like "this One," "the Person," or "the same" (our versions), although these equivalents are not as smooth and as idiomatic as οὗτος is in the Greek. Verse 2 does not intend to add a new feature regarding the Logos; it intends, by repeating the two phrases from the first two sentences, once more with the significant ἦν, to unite into a single unified thought all that the three preceding sentences have placed before us in coordination. So John writes "this One," re-emphasizing the third sentence, that the Word was God; then "was in the beginning," re-emphasizing the first sentence, that the Word was in the beginning; finally "with God," re-emphasizing the second sentence, that the Word was in reciprocal relation with God. Here one of the great characteristics of all inspired writing should not escape us; realities that transcend all human understanding are uttered in words of utmost simplicity yet with flawless perfection. The human mind cannot suggest an improvement either in the terms used or in the combination of the terms that is made. Since John's first words recall Genesis 1, we point to Moses, the author of that first chapter, as another incomparable example of inspired writing — the same simplicity for expressing transcendent thought, the same perfection in every term and every grammatical combination of terms. Let us study Inspiration from this angle, i. e., from what it has actually produced throughout the Bible. Such study will both increase our faith in Inspiration and give us a better conception of the Spirit's *suggestio rerum et verborum.*

3) The first four sentences belong together, being connected, as they are, by two καί and the resumptive οὗτος. They present to us *the person* of the Logos, eternal and very God. Without a connective v. 3 proceeds with *the first work* of the Logos, the creation of all things. **All things were made through him; and without him was not made a single thing that is made.** The negative second half of this statement re-enforces and emphasizes the positive first half. While John advances from the person to the work, this work substantiates what is said about the person; for the Logos who created all things must most certainly be God in essence and in being.

"All things," πάντα without the article, an immense word in this connection, all things in the absolute sense, the universe with all that it contains. This is more than τὰ πάντα with the article, which would mean all the things that exist at present, while πάντα covers all things present, past, and future. While the preposition διά denotes the medium, Rom. 11:36 and Heb. 2:10 show that the agent himself may be viewed as the medium; hence "through him," i. e., the Logos, must not be read as though the Logos was a mere tool or instrument. The act of creation, like all the *opera ad extra,* is ascribed to the three persons of the Godhead and thus to the Son as well as to the Father; compare the plural pronouns in Gen. 1:26.

The verb ἐγένετο, both in meaning and in tense, is masterly. The translation of our versions is an accommodation, for the verb means "came into existence," i. e., "became" in this sense. The existence of all

things is due to the Logos, not, indeed, apart from the
other persons of the Godhead but in conjunction with
them, as is indicated throughout the creative speaking in Gen. 1. "All things came into being" since the
beginning, the Logos through whom they were called
into being existed before the beginning, from eternity.
The verb "became" is written from the point of view
of the things that entered existence, while in Genesis
the verb "created" is written from the viewpoint of
God, the Creator. John repeats ἐγένετο in the negative
part of his statement and adds the perfect tense γέγονεν
in the attached relative clause. These repetitions
emphasize the native meaning of this verb. As creatures
of the Logos "all things became."

The punctiliar tense, a historical aorist, is in
marked contrast to the durative imperfect of the four
preceding ἦν. This aorist goes back to the creative
acts of Gen. 1. These acts are fundamental; for all
creatures that came into existence in the later course
of time have their origin in the creative acts of that
wonderful week recorded in Genesis. We may thus
pass down through the centuries, even to the last day
of time, and always it will be true: ὁ κόσμος δι' αὐτοῦ
ἐγένετο, "the world was made through him," v. 10,
where this significant verb is repeated for the fourth
time.

John's positive statement is absolute. This the
negative counterpart makes certain: and without him
was not a single thing made that is made. Whereas
the plural πάντα covers the complete multitude or mass,
the strong singular οὐδὲ ἕν points to every individual
in that mass and omits none. "Not one thing" is
negative; hence also the phrase with the verb is
negative, "became without him" or apart from him
and his creative power. Apart from the Logos is
nihil negativum et privativum. Yet in both the positive and the negative statements concerning the

existence of all things and of every single thing the
implication stands out that the Logos himself is an
absolute exception. He never "became" or "came into
existence." No medium (διά) is in any sense connected
with his being. The Son is from all eternity "the
uncreated Word."

The relative clause ὃ γέγονεν is without question to
be construed with ἕν and cannot be drawn into the
next sentence. We need not present all the details
involved in this statement since the question must be
considered closed. The margin of the R. V., which
still offers the other reading, is incorrect and confusing. No man has ever been able to understand the
sense of the statement, "That which hath been made
was life in him." Linguistically the perfect tense with
its present force, γέγονεν, clashes quite violently with
the following imperfect tense ἦν, so violently that
the ancient texts were altered, changing οὐδὲ ἕν
into οὐδέν, and ζωὴ ἦν into ζωή ἐστιν. But even these
textual alterations fail to give satisfaction apart from
the grave question of accepting them as the true reading of the text. So we read, "And without him not a
single thing that exists came into existence." The
perfect tense γέγονεν, of course, has a present implication and may be translated, "that exists" or "that is
made." But the perfect tense has this force only as
including the present result of a past act. The perfect always reaches from the past into the present.
The single thing of which John speaks *came* into
existence in the past and only thus *is* in existence
now. What John thus says is that every single thing
that now exists traces its existence back to the past
moment when it first entered existence. Thus the
aorist ἐγένετο is true regarding all things in the universe
now or at any time. Every one of them derives its
existence from the Logos. Since γέγονεν as a perfect
tense includes past origin, we should not press its

present force so as to separate the past creative acts
of the Logos from the present existence of the creature
world.

4)   From the creative work of the Logos John
turns to his soteriological work. He begins without a
connective and uses four brief sentences which are
joined in the simplest fashion by means of three καί.
**In him was life; and the life was the light of men.
And the light shines in the darkness; and the darkness overcame it not.** The first two statements belong together, because the two verbs, ἦν, are identical.
The third clause continues not with an imperfect
but with a present tense; and the fourth ends with
an aorist.

John uses the term ζωή fifty-four times. It is one
of the key words of his Gospel. Used here in the first
statement without the article, the quality of the word
is stressed: in the Logos was "life," life in the fullest,
highest sense, the eternal, blessed life of God. The
emphasis is on the phrase which heads the statement,
"in him" was life. This implies a contrast with all the
living beings who came into existence by the creative
act of the Logos. They all received life — it came to
them as a gift from a higher source. They all also are
capable of death, and while some escaped death (the
good angels), all the rest came under death's power.
The very attribute of the Logos is life, the life that
corresponds with his being, forever inherent in his
very essence, absolutely incapable of any hurt, subtraction, or deteriorating change. While this first statement of John's refers to the Logos only and as such
reaches no farther, it is yet not to be considered abstractly, as a piece of interesting information concerning only this great being, the Logos. It is preliminary
to the statements which follow and which pertain
most directly to us. In fact, the very terms "Logos"
and "life" look toward us and have a bearing upon

us, even as all the statements in v. 4 and 5, the first as well as the rest, are made for our sakes and for ours alone.

Because John's statement that life was in the Logos follows his statement regarding the creature world, ζωή is often taken to mean "life" in the sense of the animation of all living creatures. This is unwarranted. In v. 4, 5 John predicates nothing concerning the creatures called into being by the Logos. Many of these have no life of any kind, they are lifeless and inorganic and merely exist without living. Those that are animated received their animation when they were called into existence. Moreover, ζωή is never used with reference to mere creature life; its character is always heavenly and spiritual never physical. Enough wonderful things appear in John's Gospel without our adding thereto, and we must remember that John wrote not for speculative philosophers and lofty theological thinkers but for the church at large.

Much thought has been spent on the verb ἦν, "was," especially on the imperfect tense. John writes, "In him *was* life," and not, as we might expect, "In him *is* life," i. e., ever and always, timelessly, from eternity to eternity. A strong effort is made to regard ἦν as a historical tense, referring to a fixed period in the past. One view is that John here refers to the brief period of innocence in Paradise. A division is made between v. 4 and v. 5, placing the fall of man between them. But the mere tense of ἦν is too slender a foundation on which to base such an interpretation.

Another view has "was" refer historically to the time of Christ here on earth. It is pointed out that "was" follows the two historical aorists "became" in v. 3 and even the perfect γέγονεν with its present implication. Likewise, that "was" in the first sentence in v. 4 gets its meaning from "was" in the second sentence of this verse. The latter is then regarded as pertain-

ing to Christ's appearance here on earth. In substantiation John 9:5 is quoted, "When I am in the world,
I am the light of the world." Likewise 12:46; 12:35,
36; 3:19. Of course, we are told, the light and the
life did not depart with Christ's visible presence; now
it is the Paraclete through whom they come to us. In
spite of this argument ἦν in v. 4 is not a true historical
tense. The passages adduced come within the two ἦν
in v. 4, but no one is able to prove that they cover and
exhaust the extent of time of these ἦν. Likewise it
is impossible to prove that these two imperfects must
denote the time subsequent to the two ἐγένετο in v. 3,
and it is plain that these ἦν cannot be subsequent to
the perfect γέγονεν.

The favorite view is that the two ἦν refer back to
the entire Old Testament period. This is much nearer
to the truth. Usually, however, this view is broadened
to take in also all the natural knowledge of God left to
the pagan world and all the moral principles that still
survive among heathen nations. "There has been
much foolish speculation as to how the Word of God
in its divinity could be a light, which naturally shines
and has always given light to the minds of men even
among the heathen. Therefore the light of reason has
been emphasized and based upon this passage of Scripture. These are all human, Platonic, and philosophical
thoughts, which lead us away from Christ into ourselves; but the evangelist wishes to lead us away from
ourselves into Christ. . . . He would not have us
diffuse our thoughts among the creatures which he has
created, so as to pursue him, search for him, and speculate about him as the Platonic philosophers do; but he
wishes to lead us away from those vague and high-
flown thoughts and bring us together in Christ . . .
Therefore the light must mean *the true light of grace
in Christ* and not the natural light, which also sinners,
Jews, heathen, and devils have, who are the greatest

enemies of the light. . . . I am well aware that
all the light of reason is ignited by the divine light;
and as I have said of the natural life, that it has its
origin in, and is part of, the true life, when it has come
to the right knowledge, so also the light of reason has
its origin in, and is part of, the true light, when it
recognizes and honors him by whom it has been
ignited." Luther, Lenker's translation, *Postil*, 190,
etc. He then proceeds to show how the light of reason,
when it remains separate from Christ, becomes ex-
tinguished and dies out, how it misleads into error and
the most dangerous falsehood, how, when the light of
grace comes, a battle ensues, and, when the light of
grace conquers, it also "enlightens the light of nature
in man" and makes this what it should be. "We must
follow the streams which lead to the source and not
away from it."

Once it is clearly perceived that the very name
"Logos," borne by the Son before the world began, is
pointless save as it declares him to be God's revelation
to us who need this eternal Logos, the difficulties about
the tense of the two ἦν will disappear. We shall, of
course, not identify these two with the three ἦν in v.
1, 2, for these three extend back only from "the beginning" into infinite eternity, while the two ἦν in v. 4
extend back from Christ's incarnation across the entire
Old Testament into eternity. For John's Christian
readers it was not strange that all the works of grace
should have their inception in eternity and there disappear in mystery from our finite eyes. Just because
ἦν goes back indefinitely, it is the proper tense. An
aorist would sound historical and thus be unfit. Just
as the eternal Word *was* in the beginning, so also
in the beginning and in addition since the incarnation
this Word *was* life, and this life *was* the light of men.
John writes *was* and not the timeless *is* because he
intends to make an incision at the time of the incarna-

tion. This event and the history that follows he records
in due order. It would be a misstatement to say that the
Logos *became* or *was made* life either in time or before
time. Looking backward, no limit can be set, looking
forward, John himself sets the limit at the close of the
Old Testament or at the incarnation.

As life and light are inseparably joined together in
nature, so also they are joined in the domain of the
spirit and divine grace. Where divine, true life is,
there divine, true light is, and where light, there also
life. "In Christ is the life-light, outside is the night
of death." Besser. Yet "life" is placed first, and
"light" second. The evangelist cannot say that in the
Logos was light, and the light was the life of men.
Light is that which shines out and manifests itself;
it emanates from life which is fundamental and in its
essence a deep, mysterious, hidden power. Divine
truth is light as it shines out from him who is the
Truth; but this truth is the manifestation of the life
that underlies it even as Jesus also calls himself the
Life.

Moreover, light is a figurative term. It recalls the
sun which lights up the physical universe. So the life
that is in the Logos is intended to light up the world
and the souls of men. The term "light" always connotes its opposite darkness, just as "life" always sug-
gets its opposite death. Both "life" and "light," just
like "Logos," are human terms. They apply to us as
we are in this world where death and darkness prevail, and where we need the revelation of the Word.
In heaven these terms would either not apply at all
or would apply in a meaning so wonderful that our
minds now could not comprehend the concepts.
"Light" equals truth, and this signifies reality, namely
all the reality of God's will, purpose, and plans as they
center in his love or grace and are incorporated in the
Logos, who is Jesus Christ, our Lord. This divine and

blessed reality is composed of many facts, each of which, in turn, constitutes a reality; and when these realities are properly voiced in human language, we call them doctrines. Our soul's highest interests are thus tied up with the doctrines of Christ, the Word. Every unreality (lie), though it is trigged up in the most captivating language, constitutes a false doctrine and by its very nature works death and destruction for the soul.

In all cases where a genitive is added to designate the domain that is to be lighted, as "the light of men" or "the light of the world," the term "light" denotes not the radiance that spreads abroad, but the luminary itself from which the radiance emanates. So the sun in the heavens is the "light" of the physical world. Without this sun we should perish in physical darkness. Without the Logos and his saving life we should likewise perish in spiritual darkness. The purpose and the task of the light is to enlighten, to bestow upon men the knowledge of the truth. "For in thee is the fountain of life: in thy light shall we see light," Ps. 36:9. This knowledge is never merely intellectual, it affects the entire being and turns all who are enlightened into children of light who are born anew of the light.

5) "And the light shines in the darkness," φαίνει, a durative present tense. Here is Luther's comment: "Christ has always been the Life and the Light, even before his birth, from the beginning, and will ever remain so to the end. He shines at all times, in all creatures, in the Holy Scriptures, through his saints, prophets, and ministers, in his word and works; and he has never ceased to shine. But in whatever place he has shone, there was great darkness, and the darkness apprehended him not." The present tense of the verb "shines" has led to the interpretation that here John speaks of the New Testament presence of the

Logos. But why impose such a restriction when the general subject is still the eternal Logos, and when "the darkness" in which the light shines is not restricted to the New Testament era? It is the very nature of the light to shine, to send out its rays, to illuminate, to transfer itself? Though this is true, John is not making a remark on the abstract nature of light in general. "The light" is the one specific light mentioned in v. 4, the Logos with his life — it is he that goes on shining in the darkness.

So also the phrase "in the darkness" with its Greek article is specific, not darkness in general but in this world of ours made dark through sin and death. Between the later word σκοτία and the older σκότος no difference exists. The abstract term "darkness," which expresses a quality, is here substituted for the concrete expression "dark world" and sums up in a single word and from one angle all the hostile forces that exist in the fallen world. "Darkness," while it is a negative term like all the words for sin and death, is, nevertheless, never used in a merely negative way as denoting only the absence of light. If this darkness were no more, it would be like the physical absence of light which at once vanishes when light is supplied, i. e., when a luminary appears. The darkness of the world is a hostile power full of resistance to the true light of the Logos. The shining of the light in the darkness is, therefore, always an invasion of the territory held by the darkness, a challenge of the power of darkness, a battle to destroy this power, a victory robbing the darkness of its prey. It is thus that the light shines *in* the darkness. Far from the darkness invading the light or putting it out, the opposite takes place. Moreover, the light or luminary is never in the least affected by the darkness — this luminary is the eternal, unconquerable life of the eternal Word and as such it shines and shines in triumphant power. We see its shining in the first promise of the seed of the woman in Eden; we see its broadening, intensified radiance throughout Old Testament times; we see some of its scattered rays striking even into the dark Gentile world with which Israel came into contact; and then we see the wonderful shining like the sun in its zenith when the gospel was carried to the ends of the earth; even so it is shining now. What a wonderful fact, "And the light shines in the darkness!"

We must translate the next sentence according to the margin of the R. V., "And the darkness overcame it not." The verb καταλαμβάνειν has two meanings, "to apprehend something" in order to possess and to retain it, as in Phil. 3:12; I Cor. 9:24; Rom. 9:30; and "to pounce upon something" in order to bring it into one's power so that it shall not escape or assert itself. The analogy of Scripture is in favor of the latter meaning. This analogy embraces all the passages in which a hostile force like σκοτία is active, as for instance a demon in the case of possession in Mark 9:18; the last day as a thief in the night in I Thess. 5:4; the darkness in John 12:35; many LXX passages, like the sinner's iniquities in Ps. 40:12; the evil in Gen. 19:19; and thus constantly in the Scriptures and in other writings. We should also note that "darkness" cannot possibly "apprehend," hold and embrace "the light," it can only resist and war against it. Finally, the force of the aorist tense of the verb would clash with the durative shining of the light; this aorist would have to be a durative present: the light shines, and the darkness does not apprehend, does not appropriate it. The aorist, however, is in place when we translate, "And the darkness did not overcome the light." It made strong attempts to do so, as Jesus prophesied in John 15:18 and 16:4, as the death of Jesus attests, and the Acts report at length; but always its efforts were without success, for the light still shines on.

The A. V. translates "comprehended," which would be only an intellectual act, one that is impossible for "the darkness." The R. V. offers "apprehended," which is deeper and yet involves the same difficulty as to meaning and as to tense.

6) Verse 6 introduces the second section of the prolog which extends to v. 12. The first starts with eternity and sketches the activity of the Logos before his coming into the world. The second starts with the Baptist and sketches the Logos as having come into the world and into his own. V. 6-12 thus includes the incarnation, yet John withholds mention of it in so many words because he intends to reserve this miracle of miracles for the final section of the prolog, the climax of this mighty introduction to the body of his Gospel.

There came a man, commissioned from God, whose name was John — a few touches, and the picture of this man is complete. While the evangelist sketches the Baptist with some detail in v. 6-8, this is not done with a view to introducing to the readers a person unknown and new to them. John writes about the Baptist much as he does about the Logos. The readers know both; what John does is to lift out for each the vital and important features to which John wants the readers to give special heed. John thus presents no history of the Baptist and does not even point out his distinctive work of baptizing, either by describing this activity or by calling him the Baptist.

The very first words: ἐγένετο ἄνθρωπος, "there was (or came) a man," are in marked contrast to ἦν ὁ λόγος, "was the Word," in v. 1. The aorist is plainly historical: he came, *trat auf*, with his activity and work just like any other man. All was different in the case of the Logos. And this was "a man," a human being like other men, not an angel from the other world. Yet he differed from the mass of otherwise notable men in that he was "sent from God." The perfect participle ἀπεσταλμένος includes more than the past act of commissioning him for his special task, it covers also his standing during the entire course of that work. He was God's message bearer or ambassador. However lowly his person, his office is of the highest, with which also his name accords, "John," "God's favor." The agent with a passive verb form may be expressed, as here, with παρά. The introduction of John's name is idiomatic Greek: ὄνομα αὐτῷ Ἰωάνης, "name for him John." We may regard "name" as a nominative absolute, and the statement regarding the name as parenthetical.

The Baptist is often treated as an Old Testament prophet who was merely standing on the threshold of the New; but he really belongs altogether in the New Testament, as our evangelist's description shows, as well as that of the other Gospels, especially also Christ's words concerning him.

7) The commission received by John is now described. **This one came for witness, that he might witness concerning the light, in order that all might believe through him.** Just as in v. 2, οὗτος reaches back and grasps all that v. 6 has said about John. The aorist ἦλθεν, while it is historical and reports the past fact, summarizes John's entire career, which was "to come for witness." It may sound Hebraic to spread out first in a phrase and then again in a clause this purpose for which John came, yet the effect is that the double mention of witnessing becomes markedly emphatic. That this is the evangelist's purpose we see in v. 8, where this witness function is mentioned for the third time.

John uses μαρτυρία, μαρτύς, and μαρτυρεῖν in their native sense, "witness" that is competent, testimony

at firsthand of what the person has seen or heard,
known and experienced himself. "For witness," without a modifier, stresses this idea. John's office was
to bear witness even as he himself describes it in
language taken from Isaiah when he calls himself "a
voice." That was his function, to speak out as a voice,
to speak "for witness." We may construe the ἵνα
clause in two ways, either as being dependent on the
verb ἦλθεν and parallel to the phrase "for witness,"
merely repeating this in the longer form of a purpose
clause; or as an appositional clause, dependent on the
phrase, then it is subfinal, merely repeating the contents of the phrase. Perhaps the latter is the better.
In either case the aorist verb is constative or com-
plexive, uniting in one point all the witnessing that
the Baptist did during his brief career. But now the
object is added to the verb in the form of a phrase:
the Baptist bore witness "concerning the light," namely
that light which appeared in the Logos of which the
evangelist has informed us in v. 4, 5. While the word
"light" is the evangelist's own designation of the
Logos, it, nevertheless, expresses exactly the contents
of the Baptist's testimony. For we must not think
that the Baptist knew nothing about the pre-existence
of the Logos whom he saw in the person of Jesus.
This is a rationalistic assumption, contradicted by
the Baptist himself in v. 15 and v. 30. In connection
with the latter passage the Baptist himself testifies
how he was made sure on this point: it was by no
natural means but by direct revelation from God who
had sent the Baptist for the very purpose of testifying
as he did. The Baptist even calls Jesus "the Son of
God," v. 33, 34. Both aorists, ἦλθεν and μαρτυρήσῃ, state
that the Baptist actually executed his great commission.

All witness is intended for faith, and so the Baptist testified "in order that all might believe through

him." This comprehensive "all" includes all who went out in the wilderness and with their own ears heard the testimony. But it does not stop with these multitudes — "he being dead yet speaketh" (Heb. 11:4), and his testimony reaches out into the wide world. Just as no limitations restricted the Baptist's saving purpose when his living voice rang out in the wilderness of Palestine, so no limitations now narrow it. That all may believe is the good and gracious will of God which is universal in extent, excluding not a single sinner; it is also called his antecedent will to distinguish it from the subsequent will which becomes effective when men finally reject the gospel and is summarized in Christ's own words, "he that believeth not shall be damned."

The evangelist does not write, "in order that all might *see* the light or *know* the light," both of which would have been good. He at once employs the cardinal term "believe," trust with the full confidence of the heart. The synonymous term "receive" occurs in v. 12. "Believe" goes beyond the figure of "light" to the reality meant by this figure, which is truth, i. e., the divine truth embodied in Jesus, the Logos, shining forth in his person, words, and works. This believing, when closely analyzed, includes knowledge, assent, and the confidence of the heart. It is never a blind trust; hence it is never, like ignorance, the opposite of science and knowledge, as so many who have no experience of saving faith suppose. While saving faith is also implicit and reaches out in trust beyond what we actually know and can know, it always does this only from the vantage ground of explicit faith, the sure ground of what we do and can know. The aorist πιστεύσωσι is best regarded as ingressive, "in order that all *might come to believe*," with the thought, of course, that once having arrived at faith, this faith will continue, even as in regeneration the life once kindled lives on and on. In this production of faith the Baptist is to be the human instrument as the phrase "through him" shows. This, of course, is because of his "witness," the very nature of which is to awaken faith, even as all true testimony ought to be believed. Faith comes only through the preached Word, and God invariably honors the preachers who truly proclaim that Word. Those who leave the Word and cry, "Spirit, Spirit!" or who invent methods that discard the gospel can never hope to have it said of them that men came to faith "through them."

8)   The evangelist seems to have a special interest in defining the Baptist's person, position, and work with great exactness. We feel this especially in v. 8, and again, even more strongly, in v. 19-28; 29-34; 3:26-36; and 5:33-36. We may hazard the guess that in the evangelist's time some still thought too highly of the Baptist. Yet we find not the slightest derogation on the evangelist's part. All that he reports concerning the Baptist agrees with his noble and humble character and with his exalted mission as the forerunner of Christ. **He was not the light, but** (came) **that he might witness concerning the light.** So great was "the light" so great must it be to be "the light" indeed for all our fallen race, that no ἄνθρωπος, or any sin-born creature like ourselves, not even John, the greatest of prophets, or that other John, the foremost of evangelists, could be "the light." All that these at most can do is to testify and "witness concerning the light," and they need a special enabling even for that. Augustine writes that they are like trees and mountains upon which the sun shines, which reflect the light and show by their own brightness and beauty that a great and wonderful light, vaster and mightier than they, is shining above them. In this sense Christ himself calls the Baptist "a burning and shining light," 5:35. The evangelist is careful to follow the negative statement concerning what John was not with the

positive one concerning what he truly was, and he makes this a repetition of the clause used in 7, thus securing special emphasis.

9) After thus placing the great forerunner before us the evangelist again points to the Logos but now as incarnate and ushered in by this forerunner. **The true light, which lighteth every man, was coming into the world.** This marginal rendering of the R. V. is decidedly best. We are compelled to regard τὸ φῶς τὸ ἀληθινόν as the subject of ἦν and not as the predicate. To supply the strong demonstrative "that" as the subject (A. V.) is quite unjustifiable. This, too, is certain that ἐρχόμενον does not modify πάντα ἄνθρωπον, and that we dare not translate, "which lighteth every man that cometh into the world" (A. V.). The translation of the R. V. is rather unclear. It really makes little difference whether we regard ἦν . . . ἐρχόμενον as belonging together and forming a circumscribed imperfect (or a periphrastic future, *erat venturum*), or make the participle modify the subject τὸ φῶς. The grammars are reluctant to do the first; and it is true that John has no other example of a relative clause intervening between the two words of a circumscribed imperfect, he has only a few cases in which a few words intervene, 1:28; 3:23; 10:10 ἦν . . . βαπτίζων; 2:6 ἦσαν . . . καίμεναι Yet whichever grammatical construction is preferred, it seems quite evident that ἐρχόμενον completes the idea of ἦν. For John is not merely once more saying (v. 4) that the light *was* in existence in the indefinite past but that this light *was in the act of coming* into the world.

Here John directly identifies "the light" with the Logos and thus advances beyond v. 4, where he writes only that the life of the Logos was the light of men. "Logos" and "light" are, indeed, close equivalents, for both terms contain the idea of revelation made unto us and intended to be received by us. But here

John appends the adjective τὸ φῶς τὸ ἀληθινόν, and by
using the second article he adds as much weight to
the adjective as to the noun, R. 776. The adjective
ἀληθινόν means real, genuine, the reality corresponding to the idea, *verus,* and is thus distinguished from
ἀληθής, true, mind and word, word and deed agreeing
with each other, *verax.*

The relative clause, "which lighteth every man,"
conveys more than an activity native to "the light";
it furnishes the evidence for this being "the genuine
light." "Every man" only individualizes the comprehensive plural used in v. 4: the light "of men";
and on the other hand it corresponds with the final
phrase: coming "into the world." This light is
genuine because it is universal; every man, all men,
the entire world of men, are wholly dependent on this
one divine light. Hence also the verb φωτίζει is in the
present tense, which corresponds with the tense of
φαίνει in v. 5. As no restriction or limitation appears
in the object "every man," so also none appears in
the tense of this verb. When John writes, "which
lighteth every man," he fears no misunderstanding on
our part as though we might think that he means that
every single human being is actually enlightened by
the Logos, for both before and after making this statement he speaks of men rejecting this light and remaining in darkness. Luther has caught John's meaning, "There is only one light that lighteth all men,
and no man comes into the world who can possibly
be illumined by any other light." He also refers to
Rom. 5:18: " 'As through one trespass the judgment came unto all men to condemnation, even so
through one act of righteousness the free gift came
unto all men unto justification of life.' Although all
men are not justified through Christ, he is, nevertheless, the only man through whom justification
comes." Augustine uses the illustration of one teacher

in a city, who, then, is said to instruct all the city, meaning not that everyone actually goes to him to be instructed but that none are taught except by him.

Hebrew originals have been cited for regarding "coming into the world" in the sense of "being born" and thus as equivalent to "an inhabitant of the world." But the New Testament never uses the expression in this sense. As far as men are concerned, they never were outside of the world and thus cannot come into the world by means of birth. As far as Christ is concerned, he was already born when the evangelist writes that he "was coming into the world." This "coming" is the standard term for Christ's mission in the world, for his appearance in his office as our Savior and Redeemer. The term ἐρχόμενος is almost technical in this sense. Israel constantly expected the Coming One; and in v. 11 John writes, "He *came* unto his own," he appeared as the promised Messiah, manifesting himself as such by his word and his work, by his suffering, death, and resurrection. In v. 9, when the Baptist testified of him, he was on the point of thus coming and making himself manifest. While he came unto his own, namely unto Israel, his coming was, nevertheless, as the Savior of the entire world. Thus also ἐρχόμενον εἰς τὸν κόσμον means, "in the act of coming into the world." This, of course, involves the incarnation, yet John holds back the direct mention of this great act, saving it for emphatic mention in the final section of his prolog.

10) Verse 9 leaves us with the incarnate Logos about to enter upon his great mission when the Baptist testified of him. V. 10, 11 advance and speak of him as being fully manifest, with the tragic result that the world failed to recognize him, and that even his own refused to receive him. **He was in the world, and the world was made by him, and the world knew him not. He came to his homeland, and his home**

people received him not. The two verses are
parallels. The first verse needs three clauses, for the
second clause must point out why the world should
have known Christ — he was its Creator. The second
verse needs only two clauses, for the reason why the
Jews should have received Christ is self-evident.

In v. 9 John says of the incarnate Logos that he
was in the act of coming into the world. When he
now proceeds and says, "In the world he *was*," the
evangelist includes the entire presence of the incarnate
Logos in the world. For ἦν, as distinct from the punctiliar ἦλθε in v. 11, is durative; it spreads out the entire
presence of Christ before our eyes. "The world,"
already in v. 9 and now three times in v. 10, means
the world of men, for only for the world in this sense
is The Coming One life, light, and salvation. We must
not bring in the other creatures, nor dare we go back
to the presence of the Logos before his incarnation.
"The world" also includes the Jews, although the two
are differentiated in v. 10 and 11 but only as a wider
circle embraces one that is narrower.

"The world" should certainly have recognized the
incarnate Logos when he appeared in its midst, for
"the world was made by him," more literally, "came
into existence through him," as v. 3 has already told
us regarding the entire universe, πάντα and οὐδὲ ἕν. This,
of course, includes also the Jews. Brute creatures
might not recognize their incarnate Creator, but the
world of intelligent men should certainly have
recognized, worshipped, and adored him. And yet
the tragic fact must be set down, "The world knew
him not." The constative aorist οὐκ ἔγνω records the
summary fact. We cannot see why R. 834 makes this
aorist ingressive. The three clauses are simply placed
side by side and are connected only with two καί, much
like v. 1. Their relation to each other is left to the
reader — each clause with its deep meaning being

allowed to speak for itself. No effort is made to explain the tragic result. The fact is that no real explanation is possible; for the rejection of its Creator by the world is an unreasonable act, and no reasonable explanation can be offered for an act, the very essence of which is unreason. It is not an explanation to point out that "the world" means men dead and blind in sin; for the incarnate Logos bears the *gratia sufficiens* which is fully sufficient and able by means of the life and light of the Logos to overcome this death and blindness; yet when this *gratia* is applied, men not only reject it but are left far worse than before. Here lies the problem that remains unsolved.

11) When speaking of "the world" and considering the Logos its Creator, this is tragic enough. But within this greater tragic circle lies a lesser one in which the tragedy is much greater. "To his homeland came" the incarnate Logos, "and his home people received him not." Just as in v. 10 the phrase "in the world" is placed forward for emphasis, so in v. 11 the corresponding phrase "to his homeland." The neuter plural τὰ ἴδια and the masculine plural οἱ ἴδιοι form a play on words in which only the gender marks a difference. The words are strongly reflexive, R. 691, and denote what belongs to a person in distinction from other persons; what is his very own in distinction from what belongs to others. Thus the neuter plural often has the meaning of one's own home, and the masculine, in contrast with this neuter, one's own relatives. This established usage bars out the idea that these terms are only synonyms, parallels to "the world" in v. 10, and that v. 11 is only a synonymous duplicate of v. 10. Moreover, "the world" is never viewed as "the homeland" or "the home people" of Christ; quite the contrary, the term "world" always has a hostile connotation. Israel alone is "the homeland" and "the home people" of Christ. Not, however,

because he was born man in Palestine, for he was born here because this was his home. Israel was God's "peculiar people," Deut. 26:18; "a special people unto himself, above all people that are upon the face of the earth," Deut. 7:6; compare I Pet. 2:9. Thus Israel belonged to him who was before Abraham, who was God and was with God before Israel began; Israel's Temple was his Father's house, and the people of Israel his blood kin. During an era of more than a thousand years this chosen people had been under preparation for his coming and had been kept in expectation of that event. Therefore, too, John writes ἦλθεν, he "came" to his own, using the significant verb which is connected so completely with the covenant promises of the Messiah.

If anywhere in the world, the incarnate Logos, when he now revealed himself and thus came to his own homeland, should have been received by his home people. They should have embraced him with open arms and hearts, and the only danger should have been that they might jealously claim him as being exclusively their own, whom they would not share with any other nation. The very opposite occurred, "and his home people received him not." Here, as in v. 10, John writes αὐτόν, "him," although the antecedent of both pronouns is the neuter τὸ φῶς, "the light." These pronouns cannot be explained as presupposing the masculine antecedent ὁ λόγος, for this lies entirely too far back. The probable explanation is that with these pronouns John turns from the figure of the light to the reality of this figure, namely the person of Christ. That, too, is why John says in the second clause of v. 10 that the world was made δι' αὐτοῦ, "through him." All this is the strongest proof for the identity of the Logos, who also is called Life and Light, with the man Jesus Christ. Aside from its direct enunciation the incarnation can receive no more effective presentation.

Both expressions, the world "knew him not," and his own "received him not," two cases of litotes, negatives where positives are meant, are decidedly mild. "Not to know," in the pregnant sense here used, means to disown utterly, as in Matt. 7:23. The verb "know," which is here negatived, is *noscere cum affectu et effectu*, to know, recognize, and thus acknowledge and accept as one's own, John 10:14. What this form of disowning means is explained by Jesus himself in John 15:19-25, where he tells his disciples that the world will treat them as it treats him with hate and with persecution. The verb used for the treatment bestowed on Christ by "his own people" is of a different type though to the same effect: they "received him not," οὐ παρέλαβον. As compared with δέχεσθαι, which is often used regarding the welcome reception of a guest, John 4:45; Matt. 10:41, etc., παραλαμβάνειν, both with a personal and with an impersonal object, is used regarding a reception that includès full appropriation, a reception which intends permanent possession and communion. This, of course, is the reception Jesus sought when he came to his own, and this his own people denied him. They threw him out, turned him over to the Gentiles, had him made away with by a death of deepest disgrace. Note the strong contrast: he *came*, indeed, to his own; his own *did not receive* him. The verbs match, but the negative makes them clash. The aorist indicates the historical fact. The simplicity of expression is perfect, but it surely makes the tragedy thus expressed stand out only the more. "Hear, O heavens, and give ear, O earth: for the Lord hath spoken: I have nourished and brought up children, and they have rebelled against me. The ox knoweth his owner, and

the ass his master's crib: but Israel doth not know,
my people doth not consider.   Ah, sinful nation, a
people laden with iniquity, a seed of evildoers, children
that are corrupters: they have forsaken the Lord, they
have provoked the Holy One of Israel unto anger, they
are gone away backward," Isa. 1 :2-4.   In vain did the
Baptist call for repentance in order to prepare a true
reception.   When Jesus "came," they "received him
not."

12)   When John writes of the world and of the
Jews he allows them to take up the entire picture.   It
seems that he is not willing to make a coordination between these two on the one hand and the believers
on the other hand.   He paints the tragedy in one picture and then sets this away; then he takes another
canvas and paints the salvation.   **But as many as
accepted him, to them he gave the right to become
God's children, to those who believe in his name.**
Here is the first instance of an adversative connection, namely the adversative δέ.   The word ὅσοι, "as
many as," "those who," does not indicate whether
there were many or only a few.   Far more important
is the observation that ὅσοι denotes individuals, namely
each and every believer omitting none.   The word thus
differs markedly from "the world" and from οἱ ἴδιοι,
"his own people," both of which denote a body.   The
world as a body and the Jews as a nation rejected
Christ, only individuals as individuals accepted him.
But this means that "as many as" cannot be restricted
to individual Jews.   Since the rejection is attributed
to two bodies, the lesser of which is included in the
greater, the acceptance, now placed in contrast with
that rejection, cannot be restricted only to individuals
in the lesser body.   "As many as" means both individual Jews and individual Gentiles.   Moreover, while
John plainly refers to the time when the Logos "came"
and manifested himself, he sets no limit in the other

direction. "As many as," therefore, includes all those who accepted Jesus as the Logos since he came and manifested himself, all believers up to the time when John wrote these words and by inference all believers also after he wrote.

Still more lies in ὅσοι. First of all, that accepting Christ is an individual and not a corporate matter. Does it sound lamentable, that only single persons as individuals accept the Savior instead of an entire nation or the wide world as a whole? In reality this individual acceptance denotes universalism, "that *whosoever* believeth on him should not perish but have eternal life," — whosoever, Jew or Gentile, no matter of what nation or social and educational standing. Thus "as many as" opens the door to all men in the world. Moreover, this type of universalism comports with the very nature of true acceptance. Too often corporate acceptance is only formal. In a large body many do not assent, many others only assent, and so genuine acceptance is, after all, heavily restricted in the case of corporate acceptance. As far as the Logos is concerned, nothing whatever is lost by "as many as." We may call these the exceptions as compared with the rule indicated in v. 11. But this expresses only a superficial view. Exceptions are abnormal; they ought really not to occur. In the case of the Logos all the Jews and all the world ought to believe on him. By rejecting him these act abnormally and thus in spite of their number constitute the exception, while "as many as" act normally and thus accord with the rule.

In substance the three verbs "to know" (ἔγνω), "to receive" (παρέλαβον), and "to accept or take" (ἔλαβον) the Logos necessarily must amount to the same thing, namely to embrace by faith. It is quite evident that the simple λαμβάνειν cannot include less than the compound παραλαμβάνειν, for less was not rendered by those

who became God's children than was expected of the
Jews. The idea that the compound verb means "to
receive officially" as a King and thus solemnly to
conduct into the Temple, reads too much into the verb
as contrasted with the simple verb. Nor does ἔλαβον
need a complement in the shape of a participle to
complete its meaning, for it is sufficient to say they
"accepted," they "took" Christ, i. e., "took" him as
what he was and as what he offered himself. The
only difference between the compound and the simple
forms of the verb is that in the former the preposition expresses the purpose of full appropriation while
the latter takes this for granted. "As many as
accepted him" is placed forward as the antecedent of
αὐτοῖς, "to them," making this clause stand out in full
contrast to "the world" and "his own people" (the
Jews as a nation) more than would be the case if a
relative clause had been used, "To them, who accepted
him, he gave," etc.

All those who rejected the Logos received nothing;
they remained what they were, destitute, blind, and
spiritually dead, a condition that was the more tragic
since it might have been changed into the blessed
opposite. But to those who accepted the Logos "he
gave the right to become God's children." This is
what the others missed and lost wholly through their
own fault. John does not write: τέκνα Θεοῦ ἐγένοντο or
γεγόνασιν, "they became, or they have become, God's
children." This would be perfectly true. The objection does not hold that John would thereby say that
these persons became God's children by their own
ability. As little as ἐγένετο in v. 3 has a trace of
synergism, so little would ἐγένοντο have such a trace
of it in the present connection. And yet John writes,
"he gave to them the right," etc., placing ἔδωκεν forward for emphasis. Every time when life, pardon,
or salvation are involved, the verb "give" brings out

strongly the note of unmerited grace. The implied note of contrast is not that of synergism, as though any man might become a child of God by effort of his own or by on his part adding something toward this end. The contrast is far more obvious: the Jews, Christ's own home people, imagined they were and could be God's children without the Logos or Christ. Jesus himself had an argument with them on this very subject, John 8:42-47. They had no use for Christ because they dreamed that they could be God's children without him. That thought is what John cuts off so early in his Gospel by the wording: the Logos "gave" this right of childhood to those who received him. The two aorists ἔλαβον and ἔδωκεν occur simultaneously. The instant of accepting Christ is the instant of receiving the gift of childhood. To receive Christ is to receive life, light, and salvation.

The gift is here called "right to become God's children." Yet the infinitive γενέσθαι is an aorist and thus punctiliar and hence cannot mean that at some later time these persons would develop into God's children. This aorist infinitive expresses action that is simultaneous with that of the two preceding finite aorists ἔλαβον and ἔδωκεν — in other words, the moment of accepting Christ, which is the moment of receiving his gift, that, too, is the moment of becoming God's children, i. e., the moment of regeneration. This is called "the right," ἐξουσία (without the article, thus stressing the quality of the noun), which here means more than "possibility" and not quite as much as "power." The infinitive, "right to become," is construed as a dative, R. 1076, and is the complement of the noun. Christ's gift to those who receive him is a new relation to God, they are made God's children. Their "right" is to be such children. For this relation to God John always employs τέκνα Θεοῦ and never υἱοὶ Θεοῦ, for he always views it as the product of regenera-

tion (τέκνα from τίκτειν). The difference between
"child" and "son" is quite marked. A son may become
such by adoption, so that the word for "adoption" is
υἱοθεσία, i. e., placing one in the position of a son.
Christ, too, is never called "the Child of God," which
would leave a wrong impression, but always "the Son
of God." Cremer, *Bibl.-theol. Woerterbuch der Neutestamentlichen Graezitaet,* 10th ed. by Julius Koegel,
1073 (future references indicated by C.-K.) specifies
the difference: τέκνον as expressing relation or derivation *from*; υἱός as expressing relation *to*. A study of
the words reveals various types of interesting usage.
"Children," for instance, has the note of endearment,
while "sons" often has the note of legal standing: if
a son, then an heir, Gal. 4:7. Thus "son" and "slave"
are in contrast, and "child" and "slave" are not placed
in opposition. As regards our relation to God, the
Scriptures have no sweeter name than this that we
are "God's children" and belong to his household, Eph.
2:19.

The dative τοῖς πιστεύουσιν εἰς τὸ ὄνομα αὐτοῦ is an apposition to αὐτοῖς. This, however, is not intended to point
out the condition for receiving the right of childhood.
The fact that receiving Christ means receiving him by
faith is clear from v. 7. If, nevertheless, this thought is
to be repeated, the participle would have to be an
aorist and without the article. For the moment one
comes to faith he becomes a child of God. The articulated present participle is like a clause, descriptive
of those to whom the right of childhood has been
given. Its force is well rendered by Zahn, "and these
are they who believe on his name," i. e., who as God's
children continue thus believing. Whenever ὄνομα,
"name," is used in connections like this, "name" always
means the complete self-revelation of Christ in his
redemptive grace. At times one or the other feature
of that revelation is indicated by the context. Whether

we read: "believe in him" (Christ), or: "believe in his name," makes no difference, for we know "him" only by means of his "name," i. e., his saving self-revelation. As far as the names of Christ are concerned, the special terms by which we designate his person, these are only concentrated and thus especially valuable portions of his self-revelation. Their value consists only in their rich content which reveals to us Christ's person and his work. Thus "they that believe in his name" are they whose heart's trust and confidence extends (εἰς) to the blessed revelation they have received from him. Various prepositions are used with πιστεύειν; when εἰς is employed, this points out the direction or the relation of the confidence. The idea that "to believe on the name" indicates that a certain "name" of Christ is confessed by the believer, rests on a misunderstanding. While true faith always confesses, the phrase "on the name" in no way refers to this fact.

13) Does verse thirteen speak of "God's children" and describe their spiritual birth, or does this verse speak of the human birth of the Logos, his birth from the Virgin Mary? The question is one of the text and also one of the thought. Usually the question is not raised at all, because the accepted reading of the text seems to raise no question. The incongruities, not to say impossibilities, that result are taken as a matter of course and are smoothed out in the best way possible. The best feature about the usual reading is that it does not clash with the analogy of faith, and thus in preaching on this verse no doctrinal difficulty is encountered. **Which were born, not of blood, nor of the will of the flesh, nor of the will of man, but of God,** is treated as a relative clause attached to v. 12, describing the birth of God's children as not being due to natural generation but to a generation that has its source in God, ἐκ Θεοῦ.

The accepted reading makes v. 13 the conclusion of the second paragraph of the prolog and v. 14 the beginning of the final paragraph. Whether the division for the paragraphs is made in this way or not (some divide differently), one thing is certain: καί at the head of v. 14, once we give it adequate thought, is wholly without justification. John has used this connective nine times in the preceding account, always in order to connect facts closely related to each other. Even when these facts were opposites they could be properly combined as such. Every time a new group of facts was introduced John did this without a connective, thus indicating that he was passing on to something new. Yet here in v. 14 all this would be upset. An entirely new paragraph would begin with καί. Or, to say the least, two facts wholly unrelated, strangely diverse as to time, would be linked together with "and," namely the incarnation of the Logos (v. 14) and the spiritual birth of God's children (v. 13). The latter refers to the mass of believers living at the time John wrote, the former to the time when the Logos became flesh. The two are so diverse, even as to time, that no writer, least of all John, would connect the two with "and." Regeneration and the incarnation are not even opposites, nor does John intimate any other relation between the two. This "and" should thus cause us to pause.

The second point that should make us pause and question is that with three different statements and thus with exceeding emphasis John should deny that the spiritual regeneration of God's children is not a physical operation. Evidently, this heavy denial indicates that a wrong view is being contradicted and a right view put in its place. But who in all the church supposed that regeneration was a physical act? Even Nicodemus, whose ignorance regarding regeneration Jesus rebuked, was entirely sure that a man could not

be reborn by again entering the womb of a human
mother, by a birth that would be physical. And then,
strange to say, after this denial of regeneration as a
physical birth John would add with "and" that the
Logos was born physically in a miraculous manner!
How can such things be?

In the third place, assuming that John felt v. 12
to be incomplete (though it is certainly complete as
it stands), he could have added what he might have
desired in the simplest fashion. Here is one way,
"But as many as accepted him, to them he gave the
right to become God's children, *and they were born of
God*," etc. Again, extending the participial apposition
at the end of v. 12, "to them who are believers on his
name *and have been born of God*" (the perfect participle in the Greek). Or, if an inner causal relation
should be John's intention, revealing that regeneration
produces the τέκνα Θεοῦ, all would be clear if a relative
clause with οἵτινες would have been added, "to them
who are believers on his name, *such as have been born
of God*." Yet in no case could the three negative
phrases, denying that regeneration is a physical act,
be inserted in an addition to v. 12, for this strong
denial would necessarily imply that this preposterous
notion had advocates among the Christians of John's
time.

If we had only the accepted text, we should be left
solely to conjecture, and this at best is like a guess in
the dark. It is usually useless even to consider conjectures. The older reading, which removes all the
difficulties indicated and others that might yet be
added, has long been known. This original reading
has no relative pronoun (either plural or singular) at
the head of v. 13, and the final verb is singular: οὐκ ἐξ
αἱμάτων . . . ἐγεννήθη. V. 13 speaks not of believers
but of the Logos and of his human birth. V. 13 begins the new paragraph, the climax of the prolog.

John describes the incarnation not merely in one brief statement, "The Word was made flesh," but in two statements, the first of which is decidedly longer than the second, and thus the most natural thing in the world is for John to link the two with καί. We translate: **Not of blood, nor of the will of flesh, nor of the will of a man, but of God was he born. And the Word became flesh, etc.** The credit for first drawing attention to this reading belongs to Fr. Blass, whom Theodor Zahn followed in his various most valuable publications. We cannot enter into all the details of the ancient documentary evidence, which really belongs into works on textual criticism. We content ourselves with the following summary as being sufficient for our purpose.

The original reading appears in Tertullian, Irenaeus, and others. The gnostic Valentinians, about the year 140, changed the original singular ἐγεννήθη (without ὅ) into the plural ἐγεννήθησαν (without οἵ) in the interest of their peculiar doctrine They desired to use this passage as a description of the peculiar class of spiritual people provided for in their heretical system. In this way the verb in v. 13 became plural. The Occidentals held to the singular until the third, or possibly the fourth, century. The Alexandrians were more ready to adopt the plural and had done so by the end of the second century, but as yet without the relative οἵ. This came to be inserted in order to connect v. 13 with the believers mentioned in v. 12 and thus to shut out the Valentinian use of v. 13. This relative pronoun then found acceptance also in the Occident. For the Latins the matter of the pronoun was easier as the Latin *qui* could be used for ὅς as well as for οἵ; it was far more difficult for the Syrians, whose text had the singular verb and yet added the plural pronoun as its subject. The entire question of determining the original reading of v. 13 thus is entirely different from the usual method of comparing the readings of the codices in order to accept that reading only which the best and the weightiest codices support. This may explain why the common reading has not been challenged more resolutely by critical commentators and text critics.

The subject of v. 13 is the Logos, who constitutes the beginning, middle, and end of the entire prolog and thus needs no formal mention as John proceeds to describe his human birth. This birth was οὐκ ἐξ αἱμάτων, "not due to bloods," i. e., the mixture of blood from two human parents as in cases of ordinary human procreation. "Blood" is the material substance from which the human organism is formed. The plural "bloods" is the more necessary in the Greek, since the singular might be misunderstand. For the human organism of the Logos actually began with a bit of blood in the womb of the Virgin Mary; it was thus that she "conceived in the womb," Luke 1:31. The explanation of the plural from the analogy of other Greek expressions must be dropped. Blood that is shed in drops or in streams, animals that are sacrificed, wounds and the slain in battle, murderous acts and the like, justify the use of the plural in the Greek but are no analogy for the generation of a human being. Where a real analogy occurs, as in the reading of some texts in Acts 17:26, the singular is used in the Greek, "hath made of one blood." When the Logos became man, this was not due to, did not start with (ἐκ), the blood from two parents.

From the act of procreation in which the blood of man and woman join so that the blood of both flows in the child's veins, John advances to the impulse of nature which lies back of this sexual union, "nor of the will of the flesh." The term "flesh" denotes our bodily nature as God made it, male and female, adding the blessing, "Be fruitful and multiply, and replenish

the earth." "The will of the flesh" is thus the natural
urge and volition implanted in our bodily nature to
beget and to rear offspring. Like "bloods" this "will
of the flesh" includes both man and woman. It is
true that our blood as well as our flesh and the will of
our flesh are now corrupt because of sin and death, yet
this corruption is not stressed. The human birth of
the Logos is not due to our nature either as it now is
or as it once was. The will to beget children, implanted in man by God, had nothing to do with the
incarnation. A far higher, an entirely different will,
brought that about.

Yet the decisive will in the act of procreation is
that of the man not that of the woman, hence John
adds, "nor of the will of man," using ἀνήρ in distinction from γυνή and thus not to be identified with
ἄνθρωπος, the generic term for man as a human being
including both male and female. The three phrases
used by John in stating how the birth of the Logos
as man was not brought about are not coordinate,
merely placed side by side; nor should we subordinate
the second two phrases and regard them as merely
defining more closely the first phrase. These phrases
are like a pyramid, one placed on top of the other.
They are like three circles, the second being narrower
than the first, the third narrower than the second.
Thus the first phrase includes the other two, and the
second includes the third. Beyond the final, most pre-
cise specification John cannot go and need not go in
his negations. The Logos was born entirely without
a human father. In his conception no male parent
was active. The detailed history of this conception
and birth John's readers know from the records of
Matthew and of Luke, which John also takes for
granted. Neither v. 13 nor v. 14 can be properly
understood without the other two Gospels. What John
here does is to restate with exact precision the vital

facts contained in the full historical records of the
other Gospels.

Even those who have been content with the reading of the current text, which makes v. 13 a description of our own spiritual birth, have felt that John
here has in mind the other Gospel records which recount the miraculous conception and birth of Jesus.
They assume that John here uses the manner of Jesus'
conception and birth as a kind of type illustrating our
spiritual birth as also being miraculous in a somewhat
analogous manner. In a way they thus sensed what
the true reading of v. 13 contains. Yet John's words
offer not the least indication that he is speaking
typically, comparing our spiritual birth to the physical
birth of Jesus. In fact, the very idea of such a type
and comparison is highly questionable. The miracle
of the incarnation is too lofty to be used for the regeneration of the multitude of God's children. The
type is always less than the antitype and necessarily
must be, otherwise the antitype would be the type,
and the type the antitype. When soberly examined,
this threefold denial of a generation by blood, by the
will of the flesh, and by the will of a man, sounds trivial
when applied to our regeneration, regarding which
it is self-evident that this is altogether only spiritual;
while, when this denial is applied to the incarnation,
it constitutes a most vital confession — one necessary
for all ages of the church and most necessary for our
own day.

The preposition ἐκ denotes source or origin, and
John uses it three times in his denials as to how the
birth of the Logos was not effected, and then once
more with the positive phrase which states how this
birth was, indeed, effected, "on the contrary, of God
was he born." The incarnation of the Logos, we may
thus say, was due exclusively to God. It arose from
God alone as the source. John adds no other term

such as "of the will of God," for this might lead to the thought that God only willed the incarnation and then used some means or other for carrying his volition into effect. All such intermediate means are excluded by the three negative phrases, which leave as their one opposite only "God." In other words, the incarnation was effected without means by the direct agency of God alone.

The verb γεννᾶν means "to beget" when used with reference to the father; also "to give birth," "bring forth" when used with reference to the mother or to both parents. The fact that John is writing of the incarnation and not of the eternal generation of the Logos is made entirely certain by the preceding negative phrases, which modify the verb, just as the final positive phrase does. The tense of ἐγεννήθη is the historical aorist, and the passive accords with ἐκ Θεοῦ, not, indeed, as the usual agent with the passive, which would be ὑπό or ἀπό, but deeper than this, as the source or origin. We might translate, "was begotten," though in doing so we would have to ward off the thought that God was in some way a substitute for the human father in the begetting of the Logos. It is better to translate, "was born," using the verb in the wider sense as including all that lies in the term "incarnation." Perhaps we may derive a little help from the figurative use of the verb. The idea of sex and of the function of sex disappears entirely when God is called the Father of his people, or when one human person becomes a spiritual father to another. Fatherhood and motherhood intermingle in this form of thought. So the Logos "was born" of man by a birth due to the miraculous intervention of God wholly apart from any paternal sex function.

14) With the closing words of v. 13, "of God was he born," the connective "and" accords perfectly: **And the Word became flesh and tented among us,**

and we beheld his glory as of the Only-begotten from the Father, full of grace and truth. What lies in ἐγεννήθη is brought out by σὰρξ ἐγένετο; by his "birth" the Logos "became flesh." While this may well be called the climax of the entire prolog, the fact should not be overlooked that what is now recorded as the climax already lies in all that John writes from v. 4 onward. The Logos could not have been the life and the light of men from the beginning if in the fulness of time he had not been "born of God" and "become flesh."

Now that the climacteric statement is made, the subject is once more named: ὁ λόγος; but this name is now illumined by all that John has said of him thus far, and, in turn, what he now writes lights up and makes clearer all that he has said of him thus far. We understand the way to the goal the better after having reached the goal. And this, indeed, is the goal, for it transcends the previous statements about the shining of the light and the coming into the world (speaking of it only as a coming). Here is the INCARNATION in so many words: the Word, who *was* in the beginning, the life and the true light from eternity, this Word *"became flesh."* The aorist states the historical fact. In an interesting comparison of several aorists in the prolog R. 829 calls this aorist ingressive, because it "accents the entrance of the Logos upon his life on earth." We should rather say that this aorist marks the momentary act which made the Logos flesh, to remain flesh in the sense of man forever after. From the start the thought must be rejected that ἐγένετο here means a transformation of the Logos into flesh. The Word did not cease to be what it was before; but it became what it was not before — *flesh.* "Without controversy great is the mystery of godliness: God was manifested in the flesh," I Tim. 3:16. The identity of the subject re-

mains. *The Word* became flesh and remains in every
sense *the Word* though now made flesh. This Word,
being God, could not possibly change into something
else, for then God would cease to be God.

The mystery of how the Logos, the Creator, (v. 3)
could assume our created nature will forever challenge our finite comprehension. The tremendous fact
itself is beyond question, and for us that is enough.
Thus we have only one care, that when we ourselves
restate what John records we may in no way deviate
from the fact. It will not do, for instance, to compare
ἐγένετο as here used with γεγενημένον in 2:9, "the water
that has become wine." Of the two, the water and
the wine, the water had ceased to be; but the Word
did not cease to be — he was not turned into flesh. We
need a caution here in regard to all the uses of γίνομαι
in ordinary speech, for in all the universe no analogy
occurs for the incarnation. Hence we can find no
analogous uses of the verb. Such uses as those in
2:9; Matt. 4:3; Rom. 2:25; I Cor. 3:18; John 9:39;
16:30, are of a totally different type. The uses in
John 5:6; 5:9; 5:14; 8:33; 12:36; I Cor. 13:11; Luke
23:12, also cannot be compared with our passage. The
incarnation is absolutely unique — nothing even faint-
ly like it has ever been known. The only being with
two natures is the Son of God.

Thus we decline to say "that the divine subject
entered into the human mode of being at the cost of
renouncing his divine mode of being"; or that "he exchanged the divine state for the human"; or that "the
purely spiritual existence, independent of bodily material, . . . was exchanged for the existence of a
bodily living man." For one thing, such expressions
confuse the incarnation with the humiliation, whereas
these two are entirely distinct, and John's ἐγένετο predicates only the former. In heaven the Logos still
has his flesh but at the cost of nothing, nor by any

exchange, nor with any dependence. Stressing the "bodily material" and "a bodily living man" as decisive for the incarnation is especially unfortunate. R. 394 calls ἐγένετο in our passage a copula, which is far nearer the truth, for all that this verb does is to *predicate* what the term "flesh" contains in the moment of the Incarnation of the Logos. Note the careful way in which the church has worded this miracle of the ages in the Nicene Creed: "who for us men, and for our salvation, came down from heaven, and was incarnate by the Holy Ghost of the Virgin Mary, and was made man." Likewise the Creed of Athanasius against the Arians: "God of the Substance of the Father, begotten before the worlds; and Man of the substance of his mother, born in the world; Perfect God and perfect Man, of a reasonable soul and human flesh subsisting. Equal to the Father as touching his Godhead, and inferior to the Father as touching his manhood; Who, although he be God and Man, yet he is not two, but one Christ; One, not by conversion of the Godhead into flesh, but by taking of the manhood into God; One altogether; not by confusion of Substance, but by unity of Person. For as the reasonable soul and flesh is one man, so God and Man is one Christ." *Concordia Triglotta,* 32 and 35. For precision and exactness these confessional statements have never been excelled.

"By *flesh* we understand the whole man, body and soul, according to the Scriptures which call man flesh." Luther, who adds, "This lofty humility, which no tongue is able to express, the evangelist wanted to indicate by the little word *flesh.*" Christ's flesh was real flesh, born of the Virgin Mary, not a mere appearance of flesh (Docetism). But while the Word became flesh, he did not become sinful flesh; for the word flesh itself, as describing our nature, does not include sin. When we are raised from the dead, no

sin will be found in our flesh. Sometimes "flesh" is
identified with "body," whereas "flesh" = body, soul,
and spirit. Mary gave birth to a living son, whose
soul afterward became sorrowful unto death, who
groaned in the spirit and in death gave up the spirit
(παρέδωκε τὸ πνεῦμα, John 19:30; ἐξέπνευσεν, Luke 23:46),
commending his spirit into his Father's hands. The
manhood of Christ was thus perfect in every respect.

On the one hand, nothing dare be subtracted from
"flesh," the human nature, the perfect humanity; on
the other hand, nothing dare be subtracted from the
Word, the divine nature, the perfect divinity. These
two, each being perfect, combine in the one Person.
This person is the eternal, uncreated Logos (v. 1, 2),
who in his divine nature was with God in eternity and
was God. This person assumed "flesh," a human
spirit, soul, and body; he did not join himself to some
human being. The ego in the God-man is the ego of
the Logos. This divine ego took the place occupied in
all other men by a human ego. Hence the incarnate
Son is able to declare that he and the Father are one.
The human nature of the Logos is thus ἀνυπόστατος, without a human ego, and yet ἐνυπόστατος by possessing the
divine ego, hence not imperfect but the more perfect.
Whoever met Christ met God's Son not the person of
some man. In him were not two egos, nor was there
in him a double or a composite ego. The path between
Nestorianism and Eutychianism is narrow but perfectly straight if only we follow John and stop rationalizing and speculating, which always end by losing
either the Logos or the flesh. The marvel remains that
this great mystery should be expressed by the evangelist in such few and simple words, a mystery on
which the greatest minds have spent their most intense
efforts. Here Inspiration again becomes so tangible
that one wonders why all eyes do not recognize its

presence. No uninspired pen could ever have set down
the words, "And the Word became flesh."

The first effect of the incarnation is added by a
simple "and" in John's fashion, "and tented among
us," ἐσκήνωσεν. This recalls the Tabernacle of Israel in
which God tented and dwelt among his people. The
pillar of cloud and of fire filled and covered the Tabernacle, making visible the glorious presence of God,
Exod. 40:34-38. Compare the final dwelling of God
with his people in Rev. 21:3. This is the imagery back
of John's figurative verb "he tented among us." The
flesh of the Logos is the true Temple of God (2:21),
the tent in which he dwelt; the Logos fills this flesh
with his presence even as the Tabernacle was filled
with the Shekinah of Jehovah. Yet the verb "tented,"
as well as its historical aorist tense, indicate a temporary sojourn. The Logos remained ἐν ἡμῖν only until
his redemptive work was finished, then not to discard
the tent of his flesh but to transfer his human nature
into the Holy of Holies above by the miracle of his
glorification and ascension. John writes "among us"
without further specification since his readers know
whom he means. Comparing v. 16 "we all" and I John
1:1, etc., this pronoun "we" signifies only the chosen
ones who were called to be Christ's special witnesses
in the time to come. Some wish to extend this pronoun to include all those who beheld Christ with the
eyes of faith while he walked on earth. The fact
of their so beholding him is true enough and may
pass as such. But John is writing to a different
generation which he addresses as ὑμεῖς, "you" in 19:35,
whom also he places in clear contrast with "we" and
"our" in the opening of his First Epistle. These notable persons who "declare" what they have seen, heard,
and handled are Christ's chosen witnesses only. We
should, however, not fail to note that this important

"we" includes the Apostle John himself who thus also attests himself as the writer of this Gospel.

The second effect of the incarnation is added with another "and," "and we beheld his glory," but "we" is now in the inflectional ending of the verb. Here again the historical aorist, like the one preceding, reports what once took place and could never be repeated. R. 834 makes this aorist "effective" as marking the end of an action, as stating that finally this vision of Christ's glory was achieved. We decidedly prefer to regard this as a "constative" aorist, one which summarizes an entire course of action. For John himself reports that all along the Apostles beheld and were attracted by the glory of the God-man, beginning notably with the first miracle, 2:11, where also τὴν δόξαν αὐτοῦ recurs.

John refers to "the glory" of the Logos. This term δόξα is constantly used either to designate all the attributes of the Godhead as they shine forth in one or in another way before the eyes of men, or to indicate the manifestation of any one or of several of these attributes. Thus "his glory" may designate the radiance of the infinite love that dwelt in Christ, breaking forth again and again in word and in deed; the heavenliness of his grace, or his mercy, or his compassion; the divine depth and comprehension of his wisdom and knowledge, against which also all human cunning failed; the absoluteness of his power in all the miracles that spoke so plainly of his divinity. Any one or more of these manifestations constitute "the glory" which John and the other witnesses beheld. The verb itself, θεάομαι, is weighty and much more expressive than ὁράω, "to see." The eye and the mind rest upon the object, penetrate and absorb it; and since the verb fits only great and notable objects, it generally has the connotation of wonder and admiration. Thus John writes, "We beheld, we actually viewed, his glory." It is quite in vain to make "we beheld" mean only a beholding with the eyes of the mind, an inner experience of the soul. For that might be experienced by one who was not an eyewitness.

John repeats δόξαν, investing it with emphasis, as if he would say, "glory indeed," "glory most wonderful." And now he describes this glory, "as of the Only-begotten from the Father." The rendering in the margin of the R. V. is highly unfortunate, "as of an only-begotten from a father." These translators certainly knew that the absence of the article with nouns like μονογενής and πατήρ does not render them indefinite: *an* only-begotten — *a* father. Nouns designating persons or objects only one of which exists need no article; the English idiom requires the article. We simply must translate: *the* Only-begotten — *the* Father. Moreover, in the Greek anarthrous nouns are qualitative, R. 794; by omitting the article we are asked to fix our attention on just what the noun conveys. The sense of the margin of the R. V. is equally unfortunate. It assumes that every only-begotten son has a special glory and then informs us that God's Only-begotten Son also has such a glory. But how about the only son of a slave, or of a beggar, or of a criminal? Even if the father is a notable person and the only son a credit to his father, who would call the fact that he has no brothers "his glory"? And if such a predication should be made, who would ever think of using this human feature as illustrating the glory of God's only Son?

The term μονογενής = "Only-begotten," the Greek adjective here being used as a noun. We fail to see how the connection makes it self-evident that we supply υἱός, for "Son" has not occurred in the previous verses. Nor are we ready to reduce this weighty term to mean no more than "only child" as when it is used with reference to human parents who either have had but

one child or have only one left after the rest have
died. The term rises above all such conceptions when
we note the combination, *"glory* as of the Only-begotten." This "as" is not the common "like" of ordinary
comparisons between two — for who would be the
other? This "as" matches the reality with the idea
and thus proves and establishes. What John saw of
the glory of the Only-begotten corresponded with all
that he could possibly conceive as belonging to this
being. He also had the Old Testament to lift his
expectations exceedingly high. The glory he actually
beheld never fell short of the rightful expectation
thus formed, in fact, exceeded it in every way. We
may add that μονογενής is also far more than ἀγαπητός,
"beloved," which the LXX used as a translation for
jachid (single one, only one) in Gen. 22:2; Jer. 6:26;
etc. To be sure, the Only-begotten was the Beloved
of the Father, but the effort to make these two terms
either identical or synonymous when they are predicated of the Logos is misdirected. The one denotes
being as such, the other, ethical relation and attitude.

John alone uses μονογενής, which he coined like ὁ
λόγος, to express what in many statements Jesus said
of his relation to the Father. All but a few of the
interpreters of the last generation have taken "Only-
begotten" in the metaphysical sense and have understood it as referring to the relation of the Logos to
the Father apart from the incarnation. In other
words, μονογενής and ὁ λόγος extend back into all eternity
and belong to the Son ἄσαρκος (unincarnate) as well
as to the Son ἔνσαρκος (incarnate). The very nature
of the title "Only-begotten" involves the relation of
"Father" and of "Son," which is usually called the
aeterna filii Dei generatio. No attempt is made to
penetrate the mystery of this relation, i. e., to unveil
what lies in this *generatio.* But this, indeed, is held

as surely being revealed to us, that the First Person of the Godhead is the Father, that the Second Person is the Son, and that their relation is that the one begot and the other is begotten. Some, meaning well enough, have called this a "process," but no word of Scripture can be found to this effect. To speak of an inner-trinitarian process is either useless or tends to mislead. When accepting the revelation granted us, we must remember that these divine realities are couched in imperfect human terms, which only dimly reveal the ineffable realities. Therefore we will halt all speculation. With the church through the past centuries we will expend our efforts in guarding the revelation which we have against all the perversions that constantly enter men's minds. This, too, will aid us: God would never have revealed to us what he did concerning the Holy Trinity and the inner relation of the three Persons, because all this leaves our powers of comprehension so far behind, but for the necessity involved in his plan of salvation, the Father sending the Son, the Son executing his redemptive mission, and the Holy Spirit appropriating this redemption to us.

During the last generation efforts were made to interpret "Only-begotten" with reference to the exceptional human begetting and birth of Christ. "The Only-begotten" is said to be such only because of the peculiar relation of Christ's humanity or flesh to the Father. Others are "Children of God" by grace, by adoption, by a transfer from sin to pardon; Jesus is the Son by nature, by his very conception in the Virgin's womb, and in this sense "Only-begotten." And John first speaks of the incarnation, "The Word became flesh," and then in close connection with this statement uses what this new teaching calls the correlate concepts "Only-begotten" and "Father," whereas, in v. 1-12 nothing is said about a generation or

begetting of the pre-existent Logos. But this structure
cannot stand. If the terms "Father" and "Son" are
due to the conception that took place in the Virgin's
womb, then we have a "Father" who begot something
that was only human, for in the Virgin's womb only
Christ's human nature was begotten. Then we should
have a "Son" who is a son only in his human nature,
i. e., only a human son. Moreover, the church has
never confessed, "who was conceived *by the Father*,
born of the Virgin Mary"; but, "who was conceived
by the Holy Ghost," etc. To base the Fatherhood and
the Sonship on the human birth from the Virgin's
womb contradicts John's statement, "The Word became flesh," the Word that in eternity was with God
and that himself was God. If the Sonship is human,
and only human, "flesh," as John writes, then "the
glory" which he so emphasizes likewise becomes only
human and thus fades away. We dare not overlook
the fact that the mighty terms Logos, Life, Light,
which run through v. 1-14, are in the same class with
the terms that fill v. 14, Logos, Glory, Only-begotten,
Father, Grace and Truth, all of which reach back to
eternity, and all of them are so interlocked that not
one can be singled out and dated from some point in
time. When the Logos became flesh, and John with
the others came to see his glory, this was the glory of
the Logos — "the flesh" had no glory, save such as it
received from the Logos whose organ it became. The
objection that John beheld only the glory of the Logos
ἔνσαρκος not that of the Logos ἄσαρκος is specious. To be
sure, John did not see the unincarnate Logos. Yet
we know nothing about two different glories of the
Logos, his glory is only one. John and the others
beheld the *divine* glory of the Son as it shone forth
in his *divine* attributes manifested through the veil
of his human flesh and that flesh during the time
that it was in the state of humiliation. In due

time, in the day of exaltation, the absolute fulness
of this one glory would illumine also the flesh of the
Logos in heaven above.

The phrase παρὰ πατρός, "from the Father," literally,
"from beside," cannot be construed with μονογενής because of the verbal idea contained in the term, since
the Greek would use the genitive for this construction
or the preposition ἐκ, never παρά. Some combine
"Only-begotten from the Father" by inserting an idea
to match the preposition, "the Only-begotten *coming*
from beside the Father."   Aside from the fact that
prepositions contain no motion, this would be a superfluous idea, since the Only-begotten could come from
no one else, and we have already been assured in v.
1, 2, that he was with God. The phrase "from the
Father" is coordinate with "as of the Only-begotten,"
both equally modifying "glory." What these witnesses
beheld was "glory from the Father," a glory so great,
so truly divine, resulting from the eternal relation
of the Logos to the Father and thus shining forth in
the Incarnate Son. This was the *kabod Yaweh* revealed in the Old Testament in a variety of ways, because of which also the Son is called "the effulgence of
his glory, and the very image (impress) of his substance," Heb. 1:3.

The addition "full of grace and truth" has caused
some discussion because the apparent nominative
πλήρης seemed to depend on ὁ λόγος, thus forcing us to
assume the parenthesis indicated in the R. V., or compelling us to accept a violation of grammar by making
this supposed nominative depend either on the accusative δόξαν or on the genitive αὐτοῦ. The entire difficulty
is brushed away since the new grammars have demon-
strated that πλήρης is indeclinable. R. 1204 remarks:
"The papyri have taught us to be chary about charging John with being ungrammatical in πλήρης χάριτος
(John 1:14). These matters simply show that the

New Testament writers used a live language and were not automata." He adds: "It is doubtless true that no other writer used repetition of word and phrase as did the author of the Fourth Gospel, but no one will deny that he did it with consummate skill and marvelous vividness and dramatic power." We are thus perfectly free to regard πλήρης as a genitive modifying αὐτοῦ, or as an accusative modifying δόξαν. The former seems preferable as connecting this fulness of grace and truth directly with the person. Thus also "grace and truth" specify the attributes particularly meant by "glory."

When John writes "full" he means that all that was in him and shone forth from him was grace and truth. Once God proclaimed himself to Moses, "The Lord, the Lord God, merciful and gracious, longsuffering, and abundant in goodness and truth," Exod. 34:6. Now that the Son appeared in the flesh, the same fulness shone forth in him. There was no half measure, no fraction, but perfect completeness in every thought, word, and action. While grace and truth are especially named, this does not mean that other attributes of the Logos are excluded. These two, however, are central for our salvation. Like a stream they flow out to us poor sinners so that we may have, possess, and enjoy what they bring. "Grace" is undeserved favor. The term connotes sin and guilt on our part which this grace removes by pardon, justification, and adoption to childhood. The heart of this grace is the redemption in Christ Jesus. Grace bestows a free and unmerited gift, first the central gift of pardon, v. 12, and then all the abundance of gifts that follow pardon. Some identify grace with these gifts, but it is better to think of it as the attribute whence these gifts flow. "Truth" is linked with "grace," since the two are intertwined: grace in truth, and truth in grace. Truth is the saving light which John has mentioned repeatedly. The word ἀλήθεια means "reality," the reality itself as well as any statement of it in words. While the term is general, it is constantly used, as here joined with grace, to denote the saving realities in God and Christ Jesus. Thus the incarnate Logos is the full embodiment of saving truth, and his name thus is both Truth and Light. Again truth is the reality of God's will, his purpose and plan for our salvation, and every act of his in accord therewith. The threats and judgments of God and of Christ are also truth, and yet the term is most frequently used with reference to saving promises, every one of which is fulfilled to the uttermost. Both grace and truth intend to kindle, maintain, and increase faith and trust in our hearts. They shine forth, "that believing ye might have life through his name," 20:31. It is ungratefulness itself to be met with the fulness of grace and truth and to reply with unbelief.

15) For the great facts attested in v. 14, in corroboration of what John and his associates beheld in Christ, the testimony of the Baptist is now adduced in brief. For this reason John introduced the Baptist to his readers already in v. 6, 7, as one divinely sent to bear witness of the light. If some still thought too highly of the Baptist, they will certainly be impressed by the words which John quotes from his lips, words which he himself and his companions had heard the Baptist utter. So important is the Baptist's testimony that John presently presents it quite completely in its historical setting. Here only the pith of it is used as directly and pointedly substantiating the incarnation and the glory of the Only-begotten. Yet this brief introduction of the Baptist's testimony seems out of place to certain interpreters, who for this reason would either cancel v. 15 or transfer it to a different place, making v. 16 follow v. 14. But corroboration is always in place, as the writer may desire it to re-enforce

his own testimony, and doubly in place when this testimony deals with supernatural facts of the loftiest type. The texts are solidly for the genuineness of v. 15. **John bears witness concerning him and cries, saying, This was he of whom I said, He that comes after me is become before me, because he was first compared with me.**

The present tense μαρτυρεῖ is forceful, whether we regard it as dramatizing the past act of bearing witness, or take it that the evangelist's testimony is still sounding forth. The tense reads as if the evangelist still hears the Baptist speaking. The form κέκραγεν is the perfect; but this is one of a group of perfects which has lost the punctiliar part of the action and has retained only the notion of duration, hence must be translated with the present: "cries," or "goes on crying," R. 894, etc. The Baptist's testimony is public, delivered with a loud voice so that all may hear. Moreover, the Baptist himself states that he gave this testimony twice. The fact that he repeated it shows its great weight. Here the Baptist has ἦν, whereas in v. 30 he has ἐστίν. This is due to the attraction of thought exerted by εἶπον, which takes the speaker's mind into the past and disregards the fact that what he says is also true of the present. Similar ἦν appear in 3:23; 4:6; 10:41; 11:18. The circumstantial λέγων, "saying," "declaring," helps to mark the formal nature of the utterance now made. When the Baptist first made this utterance concerning Jesus we are unable to determine; some think it was said before Jesus' baptism and was solemnly repeated after the baptism, as is shown in v. 29-34.

The Baptist's testimony consists of three clauses: "He that comes after me — is become before me — because he was first compared with me." The first two clauses form the strongest kind of a paradox, they are like a riddle or an enigma. How can one who comes *behind* the Baptist have come *in front* of him? The adverbs of place ὀπίσω and ἔμπροσθεν are here used to indicate time. Hence: How can one who comes *later* than the Baptist have come *earlier* than he? The third clause furnishes the solution: He was *first* compared with me. We begin with the solution: ὅτι πρῶτός μου ἦν. The enigma turns on two points of time, only one of which seems possible, and yet both are declared to be actual. The solution must, therefore, also deal with time. In other words, πρῶτός μου, with its genitive of comparison, cannot denote rank. This would be out of line entirely, failing to solve the enigma and clashing with half of it, since great personages are ushered in and preceded by those of lesser rank or by their servants, and not the reverse. While the superlative πρῶτος has crowded out the comparative πρότερος when only two are being compared, this does not affect the solution of the problem. More important is the verb ἦν, which reaches back indefinitely, like the four ἦν in v. 1, 2. The solution, then, lies in the pre-existence of the person to whom the Baptist points as being present before him and his hearers, namely Jesus. That this pre-existence also involves the highest superiority in rank goes without saying and is a self-evident deduction. Yet rank is not the key to the solution of the problem. This pre-existence, to which the Baptist testified so emphatically, perfectly corroborates the evangelist's statement that the Logos became flesh and that he possessed the divine glory of the Only-begotten.

The objection has been raised that the knowledge of the pre-existence of Christ was beyond the experience of the Baptist. The evangelist is charged with putting his own ideas into the mouth of the Baptist. The same is done with regard to many of the great utterances of Christ himself. The very strangeness of the Baptist's utterance is unique. It is couched in a form that the Jews liked and because of its very form is easily remembered. The stress which the evangelist puts upon this testimony of the Baptist, both here and in v. 29-33, shows that this remarkable testimony is genuine. The Baptist uttered not only this testimony but all his preaching by revelation as one who was sent and commissioned by God. If this testimony of his is manufactured and false, then all else that is recorded of him is equally spurious, he himself becomes a figment, and the sacred records which have invented him are unreliable throughout. Even the prophets knew what the Baptist embodied in his striking saying, for they spoke and wrote by the same revelation, Isa. 9:6; Micah 5:2; Mal. 3:1; Dan. 7:13; etc.

Christ's pre-existence makes plain how one and the same person could come later than the Baptist and yet have come earlier than he; could be both his successor and his predecessor. We must note that the substantivized participle ὁ ἐρχόμενος is a standard designation for the promised Messiah. While Jesus was born about six months later than the Baptist, and the paradox would be true if this point is considered, the "coming" of which the Baptist speaks is that of entering upon his appointed office as the Messiah. Jesus assumed his office later than the Baptist, for the latter ushered him into that office by baptizing him. And yet this wonderful person also preceded the Baptist; ἔμπροσθέν μου γέγονεν. This verb, when used with an adverb of place, has the sense of "come," (hin)kommen, gehen, as in 6:25. As in v. 6, the verb speaks of appearance, hervortreten, being in action. The perfect tense is especially important, reaching back, as it does, indefinitely into the past, whereas the aorist ἐγένετο would indicate only a fixed period in the past. For we must note that in the solution of the paradox this γέγονεν merges into ἦν (has been coming before me; for he *was* first compared with me). These two tenses should not be restricted to the Old Testament era and to the presence and the operation of the Logos during that time but should be understood in the sense of Micah 5:2, "whose goings forth have been from of old, from everlasting." The Baptist's paradox deals with the mystery of the incarnation. Like the evangelist and like all of the Scriptures he shows us the eternal Son of God who became flesh, dwelt among us, and manifested forth his glory. The relation of this Son to the Father goes back to all eternity; that of the evangelist, the apostles, the prophets, and all men of God begins in time. Those who reject the *Zweinaturenlehre,* or by a kenosis empty the Logos of his divine attributes, or who make Jesus divine only morally thus reject the solution of the Baptist's paradox instead of solving it.

16) The old church made v. 16 a part of the Baptist's statement, so that "we all" in the Baptist's word would mean himself and the ancient prophets. But this cannot be correct. The Baptist's paradox and his solution stand out as something complete in itself. Then also ἡμεῖς πάντες plainly refers back to v. 14: ἐν ἡμῖν and ἐθεασάμεθα. **For of his fulness we all received, and grace for grace,** takes up the thought of v. 14 and thus continues the evangelist's own testimony. V. 15 is inserted only as a most effective corroboration. That, too, is why John uses ὅτι and not καί as the connective. The latter would coordinate with v. 15; but v. 16 is not coordinate with v. 15, unless in v. 16 the Baptist is still speaking. "Fulness" and "grace" evidently take up the corresponding terms in v. 14, and "we all received" evidently advances the thought started by "we beheld" in v. 14. Thus ὅτι intends to establish more completely what v. 14 contains and what v. 15 has corroborated in an objective way. In a way, the fact that the Word became flesh, that the

Baptist's successor, Jesus, was his predecessor in the indefinite past, needs no subjective proof. And yet it is bound to have also this kind of proof. There would be eyes to see the glory of this Person, glory as of the Only-begotten, glory as from the Father, showing him to be full of grace and truth. And this seeing and beholding would not be only an external view, it would be connected with an internal receiving, a personal and abiding enrichment.

"Of his fulness" or "from his fulness," ἐκ, takes up the adjective "full" ,in v. 14. No modifier is needed with "fulness," for we already know that this consists of "grace and truth." Col. 1:19, "For it pleased the Father that in him should all fulness dwell." This is the "riches" of the Lamb, Rev. 5:12; "the unsearchable riches of Christ" which Paul was counted worthy to preach to the Gentiles, Eph. 3:8; "the riches of his grace," Eph. 1:7. Luther pictures the inexhaustible nature of this fulness: "This spring is inexhaustible, it is full of grace and truth from God, it never loses anything, no matter how much we draw, but remains an infinite fountain of all grace and truth; the more you draw from it, the more abundantly it gives of the water that springs into eternal life. Just as the sun is not darkened by the whole world enjoying its light, and could, indeed, light up ten worlds; just as 100,000 lights might be lit from one light and not detract from it; just as a learned man is able to make a thousand others learned, and the more he gives, the more he has — so is Christ, our Lord, an infinite source of all grace, so that if the whole world would draw enough grace and truth from it to make the world all angels, yet it would not lose a drop; the fountain always runs over, full of grace."

The terseness of the phrase "out of his fulness" is matched by the terseness of "we all received." By adding no object for the verb the contrast between the fulness and the receiving is enhanced. "We" have nothing — Christ has the inexhaustible abundance. He is the Giver — we are the recipients, and that is all that we are or could be. It was so in the case of John and his fellow-witnesses who directly beheld the Savior and are the persons included in "we all"; and it is so still in our case who now behold the Savior in the inspired testimony of these original witnesses. The verb λαμβάνω has an active sense, "to take"; but it is used throughout, whenever our relation to Christ, to God, or to the Spirit of God is mentioned, without a hint of meritorious activity on our part. God's gift, offer, call, etc., always come first and not only make possible our receiving but induce, effect this receiving. So we take, as a poor, helpless patient takes the medicine put to his lips by the physician; as the blind mendicant takes the coin dropped into his hand by the charitable giver; as the eye takes in the sunbeam falling from on high, or the sound that strikes its membrane; yea, as the dead Lazarus takes the life conveyed to him by the word of him who is the resurrection and the life. This is especially true of our first taking or receiving from Christ. But even when the gift and the grace of Christ have filled us with faith, so that we ourselves come to him for replenishment and ourselves beg for his saving gifts, this very energy and activity of coming and seeking is a gift of his to us, namely the constant drawing which his fulness exerts upon us and any measure of faith that we may have. Thus in its fullest sense it is true: "What hast thou that thou didst not receive? Now if thou didst receive it, why dost thou glory, as if thou hadst not received it?" I Cor. 4:7. And the Baptist himself said, "A man can receive nothing, except it be given him from heaven," John 3:23.

The connective καί in "*and* grace for grace" marks "an explanatory addition," "epexegetic or explicative,"

R. 1181. The preposition ἀντί denotes exchange. "As
the days come and go a new supply takes the place of
the grace already bestowed, as wave follows wave
upon the shore. Grace answers to (ἀντί) grace," R. 574.
Hence "grace for grace" is not the grace of the New
Testament for that of the Old; not ordinary grace
followed by charismatic grace; not merely one individual gift of grace followed by another individual
gift — but grace ever new and greater. One measure
of it assures another. It is like a stream flowing constantly; every day, every hour its banks are full, ever
fresh volumes coming down from above, so that no
longing for grace in our hearts is left without immediate and complete supply. We may specify justification, peace with God, consolation, joy, enlightenment,
love, hope, etc., Rom. 5; Gal. 5:22; Eph. 5:9. Grace
for grace is according to the divine rule, "Whosoever
hath, to him shall be given, and he shall have more
abundance," Matt. 13:12. This doubling of the word
"grace" reveals what is meant by "his fulness" and
casts a wonderful light upon our receiving. "Are there
sinners here? Certainly, many. But here, too, is the
malefactor's grace for the sinner's heart, and it
cleanses and saves. Are there sorrowing and heavy
hearts here? Lay down your bundle of cares, take
instead grace for grace. Are there poor people here?
Here is he who by his poverty makes us rich. Nothing but his grace makes us rich amid all outward
poverty, consoles us amid all sadness, strengthens us
in all our weakness, gives us the power of life and the
fulness of life." Schoener who writes once more:
"Grace is a treasure to which none others can be compared. Carry together all the treasures of earth, and
all together they will not balance what lies in the one
word grace. Grace is the blood-red mark which cancels the handwriting against us; the star of hope
which sends its rays into this earth-life darkened by

sin; the ladder which leads us upward; the immovable pillar which shall stand, though hills and mountains pass away, and shall support the covenant of peace; the staff to which we can cling in our weakness; the guide who leads us safely through sorrow and death into the open portals of eternal blessedness."

The concept χάρις has already been defined in v. 14. We may add that "grace" is the effective manifestation of God's undeserved love toward sinful men, offering to all the salvation obtained by Christ, by this offer working faith to accept it, justifying us without any merit of our own, sanctifying and glorifying us. Grace is the chief characteristic of the entire gospel of Christ, of the entire Christian religion, the center of the mystery, unknown to the world, revealed in Jesus Christ. The fact that in emphasizing "grace" John has by no means forgotten "truth," which he added in v. 14, is shown by v. 17.

17) The ὅτι in v. 16 answers the question, why John could in v. 14 say, "we beheld." It is because "we actually received." The ὅτι in v. 17 goes deeper, from the subjective reception to the objective coming into being of what was received. Here the question is, why John could say both "we beheld" and "we received." It is because grace and truth came through Jesus Christ. To enhance the great historic fact thus offered as a reason a comparison is made between the two mediators (διά), the human and the divine, Moses and Jesus Christ. **For the law was given through Moses; grace and truth came through Jesus Christ.** A threefold antithesis is brought out in this double statement: 1) the law — grace and truth; 2) was given — came; 3) Moses — Jesus Christ. The three pairs are opposites but opposites that correspond. One likeness is included, namely the idea of mediation in διά, which is used with respect to both Moses and Jesus

Christ.   The form is that of the Hebrew *parallelismus membrorum*.

"The law," ὁ νόμος (with the article), is definite, the moral and the ceremonial law as Israel had it on the tables of stone and in its elaborate worship and in its civil and social regulations.   This law was no mean treasure; by possessing it Israel was greatly blessed. Yet it was not the actual "fulness" from which one could receive grace for grace.   The law was only preparatory.   It revealed the holy will of God and thus man's exceeding sinfulness and the depth of our lost condition.   At the same time we must add that the law was full of types and figures of deliverance from sin, and it even mediated a deliverance but one based on the great atonement that was to come.   Of course, the law itself thus indicated that everything depended on that future perfect atonement.   The law itself contained no availing atonement, it could only point forward, awaken the longing for it, picture and foreshadow it in advance, and, like a παιδαγογός, lead to it. *Lex iram parans et umbram habens,* Bengel. The law was much, but more had to follow even to make the law what it was.

It "was given," ἐδόθη, is a historical aorist.   God gave it, and it came wholly as a gift, although remnants and traces of the holy will of God were still found in human hearts.   The Israelites esteemed the law as a divine gift even when they failed to see its relation to the gospel.   It "was given" expresses exactly the historical manner of its bestowal.   It was not a human development, an outgrowth of the religious genius of the people of Israel, or a product of its great leader or of a number of its leaders (Moses and the prophets.)   This speculative idea of modern students of history is contradicted by our evangelist. In spite of all evolutionary ideas the sober fact remains that no human wisdom, genius, or development could possibly produce "the law" either in Israel or in any other nation since Israel's time, this wonderful system, every feature of which points beyond all human calculation, into the far future, to the coming Messiah, the Word made flesh and his redemptive work for all the world.

The law was given "through Moses"; διά after the passive verb plainly indicates that Moses was only God's instrument. God could easily have used any one of a number of similar instruments. We know how God used Moses to receive the two tables of stone, to construct the tabernacle and all it contained after the pattern shown him on the mount, and to inaugurate the entire worship under the law as directed by God. Moses was not the law, as Christ is grace and truth; he was only its minister and servant, as much under it, subject to it, taught by it, blessed by it as were the people to whom he ministered. With Christ, as regards grace and truth, quite the reverse is true.

"Grace and truth" are the same as in v. 14, each marked as such by the article of previous reference, each thus also marked as distinct from the other. While they are distinct, the two are most intimately joined, for grace is proclaimed by truth, and truth is the revelation and the doctrine of grace. Both have already been defined in v. 14. We may add that for us both are objective, for of both John writes that they "came," ἐγένετο. So also in v. 14 it is the incarnate Logos who is full of grace and truth. Yet both are intended for our subjective appropriation. That is why the two "came." And when it is thus appropriated, grace always forgives and gives, and truth reveals and assures both the forgiveness and the gifts.

The verb ἐγένετο is used like γέγονεν in v. 15, grace and truth "came." Here again the choice of words

evidences the guidance of Inspiration. Grace and truth
"came"; they were not "given" like the law. No Giver
used a human instrument and made grace and truth a
gift. These two are too great and high. They are in
their root divine attributes. Thus they were embodied
in Jesus Christ, they "came" in his incarnation and
his mission. God did not merely tell us about grace
and truth, so that he could have used another Moses
or an array of prophets. Jesus himself was grace and
truth. His own person and his work constitute the
very substance of grace and truth. The Lord who
passed before Moses, "abundant in goodness and
truth," Exod. 34:6, whom the Psalmist praised, "The
Lord is good; his mercy is everlasting, and his truth
endureth to all generations," Ps. 100:5, he it is "who
of God is made unto us wisdom, and righteousness,
and sanctification, and redemption," I Cor. 1:30 in the
incarnate Son, Christ Jesus. Yet grace and truth
"came" thus not in an absolute sense as though now
for the first time they sprang into existence but relatively as far as the actual work of redemption and
its historical execution are concerned after existing for
a long time in the thought of God and after being conveyed to men by promise.

Not until this place does John mention the historic
name of the incarnate Logos, the name that is above
every name: grace and truth came "through Jesus
Christ." What a glory is shed over it in all that John
has said before! It is like the sun rising in the east
and lighting up all the earth with its diffused light
while films of clouds still spread before it until suddenly it breaks through, and we see the great majestic
light itself. "Jesus" is the name of the person,
"Christ" or Messiah is a designation of the office. But
here διά is not used with a passive verb, hence it does
not introduce an instrument or a tool as a medium.
This διά is as lofty as the verb of being which it

modifies. He who himself is grace and truth mediates these attributes and all that they effect and bestow.

18) The line of thought from v. 14 onward is quite straight; the incarnate coming of the Word who is the Only-begotten, attested as pre-existent by the Baptist. Being full of grace and truth, we received from him grace for grace, for, as compared with Moses, grace and truth actually came by him, in fact, could come by him alone, who being the Only-begotten in the bosom of his Father alone could bring us the ultimate revelation. In particular, v. 18 expounds the ἐγένετο of v. 17 and helps to show how the Logos "came." V. 14 shows how he arrived, he was born in Bethlehem; v. 18 shows whence he arrived and thus how he could bring what he brought. In form v. 18 is an advanced parallel to v. 17, each with a negative and with a positive part. The advance is from the gifts (law, grace, and truth) to the source of these gifts (the law not requiring the sight of God, grace and truth requiring even more, that the bringer be even in the bosom of the Father). Because v. 17 and 18 are such parallels, therefore v. 18 is simply set beside v. 17 and has no connective word. **No man hath seen God at any time; God Only-begotten, who is in the bosom of the Father, he did declare him.**

The emphasis is on "God," "*God* no one hath seen at any time" no matter whom or what else he may have seen. The absence of the article with Θεόν has no special significance, the word itself means "God" in his actual being as distinguished from the theophanies when God assumed certain mediums for appearing unto men. The verb ὁράω means simply "to see" with the eye and thus denies even this much in regard to God: no man ever *even saw* him, to speak of nothing more. This, of course, is in contrast with the Logos who not only saw God but was in the bosom of his

Father. John uses many perfect tenses, all of which are highly expressive. Here he has ἐώρακε, which with πώποτε, "hath seen at any time," is an extensive perfect, R. 893, but of broken continuity, R. 896, 906 : . . . > . . . ; meaning that in all the extent of the past no one ever at this or at that moment had a glimpse of God. The denial is general and absolute, including Moses as a matter of course: but also all others whoever they may be. In Exod. 33:11 the Lord, indeed, spoke to Moses "face to face." "Face to face" = "mouth to mouth," Num. 12:8, and thus does not imply that Moses *saw* the face of God. God communicated with Moses in the most direct way, and in the directness of this communication Moses excelled all others save Christ, though God never appeared even to Moses *in solida sua gloria* (Calov). Luther says, the Lord showed Moses his back and mantle; "thus Moses saw the mercy of God from behind as in the divine Word."

Against this strong background of negation is placed the still stronger affirmation that the Word made flesh has more than seen God. The question of the true reading is no longer in doubt. It is μονογενὴς Θεός and not ὁ μονογενὴς υἱός, nor ὁ μονογενής without a substantive. The article in the variant ὁ μονογενὴς Θεός would even be misleading as indicating that there are several Θεοί, one of whom is Only-begotten. The absence of the article bids us stress the qualitative force of the terms, and the adjective μονογενής is attributive, R. 856. We have already rejected the interpretation that "Only-begotten" refers to the human conception in the womb of the Virgin, and that only in this human sense the Logos became the Only-begotten. Here the addition Θεός makes this certain beyond question. "*God* Only-begotten" cannot date from a point in the course of time, for this would be a contradiction in the very terms, the one term "God" being timeless, eternal, the other term "Only-begotten" being 1900 years old. "God Only-begotten" is such from all eternity, and the adjective predicates the inner Trinitarian mystery of the *generatio aeterna,* describing the eternal metaphysical relation of the Father and the Son. The objections raised against this evident sense are futile. The chief one is that John speaks of the revealed Savior, hence he says nothing about the relation of the divine persons. The simple truth is that John is revealing to us who Jesus Christ really was: the Logos, true God, begotten of the Father from eternity. He reveals this much, though it exceeds our finite powers of comprehension, because we must know at least this much, i. e., the fact thus stated, in order properly to understand and value what the Logos has done. The objection based on the glory (v. 14) of the Only-begotten, that this is only the glory of his personal revelation, dating only from the incarnation and embodied in the incarnation, is answered by the simple fact that this was no human glory, however great it may be made, but the divine glory, the manifestation of the divine nature of the Logos. Many of the German theologians who thus lower the term "Only-begotten" still hold that Jesus was the pre-existent Logos and thus in the true sense Θεός, but others have gone much farther. The breach made by removing eternity from "Only-begotten" is widened. By way of the kenosis Jesus loses also all that lies in the concept Θεός. He has now only "one nature," the *Zweinaturenlehre* is a relic of the past. We have only a divine man, differing only in degree from other godly men, a beautiful ethical example and no more. This ends with the statement that we have lost nothing in regard to Jesus, yea, have gained ever so much, for is not Jesus hereby brought much nearer to us?

At this point John goes beyond "Only-begotten" which he has here added to the Logos as being "God."

He pours out the fullest measure of revelation: God
Only-begotten "who is in the bosom of the Father."
The interpretation of this participial clause is misdirected when "Only-begotten" is made temporal
instead of eternal. The present participle ὤν is timeless as Luther already perceived: "is — ever and
ever is." It is thus more than if John had written
ὅς ἦν, "who was," for this would only reach backward;
also better than ὅς ἐστι, which would sound like a statement merely about the present when John was writing.
The participle expresses only durative being and thus
more easily becomes timeless. The article ὁ ὤν does
only one thing: it attaches the participle to "God Only-
begotten" after the manner of a relative clause and
describes this wonderful person for us. In no way
does the article change or limit the timeless force of
the participle. This would, indeed, be greatly changed
if "God Only-begotten" dates only from the Virgin
birth, for then any further modifier would be equally
limited. Without the article the participle, though it
is separated from the main verb by ἐκεῖνος, would tend
to become adverbial, either temporal, "when he was in
the bosom," or causal, "since he was in the bosom";
and thus instead of the timelessness we should have
the mere historical time indicated by the constative
(R. 829) aorist ἐξηγήσατο. These are the assured grammatical facts regarding ὁ ὤν, which we should not
yield when they are modified in the interest of a
wrong view of the person who is truly "God Only-
begotten."

The view of the ancient church was that ὁ ὤν extended back from the time when Christ appeared on
earth, back to all eternity. Since the present participle may stand also for the imperfect tense, this
view has some justification grammatically. So understood, this participle would resemble the repeated ἦν
in v. 1, 2. While thus the participle would predicate

nothing concerning Christ since the time of his earthly appearance, by an easy inference at least we should be able to conclude that Christ as "God Only-begotten" is also now and, indeed, is forever in the Father's bosom. So the ancient interpretation can hardly be called wrong. The objection that the being with God of the Logos in v. 1 and his being in the world in v. 10 are exclusive opposites is untenable; these two do not exclude each other, for the second is an addition to the other, even as the title "the Word" in v. 1 already points to the revelation to be made to the world in v. 10. A second view that Christ was in the bosom of the Father only during his earthly life is shut out by the very language and is usually understood to mean only an intimate communion of the man Jesus with his God, which negatives "God Only-begotten." The view that Christ is in the bosom of his Father only since his exaltation to heaven clashes with the very point at issue in v. 18, which is how and why Christ could perfectly declare God to us *before* his exaltation.

It is surprising that in spite of all the information available through the recently discovered mass of ostraca and papyri, presented in all the newer grammars, for instance, also by R. 535, 586, and 591, etc., at some length, any recent first-class exegete and linguist should still insist that with ὤν we must regard εἰς as distinct from ἐν, as denoting a movement toward the Father's bosom ending with rest in that bosom. This is the old explanation of the use of εἰς with static verbs and verbs of being and was made when the Koine was not understood on this and on many other points. Let the student read the entire story of the rise of εἰς after ἐν had the field alone; how εἰς first divided the field with ἐν by taking over all the verbs of motion; how εἰς then began its invasion of the territory of ἐν, namely by starting to be used with verbs of being and condition, just as we see this in the New

Testament, with a case right here in ὤν εἰς; and how this use went on until in the modern Greek vernacular ἐν is dead and εἰς rules. We must translate, "*in* the bosom" just as if ἐν were used and not εἰς. The preposition denotes place, and since persons are referred to, it denotes their union and communion, whereas πρός in v. 1 and 3 denotes reciprocity The term κόλπος is figurative and brings out the idea of greatest possible intimacy. God Only-begotten and the Father could not be in closer union. They do not only "see" each other, "know" or "speak with each other"; they are in each other's embrace. This is only one step removed from the word of Jesus himself when he says that he and the Father are one.

Hitherto John has written "God" and "the Logos" when distinguishing the two persons, though at once he also called the latter "God." Here he writes "the Father" and "God Only-begotten," by the former making fully clear in what sense "Only-begotten" is to be understood. This thus is the first instance in which the word "Father" is used distinctively with regard to "the Son" to express a relation that is far superior to that which we have in mind when we speak of the Father and regard ourselves as "God's children," v. 12, or as "God's sons," Gal. 3:26; 4:6, 7. Jesus never unites himself with us by saying "our Father." When he says "my Father" he distinguishes himself, the essential Son, from all others who are only adopted sons. This is made evident with greatest clearness in 20:17, "I ascend unto *my* Father and *your* Father, and *my* God and *your* God." It will not do, then, to see in this distinctive term "Father" only the character and the scope of what Christ revealed to us, that in a sense God is truly *our* Father, or that he is Christ's Father by virtue of the incarnation. "God Only-begotten" and "the Father" are the correlatives of the Son by virtue of their eternal relation through the *generatio aeterna*. And this relation is immutable, grounded in the divine essence itself, unaffected by the incarnation, though our human reason is able to fathom neither the unincarnate nor the incarnate side of it.

The wonderful person thus described to us can, indeed, and did, indeed, bring us the ultimate revelation, "he did declare him." The demonstrative ἐκεῖνος is resumptive and emphatic, taking up "God Only-begotten" together with the appended relative clause, R. 707 and 708. The verb ἐξηγήσατο is choice and impressive and is not used otherwise by the evangelist. It goes far beyond what any man could do, assuming even that it were possible for him to see God and then to tell us what he had seen. The tense is the historical aorist, summing up all that Jesus "did declare" concerning God not only by his words and his deeds but also by his very coming and the presence of his person. The Logos is the supreme exegete, the absolute interpreter of God. The verb means more than *erzaehlen,* "to narrate or tell"; it means "to expound" or "set forth completely." The Greek is able to dispense with an object, but the English cannot imitate this brevity. So some supply "it," which is too weak and means too little; others, what he beheld while being with God, which is well enough in substance but too long in form; "him" is best of all. "Christ did not receive the revelation in time, like the Old Testament prophets, by means of the inspiration of the spirit of God, passing it on to others; he is himself the eternal Logos and the essential truth. He made known on earth what he beheld with the Father and heard from the Father as the Son of God before the foundation of the world, John 3:32; 6:46; 8:26, 38, 40; 12:50 (compare the analogous expression concerning the Holy Ghost, 16:13). And this which he received and obtained not merely in time but beheld

and heard before his incarnation in eternity he sees
and hears also continuously as man, since it is an
eternal seeing and hearing and not subject to the
change of time. For as we have already learned, he
is the exegete of the Father, as the one who *is* in
the bosom of the Father, and he knoweth the Father,
as the Father knoweth him, John 8:55; 10:15. And
as he knows the Father, so he knows also men, his
brethren." Philippi, *Glaubenslehre*, IV, 1, 443. Thus
also the last word ἐκεῖνος ἐξηγήσατο re-echoes and joins
again the first word ὁ λόγος: The Word — *he* did
declare. And this ushers in the historical account,
setting down for us what "he did declare."

CHAPTER I — Continued

THE ATTESTATION OF JESUS CHRIST AS THE SON OF GOD IN HIS PUBLIC MINISTRY
1:19-12:50

I

The Opening Attestation as his Ministry Begins, 1:19-2:11

The sections here grouped together evidently constitute the first great chapter in the body of the book. The sections are all linked together with references to time: v. 29 — 35 — 43 — 2:1. This group of events marks those occurring on four successive days and another that happened three days later, thus coming to pass in one week of just seven days. Jesus emerges from the quiet life in Nazareth and now takes up his public ministry. We may divide into two parts: The Baptist's Attestation of Christ as the Son of God, 1:19-42; The First Testimony of Jesus Himself, 1:43-2:11.

The Attestation of the Baptist, 1:19-42. — All four evangelists begin their accounts of the Messianic ministry of Jesus with a reference to the appearance and the activity of John the Baptist as the promised herald who was to prepare the Messiah's way. John's Gospel, however, takes the general history of the Baptist for granted; his Christian readers have it in the earlier Gospels. John is satisfied to use only the specific testimony which the Baptist gave to Jesus as the Messiah and Son of God. The other details of the Baptist's preaching John passes by as not being pertinent to

(103)

his theme. He selects the most notable testimony offered by the Baptist on three consecutive days: 1) before the commissions sent to him from Jerusalem; 2) before his own disciples; 3) before two of his disciples who then follow Jesus. The three episodes are exact, detailed, and circumstantial, recorded in a way which indicates the indelible impression made upon the heart of the writer, changing his entire life most completely. Here began the faith of the first believers in Jesus, and thus Christian faith, in the specific sense, in general.

19) **And this is the witness of John when the Jews from Jerusalem sent to him priests and Levites, in order to inquire of him, Who art thou? And he confessed and denied not; and he confessed, I am not the Christ.** To begin an entirely new section, in fact, the body of John's Gospel with καί is Hebraistic, entire books and many independent parts of books beginning with *vav*, "and." This eliminates the idea that "and" here intends to connect with v. 15 as though the summary testimony of the Baptist introduced in v. 15 is now to be furnished in detail. A close reading of the entire paragraph, v. 19-28, shows that this paragraph deals with a different time and a different occasion entirely. It is the next paragraph, v. 29-34, which tells the story of the testimony quoted in v. 15. If this introductory καί could connect with anything preceding, we should choose v. 7, where the Baptist is introduced as the witness, connected with which we would be told how he gave this witness. But this καί is merely formal and connects with nothing. As such it not only belongs to the entire sentence, including the ὅτε clause, but is even repeated at the head of v. 20. This repeated καί at the head of v. 20 is often ignored, yet it is just as prominent as its original at the head of v. 19. This second καί also bars out the suggestion that καὶ αὕτη ἐστὶν ἡ μαρτυρία τοῦ Ἰωάνου forms

a kind of heading for the three paragraphs which follow, "And this is the witness of John." A new sentence would then begin with ὅτε, "When the Jews . . . , he confessed," etc. John, however, wrote, "*and* he confessed," etc.

Without further ceremony we are introduced to the Baptist at the very height of his ministry and his influence. Not a word is added describing the Baptist's person and his appearance, his mode of life in the desert, his message in general, and his Baptism. We are supposed to know in advance also how the excitement grew to huge proportions among the people until they flocked in thousands to the lonely desert region, and until even the central authorities of the nation at Jerusalem felt constrained by the volume and the character of the reports to send out an official committee to make a firsthand investigation. The evangelist at once places us at the dramatic moment when before the gathered multitudes out in the wilderness this official committee faced the Baptist and received his telling answers to their questions. The evangelist was there, saw and heard it all and has left to us the record of what occurred. We see that for him the Baptist's μαρτυρία is the essential thing. All else his readers may gather from the other evangelists; this "witness" indeed, is also recorded by them, yet our evangelist wishes to make full use of its great weight in this new Gospel which is to record the attestation that Jesus is the Son of God.

"The Jews," οἱ Ἰουδαῖοι, first meant the members of the tribe of Judah. After the exile when Judah and Benjamin returned, the nation as such was called "the Jews," and the term "Israel" or "the Israelites" marked its religious character. John uses the term in this general sense, but as the narrative proceeds often with the note of hostility to Jesus. In certain contexts "the Jews" reads like "the enemies of Christ" although this is due to what must be reported concerning them. Just what persons are in each instance intended by the term the context makes plain. In this first mention "the Jews from Jerusalem" are evidently the Jewish authorities, namely the Sanhedrin, consisting of ἀρχιερεῖς, γραμματεῖς, and πρεσβύτεροι, high priests, scribes, and elders, who had their seat in the Holy City. It is perfectly in order to use "the Jews" when the Sanhedrin is referred to, for this ruling body was the highest legal representative of the nation; its findings and decisions counted for the nation as such. We, of course, must assume that the movement produced by the Baptist had stirred the Sanhedrin into action, in particular the surmises and reports that this man might be the long expected Messiah. To make an official firsthand investigation was not only within the province of the Sanhedrin, it was really obligatory for this authoritative body to investigate and then to take such action as the case might warrant. The matter of a false Messiah, inflaming the people to fanatical action, might prove a very serious thing. So the commission is sent. The phrase "from Jerusalem," as its position shows, is not to be construed with the verb, as the English versions have translated it, but with the noun, "the Jews from Jerusalem." We note two forms for "Jerusalem," the indeclinable feminine Ἱερουσαλήμ (LXX), which merely transliterates the Hebrew, and the neuter plural Ἱεροσόλυμα, which has more of a Greek dress.

The commission consisted of ἱερεῖς καὶ Λευῖται. The former were common priests not ἀρχιερεῖς, high priests, a term which includes the reigning high priest and those who had held the office before him or belonged to his family. John uses ἱερεῖς only in this one instance. The Levites, members of the tribe of Levi, performed the menial and the police work in the Temple and in the latter capacity were marshalled under the στρατηγὸς τοῦ ἱεροῦ, the Temple captain with his lieutenants. A detachment of Levites was sent along with the committee of priests first, on account of the dangers of the road from Jerusalem to the Jordan wilderness and, secondly, to lend a more official character to the committee of priests when it appeared among the great multitudes that were gathered about the Baptist. The verb ἐρωτάω used in the purpose clause refers to a formal and a dignified inquiry and hence reflects the importance which even the Sanhedrin accorded the Baptist, "in order to inquire of him"; the translation "to ask" in our versions is too light.

The narrative is compressed, for what this committee was to inquire and what it did inquire when it arrived on the scene is combined. The actual question: Σὺ τίς εἶ; is retained as the object of ἐρωτήσωσιν in the purpose clause. The question itself cannot be considered as hostile or even inquisitorial, although it is legally formal and betrays no trace of longing or desire either on the part of the Sanhedrin or on the part of its committee. The emphasis is on σύ, *"Thou, who art thou?"* The Baptist was proclaiming the coming of the Messianic kingdom and was baptizing great multitudes as a preparation for this kingdom. Now Deut. 18:21, etc., implies that Israel should examine and test any prophet who might thus appear. Naturally, the Sanhedrin would act as the executive of the nation in the matter.

20) The striking feature is the elaborate way in which John introduces the Baptist's reply, "And he confessed and denied not; and he confessed" — positive — negative — then again positive. Why this apparant redundancy? Not for one moment could we entertain the suggestion that this question contained a temptation for the Baptist to make himself more than he actually was, to play, at least in his mind, with the thought that he himself might be or might become

the Messiah. The entire character of the Baptist, every act and word of his, bars out the idea that either now or at any time he felt tempted in this direction. No; this elaborate preamble reflects not the Baptist's state of mind but that of the evangelist. It is as if John would say, "I myself heard him confess and not for one instant deny — and this is what he confessed." The Baptist answered readily enough, but the evangelist intends that we, like himself, shall feel the full weight of the testimony that this answer contained. This, too, is why he uses these verbs "to confess" and "to deny" instead of the ordinary "to reply," which is all that is needed to match "to inquire." The Baptist's reply was more than a reply, it was a full, complete, clear-cut confession; it withheld nothing, hence had no trace of denial. This solemn preamble thus introduces all that the Baptist said in the entire dialog that follows and not merely the first brief word, "I am not the Christ."

The evangelist retains the direct dramatic form of the original scene, indicating that he writes as an eye and ear witness. We shall meet this vivid directness again and again in our Gospel. Those who deny John's authorship ignore or minimize this strong feature or explain it away by making the supposed author play the part of a novelist-historian who invents his own scenes and paints in the details from his own imagination. The Baptist might have answered the question addressed to him in a positive form by stating his name, parentage, and divine commission. Instead of this he answers the implication that lies in the question and thus from the start meets it squarely and directly. In all his proclamation to the people he had said nothing about himself. He himself was only a minor figure, one who came to point to Another far greater than himself, which all who heard him could have no difficulty in perceiving. When he is now asked directly who he himself really is, he replies in the same way, pointing away from himself to this Greater One. That is what makes his reply a confession (v. 20) and a testimony (v. 19).

After the ὅτι recitativum, which is the equivalent of our quotation marks, the oldest texts read: Ἐγὼ οὐκ εἰμὶ ὁ Χριστός and place ἐγώ forward to match the emphatic forward σύ of the question; later texts read: Οὐκ εἰμὶ ἐγὼ ὁ Χριστός. *"Thou, who art thou?"* *"I,* I am not the Christ," since this is really what you wish to know. The emphatic ἐγώ is proper where there is a contrast with another person. Ὁ Χριστός with the article is appellative, "the Anointed One," whoever this may be. In v. 17 "Jesus Christ" names the specific person. This prompt and pointed denial when the question itself was not, *"Thou,* art thou the Christ?" indicates that the rumor was abroad crediting the Baptist with being the promised Messiah, the Christ. One thing is certain, the Baptist himself had given no occasion for such a rumor. It sprang from the general expectation that was abroad, from the intensification this expectation received through the Baptist's preaching and work, and from the imagination that went beyond the bounds of the Baptist's own words.

21) Sent by the supreme authorities to probe the matter to the bottom, the spokesman of the committee, speaking for all, makes further inquiry. **And they inquired of him, What then? Art thou Elijah? And he says, I am not. Art thou the prophet? And he replied, No.** The second question with οὖν builds on the Baptist's answer, "What then?" i. e., if thou art not the Christ, and is at once followed by a more specific question, "Art thou Elijah?" Whether σύ is placed at the head or at the end of this question makes little difference, as in either place it would carry emphasis. The question itself rests on Mal. 3:23 (in

the English and the German versions Mal. 4:5) as understood by the rabbis regarding the return of Elijah in person to prepare the Messianic kingdom. Perhaps something in the stern preaching of repentance by the Baptist, aided by his austere dress and mode of life, may have prompted the surmise that this rabbinic expectation was fulfilled and that the Baptist actually was Elijah returned to life. In this sense the Baptist utters his denial: οὐκ εἰμί, "I am not," omitting any pointed ἐγώ, which would add the wrong implication: *I* am not, but *another* is or will be. The Baptist's denial, therefore, does not clash with what was promised regarding him in Luke 1:17, and with what Jesus afterward said of him in Matt. 11:14; 17:11, three statements which correctly interpret Malachi.

Without connecting words, as in drama, the third question follows with its briefest answer, "Art thou the prophet?" and we must note the article in the Greek: ὁ προφήτης, hence not "a prophet" (Luther) but *"the"* specific prophet, the one mentioned in Deut. 18:15 and 18, 19, and conceived to be, as 7:40 shows, a special prophet who would precede the Messiah. When the article is thus used with the predicate, it is both definite and treated as identical and interchangeable with the subject, R. 768. The apostles afterward understood correctly that in Deuteronomy the prophet like unto Moses is Christ himself, Acts 3:22; 7:37, which also is the understanding of the Galileans in John 6:14, etc. The Baptist answers the question in the sense in which it is put to him without stopping to correct the views of the questioners. His "No" is categorical. Note the progressive bluntness of the Baptist's denials, until οὔ comes out flatly at the last, R. 1157. The assumption, attached to Matt. 16:14, that the questioners here have in mind Jeremiah who is supposed to return in person is really only a legendary notion drawn from II Macc. 2:4, etc.

22) The results obtained thus far by the committee are negative, though they are valuable as far as they go. Various ideas concerning the Baptist have been eliminated, some of which the questioners had in mind when they began, "Thou, who art thou?" So they begin again with a more elaborate question: **They said, therefore, to him, Who art thou? that we may give an answer to them that sent us. What dost thou say concerning thyself?** If instead of εἶπον we read εἶπαν, this is only the Alexandrian form which a certain group of texts follows. The addition of οὖν after εἶπον indicates that what is now asked is the outcome of the previous questions. Hence also the very general form: Τίς εἶ; which merely asks for information about the Baptist without reference to someone who he might be.

A natural ellipsis occurs before the purpose clause, "in order that we may give an answer," etc., namely, "Tell us, in order that," etc. The questioners here urge the Baptist to consider their position as a committee. The mere negative reply that he is not the Christ will not suffice the Sanhedrin nor the mere denials of various suppositions held by the people. They must bring more or receive heavy censure for having left the main part of their task undone. The "answer" they thus request from the Baptist is one that is positive, "What dost thou say concerning thyself?" The question thus put naturally reveals no personal concern or interest in regard to the Baptist and his mission. These men think only of the answer they are expected to bring to the Sanhedrin. It may, indeed, be quite true that their personal thoughts and desires went no farther, that personally they were left quite cold by what they saw and heard out here in the wilderness. But all this is beside John's narrative.

He reports only what was said by these men and goes no farther.

23)   Thus approached, the Baptist complies. **He said, I am a voice shouting in the wilderness, Make straight the way of the Lord, as said Isaiah the prophet.** The Baptist uses Isa. 40:3, and himself mentions the prophet whose words he uses when characterizing himself. Compare the author's *The Eisenach Old Testament Selections,* 66, etc. The claim that the Baptist here merely appropriates Isaiah's words and does not mean to say that he and his work are the fulfillment of Isaiah's prophecy would certainly be remarkable if true. Matt. 3:3; Mark 1:3; Luke 3:4 interpret Isaiah's word as actually being fulfilled in the Baptist and in his work. Even without this decisive evidence no other conclusion can be drawn from the Baptist's answer to the committee of the Sanhedrin. He furnishes this committee with more than they had asked when they requested, "What dost thou say concerning thyself?" He supplies them with a divinely inspired statement from the greatest of their own prophets concerning his person and his work. Isaiah's words do not merely happen to fit the Baptist's thought, these words constitute the authority for his work.

The fact that the Baptist quotes in a free and an abbreviated way is entirely immaterial. This liberty is constantly used by those who quote. Isaiah writes, "Voice of a crier, In the wilderness prepare ye the way of the Lord, make straight in the desert a highway for our God!" The Baptist declares not that he is such a voice, not that this picture of a voice in some way fits him also; but that he himself is this voice. He even imitates the Hebrew when he says, literally, "I — voice of a crier." While the parallelism of the Hebrew lines induces us to connect the phrase "in the wilderness" with the verb prepare instead of with "the voice" (A. V.), this makes little difference. The Baptist evidently understands Isaiah to mean that both the voice and the highway are "in the desert," and, surely, the fact of the fulfillment shows that this is correct. The synoptists follow the LXX in the translation ἑτοιμάσατε, "prepare," "make ready," and εὐθείας ποιεῖτε (τὰς τρίβους); "make straight." The Baptist spoke Aramaic and may have used the Aramaic for the second of these two verbs, which the evangelist translates into Greek without following the LXX, using εὐθύνατε which only approaches the LXX. Here we have a plain case which shows that John was quite independent of the LXX. Whereas the prophet has two poetic lines in a synonymous parallelism, the Baptist uses only one. Such condensation and abbreviation are constantly employed when quoting.

In the Baptist's reply the entire stress is on his work and office, none on his person. He is merely a voice with a message. The absence of the article with φωνή and also with βοῶντος beautifully recalls the original Hebrew: *qol qore'*, "voice of a crier!" the two Hebrew words being like an exclamation. In the Greek this absence of the articles emphasizes the idea of each word: the Baptist — a voice — shouting. We need not picture God as the one who uses this voice and shouts. The voice is the speaker's own, and he does the shouting. Yet βοῶντος connotes a herald making a public proclamation, which is necessarily done with a loud voice in order to reach the multitudes. This, too, suffices to show that what the Baptist uttered was not his own but the message of one greater and higher than himself.

By thus incorporating the message itself into his reply to the committee the Baptist actually does his work also upon these men, whether he used a loud voice in so doing or not. He is actually calling upon them also to make straight the way of the Lord, Κύριος,

Jehovah of the old covenant. He came in Jesus Christ. The figure in Isaiah's words is that of an oriental king with his retinue for whom the roads are prepared when they are making a royal passage in state. So Christ, now assuming his office, comes. "Such preparation is spiritual. It consists in deep conviction and confession that you are unfit, a sinner, poor, damned, and miserable with all the works you are able to do." Neither the prophet nor the Baptist are to be understood as intending that men should by their own natural powers make straight the way of the Lord into their hearts, for this would demand the impossible. The power for this spiritual preparation the Baptist himself offered in his preaching and his Baptism, i. e., in these means of grace.

24) With the textual question settled that John wrote: καὶ ἀπεσταλμένοι ἦσαν ἐκ τῶν Φαρισαίων, various difficulties are removed. We must also note that ἐκ τῶν Φαρισαίων is partitive (ἐκ and ἀπό are frequently so used) and the phrase = "some Pharisees," which may be either the subject or the predicate in a sentence. We must, therefore, translate: **And some Pharisees had been commissioned** and correct Luther, both of our versions, and the margin of the R. V. "They *which* were sent," etc., assumes οἱ before the participle, which reading is that of a faulty text. "Had been commissioned from the Pharisees" or "from among the Pharisees" misconceives the final phrase. John deviates from the genuine Greek idiom and writes in a Jewish way, although what he says is entirely plain. The reference thus is no longer to the committee of priests and Levites sent by the Sanhedrin. It would be strange, indeed, if after characterizing this committee in v. 19, at this late point a new characterization should be incidentally introduced. The leading men in the Sanhedrin were Sadducees, and it would be remarkable for them to send out a committee composed of

Pharisees, especially on a mission relative to the Messiah concerning whom the Sadducees and the Pharisees held different views. The Pharisees were attached to the Rabbis, and we lack any intimation that the priest were Pharisees, on the contrary, being dependent on the high priest and the Sadducees, they very likely followed their lead.

The real situation, then, is that the committee of the Sanhedrin had ended its inquiry and stepped aside. In addition to this committee the Pharisaic party in Jerusalem had sent a representation of its own. These men had stood by while the committee from the Sanhedrin had made its inquiry. When these were through, the Pharisaic representatives speak. The explanation that the men who now speak are Pharisees is necessary for the understanding of the question which they put to the Baptist. They were of the party which laid utmost stress on the strictest outward observance of the law, around which they had also built up a forbidding hedge of traditions and human commandments. They were utterly self-righteous and cultivated a formalism that was ostentatious to a degree, especially in observing ceremonies, fastings, almsgiving, long prayers, tithes, etc. The Sadducees were freethinkers, skeptics, usually men of wealth and prominence, and given to loose and luxurious living. The people reverenced the Pharisees for their supposed holiness and for their zeal regarding the law; and even the Sadducees had to accomodate themselves to their demands in many ways.

25) The question now asked is one that would naturally occur to Pharisees. While the committee of Sadducees is silent and has nothing more to say, these Pharisees note what seems to them an unauthorized and thus illegal act on the part of the Baptist. **And they inquired of him and said to him, Why, then, baptizest thou if thou art not the Christ, neither Elijah,**

neither the prophet? The condition is one of reality and thus has οὐ as is usual in such conditions in the Koine, R. 1160. The Baptist himself had just acknowledged that he was none of the persons mentioned. Taking him at his word, how, then, dared he baptize? With οὖν, "then" or "therefore," the question is based on the admission all have heard. Incidentally the fact is here brought out that John was engaged in baptizing; the evangelist takes it as a matter of course that his readers know what is necessary to know on this point.

Passages like Ezek. 36:25; 37:23 led the Jews to expect a lustration and cleansing of the people. That this should be accomplished by way of a baptism would seem quite in order. But they expected that it would be the Messiah himself who would thus cleanse the people, and, if not he, then at least his forerunners as they imagined them. When John denied that he was one of these, they naturally asked how, then, he came to be baptizing. Their wrong preconceptions concerning the Messiah's forerunner blinded them to such an extent that, when they had the real forerunner before their very eyes, they failed to recognize him. In a way this scene with its question to the Baptist resembles the scene in the Temple with its similar question to Jesus 2:18; for in both cases the Jews ask, "On what authority art thou acting?"

26) John answers the Pharisees as readily and as succinctly as he had answered the Sadducees. **John answered them, saying, I baptize with water: in your midst stands one whom you yourselves do not know, even he that comes after me, the latchet of whose shoe I am not worthy to unloose.** This answer is straight and true. First, by pointing to what he was actually doing, namely baptizing with water, the Baptist clears up and clears away the misconceptions

in the minds of his questioners concerning the expected lustrations, which they looked for either from
the Messiah or from their expected Elijah or special
prophet. This confusion is cleared up if these Pharisees will only observe what the Baptist is actually
doing, *"I* (emphatic) am engaged in baptizing with
water." This "I" is like the one in v. 20 and is set
in opposition to another, namely Christ. To baptize
with water simply says that John is using a means
of grace. This both marks his person and defines his
work. The Messiah will both be a far greater person
and will do a far greater work. As the God-man he
will redeem the world and will furnish a cleansing
that is far beyond any cleansing that any mere man,
be he Elijah, that prophet, or the Baptist himself, could
provide. Christ's redemption is the basis of the means
of grace. Without this redemption no means of grace
would exist. Thus with the simplest kind of statement
the Baptist conveys the thought that he is nothing but
a man, and that his work consists in applying a
means of grace that rests on a far mightier act.

This clears away the confusion that commentators
have introduced into the Baptist's simple words. They
are apt to overemphasize ἐν ὕδατι. Some stress the preposition in the interest of immersion and do not observe that, even if ἐν were εἰς, immersion would not
follow and would not be the point stressed by the
Baptist. Some stress "with water" as being opposed
to "with the Spirit." The Baptist has no such contrast here. Where he does have it, as in Matt. 3:11;
Mark 1:7; and Luke 3:16, the Baptism with the Spirit
is also one with fire. In these passages the simple
work of applying a means of grace is contrasted with
the miracle of Pentecost, the only instance in which
the Spirit and fire are associated. And this contrast
means that all that a person like the Baptist could do
in his office was to use a means of grace, to baptize

with water, while Christ who would work our redemption could and would crown that work by pouring out the Spirit from on high in a Baptism rightly called one of Spirit and of fire. Thus disappear all derogations of what has been called "water Baptism" with the understanding that this could be only a water ceremony, an empty sign, devoid of power and of grace. These derogations have been applied especially to John's Baptism, making it a mere ceremony devoid of Spirit, although Mark so clearly says that John preached "the baptism of repentance for the remission of sins," Mark 1:4; and Luke 3:3 repeats that statement. Such a Baptism, connected with repentance and effecting remission of sins, cannot be conceived without the presence and the gracious operation of the Spirit, John 3:5.

When the Baptist replies, *"I* baptize with water," he declares: *My* work is to apply this means of grace. And this must be taken in connection with the following statement that the Messiah is right "in your midst," already actually at hand and about to manifest himself. So the Baptist's first statement also means: *I* who thus baptize am this Messiah's true herald and forerunner. Thus all the uncertainty regarding what John meant when he said, "I baptize with water," disappears, and the full pertinency of his reply comes to view. The questioners referred only to the Baptism not to John's preaching. Hence the reply also restricts itself to this sacrament. In reality, as the references to Mark 1:4 and Luke 3:3 show, the preaching and the sacrament go together. The answer John gave to the priests and Levites when he called himself a voice crying in the wilderness, a herald going before his King, must not be forgotten in the present connection. That answer is valid also for the Pharisees. The Baptist preached in order to bring the people to true repentance and to a baptism for the remission of their sins, and he baptized those who were converted by his preaching.

The tense of the verb means, "I am engaged in baptizing." The preposition ἐν is instrumental and merely indicates the earthly element employed, "with water." The verb βαπτίζω has a wide range of meaning, denoting any application of water, and it cannot be restricted to immersion. It is traditionalism when the commentators continue to speak of the "plunges beneath the water," the *Vollbad*, etc., as being the mode of John's Baptism. The mode that John used is nowhere indicated, but no single indication points to the mode being that of immersion. The lustrations common in Jewish practice were not administered by complete immersion, many were mere dipping or sprinkling. The πολλὰ ὕδατα at Ænon, where John also baptized, were springs and rivulets of water. This place was chosen because it afforded good drinking water which is so necessary where many people are gathered together. The vast multitudes which John baptized during his short ministry could not have been immersed without his living an aquatic life. Clement F. Rogers, M. A., has made an exhaustive study of the original mode of Baptism in the pictorial representations, *Baptism and Christian Archæology*, Oxford, Clarendon Press, and has found not one that depicts immersion; even the ancient fonts were shallow, making an immersion impossible. While no one is in a position to say in just what way the Baptist proceeded, the nearest we can come is to say that he took a bunch of hyssop or a twig, dipped it into the water, and then sprinkled those who were to be baptized.

John's Baptism was the true and complete sacrament, of the same nature and efficacy as our present Baptism. Jesus took up and continued John's Baptism, 3:22; 4:1, 2, and after his resurrection instituted it for all nations. To consider John's Baptism as a mere symbol in the face of Mark 1:4 and Luke 3:3 is unwarranted. The remission connected with John's Baptism cannot denote a future remission but, as surely as the repentance led to the Baptism, a forgiveness then and there. When Jesus speaks to Nicodemus about Baptism, this must refer to John's Baptism, which makes plain that it had the Holy Spirit and the power of regeneration, for of these Jesus speaks to Nicodemus. None of Christ's Apostles received a baptism other than that of John, yet Peter who was thus baptized declares that Baptism "saves," I Pet. 3:21. The baptism referred to in Acts 19:1-7 was invalid because it had been administered not by the Baptist but by faulty disciples of his, who had declined to follow Jesus and had proceeded on their own account and were not even able to teach as much as the existence of the Holy Ghost. What they had received was not Baptism, hence Paul instructed and baptized them — just as we would do today in an analogous case. As far as differences can be indicated: John's Baptism rested on the preliminary revelation made to John, Christ's on his own full and complete revelation. John's made followers of the Christ to come, Christ's made followers of the Christ who had come. John's Baptism bestowed the forgiveness about to be bought, Christ's the forgiveness that had been bought. John's was thus for Israel alone, Christ's for all nations.

After clearing up the matter regarding his baptizing John clears up the matter regarding the Messiah and shows how he is connected with this Messiah. His reply may be divided into three statements: 1) Unknown, the Messiah is already in your midst; 2) He is already in the act of coming after me; 3) And he is infinitely great. Thus John more than answers the question put to him. His work is not only legal in the narrow Pharisaic sense, it is legal in a far higher sense and has the stamp of approval from the present Messiah himself.

In μέσος the Greek has an adjective which we are able to produce only by a phrase, "in your own midst," the pronoun being quite emphatic as it is again in the subject clause. The absence of a connective makes the two statements, the one regarding John himself (ἐγώ) and the one regarding the Messiah, stand out prominently. "Whom *you* (yourselves, for your part) do not know," i. e., people like you, is the subject of στήκει a later verb formed from the perfect ἕστηκα, of ἵστημι. "He stands in your very midst" although *you* do not see or know him as yet while *I* certainly do, means more than that the Messiah "is" already in their midst. "He stands" means: ready to begin his great Messianic work. These Pharisees, too, will presently "know" him after a fashion; the Pharisaic mind will never really know him.

27) The addition, "even he that comes after me," modifies the subject clause, "whom you do not know," but really helps to explain the verb "stands." This wonderful person stands ready to carry out his great work, and this person is to be John's great successor, to perform the Messianic task of which John's work was only the herald. With the Messiah thus on the very point of succeeding John, it is foolish to question his right to baptize, in fact, his right both to preach and to baptize. This close connection between John and the Messiah seals John's work as being divine. In this testimony of John to Jesus a note of joy and mighty satisfaction throbs. To usher in Jesus — what more blessed task could be assigned to any man! And does anyone question John's work? Jesus is its justification and seal. When John tells these Pharisees that *they* do not know though *he* does, and that Jesus is on the very point of taking up his great

work, he suggests to these men that they on their part should also desire to know him and should ask to have him pointed out to them. But this suggestion falls on deaf ears, after hearing John's reply they, too, step aside. Even the final statement about the supreme greatness of this wonderful person awakens no response in their hearts.

The participial clause is a duplicate of the one used in v. 15, and it occurs again with a finite verb in 30, showing that the Baptist more than once used it with reference to Jesus. Throughout the verb forms ἐρχόμενος and ἔρχεται are significantly Messianic and must have been so understood by those who heard John speak. This Coming One is vastly greater than John, which shows how seriously mistaken they were who thought John might be he, "the latchet of whose shoe I am not worthy to unloose." The sandal was fastened to the foot by a leather strap, ἱμάς, "latchet." When an honored guest or the master of the house himself entered, it was the task of the humblest slave in the house to unfasten the straps, remove the shoes, bathe the feet, and cleanse the shoes. With this imagery John compares himself and Jesus. Did many consider John wonderfully great? He himself says that he is nothing compared with Jesus. Picture Jesus, the Coming One, either as come unto his own (v. 11) as the Master of his own home, or as the most exalted Guest at the home of his nearest kin and friends, the Baptist is not great enough to perform the menial service indicated — John being only a sinful man — Jesus, the very Son of God (v. 34).

In v. 31, etc., John tells us that he himself at first did not know that Jesus was, indeed, the Messiah and Son of God. He had always known Jesus and he may well have had his convictions concerning him. But when he spoke as God's prophet he had to have more than these. He received more, the fullest revelation

through the Father and the Spirit, on the occasion
of the baptism of Jesus. This had come to him prior
to the arrival of the two delegations from Jerusalem.
Constructions like ἄξιος with the non-final ἵνα are quite
usual in the Koine, especially in our Gospel. About
half of the infinitives are thus crowded out; ἵνα λύσω =
λῦσαι.

28) The remark is sometimes made that the evangelist fails to finish and round out so many of his narratives, and the present incident is pointed to as a case
in point. Yet, what more should the evangelist have
added? He is concerned with the testimony which the
Baptist uttered concerning the person and the office of
Jesus. Most graphically and completely he has
recorded the testimony offered on this occasion. What
more was there for him to say? The two delegations
left, which is rather self-evident. The Baptist went
about his business — should that be told? Has anyone
this or that curious question he would like to ask?
None of the evangelists attempt to answer such questions. John's first historic incident is surely quite
complete.

As in 6:59 and in 8:20, the evangelist mentions
the place of the incident at the end of his narrative.
Shall we say that this was a way he had? This naming the place of the occurrence seems to be more than
an appended piece of information; it sounds as though
John recalls the exact locality because the importance
of what transpired there impressed him so deeply at
the time. **These things took place in Bethany
beyond the Jordan, where John was, engaged in
baptizing.** "In Bethany" is the assured reading but
the addition "beyond the Jordan" should not be overlooked. The latter phrase is written from the point
of view of Palestine proper, the country between the
river and the sea. Incidentally this marks the writer
of our Gospel as one who was a native of Palestine,

who thus thinks of the land east of the Jordan as being "beyond the Jordan." There is another Bethany near Jerusalem which has the Mount of Olives between it and the city; this was the home of Martha, Mary, and Lazarus. Origen found the variant reading "in Bethabara" and helped to pass it on; but it cannot be regarded as genuine. This little place cannot now be located, but it lay not in the hot gorge at the riverside but away from this, yet in such a way that from it the river could easily be reached.

It seems, too, that we should not picture the Baptist as camping out in the open in all sorts of weather and in all seasons, or as resorting to some cave beside the river while he was doing his work. The same is true regarding the multitudes. It is more preferable to think that he used a house, and that his disciples did likewise, and that from time to time all went to the river whenever anyone was to be baptized. In 1:38 Jesus who was then with the Baptist has a house as shelter, to which he invited the inquiring disciples of the Baptist. There is no apparent reason why ἦν βαπτίζων should be a circumscribed imperfect which would greatly stress the durative idea of continuous baptizing. It seems more natural to regard ἦν as the verb, "where John was," and to regard the participle as modifying "John," "engaged in baptizing."

29) The very next day after the appearance of the two delegations the Baptist made a double notable statement concerning Jesus: v. 29-31; 32-34. This was made before his disciples, as we must conclude from 3:26, where John's disciples refer to this testimony and regard it as something for which Jesus should be grateful. Many others must also have been present, especially people from the neighborhood, as we must conclude from 10:41; for, when a long time after this Jesus again came to this locality, the people there recalled the Baptist's testimony. Since the evangelist

is concerned only with the testimony itself, he adds very little, centering our entire attention upon the Baptist's words, which certainly also deserve all the attention we are able to bestow. **On the morrow he sees Jesus coming towards him and declares, Behold, the Lamb of God, which takes away the sin of the world.** Since this occurred on the very next day, the place must also be the same. We may picture the Baptist somewhere in the neighborhood of the village in the midst of his work. John's record is strictly historical. He uses two finite verbs: John "sees" and "declares," instead of reducing the first verb to a participle: he "seeing . . . declares." He would lay equal stress on the two actions. The two present tenses are the dramatic present, reckoned, however, as aorist in force since they intend to record only the fact of the actions, although in a realistic and vivid way, as if the reader were witnessing what transpires. These tenses are touches in the narrative which make us feel John's deep personal interest: as he writes "sees" and "declares" the entire action is before him although it lies decades in the past.

Only the fact of Jesus' approach is mentioned, for this much is needed for the Baptist's words, who could not well say, "Behold, the Lamb," etc., unless Jesus were near. The surmise that Jesus was coming to be baptized is incorrect, for the Baptist's testimony on the previous day rests on the revelation that immediately followed Jesus' baptism. Likewise the surmise that Jesus was coming to say farewell; for he remained the entire following day, v. 35. Most likely the purpose of his coming was to win disciples, for this is what he actually did as the following episode shows. The present participle pictures Jesus as he gradually comes toward the Baptist. While he is busy with his work the Baptist looks up and sees Jesus coming, βλέπει indicating a momentary glance with the impression it registers (not ὁρᾷ, indicating comprehension and activity of the mind). While Jesus is still a way off, these words fall from the Baptist's lips while, as we may suppose, his outstretched arm indicates the approaching figure. They are deathless words, after all those years that intervened before John places them in his Gospel still freighted with meaning infinitely richer than the mind of John grasped at the moment when these words first fell upon his ears and penetrated to his heart.

The imperatival interjection "Behold!" is dramatic, pointing out Jesus, riveting all eyes upon him, opening all ears for what the speaker will say of him. Here we have a sample of the perfect reproduction of the words originally spoken. After all the intervening year the evangelist might have reproduced the Baptist's words in a much cooler form. Indelibly impressed upon his heart, where the Spirit kept them unchanged, he records them exactly as they were spoken. "The Lamb of God," ὁ ἀμνὸς τοῦ Θεοῦ, with its significant article point out Jesus as the one particular Lamb of God, the Lamb in the most eminent sense of the word. Compare *"the* prophet" in v. 21 and similar uses of the Greek article. The genitive is a true possessive: the Lamb which belongs to God, *his* Lamb, i. e., which he ordained as a sacrifice for himself. This is far better than to make the genitive: the Lamb which comes from God (origin), or which God presents to the world. The word "Lamb" connotes sacrifice, the Lamb whose blood is to be shed. Thus also and especially in the full title, "Lamb of God," lies the idea of being without blemish, i. e., sinlessness, and joined with this the divine purpose and aim of substitution, expiation, and redemption. A truer and more expressive title could hardly have been found for the Savior; he was, indeed, "the Lamb of God." In his *Westminster Sermons* Trench has well said, the Baptist's title for Jesus should not be referred back to this or that particular "lamb" mentioned in the Old Testament rituals, but rather to all of them, since each could typify and illustrate prophetically only some part of the stupendous work God's own Lamb would perform.

The attributive participle describes this Lamb, "which takes away the sin of the world." The present tense ὁ αἴρων is frequently used to furnish a characterization of a person: this is the kind of a Lamb Jesus is. The verb itself may mean either "to take up and bear" or "to take away," "to remove." For the latter compare John 11:48; 15:2; 17:15; 19:31 and 38, passages which show that this meaning is beyond doubt. If the meaning "to take up," "to bear," is preferred, the force of the present tense would be peculiar: the Lamb in the act of taking up. Something would have to be supplied, namely, the very thought brought out by the other meaning. For this Lamb will not again lay down its burden, will not carry its burden indefinitely, but will take it completely away. So we correct Luther's version *traegt* and abide by our English versions, "taketh away." Nor is it necessary to make ὁ αἴρων a timeless present, one that indicates only the quality of the action irrespective of the time that may be involved. Cases occur in which the time feature practically disappears. But here Jesus at this very moment is engaged in removing the sin of the world. He had just assumed this burden by assuming the office of mediation at his baptism; and his baptism itself signifies that, though he is sinless himself, he ranges himself alongside of sinners to take on himself and bear away the load they never could bear.

The thing to be taken away is named "the sin of the world," τὴν ἁμαρτίαν τοῦ κόσμου (world of men). This is one of those great collective singulars, so easily

pronounced by the lips without proper comprehension
by the mind. The idea is that of a mass, all sins as
one great body are called "sin," *una pestis, quae
omnes corripuit,* Bengel. Like most of the terms for
sin, this term, too, is negative, "missing the mark,"
i. e., the one set by the divine law, missing it by
thought, word, or deed, yea, by our very condition
which is corrupt by nature. As many men as there
have been, are now, and will be in the world, each
with his daily life stained with many sins, so many
individual masses of sin are formed, and all these
masses are combined in one supermass, "the sin of
the world." Isa. 53: "He laid on him the iniquity
of us all" . . . "for the transgression of my people was he stricken" . . . "thou shalt make his
soul an offering for sin" . . . "he bare the sin
of many." We may unfold this collective by taking
the law and dwelling on all the many kinds, types,
forms, and effects of sin. Again we may set forth
the deadly, damning power of a single sin, and then
multiply this power a million fold and again a million
fold. Yet we should not make the rather specious —
merely abstract — distinction between the "sin" itself and the "guilt" of sin, for sin exists nowhere
apart from its guilt, and guilt nowhere apart from
its sin. The same is true with regard to "sin" and
its "consequences." As the guilt inheres in the sin,
so the consequences stick to the sin, closer than a
shadow. Neither the guilt nor the consequences are
taken away, really taken away, unless the sin itself
is taken away. With the sin also its guilt and consequences are cancelled. "World" means the universe
of men from Adam onward to the last babe born just
before the judgment breaks. "That taketh away the
sin of the world" includes the entire work of Christ,
especially and most directly his sacerdotal work, his
active and his passive obedience.

It is idle and nearly always misleading to ask regarding the Baptist or regarding his disciples, to what extent they comprehended the testimony here uttered. The Baptist spoke by revelation, he uttered thoughts which towered above his own mind. They still tower above ours although we now have the full New Testament light. And yet, as in the case of Simeon, Anna, and the long line of Old Testament prophets (Isa. 52:15; 42:6, 7; 49:6, 7), the Baptist uttered no empty sounds as far as his own mind and heart were concerned, no riddles or enigmas without key or solution, but glorious truth which his own mind beheld as truth, absorbed and penetrated more and more, in which his own heart trusted with ever-increasing joy. One thing is certain, that the Baptist understood his own words far more perfectly than many who are today regarded as great theological leaders and interpreters in the church. Nor should it be thought that the evangelist here puts his own later thoughts into the Baptist's mouth. The Baptist's word to his disciples is not treated as a thing unheard of, an impossible extravagance; it does not repel but attracts these men to follow Jesus as being, indeed, the Lamb of God.

The Baptist's word has passed into the confessions of the church, also into the catechisms for instruction, as one of the clearest proofs for the universality of the atonement and the redemption. It has likewise passed into all her devotional literature, especially also into her hymns for public worship: "O Christ, thou Lamb of God" (*Agnus Dei*) in the Communion service; "Lamb of God, O Jesus"; "Lamb of God, without blemish"; "A Lamb bears all the guilt away"; "Lamb of God, we fall before thee"; "Not all the blood of beasts"; endless other incidental references, often combined with the thoughts of Rev. 5:6; 13:8; 12:11; 22:1. Luther: "Sin has but two places where it may

be; either it may be with you, so that it lies upon
your neck, or upon Christ, the Lamb of God. If now
it lies upon your neck, you are lost; if, however, it lies
upon Christ, you are free and will be saved. Take now
whichever you prefer."

30) **This is he of whom I said, After me cometh
a man who is become before me, for he was first
compared with me.** This paradoxical description
with its solution is identical with v. 15 and is here
recorded in its historical setting, whereas in v. 15 it
is quoted merely for the sake of its thought. The
verbal variations are only formal: ἐστίν for ἦν, for
Jesus is now present in person; ἔρχεται ἀνήρ ὅς for the
masculine ὁ ἐρχόμενος. Here is a beautiful example of
what Verbal Inspiration really means. It is not a reproduction of so many letters, syllables, and *Woerter,*
but a reproduction in which every word and expression are true to the intent and the thought of the divine
Spirit. It is not mechanical but dynamic, living, and
hence free in form; but never imperfect, inadequate,
or faulty, but inerrant in every expression. The exposition of this verse is found under v. 15.

31) All that follows in v. 31-34 is really one piece
which forms the full and complete answer to the question that would naturally arise in the minds of the
Baptist's hearers as to how he could be so sure of the
great things he was saying about Jesus. This certainty he did not have of himself, but being the chosen
instrument through whom God purposed to make Jesus
manifest to Israel, the great revelation was granted to
him which establishes the certainty forever. And that,
too, is why the evangelist recorded the Baptist's testimony regarding the revelation to him and regarding
the resultant certainty for him. This record is more
than a recital of the history of Jesus' baptism; it is
the Baptist's own exposition of that history, showing
what it meant for him. **And I knew him not, but**

that he should be made manifest to Israel, for this came I baptizing with water. Twice the Baptist freely admits, "I knew him not," which in its connection means, "him" in his divine greatness. The Baptist had known Jesus personally since childhood and may have had his own personal convictions regarding who Jesus really was. All this is here brushed aside, for a prophet's certainty must come from a higher source, from one that is beyond all question. We may note the three successive καγώ, "and I," here and in v. 33 and 34. For none of them we need "even I," since ἐγώ is emphatic enough, and "even" would introduce a comparison where none is intended. While ἤδειν is pluperfect in form, it is one of those forms in which the durative idea alone is left and thus is used exactly like the imperfect: all along in the past the Baptist was without the knowledge that was eventually vouchsafed to him in such a wonderful manner.

But the Baptist could not be left in this ignorance and uncertainty, for God had sent him as the Messiah's forerunner in order to make the Messiah known to Israel. The absolute certainty regarding who and what the Messiah was thus had to be given to the Baptist. Thus ἀλλά = "but" in the sense of *aber* (not *sondern*, Luther), it is an ordinary adversative not one in contrast with a preceding negative. The ἵνα clause is placed forward for emphasis and is made doubly emphatic by the summary of it in διὰ τοῦτο: for this very reason that he should be made manifest did John come baptizing. The aorist φανερωθῇ denotes a purpose actually accomplished not one merely attempted. The verb itself is defined by what the following verses relate: the Baptist was granted the experience to see and to know who Jesus really was, and through the Baptist this knowledge and certainty was to be communicated "to Israel." This is the course followed by God throughout: chosen witnesses are granted undoubted revelations, and their testimony communicates these revelations to the world. Our entire Gospel constitutes such a communication; it consists entirely of such testimony. Note "we beheld" in v. 14; "John bears witness" in v. 15; "this is the witness of John" in v. 19; "and says" in v. 29. God's way is not to the liking of many: instead of answering the divinely offered testimony which makes Jesus manifest as he actually is by ready and joyous faith, they dictate some other way to God, treat his testimony accordingly, and end in a maze of false "certainties." Behind the passive "should be made manifest" is the agent of the action, God. The correlative of "to manifest" or "to make manifest" is "faith" on the part of those who receive the manifestation.

Though Jesus as the Lamb of God takes away the sin of the world, the Baptist's mission was restricted to Israel, and his task was to make Jesus manifest only to his own nation. But this in the sense that Israel was to be only the first to know him; God had his own way for making Jesus manifest to all nations both by other witnesses and by using the Baptist's witness through these others, even as it is here used for the wide world through the evangelist. The verb "came," *trat auf,* is the same as in v. 7 and denotes coming on a mission, but here ἐγώ makes the subject emphatic like οὗτος in v. 7, "*I*," whom God chose for this great purpose. The fact that the Baptist's mission is referred to is evident from the addition, "baptizing with water." The way in which the participle is added to the verb "came": "came baptizing," parallels v. 28, "was John baptizing." This addition, "baptizing with water," does nothing more than to describe the distinctive feature of the Baptist's mission as the one to prepare the way for Jesus, as has been shown at length in connection with v. 26, "I baptize with water." The repetition of this expression in our verse fortifies the interpretation given in v. 26. It is out of line in these connections to regard "with water" as being in contrast with "with the Spirit," or to think that "with water" means "with nothing but water." The Baptist was commissioned to use this mode of lustration as an actual and an efficacious cleansing necessary for all Israelites who would receive their Savior by true faith.

32) In one respect v. 29, 30 stand out as a testimony by itself. So also v. 32-34. But the two are linked together by v. 31, so that what is said in v. 29, 30 rests on what is attested in v. 32-34. All that is contained in v. 29-34 was spoken at one time. The reason the evangelist inserts a little preamble in v. 32 is merely to emphasize that what now follows is the testimony that comes from the Baptist's own lips and constitutes the ultimate basis of all that he attested concerning Jesus. That, too, is why the verb ἐμαρτύρησεν is placed emphatically before the subject, "He bore witness," this man John, "when he said" what follows. The ὅτι is recitativum, the equivalent of our quotation marks. **And John bore witness, saying, I have beheld the Spirit descending as a dove out of heaven, and he remained upon him.** The verb τεθέαμαι, one of the extensive perfects loved by the evangelist and well explained by R. 893, pictures what the Baptist beheld some time ago, when he had baptized Jesus, as a vision that is still before his eyes. The act is past and could prosaically be recorded by the aorist, "I did behold"; but this act was so effective that a "continuance of the completed action" may be predicated of it; hence this highly vivid perfect; compare another in v. 41. The verb denotes here, as well as in v. 14, a beholding filled with wonder and astonishment.

It is surely remarkable with what clearness and definiteness τὸ Πνεῦμα, the Third Person of the God-

head, is thus early named by the Baptist before his
disciples and before the people in general without the
addition of an explanatory remark. They seem to
know who is referred to. No one raises a question.
The same is true regarding ὁ υἱὸς τοῦ Θεοῦ in v. 34. The
account of the other evangelists adds the detail that
the Father was speaking from heaven and calling
Jesus his Son. Those who deny that the Old Testament revealed the Trinity to the Jews, or who claim
that it revealed the Trinity only dimly and imperfectly,
have no explanation for the way in which the Baptist
names the persons of the Godhead as being fully known
to his Jewish hearers. Whence had they such knowledge? Later on the Jews object only to the fact that
the insignificant looking Jesus calls himself God's Son
and never raise the issue that God is but one person
and not three. The old Jews must have read their
Testament with clear eyes. As for the Baptist, he
even "has *beheld* the Spirit."

There is no need to speculate as to how fully the
Baptist grasped the reality of the three divine persons, as though the measure of his personal perception
in any way might limit what he uttered by revelation.
We ourselves utter many mighty natural facts, the
full inner nature of which is not known to us. To
rate the Baptist's personal knowledge low is unfair
to this man of God. Because of his very nature the
Spirit is invisible, but God never had difficulty when
he wished to appear to the fathers. So here we are
told how the Baptist could behold the Spirit by the
participial modifier, "descending as a dove out of
heaven," for which Luke has, "' in a bodily form as a
dove." Both the form and the descent were visible
to the Baptist's eyes. The verb, "I have beheld," like
the same verb in v. 14, cannot mean merely an inner
beholding with the mind or the soul, an ecstatic vision,
or anything else that excludes perception by the natural

sense of sight. We are not told that the Baptist saw "a dove"; what he saw was "*as* a dove," a bodily form, indeed, but one that was "as" a dove. How did the Baptist know that this descending form was the Spirit? This was not his own surmise but the miracle announced to him in advance by his divine Sender, who thus not only prepared the Baptist for the miracle but gave him in advance the full significance of the miracle, v. 33. This, by the way, is always God's method: any special revelation he is pleased to make to a chosen witness is by God himself put beyond all doubt for that witness.

The question is constantly raised, "Why this form for the Spirit?" Luther's answer is: "God the Holy Spirit comes in a friendly form, as an innocent dove, which of all birds is the most friendly and has no wrath and bitterness in it; as a sign that he would not be angry with us but desires to help us through Christ, that we may become godly and be saved." Others point to purity, innocence, and meekness as being symbolized by the dove. It is easy to run into all kinds of fancies by picking up cues here and there regarding the term "dove." Gen. 1:3 is the only place in which an expression somewhat analogous occurs concerning the Holy Ghost. We may content ourselves by saying that the dovelike form intended to convey the idea of the graciousness of God's Spirit. The present participle καταβαῖνον describes the act of coming down in its progress, and what occurred when the dovelike form reached Jesus is then added, "and he abode upon him." The phrase "from heaven," without the Greek article, is as definite as our English equivalent (R. 792), and John always has the singular "heaven" (408). The grammarians (R. 440; B.-D. 468, 3) note that in v. 33 two participles are used, "descending and abiding upon him," whereas in our verse we have, "descending, and he abode upon him."

This change from the participle to a finite verb is usually explained as a desire to make the narrative more lively, or to turn the second action into a statement uttered by the Baptist. But the two participles are as beautiful and vivid as they well can be, and all that is said is stated by the Baptist. The difference is that in v. 33 the two durative present participles, "descending and abiding," are brought to a point of rest by the clause, "this is he," etc., i. e., conviction for the Baptist of the identity of Jesus. While in our verse the durative "descending" comes to rest in the finite punctiliar aorist, "and he did remain upon him," which leaves the matter at an end. This is the grammatical solution. In both cases we have what the Baptist saw. How long the dovelike form remained upon Jesus, who can say, and why should we ask? To strain ἐπ' αὐτον because of the accusative is unwarranted, since this case occurs also with verbs of rest.

All figurative interpretations of the dove must be rejected. Likewise, the view that an ordinary dove happened to circle over Jesus' head and flew down toward him. Equally to be rejected are the ideas of two kinds of vision, one of the senses and one of the spirit, namely, that what Jesus and the Baptist beheld was seen in the spirit and was only symbolized for their eyes (and ears, viz., the Father's speaking from heaven). As the shepherds actually saw and heard the angels, so the Baptist and Jesus (no reference occurs to any others as being present) saw and heard what here occurred when the Spirit came down and the Father spoke from above.

33) God told the Baptist in advance what he was about to behold and in advance informed him regarding the full meaning of what he should thus behold. This, too, the Baptist states in his testimony. **And I knew him not; but he that sent me to baptize with**

**water, he said to me, Upon whom thou shalt see the
Spirit descending and remaining upon him, this is he
that baptizes with the Holy Ghost.** The Baptist's
testimony deals only with his own official interest in
the wonderful event he witnessed, because his great
Sender made this interest vital for him. Hence he
says nothing concerning what the Spirit's bestowal
meant for Jesus and his work; it is enough that this
bestowal points out Jesus to him as the Messiah, shows
him the divine greatness of Jesus, and indicates to him
the Messianic climax of Jesus' work.

So he again states that before this time he did not
know "him," i. e., that Jesus actually was the Messiah
(see the comment on v. 31). God himself removed
this uncertainty: *I* did not know him, *God* did and
made him known to me in a way that was beyond all
doubt. If one should be bold enough to ask why God
did not simply tell the Baptist, "Jesus is the one,"
since he spoke to the Baptist; the answer is evident:
God desired to do more than merely to point out the
person, for which a word would have sufficed; he
desired to display to the Baptist the divine character,
the divine qualification, and the final saving act of
Jesus as the Messiah. God is described as "he that
sent me to baptize with water," the substantivized
aorist participle characterizing God by means of the
one act of sending. But this designation connects
what God now does with God's original act of commissioning the Baptist. Just as the Baptist once received his mission, so he now receives this vital communication during his mission. Just as he accepted
that original mission and labored in it, so he now
accepts this communication and uses it. "To baptize
with water" means exactly what it does in v. 26 and
v. 31: to use this means of grace in preparing Israel
for the coming of the Savior. When it happened that
God spoke to the Baptist is not intimated; we can-

not even conjecture how long the interval lasted between the divine communication and the event which it foretold. How God spoke to the Baptist is also left untold, although we know that God is never at a loss to find ways of making known to his servants what he desires; he has many ways.

John quotes his Sender's words verbatim, "Upon whom thou shalt see," etc. As far as firsthand competent testimony is concerned, this as well as all else that the Baptist states meets every test. The modal ἄν may be absent in the Koine, and when it is used with a relative it may also be ἐάν. The futuristic subjunctive implies that presently the Baptist shall see even as he did. On the two participles "descending and remaining" we have already said what is needed in v. 32. Since the relative phrase "upon whom" cannot well be repeated with the second participle, the pronoun is used instead, "and remaining upon him," R. 724. The resumptive and emphatic οὗτος (see v. 2) picks up the full description of the subject, to which the predicate is then added. Since this is a substantivized participle, it needs the article in the Greek: This is "the one baptizing with the Holy Ghost."

Here baptizing with water and baptizing with the Holy Spirit form a kind of contrast, although only incidentally, as John states the features of his humbler mission, and as God himself states the supreme mission of his Son Jesus. The Baptist is called to administer that means of grace which employs water, Jesus will eventually miraculously pour out the Holy Spirit to carry on his saving work in all the world. The Baptist can only begin the great work and do only part of it, only assist to prepare men for the great Savior and for receiving the benefit of his supreme work. Jesus will perform the mighty work, and when redemption has been won, he will make this redemption accessible to all men by sending the Spirit to make this redemption their own. The commentary on our passage is Acts 1:5, "For John truly baptized with water; but ye shall be baptized with the Holy Ghost, and not many days hence," namely on the day of Pentecost, Acts 2; and the extension of this in Acts 11:16, the case of Cornelius and his relatives. None but the Messiah could baptize in this manner, and this Baptism with the Holy Ghost, once accomplished, cannot be repeated. The crucifixion and the resurrection, and the Spirit's outpouring, because of their very nature cannot be repeated.

In John's statement the major emphasis should not be placed on the two phrases "with water" and "with the Holy Spirit," thus making John's Baptism devoid of the Spirit and changing Jesus' act into something that is not suggested by the words. Let us note that all the faith and the godliness found in the Old Testament was wrought by the Spirit. All that the Baptist did by his preaching and his Baptism when he brought men to μετάνοια εἰς ἄφεσιν ἁμαρτιῶν (Luke 3:3) was wrought by the Spirit, for no true repentance and no real remission is possible apart from him. But until the day of Pentecost this work of the Spirit was limited, and that in two ways: in extent, it did not yet apply to the whole world; hence also in its nature, it was waiting for and pointing forward to the promised redemption to be accomplished in the great work of the Savior. Finally the miraculous Baptism with the Holy Ghost and fire took place on Pentecost, and now all restrictions were removed, the Spirit would now work among all nations and in all languages, Acts 2:8, etc., and would now make known all the revelation Jesus had brought. Since Pentecost the Spirit, once poured out, flows on and on through the world in the blessed stream of the means of grace. He is present and works with all his power wherever the Word is truly preached, wherever the two Sacraments are administered according to Christ's institution. Through the Word and the Sacraments the Spirit is given, and through these means alone. Through these means we today receive the Baptism of the Spirit. There is no other "Baptism by the Spirit." It is utterly impossible for any soul to come into contact with the Spirit save through these means. By these means he works regeneration, conversion, justification, and sanctification. No sudden seizure by the Spirit without these means takes place; no total instantaneous "sanctification" is thus wrought; no "second blessing" is bestowed. These views and their products are pathological human autosuggestions that may seem spiritual but lack the Spirit. In v. 33 we have only "Spirit," but here the full title "Holy Spirit" is used.

34) The Baptist rounds out and completes his testimony by a final statement. **And I have seen and have witnessed that this is the Son of God.** As one who himself saw, the Baptist is a competent witness. He did not merely see, God enlightened him in advance in regard to what he came to see, which makes his witness competent in the highest degree, for he saw with eyes enlightened by God's own revelation. The two perfect tenses are again extensive perfects as in v. 32, "I have seen," and the vision is still before my eyes as though I were still seeing; "I have witnessed," and my testimony stands as though I kept giving it continuously. Again ἐγώ is emphatic, "*I*," whom God chose for this purpose. The verb is varied from that used in v. 32: θεάομαι, "to behold" with a long look of wonder and astonishment; but now ὁράω, "see" with understanding and comprehension.

This meaning of the verb is matched by the object in the ὅτι clause which, of course, belongs to both verbs. What the Baptist "beheld" he states in v. 32; what he "saw" in what he thus beheld and what accordingly he testified he now states, "that this is the Son of God." This, however, is not a deduction made by the Baptist, one which we should thus feel we must test for ourselves before we accept it. In this summary the Baptist repeats what the Father's voice declared from heaven, "This is my Son beloved, in whom I was well pleased," ὁ υἱός μου ὁ ἀγαπητός, Matt. 3:17. Here the Baptist corroborates the evangelist's "God Only-begotten," v. 18, and agrees with all the other evangelists who make the attestation in the same connection. All efforts to reduce the term "the Son of God" to something less than essential Sonship, something less than "very God of very God" (Nicene Creed), by the contention that this title is one of the outworn ancient "categories of thought" beyond which we moderns have progressed, are less than Arianism and its allied denials and are but the old rationalism garbed in a somewhat modern dress. Since the Baptist quotes God himself when calling Jesus "the Son of God," the plea that this is an outworn category of thought makes the charge that the Eternal is guilty of using such a category. The other alternative is that the Gospel records themselves are false, and that God never called Jesus "my Son." The further comments made in connection with v. 32 on "the Spirit," in regard to the Baptist's own understanding of his words and in regard to the Jews and their knowledge regarding the Three Persons of the Godhead from the Old Testament, apply here as well as in v. 32.

Be placing the name "the Son of God" last the evangelist brings this testimony of the Baptist to a grand climax. All along the evangelist presumes that his readers know the historical fact of the baptism of Jesus and of the outpouring of the Spirit upon Jesus, as well as Luke's account of the Pentecost miracle. Hence these histories are not retold, nor are any new features of these histories brought forward by the evangelist. The great thing he does in the present record is to bring to our attention in the testimony made once for all by the Baptist the essential reality that stands out for all time, unchanged and unchangeable, in what occurred at the river Jordan when Jesus came unto John.

35) **On the morrow again John was standing and two of his disciples.** The three datives of time "on the morrow," τῇ ἐπαύριον (ἡμέρᾳ), which head three consecutive paragraphs, are all alike, each refers to the day that immediately succeeds the one mentioned before. To insert one or more other days at any point between these "morrows" is without warrant. When John here adds "again" he means to say that in a manner what the Baptist said on this day is a repetition of what he said on the day before. Here was the Baptist "again" standing in a prominent place and "again" proclaiming Jesus as the Lamb of God. The pluperfect form ἱστήκει (also written εἱστήκει) is like the similar form in v. 31 (which see), an imperfect in meaning, and while here it is coordinated with the following λέγει, it is after all circumstantial, since the chief thing is not the standing but the testimony here once more uttered by the Baptist. The finite form "was standing" makes this action more prominent than a mere participle would do.

In a simple way the person of "John" is distinguished in the scene here sketched, namely by placing the verb first and by using the singular and by placing the Baptist's name immediately after it. Two other persons, not yet named, also "were standing," but they are secondary as compared with the Baptist, hence are merely added, "and two of his disciples," ἐκ in the partitive sense in place of the genitive. Not incidentally, say somewhere along the path over which these three had come, did the Baptist repeat his great testimony concerning Jesus; no, he waited until he reached the spot where he had made this proclamation

on the day before. There he once more "stood" as the
great herald of the Messiah. We must not miss the
impressiveness of what the verb conveys. This, too, is
a touch that marks the writer as an eyewitness. Other
details, such as what the Baptist was doing at this time,
are irrelevant.

36) Now comes the chief feature: the Baptist
looks up, sees Jesus walking some little distance away,
and at once solemnly repeats his testimony of the day
before. **And he looked upon Jesus as he was walking and declares, Behold, the Lamb of God.** The
aorist participle ἐμβλέψας merely records the fact, and
the dative object is regular with this compound verb.
The Savior is described as "walking." That is different from the scene of yesterday when Jesus came
directly to the Baptist, v. 29. We have no intimation
that the participle "as he was walking" is meant in
a figurative sense: engaged in his calling. Jesus, indeed, had assumed his office and Savior work, yet the
mere statement of his walking imparts nothing on that
point. We are not even told whence he came or in what
direction he was going. We may surmise from what
follows that he was proceeding to the place where he
lodged at this time. What had brought him close to
the Baptist's preaching place we cannot say, except
that the whole narrative shows, that he was ready
to gather the first disciples about him — that at least
is what he actually began to do on this memorable day.
Thus the Baptist looked upon Jesus as he was walking
and, seeing him, "declares." The tense is the present,
λέγει, explained in connection with v. 29. The Baptist's
words still sound in his ears although they were
spoken decades ago.

The words themselves, "Behold, the Lamb of God,"
are identical with those of the day before and, although
they stop short with this exclamation, evidently intend to recall the fuller statement of the previous day.

Still more must be said. The full testimony of the previous day was addressed to all those present, all of the Baptist's disciples (3:26) and the multitude (10:41); see v. 29. The situation is now different. Only two of the Baptist's disciples are present, and thus this renewed testimony is directly addressed to them. They have had time to meditate on what they heard yesterday. Perhaps they had begun to feel what lay in the words as far as they were personally concerned. If Jesus was the Messiah, if their own master, the Baptist, attested him as the Messiah and that by divine revelation, then they must follow that Messiah. Did not the call to do that lie in the very first announcement of their master? And now the word is repeated — in a brief, pointed, almost challenging manner, "Behold, the Lamb of God!" Now it did penetrate. Some think that others besides the two disciples were present, but the record has no trace of others. These two, personally addressed by their master, at once proceed to act. Their master had rendered them the very highest service: he had given them God's call to follow Jesus.

The exposition of the words, "Behold, the Lamb of God!" is found under v. 29.

37) **And the two disciples heard him speak and they followed Jesus.** Two simple aorists record the great facts. Here is an example of the Word rightly heard. And why speak or think of man's natural powers when the Word is present with its efficacious power of grace? When the Baptist uttered the same words on the previous day, these two disciples also heard and yet they did not act. It is idle to speculate; yet we may recall in our own case how we, too, often need a second or a third invitation. Verbs of hearing are followed by the genitive to indicate the person heard, while the thing heard is placed in the accusative.

Faith comes by hearing, Rom. 10:17. There is but one right answer to the truth — faith.

"They followed Jesus" here, of course, means that the two disciples left the Baptist where he was standing and started to walk after Jesus. This was exactly what the Baptist desired, "He must increase, but I must decrease," 3:30. Yet beneath this obvious outward meaning lies a hint of something more. We know to what this following led in their case, and how the very word was afterward used by Jesus himself when calling men to discipleship, v. 43. "They followed Jesus," thereafter never to turn from him.

38) They surely did not go very far until, in John's simple way of telling it, Jesus turned and spoke to them. **Now Jesus, having turned and having beheld them following, says to them, What are you seeking? And they said to him, Rabbi (which is to say, when interpreted, Teacher), where art thou staying?** The minor actions of turning and of beholding are expressed by participles, and their aorist tense indicates merely the fact and the thought that it preceded the speaking. After θεασάμενος the accusative pronoun and its present participle: having beheld "them following," is altogether regular. How aoristic λέγει is we see in the sequence: λέγει (present) . . . εἶπον (aorist) . . . λέγει (again present). We might well translate, "he said . . . they said . . . he said." On this aoristic present see v. 29.

The Baptist urges these two men to go to Jesus, and Jesus opens his arms to receive them. Jesus first speaks to them who might have been too timid themselves to address him. Since their following him shows that they seek him, Jesus does not inquire *whom* they seek but, *"What* are you seeking?" This first word spoken by Jesus is a master question. It bids them look searchingly at their inmost longings and desires. "We are accustomed to seek what we have lost, or what otherwise is beneficial or desirable for us. But what was there more desirable, more longed for during forty centuries past on the part of so many illustrious men, the patriarchs, judges, kings, prophets, and all the saints of the Old Testament, than this Lamb of God, which John's testimony on the heights between the Old and the New Testament declared to be present at last?" Calov. Many are seeking what they should not, and others are not seeking what they should. Let us, too, face this question of Jesus in order that we may cast out all self-seeking, all seeking of ease in Zion, all worldy ambition even in churchly things, all unworthy aims, and rise to the height of our calling both as believers and as the called servants of the Lord, and let us help to confront others with this same question that they, too, may find in Jesus what he came to bring. For a hidden promise lies in the question, "What are you seeking?" Jesus has the highest treasure any man can seek, longs to direct our seeking toward that treasure in order that he may bestow it for our everlasting enrichment. Note how this verb "seek" corresponds to the verb "we have found" in v. 41 and 45.

The answer of the disciples is a question, "Rabbi, where art thou staying?" They address Jesus with the usual respectful title given to Jewish teachers. The Hebrew *rab*, an adjective meaning "much, great, mighty," was made a title: *Oberster* or "Master," the Greek equivalent for the honoring title "Teacher" (margin, R. V.). By a parenthetical relative clause John himself interprets the Hebrew title for his Greek readers and retains the vocative, though it is the predicate: Διδάσκαλε, R. 416, 432, 465. With the Hebrew suffix for "my" we have *rabbi* or *rabbei*, although this possessive was hardly more than formal. Jesus accepts this title even to the last, as we see in 13:13,

although Κύριος, "Lord," soon came to be used more
frequently by his disciples. The two disciples of the
Baptist do not venture to use a title derived from
their own master's designation of Jesus as "the Lamb
of God" or "the Son of God," v. 34. These designations certainly had their illuminating effect upon them
and yet were not of a kind to lend themselves to personal address in conversation. In the question, "Where
art thou staying?" lies the desire to have a private,
undisturbed conversation with Jesus regarding the
high thoughts and hopes which had begun to stir their
hearts. One cannot say whether they expected to confer with Jesus at once or meant merely to find out
where he lodged in order to meet him later. They
probably intended to leave that to Jesus.

39) They are invited at once. **He says to them,
Come, and ye shall see. They came, accordingly,
and saw where he stayed; and they stayed with him
that day. The hour was about the tenth.** Jesus
places himself and the humble place where he lodges
at their service without delay. This readiness is
generous on his part and kind and satisfying for
them. There never was a time when Jesus was not
eager to satisfy hearts that truly sought his blessings. His answer is, "Come, and you shall see." They
would have been happy if Jesus had said, "Come to-
morrow or the next day and see me." But he opens
the door to them on the instant just as if he had been
waiting for them. Kings and the great men of the
earth hedge themselves about with servants and ceremony, so that it is difficult to reach them and get
speech with them; one must arrange an interview in
advance to secure audience at all. Nothing is easier
than to get an audience from the King of kings at
once.

The words are exceedingly simple — just a kind
invitation, "Come!" and a promise attached, "And you

shall see." But what significance lies in these few
words! "Come!" meant, of course, to the lodging
of Jesus; yet who that knows Jesus fails to read
in this gentle imperative something of the meaning
of those other invitations by which Jesus bade those
that labor and are heavy laden to come unto him —
to come from sin, from the world, from darkness,
misery, damnation — unto him, unto pardon, peace,
rest, and salvation? The present imperative ἔρχεσθε
is here linked with the volitive future ὄψεσθε, which
not only has some imperative force (R. 875) but even
more, the note of assurance. To be sure, if the disciples would come, they would see the little place
where Jesus stayed. But their desire went far beyond
seeing this place. The entire conversation deals with
deeper things. "You shall see" means: the place where
you can speak to me and learn from me and about
me all that prompts your hearts to follow me. The
promise is broad, but the sequel shows that it was fully
redeemed. We have an echo of this invitation and
promise of Jesus in Philip's word to Nathanael, "Come
and see!" v. 46.

Two simple historical aorists report the next facts,
"They came, accordingly, and saw where he stayed,"
μένει, literally, as the Greek idiom requires, "where he
stays." This was, perhaps, a house in a nearby hamlet
or in Bethany itself, v. 28; or a temporary booth of
wattles, covered, perhaps, with the striped aba, the
usual cloth worn in the east (Farrar, *The Life of
Christ*). To come — to see — to abide with Jesus has
well been called an epitome of the entire Christian life.
Another aorist completes the story, "and they stayed
with him that day," the accusative of the extent of
time. The prolonged stay is eloquent regarding the
impression made on the heart of John and of his companion when they sat together with the Savior for the
first time. We at once feel that these words relate one

he is personally concerned, to the other man, Andrew
— he was the first in the matter of this finding. In
ὁ ἴδιος we have a strong possessive which is quite
emphatic and convertible with the reflexive ἑαυτοῦ,
although at times the adjective was used in an "exhausted" sense; see the discussion in R. 691, etc.

"He findeth" and "tells" are the vivid present in
historical narrative, the action being very present to
John's mind as he writes — of course, not only
Andrew's action but also his own. From the verb
"finds" we cannot determine whether Andrew and
also John sought his brother or only happened upon
him after leaving Jesus. But the situation itself as
here portrayed, especially the deep impression made
by Jesus on the hearts of the two visitors, leads us
to think that both forthwith sought and found their
brothers. They could not refrain from imparting
what they had found in Jesus. We may also remember that Simon and James were likewise disciples of
the Baptist, and if he directed Andrew and John to
Jesus, he certainly wanted their brothers to follow the
same course, namely likewise to attach themselves to
Jesus.

Mark the word "findeth." It keeps recurring in
a significant manner, twice in v. 41, and again in
v. 43 and 45. So the man in the field "finds" the
treasure, and the merchantman "finds" the pearl of
great price. At best our seeking is only like a blind
groping which would be useless if God in his mercy
did not lay the great treasure so near us, direct our
groping hands and blind eyes to it until, touching
it at last, lo, we find it! Andrew's finding his own
brother, John's finding his, is an excellent example
of home mission zeal. Also from the very start we
see a communion of saints in the following of Jesus:
first two, whose faith is so blended together in
the moment of its origin that we cannot tell which

was the first, that of John or that of Andrew. And at once the number doubles, and the two are increased to four with two more immediately to join the four. This is how the church has grown and still grows to the present day.

The word with which Andrew greeted his brother is remarkable: "We have found the Messiah," which John interprets for his Greek readers, translating the term with "Christ." In v. 38 the case is preserved, "Rabbi," Διδάσκαλε, both vocatives; here the accusative "Messiah" is rendered by the nominative "Christ." In both cases the neuter ὅ refers to the word only as a word, and the participle may be combined with the copula to form a circumscribed present, or, since we have no call for this here, may be read as a modifier, "when interpreted," which we prefer. Andrew has the plural verb, "we have found," not the singular with inflectional "I." The church loves to make joint confession. Of course, the agreement in this quiet "we" means to strengthen the assurance for Simon. If John had had doubts or had hesitated in seconding Andrew, Simon would have been far less impressed. Here again we have the extensive perfect εὑρήκαμεν, "we have found," see v. 32 for the explanation of the tense, R. 893, and compare v. 34 and 45. The act of finding lies in the past, but the effect and result continue to the present. This is Andrew's glad news. "We have found him whom all Israel has been looking for!" Let us not miss the tremendousness of the announcement. The verb states a fact not a supposition, not a surmise, not a deduction, but an unqualified fact. Andrew did not *think* he had found; he *had* found and he *knew* he had.

John retains Andrew's "the Messiah" in the Aramaic just as he keeps "Rabbi" in v. 38, and writes Cephas in v. 42, though in each case he translates for his Greek readers. He writes as an original witness;

and these distinctive terms have a value of their own which ought to be preserved. It was natural for Andrew to use the title so familiar to the Jews, "the Messiah" — he in whom all their hopes and aspirations centered. The Messianic hope had in the first place drawn these men to leave their fishing nets up in Galilee and to come down to the lower reaches of the Jordan where the Baptist, the great herald of the promised Messiah, was baptizing. They had not been disappointed in him although he was only the advance herald. Now, however, their highest hopes were coming to fulfillment: they have found the Messiah himself. The Baptist had called him "the Son of God," v. 34, and most emphatically "the Lamb of God." This Andrew now restates in his own way just as Philip does a little later in v. 45. The Hebrew *Mashiach,* Aramaic *Meshiha,* is the Greek *Christos,* a verbal adjective made a noun, signifying "the Anointed One." The Greek name is derived from the ceremonial verb χρίω, "to anoint," as contrasted with the common verb ἀλείφω, any smearing with oil. The term is appellative, is like a descriptive title and designates the high office of the Promised One, whoever he may be. When this person was known as Jesus, the title "Christ" was used directly to name him, yet it always retained the original reference to the office involved. So also Andrew declares that he and John have found the person who is the Messiah.

To determine the nature of this office we must combine all that the Old Testament promised concerning the coming Savior, his prophetic, high priestly, and regal work. For that combined work he would be anointed, and by the anointing he would be formally invested with that work. As high as was this mighty office, so high, we know, was the act of anointing — God himself sending the Holy Spirit (not merely a few of his gifts) upon his chosen Servant. Again

the question is raised as to how far the knowledge of
Andrew reached regarding the Messiahship of Jesus.
It is enough to know that Andrew was making the
right beginning — Jesus himself would develop this
unto the fullest fruition. Whether John, when he met
his brother James, used the same designation for Jesus
— who can say? Of one thing we can be sure, he did
not employ a term that said less; and James, too, at
once followed Jesus.

42) **He brought him unto Jesus** with its historical aorist simply states the fact, which was certainly weighty enough in itself. It must have occurred
that very evening, for John carefully marks the days
in this section of his Gospel and does not write "on
the morrow" until we come to v. 43. Thus John also
rendered the same service to James that very evening
right after Andrew had done so. Peter became the
third disciple of Jesus, James the fourth, all of them
becoming disciples on that day. When they were
"brought" to Jesus they naturally were introduced to
him. We learn how Jesus received Simon and conclude that in some equally effective way he received
also James. One might stop with the outward act
of ἤγαγεν, "brought," but surely here is a hint that
Simon (and then James) was also brought spiritually to Jesus, brought so as to believe in him and
to follow him. That is what the following narrative
implies.

**Having looked upon him, Jesus said, Thou art
Simon, the son of John: thou shalt be called Cephas,
which is interpreted Rock.** The absence of a connective makes this narration stand out as an independent incident. Jesus lets his eyes rest on Simon
for a little while. John paints the scene by means of
the circumstantial participle ἐμβλέψας, compare v. 36,
also 29. John remembered that look of Jesus. The
attractive   interpretation   is   offered   that   before

Andrew, when bringing Simon to Jesus, could say
a word, Jesus after one good look at Simon miraculously told who this man being brought to him was
and what he would become, thus in a double way displaying his omniscience. The verb forms and the
tenses make this interpretation unlikely. John would
have had to write in one connection: ἄγων . . .
ἐμβλέψας . . . εἶπε, "while bringing him to Jesus,
after Jesus had looked upon him, he said," etc. But
John writes ἤγαγεν, which is wholly disconnected from
the next two actions. He makes two sentences without even "and" to join them. He connects only
ἐμβλέψας with εἶπε, this participle modifying the finite
verb. "He brought," an aorist verb, is an action complete in itself: Andrew actually and completely
brought his brother Simon. Then Jesus looked at
Simon and spoke as he did. Moreover, just to name
a stranger after one good look, even if it is actually
done, is too much like the tricks of charlatans to be
accepted by sober men as evidence of supernatural
power, to say nothing of omniscience. Even when
the thing is done in order to mystify, we have the just
suspicion (as in the case of spiritistic mediums) that
the name was secured in some secret and perfectly
natural way. Whenever Jesus makes revelations he
bars out all such impossibilities. As far as Simon's
name is concerned, Andrew as well as John may have
in their long interview with Jesus mentioned the fact
to him that they and their respective brothers (naming them) had come from Galilee to attach themselves
to the Baptist as disciples. Then ἤγαγεν would mean
that Andrew presented Simon saying, "This is my
brother." Or, if Jesus had not been told about this
brother in the interview, Andrew now "brought" him
to Jesus by saying, "This is my brother Simon, the
son of John." In general, we are constrained to follow the rule of interpretation which finds miraculous

action only where the text plainly demands it; *Wunder-sucht* is a mistake even in the case of the many miracles of Jesus.

After Andrew has made his introduction, Jesus looked at Simon. The participle ἐμβλέψας is sometimes misconceived as indicating a look that penetrated into the real character of Simon, so that Jesus now reveals that character when he renames Simon by calling him "Rock." The fact is that Simon had an impetuous character, and his impetuosity often led him into wrong actions. Thus he often shows anything but a solid and rocklike character. When Jesus renamed him he prophetically foretold what he would make of Simon by his grace.

The two statements, "Thou art Simon, the son of John," and, "Thou shalt be called Cephas," are parallels and direct opposites, each marked by the emphatic σύ, "thou." The one says what the man now is; the other, what he shall become and thus be called at some future time. "Simon, the son of John," is only the ordinary ancient way of stating a man's name in full by adding that of his father. It is the pointed contrast with the other name that this man shall come to bear which makes "Simon, the son of John," here mean: this is all that you are by natural birth and parentage; presently you shall be far more, something far higher, by the new power that will work upon you — you shall be called "Rock." Here, and in 21:15, etc., the faulty reading "Jonah" has been introduced in some texts from Matt. 16:17, which the margin of the R. V. unfortunately still passes on. Then fancy plays with "Jonah" = "dove," combining this with "Rock": from the son of a dove Simon shall become the rock where the dove finds refuge. This fancy also violates Πέτρος, a single boulder not a rocky cliff, which would be πέτρα, a feminine.

When Jesus declares, "Thou shalt be called Cephas," the verb means that he shall be called what he then shall actually be. Jesus here speaks with full authority and not like the Baptist who first had to receive a revelation. Here, too, Jesus is attesting himself as he continues to do in the next paragraphs. Here, however, the effect is not immediate. Jesus is ready to wait until Peter shall, indeed, have become what he now so positively promises him. The Hebrew *keph,* Aramaic *kepha,* is here rendered Πέτρος, since a single person is to bear this name: a boulder of rock, a large stone, and not πέτρα, a cliff of rock. Hence also: ὃ ἑρμηνεύεται, "which is interpreted," i. e., not, "which is translated." In v. 38 and 41 John writes μεθερμηνευόμενον, "when translated," although in v. 38 "Teacher" is not a real translation of "Rabbi," and some texts offer ἑρμενευόμενον, "when interpreted." The best interpretation of the name "Peter" Jesus afterward gave in Matt. 16:18, "Thou art Peter (Πέτρος), and upon this rock (ἐπὶ ταύτῃ τῇ πέτρᾳ) I will build my church," i. e., the confession of Christ which Peter had just made. Hence, not his original character or one later developed in Peter led Jesus to name him "Rock," but what Peter should become for others, i. e., for the church, which is "built upon the foundation of the apostles and prophets, Christ Jesus himself being the chief cornerstone." In this foundation Peter with his confession of Christ would be one of the apostolic foundation stones. His name Cephas indicates his future historical place in the church not his future personal excellence. Even as late as Gal. 2:11 we see Paul solid as a rock and Peter wavering again to such an extent that Paul had to rebuke him.

This rounds out the Baptist's testimony, recording not only that he made it but also that it proved effectual for its purpose: four of the Baptist's disciples believed in Jesus and became Jesus' disciples.

The First Attestation of Jesus Himself, 1:43-2:11.—
The testimony of the Baptist and that of Jesus link
into each other as the previous section shows. But
there the word of the Baptist still dominates, "Behold, the Lamb of God!" In what now follows we, indeed, have further effects of the Baptist's words, but
he himself is no longer before us. We now see Jesus
himself in full action. For the first time we hear the
significant call, "Follow me!" It carries the tacit implication that the first four who had come to Jesus
were already following him, i. e., had permanently
attached themselves to Jesus as their Master. Thus a
little band of men had been gathered. A few days
later we find them in Cana of Galilee. And now the
testimony of Jesus appears in the form of the first
miracle, the account of which closes with the words,
"and his disciples believed on him."

43) For the third time John writes "on the morrow" at the head of a paragraph. We thus have four
consecutive days beginning with 1:19. In 2:1 "the
third day" makes the first break. Therefore, Andrew
and John brought their brothers to Jesus on the evening of the previous day. Whatever the details of the
movements might have been, we abide by the days as
John indicates them, whether our imagination is able
to fill in the details with readiness or not. The view
that Andrew and John stayed all night with Jesus and
brought their brothers the next morning contradicts
what John writes when he now says "on the morrow."
**On the morrow he decided to go forth into Galilee
and he finds Philip. And Jesus says to him, Follow
me.** The aorist ἠθέλησεν implies that the intention
was carried out, otherwise the imperfect would be
used. The aorist infinite ἐξελθεῖν summarizes the entire
journey from Bethany beyond Jordan to Galilee. It
seems that Jesus announced his decision to the four
disciples who had attached themselves to him. Much

of his Messianic activity was to take place in this land despised by the Judean Jews. Galilee was less given to bigotry and narrowness. Matthew applies to this going of Jesus into Galilee the prophecy: "The land of Zabulon, and the land of Nephthalim, by the way of the sea, beyond Jordan, Galilee of the Gentiles; the people which sat in darkness saw great light; and to them which sat in the region and shadow of death light is sprung up," Matt. 4:15, 16.

At this point Jesus "finds" Philip. Note how this verb keeps recurring. So Christ, the gospel, and the gospel messengers keep finding men. It often seems accidental but it is all in the gracious plans of God. Commentators think that Philip must have come into contact with Jesus prior to this apparently sudden call. Strictly speaking, this is not correct, for the whole previous story, as John tells it, leads to the conclusion that he and Andrew were the first who came into direct contact with Jesus. But the indications show that John and Andrew, who first visited Jesus, reported what they had found not only to Peter and to James but also to Philip. The five were associated with each other as disciples of the Baptist; they came from the same city; and Philip's reply to Nathanael, "Come and see!" recalls Jesus' invitation to John and to Andrew. Why Philip did not at once with Peter and James go to Jesus that first evening we do not know. Perhaps he did not hear the news until late that night, until the four finally came away from Jesus. The call, "Follow me!" is so much like the other calls of Jesus that we must class it with them as a call to nothing less than discipleship. Not as a mere attendant on the way back to Galilee but as a permanent follower of Jesus, Philip is to join the little band. The present imperative, 'Ακολούθει μοι is durative to express a continuous course of action. What Philip replied is not recorded, we know from what follows that he joy-

fully obeyed.   Philip's call is mentioned only incidentally as an introduction to the story of Nathanael
and to testimony Jesus uttered in connection with his
call.

44)   **Now Philip was from Bethsaida, out of the
city of Andrew and Peter.**   This is a parenthetical
explanation, showing the close connection between the
men named and, as usual, is introduced by δέ.   The
preposition ἀπό is like the German *von,* and ἐκ, *aus,* is
usual with πόλις, a variant of ἀπό for designations of
home localities.   Bethsaida, "House of Fish," lies west
of and close to the Lake of Galilee, near Capernaum
and Chorazin, its site at present is lost.   On a recent
visit to the Holy Land no trace of the place could be
pointed out to us.   The evangelist names only Andrew
and Peter although Bethsaida was also his own home.
If Philip's Greek name was derived from the Tetrarch
Philip, he would be less than thirty years old.   In
the lists of the Apostles he is placed fifth, joined with
Bartholomew and Thomas.   Tradition reports that he
afterward labored in Scythia and Phrygia and died in
Hieropolis as a very old man.

45)   Before the start to Galilee is made **Philip
finds Nathanael and says to him, Him of whom
Moses wrote in the law, and the prophets, we have
found, Jesus, son of Joseph, from Nazareth.**   Twice
we here meet the significant verb "find," once in John's
narrative, again in Philip's discourse; compare v. 34
and 41.   Andrew's and John's finding is here repeated.
Philip finds Nathanael by himself and at once pours
out to him what now fills his heart.   Nathanael =
Theodore = God-given and is taken to be identical
with Bartholomew, which is merely a patronymic.   His
home was Cana in Galilee whither Jesus was now going.   It is but natural to suppose that he, too, was one
of the Baptist's pupils and thus closely associated
with the five who had already found the Christ.   The

legend that he served as the conductor of the bride at
the wedding in Cana is a fancy.   Philip puts the
object both in front of the verb and back of it, the
latter by means of an apposition.   Thus the entire
emphasis rests on the object as if Philip says, "Just
think *whom* we have found."   He uses a descriptive
clause to designate Jesus, "Him of whom Moses wrote
in the law, and the prophets" but means exactly what
Andrew said with the one word "Messiah."   Philip's
description of the Messiah is exactly to the point.
In the closing apposition he names the person whom
he has in mind, "Jesus, son of Joseph, from Nazareth."

"Moses and the prophets" often designates the Old
Testament as such; it is sometimes also briefly called
ὁ νόμος, the law.   Here Philip separates the two terms:
of whom Moses wrote in the law, in the Torah or
Pentateuch, and (of whom) the prophets (wrote in
their books).   Moses is here said to be the author
of the Pentateuch, which fact Jesus corroborates in
5:45, 46 and Luke 24:27.   In his writings Moses transmitted the promises to the patriarchs; he gave Israel
the law which with all its symbols and types points
so directly to Christ; and in passages like Deut. 18:15-
18 renewed the divine promise concerning the great
Mediator Prophet to come.   The entire history of
Israel contained in the Pentateuch is senseless and
purposeless without the Messiah, so that all that Moses
wrote in the law actually refers to Christ.   The prophets were the expounders of the law whose special
duty it was not only to drive home the requirements
and the threats of the law in the hearts of the people
but also to hold out to them the glorious and comforting hope of the Deliverer to come, of whom they at
times spoke directly as in Isa. 53.   The Baptist continued this work in the most effective way, and we
here have men trained in the Baptist's school, who
naturally reveal their training.   Philip spoke truly

when he said that the picture of the Messiah was found in Moses and in the prophets. It has always been there though the nation of the Jews eventually refused to "find" and to see it, and modernism denies that Moses "wrote" his five books and treats the prophets and their writings with the same destructive criticism.

When Philip designates the promised Messiah as "Jesus, son of Joseph, from Nazareth," this should not be pressed to mean that Jesus was born in Nazareth. Having lived in this town so long, naturally when anyone wanted to say from what place Jesus came he would say "from Nazareth," ἀπό as in v. 44. The fact that Jesus' home was in Nazareth may have been mentioned to his first followers by Jesus himself. He still called himself "Jesus of Nazareth" in Acts 22:8. As far as the wondrous conception of Jesus is concerned and the actual place of his birth, Jesus preferred that his disciples should first discover for themselves his divine origin and nature and then learn the mighty fact that he was conceived by the Holy Spirit and born of a virgin. This applies also to the designation "son of Joseph." Joseph was undoubtedly dead at this time, probably had been for some years, since we hear nothing at all concerning him after that memorable visit to Jerusalem when Jesus spoke so plainly of his real Father and of that Father's business. Yet the fact is that Jesus actually was a "son of Joseph," namely legally; otherwise how could Joseph's name occur in the genealogy of Jesus, Luke 3:23; Matt. 1:16? To be sure, there is much more to the story of Jesus, much that none of these disciples could know thus early. But to say with Calvin that Philip here uttered an error, yea two, is unwarranted. Philip uttered facts, actual facts. He did not as yet know all the facts, but when at last all would be known to him, the last facts would illumine the first and not overthrow them.

Philip uses "we have found" exactly as Andrew did in v. 41; the tense is explained in v. 32, compare v. 34 and 41. The plural "we" now includes five and will impress Nathanael more than if Philip had said, "I have found." This plural also denotes the communion and fellowship of faith combined with joint confession. To say that Philip should have turned matters around, saying instead of "we have found," "we have been found," is only substituting one form of expression for another, both of which are true, although only the former fits here. No trace of synergism, of credit for himself, is found in Philip's, "we have found."

46) **And Nathanael said to him, Can any good thing come out of Nazareth? Philip says to him, Come and see.** Nathanael is not greatly impressed by Philip's enthusiastic, "we have found." He voices his doubt. Here the aorist εἶπεν is used beside the present λέγει, showing that the two are about equal in force, the latter adding a more vivid touch. Nathanael's question has bothered the commentators a good deal. "Any good thing," τὶ ἀγαθόν, is general but thus of necessity includes the good thing that Philip declares he and the others have found, the greatest possible Good Thing, the Messiah himself. If nothing good is to be expected out of Nazareth, how can the greatest good originate there? Nathanael can hardly be thinking of the smallness of Nazareth. We know nothing of evil reports concerning the place, and simply to surmise them is gratuitous. The later unbelief of the inhabitants cannot be referred to here; moreover, this was of the same kind as that which Jesus met with even in the very capital — Jerusalem. The fact that Nazareth cannot be reckoned with because it was

a town of the "Galilee of the Gentiles," a country despised by the men of Judea on this account, would require a mention of Galilee and a reference to Gentiles. The best explanation of Nathanael's doubting remark is that he knew nothing of any mention of Nazareth with regard to the Messiah in the law of Moses and in the prophetic promises to which Philip had made such strong references. We need not bring in Matt. 2:23, "He shall be called a Nazarene," for this is a play on words not a prophecy regarding Nazareth as being the home of Jesus; see Fausset, *Bible Cyclopedia*, 496, 3; Smith, *Bible Dictionary*, III, 2070.

Philip gives the finest kind of an answer, one that recalls the word of Jesus himself to John and Andrew, "Come and see!" The present imperative ἔρχου is combined with the aorist imperative ἴδε, thus differing from v. 39. This is excellent Greek, the first tense moving the action along until the action of the second tense brings it to a proper stop. To regard these two imperatives as equivalent to a condition, "If you come, you shall see," is to change the thought and to weaken its expression in spite of R. 949. Bengel calls this reply: *optimum remedium contra opiniones praeconceptas*, the best remedy against preconceived opinions. The answer was probably far better than Philip himself realized, for the only way to learn aright who Jesus is, is not to argue about him, about Nazareth, or about any other point that doubt may try to raise, but *to come* directly to Jesus himself (now in his Word, where he stands ready to meet us) and thus *to see*. This is the way Jesus led all his disciples, and they came, they saw, they were satisfied to the uttermost.

47) "Come and see!" is a call and an invitation, and while it is extended through Philip, it comes from Jesus himself who uses us to call others. In spite of

his doubts about a person from Nazareth being the Messiah Nathanael comes to see. **Jesus saw Nathanael coming to him and declares concerning him, Behold, truly an Israelite, in whom is no guile!** Accompanying Philip, Nathanael was approaching Jesus who thus "saw" him coming; εἶδεν merely notes his approach, thus differing from θεασάμενος, "having beheld," in v. 38, and from ἐμβλέψας, "having regarded," in v. 36 and 42. Jesus speaks to the four disciples about him, "concerning" Nathanael, not to Nathanael himself, yet he does this in such a way that Nathanael hears what Jesus says about him. Jesus expresses his joy at Nathanael's coming. Other instances similar to this one we note in the case of the Canaanitish woman who cried after him, in the case of the centurion's humble and implicit faith, in the case of the sinful woman in Simon's house, in the case of Zacchaeus' confession, in the case of the malefactor's repentance. "They are not all Israel, which are of Israel," Rom. 9:6, but Nathanael was one of them.

The adverb ἀληθῶς, "truly," "in truth or verity," modifies the entire statement, "Behold, here is in truth an Israelite, in whom is no guile." Some connect the adverb with the noun, but then an adjective should have been used, "Behold, a true Israelite." Then, too, the relative clause would merely define the adjective: true because without guile. This would connote that other Israelites were not true because they were full of guile, a contrast that is entirely out of place here where such Israelites are not thought of. Still less can we draw the adverb to the relative clause, "in whom truly is no guile," which ignores the position of the word and removes the strong emphasis on "an Israelite." This word of Jesus concerning Nathanael can be understood only in connection with the conversation of Philip with Nathanael. In his divine way Jesus knew what the two had said and how Nathanael,

instead of stiffening himself in his doubt about Nazareth, yielded to his desire for the Messiah and came
along with Philip. It cost Nathanael some effort to
come to a man from Nazareth; Jesus knows what it
cost him, and this rejoices his heart. Thus we cannot reduce this word of Jesus to mean merely that
Jesus sees the character of the man Nathanael; we
must elevate it to mean the character and quality of
his being an Israelite, a man who is absolutely sincere
about Israel's hope and salvation, so sincere that he
does not allow the mention of Nazareth to turn him
away from Jesus. Jesus' word does not mean that in
some way Nathanael will prove himself an Israelite,
indeed, as Simon would eventually be a Rock, but that
right here and now Nathanael is truly what he is.

The relative clause, "in whom is no guile," elucidates the adverb ἀληθῶς, and δόλος is cunning or deception as when one uses bait to catch fish or some cunning means to secure personal advantage. Nathanael
was without duplicity, altogether sincere. David calls
such a man blessed, Ps. 32:1, 2. Most men lack this
complete sincerity. Professing love to Christ, they
still secretly love the world and the flesh; promising
faithfulness, the promise does not fully bind their
hearts. This δόλος kept the Jewish nation from Christ,
proved the curse of Judas, almost wrecked Peter.
Church men and entire church bodies, while making
loud profession *sonoro tono,* yet squint secretly at
popular opinion, human authorities, supposed advantages, and with fair sounding excuses deviate from the
Word. "Blessed are the pure in heart, for they shall
see God," Matt. 5:8.

48) The implication of the narrative is that
Nathanael had never met Jesus before, also that Philip
had no opportunity to tell Jesus about Nathanael. No
wonder that, when Jesus touched the very center of

the desires and hopes of Nathanael, and did this even
before this unprepared meeting, this filled him with
astonishment. The question admits that Jesus knows
Nathanael. The verb γινώσκεις is the present tense,
speaking of the knowledge Jesus has just displayed
in his words. Moreover, this verb signifies the true
knowledge of insight or of experience. The aorist
would be, "Whence didst thou come to know me?" and
it would be out of place here. This question, at once
coming to the lips of Nathanael as a genuine response
to the words of Jesus, itself proves the man's utter
sincerity as an Israelite, the very fact Jesus had expressed. Strike a beautiful bell, and it gives forth its
sound on the instant.

**Jesus answered and said to him, Before Philip
called thee, when thou wast under the fig tree, I
saw thee.** The importance of this brief reply is
shown by the two finite verbs in the preamble,
"answered and said," which is stronger even than,
"answered saying." The aorist passive ἀπεκρίθη is used
as a middle to express replies of all kinds, as these
are required not only by actual questions but also
by actions and by situations. The answer of Jesus
goes far beyond what Nathanael asked and what he
expected. Jesus does not say, ἔγνων σε, "I knew thee,"
but, εἶδόν σε, "I saw thee," I perceived, noticed, observed
thee. By this seeing Jesus knew. Nathanael asked
in regard to the present, "Whence knowest thou me?"
Jesus reaches into the past, "Not only do I know thee
at this moment, I knew thee ere this, yea, saw thee."
Since the reply, "I *saw* thee," answers the question,
"Whence *knowest* thou me?" this seeing at a distance
with supernatural powers of sight is evidence for
the power to look also into men's hearts. Here is a
case like that of the woman at Jacob's well, "He told
me all things that I ever did," 4:39. Another case
is that of the paralytic let down through the roof

whom Jesus first absolved before he healed him, seeing that his chief ailment was spiritual. "Lord, thou hast searched me and known me," Ps. 139:1. In his state of humiliation Jesus did not constantly use his divine attributes according to his human nature, but he used these attributes, in which his human nature shared, whenever he deemed it necessary for the purpose of his office and work. To place Jesus, in the present case, on the same level with the prophets, saying that Jesus "saw" as they "saw," is to deny the union of his two natures, i. e., to make of the God-man what he never was and never could be.

What lies in the meaning of the verb εἶδον and its tense is brought out more clearly still by the two modifiers, one of time and one of place, "before Philip called thee, when thou wast under the fig tree." The subordinate clause of antecedent time is neatly expressed by πρὸ τοῦ with the infinitive, which takes the place of πρίν with the infinitive, R. 621 and 766. This clause modifies εἶδον and states *when* Jesus saw Nathanael. The participial clause, "when thou wast under the fig tree," modifies the object of εἶδον, "I saw thee, when thou wast," etc., literally, "thee being under the fig tree," and states *where* Jesus saw him. The supposition that ὑπό with the accusative must refer to motion like taking refuge under must be dismissed as being due to ignorance of the Koine, R. 634-5.

Who would not wish that the evangelist had told us more fully what actually happened under the fig tree when Nathanael was there before he met Philip? Something apparently disproportionate lies in the connection of this simple statement of Jesus and the instantaneous, magnificent confession of Nathanael who but a moment ago was filled with serious doubt; but we know that the disproportion does not really exist. As far as the fig tree itself and Nathanael's being under it are concerned, this was nothing unusual, since it was the custom of pious Jews — a custom encouraged by the Talmud — to study their office of daily prayer in some secluded place. Even here, away from Cana, his home, while lodging in some temporary place, Nathanael may well have had his place for quiet retirement, in this instance the shade of a fig tree. What Jesus refers to is not this custom merely but something of a deep personal nature, known only to Nathanael and to his God, that occurred say a day or two before when he had again sought seclusion under that tree. For the reference of Jesus literally strikes home in Nathanael's heart. He sees that what transpired in his inmost soul lies open to Jesus' eyes. "Under the fig tree" unlocks all that ever stirred within him regarding Israel's hope and deliverance. Imagination seeks to supply something that would be great enough to justify the great confession that rose to Nathanael's lips, such as wrestling in prayer for fulfillment of God's promise; resolve to be baptized by the Baptist; prayer victory over some temptation; perhaps, a direct response from God like Simeon's, Luke 2:26, promising him that he should see the Christ. We leave the mystery as John left it to us.

49) Almost involuntary is the instantaneous response. **Nathanael answered him, Rabbi, thou art the Son of God; thou art King of Israel.** So spoke this true Israelite heart, and his words were even truer than he himself knew. Jesus had attested himself to Nathanael, and Nathanael believed the attestation. The title "Rabbi" is the same as in v. 38. The double unqualified designation ὁ υἱὸς τοῦ Θεοῦ and βασιλεὺς τοῦ Ἰσραήλ comes as a surprise, especially when we remember how the Jews hated all deification of men. The second title, "King of Israel," furnishes the clue for the source from which Nathanael drew both, namely Ps. 2, "Thou art my Son," and, "Yet have I set my King upon my holy hill of Zion."

The entire Psalm speaks of the enthronement of the
Messiah who is the Son of God. Another view would
trace Nathanael's confession to the Baptist, v. 33; but
the Baptist's testimony lacks the significant title
"King of Israel," which then would be only Nathanael's own deduction from the other title, "the Son
of God."

It is no mean proof of the divinity of Christ that
men like Nathanael at once felt impelled to acknowledge him as "the Son of God," and having done so,
remained true to him as such, and in all their later
daily, familiar intercourse with him never changed
their minds, telling themselves that they had been carried away in a moment of enthusiasm and now in the
light of a more sober knowledge must revise their
estimate. Later impressions made these men second
Peter's great confession, "the Christ, the Son of the
living God," Matt. 16:16; John 6:69; compare Matt.
14:33; Luke 9:20; John 11:27; 20:28. What this
means in regard to the revelation of the Trinity in
the Old Testament and in regard to the knowledge of
the Jews concerning the Trinity is stated in connection with v. 32. Men like Nathanael understood Ps. 2
and Ps. 110 and other pertinent parts of the Old Testament quite well. "Son of God" seems too far-reaching
an expression even for many who admit Christ's Sonship; hence they tone it down to mean "an exceptional
relation between Jesus and God" and point to Nathanael's emotion when he made the declaration. But
John never would or could have used Nathanael's word
if it had amounted only to so little.

We need not deny that in afterdays clouds arose
to dim the clear vision of Jesus which Nathanael had
at the very beginning of his discipleship. Yet the fact
also stands out that the light always conquered, and
the clouds disappeared, and every doubt was swallowed
up by greater light and faith; for the glory that shone

forth from the Only-begotten never waned for a single moment. "Son of God" rightly stands first as expressing the true relation of Jesus to God; "King of Israel" rightly stands second as expressing the true relation of Jesus to Israel. Nathanael places the two on a parallel, but in Jesus both predicates are joined. To make "King of Israel" alone mean Messiah is verbal play, for the only Messiah is Jesus who is both "Son" and "King."

50) Jesus might have said nothing more and might have continued his journey. But where he meets faith like this he praises and rewards it. **Jesus answered and said unto him, Because I said to thee, I saw thee underneath the fig tree, thou believest. Something greater than this shalt thou see.** Again the two verbs "answered and said" as in the case of the previous speech of Jesus in v. 48. Can we follow our versions and others in regarding the first statement of Jesus as a question, "Because I said, etc., . . . dost thou believe?" A question seems to be stronger and livelier than a declaration, but it is liable to be taken in a wrong sense, thus, "Believest thou already on such little evidence?" or, "Believest thou already? — I hardly expected it"; or, "Believest thou — art thou sure thou believest?" No; Jesus declares with joy, "Thou believest!" The grounds are sufficient, indeed, "Because I said unto thee, I saw thee underneath the fig tree." When Jesus said that he intended it to be fully sufficient to produce faith — it did, and Jesus acknowledges this. So here he first *praises* and secondly rewards faith. The reward lies in the promise, "Something greater than this shalt thou see." The neuter plurals μείζω (contraction for μείζονα) and τούτων are not intended as plural occurrences, for the latter plainly refers only to the fig-tree incident, and the former is explained by v. 51. Such neuter plurals are mere idioms; we should use

the singular. There is a contrast between the terms, "I *said* to thee," and, "thou shalt *see*"; and again between, "*I saw* thee," and, "*thou shalt see.*" Nathanael accepts the word of Jesus — he shall receive even more — as Jesus saw wondrously, so shall he. The verb may be written ὄψῃ or ὄψει, according as the editors contract -εσαι into η or into ει.

51) What "greater thing" Jesus means by his promise to Nathanael he now states clearly and fully. **And he says to him, Amen, amen, I say to you, you shall see the heaven opened, and the angels of God ascending and descending upon the Son of man.** The interruption of the evangelist, "And he says to him," is like that in v. 32, and is intended to draw special attention to the words of Jesus that follow. "To him," Nathanael, and yet in what Jesus says he uses the plural as a reference to all six disciples present. This was necessary, for they all "shall see" what is here promised.

This promise is introduced by a formula of assurance which Jesus often used: a double "amen" as a seal of *verity* and, "I say to you," as the stamp of final *authority*. In "Amen" we have the transliterated Hebrew word for "truth" or "verity," an adverbial accusative in the sense of ἀληθῶς, "verily," and so rendered in our versions. In Hebrew it is placed at the end to confirm a statement or to seal an obligation, it is like our liturgical Amen. "All search in Jewish literature has not brought to light a real analogy for the idiomatic use of the single or the double ἀμήν on the part of Jesus." Zahn, *Das Evang. d. Matthaeus,* 361. This means the use at the head of statement. The best one can say is that Jesus used the double "Amen" when he spoke Aramaic, just as John reports; and that the synoptists, when reporting this in the Greek, deemed the single ἀμήν sufficient for the readers. The supposition that John's double ἀμήν is intended to produce the sound of the Aramaic words for "I say" is unlikly and leaves unexplained why he still adds to the two amen: λέγω ὑμῖν. In our Gospel the double amen occurs 25 times and always introduces statements of the greatest weight.

The word "hereafter," ἀπάρτι, dropped in the R. V., does not change the sense of Jesus' words but accords well with them. The Greek texts which omit the word seem to do so because they interpret the promised vision of angels as a reference to the actual appearance of angels, which, of course, occurred much later and not "from now on." While the future tense ὄψεσθε might be punctiliar, "you shall see once," here the durative sense is indicated, "you shall see again and again." These disciples, in fact, had the first vision of this kind three days later in the miracle at Cana. The tense also furnishes positive assurance, a definite promise and glorious prophecy, "you shall see, indeed," it will come to pass. We must also note that "you shall see" corresponds to "thou shalt see" in v. 50, the verb being identical, and the promise in v. 51 an elaboration of the one in v. 50. In both cases the verb denotes actual seeing with the eyes, and this seeing is in contrast to what Jesus has just *said* to him regarding the fig tree. The latter indicated the supernatural *knowledge* of Jesus; to this shall be added visions of the supernatural *works* of Jesus, beginning with the miracle in Cana. These works the disciples shall actually *see* and behold in them the divine power of Jesus. This seeing, then, is like that of v. 14, "we beheld his glory," etc.

They shall see "the heaven opened, and the angels of God ascending and descending upon the Son of man." The perfect participle ἀνεῳγότα means that heaven, once opened, continues thus, and thus it differs from the opening of the heavens after the baptism of Jesus, for which Matt. 3:16 and Luke 3:21 have the aorist, indicating one act, a momentary opening. What the disciples shall see is heaven permanently open over Jesus. In all his miraculous works they shall see that no bar exists between Jesus and God, between him and the heavenly world, as this is the case with us all who are subject to sin. When Jesus adds, "and the angels of God ascending and descending upon the Son of man," this vividly recalls the dream of Jacob, Gen. 28:12, although no medium like a ladder is mentioned. For the sinner Jacob such a medium (Mediator, the ladder typifying Christ) was needed; not for God's own Son. "The angels of God" are just what the words say and not figures, types, symbols of some kind or other, such as "the symbol of living communion between God and the Messiah," "divine perfection," "personal forces of the divine Spirit," etc. The order of the participles "ascending and descending" is the same as in Genesis, but here they are used in the sense of a constant going and coming — while some go, others come. When R. 423 calls this order of the participles a hysteron proteron, "a natural inversion from our point of view," we do not share his view. Only to sinners angels must first come down not to the Son. When they went up to God from Jacob and then came down, this was due to the fact that he was already in God's favor, the dream assuring him of that fact.

To understand the import of these movements of the angels we should not overlook the contrast implied in the terms "the angels *of God*" and "the Son *of man*." When God's Son dwelt on earth as the Son of man, heaven itself was here among men, the very angels of God, like an army, waited upon his least beck and call. Though he came as the Son of man, God's own angels were at his command. Recall Matt. 26:53, "Thinkest thou that I cannot now pray my Father, and he shall presently give me more than twelve

legions of angels?" The centurion in Matt. 8:9 made
a true comparison when he remarked that he had but
to say "Go!" to one of his soldiers, or to say "Come!"
and he would instantly be obeyed. Thus all power in
heaven and in earth was given to this Son of man.
We thus dismiss the ancient interpretation which held
that these six disciples would see the actual appearances of angels, for these were but few, and only at
the ascension of Jesus did two angels appear to the
disciples. We likewise decline to accept the interpretation that the angels bore Christ's prayers to the
Father and returned the Father's answer, for no such
angelic mediation is indicated anywhere, nor would
it fit the close communion of the Son with the Father.
As God uses the angels for his purposes, so did the
Son of man. His mighty works would make these disciples see that. As the angels are sent forth to minister unto those who are the heirs of salvation, so they
will minister to the will of him who is the author of
this salvation, the great original Heir. In a way far
higher than was possible in Jacob's case the ascending and descending angels would serve Jesus. The
final phrase with ἐπί does not mean "resting upon
Jesus," which is excluded by the very nature of what
is described; or bringing divine powers upon Jesus,
for the very Spirit of God had already been made
his for his work. This ἐπί is in relation to "heaven"
which stands open above Jesus, hence the descending of the angels at Christ's beck and call would
be ἐπί, "upon" him, a coming to his great person.

Here for the first time Jesus uses the designation
"the Son of man," found nine times in John's Gospel
and over fifty-five times in the four Gospels. This title
is used exclusively by Jesus himself, except in 12:34
where, after his using it, others ask its meaning; and
in Acts 7:56, which reflects Matt. 26:64. It is clear
that this title was coined by Jesus himself, was un-

known before he used it, was by the disciples restricted to use with reference to Jesus, and did not come to be used in the church until quite late. Jesus always uses it as a subject or as an object, always in the third person, never as a predicate; he speaks in the full consciousness that he is "the Son of man" yet never says, " I am the Son of man." The title is always ὁ υἱὸς τοῦ ἀνθρώπου, with the two Greek articles, which is quite distinct from "a son of man," i. e., a human being. There is a mystery in the title which is still felt as we read the record of its use by Jesus, which is clearly evident also when in Matt. 16:13, etc., Jesus first asks who the people say is "the Son of man" and who the disciples say he is.

"Of man," never the plural "of men," is generic; not descending from some man but having the nature of man, a son of mankind. The fact that the human nature of Christ is expressed in the title is beyond question. But "the Son" of man lifts out this one man from all men as being one who has this human nature in a way in which no other man has it, who while he is true man, indeed, is more than man, who accepts the designation ὁ υἱὸς τοῦ Θεοῦ τοῦ ζῶντος, "the Son of the living God." This is very clear from the mighty acts attributed to "the Son of man" which prove that, while he is man, he is also infinitely greater than man. Hence "the Son of man" is not merely "the ideal man," *homo* κατ᾿ ἐξοχήν, the flower of our race, toward whom all creation tended; but "the Word made flesh," the Son ἄσαρκος who became ἔνσαρκος, who to his divine nature joined our human nature, the Son of God who assumed our human flesh and blood. In the use Jesus makes of this title two lines of thought converge: the one is lowliness, suffering, etc.; the other greatness, power, and exaltation beyond that of men. Once the title is properly conceived, both lines of thought are seen to be clearly involved in this designation. It will also be noted that this title fits Jesus in an eminent way while he sojourned on earth and was thus used by him as early as his meeting with Nathanael. To give it an exclusively eschatological sense because Jesus calls himself "the Son of man" also in connection with the consummation, is to generalize from a few facts instead of from all.

Nathanael has just called Jesus "the Son of God," and now, it seems as though to counterbalance that true title, Jesus adds this other one as also being true, "the Son of man." The two belong together. Nathanael has just called Jesus "King of Israel," which again is true in the fullest sense. Yet the theocratic relation to Israel which Jesus himself stresses, 4:22; Matt. 15:24, is not enough, for he takes away "the sin of the world," he is the Savior of all men, and in his title "the Son of man" this great universality is brought out. So the narrow and the broad titles belong together. Here we may also note that Jesus carefully avoids the use of any title that might be taken in a political sense. Nathanael calls him "King of Israel," but Jesus does not adopt this as the usual designation for himself. When questioned by Pilate, he carefully defines his kingship as being not of this world, and when Pilate in the superscription on the cross calls him "the King of the Jews," he does this only to taunt the Jews because of their charges not because of a title that Jesus had given himself. This pertains also to the title "Messiah," which the Jews understood in a national and political sense. To the Samaritan woman Jesus reveals that he is the Messiah (4:26), but he does not make this title common when denominating himself. We may say that by most frequently calling himself "the Son of man" he desired to do what he could to denationalize his Kingship and his Messiahship and to lift it to its true universal plane.

Whence does Jesus derive this title? The answer
is: from Dan. 7:13, 14: "I saw in the night visions,
and, behold, one like the Son of man came with the
clouds of heaven, and came to the Ancient of days,
and they brought him near before him. And there
was given him dominion, and glory, and a kingdom,
that all people, nations, and languages should serve
him: his dominion is an everlasting dominion, which
shall not pass away, and his kingdom that which shall
not be destroyed." Efforts are made by von Hofmann,
C.-K., Zahn, etc., to reduce "one like the Son of man"
to a symbolic figure (like the "beast" in the previous
verses), this figure symbolizing Israel. But the words
of Daniel will not yield such a sense. The Hebrew
ki, ὡς, "like," is taken to mean that this person only
resembled a man but *was* not a man, overlooking Rev.
1:13; 14:14, where this "like" is carefully retained
in using the Daniel passage. Again, in Matt. 24:30
and 26:64 the Son of man comes in the clouds, exactly
as in Daniel's description. Only God uses the clouds
as his vehicle, hence "one like the Son of man" is
divine. Yet Daniel sees him "like the Son *of man,*"
which, although it does not directly call him "man,"
intimates clearly enough that the grand figure
described was also a man. See the thorough exegesis
of Keil in *Bibl. Com. ueber den Propheten Daniel,* 197,
etc., and 228, etc. Too indefinite is the explanation
that Jesus drew the title "the Son of man" from the
general references of the Old Testament to the *bene
adam,* or *ben adam,* Aramaic *bar enasch,* "children of
men," "children of man," "child of man," and that only
in this general sense are Dan. 7:13; Ps. 8:5 evidence.
How from such general terms, which denote only
men as men, a title could be drawn which denotes the
one unique man who is the very Son of God, is difficult
to see.

Dan. 7:13, 14 pictures the Messiah, yet the Jews had not drawn a title for the Messiah from it. This Jesus himself did. Hence when he kept using this title, it seemed strange, and the question could arise as in John 12:34, "Who is this Son of man?" Hence also no political ideas could attach themselves to this title. In Daniel, too, we observe the universality that inheres in the original description, which presents one who rules all people, nations, etc., in an everlasting kingdom and judges all the world. In Daniel the term is eschatological; Jesus uses it in the same way in Matthew 24:30 and 26:64, which is done also in the Revelation passages. But this Judge at the great consummation cannot be the judge only then, his work must reach back much farther, through the entire process of redemption, the consummation of which is the final judgment. Very properly, thus, Jesus expands the title and uses it with reference to his person in the days of his humiliation. Even when speaking to these first six disciples, however, he refers to the heavenly glory of his person and to the angels at his command who shall also function so prominently in the judgment. Matt. 25:31; Mark 8:38. What Aramaic expression Jesus used for "the Son of man" no one is able to say. To search in Jewish literature for this title is hopeless. The references in the book of Enoch, even if the sections concerned are genuine, lead to nothing. The surmise that, since Jesus also spoke Greek as for instance to Pilate, he may himself have employed the Greek ὁ υἱὸς τοῦ ἀνθρώπου, may be quite correct, although the Gospels, Revelation, and Acts are wholly sufficient.

Modern criticism attacks the historical character of John's account regarding the call of these first disciples by making them contradictory to Matt. 4:18, etc., and the parallels. But these two calls are essen-

tially different.   John describes the first attachment
of these six men to Jesus when he gathers them as
believers; Matthew describes a later event, the pre-
requisite of which John furnishes us.   When these men
left house, home, and their old calling in life, they
already knew Jesus.   John describes how they were
first drawn to him.

CHAPTER II

The First Attestation of Jesus Himself, Continued,
2:1-11. — By the power of his personality and by his
divine knowledge and words Jesus had attested himself as truly being the Messiah of whom the Baptist
had testified, as the Son of God and the Son of man.
To the attestation through the word is now added
that of the deed, which was made evident in the first
miracle.

1) **And on the third day a wedding took place**
in Cana of Galilee; and the mother of Jesus was
there. Now there was invited also Jesus and his
disciples to the wedding. John counts from the day
(1:43) when Philip and Nathanael became his disciples. The third day after that day means that
two nights intervened. On this third day a wedding
ἐγένετο, "took place." While the verb does not mean
"began" and mentions only the occurrence of the wedding, which usually consumed seven days, yet to say,
"occurred on the third day," must refer to the start
of the wedding. This wedding must be thought of in
the Jewish fashion. In the betrothal bride and groom
were pledged to each other in a way that truly made
them man and wife, although the two did not at once
live together following this ceremony. An interval,
longer or shorter, followed, and then the γάμος or γάμοι
took place. The groom with his companions brought
the bride with her companions to the groom's home,
and there without any further pledge the celebration
began, starting toward evening with a feast as grand
as possible and continuing for a week, the couple now
living together.

(183)

John's words have been scanned most carefully for all possible minor points. The fact that he writes "Cana of Galilee" is to inform his first readers in Asia Minor, where his Gospel was published, that the little town was located in the province of Galilee and not in order to distinguish it from some other Cana located elsewhere. For the Cana near Sidon did not belong to the Jewish land at this time. Names of provinces were also frequently attached to names of towns in cases where the towns were well known and were the only ones with that name. Even so we are unable at present to identify with certainty just what place John, refers to with the name Cana, whether it is Khirbet Kana, also called Kanat el-Dschelil, five hours' walk from Nazareth, or Kephar Kenna, two hours away, or Ain Kana, a half hour away, a spring by this name near the village er-Reineh. The traditional site is the second place, to which the commentators incline, but too many traditional sites in Palestine are uncertain or openly spurious.

The fact that Jesus and his six companions could make the journey from Bethany beyond the Jordan to any one of the three places indicated as Cana in the time limit of three days is assured. Yet a number of questions are left open by the brevity of John's narrative. Does he mean to say that the company arrived for the opening of the wedding feast on the evening of that third day, or that they arrived later during the progress of the wedding? Did the miracle occur on the evening of that third day or on a later day of the celebration? How and when did Jesus receive his invitation to attend the wedding with his disciples? The only clue we have is the fact that in the preceding paragraphs, 1:29, 35, and 43, the designations of time "on the morrow" fix each of the occurrences described in these paragraphs as taking place on the day indicated. The natural supposition, then, is that what is now recorded also took place "on the third day," since this designation of time is placed at the head of this new paragraph exactly like the preceding datives "on the morrow." We, therefore, take it that the miracle occurred "on the third day."

John tells us that "the mother of Jesus was there" because the story turns on her action and also because this in a manner explains how Jesus came to be invited. John does not mention her name either here or elsewhere in his Gospel. He refrains from naming himself and all other relatives of his among whom we thus must include Mary, possibly the aunt of John, the sister of his mother Salome. On the question regarding this relationship compare the remarks on 19:25. The adverb "there" means at the wedding and not merely in the town, for we hear what Mary did at the wedding. The verb ἦν contrasts with ἐκλήθη used regarding Jesus and marks a difference, which is also borne out by what follows. Mary was not present, like her son, as an invited guest but as a friend of the groom or of the bride or of both in order to aid in the feast. Perhaps she was related to one of the bridal couple. This would explain how she knew about the lack of wine and why she took steps in the matter.

2) Jesus was formally invited. The connective δέ adds this statement to the one regarding Mary and at the same time indicates that this is a little different. We have no connective with this delicate force in English. The point of difference lies in the verbs: Mary "was" there as a matter of course; Jesus "was invited" in a formal way. The tenses add to this, as well as the forward positions of the verbs, the one durative, ἦν, the other aorist to designate the one act of giving the invitation, the aorist also indicating that the invitation was effective — Jesus accepted. The verb is singular and thus lifts Jesus into prominence

over his disciples: *he* was invited and they, too, but
not on an equality — they only on account of Jesus.
The word μαθητής, as correlative to διδάσκαλος, means
more than pupil or scholar, namely a follower and
adherent, i. e., one who accepts the instruction given
him and makes it his rule and norm. While used,
as here, with reference to beginners, in its full sense
μαθηταί are those who have truly imbibed the spirit
of their master. The term thus came to mean the
true believers. When these were invited, we are unable to say; the tense of the verb records nothing but
the fact. As regards what follows we may also bear
in mind that, while Jewish weddings usually were
celebrated for a week, some even for two weeks, we
cannot be sure that this wedding lasted that long.
The impression left by the entire narrative is that
the present wedding, perhaps because the couple was
poor, lasted only the one evening and was celebrated
only by one feast, made as fine as possible by the
means of the groom.

3) With the situation thus briefly sketched, the
real story begins with the simple connective "and."
As regards the variant readings, which leave the sense
unchanged, we abide by the one that shows the greater
textual authority. **And when the wine began to
fail, the mother of Jesus says to him, They have
no wine.** The aorist participle in the genitive absolute is best regarded as ingressive, "began to fail."
The decline of the wine would be discovered before
the last of it was used. The usual explanation is
that the sudden addition of seven guests caused this
giving out of the wine. Yet this assumes that the
invitation was given so late that additional provisions
could not be secured. And why should only the wine
fail and none of the food? Had the amount of wine
been calculated so closely that it would have just
reached if these seven guests had not appeared? When

explanations are too easy they are sometimes wrong. In Palestine a universal drink such as wine would be provided even by a poor groom in such abundance that, instead of running short, the supply would leave plenty over. John simply records the fact, the wine began to run short; let us stay with that. God's providence thus provided "the hour" for Jesus. If we must have explanation, let it be that somebody had blundered by not obtaining enough wine — not enough for the company to be served counting also Jesus and his disciples.

Since Mary takes the matter in hand she must have been one of those who helped with the serving, in fact, the one who oversaw and managed affairs as also her word to the helpers indicates. It is she who thus turns to Jesus. Now here again some follow a course of explanation that is a little too obvious and easy. They think that by coming to her son she followed only the ordinary impulse of the long previous years when in any difficulty in her home life in Nazareth she turned to him. We are told positively that Mary never dreamed of a miracle when she came to her Son and said, "They have no wine," i. e., they are running short of wine. But what *did* Mary expect? Having just come from afar, in a village new to him, where he appears only as an honored guest, whence and how could Jesus at a moment's notice supply more wine? The sensible thing for Mary would have been, since she had come early to help and to manage, that she should have used her own resources or should have called in the aid of other helpers who lived in Cana, some neighbor or some friend of the groom who had a supply of wine close by. No; she goes to her Son Jesus! The old commentators are right — here is more than an ordinary appeal for help.

Here are the items that count. Jesus had left his home to begin his career as the Messiah; he had been baptized by John and had returned with six disciples; the report of what had transpired right after his Baptism together with the testimonies of the Baptist, of the six disciples, and of Jesus himself, reached Mary's ears first of all. These things brought back to her mind the great facts connected with her Son's conception, birth, etc. We know this woman's character, the depth of her nature, the clarity of her knowledge and intuition. She knew her son was the Messiah of whom wondrous things were to be expected. Like Mary of Bethany, who foresaw Jesus' death by violence and grasped the moment at the feast made for him by his friends and anointed him for his burying, 12:1-8, so Jesus' mother turns to her son at this critical moment during the wedding feast. Just what she did expect of him — was it fully clear to her own mind? The answer: ordinary help, fails to meet the case entirely. The answer must be: extraordinary, wondrous help. This touch, too, is true regarding Mary — she asks nothing, not even, "Can or will you do something?" She simply states the difficulty and humbly leaves all else to Jesus. To offer the suggestion that, since Jesus brought six extra men and thus caused the shortage, he had best leave at once and thus induce others to leave also, resolves the predicament mentioned by Mary in a rather trivial manner.

4) The answer of Jesus to his mother creates surprise. **And Jesus says to her, What is that to me and thee, woman? Mine hour has not yet come.** The question: τί ἐμοὶ καὶ σοί; is idiomatic, compare Matt. 8:29; Luke 8:28; Mark 1:24; 5:7, a fixed formula, well rendered by Luther, *"Was habe ich mit dir zu schaffen?"* It is elliptical, indeed, but not in the sense, "What have we to do with that?" meaning colloquially, "Never mind!" (R. 539). The literal thought is, "What is there for me and thee?" i. e.,

in common for us in this matter. Yet not, "This is not my concern but thine"; but the opposite, "This is my affair not thine." Thus already in this question a hidden promise is included. The other thought is that Jesus thrusts his mother away — gently but firmly. She comes to him with the expectation that in the present difficulty he will show his Messianic powers by doing something very much out of the ordinary. This he does not refuse to do but he declares that it is his own affair entirely, and that even his own mother must leave it altogether to him. Having entered on his great office, the old relation obtaining at Nazareth when he obeyed all her wishes like any ordinary dutiful son, is forever at an end. He has assumed his higher position, and even his mother must recognize that fact. "Although there is no higher power on earth than father's and mother's power, even this is at an end when God's word and work begin." Luther. The address γύναι, "woman," sounds harsher in translation than it is or was meant to be in the original. It is of a piece with the question itself. To see and to feel that it contains no trace of disrespect recall 19:26, where Jesus uses the same word in committing his mother to John. He does not say "mother" but "woman," for, while Mary will forever remain his mother, in his calling Jesus knows no mother or earthly relative, he is their Lord and Savior as well as of all men. The common earthly relation is swallowed·up in the divine. Matt. 12:46-50.

What the question tells Mary the additional statement makes still clearer, "Mine hour has not yet come." In ἡ ὥρα μου the possessive must not be overlooked. This expression is not a mere reference to time, as though Jesus only bids Mary wait a little. Nor is it only like καιρός, the time proper for something, the season for it. We often meet the expression with reference to Christ, his death, his resurrection,

etc. His enemies cannot triumph over him as long as
his hour has not yet come; not until then will be their
hour and the power of darkness, Luke 22:53. Note
the similar expression ἡ ἡμέρα τοῦ Κυρίου. Jesus' hour
is the one appointed for him by the Father; it may
be the hour for this or for that in his Messianic work.
When it comes, he acts, and not until it comes. So
Jesus never hurries, nor lets others hurry him, he
waits for his hour and then meets it. He is never
uneasy or full of fear, for nothing can harm him
until his hour comes; and when it comes, he gives his
life into death. Here the hour is the one arranged
for the first miraculous manifestation of his glory.
In performing this miracle he will not be importuned
even by his mother. In "not yet come" lies the
promise that his hour will, indeed, come. Mary also
thought that οὔπω, "not yet," intimated that the hour
was close at hand. Compare the author's *His Footsteps*, 100, etc.

5) If the coming of Mary to Jesus in the first
place is extraordinary in its motivation and its purpose, and if the answer of Jesus is still more extraordinary in its signification and implication, both the
coming and the answer are matched by the sequel:
**His mother says to the servants, Whatever he shall
tell you, do!** Mary's mind responds fully to that of
her great son. What his question, his form of address,
the word about his hour, mean flashes instantaneously
through her mind and heart. We need not suppose
that John abbreviates the dialog, and that Jesus really
said more than is recorded. Other women may have
required more, may have answered back with some
querulous question or remark — not this woman. It
sounds almost humorous when a commentator remarks
about her "genuinely feminine quickness," with which
she sizes up Jesus as following "a man's way" of
rebuffing a suggestion coming from a woman. The

idiosyncracies of sex play no part with the mother of Jesus whose clear spiritual insight here comes to view. Of a piece with the suggestions noted is the surmise that Mary's direction to the servants means that she expects Jesus to order the servants to go out to get some wine from a place near by. Mary could have done that herself. How could Jesus do that as a guest? Whither would he send the servants in a place strange to him? And is this all that "his hour" means?

Mary speaks not to Jesus but to the διάκονοι. This means that she is wholly satisfied with her Son's reply, which also is evidenced by what she tells "the servants." These evidently had not heard her conversation with Jesus. The term διάκονοι is significant. They are not δοῦλοι, "slaves" or "servants" in the lowest sense of our English word, who just obey orders and no more. These are voluntary assistants, come in to help in a friendly way with the work at the wedding feast. They work for the help and the benefit their work brings to the young people and to their festive guests. They lay hand to what is needed of their own accord or at the request of those who manage affairs. Now Jesus was a guest and had no hand in managing affairs; hence to receive orders from him would sound strange to these διάκονοι. On the other hand, Mary's word to them shows her insight in expecting from Jesus an order that itself would sound extraordinary to persons bidden to carry it out. These voluntary assistants might thus hesitate and shake their wise heads, even smile and refuse to act. So as the one who manages the work and directs these assistants come to lend a helping hand Mary gives them positive directions.

These evidence her faith in her Son's implied promise and meet the situation regarding the servants so exactly that Jesus, too, accepted her order to them on his part and used those servants when working his miracle. "Whatever he tells you," is like the indefinite relative clause in 1:33, which see. The aorist imperative is peremptory, "Do at once! do without question!" However strange the act may seem to you, foolish even to your wise eyes, useless, trivial, whatever it proves to be — do it! If only more of us would obey Mary's word, "Whatever he tells you, do!"

6) Here John inserts a necessary parenthetical remark, hence δέ. **Now there were six waterpots of stone set there after the Jews' manner of purifying, containing two or three firkins apiece.** These were stoneware jars, amphoræ, such as are still used in Syria. We do not regard ἦσαν . . . κείμεναι either as a circumscribed imperfect or as "a past perfect in sense" (R. 906) ; B.-D. is right, in John the participle is nearly always independent, compare 1:9 and 28. This is especially true when the words are as widely separated as is the case here. John tells us that the waterpots "were there" and then adds how they came to be there, "having been set there in accord (κατά) with the Jews' manner of purification" (κεῖμαι is generally used as the perfect passive of τίθημι). Just where they stood no one can say, but it was certainly not where the feast was spread. From v. 9 we gather that they stood where the guests could not see them, and the entire action of filling up these pots was known at first only to Jesus himself and to the servants who did the work, probably also to watchful Mary and to a few others.

"In accord with the purification of the Jews" is added by John for the sake of his Greek readers. The old regulations for purification were greatly extended in unauthorized ways during the post-Babylonian period, so that also cups, pots, brazen vessels were

washed ("baptized") as a matter of ritual observance,
Mark 7:4, and some texts add couches, those on which
a person reclined when dining. The washing of hands,
especially before eating, Mark 7:3, was done only in
a formal way, merely by dipping the finger into water.
John adds that the number of pots was six and tells
us how much water each (ἀνά, distributive) could hold,
namely two or three "firkins." The Attic μετρητής is
estimated at over 8½ gallons (Josephus) and answers
in general to the Hebrew *bath*. The Rabbinists, however, make the *bath* equal to a little less than 4½
gallons. Which estimate John has in mind is hard
to decide, see Smith, *Bible Dictionary* for all the available data. The higher and more probable estimate
reaches at least 110 gallons, the lower and less probable
about 60 gallons. John is at pains in his brief narration to let us know about the great quantity of wine
which Jesus created, giving the number of the vessels
and what amount of water they held, χωροῦσαι, literally,
"giving place to," i. e., containing. But it has been
asked, "Was so much water necessary for purification
purposes on this occasion?" If we ourselves could
have attended the wedding, counted the number of the
guests, and watched just how the water was used, we
could answer this question in detail. As it is, we can
only say that, even if the young couple was poor, the
company of guests seems to have been a considerable
number. As far as the addition of seven more persons by the coming of Jesus and his disciples is concerned, this cut but a small figure in general and none
at all in explaining the shortage of wine. The wash-
ings, too, which the Jews practiced seem to have included much more than is usually assumed. The six
pots of wine which Jesus created correspond in a
striking way to the six disciples with whom he appeared at this wedding and recall the miracle of the

loaves when twelve baskets of fragments were left
over, one for each of the twelve disciples with Jesus,
Matt. 14:15-21.

7)   Now Jesus acts.   **Jesus says to them, Fill
the waterpots with water.   And they filled them to
the brim.**   Jesus' hour had come.   The supposition
that Jesus waited until the wine provided for the wedding was actually used up, until the moment when
it would have to be announced to all the guests that
no more wine could be served, may be in accord with
the facts, since the ingressive aorist in v. 3: ὑστερήσαντος
οἴνου, "wine having begun to give out," points to a
total lack that would presently set in.   Jesus might
have ignored Mary's order to the helpers, but he uses
it and thereby honors his mother.   The gender of
αὐτοῖς, "them," easily refers back to τοῖς διακονίοις in v. 5.
The aorist imperative γεμίσατε is strong like ποιήσατε in
v. 5, a straight, authoritative order.   Verbs of filling
take the genitive, here ὕδατος, "with water."   If Jesus
reclined at the feast with the other guests, we may
assume that he quietly arose and went out to where the
pots stoods and the helpers were busy.   So Mary, too,
when she first spoke to Jesus, may have beckoned him
to come to her and then made known to him the impending lack of wine.   Were the pots empty when
Jesus gave his order?   John skips such details.   But
we may well assume that nis order meant that the pots
should be filled with entirely fresh water.   The order
is carried out by the helpers with alacrity, which implies that a well or spring was not far off.   One
wonders what the helpers thought while they were
filling up those jars.   John adds only the little touch
ἕως ἄνω, "to the brim."   Did managing Mary insist on
their obeying orders promptly and strictly?   Well,
they would!   Did the helpers smile at each other
when they carried all that water to the pots and
crack jokes with each other about this Rabbi who

would give the guests this precious water as a new
kind of wine?

8) The job is done, the pots are full, the eye of
Jesus watching until the last one was filled. Was
Mary in the background also looking on? Now comes
the second order, as astonishing at the first. **And
he says to them, Dip out now and go on bringing
to the steward of the feast. And they brought.** The
miracle had been wrought, the water was now wine.
Crashaw has the beautiful poetic line:

> *Lympha pudica Deum vidit et erubuit.*

Note the tenses, first the aorist ἀντλήσατε, for a quantity
is to be dipped out into some fair-sized vessel; then the
durative present φέρετε, "go on bringing" as wine may
be needed at the tables for the guests. R. 855 is correct when he says that in the midst of the aorists in
v. 5-8 this present tense stands out; but when he explains it as being "probably a polite conative offer
to the master of the feast," he regards this tense as
an aoristic present. The durative sense is far more
natural in this connection. What Jesus ordered the
helpers did. The ἀρχιτρίκλινος was the manager of the
feast, whether he himself was one of the guests selected
for the office by the groom or one who did not dine
with the rest as a guest, is hard to say. One of his
functions is incidentally mentioned, namely that of
tasting food and drink before these were offered to the
guests. He is named from the *triclina,* couches for
three persons each, three of them usually placed on
three sides of a low table, for the guests to recline on
while dining.

9) John reports in detail what happened. **Now
when the steward of the feast tasted the water that
had become wine and knew not whence it was (but
the servants knew, who had dipped the water), the
steward of the feast calls the bridegroom and says**

to him, **Every man sets on first the good wine, and
when they have drunk freely, the worst; thou hast
kept the good wine until now.** The first δέ continues
the narrative, the second indicates the parenthesis.
We must read as one concept τὸ ὕδωρ οἶνον γεγενημένον,
"the water having become wine," οἶνον without the
article being marked as the predicate of the participle.
This perfect participle has its usual present implication: the water once turned into wine remained wine.
The addition, "and knew not whence it was" (ᾔδει,
see 1:31), explains the steward's subsequent action.
Busy with his duties, he had not observed what had
been going on elsewhere. We infer that if he, whose
business it was to watch all the proceedings, did not
know, then also none of the guests knew. But the
διάκονοι "knew," knew at firsthand, even also as John
now adds the attributive participle, "who had dipped
the water," οἱ ἠντληκότες, not an aorist to indicate the
one act, but the perfect tense, describing these servants as what they continued to be. It seems that at
the moment they said nothing but allowed the triclinarch to proceed. It also took them a while to
realize fully what had occurred under their very eyes
and hands. When they awoke to the situation they
surely talked volubly enough.

10) The moment the triclinarch tasted the wine,
it flashed into his mind that someone had made a
grand mistake in regard to the wine. He hastens to
call the bridegroom, and John reports this detail first
in order to indicate the actuality of the miracle:
water turned into wine; and secondly, to indicate the
quality of this wine. Note this: as Jesus made a
great quantity of wine, so he also made this of the
greatest excellence. The triclinarch points out the fact
that the bridgroom has made a serious mistake. He
has allowed the poor wine to be served first and kept
this excellent (καλόν) wine until the last; whereas

everybody, when he is compelled to use two such qualities of wine, does the reverse. The groom, of course, is even more astonished than his steward, for he knew of no such good wine. No doubt he, too, at once tasted it and thus saw the situation for himself.

In describing the usual custom the steward uses the clause: καὶ ὅταν μεθυσθῶσιν, aorist passive subjunctive to denote the definite future fact. Some are overanxious regarding the verb μεθύσκω, "to make drunk," and the passive used in the same sense as the middle, "to become drunk," as if this steward here implies that the wedding guests were really drunk, and this excellent wine was thus utterly wasted on them. The entire context and the entire situation obviate this anxiety. The context implies only that after some time of drinking the sense of taste is blunted and does not readily distinguish the exact quality of wine. The steward is stating a general rule followed at feasts; it would be wholly untrue for him to say, when stating this rule, that the participants at such feasts always became drunk and were then fooled by having cheap wine passed to them. The situation here, as far as any application of the steward's rule to the guests at this wedding is concerned, on its very face bars out all excess. The steward cannot mean that the guests are drunk, and therefore this excellent wine will be lost upon them. It is utterly impossible for us to imagine Jesus being present in a tipsy crowd, to say nothing of aiding such carousing by his first miracle. The very thought could be entertained only by those "eager to mar, if by any means they could, the image of a perfect Holiness, which offends and rebukes them," Trench.

The word of the steward has frequently been allegorized. The wine that is worse is made to mean all that the world offers us, or again all that the false

Judaism of the day offered; while the excellent wine which Jesus created is made to mean the gospel and its true riches and joys. The text itself contains no such thoughts. The word on which these thoughts are based is not even a word of Christ but of an ordinary Jew who voiced a common observation. Allegory, especially in preaching, easily misleads. It only superimposes our own thoughts on words of Holy Writ. If it is used at all, it should be used with great care and always in such a way that our own thoughts remain clearly distinguished from what the written words actually state.

John's account is criticized as being incomplete. Such incompleteness is charged against him in quite a number of cases. We are told that he only furnishes "sketches." But this is a misconception of the evangelist's chief purpose, which is never to tell all that is interesting and all that we might desire to know about this or that great event but simply to present the attestation which reveals the Savior as the God-man. Viewed from this point of the evangelist's own purpose, the account of this miracle is perfect and complete.

11) John himself corroborates this when he closes his account as follows. **This did Jesus as a beginning of the signs in Cana of Galilee and manifested his glory; and his disciples believed in him.** The account as written by John purposes to show this first miracle as a sign, i. e., as signaling or manifesting Jesus' glory. Hence no name of bride and groom and no details about the minor persons, and no record as to what they thought or did during or after the wedding. All centers on Jesus and this "sign" and is used in the account only as helping to direct our attention to that center. We must read ταύτην by itself, namely as τοῦτο, which is attracted to the gender of the following ἀρχήν, "this . . . as a beginning

of the signs," etc. Our versions translate as if the text were: ταύτην τὴν ἀρχήν (at best an inferior variant), "this beginning," etc. After telling us in v. 1 that this miracle was wrought in Cana of Galilee, it would be a lame repetition again to say this at the close of the account. What John in closing tells us is that this miracle which was the first of all the miracles was done in Cana of Galilee. John wants it impressed upon us — not in Judea but here in Galilee the signs began. This is again emphasized in 4:46 and 54.

To designate these deeds John uses σημεῖα (σημαίνω, to make known by a σῆμα), "signs," deeds that indicate something, that convey a great meaning to the mind and to the heart. The translation "miracles," deeds which produce wonder, is inadequate; for it loses the ethical force of "signs." These point beyond themselves to something which they accredit and attest, first of all to the person who works these signs and to his significance; by that, however, also, in the case of Jesus most directly, to the new era he is ushering in. The ethical side, then, is that signs always require faith in what is signified, coupled with obedience on the part of those who see the signs. Unbelief and disobedience thus become the great crime against the signs. The term as well as its sense were well known to the Jews from the Old Testament, were constantly used in the apostolic church, and, doubtless, were used by Jesus himself to designate his own works. John's Gospel naturally uses this term in the sense of the strongest and the most tangible testimony for Jesus' divinity, always counting those guilty who meet the signs with unbelief. A few days before the wedding Jesus had attested himself by his words to the men who then became his disciples; these attestations were the prelude to the sign now wrought, one of those deeds of which he himself afterward said that no other man before him had wrought such works, 15:24. We often find σημεῖα linked with τέρατα (τέρας), "wonders," startling, amazing portents; but the latter is never used alone but always in conjunction with other terms that bring out their difference from the pagan portents. Frequent, too, is δυνάμεις, indicative of the divine power in the deeds. Next ἔνδοξα (neuter plural) as revelations of the divine glory; παράδοξα, strange things, only Luke 5:26; θαυμάσια, provoking wonder, only Matt. 21:15, though we often have θαυμάζω as a result of miracles.

"And he manifested his glory," is John's own description of what Jesus really did in this sign at Cana. The δόξα is the sum of the divine attributes or any one of these, shining forth to the eyes and the hearts of men; compare 1:14.

To the inner significance John appends the effect, "and his disciples believed in him." On the verb compare 1:12. The aorist states the fact: they rested their confidence in him as the Messiah and did this in consequence of the sign here wrought. Following their original acceptance and faith, as recounted in the previous chapter, ἐπίστευσαν here implies an increase of faith. It was, indeed, faith in the true sense of the word and yet it was only initial, needing more revelation and strength for its full development. On the term μαθηταί see v. 2.

This pericope opens up the entire question of miracles in the sense of the Scriptures, to which rationalism and a certain so-called "science" have always objected and will always object. The effort to believe the sacred record and at the same time to explain the accounts of the miracles so that they become only natural occurrences, must in the nature of the case always fail. The alternatives are exclusive, and only self-deception of a strong kind is able to hide that fact.

Minor thoughts are that by his first sign Jesus honors marriage and the family relation. By the great quantity of excellent wine he actually makes a valuable wedding present to the couple at Cana. The prohibition movement looks askance at Jesus who not only himself drank wine but presented such a quantity at Cana. The plea that, if Jesus had lived in our time, he would never have wrought this sign, virtually attacks the moral character of the Savior and of God who made wine to gladden the heart of man. The fact remains, the Scriptures nowhere condemn wine and its right use but only any and all forms of its abuse.

II

The Public Attestation Throughout the Holy Land, 2:12-4:54

The attestation by the Baptist and that by Jesus himself, as recorded hitherto, are preliminary. Even the first sign is wrought in a family circle. The evangelist now shows us the public ministry of Jesus in its full swing, grouping together a number of most notable attestations to his divine Sonship. First, The Cleansing of the Temple with its Further Effect, 2:12-25; secondly, The Conversation with Nicodemus, 3:1-21; thirdly, Jesus in Judea and the Last Testimony of the Baptist, 3:22-36; fourthly, Jesus in Samaria, 4:1-42; fifthly, Jesus in Galilee, 4:43-54.

The Cleansing of the Temple with its Further Effects, 2:12-25. — Quite simply the events are connected: after the miracle at Cana Jesus moves his home to Capernaum and from there he attends the festival at Jerusalem. **After this there went down to Capernaum he himself and his mother and the brothers and his disciples; and they remained not many days.** In John's Gospel the singular μετὰ τοῦτο connects quite closely in point of time, while μετὰ ταῦτα bridges a longer interval. The verb is singular to match the first subject, which is, therefore, also expressed by αὐτός and is followed by the other subjects. The force is: "He went down to Capernaum, and when I say 'he' (Jesus), this means he with the family and with the disciples." So the family changed its residence from Nazareth to Capernaum. Since the fact is known to John's readers from the other Gospels, he does not need to say that after the wedding all went back to Nazareth, packed up, and moved. Whether "the brothers" were at the wedding is not indicated; if they were, John finds no occasion to mention this fact. Yet we see that the disciples remained with Jesus. There is no discrepancy with Matt. 4:13, for Matthew omits what lies between the temptation in the wilderness and Christ's return from Jerusalem to Capernaum, hence he reports only that Jesus made his home at Capernaum on his return from Jerusalem. John supplements this by stating just how early the transfer was made.

It remains an unsettled question as to who the ἀδελφοί were, whether they were sons of Joseph and Mary born to them after Jesus; or sons of Joseph by a former marriage; or only cousins of Jesus through Clopas, the brother of Joseph. Each supposition has some proof but also some undeniable disproof. This, of course, is true also regarding the sisters, who are not mentioned here, since in all probability they remained in Nazareth, being held there by their marital ties. Capernaum on the shores of the Sea of Galilee was a populous place, through which passed the caravan trade route from Damascus to the Mediterranean. Here John and James had their home with Zebedee and Salome, their parents; and Peter lived here with his mother-in-law, Mark 1:29, etc. Just why Jesus made the transfer is hard to say, except that it was possible for his disciples to be near him without all of them forsaking their homes, and for the future it offered a field that was better suited for Jesus' labors than the small and retired Nazareth in the hills. When John adds that "here they remained not many days," he includes all the persons mentioned and implies in the sequel that at the end of these days all of them went to attend the Passover at Jerusalem. In v. 13 John reports this regarding Jesus, but in v. 17 we see that the disciples were with him at the festival. It is entirely in order to think that Mary and the brothers were also there. During this first brief stay in Capernaum Jesus lived quietly in contact with his disciples, away from the excitement his miracle had caused in Cana. Even now Jesus knows how to wait.

13) **And the Passover of the Jews was near, and Jesus went up to Jerusalem.** The approach of the Passover marks not only the time but indicates also the motive for the journey. This is the first Passover since Jesus assumed his ministry. The festival lasted seven days. Its crowning glory was the eating of the roasted lamb by a party numerous enough to consume it together with the bitter herbs. Every man of the Jews from twelve years up was supposed to attend this festival at Jerusalem, which overflowed the city with pilgrims. The addition "of the Jews" shows that John is writing for general readers. On the use of this term by John see 1:19. Invariably the Jews "went up to Jerusalem," no matter how elevated the locality from which they started. The verb, often enough true physically, (the Lake of Galilee lies 600 feet below sea level), is really meant ethically and spiritually. The hour has come for Jesus to step forth publicly before his nation. His first great public act would take place in the capital, yea, in the Temple itself. The great Paschal Lamb, of whom the Baptist had testified to his disciples, attends the

great Paschal Feast and there foretells his own death and sacrifice.

14) Without a single further word the evangelist presents the account which he wants his readers to have. **And he found in the Temple those that were selling oxen and sheep and doves, and the money-changers sitting.** The verb merely states the fact, not — as has been said — an occasion God offered for his Son's work. The condition of the Temple at this time was the work of men; it was what they had made of the Temple that Jesus "found." The part of the Temple here referred to is the court of the Gentiles, the ἱερόν. About the sanctuary proper (ναός) were four courts, that of the priests surrounding the building, that of the men toward the east, that of the women likewise, beyond that of the men. Around these three was an extensive court, called that of the Gentiles, since Gentiles were permitted to enter it. The outer side consisted of magnificent colonnades. "There, in the actual court of the Gentiles steaming with heat in the burning April day, and filling the Temple with stench and filth, were penned whole flocks of sheep and oxen, while the drovers and pilgrims stood bartering and bargaining around them. There were the men with the wicker cages filled with doves, and under the shadows of the arcade, formed by quadruple rows of Corinthian columns, sat the money-changers, with their tables covered with piles of various small coins, while, as they reckoned and wrangled in the most dishonest of trades, their greedy eyes twinkled with the lust of gain. And this was the entrance-court of the Most High! The court which was a witness that that house should be a House of Prayer for all nations had been degraded into a place which for foulness was more like shambles and for bustling commerce more like a densely crowded bazaar; while the lowing of oxen, the bleating of sheep, the babel of many

languages, the huckstering and wrangling, the clinking of money and of balances (perhaps not always just) might be heard in the adjoining courts, disturbing the chant of the Levites and the prayers of the priests!" Farrar, *The Life of Christ*, 455, etc.

The cattle and the doves were a necessity for the prescribed sacrifices, but to make of the great court a stockyard was the height of abuse. The little banks were also necessary, for a tax was taken from every Israelite who was twenty years old, Exod. 30, 11-16. This tax was collected during the month preceding the Passover and was either sent in by those at a distance or paid in person by those attending, who then, however, had to have Jewish coin, compelling all who came from foreign parts to have their money changed. For this a small rate was charged. A κερματιστής (from κέρμα, that which is cut off, i. e., a small coin) is one who deals in coins; and καθημένους describes these bankers "sitting" crosslegged behind low stool-like τράπεζαι on which their stacks of coins were ranged — open for business.

15) Jesus makes short work of this abuse. **And having made a scourge of cords, he cast all out of the Temple, also the sheep and the oxen, and he scattered the coins of the money-changers and upset their tables; and to those selling doves he said, Take these things hence! Stop making my Father's house a house of merchandise.** The public ministry of Jesus begins with an act of holy wrath and indignation. The Son cleans his Father's house with the lash of the scourge. No halfway measures, no gradual and gentle correction will do in a matter as flagrant as this. Here at the very start is the stern and implacable Christ. The aorists of the narrative are impressive; they state what was done, done in short order, done decisively and completely, begun and finished then and there.

Without speaking a word Jesus picks up a few pieces of rope, such as were ready at hand where so many cattle were tied. The aorist participle ποιήσας marks this as the preparatory action. He twists these into a scourge. Tender souls have imagined that Jesus only menaced with the scourge, at least that he struck only the animals. They are answered by πάντας ἐξέβαλεν, and πάντας is masculine, its antecedent being τοὺς πωλοῦντας and τοὺς κερματιστάς the men who were selling and the money-changers. With fiery indignation Jesus applied the scourge right and left to these men. Then also to the sheep and the oxen. John never uses τε . . . καί in the sense of "both . . . and," so that here we might read: he drove out "all, *both* the sheep *and* the oxen." This is shut out also by John's reversing the order, now placing the neuter πρόβατα first, whereas in v. 14 he has this word second. We must translate: he drove out "all" (the men), "also the sheep and the oxen." The verb ἐξέβαλεν refers to the three objects alike, and the participle ποιήσας which is to be construed with this verb explains that he drove all these men and these beasts out by means of the scourge he had made. Ethically nothing is gained for Jesus by making him only threaten to strike either the men and the beasts or only the men; for ethically, to threaten is equal to carrying out the threat. The scourge was no mere sham.

The same summary proceeding drove out the money-changers. The κόλλυβος is the small coin paid for exchange, hence κολλυβιστής is the banker who makes the exchange. Jesus "poured out" or "scattered" their κέρματα or "coins," perhaps with a flip of the scourge. But he also upset their τράπεζαι, the low little tables behind which they squatted. This reads as if he kicked them over. Short work, thorough and complete, a general scatterment and stampede.

16)   Fancy has stepped in to say that Jesus dealt more leniently with the doves and their sellers, either because the doves were gentler (forgetting the gentle lambs), or because the doves were the offering of the poor (forgetting that the poor paid also the half shekel Temple tax), or — more strangely still — because the dove is the symbol of the Holy Ghost (forgetting that the lamb certainly symbolized Christ himself). The doves were in closed crates. To get rid of these crates they had to be carried away; hence the peremptory aorist, "Take these things hence!" with the derogatory ταῦτα referring to the crates and their contents, which have no business to be here. It is invention to say that when Jesus came to the doves he suddenly regained his self-control. During the entire proceeding Jesus never lost his self-control; if he had, he would have sinned. The stern and holy Christ, the indignant, mighty Messiah, the Messenger of the Covenant of whom it is written: "He shall purify the sons of Levi, and purge them as gold and silver, that they may offer unto the Lord an offering of righteousness," is not agreeable to those who want only a soft and sweet Christ. But John's record here, and that of the second cleansing of the Temple (Matt. 21:12, etc., and the parallels), portray the fiery zeal of Jesus which came with such sudden and tremendous effectiveness that before this unknown man, who had no further authority than his own person and word, this crowd of traders and changers, who thought they were fully within their rights when conducting their business in the Temple court, fled pell-mell like a lot of naughty boys.

In peremptory fashion, without a connective, comes the second command, "Stop making my Father's house a house of merchandise!"   The present imperative in negative commands often means that an action already begun is to stop; so here, R. 861, etc.   While this follows the command to the sellers of doves, it is evidently intended for all the traffickers. This is not the voice of a zealot vindicating the holiness of the Temple, nor of a prophet speaking in the name or Israel's God; this is the voice of the Son of God himself to whom the Temple was "my Father's house." As God's Son, who has the Son's right in this house and the Son's power over this house, Jesus uses his right and his power. And the Father supports his Son by lending his act power to drive these Temple desecrators out through the Temple gates in wild flight. By this word, "my Father's house," Jesus attests both his Sonship and his Messiahship. "And the Lord, whom ye seek, shall suddenly come to his Temple, even the Messenger of the Covenant, whom ye delight in: behold, he shall come, saith the Lord of hosts," Mal. 3:1. Thus Jesus again attests himself, and this time publicly.

There is strong contrast between "my Father's house" and "a house of merchandise." This Father and any house of his have to do with prayer, worship, true religion. What a desecration to make his house deal with ἐμπορία, trading, gain-getting, which is so much mixed with unjust dealing and at best is only secular, even if it is here conducted on the plea of providing things that were necessary for worship. Have we not enough places for buying and selling — "emporiums" as our time loves to call them — without invading the place that should be sacred because it is dedicated to God?

But why did these men not resist since they were conscious of their vested rights, having paid the Temple authorities for their concessions? Why, if at first they were startled, did they not presently recover but actually allow themselves to be driven out? Jesus was lone handed, they were many. Not even a show of resistance was offered. The answer is not to be found in their moral cowardice, in the inherent weakness of a sinful course, and on Jesus' part in the conviction of the righteousness of his cause. Sin is not always cowardly but is often bold and presumptuous. When money is at stake, wrong is often arrogant. Besides, this case is wholly extraordinary, beyond the usual clash of sin and righteousness. One explanation alone is adequate to account for this: the Son of man wielded his *divine* authority. Another question is: "Of what good was this outward cleansing as long as the hearts were not cleansed? Of what good was it to shake off a few rotten fruits while the tree itself remained corrupt?" If the object of Jesus' zeal was only these merchants and these bankers, Jesus would sink to the level of our modern reformers who try to mend the leaking ship by repairing the rigging. This question, contrasting the inward with the outward, is not correctly stated. The Temple was the very heart of the Jewish people. Luther is right when he here sees Jesus doing a part of Moses' work. The law must be applied, especially in flagrant cases, on the basis of the light and the knowledge which people have at the time. This Jesus does with his word, "Stop making my Father's house a house of merchandise." On the score of the law alone he corrects the open abuse, so that the gospel with its loftier motive may follow.

17) We now learn, incidentally, that the disciples were with Jesus and witnessed his astounding act although themselves taking no part in it. **His disciples remembered that it had been written, The zeal of thine house shall eat me up.** The aorist "remembered" is like those that precede and those that follow and tells what happened at the time: they remembered this word of Scripture when they beheld what Jesus did. In v. 22 the temporal clause records that, when Christ had risen from the dead, they re-

membered his word about destroying and rebuilding
the Temple.   The Greek retains the present perfect
"has been written" after the aorist "remembered,"
whereas the English would use the pluperfect "had
been written," or the past tense "was written" (our
versions) ; γεγραμμένον ἐστίν is the circumscribed perfect to designate the completed act that stands as
such.

Ps. 69, repeatedly quoted as being typical of Christ,
expresses what David was made to suffer in his zeal
for the Lord.   Thus in v. 9, "The zeal of thine house
hath eaten me up," is explained by the next line,
"And the reproaches of them that reproached thee
are fallen upon me."   His zeal netted him reproach,
hatred, and persecution.   The fear comes into the
heart of Jesus' disciples that the same thing will happen to Jesus.   They thus apply Ps. 69:9 to Jesus, the
application appearing in the change of the tense of
the verb.   In the Hebrew, David has the perfect tense
which is rightly rendered with the aorist by the LXX,
for David spoke of his past experience.   The disciples
think of what the zeal of Jesus will lead to for him
in the future, hence they use καταφάγεται, "will eat
up."   The very word of Jesus about "my Father's
house" involuntarily recalled the Psalm passage to the
disciples' mind.   They did not think of an inward
consuming that uses up one's strength and vitality,
which is suggested neither by the Psalm nor by the
act of Jesus, but of a consuming that is due to opposition and harm inflicted by others.   Here appears the
limitation of the faith of the disciples.   Though they
believed Jesus to be the Son of God, having beheld
his glory (v. 11), and though they again heard the
attestation of his Sonship in "my Father's house," they
were yet afraid that Jesus might come to harm and
his work to a stop through human opposition.   That
is why John puts into his record this remark, as if

he would say, "And we foolish disciples became
frightened for Jesus, remembering what once happened to David." We need not assume that they at
once thought of a violent death for Jesus; their
thoughts did not go that far. The fact that Jesus
had no illusions on this point, v. 19 reveals. The
genitive zeal "of thine house" is objective and thus
may be rendered "for thy house"; the object of the
zeal is God's house.

We need hardly say that we hold, with the best
commentators over against the critical schools, that
Christ cleansed the Temple twice, once at the beginning and once at the close of his public ministry. The
first has been termed an act of grace, the second an
act of judgment; but both are manifestations of grace,
judgment descending on the wicked nation and its
Temple at a far later time. Christ's act is often
viewed as being symbolic: as he here purified the outward Temple, so his mission was to purify it inwardly,
hence not to purify the Temple alone but also the hearts
of the nation. This is quite legitimate, and it opens up
a wide range of application for all time.

18) The commotion caused by Jesus and the quick
report of his unheard of procedure brought the authorities down upon him. John is not concerned with the
dramatic story as a story, hence he abbreviates this so
as to bring correctly only the great testimony elicited
from Jesus. **The Jews, accordingly, answered and
said unto him, What sign showest thou to us, since
thou doest these things?** The fact that ἀπεκρίθησαν is
used to "answer" situations as well as questions, and
that doubling the two finite verbs "answered and said"
(instead of making one a participle) is more formal
and adds more weight, has been shown in 1:48. John
conveys the thought that the demand of the Jews was
formal and serious. John likes the resumptive οὖν,
"accordingly," which, after the remark in v. 17, re-

verts to the situation as it was left in v. 16: "accordingly," after the sellers and the truck had been removed, these official interrogators appear.

John merely calls them "the Jews" as though he cared to give them no higher title; see 1:19, where the term is explained and where its first use by John already has an unpleasant sound. Here the hostile attitude is quite marked. We infer from their formality and from their words as also from the character of Jesus' reply that these were Sanhedrists who were accompanied by some of the Temple police. They speak as men who have full authority and demand that Jesus show his credentials *to them,* ἡμῖν emphatically at the end. The question put to Jesus is based on the assumption that he has no official authority to proceed as a public reformer of the established Jewish customs. An unknown layman and mere visitor cannot be allowed to take matters into his own hands. A second thought behind the question put to Jesus, one that may in some part also help us to understand why Jesus met no resistance from the traders and the money-changers, is the general Jewish expectation of a "reliable prophet" who, when he would come, would either confirm their cultus arrangements or appoint better ones. For this reason also many of the rabbis attached to their decisions the formula, "until Elias comes." The same thought lies behind 1:21. These authorities, therefore, are quite careful in their proceeding against Jesus. They demand his credentials and take it that these must consist in some "sign" of a nature to vindicate his right to interfere in the Temple arrangements. We may read "what sign" or "what as a sign"; and ὅτι, "since," may be called elliptical: this we ask since, etc. Also "these things" implies that Jesus may attempt to go farther and to upset more of the Temple arrangements. On σημεῖον see 2:11.

19) The simple, quiet Jesus who had spent his days in little Nazareth is not in the least flustered by this clash with the supreme authorities of the nation — he meets them as their superior. **Jesus answered and said unto them, Destroy this sanctuary, and in three days I will raise it up.** John retains "answered and said" when introducing the reply of Jesus, thus marking its great weight. This reply is a flat refusal to furnish the kind of a sign demanded by these Jews. The explanation that, instead of considering the inner justification for the act of Jesus, these Jews ask for outward credentials, is insufficient. The same is true regarding the observation that an unspiritual outward miracle is demanded for a deed that appealed inwardly to the conscience, and that such a course could keep on with its demands for a sign and would never be content. More must be said, much more.

This is unbelief that demands a sign. Whenever unbelief asks a sign to convince itself, it does so only in order to reject every sign that could be given it, save one. So whenever unbelief made its demand for a sign on Jesus, he did the only thing possible, he pointed to that one sign which even unbelief will have to accept: the sign of the judgment. Jesus did signs enough, signs of grace, but these leaders, even while they admitted their occurrence (11:47), accepted none of them. Only when at last the Temple would fall about their ears, and the wrath of God visibly descend upon their guilty heads, then, too late, they would have their convincing sign and would by *that* sign know that Jesus was the Messiah indeed. And this explains another point that all the commentators whom the author has examined overlook: why Jesus answered by a veiled reference to the judgment. The unbelief that rejects the proffered grace and its signs is bound to stay in the dark, God intends to leave it there. So, indeed, it is pointed to the sign that shall crush it at

last but never as though that sign could or should
change such unbelief into faith. When that sign
comes, it will be too late for faith. Even the premoni-
tions of the sign of final judgment, which faith is only
too glad to heed, unbelief scorns as it does all the
signs of present grace as not being sufficient to meet
its exacting demands.

The reply of Jesus, therefore, fits the men who
make the demand. They want a convincing sign, one
that will convince *them*. Well, Jesus has one, of
course, only one. They cannot have that now, but in
due time they shall have it. What that sign is they
are told in a way that piques their curiosity. If it
were told outright, they would only resent the telling;
but since it is told in the way in which Jesus tells it,
his words will stick in their minds and secretly haunt
them with their mysterious, threatening meaning.
Jesus could the more easily do this since the Semitic
mind loves mysteries and often uses enigmatical words
which require either that the hearer have the secret
key or go in search for it and find it. These Jews
could have found the key to the enigma given them
here if they had allowed the grace of Jesus to enlighten
their hearts during their day of grace. The disciples
found that key as v. 22 shows, but the Jews, because
their unbelief grew only more intense, never found it
(Matt. 26:61; 27:40; Mark 14:57; 15:29).

Like a flash of lightning the answer of Jesus
illumined an awful abyss and cast a glare into regions
which still lay in darkness for every mind except his
own. The word about destroying the Temple reveals
the inner character of the whole Jewish treatment of
Jesus; and the following word about the raising up of
that Temple unveils in all its greatness the work
Jesus had now begun. The form of statement is the
mashal, a Hebrew term that is similar to the German *Sinnspruch,* a veiled and pointed saying, which

is sometimes equal to a *chidah* or riddle. The history
which follows shows that this first word of Jesus to
the Jews did its work, sticking to their minds to the
last and plainly causing them no small discomfort
despite all their violent unbelief. "Destroy this Sanctuary, and in three days I will raise it up" — that is
the one sign *for them*. The aorist imperative to express the one decisive act is followed by the future
indicative which is also punctiliar, the second action
being contingent on the first. The word ναός refers
to the Sanctuary proper, comprising the Holy Place
and the Holy of Holies, as distinct from ἱερόν which
included the entire Temple area with its various extensive courts and structures. What follows shows
that *"this* Sanctuary" could not have been spoken
by Jesus accompanied by a gesture pointing to his own
body. Jesus speaks of the Sanctuary before the eyes
of all, the material building with its white marble
walls and its gilded roof and pinnacles sparkling in
the sun.

**20) The Jews, accordingly, said, Forty and six
years was this Sanctuary built, and wilt thou raise
it up in three days? But he was speaking of the
Sanctuary of his body.** The connective οὖν joins this
reply with Jesus' word of mystery. The temporal
dative "forty and six years" views the entire time as a
unit, R. 527, which corresponds with the constative
aorist "was built," the entire extended work being
summarized as one past act, R. 833. In the phrase
"in three days" the preposition lays stress on the
length of the time, here, of course, by comparison so
brief a length. The imperfect ἔλεγε in v. 21, "he was
speaking," dwells on what Jesus was saying, as one
turns over in his mind the meaning of what one is
uttering, for the hearers to do the same thing.

The Jewish Temple was originally built by Solomon
and was destroyed by Nebuchadnezzar. It was rebuilt

on the ruined site by Nehemiah and Ezra.   While it
was not again destroyed, its inferior condition led to
a gradual rebuilding from the foundations up, on a
grander and more elaborate scale, under Herod (hence
it was also called Herod's Temple).   About 2 years,
beginning 20 or 19 B. C., were spent in preparation,
$1\frac{1}{2}$ in building the Porch and the Sanctuary with its
Holy of Holies (16 B. C.) ; 8 years later the court and
the cloisters were finished (9 B. C.) ; other repairs
followed until the time of the present visit of Jesus.
The whole work was not considered as completed until
A. D. 64.   The 46 years $=$ 20 until the Christian era
(when Jesus was 4 years old), plus 27 until the beginning of Jesus' ministry, thus making 46 to 47 in
all.   The questions of chronology that are involved
are more or less intricate.   Compare Josephus, *Ant.*
15 ; 20, 9, 7, where we are told that in the final stages
more than 18,000 workmen were employed.

The Jews, of course, did not grasp what Jesus
meant, but their misunderstanding did not lie in applying his words to the Sanctuary, as though Jesus had
not referred to that building.   Their error lay in applying Jesus' words to this building exclusively.   Their
unbelief saw only this building and nothing of its true
significance and higher connection.   The unbelief of
modern critical minds which rejects "the two nature
theory" regarding Christ's person fares no better with
regard to this word of Jesus than these Jews.   Now
the Sanctuary, the house in which God dwelt among
Israel, was the type of the body of Jesus in which
the Godhead dwelt and tented among men, 1 :14.   The
Sanctuary and Jesus thus belong insolubly together,
the one is the shadow of the other.   This is what the
key to the *mashal* conveys, "But he was speaking of the
Sanctuary, of his body."

The command to destroy the Sanctuary sounded
blasphemous to Jewish ears, for what Jew would think

of such a thing, especially now, when so many years had already been spent in the rebuilding? Mark that Jesus does not say that *he* will destroy it, nor that he *wants* the Jews to do this terrible thing. His words imply the very opposite, namely that he is trying to restrain the Jews from doing this frightful thing but that for some reason and in some way they are bent on doing it in spite of him. He also implies that he knows what secret force impels them to the desperate act: their unbelief and their opposition to the true Messiah, the divine reality for which the Sanctuary stood, without whom it would be an empty, useless shell. Thus the command of Jesus signifies: "Go on in your evil course, since nothing will deter you, and you will have the sign for which you call, the sign that will really convince you!" The imperative is not merely concessive: *If* you destroy. It reckons with the unbelief of the Jews as a deplorable fact that cannot be changed, just as Jesus reckoned also with the treachery of Judas when he gave the command, "That thou doest, do quickly," 13:27. We have a third command of this kind, "Fill ye up the measure of your fathers," i. e., since you are determined to do so, Matt. 24:31. This monstrous deed of destroying their own Sanctuary the Jews will perform by rejecting and killing him who was the divine reality for which the Sanctuary stood, whom it was to serve with all its services.

21) By means of "his body" Jesus dwelt among men. Because of his human nature God's Son became one with us and our Savior. "His body" is thus the "Sanctuary" in and by which we have this Savior. That body of Jesus was prefigured by the material Sanctuary of the Jews. It was a kind of substitute for it until the fulness of time should come. It was a promise of the true and everlasting connection which our Savior-God would make with us sinners by means

of a more sacred Sanctuary or dwelling place, namely our own human nature which was assumed even in a material body but in altogether sinless form when he became man for our sake. At this time when Jesus had cleansed the Temple and was confronted by the guardians of the Temple, there stood side by side the beautiful type and the heavenly antitype: the earthly Sanctuary and the Son of God in his human body. The promise had been replaced at last by the fulfillment. But instead of being impressed by the Savior whom their own Sanctuary had pictured to them for so long a time, they met him in the courts of that Sanctuary with an incipient hostility which would grow into violent rejection. Can they have the type when they reject the antitype? Can they keep the promise when they spurn the fulfillment? What is the use of a beautiful photograph of father or mother when the moment the person himself appears he is thrown out with abuse? By killing the body of Jesus the Jews would pull down their own Sanctuary. It was impossible for the Sanctuary to go on pointing to the human body of the divine Savior when that Savior had come and had been finally rejected. The rejection of the Savior involved judgment (Matt. 26:67) and thus also the taking away of the Sanctuary.

This also explains the promise, "and in three days I will raise it up." The manner of the rebuilding must match the manner of the destruction. If, then, the Sanctuary is destroyed by the killing of the person of the Messiah, it must also again be erected in the resurrection of the Messiah. As his body is killed, so his body will be raised up. And Jesus himself will effect this raising up. The Scriptures use both expressions when speaking of this *opus ad extra*. God raises him up; Jesus himself rises. Thus the sign

the Jews demanded will be theirs indeed: a sign of
infinite grace for all believers but a sign of final judgment for these enemies. All the Jewish efforts to
maintain their Sanctuary and Temple in opposition
to all for which it stood would be in vain. To this
day it has not been rebuilt. The Mohammedan Dome
of the Rock occupies the ancient site. The Temple of
the Jews served its last purpose with its destruction.
It is still the sign that answers unbelief once for all,
the type of the judgment to come. The resurrection
of Jesus wrought the new spiritual temple of God's
people with a new cultus in spirit and in truth (4:21-
24), it needed no more types and symbols since in
Christ we have the promised substance itself. Zech.
6:12, 13; Heb. 3:3.

22) The Jews not only did not understand what
the *mashal* of Jesus meant, they did not want to understand. They wholly ignored its first half and fastened
only on the second half, that Jesus would in three days
erect a building that it had taken forty-six years to
erect. Later, at the trial of Jesus, they boldly falsified
that troublesome first half, making Jesus say, "I am
able to destroy the Sanctuary of God" (Matt. 26:61),
or, "I will destroy this Sanctuary" (Mark 14:58).
From the start the Jews must thus have felt the sting
in that command, "Destroy it by your evil, vicious
practices!" So also the second half, the Jews could
tell themselves, did not mean and could not mean that
Jesus would erect this great complex of a stone structure "in three days." Though they clung to this even
at the trial of Jesus, Mark's rendering, "and in three
days I will build another *made without hands,*" indicates that they had an inkling that the Sanctuary Jesus
intended to build was something other than another
structure of stone. The one point, however, that mystified the Jews completely and was intended by Jesus

to do so was the phrase "in three days." This reference to the resurrection of Jesus was absolutely beyond the Jewish unbelief.

This phrase exceeded also the faith of Jesus' own disciples. Whatever they made of the destruction and of the raising up of the Sanctuary, the "three days" were beyond them. They, to be sure, kept their Master's saying inviolate and in their thoughts neither ignored its first half nor falsified it as the Jews did. But John tells us that they did not understand it until Jesus was actually raised from the dead. **When, therefore, he was raised from the dead, his disciples remembered that he was saying this, and they believed the Scripture and the word which Jesus spoke.** Not until that time did John discover the key and realize that Jesus was speaking of his own body, v. 21. Especially also the "three days" were solved when Jesus died on Friday and arose on Sunday. What kept Jesus' word dark for them was their unwillingness to believe that Jesus would actually die as he kept telling them he would, i. e., that by killing him the Jews would wreck their Sanctuary. Thus they also never caught what Jesus said of his resurrection even when he added that this would occur on the third day after his death. But they remembered at last when the risen Savior stood before them. After the active "I will raise up" John now has the passive "he was raised up." Both are true and both are freely used, one indicating Christ's agency, the other that of his Father. The phrase ἐκ νεκρῶν denotes separation and nothing more, R. 598. The absence of the article points to the *quality* of being dead not to so many dead individuals that are left behind; and the sense of the phrase is, "from death." In the interest of the doctrine of a double resurrection the effort has been made to establish the meaning, "out from among the dead." Linguistically and doctrinally this is untenable. When it is applied to the unique resurrection of Jesus, this is at once apparent; the idea is not that he left the other dead behind but that he passed "from death" to a glorious life. No wonder ἐκ νεκρῶν is never used with reference to the ungodly. The phrase is used 35 times with reference to Christ, a few times with reference to other individuals in a figurative way, and twice with reference to the resurrection of many, Luke 20:35; Mark 12:25, where the phrase cannot have a meaning different from that which it has in the other passages.

John has the imperfect ἔλεγε, "he was saying this," as in v. 21, and here it is set in contrast with the aorist εἶπεν, "which Jesus did say," noting only the past fact as such. Then at last, when Jesus had risen from death, the disciples properly connected the word of Jesus that had stuck in their minds all this time with the Scripture, ἡ γραφή, namely with passages like Ps. 16:9-11; Isa. 53; the type Jonah; etc.; compare Luke 24:25, etc.; John 20:9; Acts 2:24-32; I Cor. 15:4. Thus at last with full understanding the disciples "did believe the Scripture and the word which Jesus (once) spoke." The thought is not that they had disbelieved or doubted either of the two before but that now their implicit faith became explicit faith. A statement like v. 22 which gives us a glimpse into the inner biography of John and of his fellow-disciples bears the stamp of historical reality in a manner so inimitable that only the strongest preconceptions can ignore its implications. No pseudo-John living in the second century could invent this ignorance of the apostle regarding a saying of Jesus that he himself had invented. The critics who make such a claim, as Godet well says, dash themselves against a sheer moral impossibility.

23) The brief glimpse of the effect of the first public activity of Jesus presented in v. 23-25 rounds

out the preceding account of the cleansing of the
Temple and forms a transition to the conversation with Nicodemus, furnishing us with the historical background and the general attitude of Jesus.
**Now while he was in Jerusalem at the Passover dur-
ing the feast many believed in his name, seeing his
signs which he was doing.** **Jesus on his part, however, was not entrusting himself to them on account
of knowing them all, also because he was not in
need that anyone should bear witness concerning this
or that man, since he was aware what was in the
man.**

We hear nothing more about the authorities who
challenged Jesus to produce his credentials. They had
received their answer, and as far as John is concerned
are thus dismissed. The two modifiers "at the Passover" and "during the festival" are not tautological,
for the Passover was observed on the fourteenth of
Nisan, and the festival lasted the whole week following. Jesus remained for the entire time. What he
did John records only incidentally, for his purpose
is to inform us that at this first public appearance of
his he gathered no close disciples as he did down at
Bethany beyond Jordan after his Baptism, and we also
learn the reason why. The fact that by his attendance Jesus meant to step out into public view and to
begin his public Messianic work right here in the
capital of Judaism and right at this greatest festival
of Judaism, should not be denied by making his cleansing of the Temple the sudden impulse of the moment,
and his further activity during the week only incidental
to his presence here at the time. The great hour for
his public labors had come.

While the authorities from the first met him with
unbelief and a show of hostility, this was not the case
with "many" of the pilgrims who had assembled for
the festival. They "believed in his name," i. e., re-

ceived the revelation he made of himself with faith and trust; compare the remarks on τὸ ὄνομα αὐτοῦ in 1:12. John, however, prevents us from regarding this definite statement with its historical aorist as meaning that thus quickly Jesus gained many true disciples who were like the six that believed on him beyond the Jordan. He does this by describing the nature of their faith, "seeing his signs which he was doing." This was the only basis of their faith, not the attestation in the words of Jesus which had kindled the faith of those first six disciples and which was then confirmed by the first miracle of Jesus at Cana. Yet we must not regard this remark about the character of the faith of these many believers as implying that the signs Jesus wrought were not intended to produce faith, which would conflict with their character as "signs" and with passages like 5:36; 10:37, 38; and 14:11. Faith may well begin by first trusting in the signs. But the signs and the Word belong together like a document and the seals attached to it, as the passages just mentioned show. The seals alone eventually amount to nothing. Some advanced from the signs to the Word and thus, believing both, attained abiding faith. Others saw the signs just as clearly but refused the Word and remained in unbelief. When some today would take the Word and yet discard the signs, they invalidate the Word itself, a vital part of which the signs remain, and also fail in faith. The signs so establish the Word that all who began and who now begin with the Word and then accept the signs attain true and abiding faith. The "many" in Jerusalem still hung in the balance with such inadequate faith as they had.

While the incidental object "his signs" only intimates that during this week Jesus wrought such signs for the public, the added relative clause with its imperfect tense ἐποίει, "which he was doing" or "kept doing," declares positively that Jesus wrought a goodly number of such signs. Yet John relates none of them; in his Gospel he records only certain select miracles, such as most clearly and directly serve his purpose. We have seen one of these, that at Cana. By telling us that the "many" in Jerusalem rested their faith only on the signs which Jesus kept doing John does not need to add that during this week Jesus added to the signs by also testifying by his teaching. This the "many" passed by, giving it little, too little, attention.

24) The addition of αὐτός to ὁ Ἰησοῦς intensifies the subject; yet it does not mean "Jesus himself," which would wrongly contrast him with others, but means "Jesus on his part," contrasting his *action* with the other *action* just reported, with adversative δέ, "however," pointing this out. The contrast lies between ἐπίστευσαν in v. 23 and οὐκ ἐπίστευεν αὐτόν (some prefer αὐτόν, R. 688): they "trusted," he "was not entrusting himself." Πιστεύω with the accusative means "to entrust," R. 476. This contrast extends to the tenses: the first is an aorist to indicate the closed act, "trusted," which trust, however, rested only on the signs; the second is an imperfect, leaving the eventual outcome open, "was not entrusting himself," i. e., waiting to see what the faith of the "many" would prove to be. To the six disciples Jesus fully entrusted himself; from the many at the festival he held aloof, formed no closer union with them as being people who were really committed to him.

This was wholly an act on the part of Jesus and in no way dependent on information he received about these people from either his six disciples or from other sources. In this connection John informs us about the power of Jesus to read the very hearts of men. We must know about it; Jesus had already used it in the most astonishing way in the case of Peter and of Nathanael (1:42 and 47, 48), and he constantly used it, notably also in his dealings with his foes. These are never able to deceive him; all their cunning schemes lie open before his eyes. Thus here, too, Jesus holds aloof from the "many," whereas an ordinary man would have been deceived by their first flash of faith and would have wrecked himself by injudiciously relying upon it. John has διά with the articular infinitive (this infinitive is rare in John's writings, R. 756), "on account of knowing (them) all." Since πάντας refers specifically to πολλοί in v. 23, it refers to all of these "many" not to "all men" in the world. During his humiliation Jesus used his supernatural knowledge when and where it served the purpose of his saving work and not beyond that. Note the present tense in τὸ γινώσκειν, not an aorist: he was intimately acquainted with them all, and this continued in the case of not only the new additions as the number grew from one day to another but also in the case of each individual and of any change that developed in his heart. This is a sad word — "all," for it means that among the "many" Jesus found not one with whom it would have been safe to form closer contact.

25) The διά phrase includes only the "many." From this we ourselves might generalize, that as Jesus knew these so he would know others also. John does this for us, because he wants it kept in mind as we read on, for instance immediately in the story of Nicodemus and that of the Samaritan woman. So John coordinates (καί) the second reason, which also helps to elucidate the first, "also because," etc. The durative imperfect εἶχεν says that this was always the case with Jesus, "he was not in need (at any time) that anyone should witness concerning this or that man," as we so often are when we do not know what to make of a man and feel that we must ask for the judg-

ment of someone who knows him more intimately. Here ἵνα with the subjunctive crowds out the classical infinitive, a construction found frequently in John and in the Koine, and, as here, with impersonal expressions, B.-D. 393, 5. The article in the phrase περὶ τοῦ ἀνθρώπου is scarcely generic but rather specific, "this or that man," anyone who approaches Jesus with a confession of his name, with hostility, or in any other way.

The reason Jesus needed no testimony from others is added in order to make the information complete, "for he was aware what was in the man," i. e., the one in question, the article taking up the one found in the περί phrase. The imperfect ἐγίνωσκε states that Jesus always knew, in every single case. What he knew was "what was in the man," in his very heart and mind, better even than he himself knew. Here ἦν is accomodated to the tense of ἐγίνωσκε, which is sometimes done in the Koine after a secondary tense (always in English), although ἐστί would suffice, R. 1029, 1043. The glorified Christ sees to the bottom of every heart, detects every superficial confession, every trace of indifference or hostility.

CHAPTER III

The Conversation with Nicodemus, 3:1-21. — This conversation connects naturally with 2:23, 24, Nicodemus being one of the "many" there mentioned as believing because of the signs, to whom Jesus would not entrust himself. Yet the conversation with Jesus did not yet bring this man to faith. But the story of Nicodemus is not John's real concern. As far as that is concerned, the sequel appears in 7:15 and 19:39. Here John's interest is in the *teaching* of Jesus as the counterpart to the signs (2:23). Though it is conducted in private, this conversation was a part of Jesus' public ministry, just as was the conversation with the Samaritan woman. John records this conversation because it really constitutes a *summary* of Jesus' teaching, dealing, as it does, with the kingdom, regeneration, faith, the Son of man, God's love and the plan of salvation, judgment and unbelief. The observation is correct that, as in the forefront of Matthew's Gospel the Sermon on the Mount presents a grand summary of Christ's teaching on the law as related to the gospel, so here in the opening chapters of John's Gospel this conversation with Nicodemus presents a grand summary of the gospel itself.

This also explains the way in which John records the conversation. Only the first part is dialog (2-10), and the rest is a discourse of Jesus. What else Nicodemus may have asked or said is immaterial for John's purpose; hence he omits it. In this respect the record of the conversation with the Samaritan woman is different, wherefore also the form of dialog is continued to the end. In the second half of this chapter we

have a record only of what Jesus said. We may take
it that the conversation continued much longer than
the few moments required to read John's report of it,
and that thus toward the end John simply reports
the chief and essential things which Jesus told Nicodemus. We have every reason to think that not only
John but also the other five disciples (see 1:35-51)
were present at the visit of Nicodemus, just as they
were also silent witnesses in 2:17. The historical
character of John's report is beyond question. And
this is true not only for the first but also for the
last half of his account; for all that Jesus said exactly
fits the condition and situation of Nicodemus. The
historical character of John's report should, therefore,
not be questioned.

1) **Now there was a man of the Pharisees,
named Nicodemus, a ruler of the Jews.** The report
is introduced by the transitional δέ; R. 1185 has a different view. Nicodemus is described at length. His
party connection, his actual name, his official position
are stated. First we are told that he belonged to the
Pharisees (with the partitive ἐκ), which fact is made
emphatic by being placed ahead of his name. On the
Pharisees compare 1:24. All that follows is governed by the Pharisaic character of Nicodemus; a conversation such as this would have been impossible
with a Sadducee or a mere Herodian. John is somewhat chary about mentioning names. He records that
of Nicodemus, it seems, because of the subsequent acts
of this man; the Samaritan woman he leaves unnamed.
The Greek has the parenthetical nominative, "Nicodemus name for him." The fact that Nicodemus was
"a ruler of the Jews" must here, in Jerusalem, mean
that he was a member of the Sanhedrin; as such he
appears also in the session of this body in 7:50. Combined with his being a Pharisee, this means that Nicodemus was one of the "scribes," a rabbi learned in

the Old Testament Scriptures; for the γραμματεῖς that
were in the Sanhedrin were Pharisees, the entire
body of some seventy consisting of high priests, elders,
and scribes.   In v. 10 Jesus directly calls Nicodemus
"the teacher of Israel."   Incidentally we see how high
the first public work of Jesus reached — into the
very Sanhedrin itself, I Cor. 1:26 ("not many," but
some).

2)   **This man came to him at night and said to
him, Rabbi, we know that from God thou art come
as a teacher; for no one can do these signs that thou
doest except God be with him.**   With οὗτος, in the
Greek fashion, all that is said in v. 1 is picked
up: "this" is the man who did and said what is
here told.   Two points are implied: he had seen some
of the signs, and he had heard some of the teaching.
The impression made on him had been so strong that
he risked this visit "at night," νυκτός, the genitive of
time within which something takes place.   Both this
impression and the venturesome visit it produced are
part of this man's attitude toward Jesus, an attitude
produced *in toto* by Jesus himself, in fact, a vital part
in the course of his conversion.   Caiaphas, other Sanhedrists, kept aloof from Jesus, thrust every favorable impression aside — and were never converted.
Their attitude was due wholly to themselves, it was
an abnormal, wilful resistance, 1:11.   The fact that
Nicodemus came "at night" was, of course, due to
fear lest he be seen, and thus his standing be com-
promised.   Yet this is not cowardice but rather careful caution, for, although Jesus had made an impression on Nicodemus, the man was not sure about this
young Rabbi from Galilee who might turn out a disappointment after all.   So he cautiously investigates.
The fact that Nicodemus "came to him," taking the
risk involved, shows his seriousness, shows how deeply
Jesus had gripped his heart.   He did not ignore or

wipe out the impression made on him. He took a step that was certainly decisive. In the study of conversion Nicodemus, like the Samaritan woman, will always stand out as an illuminating example.

He addresses Jesus with the respectful title "Rabbi" as Andrew, John, and Nathanael had done, see 1:38. The plural "we know" refers not to other Sanhedrists but to the preceding πολλοί, "many," in 2:23. He, however, does not come as a representative of these others but only for his own sake; yet the fact that others were impressed like himself means a good deal to him. Of what he and others are convinced is, "that from God thou art come as a teacher," the perfect ἐλήλυθας with its present implication meaning "hast come" and thus art now here. The phrase "from God" is to be understood in the sense, "commissioned by him and thus sent forth from him." It does not intend to express the divine nature of Jesus but the conviction that Jesus has assumed his office and work not on his own accord but by God's direction, like the prophets of old. The statement is true as far as it goes. Yet behind this admission lurks the question whether this man Jesus, who evidently has come from God, may not prove to be the Messiah. This is the real purpose of Nicodemus' coming, the thing he would like to discover.

On what grounds Nicodemus rests the cónviction that Jesus is "a teacher come from God" he himself states, "for no one can do these signs which thou doest except God be with him." Nicodemus, too, saw "the glory" (1:14) in these signs; what they indicated to him he states. Both ποιεῖν and ποιεῖς are durative, "can be doing" and "thou art doing," and thus include the signs already done and any others Jesus might still do. The noteworthy point, however, is that Nicodemus connects these signs with the teaching of Jesus. On σημεῖον see 2:11. As a διδάσκαλος Jesus presents these signs; they are his credentials. Nicodemus regards these credentials as proving that this teacher has surely come from God, for who could do such signs "except God be with him?" μετ' αὐτοῦ, in covenant or association with him; σύν would mean "with him" to help him. We see just how far Nicodemus has progressed. The signs loom up in his mind, the contents of the teaching is not mentioned and seems not to have entered far into his mind, although he connects the two. This explains the course of Jesus' instruction: since Nicodemus accepts the signs, Jesus unfolds to him the teaching which these signs accredit and attest. And this teaching centers in Jesus' person in such a way that Nicodemus at once has also the answer to the question that troubles him — he learns who Jesus really is.

3) **Jesus answered and said unto him, Amen, amen, I say to thee, Except one be born anew, he cannot see the kingdom of God.** On the use of ἀπεκρίθη and the doubling of the verbs "answered and said," see 1:48. Jesus saw what was in the man (2:25) and thus told him what he needed; and the two verbs show that this is highly important. When Jesus "takes the word" (ἀπεκρίθη) he does not begin with his own person although Nicodemus had put this forward. In due time Jesus will cover that point. Jesus begins with the kingdom of God and the entrance into that kingdom. And we must note that this kingdom and the coming of the Messiah belong together, for he is the King, and only where he is the kingdom is. Nicodemus, too, understood this relation and, like every serious Israelite, desired to see (ἰδεῖν) this Messianic kingdom, i. e., as a member entitled to a place in it. This is the background of Jesus' statement. So he begins with the solemn formula, explained in 1:51, "Amen, amen (the assurance of verity), I say to thee" (the assurance of authority) and follows with a state-

ment regarding what is essential in order to see the kingdom as one of its members.

This word of Jesus, as also its elaboration in v. 5 and 11, goes back to what the Baptist had preached when he declared the kingdom at hand and called on men to enter it by the Baptism of repentance and remission of sins, meaning the kingdom in its new form with redemption actually accomplished by the Messiah, the Lamb of God, i. e., the new covenant that would supersede the old. This grand concept ἡ βασιλεία τοῦ Θεοῦ must not be defined by generalizing from the kingdoms of earth. These are only imperfect shadows of God's kingdom. God makes his own kingdom, and where he is with his power and his grace there his kingdom is; whereas earthly kingdoms make their kings, often also unmake them, and their kings are nothing apart from what their kingdoms make them. So also we are not really subjects in God's kingdom but partakers of it, i. e., of God's rule and kingship; earthly kingdoms have only subjects. In God's kingdom we already bear the title "kings unto God," and eventually the kingdom, raised to the nth degree, shall consist of nothing but kings in glorious array, each with his crown, and Christ thus being "the King of kings," a kingdom that has no subjects at all.

This divine kingdom goes back to the beginning and rules the world and shall so rule until the consummation of the kingdom at the end of time. All that is in the world, even every hostile force, is subservient to the plans of God. The children and sons of God, as heirs of the kingdom in whom God's grace is displayed, constitute the kingdom in its specific sense. And this kingdom is divided by the coming of Christ, the King, in the flesh to effect the redemption of grace by which this specific kingdom is really established among men. Hence we have the kingdom before

Christ, looking toward his coming, and the kingdom after Christ, looking back to his coming — the promise and the fulfillment to be followed by the consummation — the kingdom as it was in Israel, as it now is in the Christian Church, the *Una Sancta* in all the world, and as it will be at the end forever. It is called "God's" kingdom and "Christ's" kingdom (Eph. 5:5; II Tim. 4:1; II Pet. 1:11) because the power and the grace that produce this kingdom are theirs; also the kingdom "of heaven" or "of the heavens" because the power and the grace are wholly from heaven and not in any way of the earth. The Baptist preached the coming of this kingdom as it centers in the incarnate Son and his redemptive work.

Jesus tells Nicodemus the astonishing fact, "unless one is born anew" he cannot enter this kingdom. He makes the statement general, "one," τίς, not singling out Nicodemus as though making an exceptional requirement for him. Not until v. 7 do we hear "thou," although the application to Nicodemus personally lies on the surface throughout. The requirement of a new birth is universal. The form ἐάν with the subjunctive shows that Jesus counts on some entering the kingdom, i. e., that the new birth will be received by them. While ἄνωθεν may mean "from above" (place, local), here it must mean "anew" (time) ; for in v. 4 we have δεύτερον, "a second time," in the same sense. Nor is ἄνωθεν the same as ἐκ Θεοῦ (in John's First Epistle), for while God bestows this birth, the means by which he does so do not descend "from above" (Word and Sacrament), for which reason also what Jesus says of the new birth belongs to the ἐπίγεια, "earthly things" (v. 12). Not new and superior knowledge is essential; not new, superior, more difficult meritorious works; not a new national or ecclesiastical or religious party connection that is better than the Pharisaic party; but an entirely new birth, the beginning of a newly born life, i. e., the true spiritual life.

This rebirth is misconceived when the Baptist and Jesus are separated and it is thought that the former was unable to bestow the Spirit. On this subject compare the comments on 1:26. The Baptist's requirement is identical with that which Jesus makes. The Baptism of repentance and remission of sins bestows the new birth even as it is and can be mediated only by the Spirit. Jesus is not telling Nicodemus, "Go and be baptized by John and then wait until the Messiah gives thee the Spirit (how would he do that?), and thus thou wilt be reborn." True repentance, the Baptist's μετάνοια, consists of contrition and faith; and these two, wrought by the Spirit, constitute conversion which in substance is regeneration. All these focus in Baptism: every contrite and believing sinner whom the Baptist baptized was converted, was regenerated, had the Spirit, had forgiveness, was made a member of the kingdom, was ready for the King so close at hand to participate in full in all that the King would now bring. The Baptist stressed repentance and forgiveness in connection with his Baptism because these mediated the great change; in this first word to Nicodemus Jesus names only the great change itself and its necessity, "born anew." In a moment Jesus, too, will name the means.

Jesus' word regarding the new birth shatters once for all every supposed excellence of man's attainment, all merit of human deeds, all prerogatives of natural birth or station. Spiritual birth is something one undergoes not something he produces. As our efforts had nothing to do with our natural conception and birth, so, in an analogous way but on a far higher plane, regeneration is not a work of ours. What a blow for Nicodemus! His being a Jew gave him no part in the kingdom; his being a Pharisee, esteemed holier than other people, availed him nothing; his membership in the Sanhedrin and his fame as one of its scribes went for nought. This Rabbi from Galilee calmly tells him that he is not yet in the kingdom! All on which he had built his hopes throughout a long arduous life here sank into ruin and became a little worthless heap of ashes. Unless he attains this mysterious new birth, even he shall not "see" (ἰδεῖν) the kingdom, i. e., have an experience of it. This verb is chosen to indicate the first activity of one who has passed through the door of the kingdom.

4) **Nicodemus says to Him, How can a man be born when he is old? He certainly cannot enter a second time into his mother's womb and be born?** These questions of Nicodemus have sometimes been misunderstood. This is not mere unspiritual denseness that is unable to rise above the idea of physical birth; nor rabbinical skill in disputation that tries to make Jesus' requirement sound absurd, which Jesus would never have answered as he did; nor hostility to the requirement of Jesus. Nicodemus simply puts the requirement laid down by Jesus into words of his own; and by doing this in the form of questions he indicates where his difficulty lies. He thus actually asks Jesus for further explanation and enlightenment, and Jesus gives him this.

When Nicodemus says γέρων ὤν he is thinking of himself, although his question would apply to one of any age, even to a babe. This touch indicates both that the conversation is truly reported, and that one who saw the old man when he said "being old" remembered and wrote it down. The second question elucidates the first. We must note especially the interrogative μή, which indicates that in the speaker's own mind the answer can only be a no. This completely exonerates Nicodemus from the charge that he under-

stood Jesus' words only as a reference to physical
birth; or that he tried to turn those words so that
they referred only to such a birth. The fact is that
he does the very opposite as if he would say, "I know
you cannot and do not mean that!" or, "That much I
see." He clearly perceives that Jesus has in mind
some other, far higher kind of birth. But "how can
such a birth take place?" He might also have asked,
"*What* is this birth?" and the "what" would probably
have explained also the "how." He did the thing
the other way, he asked, "*How,*" etc., and the manner, too, involves the nature — "how" one is thus born
will cast light on "what" this being born really is. As
in the word of Jesus, Nicodemus also retains the
passive, here two infinitives, γεννηθῆναι, the second after
δύναται. The term κοιλία denotes the abdominal cavity
and thus is used for "womb."

Although Jesus' word must have struck Nicodemus
hard, being uttered, as it was, by a young man to one
grown old and gray as an established "teacher" (v. 10),
Nicodemus shows no trace of resentment. He neither
contradicts nor treats Jesus' statement as extravagant
and ridiculous. He takes no offense although he feels
the personal force of what Jesus says. He does not
rise and leave saying, "I have made a mistake in coming." He quietly submits to the Word. This attitude
and conduct, however, is due to the Word itself and to
its gracious saving power. Changes were gradually
going on in this man's heart, some of them unconsciously; not he but a higher power was active in producing
these changes. He was not as yet reborn, nor do we
know when that moment came. Enough that Jesus
was leading him forward, and Nicodemus did not run
away.

5) **Jesus answered, Amen, amen, I say to thee,
Except one be born of water and the Spirit, he cannot enter into the kingdom of God.** In no way does

Jesus rebuke or fault Nicodemus — clear evidence that he who knew what is in a man (2:25) regards the questions of this man as being wholly sincere. Jesus explains his former word — again evidence that Nicodemus really has asked for an explanation. Jesus repeats his former word exactly, adding only one phrase and substituting "enter" for "see," a mere explanatory detail, for only they who "enter" "see" the kingdom. The preposition ἐκ denotes origin and source. The exegesis which separates ἐξ ὕδατος καὶ Πνεύματος, as though Jesus said ἐξ ὕδατος καὶ ἐκ Πνεύματος is not based on linguistic grounds; for the one preposition has as its one object the concept "water and Spirit," which describes Baptism, its earthly element and its divine agency. The absence of the Greek articles with the two nouns makes their unity more apparent. The making of two phrases out of the one is due to the preconception that the Baptist's Baptism consisted only of water and that figuratively the Messiah's bestowal of the Spirit can also be called a Baptism — yet leaving unsaid how and by what means the Messiah would bestow the Spirit. The fact that Jesus thus also postpones the very possibility of the new birth for Nicodemus (and for all men) into the indefinite future, when he and others may already have been overtaken by death, is also left unsaid.

In the Baptist's sacrament, as in that of Jesus afterward, water is joined with the Spirit, the former being the divinely chosen earthly medium (necessary on that account), the latter being the regenerating agent who uses that medium. When Jesus spoke to Nicodemus, the latter could understand only that the Baptist's sacrament was being referred to. This was entirely enough. For this sacrament admitted to the kingdom as completely as the later instituted sacrament of Jesus. Therefore Jesus also continued to require the Baptist's sacrament, 3:22 and 4:2, and after his resurrection extended it to all nations by means of his great commission. No need, then, to raise the question as to which Baptism Jesus here had in mind, or whether he also referred to his own future sacrament. It was but one sacrament which was first commanded by God for the use of the Baptist, then was used by Jesus, and finally instituted for all people. Tit. 3:5 thus applies to this sacrament in all its stages. Jesus tells Nicodemus just what he asks, namely the "how" of regeneration. How is it possible? By Baptism! But Jesus cuts off a second how: How by Baptism? by using the description of Baptism, "water and Spirit." Because not merely water but God's Spirit is effective in the sacrament, therefore it works the new birth.

Jesus here assumes that Nicodemus knows about the preaching as well as about the baptizing of John. In passing note that the Holy Spirit is here mentioned, and that Nicodemus accepts this mention and all that follows regarding the Spirit without the slightest hesitation, as though he knew this Third Person of the Godhead; compare 1:32. Thus this reference of Jesus to Baptism is not understood by Nicodemus as an *opus operatum,* a mere mechanical application of the earthly element with whatever formula God had given the Baptist to use, but as being in the Baptist's entire work vitally connected with μετάνοια or "repentance." Strictly speaking, this repentance (contrition and faith) itself constitutes the rebirth in all adults yet not apart from Baptism which as its seal must follow; for the rejection of Baptism vitiates repentance and regeneration, demonstrating that they are illusory.

6) Without a connective Jesus takes up the remark of Nicodemus regarding the impossibility of a physical rebirth and carries this to its ultimate limit

— even if it were possible, a rebirth in the flesh would reproduce only flesh. Jesus formulates this as a general principle which is self-evident and final in its clearness and then sets beside it the opposite, the Spirit birth, again as a principle with the same evident finality. And the parallelism of the two principles once more brings out the necessity Jesus has twice stated, that only by this latter birth a man can enter the kingdom. **That born of the flesh is flesh; and that born of the Spirit is spirit.** The Greek has the neuter τὸ γεγεννημένον, which states the thought abstractly, by this form emphasizing the fact that a principle is being established, and one without a single exception: anything whatever that is born thus, certainly also including man. In the elaboration Jesus has the masculine ὁ γεγεννημένος, "he that is born." The perfect participle has its usual force: once born and now so born.

Any birth from flesh produces only flesh. A stream never rises higher than its source. The fact is axiomatic. Its statement is its own proof. There is a contrast between σάρξ and πνεῦμα, and this determines that the former does not refer merely to the human body or to nature, or to this with its connotation of weakness and mortality, but to "the flesh" in its full opposition to "the spirit": our sinful human nature. Thus σάρξ includes also the human soul, the human ψυχή and the human πνεῦμα, for sin has its real seat in the immaterial part of our nature which uses the gross material part as its instrument. A hundred rebirths from sinful flesh, whether one be old or young, would produce nothing but the same sinful flesh and leave one as far as ever from the kingdom. This is not later Pauline theology, which the evangelist puts into Jesus' mouth and which is thus beyond the mind of Nicodemus. We meet this same thought already in Gen. 6:3; Ps. 51:5; Job 14:4. In fact, it is so simple that it is clear to any man who has the least idea of what flesh means.

In the second member Jesus does not say, "that born of the water and Spirit," but only, "that born of the Spirit," although he refers to Baptism. In this sacrament the regenerator is not the water but the Spirit who uses this medium. This also settles the question as to whether we must regard this second principle in a way that is wholly abstract, "that born *of the spirit* is *spirit*," or more concretely, "that born *of the Spirit* is spirit." The entire context decides for the latter, especially also the interpretative expression in v. 8, "one born of the Spirit" (not, "of the spirit"). In addition, the other translation would produce a false contrast, namely that of human flesh and that of the human spirit. Nor is there such a thing as a birth of the human spirit — in English we should say, soul — apart from and in contrast with the human flesh. Only God's Spirit produces a spiritual birth, a new nature and life, one that is πνεῦμα, the opposite of σάρξ. Underlying both axiomatic statements is the thought that "the flesh," our sinful human nature, cannot possibly enter the kingdom but that only the "spirit," the new life and new nature born of the Spirit, can do so. This, too, casts light on the kingdom itself, on its nature, and on the people who alone are partakers of it.

7) Perhaps astonishment was written on Nicodemus' face, or a movement and gesture betrayed his thought. It all sounded very strange to this old Pharisee who all his lifelong was set on works — works — works and was admired by the mass of the nation for this very fact, to hear from Jesus: birth — birth — birth by the Spirit, by Baptism, which would bring forth "spirit," an entirely new nature and creature. The objective tone of Jesus, therefore,

takes a subjective, pastoral turn. Jesus lights up the mystery of this birth by describing one who is actually reborn by means of an analogy. **Marvel not that I said to thee, You must be born anew. The wind blows where it will, and thou hearest its sound but knowest not whence it comes and whither it goes — thus is everyone that is born of the Spirit.** In prohibitions for the second person the Greek has the aorist subjunctive instead of the aorist imperative, hence μὴ θαυμάσῃς, "Do not marvel!" What Nicodemus marvelled at is this new birth on which Jesus insisted instead of urging something else. Jesus uses the plural, "You must be born anew," for the principle applies to all men alike, of course, including Nicodemus, holy as he, the Pharisee, deemed himself because of his close observance of the law. To be sure, in itself this new birth is marvelous enough, transcending even the wonder of our physical conception and birth. But merely to marvel at it may lead to unbelief and to denial of its possibility. A thing may be marvelous, mysterious, even incomprehensible and yet it may not only be possible but actual, an indisputable fact.

8) Jesus furnishes a striking and pertinent example which was apparently suggested by the two meanings of πνεῦμα, which are found also in the Hebrew *ruach* and the Aramaic *rucha*, namely "wind" and "spirit" ("Spirit"). Take the wind, Jesus says to Nicodemus, *the reality and fact* of it is beyond question, for you hear its sound, you know it is there as a fact; but whence it came, and whither it goes, how it starts, how it stops, these and many other facts "thou knowest not." With the verbs ἀκούεις and οἶδας Jesus addresses Nicodemus personally. Was there, perhaps, a sound of wind outside as Jesus was speaking? The two clauses "whence it comes" and "whither it goes" do not refer to the mere direction of the wind,

north or south, east or west, for this anyone can know; but to the original origin and source of the wind, this vast mass of moving and often rushing air, and to its ultimate goal, where it piles up and stops. Despite all our wise modern meteriological knowledge we still do not know this "whence" and this "whither," how this vast volume of air leaves one place and goes to another. In both the LXX and the New Testament ποί, "whither," is replaced by ποῦ, "where," R. 548; which means that we must not read the latter as though it also meant to indicate where the wind comes to rest.

The application which Jesus makes of this illustration comes as a surprise. He does not say, "thus also is the Spirit of God." This is one of the numerous and interesting cases, occurring in the sayings of Jesus as well as in the writings of the Apostles, where the thought overleaps an intervening point and at once presents the final point. So here the intervening point is *the fact and reality* of the working of God's Spirit. This is taken for granted because it is involved in *the fact and reality* of the result of this working, namely every man who is actually reborn of the Spirit. In the present case Jesus has to make the comparison in this way. The two features that are alike, one in the wind, the other in the Spirit, must be such as we ourselves can verify. If the wind did not affect our senses, we should never know its blowing; if the Spirit did not produce reborn men, we should never know his presence and his activity. Thus the fact and reality of the wind that *we hear* in its activity and its effect illustrates the Spirit whom *we observe* in his activity and his effect (the regenerated man). Jesus takes only this one effect of the wind, the sound of it that we hear in the rustling breeze or the roaring storm. So also he matches it by only one effect of the Spirit, the regenerate man who himself knows the great transformation that has taken place within him, and whose transformation others likewise can observe and know. To be sure, the wind works also other effects, and the Spirit performs also other works. Jesus has no call here to enter on these points. The illustration as he uses it fully meets his purpose.

Sometimes this illustration has been misapplied by commentators because they fail to discover the point of comparison. They find three such points, whereas every true comparison has but one. This is also done by those who stress the clause, "wherever it will," and then speak of the free and unrestricted working of the Spirit. This misconception often becomes serious, for it easily leads to the false dogmatical idea that the Spirit regenerates this or that man at random, passing over the rest. It may also lead to the error that the Spirit works without means, suddenly seizing a man to convert and regenerate (or sanctify) him, whereas the Scriptures teach that the Spirit always and only works to save through his chosen means, the Word and the Sacraments, and through these means equally upon all men whenever and wherever these means reach men. The fact that all who are thus reached by the Spirit are not reborn is not due to a lack of saving will on the part of the Spirit, or to a lack and deficiency in the means the Spirit employs, but to the wicked and permanent resistance of those who remain unregenerate. Matt. 23:37; Acts 7:51-53; 13:46.

Little needs to be said regarding the interpretation that would take these words of Jesus to speak of the Spirit instead of the wind, "the Spirit breathes where he will," margin of the R. V. and a few expositors. This is done because the ordinary word for "wind" is ἄνεμος, because only here in the New Testament πνεῦμα would denote "wind," and also because the wind has no will. As to the latter, the expression "wherever

it will" predicates no intelligent will when it is used
with reference to the wind but conveys only the idea
that now it blows one way, now another without
apparent control. But this interpretation cannot be
carried through consistently. When it is read in this
manner, the entire sentence remains confused. Comparisons are intended to clarify. This comparison
greatly clarifies when it is thought of as referring
to the effect of the wind; it does the opposite when
it is regarded as a reference to the Spirit. In v. 6
πνεῦμα is rightly taken once in one sense, once in another. The fact that in v. 8 Jesus uses πνεῦμα, "wind,"
instead of the commoner word, is due to the entire
connection in which this word has repeatedly been
used. Finally οὕτως, "thus," makes a comparison; and
how the Spirit can be compared with a reborn man, or
how the action of the Spirit can be so compared, has
never been clearly shown.

9)   **Nicodemus answered and said to him, How
can these things be?** Nicodemus has progressed —
a little. In v. 4 his "how" questions the possibility
itself, especially for an old man like himself. In v. 9
his "how" admits the possibility but questions the manner. "These things" admits that they exist — so much
Jesus has attained. And yet Nicodemus does not believe (v. 11 at the end). Why? Because, after Jesus
has so clearly pointed him away from the mystery
of the manner, especially by the illustration of the
"wind" and has told him that the essential point is
the fact and reality of the Spirit birth, Nicodemus
still harps on the manner with this second "how."
He is like a man who is told that he must eat yet holds
back from eating because he cannot see "how" the
food will be digested and assimilated. The fact that
the Spirit works the rebirth *somehow,* and that it is
enough for the Spirit to know *just how,* is not enough
for Nicodemus — he, too, must know and thus does

not come to faith. That explains the reply of Jesus which scores the man's unbelief.

10)   Jesus answered and said to him, Art thou the teacher of Israel and understandest not these things?   Amen, amen, I say to thee, We are uttering what we know and are testifying what we have seen; and you receive not our testimony. The two double verbs "answered and said" in v. 9 and 10 (see 1:48) indicate that both statements thus introduced are weighty — a kind of climax is reached. In v. 4 we have only "says." The question of Jesus is one of surprise. The article with "teacher" cannot mean that Nicodemus was *the* teacher, was superior to all others, which would have given an undue sting to the question; but the well-known and acknowledged teacher who even has a place in the Sanhedrin. Of a lesser man less might be expected; of a man who knows his Old Testament as such a teacher does certainly so much at least could be expected. Jesus says: the teacher "of Israel," using the honor name to designate the nation: the people of God to whom God had given his Word of revelation and his Spirit in and with that Word. Could "these things" still be hidden from Nicodemus, that the fact and reality of the Spirit's work in its results is the essential and not the manner in which he brings the results about? The verb γινώσκεις means more than intellectual comprehension, which, even if it were possible in a man like Nicodemus, would be valueless; it means inner apprehension, a knowing which embraces and appropriates in the heart. Knowing what Nicodemus did from his study of the Old Testament, plus what he knew of the teaching of the Baptist, plus what Jesus had just so emphatically and so clearly set before him, Nicodemus still did not understand in his heart. He still laid the stress on the how instead of on the fact; he still let the mystery of the how block his joyful appropriation

of the undeniable reality of the new birth. This question of surprise on the part of Jesus is to shake Nicodemus from his foolish how.

11)   The surprise is followed by solemn assurance
which directly names unbelief as the cause of Nicodemus' ignorance (7:17). Jesus uses the same formula
as he did in v. 3. The plural "we" refers to Jesus
and the Baptist. By thus combining himself with
the Baptist Jesus acknowledges and honors him. Jesus
never uses the majestic plural, and in v. 12, where
he refers to himself alone, he uses the singular. The
disciples had not yet testified publicly, and the prophets are too far removed from the context. The
Baptist was still in full activity, and Nicodemus knew
a great deal concerning him; so he at once understood this "we." The two great witnesses to Israel at
this moment were Jesus and the Baptist.

The two statements, "we are uttering what we
know," and, "we are testifying what we have seen,"
are the same in substance. The doubling is for the
sake of emphasis. Yet to tell what one knows is augmented by the statement regarding testifying what
one has seen. Each pair of verbs also corresponds,
and those in one pair also correspond to those in the
other pair. One naturally tells what he knows; but
in order to testify he must have seen. To know is
broader than to have seen and thus also more indefinite; hence the more specific having seen is added,
concerning which one cannot only tell but actually
testify. The tenses harmonize with this, "we know,"
second perfect always used as a present; "we have
seen," regular perfect; "seen once and still have before our eyes." To tell is less than to testify. In
both statements the singular ὅ should be noted, for
it points not to a number of things told and testified
but to the one thing noted in the context, the fact
and reality of the new birth. The Baptist knew and

had seen this even as he told and testified of it in preaching and in Baptism; Jesus likewise, even now telling and testifying to Nicodemus. Both knew and even had seen the Spirit who works the new birth. Both, too, were sent to tell and even to testify which includes, of course, that God who sent them intends that they who hear shall believe and thus receive the saving grace which is the content of this testimony.

But what is the result? It is added with καί although its substance is adverse, "and you receive not our testimony." The inflectional plural is unemphatic yet it includes all those who remain unbelieving. This plural is a gentle touch for Nicodemus, allowing him to include himself in this class if he is determined to do so. It almost sounds as though Jesus pleads that he shall not do this. Here, then, is where the trouble lies: clear, strong, divinely accredited testimony, and yet for one reason or another men decline to receive and to believe it although believing it would work in them the wondrous new birth. The full seriousness of unbelief in the face of such testimony Jesus brings out in v. 19.

12) It should have been easy for Nicodemus and the others to believe this testimony regarding the new birth wrought by the Spirit, for this belongs to the lesser parts of divine revelation, to the *abc* of the gospel. The greater is the guilt for not believing. Far greater and higher things are included in the gospel and must also be told and testified. If the lesser are met with unbelief, what will happen in the case of the greater? **If I told you earthly things, and you do not believe, how, if I shall tell you heavenly things, shall you believe?** Here Jesus confronts the "how" of Nicodemus with a "how" of his own. For that of Nicodemus the answer is always ready, for that of Jesus none exists. Now Jesus omits

reference to the Baptist and speaks of himself alone, hence we have the singular in the verb forms. This does not imply that we need to press the point so as to shut out the Baptist from knowing any of the heavenly things or anything at all about them. He had the measure of revelation which he needed regarding these things. Yet he could not testify of them as one who had directly seen them (v. 13 and 1:18)

We now have the plurals τὰ ἐπίγεια and τὰ ἐπουράνια, which, of course, are not general: any and all earthly and any and all heavenly things; but specific, those pertaining to the kingdom. Nor are the earthly and the heavenly opposites but are most intimately related, are actual correlatives. The kingdom has an earthly and a heavenly side; the earthly side has an exalted heavenly background. To the earthly belong contrition and faith (μετάνοια, "repentance"), Baptism and regeneration, and many things of like nature. If these are to be fully and properly understood and received, the heavenly must be added, those things which occurred in heaven in order to establish the kingdom on earth: the counsel of God's love for our salvation (v. 16), the sending of the Son and of the Spirit; and all this not merely for the consummation of the kingdom but equally for its establishment, progress, and continuance to the end.

The first is a condition of reality, "if I told you . . . , and you do not believe." It expresses what is a fact. The second is a condition of expectancy, "if I shall tell you . . . , how shall you believe?" Jesus expects and reckons with this future unbelief. Yet it would be a mistake to think that Jesus admits some justification for unbelief in the heavenly things; or, to put it in another way, that he would more readily excuse this unbelief. The "how" of Jesus is not measuring degrees of guilt, is not justifying or excusing unbelief, but is reckoning with the likelihood of faith with this or that content of the gospel from men who, like Nicodemus, meet already the earthly things of the gospel with their "how" of unbelief.

13) Now as regards both the verity of these heavenly things and any genuine testimony concerning them a word is in place, which Jesus simply adds with "and" (not, "and yet," R. 1183). **And no one has ascended into heaven except he that descended out of heaven, the Son of man, he who is in heaven.** If any ordinary man were to become a direct witness of heavenly things, this would necessitate that he first ascend to heaven and then come down again and thus testify what he had seen and heard while he was in heaven. But "no one has ascended into heaven." The perfect tense ἀναβέβηκεν includes the past act of ascending together with its resultant effect; the one past act of ascending would apply to that person indefinitely, i. e., he could always speak as one who actually has been in heaven. The universal denial in οὐδείς, "no man," has one grand and notable exception. We are not left without direct testimony regarding heavenly things; we are not dependent only on men like the prophets and such revelations as they may receive from heaven. This exception is Jesus; εἰ μή, as so often, introduces an exception, "except he that descended out of heaven." Any other person would first have to ascend to heaven, not so this person — he was in heaven to begin with. Hence all he needed to do was to come down from heaven. And this he did as ὁ ἐκ τοῦ οὐρανοῦ καταβάς asserts with its historical aorist participle, "he that did descend" when he became incarnate, which also explains the apposition that names this exceptional and wonderful person,

"the Son of man," man, indeed, and yet far more than man; see the exposition regarding this title in 1:51.

A second apposition is added, "he who is in heaven." For it would be a misconception to think of this person as a mere man who in some unaccountable way had originated in heaven instead of on earth like all other men and then had merely changed his abode from heaven to earth by coming down to us, thus being able to tell us about the things in heaven. Not so is ὁ καταβάς to be understood. This person is God, the Son, himself, whose coming down in the incarnation is not a mere change of residence. Though he came down and now speaks to Nicodemus as the Son of man, he remains ὁ ὢν ἐν τῷ οὐρανῷ, "he who is in heaven." He cannot change his divine nature, cannot lay it aside, cannot cancel even temporarily his divine Sonship, his unity of essence with the Father and the Spirit. This is unthinkable although men have tried to think it. To think such a thing is to make also "the Son of man" an illusion, to say nothing of undoing in thought the very Godhead itself and the Trinity of immutable Persons. This person who is first ὁ καταβάς and secondly ὁ υἱὸς τοῦ ἀνθρώπου is thirdly ὁ ὢν ἐν τῷ οὐρανῷ. The participle ὤν is substantivized exactly like καταβάς, the article in each case converting the participle into a noun. The first, an aorist, names the person according to one past act, "he that *came down*"; the second a durative, timeless present, like ὤν in 1:18, names the person according to his enduring condition or being, "he that *is*, ever and ever *is* in heaven." And this designation ὁ ὤν dare not be altered into something else such as mere communion with heaven and thus with God. It denotes being. We may have communion with God, and yet who would dare to express that by saying that we ὄντες, "are," in heaven.

Verse 13, therefore, says nothing about an ascension of Jesus into heaven, which will occur in the future after his resurrection, or has occurred in the past, least of all is it to be understood in the Socinian sense of a *raptus in coelum*. These words are not figurative, meaning only that Jesus has immediate heavenly knowledge or superior, direct communion with heaven through his mind or soul. All such interpretations, which offer a *quid pro quo*, fail to grasp and to accept the real sense and offer another in its stead.

The addition of ὁ ὤν, etc., has caused a good deal of perplexity. Hence the attempts simply to cancel this addition and thus to get rid of the perplexity at one stroke. But the textual evidence is so strong that today cancellation would be arbitrary. The substitution of ἐκ for ἐν, "he who is *out* of heaven," changes the sense. Next comes the translation, *qui in coelo erat,* in old Latin versions and in recent expositions. This is based on the grammatical fact that the present participle ὤν serves for both the present and the imperfect tense, the more since εἶναι really has no aorist. While the grammatical point is correct, ὤν means "was" only when it modifies an imperfect tense of the verb and from that verb, like other present participles (all of which serve also for the imperfect tense) derives the sense of the imperfect. In the statement of Jesus no imperfect tense of a verb appears to which ὤν could be attached.

Some interpreters regard ὁ ὤν ἐν τῷ οὐρανῷ as the equivalent of a relative clause, which is then sometimes attached to ὁ καταβάς as a mere modifier, more frequently to ὁ υἱὸς τοῦ ἀνθρώπου. The article in ὁ ὤν is thus explained as indicating that the participle is attributive. The fact that Jesus "was" in heaven lies fully and clearly already in the previous participle, "he who came down out of heaven"; for no one can come out of a place unless prior to the coming he *was* in that place. Others see that the participle must be present, even though it be a timeless present; yet they cling to the idea of a relative clause, a mere modifier. This brings them to the thought that the modifier describes only a quality of the Son of man: having come down from heaven, he has a heavenly nature and character, he *is and remains* (ὤν) an ἐπουράνιος. This appears to be an escape from the imperfect tense, "who was in heaven," but it only appears so. For the Son of man so described can have this character only because prior to his incarnation he was in heaven; that he *is* there now, even while speaking to Nicodemus, is the one thing that, so many think, must be eliminated.

And this brings us to the dogmatical bias back of this interpretation of ὁ ὤν. What is so evident, namely that Jesus here uses three coordinate titles for himself: he that came down — the Son of man — he that is in heaven, is not seen. In other words, that "the Son of man" is an apposition, and that "he that is in heaven" is likewise an apposition. Again in still other words: he that came down is now here as the incarnate Son of man, and yet, having come down, does not mean leaving heaven — he is both here and is still in heaven. Impossible! is the reply. Why? This would destroy the unity of Christ's person and the unity of his self-consciousness! In simple language this dogmatical objection declares: We do not see and understand how one can be in heaven and on earth at the same time, hence such a thing cannot be — Jesus *must* mean something else; and then the search begins for what he must mean. Thus the story of Nicodemus is here repeated when in v. 9 he asked, "How can these thinks be?" and was told that his question meant nothing but plain, persistent unbelief. Jesus *is* in heaven though as the Son of man he walks on earth — that fact stands whether it staggers our reason and powers of comprehension or not. Preconceived dogmatical considerations have always been the bane of exegesis. They have vitiated the plainest grammatical and linguistic facts. The plea about the unity of person and consciousness transfers what would be true of an ordinary human being with only one nature to Christ, the unique divine Being who after his incarnation has two natures. The further plea that from John's prolog onward Christ's being on earth or in the world and his being with God (1:1, 2, and 1:10) form an exclusive contrast, reveals how far back this dogmatical preconception reaches and how it misunderstands the prolog. It will do the same with other statements in our Gospel, such as 10:30; 17:11 and 22. When the Spirit in the form of a dove came down out of heaven upon Jesus, he did not thereby remove his person and presence from heaven, nor did he do this when he was poured out upon the disciples on Pentecost. The same is true of Jehovah when he appeared to Abraham, to Moses in the fiery bush, and when he descended on Sinai, to mention only these.

The interpretation that "who is in heaven" is an insertion by the evangelist and means that now, as he writes, Jesus is again in heaven, destroys the entire historical character of John's Gospel.

Did Nicodemus understand what Jesus here tells him? The same question arises as the discourse moves on. The answer lies in v. 10. He understood and did not understand. But the end toward which Jesus is working with Nicodemus is furthered by the strong impression the words create as Nicodemus now hears and later on as he ponders these words. Jesus counts not on the passing moment alone but on the future when the little that Nicodemus now grasps will grow into fuller insight until faith arrives, and increasing faith learns to see more clearly still.

14) From the great person who came from heaven and can testify to the heavenly things Jesus advances to the great salvation coming through this person. For he shall be far more than a witness, he is the Savior himself. Thus Jesus seeks to kindle faith in Nicodemus, faith in the divine salvation offered him. **And as Moses lifted up the serpent in the wilderness, thus lifted up must be the Son of man, in order that everyone believing may in him have life eternal.** When describing this salvation in and through the Son of man Jesus employs one of its Old Testament types, Num. 21:8, 9, placing beside it the great antitype, thus aiding Nicodemus both in understanding and in believing what is now told him. To chastise the people who murmured against God he sent fiery serpents among them, from the bite of which many died. When the people came to their senses and repented, God directed that a brazen serpent be put up on a pole and promised that all who would look upon it when bitten would be cured. The Book of Wisdom 16:6 calls this serpent σύμβολον σωτηρίας, and in church decotions it is constantly used to picture Jesus. Ideas such as that like cures like, or that the serpent was a symbol of blessing for the ancients (a notion that is wholly pagan), darken the miracle instead of casting light upon it. Jesus makes the reference to the type brief, not adding the statement that by merely looking every bitten person should live. Yet v. 15 implies that he includes this in his reference. Jesus here places the stamp of verity on the act of Moses and on the record that recounts that act. The miracle of the healing by a mere look on a brass serpent is so real for Jesus that it typifies a still greater reality.

The point of comparison lies in the verbs ὕψωσεν and ὑψωθῆναι, wherefore also the latter is placed before δεῖ, "lifted up must be," and not, "must be lifted up." But these two upliftings are here not compared abstractly, merely as such, but in their saving significance. This is not a second point in the comparison but the heart of the one point on which type and antitype turn. Debate arises regarding what Christ's being lifted up includes: the crucifixion? the ascension to heaven? or both? If both are included, the passive infinitive would have to refer to two diverse agents: the wicked men who crucified Jesus and God who lifted him to heaven, Acts 4:10. The parallel with the act of Moses holds us to the one act of raising Jesus up on the cross. In 12:32, 33 Jesus himself confines his being lifted up to "the manner of death he should die"; compare 8:28. Both acts, too, lift up physically, one on a pole, the other on the wooden cross. The mystery of the sacrificial nature of Jesus' elevation on the cross is not yet revealed to Nicodemus and to the disciples who stood by listening. In 12:33 John appends the remark that the crucifixion is referred to, much as he does in 2:22. After the lifting up had actually occurred, many of the words Jesus had spoken became fully clear to the disciples. Then, too, Nicodemus fully understood.

The tendency to elaborate the type in allegorical details should be resisted. Thus the brazen serpent itself is made to picture Jesus, the former being without poison, the latter without sin. Luther: *Doch ohne Gift und aller Dinge unschaedlich.* Also the dead serpent and the dead Jesus are compared, although the serpent never was alive, and Jesus was when he was uplifted. Again, the serpent signifies "the old serpent, which is the devil and Satan," Rev. 20:2, dead and helpless like Satan whom Jesus conquered on the cross. Suffice it to say that the brazen serpent is thus allegorized nowhere in the Scriptures. We must leave both type and antitype without allegorical embellishments of our own. The type, the brazen serpent on a pole, was held up to the eyes of the Israelites as the symbol of their own serpent plague, which had come on them through God's just wrath. It was thus held up so that by obediently looking up to it they might acknowledge their sin and God's just wrath in true repentance. Wise fellows among the Israelites may have argued, "How can looking at a brass serpent stuck up on a pole cure poisonous snakebites?" Reason, science, philosophy, ordinary human experience, all support this impenitent how; compare that of Nicodemus in v. 9. The antitype, Jesus hung on the cross, not in a symbol but as the Son of man and Lamb of God himself, holds up to the eyes of the whole world of sin the wrath of God for its sin in him who bleeds to death in order to atone for all this sin. And again, the antitype is held up thus for all men to look upon, that seeing what their sin did to Jesus, they may bow in repentance and faith and thus escape. No allegorical elaborations are needed where the facts themselves are so full of weight. All types of necessity are expressed by δεῖ with the infinitive, our English "must," or "it is necessary." The "must" here meant is that of v. 16, the compulsion of God's purpose of love.

15) This being lifted up and its divine purpose constitute a unit; neither could be possible without the other. When considering both type and antitype this must be retained, "lifted up, in order that." The universality that lies already in the title "the Son of man" (see 1:51) comes out with wonderful clearness in πᾶς ὁ πιστεύων, "everyone." This "whosoever" of our versions is like a check or a deed, signed by God himself, with the place for the beneficiary's name left blank, thus inviting each one of us (here Nicodemus) by the act of faith to write in his own name. Note the singular: faith, life, salvation are personal. "To believe" (see 1:12) is to have the true confidence of the

heart, kindled by the Word, even as this was seeking
with its power of grace to win the heart of Nicodemus.
The present tense ὁ πιστεύων describes the person by its
durative action.

The reading ἐν αὐτῷ is textually assured. But since
John always uses εἰς αὐτόν when he employs a phrase
with πιστεύω, we should here not construe, "believing
in him," but leave the participle absolute, "every believer." In the New Testament πιστεύω ἐν is infrequently used. On the other hand, ἔχειν ἐν appears in 5:39;
16:33; 20:31. So we read, "may have in him life
eternal," i. e., in union or in connection with him. The
objection is ill-advised that the Israelites did not have
healing "in" the brazen serpent but in the kind will
of God; for they, too, had it only in connection with
that serpent — whoever failed to look at it died. The
verb ἔχῃ matches the durative πιστεύων. The believer
has life the moment he believes and as long as he
believes; he is not compelled to wait until he enters
heaven.

On ζωή compare 1:4. John has "life eternal" seventeen times. This is the life-principle itself which
makes us alive spiritually. Its beginning is the new
birth or regeneration of which Jesus spoke to Nicodemus. Nothing dead can give itself life, least of all
that life which has its source in the Son of God himself. He bestows it, he alone, but he does this by
kindling faith in us. Thus faith has life, and life is
found where faith is. The faith that clasps the Christ
uplifted on the cross makes us alive in and through
him. A thousand evidences show the change from
death to life, namely every motion of that life Godward,
Christward, against sin, flesh, world. And this life
is "eternal," it goes on endlessly unaffected by temporal
death, except that then this life is transferred into
the heavenly world. While its nature is "eternal" and
deathless, it may be lost during our stay in this sin-

ful world, but only by a wilful and wicked cutting of
the bond "in him," a deliberate renunciation and
destruction of faith.

16)   Why a new paragraph should begin at this
verse is hard to see since the connection with γάρ both
here and in v. 17 is close. The fact that the dialog
stops, also all forms of personal address such as "thou"
to Nicodemus, is naturally due to the simple didactic
nature of what Jesus says and begins already at v. 13,
where, if for such a reason a paragraph is to be made,
it might be made. The idea that a new paragraph
starts with v. 16 because Jesus' words stop here and
John's own reflections are now added, is contradicted
by the two γάρ, by the close connection of the thought,
which runs through to v. 21, and by the absence of
even a remote analogy for a conversation or a discourse that goes over, without a word to indicate this,
into the writer's own reflection.

Jesus tells Nicodemus that the Son of man *must*
be lifted up for the purpose indicated. This δεῖ is
elucidated in v. 16, hence γάρ which so often offers
no proof but only further explanation. **For thus did
God love the world, that he gave his Son the Only-
begotten, in order that everyone believing in him
should not perish but have life eternal.** The "must,"
the compulsion, lies in the wonder of God's love and
purpose. By telling Nicodemus this in such lucid,
simple language Jesus sums up the entire gospel in
one lovely sentence, so rich in content that, if a man
had only these words and nothing of the rest of the
Bible, he could by truly apprehending them be saved.
They flow like milk and honey says Luther, "words
which are able to make the sad happy, the dead alive,
if only the heart believes them firmly." What a revelation for this old Pharisee Nicodemus who all his lifelong had relied on his own works! And this testimony
concerning what was in the heart of God comes from

him who came down from heaven, came down so that
he still is in heaven, from the Son of man and Son
of God himself, the only ἐπουράνιος, who alone can declare
the ἐπουράνια at firsthand, 1:18 and 3:12, who thus in
the very highest degree deserves faith.

The word οὕτως, "thus," denotes manner and degree,
"in this way" and "to such an astounding degree"
did God love the world. No human mind would have
thought it, could have conceived it — God had to
reveal it, the Son had to attest it. The verb ἠγάπησεν
is placed ahead of the subject and is thus made
emphatic, not: *God* loved the world; but: God *loved*
the world. The verb ἀγαπάω denotes the highest type
and form of loving, as distinct from φιλέω, the love of
mere affection, friendship, and ordinary human relation; compare the distinction made between the verbs
in 21:15, etc. In ἀγάπη lies full understanding and
true comprehension, coupled with a corresponding
blessed purpose. How could God *like* the sinful, foul,
stinking world? How could he embrace and kiss it?
He would have to turn from it in revulsion. But he
could and he did *love* it, comprehending all its sin
and foulness, purposing to cleanse it and, thus cleansed,
to take it to his bosom. We see this force of ἀγαπάω
whenever it is used, for instance in the command to
love our enemies. We cannot embrace and kiss an
enemy, for he would smite, revile, thrust us away, as
the Sanhedrists did with Jesus at last; but we can see
the baseness and wickedness of his action and by
the grace of God we can do all that is possible to
overcome this enmity. We may fail in this purpose,
as Jesus did in the case of the Sanhedrists, but to
have it and to adhere to it constitutes "love" in the
sense of ἀγάπη.

The attempt is made to deny this distinction between ἀγάπη and φιλία on the ground that Jesus spoke
Aramaic which has only one word for all types of

love. The answer is that we have only a limited knowledge of Aramaic, and even if we knew all its forms of speech and found there only the one word, there would certainly be other ways of bringing out a difference in the character of love. But in the inspired Greek which God gave us this distinction is so marked that in scores of cases the two words ὀγαπᾶν and φιλεῖν could not be exchanged; especially would it be impossible here to substitute the lower form of love and say, "Thus did God *like* the world." Jesus uses the aorist tense because the manifestation of his love toward the world was an accomplished fact. We may call this aorist constative; it reaches back into eternity and culminates in Bethlehem. "God," here the Father, as the mention of the Son shows, like proper nouns in the Greek may or may not have the article — here it has the article but not in v. 21. There is no real difference but only a slight grammatical variation in certain connections. In this discourse of Jesus with Nicodemus the entire Trinity is mentioned as a subject that is well known (the Spirit from v. 5 onward, Father and Son now). On what this means for the Old Testament and for the Jews at this time see 1:32.

The universality already expressed in the title "the Son of man" (1:51; 3:14) and in "everyone who believes" (v. 15), is brought out with the most vivid clearness in the statement that God loved "the world," τὸν κόσμον, the world of men, all men, not one excepted. To insert a limitation, either here or in similar passages, is to misinterpret. We know of nothing more terrible than to shut out poor dying sinners from God's love and redemption. But this is done by inserting a limiting word where Jesus and the Scriptures have no such word. Thus "world" is made to mean only *omnes ex toto mundo electos*; and "all men" in I Tim. 2:4, *omnis generis homines*; and again, *Nul-*

*lum mundi vel populum, vel ordinem a salute excludi,
quia omnibus sine exceptione* (i. e., to all nations and
orders and in this sense only "to all without exception") *Evangelium proponi Deus velit.* Thus "the
world," "all men," is reduced to signify only that no
nation, no class, as a nation or as a class, is excluded;
God offers his love and the Savior only to *all kinds*
of men — not actually to all men as such.   The
reason for this misinterpretation of the universal
promises of God is that the divine *voluntas benepla-
citi* is placed above the divine *voluntas signi* or *revelata,* and the latter is interpreted by the former.
In other words, the real will of God is said to appear
in his acts, in what we see him do, not in what he
plainly says in his Word.   So we see him damning
some men.   Hence we are told to conclude that he
never loved these men, never gave his Son for them,
never intended to save them.   Hence we are told to
limit all such expressions as "the world" and "all
men" in the written will (*voluntas signi sive revelata*).
But this view disregards the fact that we are able to
see God's will only partly, dimly, imperfectly in his
acts; we often only think we see it, for as we look
at his acts, they are often full of mystery.   But the
will as revealed in the Word is always clear.   Hence
we dare never to interpret what God clearly says in
his own Word by our conception of what he does.   We
must do the exactly opposite: interpret what we see
him do or think we see in the light of the Word; and
when the two do not seem to us to square, we must
abide by the Word, never change it in one iota, and
leave what is dark in the acts of God to the light of
the future world.   Always, always and only, *Scriptura
ex Scriptura explicanda est* and not by anything *extra
Scripturam.*

Even after carefully defining "love" no human
intelligence can fathom how God could thus love the

world. The revelation of this love distinguishes the Christian religion so radically from all others, that no bridge can possibly connect the two. The former is divine, the latter only human. And this love of God is the pinnacle of his glory, the crown of all his attributes. It makes God supremely attractive to every sinner needing this love, a most efficacious call to trust this love and thus to have all it gives.

"So . . . that" indicates correspondence: the love and the gift tally. And ὥστε with the indicative expresses the attained, actual result (R. 1000); with the infinitive it would be only the intended result, one toward which this love would tend. The gift was actually made; the aorist marks the past fact. God's own Son sat before Nicodemus at that very moment. Jesus does not again use "the Son of man" as in v. 13, 14. There it fits as describing what he who came out of heaven became here on earth. Here the divine act of love takes us into heaven and shows us the gift of that love as it was when the act of giving occurred. That gift was "his Son the Only-begotten." On the repetition of the article in the Greek see R. 762, 770. This repetition lays equal weight on both terms; it bids us consider "his Son," secondly, in the same way "the Only-begotten." The addition of the second lifts this "Son" above all others who in any sense may also be called "sons." On the meaning of the title "the Only-begotten" see 1:14 and 18.

Strange reasoning argues that because John uses this title in the prolog, therefore this section, v. 16-21, is John's composition not Jesus' discourse. This assumes that John himself coined the title "the Only-begotten." Even when this section is regarded as Jesus' discourse, its wording is often supposed to be so peculiarly John's language that he inserted, here and in v. 18, the designation "the Only-begotten," which Jesus himself never uttered. This strange reasoning must be reversed. This title is so strange, striking, unique, exalted, that it is easier to believe that Jesus coined it, and that John adopted it from Jesus, than to think that John himself coined it. This title is so distinctive and striking in every way that we must say: if Jesus did not use it in this discourse, if it originated in John's mind during John's later years, then the fact that John inserted it here as though Jesus used it is unbelievable. Whatever wording of John's own is found in this discourse must be minor and must leave intact the distinctive terms and expressions that Jesus actually used, quite a number of which may be noted: loved — world — believe — perish — life eternal, etc. Among the grandest, the most unusual is "the Only-begotten." If Jesus here used it, John had to preserve it, and he did; if Jesus never used it either here or elsewhere, John would not dare to insert it here, and that twice. All is normal if John here heard Jesus say, "the Only-begotten" and thus placed this title in his prolog; all is abnormal if Jesus never used the expression and John yet writes as he does.

What is said when expounding 1:14 and 18 in regard to the meaning of the title and the fact that it cannot refer to the exceptional human birth of Jesus but must express the eternal relation of the Son to the Father, the *generatio aeterna,* is made inevitable by the way in which Jesus himself here uses this title. God's gift of love must here name this gift as it existed in heaven before the time of the giving and at that time. There with the Father in heaven was "his Son the Only-begotten" who was such from all eternity, and as such God gave him to the world. So great, so tremendous was the gift, and so astounding the love that made this gift. Luther's word must stand, "true God, begotten of the Father from eternity," expressing, as it does, the conviction of the church of all past ages.

The aorist ἔδωκεν, "did give," denotes the one historical past act. Jesus speaks objectively throughout, using the third person when speaking of himself and general expressions like "world," "he that believes," etc., when speaking of other persons, and thus he here uses the aorist. This verb "gave" really refers to an act that took place in the other world, where any consideration of time would be inadequate, meaning only that we are in a poor human way speaking of things beyond us. Keeping this in mind, we may say that "gave" neither refers to the death on the cross nor to the incarnation alone but to these and to all else by which God bestowed his Savior as a gift. No indirect object follows "gave" — significant omission, for Jesus could hardly say that God gave his Son "to the world," because the world as such did not on its part receive the Son (1:10). Nevertheless, all is clear when we hear what purpose God had by giving his gift, "in order that everyone believing in him should not perish but have life eternal." This repeats the purpose clause of v. 15, which see for the explanation. The repetition links the verses so closely that no new paragraph is in place at v. 16. The gift is a unit act, but the purpose attached to it holds until the end of time. The repetition stresses this purpose clause, even as repetition constantly marks emphasis. Jesus virtually says: Note well once more this *fiducia* of believing, this personal singular, this universality, this possession, this wondrous life.

But as is the case in many such emphatic repetitions, the emphasis is enhanced by an addition. The object of faith is indicated by John's usual εἰς αὐτόν, "in him," where, however, εἰς is not to be stressed as including

motion. In the Koine especially this would be a
linguistic anachronism, for εἰς here follows verbs of
rest and even verbs of being as an ordinary idiom;
cf. R. 591, etc., on its static use. John does not need
to repeat that the believer "should have ἐν αὐτῷ, in him,
life eternal," for this is clearly implied in the other
phrase. In εἰς αὐτόν, "him" includes all that has been
said of the Son in v. 15, 16. This wonderful Person
is the object of faith. The real amplification lies in
the addition of the negative, "should not perish" to
enhance the positive, "but have life eternal," using
the strong adversative ἀλλά. "To perish" denotes total
and eternal rejection by God, and it is so used especially in the middle voice by John and by Paul, C.-K.
788. The word never means to suffer annihilation.
Here the aorist subjunctive μὴ ἀπόληται is in place to
indicate the one final act of perishing in contrast with
the present subjunctive ἔχῃ to indicate the present and
enduring having of life eternal. Not to perish is to
have; not to have is to perish. To perish is defined in
what follows as the opposite of being saved (v. 17), as
being judged (v. 18), and as being reproved or convicted (v. 20). In this negative "should not perish"
Jesus touches the first great warning for Nicodemus:
God does not want him to perish — does he himself
mean to perish, nevertheless? He surely will if he becomes obdurate in unbelief.

17) With γάρ this verse links into v. 16. The
giving of the Son is wholly an act of love not of justice
and judgment, wholly in order that men should escape
judgment and be saved. **For God sent not the Son
into the world in order to judge the world but in
order that the world should be saved through him.**
The explanation introduced by γάρ extends to details.
Thus the giving of the Son is now expressed by the
aorist: God "did send"; he gave by sending. The gift
is the mission. As being thus sent Jesus was before

Nicodemus at that very moment. The briefer designation "the Son" means the same as the fuller "his Son, the Only-begotten." With the new verb the addition "into the world" makes the action of God clearer, whereas with the verb "gave" such a modifier could not be added. The way in which God "gave" his Son was by "sending him into the world."

We may say that in order to judge the world God would not have needed to send (certainly not to give) his Son. He could have sent another flood, or fire, or some other cataclysm. The verb "to judge" is a *vox media*, it means simply to pass a decision. But since the world was lost in sin and unbelief, this could be only a condemnatory decision. Hence the interpretative translation of the A. V., "to condemn the world," is not really incorrect although Jesus used only the simple verb "to judge." Its aorist tense implies a final act of judging.

But God's purpose was not the judgment of the world, worthy of condemnation though it was, but the salvation of the world; hence he sent a Savior into the world. "Not . . . but," or "on the contrary," forms the ·strongest kind of an antithesis. The same is true regarding the two ἵνα and the verbs, "in order to judge," and, "in order to save," ·which are made stronger by placing the verbs forward. The effect of the whole is heightened by thrice repeating "the world."

The passive "should be saved" involves God as the agent; but "through him" shows that God will use a Mediator, namely his own Son, διά here and so often being used regarding mediation, the use of a personal or other medium. The verb itself, like the equivalent adjective and the nouns, carries with it the imagery of rescue from the terrible danger referred to in the previous term "perish." In fact, the passive "to be saved" is the opposite of "to perish." But the verb always has the strong connotation: to keep sound, uninjured; to preserve sound and safe. Thus "to be saved" = "to have life eternal," to enjoy eternal safety. The aorist matches that of "to judge." God's purpose was actual, complete salvation for the world. By combining the negative and the positive Jesus throws into bold relief the great purpose of God's love and at the same time intensifies the call to faith for Nicodemus.

18) With God's purpose of love thus clearly stated, the manner of its realization is again emphasized. But this is altogether personal, for each one as an individual, hence the singular is used in this sentence. While Jesus still speaks objectively, in the third person, he yet aims directly at Nicodemus who would involuntarily turn this third person into the second and regard it as being addressed to him personally. **He that believes on him is not judged; he that believes not on him has already been judged, because he has not believed in the name of the Only-begotten Son of God.** Though no connective is used, none being needed, what the previous verse states in general in regard to being judged and in regard to being saved is here made personal, and the decisive factor in this is faith. Hence these striking opposites, "he that believes on him"—"he that believes not on him" ($\mu\acute{\eta}$ being the regular negative with a participle). Both substantivized participles are durative as in v. 15 and 16; continuous believing marking the one man, continuous non-believing the other. The whole world is divided into these two.

Jesus might have used the positive verb "to be saved" in connection with v. 17 and might have said: The believer "is saved," the non-believer "is not saved." Instead he takes up the negative verb from v. 17 and says: The believer "is not judged," the non-believer "has already been judged." This verb has the stronger tone of warning. Nicodemus must know that escape is accomplished by faith alone, escape now at this very moment, for the tense is present, "is not judged." He must know that lack of faith is the destructive force, destructive from the very start, for the tense is the perfect, "has already been judged" and thus now stands as one already so judged. In a way this explains why God did not need to send his Son to judge the world. By sending his Son to save the world the judgment takes care of itself. The believers need no judgment. Being saved, they belong to God as his own. He will institute no trial for them as if he had to decide their case pro or con either now or at any time including the last day. This also is true with regard to the nonbelievers. Their refusal to believe already judges them; they already have their verdict which, as the perfect κέκριται shows, stands indefinitely.

That is why Jesus uses the indeterminate verb κρίνεσθαι, "to be judged," instead of the verb κατακρίνεσθαι, "to be condemned," which, by the way, is not found in John. Even such an act as judging is not at all needed. But will not a grand final judgment take place at the last day? Not in the strict sense of the word. Then all men will already have received their judgment even as Jesus tells Nicodemus at this moment. Immediately after they are raised from the dead they will be ranged either on the right or on the left of the Judge by the angels. That could not be done if they were not already judged. What follows is the public announcement of the verdict which was long before this determined by the Judge, and with the verdict the evidence on which it rests.

Since the believer is not judged, nothing more needs to be added concerning him. He is not judged — that is all. But since the non-believer has been

judged, Jesus states the charge against him, using the
actual form of a legal indictment. Unfortunately this
is lost in our English translation because we have only
one negative while the Greek has two, one objective,
regarding the fact presented as such, one subjective,
regarding the opinion of the speaker. Jesus uses the
latter. If he had used οὐ, he would simply have stated
the fact regarding the unbeliever: *quod non credidit*,
nothing more. By using μή he states the charge
against the man as God would make it: *quod non
crediderit*. So stated, it includes what God or Christ
think and hold against the man. In fact, we may
call it more than a charge, for this charge becomes
the verdict of God on the man, R. 963. That, too, is
why this is stated in such a full and formal way. We
need to add only one implied word: Guilty "because
he has not believed in the name of the Only-begotten
Son of God!" The crime is thus solemnly named.
The perfect μή πεπίστευκεν matches the preceding perfect κέκριται, for they are concurrent as to time, setting in at the same instant and continuing on equally
after that.

When stating the charge and the verdict, we again
meet τὸ ὄνομα (compare 1:12): he has not believed
"on the name" of the Only-begotten Son of God. In
all such connections "the name" denotes the revelation
of the Son that is made to a person. Jesus was now
making this revelation to Nicodemus. "The name"
is thus the Word (v. 11). It tells all about this wonderful Savior and his grace and his work for us.
"The name" is thus used in these connections because
it contains the trust-producing power. Here all the
greatness of this name and revelation is brought out
by the genitive: the name "of the Only-begotten Son
of God." Can there be a greater? Could God come
to your soul with a more effective trust-producing
power? Hence the outrageousness of the crime named

in this indictment. It is not hard to imagine the impact of these words of Jesus on the soul of Nicodemus. Those who regard these words as mere objective reflections of John himself miss the personal urge that throbs in them. We also need not wonder that we have no more dialog, for we can well imagine the significant silence of Nicodemus as he sat there with such words gripping his soul. That, too, is why John placed this discourse into his Gospel: Jesus is making a wonderful revelation of himself, his attestation to his divine nature and his work could hardly be stronger.

19) The connection is close. Speaking of coming not to judge the world (v. 17), then of one man not judged and of another already judged (v. 18), the question is vital: "Just what is meant by this judgment?" Jesus gives a direct answer. **Now this is the judgment, that the light has come into the world, and men did love the darkness rather than the light; for their works were wicked.** This is the κρίσις or decision of which Jesus is speaking. If all men believed, no κρίσις like this would be necessary (v. 18a). Because men refuse to believe, this "judgment" sets in in the very nature of the case. But in defining this judgment as Jesus here does two revelations are made conjointly: the full inner justice of this judgment together with the inner moral wrong that makes this judgment just and thus inevitably brings it on the guilty man.

Since this description of the judgment is somewhat like a parenthetical statement, we have δέ, "now," R. 1184. Also the ὅτι clause is in apposition with αὕτη, "This . . . that," etc., R. 699; and is not causal as some have supposed, R. 964. "The light" with its significant article really means "the Spirit," the Son himself (1:4, 5) who as "the Truth" (14:6) brings the complete revelation of God (1:18; 3:11) and makes it shine into men's minds and hearts. In Jesus all the divine realities (this is the meaning of ἀλήθεια or "truth") concerning God, his grace and his love, his power to redeem and to save, lie open and bare so that men must see their shining. This Light "has come," and the perfect tense implies that it is now here and continues thus. In the person, signs (v. 3), and words of Jesus it was shining into Nicodemus' heart at this very moment. Normally, one would expect that by being made to see these realities men would be led to act accordingly. But no; deliberately they do the very contrary.

"And men loved the darkness rather than the light." This καί, like so many others in John, should not be taken to mean "and yet" as R. 426 would have it; it simply places side by side the unspeakably blessed fact of the coming of the Light into the world and the unspeakably tragical fact that men preferred the darkness to the Light. This coordination is finer than any disjunction would be. The verb ἠγάπησαν is placed first for emphasis. The aorist states the simple fact. Jesus could use this tense thus early in his work. We need not make it prophetic. It matches the subject "men," *die Menschen* (the generic article). Jesus speaks of his relation to men in a general way not merely specifically regarding what men had already done. This ἠγάπησαν is the answer of men to the ἠγάπησεν of God (v. 16). Note the identity of the verb. "They loved" with the love of intelligence and of purpose. "They loved," making a deliberate choice for a deliberate purpose. This purpose is stated in v. 20. Jesus says οἱ ἄνθρωποι although he does not refer to all men, for he has already spoken of those that believe, and his words cannot be misunderstood.

While it is true that with disjunctives ("rather . . . than") the nouns naturally have the article, R. 789, here they are needed also for another purpose: "*the* Light" and "*the* darkness" are both decided-ly definite. "The darkness" (compare the remarks on 1:5) is not the mere absence of light but is always conceived as a hostile power. It is the specific power of sin and death that actively wars against the Light. As the Light is the actual reality concerning God, his love, etc., so the darkness is the direct opposite, all the unreality that men imagine and invent in their folly regarding God, their souls, and eternity. Not a bit of it is true, yet they stake their very souls upon it and that in the face of all the light which displays the real facts to them. This choosing of the darkness instead of the light is the utterly unreason-ing and unreasonable folly of men. Eventually, when they are asked why they chose thus, they will remain dumb. We must construe μᾶλλον . . . ἤ with the nouns not with the verb, R. 663, because the nouns are placed in contrast, "the darkness rather than the Light." This, too, is a sad miosis, a soft way of saying that they *hated* the Light.

Jesus exposes the inner motive for this choice. This is not one which in any degree excuses the choice but one which more fully reveals its utter base-ness, "for their works were wicked." The order of the words in the Greek rests the emphasis on both "works" and "wicked." "Their works" are not scat-tered, individual deeds but those that make up and display their real inner nature and will, the net sum of their lives. And πονηρά is always meant in the active sense: doing evil, putting it forth, set on wicked-ness. To get the force of the adjective we must not think merely of gross immoralities but especially of all forms of ungodliness, all self-righteousness, all reli-gious perversions, carnal and material religious hopes, with every action and practice that displays these inclinations. The implication is not that men help-lessly lie in the toils of wickedness but that, when the saving power of the Light comes to them and battles to free them, they fight the Light, hug their wicked works, and continue to make them the sum and substance of their lives.

Jesus here reveals the terrible moral inwardness of all unbelief, laying bare the cold facts. Unbelief never means that a man "cannot see the Light." The Light cannot be charged with deficiency or weakness. God's grace is always *gratia sufficiens*. The trouble is not intellectual but moral. Paul learned this from Jesus. When he describes the heathen ungodliness he, too, goes back to the ἀδικία, "unrighteousness," the moral motive, Rom. 1:18. Every man who rejects the divine light of truth when it comes to him to draw him from evil unto God and instead determines to hold to the darkness of untruth and lies, does this at bottom for a moral reason, namely because he will not part from the evil that he loves and that thus marks his soul and his life.

20) In v. 19 γάρ establishes the reason why the evil choice is made. In v. 20 γάρ elucidates the reason stated in v. 19. This is quite necessary, for the case is not that when a man chooses the darkness in preference to the light he then leaves the light alone. The moral reason that prompts that choice, i. e., the evil work from which he will not separate himself, does not let him rest but makes him hate and war against the light. **For everyone that practices things worthless hates the light and comes not to the light lest his works should be convicted.** Here again, as in v. 18, Jesus individualizes and for the same reason. This moral baseness and the hatred it produces is personal, and the ensuing guilt is personal. The singular thus grips Nicodemus personally, who surely must think of himself as he hears these words.

A radical and far-reaching difference separates the two interpretations of v. 20, 21: the one that Jesus here describes two men who have come into decisive contact with the light that Jesus brings, the one accepting, the other rejecting that light; and the other interpretation that Jesus here adduces only a general rule, namely that any man who does wrong likes to keep it dark while any man who does right is not afraid to come into the light. The words of Jesus can be made to express the latter very ordinary thought only by altering a number of the concepts which Jesus uses in their distinctive sense. Thus "the light" is not daylight or the public light but the light that is Jesus and in Jesus, the light that has come into the world. This is also true with regard to the other expressions. This view leads to the false notion that, to begin with, "the world" is composed of two classes of men: the one inwardly false and hypocritical who forever remain so and thus are not converted; and the other a better class, better from the very start, upright and honest, who before Jesus is brought to them already follow the light and the truth that are found in natural revelation and then embrace Jesus and become converted. Rom. 2 and all that the Scriptures teach concerning man's sinful condition contradict this view. Jesus' own words in these two verses shut it out most decidedly.

"Everyone that practices things worthless" refers to all those who have spurned the light and have definitely chosen the darkness instead. Verse 19 puts this beyond question. Jesus characterizes this kind of a man according to his works not according to his act of preferring the darkness to the light, because in v. 19 the inner motive of this preference has been revealed, the determined love of wicked works. The substantivized present participles ὁ πράσσων and, in v. 21, ὁ ποιῶν are exactly like ὁ πιστεύων in v. 15, 16, and 18. The continuous action indicated describes the man referred to in each case. The variation be-

tween ὁ πράσσων in v. 20 and ὁ ποιῶν in v. 21 is slight,
and yet the difference may be noted. The one verb
has the idea of aim: *wer treibt, agit*; the other has
the idea of effecting: *wer tut, facit*. Hence also the
addition in v. 21: that his works "are wrought" in
God, εἰργασμένα. In v. 19 the evil works are called πονηρά,
"wicked" (actively so), now Jesus uses φαῦλα, "worthless." Trench, *Synonyms*, II, 169, etc.: "That which
is morally evil may be contemplated on two sides,
from two points of view; either on the side of its
positive malignity, its will and power to work mis-
chief, or else on its negative worthlessness, and, so to
speak, its good-for-nothingness. Πονηρός contemplates
evil from the former point of view, and φαῦλος from
the latter." Thus the one term amplifies the other.
The latter brings out the utter folly of him who
chooses the darkness, for the deeds for which he wants
this darkness are absolutely worthless and net him
nothing for his life.

But having made his choice for the reason indicated and now practicing such worthless things, he
"hates the light and comes not to the light." Jesus
repeats "the light," which thus plainly, even emphatically, takes up v. 19, reaches back to 1:4, 5, and forms
one of the cardinal terms in John's Gospel. This
is the light of the divine truth which always displays
everything as it really is. This light, once being
definitely rejected for the darkness, this man is bound
to "hate"; he cannot tolerate it, he "comes not to
the light," will not let its truthful, revealing rays fall
upon him. The light is there, and he knows it is
there; it is there for him, and its rays go out to reach
him. Deliberately he avoids it. Coming to it would
mean that he is attracted by it and by what it does;
not coming means that he recoils from it, dreading
what it does.

Instead of stating the cause or reason for this hate and avoidance Jesus indicates the purpose, which also is negative, ἵνα μή, "lest" or "in order that . . . not." Rejecting the light is negative; the following worthless works are negative; hating and avoiding the light is negative; trying to run away from conviction is negative. "Lest his works should be convicted," ἐλεγχθῇ, not merely, "reproved," our versions, and still less "discovered," A. V. margin; but shown up as what they actually are, evil, worthless, fit only for "the darkness." And "his works" are here again not merely certain individual deeds but the works that sum up and characterize the man as what he really is. Here we see the inner, hidden self-contradiction and self-condemnation of all such doers of evil who in unbelief act contrary to Christ and the gospel. They choose the worthless but they do not want its worthlessness revealed. They want to be undisturbed in thinking the worthless valuable. This they can do only in "the darkness" where they themselves and others cannot see. Where religious error prevails, as in the delusion of Pharisaic work-righteousness, or in any other aberration, this self-deception literally becomes tragic. When speaking of the wicked and worthless works Jesus is certainly not excluding those that transgress the second table of the law, but just as certainly he has in mind especially those that transgress the first table. The supreme issue for him is and remains faith or unbelief and the works only as evidence and fruit either of the one or of the other. Moreover, the thought behind being convicted is not mere condemnation of the worthless works but a condemnation that produces contrition and repentance and thus turns the heart from these works unto faith and the works that flow from faith.

21) Strong in warning in the last statements, the discourse of Jesus ends with a note of blessedness

and joy. Over against the negative Jesus sets the positive. The matter must be made complete. Besides, each casts light on the other. Many may reject the light, but by no means all do so. God's Only-begotten cannot fail. **But he that does the truth comes to the light, that his works may be made manifest, that they have been wrought in God.** No need to repeat πᾶς which is understood without the repetition. The surprising feature is that in describing this man Jesus does not say, "he that does things good," but that he at once penetrates to the one and only source of all things really good in the sight of God: he that does "the truth." To do the truth is a pregnant expression and means that one puts the truth which he has received in his heart into his life and actions, so that thus the truth stamps him as "one that is of the truth," 19:37. Only a believer who has the truth in his heart can do the truth, i. e., live according to it in his life. In this doing the truth the first table of the law will have the first place, and the second will, of course, not come short.

"Truth" sounds very general, and many are thereby misled. On the lips of Jesus who called himself the Truth, being its very embodiment, the word here can mean only one thing: the saving truth of God's grace in Christ Jesus as it shines forth in both Testaments. Any wider sense, such as the truth in nature, is shut out by the entire context and by the statement that the works of the doer of the truth (note the article τὴν ἀλήθειαν) are such because they "are wrought in God," i. e., in union and communion with God. In no other way than through faith in the Messiah can even a single work be wrought in God. Here, then, is a man to whom "the light" came as to the other mentioned in v. 20. He, too, up to that time was doing things wicked and worthless like the other. But when the light began to shine into him and to draw him, he did not wrest himself willfully away and cover himself up completely in "the darkness." The light did its work in him; it entered his will and began to control it — he began to do the truth. The result was "works wrought in God," works of the gospel, works of faith. The first of these will always be contrition and repentance for all past evil works, confession of faith, and the continuance of these from day to day, to be followed by the entire range of good works. A perfect and complete doing of the truth will not at once be achieved; weaknesses, faults, sins enough will appear. But the doing has begun and by the help of the truth will go on.

What of this man? He "comes to the light." Once the light came to him, now he is able to come to it. There is no need to specify that this man "loves" the light, whereas the other "hates" it. His coming to the light proves his love for the light. This man has no reason whatever to fear this divine light of truth when it shows up the inward realities of his heart and his life. The idea is not that this light will find nothing to convict in him. It will show up sins, weakness of faith, and faults enough. But this man wants to be rid of these and gladly submits to the healing power of the light. Jesus passes this feature by, but we may well add it to his brief words. The purpose which Jesus names for this man's coming to the light is, "that his works may be made manifest, that they have been wrought in God." To translate ὅτι "because" gives a wrong turn to the thought. The verb "manifest," applied to this man's works, requires that *what* is made manifest be stated. This is "that (declarative ὅτι) they have been wrought in God," ἐστιν εἰργασμένα, the perfect tense saying that, once so wrought, they stand permanently as such. This is what the light of grace already now does for all such works. It is a kind of judgment of grace. It helps, encourages, confirms, and strengthens us day by day as we fight the darkness that still assails us. What a glorious manifestation that will be when on the last day the unerring "light" seals this approval before the whole universe of angels and men!

Did Jesus say any more? We need not know. The attestation in the words which John reports is full and complete. What did Nicodemus say or think? John is not making this a story about this man but a report of the testimony of Jesus to himself. To say that John's account is incomplete is to misunderstand what the account really is. We may well say, however, that Jesus' words must have made an indelible impression upon the old Pharisee and must have shaken him profoundly. In due time he came to faith.

Jesus in Judea and the Last Testimony of the Baptist, 3:22-36. — The historical remarks which John inserts in v. 22-24 serve only to present the situation in which the dispute arose that furnished the occasion for the Baptist's final testimony regarding Jesus. This testimony is John's real subject; all else is incidental. **After these things came Jesus and his disciples into the Judean country, and he was tarrying there with them and was baptizing.** The plural pronoun in the phrase μετὰ ταῦτα includes all that Jesus had done in Jerusalem (2:12-3:21) although John has given only a slight hint in 2:23 as to what this included. Jesus now moves from the capital "into the Judean country." No specific locality is named as this is done in v. 23 in the case of the Baptist, probably because, while the latter had a fixed place where he worked, Jesus moved about from one place to another. The verb in the singular followed by "Jesus" as the subject, adding the disciples with "and," is like 2:2 and makes Jesus the important person. Why Jesus made this move John in no way indicates. The guess that

he was discouraged by what is called his failure in
the capital, the addition that he tried less radical
measures than the cleansing of the Temple and thus
descended to the level of the Baptist's work, is a
good example of judging Jesus according to the stand-
ards of ordinary men. He had made no mistake in
Jerusalem. There as well as here in the country
district he did exactly what best furthered his great
purpose. The imperfect tenses which state that in
the country he "tarried" or spent some time in company with his disciples (μετ' αὐτῶν) and "baptized" are
the usual duratives to indicate continued action.
The fact of his baptizing would indicate that the
locality was the neighborhood of the Jordan. On the
subject of this baptism see the remarks on 1:26.
Jesus did not baptize in person but did it through his
disciples, 4:2.

23) The other evangelists say nothing about
Jesus' baptizing. John's remark amplifies their account. Yet, lest someone should combine John's statement with those of the others in an incorrect manner
and think that Jesus did not take up this baptizing
until the Baptist's labors were ended, John adds the
remark: **Now John also was baptizing in Ænon
near Salim because much water was there; and they
were coming and being baptized.** The δέ makes the
statement parenthetical. The evangelist himself helps
us to determine only two points about the location of
Ænon (springs). The way in which the Baptist's
disciples refer to the former testimony of their master
as having been made "beyond Jordan," v. 26, shows
that now they were on its hither or western side. Immediately after the evangelist tells us that Jesus went
"into the Judean country" he names Ænon as the
place where the Baptist labored, and by adding no
name of a country he leaves our thoughts in Judea.
On the disputes about the actual site consult the Bible

Dictionaries. The place was so named on account of its springs, for which reason also it was suitable for the Baptist's work. The plural πολλὰ ὕδατα denotes either the springs themselves or the rivulets that flowed from them and not a large body of water. In the long search for the site of Ænon only such places have been considered which show such springs, and neither ancient nor modern records speak of a place that had water enough to immerse numbers of people. Nor is the consideration here only water for the purpose of baptizing but also and very vitally, where multitudes camped for some time, water for drinking purposes. The imperfect tense of the verbs, the coming and the being baptized on the part of the people, as in the previous verse, means to state that the Baptist was here carrying on his work for some time.

24) **For John had not yet been cast into the prison,** elucidates the previous statement. Readers of Mark 1:14 and Matt. 4:12-17 might question our evangelist's account to the effect that the Baptist and Jesus thus baptized at the same time. So John states that this occurred prior to the Baptist's imprisonment. This is the reason for the statement and not the self-evident fact that the Baptist's work ceased when he was cast into prison. That also is why John has the article: had been cast "into *the* prison," referring his readers to this well-known prison and the Baptist's confinement there, of which they had knowledge from the other evangelists.

25) Now follows the episode which occasioned the Baptist's final testimony. **A dispute, accordingly, arose on the part of the disciples of John with a Jew about purifying.** With οὖν, "accordingly," John indicates that this dispute arose out of the situation sketched in v. 22-24, hence was not about purifying in general, i. e., the old Jewish ways and regulations,

but about the Baptism of Jesus as compared with that of the Baptist. What the actual question of the dispute was the evangelist does not say since his concern is something more important. All we can gather from the complaint of the Baptist's disciples in v. 26 is that the Jew maintained the superiority of Jesus' Baptism over that of the Baptist, which the disciples of the latter refused to admit as it would also involve that men should leave the Baptist and go to Jesus. The dispute started with the disciples, as ἐκ shows (R. 515, ablative). This preposition is not used in the partitive sense, "*some* of John's disciples," when the construction calls for the genitive or the dative. The suggestion that Ἰουδαῖος here means a Judean not a Jew is strange, since the man's nationality is of no moment. By calling him a Jew the evangelist classes him with the opponents of Jesus, whom he steadily calls "the Jews." The man's interest in the dispute would thus be to cause perplexity and discord.

26) **And they came to John and said to him, Rabbi, he that was with thee beyond the Jordan, to whom thou hast borne witness, behold, this one is baptizing, and all men are coming unto him.** These are the disciples alone, and they go to their master who is near at hand. They lay before him not the question of dispute but the situation from which it arose, and this in the form of an aggrieved complaint. Hence they even avoid naming Jesus, they only describe him, but in a way that brings out first, their thought that Jesus is under great obligation to the Baptist and, secondly, that Jesus is showing himself ungrateful to the Baptist. In their complaint lies the question, "Is this right?" They refer to what is recorded in 1:29-34. By saying that this occurred "beyond the Jordan" they specify what testimony they refer to and at the same time indicate that they

were now on the western side of the river. They speak
as though the Baptist had done much for Jesus by
testifying of him as he did. But, behold, οὗτος (see
1:7), "this man," is now competing with their beloved master, competing with him after having received so much from him! By adding the exaggeration
that "all men" are running after Jesus these disciples
betray their state of mind. In the perfect μεμαρτύρηκας
we note the effect of the testimony as continuing in
the present.

27) The reply of the Baptist which now follows
in extenso and is our evangelist's chief concern is so
thoroughly true, so illuminating and at the same time
so demonstrative of his perfect humility that it stands
as a monument to him forever. He begins with a
general truth, one to which every child of God must
at once assent, one that applies equally to himself and
to Jesus. **John answered and said, A man can receive nothing except it have been given to him from
heaven.** The great importance of the Baptist's
statement is indicated by the doubling: he "answered
and said," compare 1:48. When men arrogate something to themselves, rob others, snatch what does not
properly belong to them, they really do not have what
they have; for it shall be taken from them, and God's
judgment condemns them. What is really our portion,
including our position, work, success, especially in the
kingdom of God, is a gift allotted to us, which we
thus receive and truly have. "Given" and "receive"
correspond. The doubling of the negatives in the
Greek (οὐ . . . οὐδέν) is common, R. 1162. On the
periphrastic perfect subjunctive see R. 907: has been
and thus remains given, punctiliar-durative.

28) Now the application of the general principle.
**You yourselves bear me witness that I said, I am
not the Christ, but that (I said), I am one that
has been commissioned before him.** The Baptist

meant and still means what he said on the occasion
when the delegation from the Sanhedrin questioned
him, 1:19, etc. His entire conduct has borne that out,
and his disciples must today give him this testimony.
He here briefly states what has not been given to him
and, over against that, what has. On that other occasion he did not use the wording, "I am one commissioned before him," but it certainly sums up what he
said in 1:23 and 26, 27. He may even have spoken
these words, either on that occasion or on another, our
evangelist merely not recording them. We regard the
perfect participle as the predicate of "I am"; ἐκεῖνος
is often used with reference to a person that is absent,
as in this case.

29) The Baptist really states only what heaven
(God) has apportioned to him, yet he does it in such
a manner that the disciples at once gather how much
more God has apportioned to Jesus. This implication continues in v. 29, 30. The Baptist's statements
through to v. 36 are without connectives, simply being
ranged side by side, each standing powerfully by itself. The second has a beauty of its own in that it
uses a figure hallowed by the Old Testament yet not
as this is used in Isa. 54:5; Hos. 2:18, etc., with reference to Jehovah and Israel, where no room would be
found for "the friend of the bridegroom," but as it is
used in the Song of Solomon and was interpreted also
by the Jews with reference to the Messiah. **He
that has the bride is the bridegroom; yet the friend
of the bridegroom, he that stands and hears him,
rejoices greatly because of the voice of the bridegroom. This my joy, therefore, has been fulfilled.**
The Baptist's meaning is transparent. Jesus is the
bridegroom who has the bride. Thus the Baptist is
the friend of the bridegroom. God arranged this relation, and for the Baptist it is blessing indeed. The

bride are all they who by faith truly belong to Jesus. If, indeed, "all men" are going to Jesus, v. 26, the Baptist cannot show the slightest touch of envy but can only rejoice in the fact.

No special task is here indicated for the friend of the bridegroom, who, as the article indicates, is the one formally functioning as such during the celebration. We should not transfer into the picture our present weddings with their wedding ceremony in which "the best man" has a function. The Jewish wedding was only a joyful feast at the groom's home, following the procession in which the groom brought the bride to his home. No special time in the progress of the wedding feast is in any way indicated, although commentators have tried to fix such a time, and some with gross indelicacy. The Baptist pictures only the relation and the proper attitude of the friend to the groom, for which alone also he uses this figure; for he intends to describe his own true relation and his attitude toward Jesus.

So he adds the apposition, "he that stands and hears him." The two participles are substantivized and united by the one Greek article and thus should not be made a relative clause. The friend's place is near the groom (ἑστηκώς is always used as a present not as a perfect). So he also hears the groom (αὐτοῦ, the genitive to indicate the person speaking) not his commands during the wedding but the voicing of his happiness and joy. With what feelings the Baptist (friend) does this he is happy to state: he "rejoices greatly because of the voice of the bridegroom." The article with the genitive points to the specific bridegroom referred to, namely Jesus, a point that is lost by translating, "the bridegroom's voice." The Hebrew infinitive absolute is imitated in χαρᾷ χαίρει by thus adding the cognate noun as the instrumental dative,

R. 94; B.-D. 196, 6; and the sense is that the action takes place in the highest degree, "rejoices greatly," literally, "with joy."

With one stroke the picture is transferred to the reality, "This my joy, therefore, has been fulfilled," or, "has been made full," R. V., American committee. The perfect tense means: and will remain thus. The Baptist's desires are satisfied to the uttermost. His joy, hitherto one in anticipation only, is now realized in actuality as he sees men flocking to Jesus. So far removed above all envy and rivalry or any other unworthy feeling is the Baptist's soul.

30) Hence also the direct reply to the wrong complaint of these foolish disciples: **He must increase, but I must decrease.** "Must," δεῖ, as the nature of the two persons and of their offices demands in the blessed will of God. The full development has not yet been reached, but much is already visible. "He must grow," refers both to the office of Jesus and to his success in winning men. His work had only begun (ἐκεῖνος as in v. 28). "I must become less" likewise refers both to the office and the followers of the Baptist. Presently his task will be entirely done. But it will stand as a great and blessed success.

31) The Baptist has thus far spoken of the relation between Jesus and himself, shutting off the foolish notions voiced in the complaint of his disciples. Now he turns to the other side, the relation of Jesus to men, which includes in particular also his relation to these complaining disciples. The Baptist wants them to follow Jesus as Andrew, John, and the others did. Their whole view of Jesus must be changed accordingly. Thus we receive the supreme part of the Baptist's final testimony to the Sonship of Jesus. **He that comes from above is above all men, he that is of the earth is of the earth and of the earth he speaks; he that comes from heaven is above all**

men. The heavenly origin of Jesus makes him supreme over all men, who are wholly of earthly origin. Both substantivized present participles ὁ ἐρχόμενος and ὁ ὢν are here used without reference to time, and ἐκ is used to express origin or source. Yet we should note that the former is a standing designation for the expected Messiah. Even now since he has come he is in the eminent sense "the Coming One." Since the entire contrast from v. 27 onward deals with persons, "above all" must mean not "above all things" but "above all men." Of him who is "of the earth" nothing can be said except that "he *is* of the earth," on a level with all others who are like him and above nobody. Hence also all his speaking, whatever utterance he makes (λαλεῖ), is of the same nature, "of the earth." On the other hand, "he that comes from heaven" (now using this elucidating phrase) "is above all men" not merely in his speaking but in everything. The two πάντων show that the contrast is here not between Jesus and the Baptist only but between Jesus and all men in general. This mighty contrast these disciples must know and keep in mind.

32) With this clear, the Baptist proceeds to the speaking of Jesus, save that λαλεῖν is too ordinary a verb to apply to him. **What he has seen and did hear, of that he bears witness; and no man receives his witness.** That this is, like his origin, testimony of things seen and heard in heaven goes without saying (1:18). Grammarians have difficulty with the two verbs, one a perfect, the other an aorist, "has seen," "did hear." They ask whether the perfect is aoristic, or the aorist is used in the sense of the perfect. They certainly can be understood most easily just as they stand. The perfect is extensive: what Jesus has seen in heaven all along; the aorist is punctiliar noting the past fact (historical). Jesus "has seen" all there is to be seen in heaven and can testify accordingly. The

aorist "did hear" is not added as a duplicate of all that
Jesus also heard in heaven, all the lovely music and
the heavenly language in the conversations with God.
This aorist is specific and refers to the punctiliar word
or commission which sent the Son forth into the
world.   It indicates the counsel of God for our salvation, the loving commands of the Father, 7:16;
8:28; 12:49, 50; etc.   Of these things Jesus came
to testify.

The καί coordinates two contrary acts: this superlative testimony and its rejection.   Not by mere revelation does Jesus speak as did the prophets of old, but
from actual presence in heaven he "bears witness" at
firsthand, absolutely directly.   Nothing truer and more
trustworthy can ever reach men.   And the things he
testifies thus are the very ones men need most
of all, the facts and realities about God in heaven,
his will, purpose, and plans concerning men.   "And
his testimony — this wondrous testimony — no one
receives."   The very coordination of the statements
lets us feel the enormity of the guilt implied, as in
1:10, 11.   To receive testimony = to believe it; not
to receive it = to disbelieve it, refuse to trust it, treat
it as a lie.   The fact that the negation is not meant
to be absolute the very next words show.

33)   **He that did receive his witness did seal
that God is true.**   At this point and through the
next verse commentators present views with which
we cannot agree.   Who is this that received Jesus'
witness and sealed that God is true?   The Baptist
here does what he has done in his previous statements,
he allows us to infer to whom he is referring.   Both
the aorist participle and the aorist main verb are
definite, each denoting a past act.   The Baptist refers
to *himself*.   There were, indeed, a few others besides
the Baptist who also did receive Jesus' witness.   In a
manner the words apply also to these.   But in their

full sense they apply only to the Baptist himself. As far as the receiving is concerned, he stands first and foremost and helped the first of his own disciples also to receive Jesus' witness. At this very moment he is trying to make his remaining disciples do the same. The actual situation is sometimes lost sight of, and the comment of some expositors reads as though the Baptist here utters abstract, general statements, like a man who is writing a book not like one who is talking face to face with a few men in order to move them to a definite act. The Baptist here virtually tells his disciples, "*I* did receive his witness, *I* did seal," etc. To let this aorist ὁ λαβών refer also to such as in the future will receive Jesus' witness, is to extend its force too far. Such a thought is an inference not the meaning of the word itself.

When the Baptist speaks of sealing that God is true, veracious, *verax*, he, of course, does not mean that God's being true would not be sufficiently certified without such a seal. The declarative ὅτι (R. 1034) states what the seal attests. God is true even if all men called him a liar. A seal is not intended for the person issuing a document but for the one to whom it is issued, to assure him. So God himself adds seals to his truth not for his own sake or for the truth's sake but for our sakes. What does the Baptist mean by saying, "He that did receive his witness did seal that God is true"? Here again some generalize: the seal is faith or the saving effect of Jesus' testimony. This, they say, acts like a seal or proof, helping to assure the believer and others that God is true in his revelation of Jesus. Thus again sight is lost of the actual situation: the Baptist trying to assure his disciples who were finding fault with Jesus. And how about faith and trust in error and deception? Does it, too, "seal" and make error truth? The Baptist is speaking of *himself* and by no means of himself

as an ordinary believer. He is divinely commissioned
(1:6), to him special direct divine revelation was given
(1:31, etc.). He had far more than his own personal
faith to append as a seal, he had *his word and testimony as a prophet of God, the word of the revelation
he had received.* For his disciples this seal ought to
have great weight. There were to be others like this,
namely the apostles (1:14). Their personal faith is
an entirely minor matter. The seal they present is
far higher.

34) The commentators who misunderstand v. 33
are also not clear with regard to v. 34. **For he
whom God did commission speaks the words of God;
for the Spirit gives not from** (insufficient) **measure.**
What does γάρ prove or explain? The fact that faith
acts as a seal? Impossible. The thought of v. 34
runs in an entirely different line. Only properly
related statements can be joined by "for." Therefore
v. 34 does not refer to Jesus himself but to the Baptist.
The simple story is this: John tells his disciples, in
order to convince and assure them, that he himself
puts the seal of his authority and his person on God's
truth that Jesus is the Messiah; and then, in order to
establish the weight of this statement more fully, he
explains (γάρ) that he, sent by God, utters nothing
less than the words of God, and this he can do because the Spirit gives such utterance to him in adequate
measure.

"He whom God did commission" is the Baptist and
not Jesus. The claim that only one "from heaven"
(v. 31b) can be "commissioned" is contradicted by
1:6 and 1:33, where the Baptist is the one "commissioned." In v. 31, 32 Jesus is ὁ ἐρχόμενος, "the One
Coming." Now it is true that Jesus, too, is "sent"
or "commissioned," and that he afterward tells the
Jews much about his "Sender." But here the fact
that Jesus is sent is out of line both with what pre-

cedes and with what follows. The aorist ἀπέστειλεν
indicates the past act when God sent the Baptist on
his great mission. Thus sent — let his disciples note
it well — "he speaks the words of God," literally,
"he utters the utterances of God." For λαλεῖν is the
opposite of being silent; and ῥήματα are merely utterances, whereas λόγοι are the thoughts put into statements. Of Jesus the Baptist has just said far more
in v. 32, namely that he "testifies" the actual things
he has seen and did hear in heaven. Why should he
now reduce this exalted statement? But of the Baptist
this is, indeed, the highest that can be said: God
places his words on his prophet's lips. He is in
the same class with the prophets who were sent before his day.

Another γάρ explains how the Baptist can utter
God's words, "for the Spirit gives not from (insufficient) measure." It is hard to decide from the Greek
whether God is the subject of the sentence, as our
versions take it, or whether it is "the Spirit." The
sense, fortunately, is quite the same, for the point to
be explained is the Baptist's ability to convey God's
utterances. He can do this if *God* gives him the
Spirit in proper measure; or if *the Spirit* gives him
the utterances in proper measure. Yet this γάρ clause
convinces so many that Jesus is here meant and they
do not think that it could be the Baptist. The present
tense of the verb, δίδωσι, which means "continues to
give," should give them pause. If Jesus were referred
to, this would have to be the aorist ἔδωκε, "did give,"
i. e., when the Spirit descended upon him "as a dove."
This continuous bestowal is vouchsafed to the Baptist,
as it was to the prophets before him, day by day for
his work.

Finally, οὐκ ἐκ μέτρου is taken to mean "unmeasured,"
"without measure," "not by measure," a litotes for
"in complete fulness." This misconception has led

many to refer the entire verse to Jesus. The phrase means: not in narrow or insufficient measure, as though the ordinary limits could not be exceeded. The English has no corresponding idiom; ἐκ is not our English "by." The Spirit (or if we prefer the other subject: God) gives as he wills, in richest measure, by revelation and by inspiration, the words he wants his messengers to utter. This, indeed, establishes the fact that the Baptist, as God's messenger, can and does speak God's own words when he points his disciples to Jesus. The Spirit sees to it that he is properly equipped. The disciples have every reason to believe and to obey his words as being "the utterances of God" himself.

35)   After this efficient preparation the Baptist, as one sent of God and fitted out by the Spirit in adequate measure, speaks to his disciples this weighty word of God as the climax of all that he has previously said. **The Father loves the Son and has given all things into his hand. He that believes in the Son has life eternal; but he that obeys not the Son shall not see life, on the contrary, the wrath of God remains upon him.** Let the disciples note well what the Father thinks of the Son (Jesus) as the Baptist here tells them by the Spirit. In the Baptist's own hearing God had declared, "This is my beloved Son!" Matt. 3:17. The Baptist only echoes that word just as he did that about "the Son of God" in 1:34 (compare the comment made there). The fact that here again the Baptist refers to Jesus by "the Son" is wholly evident. On the verb ἀγαπᾶν here used compare v. 16 — the highest form of love, made even infinitely high by being predicated of the Father with regard to the Son.

As this love is the basis and the adequate reason for giving all things into the Son's hands, so this supreme gift is the evidence and the proof of that

love. The extensive perfect δέδωκεν marks the gift as
once being bestowed and then becoming permanent
forever. Not in the divinity of the Son but in his
humanity must this gift be placed as we think of
Jesus. Omnipotence belongs to all three Persons of
the Godhead alike and thus cannot be given by one
Person to the other. But in and according to his
human nature Jesus could and did receive also this
gift. The evidence for his possession of this gift
lies in the miracles which Jesus wrought during the
ministry of his humiliation when he used this gift
only at times and in furtherance of his work. After
his exaltation he used it according to his human nature
without such restriction. "All things" cannot be restricted to those pertaining only to the kingdom, for
even when only the kingdom of grace is thought of,
"all things" would extend far beyond its bounds, Eph.
1:10 and 22. The things of the kingdom are the
greatest by all odds; why then should the lesser be
withheld? Compare also Matt. 11:27; 28:18; John
13:3, where also no restriction appears. "Into his
hand" means for Jesus, God's Son in human flesh, to
rule and to command at will. Did the Baptist's disciples think that their master had merely done Jesus
a favor by testifying of him as he did and had thus
placed Jesus under obligation to him? Their ideas
need a radical modification. And this also for their
own sakes.

36) These are not abstract or theoretical propositions that the Father loves the Son and has given all
things into his hands. They apply most directly to
these disciples — and to us. Since all things are in
Jesus' hands, "life eternal" is included. It is the
highest gift dispensed by the Messiah. Therefore
everything depends on each man's personal relation
to Jesus. In fact, the Baptist is here doing over again
what he did in 1:35, etc., he is urging his own disciples

to follow Jesus. So he places before them the two great alternatives: "he that believes in the Son," and "he that disobeys the Son" (the dative is the direct object, R. 540). The matter is personal, hence these singulars. Twice again "the Son" is used and not a mere pronoun; and "the" Son, this Jesus who is the Son in the supreme sense. In this thrice repeated "the Son" the climax of the Baptist's testimony is reached, and for this reason John here records the entire incident, v. 22-36.

The great personal "either — or" is made plain in the two substantivized participles, "he that believes," and "he that disobeys." For the second, the Baptist might have used, "he that does not believe." But ἀπειθέω, "not to be persuaded by the Son," involves unbelief and is a designation for it; hence "obedience of faith" in Rom. 1:5 is a description of faith. He who trusts the Son, by that very trust obeys the Son; he who will not trust the Son, by that very act of refusal disobeys him. The divine greatness of the Son makes trust and the obedience of trust our only normal and right response to him, and refusal of trust the most desperate challenge of the very character of the Son and of his words and his signs. This disobedience of unbelief is the crime of crimes.

That is why the other two contrasts are bound up in this one of believing and of disobeying. To trust the Son means not only abstractly to rely on him as being trustworthy but to rely on his word and promise concerning life eternal, i. e., to accept this gift by our trust. Hence, the moment we trust the Son we have the gift, ἔχῃ, and continue to have it even as we continue to trust. The glory and the full blessedness of this life does not at once appear, I John 3:2, but we do have this life, and in due time its glory will appear. On the terms used here compare the remarks on v. 15. Thus it means the world and all

to the Baptist's disciples that they should stop their
blind hostility to Jesus and should trust him with all
their heart in a way far beyond any trust they have in
the Baptist. Yea, unless they want to distrust the latter, they must give their very souls to Jesus, the Son,
in the trust that obtains life eternal.

If anything is yet needed to eradicate the hostility
of these disciples to Jesus and to open the way to
trust in him, the consequence of disobeying the Son
should do this. He who disobeys the Son incurs the
worst possible guilt a mortal, sinful being can incur.
This at once, by separating him from the Son, cuts
him off from life eternal, "he shall not see life" ("see"
as in v. 3), shall not "have" it and thus in any way
experience what it is, now and in the next world. This
is infinite loss. This negative result of the disobedience
of unbelief involves the corresponding positive result,
"on the contrary (ἀλλά), the wrath of God remains
upon him." His sinful state of life made him subject
to the wrath of God in the first place (Eph. 2:3), his
disobedience now fixes that wrath upon him forever
(unless he should repent). A certain type of exegesis
and all types of rationalism have assailed "the wrath
of God" as being an impossibility — which it is, indeed, if the unholy conception of it which these men
harbor were reality. Their pictures of a God angry
with the passion of a man, cruel, bloodthirsty, etc., are
inventions of their own. God's wrath is the inevitable
reaction of his righteousness and holiness against all
sin and guilt. While the term "wrath," like other
terms used in the Scriptures with reference to God,
is anthropopathic, it clearly expresses the terrible
reality that, when God is challenged by human sin and
unbelief, God in accord with his very being must cast
far from him those who persist in this desperate challenge. A holy and righteous God must come to a final
issue with all those who reject him and his saving grace

in the Son. They who will not have life by that very fact remain in death.

The Baptist's last testimony is ended. What did these disciples do? Just as little as John told us the full story of Nicodemus, so little he tells that of these disciples. The unanswered question about them leaves us with the same question concerning ourselves: "What are we doing under the impression of the divine testimony here offered also to us?"

CHAPTER IV

Jesus in Samaria, 4:1-42. — **When, therefore, the Lord knew that the Pharisees had heard that Jesus was making and was baptizing more disciples than John (although Jesus himself was not baptizing, but his disciples), he left Judea and departed again into Galilee.** The evangelist's interest in this brief preamble is to inform us how Jesus came to Samaria and thus how the great testimony culminating in v. 26, in the following paragraph, and in v. 42, came to be uttered.

"Therefore," *οὖν*, connects with 3:22, and brings the result. The two imperfect tenses in 3:22 come to the end of their action in the aorists in 4:3. How Jesus "knew" about these Pharisees is not indicated. We have no call to insert miraculous knowledge; someone brought him the information. On the Pharisees here involved see 1:24. They would be the leaders who were in the Sanhedrin, plus their followers in the capital. What they heard was not only what had become of Jesus when he left the capital, or merely what Jesus was doing since he left, but a more significant report, "that Jesus was making and was baptizing more disciples than John." The Greek retains the original present tenses in the indirect discourse, for the messengers said, "Jesus is making and is baptizing," etc. By stating that the report heard by the Pharisees included this comparison with the Baptist the evangelist implies that the Pharisees used it to cast reproach upon this entire movement. Perhaps they said that it was breaking up in competition, adding, somewhat in the manner of the Baptist's disciples in 3:26, that the very man of whom the Baptist testified in such a grandiose way was disrupting the Baptist's own work. On the term μαθηταί see 2:11.

2) For the benefit of his readers the evangelist adds in a parenthesis that Jesus was not baptizing in person but only through his disciples as his agents. This remark is, of course, not intended to mean that the disciples of the Baptist in 3:26, and now the Pharisees were wrong in their assumption of a competition between Jesus and the Baptist on the ground that Jesus himself really baptized nobody; for this ground would not hold. What one's agents do is the same as one's own act. In this final reference to this work of Jesus the evangelist merely wants his readers not to form the wrong impression that, like the Baptist, Jesus baptized with his own hands. Why he bade his disciples to act for him has been variously answered. It seems best to infer: In order that later on no one might claim that he had received a baptism superior to that of the Baptist. The claim that a baptism by Jesus' own hands would be one including the Spirit, whereas the Baptist's baptism and that of Jesus' disciples remained only "a water-baptism," is wholly specious. See the explanations of 1:26.

3) So Jesus left Judea and went back to Galilee. This means that he ceased baptizing not that he transferred the baptizing to Galilee. To think that Jesus now just changed his mind, or that he finally felt that he had made a mistake by beginning to baptize, is to make God's Son an ordinary mortal. The Baptist's work was fast coming to a close (3:30). Jesus aided it as it was approaching its end. He stopped when the hostile Pharisees turned this aid against the Baptist's work. God himself changes his actions because of men's evil acts, and we shall see that Jesus does the same as occasion requires.

4) **Now he had to pass through Samaria.** Any kind of necessity may be expressed by δεῖ, here the

imperfect ἔδει. One could, of course, go around Samaria and thus pass from Judea to Galilee, but the nearer
and more natural way necessitated crossing Samaria.
On the tense see R. 887, who also makes this verb
personal, "he must," 393, which is questionable. This
open tense is closed by the following historical present
ἔρχεται.

5) **He comes, then, to a city of Samaria, called
Sychar, near to the parcel of ground which Jacob
gave to Joseph, his son. Now Jacob's spring was
there.** The historical present "he comes," like those
in the following narration, adds vividness. The preposition εἰς invaded the territory of ἐπί and πρός, R. 596,
so that here it is used when Jesus comes only "to the
city." That this cannot be the old Shechem, now
Nablus, a mile and a half from Jacob's well, as some
have thought, is plain, because the woman could not
go that far for water, nor is the well visible from
Nablus, nor would John introduce the name of the
place by writing, *"called* Sychar," which indicates an
otherwise unknown place. In all probability Sychar
is the present village Askar, from which the well is
reached by a moderate walk, with Joseph's tomb
about a third of a mile from the well. John alone
employs πλησίον as a preposition, R. 547, 646. The
remark about the burial of Joseph is made by the
evangelist not so much to fix more closely the locality
as to enrich the references to past history in the following narrative. Compare Gen. 13:18, etc.; 48:22;
Josh. 24:32. The ground, bought by Jacob, tradition reports he gave to Joseph whose body, brought
along from Egypt by the Israelites, was then buried
there.

6) The word πηγή means "spring" and is to be
distinguished from φρέαρ, "a shaft or well," v. 11, 12.
The word refers to the water at the bottom of the
well or shaft. The author visited the place, one of the

few really assured sites in the Holy Land, in 1925. A Russian orthodox church covers the well. Through a small wooden door, down neat stone steps one comes to the well in a little chapel; there is a hole in the vaulting above to let the light shine down. The well itself is a rock-faced shaft 105 feet deep, a rectangular stone is placed at a convenient height over the well, with a hole about two feet wide in the center of the stone. A neat windlass lowers a kettle, by which the water is drawn up, and the visitor may drink from a chained cup. Candles on a tray were let down by the windlass and lit up the well down to the water, which seems, indeed, to well up like a spring. Formerly the well was partly filled with debris, it is now perfectly clean, and the water is most excellent. While one might prefer a restoration of the well to the condition that prevailed in Jesus' time under the open sky with a few ancient jars as were then (and still are) used, the well is now at least clean and neatly kept. The village, now a few houses, supposed to be Sychar, was pointed out on the hillside. Standing outside of the chapel, it was easy to conceive the scene, with Jesus resting at the well, and "this mountain" (v. 20), Gerizim, rising high not far away.

Jesus, therefore, having been wearied from his journey, was sitting thus at the spring. Jesus is introduced to us at this point of his journey. The perfect participle "having been wearied," i. e., and now in this condition, draws a vivid picture. So also does the durative imperfect "he was sitting," which bids us linger with the sitting figure. The adverb "thus" cannot intend to repeat the participle "having been wearied," for which repetition no reason appears, which also would require that οὕτως be placed before not after the verb. "Thus" = as he was, without any further preparation. Just as he came, so he sat down. The entire sketch, also this adverb, shows that the writer was an eyewitness. Here, as elsewhere in John's Gospel, the true human nature of Jesus is brought to our attention just as vividly and just as forcibly as in other places his true divine nature is emphasized. It is a mistake to think that John writes only of the latter. This man, tired, dusty, hot from his long walk as the sun rose higher and higher, and thirsty, this is God's own Son, the Only-begotten, from whom in such humility his divine glory shone forth. The evangelist even names the hour: **It was about the sixth hour,** near noon according to Jewish reckoning; see the question at issue in John's reference to the hours of the day, 1:39. By naming the hour the evangelist indicates how deeply his soul was impressed by what began here in Samaria at this notable hour.

7) The lone figure by the well is joined by another. A brief sentence tells all we need to know: **There comes a women of Samaria to draw water,** and ἐκ Σαμαρίας must be the same as Σαμαρεῖτις in v. 9, designating her as being from "Samaria," the country, not from the city by this name (called Sebaste). How came this woman to draw water at this hour? While we are not told and cannot make a positive statement, a conjecture such as, having worked in the fields and passing near the well, she desired to refresh herself, is a mere guess. We must not forget that she brought a waterpot, which indicates that she came from her home to obtain water. John's mention of the hour of the day seems to refer particularly to this woman's coming at such an hour. She also comes alone, no other women are with her, whereas oriental women like to go in companies to draw water for their homes. Piecing these observations together and joining them to what is revealed of this woman's character, we may take it that she was a social outcast. The other women would not

tolerate this woman who now lived in open adultery after a checkered career with five husbands. The more must we marvel at the condescension of Jesus who stoops to ask a favor of such a woman, and this with a love that longs to save even her miserable soul.

She would never have spoken to this Jewish stranger. **Jesus says to her, Give me to drink.** Here the Fountain asks for water, and he who bids all that thirst to come to him himself asks to have his thirst quenched. The two aorists in the request indicate two simple acts. There is no need to allegorize, "Give me *spiritual* refreshment through thy conversion." Whatever was in Jesus' heart, his words mean just what they say: he asks this woman for a drink.

8) The evangelist is even at pains to show how a kind of necessity moved Jesus to asks this *woman* for a drink. **For his disciples had gone away into the city in order to buy food.** No one was there to serve Jesus, he was alone. In later times the traditions of the Jews forbade the buying and the eating of Samaritan food; this rule evidently was not in force at this time. The supposition that only some of the disciples had gone for food, that all were not needed for this, that at least John had remained behind who then heard and afterward related the ensuing conversation, cannot be entertained, for then Jesus would have asked a drink not only for himself, nor would John have written "the disciples," without a qualifying word.

9) **The Samaritan woman says to him, How dost thou, being a Jew, ask of me to drink, being a Samaritan woman? For Jews have no dealings with Samaritans.** Thus was the simple request of Jesus denied; nor do we read in the entire narrative that his thirst was quenched. We may assume that Jesus made his request after the woman had drawn

the water not before. The aorist ἀντλῆσαι ὕδωρ in v. 7, however, does not imply this, stating only the single act of drawing water. The situation itself makes it probable that she drew up the water, that then the strange conversation followed, and that finally, when the woman hastened away, in her excitement she forgot to take the filled vessel along. The woman probably recognized the Jew in Jesus by his speech, no other mark being apparent, such as peculiar Jewish dress. The woman neither shows "a smart feminine caprice of national feeling," nor are her words "intended to tantalize." They are quite simple and self-explanatory. She puts them in the form of a question simply because she is surprised. The request is altogether unexpected, and the reason why it is unexpected lies in the relation between Samaritan and Jew. She does not say that the Samaritan is against the Jew, which, of course, would also be true; but that the Jew is against the Samaritan — this because Jesus, the Jew, asks a favor of her, the Samaritan.

With his Gentile readers in mind, the evangelist inserts the remark that the Jews "have no dealings" with the Samaritans, οὐ συνχρῶνται, no ordinary social intercourse. Some codices omit this clause, the verb of which is, indeed, unusual in the New Testament. Yet it states a fact, and, aside from textual authority, this explanatory remark is exactly like others interspersed in John's Gospel. After the return from the captivity in Babylon the Jews rightly denied any participation in the rebuilding of the Temple and in the public worship to the Samaritans, who were a mixture of former Israelites and of Gentiles, II Kings 17:24-41, and also had a mixed religion. Even after renouncing idolatry they acknowledged only the five books of Moses as the Word of God, Ezra 4:1, etc. Thus a bitter enmity existed between the Samaritans and the Jews, which continues to the present day. The handful of Samaritans that exists today at Nablus, the old Shechem, about 175 persons, neither eat, drink, nor intermarry with the Jews, nor have anything to do with them except in the way of trade. The author met their high priest Isaac Ben Omrom and visited their little synagogue in 1925. They have a dearth of girls and are thus dying out. Since others refuse brides to the Samaritans, their own girls are betrothed shortly after birth; but they are gradually dying out. Suspicion of each other divides them, so that it required three men to unlock their synagogue with three separate keys to allow our party to enter and to inspect their scrolls of the Pentateuch, to which they ascribe a fantastic antiquity, one of which is said to be 3579 years old, written by a great-grandson of Aaron, a second of which is said to come from the era of the Maccabees, and a third is said to be 1000 years old.

10) **Jesus answered and said to her** (on the combination of the two verbs see 1:48), **If thou knewest the gift of God and who it is that says to thee, Give me to drink, thou wouldest have asked of him, and he would have given thee living water.** The absolute mastery of the reply is at once apparent. In the most effective manner Jesus uses the very refusal of this woman to make her the offer of the drink she so greatly needs. This offer contains a kindly rebuke for her ungracious refusal to extend so small a favor, coupled with the assurance of a far greater gift if she would ask of him. Modestly Jesus speaks of himself in the third person. His object is to reach this woman's soul. Tired and thirsty as he is, his wants may wait if only he is able to supply hers.

"If thou knewest" — sad, deadly ignorance! Yet this is the voice of heavenly pity. So he spoke with tears concerning Jerusalem: "If thou hadst known,

even thou, at least in this thy day, the things which
belong unto thy peace! but now they are hid from
thy eyes," Luke 19:41, etc. The two cases, however,
are not parallel, for Jerusalem rejected the knowledge
so long and so lovingly offered to her, while this
woman was now for the first time receiving the offer
of this knowledge. "The gift of God," τὴν δωρεὰν τοῦ
Θεοῦ = "living water." The genitive reveals the greatness and the blessedness of the gift: it flows from
God. Yet Jesus connects it with himself as the agent
and the channel through which this gift is bestowed,
"and who it is that says to thee, Give me to drink."
This can be no ordinary person, such as the woman
had known before, not even some holy priest or
teacher in Samaria or in Jerusalem. For he who is
so significantly designated, "he would have given thee
living water," i. e., this very gift of God. Jesus does
not directly say who he is; he only indicates that he
may be the one by the reference to his request for a
drink. The woman could conclude, as she also did,
that Jesus was a great prophet, a man sent by God
to be a human mediator in the bestowal of this gift
of God. But the words of Jesus, purposely left indefinite at this stage of the conversation, may also
imply — and actually did imply — that Jesus himself
is the author and giver of this gift of living water, i. e.,
that he himself is God. The light is veiled; the woman
is led gradually to see it.

The conditional sentence is of the mixed type. The
protasis εἰ ᾔδεις, "if thou knewest," is present unreality,
while the apodosis σὺ ἂν ᾔτησας καὶ ἔδωκεν ἄν, "thou wouldst
have asked and he would have given," is past unreality.
"If thou knewest" — but thou dost not know! "Thou
wouldst have asked" — thou didst not ask. "He would
have given" — but, alas, he could not give. And yet
Jesus continues the offer. "Living water," ὕδωρ ζῶν, is
an allegorical expression, a large number of which

occur in the Scriptures. The illustration (here "water") and the reality (here "life" in the word "living") are combined, but always in such a way that the expression is self-interpretative. See Trench, *Parables,* 9, where this type of Biblical allegory is well elucidated. Unless we understand the little secret of this much-used form of figure, we shall go astray, as many have gone when interpreting "living water," saying that it means "grace and truth," "faith," *gratia renovationis,* "the Word," *"the Spirit* of the new life," or "the Holy Ghost," whereas "living water" means no more than "life," spiritual life, the life regarding which Jesus told Nicodemus that it comes by the new birth. The figure of water, which connotes drinking, intends to show that this life is a vital necessity for us and yet that it may be received so easily. But even as Jesus, physically thirsty and in need of water, remained so although Jacob's well had plenty of water, as long as no one drew and gave him of that water: so this woman, dead in sin and in need of life, would remain so although Jesus, the very fountain of life, sat there before her, as long as she would not desire, ask, and accept this life when Jesus, unlike herself with regard to the common water, unasked offered this heavenly lifewater to her.

11) **The woman says to him: Sir, thou both hast not a drawing vessel, and the well is deep. Whence, then, hast thou the living water? Art thou greater than our father Jacob, who gave us the well and himself drank of it and his sons and his cattle?** Involuntarily the respectful address κύριε, "lord," "sir," comes to the woman's lips. Those who think that her words have an ironical tinge are no doubt mistaken. This woman's question is like that asked by Nicodemus in 3:4. Told that he must be born anew, by his question about again entering his mother's womb, he really says to Jesus, "I know you cannot

mean that." This woman, told that she should have and ask for living water, by her reference to Jesus' lack of a vessel, the depth of the well, and the appended question, really means to say, "I know you cannot mean this water." The woman is sensible, her words are true. Neither Nicodemus nor this woman are so dense that they do not perceive that Jesus is speaking of something that is above the physical. And Jesus is not so bungling in his language that neither Nicodemus nor this woman are unable to see that he is speaking of something that is higher than the natural. Both state that they understand this, he with his "how" question, she with her "whence" question. Both questions are like a premise with an evident conclusion: "Thou canst not mean the natural, the merely physical; ergo, thou must mean something higher." And both are right — that *is* what Jesus means. But here: What kind of water can this be that Jesus means? and whence can he obtain this strange water? In the woman's question the emphasis is not only on "whence" but equally on the final participle τὸ ὕδωρ τὸ ζῶν (R. 777), for this reason it is added with a second Greek article, *"Whence . . . the water that is living?"* In οὔτε (οὐ + τέ, the negative plus the copulative conjunction, R. 1189), followed by καί, we simply have τέ . . . καί, "both . . . and," with the first member negated, R. 1179. Also ἄντλημα, "a drawing vessel," corresponds to ἀντλῆσαι, "to draw," in v. 7.

12) At once the quick mind of this woman leaps to a second conclusion, and again a correct one, although the mere suggestion fills her with surprise and even incredulity. If Jesus means other water than this in Jacob's well, better water than this, why, that is really saying that he is greater than Jacob who dug this well and left it for his descendants, yea, was himself satisfied with the water of this well.

The surprise and the incredulity come out in the interrogative particle μή, which in the woman's thought involves a negative answer, "Certainly thou canst not mean to say that thou art greater than Jacob?" Hence also she dwells on what Jacob did, calling him "our father" who gave us the well and who with his sons and his cattle never sought other, better water (ἔπιεν, the aorist to express the undeniable fact).

Through Joseph the Samaritans claimed descent from Jacob. Hence John's note in v. 5 on the tomb of Joseph near by and the woman's proud "our father Jacob." The point has been disputed, but compare II Kings 17:24 with II Chron. 34:6 and 9 — in Josiah's time not a few Israelites remained in devastated Samaria, so that the Samaritans became a mixed race, Israelitish and heathen elements being mingled, so that they were able in a way at least to point to Jacob as "our father." Josephus *Ant.* 11, 8, 7, reports that the Jewish element was increased by renegade Jews, who, on violating the laws and traditions of their own land, fled to Samaria. As the woman's eyes rested on the tired, thirsty, dusty traveller, it seemed incredible to her that he should be greater than the ancient patriarch.

The reasoning of this woman is typical and therefore very interesting. Her conclusions are altogether sound and yet they remain false. The good feature about them is that she, like Nicodemus, puts them into an interrogative form, thus holding her mind open and even asking for more instruction. This effect is produced entirely by Jesus. Both the woman's conclusions and her questioning are her reactions to Jesus' own words. Both also are intended by Jesus. The woman did not laugh at Jesus and call his words absurd, did not turn away and walk off with her waterpot. She thought, considered, drew conclusions, asked in surprise. Step by step Jesus enlightened her. Her conclusions were still false, because she still knew too little. Her spiritual darkness rapidly disappeared as Jesus spoke.

13) **Jesus answered and said to her** (compare on 1:48), **Everyone that drinks of this water shall thirst again; but whoever shall drink of the water that I myself shall give him shall in no way thirst forever; on the contrary, the water that I myself shall give him, shall become in him a spring of water welling up unto life eternal.** This reply of Jesus answers both questions in the mind of the woman and answers them squarely, adequately, first regarding *the kind of water* he has in mind, secondly regarding *the person* he is. This water is spiritual not material; heavenly not earthly; permanent not transient. And thus it helps to reveal who this ἐγώ, this great Giver of such water, really is.

The proposition is self-evident, "Everyone that drinks of this water shall thirst again." No material water exists that allays thirst forever. While Jesus' word refers only to the material water in Jacob's well, the inference lies close at hand that nothing material is able to quench the thirst of the soul permanently, and this is implied by the contrast which deals with the spiritual water that Jesus gives. Some, indeed, succeed in stilling their thirst but they do it in a lamentable way. In the parable of the Prodigal a citizen of that far country had gathered himself a herd of swine — significant wealth! — and was satisfied. In the parable of the Rich Fool a man was satisfied with his grain fields. These men satisfied their thirst by stifling it. Germany's greatest poet Goethe, a favorite of fortune, confesses that he was seldom happy. Augustine is right, the soul, created for God, will not rest until it rests in God.

14) The corresponding opposite is just as true and self-evident, "But whosoever shall drink of the

water that I myself shall give him shall in no way thirst forever." Jesus accepts the challenge of every man, no matter who he may be and what he may have to offer. And the test shall be only this: the true and permanent quenching of the thirst of the heart. But not in theory, not in argument; on the contrary, in actuality, in actual experience, "whosoever shall drink" — actually "shall drink," "shall in no way thirst forever" — actually never thirst. The indefinite relative clause: ὃς ἂν πίῃ is like a condition of expectancy and is thus followed (regularly) by the future indicative: οὐ μὴ διψήσει. The implication is that some will so drink and will then never thirst again. The aorist subjunctive πίῃ expresses one act of drinking, which is never repeated. Note οὐ μὴ as the strongest negation with the future indicative (also with the subjunctive).

Jesus retains the figure throughout. As the water is *life,* so the drinking is *faith,* i. e., its inception. The interpretation that the drinking is the *continued* use of the Word and the Sacraments goes beyond the words of Jesus when he says that *one act* of drinking removes the thirst forever. To bring in prayer and intercourse with God's children is irrelevant. No prayer of ours and no association with Christians have life in them to bestow on us. Christ alone has and bestows that life. The thought must here be ruled out, that, once we have life, we must feed, nourish, replenish it by Word and Sacrament. While this is true, Jesus here speaks only of the bestowal of life, which, the moment we obtain it, becomes a permanent possession. He does bring the dead to life day after day. Once made alive, we live on. Once born anew (Nicodemus), we need not be born again. Twice, for emphasis, Jesus says, "which I myself shall give him." The pronoun ἐγώ is strongly emphatic, which we attempt to convey by translating, "I my-

self." He, and he alone, gives this wonderful water.
In the first clause the relative οὗ is attracted from the
accusative to the case of its antecedent ὕδατος. The
use of ἐκ is partitive, R. 599, with a verb that requires
the partitive idea, R. 519: drink "of," i. e., "some of"
the water.

The wonder of this water's quenching thirst εἰς
τὸν αἰῶνα, "for the eon," the Greek idiom "forever," is
explained in a simple fashion, but the wonder is thereby only increased, "on the contrary, the water that I
myself shall give him, shall become in him a spring
of water," etc. This repetition, "that I myself shall
give him," involuntarily raises the question, "And
who art thou to give such water?" It is *the* question Jesus wants to raise, *the* question that must be
rightly answered, or we shall after all thirst forever. Whoever heard of a gift of a drink which, on
being drunk, forms a living spring within the person, so that he never needs to drink again! It is
wholly obvious that Jesus is not speaking of physical
but of spiritual realities. All the terms he has used
are lucid: "living," "gift of God," "water that I
shall give," "drink," "never thirst." Even natural
life, once started, lives on; more so spiritual life, which
is to have no termination whatever. The fact that it
may be lost by unbelief is not mentioned here, where
the first fundamentals alone are in place.

Jesus uses πηγή, "a spring"; φρέαρ, a shaft or cistern
that merely holds water and may also be empty and
without water, would be the wrong word, see v. 12.
Of this "spring" Jesus says, "a spring of water welling up unto life eternal." We must leave the words
in their natural order and combination and not make
"unto life eternal" a modifier of "shall become" or
even of "spring" or of "water"; it modifies "welling
up," ἁλλομένου, a middle participle, whose voice
puzzles R. 812 but it surely means "bubbling up

of itself." But "unto life eternal" does not refer
to time — continuing that long or that far. Nor
should we bring in the idea of a little stream, which
starts from the spring, flows on, and finally empties
into life eternal. Jesus uses no such figurative ex-
pansion when he says "welling up of itself unto life
eternal." This wonderful spring here differs from
the figure employed in 7:37, etc. Here it denotes
life, in the other connection the drink denotes the
Holy Spirit. The spring or life remains within the
person; the gift of the Spirit does more, it also flows
out from the person. Thus "welling up of itself unto
life eternal" = keeping the person spiritually alive
for the eternal life of heaven. Thus also in the final
concept "life eternal" all that Jesus says about this
"living" water is fully clarified.

15) **The woman says to him, Sir, give me this
water, that I may not thirst nor come all the way
hither to draw.** John writes πρὸς αὐτόν, whereas after
the verbs of saying he has had only the dative because
of the reciprocal idea in πρός. The woman is responding to what she felt was an offer and invitation on
Jesus' part, she is reciprocating by accepting. She
thus shows that she understands Jesus far better than
those commentators, who regard the future tense δώσω
in the two relative clauses in v. 14 as not to be fulfilled until Jesus gets ready to baptize with the Spirit.
This woman rightly understands that Jesus means "I
will give" with reference to a giving at any time
where he finds acceptance. As far as the Spirit is
concerned, Jesus has not mentioned him in the conversation with this woman as he did in that with
Nicodemus. Yet no sinner receives life, no sinner
obtains faith except through the Spirit. The Spirit
was bestowed through Jesus now. This woman and
many in her village came to faith and confessed their

Savior, v. 42, and no one can do either except by the Holy Spirit, I Cor. 12:3.

The entire conversation on Jesus' part is misunderstood when it is not observed that up to this point Jesus is using the gospel and that from now on he employs the law. This means that Jesus knew that the woman could not yet believe and he did not expect her to believe so soon. The law must first crush the heart in contrition, then faith can enter in, and not till then. So both law and gospel must be preached, and Jesus preaches both; the two appear here most plainly marked. Either may be offered first, or both may be intertwined, though each always remains distinct, likewise the proper effects of each. Here Jesus uses the gospel first. It is a mistake to imagine that in doing this he failed and then tried something else. Not one word of the gospel was lost upon this woman; its effect presently comes with a rush when the law begins to take hold upon her heart and to show her her sins and her tremendous need of the gospel.

The misconceptions indicated prevent a right understanding also of the woman's replies to Jesus, both up to this point and in the remainder of the conversation. The comment is wrong that Jesus has been offering her "theoretical considerations," which the woman "evaded by trifling replies." Jesus gave her pure gospel, to which the woman replied with surprise, indeed, but respectfully, seriously, with real effort to understand. That, too, was all that Jesus wanted and expected. She was not yet competent to grasp and to appropriate. When the woman now actually asks Jesus for "this water," this request of hers is the response to Jesus' offer. When after all she still clings to the thought of some wonderful natural water, which stops natural thirst permanently

and obviates coming all the way (διέρχωμαι) from her
home to this well for a supply, she only shows what is
inevitable in all who are strangers to the life of God,
namely her inability to rise from the natural to the
spiritual. Jesus does not rebuke her. Nicodemus he
had to rebuke (3:10) when he began to cling to unbelief; this woman with her response of readiness is in
advance of the learned "teacher of Israel."

16) In the case of this woman Jesus has gone as
far as he could with the gospel. He has laid the foundation and has laid it well. He now suddenly turns to
the law. **Jesus says to her, Go call thy husband
and come hither.** The imperative ὕπαγε is used with
a second imperative without adding καί, much as we
say: "go call," etc. This thrust of Jesus' is direct and
goes home. Jesus bids this woman to do what he
knows she cannot do. Such biddings are like the Ten
Commandments; like the command to the lawyer,
"This do and thou shalt live!" Luke 10:28; and like
that to the rich young ruler, "Sell all!" Luke 18:22.
Biddings and commands like these are intended to reveal to the person concerned this very inability and the
sin and guilt connected therewith. The divine law
demands perfect love and by that very demand shows
us, who lack this love, that we are full of sin. The
lawyer, ordered to do the commands he recites, by
that order is to discover that he cannot do them
and must seek a different way to heaven. The rich
young ruler, bidden to sell all and to give it away,
finds that here lay his guilt in an outwardly moral
life — he loved his possessions with an unholy love.
This woman, who cannot go and call and bring her
husband to Jesus, by that very fact is to see just what
kind of a woman she is, what a wretched, sordid, immoral life she had led.

Yet some have thought that Jesus actually regarded
this woman as one that was properly married and

that he desired the presence of her husband. The fact that in the next breath Jesus reveals the woman's whole past life is explained by supposing that suddenly between v. 16 and v. 17 God revealed these facts to Jesus. Thus in v. 16 Jesus speaks in ignorance and in v. 17, 18 with knowledge. But 1:42 and 48, etc., plus 2: 24, 25, declare that Jesus himself saw, himself knew what was in men. He is not made dependent on special revelations for this knowledge as were the prophets. To say that, unless Jesus thought the woman had a husband and could call him, he would be uttering "fiction" in his command; and that when the woman was thus bidden to go, she would have taken this chance to disappear and never to return, is to misjudge both the woman and Jesus. The fear that precipitates this judgment is the fact that certain critics charge that John's Gospel makes Jesus walk like a God on earth equipped with omniscience. But to get rid of one exaggeration we must not employ another. The Gospels and the entire Bible make Jesus God incarnate, possessing also in his human nature the divine attributes but using them only at proper times and in properly executing his office. What is Matt. 25, etc., but omniscience? yet in his human nature the Son of man does not know the time of the end, Matt. 24:36; Acts 1:7. The ancient allegorizing of the five husbands of this woman and of the man she now lived with, and the attempt to revive these fancies, needs no refutation.

17) **The woman answered and said unto him,** the doubling of the verbs marking the great importance of her reply, **I have no husband.** Jesus' bidding her to call her husband is really a call to confess her sins, to confess them voluntarily. For in saying "go call" Jesus, indeed, gives her the opportunity to pretend that she has a husband and that she now goes to call him, thus avoiding confession, and

thus also getting away from Jesus altogether. When
the bidding of Jesus to this woman is contemplated
from this viewpoint, the perfect mastery of it comes
to view. The woman makes no move to go — she is
not trying to get away. She does not lie by pretending that she has a husband, since Jesus mentions "husband." She stands there before this strange Jew and
confesses her shame, "I have no husband." Those few
words cost the woman something. Cold comment says
that she is half lying and does not understand what
it takes for a woman to reveal, even partly, her disgrace. Why fault the woman for confessing only so
much? Her quick mind surely tells her that Jesus
may probe farther, but this does not seal her lips, does
not make her evade, does not rouse her temper, does
not make her say, "What business are my private matters to thee?" No, she confesses. The fact that she
does this before this stranger is the effect of what he
has been saying to her. The gospel aids the law, as
the gospel is also aided by the law. It helps the sinner
by making him ready to confess. To Jesus, whose
lips are filled with the gospel, the sinner finds he can
confess.

**Jesus says to her: Well didst thou say, A hus-
band I have not. For five husbands thou didst have
and whom thou now hast is not thy husband. This,
a true thing, thou hast said.** Jesus accepts, Jesus
commends, Jesus completes her confession. We now
see why by doubling the verbs of saying when giving
the woman's reply John marks it as being of great
importance. The commendation lies in καλῶς and in
ὀληθές. "A husband" I have not, places the object forward with emphasis, bringing out the full contrast
that the man whom she now has is not her husband;
on ἔχειν τινά to express illegal relations compare I Cor.
5:1. Instead of wringing the rest of the confession
from the woman, Jesus makes it for her. It is a

touch of his gentleness with the sinner. So the father of the prodigal stops him in the middle of his confession — the same gentleness in a different way. How the woman came to have that many husbands we are not told and need not be told. These five were at least legal husbands, for only so can the words be understood. The lax divorce laws may help to explain, Matt. 5:31; 19:7; compare Deut. 24:1 and 3, which the Jews greatly extended, and very likely the Samaritans also. Those five were bad enough, but now she is living with a man who is not even in loose legality her husband.

It is wrong to imagine the woman as brazen and shameless in her confession. The sin had touched her conscience more than once, but she had hushed the disturbing inner voice. Now Jesus was making it speak again. The notion that Jesus at this moment received a revelation from God regarding this woman's life has already been answered. To read irony into Jesus' words when he says, "Well didst thou say," and, "This, as a true thing, hast thou said," makes Jesus receive a poor sinner's confession with irony — a thing impossible for Jesus. We must not overlook the fact that by her silence or non-denial the woman acquiesces in the confession that Jesus makes for her. Plainly Jesus is succeeding and succeeding rapidly.

19) **The woman says to him, I see thou art a prophet.** By that statement she admits that Jesus has spoken the truth about her life. Thus she really completes her confession. Nor does she qualify, excuse, or minimize. But involuntarily she also makes a confession regarding Jesus. She admits that only in a supernatural way could he know her past life; compare v. 29. The fact that she calls him only "a prophet" is natural at this stage. It never, however, entered her head that in some ordinary way this

strange Jew had discovered the things he said. This was done by men of a later age, who eliminate from this Gospel every divine trait in Jesus.

What now follows has again been misunderstood. In fact, the previous wrong conceptions culminate at this point and create confusion. Thus it is said that a gap occurs at this point, and that John skipped what lies between. Again, that the woman with quick wit here turns the conversation away from these delicate and painful personal matters to a question that Jews and Samaritans argued; that she makes a tricky dialectical evasion. But then Jesus would never have answered as he did, carefully and to the point, the very question the woman raises. He would have rebuked her and have driven in more deeply the hook of the law she would thus be evading. **Our fathers worshipped in this mountain; and you say that in Jerusalem is the place where they must worship.** The woman really asks Jesus, who are right, her ancestors or the Jews (emphatic ὑμεῖς). This she does in connection with her unqualified admission of sin and guilt. The matter is of the gravest personal concern to her for this reason and for this alone. She admits that she needs cleansing. Where is she to obtain it? Where her people say, "in this mountain," Gerizim, looming up not far from the well; or where the Jews say, in the Temple at Jerusalem? Will not Jesus send her to the latter place, to bring her sin offering and to obtain the absolution? Zerubbabel had refused the Samaritans permission to join in building the Temple at Jerusalem, and Nehemiah had driven out a son of Joiada who had married a daughter of Sanballat (a Moabite of Horonaim and a constant opponent of Nehemiah), Neh. 13:28. This man with others instituted the worship on Gerizim in Samaria, built a temple there, and established the high priesthood. This temple was destroyed 129 B. C. and was

not rebuilt, yet the worship continued and still does at
the Passover when seven lambs are offered for the congregation, at Pentecost or the Feast of Weeks, and at
the Feast of Tabernacles.

21) Jesus answers at length. **Believe me,
woman, that the hour is coming when neither in this
mountain nor in Jerusalem you shall worship the
Father.** She had just called Jesus a prophet. "Believe me, woman," links into that confession, for a
prophet's words surely require belief. This call to
believe him also ushers in another astounding statement, that at first might seem incredible, namely that
a time (ὥρα in the wider sense) is not far away when
the Samaritans shall worship neither in Gerizim nor
in Jerusalem. This prophecy, in the sense of foretelling the future, is thus another evidence of divine
omniscience used for Jesus' saving purpose. The fact
that this Jewish prophet should declare that the
Temple worship in Jerusalem was to be temporary,
was even soon to cease, must have astonished this
Samaritan woman greatly; that he should say as much
regarding Gerizim naturally surprised her less. "You
shall worship" must refer to the Samaritans and
should not be generalized to refer to anybody or to
men in general. The point in Jesus' words is that the
specific *place* of the worship is a secondary question,
whereas the true *worship* itself is the essential. Only
for the time being the place still has importance,
then it will disappear. And it did. Yet strangely
enough, Gerizim is still sacred to the handful of
Samaritans in existence today, who still worship
there; while all these centuries the site of the Temple
in Jerusalem has been in pagan and in Mohammedan
possession, and the Jews have been completely debarred from worshipping there. The Mohammedan
"Dome of the Rock" has long occupied the site of the
old Jewish Temple. Again, the Samaritans soon

dwindled to a tiny number, the Jews multiplied and spread over the world. Such are the ways of God.

A sweet gospel touch lies in the expression, "you shall worship the Father." It opens the door also to the Samaritans so that they may become the children of this Father by faith in the Son. The word "Father" here means so much more, also to this woman, than the word "God" could mean. Jesus keeps the verb προσκυνεῖν, literally "to touch with kisses," but used regarding the oriental prostration in worship and adoration of God.

22) Yet while both Gerizim and Jerusalem shall pass away as places for worship, they are not on an equal basis. **You are worshipping what you do not know, we are worshipping what we do know; because the salvation is from the Jews;** ἐκ to indicate origin or derivation. The personal pronouns "you" and "we" intensify the contrast that lies in "do not know" and "do know." With προσκυνεῖν we may have the dative of the personal object of the worship or the accusative of the impersonal as in the present instance. Jesus says, *"what* you do not know," and, *"what* we do know," for no revelation was given to Gerizim, all revelation was limited to the Jews and to Jerusalem. The facts always count, the facts alone, and not what men think or think they know. R. 713 makes the neuter ὅ refer to God, a grammatical impossibility.

And this difference between Gerizim and Jerusalem is not a mere theological dispute, it is a vital soul issue; for God's revelation contains ἡ σωτηρία, compare on the term 3:17. Though in the Greek abstract nouns may have the article as a matter of course, here "the salvation" denotes the specific and only salvation contemplated in God's promises and to be realized in his incarnate Son. This salvation is in no way promised to the Samaritans, so that it

would emanate from their midst, but to the Jews alone.
The Messiah could not be a Samaritan, he had to be
a Jew. While the Pentateuch might have made the
Samaritans "know" this, they, by rejecting all the
other books of the Old Testament containing so much
more of the Messianic revelation and by thus running
into a blind opposition to the Jews, lost this most
precious knowledge. What Jesus thus tells this woman
answers the question about the place, and in the most
effective way, namely by explaining and by holding
up to view what is essential.

23) Yet, significantly, Jesus neither says nor implies, "Thou must go to Jerusalem." He does not
even say, "The salvation is of Jerusalem." Yet we
should misread his words if we should take him to
mean, "Gerizim and Jerusalem make no difference —
just so you worship God aright." For since "the salvation is of the Jews" not "of the Samaritans," Gerizim
is plainly ruled out. The fact that the alternative,
however, for this woman is not "Jerusalem" is now
made plain by further elucidation. **Yea, the hour
is coming and now is, when the genuine worshippers shall worship the Father in spirit and
truth; for the Father also seeks such as worship him.**
Here ἀλλά is not contradictory ("but") ; it is copulative
and climacteric ("yea"), R. 1186. It reaches across
the parenthetic thought in v. 22 to the chief thought
in v. 21. This appears also in the repetition of "the
hour is coming." Both times this present tense "is
coming" states that the approach is still in progress
and not yet complete. And yet Jesus can add, "and
now is," without contradicting himself. His redemptive work is not done but is only definitely undertaken
("the hour is coming") ; but he himself is here, the
Redeemer and Savior ("and now is"). Thus all that
the Temple and the ceremonial cultus at Jerusalem
had served so long was passing away, was in a sense

already gone — would forever be done with on Easter
morning. We must note that Jesus treated the Temple
and its cultus accordingly. He brings no sacrifices
like an ordinary Jew, we do not hear that he joins
in the prayer ritual. He uses the Temple, the festivals,
the worshippers congregating there, for his own high
purpose. As the Son he uses "my Father's house"
for the last use it should serve. The rent veil in the
Temple was "the sign" that both the Father and the
Son were done with the Temple.

Thus Jesus does not compel this woman to go to
Jerusalem. Instead he explains to her the true worship which abides when the Jewish ritualism presently
disappears altogether because it is no longer needed.
The "genuine" worshippers,ιω ἀληθινοί, are those who
alone really deserve the name in distinction from all
who observe only the Jewish ritual practices. They
worship "the Father" as his genuine children in a
way that corresponds to their character. Here again
Jesus uses the significant designation "the Father,"
which connotes, first of all, that Jesus is this Father's
Son, sent to work out the promised salvation, and,
secondly, connotes that all genuine worshippers are
the children of this Father by faith in his Son, by
accepting the salvation wrought and brought by this
Son.

They shall worship the Father "in spirit and
truth." One preposition joins the two nouns and thus
makes of the two one idea. But not in the superficial
sense that genuine worshippers shall worship in a
genuine way; for they would not be such if they
used a different way. Jesus here describes what the
genuine way is. It centers in the worshipper's own
"spirit" and spirit nature (Rom. 1:9), moved, of
course, by God's Spirit (Rom. 8:14, 16, 26). We
should say, all true worship is one of the soul. But
this is not enough, for many put their very souls into

their worship and yet are only false, self-deceived worshippers. Hence the addition: in spirit "and truth." The fact that this means more than "truly," i. e., sincerely, with subjective truth, should be obvious at a glance. The essential subjective feature of genuine worship is fully covered by "in spirit." To this the objective counterpart must be added, which evidently is ἀλήθεια, "truth," in the sense of reality. So many labor over this term. They fear that if "truth" is here regarded as God's revealed truth, the reality embodied in the Word, the single phrase would become two: "in spirit" and "in truth"; i. e., that then the preposition ought to be repeated. So "truth" is made to mean: "in genuine contact with God"; or "so that the worship tallies with its object, corresponds with the essence and the attributes of God, and does not contradict them." Fortunately, Jesus is speaking to a plain woman, and "truth" to her means truth. Moreover, if a genuine contact is to be made with the Father, if the genuine object of the worship is to be reached, does this not mean that these two: the worshipper's own "spirit" and God's own revealed "truth" joined together (καί) must form the sphere (ἐν) in which this worship takes place? All that forsakes this sphere is spurious worship. Omit the spirit, and though you have the truth, the worship becomes formalism, mere ritual observance. Omit the truth, and though the whole soul is thrown into the worship, it becomes an abomination. Thus "spirit and truth" form a unit, two halves that belong together in every act of worship.

This was the case in the Old Testament Judaism, where by God's own institution ceremonies had to be observed. From Moses onward prophets and psalmists insisted, though the people often failed to heed, that the worship must be "in spirit and truth." Jesus does not here condemn this old worship on account

of its connection with ceremonies. What he does is
to foretell that these ceremonies are on the verge of
ceasing altogether. Likewise our present worship.
We assemble in churches, and the service follows a
certain outward order, now a hymn, now a prayer,
now the sermon, etc., though we ourselves now
arrange all this. This Jesus does not here condemn.
What he does is to state that not in any outward
forms but "in spirit and truth" the real worship is
rendered. For the woman this means that she need
not wait, need not go to the Temple, need not offer
a sacrifice, but can right here and now perform
the very highest act of worship, namely accept the
Father's pardon for her sins and return to him her
spirit's gratitude.

To assure the woman fully Jesus adds, "for the
Father also seeks such as worship him." "For" explains that "of such a kind" are the worshippers that
God desires. He seeks them, not as though they have
already become such by efforts of their own, but as
longing to make them such by his Word and his
Spirit. He was now doing this with this sinful woman.
The seeking is the outcome of his love. The position of καί connects it with the subject: "the Father
also," not with the verb: "also seeks." The participle is made attributive by the article: "such
as worship," i. e., such worshippers; and προσκυνεῖν
here has first a dative then an accusative personal
object.

24) Why God seeks only such worshippers is
answered by pointing to his nature: **For God is
spirit; and they that worship him must worship in
spirit and truth.** The predicate "spirit" is placed
forward for emphasis. While one might translate
"A spirit is God," this makes the predicate sound too
much like a classification of God who is "spirit" from
all eternity and uncreated, while all other, namely

created spirits, have a beginning. "Spirit" does not here classify; it only states God's nature. Jesus makes no new revelation concerning God; he only recalls to the woman what she has long known regarding God. And he does this only to show her what accordingly all genuine worship of God must be, namely worship "in spirit and truth." This deduction is not new. For δεῖ, "must," is not meant regarding a new precept, a new commandment, or worship. This "must" expresses far more, namely a necessity that is due to God's own nature and that has always held and always will hold true.

While the fact that God is spirit is not stated in so many words in the Old Testament, all that the Old Testament reveals regarding God is to this effect. Neither Jew nor Samaritan would controvert the statement for one moment. The prohibitions to make images of God, the comparisons of God with idols (for instance Isa. 40:13-26), Solomon's reminder that he whom "the heaven and heaven of heavens cannot contain" does not dwell in a house, and many other statements show how fully God's nature was understood. Even the naive anthropomorphic and anthropopathic utterances are made and can be made with such naivete only on the absolute certainty of God's infinite spirit nature. To urge these human expressions against this certainty is to hurl a pebble at a mountain, thinking thereby to knock it over. Accordingly, also the Old Testament is full of genuine worship, of its descriptions, and of injunctions so to worship and so alone. Consider the Psalms, the prayers, Daniel for instance, the many warnings that sacrifices, gifts, lip-prayers, observing festival days, etc., without a broken, contrite, believing heart are in vain. Thus the genuine worship was known well enough. The new feature which Jesus presents is that from now on this worship is enough, i. e., that the ceremonies, restrictions of time and of place, are even now to fall away. In this sense the worship will, indeed, be new.

25) The impression Jesus makes upon the woman is that she automatically thinks of the Messiah. We are reminded of Nathanael in 1:49, save that this woman does not go that far. Yet Messiah-ward her thoughts turn like the flower to the sun. **The woman says to him, I know that Messiah is coming (who is called Christ); when that one shall come, he will announce to us all things.** It is no doubt wrong to think that by this response the woman seeks to end the conversation. Then Jesus would not have replied as he did. What ideas the Samaritans held concerning the Messiah has been investigated at great pains but with small results. Their name for him was Taheb, probably meaning "the Restorer." He was to be both a great prophet and a wonderful king, although the strong political feature of the Jews seems to be absent from the Samaritan conception. In many respects the Samaritan ideas of the Messiah coincide with those of the Jews. The woman uses the Jewish name "Messiah" not the Samaritan "Taheb." Was it because she was speaking to a Jew? That the Samaritans used also the Jewish title has not yet been established. We know why John preserves the title the woman actually used, himself in a parenthesis translating it for his Gentile readers, as in 1:41: It is because Jesus testifies to this woman that he is the Messiah.

The thought that perhaps Jesus is the Messiah has not struck the woman, although she is not far from it. Perhaps she expected Jesus to state how all that he had said about God, salvation, and true worship was related to the hope of the Messiah. When she says that Messiah (without the article, as if it were a proper name) "shall announce to us all things," she voices one of the great expectations concerning the Messiah but she does more; for this thought comes to her because of the great things she has just heard from Jesus' lips. We see how Jesus' person and his words had affected this very ordinary woman who was not even a Jewess. The learned, self-righteous, exceedingly prominent Pharisee Nicodemus in the capital and this unlearned, sin-laden, ordinary unnamed woman in the country district of despised Samaria are companions. Opposites in all respects, yet both are drawn mightily by Jesus. The woman gained the goal far more quickly than did the man.

26) **Jesus says to her, I am he, (I) who is speaking to thee.** As Jesus helped the woman with her confession of sin in v. 17, 18, so he now helps her with her confession of faith (compare v. 29). To this obscure woman Jesus reveals point-blank what he had revealed to no one else. One surprise has followed another for this woman, but the climax is now reached. Nor has Jesus misjudged the woman. She does not, indeed, sink down in worship at his feet but she is ready to believe. Ἐγώ εἰμι is the good Greek idiom for, "I am he," the English requiring that the place of the predicate be filled. The substantivized participle ὁ λαλῶν σοι, "the man speaking to thee," is in apposition to ἐγώ, R. 778 and is not the equivalent of a relative clause, "I that speak unto thee" (our versions). Jesus adds the apposition because of what the woman has just said that the Messiah would do, namely announce all things. This, Jesus intimates to the woman, is just what he is doing for her right now — announcing to her the very things she needs. The person and the words are vitally joined together. They always are. And as we treat the one, so we treat the other.

Here then John has given us another great attestation of Jesus.

27) The record might close at this point just as that of Nicodemus does at 3:21; but Jesus both attests himself still further on this occasion (27-38) and also receives most notable attestation from the Samaritans (39-42). So the account continues. **And upon this came his disciples. And they were marvelling that he was speaking with a woman; yet no one said, What seekest thou? or, Why speakest thou with her?** The disciples returned from buying food (v. 8) and were not a little astonished to see their Master engaged in talking (ἐλάλει, durative, imperfect) with (μετά, with the idea of association) a woman. Jewish custom forbade that a rabbi should speak in public with a woman and most especially on matters of the law. But the reverence of the disciples for Jesus is so great that they only keep wondering (ἐθαύμαζον also imperfect and thus durative), and no one brings that wonder to an end by actually inquiring. On μέντοι see R. 1188. The first question that John thinks of is specific, τί ζητεῖς; namely, "What desirest thou of her?" which also was close to the truth, for Jesus had asked the woman for a drink and thus had started the conversation. Or, John suggests, the disciples might have asked in general why he was speaking with the woman. This, too, would have hit the truth, for it would have brought to light Jesus' saving motive.

28) **Accordingly the woman left her waterpot and went away into the city and says to the people, Come, see a man who told me all things that I (ever) did. Can it be that this is the Christ?** The connective οὖν indicates that the woman quickly left at the approach of the disciples. She would have been bold, indeed, to face all these additional strangers. And yet God in his providence had so timed her arrival at the well that her conversation with Jesus could reach the supreme point before the arrival of the

disciples. Quick-witted as she showed herself in her
answers to Jesus, she now strangely forgets to take her
filled waterpot along and in spite of her great reverence for Jesus forgets too all about his original request
for a drink. These are exquisite psychological touches
in John's narrative, indicating how deeply the words
of Jesus had gripped her heart, making her forget all
else for the moment.

This historical present λέγει beside the two matter-
of-fact aorists lends a vivid touch to the narrative.
She hurries back and without hesitation stops and
addresses the people (τοῖς ἀνθρώποις), men and women
whom she meets and who begin to congregate about
her. The interjectional adverb δεῦτε, always with the
plural, "hither," in the sense of "come hither," is
sometimes joined to an imperative as here, or to a
subjunctive, or is used independently. The woman
is wise — these people are to come and to see for
themselves, which recalls 1:39 and 46. She characterizes Jesus as "a man who told me all things that I
(ever) did" with supernatural insight into her past
life. "All things" is not an exaggeration when we
note that these things cover her entire past life since
her first marriage. With the aorist εἶπε she states the
fact. No doubt, she had to repeat just what Jesus
"did tell" her in his exact words. And the people at
once saw that this was astounding because coming
from a Jewish stranger; the facts about the woman
these people, her neighbors, knew only too well.

As wise as the woman is in calling on the people
to come and to see for themselves, so wise, too, is she
in indicating what they will find. She puts this into
a question but with μήτι not with οὐ. The English has
no such delicate distinctions, hence we must circum-
scribe, which is always bunglesome, "Can this perhaps be?" "Οὐ would have challenged the opposition
of the neighbors by taking sides on the question

whether Jesus was the Messiah. The woman does not mean to imply flatly, that Jesus is not the Messiah by using μήτι, but she raises the question and throws a cloud of uncertainty and curiosity over it with a woman's keen instinct. In a word, μή is just the negative to use when one does not wish to be too positive. Μή leaves the question open for further remark or entreaty. Οὐ closes the door abruptly." R. 1167. More briefly: οὐ heading a question = I think so, and you, too, must say so; μή = I do not think so, and you will agree; and then modified: I can hardly think so — yet it might be (so here μήτι).

30) The wrought-up condition of the woman and her astounding report had their effect. **They went out of the city and were coming to him.** The imperfect ἤρχοντο pictures them on the way and holds the outcome in abeyance. This is due to the fact that something transpires while they are on their way and must be told before their arrival is stated in v. 40, which then closes the open "were coming."

31) So we learn: **In the meanwhile the disciples were requesting him, saying, Rabbi, eat!** Strange, indeed — Jesus asks for a drink and is refused (7-9); now he is asked to eat and he himself refuses. The verb ἠρώτων denotes a most respectful request and is thus the proper word; and its imperfect tense implies repeated urging on the part of the disciples and also that Jesus did not comply. The aorist φάγε, "eat," is not "be eating," which would require the present but, "eat and finish." On "Rabbi" see 1:38. The request is full of respect and without familiarity. The disciples never addressed Jesus as "Brother," though Jesus on notable occasions called them "my brethren," Matt. 28:10; John 20:17; see also Rom. 8:29; Heb. 2:11.

32) **But Jesus said to them, I have meat to eat that you do not know.** Here we catch a remark-

able glimpse of how Jesus put his very soul into his work. Instead of doing it mechanically, in a business-like sort of way, with professional ease, he did it with all his heart. It so occupied him that all else for the time being was excluded. The exaltation of it prevented him from at once descending to lesser and lower things. It filled him with such joy and satisfaction that it acted like food and drink to his body, weariness, thirst, and hunger being forgotten. Not having been present when Jesus saved the woman's soul, the disciples could not know the βρῶσις Jesus had enjoyed.

33) **The disciples, therefore, were saying to each other, Surely, no one brought him (aught) to eat?** The imperfect ἔλεγον indicates that the disciples said this repeatedly; they could think of no other solution. The aorists ἤνεγκεν and φαγεῖν speak of actual bringing and eating. The μή in μήτις (compare μήτι in v. 29) indicates that for the disciples the only answer must be "no." Some have chided the disciples for their lack of spirituality and deeper understanding. They would be more severe than Jesus himself who did no chiding, who admitted that the disciples did not know what food he had had, who quietly went on to explain. The disciples had left Jesus thirsty and hungry and now found him refreshed and declining to eat. Someone had been there in their absence and had just left. How could they help but ask whether this person had perhaps brought Jesus something to eat? Yet they do not ask him, they question quietly among themselves. They are respectfully reticent as in v. 28 not bold to pry and to quiz.

34) **Jesus says to them, My food is that I do the will of him that did send me and that I finish his work.** Both βρῶσις in v. 32 and βρῶμα here are derivations from βιβρώσκω, the former denoting more the act of eating combined with the food, like the

German *das Essen*, the latter the food only, *Speise*.
The plural τροφάς in v. 8 = different kinds of food.
The disciples had bought and brought different eat-
ables, but one βρῶμα was all that Jesus' heart desired.
Jesus himself explains the figure, "that I do the
will of him that did send me and that I finish his
work." The double ἵνα clause is subfinal (R. 992, etc.),
exactly like a ὅτι clause, here used as a predicate
nominative: "my meat is that," etc. John uses this
ἵνα extensively. Here, for the first time, Jesus speaks
of his great Sender whom he will mention again and
again, always using the substantivized aorist participle, which names this Sender according to the one
past act of sending, ὁ πέμψας με. As such he has
a will, θέλημα, namely regarding a specific work, even
called "his work," αὐτοῦ τὸ ἔργον, the possessive being
emphatically forward. The sending or mission of
Jesus is "to do" this will, "to finish" this work, and
the aorists state actual doing and finishing. Doubling
the statement thus makes it decidedly strong. Compare 17:4, "I have finished the work which thou gavest
me to do," where the same verb is used. Also 19:28
and 30, "Jesus, knowing that all things are now
finished," etc. . . . . he said, "It is finished,"
τετέλεσται The double clause is thus a description of
Jesus' entire Messianic work. This "will" of his great
Sender is his good and gracious will regarding the sinful world, the will of his comprehending and purposeful love, ἀγάπη; this "work" is our redemption from
sin and all that belongs to it. The will and the work
were done, finished completely, when Jesus died on
the cross.

So completely are the mind and the heart, the will
and the life of Jesus taken up with this will and this
work of his Sender that they actually are his "food."
This metaphor, however, conveys not only the thought
that Jesus is devoted to this task with his whole soul

but that doing this task, accomplishing it, is a necessity for him, something he must have, as we must have food. Not only was there no other work possible for him here, but if this work would not have been given him to do, his very being here would not have been possible, i. e., the Son would not be here incarnate in human flesh (1:14). What Jesus says lies far above the thought that human talent and genius devote themselves to some special task with signal energy. It also lies above a Christian's devotion to the work of his spiritual calling. God, indeed, gives us spiritual life and powers in order to serve him; but we and our service of God — at best imperfect — are not bound together so essentially as Jesus and his work; for we could separate ourselves from our work, leave it undone, do a contrary work, but Jesus never. Thus only in a clearly modified sense could we appropriate these words of Jesus and say that our meat, too, is to do our Father's will and his work.

35) A part of this work Jesus had just been doing, and another part of it was soon to be done by him, namely the work of a prophet (Luke 4:17-21), dispensing "living water" to famishing souls. So Jesus continues. **Say you not, Yet it is four months, and the harvest comes? Behold, I say to you, Lift up your eyes and view the fields, that they are white already for harvest.** Jesus changes the metaphor of food to one closely allied, that of the harvest. Between Jacob's well and Sychar the fields had been planted in wheat or in barley. In Palestine the harvest comes in the middle of Nisan, our April. So Jesus was at the well in our month of December. The grain had been sown in November and now covered the fields with a thrifty growth of green. Jesus does not mean that his disciples are talking about the coming harvest, saying how long it will be until harvest time. He asks

an implied question, to which he takes for granted (οὐχ expects an affirmative answer) that the disciples on their part (ὑμεῖς) will say, "Yes, about four months yet until harvest" (a τετράμηνος, sc. χρόνος). Jesus says, that is what *you* would say. But I say to *you*, the harvest is already here, the grain ready to be reaped. Note the contrast: ὑμεῖς λέγετε, "*you* are saying," and: λέγω ὑμῖν, "I am saying to *you*." The contrast is thus not between the persons: you — I; for we have no ἐγώ to balance ὑμεῖς. It is between the two statements, which is indicated by the emphatic pronouns: *you* say, ὑμεῖς — I say *to you*, ὑμῖν. One statement *you* make, the other is made *to you*. And the two statements seem contradictory: "yet four months," and "already." These temporal modifiers are in the emphatic positions, the first at the head of its statement, the second at the end. This point of contrast demands that ἤδη be drawn to what precedes and not to what follows, as the R. V. margin proposes, "Already he that reapeth," etc.

Now both statements are true, that the harvest is still four months off, and that the fields are right now white for harvest, ready to be cut. It is all clear the moment the disciples do what Jesus bids them do, "Lift up your eyes and view the fields." There on the path through the young grain the Samaritans were coming, impelled by the report from the woman. We now see why John has the picturesque imperfect ἤρχοντο in v. 30 — there they were, still coming. They were the grain Jesus saw, white for harvest, ready to be gathered into the granary of the kingdom. Thus the contrast of the two kinds of "food" (v. 31 and 33) is carried over into the two kinds of "harvest." The disciples and we with them are ever inclined to see only the material and must have our attention drawn especially ("behold!") to the spiritual. It often seems less real to us than the material, yet if anything it is

more so. At least it is infinitely more important and
vital. We go into a large city and see great buildings,
a vast amount of commerce, etc., but we often fail to
see the millions of poor sinners for whom Christ died,
the "much people in this city" who may be gathered
into Christ's kingdom. Acts 18:10. We see a man's
wealth, social position, learning, power, etc., but we
often overlook the immortal soul he has to be saved.
On the other hand, we see a poor wretch, criminal,
outcast, loathsome, but again we do not see that he,
too, is a soul bought by Christ's blood and desired
by him for Paradise (Luke 23:43). To the eyes of
Christ all this is different. Our meat may be only the
earthly, his meat is the spiritual; our view may be
only concerning grain, his is concerning souls to be
gathered into his garner.

36) From the harvest the thought of Jesus extends to the reapers and backward also to the sowers
and then turns (v. 38) to the disciples personally. See
the comprehensive grasp it thus reveals and the grip
it puts on the souls of the disciples. **He that reaps
receives wages and gathers fruit unto life eternal,
in order that he that sows and he that reaps may
rejoice together.** This is not a general proposition
applicable to both material and spiritual harvesting.
Jesus speaks only of the latter. The "and" is explicative, it explains that the wages received are the
fruit gathered unto life eternal ($\kappa\alpha\rho\pi\acute{o}s$, fruit of trees
or of fields, here the latter). The wages of the
spiritual reaper are the souls gathered for life eternal
— here not necessarily only heaven but eternal life
also as a present possession reaching unto heaven.
On "life" and on "life eternal" compare 1:4 and 3:15.
How these souls can be called "wages" appears in
what follows.

God's purpose ($\H{\iota}\nu\alpha$) in thus rewarding the reaper
is that the reaper and the sower "may rejoice to-

gether." Here it becomes plain why the gathered fruit is called wages: it is because of the χαίρειν, the rejoicing. This appears partially now already: our true reward we feel and know are the souls saved through us, the holy joy we have in their salvation. It will appear perfectly in heaven, where the vanity of all other rewards fully appears, and where the joy is perfect and supreme. But this rejoicing is intended for both the sower and the reaper. Here we see that in spite of the present tenses of the participles and the verb the statement is not general with reference to the material and the spiritual but general only with reference to the latter. Materially a man may sow a field of wheat and never live to have the joy of reaping it; his laughing heir has that joy. Spiritually this cannot happen. The harvest never escapes the sower. It belongs to him as well as to the reaper.

37) **For herein the saying is genuine, One is the sower, another is the reaper.** Here ὁ λόγος = τὸ λεγόμενον, a saying commonly used. But the sense is not that in this exceptional case (ἐν τούτῳ, "herein") this common saying fits. For Jesus is not speaking of an exception but of an invariable rule in the kingdom. Nor would this common saying fit, for its common sense is that many a man is cheated out of his reward: he does the hard sowing, and another steps in for the glad reaping. That, too, is why Jesus does not say, this saying is here ἀληθής, i. e., states a true fact. This would be ambiguous. In its ordinary sense it states a fact only in the sorry experience with earthly affairs; in its ordinary sense it states no fact at all in the blessed experience of the kingdom. Jesus says, here this saying is ἀληθινός, i. e., it has genuine reality. For God never meant that any man, even in material things, should ever be cheated out of his proper reward. So even now I Cor. 9:7-10 is the

ruling thought of men. The fact that in spite of
this so many are cheated that men even formed this
saying about one sowing and another reaping, one
losing what another then gains, is due to the perverse
effects of sin. But in the kingdom the genuine divine
order prevails fully and surely. Here, Jesus declares,
the very saying which men use to express a bad
reality in their common affairs of life becomes a
"genuine" saying for the blessed reality in the purposeful divine arrangement of the kingdom, where
the sower and the reaper are never in opposition but
always joined in unity of reward and of joy. The
ordinary sense of the saying is superseded by a divine
sense.

38) But who is meant by ὁ σπείρων and by ὁ θερίζων,
"the sower" and "the reaper"? The terms are entirely
general. Jesus, indeed, has pointed to the people on
the way from Sychar, but then he uses these general
terms, which imply that he is thinking far beyond
these Samaritans, namely of all the sowing and of all
the reaping unto life eternal. More important than
ever is, therefore, the question, of whom Jesus is thus
speaking. He himself furnishes the answer. **I myself did commission you to reap that whereon you
yourselves have not labored. Others have labored,
and you have entered into their labor.** The general
statements are here made definite and concrete. The
general statements are here also made strongly personal. But neither of these is done by a special reference to the coming Samaritans. Jesus speaks of the
entire mission and work of his disciples. Here the
tenses cause dispute, the aorist ἀπέστειλα, "I did commission," and the following perfects. The "critical"
solution that John wrote these tenses from the standpoint of his old age when he penned his Gospel without noticing the incongruity that the disciples had not
yet been commissioned when Jesus spoke here at

Jacob's well, destroys all faith in John's veracity and imputes to him an error that not even a tyro would make. Others regard these tenses as prophetic past tenses, i. e., tenses which state future acts as if they were already lying in the past. But Jesus is here not uttering prophecy. But had he already commissioned these disciples, and had they already entered into other men's labor? The answer is found in 4:2. Also in 1:42 with its implication. Jesus uses only the general term, "I did commission," not "I did commission you to the world" (17:28; Matt. 18:19), which might seem strange here. The purpose in attaching the disciples so closely to the person of Jesus must from the first have been made clear to them by Jesus, and on this fact rest the later more formal commissionings.

The disciples were sent to reap. But they never could reap if others had not labored before them, κεκοπιάκατε, grown weary with arduous exertion, i. e., in doing the preparatory sowing. This plural ἄλλοι cannot be a mere plural of category and thus refer to Jesus alone. In almost the same sentence Jesus cannot possibly use ἐγώ, the strong pronoun "I" with reference to self and in the same breath the plural ἄλλοι, "others," in the same sense. The old interpretation is correct, these "others" are Jesus and those back of him, the Baptist, the prophets, Moses, etc. But it is going too far to include the priests, teachers, moralists, etc., of pagan nations among the sowers after whom the disciples could reap. By placing his own work alongside of that of God's other agents Jesus by no means cheapens it or makes it less fundamental than it is. He is the Sower of sowers without whose sowing all other sowers would be naught, whose sowing alone made that of others what it was. Yet others also sowed, and Jesus is never averse to giving credit where it belongs, Jesus thought even of the labor (κόπος, strain, effort) preparatory to his own labor. The Baptist prepared the way for him, and in a certain manner every prophet and minister of the law does the same. Jesus is adding his own work to theirs. And the apostles are as reapers entering into all this labor of others, are simply appropriating and using it, having done nothing of it themselves.

In a supreme sense Jesus is *the* Sower, for there is no reaping except after his sowing; in fact, before Jesus came, those who reaped did so on the strength of the sowing he was to do. Jesus did some reaping. He had gathered the disciples and other believers and would gather in these Samaritans. But Jesus chiefly did the sowing; he did not leave a field that was reaped bare to his disciples but a field thoroughly seeded, fast maturing unto harvest. When we compare the 500 brethren, who gathered in Galilee to meet Jesus by appointment after his resurrection, with the 3,000, the 5,000, and the ever-increasing multitude of believers in the next few years, we see, indeed, that Jesus was the Sower, the disciples the reapers. Yet, looking at the work of those who preceded and who followed Jesus, we see that one set of men always enters into the labors of another set. The apostles reaped but they also sowed, from which their pupils again reaped, and so on down the ages. So we today have entered into other men's labors. Recount their long line, their blessed names, their great exertions! But let the reaper ever be humble and remember the Sower and the sowers and not attribute the success to himself. On the other hand, if called to sow, complain not; this hard work is just as necessary, just as blessed as the reaping. Both sower and reaper shall rejoice together. When the sheaves are brought in at last, when the reapers raise the great song of praise, the sowers who began the work that proved so successful shall lead the procession, and so even they shall enter

into other men's labor, even that of the reapers who
harvested what these sowers sowed. But among them
all we shall see not one who does not altogether enter
into the labor of Christ.

39) John might at once have gone on from v. 31
to v. 39, but he records Jesus' great testimony concerning his work as an episode. **Now from that city
many of the Samaritans believed on him for the sake
of the word of the woman, testifying, He told me all
things that I did.** The aorist ἐπίστευσαν, "they believed," may be ingressive: "they began to believe,"
but even so it states the fact. This occurred at once
after the woman had testified, and while the Samaritans walked out to meet Jesus, for it precedes ὡς οὖν
ἦλθον, "when, accordingly, they came to Jesus," in
v. 40. The decisive part of her testimony is carefully
mentioned, "He told me," etc. How slowly did Nicodemus come to faith, how rapidly these Samaritans!
Both cases have been frequently repeated.

40) **When, accordingly, the Samaritans came
to him they kept requesting him to remain with
them; and he remained there two days.** The resumptive οὖν, "accordingly," connects with v. 30, as
also the aorist ἦλθον marks the end of the imperfect
ἤρχοντο in v. 30: they "were coming" — finally they
"did arrive." The imperfect ἠρώτων indicates repeated
urging and this ended with Jesus' staying at Sychar
for two days, the accusative δύο ἡμέρας denoting the
extent of time. The citizens of Jerusalem never asked
Jesus to stay; afterward he passed through Jericho,
and not a soul asked him to stay. Matt. 10:5 in no
way conflicts with John 4 and Jesus' stay in Samaria,
since that order to the disciples was temporary, and
Jesus also stopped at Sychar only in passing and did
not go from one place in Samaria to another. Matt.
28:19, etc., and Acts 1:8 cancel the temporary order of
Matt. 10:5.

41) Those were two blessed days for Sychar. **And many more believed for the sake of his word, and they were saying to the woman, No longer because of thy speaking are we believing; for we ourselves have heard and know that this is in truth the Savior of the world.** The aorist ἐπίστευσαν is the same as in v. 39. Coming after the statement that Jesus "did remain" for two days, it summarizes the entire effect of his stay: many more "came to faith" (ingressive), or simply: "did believe" (historical). These came to faith "because of his word," spoken to them during these two days. We read of no signs that Jesus wrought at Sychar, only of this pointed reference to "his word," though it was sign enough in the woman's case (v. 17, 18).

42) The καί at the head of v. 41 and the τέ in v. 42 are not coordinate; the former merely introduces the sentence, and the latter joins something "in intimate relation with the preceding" (the regular function of τέ), R. 1179. The imperfect ἔλεγον describes how these believers told the woman repeatedly that now they believed on account of what they themselves had heard. This, of course, only substantiated and corroborated the woman's word. Two kinds of faith are here distinguished: one, based on the true testimony of others; the other, based on one's own personal experience and firsthand acquaintance with the Word. The former is that of many beginners, especially also of children taught by parents and by others. It is true faith and has saving power but stands below the other and is more easy to destroy. This kind of faith should grow into the second kind, which believes without human mediators, by direct contact with Christ and his Word, and is thus far stronger than the other type of faith. In v. 39 the woman's testimony is called her λόγος by John, for the *contents* of her speaking are meant; so also the λόγος of Jesus, v. 41. The Samari-

tans speak of the woman's λαλιά, the mere *fact* of her
speaking and not keeping silence, i. e., that she told
it and did not hide it. And they say, "we are believing," using the present tense with reference to their
continuing faith.

This faith they thus joyfully confess, πιστεύομεν,
"we believe"; and this with no empty credulity but
for solid reasons, "for we ourselves have heard and
know." This is genuine confession, from the heart,
ex animo, not merely formal, by the lips. It springs
from a corresponding faith. "We ourselves have
heard" means: we, just as the woman, directly from
Jesus in person. Jesus stands before us today in
person in his Word, and we can hear him directly
and personally in that Word as if we had sat among
the listeners at Sychar. We can do this every day;
they had him only two days. They had to hold what
he said in their memories; we can examine the inspired written Word as it is fixed for all time. And
thus these believers confess, "we know." Their faith
is explicit, not ignorance, the great mark of unbelief,
but sound, genuine knowledge, the knowledge that one
attains by himself drinking the living water, eating
the bread of life, actually being reborn of the Spirit.
Argument , science, philosophical reasoning cannot
affect such faith; the true believer simply smiles and
says, "I know." Only contact with Jesus can work
this knowledge of faith, Acts 4:13, 14. All false faith
merely imitates this knowledge of true faith, it thinks
it knows and yet does not know, 9:24, compare with
9:31-33.

The assertion is advanced that here the evangelist
puts his own words into the mouth of the Samaritans
when he makes them say that Jesus is "the Savior
of the world." This charge casts reflection on John's
veracity and the truth of all that he has written.
The entire narrative depicts people who are not

bigoted, not hypocritical, nor proud. Faith found a steady entrance into their hearts. The very fact that they were Samaritans not Jews, that Jesus lodged with them and taught them, that he did not bind them to Jerusalem and the Temple, all implies that he taught the universality of God's grace and salvation. In other words, by accepting Jesus as the Messiah these Samaritans had to accept him as "in truth the Savior of the world." If Jesus accepted the Samaritans, whom the Jews ranked as heathen, whom could he reject? The fact is that John records this entire episode for one reason only, because Jesus attested himself and his work (v. 26; 35, etc.) so clearly and received an equal attestation from these Samaritans (v. 42).

Jesus in Galilee, 4:43-54. — The fact that Jesus left Sychar after "the two days" already mentioned in v. 40 is again brought to our attention — so long only in spite of his success did he linger here. Then he proceeded without further stop to Galilee, for which 4:3 shows that he started. If Jesus had prolonged his stay and his work in Samaria he would have turned all the Jews against him; and his real work was to be done with Israel.

44) **For Jesus himself did testify that a prophet has no honor in his own country.** The statement is simple enough, it is a kind of proverbial saying which Jesus corroborates from his own experience; hence, "he did testify." People show regard to a man who comes from afar more readily than to one who is merely a native like themselves. But this remark has puzzled the commentators to such an extent that one of them calls "the history of the exegesis of this passage a sad chapter."

The first question is: Did Jesus say this in connection with his second return to Galilee, or is it a word spoken by Jesus at another time and only

brought in here by the evangelist? We know that
Jesus used this saying later on in Nazareth when
his own townspeople turned against him, Matt. 13:57;
Mark 6:4; Luke 4:24. Yet it may well be possible
that in Nazareth Jesus only repeated the saying he
first uttered on his second return to Galilee. The fact
that John uses only indirect discourse without mentioning just when, where, and to whom Jesus first
spoke this word, is sufficiently explained by the connection: John uses this word only in reporting the
return of Jesus to his homeland Galilee. He thus
supplements the synoptists by incidentally informing us that Jesus made this utterance before he
came to Nazareth and that he applied it not only to his
home town but also to his homeland.

As regards "his own country," πατρίς, his father-
land, we need not hesitate long. This cannot mean
the town Nazareth, nor Capernaum, for in the entire
narrative of Jesus' return only countries are mentioned: Judea in 4:3; Samaria in 4:4; and Galilee in
4:3 and in v. 43 and 45. The mention of Sychar is
only incidental. This homeland is either Judea, where
Jesus was born, or Galilee, where he had spent his
life from childhood to manhood. The fact that Judea
is out of the question should be apparent from the
use Jesus made of this identical saying in Nazareth,
where it simply cannot mean Judea. Nor can we
assume that once when using this saying Jesus had
in mind Judea, and the next time he had in mind
Nazareth and Galilee. In comparison with the few
days of his babyhood spent in Judea the almost thirty
years spent in Galilee are decisive when Jesus now
speaks of his homeland.

But the chief difficulty is in the connective γάρ,
"for," followed in v. 45 by οὖν, "accordingly." If a
prophet is not esteemed in his homeland, how can
that be a reason or serve as an explanation for Jesus'

present return to his homeland? Would it not rather serve as a reason or an explanation why he should leave his homeland? This point is urged by those who would regard Judea as his homeland, and they add that Jesus thus far had had little success in Jerusalem and in Judea. This is the reason, they say, why Jesus, after vainly trying out Judea, now transfers his work to Galilee, where he expects greater success. Others turn the point around. Jesus is returning to Galilee just because a prophet is not esteemed in his homeland, meaning Galilee. Some say, that he now determines to win this esteem in spite of this handicap, at the cost of whatever hard effort. Some say, that Jesus intends to return to Galilee, where he will not be esteemed, because here he can in a manner retire and live quietly. But these suppositions leave out the greater facts and thus show that they labor only in some way to solve the strange "for" and "accordingly."

The facts are that after the assumption of his office Jesus had returned to Galilee only for a brief time and had wrought only the miracle at Cana. Beyond that nothing had been done in Galilee. Jesus proceeded to Jerusalem (2:12) and there began his public work. He spent from April until December (v. 35) in Judea with the result that now he was famous also in Galilee, for v. 45 reports that the Galileans received him gladly because they were impressed by the miracles they had seen him work while they, too, attended the previous Passover in Jerusalem. So now Jesus does not need to win his way in Galilee with hard effort. Also, he now comes, not for retirement, but to proceed energetically with his ministry in Galilee. Also, he has not failed in Judea but has created a mighty impression, reaching back even into and throughout Galilee. "For" explains that Jesus *now* starts his real work in Galilee; and "accordingly" corroborates this "for." Since a

prophet is not esteemed in his own land, Jesus now,
after winning his esteem in another land, comes back
to his own land and finds that esteem awaiting him.
As far as a prophet's having "honor" is concerned, it
is wrong to press the expression and to point to 5:41;
7:18; 8:50. Every prophet seeks and needs esteem
(τιμή), in order that his message may reach open ears
and, if possible, open hearts. The honor and the glory
mentioned in the other passages are of an entirely different type, namely such as men love; and Jesus
spurned all mere human glorification but never the
esteem which brought men to listen to him.

In a simple way John thus again supplements the
synoptists. They skip the eight to nine months of
Jesus' work in Judea, taking us at once from the baptism and the temptation of Jesus into his Galilean
work (Matt. 4:12; Mark 1:14; Luke 4:14). John
reports that all these important months, spent in
Judea, intervened. Yet John's plan is not to write
a chronicle of all that Jesus did during those months
in Judea just as he does not write a full account of
the following Galilean ministry. His plan takes in
only the great attestations of Jesus, and thus he selects
his material. The other Gospel writers followed other
plans.

45) **When, accordingly, he came into Galilee,
the Galileans received him, having seen all the
things he did in Jerusalem at the feast; for they also
went to the feast.** Among the many who had believed in Jesus in Jerusalem (2:23) were these pilgrims to the feast from Galilee. John, however, again
adds that they were impressed chiefly by the miracles
of Jesus; the particle is causal, "since they had
seen," etc., R. 1128. We must, therefore, remember
also 2:24, 25 with its bearing on Jesus' return to these
people. Add to this Jesus' complaint in 4:48; and
again in 6:26. This shows how we must under-

stand, "the Galileans received him," i. e., only as
their countryman now made famous by his miraculous
deeds.

46) **He came, therefore, again unto Cana of
Galilee, where he made the water wine.** He took
up the work where he had left it. The second miracle
in Galilee was wrought at the same place where the
first had been done. The first had prepared the
ground, the second builds on that. **And there was
a certain royal official, whose son was sick at Capernaum.** The report of Jesus' arrival spread rapidly
also to the larger city of Capernaum. The term
βασιλικός denotes one who in some way is connected
with the king, here Herod Agrippa, who, although
being only a tetrarch, ruling only the fourth part of
the country, was commonly given the title of king by
the Jews. Just what functions this official performed
either in the king's court or in his household we
have no means of knowing; the title βασιλικός is not
used to designate a military officer. Identifications
such as Chuza, Luke 8:3, or Manaen, Acts 13:1, are
rather useless. Because the son was sick "in Capernaum," we see that the official's home was there, hence
also ἀπῆλθε in v. 47; he hastened from Capernaum to
Cana.

47) **He, having heard that Jesus was come out
of Judea into Galilee, went away unto him and
requested him to come down and to heal his son;
for he was about to die.** All that v. 46 contains is
summarized in οὗτος: this important official who is so
distressed about his son's life. He heard the news:
Jesus is come! The Greek retains the present tense
ἥκει, "is come," whereas we after "having heard"
change it to "was come," or to "had come." Although
he is a royal official with servants at his command,
he goes in person to beg help of Jesus. Yet only his
desperate need drives him, his own free heart's desire

does not draw him. If it were not for his sick son, he would not have troubled much about Jesus. God's providence often uses our need thus to drive us to find even more than just what we think we need. The aorist ἀπῆλθε merely states the fact that the man "went away" to Cana, while the imperfect ἠρώτα, "he was requesting," holds us in suspense as to the success of his request. It pictures the man to us as torn between fear and hope. This suspense continues until the decisive word which heals the son is spoken.

The man's request is stated by the ἵνα clause, which in the Koine is a substitute for the infinitive. The request is made urgent by the additional, "for he is on the point to die," ἤμελλε followed by the infinitive. The case is nothing less than desperate. The father fully acknowledges that all human help has been exhausted, that only a miracle can save his child's life. Modern "healers" are careful not to touch such cases; when they do they fail. The fact that this royal official runs to Jesus with this case shows his faith — Jesus can save his child from imminent death, Jesus alone. The fact that he himself comes with his request shows the humility of his faith. Yet he thinks and clings to the thought (v. 49) that Jesus must come to his son's bedside to heal him and that, if the coming is not hastened, death may win the race and may make any help from Jesus impossible. This reveals the imperfection and the limitation of the father's faith.

48) **Jesus, accordingly, said to him, Unless you see signs and wonders you will in no way believe.** "Accordingly" refers to more than the mere fact of the request; it takes in all that Jesus sees involved in this request. And this extends far beyond the man who here makes his request. He is only one of the "many" we have met in 2:23 (compare 4:45), who

believed only because of the signs they saw, whose faith stopped with the signs and did not advance to Jesus' word as such, with whose faith Jesus, therefore, could not be satisfied. Jesus thus, indeed, speaks to this official (πρὸς αὐτόν) but he uses the plural, "unless you see," etc., and not, "unless thou seest," etc. This also softens the rebuke. The implication, too, is that this official (since Jesus includes him in the class indicated) is a Jew. Nor is it impossible to believe that the man was among the pilgrims who at the last Passover had been in Jerusalem and had seen Jesus work one or more miracles, little thinking that in a few months he would run to Jesus for miraculous aid for himself.

We should not emphasize the verb, "unless you *see,* actually with your own eyes *see,* signs and wonders," for the object "signs and wonders" has the emphasis. The point of Jesus' complaint is not the fact that he is asked to come down to Capernaum and to do the miracle where the man could see it done, but the fact that the kind of faith represented by this man can be kept alive only by means of miracles. The man never thought of Jesus as healing at a distance. Asking Jesus "to come down" is only incidental to the real request, which is to heal his child. So also when Jesus speaks of "seeing" miracles, this is not in opposition to hearing of them, for the effect would be quite the same. The complaint of Jesus is that so many would cease to believe in any manner, or would never believe even as they did unless he furnished them miracles on which to rest this faith of theirs. They would not advance from the miracles to faith in Jesus' person and his Word. Thus Jesus here does, indeed, refuse to hurry to Capernaum and to work the miracle under this condition. By this refusal, however, Jesus calls for and seeks to waken a better faith in the heart

of this royal official. In the refusal lies a covert
promise to help if only the man will rise to a truer and
a better faith. Compare 11:40.

The complaint is that these people have to see
"signs and wonders" (the terms are explained in
2:11). The second term is explicative of the first:
"signs" in so far as they are "wonders" or portents and
arouse excited astonishment. These people do not
read the "signs" and see their true significance, that
Jesus is the Messiah and Son of God, and that these
"signs" seal him as such; they only want to marvel
at the wonder of them. Thus they avoid the true
purpose of the signs. The strong denial in οὐ μή with
the futuristic aorist subjunctive πιστεύσητε, R. 938, etc.,
for which also the future indicative could here be
used, is to the same effect, "you will not believe at all,"
or "in no way," i. e., not even in the faulty way in
which you now believe. Jesus does not deny the poor
faith which this official had but declares that this is
not enough. His thus calling for a better faith, one
that is real, must, however, not lead us to the hasty
generalization that Jesus wrought signs only in answer
to real faith and never where faith is absent. A study
of the miracles reveals that they were used in both
ways. Jesus often calls for faith and seals faith by
a miracle, and then again he simply works the miracle
in order that faith may follow. Thus miracles, indeed,
always aim at producing faith, but as signs, not as
mere wonders, once in the one way, and again in
the other.

49) The man is not rebuffed by the rebuke in Jesus'
words. He does not turn away in sad disappointment. He does just what the Canaanitish woman does,
Matt. 15:25 — he just throws himself upon the mercy
of Jesus. **The royal official says to him, Sir, come
down ere my little child die!** We should not stress
the fact that the man again begs Jesus "to come down"

and implies that unless Jesus arrives in time even Jesus can do nothing. For in v. 48 Jesus makes no attempt to correct these limitations of the man's faith. Jesus takes only one step at a time, the true pedagogical way. He first attempts to turn this man's faith in a higher direction, namely upon Jesus' own person and his heart. And Jesus succeeds. With pleading reverence the man lays all his distress upon Jesus' heart. If we could have seen the expression on Jesus' face and could have heard his tone of voice, we could better understand his meaning and the man's response. "Unless you see signs and wonders," etc., really means, "Oh, that you would think less about the wonders and more about me!" This brings the address Κύριε, which looks up to Jesus; the renewed pleading, in the strong aorist κατάβηθι, "come down!" and the tender appeal in τὸ παιδίον μου, "my little child." On πρίν with the infinitive after a positive verb see R. 977, 1091. So much Jesus' word has produced, the first tiny advance to real faith in Jesus.

50) **And Jesus says to him, Be going on thy way; thy son lives. The man believed the word which Jesus said to him and went his way.** The plea that casts itself upon Jesus' heart is heard and in a way that is utterly surprising, far beyond the man's expectation. The two statements of Jesus are not, however, in opposition, as if the first intends to dash down, in order that the second may then raise up the more. The first does not intend to say, "No; leave me, I will not go down!" but, "Be assured and go home — thy son lives!" In other words: "It is not at all necessary for me to go to Capernaum to save thy child's life, not necessary that I should thus prolong thy suspense and anxiety — right here and now I grant thy prayer and give thee thy little son's life." Thus Jesus now corrects the man's poor notion about hurrying to the child's side and he does it with

one stroke. The power to heal lies in the person of
Jesus — where else could it lie? It is a matter of
his will and his word, not one of inches or miles. Jesus
gives the man only his word and even that in the
tersest form, "Thy son lives" — not a syllable more.
On him who speaks this little word, and on the little
word this person speaks, the man is thus bidden to
rest his faith. On paper, and as we read it from the
printed page, it does seem little — too little; yet as
there spoken by Jesus it was mighty, it bore all the
power of Jesus' will, a divine pledge, an unconditional
assurance, an absolute promise. As such it struck
upon the man's heart full of faith-kindling power.

The mild present imperative πορεύου = "just be going on thy way." Then follows the intensive present
tense ζῇ, the direct opposite of the man's fear about
his child's dying, thy son "goes on living indefinitely."
With this one pregnant word Jesus changes death into
life: the death about to close in, into life that goes
happily on. It is unwarranted to intimate or to assert
that in some way, if by no other than by clairvoyance
or telepathy, Jesus merely knew that the child's fever
was breaking just at this time, and that thus in a perfectly natural way the child would after all escape
death. These attempts of rationalism to "explain
away" the actuality of Jesus' miracles and to leave
only the appearance of miracles, turn Jesus into a
charlatan, from whom every sincere and honest man
should turn away. The fact that Jesus wrought this
miracle, as he did every other deed of his, in conformity with his calling and office and in harmony
with his Father's will, needs no saying. But to add
that in each case Jesus had and had to have a decision
or an intimation from his Father to do the deed is
devoid of Scripture support. To think that every
miracle came only as an answer to a prayer from
Jesus reduces him to the level of the ordinary pro-

phets and is contradicted by all the cases where Jesus
reveals that he acts by his own will and power. So
here, "Thy son lives" = I grant thee his life. Compare Luke 7:11, "I say unto thee, Arise!" On John
11:41, 42 see, below. It is fancy to bring in the angels
here or elsewhere in connection with the miracles on
the strength of 1:50; where angels are employed they
are mentioned.

The man believed the word of Jesus, the dative ᾧ
being attracted to the case of its antecedent (some
read ὅν). The aorist states the fact. The man had
only this "word," but now resting on that, asking no
more, he came away with a better, truer trust than the
one that first made him come. His faith was becoming
more like that of the Samaritans in v. 41. This faith
was kindled in the man's heart by Jesus and by his
mighty word, "he lives." "He believed" without
visible or tangible evidence. Yet the man had the
very highest and best evidence — Jesus' word, 20:29b.
In due time the corroborative evidence of sight follows
the decisive assurance of the Word. The inadequate
faith in so many of whom Jesus complained is such
because it clings only to the lower evidence and will
not move to the true ground on which saving faith
alone can and does rest. The imperfect ἐπορεύετο pictures the man as he was on his way and matches the
present imperative πορεύου. It also intimates that we
shall presently learn what the man found. We see
him going back hugging to his heart Jesus' word "he
lives," by that overcoming all doubts and misgivings
that very likely kept assailing his mind.

51) He did not have to wait until he actually
reached home. **Now already while going down his
servants met him, saying to him that his boy lives.
He, accordingly, inquired of them the hour in which
he became better. They, accordingly, told him,
Yesterday at the seventh hour the fever left him.**

The anxiety of the family for the boy's life is indicated by this sending of servants to report to the father the sudden change and the recovery at the earliest possible moment. John puts the glad news into indirect discourse, so that we cannot be entirely sure that the servants almost exactly repeated the word of Jesus, especially the significant verb ζῇ, "lives." It may well be that they used just that word and in the sense of Jesus: all danger of death is gone.

The father's inquiry in regard to the hour of the change sounded only natural to the servants, but the answer to that inquiry was freighted with the greatest significance to the father. Why B.-D. 328 should call the aorist ἐπύθετο "incorrect" and demand the imperfect instead, is strange, since either could be used, the aorist merely stating the fact that the father so inquired. The expression κομψότερον ἔχειν is idiomatic. The Greek likes the adverb with this verb; we use a different verb with an adjective. "One must be willing for the Greek to have his standpoint," R. 546. We say "better," the Greek prefers the comparative of κόμψος, "handsome." The aorist ἔσχε = "got better," R. 834; "better than before the word of Christ was spoken," R. 665. The servants use neither the endearing term παιδίον, which fits the father's lips, nor the weighty υἱός, which fits the lips of Jesus, but simply παῖς, "thy boy," which fits the general family relation. The father learns that the fever left the boy "yesterday at the seventh hour." Instead of the accusative ὥραν we should expect the dative to designate a point of time, or the genitive to indicate time within; but B.-D. 161 finds this accusative in the classics, and R. 470 tries to explain it: "Either the action was regarded as going over the hour, or the hour was looked at as an adverbial accusative like τὸ λοιπόν," of which, if we need an explanation at all, the latter is decidedly preferable. Note the aorists, ἔσχε in the question, ἀφῆκεν

in the answer. We meet the latter in Mark 1:31, in
a parallel case, when Jesus healed Simon's wife's
mother: ἀφῆκεν ὁ πυρετός, "the fever left her," and so
completely that she was instantly entirely recovered
and rose from her bed and "ministered unto them."
These, then, are not ingressive aorists, so that we
should translate, "began to amend" (our versions),
and the fever "began to leave." The recovery did not
merely start at the seventh hour. If that had been
all, the boy might have suffered a relapse, and it would
have been foolish to dispatch servants to the father.
An anxious wait of hours, of a day or two, would have
followed with fear lest the fever set in again. The
boy was completely restored, so completely that the
servants were at once hurried off to the father. From
the word "the fever" we are unable to determine the
exact nature of the disease, since some fevers are themselves diseases, while others are only symptoms of
diseases.

53) **The father, accordingly, knew that it was
at the hour in which Jesus said to him, Thy son
lives; and he himself believed and his whole house.**
Thus the miracle was revealed, one that was even
greater and more astonishing than the man had hoped
for. He "himself" believed with a new measure of
faith (compare 2:11). His entire household (οἰκία)
joined him in that faith. The mention of the entire
household may well indicate that in the days to come
this family, certainly an important one, being connected as it was with the king's court, took a prominent part among the members of the church. This
leads some to think that the official may have been
Chuza, but even then we have nothing but surmise.

Here we again meet the perplexing question of the
"hours" in John; see 1:39. If the seventh hour is one
o'clock (according to Jewish reckoning), the man
could easily have reached home that evening, the

distance being less than six hours' travel. If the
servants started not long after one o'clock, he and
they would surely have met at least late that same
afternoon. Yet when they meet they say, "*Yesterday
at the seventh hour*." Invention steps in and in some
way manufactures a delay long enough to extend to
the next day. The man travelled leisurely, his mind
being perfectly at ease; the servants did not start until
the next morning — both suppositions are wholly unnatural, for both would hurry. Even when father
and servants are thought to have met hours after
sundown and thus, since sundown begins a new Jewish
day, on the day after the miracle, we have too much
time with both the father and the servants hurrying
toward each other. A goodly delay has to be worked
in the account also on this supposition if John counts
the hours in the Jewish way. According to the Roman
reckoning the miracle was wrought at seven in the
evening. Then, indeed, father and servants could
meet only on the next day, and all would be clear
without inventing delays. But did John use this
Roman reckoning? Nobody knows. Our quandary
remains.

54) **This again as a second sign Jesus wrought
after having come from Judea into Galilee.** "This"
is the subject, to which is added predicatively, hence
without the article, "as a second sign"; and "again"
modifies the verb, "again he wrought." The whole is
made clear by the participial addition, "after having
come," etc. The first time Jesus came back to Galilee
he turned the water into wine (v. 46); now, having
returned a second time, he again signals his return
by a miracle, a second one to place beside the first.
During the eight or nine months spent in Judea many
other miracles had been wrought, 2:23; 4:45. Because
John does not tell us about other miracles that Jesus
wrought here in Galilee after his second return, the

conclusion is by no means warranted that Jesus remained in retirement for a considerable time. He proceeds with his public work in Galilee as all the synoptists report.

Matthew 8:5-13 and Luke 7:1-10 relate a miracle which in one point, and only in one (healing at a distance), is similar to this one. In all other points, outward as well as inward, a radical difference prevails. Nevertheless, critics identify the two, but thereby they show to what lengths they are ready to go to find their hypotheses in the sacred record.

CHAPTER V

III

The Attestation Arousing Unbelief
Chapters 5 and 6

Five and six are evidently companion chapters. The former shows how the antagonism against Jesus arose in Jerusalem among the rulers of the nation when he manifested and declared himself to be the Son of God. The latter shows a similar opposition in Galilee, where the people at first were favorable to Jesus. Both hostile movements finally resulted in the complete rejection of Jesus as the Messiah and Son of God on the part of the Jewish nation.

THE RISE OF OPEN OPPOSITION IN JERUSALEM
CHAPTER 5

1) *The Healing on the Sabbath Day, 5:1-18.* — **After these things there was a feast of the Jews; and Jesus went to Jerusalem.** "After these things" bridges the entire gap between the second return of Jesus, distinguished by the miracle upon the royal officer's son, and his return to Jerusalem as now reported. "These things" include all that Jesus said and did during this period, of which "things" the miracle is a sample.

Commentators, from the ancient fathers onward, are hopelessly divided as to what festival of the Jews John here refers to. The codices are about equally divided between the reading "a festival of the Jews" (without the Greek article) and "the festival of the

Jews" (with the article), although inner reasons would speak for the former reading. Jesus had left Judea in December (4:35) for the reason stated in 4:1-3. First there came the feast of Purim in March; next the Passover in April; fifty days later the Jewish Pentecost; in October the feast of Tabernacles. Purim we may dismiss in short order, since this festival had no connection with the Temple nor with any service there. The book of Esther was read only in the local synagogues, no work was done, and the time was spent in eating and in drinking, often to excess. Having left Judea as indicated, Jesus would not return there so soon, and surely not for the observance of a festival that compelled nobody to go to Jerusalem. So much is certain: the feast we seek to determine must be sought between the Passover of 2:12, when Jesus cleansed the Temple, and the Passover of 6:4, during which Jesus remained in Galilee. With Purim out of consideration, the choice narrows down to one of the three pilgrim feasts, Passover, Pentecost, or Tabernacles. This means that whichever of these three we choose, we must allow two years between 2:13 and 6:4. In other words, the Passover mentioned in 2:13 is followed by another, and this by the one in 6:4. It is certain that the one mentioned in 6:4 cannot be the next in order after that of 2:13. For the time from April (2:13) to December Jesus spent in Judea; late in December he came to Galilee. Then if the next April is the festival mentioned in 6:4, the feast referred to in 5:1 must be Purim, which with Jesus' return to Galilee leaves only three weeks at best till the Passover of 6:4. But in 6:4 we find Jesus in fullest activity and at the height of his work in Galilee. It is impossible to assume that his work in Galilee reached that height in so short a time, i. e., from the end of December to the beginning of April, with time taken out in March for the pilgrimage to Jerusalem for the observance of Purim. Thus 6:4 simply must be placed one year later; it is the second Passover after 2:13.

With this established, it really makes little difference which feast we assume for 5:1, the first Passover after 2:13, or the following Pentecost seven weeks later, or Tabernacles in October. The chronology remains fixed: one Passover (2:13) at which the Temple was cleansed; two Passovers following, the second of which is that of 6:4; then the next at which Jesus died — three years in all, plus the weeks or the months that precede 2:13 (Jesus' Baptism, first return to Galilee, first appearance in Jerusalem). With the choice for the festival of 5:1 thus reduced, we may eliminate the Passover (the one following the return to Galilee in December). If John had meant this Passover in 5:1, we have every reason to assume that he would have used its name instead of writing merely "a (or: the) feast of the Jews." He writes thus indefinitely because what follows did not occur at the feast, or in the Temple, nor was it connected with the feast. It took place on a Sabbath following the feast, at the pool called Bethesda. Most likely, then, the feast of 5:1 is either Pentecost or Tabernacles. The latter, by all odds, is the preferable choice. Having left Judea because of the evil agitation of the Pharisees (4:1-3) in December, Jesus would hardly return to Jerusalem in three months (April, Passover), or a few weeks later (Pentecost), but would delay till Tabernacles in October. This assumption at least meets most adequately all the data available, and, as we shall see, even the character of the miracle related in 5:2, etc. We note that Jesus then attended only two Passovers at Jerusalem during his ministry, the first and the last; and remained away for the two that intervene. Why he did not attend that of 6:4 John tells us in 7:1.

2) **Now there is in Jerusalem by the sheep gate a pool, which is called in Hebrew Bethesda, having five porches.** "Is" = is still, after the destruction of Jerusalem, when John wrote; it is not the "is" of vivid narrative, since the narration goes on with ordinary tenses. With ἐπὶ τῇ προβατικῇ supply πύλῃ, as is usual with such substantivized adjectives: "by the sheep *gate*." Besides having other names, this swimming pool had the Hebrew (i. e. Aramaic, R. 104) name "Bethesda," House of Mercy, which was most likely bestowed upon it because of the erection of the five porches for the charitable accomodation of the sick, or because of the mercy of God manifested in the supposed periodic healing. The exact location of this pool the archaeologists must determine, but we refuse to accept as the probable site the excavation seventy-five feet deep near the gate now called St. Stephen's, because it would be impossible for sick people to plunge into it except to drown. The exact location is immaterial for the narrative. John mentions the Aramaic name of the place because in this language the name bears a significant relation to the miracle here wrought by Jesus.

3) **In these was lying a multitude of sick, blind, lame, withered.** The five porches or covered colonnades were like a hospital, filled with a crowd of sufferers, four classes being mentioned, this number often being used for indicating completeness. The first group, the "sick," takes in all that are not included in the other groups. The absence of the articles draws attention to the qualities indicated by the nouns. When so many sufferers are brought together they impress us much more than when we see them singly; we then see more adequately all the wretchedness, the misery, the broken lives that form the result of sin among men.

Verse 4: "for an angel of the Lord went down at certain seasons into the pool and troubled the waters:

whosoever then first after the troubling of the water stepped in was made whole with whatsover disease he was holden," is a spurious addition. The final words in v. 3, "waiting for the moving of the water," may, indeed, state what was true, and may rest on v. 7, but are textually so doubtful that they must be cancelled. Since the details of these findings really belong not to commentaries but to works on technical text criticism, we here pass these details by. Tertullian used this spurious passage for his favorite conception of "the baptismal angel"; somewhat later Ambrose saw in it a prophecy of the descent of the Holy Spirit, consecrating the water of baptism to a mystical washing away of sin; and Chrysostom had the same conception. The spurious passage reflects only a popular notion of the time. The fresh water, bubbling up periodically, may have had some medicinal qualities. These were exaggerated as being curative for all kinds of ailments. Popular superstition did the rest. Thus shrines and fountains still attract multitudes of sick people; and since certain nervous troubles yield to strong suggestion, some sufferers find relief or cure at places of this kind and in a perfectly natural way. Catholic shrines, Christian Science, faith healers, etc., operate in this manner. In John's account Jesus completely disregards the pool, the cure the sick man hoped to find there and thought that others found.

5) **And a certain man was there, having been thirty-eight years in his infirmity.** Longer than an average term of life this man had suffered; how long he had been at Bethesda we are not told, though the implication is that he had been there for some time. His ailment rendered him helpless and may have been a form of paralysis, which was possibly due to youthful excesses (v. 14). With adverbs and adverbial expressions ἔχω = to be; here, "having been," the

present participle getting its time from the main verb ἦν.

6) **Him, when Jesus saw lying and knew that he had been thus already a long time, he says to him, Dost thou want to become well?** Jesus selects what was probably the worst case then present at Bethesda. The two aorist participles ἰδών and γνούς merely state the facts that Jesus saw this man, just described in v. 5, and that he knew about the long time he had been sick. Here ἔχει is again used with an adverbial modifier as in v. 5. Its present tense "gathers up past and present into one phrase" (Moulton in R. 879), for which we use the perfect, "has been," which after a past tense we change to the past perfect: knew that he "had been." We need assume no miraculous seeing and knowing in this case. This exceptional case would be generally known, perhaps even be paraded before visitors. It is true, the disciples are not mentioned in this entire chapter, and from this silence the conclusion has been drawn that Jesus visited Jerusalem alone at this time. But the latter is altogether unlikely. The disciples are not mentioned because John finds no occasion for referring to them. They may have drawn Jesus' attention to this man, having had their attention drawn to him by others.

The question of Jesus, "Dost thou want to become well?" could not awaken and was not intended by Jesus to awaken faith in the man. Here is a plain instance where the miracle precedes the faith, where the faith even follows some time later. Jesus merely attracts the sick man's attention (Acts 3:3) and makes him think of his sad condition and how desirable it would be to change that for complete health. Note the punctiliar aorist γενέσθαι: "be well," or "become well" at one stroke; not: gradually be getting well.

7)   The man's reply is discouraging enough; it
is only the whine and complaint of many a man who
has been sick a long while.   He does not rouse up
enough even to answer with a decided, "Yes!" or,
"Yes, I do!"   All he answers is the hopeless plaint
he had often repeated before.   **The sick man
answered him: Sir, I have no man, when the water
is troubled, to put me into the pool; but while I am
coming, another goes down before me.**   The address
Κύριε is most likely due to the dignity in the appearance and the manner of Jesus.   "I have no man"
voices the disappointed wish of past days, "Oh, if
only I had some man to help me!"   Did the look of
interest on Jesus' face, the tone of power in his voice,
perhaps lead him for a second to think that this man
would help him finally to reach the water in time,
or obtain some other man to do so?   In the clause,
"whenever the water is troubled," the aorist indicates the brief moment of the disturbance.   We may
accept this periodic welling-up of the water in a certain part of the pool as being true; but the angel is
the invention of the author of v. 4.   The man also
believed in the curative power of this freshly bubbling water and imagined it would cure him, too, if
only he could reach it in time.   What virtue the water
really had it is not in the interest of John to report.
After ἔχω the ἵνα clause takes the place of the infinitive,
B.-D. 379; although R. 960, 1011 makes it usurp
the function of a relative clause, which, however,
would be a different conception, one about the man
instead of about the action.   "To throw," βάλῃ, is summary, standing on no ceremony, losing not a second
because of gentle handling.

Always he gets there too late.   While he is still
coming, another goes down before him, pre-empts the
precious spot where the water churns for a little while,
and in the rush to get there with others he is hope-

lessly left behind. The Greek heightens the effect by the abutting of ἐγώ and ἄλλος.

8) Three mighty words from the lips of Jesus do more than this man's years of effort. **And Jesus says to him, Arise, take up thy bed, and walk.** The punctiliar aorist imperative ἆρον expresses the momentary lifting of the κράββατος or pad on which the man lay; and the durative present imperative the indefinitely extended action of walking. The two tenses are good illustrations of their use. We must regard ἔγειρε as merely being attached to ἆρον, hence no comma or καί is necessary; hence also, like other such attached imperatives, we have the usual present tense without independent tense force, and here it is aoristic because it is attached to ἆρον, R. 855; not, however, ἔγειραι, another reading, see the verb in R. 1215.

9) The effect of the three verbs is instantaneous. **And straightway the man became well and did take up his bed and was walking.** The evidence for cancelling εὐθέως is too meager. But apart from this adverb the verbs and their tenses express an immediate effect. The man was sound and well on the instant, all traces of the ailment of thirty-eight years had vanished and were gone. Strength surged through his body: he did pick up his bed (again aorist) and he was walking away (the durative imperfect). Some interpreters think that faith was necessary for the miraculous healing. Some claim that Jesus saw this faith before he spoke the words; others, that faith instantly followed the words. If not faith in the ordinary sense, then at least the faith of the man in his own ability to do as Jesus said. Thus, we are told: "The man believed that word to be accompanied with power; made proof, and found that it was so." Or, "the command of Jesus brings the courage of faith to his soul, and power into his limbs, to obey the command." On the con-

trary, the man suddenly was sound and well, and this apart from faith in any sense of the word. He no more needed to believe either in Jesus' word to arise, etc., or in his own health and strength, than any hale and hearty man does. He had the soundness, that was all. He had more; for when a man has not walked for a long time he must learn again, and this man needed not to learn. His muscles were firm and responded to his will as if they were perfectly trained and practiced. Why should not the man pick up his bed and walk away?

But did not Jesus go too far when he told the man to carry away his bed? Would it not, in view of the faultfinding it would surely arouse on the part of the Sanhedrists, have been wiser to let the man abandon his bed and go on without it? As regards the second question, it is plainly Jesus' intention to oppose, openly and positively, both the human traditions and the false spirit of the Jewish leaders. One must study their barren, legalistic, and casuistic methods of building up a hedge of human traditions or regulations around the law of God, in order to see how utterly impossible it was for Jesus to avoid clashing with the exponents of these traditions. They found thirty kinds of labor forbidden on the Sabbath and they insisted on these prohibitions, deduced by their own wisdom, in such a way as to lose sight of the law's chief requirements and true spiritual intention. Jesus could have lived in peace with these men only by submitting to their spirit and their methods, and this was an utter impossibility. So he even invites the conflict.

As regards the first question Moses had, indeed, said, Exod. 20:10, "In it thou shalt not do any work"; and Jeremiah 17:19-27 especially forbids burden-bearing. But this latter passage speaks clearly of that desecration of the Sabbath to which the Jews were ever prone, of doing business on the Sabbath and of working at common labor for gain. The prophet meant marketing and trading. Nehemiah (13:15, etc.) had difficulty with "the merchants and sellers of all kinds of ware," treading wine presses on the Sabbath, bringing in sheaves, and lading asses; as also wine, grapes, figs, and all manner of burdens. The men of Tyre brought figs and all manner of ware and sold them on the Sabbath to the children of Judah in Jerusalem. A glance is enough to show the difference between this sort of burden-bearing and that of the healed man carrying his bed. The former dishonored God, the latter glorified God and his mercy. That was done for private gain, not being satisfied with six workdays, this was done for the Master's praise. That was clearly forbidden, this Jesus himself, in perfect harmony with the law of Moses, commanded. For the miracle wrought at Bethesda was not intended only for the man upon whom it was wrought but for as many as should see this man. It was a *sign* to the Jews. As such it was intended, while in no way transgressing God's law, to run counter to the false Jewish traditions and thus to turn men's hearts — if they would be turned at all — to the true authority of Jesus, who, while upholding God's law, brought to view the mercy which both heals the sufferer's body and sets free his soul from spiritual bondage. Such was the significance of the sign set before the eyes of the men in Jerusalem: a man marvelously healed carrying his bed before men's eyes through the streets to his home, on the Sabbath!

10) The clash comes. **Now it was the Sabbath on that day. The Jews, accordingly, were saying to the man who had been healed, It is the Sabbath, and it is not lawful for thee to carry the bed.** Jesus purposely chose the Sabbath for performing this sign. As on his first visit he cleansed the Temple of traffikers, so on this second visit he seeks to cleanse the

people of their false traditions. John records this miracle for the very purpose of showing how the first preliminary clash is now followed by one that is more violent. Here we get the full hostile sense which John puts into the designation "the Jews." These were not ordinary people whom the man met on the streets as he walked along, but, as the sequel shows, men of authority (v. 16), Pharisees, some of them perhaps Sanhedrists. Their chief concern was whether a thing was "lawful," ἔξεστιν, permitted or not, *they* being the sole judges in their casuistic fashion. The verb αἴρω may mean either "to take up" or "to bear," "to carry," according to the connection; see 1:29.

The imperfect ἔλεγον describes how these authorities urged the point upon the man. John calls him, with the perfect participle, "he who has been healed," i. e., is such now. Not one word "were they saying" to the man about his wonderful healing. Significant silence!

11) The healed man knows a different authority. **But he answered them, He that made me well, that one said to me, Take up thy bed and walk.** We must read ἐκεῖνος not only as resumptive but at the same time as strongly emphatic, "that one," or "that man," *he* who did this wonderful deed, ὁ ποιήσας, the aorist to indicate the one deed. This is the man's authority for doing what he does, and this authority not only permitted but commanded the act. We are not informed whether the man put down his bed in deference to the Jews, or not; it seems that he did not do so. Pointedly he describes Jesus as "he that did make me well."

12) But this is lost upon the Jews — and yet not lost; for on his first visit to Jerusalem Jesus had wrought a goodly number of such signs and had impressed many, 3:23. These Jews had no use for such

signs; they deliberately refuse to ask this man about the great deed of healing. **They inquired of him, Who is the man that said to thee, Take up and walk?** Their minds are fixed only on the supposed transgression, on this violation of their all-important traditions. For these Jews Jesus is not the man who healed this great sufferer, who bestowed on him divine mercy, but a man who broke their traditions, who had to be punished. When they here inquire who it is that issued this unlawful command, we must not suppose that they did not from the start know that it was Jesus. They know only too well. They ask in order to secure legal testimony against Jesus. They want the man's direct testimony, in order then to take legal action against Jesus. That, too, is why they quote only the verbs "take up and walk," for these mark the crime in their eyes. The sign was before them, placed there by the master hand of Jesus, but these Jews neither read its meaning nor think of obeying its admonition.

13) **But he that was healed knew not who it was; for Jesus slipped aside, a crowd being in the place.** The very presence of the crowd made Jesus postpone the completion of his work upon the man; he would finish the task at a more opportune time. So he slipped away from the man through the crowd, ἐκινεύω, "to lean sideways," thus "to evade" or slip away; the aorist simply states the past fact, for which the English prefers the pluperfect as bringing out the time relation (see R. 840, etc.). Why such a crowd visited the place on this Sabbath is not explained. But those are evidently wrong who suppose that Jesus did not consider that the day was the Sabbath, and who say that Jesus meant to do a kindly deed in a sort of private way. An ordinary man might not think about the Sabbath in such a way, though a sincere Jew would scarcely do so. Moreover, the crowd was

evidently present because it was the Sabbath, when many visitors were free from occupation and could go to visit sick friends. But the idea that Jesus forgot about the Sabbath would make this decisive miracle of his with its consequences so vital for him a kind of accident — which we simply cannot believe. Then, with this crowd present, how could Jesus tell the man to carry his bed without at once attracting public attention? The man did not go far through that crowd before the Jews, those with some authority, stopped him. No; it was Jesus who deliberately set this sign of his before these people. Not a few must have stood around when the man was catechized.

The aorist ὁ ἰαθείς simply states the past fact that the man was healed, while the perfect in v. 10 adds to the past fact the present implication of his now being one thus healed. There is something noteworthy about Jesus' sending of this weak beginner in the faith against such powerful antagonists as "the Jews," and in his putting these antagonists to silence by the man's very weakness and ignorance. For all the man could reply to the probing of the Jews was that the man who had healed him had given him the order to carry his bed. In other words, all he could do was to reiterate the miracle (the credential and authority of Jesus) and the command that went with it (resting on that credential and authority). Because the man himself was compelled to tell about the miracle and the command he was fortified in his young faith.

14)   **After these things Jesus finds him in the Temple and said to him, Behold, thou art become well. Sin no more, lest something worse come to thee.** This finding may have occurred on the same day or on the following day. On Jesus' part it is intentional, for he now means to complete what he began with the unexpected miracle. It was a good

sign that Jesus found the man in the Temple, where the man evidently had gone in order to thank God for the great mercy he had found in the House of Mercy and to render due sacrifice.

The word Jesus addresses to the man is remarkable. First a vivid reminder of the priceless benefit, "Behold, thou art become well!" the perfect tense implying that he stands here as a well man this very moment. This is the lever whose motive power is to lift the man to a higher plane. For Jesus adds, "Sin no more!" and like a flash lays bare the man's distant past (4:18), extending over more than thirty-eight years. He had sinned, sinned in a way which his conscience would at once painfully recall, sinned so as to wreck his life in consequence. The objection that Jesus here has in mind sinfulness in general, because in Luke 13:1-5 he will not let his disciples infer a special guilt from a special calamity, cannot hold, for certain sins do entail painful and dreadful results. And if Jesus here enjoins perfect sinlessness upon the healed man, how could he ever hope to escape the worse thing? No; the man had great sins on his conscience. The bodily suffering these sins had caused him Jesus had removed. Here lay the grace of pardon — by far the best thing in the miracle for the man personally. This Jesus now impresses upon the man's soul. "Sin no more" involves that Jesus pardons the man's past sins; for if the great sins of the past still stand against this man, what would abstinence from future open sins avail?

But, alas, even after thirty-eight years of suffering the root of the old evil remains, which may now shoot up again and spread its poisonous branches. Let every man who has by divine grace conquered some sinful propensity, some special "weakness," some dangerous habit, remember that "Sin no more!" must ever ring in his ears in warning. "Watch and pray,

that ye enter not into temptation: the spirit indeed
is willing, but the flesh is weak," Matt. 26:41. But
now that Jesus has freed this man, the admonition to
sin no more comes with an effectiveness, bestowing
strength and help, such as the man had never experienced before. So it is in every case. Not by our
own unaided strength are we to fight our foe and sin
no more but in the strength which Jesus gives and is
ready to renew and to increase daily.

"Lest something worse come to thee," χεῖρόν τι
(neuter comparative of κακός), by its very indefiniteness heightens the warning — something worse than
thirty-eight years of suffering. We need not think
only of the damnation of hell, although this, too, is
meant. "Let no man, however miserable, count that
he has exhausted the power of God's wrath. The
arrows that have pierced him may have been keen;
but there are keener yet, if only he provoke them, in
the quiver from which these were drawn." Trench.
On the one hand Jesus sets the benefit received, on
the other hand the grace of warning, and between
these two the admonition to sin no more. Thus, held
by a double cord, the man will surely be found true in
the end. It is a double healing which we witness, and
the latter is the greater of the two.

15) **The man went away and told the Jews
that it was Jesus that had made him well.** This
action of the man has been misconceived as being a
malicious reporting of Jesus to the authorities. Such
a treacherous person Jesus would neither have healed
nor have treated with pastoral care after the healing. Others seek for the man's motive by supposing
that the man wanted to bring the Jews to faith, or
wanted to challenge the Jews with an authority that
was superior to theirs, or wanted to discharge his duty
to the authorities, or wanted to cover himself against
blame by thrusting it upon Jesus. We must not for-

get that Jesus set this great sign publicly before the
Jewish authorities, and that he purposely did it on
the Sabbath. The man also reports to the Jews, not
that it was Jesus who told him to carry his bed, but
that it was Jesus who made him well. The Greek indirect discourse retains the original tenses of the
direct; the man actually said, "It *is* Jesus who *did
make* me well," which the English indirect discourse
changes, "that it *was* Jesus who *hade made* him well."
Jesus wants his person and his name attached to the
sign which he himself had publicly advertised by the
bed carried on the Sabbath. Through the man Jesus
furnishes the Jews exactly what they want: direct
legal evidence that he is the man back of everything.
The man's motive is only a tool in Jesus' hands; the
motive of Jesus dominates. John reports briefly. Did
the man not tell Jesus how the Jews had stopped and
quizzed him? Perhaps Jesus actually directed the
man now to go and to tell these Jews what they
demand to know.

16) **And on this account the Jews were persecuting Jesus, because he was doing these things
on the Sabbath.** We see that by "the Jews" the
authorities are meant. The imperfect ἐδίωκον, "were
persecuting," means continuously persecuting. The
second imperfect ἐποίει, "he was doing," instead of
the aorist ἐποίησε, "he did," contains the inference
of the Jews; for from the one act of healing and ordering the man to carry his bed on the Sabbath they
rightly conclude that further acts such as this performed on the Sabbath will be regarded by Jesus as
being perfectly in order. Whether Jesus thus performed more deeds of this kind on the following
Sabbaths or not is immaterial. The Jews held Jesus
liable not merely for once breaking the Sabbath by
the one act (which would require the aorist) but for
his general attitude regarding their traditional Sab-

bath observance. This also explains ταῦτα, "these
things," a plural not because of the miracle plus the
order about the bed, but a plural to include all that
Jesus deemed proper to do on the Sabbath in contradiction to the Jewish traditions. The fact that the
persecution involved the determination to make away
with Jesus is seen from μᾶλλον in v. 18. To these fanatical Jews their own hatred, persecution, and murderous intentions were virtues, and the mercy, the
miracles of Jesus, and his showing them as signs
and seals of his divine Sonship, mortal crimes. They
broke the law in the most glaring way by their pseudo-
vindication of the law against him who never broke it
and could not break it. "And sought to slay him" (A.
V.) seems to be an interpolation from v. 18 and should
be cancelled.

17) Part of the persecution venting itself upon
Jesus consisted in charging him with violating the
Sabbath. John is not concerned with the details of
time, place, and other circumstances when these attacks
occurred, but only with Jesus' replies, filled as they
are with the weightiest attestations concerning himself. As short and striking as is the first reply, so
full and elaborate is the second (v. 19, etc.). **But
Jesus answered them, My father works till now.
Also I myself work.** That is all — not another
word. But this brief word is like a shot into the center
of the target, such as Jesus alone is able to deliver. It
absolutely and completely refutes the Jewish authorities. This time Jesus uses no *mashal*, as in 2:19, with
a hidden meaning that requires a key to unlock it,
but a word that is as clear as crystal. He does not
say *"our* Father" and thus place himself on a level
with the Jews or with men generally but pointedly
"my Father" (see 20:17). And the Jews at once
grasp the meaning that Jesus declares God to be his
Father in a sense in which no other man can call God

Father, i. e., that in his person as the Son he is equal (ἴσον) with the Father. Hence also the emphatic ἐγώ which parallels ὁ πατήρ μου. Hence also the two identical verbs: "he works — I work." The entire reply of Jesus centers in this equality of his as the Son with the Father.

The sense of this reply is so plain that the Jews could not and did not miss it. Do these Jews mean to accuse the Father, the very author and giver of the law, who, as every child knows, keeps on working (durative present tense) till this very day, stopping for no Sabbaths? Are they making God a lawbreaker? Well, Jesus says, this is my Father, I am his Son, we are equal. I work exactly as he does (again durative present). The point is that it is unthinkable that the Father and the Son or either of them, the very givers of the law, should ever break the law. When thus the Jews, as they do, charge Jesus with breaking the law, something must be radically wrong with their charge.

18) **On this account, therefore, the Jews were seeking the more to kill him, because he not only was breaking the Sabbath but was also calling God his own Father, making himself equal with God.** This verse is built exactly like v. 16, "On this account . . . because," etc. But v. 18 is a strong advance upon v. 16. The cause is greater, also the resultant effect. Jesus' word of defense and justification made matters much worse. In v. 16 the Jews charge only that Jesus was doing certain wrong things on the Sabbath; now they charge that he is breaking the Sabbath, ἔλυε, dissolving and annulling it, the imperfect meaning that he is making this his business, R. 884, not only by what he is doing on the Sabbath but by his entire claim. And not only is he busy destroying the Sabbath but on top of that he is calling (ἔλεγε, the same iterative imperfect) God his own

Father, which these Jews define as "making himself equal with God." This definition of what the Jews understood Jesus to mean by pointedly calling God "my Father" removes all doubt on the subject. All who claim that Jesus never called himself the Son of God, equal with the Father, must reject this entire Gospel as a piece of falsification. If Jesus did not mean what the Jews here understood him to say and to mean, Jesus should and could and would have said, "But this is not what I mean." Instead Jesus accepts this as being in reality his meaning. He does this not once but again and again until his final trial and even on his cross. And that is the very reason why John records this altercation with the Jews. It embodies another clear and decisive attestation of Jesus regarding who he really is.

As it is with the cause, so it is with the result. While v. 16 has the more indefinite ἐδίωκον, "they were persecuting him," we now have μᾶλλον ἐζήτουν ἀποκτεῖναι, "they were the more seeking to kill him." What is only implied in v. 16 now comes out boldly; for μᾶλλον = *magis* not *potius*. The Jews are not seeking to kill *rather than* to persecute; but are seeking to kill *even more* than they sought this before. So early the fatal issue was drawn.

In this first summary reply to the Jews Father and Son are simply placed side by side as Father and as Son. Both work, yet neither breaks the Sabbath law by so doing. When Jesus adds in regard to the Father that he works "till now" this is to make plain that the Father's work since the creation is referred to, including all the Sabbaths even to the present day; of course, no such explanatory modifier is needed when Jesus speaks of his own working. In both instances Jesus uses the unmodified verb: the Father "works" — "I work." The statement is unrestricted:

take any and every work of either Father or Son, none break the Sabbath. We have no right to limit the Father's working to his work of grace only and to justify that limitation by pointing to Jesus whose office was this work of grace. Jesus does not say: the Father and I in this work of grace do not transgress the Sabbath. The Sabbath law was, indeed, temporary (Col. 2:16, 17), but we should misunderstand Jesus if we supposed that he already abrogated, at least for himself, the divine regulations of the Sabbath law as God had given them to Israel. He does not mean that the Father and the Son are superior to this old Sabbath law, since both are God, or that he (Jesus) is free to disregard its regulations. The fact is the contrary. As the Messiah Jesus was put under the law and in his entire life and during his entire office fulfilled every jot and tittle of the law, including all the divine Sabbath regulations. Only confusion results when we bring in the Christian Sunday and when we make Jesus live according to this instead of according to the Jewish Sabbath. The entire contention of Jesus was intended to uphold the divine Sabbath law in its full integrity against the Pharisaic traditions with their vain and empty regulations which smothered even the spirit and utterly defeated the very purpose of God's Sabbath law. As the Son of God Jesus could and would not bow to these traditions or to any others the Pharisees had foisted upon the law. These "commandments of men" would make the Son, who worked only in harmony with the Father, being one with him, a slave (δοῦλος) of arrogant, blinded, perverted men. His Sonship, his Messiahship, his entire office by their very nature made Jesus challenge this attempt to make him bow as a slave to these wretched commandments. As the Father repudiated them, so did Jesus, the Father's Son.

The Attestation Regarding the Person and the Work of Jesus before the Hostile Jews in Jerusalem, 5:19-47. — The contention that Jesus appeared at this feast in Jerusalem only in the capacity of a private pilgrim cannot be correct, for no private pilgrim would work such a miracle and order the man upon whom it was wrought to carry his bed home in the most public manner on the Sabbath day. This also disposes of the contention that on this visit Jesus appeared without his disciples. They are not mentioned in chapter five, because John has no occasion to mention them. Neither in 2:13 nor in 7:10 are the disciples mentioned, yet in 2:17 we incidentally learn that they were present. Neither in chapter seven nor in chapter eight do the disciples play a part, and hence again John makes no mention of them. John writes of the miracle in our chapter as though he were an eyewitness, and he with the other disciples heard the words of Jesus' defense with their own ears.

Was the discourse of v. 19-47 uttered in one stretch, without interruption, or is it pieced together and made one by John? The more one reads this discourse, the more the impression deepens that it was spoken as it stands. The thought is closely knit together, and the force of the discourse depends on this continuity and this close coherence. The brief reply in v. 17 reads like a thesis, of which v. 19-47 are the elaboration. This creates the impression that the discourse followed the thesis, perhaps after only a very brief interval. Just as in v. 17 time, place, and other circumstances are omitted as being wholly immaterial, so here in v. 19. All we know and need to know is that **Jesus, therefore, answered and said unto them,** the hostile Jews, what now follows. The two verbs (see 1:48) mark the gravity of what follows, but here the first is the aorist middle instead of the more frequent aorist passive, the sense being the same, R. 818.

The thesis of v. 17 contains two points, and the discourse elaborates these: 1) regarding *the person and the work* of Jesus, v. 19-29; 2) regarding *the testimony* he bore concerning himself, v. 30-47.

19) **Amen, amen, I say unto you** (see 3:3) **the Son can do nothing of himself, except what he sees the Father doing; for what things that One does, these also the Son does in like manner.** The double seal of verity, "Amen, amen," is combined with the voice of authority, "I say to you." Compare 1:51. It is absolutely impossible that Jesus should ever break the law, including that of the Sabbath. It is absolutely impossible just because he is the Son, from eternity one with the Father and now the incarnate Son, come to earth to carry out absolutely nothing but the Father's will. If the Son, then, be charged by the Jews with breaking the Sabbath law, the charge would strike the Father himself. He is, indeed, "the Son," this Jesus who stands before the Jews in human flesh. The Jews were perfectly right when in v. 18 they understood that Jesus made himself "equal with God." This very relation of the Son to the Father makes it simply impossible (οὐ δύναται) that Jesus should do (ποιεῖν, now or ever) anything "of himself," ἀφ' ἑαυτοῦ, so that the thing would emanate from him alone and be done by him alone, separate and apart from the Father and thus deviating from and contradictory to the Father's will — even as the Jews charged that Jesus was breaking God's Sabbath law. Such a thing is possible for men; even Moses thus did a thing "of himself" (Num. 20:11, 12): but in the case of the Son, since he is the Son, this is absolutely excluded.

Over against this negative Jesus sets the opposite affirmative, "except what he sees (or: shall see) the Father doing," the participle ποιοῦντα after the verb of seeing. The sense is not that the Son merely *can* do this, as though he might still omit his doing. For the γάρ clause at once shuts that thought out, "for what things that One does, these also the Son does in like manner." In ἄν we merely have ἐάν, R. 190, 1018, John alone using the shorter form. The demonstrative ἐκεῖνος is strongly emphatic, "that One," i. e., the Father, R. 708. Moreover, καί is to be construed with ταῦτα, "these also," in the sense of "precisely these," R. 1181; not, "the Son also" (R. V.). Jesus even adds "in like manner": *the things* both do are identical and *the manner* of the doing by both is identical. These tenses are present throughout; they state principles inherent in this relation of the Father and the Son, enduring and without exception. Since these two are Father and Son they also continue in intimate communion: the Son constantly "sees" the Father and what the Father "is doing." This is predicated of the Son, not for the reason that he is inferior to the Father as the Son, but because it was he who assumed the redemptive mission, because it was he who was executing that mission in the incarnate state. As the Son in human flesh thus engaged in his mission his eyes were ever upon his Father, and no man will ever fathom the real inwardness of this seeing on the Son's part. Thus, however, Jesus asserts not only that he as the Son does what the Father does, all that and only that, but also that all he thus does, he does as if the Father himself does it, for it is all and in every way the Father's will and work.

In spite of the perfect simplicity and lucidity of Jesus' words their sense is often darkened or misunderstood. Jesus asserts an impossibility (οὐ δύναται, the negative even being re-enforced in οὐδέν), one

based on the very nature of this Father and this
Son. Yet some interpreters tell us that the Son might
have done something "of himself," but his love and
his obedience held him in check. We, however, believe
what Jesus says. Also, the word of Jesus is misunderstood when it is refered to the divine *concursus* of
providence, the dependence of the man Jesus as a
creature on his Creator and Preserver. Thus, we are
told, the Jews were wrong, Jesus never meant to make
himself "equal with God" and corrects this view in
v. 19 as a serious misunderstanding. The fact that
he twice calls himself "the Son" and twice refers to
"the Father" (once with the emphatic ἐκεῖνος) is
brushed aside. For the perfect union and communion
of the Father and the Son because of their equal divine
nature the creature dependence of Jesus is substituted,
the inferiority of his nature as compared with that of
his Father. Thus, we are told, Jesus only imitates
the Father, copies a superior model, moved only by his
love and obedience. We, however, still believe just
what Jesus says.

20) Jesus draws the curtain aside still farther.
**For the Father has affection for the Son and shows
him all things that he does.** One in essence, Father
and Son are naturally bound together also in affection, and this explains still further what Jesus has
said (γάρ). Here Jesus uses φιλεῖν, the love of affection,
whereas in 3:35 he uses ἀγαπᾶν, the love of full comprehension and purpose. This does not imply that the
former here denies the latter, which it does not do,
but that the former harmonizes better with the relation of the two equal persons and their consequent
affectionate intercourse. In v. 19, "what he may (or
shall) do," might refer only to some things the Father
does; here we learn that the Father shows the Son
"all things that he does," πάντα, without restriction,
which, as a matter of course, includes all that per-

tains to our redemption. The verb "shows" corresponds with the verb "sees" in v. 19. The communication between these divine Persons is perfect and complete in every way. "Shows" and "sees," because the Son is incarnate and in his humiliation on his redemptive mission. In the last clause αὐτός merely marks the fact that the Father is intended as the subject, otherwise it might be regarded as the Son. Note the undetermined present tenses: "has affection" — "does" — "shows," always, ever. The very action of Jesus in saying these things to the Jews is a reflex of the Father's will and act.

The general statement is made more specific: **and greater works than these will he show him, in order that you may marvel.** We must not miss the implication regarding the works Jesus has already done, including the healing on the Sabbath and the healed man's carrying his bed, that these were done by Jesus not "of himself" and apart from the Father but altogether in union with the Father. These were certainly great works, at which the Jews might well marvel. But these Jews are to know that for the Father and the Son, namely Jesus, these great works are only a beginning. Prophets, too, have wrought miracles and yet were only men. Jesus is infinitely greater — he is the Son. Hence in the days to come (δείξει, future) the Father will show him "greater works," which shall, indeed, reveal Jesus as the Son. "Will show" means far more than "let him see," for Jesus knows and thus already sees these works; he even enumerates them to the Jews. "Will show" implies that when the time comes, the Father will execute these works through Jesus, his Son. These greater works are the raising of the spiritually dead, the final raising of the bodily dead, and the last judgment. They are "greater" because they are fuller and loftier manifestations of the same power that displayed itself in the incidental miracles. The future tense "will show" must not be pressed as though no spiritual vivification had as yet taken place, for some had already been reborn; the tense refers to the mass of believers yet to follow before the day of resurrection and judgment. On and after the day of Pentecost, before the very eyes of these Jews, literally thousands obtained the new life.

"That you may marvel" is the intention of the Father and of Jesus. Note the emphatic ὑμεῖς, which means: people like *you*, unbelievers. These greater works are marvelous also to the disciples, but in their case the marveling is filled with faith, and in their case this faith is mentioned as the essential thing. This is true already with reference to the miracles, 2:11 for instance, and 20:31. In the case of the Jews and in the case of all unbelievers it will be empty marveling alone. They will not know what to make of these works, they will be astonished and finally overwhelmed by their progress and their power. The final exhibition of this marveling Paul describes when he tells us that at the name of Jesus every knee shall at last bow, Phil. 2:9 and 11.

21) With γάρ Jesus exemplifies and begins to describe the greater works, the μείζονα ἔργα which are parts of the one great ἔργον of Jesus as our Redeemer. They furnish the details for the refutation of the Jewish charges. So mighty is each detail that the accusers should have become terrified because they had called Jesus a lawbreaker and should have fled in consternation. But the doom of unbelief is the wicked and presumptuous blindness which leads men to war against a gracious and an almighty God to the last. **For just as the Father raises the dead and quickens them, thus also the Son quickens whom he wills.** Verses 21-25 describe the raising and the quickening of the spiritually dead. Here Jesus does

not include the raising of the bodily dead, Lazarus and others, and all the dead of the last day; and still less does Jesus here speak only of the bodily resurrection at the last day. The raising of the three dead persons were miracles and thus belong only to the great not to the greater works. The final raising of all the dead at the last day is described in v. 28 in connection with the final judgment.

Note how v. 21 parallels the Father's and the Son's work just as v. 17 had done, save that in v. 21 "just as . . . thus also" formally emphasizes the parallel actions. The equality of the work evidences the equality of the Persons. The raising and the quickening are two sides of *one* work, the one negative, the other positive; for where death is removed, life is assuredly bestowed. It is impossible to regard these as two works: first, bodily raising; secondly, spiritual quickening. For both verbs have the identical object "the dead," which cannot be divided so as once to refer to the bodily dead and then to the spiritually dead. All the present tenses used in this verse have the same meaning; they refer to these acts as being in continuous progress. We cannot refer one or the other of these equal tenses to a peculiar time. In other words, all the spiritual raising and quickening that has ever taken place (from the beginning onward), takes place now, or ever will take place, is equally the work of the Father and the Son; and we may add from the following: because they are wrought by the Father through the Son.

Only the one verb "quickens" is used in the clause with reference to the Son, to avoid a pedantic repetition of the two in the first clause. The addition "whom he wills" does not intend to mark a difference between the Father and the Son, for the Father certainly raises and quickens also only those whom he wills; and the will of Father and of Son is identical. This is the

gracious and saving will, revealed in a large number
of passages of Scripture, among which 3:16 stands
out prominently, look also at 5:24. Neither here
nor anywhere in the Scriptures are we told of a
secret, mysterious, absolute will, which governs the
bestowal of life and salvation. "Whom he will" cannot imply that in some case the Son might will contrary to the Father; their very relation excludes that
idea. The clause is added to bring out the supreme
greatness of the Son. That, too, is why Jesus here
calls himself simply "the Son," for the act here predicated of him is not restricted to the time since his
incarnation. Yet all the quickening both by the Father
and the Son is possible only because it is made so by
the redemptive work of the incarnate Son.

22) This second γάρ exemplifies still further; it
parallels the other in v. 21. Here is a second greater
work. Yet it naturally goes together with the first;
it is the outcome of the other. Since the Son quickens
whom he will, how about those unquickened? They,
too, are committed to the Son. Both quickening and
judging are in his hands. How the latter is involved
in the former Jesus explains in 3:17, etc. Jesus could
have said, "Just as the Father judges, thus also the
Son judges"; even as he could have said, "The Father
quickens no one but has given all quickening to the
Son." Jesus first simply parallels Father and Son, as
if to say: Mark that they are of equal dignity; and
then, secondly, he unites Father and Son as if to
say: Mark how they work together, the Father
through the Son. **For neither does the Father judge
anyone but has given all judgment to the Son.** The
Greek doubles and strengthens the negative, as in
v. 19. The fact that the Father judges no one does
not mean that, while the Father quickens, he does
not judge, or that the Son alone without the Father
and apart from him does the judging. This would

contradict the statement that the Son does nothing of himself, v. 19. The Father's giving the judgment to the Son shows that it is, indeed, the Father's. But he exercises it by giving it to the Son, "all judgment," the preliminary judgments in time and the final judgment at the end of time.

In order to understand the work of judging we must first understand the work of quickening. Both involve the incarnation and the work of redemption by the incarnate Son. In v. 21, where the Father and the Son are only set side by side as both quickening, no reference to the incarnation appears. In v. 22 a veiled reference is added, namely in the verb δέδωκε, "has given." The fact that this giving applies to the human nature of the incarnate Son is fully brought out in v. 27. All the greater works here mentioned by Jesus belong equally to the three equal divine Persons and in that sense are not given or received by one Person. And yet the Son alone became incarnate and performed the redemptive mission. It is thus that the Son takes from the Father the works that go with his mission. Thus the perfect tense δέδωκε reaches back into eternity but rests on the incarnation and the mission of the Son and, of course, carries with it the implication for the present: the one act constantly stands as such. As in 3:17-19, Jesus uses the *vox media,* κρίνειν, likewise κρίσις, which does not intimate whether the verdict is acquittal or condemnation. This the context decides. Because, as in the present case, the spiritually dead are referred to, "to judge" and "the judgment" refer to condemnation. The quickened do not come into this judgment.

23) First, the equality of the Persons, secondly, the equality of the works, and now, thirdly, the equality of the honor and this expressed strongly with a positive and a negative statement. **In order that all**

may honor the Son even as they honor the Father. He that honors not the Son honors not the Father that sent him. Why this is and must ever be the Father's purpose lies on the surface: the Father would deny himself if he had a lesser purpose regarding the Son. His very truth demands that where the Persons and the work are equal, the honor must be likewise. But note that this is the Father's gracious purpose, desiring that men by thus honoring the Son receive that Son's salvation. Hence Jesus does not here say, "that all *must* honor the Son." So little did the Jews misunderstand Jesus in regard to his claim to be equal with God (v. 18), so little does Jesus disavow claiming this equality (v. 19), that here in the clause, "even as they honor the Father," he asserts that equality in the clearest possible manner. Recall Isa. 42:8: "I am the Lord: that is my name: and my glory will I not give to another (a creature), neither my praise to graven images." This honor is constantly due to the Son, hence the durative present τιμῶσι, was due even then as the Son stood before those Jews in the flesh of his human nature.

Now the mighty warning in the negative statement, more forceful because it is without a connective, "He that honors not the Son honors not the Father that sent him." The negative μή with the participle needs no explanation, R. 1137, it is the regular usage. Jesus does not say, "he that *dishonors* the Son," but, "he that *honors not*," which is stronger. What is meant v. 24 shows: refusal to hear and to believe the Son. Merely to disregard or to ignore the Son is fatal. What, then, does it involve, like these Jews, to accuse the Son, to persecute, to seek to kill him? This word applies to all the followers of those Jews down to the present day. They thought that they were honoring God by contending for God's Sabbath law against God's Son and were thereby robbing God of all honor. So men today talk of "God," "the Father," "the Great Architect of the Universe," or whatever other name they use, and set aside the Son and thus rob God of all true honor. Every religious profession and practice, whether by individuals or by organizations, that does not honor the Son, our Redeemer and our Judge, has its sentence of condemnation here recorded. The attributive participle modifier: the Father "that sent him," brings out the vital point with which God is concerned and with which all men ought to be equally concerned: the saving mission and work of the Son incarnate. See 3:17 and note how often in the following utterances of Jesus he refers to "my Sender." Others, too, are sent both by the Father and by the Son but none is like the Son (1:18), very God himself, the actual fountain of salvation, through whom alone we can come to the Father (14:6), in whom alone we see and have the Father (14:9-11).

24) With the same assurance of verity and authority with which Jesus began in v. 19 he now explains what he means by saying that "he quickens whom he wills." For the figure of quickening he now uses literal terms, and the mystery of "whom he wills" is made plain by describing the persons: "he that hears and believes." **Amen, amen, I say to you, He that hears my word and believes him that sent me has life eternal and comes not into judgment but has passed out of the death into the life.** Jesus "quickens whom he wills" means that he gives life eternal to everyone that hears and believes his Word. This Word he utters and sends out, and it comes to men as the bearer of life, Rom. 1:16. The Word itself causes the hearing — men's ears perceive its invitation, offer, gift, and blessing. The more they hear, the more they perceive. As the Word impels men to hear, so it impels them to trust (πιστεύειν) as

its message is made more and more clear. The very nature of what the Word offers induces trust to appropriate that offer. The normal and natural effect of the hearing is to trust. The Word is not only itself absolutely trustworthy, it is full of efficacious power to implant truth in the heart. That trust, when wrought, is always the product of the Word not of any goodness or ability in the hearer. Yet it never works irresistibly. Man can exert his depraved will in such an abnormal way as to prevent the faith-producing power from accomplishing its purpose. Those who do this are not quickened.

The hearing and the believing go together. They are always correlatives of the Word, i. e., the latter is intended for the very purpose of being heard and believed. And these are personal acts, hence the singular, so personal that Jesus combines person and act: ὁ ἀκούων καὶ πιστεύων, "the one hearing and believing." Jesus does not say: the one believing "my Word," but: believing "him that sent me." This really states the contents of the Word, which is all about the Father sending the Son for our redemption. To trust that Sender is to trust the Word that reveals and brings him to our hearts. Jesus here uses this summary of the Word because of the accusations of the Jews which he is refuting, and by this summary he again points to his relation to the Father, which the Jews refused to admit. The key word is ὁ πέμψας με. To this day Jesus proclaims that the Father sent him; and on this Word, on the Father so having sent the Son, and on the Son so sent by the Father our faith rests.

He that hears and believes "has life eternal" (see 3:15), ζωὴ αἰώνιος, the very life itself that flows from God, is grounded in God, joins to God, leads to God (10:28). The moment one has this life he is quickened, or made alive, or reborn (3:5). Temporal

death only leads him into a fuller measure of this
life. The present tenses ἔχει and οὐκ ἔρχεται may be considered gnomic or prophetic, R. 897-8, being used regarding constant truths, irrespective of time; as such,
however, they include the immediate blessed possession of this true, spiritual, heavenly life that goes on
endlessly into eternity. The obverse is that the believer, who has this life, "comes not into judgment"
(elucidated in 3:18). Since ζωοποιεῖν and κρίνειν, both
committed to the Son Jesus, are opposites, where the
one is effected, the other is shut out. As one of God's
children, how can the believer be judged now or at
any time? No adverse sentence can ever be passed
upon him.

This is made more vivid by the statement, "but
has passed from the death into the life," the perfect
tense meaning that once having gone from the one
to the other he remains where he is, I John 3:14.
Whereas Jesus speaks of "the dead" in v. 21 he now
speaks of "the death," and the article points to the
specific death here meant, namely spiritual death that
ends in eternal death, the opposite of "the life," again
the article and again the specific life here referred
to, namely spiritual life that ends in eternal blessedness.

In saying these things Jesus utters the most
effective call to faith in the ears of the hostile Jews.
In every word the gift of life was knocking at the
hearts of his hearers, trying to break the bonds of
their death; but they held to death and wilfully rejected the gracious gift of life.

25) Once more and with cumulative effect the
voice of verity and authority rings out: **Amen,
amen, I say to you, The hour is coming and is now
when the dead shall hear the voice of the Son of
God; and those that did hear shall live.** In v. 21
everything is compressed into the brief term that the

Son "quickens." In v. 24 this is expanded by adding
the fact that life is received by means of "my Word"
heard and believed. In v. 25 this is expanded still
farther by stating that the hour for this coming to
spiritual life "is now" already. That is why the
words, "The hour is coming and now is," are emphatically forward; compare for the same expression and
in the same sense 4:23. The time referred to is that
of the New Testament era (ὥρα in the broad sense),
which, as Jesus speaks, still "is coming," since the
work of redemption is not yet complete and which
yet "now is," since Jesus is here and his saving Word
at this very moment rings in men's ears. It is thus
impossible to refer these words to the last day and
to interpret them with reference to the resurrection
at that day. The Jews to whom Jesus is speaking need
not wait till a later time, the hour to escape from
death is now right here.

Again Jesus describes the quickening. In v. 21
it is the fact that the Son "makes alive," ζωοποιεῖ, he
bestows life on the dead. In v. 24 it is the fact that
the believer *has life*, ἔχει ζωὴν αἰώνιον. Now it is the
fact that the believers *shall live,* namely on and on
to eternity. But now the figure is intensified into a
spiritual resurrection. The preparation for this is
the reference to "the death" in v. 24; to go "out of
the death into the life" means a resurrection and
no less. Thus οἱ νεκροί (plural of the category), the
spiritually dead, lie lifeless. Then there sounds "the
voice of the Son of God," identical with "my Word"
in v. 24. Note the correspondence in the terms:
"my" (subjective, personal) "Word" (objective);
"the voice" (subjective, personal) of the Son of God
(objective, because in the third person). In the
objective "Word" speaks the personal "voice" as one
stands before another and speaks to him. "My"
Word, i. e., that of Jesus in his humiliation, whom

the Jews had before their eyes; but this is no less a person than "the Son of God." Note the weight of the article τοῦ υἱοῦ, R. 781. A resurrection is to take place, and this only *the* Son of God, who as *the* Son is equal with the Father, can effect. In this entire discourse Jesus again and again calls himself "the Son" and now he calls himself "the Son of God." The modernistic claim that he never so called himself is maintained only by eliminating this and all other testimony of Jesus and of the Scriptures in general to the identity of his Person.

Twice Jesus mentions the hearing of his voice in his Word, using first the middle then the active of ἀκούειν, however with no difference of meaning in the forms, R. 356. Jesus means effective hearing, such as actually reaches the heart. In v. 24 this is expressed by two participles: "he that hears and believes." The fact that some close their hearts and refuse the hearing of faith is omitted, enough having been intimated regarding these in v. 22, 23. The future "shall hear" refers to the coming hour, although it includes also all the hearing from the present moment onward ("and now is"). The instant of the hearing is the instant of the awakening of the sleeping dead. Hearing, they awake; awaking, they hear. "Shall hear" and "they that did hear" do not denote two kinds of hearing, the one hearing only outwardly with the ears, the other inwardly with the heart. Both denote the identical act of hearing: first, this act as it follows the Son's voice (future tense), then, this act as it is followed by their living (aorist participle). The voice produces the hearing, the hearing produces the life.

The article in οἱ ἀκούσαντες is vital, "the ones that did hear," for this changes the subject, which is vital to the sense of what Jesus here says. "The dead shall hear" — "they that did hear shall live." This change of subjects focuses everything on the hearing, even on the first instant of hearing. If the article is omitted, Jesus would say, "The dead shall hear" — "after hearing they (the dead) shall live." This separates the hearing from the living and nobody would know by how long an interval: first the dead would hear, then at some time after the hearing they would live. No; the dead, the very instant they shall hear, in that instant become οἱ ἀκούσαντες, "they that did hear," and from that instant onward "they shall live." Thus the Son "makes them live" (v. 21), and each of them "has life eternal" (v. 24). The verb ζῆν cannot here mean merely *aufleben*, "come to life," but must mean "to live," i. e., ἔχειν τὴν ζωὴν αἰώνιον, v. 24. The figure of death, however, must not be pressed by bringing in omnipotence for the Son's voice, for this would result in an omnipotent and irresistible grace, which is contrary to all Scripture teaching. We must abide by the *tertium comparationis:* the dead cannot bring themselves to life, the Son alone can and does give them life; and this he does by his Word and the voice of gospel grace. The spiritually dead may resist that grace; many do. We know of no omnipotence that man is able to resist.

26) From the work Jesus reverts to the Worker. Everything depends on who he really is. "For" gives the reason why Jesus is able to do this work. This is not the evidential reason; for that would be the accomplished work itself, proving by his having done the work that he could indeed do it. This is the causal reason: Jesus, being what he is, can do what he says. **For as the Father has life in himself, thus also he gave to the Son to have life in himself.** The one fountain of life thus flows in one stream from the Father and the Son. We must remember that this is not a truth uttered in general but a refutation of the charge of the Jews that Jesus made himself equal

with God. The Jews certainly agreed that God the Father "has life in himself," i. e., not derived from or dependent on, another. They would equally agree that God the Son "has life in himself" in the same way. To explain to these Jews the relation of God the Father and God the Son in the matter of both alike having life, each in himself, would thus be utterly pointless. This already shuts out the interpretation that ἔδωκε, "he did give," refers to the eternal generation of the Son and a gift involved in that generation. This idea is again shut out by the same aorist ἔδωκε in v. 28. Both times "he did give" is the historical aorist. Both verbs refer to the incarnate Son, to a giving for his mission and work. When Jesus says that this gift was made "to the Son," he once more uses "the Son" to assert to the Jews that he, Jesus, is actually "the Son of God." After explaining at length his work of making the spiritually dead alive with a life that is eternal, of doing this by "my Word," the very Word the Jews were now hearing from his human lips, Jesus now adds the explanatory reason (γάρ) why this Word thus sounding in the ears of the Jews does, indeed, bestow life as he says. It is because of the Father's gift, made when he sent his own Son on this mission to redeem and to quicken. "He did give" thus refers to the Son in his human nature, joined as it was to the divine. The great mission of the Son was carried out through that Son's human nature. In itself this nature never "has life in itself"; in Jesus it received this gift from the Father, the Sender of Jesus. Thus Jesus sets before the Jews the answer to the question how he, being man, does, indeed, not only as the Son but equally as man, not only by one nature but by both indissolubly united in his Person, bestow life eternal.

27) And now again Jesus reverts to the other side (as in v. 22), for some reject this life. **And he gave him authority to execute the judgment, because he is man's son.** Those who obdurately remain in spiritual death the Father has not reserved for himself, he has placed them, too, in the hands of Jesus, the incarnate Son (v. 22). The two ἔδωκε go together. The second is only the negative side of the first. It is the same throughout: to believe — not to believe; to honor the Son — to dishonor him; to receive life — to reject life. Thus the Son has life in himself to bestow of himself on all who hear and believe — and authority to judge all who remain in their death.

We must note that the antecedent of αὐτῷ is "the Son" in v. 26; so that we may read, "He did give *to the Son power* to execute the judgment," literally, "*Power* did he give," etc., with the emphasis on "power." The present tense ποιεῖν refers to all judgment throughout time and on the last day; if the latter only were meant, we should have the aorist infinitive. And now Jesus adds what he left unsaid in v. 26 but what applies equally there, the statement that this act of giving on the Father's part refers to the human nature of the Son, "because he (the Son) is man's son." In υἱὸς ἀνθρώπου neither noun has the article. This designation is not equivalent to ὁ υἱὸς τοῦ ἀνθρώπου, "the Son of man," which Jesus constantly used as a title when referring to himself. Compare on this title the remarks on 1:51. The Son was born man (1:14), the son of a human being, ἀνθρώπου (not denoting sex) not ἀνδρός (which denotes a male). True, the Virgin birth is here not specifically predicated, because ἄνθρωπος may refer to either sex; and yet it is predicated, because Jesus speaks this word only with reference to his mother. What he tells the Jews is that only in one way, by a gift from the

Father, could he as man receive the ἐξουσία, the right
and the power, to act as the judge. And this only
he, the Son, could receive for *his* human nature,
joined as it was to the divine in personal union. No
other "man's son" could possibly be made the recipient of such a gift as the power to judge. So
great is this gift that any mere man would be
crushed by it.

Among the untenable interpretations are the following: "man's son" = "the Son of man"; the hidden
God cannot judge, hence he had to select a man (a
gnostic idea; the Jews always knew God as the judge);
judging came as a reward to Jesus for his redemptive work; ἐξουσία = only the *right* not also the
power.

28) Jesus now states how he will exercise the
right to judge. Thus he names and describes another
of the greater works. **Stop marvelling at this; for
the hour is coming, in which all in their tombs shall
hear his voice and shall come out, they that did do
the good things unto resurrection of life, but they
that did practice the worthless things unto resurrection of judgment.** The present imperative with μή
forbids what one is alreay doing, hence we translate,
"Stop marvelling!" R. 890, i. e., at what Jesus has
just said (τοῦτο refers to v. 24-27). In 3:7 the aorist
forbids Nicodemus to begin marvelling. People such
as the unbelieving Jews are indeed to marvel; it is
God's intention. When Jesus here tells the Jews to
stop this marvelling, this, like all that he says to them,
is his call to cease their unbelief, to grasp and to believe the truth of what he says. Hence also Jesus
states the great reason why these Jews should stop
marvelling and begin believing: lest at the judgment
they be found among those that practiced the worthless things.

As v. 25, 26 repeat and amplify v. 24 regarding the subject of life, so v. 28, 29 repeat and amplify v. 27 regarding the subject of judgment. Verse 25 and v. 28 are parallels also because both have the statement regarding the time, "the hour is coming." Yet the difference is marked, for in v. 28 Jesus cannot add, "and now is." Spiritual quickening starts now and will spread over the world when redemption is once wrought, but the universal judgment comes at the end of time. Yet "is coming" means that now, with Jesus here and redemption at hand, nothing else intervenes between this present and the final judgment day. The word ὥρα is again used in the broad sense. In what Jesus tells the Jews about this hour he states only what they themselves believed about the resurrection and the judgment (Dan. 12:2, and back to Abraham, Heb. 11:19). The only point he adds is that he connects all this with himself, the Son of God and man's son. That these Jews are most assuredly to know, they who now have the very judge before them and are seeking to destroy him.

Note the important and decisive πάντες, "all," and the attributive phrase, beyond question made such by the article, "all in their tombs," i. e., all the bodily dead. With intentional similarity to v. 25 Jesus says that these too "shall hear his voice," Jesus' voice, that of God's Son and man's son. Now the voice of grace sounds forth in Jesus' Word; spiritually dead hear it and are made spiritually alive. Then the voice of omnipotence will sound in the last trump, and all the bodily dead shall hear it, for that voice comes with resistless power, "and shall come out" of their graves, raised, all of them, from bodily death, their bodies once more being joined to their souls. This statement of Jesus' is the foundation for *one* resurrection, and that occurring at the last day. In Rev. 20:6 "the first resurrection" uses "resurrection" symbolically with reference to "soul" (v. 4). The transfer of these "souls" into heaven is called "the first resurrection." Nothing is said in Rev. 20 about "the second resurrection," but the implication is that the final transfer of the bodies of these blessed "souls" into heaven constitutes "the second resurrection." So little can Rev. 20 refer to *two bodily* resurrections that it does not even refer to one; for Rev. 20 does not imply that bodies come from graves but that bodies are transferred to heavenly glory, as their souls were previously transferred to that glory. In John 5:28 only preconception can split into two parts the one word, "All in their tombs shall hear his voice and come out," i, e., on the instant when that voice sounds.

29) But "all," thus coming out in one moment, shall appear as two classes: "they that did the good things" — "they that did practice the worthless things," the substantivized participles exactly as in 3:20 and 21, save that now they are plurals. On the difference between οἱ ποιήσαντες with reference to the believers and οἱ πράξαντες with reference to the unbelievers see 3:20, 21; also for the distinctive meaning of τὰ φαῦλα, "the worthless things," which are here set overagainst τὰ ἀγαθά, "the good things" in the sense of excellent and thus valuable. The aorist tenses of the participles sum up the entire life of each class. For the one class it is, "they did do the excellent things"; for the other, "they did practice the worthless things." The one class is marked by the good works that spring from faith; the other by the worthless works that spring from unbelief. Each class of works is specific, hence the articles τὰ ἀγαθά and τὰ φαῦλα, i. e., the well-known works that God regards as excellent and prizes as valuable in us; the well-known works that God regards as worthless. Some

of the latter men prize highly, as the Pharisees do
their formal outward observances, as men's work-
righteous, humanitarian, philanthropic works today;
see Matt. 7:22, 23. The connection of the two classes
of works, the one with faith, the other with unbelief,
is furnished by the preceding statements on hearing,
believing, having life, and the opposites of these. We
may add that ποιεῖν, so distinctively used with reference to the believer's works, accords with the idea
of obedience to God, even as we always have this verb
with reference to the obedience of Jesus to his Father's
will; while πράσσειν lacks this connotation in these connections and accompanies actions that are self-chosen,
was einer selber treibt.

The actual judgment is here compressed into two
mighty phrases: "unto resurrection of life" — "unto
resurrection of judgment," keeping the two cardinal
terms in the two genitives. Both classes "come out
unto resurrection," their bodies being made alive by
being joined to their souls. In neither case has εἰς
ἀνάστασιν the article, though our versions add it. Its
absence stresses the quality of the noun: both classes
come out to what is truly and rightly called ἀνάστασις,
"resurrection." How R. 500 can call the two added
genitives objective is a puzzle. No transitive verbal
idea lies in the noun "resurrection"; even if it could
be inserted, neither "life" nor "judgment" could possibly be the object of the transitive action. These
genitives are qualitative; each describes and characterizes. The mark of the one resurrection is "life,"
of the other "judgment." Before they arise, the classes
are already so marked; in their earthly existence the
one obtained life through faith, the other remained
under judgment because of unbelief (3:18). What
Jesus here compresses into phrases he describes at
length in Matt. 25:31-46.

So little can Jesus be charged with breaking God's Sabbath law that he does all his work as God's Son in divine intimacy with his Father. This is the first part of his answer to the Jews.

They also assailed his testimony concerning himself, saying that he lied when he made himself equal with God. Thus the second part of the discourse deals with the testimony concerning Jesus. No less than nine times does Jesus in the first part of his answer repeat his own testimony that he is, indeed, the Son. This testimony is so true that it only re-echoes God's own double testimony, that of the works he gave Jesus to do, and that of the Scripture he gave to the Jews themselves.

Does the second part of the answer begin with v. 30 or with v. 31? It is attractive to think that Jesus closes the first part as he began it by saying, "I can do nothing of myself," compare v. 19. But it is equally attractive to have him begin the second part in the way in which he began the first. What seems to mislead some is the fact that in v. 31 Jesus still speaks of his judgment; hence they conclude that this still belongs to v. 27-29, where Jesus speaks of the final judgment. They overlook the force of the present tense, "I judge," and of the statement, "My judgment is righteous." They likewise overlook the fact that Jesus says, "As I hear," I judge. He speaks of his judgment concerning himself, i. e., of his testimony that he is, indeed, God's Son.

30) **I can do nothing of myself. As I hear, I judge; and my own judgment is right, because I seek not my own will but the will of him that did send me.** The pronoun ἐγώ is emphatic, for which v. 19 has "the Son." Compare the explanation of v. 19. Both the nature of Jesus as the Son and his mission as the incarnate Son absolutely shut out even the possibility that he should ever do (ποιεῖν, durative

present) anything "of myself," apart from and conflicting with the Father. But this fundamental statement is now applied to all the testimony of Jesus,
whereas in v. 19, etc., it was applied to all his deeds
and works. Hence, while in v. 19 Jesus speaks of
seeing what the Father shows him for his great mission in the line of works, he now speaks of *hearing*,
"As I hear, I judge." The present tenses mean now
or at any time. This, of course, includes also the
final judgment. But the clause, "as I hear," now
speaks of the judging of Jesus, not as a work, but as
a pronouncement, as a verdict of his lips. Not a
single word that Jesus utters in stating a judgment,
whether it be on men, believers or unbelievers, or on
matters or subjects of any kind, or on his own person
and work, ever deviates from, or clashes with, the word
of his Father. On the contrary, it only restates the
Father's word and judgment. And "as I hear" implies
that the Son Jesus is in constant and most intimate
communion with his Father. As little as Jesus could
deny his Sonship, as little as he could repudiate his
mission as the incarnate Son, so little could he utter
one word that might be in disharmony with his
Father's word and verdicts.

Jesus merely coordinates, "and my own judgment
is right," although the relation of thought is that this
being right is the consequence of Jesus' judging as
he hears. Jesus uses the emphatic pronoun: ἡ κρίσις
ἡ ἐμή, "this judgment of mine," whatever may be the
judgment of others, in particular the false judgment
of these Jews. "Right," δικαία = in perfect harmony
with the Father's norm of right (δίκη). The word is
chosen to match κρίσις and κρίνω; in a moment, when
the judgment is defined as testimony, we have the corresponding adjective "true."

Why the judgments of Jesus are always right is
now established ethically: "because I seek not my

own will but the will of him that did send me." In
every word and judgment Jesus utters he has only
one purpose: to carry out the great mission on which
his Sender sent him. "The will of him that did send
me" means, not the faculty of willing, but the content of the Father's will, *what* he wills. Exactly
that Jesus wills. "My own will," the pronoun being
emphatic, would be *something else*, determined by
Jesus himself in contravention of what his Sender
determined. Such a "will" does not exist. When the
Son entered on his mission, all that that mission should
include and effect was determined. When the Son became man, his human consciousness and will entered
perfectly into all that had thus been determined. Jesus
and his Sender were in constant communion: "as I
hear." No possibility existed that Jesus should ever
will anything of a different nature. "I seek," is a
pregnant expression for "I seek successfully," or "I
seek and carry out."

31) After the general statement that every judgment of Jesus accords with the will and the word of
his Sender, Jesus turns in particular to the word
which the Jews claimed to be false (v. 18), making
himself equal with God. **If I bear witness regarding myself, my witness is not true.** According to
R. 1018 this means, "If perchance I bear witness,"
and looks at the matter either as a present reality or
as a future possibility (we prefer: as something Jesus
expects to do). In 8:13 the Jews say the same thing:
when a man bears witness regarding himself, his witness is not true. In 8:14 Jesus contradicts this and
says that if he bears witness concerning himself, such
witness is, indeed, true. The contradiction is only
apparent. Legally a man's unsupported testimony
regarding himself or his own case cannot stand and
be accepted as true. Yet in fact, as 8:14 shows, Jesus'
witness concerning himself is true, for he knows

about himself, the Jews do not. The contrasts in
the two passages are different. In 5:31, etc., it is
Jesus, the Baptist, and the Father — their witness
agrees. In 8:13, etc., it is Jesus and the Jews — their
witness clashes. In the one case the appeal is to two
witnesses that are competent and must be accepted.
In the other case the appeal is from the incompetent
witnesses, who do not know, and whose attempt nevertheless to witness must be rejected. So here Jesus
accepts the common rule concerning testimony in a
man's own behalf. He says in substance, "I do not
ask you to take *my* word alone concerning who I
really am."

32) Hence also the sharp contrast: **It is another that bears witness concerning me; and I know
that the witness is true which he witnesses concerning me.** The emphasis is on ἄλλος and on ἀληθής.
Not for one moment does Jesus ask the Jews to accept
his own lone testimony in his own behalf. Then,
indeed, they might appeal to the common legal rule
stated. On the contrary, Jesus has the greatest and
most competent witness imaginable. When he adds,
"and I know that the witness is true," etc., the word
"true" must be taken in the same sense as in v. 31:
"true" legally, so as beyond question to stand as true
in any court of law. What Jesus says is that he is
offering the Jews a witness of whom *he knows* that
he is legally and in every other way competent. What
the Jews will say to this witness and his mighty testimony, whether they, too, will accept it as legally competent Jesus does not here intimate. If they do, well
and good; if they do not, they condemn themselves.
The reading "you know," οἴδατε, instead of "I know,"
οἶδα, is due to the misconception regarding the word
"true," which is so often taken to mean "true in
fact." This sense of the word would make Jesus by
his testimony establish the truth of this "other" wit-

ness to whom he appeals. By that implication Jesus would himself admit that the testimony of this "other" is after all insufficient. In fact, he would thus fall back on his own testimony. This, of course, is not and cannot be Jesus' meaning. To evade it the reading was changed. The explanations of the correct reading "I know," when these are combined with the wrong sense of the word "true" as meaning "true in fact," are labored and unsatisfactory.

33) Jesus speaks of "another" as his all-competent and legally irreproachable witness but does not at once name him or state his testimony. When introducing this "other" he declares that he is not the Baptist, valid· and valuable as the Baptist's testimony is. **You yourselves** (emphatic ὑμεῖς) **have sent** (a delegation, this the sense of the verb) **to John, and he has testified to the truth,** openly and without reservation. Jesus' hearers know what that "truth" is, for some of them had helped to send that delegation, and all of them knew what report that delegation brought back, 1:19-23, namely, that the Baptist declared that he was not the Messiah, but that another was, namely, one so great that the Baptist, mighty prophet that he was, was not worthy to untie his sandal latchets. That, indeed, was "the truth." The two perfect tenses "you have sent" and "he has testified" are the dramatic historical kind, presenting a vivid and realistic view of past acts, R. 897, as in effect still standing for the present moment.

34) Jesus might, indeed, appeal to this witness of the Baptist and in a way he does — not in his own personal interest but in the interest of these Jews, whom Jesus would yet, if possible, save. **But I on my part not from a man do I take the testimony; but I say this, in order that you on your part may be saved.** As ὑμεῖς in v. 33, so now both ἐγώ and ὑμεῖς are emphatic; and "I on my part" and "you on

your part" are in contrast. The Jews even dispatched
a delegation to the Baptist to get his testimony. Jesus
can afford to dispense with the Baptist's testimony,
great though it is, because he has "the testimony"
that is far greater than his. Grimm regards λαμβάνω
as here being equal to *capto*, "to snatch at"; Ebeling
as "seek to secure." Jesus, of course, "receives" or
"accepts" the Baptist's testimony. When he here says
that he does not "take" it, the verb means: take in
order to use it against his opponents. In other words,
Jesus, as the defendant facing these Jews as his
accusers, does not call on the Baptist to bring in the
decisive testimony (τὴν μαρτυρίαν, note the article).
Jesus' great witness is God himself.

But why, then, does he mention the Baptist at all?
"But I say this, in order that you on your part may
be saved." Though the Baptist was only "a man,"
though Jesus thus very properly excels the Baptist
by at once taking his greatest witness, namely the
Father, the Baptist's testimony should greatly impress
the Jews, for among them generally the Baptist was
deemed a great prophet who spoke by revelation from
God. Among the hostile hearers of Jesus some might
be found who, remembering what the Baptist said
regarding Jesus, might be aided by his true testimony to believe what he testified and thus to "be
saved" (on the verb see 3:17). Thus as ever when
Jesus deals with his enemies, he holds out salvation
to them.

35) How highly Jesus thought of the Baptist is
made plain in the testimony Jesus now gives him and
in the way in which he scores the Jews for the treatment they accorded him. **That one was the lamp
burning and shining; and you on your part willed
to exult for an hour in his light.** A λύχνος is a port-
able lamp, which, when lit, burns and *shines*. The
article means that the Baptist was "*the* lamp" intended

by God specifically for that generation. The two participles, added attributively by one article, denote only one action: "burning and thus shining." The entire figure describes the Baptist as showing the Jews the way to salvation in the Messiah who now was come. The Baptist was, indeed, "*the* lamp," not "*the* light," (1:9). Both tenses here used, he "was" and you "willed" or "did will," imply that the Baptist was now imprisoned. If the tragic news of this event had just become known, this reference to what the Baptist was to his generation would come with greater effect upon the authorities Jesus was facing. That burning and shining lamp had now been quenched forever.

So great was the Baptist in his short career, and how wretchedly had the Jews treated him! Again ὑμεῖς is emphatic, "you on your part," in contrast with ἐκεῖνος, "that one" and all that *he* was. Your will went only so far as "to exult" in his light, ἀγαλλιασθῆναι, the passive form in the middle sense (R. 334), i. e., to disport yourselves in his light for the time being πρὸς ὥραν (by position unemphatic), πρός with the accusative indicating extent of time. Instead of repenting and believing you only ran out to see and to hear the Baptist, delighted to have again after so long an interval the spectacle of a prophet in your midst. The aorist "you did will" implies that now it was all over and done with for the Jews. When Herod laid hands on the Baptist, no popular uprising took place, no violent indignation because of this outrage upon a prophet of God was voiced, no concerted effort was made to effect the Baptist's release. The Jews let Herod do with him as he pleased, and now their interest in the Baptist was gone.

36) Jesus now proceeds to present the witness on whose testimony he relies. **But I have the testimony that is greater than John's: for the works which the**

Father has given me, in order to complete them, the very works which I do, they testify concerning me that the Father has sent me. As in v. 34, the article τὴν μαρτυρίαν designates the decisive testimony, decisive legally and in every other way. When Jesus says "I have" this testimony, he means that he has it to bring it forward in any court and thus by presenting it to establish that, when he himself says he is God's Son, his statement is the truth. The addition of μείζω without the article is predicative and equal to a relative clause, R. 789; B.-D. 270, 1: the testimony "that is greater"; and the unmodified genitive τοῦ Ἰωάννου is a common case of breviloquence, as R. 1203 states, for: greater "than that of John"; and we should not say, with B.-D. 185, 1; R. 516, that it is not clear whether we should understand: greater "than as John had it," or: greater "than that given by John." The difference between μείζων and μείζω is only that in the former contraction of μείζονα the irrational ν is used, R. 220. This disposes of the contention that the former is masculine, the latter feminine (with τὴν μαρτυρίαν) ; and that we should read the former: "I . . . as one greater than John." This would also clash with the entire context in which the Father (not Jesus) is contrasted with the Baptist, and thus the Father's testimony with that of the Baptist.

This greater testimony is that of Jesus' works, meaning all his Messianic works, his miracles, his making spiritually alive, his final judgment. Some would exclude the latter, because these Jews cannot *now* see the work of judgment and because Jesus says ἃ ποιῶ, "which I am engaged in doing." But the latter is quite general, and we should not slip in a "now": "engaged in doing now." For Jesus also says: ἵνα τελειώσω αὐτά, "in order that I complete them," the aorist signifying: actually bring them to an end. This reaches even to the final judgment. Let us recall

2:19, etc. (compare the exposition), where the judgment forms the final and convincing sign for all obdurate unbelievers. These works, Jesus says, the Father "has given to me," and by this perfect tense he refers to the giving in his mission as the Messiah, a giving which stands indefinitely. This is not a constantly repeated giving, as some think, each miracle, as it were, a new gift. The giving was complete from the start, and, once made, stands thus. Compare "he gave" in v. 26 and again in v. 27, especially also the reference in this repeated verb to the human nature of the incarnate Son. How much the gift includes in the line of works the ἵνα clause states, which we may regard as an ordinary purpose clause, or, if we prefer, as a substitute for the infinitive, but then the infinitive of purpose; hence they are practically the same. And ἃ ποιῶ states that Jesus is now in the midst of these works. Here Jesus uses the plural "the works," spreading them out, as it were, in their great number, while in 4:34 (where also the same verb is used) "his work" compresses them into one great unit.

With strong emphasis Jesus says, "the very works that I do testify concerning me," each one and all together now as they are being done and ever after. They stand up as witnesses in any court that may be called and testify. And their united, unvarying testimony is "that the Father has sent me," the perfect tense stating that, once sent thus, Jesus is now on this his mission. By saying that he can do nothing of himself (v. 30), by adding that all his works are the Father's gift to him, the testimony of all these works is presented as the testimony of the Father himself. A silent implication underlies what is thus said of the works and of their testimony, namely that they are such as admittedly no man could do of himself, in fact, no man at all, not even by way of a gift;

for no man is great enough to receive and to administer a gift that is so tremendous. "That the Father
has sent me" means: "has sent me on the Messianic
mission." The Baptist, too, was sent (1:6), and all
the prophets were sent, but the sending of Jesus
went far beyond the sending of all these. The sending of all others rested on that of the Son, while the
sending of Jesus rested on no other sending.

37) Yet Jesus here mentions this great testimony
of the Father's only in a secondary way, for it is still
in progress. Moreover, this testimony is mediate: the
Father utters it through the works, although, of course,
all the works are directly connected with Jesus, since
he in his own person does them. Jesus brings to court
a testimony that is all complete and one made immediately and most directly by the Father. **And the
Father that did send me, he has given testimony
concerning me. Neither his voice have you ever
heard, nor his form have you seen.** Purposely Jesus
reveals this all-decisive testimony only little by little,
keeping the attention of the Jews on the alert to the
utmost. Here he names the ἄλλος, left unnamed in
v. 32 and named indirectly as regards the works in
v. 36. Now the name comes with full emphasis:
"the Father that did send me, he," or "that one,"
ἐκεῖνος, the demonstrative making the name prominent.
This is the person whom Jesus brings in as his witness. To call him "the Father" is not enough in this
connection. For not merely as such is he this witness. But as "the Father that did send me," for as
the Son's great Sender this Father appears as Jesus'
witness. In other words, all his testimony is occasioned by the act and the fact of thus sending his
own Son as the Messiah, deals with his sending, prepares for it, explains it, and thus accredits that sending. By thus designating his great witness Jesus gives
an intimation regarding the character of the testi-

mony of this witness, or, we may say, what the sum
and substance of his testimony is. When Jesus calls
the Father to the witness stand, that Father appears
and testifies as the Sender of his Son.

The next feature is expressed by the perfect tense
of the verb, "he has given testimony concerning me."
This is in contrast with the present tense used in
v. 36: the works "give testimony," i. e., now and right
along as they occur and will occur. This other testimony stands complete. It was offered long ago, and,
thus offered, now stands for all time. Not yet does
Jesus say that this complete and enduring testimony
consists of the Father's own Word, although we can
almost guess that this is what Jesus means. Long
ago the Father gave his testimony regarding Jesus
and the sending that followed; long ago, then, this
testimony was known. Why, then, did the Jews know
nothing about it? Why must Jesus now at this late
date tell these Jews about this ancient testimony?

Because they do not even know this great witness!
"Neither his voice have you ever heard," although his
testimony has sounded out all along; "nor his form
have you seen," although in his testimony he has stood
before your very eyes all along. Both "voice" and
"form" are anthropomorphic and, of course, are not
to be understood literally. Both expressions: hearing
the voice and seeing the form, refer to the witness,
whom one both hears and sees when he gives his
testimony. Thus Jesus tells these Jews that they
have never met this witness, they have never been
near enough to him either to hear or to see him. In
other words, they know nothing at all about his testimony, in fact, do not know that he ever thus testified.
"Voice and form," like hear and see, are only companion terms. Both are plainly meant in a spiritual
not in a literal sense, i. e., to hear and to see with

the heart. On this sense of seeing the Father compare 14:9; 12:45.

This disposes of the labored explanation caused especially by the saying that these Jews never saw God's εἶδος or "form." The prophets and the Baptist are usually brought in, who literally heard God's voice and saw him in some visible form in a vision (Isa. 6 for instance). But what these prophets heard and saw they only told the people who themselves, even the most godly among them, never heard and saw in this way. The point of Jesus' words is lost when we are told that the blame does not begin until v. 38; for then the words of Jesus about these Jews never having heard and seen the Father become pointless. Nor is this pointlessness removed by making Jesus mean, "I know you have never been granted a direct voice and vision of God like the prophets." No ordinary Jew and no Christian today expects such a thing. Equally inadequate is the idea that Jesus here alludes to certain apocryphal expressions (Baruch 3:14-37; Ecclesiasticus 24:8-14), and that these indicate that Jesus here has in mind the Jewish institutions for teaching and for guiding the people, as a kind of embodiment of the divine authority and presence, in which they could have heard and seen God. Why take these institutions, and that on apocryphal evidence, when in the entire Old Testament the Father as the Son's Sender stood for ages as the supreme Witness for all the hearts of his people to hear and to see? The perfect tenses "have heard" and "have seen" match the perfect "he has testified," i. e., you have not in the past nor do you now.

38) With plain literalness Jesus continues: **And his Word you have not remaining in you; because whom that one did send, him you do not believe.** We must note that οὔτε . . . οὔτε . . . καί

οὐ, "neither . . . nor . . . and not," go together and form one statement, R. 1179, 1189. Three negations are thus linked together, for οὔτε is not disjunctive but only a negative copulative conjunction, "and not." While the third negation is thus added to the previous two, in substance it states what results from those two: they who have never heard the Father's voice and have not seen his form naturally have not his Word abiding in them, τὸν λόγον αὐτοῦ, the substance of truth which constitutes his Word as distinguished from the sounds by which it is uttered. The emphasis is on ἐν ὑμῖν μένοντα, which must not be divided, making only the phrase "in you" emphatic and not the participle also. Then we should have the phrase placed after the participle, and even so the two would go together. This third negation shows in what sense hearing the Father's voice and seeing his form is meant, namely, an inward hearing and seeing in the heart by faith and true understanding. For only thus by the heart and by faith does the Word remain in us. If these Jews had heard what the Father's voice speaks (but they have no ear for his voice), and if they had seen therein God's presentation of himself (but they had no eyes for his form), then through such spiritual seeing and hearing the substance of God's Word would become an abiding power in their lives. Meyer.

The ὅτι clause furnishes the undeniable evidential proof: "because whom that one (the Father) did send, him (the Son Jesus) you do not believe." The Greek is highly effective in placing side by side the three emphatic words: ἐκεῖνος — τούτῳ — ὑμεῖς: *he* (no less a person than the Father) sent him; *him* (no less a person than the Son he sent); *you* (just think what wretches you are!) do not believe. Can they who reject the ambassador when he arrives and presents his credentials (Jesus and his works) claim to honor

the announcements which tell them of that ambassador's arrival? The dative with πιστεύω means to believe the person, i. e., that what he says is true; this
is said because in v. 18 the Jews refuse to accept as
true the word of Jesus that God is his Father.

39) So the testimony of this supreme Witness is
the Father's Word, i. e., the Old Testament Scriptures,
in which God long ago and all along stood as a Witness and uttered his testimony regarding the Son
whom he would send and did then send in Jesus.
Though he stood there as concretely as possible and
spoke as clearly as possible, these Jews never saw or
heard him, and his Word and its meaning (ὁ λόγος
οὗτου) never entered and found lodgment in their
hearts. What these Jews had hitherto failed to attain
Jesus bids them attain now at last. **Search the
Scriptures, for you think in them you have life
eternal; and these are they that testify of me; and
you are not willing to come to me that you may have
life.** All the old exegetes with the single exception
of Cyril read ἐρευνᾶτε as the imperative, likewise a host
of others. More recently a number regard this form
as the indicative: "You are searching" (also the
R. V.). The question is purely one of context, since
no other evidence is available. When R. 329 con-
cludes: "probably indicative," he does so on grammatical grounds.

The imperative fits the entire situation, the indicative requires modifications, which we have no right
to make. The situation is that Jesus introduces the
Father together with the Scriptures as his all-decisive
witness (v. 37). Really, this great Witness is a
stranger to the Jews, and thus, of course, they have
never known his testimony (v. 38) although it was
given long ago (v. 37). Jesus tells the Jews: Here
is my Witness — examine him! This testimony he
gave long ago — "search it!" He could not say to

these Jews: You are already searching it. If Jesus
should want to say that, he would have to add, "You
are, indeed, searching it, but in the wrong way." And
then he would have to indicate what is wrong and
what the right way is. He does nothing of the kind.
Yet this the pleaders for the indicative have Jesus
say: "You Jews are searching only outwardly, only
the bare letter of the Old Testament, only in your
sterile rabbinical fashion." Not one word of this is
found in what Jesus says. And, of course, also not one
word of what Jesus then certainly ought to add, namely how these Jews should correct their false way of
searching.

Again, take the situation. After Jesus introduces
his great Witness with his decisive testimony, telling
the Jews to search it, he adds the reason in full why
they themselves should want to proceed to do so. We
must note, however, that this reason extends through
the three following clauses: ὅτι . . . καί . . . καί
(v. 40), which, therefore, must not be divided, or
joined only in loose fashion. Some find the reason only
in the ὅτι clause, a few advance upon this and add the
first καί clause, but the second καί clause (v. 40) is read
as a statement by itself.

The first part of the reason why these Jews should
certainly want to examine the Scriptures again is
the statement of Jesus, "because *you think* (ὑμεῖς,
emphatic) you have in them eternal life." With "you
think" Jesus plainly tells them they are mistaken.
He, indeed, does not add, "*I* think otherwise," merely
pitting his thought against theirs, which would make
no impression on these Jews. He does what is bound
to carry more weight with them. He adds a second
part of his reason. Over against the emphatic ὑμεῖς
he sets the equally emphatic ἐκεῖναι (R. 707), "*you*
think" — but just search the Scriptures, "*these*," the
very ones in which you think you have life eternal,

they are "*the* ones that testify (αἱ μαρτυροῦσαι) concerning me." And περὶ ἐμοῦ means far more than that the Scriptures only say this or that about Jesus; "concerning me" means that all their testimony centers in Jesus, centers in him so that only *by and through him* men are declared to have life eternal. Thus Jesus adds the second point to his reason why the Jews should certainly want to examine the Scriptures. And this demands that Jesus state also the third point, which is already involved in the other two.

40) For when these Jews are so sure that they have life eternal in the Scriptures, they think that they have it *without Jesus*. Therefore Jesus says, "and you have no will to come *to me* (emphatic by position) in order to have life." You think that life can be had without me. And again, when Jesus tells these Jews what they have never realized before that the Scriptures testify *of him*, i. e., of life only through him, he adds for this too, "and you have no will to come *to me* in order to have life." The threefold reason which Jesus gives these Jews as to why they most certainly should want to search the Scriptures really forms a syllogism, one that refutes the false and shallow conclusion of these Jews. They conclude: We have life because we own and accept the Scriptures. Jesus answers: You merely think you have. Major premise: To have life you must, indeed, have the Scriptures, but that means *me*, of whom they testify, *me* the fountain of life in the Scriptures. Minor premise: You do not come to *me* for life, in fact, you do not even know that the Scriptures thus testify of *me*. Ergo: You have not life; you only think so; you are sadly mistaken. This forceful reason and reasoning must stir even these Jews. They are challenged with the very Scriptures in which they proudly trust. They must meet this challenge; to refuse is to let the contention of Jesus stand. And

there is only one way to meet it: just what Jesus says: "Search the Scriptures!" The surer these Jews are that they are right and that Jesus is wrong, the more eager they will be to do just that, "search the Scriptures." Thus, only when ἐρευνᾶτε is the imperative does it fit the situation; an indicative would not meet the situation adequately. It is the same situation over again that occurs in the case of Isaiah and his opponents, Isa. 8:20.

Formally these Jews were right when they thought that life eternal is to be had in the Scriptures; and this Jesus not only admits but himself asserts with his command to search the Scriptures. Concretely, however, these Jews were wrong, for they failed to find the one fountain of life in the Scriptures, the Father's Son, whom he sent as the Messiah to bring them life. What made them wrong was not that they merely clung to the Book as a book, or merely studied it outwardly, its shell or letter, or merely went at this study with rabbinical refinement. Paul presents the matter more clearly in Rom. 10:3 and elsewhere. The Jews found the law in the Scriptures, the law alone. When they were so sure of having life eternal "in them," they based their assurance only on this law and on their diligence in its observance. They even added to this law a lot of regulations of their own, intended to support this law, among them the Sabbath rules which Jesus spurned, thereby bringing on the present conflict. They trusted in their works. They established a righteousness of their own. It was thus that they remained blind to the gospel, the very heart of the Scriptures, "ignorant of God's righteousness," the very righteousness revealed in the gospel (Rom. 1:17), the righteousness of faith in God's Son and their Savior. Hence also the one cure for the Jews was the one Jesus here applies: "Search the Scriptures!" — "they are they that testify of me."

41) The call, "Search the Scriptures!" still dominates what Jesus now adds, first on the real moral or spiritual reason for the unbelief of these Jews (v. 41-44), and secondly on the fearful consequences of this unbelief (v. 45-47). When men truly search the Scriptures to find what they say concerning his Son and their Savior, they begin to assume the right attitude toward God, the opposite of which these Jews now manifest, v. 42-44; then, too, they will escape the consequences of unbelief, into which they are now bound to run, v. 45-47.

Jesus has said: these Jews would not believe in *him* (v. 38), the Scriptures testify of *him*, the Jews will not come to *him*. Jesus reads their hearts and sees how they may think that he is motivated just as they are, that he is piqued because they do not honor and glorify him. This he cuts off at once. **Glory from men I do not take,** compare 8:50. The object is placed forward for emphasis: "glory," honor, praise, distinction "from men," in distinction from "the glory that comes from the only God" (v. 44). Even when men offered it to him (6:15) he spurned it and did not catch at it, λαμβάνω in the sense of *capto*, R. 110. Jesus took only the glory which God gave him, God directly, and God through the faith of believing men. Let not these Jews imagine that Jesus is miffed because *they* do not honor him, that this is why he is scoring them so severely.

42) The unworthy motive is not in Jesus but in the Jews, the very motive back of their rejection of Jesus, back of their misjudging Jesus, back of their misreading of the Scriptures, back also of the consequences which therefore shall come upon them. This *their* motive makes Jesus charge them as he does.

On the contrary (ἀλλά after a negative statement), **I have known you, that the love of God is not in your-selves.** Let these Jews not screen themselves behind Jesus when something is radically wrong with them-selves. The perfect tense involves the present: "have known" all along and so know now. Compare on this knowing 2:24, 25. Why R. 499 and 500 wavers regard-ing the genitive τὴν ἀγάπην τοῦ Θεοῦ is strange. This is without question the objective genitive, the Jews' love for God, not the subjective, God's love for the Jews. This is shown by οὐ ζητεῖτε in v. 44, they cared nothing for God's opinion of them but only for the opinion of men. Behind the negative, not loving God, lies the positive, loving men instead. To be sure, they may profess love to God with their lips, even think they honor God by rejecting Jesus, but ἐν ἑαυτοῖς, in their hearts, a far different motive prevails. No wonder God's testimony counted so little with them. It is so to this day. All lovers of God accept his testimony, by it quickly recognize and accept his Son Jesus, care nothing for and are influenced in no way by the opinions of men who spurn Jesus. When men do otherwise and claim to love God nevertheless, their claim is refuted by the evidence of their act of reject-ing Jesus.

43) To this undeniable evidence Jesus points the Jews. **I have come in the name of my Father, and you do not receive me; if another shall come in his own name, him you will receive.** That is how much they really love God. Note the strong contrasts, each strengthening the other: I — another; have come — shall come; in the name of my Father — in his own name; you do not receive me — him you will receive. In Matt. 23:36, etc., Jesus shows this utter lack of love on the part of the Jews from the treatment they bestowed upon all the prophets, crowning this with their treatment of his Son; here he speaks only of

the latter. To come "in the name of my Father" does not mean: by his authority or as his representative. See on τὸ ὄνομα in 1:12. "The name" here means the revelation of the Father, in other words, the testimony of the Scripture. By this Jesus is recognized as indeed coming from the Father, and by this those Jews should and could have recognized him. Having no love for God, his "name" or revelation made no impression on them, and when Jesus came, with his coming all in connection with that revelation, "the name," counted for nothing with them: "and you receive me not" (1:11). The very people to whom "the name" was given, that by it they might know him who was to come in that name, refused that name and did not receive him who came in that name. The tenses correspond: "I have come," perfect, and now am here; and: "you do not receive," present. "Not to receive," a litotes, = to reject. While the negative is milder than the positive, it really is stronger. The mere omission already constitutes the crime. As in 1:12 "to receive" = to accept in faith; hence "not to receive" = to reject in unbelief.

Jesus, so perfectly accredited by "the name," the Scriptures, their testimony, and this by the Father himself, these Jews do not receive. When "another" shall come, any other, for ἐὰν ἔλθῃ is general, "in his own name," in connection with a revelation concocted and made up by himself, hence accredited by himself alone and not like Jesus by God — though it seems astounding and incredible when looked at sensibly: "him you will receive." And yet it is not so astounding after all. Such an impostor is of the type and the character of these Jews, out for glory from men, caring not for glory from God.

The words of Jesus are a prophecy concerning all the false Messiahs and other false religious leaders that would come in the future. To generalize and to

refer to any man who is out only for his own interest
is to loose the contrast between ἐγώ and ἄλλος, between
the acts of coming, and between the two ὀνόματι. While
the statement is not that broad, neither is it so narrow as to refer only to *one* person, say to the anti-
Christ (older exegetes), or to Simon Barkochba, whom
Rabbi Akiba termed "the star of Jacob" (Num. 24:17),
and who was acclaimed by the leaders of the Jews in
the years 132-135, many giving up their lives for
him. This would require the direct statement: ἄλλος
ἐλεύσομαι, "another shall come," not the conditional: "if
another shall come." Bengel notes that up to his time
sixty-four such messiahs had come, including, of
course, the notable Barkochba. Since then more religious deceivers have been added, and the end is not
yet. II Thes. 2:11, 12. It is truly astonishing how
one coming in his own name (not long ago even a
woman!), seeking in the boldest, rankest way his own
glory, advantage, power, money, by making people
his dupes and victims, is received by thousands with
open arms. They who count the Son of God too small
to give their hearts to him, the name, Word, and revelation of God too unreliable to trust their souls to him
of whom God thus testifies, yield their hearts, their
happiness, their property, their all, to any fool who
condescends to impose upon their credulity and to use
them as his tools. The generation of the Jews never
dies out.

44) This calls forth the dramatic indignant question: **How can you come to believe, since you receive
glory from each other and the real glory from the
only God you seek not?** Jesus combines non-belief
in himself and belief in any deceiver. Both rest on
this seeking for glory not from God but from men.
"How is it possible with such people as you (ὑμεῖς) to
come to faith (πιστεῦσαι, ingressive aorist, R. 857)? It
is altogether out of the question." But the impos-

sibility is due not to God but to themselves. The participle is not equal to a relative clause, "who receive" (our versions), which would require articulation; it is causal, R. 1128, "since you receive." Jesus might also have continued with a second participle, "and since you seek not," etc. Instead he uses the stronger indicative, "and you seek not." Note also δόξαν without the article and then τὴν δόξαν with the article; the former "any glory" in the line of poor, passing honor from men, the other, "the real glory," the specific praise and commendation of God which he bestows when he calls a man his own child and heir. The former these Jews actually "receive," the latter they do not even "seek," to say nothing of "receiving" it.

The emptiness of the one over against the value of the other is brought out still more by the two opposite παρά phrases. The one is glory only "from each other," who are all on the same poor and wretched level, none of whom can give more than any other. The other is glory "from the only God," or as some texts read, "from the Only One." (Entirely wrong, "from God alone"). He, infinitely exalted above men, bestows glory indeed, here that specific glory which lifts us up as his own. In τοῦ μόνου we have an allusion to Deut. 6:4, etc., "Hear, O Israel, the Lord our God is *one* Lord." Jesus had this in mind already in v. 42, where he speaks of "the love of God"; for Deut. 6:5 continues, "And thou shalt love the Lord thy God with all thine heart," etc. These words each devout Jew prayed twice daily in the prayer called *Shema.*

Jesus scores the vanity of the Jews, by which they boasted to each other of being Jews, instead of letting God bestow on them the true glory of Israel in his Son Jesus. Jew still boasts to Jew of their mutual prerogatives and is pleased when Gentiles praise Jews and Judaism. This self-exaltation proved their abasement, Luke 18:14. A special sting lies in the designation "the *only* God," which is not in contrast with the Jews as being many but a designation for monotheism as against polytheism. The special boast of the Jews to each other was that they adhered to monotheism, and is used by them now in opposition to the Christian doctrine of the Trinity, although the Jews in the Old Testament and in the time of Jesus knew "the only God" as Triune: compare 1:32. Examples of the general Jewish greediness for honor are found in Matt. 23:5-7; John 12:43. Paul describes a real Jew as one "whose praise is not of men but of God." Rom. 2:29. So our skeptic scientists, our "critic" theologians, our gaudily bedizened lodge brothers, and others like them, still shower honors, titles, laudations, offices, and emoluments upon each other, boosting their own pride in themselves and in each other while "the real glory from the only God" they do not even seek.

Luther writes: "It is an exceedingly proud and glorious honor, when a man can boast of God, that he is God's servant, child, people, over against which all the honor of the world is as altogether nothing. But the world regards not such honor, seeks honor from men. The false apostles teach what pleases men, and this in order to have peace and the favor and applause of the mob. And, indeed, they get what they seek; for such fellows get the prize and have the thanks of everyone, Matt. 6:2 and 5. . . . If you want honor, give all honor to God alone, and for yourself keep nothing but shame. Despise yourself and let all your doing be nothing and thus you will sanctify God's name and give honor to God alone. See, as soon as you do this, you are already full of honor, which is greater than the honor of all kings and abides forever; for God adorns you and honors you with his name, so that you are called God's servant,

God's child, God's people, and the like. What now could God do more for you, who gives you so much temporal and eternal good and in addition the highest, even his own name, and the eternal honor? It seems to me, this is, indeed, worthy of our thanking him from the heart and praising him. Who is able for one of these things constantly to praise and thank God sufficiently?"

45) Now Jesus presents to these Jews the consequences of their rejecting the Father's testimony in his Word. **Think not that I will accuse you to the Father; there is he that accuses you, Moses, on whom you have set your hope.** We must not forget that Jesus faces the Jews with the consequences of their unbelief in a final effort to shatter that unbelief and turn it into faith. These last three verses are full of terrific force; either this will crush the hearts in contrition or be met with desperate obduracy, blindly set on its own destruction. We feel the force of Jesus' words when we understand how the Jews clung to their Moses, boasted in him, gloried in him, felt themselves absolutely safe in him — not, of course, the real Moses but the figure they had made of him in their own minds. With one sweep Jesus not only takes their Moses away but hurls the real Moses against them, as the one who already condemns them. The mastery with which Jesus does this must ever captivate our hearts.

"Do not think" implies that the Jews had been thinking this very thing, R. 853. We need not press the future "that I shall accuse you to the Father" as referring to the future judgment and urge that then Jesus will appear only as the judge; for this tense is in correlation with the substantivized present participle "there is he that accuses you, Moses," etc. What Jesus tells these Jews is that he does not need to accuse them, that Moses already attends to that. Why should

Jesus accuse those who are already under the strongest kind of an accusation? Moreover, the contrast is between ἐγώ and this accuser ὁ κατηγορῶν ὑμῶν (objective genitive: "he that accuses you"), whom Jesus not only names but also characterizes, "on whom you have set your hope." Any accusation Jesus might bring forward these Jews would treat lightly, thinking him only a man who makes great unwarranted claims for himself (v. 18). But Moses is their own great and acknowledged authority. More than that, they "have set their hope on him," that Moses will acknowledge them as his disciples and as faithful adherents and defenders of his law, and that thus through the mediation of Moses God will undoubtedly pronounce a favorable verdict upon them in the judgment. On the perfect ἠλπίκατε see R. 895. Proudly they say in John 9:28, 29: "We are Moses' disciples; we know that God spoke unto Moses: as for this fellow (Jesus), we know not whence he is." But by thus setting their hope on Moses and on his law they made of both something that neither was, much as the teachers of work-righteousness and of salvation by morality do today, who do not, like the Jews, stop with Moses but reduce even Jesus to the same level. When Jesus now says that this their Moses, on whom all their hopes rest, is their accuser, to whose accusation Jesus needs to add not a thing, he delivers a blow to their proud self-assurance which strikes home. They may recoil in outraged feeling, but they are bound to feel the shock. Placed first, ἔστιν has the regular accent and means "there exists."

46) **For if you believed Moses you would believe me; for concerning me he did write.** This statement cannot intend to prove at this late point why Moses accuses the Jews. The reason has already been furnished in v. 41-44, which also is full and complete. With γάρ Jesus elucidates why any accusation

of his would be superfluous when Moses already
attends to this. If these Jews would treat Moses right,
so that he would have no accusations against them,
they would treat aright also Jesus, of whom Moses
wrote, and thus, of course, he, too, would have no
accusations against them. Jesus uses "believe Moses"
and "believe me," two datives: accept Moses' and my
words as true. The condition is one of present unreality and in regular form: εἰ with the imperfect
followed by the imperfect with ἄν. This implies that
the Jews are not believing what Moses said and thus
are also not believing what Jesus says. The former
is enough and more than sufficient for accusation; so
Jesus leaves that work to Moses.

But Moses and Jesus are not merely paralleled, nor
is the Jewish unbelief against Jesus treated merely as
a case similar to the Jewish unbelief against Moses.
The two cases of unbelief are made one by the second
explanatory γάρ: "for concerning me he did write."
What Moses wrote and what Jesus has been testifying
concerning himself is identical. Thus to believe the
one is to believe the other; to disbelieve the one is to
disbelieve the other. Moses with his writing came first,
Jesus now follows. Since the unbelief is one, whether
of Moses or of Jesus, the one accusation, that of Moses,
covers the case.

"He wrote" — *Moses!* Let the critics who repudiate the Mosaic authorship of the Pentateuch face
this authoritative declaration of Jesus. It is worth
more than all the so-called "research" that has ever
been put forth and it stands overagainst these critics
as Moses overagainst these Jews, as ὁ κατηγορῶν ὑμῶν,
as "he that accuses them." Nor did Moses write of
Jesus only in a few detached places, as some suppose.
Bengel: *Nusquam non* — *nowhere* did Moses *not*
write of Jesus. Nor did Moses *also* write of Jesus;
for the whole center and substance of what he wrote

is Jesus. The entire twenty-five centuries with which he deals he views in relation to the Messiah. Ever and always faith in the Coming One decides the fate of man. Great things he touches slightly, and little things, dry genealogies, small occurrences in the lives of the patriarchs, he describes at length, because these have a bearing on the Messiah. From the story of creation onward, through all the following history, ceremony, prophecy, and promise, he is ever in the mind of Moses. Moses in person and in office is even himself a type of the Mediator to come. All this the Jews of Jesus' day did not believe, nor do the Jews believe it today. And this Jewish unbelief has been adopted by thousands of others who with the Jews count it the very height of Bible knowledge.

On "if you believed Moses." Stier writes: "The Jews believed not Moses in his account of the creation and in his testimony on the fall of man; for if they had accepted this as truth, they as sinful men would have had to seek with all earnestness the living God, as did Enoch and Noah. They did not believe him in the account concerning the fathers and their faith, else they would have followed in the footsteps of Abraham. They did not believe in the sacred earnestness of the law he delivered, judging the hearts, else their Pharisaic work-righteousness would have fallen to the ground. Finally, they did not believe him when his entire order of priests and sacrifices constantly renewed the memory of their sins and pointed in shadowy outline to a future real fulfillment, else they would have become through Moses already what the Baptist finally tried to make them, a people ready and prepared for the Lord, embracing his salvation with joy like Simeon."

47) The condition of unreality is now expressed in a condition of reality. **But if his writings you do not believe, how shall you believe my words?** The

structure of the statement is chiastic and thus places
the two objects into the emphatic positions. Not only
does Jesus say, "Moses wrote"; he now adds, "Moses'
writings," placing a double seal of authorship and
truth on the Pentateuch. The contrast is between
"his" and "my," not between "writings" and "words."
Of course, the Jews had only the *writings* of Moses
whereas they had the *words*, ῥήματα, the living audible
speech of Jesus. Though we now have the utterances
of Jesus in writing, the relation between Moses and
Jesus is still the same. In conditions of reality the
Koine uses εἰ with οὐ as the negative.

With a sad question, the implied answer to which
is negative, Jesus breaks off and says no more. His
task was done. Deep into the callous conscience of
these Jews he had pressed the sting of the law. They
pretended mighty zeal for the law, raging against
Jesus for breaking the Sabbath law. But what Moses
really wrote, what God through Moses really testified
they did not believe. So Jesus leaves them with this
gripping question. John is right in adding no remarks
of his own at the end of this discourse. Its testimony
is most effective just as it stands.

CHAPTER VI

The Preliminary Events, 6:1-21. — As chapter 5 relates the rise of opposition in Jerusalem, so chapter 6 relates the rise of opposition in Galilee. Hence only the pertinent events and discourses are selected, and these are presented only with such details as serve to bring clearly to view the attestation of Jesus and to show how it caused such opposition. **After these things Jesus went away beyond the Sea of Galilee, the Tiberian.** With the simple phrase μετὰ ταῦτα (compare 5:1) John passes over the months between the festival at which Jesus healed the impotent man (5:1, etc.) and the Passover now approaching, the third Passover during Jesus' ministry. When John says that Jesus "went away beyond the Sea," the implication is that for some time Jesus had been working in Galilee, whence he had come from Jerusalem, and that now for the events to be narrated Jesus crossed the Sea of Galilee to its northeastern side. John adds "the Tiberian" for the sake of the general reader, to make sure that he thinks of the right sea, not of the Mediterranean.

2) Without telling us in so many words, John presents Jesus at the height of his Galilean ministry. **And there was following him a great multitude, because they were beholding the signs he was doing upon those that were sick.** The three imperfect tenses picture Jesus in the full exercise of his activity at this period, including, of course, the present crossing of the Sea. The statement that the crowds were attracted by "beholding the signs he was doing"

is intended to parallel 2:23 and to show that in general the situation here in Galilee was a duplication of the previous one which occurred in Jerusalem. Not the teaching but merely the signs were the great attraction. This John wants us to bear in mind for the sake of what follows.

3) **And Jesus went up into the mountain and was sitting there with his disciples.** Jesus crossed the Sea in order to find a respite from the crowds that followed him, for the news had just come to him that the Baptist had been killed (Matt. 14:13), and because Jesus also had other business with his disciples (Mark 6:31, etc.). The view that Jesus failed to find this respite because the crowds followed him, is refuted by the imperfect ἐκάθητο, "was sitting," and it is also evident that the crowds, who had had to walk along the shoreline, arrived at the place to which Jesus had crossed by boat some hours later. Without telling us, John assumes that we know that "the disciples" are now twelve in number.

4) The connective δέ (note that it is not γάρ) is parenthetical. **Now the Passover, the feast of the Jews, was near.** The article "*the* feast" is not stressed, for in 7:2 another feast is also so designated. The apposition is intended for the general reader who is not particularly versed in Jewish matters. Of course, the mention of the Passover marks the date of this narrative, which also must be John's intention. But it does more. It does not, however, explain the flocking of the multitude to Jesus. This has already been most adequately explained in v. 2, and this applies not only to this one day but to this period in general. Moreover, the pilgrim caravans going to the Passover would not follow a route around the Sea to its northeast side, but routes leading southward. Nor is this mention of the Passover to give a setting for the final discourse on the Bread of Life. The two events

are too far apart. In the entire discourse not even
a slight reference is made to the Passover. The
idea that Jesus would dispense the Bread of Life as
a better substitute for the Jewish Paschal feast, a
better feast also as typifying the Lord's Supper, is
not only without support in Jesus' own discourse but
contrary to Jesus' own action when a year later he
celebrated his last Passover with the disciples in
Jerusalem. Not until after that event was the Jewish
Passover abrogated, because not until then was it
completely fulfilled. We must not carry thoughts, attractive to ourselves, into the Scripture and then persuade ourselves that we have found them there. The
reference to the Passover at this point in John's
narrative is intended to explain the action of the multitude when after the miracle of the loaves they conceived the plan of forcing Jesus to go with them to
Jerusalem, there to be made a king. Perhaps we may
add that the approach of the Passover and the
news of the Baptist's death foreshadowed to Jesus
his own approaching death at the Passover a year
hence.

5)   John assumes that his readers know the fuller
narrative found in Matt. 14:13-21 and in Mark 6:35,
etc., together with the briefer account in Luke 9:12,
etc. Thus John briefly sketches the situation and adds
from the conversation with the disciples what serves
his purpose in showing their helplessness to meet the
problem that was facing them. After the parenthetical remark οὖν merely resumes the narrative.
**Accordingly, having lifted up his eyes and hav-
ing seen that a great multitude was coming to him,
he says to Philip, Whence shall we buy bread, in
order that these may eat?** John is not worried in
the least whether his account of what preceded and
led up to the miracle will harmonize with the accounts
of the other evangelists, for he knows that it does

harmonize with them. John alone tells the incident about Philip, and this he does to amplify the other accounts on two points. If we had only these other accounts we might conclude that the disciples took the initiative when toward evening they asked Jesus to dismiss the multitude; from John's account we learn that Jesus thought about the needs of the multitude when the crowd first appeared, and that already then he asked Philip whence bread might be obtained for them. We thus see that the request of the disciples to send the multitude away was made after the situation had become acute, namely toward evening, when everybody was hungry. The disciples saw only one thing to be done, namely that Jesus send the multitude away at once. They act as though Jesus had forgotten to think of their needs and, therefore, also add that it is high time to act if all these people are to reach the neighboring villages and are there to buy bread. The answer of Jesus, that the people need not depart (Matt. 14:16), that the disciples should give them to eat, shows that Jesus all along had in mind that he and his disciples should feed these people. That is why he had taught and healed all this time, unworried about the eating. He had not forgotten by any means but had purposely waited until this time, when at last something had to be done. And he had purposely waited until the disciples could keep still no longer, until they felt that they must take the initiative. But now that they do so, none of them musters faith enough to think that perhaps Jesus himself intended to feed these people and that for this reason he had taught and healed until so late an hour.

The other point is the explanation of Mark 6:37, where the disciples ask, "Shall we go and buy two hundred pennyworth of bread," etc.? Why did they think of this sum and of asking this question? John

tells us: because when Jesus first saw the crowds as
they were coming (ἔρχεται), he had first raised the
question of getting bread for so many, asking Philip,
"Whence shall we buy bread," etc.? Philip had told
the others about this question and about the answer
he gave. The other evangelists omit this detail in
their accounts, John adds it. The subjunctive
ἀγοράσωμεν (always in the first person) is used in
a question of deliberation when one asks himself or
himself and others what to do. The aorist indicates
the single act of buying.

6) **Now this he was saying as testing him;
for he himself knew what he was about to do.**
As δέ shows, this remark is parenthetical. We should
not wonder why Philip was selected for this testing
(πειράζω, "to try out," thus also in an evil sense "to
tempt") and then try to find a reason in the disposi-
tion and the character of Philip. Jesus selects Philip
merely as being one of the entire number of the
Twelve. If the others stood by and listened or if
presently Philip told them about the question and
of his answer, the test was intended for all of them.
The fact that they passed this test no better than
Philip we see from Mark 6:37, where they ask whether
they shall go and buy bread, putting Philip's answer
to Jesus into the form of a question. None of them
rose higher than Philip's low level.

Now Jesus asked Philip when the multitude was
first gathering. Philip and the Twelve thus had hours
of time in which to think over what Jesus might have
intended with his question. Yet towards evening, as
we learn from Mark, they still think that Jesus had
actually contemplated only buying bread for all these
people. Note, too, how by this question Jesus raised
the problem of food from the very start and bade the
disciples solve it. When then he proceeded entirely
unconcerned, as though the problem did not exist,

until evening was approaching and everybody, the Twelve included, grew real hungry, the disciples could have guessed that Jesus, who saw the problem long before the disciples did, must have had in mind an adequate solution. Yet none of them thought of the wine furnished in Cana, nor of the "hour" for which Jesus there waited. The fact that Jesus knew all along (ᾔδει, used as an imperfect) what he was about to do, John reports as something that he discovered later. Only afterward he saw why Jesus spoke to Philip so early and yet continued until evening, until the Twelve could stand it no longer and felt that they must tell Jesus what to do. The imperfect ἔμελλε is due to indirect discourse, R. 1043, 1029; and the present infinitive following it indicates the course of action in Jesus' mind.

7) **Philip answered him, Two hundred pennyworth of bread is not sufficient for them, for each to take a little something.** Philip thinks only of buying and answers only regarding that. He mentions the lowest possible amount, one that would give only "a little something" to each person, not by any means enough to satisfy the appetite. Contrast with this v. 12, "they were filled," and v. 11, "as much as they would." To provide only "a little something" would cost two hundred δηνάρια (at 17 cents this would amount to $34), a sum far beyond the balance in the joint treasury of Jesus and the disciples. The genitive is one of price. Jesus, of course, wants to bring out the hopelessness of buying food for all these people. Philip stops at the prohibitive price; he might have added that no place to buy such a quantity of food was at hand. One impossibility is enough. The idea that the realization of this impossibility should turn Philip's thoughts into an entirely different direction, and that by means of his question Jesus tried to turn them thus, never occurred to Philip.

8) Evening is coming on, no food is in sight, the case is reaching the acute stage. The disciples tell Jesus to send the multitude away. Jesus replies that they need not depart (Matt. 14:16). He tells the disciples to give them to eat. Even this does not awaken in their minds an inkling of what Jesus has in mind. All they know is to ask whether Jesus at this late hour wants them to go and to scour the country to buy the least amount for these many mouths (Mark 6:37). To this Jesus replies by telling them to go and to see how many loaves they have. They do this, and a report is quickly made (Mark 6:38). Here John adds more detail. **One of his disciples, Andrew, Simon Peter's brother, says to him, There is a lad here who has five barley loaves and two fishes; but what are these for so many?** Whereas the other evangelists mention only the disciples, John says that their spokesman was Andrew, whom we met in 1:45, whose relation to his brother Simon Peter is again noted. This was perhaps done because Andrew was one of the first two who became disciples of Jesus. The deduction that Andrew was a practical man and that thus he made this investigation, falls by the board, for Jesus told the disciples to go and to see how much bread was there.

John also adds Andrew's hopeless expression, which has often been repeated since, "What are these for so many?" As was the case with the first question to Philip, so also with regard to this order to the disciples, these men think only that Jesus has in mind by means of purchase or by means of gathering up the supplies still available, to feed this vast crowd. So both times Jesus is told that his suggestions are hopeless. The παιδάριον or "lad" seems to have been a boy who tried to make a little money by selling to the crowd such supplies as he could carry. Barley bread was much used by the poorer classes. In the present instance ὀψάρια, the diminutive plural of ὄψον or "cooked food," are fish, since this was a great fish country, and prepared fish was eaten with the thin, flat cakes of bread. The singular ἄρτος means "bread," bread as such or a sheet of bread, which nobody thought of cutting since it was so easily broken for the purpose of eating. The Greek has the plural ἄρτοι, "breads," which the English lacks, so that we substitute "loaves," but should think of flat, round sheets. On ταῦτα τί as also being classical see R. 736.

10) According to Matthew, Jesus orders the bread and the fishes to be brought to him, which means that they are to be bought from the lad. Did the disciples think that Jesus intended to secure this food for himself, so that he and a least some of his disciples should not go hungry? At the same time **Jesus said, Make the people sit down. Now there was much grass in the place. Accordingly, the men sat down as to number about five thousand.** Note the peremptory aorist in the command and the aorist which states that the command was carried out. What did the Twelve now think — all these people sitting down as if to dine, and only this bit of food in sight? In the command οἱ ἄνθρωποι includes the women and the children in the count, οἱ ἄνδρες counts only the men, compare Matt. 14:21, "besides women and children." Mark 6:40 lets us see how the count was made: "they sat down in ranks, by hundreds, and by fifties." Matthew, too, mentions the grass, but John states that the place was covered with grass, both writing as eye-witnesses in distinction from Mark and Luke who were not present. All are seated in orderly fashion with lanes between the groups to enable proper serving. The impressiveness of the miracle is thus also brought out, for over five thousand at one meal is quite a host;

τὸν ἀριθμόν is the adverbial accusative, R. 486, and ὡς, "about," states that absolute exactness was not intended.

11) The miracle itself is described in the simplest manner by mentioning only the actions of Jesus. In points such as this the control of inspiration is tangible, for an ordinary writer would certainly elaborate on this great climax of the account. **Acoordingly, Jesus took the loaves and, having given thanks, distributed to those sitting down; likewise of the fishes, as much as they would.** Not even a single exclamation! Not one word beyond the bare facts that John saw and heard! We are not even told that a miracle was taking place; not even that the food kept multiplying as it was being handed out, or how many each sheet of bread and each fish served. Our familiarity with this account should not blind us to all these features.

"Jesus took the loaves" probably as they were together with the fishes in the lad's basket. Then he "gave thanks" or said grace by using a customary table prayer or perhaps a new form for this occasion. If the prayer was unusual, one of the evangelists would have intimated this fact; none does so. Matthew adds κλάσας, "having broken," which John covers by διά in the verb, "he distributed"; the bread was about an inch and a half in thickness, baked thus for the purpose of breaking. The other evangelists state that the pieces were taken by the disciples, probably in baskets, collected from people who had carried something in them. Thus loaded down, the disciples functioned as the waiters on this grand occasion. Jesus gave and gave and gave, and as he gave, there was always more to give. He did not stint, as Philip and the others thought to do by purchasing only two hundred pennyworth of bread, omitting anything to go with the bread. The fact that Jesus did not stint is mentioned in connection with the fishes; each person could have as much as he wanted, to go with his bread. The imperfect ἤθελον is used because of the repetition.

12) **And when they were filled, he says to his disciples, Collect the superfluous broken pieces, in order that nothing may be lost.** Only incidentally, as it were, in a subordinate temporal clause, the great fact (aorist) comes out that all these people "were filled," each having eaten all he could eat. But now, after all this prodigality, Jesus becomes exceedingly saving. A comparatively few had taken more than they could actually eat. Jesus will not have these left-over pieces wasted and thrown away — certainly a lesson for us. Yet here is more. The great sign has been wrought, its significance is plain to all who will read. It does *not* mean that Jesus will thus keep on feeding the people with exhaustless supplies of earthly food; he has come on no such mission. We should misunderstand this sign, if we thought that Jesus merely stepped in to meet an unexpected, great bodily need. Verse 6 eliminates that thought. Jesus purposely let the need develop until toward evening it became acute, because from the beginning he intended to work this sign. He could easily have obviated the need. Any man could foresee that presently all these people would be hungry and, using his common sense, could have sent them away betimes to places where they might find food. But Jesus deliberately detains them, "for he himself knew what he would do."

13) **Accordingly, they made the collection and filled twelve baskets with broken pieces from the five barley loaves which were left over to those having eaten.** A κόφινος is a small basket used by travelers for provisions, etc. More was left over than Jesus began with, as John intimates by mentioning side by

side "twelve baskets" and "the five barley loaves."
Each of the Twelve came with a basketful. It seems
that Jesus did not forget that his disciples, too, must
be hungry. How about himself? Why not one more
basketful, one for him? May we say that Jesus
expected the Twelve to share their abundance with
him? He still pours his abundance out to us and
expects us to remember him in the poor and needy and
in the support of the church.

14) John amplifies the account of the synoptists,
Matt. 14:22, etc.; Mark 6:45, etc., but in accord with
his purpose. They report only that Jesus sent his disciples away to sail back across the Sea, while he dismissed the multitude and retired into the mountain to
pray. John reveals the cause for this action in accord
with his purpose to show how also in Galilee the opposition to Jesus now developed. **The people, therefore, having seen the signs which he did, were saying, This one is truly the prophet that is coming into
the world.** The reading varies between the plural
"signs" and the singular "sign"; in any case the last
sign just narrated is the decisive one, which precipitated what follows; σημεῖον is explained in 2:11. In
the relative clause ἃ ἐποίησε σημεῖα the antecedent is
drawn into the relative clause, R. 718. The imperfect tense, "they were saying," describes how this
word circulated and was repeated and at the same
time intimates that something follows in consequence.
"The prophet" these people have in mind is the one
promised by Moses in Deut. 18:15, whom some conceived as the great forerunner of the Messiah
(1:21), and others as the Messiah himself. Note
the Messianic designation in ὁ ἐρχόμενος, "he that is
coming."

15) **Jesus, therefore, having realized that they
were about to come and kidnap him in order to
make him king, withdrew again into the mountain**

himself alone. The acclaim of the multitude was about to eventuate in action. We need not spend time explaining γνούς, for the purpose of the multitude was obvious, and the powers of perception on Jesus' part were beyond question (2:24, 25). Their plan was "to come and kidnap" or "snatch him away," whether he would consent or not, "in order to make him king," βασιλέα, predicate accusative with αὐτόν. They would carry him to Jerusalem at the coming Passover (v. 4) in a grand, royal procession, gathering increasing adherents on the way, sweeping the capital off its feet in universal enthusiasm. This scheme Jesus frustrates by withdrawing again into the mountain from which he "went forth" in the first place (Matt. 14:14) to meet the multitude. But this time he slips away "alone," thus it will be harder to find him in the approaching darkness.

16) John writes for readers who have Matt. 14:22-34 and Mark 6:45-51 before them, who thus know to what he refers (v. 17) and are able to combine the new features he offers with the accounts they already know so well. **Now when evening came, his disciples went down to the Sea.** They lingered until evening (ὀψία, supply ὥρα), not the so-called first evening, from 3 to 6, but the second, from 6 until dark, for we hear that darkness soon set in. "They went down" means from the place where the 5,000 had been fed, where Jesus left them with strict orders ("constrained," Matt. 14:22) as to what to do, namely to sail for Capernaum without him a little before dusk.

17) **And having embarked in a boat, they were proceeding beyond the Sea to Capernaum. And darkness had already come, and Jesus had not yet come to them.** The boat was the one in which they had come (v. 1), the only one on that shore (v. 22). The descriptive imperfect ἤρχοντο pictures the disciples

sailing away, withholding for the moment the information as to how their voyage turned out. "Beyond
the Sea" states their general and "to Capernaum"
their specific destination. We catch the intention of
their Master in this way to remove them from the
foolish multitude and its plans to make him an earthly
king. In a little while he would show them and also
let the multitude infer what kind of a king he really
was. In the meanwhile we see the little vessel in its
progress toward the setting sun. All is calm and
beautiful. The experienced sailors in the boat anticipate no difficulty in reaching their destination not
long after dark.

When, after thus picturing the disciples as proceeding on their journey, John remarks that darkness "had
already come" and furthermore that "Jesus had not
yet come to them," he refers in advance to what his
readers know from the accounts of Matthew and of
Mark. The two pluperfect tenses are well explained
by R. 904: "The verb in the sentence before is
ἤρχοντο (descriptive), and the verb following is διηγείρετο
(inchoative, the sea was beginning to rise). The time
of these imperfects is, of course, past. But the two
intervening past perfects indicate stages in the going
(ἤρχοντο) before they reached the shore. Both ἤδη and
οὔπω help to accent the interval between the first darkness and the final appearance of Jesus which is soon
expressed by the vivid historical present θεωροῦσιν
(v. 19). Here we have a past behind a past beyond
a doubt from the standpoint of the writer, and that
is the very reason why John used the past perfects
here." R. is right when he adds that these tenses
"form a very interesting study," that John often uses
them to take us "behind the scenes."

The gathering storm very likely hastened the darkness. John writes from a very vivid recollection. The
puzzling of the commentators about the statement that

"Jesus had not yet come to the disciples" is solved, likewise their proposed solutions, such as that the disciples had some kind of an expectation that Jesus would come to them either before they sailed or while they were sailing, or that Jesus had made them such a promise. Nor can the supposed puzzle be solved by charging John with contradicting the synoptists. With "not yet" John merely refers to the coming of Jesus which his readers know from Matthew and from Mark; as Robertson puts it, John's reference is "beyond a doubt from the standpoint of the writer." The disciples were sailing on Jesus' orders. What he intended to do he had kept to himself. Darkness and storm were upon them — and they were alone. John and his readers know that Jesus came to them, but John says: here they were in this position — Jesus had not yet come.

18) **And the sea, a great wind blowing, was beginning to rise.** On τέ see R. 1179. The inchoative imperfect means that the sea was rising more and more. The genitive absolute, "a great wind blowing," states the reason. Matthew writes that the boat was distressed by the waves, the wind being against them. Mark says the disciples were distressed with the rowing. At the start they had used their sail, since the boat was large enough to hold so many passengers and was fitted with a sail. But the contrary wind, as well as its violence, with the darkness complicating the situation, soon made them resort to their oars, thus trying to keep the boat head on against the raging waves — a distressing task, indeed.

19) **Having rowed, therefore, about twenty-five or thirty stadia, they behold Jesus walking on the sea and drawing nigh unto the boat; and they were affrighted.** The other evangelists mention the time when Jesus came to the boat, about the fourth watch of the night, i. e., toward morning, between 3 and 6,

showing that the disciples had fought against the storm all night long. John adds to this information the short distance they had covered by all this work of rowing against the storm, $3\frac{1}{8}$ to $3\frac{3}{4}$ miles, a stadium being $\frac{1}{8}$ of a Roman or English mile. As to their location with reference to Capernaum or to any part of the shore we have no intimation, and it is safe to assume that, rowing as they did in the dark and in the open lake, the disciples themselves did not know. Only one thing is certain, they were still far from their destination.

John reports the miracle itself only in a summary way, "they behold Jesus walking on the sea and drawing nigh to the boat." The only touches are the dramatic present tense "they behold" and the descriptive participles "walking and drawing nigh." John writes "Jesus," but at first they could have seen only the indistinct figure on the water moving toward them. Mark adds this point, together with the superstitious thought of the disciples that they were seeing a "phantasm" or ghost. The darkness, the hour of night, the storm and the danger still in full force, the exhausting battle with the oars, all combined to make the disciples give way to the superstitions still lurking in their minds. What would some who now smile at superstition have felt and said if they had held an oar in that boat? Mark adds that Jesus was about to walk past the boat; John reports only his drawing nigh. Jesus was giving the disciples time to recover from their fright, also time to ask him to enter the boat. When trying to imagine Jesus walking on the sea, we must not overlook the storm and the raging waves. These howled and dashed about him, but they did not affect him in the least. He was not tossed up and down; his clothes and his body were not wet with spray. Before him as he moved his feet a smooth, apparently solid path lay, on which he walked as on ordinary ground. He did not move as a specter is supposed to move; no unearthly light played around him, as painters often imagine. It was simply Jesus as they had left him the evening before — only now he was walking on the storm-tossed sea. One might inquire whether he had walked all the way from the shore to the boat or had suddenly transported himself to the spot where the disciples first saw him. Curious questions, for which no sign of an answer exists, should not be raised. The aorist "they were affrighted" states the mere fact, and the verb includes all of the Twelve.

20) **But he says to them, It is I — stop being afraid!** This was done to calm the disciples' superstitious fear. "It is I" = and no specter. "It is I" = your Lord and Master whom you know so well. The other evangelists report that Jesus' first word was, "Be of good cheer!" assuring them that all their troubles were ended. And Mark 6:52 adds that despite the wonderful feeding of the 5,000 the disciples failed to understand with their hardened hearts. These obdurate hearts Jesus now tries again to penetrate with faith. The present imperative often forbids what one is already doing; so here $\mu\grave{\eta}$ $\phi o\beta\epsilon\hat{\imath}\sigma\theta\epsilon$ = "stop being afraid!" John makes no reference to the incident regarding Peter but tells us about the landing.

21) **They were willing, therefore, to take him into the boat; and immediately the boat was at the land to which they were going.** Overagainst the dreadful fear that they were seeing a ghost, a portent presaging that they were all doomed to destruction, John sets the durative imperfect $\mathring{\eta}\theta\epsilon\lambda o\nu$, "they were willing" to take him into the boat, which describes the new feeling and desire: instead of paralyzing fright, this desire and this willingness. If John had written the aorist, he would have expressed the will only as a single act; he chose the imperfect in order

to describe a new state of will. True enough, this imperfect does not itself indicate that the will to take Jesus into the boat was carried into effect. That, however, lies in the following aorist ἐγένετο, "immediately the boat *was* at the land." For no reader for a moment would think that Jesus was left out on the sea while the boat with only the disciples in it was at that instant at the land. Besides, John counts on his readers knowing what the other evangelists had recorded long ago, how Jesus did enter the boat and also lifted Peter into it. Thus all the worry about the tense of ἤθελον is brushed away. John neither "differs from" the other evangelists nor "contradicts" them. On the other hand, we need not insist on making the imperfect tense of this verb exceptional, as including the execution of the wish. Least of all will we resort to the supposition that Jesus walked past the boat after calling to the disciples, then suddenly disappeared, and finally came to the disciples after they had landed.

John now mentions something that the other narrators omit. They report only that Jesus entered the boat, and that the storm then instantly ceased, due, of course, to the will and the power of Jesus. John adds the detail that "immediately" the boat "was at the land to which they were going." In other words, the exhausted disciples were not compelled to begin their rowing again in order to cover the considerable distance to the shore. We now see why John notes the distance covered during the stormy night voyage, some 25 to 30 stadia. He means to say that the boat was still far from shore when Jesus came to it. That distance melted away the moment Jesus stepped into the boat.

By "the land to which they were going" the reader will understand Capernaum, even as v. 17 indicates. This is made certain by the following references, that "on

the morrow" the multitude crossed by boats to Capernaum and there found Jesus teaching in the synagogue
(v. 59). Besides this the situation requires that the
discourse on the Bread of Life be spoken immediately
on the day after the feeding of the 5,000, for it is
addressed to those who were thus fed and who certainly would not have remained together for a couple
of days waiting in Capernaum for Jesus, but, coming
as they did "from all the cities" (Mark 6:33), would
have scattered again to their homes in those cities.
John's account is too compact and too closely knit
for us to insert at this point Matt. 14:34-36, and
Mark 6:53-56, letting Jesus and the disciples land
on the plain of Gennesaret on the morning after the
storm, spending one or more days among the people
of this region, and then finally going to Capernaum.
The two aorist participles in Matthew and in Mark,
"having crossed over," are quite general and do not
compel us, like the close reference in John, to connect the visit to the region of Gennesaret with the
journey by boat through the stormy night. This visit
must be set at a later time. The assumption that
6:59 occurred on the Sabbath, because Jesus was
teaching in a synagogue at Capernaum, coupled with
the observation that the multitude would hardly have
taken so long a journey by boat on the Sabbath in
trying to find Jesus, overlooks the action of Jesus and
of his disciples. For if the day after the feeding of
the 5,000 was a Sabbath, that Sabbath began the very
evening when Jesus himself ordered the disciples to
sail the identical distance to Capernaum and would
include the night of the storm during which the disciples labored to exhaustion. Assemblies, however,
were held in the synagogues not only on Saturday
but also on Monday and on Thursday. We are not
compelled to think of a Sabbath every time we find
Jesus in a synagogue. The statement in 6:4 that the

Passover was near is too indefinite to justify a dating of the day of the miracle. It is useless to figure the day of the Passover of this year as being Monday, April 18, in the year 29; and then to set the date of the miracle on the day before, and thus to fix the date of the discourse in the synagogue on the Monday of this Passover.

John narrates the two miracles, that of the feeding of the 5,000 and that of Jesus' walking on the sea not merely in order to inform us that these great miracles occurred but for a much higher purpose. They constitute the divine prelude and preparation for the attestation of Jesus in the discourses on himself as the Bread of Life. By placing these miracles into this vital connection John gives us far more than the other evangelists, who say nothing of the teaching on the Bread of Life and content themselves with the miracles as such. In John's Gospel they are introduced as aids given in advance to faith in order that all concerned might believe that Jesus is the Bread of Life and thus might have what is far greater than earthly help.

The Decisive Discourse on the Bread of Life, 6:22-59. — Its three parts are not coordinated in the ordinary fashion, but the second advances beyond the first, and the third beyond the second. The structure is like that of an inverted pyramid: 1) Jesus gives to him that believes the Bread of Life; 2) Jesus gives to him that believes himself as the Bread of Life; 3) Jesus gives to him that believes his flesh as the Bread of Life.

Jesus Gives the Bread of Life, 22-40

22) **On the morrow the multitude which was standing beyond the Sea saw that no other boat was there except one and that Jesus did not enter with his disciples into the boat, but his disciples**

alone went away. Instead of combining the thoughts of v. 22-24 in one balanced period in the Hellenistic style of writing, John strings them together in the Hebraistic fashion, which results in less smoothness. The perfect participle ἑστηκώς is always used as a present: the multitude "which stands." It is the situation described in the two ὅτι clauses, the situation produced already the evening before, that John tells us the multitude "on the morrow saw." We thus need not change εἶδον into the participle ἰδών (a far inferior reading), to throw the seeing back to the previous evening; nor need we put a pluperfect sense into the simple aorist. It was not until the next morning that the multitude really "saw" the situation: first, that yesterday (hence ἦν and not ἐστί, R. 887) no other small boat (πλοιάριον) was there except one, i. e., the one in which Jesus and the disciples had crossed; and secondly, that Jesus yesterday did not go into that boat with his disciples (hence the article εἰς τὸ πλοιάριον), but the disciples yesterday went away alone. How much of this the multitude had seen yesterday does not matter to John, but that "on the morrow they saw" this is the point for him, for not until now does the multitude begin to put two and two together. When we understand John thus we need not, by resorting to ἰδών, regard v. 22-24 as an awkward anacoluthon or broken sentence, just because *we* think that the multitude should have seen all this already during the evening.

23) The next statement is parenthetical, explaining how boats arrived in the morning on which the multitude could also cross to Capernaum. **But there came boats from Tiberias near to the place where they ate the bread after the Lord had given thanks.** None came from Capernaum, for in the morning Jesus was found there together with his disciples. John does not state for what purpose these boats from Tiberias

crossed the lake. It is a fair guess to say, because the boatmen knew that the multitude could not long stay on this lonely shore, and many would want to ride back instead of once more going the long road around the upper end of the Sea. These boats, it seems, brought no passengers, for they are now ready to take on passengers and to carry them just where these want to go. If the boats had come from Tiberias loaded, they could not have helped the multitude to cross and would, of course, have taken only their original passengers back to Tiberias.

Tiberias had been built on the southwest shore of the lake by Herod Antipas, the murderer of the Baptist, and was named in honor of the emperor Tiberius. We have no record that Jesus ever visited that city, for its character was strongly pagan. Outside of the two designations of the sea as being that of Tiberias (6:1; 21:1) the city is mentioned only here and that quite incidentally. Until the fourth century it was the seat of the rabbinical school which produced the *Mishna* or Jerusalem Talmud and the *Masora*. In 1925 the author found it a small town, with two ancient towers at the water's edge, while practically no assured trace can be found of even the location of Capernaum, Bethsaida, and Chorazin (Matt. 11:20, etc.; Luke 10:13, etc.). Note that here for the first time in his Gospel John himself calls Jesus "the Lord."

24) **Accordingly, when the multitude saw that Jesus was not there nor his disciples, they themselves entered the boats and came to Capernaum, seeking Jesus.** They evidently first made a thorough search. The Greek preserves the tense of their present finding ἐστί: "Jesus *is* not here"; compare ἦν to express the absence of any other boat on the previous day, v. 22. They also made sure that the disciples whom they had seen sail away in the evening had

not returned during the night. The singular εἶδεν treats "the multitude" as a collective, while εἶδον in v. 22 and the two plurals in v. 24 refer to the individuals. As a body they "saw" that Jesus and the disciples were not there, but they embarked and went away as so many individuals. They were still a large number, but hardly any longer 5,000; many, we must suppose, had left the evening before, and others in the morning. Those that secured passage in the boats go to Capernaum, either following a guess that this was the most likely place to find Jesus, or because someone of their number had heard Jesus tell the disciples to sail to Capernaum.

25) It was not long before they found him. **And having found him beyond the Sea, they said to him, Rabbi** (see 1:38), **when hast thou come hither?** It is grace on Jesus' part that he allows these people to find him; he is still willing to work upon their souls. Their question is full of curiosity and yet entirely natural, surmising something miraculous, as John's elaborate explanations in v. 22, 23 show. They ask "when," since the time was so short and the way around the shore so long. This "when," therefore, also includes a "how." The perfect tense "hast thou come" = and thus art here, R. 896. Let us note that this question could never have been asked a day or two later, for then Jesus would have had more than enough time to get back to Capernaum in the ordinary way. This again shuts out the view that Jesus and the disciples landed south of Capernaum in Gennesaret and remained there a day or more.

26) While the question hints at a new miracle, it comes from hearts that are eager only to see miracles and not to understand them aright. Hence Jesus does not tell these people when or how he came across so mysteriously but in his answer rebukes their wrong spirit. Many answers of Jesus are on this order. He

replies to men's hearts not merely to their words. He would give what men need not merely what they would like to have. **Jesus answered them and said** (see 1:48), **Amen, amen, I say to you** (see 1:51), **you are seeking me, not because you saw signs, but because you ate of the loaves and were filled.** The two verbs in the preamble mark the reply as being weighty, likewise the two "amen," which stamp the reply with verity, and "I say to you," which stamps it with authority. They ask about *him*, he answers about *them*. What he tells them is the plain truth. People do not like to hear what their real spiritual condition is. Shams are so popular, but verity alone saves, even though it is bitter.

"Not because you saw signs" means that these people only saw *wonders* and never saw *signs* at all, i. e., signs full of great meaning. We need not make the plural "signs" one of category in order to make it cover only the feeding of the 5,000; for v. 2 reports that Jesus healed many sick at the place where presently he also fed the multitude, and these healings, too, were "signs" full of significance. On the term "signs" see 2:11. These people failed to see what was so gloriously pictured to them, the divinity of Jesus, his ability to feed their souls as he had fed their bodies, his Savior qualities as the Messiah sent of God. They had held the wonder bread in their hands, had eaten it with their mouths, but had never understood its true meaning with their hearts.

Overagainst the negative Jesus puts the positive, "but because you ate of the loaves and were filled." Jesus drives this home by using the coarse word χορτάζω, from χόρτος, fodder or hay; they were satisfied like the ox when his belly is full of fodder. That is all these people obtained ἐκ τῶν ἄρτων (note the article), "out of the bread" that meant to give them so much more. It is easy to see how coarse and low

were the desires of these people; but thousands today
have no higher desires.

27) As stern as is the rebuke, so strong is the
renewed call of grace. **Work not for the eating
which perishes but for the eating which remains
unto life eternal, which the Son of man shall give
you; for him the Father did seal, even God.** The
pivotal word is the imperative, "Work for," which
was selected so as to fit the two kinds of "eating,"
βρῶσις, that which perishes and that which remains.
On the distinction between βρῶμα and βρῶσις compare
4:32 and 34; the latter signifies both the food and
its eating. We are to exert ourselves so that we may
have not merely earthly food to eat but spiritual and
heavenly food to eat. But "work for" excludes every
Pelagian and synergistic sense. Even earthly food
for bodily eating we do not produce by any "working"
of ours, it is God's creature and gift; witness every
earthly harvest, also the miracle of the feeding of
the 5,000. In a far higher sense the spiritual food
for our eating is that "which the Son of man shall
give you." The entire subject is perfectly elucidated
in *Concordia Triglotta*, 901, 48, etc. Here the quest-
tion is answered, "How we should conduct ourselves
towards these means (Word and Sacraments) and use
them" (48). In brief: 1) *"go to church and hear"*
(53); 2) "be certain that when the Word of God is
preached purely and truly, according to the command
and will of God, and men *listen attentively and
earnestly and mediate upon it,* God is certainly
present with his grace and grants, as has been said,
what otherwise man can neither accept nor give from
his own powers" (55). When Jesus bids the people
at Capernaum to "work" thus, he implies that they
have not as yet done so. They, indeed, had come and
had heard, but altogether superficially, with their ears
not with their hearts. They had clung to the tem-

poral and transient, and every effort of Jesus to
give them the eternal they had passed over coldly and
indifferently.

Note the utter folly of working for τὴν βρῶσιν τὴν
ἀπολλυμένην, a food and eating the very nature of which
is that it perishes. Here is a true description of all
earthly food and bodily possession and satisfaction —
it "perishes." True, this food, etc., is also one of God's
blessings — did not Jesus himself feed the 5,000?
For it, too, we may work; for the command, "Work
not!" is meant relatively, i. e., do not make earthly
food, etc., your life's chief concern. But ever we must
know that because of its very nature all we thus obtain "perishes." When life is done, what is left of it
all for us? Nothing, absolutely nothing.

In striking contrast with this perishable food Jesus
places "the eating which remains unto life eternal."
This is the food and eating which truly satisfies the
heart and soul, the very nature of which is that it
does not perish or come to nothing but remains forever
with its blessed effect. The phrase "unto life eternal"
should not be construed merely with the participle,
as though this food endures to a future period called
life eternal, but with the entire expression. For the
εἰς phrase denotes purpose with the idea of result,
R. 897. This abiding food and eating is "unto life
eternal," it produces life and salvation here and hereafter. How few are those who seek this eating, knowing what it brings forth! This wonderful βρῶσις has
been defined as the Word of God; as grace and truth;
as a treasure which Jesus bears in himself and gives,
namely eternal life; or simply as Jesus himself. But
in v. 32 Jesus interprets βρῶσις as "the true bread out
of heaven"; in v. 35 and 48, "I am the Bread of
life"; in verse 51; and in verse 55, "my flesh is meat
indeed, and my blood is drink indeed." Summing up
these statements, we have as the βρῶσις: Christ who

is sacrificed for us. But the term implies also that by faith we eat this βρῶσις and thus have and enjoy "life eternal," see 3:15.

In the relative clause, "which the Son of man shall give you," the verb "shall give" removes every synergistic notion from the command, "work for." For this food and its eating is entirely a gracious gift of Jesus as "the Son of man," the divine incarnate Messiah (on this title see 1:51). The reading "shall give" has more authority than the present "gives," although the sense is quite the same. The future "shall give" is relative to the present tense "work for," in the sense that the moment we are moved to want this gift Jesus bestows it by his blessed grace.

The explanatory clause, "for him did the Father seal, even God," shows how this Son of man is able to do this wonderful giving. This time Jesus does not say merely that the Father sent him, but that the Father "sealed him," i. e., sent him and confirmed or attested him as one so sent to give this enduring food unto life eternal. The addition "even God" is placed emphatically at the end. The Father as "God" is the highest possible authority, beyond which no man can go. His seal should at once be recognized and accepted without question. The seal he affixed to Jesus these people had seen on the previous day in the miracles he wrought, especially in that of the bread. This seal should at once produce faith, and Jesus now refers to it in order to call forth faith from these people now. Luther writes: "It is a Hebrew way of speaking to say that our Lord God has a ring, a signet and seal on his thumb, with which he stamps when he writes and sends out a letter. Such a seal Christ is to be, and no one else; he thereby rejects and condemns all other seals. This is a strong word, which reaches exceedingly far, that whoever would live forever must have this meat which the Son gives

and must be found in the Son who is sealed; otherwise, if he has him not, he will miss eternal life, for
here is the seal and testimony attached. See now
what you have in this text; there you find clearly:
the Father has given his seal to the Son. With this
word he snatches away from all other teachers, who
would nourish me eternally, their honor and merit, and
admonishes us to remain with Christ alone. Therefore go and see whether God the Father has sealed
what is preached to you and you are asked to believe;
if not, tear the seal away."

28) **They, accordingly, said to him, What shall
we do in order to work the works of God?** Jesus
secures a response, but what a response! Remember
the response of blind Nicodemus and that of the
Samaritan woman. Yet note the deliberative subjunctive in the question, which suggests doubt on the
whole subject, or a wish to do something, not being
certain what that ought to be; this is quite different
from the present indicative, R. 923, etc. The subjunctive would take Jesus' answer under advisement;
the indicative would ask for Jesus' orders. The
tenses, too, must be noted, "what are we to be doing,
in order to be working," etc.? The worst part of the
answer, however, lies in the use of the plural: in
order that we may be working "the works of God,"
those commanded by God. These people imagine that
there is an entire scale of such works, a multiplicity
of meritorious deeds to be done by them. Moreover,
they imply that if they knew just what these works are,
they may with powers and efforts of their own decide
to do them. They think that the "giving" of which
Jesus speaks is like the bestowal of wages for such
works. Thus these people completely lose sight of
the meaning of the miracle of the past day when
Jesus gave them a free gift, which was to signify
a still greater free gift to be received by them through

faith. Jesus speaks of grace; they think only of work-righteousness.

29) The answer of Jesus is a masterpiece. **Jesus answered and said to them** (the two verbs mark the weightiness of the reply), **This is the work of God, that you believe on whom he did send.** He keeps the term "work," the verb for which he used in v. 27, and by one stroke corrects the wrong idea put into it by these people. He turns their wrong plural, "the works of God," into the correct singular, "this is the work of God." He makes the genitive "of God" mean, not "commanded by God," but "wrought by God." And then in the ἵνα clause, which is in apposition to "this," R. 400, he plainly defines just what work God works in us. Faith is here called a "work" in a peculiar sense, differentiating it entirely from "works" as righteous acts of ours. We, indeed, must do the believing, but our believing is the work of *God. We* trust, but *God* kindles that trust in us. Compare v. 37, "All that the Father giveth me shall come unto me"; v. 44, "No man can come to me, except the Father which sent me draw him." Faith is "of the operation of God," Col. 2:12. Hence faith is not "the fundamental virtue" from which the other works flow. Faith is the opposite of all other works. For faith receives from God; the other works make return to God. All law works (works of unregenerate men) are the very opposition of faith, for by such works men would climb to heaven on their own merit, without a Savior and without faith. All Christian good works do, indeed, spring from faith, like fruit from a good tree, but always and only from a faith which already has Christ, salvation, life eternal, and needs no good works to merit these treasures which never can be merited.

The present subjunctive "that you believe" means continuous believing; compare the verb in 1:12:

trust or *fiducia*, relying for salvation wholly on Christ. No man can trust anyone of himself; the person whom he trusts by his character, words, acts, etc., always instills the trust. This Jesus ever sought to do by his person, words, deeds, and by his Father's mighty attestation. Thus *we trust*, but at the same time this *trust is wrought in us*. Only to him who trusts Jesus can he give salvation; all who refuse to trust him would not accept the gift from him but think they can obtain it elsewhere. Thus also Jesus at once designates himself as the one who is absolutely trustworthy: believe "on whom he did send." This summarizes his Messianic mission and at the same time points to his exalted person. Only then dare any man refuse to trust Jesus if Jesus is not the person he says he is, and if he is not sent by God as he says, and if God's attestations of Jesus are false. The relative "on whom" has the antecedent drawn into itself: "on him whom," etc.; and ἐκεῖνος is emphatic: *he*, the Father, God! Note how faith recurs in this discourse: v. 35, 40, 47, and figuratively: v. 50, 51, 53, 54, 56, 58. Also in the confession of Peter, "We have believed," v. 69.

30) **They, therefore, said to him, What, then, art thou doing as a sign that we may see and may believe thee? What art thou working?** Both John's οὖν and that in the question itself bring out the idea that this question is intended to be a legitimate deduction from what Jesus has just said. Asking so much of *us*, they say, what art *thou* doing to justify that? Note the emphatic σύ placed after the verb. They keep both of the verbs they used in v. 28 and thus emphatically give Jesus back his own demand: "what art thou *doing?* what art thou *working?*" i. e., now or at any time. What they mean comes out in the predicate accusative: what art thou doing "as a sign"? They thus cast the blame back on Jesus him-

self. If *he* would do more, *they* would respond with
more. When Jesus fed them miraculously the day
before, had they not wanted to make him king? If
Jesus wants them to do more, he himself will have
to do more in the way of a sign. They fail entirely
to see that they had not understood the meaning of
the miracle they had witnessed. If Jesus had given
them a list of works to do, they would have been
ready to attempt them; but this insistence of his on
faith only makes them balk. Not grasping what
Jesus means by this faith, they catch only that he
means more than they have done and so ask for more
from him.

The two aorists in the *ἵνα* clause are not ingressive,
"come to see and come to believe," as R. 850 states;
their force is, "that we may actually see and actually
believe." The latter verb is construed only with the
dative, "believe thee," i. e., what thou sayest.

31) To re-enforce their counterdemand that Jesus
do more if he demands so much, these people point
to what Moses had done. **Our fathers did eat the
manna in the wilderness, as has been written, Bread
out of heaven he did give them to eat.** The periphrastic perfect "has been written" implies: and is
now on record. In Ps. 78:24 the LXX has "bread
of heaven," but these Jews revert to the Hebrew
"bread out of heaven." Exod. 16:4 reads, "I will rain
bread from (out of) heaven for you," the prepositional
phrase modifying the verb. In the quotation the
emphasis is on the character of the bread not on the
manner of giving, hence the wonderful gift is termed
"bread out of heaven." That, these people mean to
say, was a sign far greater than what they had witnessed yesterday. Jesus only multiplied some bread
he already had, but Moses gave the fathers bread
right out of heaven. What had Jesus to compare with
that? A shrewd kind of reasoning is thus offered which

is apparently sound yet is false in its very premises.
As they put it, Moses is far greater than Jesus — why,
then, does Jesus claim to be so exceedingly great?
If he is, let him bring on a sign that is greater than
this one of Moses'.

32)   This demand Jesus ignores because it is met
the moment these people are shown what "the true
Bread out of heaven" really is. **Jesus, therefore,
said to them, Amen, amen, I say to you, Moses did
not give you the bread out of heaven, but my Father
is giving you the genuine bread out of heaven. For
the bread of God is that which comes down out of
heaven and gives life to the world.** Only in a superficial sense could the manna in the wilderness (as is
done in the Psalm) be called *dagan shamajim,*
"heaven-bread," for after all it was only like other
earthly bread, satisfying only the body from day to
day. So again with the seal of verity and authority
(see 1:51) Jesus corrects these people. The point of
the correction lies in the twice used term "bread out
of heaven," which is then defined at length as "the
bread of God," actually "coming down out of heaven
(origin) and giving life to the world" (exceeding
great effect). Note the constrasts: Moses — my
Father; did not give — is giving; bread out of heaven,
as these people understand it — bread out of heaven,
as Jesus understands it; out of heaven, not applicable to the manna, which never was in heaven — out
of heaven, applicable to the genuine bread, which
actually was in heaven and actually comes down out
of heaven. This genuine (ἀληθινόν) bread Moses could
not give, nor even God through Moses. Since Jesus
speaks of this bread he says nothing about the fathers
but uses the pronoun "you" in both clauses.

33)   The γάρ clause makes Jesus' meaning plain
by stating just what "the bread out of heaven" is.

It is "the bread of God" — *"bread,"* indeed, always "bread," because we are to receive and to eat it and thus to obtain what it conveys. But actually bread *"of God,"* derived directly from God himself, *das wesenhafte Brot Gottes.* What lies in this weighty genitive is expressed in the predicate, the two present participles being combined under one article and thus made a unit. These participles describe the character and the quality of this bread of God, hence are really timeless. Like no other bread that ever existed, not even the manna, this bread is such as actually "comes down out of heaven" from God himself in heaven and thus is such also as "gives life to the world." This ζωή (1:4; 3:15) is the life principle itself. It does not only keep the life that one already has alive by nourishing it, it actually brings and gives life, the true and eternal life, to those who are dead and have no life. In this sense it is "the bread of God," and a bread that does this is not a mere creature of God like other bread and like the manna, it descends from God's own being out of heaven where God is. And being such bread, its effect is for no limited number but actually for "the world," for the universe of men. The manna fed only "the fathers," only for a few years, and only their bodies which perished in the wilderness. Think, then, by comparison, what this "bread of God" is. The sentence reads naturally with "bread" as the subject and the articulated participles as the predicate. Some would invert this and would make the articulated participles the subject, regarding them as substantivized, "he that comes down and gives is the bread of God," i. e., proving by coming down and giving (the effect) that he is the bread of God (the cause). But this inversion is unnatural, and no reader would make it of his own accord. The fact that this bread is a person descended from God in heaven on a mission to bestow life on the world, is still not revealed but will be most clearly stated in a moment.

34) So captivating is this description of the bread of God that it draws even from these unspiritual people the request that Jesus give them this bread. **They said, therefore, to him, Sir, evermore give us this bread.** This case is identical with that of the Samaritan woman in 4:15. The respectful address "sir" or "lord" shows that no irony is intended as though these people mean, "We do not believe there is such bread, but since you claim there is, give us some of it!" They do really want this bread; they are impressed by its great desirability. But the emphatic adverb "evermore" betrays the fact that they still think only of bodily bread that will obviate their baking and their buying from time to time, that they can eat constantly without effort whenever they grow hungry.

35) Right through this unspiritual denseness flashes the reply of Jesus, destroying once for all every notion of bodily bread and bodily eating. **Jesus said to them, I am the Bread of Life. He that comes to me shall in no way hunger, and he that believes in me shall in no way thirst ever.** Here is one of the great *I AM* statements of Jesus, shining like the noonday sun. Jesus is this bread. Who now can any longer think of mere bodily bread? He it is who came from God out of heaven and gives life eternal — he, sent of God on this mission for the world. To him men must come, in him they must trust, and thus men eat and drink him with the result that they shall never again hunger or thirst. No reply, in words so few, could be more to the point once for all to set these people right.

"The Bread of Life," like "the water of life" in chapter 4, is Biblical allegory which unites the figure

"Bread" with the reality "Life" and thus always interprets itself; compare "living water" in 4:10. In 14:6 the allegory is dropped and only the reality is predicated, "I am the Life." Compare Gen. 3:22; Rev. 22:2 and 17. The figure "Bread" connotes eating, which in the reality "Life" means coming to Jesus and trusting in him. It is especially necessary to note that the predicate has the article. Jesus does not say, "I am Bread of Life," which would mean that others, too, are such Bread; but, "I am *the* Bread of Life." Subject and predicate are indentical and thus interchangeable (R. 768, read at length), so that Jesus could also say, "The Bread of Life is I." He and he alone is "the Bread of Life"; apart from him no such Bread exists. Other "I am" statements of Jesus are of the same type, such as, "I am the Light of the world"; "I am the vine"; etc.

As clear as is the brief word on the Bread, so clear also is that on the eating. This statement resembles the parallelism of Hebrew poetry:

> "He that comes to me shall not hunger,
>   And he that believes in me shall in no way thirst ever."

The present participles are substantivized by the articles, with the present tense indicating only quality; and the second elucidates the first, for only he comes to Jesus for this Bread who trusts him. "Coming" is often used for believing, but here, in order to obtain the greatest clearness, both are placed side by side. In the two phrases with the participles the textual authority is in favor of πρὸς ἐμέ and εἰς ἐμέ, the emphatic pronouns instead of the enclitic forms of these pronouns; which also harmonizes with the emphatic ἐγώ: "*I* am . . . comes to *me* . . . believes in *mē*." A striking point for correcting the notion of mere bodily eating is that Jesus without a word of explanation adds the idea of drink to that of bread. Faith is both eating and drinking, so that either may be used or both; compare 4:10, etc. Thus to eat and to drink, Jesus says, abolishes hunger and thirst forever, 4:14, which corrects the request, "Evermore give us this bread." Life, once given, lives on and on, even natural life, although this has a terminus, while spiritual life (unless it is destroyed by unbelief) has none. In both statements note the strongest form of negation in οὐ μή, first with the aorist subjunctive, "shall in no way hunger," and secondly with the future indicative, "shall in no way thirst," to which is added the adverb "ever."

36) To the Jews at Jerusalem Jesus had to say, "You will not come to me, that you may have life," 5:40. To these Jews in Galilee Jesus must now say the same, **But I said to you that you have both seen me and do not believe.** With "I said to you" Jesus refers to v. 26, where he told these people of their guilty unbelief; and here, where his self-revelation is so vivid and clear, this unbelief still persists. These Galileans now know both the Bread and the eating; but *this* Bread does not attract them, *this* eating they refuse. "Both . . . and," καί . . . καί here connect opposites: instead of "you have both seen and do believe," Jesus is compelled to say, "you have both seen and do *not* believe." The perfect "have seen" implies that what they saw is still before their eyes, i. e., the miracles of the past day together with all that Jesus reveals to them. The present tense, "and do not believe," matches this perfect; they still go on without trusting Jesus. Here the guilt of unbelief becomes evident. When the blessed reality of life and salvation in Christ is placed before the eyes and the hearts of men, so that they are made to see them, and when they then refuse to believe and to accept these gifts, their guilt is on their

own heads. But Jesus points these people to this their guilt, not in order to cast them off forever (although they deserve that), but in order to drive fear into their conscience.

37) The Jews of Jerusalem had turned against Jesus, and now these Galileans were doing the same. But Jesus is not a mere man, operating alone as best he can with his human wisdom and his strength. He tells these Galileans plainly who is behind him, and how, therefore, his work will reach its glorious goal without the least question. But by saying this to these people and by telling them how he will carry out the Father's gracious will in all who believe by giving them eternal life and by raising them up on the last day, Jesus raises the question for them: how about themselves? Do they mean to turn against the Father, contradict his saving will, and thus, as far as they are concerned, by their own folly shut themselves out from life now and hereafter? Thus once more Jesus grips their hearts, drawing them from unbelief to faith. The absence of a connective need not indicate a pause on the part of Jesus; it is sufficiently explained by the turn of the thought. The Galileans are not believing; from them Jesus turns to the great host that will believe. **All that the Father gives to me shall get to me; and him that comes to me I will in no wise cast out.** First the mass: "all that," etc.; then each individual: "him that," etc. The neuter singular is used as an abstract expression and as such sums up the whole mass of believers of all ages and speaks of them as a unit (R. 409); it is even stronger than if Jesus had used a masculine plural. Yet beside this unit mass Jesus places each believer as an individual, for all faith is highly personal.

When Jesus says of this unit mass that the Father "gives" it to him, he describes the gift as being in

progress, as more and more of this mass is being
made Jesus' own. In v. 39 Jesus uses the perfect
tense: all that the Father "has given to me," which
describes the gift as having been made once for all
and as now being permanent as such a gift. The
difference between the tenses lies only in the point
of view, which is brought out in the respective predicates. For all that the Father "gives to me," Jesus
says, "shall get to me." He sees the gift flowing to
him in a great stream through the coming ages; and
although the gift is so great, running through so long
a period, all of it shall reach him, not even the slightest
part of it shall fail to come into his possession. That
is the case, of course, because the Father's gift cannot
possibly fail. To match the neuter πᾶν Jesus uses ἥξει,
"shall get to me"; not ἐλεύσεται, "shall come to me." The
former does not suggest a voluntary action on the part
of the mass, because πᾶν indicates mass only as such.
When it comes to the individual, we see that each is
described as ὁ ἐρχόμενος, "he that comes to me." In
v. 39 the perfect tense, "all that he has given to
me," pictures the gift from the viewpoint of the last
day when Jesus will appear and will not have lost
any part of this gift and will then put it beyond all
possibility of loss by raising the entire mass of believers from their graves.

But in these expressions, "all that the Father
gives," and, "all that he has given," Jesus speaks of
all believers of all ages as already being present to
the eyes of God, he also thus is giving them to Jesus.
This Jesus does repeatedly: v. 65; 10:16 and 29;
17:2 and 9 and 24. There, however, is not a fixed
number, in some mysterious way chosen by an absolute decree of God to be such a gift to Jesus. Such
an exegesis is wholly dogmatic and carries into what
Jesus says a thought that is not contained in his
words. On the other hand, equally dogmatic is the

view that those who constitute God's gift to Jesus are those who in the first place are morally better than the rest, or who at least act better than the rest when the gospel is brought to them. These words of Jesus are without a trace of either predestinarianism or synergism. God's grace is universal. He would give all men to Jesus. The only reason he does not do so is because so many men obdurately refuse to be part of that gift. On the other hand, God's grace is alone efficacious. Every man who believes does so only and wholly by virtue of this grace. Thus the words of Jesus concerning the Father's gift to him and its getting to him raises the question for these Galileans, "Do they want to be a part of this gift, or do they mean to exclude themselves?" "Shall get to me" implies that Jesus accepts the gift.

"Him that comes to me" makes the matter individual, personal, and a voluntary act. The Father's drawing (v. 44) is one of grace alone, thus it is efficacious, wholly sufficient, able to change the unwilling into the willing, but not by coercion, not irresistibly. Man can obdurately refuse to come. Yet when he comes he does so only through the blessed power of grace. Him that comes thus (the present participle only describing the person as such) Jesus "shall in no wise cast out," a strong litotes for "shall most certainly receive." The Son could not possibly contravene the will of his Father. Back of the individual's coming to Jesus lies the Father's giving (and having given, v. 39) that individual to Jesus. And in the same way getting to Jesus means complete reception by Jesus. And this reception is made so strong, not because Jesus would refuse no one coming to him, but because Jesus could not possibly deviate from his Father's will.

Observe how subject and predicate are reversed, so that each becomes emphatic: *gives* to me *the*

Father. Likewise, "all that," etc., is emphasized as being the object by being placed in front. And again, "to me *shall get*," places the stress on the verb. These points are unfortunately lost in translation. The strong negative οὐ μή, "in no wise," is the same as that used in the previous sentence in v. 35. Also, ἐκ in the verb is strengthened by the appended adverb ἔξω. "To throw out outside" means out of the blessed circle of those who belong to the Son: "outside," into outer darkness.

38) The perfect agreement of Jesus as the Son with the Father he now states in the most direct way. Then in v. 39, 40 he adds the sum and substance of the Father's will which alone is normative for Jesus as the Son. By thus putting himself back of the Father, Jesus makes plain to these Galileans that their unbelief is really opposition to the Father and to that Father's gracious will which Jesus is carrying out in his work with them; and that faith in Jesus alone makes them true to the Father. The stress is on the unity of the Father and Jesus as his Son. **For I have come down from heaven not in order to be doing my own will but the will of him that did send me.** While the stress is on the purpose clause, which, therefore, also is expressed both negatively and positively, we must not overlook the main clause, in which Jesus says in so many words: "I (the Father's Son) have come down (perfect tense: and thus am now here) from heaven (ἀπό, elucidating ἐκ, 'out of' in the previous verses)." And "I have come down from heaven" states in most literal fashion what in v. 33 Jesus says of himself as "the Bread of God," that this "comes out of heaven." Standing there in human form before his hearers, Jesus tells them whence he came: "from heaven" to earth. He himself thus enunciates the Incarnation in the simplest and most matter-of-fact way. The fact that these people

understand Jesus to say just this their own questioning in v. 41, 42 shows beyond a doubt. Here in Galilee the same issue regarding the identity of Jesus as
the Son of God is raised as was controverted in Jerusalem, 5:19-47. And here in Galilee unbelief again
turns on this supreme issue. It has always done so,
and it always will.

But the Person is wholly tied up with the purpose of his coming from heaven. This is not and
never could be the doing of his own will, i. e., one
different from that of the Father, a will with voli-
tions conflicting with those of the Father. "My own"
is the possessive adjective, added by a second article
in the Greek, thus has as much emphasis as the noun
"the will" to which it is attached. This negation is
made so strong because it constitutes the real basis
of all unbelief. Only then is unbelief in Jesus justified when it is able to prove that Jesus is doing only
his own will and not the Father's will. In fact, all
who still claim to believe in God and yet reject Jesus
thereby assert that he was false to God. The
other way out is for unbelief to alter and to falsify
God's will and then to say that Jesus performs this
altered will (to be nothing more than an example
for men to copy), which, however, is nothing but
rejection of God and his Son by one and the same per-
versive act. And this thought, too, Jesus meets in the
next two verses.

After a negative ἀλλά brings in the contrary: "on
the contrary, I have come down from heaven in
order to be doing the will of him that did send me,"
and we might translate the substantivized aorist
participle: the will "of my Sender." Having come for
this purpose and for this alone as the Son from the
Father, how could this Son possibly be untrue to his
Father? He would have to repudiate his mission,
repudiate his Father, whose mission he came to carry

out, repudiate his own Sonship. Do these people mean
to say that Jesus is guilty of such an act? Only then
would their unbelief in him be justified. It rests on
an utter and a monstrous impossibility. Jesus convicts
the unbelief of his hearers and once more presses them
to believe in him.

39) Jesus says "the will of my Sender," and this
must be defined, for everything depends on what this
will is. Thus Jesus twice over defines this will.
**Now this is the will of him that did send me, that
all that he has given me I shall not lose any of it
but shall resurrect it at the last day.** Once more
(v. 37) the neuter πᾶν, "all," is used as a designation
for the whole mass of believers. But now, since
Jesus is thinking of the consummation at the last day,
he uses the perfect tense "has given to me." This
tense reaches back to the point where the Father "did
send" his Son on his saving mission "from heaven."
Then the gift was first made, and it stands as such
since then. It was made by virtue of the infallible
foreknowledge of God, to which all who would ever
be brought to faith were present before they came
into existence. In the mind of God, the giver, and of
his Son, the receiver, no uncertainty ever existed
about those who in all ages are made his own by grace
through the gospel and by faith.

The subfinal ἵνα clause is in apposition to "the will
of him that did send me" (R. 992) and states the
contents of that will. This will, however, has two
parts, one that pertains to acts of Jesus (v. 39),
and another which pertains to the blessing of believers
(v. 40). The construction is anacoluthic, B.-D. 466, 3,
and R. 718. We may regard πᾶν, etc., as either a
nominative or an accusative absolute that, after the
two verbs, is resumed first by the phrase ἐξ αὐτοῦ,
secondly by αὐτό. The Father's will is (negatively)
that Jesus shall lose no part of this great gift to him

but shall bring the whole of it to the consummation
of the resurrection at the last day. Regard ἐξ αὐτοῦ
as partitive: not lose "out of it" any part; and αὐτό
as the opposite: resurrect "it," all of it. The verb
ἀπόλλυμι occasionally means "to lose," and the aorist
tense (here, of course, the subjunctive) is constative:
in all that Jesus does from the beginning to the final
consummation of his mission he is not to lose any
part of all that the Father has given him. This
blessed and gracious will Jesus will most certainly
carry into effect. Let none of these Galileans for a
moment suppose that in his dealings with them he
is making a single mistake and losing a single soul
that otherwise could be won. All who are lost are
lost altogether through their own perverse and unnatural unbelief.

Not to lose = to keep, and that forever. This
includes the final act of Jesus' mission: "on the contrary," the Father's will is "that I shall resurrect it
(all of it) at the last day." After ἵνα the Koine permits the future indicative, especially when a second
verb is used. Even the bodies of those given to Jesus
shall not be lost through the power of death. Jesus
says, "I shall resurrect *it*," i. e., *"all* that he has given
to me"; and again in v. 40, "I shall resurrect *him*."
The verb ἀναστήσω (from which we have ἀνάστασις,
"resurrection") is too definite to think of anything
save the bodies of believers. *We* are resurrected when
our bodies are called out of the grave and are united
with our souls and are glorified as are they. Souls
cannot be resurrected. As the very body of Jesus
was raised from the tomb, so our very bodies shall
be raised from their dust and decay. As an act of
omnipotence, like the creation, the resurrection of
our bodies is utterly beyond human conception.

This resurrection of believers, of all of them, shall
take place "at the last day." Then time shall be no

more. This surely is a specific date and is in perfect
harmony with 5:29. Those who speak of a double
resurrection, one at the opening of the millennium
and one at its close, place the resurrection of the
godly first, that of the rest last. Here Jesus says
nothing about the latter, but he says most clearly
that *"all* that he (his Sender) has given him" he
shall resurrect "at the last day." No other day shall
follow. No further resurrection shall follow. The
godly shall not be divided into two or more groups.
All of them shall rise "at the last day," all of them
at the same time. The dream of a millennium is thus
shut out.

40) What the Father's will is regarding the acts
of his Son cannot be fully understood unless we further
know what his will is regarding those who believe
in Jesus. Thus v. 40 is added to v. 39 by an explanatory γάρ. **For this is the will of my Father,
that everyone that beholds the Son and believes on
him shall have life eternal; and I myself will
resurrect him at the last day.** In v. 39 we have the
Father's will concerning Jesus and his mission, hence
the designation: the will "of him that did send me."
We have no such mission, hence now: the will "of
my Father." In v. 39 we have the mass as an undivided whole: "all that he has given me," just as
in the first part of v. 37. Now we have each and
every individual composing this mass: "everyone that
beholdeth," etc. But note that not one is left out.
So in v. 37, too, the mass was individualized. But
there the description was only general: "him that
comes to me"; now this coming is fully described by
two characterizing or qualitative present participles:
"everyone that beholdeth the Son and believeth on
him." To come to Jesus is to behold the Son and to
believe on him. The two participles really refer to
one act, involving the intellect which by beholding

aright recognizes truly, and the heart or will which in that moment of true recognition gives its trust or confidence. In order to behold, someone or something must be brought to our vision; and in order to believe or trust, someone or something must come to us that is able to awaken and arouse such trust. Here it is "the Son," purposely thus named, the Son of the Father, more trustworthy than whom no one can be named. Our beholding and our trusting are the normal effect of the Father's showing us his Son and bringing us into contact with him. It would be the height of abnormality, of flagrant perversity, of senseless unreason to have the Son thus brought to us and for us to turn from him in distrust.

Jesus does not say that it is the Father's will for us to behold the Son and to trust in him. Instead he passes by these subjective means and at once names the goal, which is that every believer "shall have life eternal," touching the intervening means only lightly. Yet he who desires the end must necessarily desire also the means. Hence we may say that the Father's will is that we behold the Son and believe in him. But only to this end: that we "shall have life eternal," ζωή, the principle or very substance that constitutes life. Beholding and trusting in the Son puts us into true inward contact with him, and since he is the Bread of Life, or literally Life itself, this inner contact with him fills also us with life. His life enters our souls, and so we "have life." The present subjunctive (3:15, 16) ἔχῃ = "shall be having" from the instant of beholding and believing on and on forever. This spiritual life, like our physical life, is itself invisible but is strongly manifested by its activities. The believer does a thousand things that unbelievers cannot possibly do. To say that the believer "has life eternal" is to say that the unbeliever lacks this life, in other words, is spiritually dead, far from the

source of all the light, joy, and blessedness that goes
with life. Shall this blessed will of the Father be
done in these Galileans, or do they mean by guilty unbelief to frustrate that will?

This life of the believer is not merely to pass unharmed through temporal death and to last forever
as the believer's possession, it is to fill also his body
as well as his soul. Thus the Father's will is that
our bodies should be raised from the grave and be at
last made full partakers together with our souls of
this life in all its final glory. Thus Jesus adds, not
now as an expression of his Father's will, not in a
second clause after ἵνα (as in v. 39), but in a coordinate separate statement of his own, "and I myself will resurrect him at the last day." That he
shall do this as the consummation of his mission is
his Sender's will. That he will do this is his own
personal promise to every believer. Hence he now
says ἐγώ, using the emphatic pronoun, "I myself,"
which is absent in v. 39. We may imitate the Greek
emphasis, primary on the verb, secondary on the pronoun: "and UPRAISE him will *I Myself*." All that
this means for the believer's body, for the date of this
act, etc., has already been shown in v. 39 and should
again be considered here.

Jesus Gives Himself as the Bread of Life, 41-51

41) The offense in Jesus' words is practically the
the same as that in his words spoken to the Jews at
Jerusalem, 5:18. **The Jews, therefore, were murmuring concerning him, because he said, I am the
Bread which did come down out of heaven. And
they were saying, Is not this Jesus, the son of
Joseph, of whom we ourselves know the father and
the mother? How now is he declaring, Out of
heaven have I come down?** Here John calls these
Galileans "the Jews," a term which he uses so con-

stantly in combination with the hostility to Jesus. The two imperfects describe their grumbling and their talking to each other after Jesus had stopped speaking. They fastened their objection on the statement of Jesus that he is the Bread "which did come down out of heaven." For in v. 33 they substitute the aorist participle which refers to the single act of thus coming down out of heaven. In this they were right, for only this past act lends this quality to Jesus.

42) Over against this declaration of Jesus these Jews place what they themselves (emphatic ἡμεῖς) know about him. They are acquainted with his parentage: "Is not this Jesus," etc.? "It most certainly is!" With οὗτος they use a contemptuous tone, R. 697. Only Galileans from the neighborhood where Jesus lived so long could thus speak of his father Joseph and of his mother. The mention of Joseph is no evidence that he was still alive at this time. The final question specifies the point of the objection, how the son of parents they knew so well can stand before them and expect them to believe his declaration, "Out of heaven have I come down." That, indeed, is the vital point in all that Jesus said to them. It has ever been the stumblingblock and rock of offense for unbelief.

43) Although nothing was said directly to Jesus, he interrupts their grumbling, understanding it completely (3:23, 24). **Jesus answered and said to them** (1:48), **Stop your murmuring.** The present imperative refers to the preceding imperfect and thus bids the action that was going on to stop, R. 851.

Only in one way can the question raised by these Jews be effectually answered. Not by the way of the mere intellect, but by the way of actual experience. The former is hopeless in man's sinful state. Tell the intellect that this man Jesus is the incarnate Son and gives eternal life; forthwith the intellect with its theoretical reasoning and argument will deny the one, or the other, or both statements. That is why the gospel is not an argument, a piece of pure reasoning, a set of logical propositions and religious theory or hypothesis like those of science, or anything else addressed only to the intellect. It is *"the power of God* unto salvation," Rom. 1:16, "that your faith should not stand in the wisdom of men, but in *the power of God,"* I Cor. 2:5. Like any power, this divine power is not merely *known* theoretically or intellectually but is *realized in the actuality of experience* in a man's own life. He alone knows that power who has undergone its operation in himself. See the case of the Samaritan woman in 4:29 and of her townspeople in 4:41, 42. A fine example is the blind man in 9:30-33. Hence Jesus does not here commit the folly of explaining his Incarnation to these grumbling Galileans, for that would be the surest way of confirming them in their unbelief. Here, as always, Jesus follows the other way. He keeps applying the power that saves the sinner by changing his spiritual death into spiritual life eternal. Once this power actually enters a soul, that soul is taught of God and has learned of God by the actuality of its own experience. Its intellect is more than satisfied, because the soul itself is satisfied. It knows that Jesus did, indeed, come down out of heaven, even as he says, because it has as a most blessed gift the very life he brought us out of heaven, the life that shall live in heaven forever.

44) This is why Jesus continues his reply as he does. **No one can come to me unless the Father who did send me shall draw him; and I will resurrect him at the last day.** Luther has put these words into classical form: "I believe that I cannot

by my own reason or strength believe in Jesus Christ, my Lord, or come to him; but the Holy Ghost has called me by the gospel, . . . and will at the last day raise up me and all the dead, and give unto me and all believers in Christ eternal life. This is most certainly true." Here Jesus explains the Father's "giving" mentioned in v. 37 and 39: he gives men to Jesus by drawing them to him. This drawing (ἑλκύειν) is accomplished by a specific power, one especially designed for the purpose, one that takes hold of the sinner's soul and moves it away from darkness, sin, and death, to Jesus, light, and life. No man can possibly thus draw himself to Jesus. The Father, God himself, must come with his divine power and must do this drawing; else it will never be effected.

But significantly the Father is here again called the one "who did send me." Only as the Sender of Jesus does he draw and as such he draws to Jesus. His drawing power is exerted altogether through the mediation of Jesus, whom he sent for this purpose. The drawing is here predicated of the Father; in 12:32 it is predicated of Jesus, "And I will draw all men unto myself." Like all the *opera ad extra,* this, too, belongs equally to all three Persons. The Sender of Jesus is here mentioned because of the unbelieving Galileans; they are to understand that it is God himself who is now dealing with them through Jesus whom he has sent. The power by which these Jews are at this very moment being drawn is the power of divine grace, operative in and through the Word these Jews now hear from the lips of Jesus. While it is power (Rom. 1:16), efficacious to save, it is never irresistible (Matt. 23:37, "and ye would not"). Nor is this power extended only to a select few, for in 12:32 Jesus says, "I will draw all men."

The power of the gospel is for the world, and no sinner has fallen so low but what this power is able to reach him effectually.

The promise in v. 40 is renewed with only the shift of ἐγώ from one emphatic position to another that is equally emphatic. By this emphatic pronoun the Sender and the Sent are again placed on the same level. In v. 40 Jesus summarizes what he says in v. 37-40, inserting only the elucidation concerning the Father's power which does the drawing. This is why the promise concerning the final consummation in the blessed resurrection is added to the work of drawing. The beginning of the work in the Father's drawing is coupled with the crowning of this work in the Son's resurrecting those drawn.

45) Whereas Jesus first uses διδόναι, "to give," in v. 37 and 39, he adds ἑλκύειν, "to draw," in v. 44. He now takes the next step and makes fully clear how this giving and drawing to Jesus is effected by the Father. **It has been written in the prophets, And they shall all be people taught of God. Everyone that did hear from the Father and did learn comes to me.** "It has been written" (periphrastic perfect) and is thus still on record, "in the prophets," in that portion of the Old Testament which the Jews commonly designated "the prophets." Isa. 54:13 (compare Jer. 31:33, 34; Joel 2:28; etc.) describes the blessed condition of Jerusalem's children after accepting the sacrificed and glorified Messiah (Isa. 53) in repentance and faith. Among these blessings is this: all will be people taught of God, and great the peace of thy children. The emphasis is on the genitive "of God," which is subjective, naming God as the teacher; R. 516 makes it ablative "by God." All that they hold and believe is God's own teaching, none of it comes from themselves or merely from men. Thus we see what it means to be drawn by the Sender of

Jesus, namely to be "people taught of God." The verbal διδακτοί is used as a noun, the predicate of "shall be." This plural Jesus resolves into its component individuals: "everyone that did hear from the Father and did learn," he, and he alone, belongs to these people taught of God. The two aorist participles are really timeless (R. 859), but as qualitative aorists they describe actuality, actual hearing and learning. They also belong together as a unit idea, effective hearing resulting in actual learning; for the two participles have but one article. The fact that some, like these Galileans, hear with deaf hearts and ears and refuse to learn is here not considered by Jesus. This hearing and learning from God denotes reception from God who gives by means of teaching his Word; we receive when that Word makes us hear and learn. By attaching the phrase "from God" to the first participle this phrase has the emphasis; then by adding the unmodified second participle this participle receives emphasis. What we receive is *from God* by way of *actual learning*.

The result of this teaching and this learning is not by any means merely intellectual. We have already heard that God thus *draws* us by teaching us. Hence everyone so taught "comes to me." The participles "everyone that did hear and learn" are without an object, yet the great teacher is the Sender of Jesus, and the effect of his teaching is that everyone so taught comes to Jesus. This teaching and this learning thus deal with the coming to Jesus as to the Son sent by the Father to give life. To come thus means to believe and to receive life.

46) The quotation from the prophets, "people taught of God," and the interpretation, "everyone that did hear from the Father," παρὰ τοῦ πατρός, need further elucidation. How does God as a teacher meet his pupils? How do we get to his side (which is the

thought in παρά), so as then to hear "from this Father" as his children? Not in an immediate way but mediately through his Son. **Not that anyone has seen the Father, save he that is from God, he indeed** (οὗτος, emphatic) **has seen the Father.** The Old Testament is very plain regarding the impossibility of mortal, sinful man while remaining in this state seeing God. So that notion is shut out completely. When the prophet spoke of that most blessed future period, saying that then Israel should be a "people taught of God," he referred to the coming of God's Son in human flesh. In this Son the Father would actually come to his people and would so teach them that they would actually hear him speak, as one person speaks to another. The Son is, of course, the one exception (εἰ μή). He is, therefore, characterized as ὁ ὢν παρὰ τοῦ Θεοῦ, "he who is from God," he who has this characteristic mark. Note how the παρά phrase "from the side of God" explains the previous ἐκ phrases: "out of heaven." The demonstrative οὗτος takes up the previous characterization: he who is from God, "he indeed" has seen the Father. Both times we have the extensive perfect "has seen," so that the effect of that seeing is still present to him.

The entire statement has one purpose: if no one ever saw God, and Jesus alone has seen him because he comes from him, it is Jesus who makes us "people taught of God," for through him we hear and learn from the Father. This explains completely how the Father draws to the Son, and how by his drawing he gives to the Son. The question for these Galileans was: "Has this been done in us? are we people thus taught?"

47) After all this has been made plain, Jesus again turns to the main thought, the call to faith. He is even now executing the drawing of the Father,

and none who hear him can ever say, when they refuse to come to him, that they have not been drawn. **Amen, amen, I say to you, He that believes has life eternal.** Once more Jesus uses the double seal of verity and with it that of his final authority. The Father's giving (v. 37 and 39), drawing (v. 44), and teaching (v. 45), making us "hear and learn," is accomplished as to its purpose and its effect when faith is kindled in the heart. Hence the subject of the emphatic statement is ὁ πιστεύων, "he that believes," the qualitative present participle describing the person as one animated by confidence and trust. By adding nothing further to the substantivized participle the weight of thought rests on the believing as such. Of course, just as in the drawing, teaching, hearing and learning, so also in the believing, a corresponding object is implied, yet here the thought turns on the participle, i. e., on the person who is described as one marked by faith. He, and he alone, "has life eternal," as already explained in v. 40. The participle also has the force that this person has life eternal from the first instant of his believing onward and as long as he believes. The moment he would cease to believe, that moment he would cease to have life. It is believing or trusting that joins him to Jesus and thus to life eternal. Faith *has* life and, we may also say, *is* life. It *has* life because it is the constant reception of that divine grace and gift which frees us from death and makes us one with God. It *is* life because faith is the divine spark or flame which animates the soul and distinguishes us from the spiritually dead (5:24-26).

48) With this statement Jesus has returned to his central theme: **I am the Bread of Life,** i. e., the Mediator of that life, v. 35. The repetition is, of course, emphatic, but here it also introduces a fuller elaboration. We also see that the human figure of

bread is strained in order to convey the greatness and the fulness of the thought for which it is employed. This is often the case with the figurative language used in the Scriptures, for all human illustrations are weak when it comes to portraying spiritual realities completely. Ordinary bread only *sustains* physical life, but Jesus as the Bread of Life not only *sustains* spiritual life but even *gives* us this life. Hence also he is not merely "bread" or "bread of life" but actually "living Bread" (v. 51), i. e., Bread full of life, the reception of which gives and sustains life.

49) This is made exceedingly clear by reverting to the manna mentioned in v. 31-33. When the Galilean Jews pointed Jesus to the manna which Moses gave them, Jesus replied on the point of origin: the manna never was in heaven and never came down out of heaven whereas Jesus both was in heaven and came down out of heaven. Now to the point of origin that of the effect is added. **Your fathers did eat the manna in the wilderness, and they died. This is the Bread that comes down out of heaven, in order that one may eat of it and not die.** The comparison is striking indeed. Pointedly Jesus says "your" fathers and does not include himself among these Jews by saying "our" fathers. In the same pointed way he speaks of "my" father in v. 32; compare the elucidation of that verse. The two aorists are historical and state the undeniable facts: "they did eat" and "they died." So after all, though it was miraculously given, the manna was not superior to other earthly food. It only sustained the bodily life temporarily; it could never be called "the Bread of Life" in the full sense of the word. "And they died" means only that they were at last overtaken by temporal death, including Moses himself. We have no right to make the verb mean eternal death. It is true enough that the Israelites perished in their sins (Acts 7:42 and 51;

Heb. 3:16-19, R. V.), but ἀπέθανον does not include that fact. What Jesus says is that the manna was only like other earthly bread, including the bread with which the 5,000 had been fed on the previous day. Those who get no better bread eventually die. They will have lived only the common earthly life with no higher life in them, and so their dying is a sad end, indeed. The only life they have they then lose, for the only bread they have eaten is one that thus lets them die at last.

50) But look at "the Bread of Life." Its very character is different, for it "is the Bread that cometh out of heaven." The present participle does not refer to a constant descent out of heaven but describes the quality of this Bread as being something constant. By having descended out of heaven, by having become incarnate, and by assuming his saving mission, Jesus is the Bread that has this wonderful quality of being derived from heaven. All that can be predicated of the manna lies on the plane of the natural life; all that can be predicated of the Bread of Life lies on the plane of the spiritual life. Hence the purpose clause governed by ἵνα, which modifies the entire statement: "in order that one may eat of it and not die." God's intention is that we shall eat of this Bread, and the intended result of this eating is that we shall escape death. As the food, so the eating and its effect both in the case of the manna and in the case of the Bread of Life. Those who eat only the earthly bread prolong only their earthly life and finally die in temporal death and never attain more. Those who eat of the Bread of Life obtain the spiritual and heavenly life, which passes unharmed through temporal death and enters into eternal blessedness. "He that believeth on me, though he die, yet shall he live; and whosoever liveth and believeth on me shall never die," John 11:25,

26. "And not die" refers to spiritual and eternal death. This death we who eat of the Bread of Life escape; this death they who spurn the Bread of Life fail to escape. Note the strong contrast in the two verses 49 and 50: "and they died" — "and (shall) not die."

51) The facts stressed in v. 48-50 are now restated with modifications and additions, so as to make them clear beyond all question. **I am the living Bread that did come down out of heaven. If one shall eat of this Bread he shall live forever; and the Bread, moreover, which I will give is my flesh, in behalf of the life of the world.** First, a restatement of v. 48, again focusing everything upon Jesus with the emphatic pronoun ἐγώ, "I," "I myself, and no other." And now "the Bread of Life" is explained by "the living Bread," or "the Bread that lives," for the participle is made as emphatic as the noun itself by having the article repeated: ὁ ἄρτος ὁ ζῶν. "The Bread of Life" = the Bread which belongs to the true Life; "the Bread that lives" = the Bread that is full of the life it is intended to impart; the Bread, the very quality and character of which is that it lives and makes him alive who partakes of it. In literal language, Jesus is full of Life and the Giver of Life. A second attributive participle is added by another article: "that did come down out of heaven." This time the participle is the aorist, declaring the historical fact of thus coming down. On this fact rests the quality of this Bread expressed in v. 50, as in v. 33, by the descriptive or qualitative present participle "coming down." Thus once more in the clearest and simplest way we are shown just what Jesus is for us.

The figure in "Bread" always connotes eating; and thus Jesus once more speaks of the eating. To eat = to believe in Jesus, v. 47. In v. 50 we are told that it is God's purpose that we eat this Bread, or literally that we believe in his Son (v. 40). This purpose will, of course, be carried into effect, and thus Jesus now adds, "if one shall eat of this Bread." He uses the condition of expectancy: there shall be those who eat. Some will refuse to eat, but many will be moved to eat. In v. 50 the negative effect of this eating is stated: he that eats "shall not die"; now the positive effect is placed beside the negative: "he shall live forever." The one, of course, always implies the other: not to die = to live forever. The aorist φάγῃ means "come to eat." One act of eating bestows life (4:14; 6:35). The phrase εἰς τὸν αἰῶνα, literally "for the eon," views eternity in human fashion as a vast extent of time and is the Greek way of saying "forever"; compare the corresponding adjective αἰώνιος, "eternal." See also on 14:16. We must place side by side the Bread of Life, τῆς ζωῆς; the Bread that lives, ὁ ζῶν; he that believes has life eternal, ζωὴν αἰώνιον; and shall live forever, ζήσεται εἰς τὸν αἰῶνα — each expression illuminating the other.

Thus the entire thought is rounded out and made complete, the wonderful circle of salvation is closed. Jesus, the Life, is the center. All who are made one with him by faith are joined to him and are made full partakers of his life, not only of something which he has, or of something which he does (we following his example), but of what he himself is.

But in this figure of the Bread lies a still deeper meaning, one which shows us completely just *how* Jesus is, indeed, the Bread of Life and also just *how* we eat of this Bread by faith. And so, with one circle of thought complete and closed, at once another, reaching out still farther, is started. The first centers in the origin of Jesus, in his being Life itself descended out of heaven from the Father on his sav-

ing mission into this world of sin and death. The
second centers in this mission, or rather in its vital
and central act, namely in his sacrificial death. The
new distinctive terms are thus "my flesh," or more
fully "the flesh of the Son of man and his blood (v.
53), and corresponding with these expressions our
"eating" his flesh and "drinking" his blood by faith.
This second circle of thought is joined to the first
when Jesus now adds, "and the Bread, moreover,
which I will give is my flesh, in behalf of the life of
the world."

The reading with the two connectives καί . . .
δέ is assured, not, however, in the sense of "but also,"
which in no way fits the thought, but in the sense of
"and . . . moreover"; for καί tells of an addition
that is made, and δέ presents this addition as something that is new and different from what precedes.
The new feature is "my flesh." Before the ὑπέρ
phrase some important texts add the relative clause
ἣν ἐγὼ δώσω, "which (flesh) I will give for the life
of the world," A. V. While the weight of textual
evidence is against this clause, its thought is in harmony with what Jesus here says. In the turn which
the thought here takes too little attention has been
paid to the emphatic ἐγώ: "and the Bread which *I*
shall give is my flesh." In what Jesus now states
the contrast is not between the Bread which he *is*
and the Bread which he *gives* but between the gift
the Father gives and the gift which *Jesus himself*
shall presently give. The former is the Bread of
Life coming down out of heaven, i. e., the incarnate
Son in his entire saving mission. As regards this
gift the Father is the Giver, yet so that the Son, too,
is called the Giver (v. 27 and 32, 33). When the
gift is viewed as coming down out of heaven, the
givers are the Father and the Son. But in this mission of the Son an act of giving is involved which

belongs in a peculiar way to Jesus alone as the incarnate Son. This gift Jesus had not yet made, hence the future tense, "which I shall give." It is the gift of his flesh and his blood in the sacrifice upon the cross. This gift Jesus himself will make. "The Son of God gave *himself* for me," Gal. 2:20. "Christ hath given *himself* for us," Eph. 5:2. "I lay down *my life*," John 10:17. "The Son of man came to give *his life* a ransom for many," Matt. 20:28. In this sense Jesus says, "the Bread which I shall give is *my flesh*." This specific gift lies within the comprehensive gift. And this specific act of giving on Jesus' part is the vital part of the comprehensive gift, namely that act which truly makes him for us the Bread of Life, enabling us to eat and to drink by faith.

Since both subject (ὁ ἄρτος) and predicate (ἡ σάρξ μου) have the article, the two are identical and convertible, R. 767, etc. Thus the contention that we must here reverse the order and read, "my flesh (subject) is the Bread (predicate)" is untenable. The proposition is true either way. Yet the argument, that because the Bread has been mentioned before, therefore it must be the predicate, is specious; for the reverse holds good: since Jesus has repeatedly spoken of the Bread, he now tells us what it is, namely "my flesh." More important by far is the question, whether the word "flesh" here, and "flesh and blood" in v. 53, connote and imply the sacrificial death of Jesus on the cross. This has been emphatically denied. It seems that for this reason, too, the addition "my flesh *which I will give* for the life of the world" is repudiated. We dare drop these words for no such reason. The Scriptures know of no gift of Christ's "flesh," or, as these objectors put it, Christ's humanity or *Menschlichkeit* in behalf of the world apart from and without his sacrificial death on the cross. Take away the death, and the flesh of Christ ceases to be the Bread of Life for us. With the cancellation of the sacrificial death any participation in the flesh and the blood, any eating of his flesh or drinking of his blood, becomes an impossibility. The future tense δώσω demands the death, for this gift is yet to be made on Calvary. If "my flesh" refers to Jesus' humanity without or irrespective of his death, the tense would have to be an aorist, or at least the present, for then the gift of the flesh must refer to the Incarnation, a gift already made. Yet such a gift would be no gift, for the Incarnation without the sacrificial death would not bring life eternal to the world. Ideas such as that the flesh of Jesus, when it is imparted to us, becomes in us "a tincture of immortality," at last vivifying our flesh in the resurrection, or that by means of Jesus' flesh a germ is planted into our bodies and is kept alive and fed by means of the Lord's Supper to grow forth from our dead bodies in the resurrection, are completely shut out when the flesh of Jesus is rightly viewed as the Bread of Life in connection with the sacrificial death upon the cross.

If we adopt the text: my flesh "which I will give for the life of the world," the construction as well as the sense are plain. But we must drop the relative clause for textual reasons and must read: "the Bread which I will give is my flesh, in behalf of the life of the world." In this reading the ὑπέρ phrase cannot be construed as a modifier of "my flesh," for the copula ἐστίν intervenes. The article would have to be repeated before the phrase in order to make it a modifier of "my flesh," or the phrase would have to be converted into a participial or a relative clause. The construction, then, must be that the final phrase is an adverbial modifier of the predicate, and since the subject and the predicate are interchangeable, this adverbial modifier belongs to the entire sentence. In other words, when Jesus shall give as the Bread his flesh in the sacrificial death, this "is in the interest of the life of the world." While the phrase is brief and compact it is entirely clear: the Bread, the flesh, the future act of giving, all together have one purpose or object, they intend that the world may have the true heavenly life. It is mere quibbling to pit the one expression, "giving into death," against the other, "giving for us to eat," and to stress this difference as excluding the death in this statement of Jesus and in the others that follow. True enough, the two acts may be distinguished: it is one thing for Jesus to give himself into death, and it is another to give himself to us as the Bread of Life. Yet the two are indissolubly joined together: by giving himself into death Jesus gives himself to us as the Bread of Life. In v. 53 the blood is placed beside the flesh to indicate the more that Jesus is speaking of his death. Now this blood, once shed on Calvary when Jesus gave himself into death, is ever after the fountain of life for the world. By being given in the one atoning act on the cross it was given as the source of life for all sinners, I John 1:7; Heb. 9:14; Rev. 7:14; and I Pet. 2:24, where "stripes" are used for flesh and blood in conformity with Isa. 53:5. In v. 33 Jesus says, "The Bread of God . . . gives life to the world." This universality is now again emphasized: "in behalf of the life of the world." This living Bread, the flesh of Jesus sacrificed on the cross, is so full of life and salvation that all the world may take and eat and live forever.

Jesus Gives to Him That Believes His Flesh as the Bread of Life, 52-59

52) The Jews, therefore, were contending with each other, saying, How is this one able to give us

his flesh to eat! The moment Jesus mentioned his flesh contention arose among his auditors, whom John again designates as "the Jews," a term used by him to indicate their hostile temper. The imperfect ἐμάχοντο describes the passionate exchange of words among themselves, no longer spoken in undertones like the previous murmuring mentioned in v. 41, but in open exclamations. The verb shows that they were divided; yet this does not mean that some supported Jesus while others contradicted them, but that some raised one objection while others clashed with them in raising a different objection. Thus there was a battle among them. The objection of all of them is summarized in what is rather an unbelieving exclamation than a question, "How is this one able to give us his flesh to eat!" The derogatory οὗτος has a touch of scorn: this man, the son of Joseph, whose father and whose mother they knew, v. 42. In spite of his miracles they persist in regarding him as a mere man; and thus it appears wholly preposterous to them that he should be able to give them his flesh to eat.

The article τὴν σάρκα has the force of the possessive pronoun "his flesh." These Jews understand Jesus correctly when they exclaim regarding his giving them his flesh "to eat," for this is exactly what Jesus means (v. 53). If the Bread he will give is his flesh, then the connotation of eating that lies in "Bread" extends also to "my flesh." On the assumption that Jesus is a mere man the eating of his flesh would be nothing but a horrible cannibalism — an outrageous idea. They say only, give "us" to eat, whereas Jesus said, in behalf of the life "of the world." The fact that Jesus himself has thus shut out their preposterous notion of masticating his physical flesh with their teeth and digesting it in their stomachs, their blindness fails to note. What these Jews voice here in

Capernaum has come to be called "the Capernaitic mode" of eating. For the old Jewish unbelief still persists, justifying itself by holding to the idea that the flesh of Jesus could be eaten only in the gross physical way, thus rejecting not only what Jesus says in this discourse on the Bread of Life, but also what he says when instituting the Lord's Supper, telling us to take and to eat his body and to drink his blood.

Both the spiritual eating by faith here meant by Jesus and the sacramental eating of Christ's body and blood in the Lord's Supper are *toto coelo* removed from all Capernaitic eating, which rests on a false conception of the person of Jesus and on the denial of the personal union of his two natures, the human and the divine. Luther lays his finger on the little word *my* flesh: "With great, mighty letters we ought to engrave what Christ says: MY, MY flesh. But they will not look at this *my*. The fanatics cannot grasp this word *my*. But with the word *my* he distinguishes and separates himself from all other flesh whatever it may be called. For here *my* flesh is as much as, I am God and God's Son, *my* flesh is filled with divinity (*durchgoettert*) and is a divine flesh. His flesh alone will do it. To this God would have us attached and bound fast. Apart from the person who is born of Mary and truly has flesh and blood and has been crucified we are not to seek nor find God. For we are to grasp and find God alone by faith in the flesh and blood of Christ and are to know that *this* flesh and blood is not fleshy and bloody, but both are full of divinity." On the different modes of the presence of Christ's body see *Concordia Triglotta*, 1005, etc.

53) **Jesus, therefore, said to them, Amen, amen, I say to you, Unless you eat the flesh of the Son of man and drink his blood, you have not life in your-**

selves. Instead of softening his words regarding the eating of his flesh Jesus, we may say, hardens them. On "Amen," etc., see 1:51. Yet this hardening is only a fuller and more explicit statement. It is impossible for him to retract a single word, for that would put falsehood in place of truth. Jesus had abundantly prepared these Jews and now reveals the truth in its fulness. He can do nothing else. If the truth, fully and clearly presented, does not produce faith, nothing else will.

The Jews exclaim, *"How* can this one give us his flesh to eat!" Some commentators think that this question is altogether wrong, having in mind not merely its Jewish or unbelieving feature but all inquiry as to the how. Likewise, the reply of Jesus is regarded as a simple declaration of *the necessity* of eating his flesh and as a refusal to explain *how* this eating can be accomplished. But this is a misconception. If we are to eat Jesus' flesh in order to have life we must surely know how this is to be done. If he gives us his flesh as the living Bread, we must know how this Bread is to be eaten, in order that we may receive it. Jesus answers this question but does so in his own way by combining the manner with the necessity. Of course, he does not satisfy either unbelief or curiosity, but he does open the way to faith. The speculation which would unravel all mystery will not be satisfied, but the soul that hungers and thirsts for life and salvation will know both how he gives us his flesh to eat and thus also how we may eat it and live. The case is somewhat like that of Nicodemus who also asked about the how in regard to regeneration (3:4). There as well as here Jesus uses the solemn assurance of verity and authority, "Amen, amen, I say to you," in order to overcome unbelief and doubt and to emphasize the importance of his words. There as well as here he

repeats his former statement but with the necessity
he combines the explanation needed for faith.

He begins with the negative side, as in v. 50; but
at once (in v. 54) adds the positive side, as in v. 51.
"Unless you eat the flesh of the Son of man" is a
protasis of expectancy, ἐάν with the subjunctive, for
Jesus expects that some will eat. Yet οὐκ ἔχετε, "you
have not life in yourselves," is an apodosis of reality,
as if Jesus reckons also with unbelief and its loss of
life. Jesus adds his own Messianic title "the Son of
man," he who is man, indeed, and thus has flesh and
blood but who at the same time is far more than man,
namely God's Son in human flesh sent for our redemption. On this title see the exposition in 1:51. The
addition of this title is of the utmost importance. By
thus naming himself, Jesus declares that if he were,
indeed, a mere man, he could not give his flesh to
men to eat; but since he is "the Son of man," the God-
man, sent as the Messiah from heaven itself, therefore he can so give his flesh. The premise of unbelief
is false, and that fact annuls its logical conclusion.
Here the how of these Jews receives its first decisive
answer.

The second lies in the significant addition "and
drink his blood." The spirit of Jesus is misconceived
when we are told that he made this addition "in order
to increase the offense." Jesus never sets out to give
offense. When men take offense they do so wholly
without cause. Unbelief always takes offense at the
truth, but always does so without reason. The more
truth unbelief meets, the more it takes offense, revealing its true nature, its folly of unreason, and its inexcusable guilt. Yet truth alone can turn unbelief into
faith, and the greater the measure of truth, the greater
its power to convert offended unbelief into satisfied
faith. To say that the addition about drinking the
blood of the Son of man is without special significance,

that it only helps to describe the humanity of Jesus, is to cancel from this final and fullest declaration of Jesus the very feature which is distinctive and most explanatory. For to parallel the eating of the flesh with the drinking of the blood of the Son of man, as Jesus parallels them here, is to point in the clearest way to his own sacrificial death. This parallel explains what eating and drinking really mean, namely participátion in the sacrifice. By the death of the Son of man his blood is shed in sacrifice. It is folly, then, to think for one moment of drinking that blood in a physical (Capernaitic) manner. To drink the blood thus shed is a spiritual act *in toto,* an acceptance by the soul of the efficacy of that blood once shed and of the atonement and expiation wrought by its being shed. "Flesh and blood" is here not a unit as in Matt. 16:17 and Heb. 2:14, but "flesh" is separated from "blood," and "blood" is separated from "flesh" by means of the sacrificial death. On having life see 3:15. The present tense is noteworthy, since the negation refers to present possession and to its continuance. In the protasis the two verbs "eat" and "drink" are properly aorists, because only one act of reception secures life. The addition of the phrase "in yourselves" emphasizes the idea of permanent possession in the verb, "have not in yourselves."

54) The tremendous importance of eating the flesh and drinking the blood of Jesus is pressed upon these Jews by the addition of the positive statement to the negative: **He that eats my flesh and drinks my blood has life eternal; and I will resurrect him at the last day.** The English is unable to render the peculiar force of ὁ τρώγων, which is more realistic than the verb ἐσθίω, "to eat," the aorist of which is used in v. 53 (φάγητε). It is the German *knabbern,* audible eating, *manducare* or *mandere.* The two present

participles are qualitative and merely characterize the person, one article combining the two. We may read ὁ τρώγων καὶ πίνων like ὁ πιστεύων with regard to a quality conveyed by continuous action: eating and drinking and going on in these actions; or like ὁ καταβαίνων in v. 33 and 50 with regard to a quality impressed by the single act of eating and drinking once only, this one act producing a permanent character (compare with v. 33 and 50; the aorist for the same act in v. 41 and 51; and the perfect in v. 38 and 42.)

It is in vain to argue against what is so evident, that the present statement is only another form of v. 47 (compare v. 40), "He that believes has life eternal." The gospel knows of no way except believing by which I may "have life eternal." Some recent commentators are led astray by a misconception of faith, which they conceive as an act of man's own free will, something that God requires of us, "a moral obligation," "an ethical deed." This leads them to conclude that eating the flesh and drinking the blood of Jesus cannot denote faith, for so to eat and to drink is to receive something not to render something ourselves. But the essence of faith is exactly this, that we receive from Jesus, that we abandon all else and let him give himself to us, his blood-bought merits, his flesh and his blood sacrificed for us. The ancient saying is true: *manducatio est credere.* No truer and richer definition of faith can be given than this: faith = to eat Christ's flesh and to drink Christ's blood. It is idle to charge that "no sensible man would entertain the thought" that believing can be an eating and a drinking. Like this discourse on the Bread of Life is the word of Jesus in Matt. 5:6, "Blessed are they which do hunger and thirst after righteousness; for they shall be filled"; also John 7:37, 38, "If any man thirst, let him come unto me

and drink. He that *believeth* on me," etc.; also John
4:10, etc. If the point of comparison is asked for,
it is simply that eating and drinking, like believing,
is a receiving of the most intimate and vital kind.
As eating and drinking receive food to be assimilated
in the body, so believing receives Christ with the
atonement made through his sacrificial flesh and blood.
But the figure is less than the reality, for bodily eating
only sustains life already present while spiritual eating or believing expels death, bestows life, and sustains that life forever.

For the second time Jesus pointedly parallels his
flesh and his blood as sacrificial gifts and even continues this parallel in the next two verses. How his
death is connoted by the term "flesh" or σάρξ appears
in I Pet. 3:18, "being put to death in the flesh";
in Eph. 2:15, "having abolished in his flesh the
enmity"; in Col. 1:22, "in the body of his flesh through
death"; and in Heb. 10:20, "through the veil, that is
to say, his flesh." To these add the following concerning the blood, which point even more directly to
the death, and this a sacrificial one: Lev. 17:11, "For
the life of the flesh is in the blood: and I have given
it to you upon the altar to make an atonement
for your souls: for it is the blood that maketh an
atonement for the soul." Heb. 9:22, "Almost all
things are by the law purged with blood; and without shedding of blood is no remission." I Pet. 1:18,
Ye were redeemed "with the precious blood of Christ,
as of a Lamb without blemish and without spot."
Acts 20:28, "the church of God, which he hath pur-
chased with his own blood." Add Heb. 9:14;
Eph. 1:7; Rev. 5:9. This more than answers the
claim that flesh and blood are here used only
for the *Leiblichkeit* of Jesus as in Matt. 16:17;
Gal. 1:16; I Cor. 15:50, without reference to Jesus'
death.

In order to make fully clear what kind of "life" this "eating and drinking" convey and what it means "to have life eternal," Jesus repeats his promise from v. 40, "and I (emphatic ἐγώ, I myself) will resurrect him at the last day"; compare the explanation in v. 39 and 40. This "life" or ζωή not only passes unharmed through temporal death, it also assures the body that is stricken by this death of a blessed resurrection at the last day of time. "To have life eternal" means the restoration even of the body at the last day in the resurrection of the blessed. This resurrection was a well-known article of the Jewish faith, 11:24. What the Jews did not know is that the life which comes to us by faith in Christ's death alone guarantees the blessed resurrection to us. In order to be raised up in glory at the last day we must eat the flesh and drink the blood of Jesus, i. e., partake of the Bread of Life, believe. Note especially the ἐγώ in this mighty promise. It is the answer to the derogatory οὗτος in v. 52. He indeed, who is able to say, "I myself will resurrect him," is able also to give us his flesh to eat so that we may have life even as he declares. Will not these Jews finally see with whom they are dealing?

55) With γάρ Jesus explains why the eating of his flesh and the drinking of his blood bestow life eternal and include the resurrection of the blessed. **For my flesh is real food, and my blood is real drink.** Both are ἀληθής, deserving that epithet in the fullest sense of the word, a βρῶσις or food that is eaten and will then do exactly what Jesus says, a πόσις or drink that is drunk and will then do exactly what he declares. Other meat and drink was offered in Old Testament times (for instance that mentioned in I Cor. 10:3, 4), and men have always had earthly food and drink. None of these deserves the predicate "real." The

sacred meat and drink of the old covenant could only typify and promise the "real" food that was to come, and all other meat and drink is but for a day and has in it no abiding vitality (v. 26, 27). The flesh and the blood of Jesus alone are able to bestow "life eternal" and the resurrection unto glory.

The word ἀληθής, "real" or "true," cannot be used to support the view that Jesus is here speaking of the Lord's Supper (some versions have the adverb ἀληθῶς, "really," "truly," which changes the thought only slightly). For here Jesus answers the Jewish objection that his flesh cannot possibly be the Bread of Life or be given to us to eat. To men of this mind Jesus asserts that his flesh and his blood are real food and drink which will do what he says; not an imaginary, or worse, a false and deceptive food and drink.

56) The previous explanations answer the question as to how Jesus can give his flesh to us to eat by pointing to himself as the Son of man, by placing his blood beside his flesh, and by emphasizing that these are real food and drink. The answer thus far deals with the gift itself. When we understand the gift properly we shall no longer doubt or deny that it can be given. But the gift is to be received. The Jewish unbelief denied not only that Jesus could give his flesh but also that they, the Jews, could receive or eat his flesh. "How can this one give *us his flesh to eat!*" So complete is Jesus' reply that he fully covers also this vital point. **He that eats my flesh and drinks my blood remains in me, and I in him.** Compare the allegory of the Vine and the Branches, 15:1, etc. To eat and to drink means to be spiritually joined to Jesus, the Son of man. Our souls embrace him and his sacrificial death in faith and trust, and he embraces us as now drawn to him (v. 44) and given to him (v. 37 and 39). That is why Jesus

once more speaks of "my flesh" and "my blood," his sacrificial death, and of our eating and drinking, which denote the reception of this death and sacrifice by faith. By this gift from him and its reception in us he and we are joined inwardly: ἐν ἐμοί . . . ἐν αὐτῷ. As long as we remain apart from Jesus and inwardly separated from him we are in spiritual death; the moment we are inwardly joined to him we are freed from this death and have life eternal.

This effect of faith is usually termed the *unio mystica,* or mystical union of the believer with Christ. It is pictured as an indwelling (μένει) by means of the figures of a house, a household, a temple, the marriage relation, a body and its members, a garment, etc., in a great variety of passages, the fundamental form of which is Jesus in us, we in him. Both expressions "in us" and "in him" designate our benefit and ours alone; both denote our salvation. When it is said that he abides in us, he is our life, light, joy, pearl of great price, peace, crown. "He in me, and I in him" = 1) Jesus the life element in which we life and move and have our being spiritually; 2) Jesus the life center, preserving, molding the spiritual life within us. A false mutuality and reciprocity are introduced when Jesus is made the beneficiary with us, when it is assumed that he cannot exist as the head without us as the members, or that, when he makes us his body, we in turn make him the head. For this entire discourse a caution is in place, namely to curb the imagination lest it run into a spurious and an overdone spirituality and seek unknown depths which prove mazes of error.

57) Eating and drinking (believing) join to Jesus and thus give us life. Just how this effect is brought about is also clearly explained, and in this part of the explanation the climax of the entire discourse is reached. **Even as the living Father did send me,**

I myself also live because of the Father; and he that eats me, he also shall live because of me. While this explains all the previous statements on the believer's having live eternal even as the pivotal terms are "living," "live," and "shall live," this declaration summarizes all that precedes. Once more it reveals who Jesus really is, how we can thus be joined to him, and how as a result we can have life forever.

The life we receive through faith is traced back to this ultimate source, "the living Father," who as such has life in the absolute sense, as an essential attribute, whose life is not derived from another, from whom all other life is derived. When Jesus says that the living Father "did send me," by that weighty participle "living" he describes his mission as being one that is intended to convey life to us who had lost it through Adam's sin. As the one thus sent to bestow life Jesus is "the Bread of Life."

The second point in this explanation is: "I myself also live because of the Father." The emphatic ἐγώ = "I," who was thus sent to be the Mediator of life to men, Jesus, as he stood there in human flesh before his hearers; compare "the Son of man" in v. 53. "Even as . . . also" combines the living Father and Jesus who "lives" in a special manner. For καθώς is to be construed with the first καί (κἀγώ) not with the second (καὶ ὁ τρώγων). Our versions and many commentators translate the second καί "so," which is not correct and would require οὕτως. The thought expressed by this translation is also incorrect; for the similarity expressed by καθώς is one that exists only between the Father and Jesus, not one that obtains between the Father and us. We can never "live" καθώς, in the same manner as the Father. This is true only of Jesus, as 5:26 has made plain with ὥσπερ . . . οὕτως.

Here Jesus is speaking as the Son of man (v. 53),
with reference to his human nature. He is meeting
the objection of the Jews who see in him a mere
man (v. 42), who, therefore, could neither give them
his flesh to eat, nor impart to them life eternal. To
these objectors he declares that as the one sent by
the living Father, standing thus before them incarnate
in his human nature, he "too lives," even as the living
Father sent him to convey life to us. In 5:26 he says
that the Father, who has life in himself, "did give"
him to have life in himself also, i. e., in his human
nature, that nature which he uses as the medium for
bestowing life upon us ("my flesh," "my blood," "to
eat and to drink"). The same thought is here expressed by the phrase διὰ τὸν πατέρα, "because of the
Father," his Sender. This phrase states the reason or
the ground for his having life even as his Sender has
life. If only his divine nature and not his human
nature had this life, he could not convey life to us by
means of his sacrificial flesh and his sacrificial blood,
which belong to his human nature. To make his flesh
and his blood the means for bestowing life on us, life
had to be in them, just as life is in the divine nature
of Jesus and in the living Father who sent him. In
the divine nature of the Father and the Son life dwells
as an essential and absolute attribute irrespective of
us; in the human nature of Jesus this same life
dwells as a gift (5:26) by reason of the Father who
sent Jesus (διὰ τὸν πατέρα) with respect to us, in
order that through his flesh and his blood and his
sacrifice on the cross life eternal might be imparted
to us.

"And he that eats me," me, who lives because of
the Father, me, whom the Father made the source of
life for men by sending me on the mission that culminates in the sacrifice on the cross ("my flesh," "my
blood"), "he, too, shall live because of me." It is true

that Jesus abbreviates when he says "he that eats *me*"; for to eat *him* means to eat his flesh and to drink his blood by accepting his sacrifice in faith. This pronoun "me," however, includes much more than the flesh and the blood of Jesus. In the first place it reverts to the pronoun "me" in the previous statement: "the living Father did send *me*," and to the two pronouns in v. 56: "he remains in *me*, and *I* in him." Thus "me" denotes the entire person of Jesus with both of his natures. We are joined by faith to the entire person of our Mediator Jesus. Yet this union with him takes place only through his human nature or the reception of his flesh and of his blood. These are the one door by which he in his entire person comes to us, and we to him.

The emphatic repetition of the subject in κἀκεῖνος, "*he* also," has the force of "he alone and no other" shall "also live." The future tense "shall live" is not in contradiction to the present tenses "has, have life eternal, remains in me" (v. 47, 53, 54, 56), but like the future tense in v. 51, relative to the moment of eating; "shall live" the moment he eats. The final phrase, shall live "because of me" receives special force since it parallels the phrase "because of the Father." The former, like the latter, states the ground or reason for our living. This is not the mere act of our eating; it is the person to whom we are joined by this eating. The living Father's life reaches down to us through his Son, but through his Son as fitted out with flesh and with blood, by these and by these alone being enabled to make contact with us dead sinners. When this contact is made, the entire Son with his life is ours, "in us," and so we live "because of him," by reason of having no less than him. While the two διά phrases are parallel, this parallel must not be pressed. This is done by those who translate the second καί "so"; for they make us live because of

Jesus, just as Jesus lives because of the Father. Jesus shuts this out by emphatically stating, "he that eats me he also (he alone) shall live." Our living is conditional on our receiving Jesus; the moment the condition ceases in that moment our life is gone. No such condition exists for Jesus. He lives as the Mediator of life for us by virtue of the living Father's mission. The every essence of the divine life of the Father is the human nature of Jesus. We live because of him in a different way, not by also receiving the essential divine attribute of life, but by having that attribute touch our souls and by this touch kindling spiritual life in us. His is the divine essence of life itself, ours is the product, a creation, of that life, II Cor. 5:17; Gal. 6:5; Eph. 2:10.

58) The concluding statement merely rounds out the entire discourse by once more contrasting the transitory effect of the earthly manna and the permanent effect of the Bread that came down out of heaven. **This is the Bread that did come down out of heaven, not as the fathers did eat and did die. He that eats this bread shall live forever.** Jesus means to say: I have now told you fully about this Bread that actually came down out of heaven (καταβάς as in v. 41 and 51; compare the other tenses in v. 33 and 50, and in v. 38 and 42) and how it differs from the manna which left the fathers to die (v. 49). The final thought which Jesus impresses upon his hearers is the blessed effect of eating this Bread: it makes him who eats it live forever (the εἰς phrase as in v. 51 and in 14:16). The discourse thus closes with an implied invitation. Do these Jews want to live forever? Let them come and eat of the Bread of Life!

59) **These things he said by way of teaching in a synagogue in Capernaum.** This remark intends to separate what follows from the discourse just completed. We must combine "teaching in a synagogue,"

and not "he said in a synagogue." Note that "synagogue" is without the article. John means to tell us
that this discourse was spoken by way of public synagogue teaching before all who had gathered there.
What follows was spoken elsewhere and thus somewhat later and only to those who had begun to be
Jesus' disciples. On the point that this teaching of
Jesus in a synagogue does not imply that the day was
necessarily a Sabbath see v. 21. The final phrase "in
Capernaum" does not intend to repeat what we gather
already from v. 24, for this would be quite unnecessary. Placed at the end, the phrase is made emphatic.
John means to convey to us that Capernaum repeats
what Jerusalem (5:1, 2) began, namely unbelief and
opposition to Jesus. Chapter six is the counterpart
to chapter five.

We must now answer the question whether this
discourse deals only with the spiritual eating of faith
or with the oral sacramental eating in the Lord's Supper. We reply, only with the former. The eating of
which Jesus speaks throughout (note for instance
v. 53) is absolutely necessary for salvation. Yet all
the saints of the old covenant were saved without the
Lord's Supper, so was the malefactor on the cross,
so are all babes and children in the new covenant.
This fact alone is decisive. It has never been answered
by those who maintain the contrary concerning John 6.
The old principle holds true: only the *contemptus*,
never the *defectus* of the Supper condemns. —
Secondly, the eating of which Jesus here speaks is
always and without exception salutary (see for
instance v. 54). It is impossible to affirm this of the
oral eating in the Sacrament. — Finally, it is inconceivable that Jesus should urge upon these unbelieving
(v. 36) Galileans a sacrament not yet instituted and
urge upon them the sacramental eating of which no
one could know until the institution had taken place.

It is in vain to point to Nicodemus upon whom Jesus urged baptism; for the Baptist baptized thousands, Nicodemus knew of this sacrament, and Jesus explains its effects to him.

Recognizing the force of these facts, some seek a compromise, admitting that primarily this discourse does not deal with the Lord's Supper, yet maintaining that secondarily or indirectly it does. They claim that Jesus so expressed himself that his words find their ultimate and most complete fulness in the Lord's Supper. These are divided among themselves as to the way in which they suppose that Jesus here refers to the Sacrament. Some hold that the words of Jesus constitute only a preparatory prophecy of the Supper; others, that the idea of the Supper is included, the feeding of the 5,000 being "a significant prefigurement" of the Supper; still others, that the Supper is included by way of inference. All these generally make much of the fact that John's Gospel reports neither the institution of Baptism after the resurrection of Jesus nor the institution of the Supper; and they assume that John reported the conversation with Nicodemus in lieu of the former, and the discourse on the Bread of Life in lieu of the latter. The general answer to these views is the old hermeneutical rule of Hilary: the true reader of the Scriptures is he who expects the passages of Holy Writ themselves to furnish their meaning, who carries nothing into them, who takes out only what they bring, and is careful not to make the Scriptures say what he thinks they ought to say. The specific answer to these views is, that they confuse the spiritual eating by faith, which is to take place equally with regard to the three means of grace (Baptism, the Word read, taught, and preached, and the Lord's Supper) with the oral eating peculiar to the Supper, which invariably takes place. All ought to eat and to drink by faith when they are baptized, when they hear and read the Word, when they receive the Lord's Supper; but all do not so eat and drink by faith, many use these means of grace so as not to receive life eternal through them. But no one ever partook of the Lord's Supper who did not eat and drink orally, with his mouth, the consecrated bread and wine, and in, with, and under this bread and wine the body and the blood of Christ conveyed to him by the earthly elements. To eat and to drink by faith is an inward spiritual act that is always salutary; to eat and to drink the elements of the Supper orally is an outward act which sometimes is not salutary but unto judgment, I Cor. 11:28, 29.

The Result of the Discourse on the Bread of Life, *6:60-71.* — Jesus left the synagogue, and most of "the Jews" scattered. Only those who counted themselves among his "disciples" remained with him as he walked away. We now learn what occurred in the case of these. **Many, therefore, of his disciples after hearing (this) said, Stiff is this statement. Who is able to listen to him?** The "disciples" were Galileans who had begun to follow Jesus, and their number was considerable. A severe sifting now takes place among them. Many of them spoke as here indicated, yet not all. Comparing v. 66, we see that a number remained true, which explains how eventually five hundred brethren assembled to meet the risen Savior in Galilee, I Cor. 15:6. The aorist particle ἀκούσαντες, "having heard," or "after hearing," means to say that after the services in the synagogue were over, the more these disciples thought of what they had heard Jesus say, the more their objection grew. The verb εἶπον means that they voiced their thoughts to themselves.

These disciples find what Jesus says σκληρός, "stiff," dried out and hard, like a twig that has become brittle.

The word does not here mean dark and difficult to
understand but objectionable, offensive, impossible to
accept and to believe. By οὗτος ὁ λόγος we must understand the entire discourse on the Bread of Life, even
also as it is a closely knit unit. The objection that
began in v. 30, 31, that came out in the murmuring
in v. 41 and in the open contention in v. 52, here
continues. Some think that it refers especially to the
idea of the bloody death in the way in which Jesus
spoke of his flesh and his blood; others, denying that
Jesus had such a death in mind, think of the carnal
hopes and expectations of these disciples, which find
no support in the words of Jesus; still others suppose
that these disciples think only of a gross and carnal
eating of the flesh of Jesus and of a similar drinking
of his blood. Those, finally, who think that Jesus
spoke only of his *Leiblichkeit* or *Menschlichkeit* in
general imagine that the objection lies in the idea
of eating and drinking the human nature of one
whom these disciples saw standing before their eyes
like any other man. These attempts reflect the various
interpretations which the different commentators have
applied to the cardinal points in the discourse itself,
some of them being decidedly wide of the mark. These
disciples objected to the entire discourse: that Jesus
should call himself the Bread of Life, descended out
of heaven, whose flesh they must eat and whose blood
they must drink as the real food, full of life, and
thus giving them life eternal and the resurrection of
blessedness. The whole of it these disciples find
σκληρός, intolerable. Hence they exclaim, "Who is
able to listen to him?" If αὐτοῦ is to refer to λόγος,
we should expect the accusative αὐτόν. Yet the old
rule: the genitive to indicate the person heard and
the accusative the thing heard, is not strictly observed. These disciples, however, turn away from

Jesus (v. 66) and refuse to hear him any longer, so we translate, "Who can hear him?" and not, "hear it?"

61) Jesus does not need to be told what is passing through the minds of these disciples. To some extent the way in which Jesus saw them acting and talking together betrayed to him what was wrong. But by his higher powers Jesus perceives all that is in the hearts of these disciples (3:24, 25). Like his omnipotence in the miracles, so he uses his omniscience again and again in dealing with men to the extent that this was necessary in his mission. **Now when Jesus knew in himself that his disciples were murmuring concerning this, he said to them, Does this entrap you?** The phrase ἐν αὐτῷ means: in his own mind, R. 587. And "concerning this" refers to the matter about which these disciples were complaining, it is thus identical with "this" in the second question. What is meant does not need to be specified, since those concerned know. The verb σκανδαλίζειν means to serve as a σκάνδαλον, the crooked stick to which the bait is fixed in a trap and by which the trap is sprung; thus, literally, "Does this entrap you?" The idea is: "Does this prove fatal to you?" A trap that is sprung kills its victim. This point is lost in the translations of our versions, "cause you to stumble" (R. V.), "offend you" (A. V.), neither of which need be fatal. On stumbling, even on falling, one may arise again; so also one may be offended and get over it. But a dead-fall trap kills.

62) With a second question Jesus points these murmuring disciples to the great key which unlocks the difficulty that was entrapping and holding them in unbelief. It is the same key he had offered his hearers from the start when in v. 27 and then again in v. 53 he had called himself "the Son of man," as now also he again does, adding in v. 40 "the Son";

and when he said of the Bread that it comes down
out of heaven (v. 33 and 50), that it came down
out of heaven (v. 51 and 41), and that he himself
who is this Bread "has come down from heaven"
(v. 38), which the Jews repeat, changing only the
preposition. **If, then, you shall behold the Son of
man going up where he was before — ?** The
protasis stands alone, naturally with a rising inflection like a second question, leaving the apodosis to
be supplied by the hearers, "what then? say it yourselves!" This is a case of aposiopesis, which differs
from ellipsis or mere abbreviations by the passion or
feeling put into the words. "One can almost see
the gesture and the flash of the eye in aposiopesis,"
R. 1203.

By calling himself "the Son of man" for the third
time and by now adding his ascent to heaven to the
descent out of heaven, which he has mentioned
repeatedly, he once more in the plainest way tells these
disciples who he actually is. The key to the entire
discourse on the Bread of Life is Jesus, the Father's
Son (v. 40), sent out of heaven on his saving mission and thus now incarnate, the Son of man (see
1:51), standing as man before these disciples. The
mention of his ascent only completes the picture of
himself which he wants these disciples to have; for he
descended out of heaven only on his mission, and thus
evidently will again ascend when that mission is performed. The participle ἀναβαίνων is only the counterpart to καταβαίνων (v. 33 and 50) and καταβάς (v. 41
and 51). They are even connected by the clause,
"where he was before," which Jesus uses instead of
"to heaven." To the very place from which he
descended he will again ascend. Jesus thus tells these
disciples: "You are right, indeed, if I were only a
man like other men, no matter how great a man, I
could not be the Bread of Life out of heaven, could

not give you my flesh nor my blood, nor could you eat
that flesh and drink that blood, and, of course, you
could not thus have life eternal, nor could I resurrect
you at the last day; but I am the God-man, and thus
all that I say is true."

We thus see that Jesus is not increasing the offense
for his hearers but making the fullest effort to remove
the offense they had taken. Nor is he raising a new
point, which may cause new offense, but is stating the
key point over again and more clearly. The implication is the same as it was in the entire discourse:
How can unbelief find justifiable room when men are
shown who Jesus really is? "When you shall see the
Son of man ascending where he was before — ?" what
then? how then can you maintain unbelief? We need
not enter the debate regarding what "ascending" here
means. It certainly refers to the Ascension not merely the visible rising of Jesus' human form from the
earth until a cloud withdrew it from sight (which is
only the first part) but, as the addition "where he was
before" shows, combined with the visible also the
invisible part when beyond the cloud the earthly form
of Jesus was transferred in a timeless instant to the
glory of heaven. It is useless to make this ascending
refer to the "dying," or to bring in the general offense
always connected with the cross. Likewise, instead
of the ascent hindering faith in that it removes the
body of Jesus to heaven, it constituted a strong help
to faith by that very removal; for, like all the previous
references to Jesus as the God-man, this ascension of
his body to heaven leaves us most decidedly with the
one sacrificial act which makes his flesh "real food"
and his blood "real drink" (v. 55) such as can be
received spiritually by faith alone and thus shuts out
every carnal mode of reception.

The condition ἐάν with the subjunctive is one of
expectancy; hence we should translate, "if you shall

see" (A. V.) and not "if you should see" (R. V.). The point to be observed in all conditional statements is that they present to us only the speaker's or the writer's thought about the matter, how he wants us to look at it, and not the actuality as it is or as it will be (if it is future). So here. Jesus knows that he will, indeed, ascend. He might say so directly. But that would be like a challenge to these already unbelieving disciples, provoking their outright denial. By using the condition of expectancy Jesus obviates such a clash. He secures their consideration of his ascension as a solution of their difficulty, as again revealing the divine nature of his person. We need not disturb ourselves about the verb "shall see" addressed to these disciples. Even the Eleven saw only Jesus' departure from the earth and not his entrance into heaven. This entrance the Eleven and all believers "see" in the same way, by faith in the Word and by his rule at the right hand of his Father in his church and over all the earth. The verb θεωρέω includes the seeing with the mind and the soul not only that with the physical eye.

63) As the statement on the ascension of Jesus is formulated so as to call out faith, so also are the next two statements: **The spirit is that which makes alive; the flesh profits nothing at all. The utterances which I have spoken to you, spirit they are, and life they are.** Verse 62 deals with *the source*, the divine person of Jesus; v. 63 deals with *the effect*, the life bestowed by this divine person. These two, the person as the source, the life as the effect, form the framework of the entire discourse. This is true even of the concentrated statement, "I (person, *source*) am the Bread of Life (life eternal, *effect*)." The discourse answers the question as to how we dead sinners may obtain life eternal (the effect). It answers: through the God-man alone via his flesh and his blood (the source). Hence, like the

discourse itself, any added explanations seek solely
to make plain these two: the source and the effect.
Thus the way to faith is opened, and all real cause for
doubt and unbelief is removed.

When this object of v. 62 and 63 is clear, we see
that the latter removes all false conception regarding
the life (the effect) as wrought by the person (the
source) through the medium of his flesh (including,
of course, his blood, here left unnamed only for the
sake of brevity). The proposition Jesus presents is
general, an axiom that needs no proof: the spirit not
the flesh makes alive. Leave out the spirit, and all
the flesh in the world, including that of Jesus, could
not kindle a single spark of life; the spirit alone
quickens and makes alive. This holds true even for
physical life (Gen. 2:7) and certainly also for spiritual and eternal life (Eph. 2:5). A flood of light
thus illumines the discourse. When Jesus spoke so
pointedly about his flesh and his blood bestowing life
eternal on all who eat and drink, how could anyone
dream that he meant flesh only as flesh and blood only
as blood? Did not Jesus constantly say "*my* flesh,"
"*my* blood," and add, "he that eats *me*," and name
himself as "the Son" (v. 40), and "the Son of man"
(v. 27 and 53, God's Son sent by the Father and
thus in human flesh)? Did he not tell these disciples
that his flesh is "the *living* Bread" (v. 51) and thus
"the *real* food" (v. 55), and that eating his flesh and
drinking his blood make us abide in *him*, and *him*
in us (v. 56)? Let the other Jews miss all this, of
these Jews who counted themselves disciples of Jesus
he certainly had a right to expect that they would
understand what he said so clearly, that *his* flesh and
his blood, sacrificed for us, unite us with *him* and the
divine spirit of life that dwells in him — thus and
thus alone giving us life eternal.

This abolishes the old error that when Jesus says, "the flesh profits nothing at all," he includes also his own flesh. Doing this, Jesus would deny every statement concerning his flesh made in his previous discourse and would assert that when he says "flesh" he means the very opposite, namely "spirit," thus turning his entire discourse into nonsense. The flesh of Jesus, given into death for us and lying in the tomb until the third day, was quickened again (I Pet. 3:18) and became the means by which Jesus himself with his spirit enters our souls and quickens us to spiritual life. The notion that "spirit" here means the true spiritual sense of the words of Jesus, and that "flesh" here means the carnal or Capernaitic sense held by the Jews, introduces figures of speech where no figures are indicated. As to the word "spirit" we must say that, as the opposite of "flesh," it cannot denote the Holy Spirit. When the general principle here enunciated by Jesus is applied to him, "spirit" means Jesus' own spirit and is identical with his person and his being. Those who press the figure of the Bread in the discourse to refer only to food for nourishment to sustain life already present overagainst the bestowal of life, are answered by τὸ ζωοποιοῦν, "that which quickens," which makes alive (see the remarks on v. 48).

When Jesus adds, "The utterances which I have spoken to you, spirit they are, and life they are," he continues his tone of rebuke to those disciples. Just as they should long have known that the flesh by itself never quickens, so they should have known the nature of every utterance that falls from Jesus' lips. The pronoun ἐγώ is emphatic: because *I* make these utterances they are what I say. The better reading is the perfect, I "have spoken," although the present, I "speak," does not alter the sense, for Jesus refers to all his utterances which include his recent discourse on the Bread of Life.

Both τὰ ῥήματα and the corresponding verb λελάληκα denote the vehicles which Jesus employs for communicating with his disciples, namely the terms and expressions he chooses for the speech that falls from his lips; λόγος and λέγω would refer more to the thought. Jesus thus refers to such terms as "bread," "flesh," "blood," "to eat his flesh," "to drink his blood," and, in fact, to every form of expression employed in the recent discourse and at other times. His disciples should surely by this time know that not one of these expressions coming from *his* lips is hasty, ill-considered, extravagant, or faulty in any way. On the contrary, the vehicles Jesus employs are perfect, and that in the highest possible sense: "spirit they are, and life they are." Note how the two predicates are kept apart, so that each stands out by itself. The sense is made trivial by those who interpret: My words are of a spiritual kind and the expression of my spiritual life. We must connect "spirit" and "life" with the preceding statement, "The spirit is that which makes alive." Thus every term and expression that falls from Jesus' lips is full of his own divine spirit and, therefore, full also of his own divine life and thus reaches out to us in order to enter our souls. This, however, cannot mean that now suddenly Jesus is substituting these ῥήματα for his flesh and his blood as conveyors of life to us, which would simply cancel his entire previous discourse. Nor can he place his "utterances" beside his flesh and his blood as a second means for bestowing life on us, which would again contradict that discourse (see its summary in v. 53). Cast aside all such dual notions. The ῥήματα and the realities are one; we have neither without the other; the identical spirit and life are in both. Take the ῥῆμα or vocable "the Son" in v. 40 — it is

vacuous without the actual Son. Take the actual Son
— he remains nothing to us until this word comes to
us and tells us that he is "the Son."

64) What Jesus says about his ῥήματα being spirit
and being life connects not only with the fact that
the spirit is the quickening power but also with the
other and very sad fact: **But there are some of
you that do not believe,** which John elucidates (γάρ)
by adding: **For Jesus knew from the beginning
who they were that did not believe and who he
was that would betray him.** The fault does not lie
with the expressions which Jesus uses, every one of
which is so filled with spirit and with life that it can
be said to be spirit and to be life. No mind can suggest more adequate expressions for transmitting the
spirit and the life to the hearers of Jesus. The fault
lies with some of these disciples and hearers, who,
indeed, hear these expressions but refuse to accept
what they are and contain, namely the blessed realities,
the spirit and the life. They understand Jesus well
enough; they see what his ῥήματα bring; but this is
what they do not want and will not have. They seek
earth, and when heaven is urged upon them, they turn
away in disappointment; in fact, the more they are
made to see heaven in Jesus, the more they determine
not to have it.

When Jesus here charges these disciples with unbelief, John feels compelled, because of what Jesus
presently adds concerning Judas in v. 70, to inform us
that Jesus became aware of this unbelief, not by the
evidence it furnished of its presence by murmuring
and raising objections, but that he knew of it "from
the beginning"; and in this knowledge of Jesus John
includes also the future traitorous act of Judas. The
phrase ἐξ ἀρχῆς is definite as such, without the article,
R. 792; but what point of time is referred to? John's
statement is general and not restricted to the unbe-

lief of these Galilean disciples alone. The Greek, unlike the English, does not change the tenses after
the main verb "Jesus knew" but retains the tenses
that indicate the moment when this knowledge first
began: "who they *are* that *do* not believe, and who
he *is* that *shall betray* him" .(English: "who they *were*
that *did* not believe, and who he *was* that *would betray* him"). We see that this is the same supernatural
knowledge, used by Jesus as needed in his mission, as
that with which John acquaints us in 1:42, etc., and
in 2:24, 25. We are thus led to say that Jesus knew
what course any man's heart would take from the first
moment when Jesus came into contact with that man.
The effort to make "from the beginning" mean only
from the moment when unbelief actually begins in
one attached to Jesus, is due to the desire to escape
what some consider a grave moral difficulty. They
usually exemplify by a reference to Judas: If Jesus
knew when he first met Judas that Judas would be
his betrayer, how could Jesus, having that knowledge,
nevertheless choose him as one of the apostles? A
moment's thought, however, shows that we fail to
escape this question with its difficulty when we
assume that Jesus did not know at the time he chose
Judas that Judas would betray him but discovered
the secret unbelief at a later time, i. e., not until that
unbelief actually arose in Judas' heart. For then
the question would be cast into a new form: Knowing the unbelief of Judas and to what it would
lead, how could Jesus retain Judas as one of the
apostles?

In the first place, the future participle ὁ παραδώσων
αὐτόν blocks any escape by dating the knowledge of
Jesus only from the moment when unbelief actually
enters. For ὁ παραδώσων αὐτόν refers to a future
definite act: Judas is he who shall betray Jesus. The

articulated future participle is futuristic not volitive, R. 878, note also B.-D. 356. It states what shall take place, not what one wills to do. In other words, Jesus knew that Judas would turn traitor long before Judas exercised his traitorous volition. How far in advance Jesus knew this, therefore, makes no difference. Moreover, this exemplification by means of Judas must not be allowed to mislead us. For the question here raised is far older than Judas. It begins with Adam and includes a large number of others. How could God create Adam when God knew that Adam would fall? or create those of whom he knew that they would be damned? or receive into the church those of whom he knew that they would turn out hypocrites and renegades? In fact, how could God create Satan knowing what Satan would become? As regards Judas: Jesus chose him *not for the purpose* of betrayal but only *with the knowledge* of that betrayal. No act of God's or of Jesus' shut the door of grace for Judas, their foreknowledge did certainly not do so. This foreknowledge rested on the act of Judas, not the act of Judas on the foreknowledge. If the act had been the reverse, the foreknowledge would have accorded with the reversal. The human mind cannot penetrate the profundity of the divine mind in these questions. All we can say is that Jesus bowed to the Father's will and did this perfectly also in the grace he vouchsafed to Judas to the very last. Furthermore, even if Judas had never existed, the deadly wickedness of sin in man would have turned in murderous opposition to Jesus when the holy Son of man came to draw them to heaven, and a tragedy like that of Calvary would have been the result. One thing more must be added: when the wickedness of any man becomes unchangeably fixed, God takes it in hand and in his providence uses it for his own purposes. In the face of Mark

14:21 the intimation that the moment Judas felt the enormity of his crime, this may yet have become his salvation, must be rejected.

65) **And he was saying, On this account I have said to you, that no one is able to come to me except it have been given to him of the Father.** Jesus made no pause or break in his words; "and he was saying," with the descriptive imperfect ἔλεγε, merely informs us that Jesus went on speaking, the tense asking us to dwell on what he says. In v. 44 Jesus had said, "No man can come unto me except the Father which sent me *draw* him"; and in v. 37, "All that the Father *gives* to me shall get to me." To these two statements Jesus again refers, only changing the active form into the passive, "have been given to him." To come to Jesus is to believe in Jesus; and the ability to come is never without the coming. In our abstract thinking we must never separate the two and imagine that the Father grants the ability and that we then may decide whether we will use this ability or leave it unused.

The best commentary on this giving and this drawing is furnished in *Concordia Triglotta* 1087, etc.: "The Father will not do this without means, but has ordained for this purpose his Word and Sacraments as ordinary means and instruments; and it is the will neither of the Father nor of the Son that a man should not hear or should despise the preaching of his Word and wait for the drawing of the Father without the Word and Sacraments. For the Father draws, indeed, by the power of his Holy Ghost, according to his usual order, by the hearing of his holy, divine Word, as with a net, by which the elect are plucked from the jaws of the devil. Every poor sinner should therefore repair thereto, hear it attentively, and not doubt the drawing of the Father. For the Holy Ghost will be with his Word in his power and work by it; and that is the drawing of the Father. — But the reason why not all who hear it believe, and some are therefore condemned the more deeply, is not because God had begrudged them their salvation; but it is their own fault, as they have heard the Word in such a manner as not to learn (v. 45) but only to despise, blaspheme, and disgrace it, and have resisted the Holy Ghost, who through the Word wished to work in them."

Where the ability to come and the coming are not given, this is not due to the will or the effort of the Giver but to the contrary, hostile will and obdurate, resisting effort of him who should be the recipient, Matt. 23:37, "ye would not." "On this account," διὰ τοῦτο, refers back to the statement, "But there are some of you that do not believe." Faith and coming to Jesus is not theirs and is not given to them because in their persistent preference of unbelief they are determined not to receive it. Their lack of faith is not excused by any inactivity on the Father's part, for this does not exist; their non-faith is blamed onto them because they nullify the Father's activity of giving and drawing. "Judas would have liked nothing better than for Jesus to have allowed himself actually to be made a king by the Jews; that would have been a Messiah for his avarice, for his earthly-mindedness." Besser.

66) **In consequence many of his disciples went back and were no longer walking with him.** The phrase ἐκ τούτου is not temporal, although some think it is; for τούτου has no antecedent of time. Likewise, we cannot accept the view that "this" refers only to the hard statement of the discourse in the synagogue and not to the words spoken in v. 61-65. These disciples did not leave Jesus as they were departing from the synagogue, they left after Jesus once more spoke with them. The view that only the discourse in the

synagogue furnished them their reason for leaving, and that what Jesus said afterward furnished no such reason, misconceives the latter statements of Jesus. By charging these disciples with not believing (v. 64) and not receiving the Father's gift ·Jesus intimates that he does not consider them his disciples. "This" caused the break. "Due to this" they dropped Jesus. Jesus labors faithfully, patiently, and long, but eventually calls for a decision. This withdrawal from Jesus should have included Judas, but, covering his inward defection with hypocrisy, he remained one of the Twelve.

The aorist "they went away" merely states the fact in a summary way. Inward separation ends in outward separation. But these are not losses, because, as John indicates in his remark in v. 64, Jesus never counted the presence of such disciples as gains. We need not assume that all of the "many" left in a body but rather that they dropped away in successive groups. When John says, "they were no longer walking with him," he intimates that hitherto they had done this, all of them following Jesus about from place to place, always returning to him, when for a little while it had been necessary for them to leave. This apparently promising custom now ceased. The phrase εἰς τὰ ὀπίσω, literally "to the things behind," means that they went away from the things Jesus was offering them, back to the things that had occupied them before, their common everyday affairs. These transient, empty affairs still seem to be the real values of life to many.

67) When these withdrawals had thinned the ranks of Jesus' followers and were about complete, which must have taken place some days after the discourse in Capernaum, Jesus spoke also to the Twelve. John assumes that his readers know how Jesus had chosen them in order to train them as his special mes-

sengers or apostles. **Jesus, therefore, said to the Twelve, You, too, surely will not also be quietly leaving?** The connective οὖν marks this question as the outcome of the withdrawal of so many others. The interrogative particle μή implies that Jesus expects a negative answer. This he actually received. Yet we must note that the shades of expectation suggested by μή vary greatly according to the emotion involved: protest, indignation, scorn, excitement, sympathy, etc., R. 917 and 1175. Here the feeling of assurance prevails. We may note that θέλετε is used as an auxiliary and, for one thing, gives the question a polite form. To what extent this verb refers to the will and volition of the Twelve may be questioned as it is used also for indicating only the future. Thus the question may be, "Are you, too, about to leave," or, "Do you, too, intend to leave?" To be sure, remaining with Jesus is without compulsion, entirely voluntary. Note, however, the difference between ἀπῆλθον and ὑπάγειν, the former denoting open withdrawal ἀπό or from Jesus, the aorist stating the past fact, the latter denoting secret or quiet slipping away, ὑπό, under cover, perhaps of some excuse, the present tense describing the proceeding. Jesus does not ask this question on his own account as though seeking comfort for the loss of the many in the faithfulness of the Twelve; but for the sake of the Twelve themselves, whom the defection of so many is to help to establish the more in faith and in the true and intelligent convictions of faith. Since this is the purpose of the question, we must drop ideas such as that Jesus here "sets the door wide open" and says, "if you will, you may depart."

68) **Simon Peter answered him, Lord, to whom shall we go? Utterances of life eternal thou hast; and we on our part have believed and have realized that thou on thy part art the Holy One of God.**

John agrees with the synoptists in picturing Peter as the leader and on notable occasions the spokesman of the Twelve. The critical view that throughout John's Gospel another disciple, one who remains unnamed in the Gospel, (meaning John himself) is put into greatest prominence ahead of Peter, is deprived of its support both in 1:40, etc., where Peter is first introduced, and here where John reports Peter's grand confession for the Twelve as a body. Undoubtedly, John called him only Simon in daily intercourse with him, but when late in life he writes this record for the church, he here adds the name the Lord bestowed upon Simon and writes "Simon Peter"; he does so also in 6:8 and elsewhere where "Simon" alone would suffice.

The question of Jesus, which betrays emotion, evokes deep feeling on Peter's part, which is at once revealed when he has his reply begin with a counter-question, "Lord, to whom shall we go?" Unjustified thoughts are read into this emotional question when the addition is made, "now or ever," for Peter's response refers to the question of Jesus and a definite going away such as that which the Twelve had witnessed in the unbelieving disciples. Peter's question is misunderstood when it is taken to mean that he and others had left the Baptist and had substituted Jesus for him, and that Peter's question contemplates the possibility of again substituting another master in place of Jesus. Peter had *not* left the Baptist in any vital sense but was following the Baptist's own instruction and direction by following Jesus (see 1:35, 36). Those disciples who had forsaken Jesus did not choose another master whom they preferred to follow instead of Jesus, they only disowned Jesus. Thus Peter also continues by stating why he and the Twelve cannot possibly follow a like course and also disown Jesus. Those others preferred to shift for themselves, and this, as Peter declares, the Twelve cannot do.

In the succinct statement of the reason why the Twelve cannot leave Jesus as others had left him, "Utterances of life eternal thou hast," there is no σύ as a contrast with πρὸς τίνα. Thus there is not a contrast between Jesus and some other possible master to whom the Twelve would go if they could find such a better master. The emphasis is on the object "utterances of life" which is placed in front of the verb. Since Jesus has *these*, they cannot leave him. Because Jesus has these utterances, the Baptist bade his own disciples to follow Jesus; he himself also followed Jesus as all his attestations show, although by God's arrangement he had his own office and was not to become one of the apostles. When Peter uses ῥήματα he borrows this term from the words of Jesus in v. 63 and uses it in the same sense (see the elucidation above). Of the two predicates: "spirit they are, and life they are" (v. 63), Peter chooses the second, but by no means as though he were avoiding the first, for the second includes the first; for Jesus himself binds them together when he says that the spirit (agent, cause, source) makes alive (effect). The "utterances" of Jesus are the vital vehicles of language for the divine realities (Bread of Life, my flesh, my blood, etc.) by which "life eternal" is brought to us, that hearing these "utterances" we may appropriate the realities they name and thus have what they convey, namely "life eternal." When Peter says thou "hast" he means that these "utterances" form the treasure which Jesus dispenses to all who come into contact with him and hear him speak.

69) The counterpart is the next statement, "and we on our part have believed and have known that thou on thy part art the Holy One of God." The utter-

ances of Jesus were spurned by those who left Jesus as being a stiff and objectionable λόγος (combining the utterances with the realities they express) but they won the hearts of the Twelve. The emphatic pronoun ἡμεῖς balances only the equally emphatic following pronoun σύ: "we on our part" have believed, etc., that "thou on thy part" art, etc. Of course, what Jesus has (and bestows) is balanced also by the reception wrought in the Twelve, but this balance lies in the thought as such not in any pairing of terms. Yet "utterances" are fittingly followed by the verbs "believe" and "realize," for they are intended to be received in confidence and trust, with full reliance of the heart, and in true understanding of just what they mean, with full realization of the heart as to what they bestow ("life eternal," v. 68). The perfect tenses reach back into the past, to the moment when this faith and this realization first began, and at the same time they reach to the present, in which both actions continue. Thus Peter confesses that the Twelve have long believed, etc., (in fact, from 1:42 onward), and all that Jesus has said has only confirmed their faith.

R. 423 is right when he says that the order of the verbs is just as true here as the opposite order in 17:8. A certain kind and amount of knowledge precedes actual faith and trust and is usually also considered an integral part of it; for no one can possibly trust a person or a truth of which he does not know. On the other hand, a certain kind of knowledge always follows faith and confidence, a knowledge that is possible only as a result of this confidence. This is the knowledge of actual experience, here the experience which the Twelve had with Jesus during the two years and more of their contact with him. This knowledge is impossible for those who refuse to trust Jesus. The verb γινώσκειν invariably means "to know," but when it is used regarding spiritual knowledge, its meaning is intensified, and its sense is expressed by "to realize" with a knowledge that truly illuminates and grasps what it has learned.

The assured reading is: "that thou on thy part art the Holy One of God." This designation of Jesus is so exceptional that it is not surprising to find a commoner title in place of it in many texts, and this substitution has some variations; this is especially to be expected since Matt. 16:16; Mark 8:29; and Luke 9:20 (which describe another occasion when Peter confessed for the Twelve) contain more ordinary terms. Thus in the A. V. "that Christ, the Son of the living God" is derived from Matt. 16:16. We need not collect the Old and the New Testament passages in which ἅγιος is applied to other servants of God, for in Peter's confession it is used regarding Jesus in the supreme and the Messianic sense, in which no one save Jesus can be called "the Holy One of God." Jesus himself helps us to interpret this title when in 10:36 he designates himself as the One "whom the Father sanctified and sent into the world." He is "the Holy One of God" as the God-man sent on his saving mission into the world. As such he is ἅγιος, separate unto God. This includes the two thoughts, that Jesus is wholly separate from the world, which is unholy because of sin, yet that he comes from God to rid the world of its unholiness and sin and to separate men in true holiness unto God. The fact that Jesus in his person and his life is also himself sinless and "holy" in this sense is a self-evident but entirely minor thought. The genitive Holy One "of God" is possessive. A study of the adjective ἅγιος in C.-K. 34, etc., yields highly valuable results for all passages

in which this term or any of its derivatives are
employed.

70) Great joy fills the heart of Jesus on hearing
this adequate and earnest confession on the part of
Peter. But this joy is combined with deep pain, for
Jesus knows what Peter could not know, namely that
not all of the Twelve believed in their hearts as he
had confessed. **Jesus answered them,** since Peter
had spoken for all of them, and all had given silent
assent to Peter's words, **Did not I elect you the
Twelve for myself? and of you one is a devil.** The
question with its implied affirmation is rhetorical and
expresses the feeling of Jesus. Both pronouns are
emphatic and are made more so in the Greek by being
abutted: "I you" did elect. The middle voice "did
elect for myself" conveys the thought with sufficient
clearness, namely to be my followers in a special
sense, to be trained as my apostles for your great
future work. The apposition "the Twelve" is without
emphasis and yet has its significance. John felt it
deeply when in v. 71 he repeats: "one of the Twelve."
This number is symbolical, dating from the twelve
patriarchs and the twelve tribes of Israel, so often
used with reference to the apostles, and with the constant tragic meaning that Judas was "one of the
Twelve," finally in Rev. 7:4, twelve times twelve
thousand (144,000), 12:1, twelve stars, and 21:12-
22:2, six times in the description of the new Jerusalem.

By his own act (ἐγώ) and for himself (middle
voice) Jesus made this election of "the Twelve." John
is certain that his readers know the account of this
act from the other Gospels. With a simple "and" the
terrible adversative fact is added: "and of you (partitive use of ἐκ) one is a devil." All efforts to modify
διάβολος so that it means only a slanderer, adversary,
enemy, or traitor, break down before the analogy of

Scripture wherever this word is used as a noun. It is stronger and intended to be stronger than "devilish," or "son and child of the devil" (8:44; I John 3:10) ; it is as strong as the term "Satan," which Jesus once applies even to Peter, Matt. 16:23. "Devil" designates the real moral nature of Judas and the mind that had finally developed in him. Those other disciples who did not believe in Jesus left him, and nowhere are such men called devils; but Judas remains, remains even as one of the Twelve, remains and consents to Peter's confession, not with ordinary hypocrisy, but with lying deceit such as Jesus predicates of the very devil himself in 8:44.

So early Judas had completely broken with Jesus. "*Is* a devil" means now, at this time when Jesus says so, not that he already *was* a devil when Jesus chose him. When Judas lost his faith we are not told. Now that he has lost much more, we are told of it. This should suffice as the explanation as to why Jesus here makes this revelation. Usually it is assumed that Jesus means to utter only a pastoral warning to the Twelve not to think themselves safe just because he had elected them as apostles; but this is superficial and cannot be established by αὐτοῖς, namely that Jesus here speaks to all of them. He tells them about this "one" at this early time, so that a year from now they may remember how their Master foreknew all that Judas would do. Secondly, Jesus intends his revelation for Judas personally. This man is to know that Jesus knows him absolutely as just what he is, "a devil." He deceives his fellow-apostles but not the Son. With all his might Jesus strikes a blow at the conscience of Judas by this word "devil." In his dealings with this human devil Jesus omits nothing that may frighten him from his course and turn his heart from Satan to his Savior. So great is grace that it goes on with its blessed efforts even where foreknowledge infallibly makes certain that it shall fail. This, too, the Eleven are to remember after Jesus has died and has arisen and they go out on their mission.

71) The fact that Jesus secured this effect of his revelation John shows in his closing statement. **Now he was speaking of Judas, the Son of Simon Iscariot; for this one would betray him — one of the Twelve.** John gives us the full name of the traitor: "Judas, (son) of Simon Ish-Kerioth" (man of Kerioth, a town in Judea, Josh. 15:25). Some texts have an accusative instead of the last genitive: "Judas Iscariot, (son) of Simon." The traitor is thus distinguished both from the other Judas among the Twelve and also from the other eleven all of whom were from Galilee. The reflection that he hailed from Judea not from Galilee and thus became the traitor, is rather meaningless. The demonstrative οὗτος fixes our attention upon him in the explanatory remark that he was to become the traitor. The imperfect ἤμελλε with the present infinitive circumscribes the future tense but is able by means of the imperfect tense of the auxiliary to place this future back to the time when Jesus spoke as he did; the delivering Jesus into the hands of his enemies (παραδιδόναι) was future at that time. John usually reports without a show of feeling on his part. This makes the feeling, here expressed in the final apposition "one of the Twelve," the more effective. With this tragic apposition John closes the two chapters (five and six) in which he describes the rise of the Jewish opposition to Jesus, first in Judea, then in Galilee, and points in advance to the fatal deed which precipitated the final tragedy. This unspeakable deed was the act of "one of the Twelve."

CHAPTER VII

IV

Jesus' Attestation in Open Conflict with the Jews, Chapters 7-10

The entire fourth part of John's Gospel deals with the ministry in Jerusalem and includes two Jewish festivals, the Feast of Tabernacles and the Feast of Dedication. Comparing 6:4 and 7:2, we see that the interval between chapters six and seven is a little more than six months, from early April to the second half of October, thus about six months before the final Passover. We may divide this part into ten sections.

I. *Jesus Goes to the Feast of Tabernacles,*
        7:1-13

1) **And after these things Jesus was walking
in Galilee; for he was not willing to walk in Judea,
because the Jews were seeking to kill him.** The
three imperfect tenses point to continuous situations.
Instead of remaining in the populous Lake region in
Galilee Jesus went to the more distant parts of the
country, as far as the Phoenician border in the north-
west, down into the region of the Ten Cities (Deca-
polis) in the southwest, and up to the extreme north;
Matt. 15 and Mark 7:1-8:10. Thus Jesus prudently
avoids the opposition that developed in Capernaum
and in the populous Lake region. The murderous
temper of the authorities in Jerusalem (5:18) is mentioned as the reason why Jesus avoided Judea also.
This had developed a year ago, at the preceding Feast
of Tabernacles (see 5:1), when Jesus had last been
in Jerusalem. Jesus knows that the determination to
kill him has not changed in the capital; when he returns thither he knows the danger he will expose himself to. When we now see him, nevertheless, visiting
Jerusalem on two festival occasions, this means that
his attestation at the capital has not yet been completed and that in spite of the danger he intends to
finish also this task. But he is prudent enough to
choose two festival occasions when the crowds of pilgrims from all over the land fill the city and afford
a measure of protection for him; for large numbers
of these visitors were at least favorably inclined toward Jesus, and the authorities at Jerusalem hesitated
to outrage them by laying violent hands on him.

2) **Now the feast of the Jews was near, the Feast of Tabernacles.** John had no special reason for naming this festival in 5:1, but now he adds the name, because in the words of Jesus which he intends to report reference is made to certain customs connected with this particular festival (7:37, etc.; 8:12; 9:7). "Tabernacles," ἡ σκηνοπηγία (σκηνή, "tent," plus πήγνυμι, "to join or build"), was celebrated from the 15th to the 22nd of Tisri, our October, in commemoration of Israel's passage through the desert, and was made a festival of thanksgiving for the season's harvest of grain, fruit, and wine. The men were required to attend it at Jerusalem. Booths and tents, thousands of them outside of the walls, were occupied for a week; and in postexilic times many symbolic features were added, to some of which Jesus refers.

3) **His brethren, therefore, said to him, Depart hence and go into Judea, in order that thy disciples also may view thy works which thou art doing. For no one does anything in secret and seeks himself to stand out in public. If thou doest these things, manifest thyself to the world.** On these "brethren" compare 2:12. These relatives of Jesus urge him as they do in view of the approaching festival. Evidently they had learned from Jesus that he was making no preparation to attend this festival in the capital. They think that Jesus is largely wasting his efforts in these remote parts of Galilee, his place is on the grand stage in the heart of the nation. They say "Judea" and not at once Jerusalem, because they have in mind that Jesus should be in the midst of the great crowds of pilgrims proceeding from Galilee to Judea. This, of course, includes the grand entry into the capital city. For the Jew the great world-stage was Jerusalem. When these brethren add, "in order that thy disciples also may view thy works which

thou art doing," they do not mean that the number of Jesus' disciples in Galilee has dwindled down to negligible proportions and that he was not winning disciples of any consequence by working in the borders of Galilee. "Thy disciples" is general. Practically all of them would flock to Jerusalem for the coming festival, now more than ever drawn by the expectation of seeing and of hearing Jesus there. The implication in the ἵνα clause is that if all these disciples gathered in one mass they could really do something for Jesus in forcing through his Messianic claims, whereas nothing of consequence could be accomplished by traveling around in the borders of Galilee. Moreover, we must not miss the other implication, that the brethren of Jesus would like to see their great relative in a grand triumph at the capital with the nation bowing at his feet. They suggest that the works he is now doing are of such a kind that, if they are done on this lofty stage, will certainly bring this triumph to pass.

4) Their argument, too, is sound: "For no one does anything in secret and seeks himself to stand out in public." They see Jesus scattering his efforts among small groups of people in these remote parts and describe this as working ἐν κρυπτῷ, "in secret," in a kind of private way. This they feel is not the proper method for one whose aim is αὐτὸς ἐν παρρησίᾳ εἶναι, "himself to stand out in public." While παρρησία often means unrestrained freedom of speech; with εἶναι ἐν it means the public eye. These brethren were right: Jesus claimed to be the Messiah of the nation and had himself repeatedly said that he was sent "to the world." Then, evidently, his place and the scene of action were not in the distant parts of Galilee but in Jerusalem at this coming festival.

"If thou doest these things" is a condition of reality. Like the previous reference to "thy works which thou art doing" in v. 3 this conditional clause asserts on the part of these brethren that the works of Jesus are sufficiently great. No fault is found with them, other supposedly greater works are not demanded, for all that these brethren suggest is a grander stage, one on which these works can be displayed as they deserve to be. Hence these brethren urge Jesus, "Manifest thyself to the world!" "To the world" is the complete opposite of "in secret." Perhaps they had heard the term κόσμος from Jesus himself; for Jesus indeed intended to do nothing less: he would manifest himself to "the world" and not merely, as these relatives of his most likely understood it, to the world of Judaism but to the world of all nations and all times.

Generally this proposal of the brethren of Jesus is viewed as a repetition of the temptation offered to him by the 5,000 who wanted to carry him to the capital as king, 6:15. But the propositions are quite different. The 5,000 think of making Jesus a king by their action; these brethren say nothing about a king and urge Jesus to an action of his own. So also the response of Jesus to his brethren differs entirely from the action with which he replied to the 5,000. The fact is, these brethren, with their imperfect insight into the real mission of Jesus, are in their way not far from the plan which only six months later Jesus actually carried out in his own superior way when he made his royal entry into the capital on Palm Sunday.

5) Before giving us the reply of Jesus John explains: **For even his brethren were not believing in him.** The force of οὐδέ, "not even," R. 1185, is that, although these men were related to Jesus, they could not as yet be counted among the true believers. The imperfect tense "they were not believing" refers to more than the duration of their non-belief; the

tense is open and points to an outcome which in their
case eventuated in true faith. The way in which these
brethren are impressed by *the works* that Jesus is
doing places them in the general class indicated in
2:25; 4:45; and 6:2. In his confession Peter emphasized *the words* of Jesus (6:68), and in this the
brethren could not yet join. But they remained with
Jesus, were present with him now, and had not left
like the many in 6:66. On the one hand, they themselves do not count themselves among "thy disciples"
(v. 3), and they venture to criticize Jesus for working
"in secret"; but on the other hand, they propose plans
by which they think Jesus will succeed.

The names of these brethren are James, Joses,
Jude, and Simon, Matt. 12:46; Mark 6:3. The complete openness with which John reports their unbelief
as continuing as late as six months before Jesus' death
is noteworthy in various ways. John tells the true
facts; a fabricator would omit at least a fact like
this if he knew of it, or would alter it in some way.
In the face of the fact that these relatives of Jesus
were not among the believers, the assumption, which
is still advocated, that two of the four had been
chosen by Jesus when he selected the Twelve, namely
James and Jude, becomes untenable. Even the inferior reading ἐπίστευσαν instead of ἐπίστευον cannot alter
this conclusion; for so certainly did none of the
brethren belong to the Twelve that they are not
counted even among the "disciples" in the wider sense.
All the rest of the evidence is to the same effect, Zahn,
Introduction to the New Testament, I, 105; II, 240,
etc. What is true is the fact that all these brethren
came to faith, apparently after the resurrection of
Jesus, and that James became the first bishop of the
Jerusalem church and the writer of one of the New
Testament Epistles, and his brother Jude the writer of
another.

6) **Jesus, therefore, says to them, My right time is not yet at hand; but your right time is always ready.** We must note that Jesus does not reject the suggestion of his relatives as such, namely that at one of the festivals he enter Jerusalem as the Messiah, manifesting himself in the most public manner possible. All he does is to point out that the proper time (καιρός) has not yet come. In a manner he even excuses his brethren for urging him to proceed with this manifestation at the approaching festival. They are judging Jesus according to their own standard. Their καιρός or proper time is always ready. It makes little or no difference what time they select. They have no set mission to carry out. The case of Jesus is altogether different. The term καιρός is relative, the right time for a certain thing; the close contrast "*my* right time" and "*your* right time" also requires a parallel in the things for which these times are the right ones. This parallel cannot be the right time for going to the present festival, the fact, that the brethren were free to go at any time, but that Jesus had to wait and to go later. This restricts everything to the point of time, which is minor, and loses the main point, which is that for which the time is to be used. Likewise, the mere going to the festival cannot be meant, for this, too, is a minor action. If Jesus were going to the festival like the rest of the pilgrims, he certainly might go with them. This, however, is not what his brethren urge upon him but something decidedly greater, namely that now is the right time to make himself manifest to the world. On this point Jesus tells his brethren that for him the right time to do this has not yet arrived; but as far as they are concerned, who still belong to the world, it makes no difference when the world sees who they are.

7) That this is the thought of Jesus we see when he adds: **The world cannot hate you, but me it hates, because I bear testimony concerning it, that its works are wicked.** This is the vital difference between Jesus and his brethren, decisive also for "the right time" in regard to him and them, in v. 6. Their relation to the world (ὁ κόσμος, ungodly men as a great body or unit) is different. While the term "world" here refers specifically to its present hierarchical representatives in Jerusalem, it, nevertheless, embraces all men who are spiritually like them. In the very nature of the case it would be a psychological impossibility for the world to hate these brethren of Jesus, for they themselves were still part of the world. That does not necessarily mean that they, too, were filled with murderous hate against Jesus; but it does mean that in their hearts an opposition to Jesus lurked which was capable of being inflamed into violent action. Let us apply Matt. 5:12, etc. Even the authorities in Jerusalem at first showed only a hostile attitude (2:18) and not until Jesus' second visit advanced to violent plans (5:18). Thus, although "the world" embraces all forms of opposition to Jesus, from the silent "no" in the heart to the vociferous "Crucify!" of the mob, all these forms are essentially agreed and thus support and acknowledge each other. When, therefore, Jesus tells these brethren that the world cannot hate them, this should shock them — it so plainly implies that they still belong to the world and not to God and to his Son.

The case of Jesus is quite the opposite (adversative δέ): "but me it hates." Yet not merely because he does not and never did belong to the world, which fact also would serve as an explanation; but because of the mission of Jesus to change and thus to save the world. Jesus might have said, "yet me it cannot but hate"; he is content to state the fact only, "me it

hates." And then he points to that feature in his
mission which invariably arouses hatred when men
determine to turn against him, namely his testimony
regarding the wicked works of the world. This testimony is the application of the divine law to the sinner
(3:19, 20; 4, 16-18), which intends to crush the heart
in contrition, that it may bow to the pardon of grace.
Where this testimony is spurned, the ἔργα πονηρά remain, to be used against the world as the decisive
evidence that damns. And at the top of these wicked
works is the most wicked of all, the hate of the Savior
and all the manifestations of that hate.

When the brethren of Jesus say, "Manifest thyself to the world!" they little think what "the world"
implies for Jesus. Yes, the right time for thus manifesting himself is coming, but it means that then the
hate will rise to its highest pitch and that due to it
Jesus will die. The assumption that at this time
Jesus is still unaware of this final result is obviated
by 2:19-22; and the view that the details of the
tragedy are still hidden from him is answered by all
the advance announcements that Jesus made of his
passion.

8) Thus Jesus says to his brethren: **Do you
go up to the feast; I do not go up to this feast, because my right time has not yet been fulfilled. And
having said this to them, he remained in Galilee.**
Jesus tells his brethren to go to he feast, and they no
doubt went. As regards himself he states that he is
not going "to the feast." Yet v. 10 informs us that
he went after all, not publicly but in secret, and, as
v. 14 shows, so as to arrive in the midst of the celebration. For Jesus to say that he is not going, and
then for him to go after all, impresses many as being
a contradiction, which they then attempt to remove.
They forget the connection in which Jesus says that
he is not going. The interchange with his brethren

deals not with an ordinary attendance of Jesus at
the approaching festival but with an attendance which
would make this festival the right time for Jesus
to manifest himself to the world. The latter Jesus
declines. He tells his brethren, "You go up to the
feast!" namely in your customary way. Of himself
he says, "I do not go up to *this* feast," namely to
make "*this* feast" what you suggest. Whether he
will go at all or not is another matter. He may
stay away altogether; but if he goes, it will not be
to make of *this* feast what his brethren propose. The
pointed demonstrative "*this* feast" is in contrast with
another feast, namely the coming Passover, which will,
indeed, be the right time for Jesus to manifest himself to the world.

That this is the meaning of his words appears in
the reason why Jesus declines to go to *this* feast:
"because my right time has not yet been fulfilled."
Six additional months will fill up that measure; then,
and not until then, will Jesus carry out what at *this*
feast would be untimely. We need only to understand
what Jesus really declines to do, then even the appearance of a contradiction between his words and his subsequent act disappears.

Then, too, the proposed solutions for the supposed
contradiction are unnecessary. One of the most
ancient is a slight change in the reading, οὔπω in place
of οὐκ; as if Jesus means to say, "You go on up *now*,
I am *not yet* going but will follow *later on*." But
this change in the reading is valueless unless we suppose a contradiction and make this change in the
reading the means for its removal. The moment we
understand Jesus aright, "not yet" would refer to
the right time for the manifestation to the world —
this right time is not the present festival but another
that is not far off. Other solutions for the supposed
difficulty are less convincing. One is that Jesus

changes his mind, first deciding not to go at all, then deciding to go at least for the latter part of the feast. Another is, that the Father changes the mind of Jesus for him, ordering him to go after he himself has resolved not to go and after he had told his brethren that he would not go. But such a Christ and such a Father the Gospels do not know: a Christ who changes no to yes; but note ἐγώ — *this* festival is not the right time for him to go up as they were proposing. What Jesus declines is not an attendance at the coming feast but to make *this* feast the time for what his brethren suggest. Note that the demonstrative "this" appears only when Jesus speaks of himself.

With this correct view of the declination agrees not only the previous context but also the subsequent, the quiet way Jesus chose for going, his late arrival, and the continuance of the clash with the authorities without decisive issue. We have no reason whatever to assume that Jesus changed his mind, first deciding not to go at all, then deciding to go at least for the latter part of the feast. Or that his Father changed his mind for him, ordering him to go after he himself had resolved not to go. Since no problem exists, we need no solution.

9) Jesus, accordingly, remained behind in Galilee, the aorist merely noting the fact.

10) **Now when his brethren were gone up to the feast, then he, too, went up, not publicly, but as it were in secret.** His brethren wanted him to go as publicly as possible. This Jesus refused to do. His plan was to go as quietly as possible. So he delays until his brethren have gone with the crowds of pilgrims, until the roads are deserted, and then he goes with only the Twelve to accompany him. The emphasis is on the way in which Jesus goes up, and οἱ φανερῶς is in direct contrast to φανέρωσον σεαυτὸν τῷ

κόσμῳ in v. 4. This is even enhanced by adding the positive: "as it were (ὡς) in secret." After everyone had gone who intended to go, this was easy.

11) The situation in Jerusalem is now described. **The Jews, therefore, were seeking him at the feast and were saying, Where is that one?** These are the authorities, the members of the Sanhedrin (v. 48), as distinguished from the citizens of Jerusalem (v. 25), and also from the ὄχλος (v. 12; 20; 31, 32; 49). In what follows we must keep these three parties in mind. The rulers were nonplused by the absence of Jesus. They were well informed regarding his activities in Galilee during the past year since he had last been in Jerusalem (5:1) and had incurred their deadly hatred by ordering a man to carry his bed on the Sabbath and by making himself equal with God (5:18). They fully expected him at this festival and even instituted search for him. Note the durative imperfects "were seeking," "were saying," which at the same time indicate that the outcome will presently be stated.

12) **And murmuring concerning him was much among the multitudes. Some were saying, He is a good man; while others were saying, No; on the contrary, he is deceiving the multitude.** Perhaps John uses the plural "multitudes" because he at once speaks of two parties. The ὄχλος or ὄχλοι are the hosts of pilgrims who had come for the festival from near and far. John himself explains the extensive "murmuring" that was going on among these visitors concerning Jesus. He was the general subject of discussion, and two opinions were widespread. Those who favored Jesus called him ἀγαθός, the masculine adjective meaning "a good man," one who is excellent, in the sense that he brings benefit. This fits the type of miracles which distinguish Jesus, conferring healing, deliverance, and help. This estimate was weak

and poor enough; too weak to form the basis of faith. The fact that a large portion of the pilgrims should hold a contrary opinion comes as a surprise. These contradict the others with a flat "no" and mark their judgment as the direct opposite by ἀλλά, which after a negative has the force of "on the contrary." And, indeed, they assert that he "deceives the multitude," is intent on misleading it. They must refer to his teaching and imply that this is false and that his miracles are used only to cover up the falseness. Neither side could convince the other, and the two imperfects ἔλεγον allow the dispute to remain unsettled.

13) The fact that this talk about Jesus never rose beyond a subdued "murmur" John explains. **No one, however, was speaking with openness concerning him because of the fear of the Jews,** the rulers in the capital. This evidently refers to both parties alike. The authorities had not yet rendered an official opinion or verdict. Hence no one felt sure of himself. Here παρρησία has its more usual meaning: freedom to say anything. The genitive "of the Jews" is objective, R. 500. John's remark casts a light on the spiritual slavery in which the Sanhedrin and other Jewish authorities kept the nation. Compare v. 49 and 9:34. Woe to those who did not yield to this domination!

II. *Jesus' Testimony Stirs the Authorities to Order his Arrest, 14-36*

14) In a quiet way, without any demonstration whatever, Jesus arrives in the city. **Now when the feast was already half over, Jesus went up into the Temple and began teaching.** The genitive absolute τῆς ἑορτῆς μεσούσης (from μεσόω, to be in the middle), together with ἤδη, "the feast being already in its middle," i. e., half over with, shows at how late a time

Jesus appeared in the courts of the Temple. On the
other two occasions when he had appeared in Jerusalem
he at once made his presence felt by deeds that acted
like a public challenge, cleansing the court of the
Temple (2:13, etc.), and sending a healed man through
the streets with his couch on his shoulder on the Sabbath (5:9, etc.). On neither occasion had he assumed
the quiet role of a teaching rabbi. But this is what
he now does. The imperfect is here ingressive: "he
began to teach." What followed we are told presently.
He found some convenient place, where he sat on the
pavement under some porch or balcony, the Twelve
and a group of hearers sat cross-legged in a circle
about him, and he quietly began his instruction. On
what subject he spoke John does not state.

Among those present, perhaps standing on the
fringe of the seated group, were a few of the ruling
class. Here was the man they were seeking. But
they found him using only the ordinary privilege of
a rabbi, teaching a group of interested hearers. We
may take it that this group grew rapidly, for presently
the ὄχλος utters an exclamation, v. 20.

15) After listening awhile to the teaching of
Jesus the Jews start their interference. **The Jews,
therefore, wondered, saying, How does this fellow
know letters, not having learned?** These Jews had
never before heard Jesus teach as a rabbi. But this
wondering of theirs is not surprise because of the
ability of Jesus to teach the Scriptures although, as
they knew, he had never studied in any of the rabbinical schools. If they had felt such surprise they would
have hidden it and would never have credited Jesus
with ability along this line before a crowd of pilgrims
assembled about Jesus. Moreover, οὗτος is highly derogatory and means "this fellow." By γράμματα they
mean *litteras* in the Jewish sense, the rabbinical
study of the Old Testament writings. We need not

change the sense of θαυμάζειν into offended wondering. What surprises them, they say, is that a man who has had no proper education should presume to teach in public and palm himself off as one who is versed in Scriptural learning. Their question is a general exclamation addressed not to Jesus but to the multitude. It charges Jesus with incompetency, with utter lack of proper qualifications for being a great religious teacher. The purpose of the rulers is to discredit Jesus before his audience. The force of their question is: "This fellow does not know what he is talking about because he has never studied in any of our Jewish schools."

We meet the same charge today when any man dares to contradict the "scientific" critics of Christ and the gospel. At once he is branded by them as an ignoramus, incompetent to speak on these subjects because he is not one of their guild, who has pre-empted "scientific" learning and does not bear the stamp of their approval. The object is to impress the crowd, and the secret object is to maintain their own authority by crying down the man who challenges it. Those commentators are mistaken who think that the marvelling of these Jews is genuine and that they are really surprised at Jesus as being *"ein schriftkundiger Volkslehrer," "ein wirksamer Haggadist," "ein genialer Autodidakt."* Instead of being a self-taught genius, they make him out the very opposite: *dass er als unbefugter Pfuscher an Stelle der alleinberechtigten Gelehrtenweisheit nur eigene Einfaelle vorbringe und fuer Weisheitslehre ausgebe.* The proceeding of these Jews is the height of cunning. They seek to shift the question: How true and genuine is the teaching of Jesus? to: What great and accredited schools has Jesus attended? They also count on the fact that the teaching of Jesus differs completely from that which the people have been accustomed to receive from the rabbis, both in contents and in form. To tell the people that Jesus has never attended a school of any standing for training rabbies, that he has no degree or certificate from such an accredited school, would certainly have its effect upon the ignorant.

16) *The Divine Origin of Jesus' Doctrine, 16-24.* — Without the slightest hesitation Jesus meets the wicked charge of the rulers. And he, too, does not direct his words to these rulers in particular but to all who are gathered before him and have heard the charge. These wise Jews, Jesus intimates in his answer, have certainly heard aright: the entire doctrine of Jesus is totally different from the arid refinements and empty distinctions of the rabbis, and it is plain to any man who has ears to hear, that Jesus has never "learned" from such teachers. Nobody needs to tell the people this. **Jesus, therefore, answered them and said** (see 1:48), **My doctrine is not mine, but his that did send me.** He has in mind the substance of what he is teaching; διδαχή corresponds to ἐδίδασκε. The adjective in ἡ ἐμὴ διδαχή is stronger than the possessive pronoun would be. The wonderful feature about the doctrine Jesus taught is that it is not his own at all, in the sense that he, like some human philosopher, had himself invented, had produced it by his own human brain. On the contrary (ἀλλά after a negative), it is "his that did send me," it belongs wholly to his great Sender. Jesus is only the mouthpiece, the spokesman, of that Sender. By rejecting and trying to discredit this teaching of Jesus these Jews are by no means dealing with Jesus alone but with the Sender of Jesus, with God himself. It is no wonder that God's great doctrine is wholly different from the speculations of the rabbis. If that is any discredit to the doctrine of Jesus, he accepts the discredit; but woe unto those who offer this

discredit! See what they betray concerning themselves. They have never "learned" (v. 15; also 6:45) in God's school at the feet of the great teachers and prophets whom God sent them in the Old Testament. If they had, they would at once recognize the doctrine of Jesus as being that of God; but now they blindly slander it and try to turn others from it.

17) As far as recognizing the fact that this doctrine is of God is concerned, no difficulty whatever is encountered. Simply apply the right touchstone. It is useless merely to reason and to argue about it intellectually, if for no other reason than that man by nature is spiritually blind and cannot even know the things of God, since they are spiritually discerned. Jesus is far from submitting his doctrine to the decision of blind human reason, which, indeed, constantly endeavors to usurp the authority of a judge in spiritual things. No; the right touchstone is a living experience with the doctrine of Jesus. Such an experience at once makes plain and convinces us inwardly that this doctrine is of God. **If anyone shall will to do his will, he shall know concerning the doctrine whether it is of God or whether I am talking from myself.** The condition of expectancy has the regular form, ἐάν with the subjunctive (protasis) followed by the future indicative (apodosis). Whenever a case like this occurs, that a man wills to do God's will, the result follows, he realizes that the doctrine is of God (the article to indicate the doctrine here in question, R. 757). The present subjunctive θέλῃ indicates more than a single volition; it denotes a durative and lasting course. The Greek abuts θέλῃ τὸ θέλημα, "shall will the will," and the present infinitive ποιεῖν means "to carry out" God's will in a consistent course. "His will" is objective, *what* God wills; "shall will" is subjective, *accepting* by our will what God wants carried out by us.

This will of God is faith on our part. "This is the work of God, that ye *believe* on him whom he did send," John 6:29; compare 6:40. Before the coming of Jesus this faith was to believe the promises concerning Jesus, after his coming this faith is to believe the fulfillment of these promises in Jesus. God's will is that we believe, our willing to carry out his will is our actual believing by his grace. The entire thought of Jesus would be perverted if we should take it that God's will here refers to the law and our doing of the law; and correspondingly that our willing to do his will is our setting out to meet the requirements of that law. The doctrine of Jesus centers not in the law but in the gospel, in God's will of pardoning and saving grace. Again, it would be a perversion of the thought of Jesus if we conceived his meaning to be that we are to do God's gracious will by means of our own natural ability. Nothing is farther from his mind than that God commands us to believe and that we then obey by believing. Man's will as it is by nature cannot possibly itself resolve to do this will of God, i. e., to believe. So far is God from expecting this that ever in the very revelation of his gracious will his own divine will comes with efficacious power to set our will free and to move it to accept his will, i. e., to believe. The efficacy of his will our will may resist obdurately and persistently but always without excuse, and thus only with the most damnable guilt. When Jesus speaks of our willing to do God's will, he means that willing which God by his grace works in us through his Word and his Spirit.

This willing (believing) is the touchstone: "he shall know concerning the doctrine whether it is of God or whether I am talking from myself." "Know" means "realize," not by means of mere intellectual processes, not by reasonings and arguments but by the actual

experience of letting God's will move his will. When
God's will sets the human will free and fills it with
new power, then, and then alone, a man knows God's
will, what it really is, by having experienced in his
own will what God's will does. In no other manner
can this knowledge be attained. If your will is moved
by God's will as this will graciously reaches out and
changes your will; if your will is moved from sin
toward Christ and the salvation he brings; if, thus
moved, it finds the curse and the shackles of sin gone,
a new, heavenly power filling it and working in it:
then you will realize, indeed, that the doctrine which
brought this heavenly will to you is "of God" (ἐκ,
derived from him) and that in uttering it Jesus is
not talking (λαλῶ) "from himself" (ἀπό, from notions
he has invented).

18) But as far as the person of Jesus and his
doctrine are concerned, a more general criterion is at
hand. **He that talks from himself seeks his own
glory; but he that seeks the glory of him that did
send him, this one is true, and no unrighteousness
is in him.** To the Jews it was axiomatic that all
genuine religious teaching emanated from God, and
that therefore every genuine religious teacher must
teach as commissioned, authorized, and sent by God.
Whoever, therefore, as a religious teacher presented
anything emanating from himself instead of from
God could do so only by arrogating to himself the
glory and the honor that belong to God; he would
"be seeking his own glory." Thus Jesus says: "he
who seeks (not his own glory by offering his own supposed wisdom but) the glory of him that did send
him (as a teacher, by teaching only what he is commissioned to teach — this being God) this one
(οὗτος, only he and no other) is true (ἀληθής, *verax*,
namely, as a teacher, not false, lying), and no

unrighteousnes is in him" (he can be charged with no wrong or unfaithfulness in his office as a teacher).

The application of this axiom is easy. First, as regards Jesus. He sought only the glory of God, 5:19; 7:16. Sincere people could have no difficulty on that point. To insinuate that because he had not been educated in the rabbinical schools he is a spurious teacher is base slander. Its worst feature is the substitution of a false test for religious teachers. This slander puts the authority and the praise of the rabbis in place of God and his glory. Jesus insists on the true criterion. The moment this is applied the divinity of his teaching is established beyond question. But this axiom holds good also for the opposite. How about these Jewish rulers and their religious teaching as it is now being urged in opposition to Jesus? They are notorious seekers after their own glory and honor. They oppose Jesus for the very reason that they fear to lose their position of honor and of power among their people. Even Pilate, six months later, knew that "for envy" they had delivered him, Matt. 27:18. It is evident that as teachers they are not "true" and not void of "unrighteousness." This is the inner reason for their hostility to Jesus, the cause of their blindness to the divinity of his doctrine. Here again we touch the will as being the real domain in which the battle is fought, and in what follows we see how Jesus continues his attack upon this central citadel.

19) In verses 17 and 18 Jesus lays down axiomatic principles. The first is regarding *the doctrine*: anyone may test the doctrine and by his own experience with it convince himself that it is of God. The second is regarding *the teacher*: anyone may test the teacher. If he seeks God's glory alone (by teaching the true faith which gives all honor and praise to God

alone) he is a true teacher with no unrighteousness
to discredit him as a teacher; but if he is after his
own glory and his personal advantage he is a false
teacher and stands revealed as such. Defense and
offense are combined in the enunciation of these principles. But now, with a sudden turn, Jesus takes the
offensive. Like a bolt of lightning he drops the charge
of the grossest kind of ἀδικία or unrighteousness upon
the heads of the Jewish rulers. **Did not Moses give
you the law?** That sounds innocent but is ominous.
Of course, Moses gave them the law, all of it as comprised in the five books of Moses (the *Torah* or "Instruction") and specifically its moral regulations in
the Ten Commandments. And the great boast of
these Jewish rulers was that they sat in Moses' seat
(Matt. 23:2) as teachers and guardians of the law
and as "disciples of Moses" (9:28). This reference
of Jesus to Moses and the law is a masked battery.
Two annihilating volleys will roar out from it: these
Jews, boastful exponents of the law, breaking the law
in the most horrible manner; these Jews, supreme
teachers of the law, circumcise on the Sabbath in
order not to violate the law and yet charge Jesus
with violation when on the Sabbath he extends a blessing far greater than circumcision.

And none of you does the law by no means
asserts only that these rulers, like all men, are sinners
in a general way. For if that disqualifies them as
guardians of the law, no man could ever be a true
teacher of the law. Like the previous question about
receiving the law from Moses, this assertion about
their not living up to the law still has a harmless
look. For Moses himself, through whom the law was
given, was a sinner in the general sense of the word,
and so were all the great prophets who taught the
law. The question and the assertion have a specific
bearing.

Why are you seeking to kill me? The briefest, simplest kind of a question but devastating in its effect. Its implication is that these rulers are even at this very time plotting and scheming to murder Jesus. The question is stronger than an assertion would be. This "why" is addressed to these Jewish rulers as the exponents, guardians, and teachers of the law, into whose keeping Moses gave the law. This unanswerable "why" reveals what these enforcers of the law were doing with that law in planning the murder of Jesus, sent to them of God with the doctrine of God. Compare 5:18. Consternation sealed the lips of the Jews; silence reigned. We may imagine how the eyes of all the pilgrims turned toward and for a moment searched the faces of their rulers. This was the ἀδικία that branded them as the type of teachers they were and as the kind of teaching they offered. Is murder of God? is murder the teaching of God's law? Murder is of the devil; and murder and lying are twins, 8:44. These Jews expected to have an easy victory over Jesus by pointing out that he had no professional training. In their attack they felt secure behind the plausibility of their insistence on proper qualifications for public teachers, behind the secrecy which hid their real motive for attacking Jesus. In a flash they now stand exposed as criminal law-breakers.

20) The citizens of Jerusalem, at least those in touch with the rulers, know of the plot against Jesus, v. 25. But the pilgrims that came from all parts of the country are entirely innocent. When Jesus suddenly and publicly casts into the face of the rulers their scheme to kill him, these pilgrims are astounded and horrified. **The multitude answered, Thou hast a devil! Who is seeking to kill thee?** The adjective δαιμόνιον, here used as a noun, means some kind of evil spirit. The exclamation does not voice ill will

but impatient surprise that a man like Jesus, whom so many of the ὄχλος admired, should utter a charge involving what seemed to them a moral impossibility. Surely, some evil spirit must be clouding his mind with the mental aberration and fixed idea that he is being persecuted. The added question shows how unthinkable it seems to the pilgrims that their rulers should be seeking to kill Jesus. But — the rulers stand there silently, with the eyes of the crowd searching their faces. That silence speaks loudly.

21) In v. 19 Jesus addresses only the rulers; now he ignores them — he is done with them. **Jesus answered and said unto them,** αὐτοῖς, plural because of the collective antecedent ὁ ὄχλος. On the use of the two verbs see 1:48; also note that ἀπεκρίθη = *er nahm das Wort*. This does not imply that Jesus makes a direct reply to the question of the multitude. In no way does Jesus qualify or alter the charge that the rulers are seeking to kill him; on the contrary, he involves also the multitude to a certain degree, because they, too, were angry with Jesus because of the miracle wrought on the Sabbath. That miracle, wrought a year ago (5:2, etc.), which first caused the rulers to plot his death (6:18), Jesus now discusses. **One work I wrought, and you all wonder because of it.** Jesus means "one" especially that still causes wonderment; many other miracles of his produced no such effect. It is not the greatness of the deed that causes this wondering as compared with other miracles of Jesus. We must construe: "you all wonder *because* of it," διά. We need not here bring in the constructions of θαυμάζειν with ἐπί or περί, because these prepositions place the surprise or wonder on the thing itself that is wrought. In this instance it is not the fact that Jesus healed a man impotent for thirty-eight years that causes the marvelling. It is not in any sense the miracle itself but something

connected with the miracle, hence the preposition διά,
"because" Jesus performed this deed on the Sabbath, and "because" he made the man carry his bed
on the Sabbath. The thought is not complete, not
even correct, without the phrase διὰ τοῦτο, "because
of this."

The moment this is understood we shall not connect this phrase with the next sentence, as is done
by a number of codices, by the ancients, by some of the
moderns, by our versions, and by others. The claim
that the phrase is superfluous when it is attached to
v. 21 arises from the fact that its sense is not understood; for "you all are marvelling" is not what Jesus
wants to say but "you all are marvelling *because of
this,*" i. e., the feature that you fail to understand and
that upsets you, that I should do such a work on the
Sabbath.

22) **Moses has given you the circumcision (not
that it originates with Moses but with the fathers),
and you circumcise a man on the Sabbath.** The
emphasis is on Moses, on this great authority to whom
all Israelites bowed. Jesus holds up Moses to the pilgrim crowd, as a moment ago he pointed their rulers
to this same Moses (v. 19). If, however, we draw
the phrase διὰ τοῦτο to v. 22, the emphasis would be
transferred to this phrase. Instead of saying: "*Moses*
(no less an authority) has given you the circumcision, . . . and you circumcise a man on the Sabbath," Jesus would say: "*For this reason* has Moses
given you circumcision, not because it originates with
Moses, but with the fathers; and you circumcise," etc.
But if this were the sense intended, the sentence should
read: "*Not* for this reason has Moses given you
circumcision, *that* it originates with him *but that*
it originates with the fathers," etc., οὐ διὰ τοῦτο
. . . ὅτι . . . ἀλλὰ ὅτι, and the second ὅτι could

not be omitted. Such a statement, however, would not be true. The Jews did not circumcise on the Sabbath because this rite *originated* with the fathers and not with Moses. The historical origin of circumcision (ἐκ) is a side issue; i. e., the fact that the rite is older than Moses. Nor did Moses embody circumcision in the law because the patriarchs already had the rite but because God wanted him to command it in the law. If the point of origin and age were urged by Jesus, he would have said that the Sabbath goes back much farther than circumcision, to God himself and to the very week of creation. What Jesus does point out is that *Moses* gave the Israelites circumcision, *Moses* as the agent of God, and that thus — very properly — they circumcise on the Sabbath whenever the eighth day after birth happens to occur on a Sabbath.

The statement, however, that no less an authority than *Moses* gave circumcision, requires an explanation lest it be misunderstood. Jesus is not speaking historically but from the legal standpoint. Historically the fathers, i. e., the patriarchs, already had circumcision prior to Moses. Its origin dates back thus far. But legally the Israelites were held to this rite since the time of Moses, the great lawgiver of Israel. Hence the statement, "not that it is of Moses but of the fathers," is parenthetical, in the nature of an elucidation. This shows that in the main clause the emphasis on "Moses" dare not be shifted as it would be by placing the phrase before "Moses." But we also should not find other thoughts in the parenthetical statement, either that circumcision has more weight than the law because it antedates the law and because it is derived from the fathers; or that it has less weight than the law because it consists only of a tradition from the fathers. Such notions confuse the plain sense of what Jesus desires to convey.

The examples adduced for the use of διὰ τοῦτο at
the head of a statement, such as 5:16 and 18; 6:65;
8:47; 10:17; etc., have no bearing on the present case
because they all have ὅτι following: "for this reason
. . . that," etc. Really analogous examples are
those that illustrate οὐχ ὅτι . . . ἀλλά, such as
6:46; 12: 6; II Cor. 1:24; 3:5; 7:9; Phil.4:11 and
17; II Thess. 3:9.   All these are parenthetical in their
very nature. On the formula οὐχ ὅτι see R. 1429. To
regard the parenthesis as superfluous is an indication
that its purpose is not fully understood. It makes
clear that circumcision is binding only as a legal
requirement irrespective of its origin. The effort
to explain διὰ τοῦτο as an ellipsis is unfeasible: "For
this reason *I say to you*, Moses has given," etc.; or:
"For this reason *hear*, or *know*, Moses," etc. Jesus
is here not making an authoritative announcement but
is only repeating admitted facts, that Moses has given
the circumcision (the article pointing to the rite as
one that is well known), and that circumcision is performed on the Sabbath.

23)   Now just as these facts are beyond dispute,
so should be their application to the deed of Jesus.
**If a man receives circumcision on the Sabbath, in
order that the law of Moses may not be broken, are
you angry with me because I made a man completely well on the Sabbath?** Jesus puts the
application in the form of a question, in order the
more effectively to appeal to the judgment of his
hearers. This question brings out the true point which
ought to be decisive for the judgment of his hearers.
It appears already in v. 22 when Jesus says that
Moses "has given" you the circumcision. This rite
was a good gift from God through Moses, not a burden, not an infliction, not a work done for God. So
Jesus now continues and asks, if a man "receives"
the circumcision on the Sabbath, receives this gift or

blessing. Jesus does not ask, "if you circumcise a man on the Sabbath," for this is not a question of so much labor in administering the rite. He also adds the purpose clause, "in order that the law of Moses may not be broken," for it is the law itself which requires that the gift be bestowed even if the day be the Sabbath, Lev. 12:3. In other words, to withhold the gift because the day happens to be the Sabbath would be a violation (λυθῇ, a dissolution) of this law. The emphasis is again on "Moses" and it shows that in v. 22 "Moses" is the emphatic word. "If" (εἰ with the indicative) is a condition of reality; for Jesus takes it that the rite is thus received as a blessing, and his hearers certainly agree with him.

Now the path is clear for the application to the healing of the impotent man on the Sabbath. The emphasis on the genitive "of Moses" is matched by the emphasis on the dative "with me," and for this reason the two are abutted in the Greek. What is an inviolable law in the case of *Moses,* can that be a cause for anger with *me?* In v. 21 Jesus uses only the verb "wonder," here he now employs the stronger term "to be angry." These people wonder that Jesus should heal a man on the Sabbath and are gravely displeased with him as a result. Yet Jesus had done a deed that was essentially identical with what Moses had commanded and the Jews practiced as a matter of course; for just as the circumcision of the bodily member is a blessing received by the child, so the healing of the entire body was a blessing received by the impotent man. The identity, however, lies not in the sanitary features of the two blessings, the one concerned with a single member of the body, the other with the entire body. The Scriptures show no trace of hygienic or sanitary valuation of circumcision. As part of the ceremonial law this rite effects the religious purification of the organ of procreation, and thus Jesus pairs it with the restoration of the entire body of the impotent man. The identity here stressed lies in the fact that both are blessings, the one affecting a single member, the other the entire body. By ὅλον ἄνθρωπον, "an entire man," Jesus does not refer to both body and soul but to the body alone. What Jesus did for the impotent man's soul by warning him not to fall into sin again was unknown to the Jews and may not have been done on the Sabbath at all, nor would such a warning have transgressed their conception of the sanctity of the Sabbath.

The argument is thus quite simple: on the one hand, a beneficial act involving one member; on the other hand, a beneficial act involving the entire body. The force of the argument, however, is increased in two ways. Whereas Moses *commands* circumcision also on the Sabbath, these Jews will not so much as *permit* a healing on the Sabbath. The conferring of a benefit means *so much* to Moses that he will not let even the Sabbath stand in the way; the conferring of a benefit means *so little* to the Jews that they misuse the Sabbath and force it to stand in the way. This point in the argument operates *a majori ad minus*. On the other hand, the benefit for the bestowal of which Moses commands that it be conferred even on the Sabbath is *small* (one bodily member), whereas the benefit for the bestowal of which these Jews forbid its being conferred on the Sabbath is by comparison *great* (the entire body). This point in the argument operates *a minori ad majus*. The combination of the two points in the presentation of the argument is unusual and utterly convincing. It goes to the very root of the matter and does not, after the fashion of the rabbis, deal merely with the superficial wording of the law. If the multitude would only use Moses it would not abuse Jesus.

24) Therefore the closing admonition: **Do not keep judging according to appearance but render the right judgment.** This is not a general injunction against forming superficial judgments but a demand to render the right judgment in the present case. Hence the article τὴν κρίσιν. We may also translate the present imperative, "Stop judging superficially!" for it forbids what these people were already doing. The preposition κατά indicates the norm, namely the mere appearance of the act Jesus had performed. Looked at only from the outside, this act might seem to be in contravention of the law. But mere appearance is never to be the norm for directing our verdicts. The very law itself, which these people cited against Jesus, should teach them to follow a different course.

In the second clause the correct reading is the aorist κρίνατε, which also matches the article τὴν δικαίαν κρίσιν (an accusative of inner content, or cognate accusative, R. 478): "judge the right judgment" in this case, the one governed by the norm of right (δίκη). This aorist plus the article restricts the command to the case in hand. The reading κρίνετε is due, it seems, to the use of the same present tense in the first clause and to the idea that Jesus here voices a general rule for deciding any and all cases. Righteous judgment will see in the man carrying his bed no violation of the Sabbath law but a publication of the astounding blessing he had received on the Sabbath through the grace of God.

The answer of Jesus is misconceived when circumcision and the miracle of Jesus are considered exceptions to the sabbatical law. The law itself demanded circumcision also on the Sabbath and not by way of exception. Circumcision on the Sabbath was as much a law as the observance of Sabbath rest. And the miracle is placed on a par with the former. Likewise, Jesus does not abrogate the Sabbath by his miracle. Jesus keeps the Sabbath law as given by Moses, but he refuses to be bound by the rabbinical regulations which had been added to the Mosaic law. These were unwarranted human additions, to which Jesus could never bow.

Moses upholds Jesus, and Jesus Moses. Both are here shown to be true teachers of God, teaching nothing of their own but only what he who commissioned them gave them to teach; and thereby they honored him in the highest degree. But "the Jews" (rulers), who opposed Jesus and only imagined that they were supporting Moses, who even planned to murder Jesus in flagrant violation of Moses; and in lesser degree "the multitude" (pilgrims), who were displeased with Jesus — are shown to be gravely in the wrong.

25) *The Divine Origin of Jesus' Person, 25-30.* — After dealing with the rulers and then with a crowd of pilgrims Jesus answers also a number of the citizens of Jerusalem, who raise the question regarding his person and tell themselves that he cannot be the Christ. **Some of the citizens of Jerusalem accordingly were saying, Is not this he whom they are seeking to kill?** These "Jerusalemites," as John calls them, live in the city. "Accordingly" connects what these citizens say with what they are witnessing at the moment. They are a part of the crowd that confront Jesus. No interval occurs between v. 24 and v. 25. The imperfect ἔλεγον is descriptive; they were most likely a little group and were speaking quietly to each other, certainly not so that either the pilgrims or the rulers heard their remarks.

These citizens are better posted than the pilgrims who live elsewhere and visit the city only on great occasions. So they are well informed about the intention of the rulers to kill Jesus, while the pilgrims are shocked to hear of this intention (v. 19). But the situation these citizens are witnessing puzzles them. "Is not this he whom they are seeking to kill?" They feel sure that this is, indeed, the man (οὐ at the head of the question).

26) **And behold, with openness he speaks, and nothing to him do they say. Can it be that the rulers have, indeed, realized that this is the Christ?** First the astonishing fact, then an explanation that would, indeed, explain the fact but that is presented as certainly being out of the question. Here to the astonishment of these citizens is Jesus speaking in public (παρρησίᾳ), and here are some of the rulers (οἱ ἄρχοντες), and they do not say a thing (οὐδέν) to him, namely to apprehend him and to carry out their determination to kill him. The rulers had, indeed, said something (v. 15), but Jesus had promptly closed their mouths, and they had kept them closed. "Nothing to him do they say?" means nothing to prevent him from speaking with freedom, nothing like declaring him under arrest, nothing like a criminal charge to justify arrest.

The possibility flashes into the minds of these citizens that their rulers have changed their minds about Jesus. The very clash, however, which they have just witnessed (v. 15-19) settles any such possibility. The very question in which they utter it carries in it their own denial, for μή implies a negative answer in their own minds: "Can it be ever (μήποτε)?" No, it cannot be. The Greek has the aorist ἔγνωσαν, "did come to realize," whereas the English idiom prefers the perfect tense; see the excellent discussion in R. 843, etc. This is due to the fact that in the Greek the perfect does not like the English perfect indicate an action just *recently* completed. The sense of ἀληθῶς is "indeed," or "really"; but the second ἀληθῶς in the *textus receptus* (A. V.) must be cancelled: "that this is the *very* Christ" ("is *truly* the Christ"), the promised Messiah. All the evidence is to the contrary — the rulers have not changed their minds about Jesus.

27) Moreover, these citizens agree on this point with the rulers. **On the contrary, him we know, whence he is; but the Christ, when he comes, no one will know whence he is.** The negation in the minds of the citizens (μήποτε in v. 26) is matched by the adversative (ἀλλά) at the head of v. 27: No, the rulers have not realized, etc.; "on the contrary," they could not, for even these citizens know that Jesus cannot possibly be the Christ. Why not? The mighty evidence of his miracles, all the power of his teaching, and the impact of his personality inevitably felt in both, count for nothing with these men of the metropolis, who refuse to be impressed as were the pilgrim crowds, especially those from Galilee. They have their own little criterion for rejecting Jesus' claims. "Him we know, whence he is; but the Christ, when he comes, no one will know whence he is." This Jewish notion about the expected Messiah, with which in the minds of these wiseacres Jesus does not accord, they imagine keeps them from being deceived by Jesus. We have no evidence that the rulers use the same line of argument. On the contrary, like some of the multitude (v. 41, 42), the rulers apply a different criterion, namely, that Jesus hails from Galilee whereas the Scriptures say that the Messiah will be born in Bethlehem, of the seed of David, in Judea (v. 52).

The efforts to trace the notion of the citizens in Jewish literature have produced no satisfactory results. In the middle of the second century Justin puts into the mouth of the Jew Tryphon the opinion: "But the Messiah, even when he is born and exists somewhere, is unknown and does not even know himself, and has no power until Elijah anoints him and makes him know to all." Jewish literature, however, nowhere makes Elijah anoint the Messiah. Justin's version of Tryphon's opinion makes no reference to the origin of the Messiah, "whence he is," but states only that neither the Messiah nor anyone else will know him as the Messiah until Elijah anoints him. The assumption that the notion of the citizens is derived from the low state of the house of David at the time, supported possibly also by Scripture statements like Isa. 53:2 and 8; Mal. 3:1, "shall suddenly come to his Temple," is too farfetched to merit consideration.

The citizens think that they are fully informed "whence" Jesus is. They have found out all about his long residence in Nazareth, his family connection (1:45; 6:42), especially also his career in Galilee during the past year since his last visit to Jerusalem. Thus they feel that they know all about him. No reason appears for restricting "whence" to the family of Jesus exclusive of his home and his residence, for the two always go together. But this very information is proof to them that he cannot be the Messiah. For their picture of the Messiah — however they may have obtained it — is that "when he comes, no one will know whence he is," i. e., from what town and province and from what family. Not that his origin will forever be shrouded in mystery, but that it will be unknown "when he comes," or at the time of his public appearance. This type of reasoning has often been followed by men who imagine themselves to be superior to others. They pick some flaw and fasten on that and refuse to consider the real and decisive facts, however great and convincing these may be.

28) The cool and self-satisfied way in which these citizens dispose of Jesus arouses him to make the most energetic reply. **Jesus, accordingly, cried out, teaching in the Temple and saying, Both me you**

**know and know whence I am?! And (yet) I have
not come of myself, but one that is real is he that
did send me, whom you do not know.** With a loud
voice, showing how deeply he was affected, Jesus
cried out. What moves him is not the argument
of these citizens but the superficiality and shallow-
ness which satisfies them for disposing of his person
and his office. The position of the subject, ὁ Ἰησοῦς,
between the two participles διδάσκων καὶ λέγων shows
that the phrase "in the Temple" is not to be drawn
to the main verb: "he cried out in the Temple," but
that it must be drawn to the two participles: "teaching in the Temple and saying." The participles, however, cannot indicate the time: while still teaching
and speaking in the Temple; or: before he left the
Temple court. For v. 14 has already given us this
information, and no reason appears for repeating it
here. These are modal participles, describing the loud
crying of Jesus. "He cried out" draws attention to
the fact that he was deeply moved thus to raise
his voice; the participles add that he did this as
teaching and making a declaration (λέγων) here in the
Temple, the central place designed for this very purpose. In this loud cry we are still to hear the teacher
and speaker engaged in his Temple work. John writes
this preamble to Jesus' words as a witness who was
present, who heard and saw what took place.

The fact that Jesus cried out as he did should
dispose of the idea that Jesus merely acknowledges
what the citizens claim to know, namely, whence he
is, which naturally involves also who he is: "You
know both me and know whence I am." Why should
Jesus lift up his voice in order to make such an
admission? His ordinary tone of voice would have
sufficed for that. The emotion indicated on the part
of Jesus makes it quite certain that his first words
are an exclamatory question. In fact, Jesus cannot

admit that these citizens really know him, for their
own little argument shows that they do not, and Jesus
tells them in no uncertain way that they do not.
Note the emphasis brought out by the two *καί*:
"Both *me* you know and *know* whence I am?!"
This matches exactly the words of these citizens. Not
that Jesus actually heard what they said to each
other; he understood of his own accord exactly what
they said. They claimed to know "him, whence he is,"
him, that he cannot possibly be the Christ, that he
must be an imposter, deceiving the people (v. 12),
not sent of God, but foisting himself upon the people;
and this because *they know* his home town and his
family and are sure because of this knowledge of
theirs. The force of Jesus' cry is: "So you think
you know *me* since you are sure you *know* my home
and family!" The question is debated as to whether
these words contain a tinge of irony or not. The
blanket denial that Jesus never employs irony is
untenable. Equally unwarranted is the claim that
irony is incompatible with a loud tone of voice, for
many an exclamation is even sarcastic. In the present
case the irony is sufficiently marked by the fact that
these wise citizens treat as supremely significant something that has no significance at all.

The fact that Jesus grew up in Nazareth in the
home of Joseph and Mary reveals nothing about his
true origin and mission, and the assumption of the
citizens that it reveals everything only demonstrates
their foolish ignorance. With a third *καί*, used advers-
atively, Jesus himself testifies "whence he is": "and
I have not come of myself, but one that is real is he
that did send me, whom you do not know." The
emphasis is on the positive clause, which the negative
clause only aids in stressing. And in this positive
clause the point is the reality of the great Sender of
Jesus: "he is *real* that did send me." The predicate

ἀληθινός opposes the idea which these citizens hold, that Jesus has come on his own initiative, that at best he only imagines that he is sent. His Sender, he testifies, is not a phantasy of his mind, a being whom he has invented, but One who is actual and real. This evident contrast, furnished by the negative clause, dare not be altered. Jesus is not comparing two senders, one who is such in the highest degree and one in an inferior degree; or one who has genuine authority to send and another whose authority may be called in question. Likewise ἀληθινός does not mean ἀληθινὸς Θεός: he that did send me is "the true God." While Jesus refers to God, the predicate "real" states only that as a Sender the person of whom Jesus is speaking is "real," One who actually exists.

The full impact of this testimony lies in the relative clause, "whom you do not know." We must note the emphatic pronoun ὑμεῖς, "you," such as *you* are. These citizens boast of their knowledge: "him we know whence he is." This supposed knowledge Jesus first calls in question: *"Me* you know?! and *you know* whence I am?!" meaning: You do not know *me,* nor do *you know* whence I am! Then Jesus denies this supposed knowledge: this Sender, who is real, "whom *you* (being what you are) *do not know."* In spite of the Scriptures which these citizens had they do not know God (5:38), proof of which is the fact that, when God sent them his own Son, they failed to recognize that Son and the fact that God had sent him. They know a couple of minor and external things about Jesus, his home town and his family; with this shallow knowledge they could never know either his person or his mission. To know these they would have to know God, as God actually had revealed himself — and him they do not know.

29) These citizens are blind regarding the vital point; not so Jesus. **I know him because I am from**

him; and he did commission me. The reading with δέ has insufficient support: "Yet I know him." This means that ἐγώ is not meant to be in contrast with the preceding ὑμεῖς, but in contrast with the following ἐκεῖνος: "*I* know him, . . . and *he* did send me." It is true that Jesus places his knowledge overagainst the ignorance of these citizens. But we must add that the knowledge Jesus has is of an entirely different kind from that which these citizens might have had and failed to have. They could and should have known God from his Word, but Jesus was not dependent upon this source for his knowledge of God. He knows God in an immediate manner: "because I am from him." In παρ' αὐτοῦ lies an original παρ' αὐτῷ. He who is "from God" was originally "with God." Compare 1:18; 3:13; 6:33, 38, 46, 50, and 58. Before his incarnation Jesus was with God in heaven and thus he now says of himself, "I am from God." The knowledge he has of God is that which he brought with him from heaven (1:18).

Certain texts have: ὅτι παρ' αὐτῷ εἰμι, "because I am with him." The textual evidence has not established this as the true reading. The claim that παρ' αὐτῷ was changed into παρ' αὐτοῦ because the former conveys an "inconvenient" meaning is unwarranted; for Jesus utters the same thought in 3:13 (the last clause: "he who is in heaven"; see the explanation of these words), and, of course, might use it again. The "inconvenience" of this thought is rather in the minds of the moderns, who do not admit that Jesus can at the same time be present both on earth and with God in heaven. For this reason they eliminate this thought from 3:13, and the παρ' αὐτῷ in the present passage they refer to the communion of Jesus with God, supporting their view by a reference to 8:29, μετ' ἐμοῦ, God's communion with Jesus — although the prepositions as well as the contexts

differ. In order to clear up the matter we must
note that the primary question at issue is πόθεν ἐστίν,
"whence Jesus is." In v. 27 this indirect question is
twice repeated by the citizens, and in v. 28 Jesus takes
it from their lips. When answering this question
Jesus brings in the point of knowledge; because the
citizens do not know God, therefore they know neither
Jesus nor whence he is; Jesus, however, knows God
because he is "from him," παρ' αὐτοῦ, even as also God
sent him. We thus see that it is not enough for Jesus
to say that he is "with God," for, while this would
show that he knows God, it would not state "whence
he is." Therefore Jesus says that he is "from God,"
which does both, namely, proves his origin from
heaven and thus his direct knowledge of God.

When Jesus testifies that he is "from him" he
already declares his mission, namely, that he is sent
as the Messiah. But he states this directly, "and he
did commission me." This is an independent statement which is no longer governed by ὅτι. It forms
part of the answer to the question "whence" Jesus
is. Note how ἐγώ and ἐκεῖνος are emphatically balanced:
"*I* am from him; *he* did commission me." In other
words, this God, whom these citizens do not know,
Jesus knows so well, for Jesus came from him, and
that God did himself send and commission Jesus. In
the completest way the question, whence Jesus is, is
thus answered. And at the same time these citizens
are shown why they know nothing of Jesus' origin
although they think they know everything, and why
Jesus knows what is hidden from them. The issue
is squarely drawn: on the one side utter ignorance
and empty boast of knowledge, on the other complete
and self-evident knowledge; on the one side a spurious
deduction, on the other firsthand testimony to the
fact; on the one side vain and empty denial that Jesus
is the Christ, on the other the assured reality that he

is, indeed, the Christ. While it is brief, this testimony
of Jesus is most direct and to the point and at the
same time highly dramatic.

30) It intensifies the hostility of the citizens.
Therefore they were seeking to arrest him; and no
one laid his hand upon him because his hour had
not yet come. No change of subject is indicated.
The irritated citizens of Jerusalem (v. 25), passively
averse to Jesus up to this point, are now filled with
the desire to aid the authorities in apprehending
the man who had contradicted them. The imperfect
ἐζήτουν leaves the outcome of this desire open; the
following aorist οὐδεὶς ἐπέβαλον reports that the desire
proved abortive. No one had the courage actually to
lay his hand on Jesus. The scene is overdrawn when
these citizens are made to press in on Jesus "in wild
rage" in order to drag him to prison. We are told
only what was in their hearts. When it came to
action, they hesitated. So also we read nothing about
"an invisible wall of protection surrounding Jesus"
so that he "remained untouched in the midst of his
raging enemies." But instead of reporting the secondary reason why no one laid his hand upon Jesus, John
at once points to the primary reason why these citizens
were restrained from carrying out their desire. "His
hour had not yet come," the time set by the Father
for Jesus to be delivered into the hands of his enemies.
On this occasion the invisible hand of God restrained
his foes by opening no way for them to carry out
their design. We may take it that the citizens were
afraid of the pilgrim multitudes who thronged the
Temple courts during the festival. It was God's
hand that protected Jesus, but that hand used natural
means.

31) *Jesus Warns the Jews regarding his De-*
parture, 31-36. — The encounter sketched in v. 14-24
took place on the day in the midst of the feast when

Jesus first appeared in the Temple. The clash with the citizens seems to have followed almost immediately on the same day. Verse 37 takes us to the last day of the feast. The intervening paragraph, v. 31-36, evidently reports an incident that occurred on one of the days between these two events. For the Sanhedrin has had time to call a meeting and to issue an order to the Temple police to take Jesus into custody. We must begin a new paragraph with v. 31. This verse states what moved the Pharisees to stir the Sanhedrin into action with the result that Jesus publicly warns all concerned that he will soon return to his Sender, at which announcement the rulers scoff.

But of the multitude many believed on him; and they were saying, The Christ, when he shall come, certainly will do no greater signs than this man has done? Not all, but a goodly number of the pilgrims gathered for the feast, believed in Jesus. The connective δέ contrasts these with the citizens of Jerusalem who had advanced to decided hostility. But we cannot conclude from the fact that Jesus only taught on this visit to Jerusalem and wrought no miracles that the faith of these pilgrims was the result of his words. We are compelled to connect the character of the faith of these people with the confession they make, and this shows that their faith as yet rested only on the signs and had not yet embraced the teaching of Jesus. It resembled the faith of those mentioned in 2:23; and again in 4:45; and was inferior to the faith of those mentioned in 4:41. The imperfect ἔλεγον describes how they question one with another. Note how ὁ Χριστός is placed emphatically forward. The question is really abstract; it supposes the coming of the Christ and then asks whether he could do greater signs than Jesus had already done. We must regard πλείονα, not as a reference to mere number: "more signs," but to

a *plus qualitate,* as S. Goebel states: "greater signs."
For this use of the term compare Matt. 6:25; 12:41;
also Matt. 21:36; Heb. 3:3; 11:4; Rev. 2:19. The
question with μή indicates that in the minds of these
pilgrims the supposition must be denied. They cannot imagine that the Messiah, whoever he may be,
would work signs that exceeded those Jesus "did
work," the historical aorist to express the past fact.
Among those present there must have been many who
had seen some of these signs, and, no doubt, they told
of them and exchanged reports. In ὧν the antecedent is drawn into the relative, and the case of the
antecedent is retained: τούτων ἅ, R. 720.

32) For fear of the rulers no open demonstration
was made in favor of Jesus, proclaiming him as "the
Christ"; the pilgrims contented themselves with quiet
talk. **The Pharisees heard the multitude murmuring these things concerning him; and the chief
priests and the Pharisees sent officers in order to
arrest him.** The Pharisees (see 1:24) were the great
guardians of the law. Some of these moved among
the pilgrims and heard this quiet talk. The genitive
indicates the persons heard and is here modified by a
predicative participle: τοῦ ὄχλου γογγύζοντος. These Pharisees at once reported to the rulers and stirred them
to action. The term "Pharisees" denotes a numerous
party among the Jews (see 1:24), but "the chief
priests and the Pharisees" is John's designation for
the Sanhedrin, the highest court of the nation, 7:45;
11:47, and 57; 18:3. Some of Pharisees who brought
the report concerning the talk among the pilgrims
may also have been members of the Sanhedrin. John
sketches only sufficient of the situation to permit his
readers to understand the following words of Jesus
and the reaction which they caused. So he reports
only that the Sanhedrin sent its police officers to arrest
Jesus. Whether the Sanhedrin just happened to be

in session, or whether a special meeting was called, and what the deliberations were that ended in the order of arrest, is omitted. This legal and official order, issued by the proper court of jurisdiction to its lawful police force, marks a definite stage in the proceedings of the authorities against Jesus. In 5:18; 7:1 and 20 we learn only that the Jewish leaders "were seeking to kill" Jesus, i. e., that this was their desire and design. Now they take the first official and legal steps toward that end. As the sequel shows, this order of arrest is not peremptory, to bring Jesus in forthwith. The officers are to watch for their opportunity; for the Sanhedrin fears to enrage the pilgrims who are favorable to Jesus. This might prove dangerous. The Sanhedrin generally reckoned with the consequences.

33) The order is issued. The connective οὖν shows that in some way Jesus is fully aware of the serious move. Before him are the ὄχλος, as usual, some of the Ἰουδαῖοι or members of the Sanhedrin (v. 35), and the ὑπηρέται or police watching their chance. **Jesus, therefore, said, Yet a little while I am with you and I am going away to him that did send me.** We must cancel αὐτοῖς: he said "to them" (A. V.). While "the Jews," namely the Sanhedrists present, make a response (v. 35), this is not addressed to Jesus but to each other, it is a kind of scoffing uttered only so that Jesus, too, shall hear and be wounded the more. We may then say that the words of Jesus are intended for all present, in particular for "the Jews." With perfect calmness and assurance Jesus delivers his answer to the move that has been made against him, but a sorrowful tone of deep pity vibrates through his words.

Jesus speaks as one whose course is fully planned and will be completed in due order. He will yet remain with these people for a short time; then his task

will be finished, and he will go back to his great
Sender. The underlying thought is that nothing which
these Jews, his enemies, may do will change that pro-
gram in the least. In a short time he will complete
his mission and return to his Sender to make his
report. The emphasis is first on "little" (actually only
six months remain) and next on "I am going away."
Jesus says that he himself will stay yet awhile and
then will leave. As far as the Jews are concerned,
their actions do not count. There is something majestic
in the words. When he again mentions "him that
did send me" he speaks as the Messiah engaged in
his Messianic mission, back of which is God himself.
The other thought is that the Jewish authorities want
to be rid of Jesus, at once if possible, and that their
wish will, indeed, be fulfilled by Jesus himself,
though not at once. But his leaving will not be as
they desire. It will not be a mere killing him as a
man and thus an ending of his career. Jesus will complete his mission and then, after everything has been
finished for which he came to earth, he will return to
his Father in heaven.

34) But this leaving has another side, one pertaining to the enemies of Jesus, one dreadful to contemplate. **You shall seek me and shall not find me;
and where I am you cannot come.** Luther writes,
"These are terrible words, I do not like to read them."
Back of them lies the rejection of Jesus, God's Messiah, by the Jewish nation. "You shall seek me"
cannot refer to a *hostile* seeking, for Jesus will be
exalted at his Father's right hand. It cannot refer
to a seeking *for help* to alleviate the calamities that
will descend upon the nation, for Jesus nowhere intimates that he is a political or a military deliverer. A
repentant seeking is also excluded, for Jesus adds,
"and you shall not find me," and elucidates this in
8:21, "You shall seek me and shall die in your sins."

This is the seeking of *despair* which always comes
too late. Amos 8:11, etc., describes it: "Behold, the
days come, saith the Lord God, that I will send a
famine in the land, not a famine of bread, nor a thirst
for water, but of hearing the words of the Lord. And
they shall wander from sea to sea, and from the north
even to the east, they shall run to and fro to seek
the word of the Lord, *and shall not find it.*" Again
Prov. 1:24, etc.: "Because I have called, and ye
refused; I have stretched out my hand, and no man
regarded; but ye have set at naught all my counsel,
and would none of my reproof: I will also laugh at
your calamity; I will mock when your fear cometh;
when your fear cometh as desolation, and your destruction cometh as a whirlwind; when distress and anguish
cometh upon you. Then shall they call upon me, but
I will not answer; *they shall seek me early, but they
shall not find me:* for that they hated knowledge, and
did not choose the fear of the Lord: they would none
of my counsel, they despised all my reproof. Therefore they shall eat of the fruit of their own way, and
be filled with their own devices." This terrible seeking comes when the day of grace is past. "Today if
ye will hear his voice, harden not your hearts as in the
provocation," Heb. 3:15. Note the juxtaposition of
ἐγώ and ὑμεῖς — in heaven and blessedness, *I, you* amid
death and damnation.

35) While Jesus addresses those present in the
most direct way, no direct reply is made to him. Only
the rulers speak, but to each other not to him. They
had not fared very well in their last attempt (v. 15)
when Jesus had promptly silenced them (v. 16-19).
**The Jews, therefore, said to themselves, Where is
this fellow about to go that we shall not find him?
He certainly is not about to go to the Dispersion
among the Greeks and to teach the Greeks? What
is this word which he said, You shall seek me and**

shall not find me, and where I am you cannot come? The phrase πρὸς ἑαυτούς, "to themselves," means "to each other"; πρὸς is reciprocal. These Jews want the crowd to understand that they do not deem Jesus worthy a reply. What they remark to each other is intended as insulting mockery. They act as though they did not hear the words, "to him that did send me," with all that these words implied. They heard well enough and understood fully. But in order to mock Jesus and to ridicule the prophetic threat in his words, they pretend to be mystified. So he is going to run off somewhere and hide where they will not find him? On ποῦ for "whither" see R. 299 (*b*); ὅτι is made causal, B.-D. 456, 2; R. 1205 "probably"; consecutive is much better, R. 1001. Well, about the only place that could be would be the Diaspora among the heathen Greeks, some distant country where scattered Jews live among the heathen Greek population. Smaller and larger groups of Jews were scattered far and wide over all the Roman Empire; see the list in Acts 2:9-11. The genitive "of the Greeks" is called objective of place, R. 495, 500, etc., and is translated "among the Greeks." These genitives look like simple possessives: the Diaspora which the Greeks have. The form of the question implies a negative answer. Yet this does not mean that the Jews suggest "no" as the answer. Their question is intended as a sneer, and its negative turn with μή intends to make the sneer more cutting.

This is brought out by the addition, "and to teach the Greeks," τοὺς Ἕλληνας, pagan Greeks, not Hellenized Jews, which would be Ἑλληνισταί. The thought in the negative question is that Jesus, rejected by the acknowledged Jewish authorities at the capital, might turn to the Jews scattered in other lands, and, finding himself rejected also by these, would have left only pagan Greeks among whom to play the Messiah. Thus for the statement of Jesus that he will soon go away to his Sender the Jews would substitute the wild notion that, if he does go away, the only choice he would have is to go to the pagan world. This sneer intends to reduce the Messiahship of Jesus to a bald absurdity. We, therefore, do not need the explanation that the Jews did not understand Jesus when he spoke about his Sender; or that these Jews were other individuals who had not faced Jesus before. Nor is the claim warranted that Jesus never uttered the phrase "to him that did send me," but that John added it of his own accord. It is correct, however, that John records this sneer of the Jews because the gospel afterward took exactly the course sneeringly suggested by these Jews. Paul carried it to the Dispersion and to the Gentiles, and John himself labored in Ephesus and wrote his Gospel in the very language of the Greeks.

36) When the Jews inquire of each other, "What is this word which he said?" etc., they merely continue their pretense of being mystified, and this is the reason why Jesus pays no further attention to them. The police officers stood by but received no hint to step in and to take Jesus into custody. Whether this inaction was due to the effect of the calm and deliberate attitude of Jesus and to the force of his words or merely to the outward situation, the presence of too many friends of Jesus in the multitude, who will say?

III. *Jesus' Testimony Impresses the Police Sent for His Arrest, 37-52.*

37) **Now on the last day, the great day of the feast, Jesus was standing, and he cried, saying, If anyone thirsts, let him come to me and let him drink.** The question whether this last and great day of the feast is the seventh or the eighth day is of

minor importance. John specifies the day, not merely because he vividly remembers it but evidently because the significance of the day and of the ritual connected with it are reflected in the words of Jesus. We join the majority in deciding for the eighth day, although the question is still being debated. The details of the argument deal chiefly with Lev. 23:36; Neh. 8:18; Josephus, *Ant.* 3, 10; and the Mishna treatise entitled *Succa.* The fact that the festival commonly comprised eight days ought no longer to be contested. The chief point, as all acknowledge, is the greatness of the day in question. Those who contend for the seventh must show that this exceeded the eighth. Yet it lacked the convocation which distinguishes the eighth day. The greatest number of sacrifices were offered on the first day, and this number decreased day by day, so that on the seventh day very few were offered. The eighth day had the special distinction that it was the last festival day in the entire Jewish church year and was called "the last good day" (*Succa* IV, 8), "the sacred close of the year" (Josephus), ἐξόδιον (LXX), a free translation of '*Atzerch,* "Festive Convocation" (Lev. 23:36; Num. 29:35; Neh. 8:18). At least since the time of the Maccabees (II Macc. 10:6) the eighth day accords best with John's designation, "on the last day, the great day of the feast."

The action of Jesus accords with the greatness of the day. "He was standing and he cried" (compare v. 28). He now performed the role of a public herald, no longer that of a teacher, who usually was seated. The pluperfect εἱστήκει is imperfect in sense and describes the action of standing, while the aorist ἔκραξε notes the fact that Jesus shouted. Both are finite verbs and thus make both actions equally important. The crowds surging in the Temple court made it necessary for Jesus to seek some prominent place where he could stand above the people and be gen-

erally seen and to lift up his voice so that as many
as possible might hear him. Oriental orators still sit
while they are speaking. In the great mosque at
Damascus and again in the mosque of the dancing
dervishes in Constantinople the author heard the
Koran expounded by speakers who were seated cross-
legged on a small elevated platform, the audience being
seated cross-legged on the floor around them.

Jesus shouts into the ears of the great crowd,
"If anyone shall thirst," etc., (present subjunctive,
"shall be thirsting"). The condition of expectancy
implies that some will, indeed, thirst, yet the indefinite singular sounds as though Jesus does not
expect that many will thirst. He refers to *spiritual*
thirsting (4:14; 6:53-56), which, however, does not
emanate from ourselves but, like the coming and the
drinking, is the effect of the presence of Jesus, of his
call and offer of living water (grace and salvation).
He awakens the desire for spiritual satisfaction, even
as he also satisfies this desire.

Each morning during the seven days of the
feast, at the time of the sacrifice, a priest proceeded to the fountain of Siloah with a golden pitcher,
filled it with water, and, accompanied by a solemn
procession, bore it to the altar of burnt sacrifice,
pouring the water, together with the contents of a
pitcher of wine from the drink offering, into two per-
forated flat bowls. The trumpets sounded, and the
people sang Isa. 12:3, "Therefore with joy shall ye
draw water out of the wells of salvation." Compare
the author's *Eisenach Old Testament Selections*, 701,
etc. Late Jewish authorities report that this was
done also on the eighth day. In the debate as to
whether Jesus has this ceremony in mind when uttering his cry we need not be in doubt. It commemorated
the water that gushed out of the rock at Meribah
and that was intended to quench the *thirst* of the

multitude in the desert, although the symbolic ceremony in the Temple repeated only the pouring out. Symbols seldom re-enact every feature.

Water is not directly mentioned but is certainly implied in thirsting and in drinking. This water is usually identified as the Word. But 4:10 (which see) shows that the water which Jesus has in mind is life, and thus his Word is the means for bestowing it. Coming and drinking are merely two sides of one action, namely, believing in Jesus. This call to come and to drink is full of efficacious drawing power. Whoever does come and drink is moved thereto by the Word and the gift held out to him. The two present imperatives ἐρχέσθω and πινέτω are aoristic presents not durative or linear actions; see R. 864, etc., especially the three examples of imperatives in Luke 7:8, at the bottom of 865, under "specific presents." We are to come and to drink once only — then we shall never thirst again. Life, once received, lives on and on; we need not receive it over and over again. The figure of birth (3:3-5) is more adequate in this respect, as natural birth is without repetition. In the case of eating and drinking the explanation must be added that repetition is not necessary (4:14; 6:35) because in nature hunger and thirst recur, and we are compelled to eat and to drink daily.

38) The lack of a connective between v. 37 and v. 38 is sufficient ground for assuming that the two verses are independent statements, not uttered consecutively but taken from separate parts of a longer discourse. That Jesus said more on this last day when he stood in a prominent position and cried out may well be assumed, compare "these words" in v. 40. Verses 37 and 38, however, are too closely related in thought to be separated from each other. If anything at all intervened, it only expanded v. 37 and retained

the inner connection with v. 38. He who comes to Jesus not only finds his own soul satisfied but also becomes a medium for conveying the same spiritual satisfaction to others — this, of course, when the work of Jesus shall be finished and the Holy Spirit given to believers after Pentecost, v. 39.

He that believes in me — even as the Scripture has said, out of his belly rivers of living water shall flow. The sense will not allow us to draw "he that believes in me" to v. 37, for Jesus bids the thirsty to come and to drink and not him who already believes and has his thirst quenched. It is equally impossible to refer αὐτοῦ, out of "his" belly, to the pronoun "me" in v. 37 and thus to have Jesus say that out of "his" belly these rivers shall flow. The anacoluthon is quite simple and fairly frequent, beginning the sentence with a nominative (a suspended subject, R. 437; a *nominativus pendens,* R. 459, 1130) and continuing with another subject while a genitive takes up the first. "He that believes in me" is literal and thus makes clear what the figurative coming to Jesus and drinking mean, namely to become a believer. The present substantivized participle ὁ πιστεύων characterizes the person as one who continues trusting in Jesus. To the person thus described an astounding promise is held out, one mentioned in the Old Testament Scriptures and now restated by Jesus.

"Even as the Scripture did say" (the English requires "has said") is not the formula for introducing a direct quotation from the Old Testament but one that reproduces Scripture thought. We may consider Isa. 58:11: "And the Lord shall . . . satisfy thy soul in drought, . . . and thou shalt be like a watered garden, and like a spring of water, where waters fail not"; Zech. 14:8: "And it shall be in that day, that living waters shall go out from Jerusalem," this plural being individualized by Jesus; and other

passages verbally close. A point that is often overlooked is the question why Jesus fortifies what he here
promises the believers by anchoring this promise
in the Old Testament Scripture. He does the same
in 5:39; 5:46, 47; and 7:22. His entire mission and
work, together with all the blessings he has come
to bestow, are the fulfillment of God's ancient
promises, which fact proves beyond question the
genuineness of his Messiahship. This reference to
the Scripture is another direct answer to the rulers
who scoff at his claims. The fact that through Jesus
every believer actually attains what God promised
ages ago by the mouth of his holy prophets is the
subjective evidence for the truth of Christianity. In
the present case, however, the festival with its rites
renews the old promises of God to the people, and
what Jesus shouts to the multitude interprets and
shows the fulfillment of these promises. This is the
real bearing of the reference to the Scripture.

The emphasis is on ποταμοί (placed forward) and
on ὕδατος ζῶντος (placed at the end), which the English
cannot imitate. Actual "rivers" not mere trickles
shall flow forth; and these shall consist of "living
water" (4:10). It is commonplace to remark that
"living" means "flowing" as opposed to stagnant, for
rivers always flow. "Living water" is one of the allegorical expressions frequently used in the Scriptures,
in which the figurative term is at once expounded by
the non-figurative (see 4:10). We may analyze as
follows: the fountain = Jesus ("let him come unto
me"); thirsting, coming, and drinking, taken together = believing; the κοιλία receiving the water =
the inner man; the water = true life; the flowing
rivers = life-giving influence on others. The abundance of the latter is indicated by the plural "rivers,"
saving influences in various directions and of different
kinds. The ancients felt no impropriety in using

κοιλία, which denotes the abdominal cavity and its contents, in a figurative way. The American Committee of the R. V. translates "from within him" instead of "out of his belly"; but for the modern imagination the gain is small. "Belly" merely continues the figure already used in thirsting and in drinking (v. 38) and extended to "water." All four expressions are to be understood spiritually.

In the figurative language of Jesus we must note certain features that are sometimes misunderstood due to the greatness and the strangeness of the realities that are pictured. At times the figure falls short, its imagery will not cover the reality; hence it is frankly abandoned and the reality itself is finally also stated, as in Matt. 25:30, "the outer darkness," "the weeping and gnashing of teeth." Again, the figure is utterly improbable, as in Matt. 21:37; no man would send his son under circumstances such as are narrated. Finally, a second figure is used to help out the first, as in Matt. 21:42-44, that of the stone (note the astonishing use in v. 44) completing that of the husbandmen. On this order is 4:14, one drink and a ceaselessly flowing inner spring — the entire realm of nature has no phenomenon like that. Similarly here, one drink to quench spiritual thirst; then rivers of water full of spiritual life flowing out in different directions. Whoever heard of one mouthful of water producing even one river? and whoever heard of one source sending out a number of rivers? This breath-taking boldness in using imagery, with a single turn going from a drink to a number of rivers, subordinates the figures to the reality and at the same time impresses that reality in an unforgettable way. The idea of water is thus used in the fullest manner, being based on that drawn from Siloah and poured out at the altar.

In 4:14 the figure of the "spring" pictures only
the fact that the believer will never thirst again;
here the "rivers" picture the fact that the believer will
resemble Jesus himself in that he will help to quench
the thirst of many others. The story of the Acts
has been scanned to find the fulfillment of the promise
here made by Jesus. "What is the apostolic Word itself through which we believe (John 17:20); what are
the confessions of the church, in harmony with which
we believe; what are her hymns, her prayers, her sermons, all the testimonies of the faith and love in saving word and sacred conversation — what are they but
rivers of living water flowing from the body of the
church?" Besser.

39) John adds an explanation for the instruction
of his readers. **Now this he said concerning the
Spirit whom they that believed in him were about
to receive; for the Spirit was not yet present because Jesus was not yet glorified.** The connective
δέ indicates that this is a parenthetical remark.
Πνεῦμα is used with and without the article after the
manner of proper names. John is not elucidating the
figurative language of Jesus; the rivers of living
water are not identical with the Spirit, nor is the
water of life that quenches spiritual thirst. Nor dare
we suppose that those who at this time believed in
Jesus, like the apostles, did so without the Spirit. The
translation for οὔπω ἦν Πνεῦμα, "not yet did the Spirit
exist," is entirely too strong. The Spirit wrought
throughout Old Testament times, in the work of the
Baptist, and in the work of Jesus. And yet the
believers "were about to receive" the Spirit; he "was
not yet present," as presently he would be, i. e., was
not yet present thus. The reason is that "Jesus was
not yet glorified." That glorification would give them
the Spirit.

The redemptive work of Jesus must first be completed, he must return to his Sender (v. 33), rise from the tomb, and ascend to heaven. Then, after all this work of Jesus was completed, he could at Pentecost send the Spirit upon his believers. And that Spirit would make rivers of living water flow from the believers throughout the New Testament era. Acts 1:8, "But ye shall receive power, when the Holy Ghost is come upon you; and ye shall be my witnesses," etc. No believer was ready or able to function as Jesus wanted him to function as long as he did not understand the sacrificial death of Jesus and his glorification. Prior to that completion of Jesus' work all faith was like that of the Old Testament saints, a trust in the promise. Jesus' glorification would fulfill that promise. Then, too, he would send down the Spirit; things were not ready so that he could send him before that time. From that great day onward, even as the Acts report at length, salvation would flow out in great streams to the ends of the earth. The reading should be the aorist οἱ πιστεύσαντες not the present participle; and the observation of R. 859 is valuable: this constative aorist is timeless, designating not merely those who up to this time, when Jesus spoke in the Temple, had believed, but also those who in future ages would believe in him.

40) John has finished his account of the testimony which Jesus delivered at the Feast of Tabernacles; he now records the effect in detail. **Some of the multitude, therefore, who had heard these words were saying, This is of a truth the prophet.** Here ἐκ is partitive for "some," these constituting one class or one side. We see that an advance from v. 31 has been made, where the signs convince many in regard to Jesus; now the deciding factor is the words of Jesus, and nothing is said about the signs. "These words," here the genitive (which is infrequent to indi-

cate what is heard), are usually taken to mean the ones recorded in v. 38, 39, and, because they are so brief, it is assumed that John has greatly abbreviated the address of Jesus. Even then, since this chapter reports other words of Jesus, also uttered before the multitude (v. 16, etc.; 28, etc.; 33, etc.), these others should be included. The reaction of the multitude is thus indicated in v. 20; in v. 31; and now as final in v. 40-43. In distinction from the pilgrim multitude the citizens of Jerusalem totally reject Jesus, v. 25-27; certain ones in the multitude show the same vicious temper, v. 44 (compare v. 30).

The verdict of this first class is expressed with great earnestness, ἀληθῶς, "truly." But when they call Jesus "the prophet," this cannot mean "the Christ," since another part of the multitude sets up this claim in contradiction to those first mentioned. Here, as in 1:21, "the prophet" is conceived to be a forerunner of the Christ. The Old Testament basis for the expectation of such a prophet is Deut. 18:15 and 18, 19. In John 6:14; Acts 3:22; 7:37, this prophet is identified with the Christ. By thus rating Jesus as "the prophet" this part of the multitude is at least deeply impressed and decidedly favorable to Jesus, although it is still far from the truth.

41) **Others were saying, This is the Christ,** the promised Messiah himself. The statement is positive and without qualification. These are believers, of course, with faith of varying degrees and quality. We see their helplessness when an objection is raised, which they seem unable to meet.

Some were saying, Why, out of Galilee the Christ certainly does not come? Did not the Scripture declare that the Christ comes out of the seed of David and from Bethlehem, the village where David was? The first group (ἐκ τοῦ ὄχλου) and the second (ἄλλοι) are placed side by side since their convictions merely vary. The third group (οἱ δέ) is placed in opposition to the second as though this had been designated by οἱ μέν. They offer an argument for their conviction that Jesus cannot be the Christ which is couched in two questions, the first with μή implying a negative answer, the second with οὐ implying a positive answer. The insertion of γάρ (R. 1190), translated "why," points to the proof that "out of Galilee" the Christ does not come, as all will admit. Over against this negative they place the positive, the assurance derived from Micah 5:2; Isa. 11:1; Jer. 23:5, and from their synagogue instruction, that the birthplace of the Messiah must be Bethlehem. "The Scripture" is a comprehensive singular designation for the Old Testament canon, the final authority beyond which no Jew could go. The Davidic descent of the Christ is added in natural connection with Bethlehem which was also David's birthplace.

Because of the long residence of Jesus in Nazareth he was commonly supposed to have been born there. Closer inquiry was not made. By recording without comment the appeal to the Scripture which these men make in regard to Bethlehem John intimates that their idea is correct. If their interpretation of the Scripture were incorrect, John would have pointed that out. He, too, accepts both the Davidic descent and Bethlehem as the birthplace of Jesus, but he knows that both are facts in regard to Jesus, of which these objectors, however, are not aware. "Where David was" refers to his stay in his father's home in Bethlehem before he left that place in later years.

43) The three descriptive imperfects ἔλεγον in v. 40, 41 show us the discussion as it went on, each of the three parties making its claim. The aorist that now follows states the outcome. **Accordingly there came to be a division in the multitude because of him.** Neither party convinced the others; they were

hopelessly divided. "In the multitude," however, shows that the three parties consisted entirely of pilgrim visitors. The argument of the third party in regard to Bethlehem thus differs from that of the citizens of Jerusalem in v. 27, where the claim is made that the Messiah's place of origin will not be known at all.

44) **Certain ones of them, however, would have arrested him, but no one laid his hands on him.** This fourth class must have been quite small ($\tau\iota\nu\acute{\epsilon}\varsigma$), yet they were also pilgrims, possibly adherents of the Pharisees who had instigated the move to take Jesus into custody. The imperfect $\mathring{\eta}\theta\epsilon\lambda o\nu$ points to a will that was not carried into effect, as also the following aorist states. These violent opponents would like to have arrested Jesus and handed him over to the authorities, but, like the citizens in v. 30, they failed to act. Why, John does not say, but evidently for the same reason as that mentioned in v. 30. John varies his expressions slightly: in v. 30, "his hand," now "his hands." This closes the account of the effect of the testimony of Jesus on the pilgrim crowds who attended the feast. Note the extremes: some believe, others are ready to aid in killing Jesus.

45) At this point John reports how the order of the Sanhedrin to the Temple police to arrest Jesus broke down completely, so that the order was quietly dropped, and Jesus could remain in Jerusalem for some time after the feast was over. **The officers, therefore, came to the chief priests and Pharisees; and these said to them, Why did you not bring him?** The connective $o\mathring{\upsilon}\nu$ reverts to the inability of others besides the officers to lay hands on Jesus, though they are prompted by their own strong desire to do so. The officers were prompted only by the orders they had received. They now return to make their report.

We may suppose that this occurred in the late afternoon of the eighth festival day. By the next day the
pilgrims would be on their homeward journey. The
authorities thought that the arrest would have to be
effected before the festival closed, assuming that otherwise Jesus, too, would leave together with the crowds.
Thus we find the Sanhedrin in session, expecting that
finally Jesus would now be brought in. The time for
effecting the arrest having expired, the officers feel
constrained to come and to make a report. They
appear without Jesus and are at once faced with the
peremptory question as to why they have not carried
out their orders. In this verse one Greek article combines *"the* chief priests and Pharisees" as one class
or one body, while in v. 32 two articles are used, *"the*
chief priests and *the* Pharisees," since the Pharisees
were the ones that instigated the order for the arrest
(v. 31) and thus appear as a distinct group of the
Sanhedrin.

46) **The officers replied, Never did a man so
speak as this man.** Some texts abbreviate this reply, "Never did a man speak thus." The longer form
seems the more likely in the mouth of men like these
officers. Their reply is truly remarkable. They could
truthfully have stated that they had failed because
of the danger they would have incurred from the
friendly part of the multitude always clustering about
Jesus. The Sanhedrin itself feared these pilgrims,
and, on receiving such a reply from their subordinates,
could hardly have administered more than a mild
rebuke. But whatever was the truth as regards the
multitude, these officers had been restrained by something else, something that had made so deep an impression upon them that they openly avow it before
the whole Sanhedrin, although they know in advance
that they will be severely reprimanded and very likely
even punished for admitting what they feel they must

admit. We must note these two points: the impression which lamed the hands of these officers, and then the impulse not to hide but openly to confess this impression. Both are due to Jesus.

The emphasis is on οὕτως, the manner in which Jesus spoke, and the verb ἐλάλησεν omits any reference to the substance of the thought that Jesus uttered. The authority, majesty, and power of the speaker restrained these officers, contrary to explicit orders; compare Matt. 7:28. They acknowledge that the manner of Jesus is superior to anything ever found in any other man. They are only one step from saying that this manner is superhuman, yea divine. Much as these officers felt constrained to obey their orders, a stronger influence had come over them — they simply could not and would not lay hands on a man who spoke as this man did. Thus another strange thing appears: the very tools through which the rulers planned to bring Jesus to prison and to death, by making this honest confession, disrupt the unity of the Sanhedrin and thus cause their own plan to be dropped. The means defeat the end. God often plays with his enemies and makes their schemes ridiculous.

47) The rage of the Pharisees in the Sanhedrin now breaks loose. **The Pharisees, therefore, answered them, Certainly you, too, have not been deceived?** The emotion displayed in these μή questions is indicated by the context: protest, indignation, as here, scorn, excitement, sympathy, etc., R. 1175. While in the mind of the questioner the form with μή implies a negative reply, this very form often conveys the fear or the suspicion that the real reply will be the very opposite. Hence here we have the perfect tense "have been deceived" and thus are even now in this condition. Note also the emphatic καὶ ὑμεῖς, "even *you* — *our own officers,* who ought to stick to

us and listen to us and not to the wily tones of another,
one whom we despise.   In this manner these Pharisees
twist the reply of the officers, who say that never did a
man speak *so,* οὔτως, by insinuatingly implying "so
wily, with such cunning deceit."

48)   This they follow up.   **What, did anyone of
the rulers believe in him or of the Pharisees?   But
this multitude, which knows not the law, — accursed are they!**   This time μή takes the negative
answer˙ as actually being granted.   Observe the
superior tone of these rulers over against their petty
subordinates.   What business have these dependents
to follow impressions and thoughts of their own?   The
aorist of the verb marks the past fact: not for one
moment did any of these superior men put confidence
in Jesus.   So old is the argument, which still is current, that in religious matters men of power, authority, and learning cannot err, and that all humbler people ought to be guided by them without question.   It
was the argument which the lone monk of Wittenberg
had to face.   Could he alone be right when the pope,
the emperor, and all the prelates and the princes held
the contrary view?   Could he alone be right, and they
all be wrong?

49)   This argumentative question is followed by
a fierce invective: "But this multitude," etc.   The
strong adversative ἀλλά is often equivalent to our No!
We may translate with Zahn, "No; only this rabble,"
etc.   Likewise, in this connection where it is contrasted with the rulers, ὄχλος seems to be the equivalent
of the Hebrew *'am haaretz, die breite Schicht der
Landbevoelkerung* (Koenig, *Hebraeisches und ara-
maeisches Woerterbuch*), the country rabble, a scornful designation for the ordinary people, here the pilgrims from outlying parts.   What are they over
against the high and holy Pharisees, especially those
in the great Sanhedrin?

"Which know not the law" = is so ignorant as not even to know the law much less carefully to observe it. But the holy Pharisees make this their absolute specialty. They are the authoritative custodians of the law; they *know*. And here these fools of officers were following that miserable, ignorant rabble instead of these high representatives and guardians of the law!

But the heat of the enraged Pharisees almost makes them blurt out what they certainly do not wish to admit. Their invective starts as though they would say, "But this multitude, which knows not the law, *it believes in him*." A sudden shift avoids this damaging admission: " — accursed are they!" But by this veering even the sense is wrecked; for mere ignorance of the law on the part of common people who do not enjoy the advantages of the Pharisees cannot make them accursed. The real reason for cursing the multitude is not their ignorance but their listening to Jesus and their believing in him. Thus the Pharisees after all betray themselves. No measures were as yet taken against people who believed in Jesus, but note 9:22. The Pharisees soon tried to make good their curse. We hear no more about the officers. They seem to have escaped with the rebuke they had received.

50) But now the Sanhedrin hears another voice. **Nicodemus says to them (he that came to him aforetime, being one of them), Surely our law does not judge the man unless it first has heard from him and has come to know what he does?** If the avowal of the officers causes surprise, the objection of a member of the Sanhedrin itself must cause consternation. John's λέγει, too, is vivid. The parenthesis makes us recall 3:1. A textual question is raised in regard to the words: "he that came to him aforetime," especially also since the codices present different readings. Yet

the interference of Nicodemus cannot be understood unless we recall his former meeting with Jesus. Merely to identify Nicodemus as "being one of them," i. e., a ruler and a Pharisee ("of them" = the Pharisees, v. 47), would leave unexplained why he spoke out at this critical moment. It was not because he was one of them, for as one of them he would have remained silent; it was because he had been with Jesus.

51) Immediately after the Pharisees asserted so confidently that not one of their own exalted number believes in Jesus, Nicodemus, one of their number, speaks in defense of Jesus. Immediately after they boasted about themselves as being the great guardians of the law, one of their own number points out that they are violating that law. These clashes are highly dramatic. As a judge Nicodemus had both the right and the duty to remind his fellow-judges of the requirements of the law when they were forgetting them. He avoided every discourtesy, every appearance of arrogating to himself a judgment of his fellow-judges, by merely raising the question, thus allowing all to join in the answer. Yet it evinces courage for him to do even so much. Some have called him timid, but this is a mistake; timidity would have closed his lips. By employing a question instead of making an assertion Nicodemus shows wisdom. Some questions answer themselves, and this is one of that kind. By using μή Nicodemus indicates what he on his part thinks the answer must be, but only so that he intimates that all the rest will agree with him. Actually they could not disagree. He, indeed, had to betray his friendliness toward Jesus by asking even this question that suggested so self-evident an answer. Whatever odium may result to him from his colleagues he is ready to bear. He is a noble figure at this turn of affairs. By overplaying their hand the Pharisees in a manner force Nicodemus to the

front. He probably would have preferred to say nothing, but his contact with Jesus had opened his eyes sufficiently to see the real character of what was now being enacted, and that gave him courage to speak. By speaking he was brought one step nearer to faith.

It is a mistake to think that Nicodemus uses "the law" as a pretext behind which he may hide. Quite the contrary; the Pharisees had mentioned "the law" and had cursed the people for not knowing it. For this reason Nicodemus refers to "the law." The legal provisions in question are Exod. 23:1 and Deut. 1:16, etc. Moreover, these legal requirements are broader than "the law" as it was laid down for the Jews by God, they are part of the commonest human justice, which is followed even in pagan courts. Here we may remark that fanatical religious zeal on the part of men who claim great holiness for themselves often blindly violates the commonest ordinary justice when dealing with religious opponents. The scene occurring in the Sanhedrin this day has often been repeated since, and often without a Nicodemus to call a halt.

No, the law does not render a verdict on a man, κρίνει, until that man (the one in question, τὸν ἄνθρωπον) is first heard in person by the court, and the court thus itself knows what he does. The verb κρίνει is indeterminate — according to the finding (γνῷ) the verdict may result either in acquital or in a fitting sentence of punishment. There must first be a proper trial. The man charged must first be heard, i. e., given an opportunity to make his defense. Only after all the evidence is in, including that of the man himself, after the court knows and has been able to make a just finding in the case, is the verdict rendered. The aorists ἀκούσῃ and γνῷ indicate actuality. Both are legal terms, as is also κρίνει. "What he does," τί ποιεῖ, = what the

real character of the man's deed is, the court rendering a verdict accordingly. All this, Nicodemus implies, still holds for the Sanhedrin, whether the ὄχλος
or Jesus be brought before its bar. The question
arises whether Nicodemus was present when the order
for the arrest of Jesus was issued, v. 32. We must
assume that he was absent. Since so many judges
made up the court, it no doubt frequently occurred
that one or more were not in their places when a
meeting was held. Some suppose that in spite of
the full title "the chief priests and the Pharisees" in
v. 32 only the executive managers had issued the order.
This is possible but doubtful.

52) The answer which Nicodemus receives is as
passionate as that given to the officers. **They answered and said unto him** (see 1:48), **Surely thou,
too, art not of Galilee? Search and see that no
prophet arises out of Galilee.** Of course they
know that he is not a Galilean, but by their question introduced with μή they insinuate that only on
this supposition could they possibly understand his
appeal to their legal obligations. Jesus hailed from
Galilee, there, too, he had risen to great fame, and the
Galilean pilgrims were the ones who especially acclaimed him at the festival. So the Pharisees, having no possible defense for their illegal procedure,
substitute an insulting attack upon the motive of their
monitor, namely, that he talks as though he, too, were
from Galilee. To this usual interpretation we must
add, that since all the Galileans at the feast are members of "the multitude," the Pharisees imply that
Nicodemus must be no better and stand no higher
in trying to defend the legal rights of the multitude
and of Jesus. Does he want them to think that he
is as ignorant as the multitude? Does he want to
share the curse they had pronounced upon this ignorant rabble?

That is why they add the admonition that Nicodemus search and see for himself that no prophet arises out of Galilee, to say nothing of the Messiah himself. This reference to the gross ignorance of Nicodemus must be coupled with the charge of ignorance against the multitude, among which so many were friendly to Jesus. At the same time this is their return slap at Nicodemus, calling him desperately ignorant for having intimated ignorance of the law on their part, while they thus vindicate their own pretense to knowledge. The aorist imperative "search" enjoins a search that will go to the bottom of things and obtain the actual facts. They do not say whether Nicodemus is to search the Scriptures or only history in general. "See" means: "convince yourself!" The emphasis is on the phrase "out of Galilee." The present tense ἐγείρεται, "arises," reads like the general proposition that at no time Galilee can furnish a prophet. Some texts have the perfect ἐγήγερται, "has arisen," which restricts the claim to the past and says nothing about future possibilities. "Arise," whether the present or the perfect was used, is wider than to be born. It seems almost incredible that these Pharisees did not know that Jonah hailed from Galilee, II Kings 14:25, and that most likely also Nahum and Hosea came from that country. If the present tense is taken in a restricted sense as excluding the past and the three prophets named, Isa. 9:1 (compare Matt. 4:15, 16) is in the way. As so often, blind passion made these men set up false and unwarranted claims which contradicted their own better knowledge. Whether Nicodemus further discussed the point we do not learn. The upshot of the proceedings was that at this time the Sanhedrin took no further action, so that Jesus, who remained in Jerusalem after the feast, continued his work.

CHAPTER VIII

IV. *Jesus Proves his Testimony True and Warns his Opponents, 8:12-30*

7:53-8:11 is not an integral part of John's Gospel but part of the early oral tradition (antedating the year 70) ; it was very early put into written form, and one of its two versions was eventually inserted into John's Gospel. These findings of the text critics must be accepted as facts. Between 7:52 and 8:12 nothing intervenes. The spurious section is foreign to John's Gospel, fits nowhere into the plan of this Gospel, and is easily recognized as an interpolation in the place which it occupies. The language differs decidedly from that of John's own writing. Yet this spurious section reports quite correctly an actual occurrence in the life of Jesus. Every feature of it bears the stamp of probability, although we are unable to say at what point in the story of Jesus it should be inserted. Since John did not write this section, we give no exposition of it.

12) The Feast of Tabernacles is ended. We hear nothing more about the ὄχλος, all the pilgrims have departed. **Again, therefore, Jesus spoke to them saying, I am the light of the world. He that follows me shall in no way walk in the darkness but shall have the light of life.** The movement to arrest Jesus had proved abortive, "accordingly," οὖν, he goes on delivering his testimony. When John writes, "again, therefore, Jesus spoke to them saying," πάλιν refers back to 7:35, where he stood and cried out to the multitude. He now again speaks after a brief interval. The verb ἐλάλησεν (λαλεῖν, the opposite of be-

ing silent) conveys the thought that Jesus simply continued with his public utterances as he had done before, and αὐτοῖς, "them," has as its antecedent the Pharisees (7:47), who also in v. 13 are named as making a reply. That others, too, are present it self-evident, compare "many" in v. 30, all of whom certainly were not Pharisees. The Temple was the most public place in Jerusalem, where crowds constantly gathered. The Pharisees, those that were members of the Sanhedrin, and others of their numerous party kept close watch on Jesus to note anything he might say or do.

This is the situation when Jesus now again speaks and declares (λέγων), "I am the light of the world." The emphatic ἐγώ means I and I alone, I and no other. When the predicate has the article as it does here: τὸ φῶς, it is convertible with the subject; in other words, the predicate is identical with the subject, R. 768. The question is asked as to how Jesus comes to use the figure of light just at this time. Because the context furnishes no hint, some say that no special reason or occasion suggests the figure; that Old Testament references such as Isa. 9:1; 42:6; 49:6; 60:3; etc., are basis enough for its use on this occasion. Others find a connection with a notable ceremony that was observed during the festival that has just ended. Grand candelabra with four vessels of oil were placed in the inner court. Young priests climbed ladders and lighted the wicks, and a grand torch dance was staged by the people, even men like Hillel priding themselves on their skill in taking part. We are told that the bright light shone all over the city. Maimonides states that this ceremony took place every evening during the feast, others are sure that it occurred only on the first evening. The main difficulty in connecting the word of Jesus with this ceremony is that it leaves out an essential part of the figure. Those candelabra were stationary, and men danced in the courts, while Jesus speaks of a movable light: "he that *follows* me." We may say more. In 7:37, when Jesus calls those that "thirst" and bids them come to him and "drink," he does not stop with the ceremony of drawing water from Siloah and pouring it out at the altar, in which no quenching of thirst by drinking is pictured; he reaches back to the original blessing received at Meribah where the thirsty actually received water to drink. He does the same here. One of the great blessings during the desert sojourn of Israel was the pillar of cloud and of fire, evidence of the presence of Jehovah with his people. As the entire feast, with Israel for a week dwelling in booths, commemorated the sojourn in the desert, so the shining candelabra pictured the pillar of fire that dispelled the darkness of night during the desert journey. Israel followed that pillar and camped in its light every night. What that pillar was for Israel in days gone by Jesus is for the whole world. That pillar was Jehovah, Jesus is God's own Son.

Following this word of Jesus that he is the light of the world, John in his prolog, 1:4-9, described the Logos as "the light." When speaking to Nicodemus on faith and unbelief (3:18), Jesus said that "the light is come into the world," and that the believer comes to this light while the unbeliever shuns it (3:19-21). Here we now have the basic word, "I am the light of the world." The idea in "light" is that of an active power which conquers the opposing power called "darkness." Each constitutes a power, each stands opposed to the other, and the light triumps, over the darkness. Note the article τῇ σκοτίᾳ, *the* darkness," not merely "darkness" in general. The best analysis of both is that of S. Goebel: divine truth, clear as light, over against human falsehood and ignorance; divine holiness, pure as light, over against human sin and impurity; divine blessedness and glory, radiant as light, over against the night of human woe, to which we would add death. In the various connections in which the term light is used one or the other of these features may be more prominent. Here where Jesus speaks unconditionally all three are combined. "I am the light of the world" means to say: "In the human person of Jesus, as in a focus of radiant light, the shining image of divine truth, holiness, and blessedness has appeared in the human world, by its victorious radiance to penetrate the darkness of the word and to deliver it from the night of falsehood, sin, and woe."

Like the pillar in the desert, Jesus as the light of the world must be followed: "he that follows me." While actual outward attachment is meant, even as many at that time followed Jesus about and kept in his company as much as possible, following Jesus here as elsewhere in the Gospels means permanent spiritual attachment (see 1:43). Of its own accord this gracious gift of God, this light, shines into the world's night. Its glorious, saving radiance attracts all whom it meets and draws them to remain with this light. Everyone who yields to this drawing power "shall not walk in the darkness," shall escape from its deadly power, shall no longer be lost, eventually to perish in the world's desert. This negation, however, and its individual formulation intimate that some whom the light reaches and begins to draw to itself will turn from it and prefer the darkness, 3:20. This is the tragedy that is connected with the coming of the light. Yet the positive "he that follows me" intimates also that some will truly follow Jesus, and the effect shall be that each of these "shall *have* the light of life." As so often in the words of Jesus, the positive is not made the mere counterpart of the negative. Jesus says more than that "he shall *walk* in the light." To be sure, he shall do this too, but he shall do it because this light shall actually penetrate him and shall become his personal possession. This is another case where the figure used is really inadequate to express the spiritual reality, it only approximates that reality. Natural light never becomes part of our inner being, it only shines outwardly round about us. Jesus, the light of the world, shall do far more.

"He shall have the light *of life*" states more than this inner penetration and personal possession; it adds the inner and permanent effect of the possession, which is life, ζωή, the spiritual life, abiding union with God who is the essence of life. Here we have the same combination of life and light as in 1:4. As the two go together in nature, so also in the world of the spirit. By implication the opposite is suggested: darkness and death likewise go together. The absolute mastery of expression used by Jesus must not escape us. Words so few, so simple in themselves, in such lucid combination, to express realities so profound, so exalted, so heavenly, that our minds stagger in the effort to apprehend them. God, who is life and light, sent his Son Jesus as the source of light and life to all the world, to fill each individual soul with truth, holiness, and blessedness, and thus to give it life eternal. Note the universality in "the light of the world," combined with the personal individuality in the singular "he that follows me." Both reach out to the universe of men, far beyond the bounds of national Judaism. When we visualize the lowly Jesus in the Temple court uttering these words, astonishment overcomes us. But two thousand years of Christianity have verified these words in millions of individuals in all the "world."

To follow Jesus as the light keeps to the figure and yet indicates all of the reality by one simple verb form. The light does all the drawing to itself, not we;

it makes us follow. Only wilful resistance, the most unreasonable and unaccountable perversion, breaks away from that drawing and chooses the deadly darkness instead of the light which brings life, yet not "to follow" darkness but to remain in it. To follow Jesus is to believe and trust him. How can anyone trust the darkness? He must mistrust and flee from it when the light shines over him. How can anyone mistrust and flee from the light when it shines over him? We are made for this light and its life, our whole being responds to it. How can it help but draw, hold, and fill us? While to follow means to believe and to trust, it means this in its fulness, even as the verb "to have" indicates. To follow is to believe and to obey, i. e., to walk in the path of this life. To follow means to unite inwardly with Jesus — he in us and we in him, "to have" in the *unio mystica*. The genitive "the light of life" is not appositional, so that "the life" is identical with "the light." Nor is it the genitive of origin, so that "the light" proceeds from "the life" (Jesus). This is the simple possessive genitive, "the light" which belongs to "the life" and is invariably connected with it. Thus light and life are distinct concepts. The former is here identified with Jesus, the latter is elsewhere also identified with him. By making the second a genitive the two clasp hands in this case: Jesus is the light, and this light is always linked with life. Shall we ever be able to penetrate the depth of these simple words?

13) As soon as Jesus has uttered this great I AM, the Pharisees, some of whom are present among the auditors, object. **The Pharisees, therefore, said to him, Thou art testifying concerning thine own self; thy testimony is not true.** They pay no attention to what Jesus says of himself and to his promises to his followers. Their ears are deaf to anything of that kind. They are completely satisfied with themselves

and care nothing for who he is and what he bestows. They are bent only on catching at any reason for rejecting him and for discrediting him, no matter how flimsy it may be. So now they fasten on "I am" and raise the formal objection that Jesus is testifying in his own behalf, and that such testimony "is not true," i. e., cannot be accepted as true before a judgment bar. Jesus had met this objection a year ago when in 5:31 he acknowledged the formal principle and made his own testimony legally competent by adducing his Father as a second witness, who had given the Jews his testimony in his Word, 5:37, etc. Here he does the same, v. 18.

14) But before he adduces his supporting witness he qualifies himself as a competent witness. **Jesus answered and said unto them (1:48), And if I do testify concerning myself, my testimony is true, because I know whence I came and where I am going; but you do not know whence I come or where I am going.** We cannot admit that Jesus here contradicts what he says in 5:31, although it be only formally. For in verse 17 Jesus himself enunciates the old principle of the law, which requires at least two witnesses, the very principle he admitted in 5:31 and met in 5:37, just as here he again complies with it in verse 18. Why the notion of at least an apparent contradiction persists, is hard to understand. To be sure, a second witness is necessary, and Jesus has that second witness. For that very reason the self-witness of Jesus must be accepted as being legally perfectly competent. While, if offered alone, it would amount to nothing before a court of law, corroborated by a second witness, it stands. So Jesus qualifies as a witness in his own case. "And if I myself (ἐγώ) do testify concerning myself, my testimony is true." Why? "Because I know whence I did come and where (ποῦ for "whither," R. 298, d) I am going." He is con-

versant with the facts, namely those concerning his coming into the world from heaven for his saving mission, and his return to heaven, whence he came, after completing his mission. Knowing these facts, though they concern himself, he is competent to testify concerning them.

It is, therefore, a misconception to say that "the ordinary rule of law does not apply to Jesus"; the contrary is true. Nor does Jesus here appeal to his divinity or to his holiness as a guarantee of his truthfulness. He says not one word about either of these. He declares his testimony to be true for the simple reason that it states the true facts regarding himself. That this testimony of his must be accepted as being legally competent is due to the fact that it is corroborated by a second unimpeachable witness, namely the Father, v. 18. Jesus claims no exemption of any kind for himself; on the contrary, he gladly and completely submits to every legal requirement regarding the admission of testimony. How could he hope to have his testimony accepted by anybody if he proceeded to set aside the very law concerning testimony? It tends to confusion to talk about "the consciousness of Jesus" in connection with the verb οἶδα, "I know." How far this confusion may lead appears in the assertion, that "Christianity is entirely based upon Christ's consciousness of himself," and in the admonition about "the heroism of faith" on our part in resting on that consciousness. Like any witness, Jesus tells what "he knows," knows by firsthand, direct, personal knowledge, not what he has heard from others at second hand, not what he merely thinks or imagines. "I know" — that marks the genuine witness. "Whence I did come" is a fact which he most certainly does know. Why would he be ignorant of it? "And where I am going" is a second fact of the same kind. Who can bring evidence that Jesus does not know either or both of these facts? He is not a witness who is not in a position to know and thus to testify in regard to these facts. Here Jesus does not specify the place that is referred to. He has already done that, more than once, and his hearers have heard it a long time ago. All that he now needs to do and all that he does, is to insist that he is doing the true part of a genuine witness: telling what he actually knows. That is all that anyone can ask of a witness. And when a witness tells this, all men who are true and honest will believe his testimony — provided, of course, that it is duly corroborated (v. 18).

We do not believe that κἄν (καὶ ἐάν) is concessive in this case in the sense of "although" I testify, or "if also," or "if perchance" (R. 1018) ; for Jesus does actually testify that he is the light of the world. In fact, he keeps testifying so often that one of his titles is "the faithful witness," or "the faithful and true witness," Rev. 1:4; 3:14. His bearing witness is not an incidental function but one of the chief functions of his office. R. 1010, 1018, and B.-D. 372, 1 (a) think that κἄν μαρτυρῶ (as in 5:31) may be the indicative and not the subjunctive; and B.-D. offers the explanation that ἐάν is used for εἰ, calling the construction a vulgarism. Whatever the real explanation of ἐάν with the indicative may be, an indicative would here indicate actuality, and a present indicative iterative actuality: "and if I do keep on testifying," *wenn immer* (B.-D.) ; but certainly not: "if I *perchance* testify" (R.). The subjunctive would indicate future iterative testifying: "if I shall keep on testifying, as I expect to do."

By repudiating the testimony of Jesus on legal grounds the Pharisees arrogate to themselves the position of legal judges in Jesus' case. They love to do that sort of thing, deeming themselves the great guardians of the law. Therefore, after establishing

his own competency as a legal witness, Jesus establishes the incompetency of these self-constituted
judges: "But you do not know whence I come, or
where I am going." Whether we read δέ or not, this
statement is not a continuation of the proof that Jesus
is a legally competent witness. The ignorance of the
Pharisees in no way helps to qualify Jesus as a witness. Such qualification inheres and must inhere in
Jesus alone; it cannot inhere partly in other men. Nor
does this statement about the ignorance of the Pharisees mean to say that because of their ignorance they
are dependent on Jesus for any testimony regarding
whence he comes and whither he is going. A thought
of this kind would be entirely out of line with what
Jesus presents. The statement about the ignorance
of the Pharisees is the preamble to their disqualification as judges in Jesus' case. It goes together with
what follows on this point in v. 15. We see at a
glance that in the clause, "whence I come," ἔρχομαι
is identical in thought with the same clause that precedes, "whence I did come," ἦλθον. This is the aoristic
present, which expresses the fact in a timeless manner; R. 865, etc., calls it "the specific present." Here
Jesus uses "or" between the object clauses, drawing
separate attention to each of the two.

15) Since the Pharisees labor under this ignorance they are rendered totally incompetent to make
a legal pronouncement as judges concerning Jesus as
an inadmissible witness. **You are judging according to the flesh.** That is all they are able to do in
Jesus' case when they arrogate to themselves the position of judges. Note the article in κατὰ τὴν σάρκα. All
they see and know is "the flesh" of Jesus, his human
appearance. They have no other norm (κατά) for
judging him. Who this person really is, whence he
came, or whither he is going, is hidden from them.
This ignorance disqualifies them. Deprived of the real

data for pronouncing a valid judgment on Jesus, in particular as to whether he is a competent witness, they fall back on a superficial datum (his flesh) and thus render an invalid, spurious judgment, showing that they are unfit to serve as judges. These Pharisees, however, have had many followers. "The flesh" is specific and refers to the flesh of Jesus; without the article, κατὰ σάρκα, "according to flesh," would state only a general principle, that of customarily judging only in an outward way. How these Pharisees customarily judge is not the point here but how they judge in this specific case of Jesus.

The Pharisees made a profession of judging; see the shallow judgment in 7:15, and the intemperate judgment in 7:49. Jesus contrasts himself with them. **I judge no one,** ἐγώ in contrast with the preceding ὑμεῖς. But in the next breath he adds, "And if I do judge," etc. Many seek to remove what to them seems like a contradiction. So some add, "I judge no one according to the flesh," or "like you," which the very sense of the phrase forbids. Others stress the tense, "I judge no one now," meaning that he will eventually judge at the end of the world; but the following, "if I do judge," also refers to the present time. Still others stress the pronoun "I" and let it mean "I alone," "I in my human individuality," as if John had written ἐγὼ μόνος, which he has not. Finally, "no one" is stressed as a singular: he judges no individual but does judge "the moral state of the people." Those are right who supply nothing, find no appearance of contradiction, and stress neither one nor the other of the words. What Jesus says is this: "I am engaged in judging no one." The mission on which God sent him is not to act as a judge but as a Savior, 3:17. Here the context points to the contrast between judging and testifying. His great function is to testify to the truth and thus to save. He is the light of the world, sent to bless with enlightenment and salvation. Luther puts it tersely, "He here indicates his office."

16) But this very office with all its great saving purpose and in the very prosecution of that purpose necessitates the secondary function, a certain kind of judging. Luther continues: "If you will not have the Lord God, then keep the devil; and the office, which otherwise is not established in order to judge but to help and to comfort, this is compelled to judge." This does not mean that unbelief turns the testimony of Jesus into judgment for itself but that Jesus himself does utter judgment on certain men in the prosecution of his office. **And if, nevertheless (δέ), I do judge, my judgment is genuine, because I am not alone, but I and the Father that did send me.** Here καὶ ἐὰν κρίνω is exactly like κἂν μαρτυρῶ in v. 14, present actuality (if subjunctive). The emphatic ἐγώ = "I," who am sent to testify not to judge. This moves δέ back to fourth place in the sentence, which is unusual; it marks the contrast with the previous statement. When this necessity of judging, nevertheless, arises, Jesus says, "my judgment (note the emphatic possessive: *my* in contrast with *your* judgment) is genuine," ἀληθινή, worthy to be called a judgment. His judgment will not be only ἀληθής, "true," rendering a correct verdict by some means or other, but "genuine," coming from one who is in every way competent to act as a judge, who does not only happen to hit the right verdict but penetrates to all the facts in the case and pronounces accordingly. That kind of a judgment is, indeed, genuine, far beyond the judgment of these Pharisees on Jesus, who saw only his flesh.

As Jesus has qualified as a witness, so he now qualifies as a judge: "because I am not alone," a mere man, as these Pharisees think, left only to the penetration and wisdom of his human abilities. Such a judge may err, even with the best intentions, and in many cases his judgment may not be "genuine," worthy of the name. When Jesus judges, sent as he is by his Father from heaven on his saving mission, his judging must be infallible, hence his qualification as a judge must be according, far above those with which we are satisfied in mere men. Jesus has this qualification: he is not alone, "on the contrary (ἀλλά after a negation), I and he that did send me, the Father" (πατήρ omitted in some codices), i. e., we two are always together. By thus pointing to his Sender in connection with his judging Jesus declares that his judging is in connection with his mission. We may compare 5:19 and 30, also 8:26. Also in his judging Jesus never acts apart from, or contrary to, his Sender. The judgments of Jesus are thus identical with those of his Father, unerring and divine. In all the verdicts of Jesus these Pharisees have the verdicts of God himself. A note of warning to the Pharisees lies in these brief statements which reveal the kind of judge that Jesus is.

17) What Jesus says of himself as a judge is only incidental, elicited by the action of the Pharisees in usurping judicial authority by calling the testimony of Jesus illegal and void in a court of law. Therefore, after briefly contrasting his genuine judging with the spurious judging of the Pharisees, Jesus reverts to the main issue, that of the legal competency of his testimony regarding himself. In v. 14 only the preliminary point is settled, that when Jesus does testify he testifies from actual and direct personal knowledge. Now the main point is taken up. **And in your own law, moreover, it has been written, that the testimony of two men is true.** Here καί . . . δέ is not the same as in v. 16; it is not "and yet," or "and . . . nevertheless" (with δέ adversative), but as

in 6:51 and in I John 1:3: "and . . . moreover"
— καί adds, and δέ marks the addition as something
different from v. 14. Jesus himself cites the law on
the point at issue, formulating it himself from
Deut. 17:6 and 19:15. He knows that law perfectly.
"It has been written" means that it stands thus indefinitely (this being the force of the tense). Jesus
pointedly calls it "your own law." Jesus thus points
these legalists to their own supreme legal authority.
But not with the implication: This is *your* law not
mine; for Jesus was put under this law (Gal. 4:4),
came to fulfill the law (Matt. 5:17), and did fulfill
all its requirements. Yet Jesus cannot say *"our* law,"
even as he must distinguish *"your* Father" from *"my
Father"* and can never say *"our* Father." His relation to the law differed from that of men. The law
bound all Israelites since it was given for them. Jesus
placed himself under this law only for the sake of
men; he was the Son, thus the lawgiver himself, and
the law was never given for him. This vital disparity
between Jesus and men is here brought out. Therefore, too, the possessive "your own" in no way dis-
parages the law; Jesus always honors the law.

Now in Deut. 19:15, etc., the law demands that
there be more than just one witness; there must be
at least two. Each must corroborate the other. Our
state laws contain the same proviso. Testimony by
at least two witnesses stands as "true," ἀληθής, must
be admitted as true. The fact that one of the two witnesses may be testifying in his own case makes no difference. When citing this law about legally competent
testimony Jesus uses the genitive: the testimony "of two
men," (ἄνθρωποι), whereas Deuteronomy has "of two
witnesses" (μάρτυρες). This difference in terms might
be only accidental, since Jesus is not actually quoting
the law in a set form, if the case at issue were one
involving only a man and ordinary men as witnesses.

Here, however, where Jesus is on trial and where he and his Father are the witnesses, the change in terms is evidently intentional. In any human court "two men," two human witnesses, would be enough; for these Pharisees Jesus adduces two divine witnesses. So fully does he meet the requirement of the law that he greatly exceeds that requirement.

18) **I am he that testifies concerning myself, and the Father that sent me testifies concerning me.** In the Greek the statement is chiastic; the subjects are placed first and last, and the predicates are placed in between, an arrangement that is highly effective. Thus, indeed, we have two witnesses as the law requires. Both testify to the same facts concerning Jesus. This, however, shuts out the idea that the Father's testimony is already contained in that of Jesus, that when Jesus testifies, the Pharisees already have also the Father's testimony. The two are independent witnesses and stand as two; otherwise the provision of the law would not be met. Jesus does not need to state what the Father's testimony is because he did this a year ago when the same point was discussed, 5:31, etc., and the Pharisees have by no means forgotten. But the question is raised whether Jesus now includes in the Father's testimony both the works which he gave him to do (5:36) and the Old Testament prophecies concerning Jesus (5:37-47), or only the former. The present tense μαρτυρεῖ, "he testifies," is stressed as pointing only to the works. Yet the perfect tense μεμαρτύρηκε in 5:37, which is there used concerning the writings, has a present implication. Here, where the Father's entire testifying is summed up in "he testifies," the writings certainly cannot be excluded; and this the less since the presentation of the Father's testimony made in 5:31, etc., is assumed still to be in the minds of the Pharisees.

19) **They were, therefore, saying to him, Where is thy Father? Jesus answered, Neither me do you know nor my Father. If you knew me you would know also my Father.** The imperfect ἔλεγον may mean that different ones of the Pharisees put this question at Jesus. Their "where" question has a mocking tone. If God is, indeed, the father and Sender of Jesus, and if this God is to be the second witness, with his testimony to corroborate that of Jesus concerning himself, then let Jesus present this Father, that he may be interrogated as a witness, so that these Pharisees may see whether his testimony agrees with that of Jesus. A silly shrewdness lies back of this question: the certainty that Jesus cannot produce this second witness in the way they intimate. In this demand on Jesus to present his second witness these Pharisees repeat their proceeding of v. 13: they dodge the main issue by raising a minor one that is wholly immaterial. The main issue is: Does God testify as Jesus says, or does he not so testify? In 5:36, etc., God's testimony was given to the Pharisees: the works of Jesus and the Old Testament declarations concerning Jesus. This double testimony is undeniable and incontrovertible. These men brazenly set it aside and instead fasten on the point that Jesus should produce this second witness in person before them.

But by foolishly asking where this second witness is these Pharisees betray a second piece of fatal ignorance. The first Jesus points out in the last clause of v. 14; the second he now states in the same categorical way: "Neither me do you know nor my Father," i. e., the true God. Their question is evidence for this their ignorance. People who ask *where* the Father is, who want him produced so that they can place him on the witness stand, thereby demonstrate that they do not know him at all, and no wonder, then, that they also do not know him whom God has sent. God is always on the witness stand of his written Word, where all who will may hear his testimony in full and thus also learn to know him most intimately and adequately. Those who reject this testimony know neither the Father nor the Son — and the guilt of this ignorance is theirs alone.

In the statement regarding the ignorance of the Pharisees Jesus uses "neither . . . nor," disjunctives, placing each person by himself beside the other. In the following conditional sentence "also" (καί) connects the two persons. Why Jesus puts himself first and the Father second is apparent from the latter: "If you knew me you would know also my Father" (present unreality, εἰ with the imperfect followed by the imperfect with ἄν; ἤδειτε, pluperfect, always used as an imperfect). If Jesus had placed the Father first he would thereby have pointed to the Old Testament revelation as the means of knowledge, i. e., that by showing us the Father the Old Testament shows us also the Son. This the Old Testament, indeed, does. By placing himself first a different thought is expressed, namely that Jesus is the medium for knowing the Father aright. For although the Father speaks clearly enough in the Old Testament, he speaks more clearly still through his Son (Heb. 1:1, 2), his person, mission, word, and work (14:6, 7). He who knows the Son, he, and he alone, knows als the Father. Thus these two, who may be placed side by side ("neither . . . nor"), belong together ("also," καί), 14:9. The question of Philip in 14:8 is only apparently like that of the Pharisees.

The conditional form of the sentence shuts out the possibility of regarding it as an inverse deduction, in the sense that ignorance concerning Jesus is conclusive evidence that the Pharisees are ignorant also regarding the Father. Such a deduction appears in 5:38, where not believing in Jesus proves that the Father's word is not in the Jews. If Jesus had desired a deduction of this type he would have said, "Because you do not know me, therefore also you do not know the Father"; or, "You do not know the Father, for you do not know me." What he does say is that knowing the Father depends on (εἰ) knowing Jesus. Where this condition is absent, the conclusion is also absent. The implication is that it should be easy to know Jesus, who also has come to show us the Father and in and through whom the Father reveals himself.

20) This ends the present clash. The Pharisees have no reply and possibly walk away. **These words he spoke at the treasury while teaching in the Temple; and no one arrested him because his hour had not yet come.** Just what place is meant by "the treasury" is disputed. In the court of the women stood thirteen treasure chests with funnel or trumpet-like receptacles, into which the gifts were thrown; while near the hall in which the Sanhedrin met was the room in which the Temple funds were kept. The purpose in mentioning the place is to indicate that it was public, under the very noses of the authorities. Moreover, Jesus made not only the utterances here recorded but was engaged in teaching. Yet (καί for joining an adversative thought) no one, not even these Pharisees, who had again been refuted in public, ventured to make a move to arrest Jesus. No secondary reasons are mentioned why he was let alone. The supposition that the consciences of the Pharisees had been touched, making them cowardly for the moment, is improbable. The primary reason is the same as that assigned in 7:30, which see.

21) A second and much sharper clash follows the altercation which John has just marked as being

finished (v. 20). There cannot have been a long interval between the events recorded in these two verses. **He said, therefore, again unto them, I am going away, and you shall seek me and shall die in your sin. Whither I go, you cannot come.** The connective οὖν, "therefore," refers to v. 20: since no one had arrested him, his hour not having come. "Again," once more (compare v. 12) he thus spoke to them, this time in most serious warning. The persons addressed are the same, although John now calls them "the Jews," such as belong to the hostile ruling class. Jesus reiterates what he said to these men in 7:33, 34, but with important modifications. He points in warning to what their wicked unbelief must lead. This time the preamble, "Yet a little while I am with you," is omitted. In 7:33 it was added because the police officers had been sent out to arrest him before the festival was ended; no police are now watching to effect an arrest. This time, however, an emphatic ἐγώ precedes the verb: "*I*, of my own accord, am going away" entirely irrespective of what you Jews may plot and plan. Jesus' mission is approaching its end; then he will leave (ὑπάγω, the futuristic present, R. 870). There is no need to repeat from 7:33 that he is going to the Father, his Sender. Then what about these Jews who are now so keen to be rid of Jesus? Strange to say, then when they have what they wish, they will not wish what they have — then: "you will seek me," too late, with the seeking of despair; compare the explanation of 7:34. When the calamities of judgment will set in, the Jews will cry in vain for a deliverer.

In 7:34 only the negative is presented: "you shall not find me," i. e., I shall not deliver you; here the positive is stated: "you shall die in your sin," ἁμαρτία, the collective singular. To die in one's sin is to re-

ceive the eternal penalty of sin after death. For
to die in sin is to die without repentance and saving
faith. To die thus is to perish, 3:16. Wanting to
be completely rid of Jesus, these Jews shall be rid
of him forever. "Whither I go, you cannot come."
The blessed presence of the Father, to which Jesus
returns after he has completed his mission, will be
closed to his enemies after death overwhelms them.
This is what their unbelief will at last lead to.

22) This renewed, most positive warning the
Jews again answer with mockery. **The Jews, therefore, said,** not addressing Jesus but speaking of him
in the third person as in 7:35, 36, **Surely, he will
not kill himself since he declares, Whither I go
you cannot come.** They state the question with
μήτι as if they have in mind a negative answer yet see
no other way but to answer positively. The ears
of these Jews are keen in a certain way, for they catch
the force of the emphatic "I": *"I myself"* am going
away, and tack their answer onto that. This "I" is
absent in 7:33, which accounts for the fling the Jews
there employ, fastening it only on the verb ὑπάγω. In
the present case the thrust that Jesus must be contemplating suicide is more vicious than the sneer about
his going among the pagan Greeks in 7:35. We may
here regard ὅτι as causal, "since," but compare the
ὅτι in 7:35. The Jews here persist in their trick of
catching at some one word or expression in the utterances of Jesus, turning their venom on that, and
blindly ignoring the grave substance of what Jesus
says. So here they are deaf to the warning that they
shall die in their sins with all the horror that lies in
this statement; they pick up only the expression that
Jesus himself is about to go away. The fact that a
man who kills himself lands in hell, and that these
Jews do not intend to go there, is not implied in their

mocking question, although some have thought so. If this were the point in their sneer, something in the wording would indicate as much.

23) Jesus pays no heed to the mockery just uttered. To ignore is also to answer, and often more effectively than to use words. **And he was saying to them,** means that he added the following to what he had already said: **You are from below, I am from above; you are of this world, I am not of this world.** This double contrast is only the preamble to the warning, combined with the call of grace, which follows in v. 24. Jesus thus repeats and expounds more fully what he has said in v. 21. The four ἐκ denote origin. "From below" = "of this world"; likewise "from above" = "not of this world." The contrast in positive form is elucidated by the contrast in negative form. The origin of the Jews is *not* the origin of Jesus. Moreover, the emphasis is on the two second members of the contrast, i. e., on the origin of Jesus. He and he alone is the exception. That the Jews, like all men, are "from below," "of this world," is an ordinary fact, universally acknowledged. That Jesus is totally different in his origin is the exceptional fact, denied by these Jews but a fact, nevertheless, and, as v. 24 shows, decisive for these Jews, whether they shall die in their sins or escape from this death.

While "this world" defines "below," the latter also helps to define the former; the same is true of the opposite phrases. This means that the Jews are of mundane origin, but Jesus of supermundane, heavenly, divine origin. In the Biblical concept "world" mankind holds the dominating place, and "this world" indicates the present actual condition of the earth with its human inhabitants, with its corruption of sin and death. The effort to dissociate sin and death from "this world" as used here by Jesus fails because both are mentioned in the next breath (v. 24). Yet this is true, Jesus does not here operate with the contrast: the Jews are sinful, he is sinless. This would only place a gulf between him and them. To be sure, the Jews are sinful because of their origin, and Jesus sinless because of his. This goes without saying. But Jesus, who is from above, is now amid those who are from below in order to lift them to his side. He who is not of this world now stands among those who are of this world in order to deliver them from the sin and the death in this world and to raise them to heaven. This preamble, therefore, intends once more to usher in for the Jews the way of escape through faith in Jesus.

24) Now follows the main statement. **I said, therefore, to you, that you shall die in your sins; for unless you come to believe that I am (what I say) you shall die in your sins.** Here is the full presentation of the briefer warning of v. 21. Its main point is that a way of escape from death is open. Hence the weight of οὖν rests on the clauses about Jesus in the preamble: "I am from above, not of this world." Since Jesus is such a Savior he can help these Pharisees so that they shall not die in their sins. Only secondary weight attaches to the first clauses in the preamble, that the Pharisees are from below and of this world; for this is obvious and accounts for their state of sin. This made it necessary, in the grace of God, that Jesus should appear in their midst, he who is from above, not of this world, divine, with power to deliver from sin and death. The reason, then, why Jesus told these Pharisees that they would die in their sins is not that, like all men, they are sinners. Note the thrice repeated phrase: die *"in* your sin" or "sins" (spreading out the collective singular in the plural). Though they have sins, they need not "die in them," for here is the divine

Savior from heaven come on his mission to free them from their sins.

The explanatory γάρ thus puts the warning in this form: "Unless you come to believe, you shall die in your sins." The sins of these men will destroy them by robbing them of life eternal only if they refuse to believe in Jesus. The "if" clause is pure gospel, extending its blessed invitation anew. Yet it is again combined with the warning about dying in sins. This note of warning with its terrifying threat persists because these Jews had chosen the course of unbelief. Yet the "if" opens the door of life in the wall of sin. The divine threats are conditional. You shall die if you do not come to faith (πιστεύσητε, ingressive aorist), come to accept, trust, and cling to the divine deliverer. That is why in v. 24 ἀποθανεῖσθε, "you shall die," has the emphatic forward position while in v. 21 "in your sins" has this position. In v. 21 Jesus says, *the sins* will bring on death; now he says, *death* will be brought on by the sins. The emphasis is shifted to death because of the implied contrast with escape from death in the "if" clause. Unfortunately, this shift in emphasis with its important meaning is lost in translation.

Jesus might have said, "unless you come to believe *in me*." Instead of the mere pronoun he uses the far more significant object clause ὅτι ἐγώ εἰμι with its strong emphasis on "I" — "I" alone and no other. The ellipsis in "that I am," the omission of the predicate, is idiomatic in the Greek and quite common; see 4:26; 6:20; 9:9; 13:19; 18:5, 6 and 8 in John alone. The Greek mind is nimble and finds no difficulty in each instance in supplying the predicate from the context. So here "that I am" means: "that I am, as I say, from above, not of this world," i. e., divine, the Son of God, come from heaven on the mission to save sinners who are from below and of this world.

This is the substance of the faith that affords escape
from death. Some would supply: "that I am the
Messiah," or "God," etc.; but this disregards the context which alone supplies the predicate that the
speaker has in mind. In English this Greek idiom
cannot be reproduced; we must in some way fill the
place of the predicate: "that I am he"; "that I am
what I say"; *dass ich es bin.* Note also that Jesus
uses ἐάν, the condition of expectancy, and not the condition of present unreality: "if you would come to
believe." He does not imply that he thinks they will
not believe but rather that he hopes and expects that
after all they may come to believe. Thus ἐάν has
the kindly note of grace, it is like an efficacious invitation.

25) The reply of the Jews pointedly repudiates
both the warning and the invitation. **They were,
therefore, saying to him, Thou, who art thou?** The
descriptive ἔλεγον bids us contemplate this reply. Its
tone is contemptuous. These Jews are not asking who
Jesus is; they are sneering at him for making such
claims for himself: "How dost *thou* (note the
emphatic σύ) come to assume a role like this?" B.-D.
300, 2.

The reply of Jesus constitutes one of the most disputed passages in the New Testament, on which much
research and ingenuity has been spent without attain-
ing anything resembling unanimity.

Without question, τὴν ἀρχήν is an adverbial accusative and because of its forward position strongly
emphatic. Aside from the possibility that τὴν ἀρχήν
ever means "from the beginning" (our versions) this
meaning is here excluded by the present tense λαλῶ;
the A. V. changes it to "said" (aorist), and the R. V.
to "have said" (perfect or possibly aorist). It is
also excluded by the sense of λαλῶ; we should expect
to find λέγω used here, or rather the aorist εἶπον. In

other instances where John desires to say "from the
beginning," he invariably uses ἐξ ἀρχῆς, 6:64; 15:27;
16:4; and in the epistles.   Finally, why the strong
emphasis on a phrase like "from the beginning"?
Luther's *erstlich*, "in the first place," "principally,"
is without another example in the Greek; nor does
any other statement follow in regard to who or what
Jesus is.   The suggestion to draw the adverbial accusative to v. 26:   "First of all, since I am still speaking to you, I have many things to speak and to
judge concerning you," likewise attributes a wrong
meaning to τὴν ἀρχήν and duplicates λαλεῖν in the same
sentence in a helpless manner.

More prominent authorities propose "at all" as
the translation.   Thus the margin of the R. V., "How
is it that I even speak to you at all?"   B.-D. 300, 2 and
R. 730, "Do you ask, why I speak to you at all?" or,
"Are you reproaching me that I speak to you at all?"
and Zahn's exclamation, "To think that I yet speak
to you at all!"   *Dass ich ueberhaupt noch zu euch rede!*
The sense of these renderings is that by their hostile
interruptions the Jews have about made it impossible
for Jesus to go on speaking to them.   But this leaves
no adequate emphasis on τὴν ἀρχήν; in fact, this adverbial accusative should appear after ὅτι not before
it.   The thought, too, is unparalleled in the speech
of Jesus.   Aside from the fact that he goes right on
speaking to the Jews, why should Jesus intimate that
he is wasting his effort by saying anything further to
these Jews when in a moment John reports (v. 30)
that many believed on him?

Far more acceptable is the rendering, "Altogether
(in every respect) I am what also I am telling you"
(compare Thayer).   The exact force of τὴν ἀρχήν
is ὅλως, but in the sense of *ueberhaupt* (C.-K. 176):
**In general (I am) that which (ὅ τι) I also am telling
you,** καὶ λαλῶ, not holding anything back in silence.

Jesus thus meets the question, "Thou, who art thou?" This he invariably does, no matter how contemptuous or hostile the questioners may be. But Jesus cannot here allow any implication as though he has been silent on any vital point regarding himself. He has spoken fully and not kept silent, in fact, is now speaking clearly (καὶ λαλῶ), v. 12; 23, 24. And these Jews have heard his testimony, for they refused and still refuse to accept it (7:19, etc.; 7:30, etc.; 8:13, etc.). This same testimony concerning himself, Jesus intimates (λαλῶ), will go on — he will speak and not remain silent. By thus holding the Jews to what he is constantly saying concerning himself Jesus rebukes their question as being altogether uncalled for. Why ask a man who he is when he keeps on telling you? The claim that in this rendering εἰμί would have to be written out after τὴν ἀρχήν is invalid, for we do not really need it even in the English, "In general, that which I also am telling you."

26) With this reply the contemptuous question of the Jews concerning Jesus is both answered and dismissed as uncalled for. While Jesus will keep on telling these Jews in due order who and what he is, just as he has done up to this moment, he now informs them: **Many things have I to tell and to judge concerning you. Now he that did send me is true; and what things I did hear from him these I am telling in the world.** In 7:33, 34 and again in 8:21 Jesus tells these Jews something not only about himself, but also about themselves, something of a terrible nature, amounting to a prophetic judgment. Instead of heeding these utterances about themselves the Jews deliberately ignored them and by their contemptuous rejoinders tried to shift all the attention to Jesus. But Jesus has an answer for them. He has "many things to tell concerning them," using the same verb as in v. 25, λαλεῖν, things about which

he cannot keep silent. Significantly he adds, "to tell
and to judge concerning you," the second verb being
in explanation of the first. Their unbelief turns this
telling into judging; compare v. 16. Jesus does not
say "to tell *you*," he says only "concerning you."
They may or may not hear this telling and judging,
that makes no difference, Jesus will certainly not be
silent.

As in v. 16, Jesus places his Sender back of everything that he will tell concerning these Jews. Here
ἀλλά is not adversative, "but"; it adds only "an acces-
sory idea": "and," "yea," "now," R. 1185, etc. First
the preamble, "And he that did send me is true,"
ἀληθής, whose very nature is verity, and whose every
word thus expresses reality and truth. Being what he
is, he cannot possibly say anything false or untrue.
The designation "he that did send me" connects Jesus
and his entire mission with this supreme author of
truth. This again appears in the main statement,
attached to the preamble with καί, "and what things
I did hear from him these I (ἐγώ, I myself, emphatic)
am telling in the world." Compare 5:30. All that
Jesus tells on any subject emanates not from himself
but from the Sender. This, of course, includes the
"many things" he has to tell and to judge concerning
these unbelieving Jews. Let them understand that in
every word of warning and of judgment from the lips
of Jesus they hear the word and the verdict of his
great Sender. Will their conscience still remain callous? The breadth of Jesus' statement covers also his
offers of grace and escape from sin and death (v. 24).
Back of these, too, is the Sender of Jesus. Will the
hearts of these Jews still refuse faith? The aorist
ἤκουσα is explained by v. 23, "I am from above, not of
this world" (compare 1:18). The tense refers to the
same time as that expressed by ὁ πέμψας. The Son
heard when he received his great commission. We need

not put into this tense the present constant communion of Jesus with his Sender, expressed for instance in 5:30, "as I hear," and in 8:16, "I am not alone." Since Jesus here includes all his speaking, he says, "these things I am telling in the world" and not merely to these Jewish rulers. We need not worry about εἰς and try to make it "into" or "unto." This is an ordinary case of the static use of εἰς, "in," on which see the discussion R. 591, etc.

The old idea that ἀλλά is always adversative, "but," has led to a complete misunderstanding of what Jesus says. He is thought to say, that, although he has much to tell and judge concerning the Jewish rulers, nevertheless (ἀλλά), he will refrain and restrict himself to telling what he has heard from the Sender. Instead of spending his time in rebuking these Jews he will devote himself to his real mission. The moment ἀλλά is properly understood (R. 1185, etc.) ideas such as this fade away.

27) In order that we may understand why Jesus continues his discourse in the way in which he does in v. 28, 29, John introduces an explanatory remark. **They did not realize that he was speaking to them of his Father.** The Jews must have indicated their ignorance by some exclamation or objection which John does not record, preferring to state what their minds lacked. In ἔλεγεν we have a case where the Greek, like the English, accomodates the tense of the indirect discourse to the secondary tense of the main verb, here using the imperfect ἔλεγεν instead of the present after the aorist ἔγνωσαν, R. 1029.

The point of John's remark is not that the Jews failed to understand the expression "he that did send me" as a designation for the Father. Verses 17-19 are too plain to be misunderstood; moreover, the expression itself would be clear to any Jew. Of course, the obduracy of the Jews blinded them, but not to the extent that they understood none of the references to the Father, for then John's remark about their ignorance should have been made much earlier. The ignorance here meant refers only to v. 26, and in this verse only to the one point in the mission of Jesus, that every word he utters (λαλῶ) is in reality the word of the Father himself and thus verity in the highest degree. The Jews, indeed, heard Jesus say this, and the words he uses were quite intelligible to them. What their obduracy hid from them was the force of these words as pertaining to the Father. The verb γινώσκω denotes an inner grasp and realization, which is often lacking even where the intellect is active enough.

28) Jesus, of course, perceived that his mighty word about the Father's relation to every one of his utterances had not registered with these Jews. In fact, obdurate as they are, it would not register; they would not "realize" even if he repeated this statement about his Father. Therefore Jesus turns to prophecy. **Jesus, therefore, said** (giving a prophetic turn to his statement), **When you shall lift up the Son of man, then you will realize** (what now your obduracy will not let you realize), **that I am (what I say), and that from myself I do nothing, but, just as the Father taught me, these very things (and only these) I tell.** We see that Jesus does not expect these Jews to realize just what the force of his words is even after this restatement. They will go on treating them lightly, as if no real verity is back of them. But the time will come when this will change. Not indeed, as some have thought, that finally their obduracy will cease and turn to repentance. They will remain as they are, but God will speak another language to them, one that will crash through even their hard hearts — crushing them in judgment. Yet the purpose of uttering this prophetic warning now is

still one of grace, that ere it be too late these Jews may yet turn, realize indeed, and repent.

Jesus uses a condition of expectancy in pointing to that future time, ὅταν with the subjunctive in the protasis, and the future indicative in the apodosis. His mind vividly conceives the coming time of his crucifixion. The verb ὑψοῦν, "to lift up," refers to the elevation on the cross, just as in 3:14; compare also 12:32. Since Jesus ascribes this act to the Jews, the debate should end as to whether the crucifixion is referred to or the exaltation in heaven, or possibly both combined in some way. Moreover, the crucifixion is here brought in as the final act by which the Jewish rulers will repudiate Jesus and all he came to bring. Here Jesus once more calls himself "the Son of man," using the Messianic title he loves: he who is a descendant of man, the incarnate Son of God. See 1:51. In the crucifixion of Jesus the doom of the Jews would be sealed; not, indeed, in an absolute way as by the perpetration of this act alone, but in a factual way as the final rejection from which the Jews as a nation would never recede in repentance. Thus that act will open the floodgates of judgment, bringing on the destruction of Jerusalem, the permanent exile of the Jews from their native land, their miraculous preservation as a foreign element scattered among all other nations of the world as a sign until the end of time. Then will be fulfilled what Jesus says in v. 21, 24, "You shall die in your sins."

"Then," Jesus says, "you will realize." Some connect this "then" too closely with the "when" clause, as if hard upon the crucifixion the realization of what Jesus here says will break in upon these wicked Sanhedrists and the unbelieving Jews generally. We must, however, abide by the context. Verse 28 is an elucidation of verses 21 and 24. Every unbe-

lieving Jew, upon whom the fate of his nation makes
no impression when he finally dies in his sins, will
realize too late just what Jesus says. First, ὅτι ἐγώ εἰμι,
a repetition from v. 24 and to be understood in the
same sense, "that *I* (and I alone) am" what I tell
you, namely "from above not of this world" (v. 23).
We see how this reference knits the entire discourse
(v. 21-29) together as a unit. Too late all these ill-
fated Jews will "realize" by their own experience of
the divine judgment that what Jesus kept telling them
concerning himself is verity indeed. Secondly, they
will "realize" in the same way the verity connected with the Father, already stated in v. 26 and
now repeated and amplified, "and that from myself
I do nothing (5:19, etc.), but, just as the Father
taught me, these very things I tell (5:30, etc.)." Back
of every act and thus also of every word of Jesus is
the Father and his verity ("he that did send me is
true," v. 26). Word and deed of Jesus go together, although here the emphasis is on the word;
and this means the threat and the warning as well
as the call and the offer of grace (v. 24) at present still
held out.

"That I am" is a repetition from v. 24; and the
predicate that is to be supplied is the same. The
aorist "he taught" is historical, just as the aorist
"I heard" in v. 26; both refer to the time indicated
in ὁ πέμψας με, "he that did send me," in v. 26 when
Jesus went forth from God on his mission. We must
note that καθώς . . . ταῦτα correspond: "even as
. . . these very things"; and ταῦτα is resumptive
for the clause "even as the Father taught me." But
from the manner "even as" Jesus turns to the substance, "these very things," instead of keeping to
the manner, "thus also" (οὕτως). This is lost in
our versions which translate, "I speak these things,"
as though Jesus refers only to what he just now says.

29) Jesus prophesies that the obdurate Jews will come to realize too late what they ought to realize now, namely that Jesus is what he says, and that every word of his has back of it the Father and his verity. From the Jews he now turns to himself. They shall die in their sins, but Jesus, being what he is, doing and saying what he does, is sure of his Father and that Father's support. **And he that did send me is with me; he did not leave me alone; because the things pleasing to him I for my part am doing always.** The observation is correct that these three brief statements are closely united and are understood only when taken together. The first is positive: the Sender is with him whom he sent; μετά here conveys the idea of help or aid, R. 611. While Jesus uses the present tense "is with me," this tense receives its force from the subject, "he that did send me." For in the entire mission of Jesus from its start to its finish the Father is with Jesus.

The positive statement is followed by the negative, "he did not leave me alone." The absence of a connective lends it greater force. Here Jesus uses the aorist ἀφῆκεν, "he did not leave" me alone. Like the present tense "is with me," this aorist receives its force from the subject, "he that did send me." The sense cannot be that the Father did not leave his Son only at the moment when he sent him. Some regard this aorist as constative: from the moment of the sending up to the present moment the Father did not leave the Son he sent. This is conceived as an expression of the consciousness of the Father's presence which Jesus has enjoyed until this very time. That, too, we are told, is why the hostile Jews with all their number and their power were unable to destroy Jesus as they planned to do — Jesus was not alone. Only by way of a deduction the thought is added, that as hitherto the Father did not leave his Son alone, so also

he will be with the Son until the end. We need make
no deduction whatever, the aorist itself covers all that
is added by the deduction. The Father who sent
the Son on his mission "is with him" during that
entire mission and "did not leave him alone" during
any part of that mission. "He that did send me,"
repeated so often by Jesus, is true regarding every
moment when Jesus utters this designation, applies to
every moment until his mission is completed and he
returns to his Father.

Jesus is here thinking and speaking of the close
of his mission, "I go away" (v. 21) ; "When you have
lifted up the Son of man." The crucifixion is in his
mind. With that before his eyes he utters the words
of verity and assurance that his great Sender is ever
with him and did not leave him alone. This is substantiated by the reason which Jesus assigns for the
constant presence of his Sender in his mission: "because the things pleasing to him I am doing always."
Jesus is not speaking only of what he is doing at the
moment. "I am doing always," the adverb made
strongly emphatic by being placed at the end, covers
the entire mission of Jesus. Most pleasing of all, indeed, "an odor of a sweet smell" (R. V.) for his Father,
is his passion when he prayed, "Thy will be done!"
and drank the bitter cup of death. "Always" looks
also to the cross.

When in v. 28 (compare 5:19 and 30) Jesus says
that he does nothing "from himself," he means that
in his entire mission *he* never disowns but always
acknowledges his Father. The counterpart of this is
the fact that in his entire mission the Father is "with
him" and never "leaves him alone," i. e., *the Father*
never disowns Jesus but always acknowledges him.
Both thoughts meet in the expression "the things
pleasing to him," the adjective having "a distinct personal flavor," R. 537. Jesus ever pleases the Father,

and the Father is ever pleased with Jesus. Thus the two are bound together with never a break in the tie. This holds true even with regard to the agony on the cross; in fact, holds true there in the highest degree. For there, if anywhere, Jesus did not his own but his Father's will; there, if anywhere, Jesus did what pleased his Father; there, if anywhere, the Father was pleased in his Son. "With me" and "did not leave me alone" (οὐ ἀφῆκεν) holds true with regard to the cross. And yet God forsook Jesus on the cross. But the verb ἐγκατέλιπες, "Why didst thou forsake me?" (Matt. 27:46; Matt. 15:34) means something entirely different, namely that Jesus trod the winepress alone, drank the cup of wrath for our sins alone, paid the penalty for our guilt alone. This was the Father's will; and Jesus did it. Yea, for this he had come (12:27; compare 10:18) and, though it wrung the bitter cry from his soul, he carried it through. He could perform this part of his mission only in this way — alone; no one could share the extreme agony with him. But paying the ransom (λύτρον) and the price (τιμή) alone does not mean that at that supreme hour Jesus acted "from himself," disowning his Father and his Sender's mission, or disowned by his Father and Sender. In that very hour the hardest part of his mission was accomplished (Phil. 2:8).

We may say that the emphatic pronoun ἐγώ, "I on my part," is in contrast to the Jews and to all of us as sinners, for none of us do what is pleasing to the Father. Yet this is a minor point. For "the things pleasing to him" signify all that belongs to Jesus' mission. These Jesus did "always" without a single omission. While thus the reason for the Father's ever being with Jesus can be called ethical, this reason is not ethical in the usual sense as obeying the divine law but in the far higher sense of voluntarily assuming the mission of redemption and executing that mission with absolute fidelity. The opposite of doing "the things pleasing to him" is, therefore, not the doing of some sin displeasing to God — a thought that is foreign to the connection; but of after all giving up the voluntarily assumed redemptive mission and of thus allowing it to remain unfulfilled. The perfect sinlessness of Jesus is only mediately involved in "the things pleasing to him" as one of the personal qualifications (as, on the other hand, the divinity) for the redemptive mission.

30) **As he was uttering these things many believed in him.** It makes little difference whether we add this sentence as the close of the previous paragraph or make it head the new paragraph. "These things" points backward, yet v. 31 mentions believing Jesus, and v. 30 accounts for them. The aorist ἐπίστευσαν merely states the fact that many "believed." Amid all the hostility that Jesus faced he won this victory.

V. *Jesus' Testimony Culminates in an Effort to Stone Him, 31-59*

31) **Accordingly, Jesus was saying to the Jews who had believed in him, If you remain in my word you are truly my disciples and you shall know the truth, and the truth shall set you free.** When editors of the text and commentators make a paragraph at v. 30 or 31, this does not imply that we are to insert an interval, either of hours or of a day, between the paragraphs, as is generally done. John connects v. 30 with what precedes by means of ταῦτα and the genitive absolute, "while he was saying these things," and v. 31 with v. 30 by means of οὖν, "accordingly, Jesus was saying" to these believers. Any interval is shut out. John's remark in v. 30 and in

the preamble of v. 31 are merely explanatory of the words which Jesus now utters, for they are words intended only for believers, and we must be told that and how such believers were present. John's explanatory remark is exactly like the one he inserted a moment ago in v. 27 in order to make plain to us why Jesus turned to prophecy in v. 28.

Once this is clear, we shall not think that τοὺς πεπιστευκότας αὐτῷ Ἰουδαίους is an exceptional expression in John's Gospel. It is as natural as it can be in this its proper place. Nor shall we place the emphasis either on the noun "Jews" or on the attributive participle "having believed," for neither term is emphatic. We shall also not entertain such notions as that John means to convey to us the thought that the people here named have a double nature, the old Jewish nature still persisting beside the new nature of faith. This idea is introduced in order to explain v. 33, "they replied to him"; the unspecified subject of ἀπεκρίθησαν is taken to be these believing Jews, whose old Jewish nature is supposed to be cropping out in objecting to what Jesus says. But the moment this is done, all that follows likewise refers to these believing Jews. Jesus would be telling them that they are seeking to kill him, that they are of the devil, etc. In fact, then the most scathing utterances of Jesus in this entire chapter would be hurled at these believing Jews. But so monstrous a situation is incredible.

From v. 21 to the end of the chapter is one uninterrupted narration. The persons participating are the same throughout, Jesus and a crowd of Jews. At first all are hostile to Jesus, but by the time we reach v. 29 a goodly number are actually won to believe in him (note the statement of this as a fact by means of the aorist ἐπίστευσαν in v. 30), not through miracles, but through the words of warning coupled with grace which these men have just heard. In some way or other, not indicated by John, these believers manifest their change of heart. At once Jesus has a word for them in particular. No sooner does he utter it than the hostile crowd of Jews raises further objection. They act just as they did from the start: they pick at some point to which to object (compare v. 22 and 25; also v. 13 and 19). John does not need to say in v. 33 who these objectors are, for we have heard them from the very start, and their objection is of the same type as before. Jesus answers them in v. 34, etc. But they go on. The clash becomes more and more intense until these Jews take up stones, and Jesus leaves them.

The imperfect ἔλεγεν is like the imperfect in v. 23 and 25, little more than a variation from the aorist; note that in the following exchanges the aorists introducing them are interrupted by one present tense, λέγει, in v. 39. After faith has been kindled in the hearts of a goodly number of the present audience of Jesus, the great need is that they continue in the blessed course upon which they have entered. The condition of expectancy (ἐάν with the subjunctive), "If you remain (or shall remain) in my words," counts on such continuance as the normal thing. The pronoun ὑμεῖς is emphatic, "If *you on your part* remain," etc., i. e., "you" as having come to faith. This singles them out from the rest of the Jews. We must not overlook the implication in the verb "remain" in my word. Jesus acknowledges that these men *are* now in his word; in other words, that they now embrace his word by faith. He uses the aorist subjunctive μείνητε, actually and definitely remain, be fixed and established in his word. The opposite would be to drop the word they have taken up, definitely to leave it again, namely by a return to unbelief. Jesus also uses the strong possessive adjective "word of mine," which is weightier than the genitive pronoun.

This clause sheds light on the dative αὐτῷ: who believed "him." It indicates that these Jews now believed in what Jesus had told them; to believe "him" = to believe what he says. Theirs was the genuine type of faith, resting on the word. All they needed was to become permanently fixed in that faith.

The apodosis: then "you are truly my disciples," corroborates the implication in the protasis. Jesus implies that these believers are already his disciples; on μαθηταί see 2:2. Yet there is a difference between being disciples and being truly disciples. The preceding aorist subjunctive indicates what this difference is. All are disciples of Jesus who in any way believe his word, but those are truly disciples who once for all become fixed in his word. Hence also the "if." Beginners, however genuine their beginning, may drop off again; but once they become fixed definitely to remain in the word, they will never drop off again. Note, too, that Jesus uses the present tense: then "you are truly" my disciples; and not the future tense: then "you *will be* truly." This avoids the implication that only at some perhaps future time these believers can achieve the higher status. They can become fixed and established in Jesus' word in short order. No long apprenticeship is needed. To remain in Jesus' word (aorist) carries an intensive and not merely an extensive idea. Not the amount and quantity of the word makes us truly disciples but the fidelity and the firmness with which we hold the amount of the word which has been vouchsafed to us. While these beginners in the faith must learn more and more of the precious word of Jesus on which their incipient faith rests, and while all further portions of the word, such as the portion they already possess, will tend to hold them in the faith, for them to remain in the word of Jesus means primarily what Paul puts

into the admonition, "Be ye steadfast, unmovable!"
I Cor. 15:58.

The word of Jesus (λόγος) is his teaching, the gospel; most emphatically it is "his" word. The necessity
for firm adherence to it is at once seen when we
remember that this "word" and this alone is spirit
and life, outside of which is spiritual death. Jesus
identifies himself with his word, "If you remain in me,
and my words (the one word in its different parts)
remain in you," 5:7. The word is the vehicle of Jesus,
bringing him to us, and us to him. An example of
remaining in his word is seen in the case of the 3,000
at Pentecost: "they continued steadfastly in the
apostles' doctrine," Acts 2:42. Compare Acts 13:43;
Col. 1:23; Heb. 3:14; I John 2:28 (John loves the
word "to remain," "to abide"); II John 9. Thus to
remain is not only a mark of discipleship but its very
essence.

32) "And" adds the blessed result that is immediately involved in truly being disciples of Jesus, first
the proximate, next the ultimate result. The former
is: "you shall know the truth," γνώσεσθε, "realize" it
by your inner spiritual contact with it. Of course,
intellectual apprehension is included, but much more
is involved (7:17), namely the knowledge derived
from a living experience with the blessed power of
the truth. No man who rejects the truth can possibly
attain this type of knowledge. The future tense is
constative, R. 871, like that of the same verb in v. 28;
it summarizes the entire realization following real discipleship. "Shall know" does not refer to a remote
future but to one that begins at once and continues
and grows.

"The truth" is the contents of the word of Jesus,
the substance of what he conveys to our minds and our
hearts. "I have given them thy (the Father's) Word,"
17:14; "Sanctify them in the truth; thy Word is

truth," 17:17 (see also 17:8). By "truth," ἀλήθεια, "reality," is meant, and the Greek article here indicates the specific reality and actuality that exists in God and in Jesus, and all that they give to us and do for us by divine grace. Compare the term in 1:14. It is not in any sense philosophic, so that the language of philosophy could define it. It is not an abstraction formed by operations of the intellect but divine and everlasting fact, which remains such whether men know it, acknowledge it, realize it or not. It is a unit: "the truth," although it consists of many united and unified parts. Thus also Jesus speaks of his "Word" and of his "words." It centers and circles about Jesus who, therefore, also calls himself "the Truth," 14:6. In his own person and his life Jesus embodies, incorporates the saving realities of God.

At once and in any measure that we realize the truth this follows as the next effect: "and the truth shall set you free," shall liberate, emancipate you. R. 872 calls this future punctiliar or effective. Yet we should not disconnect it from the preceding future tense, which R. acknowledges as constative. For by realizing we are set free; hence the more we realize, the more we are set free. The one action grows immediately out of the other. Any measure of inner penetration on the part of the truth produces a corresponding measure of freedom. Moreover, these results have already begun in the believers Jesus addresses; for to believe the word of Jesus ever so little means to realize the truth to that extent and to be set free correspondingly. Then, of course, to remain in the Word of Jesus, to be fixed and firm in that Word, means a realization and an emancipation fixed and firm accordingly.

This liberating effect implies that here "the truth" is viewed as an inward and spiritual power, one that

conquers an opposing, an enslaving power. The implication is also that only "the truth," or the Word of
Jesus, is able to crush that opposing power and to
set men free. Hence, all who bar out from their souls
this liberating power of necessity remain under the
enslaving power. The quick rejoinder of the unbelieving Jews prevents Jesus from adding what he
means by this enslaving power and by the bondage
from which "the truth" sets the believers free. Yet
the very implication that lies in ἀλήθεια as "reality"
reveals that the opposing power must be "the unreality," the power of spiritual lies, falsehoods, decep-
tions (all that in religion is not so), which fetter
and thus enslave the souls of men. A glorious prospect
is held out to the believing Jews by Jesus, one to
inspire them to ever greater faith in order to be free
from all delusion and spiritual bondage. Liberty!
Men have fought and died for it on the lower plane
of life; philosophers dream of it in the intellectual
life; Jesus assures it on the highest plane, that of
religion and the soul.

33) **They made answer against him, Seed of
Abraham are we and to no one have we been in
bondage ever. How dost thou say, You shall
become free men?** Instead of the regular dative
αὐτῷ (or the plural where required) John here writes
πρὸς αὐτόν, "against him," affording us this hint that
these objectors are the unbelieving Jews who again
seize on one certain expression (see v. 19, 22, 25) in
order to upset what Jesus is saying. See the discussion on v. 31. Those who assume that the believing
Jews here speak against Jesus must assume also (and
some actually do) that, believing in one instant, they
lose their faith in the next and in a moment become
more vicious than ever. One thing is beyond question,
we now hear the voice of open unbelief. Note the
passion displayed: haughty pride: "Seed of Abraham

are we!" etc.; open scorn in the emphatic σύ, as much as to say, "Thou, who art thou!?"; resentment in restating ἐλευθερώσει by ἐλεύθεροι γενήσεσθε, "you shall become free men." If the believing Jews could thus pass over into passionate unbelief because of one simple word of Jesus', he certainly made a mistake when he held out to them the sweet prospect of spiritual liberty. Had he here lost his power to see what is in men's hearts (2:25)?

Besser's paraphrase is good: "If the truth you speak of is good only for *slaves,* do not trouble us, *Abraham's seed,* with it! We are a freeborn, royal nation (Gen. 17:6, 7; 22:11) and acknowledge no one as our master save God. To him we belong as children (Deut. 14:1) and to no one else. This is the *truth* which makes us free!" The reply is headed by the emphatic, "Seed of Abraham are we!" This shuts out the notion that these Jews refer to political liberty, which also would contradict most flagrantly the facts of history, the domination of the Jews by the Babylonians, the Persians, the Seleucidae, and the Romans (these latter at this very time). It shuts out also the idea of social liberty, namely that in this nation Jews were not made slaves. "To no one have we been in bondage ever" asserts unbroken religious liberty for all Jews as God's own chosen people, compared with whom all Gentiles were slaves of idols. Talk of *them* becoming free men! These Jews understand correctly that Jesus is speaking of religious liberty, and what they hurl against him (πρὸς αὐτόν) is meant in that sense.

The name "Abraham" here broached runs on through the remainder of the conflict to the very end. It constitutes the acme of Jewish assurance and pride — does so to this day. The emphatic σύ gets its force from the feeling of outrage that Jesus should presume to say anything against *Abraham's* seed. Who art

"thou" to dare such a thing? In v. 48 these Jews disown Jesus as a son of Abraham by calling him a
Samaritan, the very antithesis of a child of Abraham.
What these Jews voice as Jews in the name "Abraham"
is found in all the sons of Adam, all of whom cling to
their unholy pride when the gospel comes to give them
true freedom.

34) Calm, quiet, direct, crushing is the simplicity
and the force of the answer of Jesus. **Jesus answered them, Amen, amen, I say to you, Everyone
who does sin is the slave of sin.** The double
"amen" is the seal of truth for what Jesus says (compare on the term 1:51); "I say to you" is the voice of
authority based on absolute knowledge and truth.
This preamble marks the weight of what follows. It
is in the nature of a moral axiom: "Everyone who
does sin is the slave of sin." The truth of the statement is self-evident. The article in ὁ ποιῶν is needed
to substantivize the characterizing present participle
and thus does not affect πᾶς as meaning "every." The
article in τὴν ἁμαρτίαν is generic, everything that is
rightly termed "sin." The man so characterized, who
does what is sin, obeys the dictates of sin, cannot
break away from them — he is beyond question a
slave of sin, in the spiritual soul-slavery of the worst
kind. This is true of men everywhere, at all times.
The effect of sinning is as certain as the mathematical
law that two and two make four. Jesus does not say
outright that all men are sinners and thus slaves of
sin, but his application to the Jews includes that
thought. "Doing sin" is to be taken in the widest
sense, doing it by thought, word, and act. Compare
II Pet. 2:19; Rom. 6:16. Even the pagans voice what
Jesus says about this slavery. Seneca declares that
no bondage is harder than that of the passions; Plato,
that liberty is the name of virtue, and bondage the
name of vice.

35) A second axiomatic statement follows and in a surprising way opens up what lies in the word "slave." **Now the slave does not remain in the house forever; the son remains forever.** To be sure, the status of the slave is such that he may be sold. He is in no sense a permanent part of the family. This again is undeniable. Not "the slave" but "the son" (both articles being generic) remains forever, namely by virtue of his relation and position as son and hence heir. Probably in order to avoid an incongruity the genitive τῆς ἁμαρτίας in v. 34 was dropped in some codices, so that the clause reads, "is a slave," and not, "is a slave of sin." The idea of the codices seems to be the avoidance of two masters, first "sin" as the master of this slave, and secondly he who is the head of "the house" together with "the son." But no father or head of the house is mentioned. Jesus is not narrating a parable in which all the figurative details have their place. The illustration turns only on the correlative points: slave and son, or, we may say, slavery and freedom. We really do not need the usual explanation that this slave, made such by the domination of sin, would thus be nothing but a foreign slave in the house whose head is God, thus having even less right in the house. The figure Jesus uses is without such complication; for what would a native slave of the house be? All that Jesus uses is the status of a slave and the status of the son. In the phrase εἰς τὸν αἰῶνα the noun αἰών denotes unlimited time and thus eternity, here with εἰς eternity *a parte post* (from now forward), C.-K. 93.

36) What Jesus means appears in the application which he makes of the figure. **If, therefore, the Son shall set you free, you shall be free men in reality.** The application retains the figure, now plainly joining it to the reality. Jesus goes back to his first utterance concerning those who are truly his disciples and are

set free from bondage. He even combines his own word "shall set free" (v. 32) with that of the Jews, "shall become free men" (v. 33), for which Jesus substitutes "shall be free men." What Jesus said regarding the truth in v. 32 he now predicates of himself. For the generic term "the son" (as opposed to "the slave") in v. 35 is now turned into the specific "the Son." This one and only Son is the embodiment of "the truth" and as such the great Liberator in his Father's house. For, not only are he and the Father one, but into his hands is laid the entire administration of the house by virtue of his redemptive and saving mission. For this reason also nothing concerning the Father needs to be provided for in the figurative terms.

Who is pictured by "the slave" is also plainly stated: "you," the unbelieving Jews. Note that the believing Jews were already set free, needing only to be fully established in their liberty. Thus Jesus vindicates his implication in v. 32 that the unbelieving Jews need emancipation from slavery and that, in fact, they are slaves, an allegation against which their ire rises. Yet fine as the figure is for the main point Jesus means to drive home, like so many other figures and illustrations taken from merely human relations, it falls short in picturing what Jesus does for those who believe in him. When Jesus sets us free, we, of course, are ἐλεύθεροι, "free men," and yet we are far more than the so-called freedmen (liberated slaves) in the old Roman Empire; we are ourselves turned into "sons," adopted into the household of God, children of the Father, joint heirs with Christ. Only the emphatic adverb ὄντως, "really," hints at this result of our emancipation by the Son. Perhaps also ἔσεσθε, "you shall be" (durative), is placed in contrast to γενήσεσθε, "you shall become" (punctiliar), used by the Jews.

Glancing back from the application in v. 36 to the figure used in the axiomatic statements in v. 34, 35, we see that already there part of the reality is interwoven with the figure. "Everyone that does sin" is non-figurative, and in "a slave of sin" "sin" is literal. Thus the figure about the "slave" only helps to bring out the axiomatic character of the statements. In v. 35 εἰς τὸν αἰῶνα, "forever," might be considered part of the figure, simply meaning that the slave does not remain "always," only the son remains "always" (compare the phrase in 13:8; Mark 11:14; I Cor. 8:13; etc.). And yet where figure and reality are combined, as is the case here, and where the fate of souls is the subject, we may well prefer to take "forever" in the literal sense. "One thing have I desired of the Lord, that I will seek after; that I may dwell in the house of the Lord all the days of my life, to behold the beauty of the Lord, and to inquire in his temple," Ps. 27:4. Again, "I will dwell in the house of the Lord *forever*," Ps. 23:6.

37) First, the point that these Jews do need liberation; now, the point that they are not "seed of Abraham." The two belong together: true seed of Abraham would, indeed, be free; these Jews are not such seed, hence they need to be set free and thus truly become Abraham's seed. **I know that you are seed of Abraham,** namely his physical descendants. No question about this point, and also the fact that it constitutes a great advantage to have a forefather like Abraham. Jesus is speaking of spiritual relationship, something that is on an altogether higher plane. Hence he lays his finger on the moral nature and character of this physical seed of Abraham: **but you are seeking to kill me because my word has not free course in you.** The question is: How does this agree with your being seed of Abraham and thus really free sons of God?

How can they as sons so treat the eternal Son? Compare 5:18; 7:19 and 25; also 8:59. With ἀλλά Jesus merely holds up the glaring contrast between the proud claim to be Abraham's seed and the criminal determination to kill Jesus, the Son. One would expect of the physical sons of Abraham that they more than all men would turn out to be also Abraham's spiritual sons and thus enter upon the spiritual inheritance of their great father. With these Jews the contrary is the case. Their real character they themselves reveal ("you seek to kill"). The gravity of what they thus reveal lies not merely in the fact that they are base enough to plot murder as such but to plot the murder of the very Son, whose day Abraham desired to see (v. 56), for whom Abraham was made what he was, to whom the Father committed his entire house (v. 36).

The reason why these Jews fell so far from their Abrahamitic descent and heritage is presented in negative form, "because my word has not free course in you." Moreover, it assigns a fact which does not stop at a halfway point but goes to the very root of their defection. With this reason Jesus also returns to the vital point which he had emphasized for those who had begun to believe him (v. 31, αὐτῷ, believe what he said), namely "my word." Those believers, he said, must remain in "my word"; of these unbelievers he says: "my word" finds no place in you. The negation is in the nature of a litotes. Not to have free course = to be barred out. In the believers the word, having entered, must remain; in these unbelievers it has found no entrance at all. The word of Jesus would make these Jews believers and thus true seed of Abraham. Instead of criminal designs against the Son the result would be loyal attachment to the Son. These slaves of sin would be turned into sons of the Father to abide with the Son forever. Thus

all that Jesus says from v. 31 onward turns on the
one point of his word. Note how much weightier
ὁ λόγος ὁ ἐμός, "this word of mine," is than ὁ λόγος μου,
"my word." The word χωρεῖ is not transitive, for then
we should have χωρεῖτε τὸν λόγον, "you make no room";
but intransitive and in the sense, "my word finds no
room in you." Every effort of that word to enter
leaves it outside.

38) The final statement is still about this word
(λαλῶ), now tracing it back to its ultimate source and
on this point placing it over against the ultimate
source of the word which controls the unbelieving
Jews. The text of the A. V. cannot be accepted.
**What things I myself have seen with the Father
I utter; and you, accordingly, what things you did
hear from your father you do.** It is hard to pronounce on all the minutiae of the readings, some of
which are altogether unimportant. The two statements are parallel but with marked differences in
detail. The main thought is that Jesus' word has one
source, and the actions of the Jews the very opposite
source. The two relative clauses are prominent,
being placed, as they are, ahead of the main verbs.
But the emphatic ἐγώ is placed in the first relative
clause, "I myself have seen," while the equally emphatic
ὑμεῖς precedes the second relative clause and forms the
subject of the main verb, "and you, . . . , you
do." Thus the pronouns are in contrast, yet each
has its own angle. Jesus was "with the Father" in
heaven (the pronoun in the relative clause); the corresponding statement would not be true of the Jews,
for they have not been with the devil in hell, their
father, (hence the pronoun outside of the relative
clause and with the main verb).

Jesus has seen the Father (properly with the
locative, παρά and the dative); the Jews have not seen
their father. He would not dare to show himself to

them. They only heard from him (properly the ablative, παρά and the genitive, R. 614). He whispered insidiously to their hearts, not showing his real self but masquerading, just as in Eden. Even the tenses add a point, the extensive perfect indicating the prolonged seeing and association of the Son with the Father while in heaven, the effect of which is still present with Jesus; on the other hand, the aorist stating only the fact: "you did hear from your father." In other connections, where no such contrast is intended, Jesus uses the simple aorist also regarding himself, "I did hear," in v. 26; the Father, "did teach" in v. 28. In the phrase "with the Father" we do not need the pronoun "my," which is added in some texts; for only one Father exists, he whose Son is Jesus; but in the corresponding phrase "from your father" the pronoun "your" is in place. Its omission in some texts has led to a decidedly different interpretation: "Do you also, therefore, the things which you did hear from the Father!" (R. V. margin.) This would be an admonition addressed to the unbelieving Jews to follow the example of Jesus. But the Jews heard something far different, as their objection shows, namely an intimation in regard to their father, that he was evil. "The things which you did hear from your father" includes their plot to kill Jesus and thus intimates other deeds of this kind.

Jesus says, "I utter" (λαλῶ), because he has been speaking of his word and on this visit to Jerusalem had confined himself to speaking and presenting testimony, doing no miracles. With his utterances of the divine truth he was conferring the greatest benefit upon the Jews. Yet for this they wanted to kill him. Regarding the Jews, however, he uses "you do," or "you perform" (ποιεῖτε), referring to their actions, including especially their efforts to kill him, these actions so openly marking their spiritual parentage.

39) Whom Jesus has in mind when he so pointedly says "your father" he does not yet state. One thing
is clear, namely that this is not the one whom he
calls his Father; yet this, too, is a father in the sense
that he confers a spiritual character that is like his
own, the opposite of that found in the heavenly
Father. Jesus thus strikes at the consciences of these
unbelieving Jews, seeking thus to convict them of
their sins. They are "in their sins" (v. 24), liable
to die in them; they are "doing sin" (v. 34) and thus
lie in slavery. It is thus that they are doing "the
things they did hear from their father," thereby betraying their real parentage. This explains their
reaction. **They answered and said to him** (the
doubling of the verbs indicating the weight they
put on their reply; see 1:48), **Our father is Abraham.** The observation is correct that by this reply
these Jews are not attempting to make Jesus speak
out more plainly in regard to whom he terms their
father. They had an inkling whom Jesus had in mind.
Their conscience was pricked. Therefore, to ward off
the sharp sting they assert the more strenuously that
they have no father, physically or spiritually, but
Abraham. Note that this reply is purely defensive,
and that all their previous replies are either altogether offensive or connect offense with defense.
Their next reply (v. 41) is also nothing but an effort
at defense; then comes vituperation, since defense
fails (v. 48), and after that the preliminaries to murderous violence (v. 52, 53; 57 and 59).

Jesus is succeeding. The first sharp stab at the
conscience is followed by a deeper thrust. **Jesus
says to them: If you really are Abraham's children
you would be doing the works of Abraham. But
now you are seeking to kill me, a man who has
been telling you the truth which he heard from
God. This Abraham did not do. You are doing the**

works of your father. Note the vivid aoristic present λέγει at this climax of the altercation and how it lends a special touch to the reply of Jesus, just as the double "answered and said" in v. 39 lends weight to the reply of the Jews. The first sentence uses a mixed condition, a protasis of reality and an apodosis of unreality (the imperfect with ἄν, although ἄν may be and often is omitted, as here). Mixed conditional sentences are perfectly in order (in all languages), according as the thought may require. Some texts have ἦτε for ἐστε (and even add ἄν), merely changing the form to an ordinary conditional sentence of present unreality: "If you were . . . . , you would." With ἐστε Jesus says: "If you, indeed, are, as you assert, children of Abraham, you would," etc. He here uses τέκνα not σπέρμα as in v. 37, with no difference in the sense. A generally admitted axiom underlies the statement, namely that children are like their father, disregarding the cases where abnormally a child differs from his parent.

40) In v. 39 Jesus really lays down the major premise of a negative syllogism. In v. 40, with the logical νῦν δέ, he lays down the minor premise. The conclusion of the syllogism is not stated. It is inevitable, left by Jesus for the Jews to draw for themselves, namely: *"Ergo,* you are not Abraham's children as you assert." This negative syllogism is irrefutable. Its effect is deadly for the claim of the Jews. It stamps their claim as a brazen lie. In stating the minor premise Jesus uses the specific act of the Jews, their seeking to kill him. This act as such could not serve as the minor premise. But the moment this one act is placed in its proper category and is viewed as marking that category, the minor premise is perfect. Therefore Jesus adds the simple apposition: You are seeking to kill me, "a man who has told you the truth which I heard from God," and sets over

against the action thus characterized and generalized the undeniable fact: "This Abraham did not do." When any man came to Abraham with the truth of God, Abraham did not try to kill him. This strong negative implies an equally strong positive: Abraham accepted that truth of God and the messenger who brought it to him.

This formulation of the minor premise lends terrific force to the entire syllogism by the simplicity with which the enormity of the crime of the Jews is indicated: trying to kill a man who brought them the truth of God! The greatest divine benefit — rewarded by the most dastardly human ingratitude! If the thing were not an actual fact, it would be utterly incredible. Just as the Jews, self-blinded and deaf to the truth Jesus brings them, know only the trick of fastening upon one certain word or expression of Jesus, perverting that into an objection to the truth, so later deniers of the Godhead of Christ fasten upon the word ἄνθρωπος here used by Jesus and try to prove by that that Jesus is not God. Indeed, Jesus is "a man," perfectly human, even "flesh" (1:14); but what a man? Why fasten upon "a man" and omit the relative clause, the final part of which repeats what Jesus constantly testifies to the Jews, for which also they first (5:18) resolved to kill him, that as God's Son he "did hear from God" and came down from God on his great mission. This divine Son is the "man" who here again testifies that he is God. Note that both λελάληκα and ἤκουσα are verbs in the first person: "I have told," "I have heard." In translation this "I" is lost in the first verb. What this "man" here says of himself applies to his person only. No other man heard directly in heaven from God and then came to tell what he thus heard.

41) But if Abraham is not the spiritual father of these Jews, then who is? To this point Jesus returns

by repeating with slight change the veiled statement
of v. 38. **You on your part** (ὑμεῖς, emphatic) **are doing the works of your** (ὑμῶν, correspondingly
emphatic) **father.** Now, however, it is clearer
what Jesus means, since he has instanced one of these
damnable works. Spiritually, then, these Jews can
claim only a father who approves and who impels to
such works.

The Jews are stung to the quick. The lash of the
law makes these sinners squirm and wince. That they
should, is just what Jesus intends, and we see that
he lays the whip on still more severely. Unless he
succeeds in crushing these hard hearts, the gospel
cannot enter them. Frantic under the veiled imputa-
tion of Jesus, they attempt no counterattack but only
hopeless defense. **They said to him, We, not of
fornication were we born   One father we have—
God!** The stress is on ἕνα, "one," followed by τὸν
Θεόν, "God." The battle is far away from the question
of physical fatherhood, abandoned already in v. 37; it
is altogether on spiritual descent. Driven from the
claim of being the spiritual children of Abraham by
the inexorable syllogism of Jesus in v. 39, 40, the Jews
now seek cover behind the passionate claim of their
supposedly impregnable standing in the theocracy of
God. For who can deny that they and they alone
properly belong in that theocracy — all other people
and nations are here shut out. God and God alone
has placed them there — he is thus their one spiritual
father.

The negation of this relation would thus be
γεννηθῆναι ἐκ πορνείας, to be born of fornication, in the
sense of having two fathers: one their real father,
who actually begot them; the other their apparent
father, in whose house they are merely tolerated.
Their real nature would be inherited from the former;
and only outwardly and nominally the second would

be deemed their father. Is this what Jesus suggests, that, while these Jews are outwardly in the theocratic house of God, they are really the product of (ἐκ) fornication, illigitimately carried into that house? They do not indicate directly, as little as Jesus had done, who this adulterous real father would be. That he could only be evil is the implication which makes these Jews so passionate. Thus ἕνα is opposed to δύο.

Usually, since the Old Testament so frequently pictures the defection of the Jewish nation from God, their running after idols in the time prior to the exile, as fornication and adultery and thus the idolatrous Jews as "the seed of the adulterer and the whore" (Isa. 57:3), this reference to πορνεία is taken to mean: born of *idolatrous* fornication. The emphatic ἡμεῖς is then regarded as referring to the present generation of the Jews in the sense: "we Jews now," we cannot be charged with idolatry, for since the days of the exile our nation has been practically free of this type of spiritual fornication. The difficulty regarding this view is the fact that Jesus in no way charges idolatry against these Jews and that he speaks only of one evil father (the devil) not of many such fathers (pagan idols or gods). To defend a point not attacked is senseless.

42) Again Jesus crushes this new vain defense of the Jews; this time not by a syllogism (although he might have put his reply in that form) but by applying the most simple axiomatic test. **Jesus said to them, If God were your father, you would love me; for I came forth and am come from God; for not of myself have I come, on the contrary, he did commission me.** The conditional sentence is the ordinary type of present unreality, εἰ with the imperfect, the imperfect with ἄν. The test is simple: true children of God would at once recognize the Son of God and in intelligent love (ἀγαπάω) would turn

toward him; it is impossible that such children should not recognize and embrace God's Son. Whereas in v. 40 Jesus speaks of himself as a man and adds the mark of divinity, here he does the reverse, stating what makes him divine (his coming forth from God) and adding the mark of his humanity ("I am come," i. e., am here). The verbs ἐξῆλθον and ἥκω are not a mere duplication; both verbs are also modified by ἐκ τοῦ Θεοῦ. "I came forth from God" = the Incarnation, God's Son became man (1:14). "I am come from God" = the mission, Jesus is standing here before these Jews, engaged in his mission, (ἥκω, present tense from a root with the meaning of the perfect, R. 881). Doubly these Jews would recognize and love Jesus if they were God's children: once as their relative, come from their God to them; again as their benefactor on his saving mission from God to them. His very person and his very work so mark Jesus as "from God" that any contact with him at once opens the hearts of God's true children. Not one of them could possibly fail in this test. To fail is to demonstrate that those who fail, however emphatically they assert their childhood, are not children at all but — liars. For the coming of Jesus from God the Greek may use ἐκ, παρά (16:27), or ἀπό (16:30), R. 579.

The fact that "I am come from God" refers to the mission of Jesus, which he is now executing before these Jews, is explained by the second γάρ which elucidates ἥκω: "for not from myself have I come," not thus am I here, carrying out a plan conceived only by myself; "on the contrary, *he* (ἐκεῖνος, God, emphatic, R. 708) did commission me" with a mission from *him.* Compare 7:17 and 28, 29; 8:28 and 42; 10:36; 11:42; 12:49; 14:10; 17:3 and 8. While the going forth from God and the mission of Jesus cannot be separated, since the latter is the one and only purpose of the former, the mission from God with all the truth it brings from God well deserves especial emphasis in the present connection. For, certainly, true children of God must at once recognize and love him who comes with God's own truth and blessings.

As an affinity with Abraham would automatically show itself in doing the corresponding works, so an affinity with God would automatically show itself in loving him who came out from God and is sent by God. The claim of the Jews perishes under this natural test.

43) So far are these Jews from receiving Jesus with intelligent love (ἀγαπᾶν) that he appears as a foreigner to them. **Why do you not understand my language, seeing that you are unable to hear my word?** "You are not able to hear" is a litotes for "you are deaf." They are deaf to τὸν λόγον τὸν ἐμόν, this "word of mine" (emphatic), i. e., *my* meaning, what *Jesus* has to say. These Jews are not deaf to what others say, that goes right into their ears, they "are able to hear" just what is meant. The ὅτι clause, "seeing that," just states a fact, a strange fact but a fact nonetheless. Jesus may present to them all the truth he pleases; these Jews "are unable to hear" a particle of it. The explanation lies in the first part of the question: they do not even *recognize* what "language" Jesus is speaking. The emphasis is on the verb; also λαλιάν and λόγον are distinct, the language used in speaking and the meaning that is put into that language. The very language of the divine truth is foreign to these Jews. The evidence that the language is foreign to them is their inability to hear what is put into that language. Jesus may as well talk to deaf men. These Jews indeed claim that thy are God's children; but when Jesus talks to them in the language of God and of God's house, they act like deaf persons, his meaning is lost upon them. That fact has only one explanation: they do not even

recognize the language, that it is that of God. That
proves that God is not their father. Children know
their father's language, it is their mother tongue.
These Jews belong to a foreign land, where a different
mother tongue is used. No need to say what land
that is.

The fact that ὅτι must be rendered as here indicated
is established by the use of this connective in 2:18;
7:35; 8:28; 9:2 and 17; 12:49; 14:10 and 22;
Matt. 8:27; Mark 4:41; Luke 4:36; 8:12; see the
grammatical explanations in B.-D. 456, 2; 480, 6;
R. calls this ὅτι consecutive, 1001. Yet the grammars
say nothing at all about our passage, although this
is the very passage most in dispute. Is it because
many translators and commentators take ὅτι to mean
"because"? This turns the passage into a question
which is followed by its answer: "Why do you not
understand my language? Because you cannot hear
my word!" But the answer is wrong. It ought to be,
"Because you have not learned that language!" Or
things ought to be reversed. "Why are you unable to
hear my word? (why are you deaf to my meaning?)
Because you do not understand my language!" To
escape the incongruity between the question and the
answer λαλιάν is translated "speech" instead of
language, and the emphasis on γινώσκετε is overlooked.
Yet even then little more than a tautology results.

The Jews had been deaf to all that Jesus had said
to them (his word, the truth). In view of this Jesus
asks whether they even *understand* his language. The
question is rhetorical; it answers itself.

44) Now comes the final crushing blow, striking
home in the conscience. The name of the spiritual
father of these Jews, withheld so long, is now hurled
straight into their faces: **You, of your father, the
devil, are you, and the lusts of your father it is your
will to do.** Note the emphatic subject ὑμεῖς. There

are children of God, but *you*, you unbelieving Jews,
are the devil's children. Of course, the devil did not
create these Jews while God created those people who
are his children by faith. The fact that moral and
spiritual relationship is referred to the clause with καί
places beyond question. The ἐπιθυμίαι of the devil are
the evil desires, lusts, and passions that fill the devil
himself and show that he is the devil. His children
are naturally inflamed with the same lusts; they get
or inherit them through their spiritual descent from
him. And yet, since the entire relationship with the
devil is moral and spiritual, these lusts of the devil
find place in his children only by their own consent
and will. Not unwillingly these Jews are what they
are. Nor are these lusts merely passive or latent in
their hearts. The devil's children always actually will
and go on willing (θέλετε) to do or to carry into
action (ποιεῖν) these lusts. The evil desire kindled
in the heart gives birth to the corresponding deed.
No evil deed is without this evil root. Thus the
deeds are prima facie proof first of the lusts, secondly
of the inward connection with the devil. With τοῦ
πατρός we need no ὑμῶν; the article alone suffices, and
really no more needs to be said. And τοῦ διαβόλου
is the appositional genitive. Among the inanities of
exegesis is the one which makes this genitive possessive: of the father "of the devil," turning the Jews
into brothers of the devil, and Jesus and John into
gnostics.

"The lusts of your father" is general, including all
of them. Two of them are outstanding, as the history
of the devil shows, and these two lusts reapppear
similarly in the devil's children. Thus Jesus specifies:
He, a manslayer was he from the beginning; and in
the truth he does not stand because truth is not in
him. When he speaks the lie, he speaks from what
is his own; because he is a liar and the father there-

of. Here is the historical moral portrait of the devil drawn by Jesus himself. The subject ἐκεῖνος is emphatic. Murder and lying are mentioned as the devil's lusts because they are that, as history shows, and because his children, the very Jews to whom Jesus is speaking, display these identical lusts. The historical reference in "manslayer" is not to the killing of Abel by Cain (I John 3:12), but, as "from the beginning" shows, to the first introduction of sin among men, by which death entered and slew our race (Rom. 5:12). "Manslayer" attributes to the devil far more than the physical murders that are committed by men; it charges him with bringing death in all its destructive power upon the whole of mankind.

Because lying was the means by which the devil murdered our race, lying is mentioned as the second lust. For the text we must rely on the text critics. Since οὐκ is at times written also before a rough breathing, it makes little difference whether we agree on οὐκ or write οὐχ before ἕστηκεν. B.-D. 73 and 91, 1 prefers to read ἕστηκεν, but also as the perfect of ἵστημι and he explains the smooth breathing in 14. So this, too, is only a difference in writing and in pronunciation. Hort makes ἕστηκεν the imperfect of στήκω, but R. 224 and 1219 leaves this idea wholly with Hort. While an imperfect would in a way match the preceding ἦν, yet no phrase such as ἀπ' ἀρχῆς accompanies the second verb; and the perfect of ἵστημι (whether written with a rough or with a smooth breathing) is always used as a present and certainly matches the following ἐστίν, which is also more closely connected with it than the preceding ἦν. Thus Jesus says, "and in the truth he does not stand." Why not? "Because truth is not in him." Since ἀλήθεια is an abstract noun, it may or may not have the article. Truth

and the devil are wholly foreign, in fact absolutely
antagonistic to each other. Take the sphere of truth
(ἐν τῇ ἀληθείᾳ) — the devil has no place in it anywhere.
Reverse this and take the devil — truth has no place
in him anywhere. The word "truth" is here objective
truth, since the truth and the devil are wholly separated; but also all that we conceive as subjective
truth is denied with reference to the devil by the
verbs used ("does not stand in," "is not in"); personally "he is a liar," etc. A wrong implication
should not be inferred from οὐκ ἔστηκεν, such as "does
not stand firm" (as though he does stand loosely in
the truth), or "does not stand permanently" (as
though he does stand temporarily in the truth). The
verb is absolute: "does not stand in any way."

The statements that follow have no connective
such as γάρ and do not mean to prove that such a
gulf exists between the truth and the devil. Their
purpose is much deeper. These statements reveal the
origin of untruth, falsehood, lies, and place that origin
in the devil. "When he speaks the lie he speaks from
what is his own," ἐκ τῶν ἰδίων. This does not mean
that he acquired or appropriated what is now "his
own," for it had no existence before him or apart
from him; "his own" is what he himself originated.
In this sense Jesus adds, "because he is a liar and
the father thereof" — a liar, not like others who
learned lying from him, but unlike others, the parent
of the lie itself. We find no difficulty in αὐτοῦ, which
goes back through ψεύστης to τὸ ψεῦδος, B.-D.282,2;R.683.
This pronoun is frequently construed without a close
antecedent, merely *ad sensum.* To think of "his (the
devil's) father" is untenable. To translate, "and his
(the liar's) father," is impossible, for this would make
him his own father since "liar" is the predicate of
"he (the devil) is." The devil is the father of the

lie; in this way he speaks "from what is his **own**" when he speaks the lie (for instance in Gen. 3:1-6; Job 1 and 2; Matt. 4:1-11).

Since ἡ ἀλήθεια denotes reality (that which is so), it exists by itself even apart from any created expression. Since τὸ ψεῦδος denotes unreality (that which only pretends to be so), it never exists by itself but only as some created mind may conceive it or give it expression. Hence "the lie" must go down before "the truth." The truth, however, is also the expression of the actual reality, as the lie is that of the pretended reality. Truth loves to express what it really is, the lie never dares to do that. The two are powers with no peace possible between them. Truth's power is eternal, because the reality cannot cease; the power of the lie is ephemeral, because its pretense is bound to be exposed. God himself is the essence of the truth; the lie is the devil's vain invention. To receive the truth is to connect with God; to yield to the lie is to be the child of the devil.

In the most decisive way Jesus here declares the existence, personality, character, and potency of the devil. Either these statements of his are "the truth," ἡ ἀλήθεια, or he himself is guilty of "the lie," τὸ ψεῦδος — no escape from this alternative is possible. To say that Jesus knew that no such being existed as he here describes, that his language is only an "accomodation" to the superstitious and false notions of his Jewish hearers, is to rob language itself of its meaning and to strip Jesus himself of his moral character. By making the devil the originator of sin the notion that evil is also an eternal principle is shut out. In the two types of evil made prominent as inhering in the devil Jesus recalls to the Jews the main chapters of Satan's activity among men as set forth in the Old Testament. Jesus has no occasion here to declare the fall of the devil. Those who think the devil's fall is implied in the tense of οὐκ ἔστηκεν misread the tense; it is a grammatical perfect but an actual present: "does not stand" in the truth. It describes the devil as he now is and says nothing about the fact that at his creation he was otherwise. The testimony regarding his fall is recorded elsewhere. How the devil could become the author of evil, or how evil first began or could begin in him, is one of the mysteries that are wholly impenetrable to the mind of man.

45) From the devil Jesus turns to the Jews, the devil's children. **But because I on my part declare the truth, you do not believe me** — proof positive that they are descendants of him who stands not in the truth, because the truth is not in him. Truth always demands faith; this is the very law of our concreated moral nature. To reject the truth because it is the truth is to turn devilish. These Jews, bent on doing the lusts of their father, the devil, trample truth under their feet. As sons of the father of lies their souls have an affinity only for lies; they believe only liars and lies (πιστεύετε, durative to express continuous conduct).

46) But this statement that Jesus "declares the truth" to these Jews must not be understood superficially as though he means only that what he tells them is true. This statement about Jesus declaring the truth is in direct contrast to what he has just said about the devil. As the devil's very nature is "the lie," so the very nature of Jesus is "the truth." When the devil opens his mouth (λαλεῖ), out flow "what are his own" — lies; when Jesus declares his thoughts (λέγω), these thoughts coming from *him* (emphatic ἐγὼ δέ) are the very expression of his being and his person — the truth. This is the connection for the dramatic and challenging question: **Who of you convicts me of sin?** *He* has convicted, is convicting *them* in the most crushing way with un-

answerable proof.   He has done this by bringing "the
truth" to bear upon them, the reality of what they
actually are.   He has specified, pointing to their murderous plot and to their open refusal to accept the
truth, irrefutable evidence of their filial connection
with the devil.   By doing all this Jesus furnishes to the
Jews equally irrefutable evidence that *he* is the very
opposite of them and of their father, the *devil*, — his
very nature is "the truth."   And what are these Jews
doing by way of reply?   Is even one of them convicting Jesus in any way whatever?   No, not one.   Are
these Jews then by their utter inability to convict Jesus
in any way not furnishing the strongest kind of
evidence as to the true character of Jesus?

To be sure, the challenging question of Jesus is
an incidental part of the truth with which he convicts
the Jews.   But not the small part which some consider it, as if all that Jesus challenges these Jews to
do is to convict him of the fact that any allegation he
is making against them is untrue, or that any allegation he is making concerning himself is false.   Then
the challenge would have to read, "Who of you convicts me of a lie?"   But Jesus uses ἁμαρτία, the generic
term for "sin."   He even omits the article, so that
we are compelled to understand "sin" in the broadest
sense of the word and not as restricted to some one sin
which may perhaps be suggested by the context.   The
effort to reduce ἁμαρτία to "fraud" or "mistake" in the
indictment of the Jews by Jesus is misspent.   "Sin"
means any and every kind of sin.   And ἐλέγχειν means
to convict by proof, to furnish genuine evidence of
guilt, not merely to accuse.   An accusation may be
false and lack grounds.   The Jews accused Jesus
violently enough, for instance at his trial, but altogether groundlessly.   Compare Trench, *Synonyms*,
1, 31, etc., on the word.   In a conviction it makes no
difference whether the person himself is convinced and

confesses his guilt or not. The Jews were convicted
by Jesus although they scorned to confess and would
not amend their ways. They stood convicted because
neither they nor anybody else could possibly show that
they were not guilty exactly as Jesus charged. Their
sole defense consisted in lies; thus that they were not
slaves (v. 33) when they were; that their spiritual
father is Abraham (v. 39) or is God (v. 41), neither
of which is true. So the challenge Jesus hurls at these
Jews defies them to bring proof of anything in him
that in any way is sin. Let them take the entire category of sin, on not a single point are they convicting
Jesus, yea, can they convict him.

Some look at this challenge only in so far as it is
addressed to the Jews: "who of you." This passage,
we are told, cannot be used as proof for the absolute
sinlessness of Jesus; for the inability of *the Jews* to
prove some sin in Jesus certainly would not establish
his entire freedom from sin. Many a criminal even,
to say nothing of a common sinner, cannot be convicted
by us simply because we lack the necessary evidence —
the crime or sin is hidden from us. So this defiance
of Jesus, challenging the Jews to prove sin against
him, we are told, is sufficient to establish only a relative
sinlessness for him not his absolute sinlessness. But
this view leaves out the main fact, namely that it is
Jesus who utters this challenge. Morally he would
convict himself of inner falseness if he knew of any
sin in himself and yet, counting on the ignorance of
these Jews regarding himself, defied them to point out
sin in himself. The fact that *Jesus* makes this challenge shuts out another mistake that is sometimes
made when it is granted that in him was "no consciousness of sin." Not to be conscious of sin is not by any
means to be sinless. Paul "knows nothing against
himself" and yet adds in all honesty, "I am not hereby
justified," I Cor. 4:4. With the same honesty David

prays, "Cleanse thou me from secret faults." The
case of *Jesus* is different, for not only does *his* consciousness reveal to him all that is in his moral being,
leaving no secret recess hidden from his inner eye, as
the very Son of God all possibility even of sin in any
sense of the word was shut out for him, and this he
knew with infallible knowledge.

The constant use which the church has made of this
word of Jesus as an assertion of absolute sinlessness
from his own lips is sound in every respect.

Since there is no sin in Jesus, everything that he
says is and must be pure truth and verity. The assertion in v. 45, that the Jews do not believe Jesus just
because he speaks the truth, is now turned into a
question to strike once more and still harder at the
callous conscience of the Jews, in order to crush them
in repentance or to convict their obduracy by reducing it to impotent silence. **If I say truth, why do
you not believe me?** The condition of reality implies that Jesus does say truth, never says anything
but truth. Jesus has already given us one answer.
Just because he presents truth, these Jews do not believe him. Their kinship with the devil is thus made
evident. These Jews never dared to assert or to prove
that what Jesus says is untrue. They do not spurn
what Jesus says because they think it is not really
true, or because they do not see that it is true. In
their case the reverse is the fact: they see and know
that what Jesus says is truth and for that very reason
spurn it. The fault is not in Jesus, that he did not
make the truth plain enough, that if he had done better in this regard, they would believe. The reverse
is the fact. Aside from the fact that Jesus did his
work of presenting the truth most perfectly, the more
these Jews were made to realize that they were face
to face with genuine truth, the more that truth stung
them to rid themselves of it at all hazard. That is

why the question of Jesus receives no answer. Any
true answer would resemble v. 45. An unreasonable
act cannot have a reasonable explanation. When
truth is rejected because it is truth, all that can be said
is that the act is the height of unreason, is vicious, and
stands self-condemned. Refusing to give this true
answer, these Jews are left dumb. On this silence
compare Matt. 22:12, also 21:27; and Luke 19:20-
22 for an attempted answer. Silence proves conviction.

47) The Jews dare not answer, hence Jesus answers for them. **He that is of God hears the utterances of God. For this reason you do not
hear because you are not of God.** The verb
ἀκούειν is used with reference to true inward hearing,
one which perceives and believes. Even the ῥήματα
of God, the expressions used for conveying the truth
of God, will thus be received as holy vessels filled
with holy contents by him who is of God, a true child
of his. Jesus employs a regular negative syllogism
(compare another in v. 30). Major premise: "He
who is of God hears God's words." Minor premise:
"You do not hear God's words." *Ergo*: "You are
not of God." The conclusion is deadly in its grip.
Here, then, is the real reason why these Jews refuse
to believe the truth which Jesus declares. They are
not of God and want nothing that comes from (ἐκ, out
of) God. Even the bitter truth Jesus now tells them
about themselves, doubly because of its bitterness, they
refuse. The more complete is their conviction.

This conviction Jesus executes by the calmest,
clearest, most deliberate and irrefutable line of reasoning — but one that presents nothing but the undeniable
realities themselves.

48) The boiling rage of the Jews breaks out in
vicious insults and vituperation — an open confession
of defeat in their war against the truth and at the

same time an involuntary and unconscious substantiation on their part of all that Jesus has said about them and their moral parentage. **The Jews answered and said to him** (1:48 for the use of the two verbs), **Say we not well, that thou art a Samaritan and hast a demon?** By the tense of λέγομεν these men convey the thought that they have right along been calling Jesus such names when speaking of him. They mean to say that by denying that they. are true children of Abraham and of God by calling them the devil's offspring, Jesus, though he is a Jew, speaks like a Samaritan, one of the hated race who would reciprocate with equal hate; and, though he is sane enough, he speaks like a demoniac, like one possessed of an evil spirit that uses Jesus' tongue to vilify these Jews, God's dear people. These vicious insults intend to wound most deeply.

49) With the calmness of complete mastery Jesus makes reply. **Jesus answered, I, I have not a demon; on the contrary, I am honoring my Father, and you, you are dishonoring me.** He simply puts in glaring contrast what *he* is doing and what *they* are doing; the pronouns are the pivots: ἐγώ . . . ὑμεῖς. This contrast speaks for itself. Jesus touches only the second epithet hurled at him, that of being possessed by a devil, because that is enough for the contrast he is bringing out between what he is doing and what they are doing. Moreover, while these Jews utterly despise the Samaritans, Jesus does not; but to be a demoniac would destroy the force of every word he has uttered. Even then Jesus denies the latter only in passing. For the emphatic ἐγώ is to be construed with τιμῶ, to match the emphatic ὑμεῖς with ἀτιμάζετε: "*I* am honoring, *you* are dishonoring." The implication is not, "*I* have no demon," meaning, "but *you* have." "Who, when he was reviled, reviled not again," I Pet. 2:23. The vicious outburst of the

Jews by which they dishonor him makes Jesus tell these slanderers what he on his part is doing, namely honoring his Father. Indeed, he honors his Father most highly when he proves that these vicious Jews are certainly not the Father's children and when he tells them just what they are. A tongue governed by a demon would never speak so.

By saying that they dishonor him Jesus means himself as he is engaged in honoring his Father. The dishonor heaped on Jesus thus falls also on his Father, 5:23. Here again the Jews show how certainly they are not this Father's children but the offspring of an entirely different being. The exclamation in 7:20 should not be paralleled with the slander that Jesus has a demon, for the former is mere incredulous surprise, while the latter is deliberate insult.

50) Jesus suffers the insult, he does not retaliate. **But I seek not my glory. There is one who seeks and judges.** Under this insult offered him Jesus commits himself to him that judges righteously, I Pet. 2:23. Again ἐγώ is emphatic. The matter of maintaining and vindicating the honor of Jesus is in other, proper hands. He uses δόξα, "glory," the highest form of honor, not merely τιμή (see τιμῶ and ἀτιμάζετε in v. 49). The person and the honor or glory of Jesus are not cheap, for men to abuse at will; even though Jesus makes no defense. A mighty Vindicator stands behind Jesus, whom he describes only most briefly. His name these Jews may tell themselves. He is the one "who seeks" the glory of Jesus, i. e., who sees to it that glory will be his. Most deeply is he concerned as the Father about his Son, as the Sender about the representative he has sent. He both seeks and he "judges." He justifies Jesus, who upholds his Father's honor; he condemns those who drag down his honor by reviling his Son and messenger.

51) **Amen, amen, I say to you** (see 1:51), **If anyone shall guard my word, death he shall not at all see forever.** This glorious gospel word, uttered with the assurance of verity and with the force of authority hard upon the stern words which convict these unbelieving Jews of sin, puzzles many of the commentators. Some assume that a pause occurred, after which Jesus begins anew; but John indicates no pause. Some think that Jesus turns from the unbelieving to the believing Jews and intends this word only for the latter. Those who think that the believers of v. 31 lose their faith in v. 33 and are called the devil's children in v. 44, also suppose that Jesus now desires to revive their faith. Still others think that Jesus here declares that his word, on account of which the Jews revile him, will be gloriously vindicated by the great Judge. Yet Jesus does not mention the Judge or any act of vindication by him in his great statement. What he does is to place the gospel beside the law, exactly as he does in v. 34-36. First he convicts of sin, then he opens the door of salvation from sin. In the wall of fire with which the law surrounds the sinner the gospel opens a wide gate of escape through faith in the Savior and his word. Never dare the law and the gospel be separated if their divinely intended result is to be achieved. In preaching either may come first; here law then gospel, but in 4:7-15 gospel then in 4:16-19 law. The two may also alternate as in v. 34-36 followed by 37-51 and further by v. 54-58 — three times law and gospel.

"If anyone" is universal and opens the door to all the sinners in the world. At the same time it is personal: each sinner must enter for himself. In the condition of expectancy (ἐάν with the subjunctive) Jesus sees that many will, indeed, guard his word and thus never see death. As in v. 32, it is *"my* word," or "*my own* word," (the possessive adjective added with the article) as against the word of anyone else. "*My* word" has this effect, mine alone. In substance "to guard" Jesus' word is the same as "to remain in" his word (v. 32). Both verbs are aorists denoting actual guarding and actual remaining in the word. Jesus loves the verb τηρεῖν, especially in connection with his word, his sayings, and his commandments (behests, ἐντολαί), 14:15-24; 15:10 and 20; 17:6. The picture in the verb is that of keeping an eye on the word, so that it is not tampered with but is kept inviolate. The English "to keep" has too much the suggestion of only retaining. Usually only two ideas are found in τηρεῖν, that of faith in the word, and that of obedience to the biddings of the word ("observe," Matt. 28:20). We should add a third, that of letting no one tamper with the word, guarding it against perversion.

He who thus guards Jesus' word, "death he shall not at all see forever." This again matches v. 32, "you shall truly be my disciples, know the truth, and the truth shall make you free." Save that v. 32 speaks of the proximate result (free from the bondage of sin), v. 51 of the ultimate result (eternal freedom from death). "Death" is made emphatic by position; οὐ μή, "not at all," is the strongest negation with a subjunctive (as here) or with a future, intensified in this case by "forever" and by the strong promise in the verb "shall see." So far and so completely shall he who guards Jesus' word be removed from death that he shall never even *see* it. Not to see death is the opposite of not to see the kingdom (3:3), the opposition being death and the kingdom. But "cannot see (ἰδεῖν) the kingdom" (explained by "cannot enter into the kingdom," 3:5) conveys the idea that the person in question shall not catch even a glimpse of that kingdom; while not to see (θεωρεῖν, to view) death conveys the thought that the person in question shall not view death as crushing and destroying him. He shall not view death by experiencing it, by partaking of it (Abbott-Smith, *Manual Greek Lexicon*). The negative thought here expressed is coupled with its positive counterpart in 5:24; see also 6:50. He who has the life (ζωή) which Jesus and his word bestow is free from death forever. Only by implication we gather that he who rejects Jesus' word shall, indeed, see death and see it forever. This negative fact Jesus here leaves unsaid. On εἰς τὸν αἰῶνα see v. 35.

52) Once more the Jews justify what Jesus says about them in v. 45, that just because he tells them the truth they do not believe him. Their one determination is to repudiate whatever he may say. **The Jews, therefore, said to him, Now we know that thou hast a demon. Abraham died, and the prophets; and thou sayest, If anyone shall guard my word he shall not at all taste of death forever.** In ἐγνώκαμεν we probably have an intensive perfect, R. 893, "know beyond a doubt," now after this last statement of Jesus'. No man in possession of his own sound mind would say a thing like this; a lying demon must rule his mind and his tongue.

The fact that Abraham died, as well as the prophets, the holiest people named in the Old Testament, brands as a lie this assertion of Jesus, that one who guards his word shall not experience death forever. The verbal change from "shall not see death" to "shall not taste of death" is unimportant, as both alike denote the experience of death, C.-K. 231. The latter is analogous to the rabbinical Hebrew and Aramaic and seems to refer to the bitterness of physical death, perhaps also to the more extended figure of drinking the cup of death. "Abraham died" is the commentary of the Jews themselves on their expression, "shall not at all taste of death." With superficial blindness they substitute physical death for eternal death and thus pervert the word of Jesus. This is the more inexcusable since he had often told them of eternal life, the opposite of the death of which he now speaks. The perversion may even be deliberate on the part of the Jews, an evidence of their wicked intention *not* to understand whatever he may say if it does not serve their purpose.

The attempt is made to deny this perversion, whether blind or deliberate, and to have the Jews and Jesus understand death in the same sense. The souls of Abraham and of the Old Testament saints, we are told, passed into the "realm of the dead"; in this way they "saw death," "died," "tasted of death." In this realm these souls remained until Jesus released them. To the New Testament saints Jesus promises a better fate: their souls shall not enter that dread realm. That is what Jesus means to say, what the Jews understand him to say and what they themselves have in mind. Their mistake, we are told, was only this that they considered Jesus a mere man and thus unable to give his believers what he promises. But this "realm of the dead," identified with the *sheol* of the Old Testament, is a fiction. The entire Bible knows of only two places in the hereafter, heaven and hell. Elijah was carried bodily into heaven; compare Gen. 5:24 on Enoch. Moses and Elijah appeared to Jesus and three of the disciples on the Mount of Transfiguration (Matt. 17:3). Did Moses come from "the realm of the dead"? And whence did Elijah come? Read Acts 2:25, etc., "that I should not be moved . . . my flesh also shall dwell in hope." And why? "Because thou wilt not leave my soul in hades," correctly rendered, "thou wilt not abandon my soul unto the house of hades," οὐκ ἐγκαταλείψεις τὴν ψυχήν μου εἰς ᾍδου (supply οἶκον).

David knows that at death his soul will not be abandoned to hades (*sheol*). Ps. 16:10. The supposition of two compartments in this hades realm of the dead, one for the damned, and one for the saints, found even in C.-K. 80 and based on a misinterpretation of Luke 16:22, etc., only embellishes this alleged realm and is as fictitious as the realm itself.

53) In the original deduction that, since Abraham and the prophets are dead, a devil must wag a man's tongue if he talks of preventing death by his word, lies a second deduction, namely that the man who talks thus must imagine himself greater than even Abraham or the prophets. This is like the deduction made by the Samaritan woman in 4:12. Yet hers led to faith while this leads the Jews to violence. **Certainly thou are not greater than our father Abraham, seeing that he died? and the prophets died. Whom art thou making thyself?** The interrogative word μή shows how certain the Jews feel of a negative answer; and ὅστις has causal force, R. 728. The break in the construction: "and the prophets died," ending the interrogative sentence with a declarative clause, is both natural and effective, R. 441. The only thing wrong about this second deduction is the assumption of the Jews that it cannot be drawn in fact but only in the imagination of Jesus. That Jesus is greater, infinitely greater, than Abraham or any mere man these Jews *will* not believe, no matter what the evidence. All the previous proof Jesus has given them in regard to his deity is non-existent for them. In the pointed question, "whom art thou making thyself?" lurks the threat that the questioners attempt to carry out in v. 59. A question such as, "Who art thou?" asked with a real desire to find out the truth, might lead to faith; but not the question they ask.

54) Jesus starts with the base insinuation that he is ascribing a fictitious glory to himself, but he proceeds not only to say who he is but also to prove that what he thus says is fact. **Jesus answered, If I shall glorify myself, my glory is nothing,** without reality, empty, talk — "I," apart from God, like a man vaunting himself. The aorist subjunctive refers to some certain act of self-glorification which Jesus may perform. What Jesus here says of himself would apply equally to any boaster. **It is my Father that glorifies me,** and the present participle ὁ δοξάζων με includes all that the Father does in glorifying Jesus, past, present, and future. Here Jesus declares who he is, the Son of his heavenly Father. This Son the Jews may dishonor, God not only honors but glorifies him.

The relative clause is masterly in the highest degree. It is directed against the Jews and their false claims of honor and at the same time defines just who the Father of Jesus is and who Jesus himself thus is: **of whom you assert that he is your God, and** (coordinating the very opposite) **you do not know him** (proving that your assertion is false). Here again (as in v. 52) the perfect ἐγνώκατε seems to be intensive (R. 893), "truly know," with the sense of the present intensified. These Jews had the fullest means of really knowing God, γινώσκω, through actual experience and the realization it brings, through the Old Testament revelation. The evidence, proving that these Jews are strangers to God, is furnished in v. 47; so here only the fact is repeated. These Jews claim the great honor of being the children of this the true God. They are the ones who are making the empty boast. This very God is the Father of Jesus, Jesus is his Son.

Hence Jesus adds: **but I do know him, and if I shall say that I do not know him, I shall be like you, a liar; on the contrary, I know him and I am guarding his word.** Three times Jesus here uses οἶδα in declaring that he "knows" God, in marked difference from γινώσκω, which he uses regarding the Jews; a difference lost for us in translation. The former fits intuitive knowledge, the latter knowledge gained by experience; thus the former reflects the very presence of the Son with the Father in heaven, and the latter the experience with God through his Word. When Jesus says, "I know the Father (οἶδα)," he means that he has been with him; when he tells the Jews, "You do not know him (οὐκ ἐγνώκατε) although you call him your God," he means that they do not realize who God really is although he has revealed himself to them through his Word. This negation does not imply that the Jews followed idols instead of the true God but that their conceptions of the true God are in conflict with the revelation God made of himself in his Word. They have only a caricature of God. C.-K. 388 adds another point: οἶδα indicates a relation of the object to the subject, γινώσκω a relation of the subject to the object. Thus in Matt. 25:12: οὐκ οἶδα ὑμᾶς, *you* have no relation to me of which I know; but in Matt. 7:23: οὐδέποτε ἔγνων ὑμᾶς, *I* have had no relation to you of which I know. Likewise here, "You do not know him (γινώσκω)" because *you* are not his children but only call yourselves so; while, "I know him (οἶδα)" because *I* bear a relation to him, *I* am his Son, and he is my Father. The knowledge here expressed by οἶδα includes also that expressed by γινώσκω, hence the latter type of knowledge is also claimed by Jesus for himself in 17:25.

In order to drive home this contrast between the Jews and himself and, if possible, to pierce their conscience, Jesus adds, "and if I shall say, (εἴπω, aorist subjunctive: in some statement) that I do not know him, I shall be like you, a liar." The condition with ἐάν in the protasis, followed by the future indicative in the apodosis, conceives the thought in a vivid and realistic manner. Jesus minces no words when he says, "like you, a liar," thus calling these Jews liars to their faces.   The vivid supposition would, indeed, make Jesus "like" these Jews. only in an opposite way: they claim to know God and yet do not; Jesus would claim not to know him and yet he does know him.

The repetition, "on the contrary (I am not a liar like you), I know him," is due to the evidential proof that is added by the coordinate clause, "and I am guarding his word." The contrasting comparison with the Jews is carried even to this vital point.   The Jews do not even "hear" God's word (v. 47), to say nothing of "guarding" it (v. 51). That proves who they are. Jesus meets this axiomatic test: he is guarding his Father's word. Here τηρῶ evidently means not only to hold to that word and to obey it but also to keep guard over it, to defend it against attack, and thus to keep it inviolate. Jesus here refers to his office as the great Witness and Prophet, but to defend and keep God's Word inviolate is the natural duty of every true child of God.

56) The charge of self-glorification is answered first, by the facts of Jesus' relation to the Father, and now, secondly, by the relation of Jesus to Abraham. **Abraham, your father, exulted to see my day; and he saw it and was glad.**   It is correct to say that "your father" here refers to the father of whom these Jews boast.   Also that in regard to Jesus this father acted very differently from these Jews who claim to be his children.   We must add that when Jesus said, "this (seeking to kill me) did not Abra-

ham," Jesus had in mind what he now says about
Abraham. But apart from these points, Jesus cannot say "our Father," for even physically Abraham is
not the father of Jesus in the same sense as he is the
father of the Jews. Invariably Jesus marks this difference in his human descent.

Two things are said of Abraham: he rejoiced that
he was to see (ἵνα, subfinal, purport, not purpose,
R. 993) ; then that he did see and was glad.   The first
is hope, the second realization. The object of both
is identical: τὴν ἡμέραν τὴν ἐμήν, "my own day." The
statement is evidently a *mashal* with a hidden meaning, like a riddle, which needs a key to solve it (like
2:19) ; for Abraham lived about 2,000 years before
Jesus came to earth.   The two words Abraham
"exulted" and "was glad" intend to fix our attention
on the central occurrence in the patriarch's life,
Gen. 17:17; 18:12-15; 21:6-8, all marked by
"laughter," even as Isaac's name itself means
"laughter."   The other two prominent verbs "to see"
and "saw" may intend to recall Gen. 22:14: "Je-
hovah-jireh," meaning, "In the mount of the Lord
it shall be seen." Moreover, it should be clear that
"to see the day" means "to live to see it" and
thus to behold the great event that distinguishes the
day referred to.

These observations put to rest the bizarre, un-
biblical notion that Abraham hopefully exulted during
his earthly life and then, when Jesus was born, in
some way saw this event in the fabled "realm of the
dead" (hades, *sheol*) and there was glad. Likewise
we must decline the view that Abraham "saw and was
glad" in paradise, "in the bosom of God," in heaven,
namely when the birth of Jesus finally occurred in
Bethlehem. Not only are all the aorists alike: "he
exulted to see," and "he saw and was glad," historical
aorists in the earthly life of Abraham, but also

"my own day" cannot mean "my own birthday," "seen" first in prophetic vision 2,000 years before its occurrence and then "seen" in some other supernatural way in hades, or in heaven, when it actually arrived here on earth. Abraham "rejoiced to see and saw" means: Abraham during this life.

Some seek the solution of Jesus' *mashal* in the typical nature of Isaac's birth. Accordingly, Abraham first rejoiced that he was to see, and then also he actually did see with joy in the birth of his son Isaac the future birth of God's Son Jesus. This sounds plausible yet proves unacceptable. Jesus does not in any way mention Isaac or hint at such a thing as type and antitype. He speaks only of Abraham and of two actions of Abraham, each of which is made decidedly emphatic by doubling the verb, and the exulting and being glad fixes the exact time in Abraham's life here meant. For the mysterious *mashal* in 2:19 Jesus gave the Jews no key; John gives it to his readers in 2:21, 22. Here Jesus furnishes the key, "Before Abraham came to be, I am." This key contains nothing of type and antitype. Such a thought would be wide of the point at issue, namely the greatness of Jesus' person as compared with Abraham.

With the key of Jesus in hand we can unlock the mystery. What caused Abraham to exult was the promise of the birth of Isaac as the son through whom the nations should be blessed. Abraham saw that son born and was glad. Then and there, in that event, Abraham saw with his own eyes what Jesus calls "my own day." Then and there the day of Jesus began. In that wonderful gift of Isaac the very person now speaking to the Jews began by an action of his a deed both astounding and infinitely blessed, his own saving manifestation. Promises had preceded, only promises. Here the first great fulfillment was wrought, a fulfillment that one could "see." It was as Jesus says, "my own day." Abraham, though a hundred years old, had lived "to see" it. He saw it and was glad. Was Jesus greater than Abraham? Is the incredulous question of the Jews comparing Jesus with Abraham answered?

57) The Jews ignore all that Jesus has told them about his divine sonship, about his having come from the Father, about having known the Father directly, etc., and regard his words as those of a mere man. **Thou hast not yet (lived) fifty years and hast thou seen Abraham?** The reading, "and has Abraham seen thee?" is discredited. We need not trouble about how old Jesus seemed to the Jews, or bother about the deductions based on the "fifty years," which are merely in contrast to the 2,000 years since Abraham lived. The question of the Jews rests on a correct conclusion, namely that if Abraham actually saw the day of Jesus, Jesus must have seen Abraham. Does Jesus actually mean to say that he is so old?

58) Not only does Jesus affirm what the question of the Jews asks, with the solemn formula of verity and authority he affirms vastly more. **Amen, amen, I say to you, before Abraham came to be, I am.** The aorist γενέσθαι (πρίν with the infinitive after a positive verb, R. 977, 1091) marks the historical point of time when Abraham came into existence as against the time prior to that point when Abraham did not exist. This aorist is in contrast to εἰμί; which Jesus predicates of his own person (ἐγώ), here a finite verb not the mere copula (R. 394). As the aorist sets a point of beginning for the existence of Abraham, so the present tense "I am" predicates absolute existence for the person of Jesus, with no point of beginning at all. That is why Jesus does not use the imperfect ἤμην, "I was"; for this would say only that the existence of the person of Jesus antedates the time of Abraham

and would leave open the question whether the person of Jesus also has a beginning like that of Abraham (only earlier) or not. What Jesus declares is that, although his earthly life covers less than fifty years, his existence as a person (ἐγώ) is constant and independent of any beginning in time as was that of Abraham. For what Jesus here says about himself in comparison with Abraham is in the nature of the case true of him in comparison with any other man, no matter how far back the beginning of that man's existence lies. "I am" = I exist. Thus with the simplest words Jesus testifies to the divine, eternal pre-existence of his person.

To speak of an "ideal" existence before the days of Abraham is to turn the solemn assurance of Jesus into a statement that means nothing. Unacceptable are also all other efforts to empty out this divine "I am" and to substitute for the fact and reality of existence before Abraham something merely mental, whether this occurred in the mind of Jesus or in that of God. Yet this "I am" is nothing new; by means of two tiny words it states only what Jesus has testified and continues to testify of himself in many other words in other connections. Thus, too, it forms the parting of the ways for faith and unbelief.

Yes, Jesus has seen Abraham — the deduction of the Jews is right in every respect, only it should go much farther.

59) As Jesus had made his meaning clear to the Jews in the first place, so also he did in this final word. They understand its full import, namely that, if the existence of the person of Jesus antedates that of Abraham in absolute continuation, he declares himself to be God. To them this is rank blasphemy. **They took up stones, therefore, in order to throw at him; but Jesus was hidden and went out of the Temple.**

The Jews, with what they deemed blasphemy ringing in their ears, proceed to carry out Lev. 24:13-16 upon Jesus, and this without formal legal proceedings but by an immediate act of popular justice. This haste and irregularity is the expression of the murderous hate in the hearts of these Jews, rushing now that they feel they have caught Jesus *in flagrante delicto* to make short work of it and to be rid of him once for all. The stoning mentioned by Josephus, *Ant.* 17, 9, 3, is of quite a different type.

Parts of the Temple were in the process of rebuilding during these and many following years, so that pieces of stone could be obtained for the deadly work. Yet a brief delay ensued as some of the Jews ran to the spot where the builders were at work and "took up" the stones. During this interval, we may take it, Jesus "was hidden." The form ἐκρύβη, a second aorist passive, might be read in a middle sense, "hid himself," since the Koine increased the number of these passive forms and used them in preference to the middle (R. 349). But here the passive sense is entirely in place (R. 807): Jesus "was hidden" from the Jews so that they could not reach him. We may suppose that he moved aside, and that his friends massed around him, and thus "he went out of the Temple." The addition found in later texts: "going through the midst of them, and so passed by" (A. V.), must be cancelled as a combination that was added from Luke 4:30 and John 9:1. This addition is also untrue in fact. For nothing miraculous took place in the escape of Jesus. "He was hidden" and "he went out" are two facts placed side by side, nor can we follow B.-D. 471, 3 in the suggestion that the second verb is used in place of a participle: "by going out he was hidden."

Inwardly and outwardly the tension between Jesus and the Jewish leaders increases and approaches the breaking point. The realism of John's narration is perfect — we see and hear just what was said and done. Always and at every point the antagonism of the leaders together with their followers is revealed as unjustified, unreasonable, due wholly to their own ungodliness. With ever greater clearness Jesus reveals to them both their own character and state and himself as the Son and Savior. He never temporizes, compromises, hesitates, or hides. He is absolutely fearless, and his victory is complete at every step. The Jews are driven from argument to vituperation and finally to desperate violence — their defeat is complete.

CHAPTER IX

VI. *Jesus Attests Himself by Healing a Blind Beggar, 9:1-12*

1) All that John reports from 7:14 onward transpired in the Temple, and these Temple scenes are now ended. "Jesus went up into the Temple and was teaching," 7:14, begins what 8:59 closes, "he went out of the Temple." For the remainder of his present stay in Jerusalem we hear no more about his appearing in the Temple. Not until his next visit to the city is the Temple again mentioned (10:21). Yet Jesus remains in Jerusalem. Soon after the altercations in the Temple he attests himself by a remarkable miracle. By this *deed* he shows himself as the Light of the world, who bestows the light of life, just as he had showed it before by his *Word* (8:12). Those who reject him remain in darkness. In this instance the Jews do not pounce upon the Sabbath desecration (5:16-18) but endeavor, though vainly, to discredit the miracle itself. This effort marks their progress in hostility and hardening. We see how the breach continues to widen as Jesus proceeds with his self-attestation.

And in passing by he saw a man blind from birth on. "And" (*καί*) merely "hooks" the new account to the one that precedes (R. 1180) and does not mean that Jesus saw the blind man on leaving the Temple. Moreover, this is the Sabbath (9:14), hardly the same day on which the Jews sought to stone him. Somewhere in the city, while walking along, Jesus came across the beggar blind "from birth on," a classical phrase found only here in the New Testament in place of the more Hebraistic "from his mother's womb on," Acts 3:2. "From birth on" is at once mentioned, because the question of the disciples turns on this point, and then also because the healing of such a case is astonishing in the highest degree. When Jesus saw the man he stopped, and very likely the beggar himself told that he had never seen during his life.

2) **And his disciples asked him saying, Rabbi, who did sin, this man or his parents, so that he was born blind?** Here for the first time in connection with this visit to Jerusalem John mentions the disciples (2:2). In the two chapters preceding this one their presence required no mention for what John records; but they must have been with Jesus all along, as they were closely attached to their Master, and a rabbi without disciples would have been unusual and not impressive in public teaching. The disciples are perplexed about this beggar's blindness. From the Old Testament the rabbis deduced that the sins of parents are punished in their children, yet the prophets said that each must bear his own sin. The disciples assume that a specific sin has been committed: "Who did sin?" ἥμαρτε, an aorist, to indicate a definite act of sin. They are at a loss in regard to the person who committed the sin. If the sufferer himself committed the sin, then, seeing that he has been blind from birth on, his punishment would antedate his sin. On the other hand, if the parents sinned and as a result had a child born blind, the worst part of the penalty for their sin would lie upon the poor child.

On "Rabbi" see 1:38. It seems needless for B.-D. 391, 5 to struggle against the idea that ἵνα expresses actual result. He even advocates a different reading in order to escape this finding. Here, beyond doubt, we have not merely contemplated but actual result: "so that he was born blind." See the confessions of J. H. Moulton and A. T. Robertson in R. 998, etc.

Even the A. V., "that he was," etc., while it is not decisive enough, is more correct than the R. V., "that he should be," etc. In noting the inroads that ἵνα has made on the infinitive we must accept the idea that it usurps the following uses and in this order: final, subfinal, consecutive (first contemplated, then also completed result).

3) **Jesus answered, Neither did this man sin nor his parents but in order that the works of God should be made manifest in him.** This, Jesus says, is not a case in which a specific sin either on the part of one or another person has produced a specific penalty. He corrects the general idea of the disciples to this extent that they must not consider every serious affliction the penalty for some equally marked and serious sin. At times this is the case (compare 5:14) but not always (compare Luke 13:1, etc.). Sin works out its painful and distressing results in many ways that are beyond our ability to trace. Jesus does not attempt enlightenment on this wide and intricate subject, either here or elsewhere. Instead, he opens up an entirely new view in connection with the particular case before him. The disciples are not in every case of suffering to look back to find a possible cause of sin but to look forward to the divine purpose which God may have in providentially permitting such suffering to come upon a person. To be sure, all suffering in this sinful world is the outcome of sin in some way or other, but this is only half of the story. The other half is that God governs even in this wide field, and in some instances we are able to trace his purpose, especially those of grace and mercy, in allowing certain afflictions to befall a man. Here, in the man born blind, we have a case of this kind.

The adversative ἀλλά is elliptical: "on the contrary, this man was born blind," etc. This time ἵνα is plainly final: "in order that," etc. For the aorist subjunctive φανερωθῇ indicates a future event: "the works of God should be made manifest"; and not like the aorist subjunctive in v. 2, γεννηθῇ, a past event: "was born." "The works of God" which Jesus has in mind are the ones now about to be wrought, not merely works of omnipotence over against human impotence, but blessed works of mercy and grace for the blind man's body and his soul. Moreover, these are to affect not only the blind man himself but are to shine out for many others to see. The verb "should be made manifest" implies that the works of God are so often hidden from general view; so this man's blindness is to serve God in making these works of his public before men.

4) **We must work the works of him who did send me while it is day: the night is coming when no one can work.** The reading ἡμᾶς δεῖ κτλ. is assured: "We" must work, etc., instead of ἐμέ: "I" must work, etc. Jesus thus includes his disciples: they, too, will have works of God to do. These "works of God" are wrought through agents, namely through Jesus and his disciples; yet they remain "God's" works. When they are now called "the works of him who did send me," we see that these are the works which comprise the mission of Jesus, for which he had appeared on earth. The share assigned to the apostles will appear after the resurrection of Jesus, on Pentecost. Here the reading is μέ and not ἡμᾶς: who did send "me." Invariably the distinctiveness of the sending of Jesus is adhered to: we have only one Redeemer. Always also the Father sent Jesus, and Jesus sends the apostles; a resemblance exists between the acts (καθώς, "as," John 20:21) but nothing more. Their sending is only an outgrowth of that received by Jesus, wholly subsidiary to his and nothing more. The idiom δεῖ is used to denote all forms of necessity, here according

to the context one that is involved in the Father's sending of Jesus. "To be working (present infinitive) the works," one by one as required, is to carry out the commission of the greater Sender of Jesus. And these works are "made manifest" (v. 3), displayed for men to see, when they are "worked," actually performed.

The emphasis is on the temporal clause, "while (ἕως, R. 976) it is day," for which reason also the thought of this clause is elaborated by pointing to the coming of the night when no one can work. The figure of the day which is terminated by the night must not be pressed beyond the point of comparison intended by Jesus, namely the time allotted to Jesus by the Father for accomplishing his mission. We may refer "the night is coming" to the death of Jesus, in harmony with his cry on the cross, "It is finished!" and with the word in his high-priestly prayer, "I glorified thee on the earth, having brought to a finish the work which thou hast given me to do," 17:4, etc. The figure is made general by the addition, "when no one can work," and thus includes also the apostles and the time allotted to them for their work. We must not bring in the work which Jesus does in his glorified state since his death, for this is of an altogether different type, a work which rests on the perfectly completed task performed here on earth. Moreover, Jesus combines his working with that of the apostles, and their work will cease at death with no continuation in an exalted form in heaven.

5) Returning from the reference to all the works he must be busy doing in his mission to the one work which is now in order upon this blind beggar, Jesus adds: **As long as I may be in the world I am a light of the world.** The use of ὅταν, which generally means "whenever" when it is construed with the subjunctive, is unusual. To say that it has the idea of

duration (R. 972) is hardly to the point. The ἐάν in the compound ὅταν rather points to the indefinite length of Jesus' stay in the world. He expects to stay for a time yet, but he withholds mention of how long this will be. In 8:12 he calls himself "the Light of the world" (subject and predicate being convertible, hence the article with this predicate), i. e., "the light absolutely and forever." Here he speaks only of the brief time that yet remains of his visible stay in the world of men. Hence the predicate is without the article: "a light." It merely states that while he remains as he now is he will shed light. As a light in a dark place he cannot but send forth the radiance of truth and grace. When he enters the glory of heaven and there shines as "the light of the world," that activity will rest on what he now does and will complete during his earthly mission.

6) At once suiting the act to the word, John reports: **Having said these things** in explanation of what he intended to do, for the beggar as well as for his disciples to hear, **he spat on the ground and made mud of the spittle and put the mud of it on the eyes and said to him, Go wash in the pool of Siloam (which [name] is interpreted, Sent).** The αὐτοῦ is to be construed with τὸν πηλόν and not with τοὺς ὀφθαλμούς. For the sake of the blind man Jesus here uses sign language. The only answer we know for the question as to why Jesus proceeded in this fashion (as also in Mark 7:33; 8:23) is that he knew best how to obtain his object. By placing the mud from his own spittle on the beggar's eyelids he lets him know that the healing power comes from Jesus. The beggar is not merely to wash off this mud, for which any place that had water would suffice, but to wash it off in the pool of Siloam, which word or name ὅ (neuter) signifies ἀπεσταλμένος, "the One Sent." For the beggar to act on this strange command with noth-

ing but an implied promise, requires some degree of
faith, which certainly also is intended to be aroused
by Jesus as in the analogous case of the ten lepers,
Luke 17:14. We may call these effects on the beggar psychological, if we will. Since the beggar is
to cooperate in the procedure of his healing by going and washing in that pool, it is ill-advised to
deny these effects on the score that they are psychological.

One is surprised at the strange ideas that have
been connected with this proceeding of Jesus. One is
that spittle was considered medicinal; but Jesus uses
mud. Another is that Jesus wished to create a delay
in order to let the crowd scatter; but no crowd is at
hand. Still another is that Jesus meant to give the
eyes time to develop sight, since this was a case where
the man was born blind; but what about the man born
with deformed limbs in Acts 3:2, etc.? Finally, we are
told that plastering the man's eyes with mud was
symbolical, adding an artificial to his natural blindness
by making him close his mud-plastered eyelids over
his sightless eyeballs. This is to symbolize that men,
who are by nature spiritually blind, are to be brought
to a realization of their sad spiritual condition.
Preachers thus often allegorize the miracles of Jesus,
because they have no other way of getting anything
out of them for their hearers. To turn simple facts,
infinitely weighty as facts, into pictures and allegory is illegitimate in preaching and even worse in
exegesis.

The indeclinable Hebrew name *Shiloach*, "Siloam,"
with its masculine genitive article τοῦ, is here translated by John for his Greek readers by the nominative
masculine perfect participle ὁ ἀπεσταλμένος, "the One
Sent," i. e., who, having been sent, has that character
and quality. This, of course, is not merely an interesting incidental philological remark that John inserts.

On the contrary, John here asks his readers to substitute "the One Sent" for "Siloam": "the pool of the
One Sent," the pool that belongs to him; for "of
Siloam" is the genitive of possession. Both the spring
and the pool it formed are called Siloam; but in the
combination "the pool of Siloam" the genitive must
denote the spring. In v. 11 the beggar repeats the
significant name, this time applying it to the pool.
What distinguishes this spring is the fact that it flows
from the Temple hill and forms its pool at the foot of
that hill. For this reason Isa. 8:6 uses Siloam and its
waters as a symbol of the blessings that flow from the
Temple; likewise, the water of Siloam was used in the
sacred rites of the Feast of Tabernacles as we have
seen in connection with 7:38. We must, therefore, say
that just as Jesus used the Temple as his own Father's
house, in which he has a Son's rights, so now he appropriates this Temple pool and its waters for his
sacred purposes. How the spring and the pool originally came to be called "Siloam" need not be inquired
into; they now became, indeed, the spring and the pool
of Jesus, the One Sent. They were appropriated by
him and used in his mission of making manifest the
works of God and thus sending out light in the world
(v. 3 and 5).

We cannot assume that Jesus selected this pool for
the beggar's washing without himself being conscious
of the meaning of its name. Too often he speaks of
his Sender and thus designates himself as the One
Sent. He never acts without the most comprehensive
insight. In this instance even the disciples may well
have caught the connection: "Wash in the pool of
Siloam — of the One sent." Even the beggar does
not afterward say merely, "Go wash!" but, "Go to
Siloam and wash!" To apply the name Siloam to the
beggar as being "the one sent" is beside the mark;
likewise, that the pool is another "one sent," com-

pleting the work of Jesus as also being "One Sent."
To think of some medicinal power in the water of this
pool that was great enough to give sight to a man
born blind is ridiculous. An elaborate allegory has
been attached to the name "Siloam." The pool is
Jesus. "Go to the pool!" means, "Go to Jesus!" The
open, sightless eyes are closed with mud to impress
the fact that man born blind by nature cannot see.
"Siloam," Jesus, gives man spiritual sight. Clay was
used because God's creative power used clay when he
made man in Eden. Into this allegorical structure is
mixed another figure, namely that the beggar's sight
pictures that Jesus is the world's light. Mud, water,
light — strange mixture! This entire structure is
shattered at the start when we see that only the name
"Siloam" means "the One Sent" in the phrase, "in the
pool of Siloam"; the pool itself might have had some
other name.

Briefly John reports: **He went away, therefore, and washed and came seeing.** "Therefore,"
οὖν, certainly excludes the notion that the beggar acted
on the word of Jesus as so many ignorant people do
who are ready to try any questionable means suggested
to them to remove some ailment. All that really
transpired in his heart, who can tell? Let us not forget that he heard what Jesus said to his disciples, that
the very presence and every word and action of Jesus
always make a deep impression, that he knew the name
of Jesus (v. 11). Possibly he had heard of some of
the miracles wrought by Jesus. The almighty power
of Jesus wrought the miracle the moment the man
washed in accord with the promise implied in the
command. The beggar merely "washed," i. e., dipped
up some water and washed the mud off his eyes. Because the use of εἰς with static verbs and verbs of
condition and being in the Koine has become known
only quite recently, the idea has long been entertained,

and some still hold it, that the beggar plunged into the pool because Jesus says: νίψαι εἰς; or in some other way the notion of "into" is retained. Jesus said, "Wash *in* the pool!" and here εἰς means nothing but "in."

8) Naturally the man went home. Jesus, too, had quietly gone on, and the beggar could not have found him. Arrived at home, great excitement ensued. **The neighbors, therefore, and they that formerly saw him that he was a beggar were saying, Is not this he that was sitting and begging? Some were saying, This is he; others were saying, No, but he is like him. He was saying, I am he.** The neighbors and others are here mentioned, because of what some of these do, namely take the beggar to the Pharisees (v. 13); we shall hear about the parents later. R. 866 makes the present participle οἱ θεωροῦντες gnomic (timeless), which is questionable; B.-D. 330 points to the adverb and to the following imperfect ἦν as turning the time of the present participle back into the past, which may suffice. Since the Greek has no imperfect participle but uses the present instead, why not apply that fact here as being the most natural explanation? All the verbs of saying are imperfects ἔλεγον, etc. When we are merely told that a statement was made, the aorist is used, εἶπεν, "he said"; but when we are to think of how the person was speaking (*Schilderung*), or when the statement of an indefinite number of persons is introduced, we have the imperfect, B.-D. 329.

The question with οὐχ shows great surprise. "Why this is the same man — incredible!" The two present participles describe the beggar as they know him, "the one sitting and begging," for which our idiom demands the past tense. On the article in the predicate see R. 768.

9) Some are sure of the man's identity, others find only a resemblance to him. The beggar himself openly and joyfully declares that he is, indeed, the man.

10) Naturally these people ask, **How then were thine eyes opened?** and the beggar narrates the story quite correctly.

11) The previous imperfects of the verbs of saying are now repeated with the simple aorist: **He answered: The man that is called Jesus made clay and anointed my eyes and said to me, Go to Siloam and wash. Having gone away, therefore, and having washed, I got to see.** We see that Jesus was a stranger to the beggar, who had heard only his benefactor's name. Too much is read into ὁ ἄνθρωπος when this is thought to mean "the well-known man." The variation in quoting the command of Jesus is insignificant and negligible. The Greek would subordinate the subsidiary actions of going and of washing by using two aorist participles and employing a finite verb only for the main action. The English would not make the distinction, saying, "So I went away and washed and got my sight." The aorist ἀνέβλεψα is ingressive, "I recovered my sight" (ἀνά, after having lost it at my birth).

12) To the further question: **Where is he?** he is able to reply only: **I do not know,** this evidently also being the reason why he had gone home.

VII. *Jesus' Attestation Through the Beggar Nonpluses his Opponents, 13-34*

13) John devotes considerable space to the story of this beggar, whose name he withholds. In chapter five only the alleged breach of the Sabbath is charged against Jesus; here this breach is repeated, yet the Pharisees make no issue of that point but endeavor

to discredit the miracle itself. This marks the advance in their wilful blindness. In chapters seven and eight Jesus shines as the Light of the world by the testimony of his word against which the Jews deliberately close their eyes. Now Jesus shines as the Light by an astonishing miraculous deed. By this deed he "makes manifest the works of God" (v. 3). It is only incidental that this deed consists in the opening of the eyes of a blind beggar. Hence we should not carry allegory into the miracle. The final words of Jesus on spiritual sight and blindness in v. 39-41, are suggested by the restoration of physical sight to the beggar, yet constitute no allegory. The words are literal and matter-of-fact and, in fact, go far beyond any allegory that might be drawn from the blindness of the beggar and the miraculous gift of sight to him.

No connective joins this account to the preceding, which indicates a lapse of time. **They bring him to the Pharisees, him once blind.** Possibly several days elapsed. We must note that ἄγουσιν has no subject. It is rather hasty to conclude that the neighbors and others who used to see the blind man begging constitute the subject. Why should they bring the blind man to the Pharisees? To answer, because their opinions were divided, and because they thus sought an authoritative decision, is conjecture; for the only difference in opinion was as to whether this was really the blind beggar or only somebody who looked like him, who had never been blind at all and was posing as the beggar. This question the beggar himself settled from the start, and if any doubt were yet possible, the man's parents had certainly removed that. Moreover, the man's identity is not at all the question brought before the Pharisees. In their investigation no such question is even touched. The effort to read something hostile into the question of v. 12, "Where is he?" is also unwarranted. John records this question and its simple answer only to prepare for the next meeting of Jesus with the beggar, v. 35, etc. We are also to see how this insignificant beggar, who had come into contact with Jesus but once in his life, stood up before the Pharisees and defended his benefactor most manfully. The account would lose an illuminating point if John had not written verse 12.

This subjectless ἄγουσιν is like the German *man brachte ihn* — somebody or other did this. The most probable view is that one or the other of the Pharisees had heard about this beggar and had the case brought to the attention of others of his party. Thus we find a gathering of "the Pharisees." They came together in some convenient place in order to look into this case. Some commentators speak only of a meeting of the Pharisees for some unknown purpose or other. They met in order to investigate this case. This accounts for ἄγουσιν — being too important for any of their standing to go after a mere beggar, they have somebody else bring him before them. During the whole proceeding with the man we hear of no neighbors or others who ask to have any question settled for them by the Pharisees. These Pharisees are the only ones who show concern, and even they do not know just what they want; for presently they themselves are divided. These Pharisees do not act as a regular court, either as belonging to the Sanhedrin, or as one of the two lesser courts in Jerusalem, each constituted of twenty-three members, or as rulers of a local synagogue. They act only as an incidental gathering of men of the influential Jewish party, just Pharisees who are bent on making their superior influence felt.

14) **Now it was a Sabbath on the day when Jesus made the mud and opened his eyes.** John does not write γάρ, "for," as though this were a

charge brought forward by somebody or the reason
why the Pharisees called in the beggar; he writes δέ,
marking this statement as parenthetical, a point he
wants us to note so that we may understand what
follows.   On the phrase ἐν ᾗ ἡμέρᾳ, literally, "on what
day," for "on the day on which," see R. 718 "incor-
poration."   To make mud on the Sabbath the Pharisees regarded as a forbidden work; to heal the sick
likewise, except in extreme cases, and this case they
would not consider extreme — it could wait until
Sunday.

15)   **Again, therefore, the Pharisees were also
asking him how he got his sight,** just as the people
about the beggar's home did in v. 10.   The imperfect ἠρώτων is like those used in v. 8, etc.   Due,
no doubt, to caution the beggar makes his answer
brief.   **And he said to them, Mud he put upon my
eyes, and I washed, and I see.**   Note the present
tense: "and I see."

16)   **Some, therefore, of the Pharisees were saying, This man is not from God because he guards
not the Sabbath.   But others were saying, How can
a man (that is) an open sinner do such signs?   And
there was a division among them.**   The imperfects
permit us to view the scene: Pharisees against Pharisees.   The conclusion of the first group is certainly
correct: one sent and commissioned by God (παρὰ
Θεοῦ, from his side) would certainly guard (τηρεῖ, as in
8:52) and observe the Sabbath law in his conduct;
but God never ordained the Sabbath traditions set
up by the Pharisees and regarded by them as more
sacred than the divine law itself.   The argument of
the second group is equally to the point.   A man who
is a ἁμαρτωλός, "an open sinner" in the sight of God
such as a breaker of the Sabbath would be, could not
possibly do such signs as this one wrought upon the
blind beggar.   In the ancient epitaphs found in Asia

Minor ἁμαρτωλός is used like ἐπάρατος, "cursed," and
ἔνοχος, "guilty," "let him be a sinner before the sub-
terranean gods," to be treated as one accursed by the
gods, Deissmann, *Light from the Ancient East,* 115;
sceleste, 322, 3.   The first group of the Pharisees thus
questions the reality of the miracle.   By saying that
this man who does not observe the Sabbath is not from
God, they mean that Jesus could not have wrought a
miracle — there must be something phony about the
case.   This the second group contradicts, accepting the
reality of the miracle — and let us note — of others
like it in spite of the alleged Sabbath violation, for
which they have no satisfactory explanation.   The
conclusion of neither group is decisive; neither one is
able fully to prove its contention.   What is suspicious
about the case?   How can the Sabbath violation be
denied?   So the division remained.

17)   Both groups are helpless to break the dead-
lock.   They know of nothing else to do but once more
to turn to the beggar.   **They say, therefore, to the
blind man again, What dost thou say concerning
him, seeing that he opened thine eyes?**   It sounds
significant for John to designate the beggar as "the
blind man" in a connection like this — these Pharisees,
who considered themselves so far removed from blindness, asking the verdict of a blind man!   There is no
need to refer λέγουσιν only to one or to the other of
the two groups indicated in v. 16.   Both are helplessly
battling with a difficulty, and so they ask the beggar
"again."   There is no need also to inquire what they
hoped to obtain from the beggar by asking him again
— they themselves probably had no clear idea.   As in
2:18, we regard ὅτι as elliptical: this we ask "since,"
or "seeing that," etc.   We must not regard "seeing
that he opened thine eyes" as an admission on the
part of the Pharisees that Jesus had actually done this
— John himself cautions us against that.   This clause

is spoken from the standpoint of the beggar and merely
repeats his testimony.

And he said, He is a prophet. It certainly took
courage to give this answer before these authoritative
persons. Here we begin to admire the man. He
might have hidden his conviction by saying, "I do not
know." He is honest and confesses. That Jesus must
be classed as a prophet of God was beyond question
to him.

18) Now that the Pharisees had the plain verdict
of the beggar, they refuse to accept it and revert to
their suspicion of some kind of a collusion between
the beggar and Jesus. Their minds cannot let go of
the thought that something must be crooked about
this apparent miracle. Someone among them hit
upon the bright idea of questioning the man's parents.
This might not at all be their blind son, or they may
know what is back of the affair. So John informs us:
The Jews, therefore, in spite of the beggar's verdict, **did not believe concerning him that he was
(formerly) blind and received his sight** (as he had
testified) **until they called the parents of him that
received his sight and asked them, etc.** John now
writes "the Jews" instead of "the Pharisees," but only
to bring out the hostility of these men. So often in
this Gospel "the Jews" has this implication. On the
tenses ἦν and ἀνέβλεψεν see R. 1029; we should write
pluperfects: "had been blind," "had received his
sight." Also ἕως ὅτου is merely a set phrase, R. 291.
Not that the Jews believed the fact of the miracle
after questioning the parents; for they got nothing
whatever from them, and "until" never itself implies
that the reverse follows afterward.

19) So the parents are brought in, and after the
beggar had been ordered out of the room, the Jews
**asked them, saying, Is this your son, of whom you
yourselves say that he was born blind? How, then,**

does he now see? The point of the first question lies in ὑμεῖς (emphatic) λέγετε. The couple might, indeed, say that this is not at all their son; but for such testimony the Jews have little hope. Hence the stress on the other point: does this couple really mean to say that this son of theirs, if he is their son, was actually born blind? And if this too is true, then the most important point of all: How in the world does he now see?

20) The parents answer each point in turn.. They are most excellent witnesses, for they testify only to what they know at firsthand. John, too, introduces their testimony with two finite verbs (see 1:48). **His parents, therefore, answered and said, We know that this is our son and that he was born blind.**

21) On the third and vital point they are more explicit, for they answer with a double statement and even add a piece of pertinent advice. **But how he now sees we do not know; or who opened his eyes we ourselves do not know.** Note the emphatic ἡμεῖς, "we ourselves," in the second statement. They know no more than these Jews or anyone else. What they have *heard*, the Jews and others have likewise heard. So they add what is certainly to the point if these self-constituted judges desire firsthand testimony: **Ask him; he has age** (is a grown man); **he himself shall speak for himself.** To be sure, that is the only correct and sensible thing to do.

22) The carefulness of the parents in assuming no responsibility of any kind before these Pharisees is explained by John. **These things his parents said because they were fearing the Jews; for already the Jews had agreed that if anyone should confess him as Christ, he should be one banned.** To such a pitch the hatred of the Jews, namely the party of the Pharisees, had already risen that by a general agreement among themselves they had determined on

the severest Jewish measures against possible believers in Jesus who should dare to confess him as "Christ," the promised Messiah. These stern measures were to act as a deterrent. The Pharisees were numerous and powerful enough to carry out their threat. Subfinal ἵνα introduces the substance of the agreement; and ἐάν reads as though the Jews expected such cases to occur. John has two accusatives with ὁμολογεῖν, the second being predicative to the first, R. 480.

To become or to be made an ἀποσυνάγωγος does not refer to one who does not dare to enter a synagogue but to one who is expelled from the religious communion of Israel, cut off from all its blessings, hopes, and promises, like a pagan or Gentile. We have no assurance that the later double ban was known in the times of Jesus, a minor ban lasting for thirty, sixty, or ninety days, and a major ban for all time. The New Testament references read as though the expulsion was permanent. Grave civil and social disabilities were as a matter of course connected with the ban. The *aposynagogos* would be treated as an apostate who was accursed, under the *cherem* or ban. No wonder these parents were careful of their words. When they refer the Pharisees to their son they seem to have known that he would be able to take care of himself; at least, he here shows that he can do so.

23) **On this account his parents said, He has age,** is a grown man; **ask him.** They have no fears for their son. Thus John points out why they added just these words.

24) Having gained nothing by their second effort and being without any other prospect of success, the Pharisees would like to close the case. **So for a second time they called the man that was blind and said to him, Give glory to God: we ourselves know that this man is an open sinner.** In all due form as before a court of law the beggar is again

brought in.   Expectantly he faces these Jews who pose
as a court, wondering what they had extracted from
his parents.   It is John who calls him "the man that
was blind" (we should say, "had been blind").   The
investigation has ended, the verdict is now handed
out, and, though it deals with Jesus, is addressed to
the beggar.   One of the Jews acted as spokesman.
"Give glory to God" is an adjuration (compare Josh.
7:19; I Sam. 6:5) to seal as the truth before God
the summary of the whole matter at which these
Pharisees have arrived and to which they demand
that the beggar should solemnly assent by himself
assuming the adjuration plus the finding to which it
is attached.   The A. V. has, "Give God the praise,"
which is generally understood to mean, "Give the
credit for your healing to God not to Jesus."   But
this is incorrect.   In their verdict the Pharisees admit
nothing about the healing; they do not even say that
God wrought it; they ignore it altogether.   What they
say is this: "Give glory to God by now telling the
truth, and this is the truth, which *we* now positively
know — and *we* are the people to know, ἡμεῖς — that
this man is an open sinner, ἁμαρτωλός (as in v. 16)."
They imply that they have sounded this thing thoroughly, that besides the man's testimony they have heard
that of others, and the only correct conclusion of the
whole case is what they now state.   They count on
their superior authority to effect submission on the
part of the beggar.   Many others have put forth the
same kind of authority and often enough have found
submission.

It seems that the second group mentioned in v. 16
yielded their opinion.   The reference to Jesus is derogatory throughout, as here "this man," never deigning
to mention so much as his name.

25)   But this beggar is a steady disappointment
and a growing surprise to the Pharisees.   Trench calls

him ready-witted, genial, and brave. Really he is far
more: honest, grateful, and entirely sincere — and
this especially differentiates him from his judges. Not
for one moment does he accept their finding as true.
The fatal flaw in that finding is the omission of his
healing. Instead of uttering the truth regarding that
and a true conclusion based on it concerning the
healer, it leaves out the healing altogether and from
some other premises draws a conclusion that is
wholly false. **He on his part** (ἐκεῖνος, emphatic subject), **therefore, answered, Whether he is an open
sinner, I do not know; one thing I do know, that
being blind, I now see.** Over against the emphatic
we know of the Pharisees this beggar puts his own
emphatic *I do know*; and in the clash the beggar
wins because his knowledge is real, that of the Pharisees pretended. There he stands with his bright,
shining eyes, looking right at the Pharisees. Can they
not see those eyes of his? Here, right before them,
just as Jesus said (v. 3) "the works of God are made
manifest." But these men deliberately stultify themselves: they will not see what so magnificently challenges their sight.

An indirect question is introduced by εἰ, "whether."
The action of the present participle ὤν is thrown into
the past by the adverb "now" and becomes, as R. 892,
1115 says, a sort of imperfect particle. By their
foolish proceeding these Pharisees start this beggar
toward doing his own simple, straightforward thinking and toward drawing his own truthful conclusions.
By trying to oppose the truth they only help to further
the cause of truth. It is often thus. When the beggar says that he does not know whether Jesus is an
open sinner he means that he has no knowledge on
this point, so that he can testify as to that. In a
moment we find him saying far more. We actually
see him growing in courage and in conviction. "One

thing" he "does know" and again testifies: once
blind, he now sees. Facts are facts. And this one
is so patent that the Pharisees themselves dare not
deny it.

26)   The verdict, with which these judges seek to
end the case, is smashed. They are back where they
were before and as utterly helpless; their state is even
worse. All they know is to ask the old questions over
again. **They, therefore,** not knowing what else to
say, **said to him** (whereas he had replied, they only
said), **What did he to thee? how did he open thine
eyes?** Are they parleying for time? Attempting
to sit as judges, they have plainly lost their hold.
Already they are admitting what they are determined not to admit, that Jesus opened this beggar's eyes.

27)   The man takes full advantage of their predicament and of the weak questions they put to him.
He answered them, and his answer was an answer.
**I told you already, and you did not hear. Why do
you want to hear again? You, too, certainly do
not want to become his disciples?** This is a telling
thrust. The helplessness of the Pharisees emboldens
the beggar. Instead of allowing himself to be put
on the defensive by having to go over the story of
his healing again before these men, whose only purpose is to catch him up in some way, he puts them
on the defensive. The tables are being turned. They,
the judges, thought to question him, the defendant; he
now becomes the judge and probes them as defend-
ants with telling questions. God helps his own in the
tests to which they are put for Jesus' sake.

"I told you already" means that they already have
the truth. "And you did not hear" means that they
did not believe that truth. If, then, they did not
believe it the first time, why do they want to hear
("be hearing," present tense) it again? Judicial

reason there can be none. Is there perhaps another
reason? Two might suggest themselves. The one
would compromise these judges badly, namely that
they are trying to upset and confound that truth. To
the honest mind of this beggar this answer does not
appeal; at least he does not voice it. He takes the
other, namely that after all these Pharisees, impressed by beholding the eyes which Jesus had opened,
would also like to become his disciples. With μή
the beggar suggests that he can hardly think this
possible but — strange things happen. He is hardly
making only an artful thrust at the Pharisees; his
artless simplicity leads him to entertain the thought
that possibly these men are willing to change their
minds about Jesus. The suggestion about becoming
disciples of Jesus is something like an invitation to
join the beggar in this; for καί, "you, too," intimates
that he is ready to be such a disciple. Alas, their will
(θέλετε) is absolutely contrary.

28) **And they reviled him and said, Thou art
that fellow's disciple; but we are disciples of Moses.
We know that God has spoken to Moses; but as
for this fellow, we do not know whence he is.** To
revile is all that is left the Pharisees — a sign of
complete bankruptcy. They caught the force of καί
in the second question of v. 27 and charge the beggar
with being a disciple of Jesus. The genitive "of this
fellow," ἐκείνου, is highly derogatory. *Hoc vocabulo
removent Jesum a sese,* Bengel. By calling the beggar
Jesus' disciple these Pharisees imagine that they are
reviling and heaping shame and insult upon him;
in reality they could offer no higher testimonial of
honor and praise to him. With an emphatic ἡμεῖς
they place themselves over against the beggar with
the proud and lofty assertion, *"We — we are the
disciples of Moses!"* Here they pronounce sentence
upon themselves, and out of their own mouth the

Lord will judge them at the last day. Moses himself, on whom they set their hope, will accuse them,
5:45. There is, indeed, a difference between Moses
and Jesus; for "the law was given by Moses, but
grace and truth came by Jesus Christ," 1:17. But
all that Moses wrote he wrote concerning Jesus, 5:46;
even the law, of which he was the mediator, was to
be for us a παιδαγωγός, a boy's slave-conductor, to lead
us to Christ. These Pharisees were the disciples of a
fictitious Moses, whom they had invented for themselves, and who did not exist.

29) And now they imitate the beggar's own
words, "I do not know — I do know" (v. 25), but they
reverse the two, *"We* — we know (emphatic ἡμεῖς) —
we do not know." In the first assertion, *"We* know!"
speaks the voice of arrogant authority, seconded by
the other assertion, "We do not know!" spoken with
the same authority. What *we* know, that alone counts;
what we do not know, regarding that nobody dares to
pronounce. And knowledge is our personal prerogative; whoever does not bow to us and our knowledge
knows nothing, and whoever presumes to know anything we do not know is a fool. Even to this day the
skeptic, the agnostic, and a certain type of scientist
take the same attitude. It pretends to intellectuality,
but at bottom the intellect is made to voice only the
attitude of an ungodly heart.

These Pharisees claim that they know "that God
has spoken to Moses," for instance in Exod. 3:2-4 and
in other cases. They lack only the essential thing, a
knowledge of what God really said to Moses ("he
wrote of me," 5:46; the Scriptures "testify of me,"
5:39). Many even know much about the Scriptures,
and yet their knowledge is empty of the real substance. This the Pharisees themselves declare when
they add, "but as for this fellow, we do not know
whence he is." The scornful accusative τοῦτον, while

it is the object of the verb, is placed forward, almost as if it were independent; and in what respect they do not know "this fellow" is added by the indirect question, "whence he is," i. e., who sent him, or by whose authority he comes. The implication, however, is not that perhaps God after all sent him but that somebody else sent him, or that as an impostor he came on his own authority, certainly without God's commission.

30) Even the simple logic of the man whom the Pharisees seek to override pierces through this flimsy armor. The two verbs: **The man answered and said to them** mark the importance of the beggar's reply. **Why, just in this is the marvel, that on your part you do not know whence he is, and yet he opened my eyes. We know that God does not hear open sinners; but if anyone be a God-fearing person and do his will, him he hears. From eternity it was never heard that anyone opened the eyes of one born blind. If this man were not from God, he would be able to do nothing.** Boldly the beggar makes an actual speech. It is precipitated by the assertion of the Pharisees that they do not know whence Jesus is, meaning that he is certainly not from God, and that certainly God never spoke to him and gave him a commission, as he did Moses. Instead of bringing their awkward case to something like a satisfactory end, the Pharisees themselves, against their own intentions, stir the beggar up to make this penetrating reply. They have actually only furthered the beggar's thinking; for while at first he is not ready to discuss whether Jesus is an open sinner or not, now he proves conclusively that he must be the very opposite, "a God-fearing person" who does God's will. The logic of the little lecture is invincible. It deals with premises which are axiomatic to all Jews, hence the conclusion is inevitable. The beggar's parents were

wise, indeed, when they told the Pharisees, "Ask him, he has the age!" The tables are completely turned. The judges are judged — and by a beggar!

On the use of γάρ at the head of a new statement see B.-D. 452, 2, and R. 1190. The thing itself is very plain, and the beggar sees it. Jesus had opened his eyes — that shows whence he is; it is a manifest (v. 3, φανερωθῇ) proof that in some way he is from God. The Pharisees refuse to see it, pretend even to deny it. This is "a marvel," an astonishing thing, indeed — although it has since occurred many times. The beggar supports his simple conclusion by an equally simple deduction.

31) This verse constitutes the major premise and is put in popular form. The point to be proven is that Jesus is connected with God. All present agree that God does not hear flagrant sinners; in fact, the Pharisees themselves had admitted this when they asserted that Jesus is an open sinner (v. 24). A man whose life and conduct are in opposition to God is not heard even if he asks divine help for some work. If God is to hear a man, he must be of a different kind, namely a θεοσεβής (opposite of ἀσεβής), "God-fearing," and this in the sense that he occupies himself with doing (present subjunctive) God's will. Such a man, we may assume (ἐάν), God will hear. This is the fundamental principle for deciding the case at issue, so certain and simple that no one would dare to deny it.

32) Now follows the minor premise, a statement of the beggar's own case in all its greatness. It declares not only that no sinner ever wrought a miracle but that no man (τὶς), *no* man of God even, ever opened the eyes of a person born blind. A case such as this is absolutely unheard of; even the Old Testament reports no miracles of this kind. The beggar's argument grows in the very statement of it.

The more the man ponders the thing, the nearer he gets to the truth about Jesus, namely that he is not only one of a class (God-fearing and a doer of God's will) but one altogether exceptional, ἐκ τοῦ αἰῶνος, "from the eon on," since the world-age began, ἐκ to indicate the point of departure, R. 597. Jesus had restored to sight eyes that were born blind, whose defect was organic as when the optic nerve is ruined, that were absolutely hopeless and beyond human skill to cure. This is the astounding thing that Jesus has done.

33) Now follows the conclusion. As the minor premise offers far more than the syllogism needs, so the statement of the conclusion with its negative form claims far less than the beggar is entitled to claim. The effect of such a presentation is the more convincing, in fact, it overwhelms. The beggar does not say, "Therefore he is of God," as many a good logician would be content to say. Or, using the negative form, "Therefore, if he were not of God he would not have been able to open my eyes," which again is sound logic. With one grand sweep the beggar takes in the deed wrought upon him and all other godly deeds great or small: "If he were not of God he could do — nothing." The conditional sentence is one of present unreality, εἰ with the imperfect (protasis), the imperfect with ἄν (apodosis, often with ἄν omitted, as here).

This beggar never intended to set himself up as a teacher of men who were his superiors in education, social position, and dignity in the church; they have driven him to it. By trying to quench the light they only forced it to shine the brighter to their own undoing. And the brighter its rays, the greater their fault in not admitting them into their hearts.

34) Now at last the Pharisees make a strong reply, strong, alas, not in truth and logic but only in

vituperation and violence. **They answered and said to him, In sins thou wast born altogether and dost thou teach us? And they threw him out of the place.** Thus they surrender the argument. Since the world began, when men have felt the sting of truth and refused to yield, they have taken their refuge to personal abuse. What the disciples thought possible, and what Jesus roundly denied (v. 2, 3), these Jews make their shameful refuge, namely that this man's affliction of blindness from his birth proved his wickedness, and that even to the present time. "In sins" is placed forward for emphasis. They call it an outrage that such a man (emphatic σύ) should pretend to teach them (ἡμᾶς, emphatic — all their dignity being stressed in the word) anything. "Characteristically enough they forget that the two charges, one that he had never been blind and so was an impostor: the other that he bore the mark of God's anger in a blindness which reached back to his birth, will not agree together but mutually exclude one another." Trench. They have found a crime that is greater than either of these two: his presuming to teach *them* — who, indeed, were beyond teaching! And so they threw him out of the building, ἐξέβαλον ἔξω, "out," so that he landed "outside" (preposition plus the adverb, idiomatic).

We have no reason to locate this incident in the Temple before the Sanhedrin, nor in a synagogue before a Jewish minor court. With others the author in *The Eisenach Gospel Selections*, p. 864, held that this throwing out was the ban mentioned in v. 22, which would make a martyr of this beggar and would lend itself to such reflections as Lightfoot, Trench, and others make. We give this view up because the verb alone is insufficient to yield this thought and because no distinctive term is added as in v. 22. That the ban was inflicted a few days later

is, of course, only supposition. The beggar, too, must
have seemed too insignificant a person to induce the
Pharisees to begin pronouncing the ban on him, and
such an act would only help to spread the news of
his healing.

VIII. *Jesus' Testimony Concerning Spiritual Sight and Blindness, 35-41*

35) When the Pharisees quizzed the beggar, he
came close to the confession that Jesus is the Son of
God. Jesus himself brings the man to that confession.
**Jesus heard that they had thrown him out of the
place and, having found him, said to him, Thou,
dost thou believe on the Son of God?** With an
aorist verb and an aorist participle John merely
reports the facts, that Jesus heard how the beggar
had fared, and that presently he found him. That
the latter occurred in the Temple is not indicated.
Both the hearing and the finding would occur in a
perfectly natural way, and yet there is a higher hand
behind these acts. The contact would not end with
the miracle; compare the case of the impotent man,
5:14. Jesus would finish the work he had begun. As
far as John's report goes, Jesus proceeds in the most
direct manner. It is taken for granted that the beggar knows that he is now looking with his eyes upon
the man who had miraculously opened those eyes. The
pronoun σύ is emphatic, *"Thou*, dost thou believe," etc.,
when so many important persons are not believing?
The question sounds as though it expects an affirmative answer. Jesus knows the readiness of the beggar to confess, but he nevertheless asks him to make
that confession.

"Dost thou believe," πιστεύεις, dost thou trust with
thy heart? The beggar could no longer trust the
Pharisees, though they were leaders in the church,

for he had seen their deliberate blindness and falseness. Yet Jesus does not ask merely, "Dost thou
trust me?" or use only some designation for the pronoun "me." He asks, "Dost thou trust in the Son
of God?" While this question does not intimate that
by "the Son of God" Jesus is referring to himself, on
the other hand, it certainly also is not abstract as
though it was without any vital reference to Jesus.
Moreover, the question is deeply personal for the
beggar, and is to be understood in the highest religious
sense, a parallel to the question whether one trusts in
God, relies on him for guidance, enlightenment, help,
blessing, yea, heaven itself.

Did Jesus say, "the Son of God," or, as good texts
read, "the Son of man"? In a way this is again a
question for the text critics, yet we cannot leave it
entirely to them. Neither term stands only for "me."
Certainly, the beggar would trust a benefactor like
Jesus — how could he help it? But this would be an
inferior trust, dealing only with benefactions such as
the one the beggar had received. A prophet (v. 17),
a holy man of God (v. 31) might obtain such gifts
by prayer to God. Jesus thus had to designate himself so that this beggar would drop all thoughts of a
holy prophet or merely human messenger sent from
God, so that he would at once lift his thoughts to the
person of the divine Messiah, the very Son of God.
For this purpose Jesus might have used "the Son of
man" if this designation had been current among
the Jews as a name for the Messiah, one that would
at once have been understood by the beggar. But it
is Jesus alone who uses this name, not even his disciples employ it (see 1:51). It has a mysterious
sound, and its real import must be searched out by
those who hear it without some previous intimation
as to its meaning. However the text critics may ex-

plain its introduction in our passage, the internal evidence is too strong for the reading "the Son of God." This the beggar at once understood, just as did the hearers of the Baptist when he called Jesus "the Son of God" (1:34).

36) **He answered and said, And who is it, Lord, in order that I may believe?** Although his knowledge of Jesus was limited, this beggar already trusts Jesus to such an extent, that he is at once ready to trust whomever he may point out as the Son of God. The "and" with which the question begins is like the Hebrew *vᵉ* and hardly connects with an unexpressed idea. Usually it is connected with the question Jesus has just asked. R. 999 makes ἵνα consecutive, contemplated result; B.-D. 483, a case of brachylogy, so that we supply *antworte*, in order that I may believe. This seems best, especially after a question.

37) **Jesus said unto him, Thou hast both seen him, and he who is speaking with thee is he.** There is no reason why the first καί should be "even"; "thou hast even seen him." Why such stress, especially when only ordinary physical seeing is in the commentator's mind? Here καί . . . καί is "both . . . and." Jesus might have said quite simply, "It is I." He has a better answer, one that calls out and encourages the beggar's faith. But it would certainly be inferior if the answer Jesus does give means no more than, "Thou both seest and hearest him." Either one would be enough. If Jesus meant to refer to the beggar's newly opened eyes, "Thou seest him" would have been the word. If Jesus had in mind only his person, "Thou hearest him," or words to that effect, might have done; "It is I," ἐγώ εἰμι, would have been better. The answer of Jesus contains far more than a reference to the physical senses. Jesus tells the beggar that he has already

seen the Son of God; and then he tells him that the person now speaking with him is that Son of God whom he has already seen.

Some do not sufficiently note the difference between the two tenses which Jesus employs: ἑώρακας, perfect, "thou hast seen," and ὁ λαλῶν, present, "he who is speaking." But John uses many perfects, and always most carefully in the sense of perfects. To be sure, the Greek has a group of perfect forms which are always present in sense, but ἑώρακα is not in this group. If Jesus here means, "thou seest him," the present tense alone is in order. Jesus might say, "he who has spoken with thee," recalling to the beggar how he heard Jesus tell him to go and to wash; but as regards physical seeing the beggar has not seen Jesus until just now. Some find a present sense in ἑώρακας because they think of physical seeing alone. The Pharisees, whose physical eyes have always been good, see Jesus thus, but do not at all see "the Son of God," concerning whom Jesus is asking this beggar. In the very next verses (39-41), where Jesus continues to speak about seeing, not physical but spiritual seeing is the topic.

With the perfect "thou hast seen" Jesus reaches into the beggar's past when his eyes were opened by the divine power of Jesus — then the beggar caught the first inner glimpse of who his benefactor really is, namely "the Son of God"; and the perfect tense implies that what there dawned upon the beggar remained with him. To arrive at faith in the Son of God requires more than physical eyes with which to look at Jesus. After this significant reminder to the beggar, connecting the miracle at Siloam and what there took place in his heart with "the Son of God," Jesus directly answers the beggar's question by adding, "and he who is speaking with thee is he." This means more than, "I am the one." That seeing at

Siloam was a revelation of the Son of God by means
of a deed, to which Jesus now by speaking with the
beggar is adding a revelation of the Son of God by
means of his *Word*. This, then, is the answer of Jesus
to the beggar's question as to who the Son of God is:
The One whom the beggar has already seen in the
miracle, the One who is now speaking to him in his
Word.

38) The beggar also answers by word and by
deed. **And he said, Lord, I believe. And he worshipped him.** His act is a definition of his word.
The verb προσκυνεῖν means to evidence prostration and
adoration, here in the full religious sense of worship
due to God. Sometimes the verb means less, namely
to pay deep reverence to some man deemed worthy
thereof. A lesser sense is shut out where the act is
directed to "the Son of God." The significance of the
beggar's act cannot be reduced by our searching out
and weighing just what "the Son of God" actually
meant to him when he fell on his knees and touched
Jesus' feet. So much is clear, that this beggar was
a Jew with a knowledge of the true God which he
had gained from the Old Testament.

39) After calling himself the Son of God, Jesus
accepts the beggar's worship as intended for that Son.
In fact, he shows that he is deeply moved by this beggar's word and act. A remarkable word comes to his
lips, one which sums up all that has occurred in the
beggar's case and that lets us feel why John wrote
this story at such length. **And Jesus said, For judgment I did come into this world, that those not seeing shall be seeing, and those seeing shall become
blind.** No one is directly addressed. What Jesus
says is intended for all who are present. When he
says that he "did come into this world" he speaks as
the Son of God, as he who became incarnate (1:14)
and thus entered upon his redemptive mission in "this

world" (see 8:23) of sinful humanity. Already in
3:19 Jesus speaks of the judgment which results from
his mission. There he calls it κρίσις, an act of judgment; now he uses κρίμα, a verdict of judgment. Both
terms are neutral, including acquittal as well as condemnation. Yet only in a secondary way does the
mission to save the world bring about a judicial verdict which divides mankind. It is only because so
many reject the Son whom God sent into the world to
save it and spurn the mission which brings them grace
and redemption.

With a subfinal ἵνα Jesus states this judicial verdict. Here it is stated in the form of a striking
oxymoron: "that those not seeing may be seeing, and
those seeing may become blind." The former are all
those who, although by nature they are without spiritual sight and light, let Jesus, who comes to them, give
them the light of life by bringing them to faith. In
them the saving mission of Jesus is accomplished. The
latter are those, who by nature are equally without
sight and light and who when Jesus comes to give
them the light of life spurn him and his gift by the
boast of unbelief that they already have sight and life.
In them the saving mission of Jesus is frustrated. The
wording which Jesus uses is suggested by the miracle
which Jesus wrought on the blind beggar by giving
him the sight of his physical eyes. Yet the miracle
is not allegorized, for the Pharisees have not been
made physically blind but are left to see physically
as well as ever. Jesus is speaking only of spiritual
blindness and spiritual sight. His words are formulated so as to fit the Pharisees most exactly as contrasted with the beggar. They are the ones who love
to call themselves βλέποντες, men who see — recall their
boast: ἡμεῖς οἴδαμεν, "we know." The beggar knows
only what Jesus has done for him and what the

Scriptures say, besides that he humbly asks that he may know and believe.

Thus the verdict is: these "shall be seeing," βλέπωσιν, present subjunctive (durative), have and enjoy spiritual sight forever; those "shall become blind," γένωνται, aorist subjunctive (punctiliar), shall arrive at a point that fixes them as permanently blind. To begin with, all are alike in the darkness of sin, none see. All would remain alike if Jesus, who is "a light in the world" (v. 5), did not come to them. It is when Jesus comes as "a light" with his enlightening power that a difference results. Some are made to realize that they, indeed, are blind; these arrive at sight, a seeing that remains. Others will not realize that they are blind and boast that they see; they are left devoid of sight, and their blindness remains. It is bad enough that by nature all men are μὴ βλέποντες and that in the course of nature they would remain such; it is infinitely worse that, when the Light has come and shines over us and seeks to enter and to give sight to our hearts, we should so oppose that Light as to become fixed in blindness forever.

40) **Those of the Pharisees who were with him heard these things and said to him, Certainly** (thou dost not mean to say), **we too are blind?** Some of the Pharisees are at hand, dogging the steps of Jesus and keeping an eye on him. They feel themselves hit by what Jesus says, although he had not addressed them. With a scornful air they repudiate what they think Jesus says as applying to them. It seemed ridiculous to them, who imagined that they were "guides of the blind, a light to them that are in darkness, correctors of the foolish, teachers of the law" (Rom. 2:19, 20), to be called "blind," so that they must come to Jesus to receive sight. This they indicate with the interrogative word μή and its implication

of a negative answer, which, if Jesus in any manner denies it, will make his words meaningless. With τυφλοί the Pharisees refer to the class designated by Jesus as μὴ βλέποντες. If they referred to the second class whom Jesus himself calls τυφλοί, their question would have to be: Have we too "become blind"? It is conscience and the prick of Jesus' second statement which makes these Pharisees touch only the first statement. Added to this is their repudiation of Jesus as the one who makes the blind to see. For: "Are *we* too blind?" means also: "Must *we* too come to thee for sight?"

41) **Jesus said to them, If you were blind you would not have sin; but now you claim, We see. Your sin remains.** Jesus turns their own words against them. He takes the word "blind" as they use it and declares that they certainly do *not* belong to that class. They are perfectly right in assuming that Jesus would not place them into that class. For this is the class that comes to see — Jesus is able to give them sight. But if they do not belong to this blessed class, where do they belong, where are they placing themselves? Why, in the only other class that is left. There Jesus had placed them; and they had deliberately closed their ears to that part of his word. With a condition of unreality Jesus again tells them where they belong and at the same time exposes their fatal guilt. "If you were blind," blind only as not seeing, there would be hope for you; but now you are not any longer blind in that sense. Then "you would not have sin," sin such as the other blindness involves, the sin of deliberately rejecting the Light, the sin of sins, unbelief, which forever shuts out from light and life; but now this sin is upon you; you have it, and it has you.

Against the unreality (the class to which even on their own testimony they do not intend to belong),

Jesus sets the reality (the class to which they do belong, whether they intend to or not) : "but now you claim, We see." Here, too, Jesus lets their own testimony speak, λέγετε, "you claim, assert, declare." As they would not dream of it to be included in the first class, so they are proud to include themselves in the second. The asyndeton makes the final sentence stand out as a verdict by itself: "Your sin remains." The sin of rejecting the light, the sin of unbelief. It "remains" with all that it involves for their other sins, lies like a curse upon their souls because they want it thus and will not let it be removed from them. This is a fearful word, spoken in advance to these Pharisees by him who will at last sit on the throne of judgment again to render that verdict. Yet as he now utters it, it constitutes another penetrating call to repentance to these men and a warning to all of us who believe in him today. Note the syllogistic form of the κρίμα with the stringency of its conclusion. Major premise: "If you were blind," etc. Minor: "But now you claim," etc. *Ergo:* That you have no sin does not apply to you — "your sin remains." In this negative syllogism the conclusion may be stated either way, negatively or positively, either equals the other.

CHAPTER X

IX. *Jesus' Testimony Concerning His Flock, 1-21*

Without a break or a pause Jesus continues to speak before this audience, namely his disciples, the formerly blind beggar, the Pharisees, and other Jews. The connection of thought is close. Jesus has told the Pharisees in his audience that their wilful blindness entails abiding guilt. That statement deals with them as far as their own persons are concerned. But they posed as men who "see" and who "know" over against the common people (ὁ ὄχλος) who do "not know" the law, and whom they thus look down upon as accursed (see 7:49), among them being this wretched beggar: "and dost thou teach *us* (9:34)?" Thus these Pharisees set themselves up as the only true teachers and leaders of the people (Rom. 2:19, 20). In reality they were pseudo-teachers and pseudo-leaders. So Jesus continues and now treats these Pharisees in their damnable influence and work upon others.

But this time he employs a παροιμία (παρά, *præter*; οἶμος, *via*), for which term we have no exact equivalent in English: a mode of teaching deviating from the usual way; a kind of extended *mashal*, containing a hidden sense. In the strict sense of the term a parable relates a definite story or case, it may be one that is ordinary, and again one that is quite beyond the ordinary; while a paroimia describes actions as they are known regularly to occur (the shepherd always uses the door; the robber always avoids the door and climbs over the wall). Moreover, in a paroimia an allegorical correspondence appears between the realities presented and the illustrative features used; in a parable no allegory is found. In explaining his own *mashal* Jesus gives us the key-

(710)

point in the allegorical statement, "I am the door of the sheep" (v. 7).

"We see!" say the blind Pharisees. Very well, Jesus puts them to the test. He presents a simple, lucid *mashal*. Do they see? Not in the least (v. 6). To tell them that they are blind makes no impression on them; perhaps this public demonstration of their blindness will accomplish more. To be sure, blind men cannot see, nor did Jesus expect these blind Pharisees to see what his paroimia means. Part of their very judgment is that they shall not see. Yet for such blind people the use of this uncommon way of teaching does at least one thing: by its very strangeness it remains in the memory and long after challenges the mind to penetrate to the true meaning. Perhaps thus at last the light will succeed in penetrating. In this case Jesus even condescends to explain his *mashal* and to elaborate it quite extensively (v. 7-18). In the case of many even this was in vain (v. 20), but others began to catch something of the light (v. 21). Read Trench, the first three chapters of *The Parables of our Lord*.

1)   Amen, amen, I say to you, He who does not enter by the door into the fold of the sheep but climbs up elsewhere, he is a thief and a robber; but he that enters by the door is a shepherd of the sheep. On the preamble see 1:51. It marks the weight of what is said. The brief *mashal* is perfect in every respect. Its obvious sense is quite axiomatic; so also is the higher reality which it describes. The picture is that of a sheepfold, a walled or fenced enclosure, where the sheep are kept at night, while during the day they are led out to pasture. The vital point is the action of the two persons in regard to the door of the fold. He who shuns the door and gets in some other way, such as by climbing over the wall or fence, that man (ἐκεῖνος, a word John loves) is a thief who means to steal what does not belong to him, or a robber who would obtain by violence what belongs to another. In contrast to a man of this kind he who uses the door to get to the sheep is a shepherd of the sheep (ποιμήν without the article, like "a thief and a robber"; not: *the* shepherd, but merely a quality), his action shows that he stands in the relation of a shepherd to the sheep.

3) At this point the paroimia might be regarded as being complete. But Jesus extends the picture to make still clearer the great difference obtaining between the true shepherd and the man who is anything but that. **To him the doorkeeper opens, and the sheep hear his voice, and he calls his own sheep by name and he leads them out.** From the night we move on to the morning. The door is naturally guarded by a keeper. We now see why the thieving robber, who comes at night, avoids the door. One who is a shepherd not only uses the door as a matter of course, he is also admitted there, known as a shepherd by the doorkeeper. The sheep, too, know him; they "hear" (ἀκούει in the sense of ειδέναι, v. 4), i. e., recognize, his voice. In the early morning hour, when it is still perhaps dark, a shepherd, coming to get his sheep, calls to them as he enters, and they know him by his voice. Several shepherds use the fold for the night; so each one "calls his own sheep" in his own way. A beautiful touch is added by κατ᾽ ὄνομα (distributive, R. 608), "by name," one name after the other; for he has a name for each of his sheep to which it trustfully responds. And so at early dawn he leads his own little flock forth. And the other shepherds who use the fold do the same.

4) This action is more fully described. **When he has pushed all his own out he goes before them, and the sheep follow him because they know his voice.** As each sheep responds to its name, the shepherd takes hold of it, sees that it is his own, and pushes it out. When all are out, he walks ahead, and the little flock follows at his heels. This is how the shepherd uses the door. It agrees with his shepherd relation to the sheep, a relation which is mutual: he

knows every one of them, they know him. More than
this: they know "his voice." See how this word "voice"
is repeated in v. 3, 4, and 5. How do we believers
know Jesus? By his voice as we hear it in his Word.

5) The contrast with any other man who is not
the shepherd is now brought out. **But a stranger
they will in no way follow; on the contrary, they
will flee from him, for they do not know the voice
of strangers.** What a stranger might want with the
sheep does not need to be said; but he could intend only
what a thief or robber would want. The picture is
now that of the sheep grazing, some being scattered at
a distance from the shepherd. The moment a stranger
approaches and tries to reassure them with his voice,
the sheep not only will not follow him, they will even
turn and flee from him. The future tenses are not
merely futuristic but volitive: they *will* not follow,
they *will* flee; and οὐ μή is the strongest form of negation with a future: "in no way." Jesus might have
used a conditional sentence; but the simple declarative
sentences are far more effective. Observe that the
shepherd goes to the door and uses the door to get his
sheep. The stranger tries to get in some other way,
without using the door. So the door is still the key.
Likewise, the last clause, "they do not know the voice
of strangers," is the direct opposite of v. 4, "they know
his voice," that of the shepherd. Of strangers, too,
there are many who seek to steal the sheep; there is
only one shepherd. As the shepherd's "voice" is
emphasized by three repetitions, so the fact that the
sheep "know" his voice is twice repeated. The two
correspond: "voice" — "know."

6) Now John adds in explanation: **This paroimia Jesus spoke to them; they, however, did not
realize what the things were which he was telling
them.** The subjects are abutted: "Jesus — they,"
and thus put in contrast. What Jesus meant by his
figurative language the Pharisees, who boasted, "We

see," failed completely to comprehend (aorist). The
entire presentation is lucid; but, of course, it requires
eyes to see through the lucid figure to the inner reality.

7) The first intention in using a *mashal* was to
demonstrate to all present that the Pharisees were
indeed utterly blind. Yet this form of teaching
impresses itself upon the mind more than any other,
and if there is any hope at all, it may eventually penetrate and enlighten. In so far as men will not see,
they, indeed, shall not see, and this is a judgment upon
them. For those who see, a *mashal* reveals the truth
still more and by its very form enters more deeply and
thus enlightens still more and opens the eyes of the
heart more fully. A purpose of grace is thus combined with one of judgment. Which is to prevail in
the end is decided by the heart of those upon whom
the truth is thus brought to act with its power. So
John writes: **Jesus, therefore, said to them again.**
One purpose was already accomplished; a still greater
purpose may yet be accomplished even in the blind
Pharisees. More light is added. If this does not penetrate, the judgment on these men will be more pronounced. If it does penetrate at last, grace and truth
will win another victory. The added light will, of
course, still more enlighten those who see. So Jesus
speaks "again." He interprets his paroimia and, as in
so many instances, adds new features to the interpretation, intensifying the power of the light to the utmost.

**Amen, amen, I say to you, I am the door of the
sheep.** Jesus begins anew, just as in v. 1, with the
same formula for verity and authority. Here is another great "I am," ἐγώ εἰμι. In the very first brief
statement, "I am the door of the sheep," Jesus offers
the key to his entire *mashal*. Even a little spiritual
sight should now see what Jesus really intends. The
genitive is objective: the door "to the sheep," not subjective: the door "for the sheep," R. 501. The article
with the predicate, I am "the door," means that the

subject and the predicate are identical and interchangeable, R. 768. All who are really shepherds of
the sheep (teachers, leaders, pastors) use Jesus as the
one and only door to the sheep, are there admitted,
acknowledged as shepherds, received as shepherds by
the sheep, taking them out by the door, and as shepherds leading them to pasture.

When thus interpreting his own paroimia Jesus
employs another type of teaching that is both highly
interesting and effective, though it is at times misconceived and criticized. He weaves together the figure
and the reality: "I am (reality) the door of the sheep
(figure)." Trench calls this "Biblical allegory." A
fine example is Ps. 23; another John 15:1, etc. As the
figure illumines the reality, so the reality brings out the
contents and the beauty of the figure.

8) Jesus now takes the key and himself begins
to unlock the door, not waiting for his hearers to do
this. **All, as many as came before me, are thieves
and robbers; but the sheep did not hear them.**
Here we learn what "thief," "robber," "stranger," and
"strangers" signify in the paroimia. With the aorist
ἦλθον Jesus speaks historically, but by adding εἰσί he
brings the history down to the present Jewish leaders,
some of whom stand before him at this moment. "All,
as many as came before me," is certainly not absolute
as already 5:39 and 45, 46; 7:19, sufficiently attest.
Moses, the prophets, and other godly leaders used
"the door," the promised Messiah. For Jesus that
needs no saying. All efforts to change the temporal
meaning of πρὸ ἐμοῦ to something else break down.
Jesus looks back to the false Jewish religious leadership that had come into control since the second Temple
and was represented especially by the Pharisees, beside
whom stood the Sadducees. No special meaning
attaches to ἦλθον, as though these leaders came by their
own authority. This is true enough, but the verb
means only that these self-seeking leaders appeared in

order to do their destructive work. Some have thought that Jesus here refers to false Messiahs who had come before his time. But this is historically incorrect and also untrue to the figure. False Messiahs would be false doors to the fold not thieves and robbers who fight shy of "the door." When Jesus adds that these "are" thieves and robbers he comes down to the present and includes the present Jewish leaders. All, past and present, "are" self-seekers.

All these are (reality) "thieves and robbers" (figure). They do not own the sheep and they are not shepherds. For their own evil purposes they attempt to get the sheep into their power. How ill the sheep would fare at their hands is left to the imagination. That they are, indeed, nothing but men who steal and rob is evidenced by the present representatives, who, like their predecessors, reject "the door."

Jesus can say, "but the sheep did not hear (figure) them" (reality), namely those who came thus. The true children of God ("the sheep") never do. Jesus does not complicate his figure by introducing people who follow false leaders: deceivers and deceived. These leaders rule by fear, 7:13; 9:22 and 34, the very opposite of the gentle care of shepherds. "Did not hear," as in the *mashal,* means: did not recognize the shepherd voice and thus gladly and trustfully follow; they only seek to flee (v. 5), lest they be hurt.

9) One point of the figure has thus been interpreted, that concerning the thieves and robbers who shun the door. The other point is now also interpreted, that concerning the shepherds who use the door. So again Jesus emphasizes the key: **I am the door** in the same sense as before, although "of the sheep" is now omitted because it is readily understood. **By me if anyone shall enter, he shall be safe and shall go in and go out and shall find pasture.** Here the reality ("by me," etc.) is again

combined with the figure ("he shall be safe," etc.).
Jesus is speaking of the shepherds who use the door to
enter the fold, who are thus entirely safe, go in to get
their sheep, go out with them, and find good pasture
for them. Whereas Jesus before speaks of the past as
it extends to the present, he now starts with the present
and looks into the future ("shall enter," subjunctive
and thus future, from the present moment on; "shall
be safe," etc., all future tenses, starting now). The
past is done with and cannot be changed; what happens from now on is another matter, and Jesus holds
it up like a delightful promise: "Use the door, use the
door! — then all will be well."

The interpretation is upset at this point when the
figure is changed from the shepherd to the sheep: "If
the sheep shall enter, it shall be saved and shall go in
and out and find pasture." What prompts this view
is the verb σωθήσεται, which is referred to the reality
instead of to the figure, in the sense of "shall be saved,"
i. e., rescued from sin and damnation. Under stress
of this idea the words of the entire verse are scanned
in order to find support for thinking of the sheep and
not of a shepherd. Thus support is found in the fact
that Jesus omits the genitive "of the sheep" and says
only, "I am the door." Yet it is obvious that if he now
intends to speak of the sheep and not of a shepherd, the
addition of the genitive would be decidedly in place.
Although Jesus again says, "I am the door" and then
with emphasis, "By *me* if anyone shall enter," we are
told that the figure is now expanded and becomes that
of the Shepherd (Jesus). Going in and going out is
made to apply only to the sheep and is denied to the
shepherd by thinking that these verbs refer to a home,
which the dweller enters and leaves at pleasure.

The verb σωθήσεται is part of the figure. This verb
means not only to be rescued and delivered but includes the condition that results, to be safe. Here the
context calls for the latter, and this is the case

whether the shepherd or the sheep are referred to. For neither is rescued, either is said only to be safe. Once this is settled, our eyes will not be closed to all else that applies only to a shepherd, leaving nothing that can be properly applied to a sheep. The subject τὶς is masculine, "anyone" (a person), and cannot refer to a sheep, the Greek for which is neuter, πρόβατον. The figure has not become that of sheep lost and scattered, of which Jesus now says that, if any such sheep enters the door, it will be saved. How else but by the door would it enter the fold? And even if such a ridiculous thing could be possible as the sheep climbing into the fold over the wall or the fence, would it not be saved and safe just as well? The image is not that of the fold as a refuge to which a sheep may flee for safety, for in the next breath Jesus speaks of going out and finding pasture. Would the sheep then be exposed again? Moreover, the entire conception of a sheep going in and out of the fold at pleasure is wrong. No sheep does that. It is led in by the shepherd and let out by him. Nor does the sheep go out and seek and perhaps find pasture for itself. This is not at all the business of the sheep but that of the shepherd, and he always makes certain of the pasture. All is out of line if we regard "anyone" as a reference to a sheep; all is perfectly in line when we refer it to a shepherd.

If the shepherd uses the door, Jesus says, "he will be safe." The opposite of entering by the door is climbing up elsewhere (v. 1); this only a thief or robber does. When doing so the criminal is never safe but in the gravest danger of being discovered and punished. The shepherd uses the door for any business he may have in the fold, and thus he is, indeed, safe. The porter knows him and raises no alarm. He may go in and out whenever he finds it necessary. This suffices for the order of the two verbs: "shall go in and shall go out." Of course, this is connected with his shepherd duties. We find the same order in Acts

1:21, but reversed in Num. 27:17; Deut. 31:2; I Sam. 18:13 and 16, and I Kings 3:7, — all with reference to men attending to their duties.   The order of the verbs is governed solely by the viewpoint.   In the shepherd's case his going in and going out is not confined to taking the sheep into the fold at night and bringing them out again in the morning, for here no phrase is added such as "before them" in v. 4; the shepherd also has other occasions for going into the fold and coming out again.   With all this the last clause agrees, "and shall find pasture" for his sheep.   This is the final touch which marks him as a shepherd whose concern is the welfare of the sheep.   The thief and robber act far otherwise (v. 10).

Yet σωθήσεται is misinterpreted even when all else is rightly interpreted.   Jesus is thought to leave his figure by introducing the reality: this shepherd himself shall be saved from damnation.   He has this in mind because he so uses this verb in 3:17 and 5:34.   The answer is that these passages are literal and without a figure.   In our passage the verb is embedded among figurative terms and is thus like them — figurative. When we are pointed to I Cor. 3:15 for a case where this verb is used literally in a figurative connection, the answer is that this is a mistake; I Cor. 3:15 is figurative throughout, verb and all, just like our present passage.   The claim that σώζειν is always used in a literal sense cannot be upheld.

10) In order to throw the character and the actions of the shepherd who uses the door into bold relief, Jesus paints the black picture of the thief. **The thief does not come except to steal and to slaughter and to destroy.**   No need to add that the thief is also a robber; no need to specify that he deals thus with the sheep.   The three aorists in the purpose clause express actuality.   He may kill the sheep right in the fold in order to stop its bleating.   The last verb is added to bring out the disastrous effect upon the

poor sheep: it is destroyed. Surely a contrast to the
shepherd — going in and going out and finding pasture
for the sheep! In this dreadful work the thief cannot
be safe (σωθήσεται).

Jesus now rounds out and completes his interpretation of the *mashal*. The coming of the thief for
his nefarious purpose is contrasted with the coming
of Jesus and his blessed purpose. **I** (emphatic ἐγώ)
**came, in order that they may have life and may
have abundance.** This statement is literal. The
two plural verbs leave the subjects unnamed; they
are the persons meant by the sheep. "I came" means:
from heaven into this world (9:39; 8:23; 3:17).
Others keep coming (the present tense used with reference to the thief for his coming to the fold) to
destroy; the purpose of Jesus is to bestow life. On the
expression "to have life" compare 3:15. Note the
durative present tense ἔχωσιν and its emphatic repetition: have as an enduring possession. The repetition
of the verb "may have" makes the second part of the
purpose stand out more independently than if Jesus
had said only, "may have life and abundance." The
neuter adjective περισσόν is treated as a noun, "abundance" or "superfluity," namely of all the blessings
which go with the true spiritual life; hence not, "may
have it (life) abundantly" (R. V.), or "more abundantly" (A. V.), for this "life" has no degrees.

In this last statement Jesus tells us literally what
he means by calling himself "the door" in relation to
the sheep. He is the mediator of life with all its
abundant blessings. We need not press this "abundance" to mean merely pasture for the sheep. It goes
beyond that and includes everything connected with
the door — and even this figure, as we shall see in a
moment, is too weak to picture it all. All who approach
the sheep by the door and remain in proper relation to
the door are true shepherds, because they employ the

mediation (δι' ἐμοῦ, v. 9) of Jesus; all others who reject
this mediation are branded as thieves and robbers.　At
this point the interpretation of the paroimia (v. 1-6)
ends.　It intends to portray just so much, and what
that is Jesus himself has set forth in clear and simple
words.

11)　The paroimia in v. 1-6 is a unit and its interpretation, v. 7-10, is another unit, the second exactly
matching the first.　Both pivot on Jesus as the door
and distinguish the shepherd from the thief by the
relation of each to the door.　But what makes *Jesus*
the door?　In other words, why is the relation of any
religious leader to this man Jesus so absolutely decisive, that if one uses Jesus he is, indeed, a shepherd,
and if he rejects Jesus he is, indeed, a thief?　The
answer to this question lies in the conception which
Jesus presents of himself as the door of the fold,
but this conception is veiled in the image.　In other
words, this figure does not and can not reveal that
vital point about Jesus.　Therefore Jesus now draws
this veil aside.　He does this by means of a new figure.
We hear no more about the door.　A new picture is
thrown on the screen.　Its center and key is Jesus as
the Good Shepherd.　Around this center and, of
course, in vital relation to it a new set of figures
appears.　While this new picture is different and thus
distinct from the one first used, it is, nevertheless,
related to the other.　We now have the one Supreme
Shepherd.　We still have the sheep, but now the hireling is introduced, plus the wolf, and the vital point is
the relation of the Great Shepherd and of the wretched
hireling to the sheep, and of the sheep to them.　Thus
all that lies back of the figure of the door is now
revealed by the allied picture.　Again, as in the paroimia and its interpretation, law and gospel are combined
in order to open the eyes of the blind and still more to
enlighten those who see.　This time the imagery and

its meaning are woven together, but in such a way that toward the end the language becomes entirely literal.

One interpretation starts with the observation that in the Old Testament kings are at times likened to shepherds and deduces that by calling himself the door and the shepherd Jesus here pictures himself as the true King of Israel over against the house of Herod as Idumean usurpers, the Asmoneans who also were illegitimate, the Sadducean high priests, and one or two pseudo-Messiahs; and the Pharisees are left out. This political conception, wholly foreign to Jesus, departs from the connection with the two previous sections which deal with the spiritual leadership of the Pharisees as teachers and say nothing about princely rule and princes. In the Old Testament no king is called "a door," to say nothing about the other impossibilities that result when princes and kings are found in the imagery of Jesus. In the Old Testament the figure of the shepherd is by no means confined to kings; in the New Testament it is certainly used only in a religious sense to refer to spiritual teachers and guides.

Twice Jesus says, "I am the door"; twice he now adds, **I am the Good Shepherd,** and the correspondence is not accidental. Here appears another great ἐγώ εἰμι, *I AM*. The linguistic points in the predicate ὁ ποιμὴν ὁ καλὸς are sufficient to free us from a number of fanciful ideas. When the predicate has the article it is identical and convertible with the subject, R. 768. Hence, this shepherd is absolutely in a class by himself; no other shepherd can ever be grouped with him. Thus we cannot attach to the article the idea of previous reference, for this Supreme Shepherd has not been mentioned before; nor the idea that this shepherd is now to be described, which is true but is not implied by the article; nor a reference to Old Testament prophecies (Ps. 23:1; 80:1; Ezek. 34:11-16; etc.), which nothing here indicates, as also the main point in the description of this shepherd is entirely absent from the Old Testament imagery of the shepherd.

Jesus does not add the adjective καλός predicatively; for this would say only that "the shepherd is good" and in the same class with other good shepherds. Jesus says far more; he is in a class by himself. He does not say ὁ καλὸς ποιμήν; for this would place the emphasis only on "good" over against "bad," or on "excellent" over against "inferior." Jesus does not here compare himself with other shepherds; he asserts far more than that he is relatively better than other shepherds, namely that he is a shepherd in a sense in which no other man can ever be a shepherd. This is the thought in making the predicate read ὁ ποιμὴν ὁ καλός. By adding the adjective with a repetition of the article both the noun and the adjective become strongly emphatic, and the latter becomes a sort of climax, an apposition to the noun by the use of a separate article, R. 776 and 468. Unfortunately, the English is unable to reproduce this weight of meaning in translation. Jesus is *the shepherd,* absolutely in a class by himself as the *shepherd;* and he is *excellent* with an excellence unique and all his own. *Der gute, der treffliche Hirte, schlechthin gedacht, wie er sein soll; daher der Artikel und die nachdrueckliche Stellung des Adjektivs.* Meyer.

At once the proof is added, the more effective because of the asyndeton: **The Good Shepherd lays down his life in behalf of the sheep.** The expression τιθέναι τὴν ψυχήν is peculiar to John who uses it repeatedly; M.-M. do not find it in the papyri. In order to understand what Jesus means it is quite necessary to take the entire predicate together: "lays down his life in behalf of the sheep," as well as at once to add what is made so emphatic in v. 17, 18 about his doing this of his own accord and about taking up his life again. One may, indeed, compare the laying down of a garment and taking it up again in 13:4 and 12, yet the resemblance is only superficial. A better analogy

appears in 13:37 where Peter offers to lay down his
life in behalf of Jesus, and in 15:13 where a friend lays
down his life for his friends; but both of these fall far
short in that neither has power to take up his life again
as Jesus has.   The act of Jesus is absolutely without
analogy.   Men may risk and even lose their lives for
others, but that is all they are able to do; they cannot
recover their lives.   Jesus lays his life down "in order
to take it up again" (v. 17).   That is not merely an
addition, a second act following the first; that shows
that the first act differs essentially from any similar
act of others.

This eliminates the idea drawn from v. 12 that
Jesus, unlike the hireling, faces the wolf and lets the
wolf kill him in defense of the sheep.   Little good that
would do the sheep, for after the shepherd is killed, the
poor sheep would be utterly at the mercy of the wolf
without a single hand to interpose.   The only deliverance of the sheep would lie in the shepherd's killing
or driving off the wolf, himself retaining his life for
their benefit.   Jesus is the one and only shepherd,
who saves the sheep by laying down and then taking
up his life again.   We see that this is another case
in which the human figure is too weak and small to
cover the divine reality.   The reality should not be
reduced to the small dimensions of the figure.   Where
the figure gives out, we must do as Jesus does (v.
17, 18), proceed without figure, with the reality alone.

The meaning of Jesus is lost because of a limited
view of the preposition ὑπέρ, of which it is said that
this preposition cannot designate substitution, and that
only ἀντί can mean "instead of."   A study of R. 572,
etc., on ἀντί and R. 630, etc., on ὑπέρ clears up the matter
completely.   We note that Abbott, *Johannine Grammar*, p. 276, finds that in almost all instances in John
ὑπέρ denotes the death of one for the many.   Robertson, *The Minister and his Greek New Testament*, 35,
etc., has an entire chapter on ὑπέρ as designating "in-

stead of" in the ostraca and the papyri. We quote: "When we turn to the New Testament from the papyri there can, of course, be no grammatical reluctance to allowing the same usage for ὑπέρ if the context calls for it. Theological prejudice must be overruled." "It is futile to try to get rid of substitution on grammatical arguments about ὑπέρ." "The grace of our Lord Jesus Christ appears precisely in this, that, though rich, he became poor that we, through his poverty, might become rich. That is substitution. The one who knew no sin God made to be sin in our stead (ὑπέρ) that we might become God's righteousness in him (II Cor. 5:21). All this and more Paul poured into the preposition ὑπέρ. The papyri forbid our emptying ὑπέρ of this wealth of meaning in the interest of any theological theory." Moulton, Deissmann, and other authorities on the ostraca and the papyri in relation to the language of the New Testament agree.

In brief, ἀντί really means "at the end of" and thus suggests contrast, succession, substitution, opposition, as the case may be; while ὑπέρ means "over" and thus comes to mean "concerning," "beyond," "in behalf of," "instead of." The context invariably decides. We may translate ὑπέρ "in behalf of," but this is no more exact than "instead of." When Jesus dies ὑπέρ the sheep and then takes back his life again, the only sense in which this could possibly benefit the sheep is by way of substitution — he dies in their stead. An ordinary shepherd might die in defense of his flock, but this would not benefit his flock in the least; after he was dead, the flock would become a helpless prey. Jesus came that the sheep may have life and may have abundance (v. 10). This is achieved, strange to say, by his vicarious and substitutionary death and by the still stranger act of again taking back his life out of death. How this death serves in winning life for the sheep is seen in Matt. 20:28 and Mark 10:45, "he gives his life as a ransom for many," λύτρον ἀντὶ πολλῶν. The idea of a ransom is not brought in here where the imagery of the shepherd and the sheep is used. But it is in vain to argue that the sheep already belong to the Shepherd and thus cannot yet be acquired by him; or that his ideal possession of the sheep cannot here be turned into a real possession. All such stressing of the figure in order to bar out the idea of substitution in ὑπέρ is beside the mark, for it bars out much more, namely the entire idea of this Supreme Shepherd with his power to lay down his life and to take it up again — something that is utterly beyond anything we know of human shepherds. When saying that he lays down his life "for the sheep," the sacrifice of Jesus, which is for the world and all men, is viewed with reference to its actual final result, which appears in the saved. This view is taken repeatedly in the Scriptures and never furnishes the least ground for the idea of a limited atonement.

The astonishing realities here clothed in the figure of the shepherd and the sheep are chiefly two: first, that instead of some sheep of the flock serving as a blood-sacrifice for the shepherd, here the very reverse takes place — the shepherd makes himself the blood-sacrifice for the sheep; secondly, that whereas all other blood-sacrifices yield their lives in sacrificial death never to regain them, this marvelous shepherd does, indeed, like them also yield his life but, absolutely unlike them, takes his life back again. A third point may be added: all other blood-sacrifices die without volition of their own, this shepherd of his own will dies for the sheep. And a fourth: no other blood-sacrifice by its death brings forth and bestows life upon others, but this is exactly what the blood-sacrifice of the Supreme Shepherd does. Only Jesus has ever used a human figure in this divine manner, and unless we rise to the realities thus actually pictured by him, we ourselves, like the blind Pharisees, remain in the dark.

Here Jesus prophesies, for only in the light of his
actual death and resurrection can these realities be
understood.   None of the hearers of Jesus understood
the full import of his words at the moment.   He speaks
for the future, just as he does in so many other
instances.   After the brief space of six months all will
be plain.   That too, we may take it, is why Jesus uses
this figurative language with its astonishing relation
to the realities, language which by its very form is
bound to embed itself in the memories of his hearers,
on which they will ponder until the final actualities
reveal all its divine meaning.

12) **The hireling, not also being a shepherd,
whose own the sheep are not, beholds the wolf coming and leaves the sheep and flees; and the wolf
snatches them and scatters — because he is only a
hireling and is not concerned about the sheep.**   It
lies on the surface that the negative picture of the
hireling is intended to throw into full relief the positive
image of the Good Shepherd.   Some think that this is
all, and thus make their task of interpretation very
easy: the hireling is an imaginary person, intended to
portray nobody in particular, and the drama of the
wolf is a mere embellishment without reality back of
the picture.   It has well been objected that this view
cannot be correct, because Jesus describes the hireling
at such length.   Everybody also, at least as far as the
author has found, forgets about the true and faithful
human shepherds, so beautifully and completely pictured to us in their relation to the sheep in v. 2-4, who
most certainly must be placed between the Supreme
Shepherd on the one hand and the hireling on the
other.   These true human shepherds are not imaginary
but godly teachers and guides of the flock; hence also
the hireling cannot be a mere shadow but must be the
opposite of the true human shepherds, a picture of all
false prophets, teachers, and guides, those of the days

of Jesus and of all other days. As the godly teachers
resemble Jesus in their love and care for the flock, so
the hireling is their very opposite. And this, too, Jesus
brings out in his picture of the hireling, and it helps us
not a little in understanding his meaning.

We should not think of the human shepherd and
teacher portrayed in v. 2-4 as being the actual owner of
the sheep, for no human teacher owns the children of
God over whom he is placed. This aids us in regard
to the hireling. We are not to think of him as a hired
hand employed for wages by the owner of the sheep
and thus serving as a substitute shepherd in care of
the sheep, let us say at least temporarily, perhaps only
for a day. He is not hired by the owner of the sheep,
he has no connection with him in any way. This
becomes clearer when we note that even Jesus is not
the real owner of the sheep. They belong to God.
Only because he is sent by God on the great mission of
redemption is Jesus placed over the sheep. "Thine
they are, and thou gavest them to me" (17:6). Only
thus does Jesus "have" the sheep (v. 16) and does he
call them "mine own" (v. 14). Then as the Father
sent Jesus to be the Supreme Shepherd, so Jesus in
turn sends all true teachers also as shepherds under
himself (17:18). This helps to show who the hireling
really is. Jesus never hired, employed, or sent him in
any way. "Not also being a shepherd," καὶ οὐκ ὢν ποιμήν,
means that the name "shepherd" does not in any sense
include him. We cannot translate, "He that is a hireling and not the shepherd" (A. V.), or "a shepherd"
(R. V.), because ὁ μισθωτός is definite, "the hireling,"
and the subject of the sentence not a predicate after ὤν.
The ὤν is merely attributive to μισθωτός (R. 764), and
καί is "also"; a hireling, as such "not also" like Jesus
and the teachers sent by Jesus, in any manner to be
classed with them as a shepherd. Observe that οὐ with
the participle ὤν makes the negation clear-cut (read R.

1136 and 1163) and means that as a hireling he is the direct opposite of a shepherd.

"Whose own the sheep are not" thus has nothing to do with real ownership but denies only the delegated ownership such as a shepherd has (v. 2-4) to whom the sheep are entrusted by the owner. Jesus never sent him or entrusted him with a single sheep. How the hireling managed to get hold of the sheep is left unsaid yet with the plain implication that it was done in an illegal way. He usurped the place of the shepherd; he stole the sheep in some way. Here the figure of the thief and the robber amalgamates with that of the hireling, and the latter amplifies the former. Neither thief nor hireling cares for the life or the welfare of the sheep, as we see this primarily in Jesus (v. 10b), and secondarily in those sent by Jesus (v. 2-4). All the hireling-thief wants is sooner or later to kill the sheep, in order to enrich himself with the flesh, hide, and wool of the sheep. In this process the poor sheep perish; they lose everything in order that the hireling-thief may gain something.

Now we see why the man thus described, first by a participial modifier and secondly by a relative clause, is termed a μισθωτός or "hireling." We must drop the meaning "hired servant" (Mark 1:20) and any hiring by Jesus. The μισθός or "pay" this man expects is not derived from Jesus, but consists of what the fellow is able to extract from making away with the sheep he has stolen. If he were a hired man with legitimate wages and thus connected with the sheep, he would in some sense at least be a shepherd, an unfaithful shepherd, indeed, for running off in the hour of danger, yet even then a shepherd; but this he is not, οὐκ ὤν. Due to the portrait here drawn by Jesus the term "hireling" has come to stand for a base type of character, one that is venal, mercenary, utterly selfish. In the portrait drawn by Jesus we have this type of character in its most fully developed form. This hireling is a hireling through and through. In actual life we often meet men who exhibit only some one hireling trait, but this does not affect the picture here drawn by Jesus, which has often enough found its complete counterpart in real life.

Beyond question, this hireling portrays all false religious teachers found in the visible church. The portrait is extreme in order to include also the worst teachers of this type. The lesser and partial types are thereby not excluded. Jesus undoubtedly had in mind the Pharisees as a class, some of whom stood before him at the moment; he had in mind the Sadducees as well, for their influence on the people was equally pernicious. The hireling character of the Sanhedrin and of its leaders is plainly brought to view in 11:48; even Pilate saw it, Matt. 27:18; Mark 15:10. Other figurative portrayals of it are found in Matt. 22:38; 24:48, 49. The objection that, if Jesus intended the thief and the robber to apply to the false Jewish leaders, the hireling, because it is a different figure, cannot also apply to them, is groundless. Not only are the two figures related, as has been shown, their very difference brings out two allied wicked features in these Jewish leaders, showing in two ways what their true character is, how far they are from God and Jesus, and how ill God's children fare at their hands. Moreover, does not Jesus also use two figures with reference to himself: the door and the Good Shepherd?

Some commentators do not seem to understand what the wolf is really intended to picture. It is true that the wolf is the natural enemy of the sheep, and that thus we here have the wolf and not the lion or the bear (I Sam. 17:34-37). If, however, the sheep signify the actual children of God, then their natural enemy cannot be a mere figure of speech without substance. This wolf does actual damage to God's children, and actual damage to actual people is not wrought by mere embellishments of rhetoric. These ways of interpreting the wolf are unrewarding.

Another way is to parallel the wolf with the doorkeeper in v. 3. Since nobody in particular is prefigured by the latter, nobody in particular is said to be prefigured by the former. True, the doorkeeper is only incidental to the door of the fold, for the thief would even prefer an unguarded door to climbing the wall, and thus the door and its keeper come to constitute a unit image. Jesus is not the unguarded door by which anybody may reach the sheep at will; he is the guarded door of the fold, and only as the guarded door does he reveal who the shepherds and who the thieves are. Let us also avoid the thought that the guarded door actually protects the sheep against all harm. The thief gets to the sheep in spite of the door and does them harm. But where is there anything that is in any way like the door, with which we might combine the image of the wolf and thus eliminate any special interpretation of the wolf? The search reveals only the more that the wolf is an independent figure and therefore portrays an actuality.

More promising is the reference to Matt. 7:15, where the false prophets in sheep's clothing appear as rending wolves, and to Acts 20:29, where false teachers as grievous wolves spare not the flock; for here the devil and his agents are identified. Yet they are not always thus identified; see I Pet. 5:8; Eph. 4:27; 6:11; James 4:7; Rev. 20:2 and 10; and other passages. The argument that, since the Pharisees are identified with the devil (even called his children, 8:44), the devil cannot here be opposed to the hireling, unless forsooth we mean to chase the Pharisees by the Pharisees, thus proves untenable. Such references to the devil only obscure the main point of the figures of Jesus, which unquestionably centers in the sheep. From the door down to the wolf the life and the welfare of the sheep are the pivot on which everything turns: "that they may have life and may have abundance." Yes, when the sheep are obscured, we see only the hireling running away from the wolf. But Jesus says that the hireling runs away from the sheep: "he leaves the sheep and flees"; Jesus makes the wolf attack, not the hireling, but the sheep: "he snatches them and scatters." Always, always the sheep are placed in the center. Thus the hireling and the wolf actually cooperate in the hurt to the sheep: the former contributes his part by running away from the sheep, and the latter his part by pouncing upon the sheep.

Surely, we all feel a tacit implication at this point. If, instead of this hireling, one of the true shepherds of Jesus were with the sheep, he would attack the wolf, if necessary, yield his life in the combat and thus prove himself a genuine shepherd. The church has had such noble undershepherds, who had learned well their role in the school of Jesus.

Many are agreed that the wolf does denote a reality. Those who deny the existence of the devil bar this being out on *a priori* grounds. They reconstruct the sacred texts according to their own assumptions, not only on this but likewise on many other points. To them the debate is no longer on exegetical questions. They are free to discard the entire Gospel of John. In seeking for the reality intended by the wolf many good Bible scholars decline to admit that this reality is the devil. They admit the devil's existence, even as the Scriptures teach, but when it comes to the wolf, without assigning any actual reason, they simply say that the devil is out of the question. They prefer some tool or tools of the devil, even saying that the devil is behind these tools. They think of the Roman power, or more indefinitely of the anti-Christian world power, of the heretics, or quite abstractly of the principle of evil. It is certainly true that the devil works through many agencies in seeking to destroy God's flock. Yet, as in this case, the Scriptures frequently leave these agencies unmentioned and speak of the archenemy of the church himself. Until sounder reasons are offered why the wolf here prefigures, not the devil himself, but only his tools, we are constrained to hold that the wolf is the devil. Nothing also does he like better than to find a hireling with God's sheep instead of some shepherd sent by Jesus and made courageous by him. Then he can complete what the hireling has begun: snatch with his fangs and kill by destroying the faith in the hearts of God's children; scatter helplessly those not at once spiritually crushed by making them shift for themselves in the wilderness of this world until he either snatches them too or until their spiritual life faints and dies out of itself.

13) Twice the wolf is mentioned; twice the hireling; even as Jesus twice declares, "I am the Good Shepherd." Note also the arrangement: in the center: "wolf . . . wolf"; on either side of the wolf: "hireling . . . hireling"; on either side of the hireling: "I am the Good Shepherd . . . I am the Good Shepherd." This pattern is by no means accidental. By the fact that they are mentioned, all three are made important. So we now revert to the hireling. Why does he act as just described? Because he is what he is: "a hireling." The word is now the predicate, whereas before it was the subject; hence we now have no article, thus stressing the quality expressed in the term — a base, abominable hireling.

When first mentioned, the hireling is characterized by his relation to the sheep; in the second mention likewise, but with a marked difference: first, Jesus never made him a shepherd and never placed him over any of his sheep; secondly, in his own heart he has no love for the sheep. Two things mark the true human shepherd: Jesus places him in charge of some of his sheep; he himself is filled with concern for the sheep in his charge. As the hireling has no inward relation to the Supreme Shepherd Jesus, so also he has no inward relation to any of the sheep for which the Supreme Shepherd Jesus lays down his life. These two negatives really are one; neither exists without the other. So the opposite positives are also one, neither being found in a man without the other. The hireling is centered only in — himself. Let the wolf rend and scatter, just so the hireling saves his own hide.

14, 15) **I am the Good Shepherd** — this testimony rings out for the second time. More sharply even than before the pure white image of the Good Shepherd stands out against the black background of the hireling. Yet this is by no means all. Jesus is contrasting himself with the false teachers and leaders of the Jews. It is their own black image that stands out the blacker against the pure white of Jesus. This contrast, terrible as we look from Jesus to the Pharisees and their allies, blessed as we look from them to him, Jesus leaves in the memories of his enemies there to do its work; to act, if possible, as a blow to crush the conscience and then as a balm to bind up and to heal; and if this be not possible, to act as a sentence of judgment and doom. They will remember — this they cannot help; they will question again and again what he meant. In six brief months the actual death and the actual resurrection of the Good Shepherd, now foretold so clearly, will re-enforce every word they have heard. No; none of these words are mere rhetorical embellishment; all of them reveal vital facts.

We have two parts, each headed, "I am the Good Shepherd." The first shows him to be that by his relation to the sheep (v. 11-13); the second, by his relation to the Father as well as to the sheep (v. 14-18). The first presents only the main act, laying down his life; the second again presents this act (v. 17, etc.) more fully and adds its connection with the Father as well as its result for the sheep (v. 14-16). The first remains on earth, the second joins heaven and earth. The wolf, the hireling, the door, the Good Shepherd are each mentioned twice, the latter two with the mighty *I AM* emphasis. The Father is mentioned three times and each time in connection with the Good Shepherd's office; the Father gave him that office (v. 18, last sentence), loves him for executing its supreme part (v. 17), knows him as owning him for his own (v. 14) — these three stated in reverse order.

I am the Good Shepherd and **I know mine own, and mine own know me, even as the Father knows me, and I know the Father; and my life I lay down in behalf of the sheep.** The very name "Good Shepherd" connotes "the sheep" that belong to him and for whom he is such a shepherd. So here again everything circles about the sheep. The figure is retained throughout, for τὰ ἐμά is neuter, not "mine own" (persons) but "mine own" (sheep, πρόβατα); but, as now used, this figure becomes completely transparent. "Mine own" sheep are all who in heart and soul, by living faith and trust belong to Jesus who dies in their stead and rises again. "Mine own" is in silent contrast to others who are "not mine own," all those who refuse to yield heart and soul in trust to Jesus and his sacrifice. Nothing further is here said con-

cerning these others, simply because they are away
from the line of thought.

Four times Jesus uses the verb γινώσκειν in its pregnant sense, which has been well defined as *noscere cum
affectu et effectu,* to know with love and appropriat-
tion as one's very own and to reveal that loving ownership by all the corresponding actions. Not to know
thus is to realize what is not one's own and to repudiate what is thus not known. When the verb is
used in this intensive sense, we must be careful not
to eliminate the idea of knowing with the mind and
intellect, for to this basic meaning the thought of
ownership, appropriation, love, and all the manifestations of love are added. While the added thought extends to the affections and the will and thus intensifies
the concept, this added thought does not eliminate
the knowing of the mind and turn it into an act of
the will. Compare II Tim. 2:19, and for the negative
Matt. 7:23. In this affective and effective way the
Father "knows" Jesus and Jesus "knows" him.
After the same manner (καθὼς) Jesus "knows" his
own, and they "know" him. The latter can, of course,
be only "as" the former, because of the disparity in
the persons. The divine persons are equal, and they
know each other accordingly. The Good Shepherd
and his own are not equal; his own are only men with
such spiritual abilities as they have acquired. Yet the
relation between the divine Savior and the human
souls he has saved is a lovely reflection of the supreme
relation between the Father and the Son. Always
and always Jesus "knows" his own and in countless
blessed ways manifests that he knows. And always
they "know" him, their Good Shepherd, and all that he
is to them. In this life their knowledge of him is
still imperfect and must constantly grow; but even in
the life to come their knowledge of him will be that
of finite creatures, while his knowledge of them is

divine. Here is the place for many comforting applications. The neuter plural τὰ ἐμά is here used with the plural verb γινώσκουσι, showing that the Koine has broken away from the Attic rule of construing neuter plurals only with singular verbs. This is done not merely because persons are referred to, the rule as such no longer holds, and liberty prevails. R. 403, etc.

The effort to connect the γνῶσις of which Jesus here speaks, together with the γνῶσις which Paul expounds in First Corinthians, with that of the pagan Hellenic mysteries, or at least to draw light from the latter for the true understanding of the former, has proven abortive. The two move in mutually exclusive spheres. The pagan idea is pantheistic, mingling him who knows with him that is known; the Christian idea is theistic, never mingling the two. Paul even ranks γνῶσις far lower than ἀγάπη and πίστις — spiritual fields into which pagan thought never entered. The character of the pagan γνῶσις is magically physical, and it is doubtful whether it ever rose to something even mental; the character of Christian γνῶσις is spiritual throughout and personal in the highest degree. The more we trust and love Jesus, the more we know him and realize just who he is and what he is to us. C.-K. 244.

While it is true enough that the hireling does not "know" the sheep, since they are not even "his own," even as the sheep do not "know" him, it is more than doubtful that Jesus still has the hireling in mind. Instead of looking downward to illustrate by means of a contrast, Jesus now looks upward to illustrate by a similarity: "even as the Father," etc. The tenses used are present, and yet they evidently refer to no specific time, being true for any and all time. Let us call them gnomic (R. 866).

When Jesus adds with καί, "and my life I lay down
in behalf of (instead of) the sheep," this repetition
from v. 11 is made coordinate with the preceding
and must not be made subordinate even in our thought,
as if Jesus means, "I know mine own, etc., *because*
I lay down my life," etc.   The true connection is:
"I am the Good Shepherd": first evidence: "and my
life I lay down," etc.   The sense of the repetition
is the same as in v. 10.   The subject lies in the verb
τίθημι and is thus in the first person, a merely formal
change.   The emphasis on "my life" (nothing less!)
is the same as in v. 10.   In both verses we have the
present tense, "I lay down," which, indeed, is futuristic, "I am laying down," i. e., will do so presently;
but not as R. 870 suggests, "covering the whole of
Christ's life viewed as a unit (constative aorist)."
This would mean that Jesus "lays down his life" for
the sheep by living his life for their benefit, whereas
what Jesus means is that he lays down his life by
dying, for he takes it up again (v. 17) by his resurrection from the dead.

16)   Because they are general and thus indefinite
the gnomic tenses in v. 14 require that something more
should be added.   After saying that Jesus knows his
own (sheep), and that they know him, he now adds
that he is thinking of all his sheep throughout all the
ages of the world.   **And other sheep I have which
are not of this fold; them also I must lead, and they
will hear my voice.   And there shall be one flock,
one shepherd.**   The word "other" is defined by the
relative clause, "which are not of this fold."   Yet
the implication is not a second fold in which these
other sheep exist.   Jesus knows only of one church or
kingdom of God.   When he spoke, this existed in the
form of the old covenant originally made with Abraham and embraced the true children of God in the
Jewish nation and the few Gentiles who had come to

the true faith and had identified themselves with this true Israel of God. Paul knows of only *one* olive tree in Rom. 11:7, from which the unbelieving Jews were broken out and into which the believing Gentiles shall be grafted. In Eph. 2:12 he writes of only *one* household and city, into which the Jews and the Gentiles are equally admitted, being not any longer two classes but one. These "other sheep," then, are the hosts of future Gentile believers.

Jesus says only that they "are not of this fold," that they did not grow up in the old covenant. He does not say that he will "bring" them into "this fold," i. e., as this is now constituted in the old covenant. The verb is ἀγαγεῖν, "to lead" as a shepherd leads his flock, not συναγαγεῖν or προσαγαγεῖν. The Gentiles are not to become Jews in order to become members of the flock. What he says is that he will lead them as the Shepherd just as he leads the believers of Israel. A new era and covenant is thus in prospect, which will be consummated under Jesus when his redemptive mission is accomplished. He speaks of these "other sheep" as already being πρόβατα or "sheep" and even says that "I have" them. It has rightly been urged that this is not a mere prolepsis; "other sheep" might possibly be, but certainly not the verb "I have." Compare similar statements in 11:52 and Acts 18:10. "I have" denotes divine foreknowledge and, we may add, predestination; but the latter not in the sense of an absolute decree, or a decree according to some mysterious principle which simply selects some and passes by others. Just as Jesus foresaw the existence of these other sheep as men, born into human life, so he foresaw the success of his saving grace in their hearts, the birth of their spiritual life as children of God. As far as predestination is concerned, this embraces all in whom the grace and gospel of Jesus succeed to the end. These God chose

for himself as his own elect even before the world
began.

With the hosts of future Gentile believers before
his prophetic eyes, Jesus says not only, "them also I
must lead," but adds the counterpart, "and they will
hear my voice." As their Shepherd Jesus will lead
them, and as his sheep they will hear his voice. The
verbs "must lead" and "will hear" correspond so closely to shepherd leading and sheep hearing and following their shepherd, that ἀγαγεῖν cannot mean "bring"
or "feed." How these Gentiles become believers is
not indicated. Why should it be, when it is in the
same way as Jews come to faith? Jesus portrays
these Gentiles as his sheep, following him as their
Shepherd, just as his Jewish believers now follow
him. The conversion is taken for granted where faith
and trust bind to Jesus. The force of ἀκούσουσιν is
not merely futuristic: "shall hear," but volitive: "will
hear." It is not that Jesus and his voice bring about
the hearing, but that these sheep, always listening for
his voice, are willing to hear so that they may follow.
Jesus says, "them I must lead" (δεῖ). Why "must"
he? Because this is his office as the Good Shepherd.
His redemptive mission will then be accomplished and
at an end, but he will remain the Good Shepherd. His
very death and resurrection a brief six months hence
will usher him into his world-wide shepherd work
during all the coming years. Brought from the dead,
he will still be "the shepherd of the sheep" in connection with (ἐν) the blood of the eternal covenant,
Heb. 13:20. Years after his glorification Peter calls
him "the Shepherd and Bishop of your souls,"
I Pet. 2:25.

Thus Jesus adds, "and there shall be one flock,
one shepherd." Eph. 4:4-6: One church, one Lord.
Whether we read the singular γενήσεται, "there shall be"
(impersonal), or the plural γενήσονται, "they shall be,"

makes but little difference, although the singular seems better. All racial, national, social, educational, and other differences are abolished. The R. V. translates "shall become," in distinction from the A. V.'s "shall be." The former may refer to a process that will not be completed until the consummation. All believers in Christ have ever been "one flock" under "one shepherd." Not in the sense of the Roman Catholic Church, one outward, visible organization but in the far deeper and truer sense of one communion of saints, all being brethren by faith under one Master, one spiritual body, the *Una Sancta*. This is the essential unity of the church. All who have faith, all who are justified and pardoned, are in this unity; all others are outside of it. "There shall be" is definite and decisive, with no degrees and nothing halfway. For this oneness Jesus never prays. It exists and needs no prayers, and it exists as perfect, with no rent or breach. In his high-priestly prayer (17:17, etc.) Jesus prays for a different oneness, namely that all his believers, who are one by faith in him, may also be one in the Word of truth (I Cor. 1:10), holding the divine truth with one mind, one in doctrine, free from all error. For every error means danger to the spiritual bond that joins to Christ and joins us to each other. Only by guarding his Word are we his disciples indeed, 8:31, 32.

A dangerous misconception in regard to "the other sheep" makes these "the God-seekers" in the pagan world, who, when Jesus comes to them, "shall hear his voice" and join his flock, while the rest turn a deaf ear. Entrance into the one flock is not thus decided in advance in pagan hearts. Some that we might call "God-seekers" spurn the gospel, and some that we may think utterly depraved in superstition and vice yield to the gospel. None are shut out in advance. As none are shut out in advance by a divine abso-

lute decree, predestinating them to hell, so none are
shut out in advance by their own sinful and depraved
state.   The gospel is full of the *gratia sufficiens,*
not merely for a certain fortunate class but for all
men alike.   This grace is not dependent upon a certain amount of aid in man, so that without that aid
it fails; its efficacy and power to save lie in itself
alone.   Rom. 1:16.

17)   The act which both makes and reveals Jesus
as the Good Shepherd has already been impressed upon
us by two statements: he lays down his life for the
sheep.   Due to this act he has the sheep whom he
knows and who know him (v. 14), also the other sheep
who together with the first shall constitute one grand
flock under him as the Supreme Shepherd.   This great
act of self-sacrifice is so important that he elucidates it
most fully.   **For this reason the Father loves me
that I lay down my life in order to take it up again.**
It is true, the various forms of οὗτος (here διὰ τοῦτο)
often refer back to what has just been said.   Here,
however, this is not the case because ὅτι follows and
as an apposition states what "this reason" is, R. 965.
The attempts to make "for this reason" refer back
to v. 16 end up by after all making ὅτι refer to διὰ τοῦτο.
This connection lies in the very nature of the statement made about the Father's love for Jesus.   Whatever may be said of love in connection with the sheep
gathered into one flock by Jesus is bound to involve the
great sacrifice by which this gathering of the sheep is
accomplished.   The Father loves Jesus, not merely because of all these sheep, but because of the sacrifice by
which he wins these sheep.

The Father, of course, loves Jesus as his Son irrespective of his mission in the world.   Not of this love
does Jesus here speak but of the love which Jesus
wins by voluntarily assuming and faithfully executing
the Father's plan for bestowing. redemption on the

lost world, a task to be accomplished only by the sacrifice of himself. Here the verb ἀγαπᾶν is fully in place, to love with complete understanding and with a purpose to match that understanding. The Father's whole heart goes out to his Son as he lays his human life down in the sacrifice of death. The Father knows all that this means for Jesus, prizes his act as he alone can prize, and uses it for the glory of himself and of his Son.

The emphasis on ἐγώ should not be overlooked: "I, I myself" lay down my life, I of my own free will. In a moment this will be made still plainer. And the act of which Jesus speaks is not merely his death. Like other blood-sacrifices to die and to remain dead, would avail nothing, would, in fact, be less than nothing — at best a heroic effort that ends in abject failure. Jesus lays down his life for the very purpose of taking it up again. Both acts are his; the two are halves of one whole. Only thus will he be the Good Shepherd his Father intends him to be; only thus will he be the one great Shepherd of the Father's one great flock; only thus can and will the Father's great plan be realized for the world. Therefore, neither grammatically nor merely in our thought dare we separate the laying down from the taking up. We must not translate, as S. Goebel points out: "The Father loves me because I lay down my life — (but I do it only) in order to take it up again." This sacrifice is like none that ever occurred before, because it indeed effects what all others could not effect, what they could only foreshadow. This sacrifice actually atones, actually redeems, and, doing that, the life laid down is not forfeited but is to be taken up again as freely as it was laid down. The human body and life, once laid down as a ransom for us, are now enthroned in glory at the Father's right hand.

18) Voluntary in the highest degree is the act of Jesus in laying down his life and, therefore, it merits the Father's love in an equal degree. **No one takes it from me, on the contrary, I myself lay it down of myself.** We need not trouble about the reading with the aorist ἦρεν: "no one took it," etc., R. V. margin, as this lacks both sufficient authority and harmony with the thought. "No one" has no reference to the Father but only to hostile powers. His enemies will, indeed, crucify Jesus, and it will seem as if they take his life from him; but this is not the fact. The very contrary is true: it is Jesus himself who of himself by a free volition of his own yields himself to their hands (18:4-11 and Matt. 26:52-54; 19:28-30 and Luke 23:46). Jesus makes this so emphatic, first for his believers, that they may remember it when the time comes; secondly, for the Jews who are so anxious to kill him, that they, too, may remember when the time comes. Both are then to recall that by his voluntary death Jesus wins the supreme love of his Father.

But this emphatic statement calls for further elucidation. Did not Jesus say in 5:19 that the Son is able to do nothing "of himself," ἀφ' ἑαυτοῦ? How, then, can he now say that he lays down his life "of himself," ἀπ' ἐμαυτοῦ? Here is the answer: **Power have I to lay it down, and power have I to take it up again. This commission I received from my Father.** Both are true: first, that Jesus can do nothing of himself, i. e., without the Father or contrary to the Father; secondly, that he can of himself give his life, i. e., as a free and voluntary act carried out by him alone. In the loving behest with which he sent his Son on his redemptive mission the Father himself gave him right, authority, and power to follow his own will. No one English word has the exact meaning of ἐξουσία here used in diverse connections; hence the

difference in translation, which seeks to keep the
same word for the two connections. "Power" fits
well for taking up the life but not well for laying
down the life; "right" or "authority" fit the dying
but hardly the rising. What Jesus means is entirely
plain: he is free to do both, lay down and take up
his life again. Note that ἐξουσία is derived from ἔξεστι,
which means "it is free"; and thus the noun shades
from the idea of the right and authority to act to
that of the power to act. While Jesus uses two
parallel statements to express his thought, it would
be a mistake for us to separate them in our minds
by speaking of his liberty to do the one act and
yet *not* the other. No such choice presents itself
to his will as to lay down his life and not take it
up again; but only to lay it down in order to take
it up again (v. 17), or to do neither. In these matters it is idle to raise hypothetical questions, and it
is worse to raise them while splitting normal units by
abstractions.

Jesus must go one step farther and state how he
comes to use his ἐξουσία as he does, how he makes the
choice, instead of keeping his life to lay it down in
order to take it up again. This is due to the "commission" he has received and accepted from his
Father. The ἐξουσία resides in Jesus himself as God's
Son — no one could compel him to lay down his
life. The Father, of course, would be the last to
think of such compulsion. If Jesus, then, lays down
his life in order to take it up again, i. e., to go through
the bitterness of death in our stead, it is, and in
the very nature of the case can be, only by his own
free volition. But something induces him to use his
free volition in this way. We might say that it is his
love for us, his desire to save the world. His motive
is far higher. It is one which is so high that it includes anything he might say regarding his love for

us. He decides as he does because he desires to please his Father. He and his Father are one in their will to save the world. Thus the Father gave him this ἐντολή to lay down his life and to take it up again in order to redeem us, and Jesus accepted it from his Father. By pointing to his taking this commission from his Father, Jesus reveals to us his deepest or, let us say, his highest, motive.

The translation "command" may mislead. Commands are peremptory, issued by a superior to a subordinate. Commands are compulsory and shut out free volition. No command of that kind prompts the act of Jesus. Such a command would rob his act of the very thing that makes it so pleasing to his Father (Eph. 5:2). Nor is this ἐντολή a moral obligation and a "command" in this sense, something that Jesus ought to do, as we ought to obey the Decalog and, failing which, he would in some way be morally remiss. Jesus is under no moral pressure whatever, either in the matter of passing through death for us, or in the first place accepting his Father's commission. He was just as free to decline as to accept. This ἐντολή is a commission which the Father requests the Son to assume and which he freely assumes because he and his Father are one in their desire to save the world. When offering this commission to his Son the Father appeals to love; by accepting that commission the Son responds with his love. Both the offer and the acceptance lie on the highest possible plane. And now we know how Jesus became our Good Shepherd by giving his live for us, and what it is that makes him such a shepherd. We have looked into both his heart and into that of his Father.

19) These wondrous words had their effect. **A division again arose among the Jews because of**

these words, just as happened temporarily in 9:16, and more decisively already in 7:40-44.

20) **And many of them were saying, He has a demon and raves. Why do you listen to him?** Compare 7:20 and 8:48. These are the majority and find no reply except to revile. That is the easiest answer, even if it is quite irrational to attribute such words of Jesus to a demon using his tongue for mad raving. The real intention of this majority comes out in their question. They evidently see that Jesus is making an impression on some of his hearers. This provokes them. They seek to turn everybody against him.

21) But their effort only provokes a telling reply from the minority. **Others were saying, These are not the utterings of one demon-possessed.** No; not the least resemblance could anyone note — only the absolutely opposite. First, an assertion like that of the majority; then, a question again like them. **Can a demon open eyes of blind people?** He certainly cannot! He could and would do only the opposite. The plural "eyes of blind people" generalizes from the one notable case, 9:6, etc. The minority is impressed by both Jesus' word and his act. And thus this visit of Jesus to Jerusalem (7:10, etc.) closes. The two imperfects ἔλεγον leave the situation hanging in the air; John lets it hang thus without adding a final aorist of any kind.

X. *Jesus' Attestation as the Messiah at the Feast of Dedication, 22-42*

22) **And it was the Feast of the Dedication in Jerusalem. It was winter.** This festival, called *Chanukah,* was instituted by Judas Maccabaeus in 167 B. C. in commemoration of the cleansing and re-

dedication of the Temple after its profanation by
Antiochus Epiphanes. The annual celebration lasted
eight days beginning the 25th of Chisleu (about the
middle of December) and was observed throughout
the country, a special feature consisting in illuminating the houses, from which fact the festival was called
τὰ φῶτα, "the Lights." When John adds to the mention
of the festival the phrase "in Jerusalem" to designate
the place, this would be superfluous if Jesus had spent
the intervening two months (7:2, end of October to
the end of December) in the city. He left shortly
after the October celebration and had now returned.
This is substantiated by what is now reported. The
new situation and the new testimony Jesus utters connect directly with the last that he spoke before leaving
the city (10:1, etc., in regard to his sheep). Where
he broke off two months ago there he now begins.
The situation, highly strained during that last visit
(chapters 7-10:21), now reaches its climax (10:39),
and Jesus leaves the city for good, not to return until
the Passover in the spring, when he will enter upon
his passion and his death. Quite in the same way the
miracle recorded in 5:2, etc., for which the Jews resolved to kill Jesus (5:18), is taken up again after
the lapse of an entire year on the return of Jesus to
the city (7:10) in his very first clash with the Jews
(7:19 and 23).

We cannot assume that Jesus spent the two months
in the city, either hid away from the Jews, or teaching in public. If he had appeared in public, the situation would have moved on of its own momentum, and
10:26, etc., could not connect, as it does, with 10:1-18.
Where Jesus spent the two months after leaving the
city John does not tell us. All that we have is recorded
in 10:40: "he went away again," ἀπῆλθε πάλιν where
the adverb intimates that he returned to the place

beyond the Jordan, i. e., that this was the locality to which he had retired.

The remark that it was winter is, of course, not intended to inform us about the season of the year but to explain the next statement that Jesus was walking in a sheltered place in the Temple.

23) **And Jesus was walking in the Temple in the porch of Solomon,** the covered colonnade that offered some protection from the weather on that wintry day. Josephus, *Ant.* 20, 9, 7, informs us that this portico was the only part of the old Temple of Solomon left standing after the destruction wrought by Nebuchadnezzar, and was thus named "the porch of Solomon." Here Jesus "was walking" to and fro for greater comfort in the cold. John again says nothing about the disciples, and the opinion is offered that Jesus is alone at the moment. This would make the ensuing encounter still more dramatic; but it is better to assume that the disciples are walking with Jesus as usual, and that John omits mention of them because they play no part in what transpires.

24) **The Jews, therefore, surrounded him and were saying, How long dost thou hold us in suspense? If thou art the Christ, tell us openly!** The connective οὖν indicates that the Jews see their opportunity and embrace it. Here Jesus suddenly again appears in their midst; he is alone except for his disciples; now they can have it out with him. By a concerted action they surround and enclose him, meaning that he shall not again get away. No friendly multitude is at hand to support him and to stay their hand. Jesus is suddenly face to face with his bitter enemies, who are now bound to force the issue. The moment is charged with the gravest potentialities.

The passion of the Jews flares out in their accusing question coupled with the decisive command. The two together act like a challenge. The Greek of the question is idiomatic: ἕως πότε, "till when" = how long; τὴν ψυχὴν ἡμῶν αἴρεις, "art thou lifting our soul," lifting or raising it in suspense. But ψυχή is not our English word "soul" but a designation for the person: "our soul" = "us" (C.-K. 1141) as animate beings subject to tension. The question charges Jesus with keeping the Jews on tenterhooks by not coming out fairly and squarely on the main question. What that question is their demand states, "If thou art the Christ," etc. "Tell us plainly" ("with openness") means: then we shall know how to act. The implication is by no means that these Jews would believe if Jesus would say in so many words, "I am the Christ." Nor is the idea this that the Jews would use such a plain statement as a political charge on which to bring Jesus to trial. Still less may we assume that the Jews are seeking to ease their own consciences in regard to their treatment of Jesus by casting the blame on him for not speaking out plainly. They are long past such scruples. The suspense to which these Jews object is that of thrusting the fact of his Messiahship into their consciences in such a way as to cause divisions in their own ranks (9:16; 10:19) yet without giving them the chance they are determined to have to bring him to book for his claim. They mean that this is now to end; *they* are determined to end it right here and now. "Art thou or art thou not the Christ?" If he says, "I am," the stones will fly.

25) The first two words of Jesus: εἶπον ὑμῖν, **I did tell you,** is a perfect master stroke. Here they are demanding a thing with such a show of suspense — and it has been told them long ago! Where had they their ears? Here they are now trying to force an issue — why, they should have forced it long ago when Jesus first told them! Why all this show and demonstration now? — they know well enough, and Jesus lets them know that he knows. More than this: Jesus

right here and now is again telling them with his first two words just exactly what they ask. So far is he from evading the dangerous issue thrust upon him that he meets it squarely and directly in his very first utterance. This quick, unexpected directness takes the Jews quite off their guard. The question is asked when Jesus had told the Jews that he is the Christ. The answer is to be found in every one of his discourses. We single out 5:17, etc., where the Jews first resolve to kill him for "making himself equal with God."

The trouble lies not, even in the least, with Jesus but with these Jews: **and you do not believe.** After all his telling, including the present word, they do not believe (durative present). All his telling is in vain — in vain through fault of theirs; is so even now.

In order, once and for all, to settle the question of his telling them properly Jesus points to that most convincing form of his telling, which is not merely by words but by deeds which substantiate his words in the highest degree: **The works which I am doing in my Father's name, these are testifying concerning me.** Words alone, mere verbal statements ever so plain and direct, however valuable and necessary they may be, could not suffice. A fraudulent Christ might say with his mouth, "I am the Christ." We know that false Christs did arise and so declare; but their works proved them liars. The works of Jesus substantiate every word of his concerning his person and his office as the Christ of God. These works Jesus is still engaged in doing, ποιῶ, their number and the force of their testimony is increasing. They not only tell, they "testify" concerning Jesus and do this right along (present tense). Like witnesses who have seen and heard personally, these works emanating from Jesus himself speak intimately and truly of him who wrought them. And this testimony we must have. If these witnesses were silent, or if they gave a different testimony from the one they so clearly and unanimously utter, then, indeed, we might be in doubt. But now doubt is folly.

Jesus says far more than that he is just doing these works; he is doing them "in my Father's name." This reference to his Father again tells these Jews that Jesus is the Christ. Once more he asserts his mission from the Father, the mission which makes him the Christ. The ὄνομα is not the authority, so that we should understand, "by my Father's authority"; nor representation, "as my Father's representative." It denotes revelation, "in connection with my Father's revelation," i. e., the ὄνομα or revelation given by God to Israel, by which they should know the Father and be able to recognize any works that emanate from him. God's revelation displays his omnipotence, grace, and mercy, these especially. And in every one of Jesus' miracles these divine attributes shine out with utmost clearness. By aiding the body they seek to lift the soul, too, to life eternal. Compare the two notable works which Jesus set before the eyes of these Jews, 5:2, etc., 9:6, etc. The cry of these works was even now ringing in the ears of these Jews.

26) How are they treating this double testimony? **But you — you do not believe because you are not my sheep.** Mark the strong adversative and the emphatic pronoun, also the repetition, "you do not believe," which places the blame entirely on them. True and sufficient testimony ought to be believed; not to believe it is both unreason and guilt. He who refuses to believe such testimony convicts himself. "Because (ὅτι) you do not believe" states the intellectual reason which explains the Jewish unbelief, not the effective cause which produces this unbelief. It brings the plain evidence, it does not indicate the secret source. The sense is, "Since you are

not my sheep you do not believe"; and not, "Since
you are not my sheep you cannot believe." The preposition ἐκ is partitive. The reference to "my sheep"
connects directly with the discourse spoken two
months ago in v. 1-18.

27) Jesus even repeats the particular characteristic of his sheep which here comes into play and which
the Jews utterly lack. **My sheep hear my voice, and
I know them, and they follow me.** Always they
hear, always he knows, always they follow. Trust-
ful hearing is meant; they know not the voice of
strangers (see v. 5). Jesus says "my voice" and
not "my word." The "word" signifies the contents,
the "voice," the tone, sound, personal peculiarity. Both
are inseparably bound together. In the shepherd's
word, wherever and whenever it is spoken, the sheep
hear the shepherd's voice, and it is inexpressibly sweet
and attractive to them. "This lovely, delightful picture you may, if you wish, see for yourself among
sheep. When a stranger calls, whistles, coaxes:
Come, sheep! come, sheep! it runs and flees, and the
more you call, the more it runs, as if a wolf were
after it, for it knows not the strange voice; but where
the shepherd makes himself heard a little, they all
run to him, for they know his voice. This is how all
true Christians should do, hear no voice but their
shepherd's, Christ, as he himself says." Luther.

To those who are not his sheep Jesus speaks of his
sheep. This is the gospel call to become his sheep. It
is combined with a hint as to what those must be
who will not be such sheep. Thus, too, Jesus once
more tells these Jews, not only what they asked, who
he really is, but also what they had failed to ask, who
they are, and what they ought to become if they
desired salvation, and what will become of them if
they remain what they are.

The first four tenses are gnomic presents and thus timeless. What they relate is true irrespective of time. Note how these four statements intertwine: *they* hear — *I* know — *they* follow — *I* give. In four short master strokes the relation between the shepherd and his sheep is pictured. Something vital would be left out if one of these four were omitted. Note that all four are simultaneous, not successive; and that while they are twined together, we still have two pairs: to hear and to follow, likewise to know and to give. The emphasis that is strongly brought out in the two κἀγώ: "I myself know . . . I myself give," runs through the entire description: *"My* sheep hear *my* voice; *I* know them; they follow *me*; *I* give to them, etc., and no one shall pluck them out of *my* hand." On the statement, "I know them," compare the comments on v. 14, in particular also on the verb γινώσκω. "I know them" simply asserts the great fact and stops with that. This is the point these Jews are to note when Jesus is compelled to tell them they are *not* his sheep. He knows all who are his sheep. The fact that his sheep know him in turn, while it is true enough, is not pertinent here.

Hearing the shepherd's voice is an inward act, following the shepherd is both inward and outward. This time the verb is plural, as in v. 14 (R. 403, etc.). "They follow me." I call, they come; I choose the path, they trust and come after; I lead, they are safe in my care; I command in love, they respond in obedience and love. If this at times means the cross, they do not waver. One cannot hear without following, nor follow except he hear. It is all so simple and natural — just as in the case of sheep and their shepherd.

28) As the two actions of the sheep correspond, so the two actions of the shepherd, each with its emphatic ἐγώ: **and I give them life eternal,** the life

already described in 3:15 (which see). This is the very principle of life which flows from God, is grounded in God, joins to God, and leads to God. Born in regeneration, it pulses in every believer, becomes stronger as faith increases, and reaches its full flower in the glory of heaven. Temporal death merely transfers this life from earth to heaven. Itself invisible, this life manifests itself in a thousand ways and thus attests its presence and its power. When the day of glory comes, its manifestations shall be glorious altogether. No earthly shepherd is able to give life to his sheep; Jesus "gives" life eternal to his sheep. By way of gift alone this life is ours — free grace alone bestows it, and by free grace "without any merit or worthiness on our part" it is our possession. This verb δίδωμι reveals all the richness, greatness, and attractiveness of our Good Shepherd. The incomparable Giver stood there before the Jews and was actually offering them his divine gift of grace. But they would have none of his greatness and riches.

The four present tenses are now followed by two futures, both negative, but with their opposite positives shining through. **And they shall in no wise perish forever, and no one shall snatch them out of my hand.** This is a double and a direct promise; the doubling increases the emphasis. "To perish" is to be separated from God, life, and blessedness forever. John and Paul use especially the middle voice of this verb in this sense, C.-K. 788. It is the opposite of being saved. Here we have the second aorist middle subjunctive ἀπόλωνται, with οὐ μή as the strongest negation of a future act, and the aorist because the act necessarily would be only one and as such final. "Shall in no way perish" would itself be enough, the modifier "forever" is added pleonastically: this dreadful act shall never occur. This promise does not refer only to the time after the believer's death, implying that then he shall be forever safe; this promise holds good from the moment of faith onward. The verb "to perish" never means "to suffer annihilation," or to cease to exist.

The first part of the promise is stated from the viewpoint of the sheep: they shall never perish. The second part is from the viewpoint of Jesus and of any hostile being that might attack his sheep: no one shall snatch them out of his hand. This promise, now stated with the future indicative, is intensified in a moment: "no one is able to snatch them out of the Father's hand." First the fact then the possibility is denied. The two promises, one referring to Jesus, the other to the Father, indicate the equality of the two persons (5:18). The blessedness of the sheep is not only great and sweet, it is also sure and certain, not like that of the world, which is bright today then gone forever. The phrasing οὐχ ἁρπάσει τις recalls what is said of the wolf in v. 12. The "hand" of Jesus is his power. His gracious power is all-sufficient to protect every believer forever. Even at this moment Jesus and his disciples are surrounded by the Jews who are bent on violence, but the hand of Jesus is mightier than they. However weak the sheep are, under Jesus they are perfectly safe. Yet a believer may after all be lost (15:6). Our certainty of eternal salvation is not absolute. While no foe of ours is able to snatch us from our Shepherd's hand, we ourselves may turn from him and may perish willfully of our own accord.

29) What lies in and back of these words of Jesus (v. 27, 28) regarding the entire relation between him and his sheep and their complete safety in his hand, is now stated most clearly and fully. In his entire reply to the Jews, from v. 25 onward, Jesus proceeds, not as the Jews demand, by simply declaring, "I am the Christ," but as he has proceeded all along, by do-

ing such works and offering such testimony that those
who see and hear must be stirred in their own hearts
to confess of their own accord, "Thou art the Christ."
If this method of procedure has put the enemies of
Jesus in suspense, that suspense is now driven to the
limit; for instead of changing to the method they propose for their murderous end, Jesus for his own purpose of grace carries his own method to the climax.
Back of all that he does for the sheep is his Father.
**My Father, who has given them to me, is greater
than all; and no one is able to snatch them out of the
Father's hand.** The Greek does not need to name
the objects "them," which the Greek reader automatically supplies from the context. Therefore the absence of the two "them" is no warrant for converting
the statements into abstract assertions by supplying
"aught": "who has given aught to me," and "to snatch
aught," etc. (R. V. margin).

The variant readings turn on two points, whether
we should read ὅ for ὅς, and μεῖζον for μείζων: "That
which my Father has given to me is greater than
everything (now also neuter); and no one is able to
snatch it," etc., (R. V. margin). This and any similar
reading has little textual support, which fact already
settles the case. In addition, it introduces a thought
that is wholly untenable. For this reading which
draws ὁ πατήρ μου, placed in front of the relative clause,
into that clause, throws a peculiar emphasis on "my
Father": "What *my Father* has given me," etc., and
thus injects the implication into the clause that besides
what his Father has given him Jesus has something
that is not so acquired. This is not true; *all* that
Jesus has comes from his Father. In addition, this
reading produces the strange thought that the sheep
are greater than everything else and on this account
are held firmly by the Father's hand. In what respect
are they "greater?" one is moved to ask. In v. 28 it

is the power and the greatness of Jesus that protect
the sheep; and so again in v. 29 it is the greatness and
the power of the Father, exceeding that of any possible
foe, that safeguard the sheep.

The Father, who sent the Son, works through the
Son, whom he sent.   It is·thus that he has given the
sheep to Jesus: "which thou gavest me out of the
world; thine they were, and thou gavest them to
me," 17:6; compare 6:37.   This shuts out the notion
that the Father merely employs Jesus to take care of
the sheep.   Likewise, it shuts out the thought that
the old keeper of Israel (Ps. 121:4, 5), who neither
slumbers nor sleeps, has gone to rest, and that
Jesus is now his successor in office.   When Jesus says
"my Father" he denominates himself as "the Son,"
and it is thus that these two are equally concerned
about the sheep: the Father through the mission bestowed on the Son, the Son in the mission received
from the Father.   "Has given," the perfect δέδωκε,
has its usual force: a past act when the Son entered
on his mission and its abiding effect as long as that
mission endures.   This Father is "greater than all,"
μείζων πάντων, and "all" must be masculine and denote
persons, for it includes the masculine τίς in v. 28 and
οὐδείς in the present verse.   While "greater" is broad,
here it must refer especially to power: the Father
exceeds in power every being arrayed against the
sheep (Satan, demon spirits, human foes however
mighty).

After thus declaring the Father's might, it might
seem superfluous for Jesus to add, "and no one can
snatch them out of the Father's hand," for this is
certainly self-evident.   The reason for the addition
lies far deeper.   Jesus deliberately parallels what he
says of himself, "no one shall snatch them out of my
hand," with what he says of his Father, "no one can
snatch them out of the Father's hand."   The fact that

he mentions the detail ("shall snatch") with reference
to himself is due to his being on his saving mission;
that he mentions the possibility ("can snatch") with
reference to the Father is due to the Father's institution of that mission. Both thus belong together:
Father and Son, fact and possibility. Does the
promise of Jesus, standing there in human form before the Jews, sound preposterous, that no one shall
snatch his sheep out of his hand? To snatch them
out of *his* hand is the same as snatching them out
of *the Father's* hand. Remember the relation of these
two hands, as this relation centers in the sheep.

30) What is thus prepared is now pronounced in
so many words: **I and the Father, we are one.**
The equal power to protect the sheep is due to the
equality of these two persons. This makes the mighty
acts of equal protection perfectly plain. "We are
one," therefore, cannot be reduced to mean only one
in purpose, will, and work. This, however true it
may be in itself, does not suffice; for the reference
is to power, namely almighty power, against which
no other being, however great his power may be,
is able to rise. To deny that equality of power is
here expressed is to deny just what is asserted. This
denial resorts to the faulty reading μεῖζον instead of
μείζων, and places the power in the sheep instead of
in the Father. Another way to reduce what Jesus
says is to point to ἕν and to assert that, if identity
is meant by "we are one," we should have εἷς, a masculine instead of a neuter. Augustine has answered
that: ἕν frees us from the Charybdis of Arianism,
ἐσμέν from the Scylla of Sabellianism. If we had εἷς,
this would mean that the two are one and the same
person, producing patripassionism and other extravagant fancies. Jesus says, "we are ἕν," "one thing,
one being, one God, one Lord," Luther. The two persons are not mingled, for Jesus clearly distinguishes

between ἐγώ and ὁ πατήρ; but these two, while they are
two in person, are ἕν, one, a unit substance, or, as we
prefer, a unit in essence.

It is fruitless to bring in analogies for ἕν in order
to reduce this oneness to something with which our
minds are conversant, which they are able to grasp
intellectually. Thus Paul says of himself and of
Apollos, "He that planteth and he that watereth are
one," I Cor. 3:8. Here, however, not persons as
persons but their activities, planting and watering,
make them one. It is certainly unconvincing to point
to I Cor. 12:12: one body composed of many members; and it is an actual descent into filth to think
of I Cor. 6:16. When Jesus prays that all who will
come to believe through the Word of the apostles
(17:20) may be one, this is so manifestly the increasing oneness of conviction and confession regarding
the one truth of the Word that it seems strange to
adduce it in this connection. Eph. 2:14 and 4:4, as
well as Gal. 3:28 speak of the spiritual oneness of
the *Una Sancta* or Communion of Saints, in which
any number may be joined. Acts 4:32 is merely the
accord of thought and will. Efforts will constantly
be repeated to follow some such analogy in thinking
of the oneness of the Father and the Son. But all
these human and earthly analogies are really not
true analogies. Among them all no oneness exists
which can be placed beside this expression of Jesus,
"We are one." Nor is this strange, for each of the
different lower types of oneness is peculiar and unique
in itself according to the subjects which it embraces.
The resemblances are only formal. Once this is perceived, we shall drop the effort to classify the oneness
of Jesus and the Father with some other oneness
of which we know.

As high and as absolutely singular as are the
Father and the Son, so high, so absolutely singular

and unlike any other oneness is that of him who is the one eternal Father with him who is the one eternal Son. Only he who has sounded the depths of the godhead of this Father and this Son could grasp what their oneness actually is. The ancient church defined the ἕν of Jesus by the great term ὁμοουσία, which retains the supreme credit of rising above all earthly categories to the actual numerical ἕν of the οὐσία (being or essence) eternal in the Son as in the Father. No truer, higher, or more adequate term has ever been furnished by the mind of the church. Unsatisfactory by comparison is the idea of a oneness of several joined merely in action or suffering (Zahn). Paul wrote Col. 2:8, 9: "Beware lest any man spoil you through philosophy and vain deceit, after the tradition of men, after the rudiments of the world, and not after Christ. For in him dwelleth all the fulness of the godhead bodily." Before the divine oneness of these infinite persons we bow down in childlike adoration and worship. As regards 14:28, this passage refers only to the human nature of Jesus.

31) **The Jews again took up stones in order to stone him.** They picked them up where the building operations of reconstructing parts of the Temple were going on and brought them to the Porch of Solomon as they had done once before (8:59). This their action is their answer. The aorist records only the fact.

32) As Jesus met their challenge (v. 25, etc.) unflinchingly, so he now stands his ground as the stones arrive. **Jesus answered them,** namely this action of theirs, **Many excellent works did I show you from the Father. On account of which of those works are you trying to stone me?** The pertinency of the assertion and the question of Jesus is lost when the emphasis is placed only on the object "many excel-

lent works" and not equally on the modifier "from the Father." The point is not merely that these many works are καλά, "excellent," *praeclara*, and that Jesus showed these works to the Jews, so that they could not but see this excellence; but that by their very excellence these excellent works show that they are and must be "from the Father." In other words, these works reveal in an actual, visible manner, that Jesus and the Father are one, just as he has said. This oneness of himself with the Father is manifested not only in the one work by which Jesus and the Father equally keep the sheep in their hand against any possible foe, it is manifested in every work of Jesus; for every one of these works wrought in his great mission, while it is done by him as the Son coming from the Father, is done equally by the Father through the Son. This is the point which makes the preamble so vital for the question. John has recorded two of these excellent works at length (5:1-9; 9:1-7), to the rest he refers in 2:23 and relies on the records of the other evangelists.

With ποῖον Jesus asks the Jews to point out a quality (R. 740) in any one of these many works which shows that it is not "of the Father," does not originate (ἐκ) from him and reveal this its origin to them. What Jesus asks is this, "Does any work that I have shown you contradict my assertion that I and the Father are one," so that this assertion of mine must be ranked as blasphemy deserving the penalty of stoning? The question is directly to the point. Those who think that Jesus is shifting the issue from his words (which sound like blasphemy to the Jews) to his works (which the Jews must acknowledge as "excellent"), miss the very point that is emphasized in "from my Father." The present tense λιθάζετε is inchoative, "begin or try to stone me," R. 880. The question of Jesus contains no irony,

which would only the more enrage the passion of the
Jews. It calmly asks them to stop and to think, to
make sure of their ground, and lays the finger on the
one decisive point. Jesus never asks anyone simply
to assent to the abstract metaphysical proposition
that he and the Father are one in essence. That would
be a serious mistake and would call out equally abstract denials. What he does is to show us the quality
of his words and of his works; these are the true
mirror of his person. He who looks into this mirror
will confess with John, "We beheld his glory, glory
as of the Only-begotten from the Father."

33) The Jews do pause and feel that they must
justify themselves. **The Jews answered him, Not
for an excellent work are we trying to stone thee
but for blasphemy, namely that thou, being a man,
makest thyself God.** Since this is nothing but
defense and self-justification, we are not to think that
the Jews here admit that all the works of Jesus are
"excellent," or that they have forgotten their deduction that, because he did some of these works on the
Sabbath, he could not be of God. All they say is that
they are not considering any work of Jesus, whether
it is excellent or not, when now proceeding to stone
him (λιθάζομεν, again inchoative present) but his
blasphemous utterance — that being more than
enough and coming squarely under the law set down
in Lev. 24:15, 16. Bent only on justifying their
action, these Jews separate the words and the works
of Jesus, whereas Jesus demands that they be combined. Never having seen the Father (whom they
did not even know, 8:19) in any of the works of
Jesus, nor heard the Father's voice (which was wholly
foreign to them, 5:37, 38) in any of the words of
Jesus, they now again are wholly deaf to the decisive
phrase: many excellent works "from the Father,"
and judge both Jesus' works and words without

true reference to the Father, who is so foreign to them.

This, however, the sharp ears of these Jews at once caught, that by saying, "I and the Father, we are one," Jesus was making himself God. They caught this because it was exactly what they wanted, a word on which to base the charge of blasphemy and thus full justification for the summary inflection of the death penalty. The fact that this penalty should be decreed only by a legal court after a fair and honest trial counts for nothing in their passionate hatred once for all to be rid of Jesus. They intend to dispense with legal formalities and to lynch this flagrant blasphemer on the spot. This Jewish charge of blasphemy must stand against Jesus to this day if he, being nothing but a man, either by implication or by some direct statement (here or elsewhere) made himself God. He could be exonerated in only one of two ways: first, by proving that he never said what all sacred records state that he did say — that these records are spurious; secondly, by proving that what these records state is not what the recorded words mean. Both methods are hopeless as far as fact and any legitimate proof of fact is concerned. If, nevertheless, we choose the first, we end by having no historical knowledge of Jesus — with the records we completely wipe out "the historical Jesus" and retain nothing but myth and legend. If we choose the second method, then no recorded word of Jesus can mean what it says — we ourselves make these words mean what we think they should mean, and again a "historical Jesus" becomes vapor.

34) Only in one way can the charge that Jesus, being nothing but a man, makes himself God be refuted: he must prove that he calls himself God because he is actually God. This is exactly what Jesus does. By taking up stones against an alleged

blasphemer the Jews appeal to their νόμος, "the law."
By use of this very law Jesus begins his refutation
(v. 34-36) and then completes it by the appeal to his
works (v. 37, 38). In this refutation Jesus not only
repeats the assertion, "I am God's Son," but defines
with simple clarity how he as the Son is one with the
Father. **Jesus answered them, Has it not been written in your law, I myself said, Gods are you? If
he called them Gods, to whom the Word of God
came — and the Scripture cannot be broken — do
you say of him, whom the Father sanctified and sent
into the world, Thou blasphemest! because I said,
Son of God am I?** The force of the circumscribed
perfect is: "it is on record" in Holy Writ. The term
νόμος need not here be restricted to "law" in the
sense of norm according to which one forms his judgments. While "law" often designates the Pentateuch, it is likewise used as a brief title (*Torah*)
for the entire Old Testament. This is the case here
where Jesus quotes Ps. 82:6. On the possessive "your"
law see 8:17.

The refutation is accomplished by means of a syllogism. Major premise: The Scriptures cannot be
broken; minor premise: The Scripture calls men
commissioned by God "Gods"; *ergo*: Jesus, sanctified
and sent into the world by God, is rightly called "God"
in a correspondingly higher sense. This syllogism
operates *a minori ad majus,* and is the more convincing because of this very form. It is hasty to
call this refutation an *argumentum ad hominem.* This
would be the case if by "your law" Jesus referred to
a law which he for his person does not accept; but
he accepts this law as fully as do the Jews. His
major premise is the fact that this law cannot be
broken, i. e., set aside in any way or by any person.
Nor is this an *argumentum ad hominem* by claiming
for Jesus as a mere man the title "God" in the way

in which the human judges in the Psalm have the title *Elohim* or "Gods." The contrast between these judges and Jesus is entirely too strong for this: they, to whom only the Word of God came; he, the one and only one, whom the Father sanctified and sent into the world. This mighty contrast *a minori ad majus* destroys any *argumentum ad hominem*. The supposition that Jesus states the *ergo* in the form *a majori ad minus* is untenable. While he might say, "I am God," he says only, "I am God's Son." In the passage from the Psalm the title "Gods" is synonymous with "children (literally: sons) of the Most High." The fact is that Jesus never calls himself simply "God," ὁ Θεός or Θεός, but always far more precisely, "the Son of God," as in all the instances where he speaks of "my Father" (never using the plural "our"). So in the present case "Son of God" denotes the Second Person of the Godhead as compared with the First.

The Psalm deals with judges and rulers of Israel, scoring them for judging unjustly. God tells them that although he himself called them Gods and children (sons) of the Most High, yet because of their wickedness they shall die like common men. Jesus quotes only these words from the Psalm: "I (Yahweh) said, You are Gods." He at once explains in what sense Jahweh called these judges *Elohim*.

35) It is because "the Word of God came to them," but not in the sense that God granted them certain revelations to communicate to Israel, or gave them his laws to administer in Israel. The Word of God that came to them is the one that appointed them as judges and placed them in their high and holy office. They were judges in a theocracy, in which Yahweh himself was the supreme ruler and judge. Though they received their office through human mediation, they actually held it by divine appointment as God's

own representatives among his people. In this sense, Jesus says, Yahweh himself called these judges *Elohim*; they were appointed by Yahweh's own word. In this respect they resembled the kings and the prophets of Israel. On the latter compare Jer. 1:2 and Ezek. 1:3; to them the appointive word came immediately, just as this afterward was the case with the Baptist, Luke 3:1.

Before Jesus brings in the conclusion he adds parenthetically, "and the Scripture cannot be broken," i. e., in any point or any statement which it contains. While it is only a parenthesis and is like a side remark, this is really the axiomatic major premise of the entire syllogism. Without it the conclusion could not possibly stand. Note that Jesus does not say οὐκ ἔξεστι λύειν τὴν γραφήν, "it is not lawful (not allowed) to break the Scripture." This would be only a subjective Jewish valuation of the Scripture. Any deduction resting only on this premise would be nothing but an *argumentum ad hominem,* binding only the Jews not necessarily Jesus or us, who might hold a view of the Scripture differing from that of the Jews. The axiom in this parenthesis is objective and absolute: οὐ δύναται λυθῆναι ἡ γραφή, "the Scripture cannot possibly be broken," no word of it be dissolved; compare 7:23; Matt. 5: 19. Every statement of the Scripture stands immutably, indestructible in its verity, unaffected by denial, human ignorance or criticism, charges of errancy or other subjective attack. Thus in the present case no power or ingenuity of man can alter Ps. 82:6, and the fact that Yahweh called his human judges *Elohim.*

36) On the premises thus laid down Jesus rests the incontrovertible conclusion. But in doing so he lifts himself far above the human judges and the reason why they were called gods. Over against the relative clause which declares why Yahweh could and

did call these judges gods, Jesus sets the relative clause
which describes the supreme nature of his own office,
"whom the Father sanctified and sent into the world."
In a broad way, like those judges of the Psalm, Jesus,
too, has an office from God and can thus be classed
with them.   But the moment his office is compared
with theirs, a tremendous difference appears.   This
centers both in the designation of the person who
placed Jesus in his office and in the action by which
this was done.   It is "the Father" who sanctified and
sent Jesus.   As "the Father" he did this, which
means that the one sanctified and sent is the Son, and
that for this office and work he could use none other
than his own Son.   Judges in Israel there could be
many, but only One could be sanctified and sent into
the world from heaven itself for the actual redemption and salvation of the world.   To such judges (and
any other men commissioned by God) he could send
his appointive word at the proper time in the course
of their lives; not so in the case of Jesus, his mission
began in the counsel between the Father and the
Son in heaven.   His very person and the work he
was to do necessitated this course, and this very course
reveals who Jesus is and what name properly designates him.

Both aorists, "he sanctified and sent," are historical.   In the nature of the case both acts precede
the coming of Jesus into the world.   Because they
take place between the Father and the Son in
heaven, we are able to conceive of them only imperfectly.   Whether the sanctifying and the sending are
distinct, or whether they are simultaneous is hard to
determine.   If we may judge from the analogy in
Jer. 1:5, the former is the case, and the act of sanctifying would consist in designating and setting apart
the Son for the blessed mission.   Yet, as taking place
between the Father and the Son, this sanctifying

would exceed that of any human prophet or apostle (Gal. 1:15), even as the Son stands infinitely above them. As regards the sending itself a similarity exists (Isa. 6:8, 9; John 20:21, καθώς "even as"); yet of no man do we ever read that God "sent him into the world" on a mission. The verb ἀποστέλλω means to send away for a definite purpose or on a specific mission, and thus differs from the wider term πέμπω, also used regarding Jesus, which denotes only transmission, C.-K. 1018. The accusative after ἀποστέλλω only occasionally indicates what the person sent becomes by being sent; thus in Mark 1:2, "I send my messenger." Quite generally the accusative states who the person is that is being sent, Matt. 21:1, "two disciples"; 21:34-37. This is especially clear when a second accusative indicates what the person sent is to be in his mission: "The Father sent the Son to be the Savior of the world," I John 4:14. Thus the claim is answered that the Son became the Son and is called the Son only by virtue of the sending, i. e., is the Son only as having become man.

Again, this sending is not merely *"to* the world" and to be dated from the time when Jesus began his public work; but a sending *"into* the world," to be dated prior to the Incarnation: "I came forth from the Father, and am come into the world; again, I leave the world, and go to the Father." The fact that God's Son is thus sent reveals the greatness and the value of his mission: *Ratio sub qua Jesus Christus agnoscendus est; missio praesupponit Filium cum Patre unum,* Bengel on 17:3. Having come thus from heaven to earth on his great mission, Jesus rightly confronts the Jews with the question: "Do you say of him, whom the Father sanctified and sent into the world, Thou blasphemest! because I said, I am God's Son"? When our excellent grammarian Robertson ventures into the field of exegesis with a reference to υἱός without the article and has Jesus claim that he is "a son of God" by way of an *argumentum ad hominem* (781), he contradicts himself when he admits that υἱὸς ἀνθρώπου in John 5:27 may mean either "*the* Son of man" or "*a* son of man." But the matter is not determined alone by the absence or the presence of the article. When Jesus calls himself, "*the* Son of man" some eighty times and then in one instance omits the article, this exception means only one thing — he now says, "*a* son of man." And when Jesus places "Son of God" beside "Father," and does that after a relative clause as plain as the one here used, by "Son" he means *the* Son beside whom no other such Son exists. See above on 5:27.

37) The Jews may well have been startled to learn that God himself called men appointed to office by him "gods." If Jesus should claim no more than that he belonged to this class, their charge of blasphemy against him would already be refuted. It is overwhelmingly crushed by the evidence that the office of Jesus is one that is infinitely above all such judges or any other representatives of God who in the course of their lives receive their appointment only by some word of God. This evidence Jesus now once more lays before them in a manner so clear that any doubt or denial is utterly in vain. **If I am not doing the works of my Father, do not believe me,** i. e., do not give me credence in what I say of myself. In conditions of reality the negative is alway οὐ, R. 1011. Note the present ποιῶ, which is not timeless but durative: Jesus is still engaged in doing these works. He has pointed to them in v. 25 and 32. In the latter passage he does it to shame the ingratitude of the Jews who seek to stone him; here he does it to show the wrong nature of their unbelief, making him a liar and a blasphemer. Jesus here refers to what he did in 5:31 and 36, and again in 8:13, etc. These Jews

claim that the testimony of Jesus is unsupported and that, therefore, they are right in refusing him credence. They can do this only by completely shutting their eyes to the works of Jesus, which absolutely substantiate his verbal testimony concerning himself as God's Son.

"The works of my Father" are the miracles of Jesus. Whether we make the genitive merely possessive: which belong to my Father; or subjective: which my Father does through me, these works show beyond question that he whose mission includes such works is the very Son of the Father who sanctified and sent him on his mission. Any other estimate of these works is inadequate and wrong and, therefore, untenable. We see this right along in the way in which these works worry the Jews. They are compelled to shut their eyes to these works (9:41); they try to pick some flaw in them (9:16; 5:18 and 7:23, 24); they never attempt a real fathoming of these works. The denial of the deity of Jesus has never progressed beyond this attitude of the Jews in regard to his works. The imperative, "do not believe me," i. e., what I say of myself, is not categorical but permissive. We must recall 4:48 with its complaint that men will not believe unless they see signs and wonders; likewise 8:14, where Jesus asserts that his word-testimony is true, irrespective of any further testimony. Thus Jesus does not forbid faith in his words alone, apart from his works. His words alone are enough for faith. In a large number of instances we do not require the legal two or three witnesses; one testimony is ample to convince us. Only where men refuse credence, the second and the third testimony, by corroborating the first, compel credence; so that, if it be still refused, the refusal is full of guilt. It is thus that Jesus here appeals to his works: "If I am not doing — actually doing — my Father's works, then you may claim that you are not bound to believe what I say to you about myself."

38) On the other hand: **But if I do them, and if you believe not me, believe the works — in order that you may come to realize and may go on realizing, that the Father is in me, and I am in the Father.** By making both conditions conditions of reality: "if I actually do not — if I actually do" my Father's works, Jesus puts the alternative squarely up to the Jews. They must choose either the nay or the yea — a third does not exist. To refuse to make the choice is to condemn themselves. That the choice must be yea, since the works are being done and cry out their testimony to all who see them, Jesus does not even need to intimate.

This time the imperative is categorical, "believe the works!" That this is the case we see from the preamble, "and if you believe not me," namely my words about myself. This condition of expectancy points to the refusal of the Jews to believe Jesus' words. At the same time it implies that the person and the words of Jesus are themselves enough to receive credence without the works; compare 6:63, etc., and 68, etc. Note the contrast between the two datives ἐμοί and τοῖς ἔργοις, the faith-inspiring personality of Jesus as it reaches out to men's hearts in his works. On "and if," in preference to "even if," see R. 1026. The thought is that the more one may hesitate to believe Jesus' words, the more he is bound to believe the works, which as actual works admit of no legitimate denial; compare 14:10, 11. The words one may connect only with Jesus, since they fall from his human lips; the works are so connected with both Jesus and the Father who sent him to do these works that he who will not believe the works sets himself in antagonism against the Father. "Believe the works!" means, "Fly not in the face of these!"

The battle of Jesus with the Jews most certainly turned on the truth and the trustworthiness of his statements, here especially the two that he and the Father are one (v. 30), and that he is the Father's Son sent into the world (v. 36). The use of πιστεύειν with the dative by no means reduces the verb to mean only assent to what Jesus thus declares concerning himself. A study of C.-K. 902-905 on John's use of this verb is highly profitable. To receive the testimony of Jesus concerning himself as trustworthy always involves on the part of him who so receives it a personal relation to Jesus in accord with that testimony accepted as trustworthy, i. e., a personal relation to him as God's Son who is one with the Father. This C.-K. define, "to acknowledge Christ and therefore to cling to him." The moment the Jews would admit Jesus to be what he said of himself, that moment their entire attitude toward him would accord with their admission. A glance at M.-M. 514 shows that in the pagan world πιστεύειν moved on a far lower plane, substantiating the abundant references in C.-K. to this effect.

This aids in understanding the purpose clause, which really modifies the entire previous statement. Jesus points to the works he is doing and calls on the Jews to believe at least these works, i. e., that they are indeed — as they can see for themselves — the works of the Father. The moment they thus believe these works as being most certainly connected with the Father, they will believe what Jesus testifies to them concerning his connection with the Father when he says that he and the Father are one and that he is the Son of God come into the world from the Father. The full profundity of this connection will

not at once be clear to them.   But this faith will effect
the purpose of Jesus and of the Father who sent him:
"in order that you may come to realize and may go
on realizing that the Father is in me, and I am in the
Father."   The verb γινώσκω, here used twice, (this
being the assured reading) means far more than intellectual knowing.   It denotes an inner spiritual realization due to the inner contact of faith with Jesus and
the Father.   C.-K. 244 are right in stating that
γινώσκω predicates an inner relation of the subject to
the object, one involving the essentials of salvation.
The aorist is ingressive: "may come to realize"; and
the present is durative: "may go on realizing" with
deeper, fuller personal insight.

The object that will thus be realized is "that the
Father is in me, and I am in the Father."   The great
fact and reality is meant, not the mode and manner
of these persons being the one in the other.   The
latter will always be beyond our mortal grasp, the
former will grow clearer and more self-evident as
our relation with Jesus and the Father becomes more
intimate.   It should be plain that Jesus here defines
what he says in v. 30, "I and the Father, we are
one."   This means far more than that the man Jesus,
who stood before the Jews, is in intimate communion
with God, that God merely fills his heart and mind;
or that as an instrument of God Jesus is in all his
official work moved by God's power and grace.   This
communion and cooperation of the Father with Jesus
is something visible to faith from the very start,
apparent in all the words as in all the works of
Jesus.   Even the beggar in 9:33 at once saw this.
The realization of which Jesus speaks follows this
basic perception of faith and is its result.   It is
summarized in the statement, "Son of God am I."
The oneness we behold in Jesus and the Father is
by no means merely "dynamic," even though a meta-

physical basis for it is acknowledged. Jesus is not merely "the effective organ," and the Father "the determining potency." This might fit "the Father in me"; it would leave untouched the second and equal statement, "I in the Father." For exactly as the Father is in the Son, so the Son is in the Father. And these two are persons, hence their oneness is that of being. This is the ineffable mystery that Jesus, God's own Son, is in essence one with his Father. "He that hath seen me hath seen the Father," 14:9. The relation of these two is an indissoluble interpenetration, equally from the Father to the Son, from the Son to the Father. For it the ancient church coined the term περιχώρησις *essentialis,* than which term no better one has yet been found. That this essential interpenetrating oneness of the divine persons should manifest itself dynamically goes without saying. An additional part of the mystery is the place of the human nature in this divine oneness. All that we may venture to say is that its part in this oneness is wholly passive and receptive through its union with the person of the Son.

39) **They were trying to arrest him again; and he escaped out of their hand.** The supposition that when Jesus concluded by saying, "The Father in me, and I in the Father," he toned down his statement made in v. 30, and that thus the Jews mitigated their violence and instead of stoning him at once sought only to arrest him, is untenable. The closing words say more, and say this more pointedly than v. 30. What stopped the immediate stoning was most probably the effective reference to Ps. 82 and the refutation of the charge of blasphemy. The Jews felt less sure on this point. So they closed in on Jesus to arrest him and to bring him to formal trial before the Sanhedrin, where the exact measure of his guilt could be determined. The imperfect ἐζήτουν = "they tried to

arrest him," and the following aorist records the outcome, in regular Greek fashion; "again" recalls 7:30 and 44.

All that John records is that Jesus escaped their hands. How he succeeded in doing so has called forth various conjectures. Those that assume some kind of miraculous action are least probable, as John would probably have indicated as much if Jesus had escaped in this way. He escaped — that is all.

40) **And he went away again beyond the Jordan to the place where John was at the first baptizing.** The final break had come — Jesus did not return to Jerusalem until Palm Sunday and the final Passover. The adverb πάλιν would intimate that Jesus went back to the place from whence he last came to Jerusalem (v. 22), where thus he had already a short time before spent about two months (the interval between the last two festivals). John does not again (1:28) name the place, but he indicates that the Baptist did much of his work here "at the first," τὸ πρῶτον, adverbial accusative. That is how the people came to make the comparison in v. 41, with the result that many came to faith. **And he remained there** until he was called to Bethany by the death of Lazarus (11:7), after which he retired to Ephraim (11:54).

41) **And many came to him and were saying, John did no sign, but all whatever John said concerning this man was true.** Only a glimpse at the activity of Jesus here in Perea is afforded us. The people flocked to him, and he must have taught them as usual. These people, in a way, compare Jesus with the Baptist, the memory of whom was still vivid among them, for they remark that the Baptist did nothing (οὐδέν) in the way of a sign, implying that Jesus did signs also in this locality. At the same time they connect Jesus and the Baptist and quite in the right manner when they remark that literally

everything the Baptist had told them about Jesus "was true," i. e., when he told it, as now they are able to see for themselves. The testimony of the Baptist was thus bearing its fruit.

42) **And many believed on him there.** The aorist may be ingressive, "came to believe," or simply historical, just reporting the fact. What the rulers at the capital reject with violence these simple people receive for their salvation. John says nothing about them and thus leaves the impression of great success in this corner of the land. Stones for Jesus in Jerusalem, faith for Jesus in Perea. With this bright picture the dark and ugly story of this part of John's Gospel (chapters 7 to 10) ends.

CHAPTER XI

V

Jesus' Final Attestation Before the People, Chapters 11 and 12

The public ministry of Jesus is fast drawing to its close; only about three and a half months are left. In 10:40-42 we catch a glimpse of Jesus' activity during this time. Now John proceeds with the great events that mark the end of this period: first the Raising of Lazarus, then the Royal Entry into Jerusalem, with the important incidents closely connected with these great events.

I. *The Attestation in the Crowning Miracle and its Effect, Chapter 11*

Lazarus is Raised from the Dead, 11:1-44

John presupposes the acquaintance of his readers with Luke 10:38-42. **Now there was a certain person lying sick, Lazarus from Bethany, of the village of Mary and Martha, her sister.** John at once strikes the keynote, "there was a certain person lying sick," the participle ἀσθενῶν being used as the predicate of ἦν. One link follows another in the story: the sickness — the message — the delay of Jesus — the death of the sick man — the return of Jesus into the territory of his enemies — the miracle — the plotting that ends in Jesus' death. God always sees the end from the beginning, whereas our eyes are holden. An example like this should teach us to trust his purposes and leadings "when we cannot see our way."

We have here the first mention of Lazarus. His name is contracted from Ἐλεάζαρος, "whom God helps." While John uses two prepositions: "from Bethany, of the village," the two express only one fact, that Bethany was the native town of Lazarus. Another "Bethany" (wrong reading "Bethabara") is mentioned in 1:28; hence the addition here: "the village of Mary and of Martha, her sister." This Bethany lies just beyond the ridge of Mount Olivet. Mary is mentioned first, although she seems to have been younger than Martha; the reason is added in v. 2 (compare 12:1, etc.). Since the sisters are already well known to John's readers, he is able to refer to them for identifying the home of Lazarus.

2) With δέ John adds a necessary parenthetical remark. **Moreover, it was the Mary that anointed the Lord with ointment and wiped his feet with her hair, whose brother Lazarus was lying sick.** In Matthew's and in Mark's account of the anointing in Bethany we read only of "a woman"; John tells us her name and connects this Mary with Martha, whom we know as her sister from Luke 10:38, etc., and with Lazarus, their brother, whom we now meet for the first time. Thus John carefully supplements the other evangelists and fits his account into theirs. John has two substantivized participles to characterize Mary's act, telling us that she not only used the ointment upon Jesus but also humbled herself by using her hair upon his feet. The aorists denote single past acts, past from the writer's standpoint. For ἦν John might have written ἐστίν: "it is" the Mary; with ἦν he carries her identity back to the time of which he now writes, when Lazarus lay sick. *Then* already she "was" the Mary of whom we *now* say that "she did anoint," etc., (aorists). So also John writes "the Lord" and not "Jesus," since this is a remark intended for his present readers and not part of the historical

narrative. The fact that Lazarus was the brother of the two sisters we learn from the relative clause which mentions only Mary: "whose brother Lazarus," etc. It is Mary whom John evidently means to distinguish. This again appears in v. 45 where she alone is named. Her importance rests on Matt. 26:13. In 12:1, etc., John himself relates the anointing of Jesus in its historical connection; when in the account about Lazarus Mary is here made so prominent, this is done because what happened with regard to Lazarus in a way led to the great and significant act of Mary. Thus it was Mary's brother of whom we hear once more ἀσθενεῖ, that he was lying sick, this repetition intimating the gravity of his condition.

3) After the explanatory remark in v. 2 resumptive οὖν goes on with the story proper. **The sisters, therefore, sent to him, saying, Lord, behold, he whom thou lovest is lying sick.** This must have been done when death began to threaten. We may imagine how the sisters called on Jehovah for help, and how their thoughts turned to Jesus who had healed so many. Alas, the wicked plotting of the Jews had driven him far away. In verses 21 and 32 we see the longing that filled both hearts alike. Finally a messenger is dispatched in haste. The message sent is remarkable. It merely states the fact that Lazarus is sick, although with "behold" it emphasizes that fact. It does not say *how* sick Lazarus is, it leaves that to be inferred. It sends no direct appeal for help; it leaves wholly to Jesus what he will do. This restraint is remarkable. Yet who will deny that the sisters hoped Jesus would restore their brother to health?

"He whom thou lovest," they say, resting the case entirely on *his* love, not on their brother's love, or on their own love to Jesus. They use φιλεῖν, the love

of affection and personal attachment, not ἀγαπᾶν, the
love of the spirit and of reason. In v. 5 Jesus uses
the latter when he tells of his love for Lazarus and
the sisters. Trench remarks that φιλεῖν might be used
by Jesus in regard to the brother but would have been
contrary to the fine decorum of the language of the
Scriptures where the sisters are included. This message with the clause "whom thou lovest" affords us
a glimpse of the affectionate friendship which Jesus
bore to Lazarus. It is friendship of the truest kind,
which, as Augustine says, only needs to know. Yet
here is what troubled the hearts of these sisters, even
as it still troubles many a Christian — to be a friend
of Jesus, embraced in his true and tender affection,
and yet to lie sick, to grow helplessly worse, to die at
last — just as if Jesus, our Friend, had forgotten!
Our answer to this is that above the φιλεῖν stands the
unfathomable and blessed ἀγαπᾶν.

4) The messenger found Jesus, and, we may
assume, supplemented the set message he was to convey with words of his own about the sad condition of
Lazarus. **Now having heard it, Jesus said, This sickness is not unto death but for the glory of God, that
through it the Son of God may be glorified.** John
does not say that this word was addressed to anyone in particular, yet unless Jesus gave the messenger
some other word to report, this must have been his
answer to the sisters. It must be noted that Jesus
does not say that Lazarus will not die but only that
this sickness is not πρὸς θάνατον — its final result and
outcome is not death. This is a statement of fact
not of purpose. With Lazarus being at the verge of
death it is the more striking. In the light of what
follows we see that Jesus here actually promises the
miracle which brought Lazarus back to life.

Here ἀλλά does not introduce the direct opposite of
"unto death." This would require a second πρός

coupled with a term to denote "life." Jesus does not need to state this opposite, for it lies in the negative — what does not end in death must end in life, for nothing lies between. Now the preposition is ὑπέρ with the genitive: "for the sake of," "in behalf of the glory of God." This states the reason why this sickness has come to Lazarus. It tells, not of the outcome, but of the purpose back of both the sickness and its outcome; this is the furtherance of "the glory of God," which, of course, cannot mean the heavenly glory, the sum of God's perfections, incapable of any increase in themselves, but the earthly manifestation of this glory as it shines out more and more fully among men and is seen more and more clearly by men. This glory could have been enhanced by Jesus' healing of the sickness of Lazarus; it was to be enhanced by an even greater miracle, by raising Lazarus from the dead. This is another case like that of the blind beggar in 9:3.

The purpose clause, "that through it the Son of God may be glorified," elucidates the short phrase "for the glory of God." The verb "may be glorified" has the same sense as the preceding noun "glory," an act which makes the divine perfection of Jesus shine out the more before men that they may see these perfections the more fully and clearly. The agent back of the passive verb is God himself: he intends to use this sickness of Lazarus (διά denotes the means) to reveal Jesus more fully as his own Son. Compare 1:48-51; 2:11. God's glory shines out before men when the glory of Jesus as God's Son appears to them, when the two are recognized, the one as the Father and the other as the Son (1:14). The shining forth of the glory of the Son of God is the shining forth of God's own glory; for: *Gloria Dei et gloria Filii Dei una gloria,* Bengel. With great plainness Jesus here once more calls himself ὁ υἱὸς τοῦ Θεοῦ (10:36; 1:34).

This world found lodgment in Martha's heart when afterward she confesses, "I believe that thou art the Christ, *the Son of God,* who comes into the world," v. 27. In the raising of Lazarus especially two of the divine attributes came to view, omnipotence and mercy. Jesus exercised these attributes and thus revealed himself as the Son of God. He exercised them in the execution of his mission from the Father; thus the Father and the Son are equally revealed in the exercise of these attributes by Jesus. Even now the revelation of the glory has begun, for Jesus speaks as one who is in full possession of the purposes of his Father and thus declares these purposes in advance. And all this glory of the Father and the Son is connected with our salvation (17:2).

5) Another parenthetical remark is now inserted, in order that we may read aright what follows. **Now Jesus was loving** (and thus acted in accord with this love in what he now did) **Martha and her sister and Lazarus,** ἠγάπα, with the all-comprehending and purposeful love of the Son of God. The order in which the three are mentioned is probably that of their ages. "And her sister" couples Mary with Martha. Lazarus lay dying — a black cloud lay over the home in Bethany, but above it shone the love of Jesus.

6) Human love would have hurried to Bethany with all speed to arrive, if possible, before death set in. Divine love acts otherwise and also has the divine knowledge for its work. **When, therefore, he heard that he was sick, then he remained for two days in the place where he was.** With οὖν the narrative is resumed. But we mark the repetition that Jesus "heard that he was sick" (the Greek retains the original present tense "is sick," v. 2), which makes the impression that Jesus deliberately remained right where he was for two entire days, i. e.,

that he purposely waited here until Lazarus actually died.

One need not assume that Lazarus was already
dead when the messenger reached Jesus, or that he
died before the messenger's return to Bethany. Both
suppositions are based on the four days during which
Lazarus lay in the tomb (v. 17), counting one day for
the messenger to reach Jesus, two days for Jesus'
delay, and one day for Jesus to travel to Bethany.
We are not sure that the messenger reached Jesus
in one day — he may not have known exactly where
to go, for John mentions no definite place where Jesus
was. The manner in which Jesus afterward announces the death of Lazarus to the disciples leaves
the impression that Lazarus had died just then, and
that Jesus knew of it by virtue of his omniscience.
The actual death of Lazarus is thus the signal for
Jesus to start for Bethany. He had no reason for
hurry. Lazarus was, no doubt, buried the day on
which he died, as was customary in that climate. On
the fourth day following, Jesus reached Bethany.
Thus Lazarus lay in the tomb part of the day on
which he was buried, two full days besides, and part
of the day on which he was raised from the dead.
The number four, here as elsewhere in the Scriptures,
indicates a certain completeness. Jairus' daughter
was raised immediately after her death, the widow's
son at Nain during the course of his funeral, Lazarus from the tomb after decomposition was under
way. The messenger returned before the death. On
his deathbed Lazarus heard the word of Jesus which
the messenger brought back. Yet death sat upon
his brow, and either that night or the next day Lazarus died.

7) **Then after this he says to the disciples, Let
us go into Judea again.** Note the antithesis be-

tween τότε μέν in v. 6 and ἔπειτα, R. 1152. The double adverbial expression "then after this" draws especial attention to the time and the delay, as if something important had finally occurred to demand a return to Judea. The subjunctive "let us be going" is hortative, R. 931. "Into Judea" is used instead of "to Bethany" because of the danger involved, as the next verse shows.

8) **The disciples say to him, Rabbi** (see 1:38), **the Jews were but now seeking to stone thee; and goest thou thither again?** The imperfect ἐζήτουν (10:39) marks the unsuccessful attempt, R. 885. Even the disciples, themselves Jews, put a hostile sense into "the Jews." They vividly recall 10:31 and 39. Will Jesus again put himself into mortal danger? The disciples say nothing about themselves; their thought is first of Jesus, yet v. 16 shows how they certainly would not let Jesus go alone, no matter what the danger.

9) **Jesus answered, Are there not twelve hours of the day? If a man walk in the day, he does not stumble because he sees the light of this world. But if a man walk in the night, he stumbles because the light is not in him.** Jesus is speaking of the ordinary working day, which extends from morning until evening and was thus divided into twelve hours. This was the popular way of counting even where otherwise the Roman method of reckoning the legal day from midnight to midnight, or the Jewish method from evening until evening, was used. The same is true with regard to the time of life and labor which God allots to a man — there are its twelve hours. Jesus implies that his own earthly working day is not yet ended, and that even if now it be the twelfth hour for him, he shall have also that hour for his work, and nobody shall be able to rob him of it by killing him

before the time. Compare 9:4: "We must work the works of him that sent me, while it is day; the night cometh, when no man can work."

Jesus says, "If a man walk," and not, "If he work," because he has just proposed a journey back to Judea. He keeps to the figure when he adds, "he does not stumble," using the present tense, as in maxims, not the future, R. 1019. The reason for not stumbling is plain: "because he sees the light of this world," daylight is all about him. Just as the twelve hours of the ordinary working day are made light by the sun in the heavens, enabling a man to complete his day's task; so the time of life granted by God to a man is full of light in order that he may accomplish the work God wants him to do. The statement is entirely general and refers to God's children in general as well as to Jesus in particular. Only Jesus saw the day of his life and every hour of it with perfect clearness, while our eyes are often clouded because of sin. He, therefore, moved amid dangers with an assurance and fearlessness that astonishes us. We can only place ourselves into God's hand, doing his will as his Word and his providential indications point it out to us; yet we, too, are to know that the time he wants us to have will surely be ours — the entire twelve hours, even if we do not know just which hour each is as it arrives.

10) The statement about "the night" is so evidently a counterpart to the one on "the day," that we do not think, either that Jesus now alters the figure, or that he now no longer refers to himself. As the day with its twelve working hours pictures the length of life allotted by God, so the night pictures death as the end of life's day. Correspondingly Jesus describes our life as "seeing the light of this world" and our death as "the light not being in us." The thought is deeper than is generally perceived, for "the light" is used in

a double way. When we are alive we see the light of this world (the sun) because our life is itself a light and is thus able to see; when we are dead, not merely the sun is taken from us, but the very light that is in us ourselves (life) is gone. This explains the stumbling, which like the walking and the opposite of walking, is used with intensive force. We should not think of walking the entire twelve hours — nobody does that; likewise we often stumble, in the ordinary sense of the word, even during the day. To walk and not to stumble means to go on with our life's work; to stumble means to come to the end of our life's work, for this is something that happens not merely when the daylight ceases, but when the light in our own eyes goes out in death.

What causes some odd interpretations is the failure to perceive that here again, as in 10:1, etc., Jesus uses Biblical allegory, i. e., weaves together figure and reality. The key is in the question, "Are there not twelve hours in the day?" Night merely ends these hours, and we are not to think of another twelve hours for the night. We lose the thread when we think that seeing the light of this world and the light not being in us are merely ornamental touches without significance; the one describes life while it lasts, the other death when life is past. The thought is again misunderstood when walking in the day is made faithfulness in our calling and stumbling in the night unfaithfulness; or the former, to remain in our calling, or to remain in fellowship with Christ (the light), and the latter to forsake our calling, or to leave Christ; or variations of these ideas. These are untenable because Jesus speaks of himself as well as of his followers. "If a man walk in the night, he stumbles," does not mean that he goes on, but now stumbling along in the dark; for Jesus does not add, "because he does not see the light of the world," but, "the light is not in him," — he is dead: "the night cometh when no man can work," 9:4.

Jesus reassures the disciples: though he returns to Judea, his enemies will not be able to cut short his life and work, as these were allotted to him by his Father; he will not die until his earthly mission is accomplished. And their own lives and labors are under the same divine control — let them not fear what men threaten to do.

11) **These things he spoke,** pausing at this point to allow the disciples to ponder a little on his significant words. **And after this he says to them, Lazarus, our friend, is fallen asleep, but I am going, that I may wake him out of sleep.** So this is why Jesus determined to go back into Judea. He calls Lazarus "our friend." This plural "our" is noteworthy, for Jesus always distinguishes between "our" and "your," and "your" and "my." Here Jesus raises the disciples to a position beside himself, into that blessed circle of which he, the Master and Friend, is the center. As the friend of Jesus, Lazarus is the friend of the disciples. So it should ever be among all the friends of Jesus.

Not the slightest indication appears that a messenger from Bethany brought the news of Lazarus' death. The very contrary is implied, for if a messenger had come, the disciples would have heard about the death from him. Here, then, is a case where Jesus uses his omniscience in his mission. This, too, is part of the miracle recorded by John. The announcement is one word: κεκοίμηται, "sleeps," the perfect denoting a present state, R. 895. "Since the days of old men on earth, and among them the children of Israel, used this euphemism in speaking of dreadful death because of the outward similarity and in order to cast a soft veil over the grave; but in the mouth of the Lord this figure of speech turns

into reality." Stier.   To speak of sleeping "is to indicate secretly the resurrection from the dead,
since they who sleep have the hope of rising again."
Luther.

"*Our* friend," but not, "Let *us* go and awake him."
"*Our* friend," but, "*I* am going, that *I* may awake
him," although the "I" is not made emphatic by an
ἐγώ.   Someone has written a little book on the striking manner in which Jesus manifested his deity by
his use of the personal pronouns.   In Bethany all is
still dark — the shadow lies heavy on the sisters'
hearts, doubts, questions, disappointment wrestle in
the gloom with faith that strives to find and to hold
the hope in the words Jesus sent by the messenger.
But beyond the Jordan the sun is already shining: "I
am going that I may awake him out of sleep."

12)   **The disciples, therefore, said to him, Lord,
if he is fallen asleep he will be saved,** i. e., from
death, by recovery.   The conclusion is the more natural
since two days ago Jesus had said that the sickness of
Lazarus was not "unto death," i. e., to have death as
its end, but for the glory of God and of his Son.
Had not Jesus healed the officer's son at a distance,
4:50-52?   Had he not during the past two days acted
as if Lazarus had been dismissed from his mind?   It
seems like going too far to charge the disciples with
"grave misunderstanding."   Of course, they do not
understand, but their lack of understanding lies in
their failure to connect the going of Jesus to Bethany
to wake up Lazarus with the sleeping of Lazarus.   For
the intimation is that, if Jesus does not go and wake
him up, Lazarus will remain asleep.   This is the intimation the disciples fail to perceive.   Any natural,
health-restoring sleep would not last until Jesus made
the long journey to Bethany.   Just how the reply of
the disciples applies to the proposal of Jesus to go
and to wake Lazarus up is not indicated by John.   Did

they mean, thinking as they do of natural sleep, that Jesus will not need to go to wake him up, that he will wake up on his own accord long before Jesus arrives? Do they include the thought that with Lazarus on the way to recovery Jesus will not need to make the journey and run into danger? Or did they think nothing at all about this proposed waking up of Lazarus and express only their gladness at his prospective recovery?

13) Here again John adds a parenthetical remark. **Now Jesus had spoken concerning his death; they, however, thought that he spoke concerning the resting of sleep.** Quite generally this parenthesis is passed over without further remark. To be sure, Jesus referred to death, and the disciples thought only of "the resting of sleep," appositional genitive, R. 498. That need not be said; every reader perceives that without being told. Then why this remark? *"They* (ἐκεῖνοι) thought" means to say: the rest — not John himself. He at once perceived what Jesus had in mind.

14) **Then Jesus said to them with plainness, Lazarus died.** Only two words. The brevity heightens the effect. The aorist simply states the fact. When did he die? The answer is: just now. How did Jesus know? The answer is: by the use of his omniscience in this important part of his mission. Both announcements, that in v. 11 and now that in this verse, read as though Lazarus had just died and as though this is the signal for Jesus to proceed to Bethany.

This first consideration which induces some to place the death at least two days earlier is the one in regard to the four days mentioned in v. 17, which we have cleared up in v. 6. Hence we need no explanation as to why Jesus either kept the fact of the death from the disciples for two days, or that he himself did not learn of the death until just now. In support of the former we are told that Jesus withheld the news because he wanted to start so late in order that Lazarus might lie in the tomb so long a time. Those who choose the latter alternative tell us that not until now the death "entered the consciousness of Jesus" by an intimation from the Father. Both are cases where a misconception introduces difficulties, for which some plausible explanation is then made. Some even suppose that a second message from Bethany brought the news of the death.

A second interpretation introduces the Father into the narrative as controlling every word and every movement of Jesus. He first informs Jesus only to the extent that the sickness is not unto death but has a higher purpose. He does not permit Jesus to heal Lazarus at a distance, or at once to go to Bethany. But now, after two days, he orders Jesus to go to Bethany, either ordering him now to raise up Lazarus, or giving this order only after Jesus arrives at the tomb. Jesus is made a tool of the Father and is placed on a level that is no higher than that of the prophets or the apostles after they were in their ministry. This is evolved out of the prayer of Jesus in v. 41, 42. John's narration is without a trace of this detailed control; in fact, throughout the emphasis is on what Jesus himself does. This control of Jesus by the Father, furthermore, involves specious ethical considerations. Lazarus dies "without the knowledge and will of Jesus." It would be wrong for Jesus to wait for his death and then proceed to act. Thus some have Lazarus die before the messenger reached Jesus, or at least before Jesus and the messenger could have reached Bethany. At any rate, the work Jesus was just now doing in Perea compelled him to stay two days, so that he *could* not go earlier — and thus Lazarus died. These complications are furthermore involved with the supposed directions from the Father. This structure with its various ramifications falls to pieces when we recall that all that happened to Lazarus certainly happened "with the knowledge and will" of the Father. Who will apply ethics to the Son which do not apply equally to his Father?

In v. 4 Jesus promises the resurrection of Lazarus. That means the death of Lazarus and the fact that Jesus will not prevent that death. On the prayer at the tomb see v. 41, 42. Both the Father and Jesus are agreed that this shall be the crowning miracle, i. e., that Lazarus shall be raised after lying in the tomb so long that his body has begun to decay.

15) It is not a word of grief but one of joy which Jesus adds to the announcement of the death: **And I am glad for your sakes, to the intent that I was not there; nevertheless, let us go to him.** This gladness emanates from far higher considerations than those which we ordinarily connect with sickness, death, and bereavement. Jesus is glad because his disciples — and not only they — shall now see the glory of his Father and of himself as the Son of God revealed in the resurrection of Lazarus. The phrase "for your sakes" is at once defined by the purpose clause, "that you may believe." No object is needed with "may believe," for faith as such is intended. The aorist πιστεύσητε may be ingressive, "come to believe," which, since they already believe, would mean a new and higher start in faith; in 2:11 "his disciples believed on him," although before the miracle they already had faith.

When the circumstance "that I was not there" is made "a divine dispensation," one which Jesus "had not willingly and purposely occasioned," the fact is overlooked that the Father and the Son never act apart from each other, yea, that Jesus here says that he himself rejoices in this "divine dispensation." Ethically it is no more wrong to occasion a circumstance than to rejoice in it when occasioned by another. Nor is Jesus guilty of dissimulation in rejoicing over what he himself helped to occasion. This confusion of thought disappears when the words of Jesus are taken together as they stand: he rejoices, not because of his mere absence from Bethany, but because of this absence in combination with what it will produce for his disciples. The emphasis is not on the clause "that I was not there" but on the phrase "for your sakes," defined by "in order that you may believe." If the Father and Jesus had arranged for Jesus to be at Bethany during the sickness of Lazarus, Jesus would have healed his friend, and the miracle would have been one of a common type; by the dispensation, in which both the Father and Jesus concur, a miracle comes to be wrought that exceeds in its revelation of the glory of the Father and the Son all the other miracles of Jesus, that brings the most wonderful blessings to those that behold and believe. God and his Son still deal thus with us. At the time of their dispensations we may feel and speak as did the sisters in Bethany (verses 21 and 32), presently, like Jesus, we, too, shall be glad.

"Nevertheless, let us go to him," is adversative (ἀλλά) to the preceding clause, "that I was not there." Now it is time for Jesus to be there and for his disciples likewise.

16) **Thomas, therefore, who is called Didymus, said to his fellow-disciples, Let us go, that we, too, may die with him.** This pessimistic response of Thomas is usually understood as our versions indicate, "Let us also go, that we may die with him (Jesus)." In v. 11 Jesus, indeed, says, "I am going," but he does not use ἐγώ, as though, possibly, the dis-

ciples might not be willing to go. The singular is
used because Jesus alone is the one who will awaken
Lazarus. When in v. 7 Jesus the first time says,
"Let us go," the disciples show reluctance, yet not
on their own but on Jesus' account. From the start
(v. 7) Jesus takes it for granted that the disciples
will go with him. Their fear in regard to himself
he fully removes in v. 9, 10. So now in v. 15 there
is no other thought than that all the disciples will
accompany Jesus. But this leaves the emphatic καὶ
ἡμεῖς of Thomas wholly in the air if it is construed
with ἄγωμεν, "Let *us too* go." Grammatically and
otherwise this is proper only if Jesus had just said,
"*I* (ἐγώ) am going," i. e., whatever *you* may decide
to do. What Thomas really says is, "Let us go, that
we, too, may die with him (with Lazarus)." As so
often in John, the emphatic words in a ἵνα clause are
placed before the conjunction. The credit for this
correct reading belongs to W. Bleibtreu.

Thomas thus appropriates the phrase of Jesus,
"Let us go *to him* (to Lazarus)." "Yes," Thomas
says, "let us — that we, too, may die *with him* (dead
Lazarus)." This is pessimistic unbelief. It is the
very opposite of what John intimates concerning himself in v. 13. Thomas does not believe that Jesus
will be able to raise Lazarus from the dead. The
veiled promise of Jesus has kindled no hope in him.
Going back to Judea, they may all run into death. The
assurance of Jesus in the allegory has not assured
Thomas. Three times when Thomas is introduced
(here and in 20:24 and 21:2) John adds the Greek
equivalent for his Hebrew name; the root of the latter
means *geminus*, "twin," as well as *duplex*. Some regard this *nomen* as an *omen* of the dual character
of this disciple, once brave, even heroic and then black
with gloom; or, referring to 20:24, a man divided,

a doubter. But it would be strange, indeed, to find one of the Twelve marked thus for life with a name perpetuating a fault in his character. Just as the Hebrew name Thomas, given to him at the time of his circumcision, was merely his name, so was its Greek translation Didymus. He may very well have been a twin child, the other of the twins not surviving. John here and elsewhere adds his Greek name, not as a mere translation, but because afterward Thomas was generally just called Didymus. Thomas addressed only the other disciples; Jesus makes no reply — his reply will come at the tomb of Lazarus.

17) Omitting any reference to the journey, John places us in Bethany. **Having come, therefore, Jesus found that he was already four days in the tomb.** On the four days see v. 6; ἔχειν with an adverb is intransitive, R. 799-800, literally, "found him being already," etc. The time spent in the tomb is here mentioned in order to show that the death occurred at the time when Jesus announced it in v. 15.

18) **Now Bethany was near Jerusalem, about fifteen stadia off.** This parenthetical remark explains for Gentile readers how the visitors from Jerusalem easily reached Bethany. The Greeks reckon the distance from the far point forward, hence ἀπό: "from" the capital to Bethany. The distance is about two miles.

19) **And many of the Jews had come to Martha and Mary in order to condole with them concerning their brother.** The term "Jews" here, too, bears a hostile note as far as the attitude of these visitors toward Jesus is concerned; note v. 46. Visits of sympathy and condolence were made to the bereaved for seven days. The fact that many Jews from the capital felt constrained to pay these visits to the sisters in Bethany is evidence of the prominence of the family,

which also seems to include wealth. It has been called "an insinuation lacking good taste" to think that these visits were anything but friendly.

20) **Martha, therefore, when she heard that Jesus was coming, met him, but Mary continued sitting in the house.** Instead of making Martha busy either outside of the house or in the kitchen, while Mary sat among the visitors, we prefer to think of both sisters as sitting in the house with the visitors. Since ὅτι Ἰησοῦς ἔρχεται reads like a quotation, we take it that this was the word that came to Martha. If some villager had spied Jesus and his band of disciples approaching the village, he would have blurted out the news to all the company. So Jesus must have sent some friendly messenger with orders to tell only Martha. He slipped in and whispered to her; she quietly stepped out, leaving Mary and the company undisturbed. She went to the outskirts of the village where Jesus was waiting to receive her alone. No move is made to proceed to the house (v. 30). No outsiders are at hand.

21) As she reaches Jesus, the thought that had again and again passed through her mind as well as through Mary's during the long, heart-breaking days of waiting, while Jesus did not come in response to the message sent him, involuntarily rises to her lips. **Martha, therefore, said to Jesus, Lord, if thou hadst been here, my brother would not have died.** Mary's first word to Jesus is identical with Martha's, v. 32. The condition is one of past unreality (εἰ with the aorist, the aorist with ἄν), with ἦς in the protasis doing duty for the aorist (R. 1015, "Sometimes ἦν is aorist"). Martha's word is neither accusation nor reproach but deep sorrow and poignant regret. When Lazarus was sick, the sisters longed, "Oh, if only he were here!" Then they sent him word, but Lazarus died, and so the regret set in, "Oh, if only he had been

here!" So many sick he had healed, and yet their brother had to die. *"If* thou hadst been here" — who will write the story of these sad, sad "ifs"?

22) The fact that no reproach is intended appears from the way in which Martha at once voices her faith in Jesus. **Even now I know that whatever thou wilt ask God, God will give thee.** "Even now!" — with my brother dead — even in the face of this — I still believe! This resembles Asaph's faith, surmounting all fears and doubts, "My flesh and my heart faileth, but God is the strength of my heart and my portion forever" — read in connection with the entire 73rd Psalm. And Job's word, "Though he slay me, yet will I trust in him," 13:15. The strength of this faith comes out in οἶδα, "I know," the verb denoting knowledge based on intuition or information, Abbott-Smith under γινώσκω. Martha is firmly convinced by all that she has seen and heard of Jesus; and her conviction holds in spite of what now seems so dark to her, so hard to explain.

In stating the sum of her knowledge two things are plain: that she did know much, but also that her knowledge fell short of the full reality. The indefinite relative clause ὅσα ἂν αἰτήσῃ is one of expectancy: Martha rises to the height where she expects Jesus to ask something of God. This hope she could base only on the positive assurance of Jesus that the sickness of her brother was not "unto death" but "for the glory of God, that the Son of God may be glorified thereby." The word ὅσα, "whatever," a distinct echo of the word used repeatedly by Jesus, is especially great, both in its wide sweep and in its indefiniteness, leaving what Jesus will ask entirely to him, not even expressing a wish on her part. The expectancy of the relative clause, based also, as it is, on the implied promise sent by the messenger, contradicts those who think that Martha does not expect Jesus to ask anything of God in this case. While ὅσα veils what Martha expects, it includes the greatest possibilities, also, if it be Jesus' will, the restoration of her brother to life. Martha's only limit is what Jesus may will to ask of God.

Yet she falls short. This is evident chiefly in her use of the verb αἰτεῖσθαι: "αἰτέω, the Latin *peto*, is more submissive and suppliant, indeed the constant word by which is expressed the seeking of the inferior from the superior (Acts 12:20); of the beggar from him that should give alms (Acts 3:2); of the child from the parent (Matt. 7:9; Luke 11:11; Lam. 4:4); of the subject from the ruler (Ezra 8:22); of man from God (I Kings 3:11; Matt. 7:7; James 1:5; I John 3:22); ἐρωτάω, on the other hand, is the Latin *rogo*, or sometimes *interrogo*. . . . Like the Latin *rogo* it implies on the part of the asker a certain equality, as of king with king (Luke 14:32), or, if not equality, familiarity with him from whom the gift or favor is sought, which lends authority to the request. . . . The consciousness of Christ's equal dignity speaks out of this, that as often as he asks or declares that he will ask anything of the Father, it is always ἐρωτῶ, ἐρωτήσω, an asking, that is, as upon equal terms (John 14:16; 16:26; 17:9 and 15 and 20), never αἰτῶ or αἰτήσω. Martha, on the contrary, plainly reveals her poor, unworthy notions of his person and, in fact, declares that she sees in him no more than a prophet, ascribing the αἰτεῖσθαι to him, which he never ascribes to himself," Trench, *Synonyms*, I, 195, etc. Martha, indeed, calls Jesus "the Son of God"(v. 27), but seeing his lowly human form, his praying to God, she still thinks of him as inferior to God.

Exception to the finding of Trench is taken by C.-K. 91, but his main point on αἰτέω remains, that Jesus does not use this verb with regard to himself. On ἐρωτάω the observation of C.-K. is correct: it is only

the refined word for a request and may be used with
regard to an inferior as well as with regard to an
equal.

Some commentators resemble Martha when in this
entire narrative they regard Jesus, not as what he
is, the Son operating together with the Father with
the fullest mutual understanding and unity of will,
but is made a kind of tool or instrument that is moved
only by the Father who is the real agent. So he is
kept in the dark until his Father tells him; he does
not know what he will do, or be able to do until the
Father orders him; in fact, not by his own power but
only by that of the Father does he act. Not thus did
the Father send the Son on his mission, not thus did
the Son execute his Father's mission. Only prophets
and apostles were in such a position.

23) Jesus' dealings with Martha are not fully
understood unless we note well that he is revising her
estimate of his person. Over against her word, *"Died
would not have my brother"* (note the word order
of the Greek) he squarely sets the promise and assurance, *"Rise again shall thy brother."* **Jesus says to
her: Thy brother shall rise again.** Purposely Jesus
does not at once declare his intention. Like a child
he takes her hand to help her up gradually, one step
at a time. This word of Jesus is not "ambiguous,"
nor does it intend to try Martha's faith. It is comprehensive and complete, truly glorious in every respect, and thus for the education and clarification of
Martha's faith.

24) **Martha says to him, I know that he shall
rise again in the resurrection at the last day.** Here
is another οἶδα (v. 22) like the first from Martha's
lips, precious as far as it goes but again rather inadequate. By eliciting this reply from her Jesus helps
Martha to reveal what she still lacks. Jesus wants
her to display her empty way of looking at the resur-

rection in order that he may fill this emptiness with himself, the very resurrection and the life itself, together with all the assurance, hope, and joy that this conveys.

Some, like Martha, find little comfort in this word of Jesus'. Their comment sounds like hers, as if now raising her brother from the tomb where he had lain only four days would be *more, much more* than the resurrection of that body at the last day unto the eternal life of glory; whereas the very reverse is true. As Hiller says, our temporal life and the joy of living it together with our loved ones is still far too precious to us compared with the eternal life which shall reach its climax for the body on the last great day in the blessed resurrection of believers. By declaring, "Thy brother shall rise again," Jesus simply lays down the first great fundamental proposition on which he then proceeds to build the next and the next until the full measure of the truth overflows the heart with comfort and joy.

25) **Jesus said to her, I am the resurrection and the life.** What Jesus said about Lazarus' rising again, and what Martha said about the resurrection at the last day as proclaimed in the Old Testament, all this is actually and literally embodied in Jesus. Here is another mighty "*I AM*," ἐγώ εἰμι. This makes every notion, such as that the Father merely grants something to Jesus at his request, disappear completely. The inadequate is set aside by the adequate. Here again the two articles with the double predicate denote that subject and predicate are identical and interchangeable (R. 768). No resurrection and no life (ζωή) exist except as they are embodied in Jesus. When he is absent, resurrection and life are absent; when he is present, resurrection and life are present.

We should not separate the resurrection and the life, should not ask which is first, which second, which depends upon the other, or produces the other. These are not two, they are essentially one, even as Jesus is one. This one concept is expressed by two words, because we lack a term great enough to serve in place of the two. We must say "life" as the opposite of death, and "resurrection" as the annulment of death. Neither is without the other.

This appears when Jesus now speaks about the possession of himself, the resurrection and the life. Martha had only a small part of the truth when she spoke of the resurrection as an occurrence only at the last day. Jesus gave her the whole truth, not only by combining the resurrection with the life, but by identifying these with himself. Now we see how this glorious treasure may be possessed as an inexhaustible fountain of joy. **He that believes in me, even if he dies, shall live; and everyone that lives and believes in me, in no way shall he die forever.** Here is not only the way of possession but the very possession itself with all it contains. The two parallel statements are not a progress in thought, so that the second flows out of the first; nor is the alternative a mere repetition, a saying the same thing twice with a few different words. The two statements radiate from the one center I AM, just as do the two terms "the resurrection" and "the life." We have two applications, a looking at the person concerned in two ways.

First is the person who dies (κἂν ἀποθάνῃ, expectancy), as Lazarus has died, as every believer will lie down to sleep in death. To him Jesus is "the resurrection," the victory and triumph over death. He shall sleep indeed, yet "he shall live," temporal death harms him not at all. Just as we do not lose a brother or another relative, and he does not lose us when he retires for sleep at night, so we do not lose him when he retires for sleep in the shadow of death. "He shall live" does not mean merely: "shall come to life in the far distant last day," but from the very moment of death on. Only a restful shadow covers him, no real death; for Jesus has taken that away. This is what the believer's death means.

26) Each of the two parallel statements illumines the other. Next the person before he dies: "everyone that lives," that has the true "life" in himself, the ζωή or life principle, which is identified with Jesus, just as is "the resurrection." Having this "life" in himself while he continues here on earth, no death in the real sense can touch him, "in no way shall he die forever" — οὐ μή the strongest negation with the subjunctive, as here, or with a future indicative. Compare 3:15, 16; 6:47; 9:51; and on the negation of εἰς τὸν αἰῶνα, 4:14; 8:35 and 51; 10:28. What a joy in the prospect that we "shall in no way die"!

Both parallels, however, mark the idea of possession in the same way: "he that *believes in me* and yet dies" — "he that lives and *believes in me*" — note the chiastic arrangement. The possession is obtained by connection with Jesus. This connection is spiritual, by the confidence and trust in the soul which clings to Jesus who is all that he says. The present participles are durative qualifications, and the two in the second clause are construed with one article. Instead of using two participles in the first clause: "he that believes and dies," Jesus marks what to us seems a kind of wrong: "he that believes — even if he dies." "Even if" he must pass through temporal death, let this not disturb us. Believing does not relieve us of temporal death even though we may think it should. By using two participles in the second clause: "he that lives and believes," living and believing are so joined that neither is without the other: to live is to believe; to believe is to live. The addition of πᾶς, "everyone," in the second statement is far from mark-

ing a contrast with the first, it leaps back and includes also the first — this is due to the fact that
πιστεύων occurs in both. It is like saying, "he that
believes . . . yes, *everyone* that believes!" It is
impossible that any believer should ever, εἰς τὸν αἰῶνα
(see 8:35), until the end of the Messianic eon, lose
what Jesus here guarantees. Only by turning from
faith are these promises lost.

Therefore the vital question, now put directly to
Martha: **Believest thou this?** To believe "this" is
to believe what he says of himself and thus to believe "in him." It is one thing to hear it, to reason
and to argue about it; and quite another thing to
believe, embrace, trust it. To believe is to receive,
hold, enjoy the reality and the power of it, with all
that lies in it of joy, comfort, peace, and hope. The
measure of our believing, while it is not the measure
of our possessing, since the smallest faith has Jesus,
the resurrection and the life, completely, is yet the
measure of our enjoyment of it all.

27) It is now that Martha rises to her greatest
height by uttering her great confession of faith in
response to Jesus' question. **She said to him, Yea,
Lord, I have believed that thou art the Christ, the
Son of God, he that comes into the world.** With
"yea, Lord" she accepts and confesses all that Jesus
has said of himself. The response is direct and without qualification. In what sense Martha addresses
Jesus as "Lord" is shown by the titles she at once
adds. In "I have believed" note the emphatic pronoun
ἐγώ. Others have not believed, others have charged
Jesus with blasphemy (10:33) for calling himself
"the Son of God" — Martha "has believed," has done
so this long while and is believing now. In stating
the sum and substance of her faith she shows that
she has apprehended the chief and true point in the
self-attestation of Jesus, which is his own person.

Hence all the predicates for "thou art" are *who* Jesus is and not merely *what* Jesus is. The *what* depends entirely on the *who*, and it is the *who* that is merely made manifest by the *what*. This fundamental *who* Martha puts into terms on which the greatest confessors of today could not improve. "The Christ" or Messiah, on the lips of this Jewess, embraces all that the Old Testament contains in its promises to Israel. When she adds the apposition "the Son of God," we dare not forget the preceding scenes in Jerusalem, as they reached a climax during the last festival (10:22-39) on the very issue whether Jesus is "the Christ" (10:24), "the Son of God" (10:33 and 36). With the emphatic ἐγώ Martha puts her faith squarely in contrast with the unbelief of the Jerusalem Jews, some of whom, it seems, were in her house at this very moment (v. 46).

It is surely unjust to the memory of this noble woman to reduce the truth of her confession by having her say that she does not really understand Jesus in regard to what he says about himself as the resurrection and the life, etc., that all she is ready to admit is that Jesus is the Messiah. It is unfair to inquire abstractly what "the Son of God" could mean to her mind and then to make it mean as little as possible by eliminating the deity of Jesus. We feel bound to say that Martha understood "the Christ, the Son of God," in the same sense in which the unbelief of the Jerusalem Jews found blasphemy in it, in the same sense in which Jesus through the messenger co-ordinated the glory of God and the glorification of the Son of God (v. 4). After all these years we ourselves do not fully fathom all that lies in these terms. She actually heaps up the vital terms for adequately designating the person of Jesus, adding as a third the apposition: "he that comes into the world." On ὁ ἐρχόμενος compare 1:9; 4:25; 5:43; 6:14, and other passages. It is always the same verb, and when used by the Jews is always in the present tense. The Messiah is ὁ ἐρχόμενος, "the One Coming." The present tense of the substantivized participle may be considered futuristic, R. 891: "the One who will come," but only as this designation was originally meant. It thus became fixed, and Martha does not change it although Jesus has now come and stands before her at the moment. Compare Matt. 11:3; Luke 7:19, 20. Those who would reduce this participial designation to a relative clause forget that the term has become a fixed title. The phrase "into the world" Martha has learned to add from its repeated use by Jesus himself, for he always says that his Father sent him "into the world," i. e., from heaven to earth. Martha's confession is in the same class with Nathanael's, 1:49; and those of Peter, 6:69; Matt. 16:16.

28) **And having said this, she left and called her sister Mary secretly saying, The Teacher is here and calls thee.** "And calls thee" shows that Martha was Jesus' messenger to Mary. We see by what title the friends of Jesus spoke of him: "the Teacher," ὁ διδάσκαλος. Jesus remained at the outskirts of the village, waiting for Mary. The adverb "secretly" is to be construed with the main verb "called," not with the merely incidental participle. The first εἰποῦσα is antecedent, the second coincident; the nature of the actions decides. A variant for the second is εἴπασα (from εἶπα). It seems to be Martha who decides on the secrecy, not Jesus. As she herself had been called secretly by the messenger, so she now does when she is the messenger.

29) **But she, when she heard it, rose quickly and was going to him.** The imperfect ἤρχετο indicates that more will be said about her going.

30) A parenthesis (hence δέ) explains the situation. **Now Jesus had not yet come into the village**

but was still in the place where Martha had met him. As he had prepared Martha for the miracle, so he desired to prepare her sister also.

31) **The Jews, therefore, who were with her in the house and were condoling with her, having seen Mary, that she got up quickly and went out, followed her, thinking that she was going to the tomb to sob there.** If Mary had risen without haste, as Martha did when she was called, the condoling Jews would have remained seated. The little circumstance that Mary goes out so quickly puts the thought into their minds that she is going to the tomb, there to mourn, and they feel that they must not allow her to go alone, that now especially she needs their support. Note the two adverbs for "quickly" in v. 29 and here in v. 31.

It is evident that Jesus desired to meet both of the sisters quietly at the outskirts of the village, also that in Mary's case a slight thing on her part frustrated this intention. Here let us note that only in those exceptional cases where we are told that Jesus used his supernatural knowledge does he control persons and events. At other times he meets events as they come to him, also those which thwart his intentions, as for instance in Mark 7:24. If we look from Jesus to God and the workings of his divine providence as regards the actions of men in relation to Jesus, we see both control of actions and events and absence of control. In some few instances the why and the wherefore are revealed to us, but in by far the greater number all remains a mystery to us. Only one thing is certain: when God and when Jesus take control, as well as when they do not, both operate in perfect accord, never at cross-purposes. Beyond this our minds cannot go.

32) **Mary, therefore, when she came where Jesus was, at sight of him fell at his feet, saying**

to him, Lord, if thou hadst been here, my brother would not have died. Mary is far more emotional than her sister. John brings out their different characters with wonderful distinctness. The little touch "at sight of him," ἰδοῦσα αὐτόν ("when she saw him"), tells us that this made her sink to the ground and then break out in sobs. Here was the great Helper for whom their heart had longed — oh, how they had longed! — and he had come far too late! The very same words that Martha had uttered rise to her lips; but Mary, bent prostrate, bursts into tears, whereas Martha struggles to express her faith and her hope amid the flood of her grief and regret. The sense of Mary's word and the motive for its utterance are the same as those of Martha in v. 21. The position of μου, in Mary's word before, in Martha's after the noun, is without significance and is apparently due to the writer's choice, R. 420, etc.; 681. Those who in this point see in Mary a deeper feeling for her brother are — straining a point.

33) **When Jesus, therefore, saw her sobbing and the Jews sobbing who had come with her he was indignant in the spirit and shook himself and said, Where have you laid him?** The verb κλαίειν denotes loud, audible weeping, hence "to sob." The verb ἐμβριμάομαι usually has a dative object and then means to turn upon someone with angry words. Here no such object is named, for τῷ πνεύματι is the dative of relation and refers to Jesus' own spirit. "He was indignant in the spirit," *er ergrimmete im Geist* (Luther), means that Jesus restrained his indignation. The only outward sign of deep emotion was the fact that "he shook himself," the verb ταράσσω used in its physical and not in a metaphorical sense ("he troubled himself"), since the emotion of indignation is already indicated. Note the recurrence of this emotion in v. 38, where ἐν ἑαυτῷ is practically

the same as the preceding τῷ πνεύματι. What John describes is a deep emotion of indignation, which produces instead of indignant words only a quivering of the body. This quivering, however, is active: "he shook himself," not passive, as though the strong emotion shook him. This must mean that the bodily quivering is the visible evidence of the inward effort by which Jesus restrained the indignant feeling.

The only cause for this highly unusual effect in Jesus is the sobbing of Mary and her friends; John indicates no other cause. It is impossible to separate the sobbing of the Jewish friends from that of Mary and to assume that their sobbing is hypocritical and thus makes Jesus indignant; yet instead of rebuking it with sharp words, as it would deserve, he compels himself to answer it only by his great deed. John coordinates the sobbing of the Jews with that of Mary; besides, her grief is so deep and apparent that it certainly is perfectly natural for her friends to weep with her. The open grief of Mary and her friends is not the evidence of their unbelief in Jesus, for Mary's word spoken to Jesus is exactly like that of Martha, and both express faith, certainly not unbelief. Moreover, Mary's tears, not any unbelief in their hearts, cause also her friends to break out in tears. Equally untenable is the idea that the indignation of Jesus is directed against the contagion of sobbing as this affects himself, that his business is not to sob with the rest but to act. Also untenable is the psychological explanation, that the will power which Jesus had mustered for effecting the raising of Lazarus was not again to be dissipated by his giving way to the enervating feeling of grief. We know of no mustering of will power for this or for any other miracle of Jesus, especially of a will power that would be weakened by way of sympathetic grief.

Yet why should this sobbing move Jesus to an indignation, the expression of which he represses? It cannot be the mere sobbing itself, it must be this effect together with its cause: the sin and the death which bring such pain even to the hearts that Jesus loves. Invariably Jesus looks beneath the surface even to the very bottom.

That is why John at once adds that Jesus demands to know where Lazarus has been laid. We must not break the link of this second καί in our picture of the scene: "*and* he shook himself *and* he said, Where have you laid him?" His action shall speak more effectively than any words can speak. His indignation against the death which plunges his loved ones into such a flood of sorrow will turn against this death itself by forcing it to give up its prey. It is best to stop at this point. The words of John do not warrant the addition that Jesus is indignant also because this greatest of his miracles will be used by his enemies to bring death upon himself.

34) **They say to him, Lord, come and see.** Several speak at once and like Martha and Mary address him with the title "Lord." They were evidently his friends (v. 45). So the entire company starts toward the tomb. The fine distinction between the present and the aorist imperative must be noted: "be coming (durative) and see (punctiliar)."

35) With gripping brevity and without a connective John writes: **Jesus wept.** Now the verb used is not κλαίειν but δακρύειν — silent tears trickle from his eyes as he walks toward the tomb with the company. It is true, indeed, that this shortest verse in the Bible answers the criticism that has been directed against the genuineness of John's Gospel as painting an unhistorical picture of Jesus, a being with nothing human about him except his outward appearance, being all Logos, all deity. The simple fact is that Jesus is both God and man and so truly man that he here weeps with those that weep. Throughout John's Gospel the human and the divine are combined, and both are equally true. No criticism can ever separate the two. No historical Jesus exists except the Jesus of the four Gospels.

The fact that Jesus wept thus should show clearly that in v. 33 he was not fighting to keep from sobbing with the rest. Jesus ever has perfect control of himself. He now wept because his heart was filled with deepest sympathy, Rom. 12:15. He wept again in keen sorrow over Jerusalem, and then once again in the darkness of Gethsemane (Heb. 5:7)

36) These are noble, manly tears. **The Jews, therefore, said, Behold, how he loved him!** They were certainly right. Naturally they speak of φιλεῖν, the love of friendship and affection, and the imperfect expresses the duration of this affection in the past and up to the present.

37) **But some of them said, Could not he, the one who opened the eyes of the blind man, have caused this man also not to die?** Sometimes these people are assumed to be hostile to Jesus and are identified with those mentioned in v. 46, who also are regarded as being hostile. But throughout the account concerning the blind beggar (9:15-34) we find that the Pharisees refused to admit the fact of the miracle, while the present questioners do the very opposite. Instead of hostility their question expresses perplexity, in fact, the very perplexity with which Martha and Mary wrestled. They, too, had used φιλεῖν in their message to Jesus. How could Jesus have such affection for Lazarus and yet somehow fail to be at hand and heal him before he died? As in the case of the sisters and their word of deep regret to Jesus

(v. 21 and 32), a degree of faith in Jesus is manifested in this question of the Jews. They here speak
of the case of the blind beggar because this was the
last notable miracle performed in Jerusalem. The
raising of Jairus' daughter and of the widow's son
occurred in Galilee and may not even have been known
to the people in Jerusalem. At least their thought,
like that of the sisters, is only regarding the preven-
tion of death not regarding a miracle performed upon
one already dead.

38) **Jesus, therefore, again filled with indignation in himself, comes to the tomb.** The οὖν connects
only the main verb with what precedes: "Jesus, therefore, comes to the tomb," and not the participle: "therefore filled again with indignation." This οὖν links into
the inquiry which Jesus made about the location of
the tomb and the answer he received when the people
told him to come along with them and to see. This
Jesus did, and "accordingly" (οὖν) he now arrives at
the tomb. This is the grammar of the statement.
Coincident with ἔρχεται is what the present participle
reports: πάλιν ἐμβριμώμενος ἐν ἑαυτῷ; in other words, as
Jesus arrives and sees the tomb, the feeling of indignation again rises in him. It is only a variation
of expression when John writes "in himself" instead
of repeating the dative "in the spirit" (v. 33). This
time John does not add the detail that this indignation showed itself visibly. This is taken for granted,
having been stated before; moreover, no one could
have known of this return of the feeling in Jesus if it
caused no visible effect in Jesus.

All this means that John in no way connects the
renewed indignation with the words of perplexity
uttered by some of the Jews. All that is recorded in
v. 35-37 occurs on the way to the tomb, before it is
reached. The indignation wells up in Jesus' heart
only as he arrives at the tomb. These facts remain

even when we now consider the words of "some of them" to be *Spottreden,* "words of mockery," which, as we have seen, they are not. As the first feeling of indignation is not caused by words of mockery, so also this second feeling. The adverb "again" makes both alike due to the same cause. Here is the tomb, the very evidence of the death that has brought all this anguish upon the hearts that Jesus loves dearly. The sight of this stronghold of death causes the former feeling of indignation "again" to rise. And this time Jesus does not put his feeling into words but promptly proceeds to action. One additional point must be mentioned. We now hear of no sobbing as the tomb is reached. Hence the indignation is now not a fight on the part of Jesus against being carried away into a paroxism of sobbing with the rest. No one attempts to explain it in this way. This proves that when the indignation first moved Jesus it was not a fight against the contagion of unrestrained grief, not a battle against a supposed dissipation of his power of will.

John inserts an explanatory remark (hence δέ) about the nature of the tomb. **Now it was a cavern, and a stone was lying against** (or upon) **it.** It was a chamber hewn into a rise of rock. In some of these tombs, very common in that rocky country, the floor is level with the outside, in others it is lower, a step or two leading down to it. The size of the hewn-out chamber would be in accord with the owner's wealth. A heavy slab of stone closed the opening, which might be quite perpendicular or slanting back; ἐπί with the dative fits either mode of closing the opening. On August 1, 1925, when the author visited Bethany, he was conducted down twenty-two big, clumsy steps, down deep into a rough, rocky cellar, now shown as "the tomb of Lazarus." Near by an open space with a few old stones from ruins, placed there to mark the site where walls are supposed to have been, was pointed out as the home of the sisters, and a few rough, pillar-like pieces of stone were called the house of Simon the leper. The place itself is composed of shabby stone hovels. Only the village site is genuine, all the rest is puerile invention.

39) Arrived at the tomb, **Jesus says, Take the stone away!** The command with its aorist imperative is short and incisive. Some of the disciples and the Jewish men are to lift the stone and to open the death chamber. The masterful command moves to action.

Martha, the sister of him that was dead, says to him, Lord, by this time he stinks, for he is dead four days, τεταρταῖος, an adjective, "one at the fourth day," whereas in English we should use an expression with an adverb or a phrase, R. 657. It is characteristic of Martha and not of Mary to exclaim thus. The addition to her name: "the sister of him who has died (and thus is now dead — the perfect participle)," when we already know of her relationship, is to give point to her exclamation — a sister would dread to look upon the already decomposing body of her brother. Lazarus, no doubt, was buried as well-to-do Jews were buried, his anointed body being swathed in linen strips with powdered spices sprinkled in the folds. There was nothing to check the natural process of decay. The Egyptians disemboweled the body and removed the brain and then soaked the body in a chemical solution for seventy days and thus prevented decay. Martha's exclamation is fully justified and reveals the greatness of the miracle about to be wrought. Yet not on this account has John recorded her words but for the sake of Jesus' reply. We need not ask how Martha's word accords with her faith as previously expressed. The astounding order of Jesus involuntarily brought the exclamation to her lips. Our

natural thinking is never swift enough to rise to the
height of our faith; and this appears most frequently
when faith is to be rewarded by actual sight.

40) **Jesus says to her, Did I not say to thee,
that, if thou shalt believe, thou shalt see the glory
of God?** Jesus is not quoting from either the original
message to the sisters or from the conversation
recorded in v. 21-27; he is only reminding Martha of
the two chief points in both the message and the conversation, that of faith (v. 26: "whoever believes,"
and: "believest thou this?"), and that of God's glory
(v. 4: "for the glory of God," etc.). Jesus speaks
only to Martha because she is the only one who uttered
the startled exclamation; yet all present may well
heed what Jesus says. The emphasis is on faith: "if
thou shalt believe," the aorist subjunctive to express
the act of believing now (the present would speak of
believing in general). The condition of expectancy
(ἐάν with the subjunctive) counts on Martha's act
of believing at this juncture. "Thou shalt see" is
a positive promise. In a moment believing Martha
did see. "The glory of God" has been explained in
v. 4. Jesus thus encourages the faith that is already
in Martha's heart; at the same time we must remember the purpose clause in Jesus' prayer, v. 42:
"in order that they may believe," for when the glory
now shines forth, this glory will impel those not yet
believing unto faith, and so these, too, will see that
glory (v. 45).

41) **They, accordingly, took the stone away.**
All eyes are strained on Jesus to see what he would
now do. **And Jesus lifted his eyes upward and
said, Father, I thank thee that thou didst hear me.
Yet on my part I know that always thou hearest me;
nevertheless, for the sake of the multitude standing
around I spoke, in order that they may believe that
thou didst send me.** The lifting of the eyes is a

natural gesture in prayer, since for us God is always above. It is the Son who here says, "Father," but the Son whom the Father "did send" on his great redemptive mission. This means that the entire prayer here uttered moves on a plane that is correspondingly high. It is God's own Son who here thanks his Father, and it is this Father who in this present case, just as in all other cases, hears this his own Son. Both the hearing and the thanks in this case and in all others deal with what pertains to the mission on which the Father sent his Son, and which the Son accepted from the Father and is now engaged in carrying out. Holding to these vital facts in relation to the Father and his Son, we shall see to what Jesus refers when he says, "thou didst hear me," and, "always thou hearest me." The prayers of the Son to the Father and the answers of the Father to the Son deal with one thing only, that which Jesus makes so prominent in his message to the sisters: "the glory of God, that the Son of God may be glorified thereby," v. 4. Compare 12:28; 13:31, 32; 14:13; 17:1 and 4. We may add that in whatever will redound to the glory of both, both the Son and the Father are always at one — a shadow of divergence between the two can never occur. This is due to the fact that the Father's conception of the mission on which he sent the Son is identical with the conception of that mission on the part of the Son who accepted that mission and is now carrying it out.

Accordingly, we dismiss as inadequate those interpretations which have Jesus ask the Father for power and authority to raise Lazarus from the dead. This reduces Jesus to the level of the prophets and the apostles who as mere men wrought miracles only in this way. Compare on this point the explanation in 4:50. We likewise dismiss the additions which are appended to this conception about "the assurance" or "the certainty" Jesus felt "in his consciousness" that "at the decisive moment the Father would not leave him without the joy and the victorious power for the execution of the deed." A further embellishment of this view is the "mighty agitation" or "excitement" of Jesus, which caused him to shout with a loud voice when the miraculous word was uttered. Jesus neither is nor acts as a mere tool of the Father. Jesus' mission is so great that it could not be executed by one who would be only an instrument in the Father's hands, to be guided by him at every step, and to be powerless except for the special power granted for every work. This mission the Son alone could execute, for it required one who in power as well as in mind and in will is wholly one with the Father. This is the sense of 5:19 and 30: Jesus can do and say nothing "of himself," as emanating from himself alone and deviating from his Father; in all he does and says he is one with the Father, because he is the Father's Son. Ever the Father "shows," ever the Son "sees"; ever the Son looks up to the Father, ever the Father "hears." Such absolute unity is possible only between these two.

42) All this is revealed on this occasion for the sake of those who are present to witness the miracle. That is why Jesus "spoke" (εἶπον) the audible word of thanks in v. 41. The purpose of the Father and the Son is "that they may believe (πιστεύσωσιν, aorist: come to believe) that thou didst send me" — me as thy Son on this saving mission. For Jesus thus to thank God aloud and to add aloud the motive that prompts him to utter his thanks, has been called a sham prayer and a mere display since God knew all this without Jesus' saying so audibly. As far as God is concerned, this objection would abolish all prayer, for God knows the heart even before it at-

tempts to formulate its thoughts, whether it utters them or not. He who would say to God only what God does not yet know would never have anything to say. The very essence of prayer is to say to God what is in our hearts. As far as those are concerned who hear us pray, the very object is that they may hear and may be impressed and affected by what they hear. Genuine prayers, uttered aloud, always have a corresponding effect. These prayers would draw also the hearts of others up to God, that they may recognize him and may also glorify him in their own hearts.

43) Thus Jesus prepared all those assembled at the tomb for the great deed they were now to witness. He had connected it with the Father and with the sending he had received from the Father. When the deed is now wrought, it will, indeed, proclaim in mighty fashion that the Father has sent him. In the face of this deed only the most obdurate unbelief will be able to deny that the Father did, indeed, send Jesus. **And having said these things,** in proper preparation, **he shouted with a great voice, Lazarus, come forth!** literally, "hither, out!" The loudness of the command is certainly not due to any excitement on the part of Jesus, caused by the strain of this supreme moment which will now show whether the Father sent him or not. It is Jesus who raises Lazarus from the dead not the Father in answer to the prayers of Jesus. A quiet order from Jesus would also have brought the dead man forth. The accepted explanation for this loudness is that it comports with the mighty power put forth, penetrating the wall that divides the dead from the living. Yet when Jesus put forth this same power in calling back to life Jairus' daughter and the widow's son, he used no loud shout. The "great voice" in the present case is not for the sake of the dead man or for the

sake of death, but for the sake of its effect upon the assembled people.

In Mark 5:42; Luke 8:54; 7:14 Jesus says, "Arise!" ἔγειρε, ἐγέρθητι; here he says, "Come forth!" δεῦρο ἔξω. The difference is due to the situations. The daughter lay upon a bed, the widow's son upon a bier; when called back to life, they would rise from their prone posture. Lazarus is in his tomb; he will not merely rise up from his prone posture but also move out of the tomb. The assumption that, when Jesus called to Lazarus to come forth, Lazarus was already alive and needed only to be asked to step out, is unwarranted, whether it involves the idea that the Father had already made him alive again, or that the mere will of Jesus had already done so. It is the voice and the word of Jesus that bring Lazarus back to life, just as "all that are in their tombs shall hear his voice, and shall come forth," 5:28, 29. This voice of Jesus with its almighty power raises the dead. As the dead child and the widow's dead son responded to that voice, so also Lazarus. It is Jesus in his own person who thus works these miracles even as we read in Mark 5:41 and Luke 7:14, *"I say to thee, Arise!"*

44) The effect of Jesus' word was instantaneous. **The dead man came forth, bound hand and foot with gravebands; and his face was bound with a sweatcloth.** First, the great fact as such in the fewest possible words; then, the description of the figure that appeared in the door of the tomb. John does not even use an exclamation. With a subject so tremendous to present he drops all attempts to make us feel its tremendousness. This is all: "The dead man came forth." The perfect participle ὁ τεθνηκώς, while it is intensive (R. 910), has lost its perfect force (R. 1117) and simply means "the dead man." If we pause to think, the statement becomes a paradox,

a contradiction — how can a dead man come forth out of his tomb? Not only alive now but wholly sound and full of vigor, hampered by the linen swathings though he was, Lazarus came forth. Without a struggle death gives up its prey. All death's ravages are undone. Here is the glory of the Father and the glorification of the Son whom he did send. Even the physical eyes of the bystanders can "see" it. Not a word, however, does John record about the excitement that surely must have overwhelmed the witnesses who beheld the man, dead and in his tomb for four days, now alive at Jesus' word.

Now the brief description, "bound hand and foot," the passive perfect participle: bound thus when entombed and now in that condition. The Greek has plural accusatives, loosely attached to the passive participle: "the feet and the hands," our idiom has "hand and foot." The κειρίαι are linen strips (note the singular σινδών in Matt. 27:59) wound around and thus binding the body. Around the head and covering the face a *sudarium*, literally "sweatcloth," was bound, no other wrappings being used. From the early days onward it was considered part of the miracle that the body thus wrapped and swathed and rendered helpless came forth from the tomb. It was supposed that the power of Jesus raised the body to its feet and made it float forward. A recent writer thinks of "the miraculous floating upward of a mummy," confusing Egyptian with Jewish swathings. Another thinks that the rock tomb was cut down perpendicularly like our graves, and that Lazarus merely rose to his feet, standing upright in the grave. "Hither, out!" would hardly fit this supposition but rather the command, "Arise!" and Lazarus would have to be lifted out. Since we do not know just how the body and the limbs were wrapped, it is best to assume that Lazarus was able to rise upright without aid and to move sufficiently to get to the door of the tomb. Quite likely Meyer is right: "The wrappings, which also held no spices, encircling the entire body, over the sindon (linen sheet) folded around the corpse, could have been loose enough, so that, stretched by the movement of the living man, they made his coming forth possible." The entire description, notably also the mention of the cloth around the head and covering the face, reveals the writer as an eyewitness of the scene. But no sheet enveloped the swathed body.

Jesus says to them, Loose him and let him go. Struck with amazement at first, no one moved, so that Jesus called on them to unfasten the binding, enabling Lazarus to walk home. "Loose him" is only preliminary to the chief command, "let him go away." Lazarus is not to stand as a spectacle for the wonder of the crowd; nor has Jesus anything more to say or to do. All is done, and even Jesus does not detain Lazarus or speak a single word of greeting to the friend whom he loved. "Let him go away" dismisses also the crowd and at the same time bids Lazarus to go to his home. The glory of God and of the Son whom he had sent had appeared to the hearts of them all — on that glory let their thoughts dwell. Jesus and his disciples also leave the place at once; note "departed thence" in v. 54.

The Effect of the Miracle wrought upon Lazarus, 11:45-57

45) First the effect upon the Jewish witnesses. **Many, therefore, of the Jews, they who came to Mary and beheld what he did, believed on him.** We must not that πολλοὶ ἐκ τῶν Ἰουδαίων is identical with v. 19 and includes all who came to condole with the sisters. All these are incorporated in the apposition: "they who came," etc. John thus

says that all of them "believed on him." So great was the effect of what these Jews beheld that for once no unbelievers were left. John does not write: "many of the Jews, of those who came" (genitive) ; but the nominative: "they who came," οἱ ἐλθόντες κτλ. The aorist "believed" is simply historical and states only the fact. The fact that they "came to Mary" is often explained by assuming that she was more in need of comfort, and that thus Martha is left out; or by assuming that Mary was better known among the Jews than her sister. The best explanation is that she is made prominent here just as in v. 1, 2.

46) The effect of the miracle, however, extended far beyond the immediate witnesses. The authorities in Jerusalem were moved to action. How this came about John explains. **But some of them went away to the Pharisees and told them what Jesus had done.** This is often explained as though the witnesses divided themselves into two groups, a majority who believed and a minority who did not believe. Yet "some of them" means a few of those mentioned in v. 45, i. e., of those who believed. In other words, from some of the direct witnesses, who believed in Jesus, the Pharisees learned what Jesus had done in Bethany. Not at second or at thirdhand but at first-hand the enemies of Jesus obtained their information. This does not mean that "some of them" went and denounced Jesus — what could they denounce? In all good faith and with all sincerity these witnesses told the Pharisees what they had seen Jesus do. Why they "went away to the Pharisees and told them" is not stated, yet we may well suppose that they went in order to convince these opponents of Jesus that they were surely wrong in their opinion about him. This would also agree with what follows when the Pharisees are worked up to say, "If we let him thus alone, all men will believe on him," v. 48. The

very fact that *all* the Jews who witnessed the miracle
in Bethany came away as believers made the Pharisees now determine on decisive action.   The success of
Jesus simply had to be stopped.

47) Action at once results.   **The chief priests,
therefore, and the Pharisees called a session and
were saying, What are we doing? seeing that this
fellow is doing many signs.**   The Pharisees together
with the chief priests, to whom they had carried the
latest news about Jesus, call a regular session of the
Sanhedrin.   The translation "gathered a council" does
not mean that a private consultation was held; for
"the chief priests and the Pharisees" is the title of the
Sanhedrin as such, and συνήγαγον συνέδριον means that
the Sanhedrin "brought together a session," a regular
meeting (συνέδριον, a common noun.)

The imperfect ἔλεγον takes us into the session and
lets us hear what goes on.   Here "they were saying"
— most likely the Pharisees (v. 40) —, "What are
we doing?" τί ποιοῦμεν;   This is not the subjunctive
ποιῶμεν, which would indicate deliberation or doubt
as to what to do; nor the future ποιήσομεν, which would
only ask for information regarding what to do; but
the present indicative, which asks what really is being
done and thus implies that actually nothing at all is
being done about Jesus.   R. 880, 923, etc.   And this,
indeed, is the fact; the Sanhedrin had talked and resolved but was actually doing nothing of consequence
toward checking Jesus.

Here ὅτι is consecutive, "seeing that," etc., not
causal, "for" or "because."   Compare 2:18; 7:35; and
8:43, where the references are given.   Always these
Jews show a distaste for the name "Jesus," substituting the derogatory οὗτος, "this fellow."   It is
somewhat startling to read the frank admission that
Jesus "is doing many signs," acknowledging the
number and the quality ("signs").   What follows

shows how "signs" is here understood, namely as revealing something about Jesus which the Sanhedrin
absolutely refuses to accept, which many of the people, however, are accepting in their ignorance.   No
effort is made to deny the reality of the miracles, now
that these men are by themselves; before the people
they were less free with their admission.   Then, too,
the Sanhedrists were at a disadvantage: it was a
little awkward to deny the resurrection of a Lazarus,
for instance, when the man was right there to testify
concerning his own death and his return to life, to say
nothing of a great number of actual witnesses.   Faith
is not a matter of so much proof or evidence for the
intellect; it is a matter of the will.   These leaders
openly admit the most glorious Messianic deeds and
yet do not dream of believing.   Quite effectively they
place what Jesus "is doing" over against the quest-
tion what they "are doing" — he so much, they —
nothing.

**48) If we shall let him alone thus, all will be-
lieve on him; and the Romans will come and remove
both our position and our nation.**   The condition of
expectancy pictures this eventuality in a vivid manner.   The adverb "thus" connects with the preceding
question and its implication that the Sanhedrin is
doing nothing while Jesus is doing a great deal, and
thus justifies ἐάν with the subjunctive.   "All will believe on him" is really not intended as an exaggeration, nor is it due to the temper of the speakers.   The
Sanhedrists actually assume that they alone are able
to counteract the influence Jesus is exerting, and that,
if they do no more than they are now doing, in a short
time all — save, of course, they themselves, will be
carried away by Jesus.

A gap in the thought must be filled in before the
conclusion of the Sanhedrists relative to the Romans
can be understood.   With the populace generally be-

lieving in Jesus, i. e., adhering to him as the Jewish Messiah, the result, to the unbelieving Jewish mind, could be only this: some fine day Jesus would set himself up as a worldly king and fulfill the popular expectation in this regard. Of course, Jesus had hitherto firmly refused to do this thing. But these Sanhedrists, themselves altogether insincere and false at heart, adjudge Jesus to be no better than they are; in fact, they are unable to imagine a Messiah in any other form — he simply had to come in earthly royal guise. The outcome of such an action on the part of Jesus the Sanhedrists can easily see: "the Romans will come" and will crush this revolt against their authority with military force and in so doing will deprive the Jews of the last trace of autonomy by abolishing Jerusalem as the capital, dissolving the Sanhedrin, and forever abolishing its power.

In ἡμῶν καὶ τὸν τόπον καὶ τὸ ἔθνος note the emphatic position of the pronoun: remove "both the position and the nation *that are ours.*" They speak as though both are a perquisite of theirs. As regards the meaning of τὸν τόπον the choice is usually between the country, the city, and the Temple; but when explanations are added they always refer to the position of domination held by the Sanhedrin, whether in the Temple as its headquarters, or in the city as the capital, or in the country as its domain. What these Sanhedrists are concerned about is their "position" as the ruling body. They use ἔθνος, the proper word for "nation," not λαός, the word for "mass of people," which is also often used to designate God's people in a sacred sense. There is not fear that the Jewish nation would lose its Sanhedrin, but that the Sanhedrin would lose the nation it dominates. This calamity must be prevented at all hazards. Observe the selfishness that is here thinly veiled behind a show of patriotism. Prompted by this motive, these leaders virtually abandon their own idea of a Jewish King-Messiah as far as any transfer of *their* power to such a Messiah is concerned. If this appears incredible, we need but recall how these Sanhedrists brazenly turned traitor to the Jewish ideal of the Messiah as a grand earthly king when they shouted before Pilate, "We have no king but Caesar." Coldly self-seeking, power and place is their one desire. Yet the plan they adopted for maintaining themselves brought on the very calamity they meant to avoid: rejecting their true Messiah, their Temple and their capital were demolished by Roman fire and sword, their nation was scattered to the ends of the earth, never again to possess their land or to be a nation like other nations.

49) **But a certain one of them, Caiaphas, being high priest of that year, said to them, You do not know a thing; nor do you take account that it is expedient for you that one man die instead of the people, and that the whole nation perish not.** The sinister condition in v. 48, "if we shall let him alone," is now made specific: Jesus must die. "A certain one of them" comes out boldly with the plan thus to end this business of letting Jesus alone. "One of them" does not place Caiaphas on the same level with the rest but places him over against all the rest, who knew only how to lament but not how to act. Caiaphas secures this credit for himself. His regular name was Joseph, as Josephus informs us. He was no less a personage than the "high priest," holding this office far longer than his predecessor, from about the years 18 to 36. We must not translate "that year" but "of that year"; the thought is not that he held office for only one year, or alternated annually with another, but that his time of office covered that notable year in which Jesus was put to death; compare also v. 51 and 18:13.

As the boldest in the assembly he blurts out, "You do not know a thing!" Discourteous, rough, and insulting in what should be a dignified assembly, Caiaphas shows that he feels his power. Josephus adds a bit of light on this Sadducee's manners when he reports of the Pharisees that they "were friendly to one another and are for the exercise of concord, and regard for the public; but the behavior of the Sadducees one toward another is in some degree wild, and their conversation with those that are of their own party is as barbarous as if they were strangers to them." *Wars,* 2, 8, 14.

50) In what respect the rest show their denseness Caiaphas specifies, "nor do you take account," etc. The problem is exceedingly simple for him: Jesus must die. Yet even this overbearing Sadducee uses an abstract form of statement in proposing the death of Jesus to the Sanhedrin in order at least in some degree to hide the criminality of the proposal. Here is a thing, he says, that all the rest have failed to take into account in their thinking in regard to Jesus. He implies that the thing they have overlooked is under certain circumstances perfectly in order and acknowledged as right and proper — hence the abstract statement that follows with a ὅτι clause as the object of λογίζεσθε, and a subfinal ἵνα clause ("in much the same sense," R. 1034) after the impersonal συμφέρει. This ἵνα does not express a purpose but states *what* "is expedient for you"; the classical Greek would use an infinitive. "It is expedient for you" means: advantageous to you as the Sanhedrin, the ruling body charged with the care of the nation, who must in the interest of the nation choose and use the best means available in meeting the responsibilities of your office. Cunningly Caiaphas identifies the personal interests of the Sanhedrists with the national interest — what is advantageous to them in

preserving their position and their power is the very thing that will conserve the nation placed in their charge.

What is this thing that is so advantageous under the present circumstances? "That one man die instead of the people, and that the whole nation perish not." It is an old trick to present two extreme alternatives in order to force acceptance of the one desired, as though no third possibility exists. Here either one man dies, or the whole nation is destroyed. What aids Caiaphas in holding the Sanhedrin to these alternatives, extreme though they are, is the inability of his colleagues in all their previous deliberations to find a feasible middle course. Thus he claims that only this choice is left: one man's death or the death of the nation. Note the correct contrast between εἷς ἄνθρωπος, "one man," and ὑπὲρ τοῦ λαοῦ, "for the benefit of the people" (the great mass), λαός being often used for "the chosen people." On the other hand, "that the whole nation perish not" has τὸ ἔθνος, that they lose not their national standing, yet preserving the idea of a great mass over against "one man" by ὅλον, "the whole nation."

The full force of the alternatives presented by Caiaphas and the fact that they exclude anything like a third choice, is evident from the preposition ὑπέρ, "in behalf of," "for the benefit of," but here plainly containing the resultant idea "instead of." The data on this preposition are given under 10:11. Robertson has shown at length that in all the pertinent connections the idea of substitution expressed by this preposition is beyond question. One "instead" of the other leaves no third choice. One "instead" of the other also removes the appearance of a forced choice between two evils. To die "instead" of another is a vicarious sacrifice — his death would save the nation, keep it alive. The only trouble is that the proposi-

tion of Caiaphas will not bear examination. For one
man voluntarily to sacrifice himself for the people
would, indeed, be not only a permissible but even a
most noble act; but for the Sanhedrin deliberately
to kill a man under the plea that he is being killed
instead of the nation's suffering extinction, is quite
another thing. For how is this "one man" Jesus to
die? Caiaphas carefully avoids even a hint on this
point. A moment's thought reveals that his abstract
proposition contemplates nothing less than cold-
blooded, judicial murder, either secret assassination
by a tool of the Sanhedrin or a mock trial with
the verdict being settled in advance. Unscrupulous
as the high priest was, he leaves this vital point in
abeyance.

Did Caiaphas encounter dissent? Luke 23:51 reports that Joseph of Arimathea did not consent to
their counsel and deed. We have no word about Nicodemus, save his former courageous dissent, 7:50, etc.
It is a fair conclusion that a minority of the Sanhedrin
protested, although to no avail.

51) **Now this he said not of himself, but being
high priest of that year, he prophesied that Jesus
was about to die instead of the nation, and not
instead of the nation only but in order that he
might also gather into one the children of God that
are scattered abroad.** This parenthetical (hence δέ)
elucidation by John reveals the divine control at this
decisive stage in the midst of the enemies of Jesus.
The negative "not of himself" is not absolute as
though he had nothing to do with his speaking but
relative: "not just of himself alone" but with another
directing the form of his utterance. He might have
voiced his wicked thought in a variety of ways, but
God led him to voice it in such a way and with such
words as expressed far more than the speaker himself
realized when he spoke.

"But being high priest of that year, he prophesied" informs us why God singled out Caiaphas, why his utterance was controlled as indicated, and not the utterance of some other man in the Sanhedrin. We must not hastily conclude that every high priest was also a prophet, for this was not the case. No; God took the high priest "of that year" (compare v. 49), the man who held the notable office which of old in the theocratic order of the first covenant was at times used for decisions vital to the people, and made him serve again, now not through the Urim and Thummim, lost long ago, but through an immediate control of his words to utter a truth absolutely vital not only for the Jewish people but also for all men in the world. "He prophesied" — God controlled his utterance. His wickedness is left wholly intact, his murderous intent and his cunning way of expressing it in order to bring the Sanhedrin to action. Caiaphas is not forced in any way, but the words that come to his lips and that say just what *he* wants to say are words that also say just what *God* wants said in this assembly of the chief representatives of the Jews. *They* want to slay Jesus for their purpose, *God* will let them slay Jesus for his purpose. In stating *his* purpose so as to win the consent of the Sanhedrin Caiaphas so formulates his words that he unconsciously states also *God's* purpose. This, John says, was not accidental but due to God. The best formulation that Caiaphas could find to meet the situation he faced was the very formulation God wanted him to find for a purpose of which Caiaphas never thought.

Here we have a peculiar case of verbal inspiration. It is peculiar in that it is unconscious. It is inspiration in that what is uttered and in the way it is uttered we have what God wants uttered and in the way he wants it uttered. The speaker (or writer) may or may not grasp what he is uttering; in I Pet. 1:10, 11 we find that even the conscious prophets of God study their own words.

When restating what Caiaphas said John interprets his unconscious prophecy for us. "That Jesus was about to die instead of the people" states the impending fact (ἔμελλεν). In the direct form the main verb would be the present tense ("he is about to die"), which here and sometimes in the classics is changed to a past tense in the indirect discourse ("he was about," etc.), R. 1029. The present infinitive "to die" is descriptive of the dying as it will occur. Whereas Caiaphas uses λαός, John substitutes ἔθνος. Caiaphas thinks of the mass of the covenant people; John interprets that Jesus will die for the Jews, not as being the covenant people (they had long forsaken that covenant), but as being a human nation. But this compels him at once to add, "and not instead of the nation only," i. e., the Jewish nation, but instead of all other nations likewise — his death will be vicarious and substitutional for all men. The prophecy of Caiaphas was only partial, although the part stated necessarily involves the remainder not explicitly stated by him. Jesus could not die for the Jews only; his dying would include all other men and nations as well.

52) But John does not stop to say, "not instead of this nation only but also instead of all other nations." He takes this thought for granted and at once states the ultimate purpose of God, which rests on the universality of the atonement wrought by Jesus' death. In this John copies the manner of his Master's deep and surprising sayings. This ultimate purpose is: "but (for all others likewise) in order that he might also gather into one the children of God that are scattered abroad." Here John brings in what lies in λαός as used by Caiaphas, the idea of

a sacred covenant people; but John again expands the term, as he necessarily must, to include all God's chosen people in the grand new covenant, gathered from among all nations and people. Although this vast host extends through generations not yet born, they are already in advance called "the children of God," as the Scriptures do this repeatedly, 10:16; 17:9 and 20; Acts 18:10. The fact that this proleptic designation rests on the infallible foreknowledge of God, which knows all his own in all ages to come, is shown in connection with 10:16. These coming believers, at first "scattered abroad" without faith (like sheep going their own way, Isa. 53:6), when they are brought to faith will by means of that faith "be gathered together into one," ἕν, a unit, one spiritual body, "one fold" under "one Shepherd," the true *Laos* of the New Testament, the great *Una Sancta* which is already one shall at last stand before Jesus as one in glory. The aorist subjunctive συναγάγῃ implies that this divine purpose regarding the children of God in all nations and in all ages will, indeed, be realized. In all the redemptive work of the Son God always looks to what we may call the net result: the souls that will actually be brought to eternal salvation.

53) **From that day, therefore, they took counsel to kill him.** The aorist is historical and reports the fact. "From that day" marks that as the decisive day. The ἵνα clause is not final but subfinal and states the subject on which they agreed "that day" and on which they then took counsel, namely on ways and means to effect the killing. Hence the present tense ἀποκτείνωσιν. Jesus brought back life to Lazarus; the Jews plan to bring death to the Lifegiver. Yet despite all their counselling they themselves never found a way — Judas had to show them the way.

54) **Jesus, therefore, was no longer walking openly among the Jews but departed thence to the**

country near the desert, to a town called Ephraim, and there he remained with the disciples. Jesus did not return to Perea from Bethany but went to a new locality, which is designated broadly as "the country near the desert," a retired section, and then specifically "a town called Ephraim," a small place, so little known that its present location is in dispute. It was probably located in northern Judea. Here Jesus remained until the approach of the Passover season.

55) **Now the Passover of the Jews was near, and many went up to Jerusalem from the country before the Passover in order to purify themselves.** "From the country" is here used in contrast to "Jerusalem" and refers to the land in general and not merely to the locality where Jesus at this time was. These early pilgrims went to Jerusalem in time to attend to the Levitical purification, which, because of some defilement, they needed in order to be fit for the Passover celebration. They took sufficient time to attend to the required lustrations, sacrifices, and other rites that were required.

56) **They were, therefore, seeking Jesus and were saying to each other while standing in the Temple, What do you think? That he will not at all come to the feast?** They looked for him thus early and, standing in groups in the Temple courts, asked each other's opinion, "What do you think?" And then, suggesting an opinion themselves, they ask: Do you, too, think "that he will not at all come to the feast?" That seemed to be the general expectation. The οὐ μή with the subjunctive is the strongest form of negation.

57) What made it seem so doubtful to these pilgrims that Jesus would come was the decree of the Sanhedrin. **Now the high priests and the Pharisees had given order that if anyone should know where**

he was, he should furnish the information in order that they might arrest him. The connective δέ is not adversative, in contrast with the questions of the pilgrims, but a parenthetical statement needed to understand the situation. Hence also the past perfect "had given orders," i. e., prior to the arrival of these pilgrims. The subfinal ἵνα states the contents of the "orders." The authorities expect that someone will know, hence the condition with ἐάν and the aorist subjunctive γνῷ, actually know. Yet nobody, it seems, knew. The purpose clause, "in order that they might arrest him," is not a part of the orders but is added to show why the orders were given. The Sanhedrin had thus settled how they would bring Jesus to death. It was not to be done by assassination but by due legal process. This was probably due to the influence of the Pharisees.

With the situation at the approach of the festival thus before us, John again turns to Jesus.

CHAPTER XII

The Anointing at Bethany, 12:1-11

At the beginning of a discussion of this chapter the observation is in place that all its sections deal with the imminent death of Jesus except the final paragraph, v. 44-50, which constitutes John's conclusion to the entire first half of his Gospel. We are now in the actual shadow of the cross.

1) **Jesus, therefore, six days before the Passover came to Bethany, where Lazarus was, whom Jesus raised from the dead.** John loves the continuative οὖν: with things being as reported in the closing section of chapter 11. "We moderns do not feel the same need for connecting particles between independent sentences. The ancient Greeks loved to point out these delicate *nuances,*" R. 1192. The orders of the Sanhedrin (11:57) did not amount to much since Jesus was not in hiding, and anyone who wanted to reach him could certainly find him. The day after the feast at Bethany he openly entered Jerusalem, and no one touched him.

"Six days before the Passover" is not in conflict with the two days before the Passover mentioned in Matt. 26:2; Mark 14:1. Neither of these two evangelists gives the date of the supper at Bethany. They report a saying of Jesus that he would be betrayed and crucified at the feast of the Passover two days hence, while at the very same time the Jewish authorities resolved *not* to destroy him at the time of the Passover. Then, without following the chronological sequence of events, these two evangelists report the supper. Matthew merely says, "now when Jesus was in Bethany," and Mark, "and being in Bethany," neither fixing the date. John supplements the others and records the date.

When counting the days the Greeks always began from the far end, here from the Passover back to the supper, and, unlike the Romans, did not include in the count the day from which they counted. In πρὸ ἓξ ἡμερῶν τοῦ πάσχα the forward position of the pre-position is not a Latinism, as has been often assumed, but is found in the Doric and the Ionic and is common in the Koine, R. 110, 424, 621. M.-M. furnish examples and state that Moulton regards the second genitive as an ablative, "starting from the Passover." This fixes the date of the arrival at Bethany. For, since the Passover began with the 14th of Nisan on the afternoon of which the paschal lambs were killed, we must begin the count backward of six days with the 13th, and thus obtain the 8th of Nisan as the day of the arrival. We cannot start the count with the 14th and place the arrival at the 9th. With the arrival fixed on the 8th, it is incredible that this should be a Sabbath; for Jesus certainly had no need to violate the Sabbath by a long journey, and the supposition that he spent the night before the Sabbath so close to Bethany that on the Sabbath he needed to walk only a Sabbath-day's journey (three-fourths of a mile) to enter Bethany, is equally incredible, since another short hour would take him to Bethany, and no place so near to Bethany is known where he could have lodged, unless he would sleep in the open.

If the 8th was not a Sabbath, neither was the 15th. The Sabbath during which Jesus rested in the tomb was the 16th of Nisan, the day of the crucifixion

the 15th, and the evening when Jesus ate the Passover with his disciples was the evening of the 14th,
the lamb being killed in the afternoon.   With this
phrase, "six days before the Passover," John thus
agrees perfectly with the synoptists and answers the
contention of the opponents of the Quartodecimans in
the second century that John clashes with the synoptists by making the Friday of Jesus' death the 14th
and the Sabbath in the grave the 15th of Nisan.   See
19:14 and compare Zahn on the question.   On Friday
morning the 8th, after a night spent in the home of
Zacchaeus, Jesus left Jericho and arrived in Bethany
that afternoon.   The supper was not given that evening; for v. 12 reports that "on the morrow," i. e., the
morning after the supper, Jesus made his royal entry
into Jerusalem.   The Sabbath began at dusk on Friday.   That Sabbath Jesus spent quietly with his beloved friends in Bethany.   On Saturday, when the sun
set and ended the Sabbath, the supper was prepared.
John writes: Bethany, "where Lazarus was, whom
Jesus raised from the dead," in order to recall the
events recorded in chapter 11 with their bearing on
what now follows.   The other two evangelists omit
mention of Lazarus.   The best reading omits the
ὁ τεθνηκώς of the A. V.   On ἐκ νεκρῶν see the exposition in 2:22.

2)   **They, accordingly, made him a supper
there.   And Martha was serving, while Lazarus
was one of those reclining with him.**   "Accordingly" hints at the fact that the friends of Jesus embraced
this opportunity to honor Jesus.   The δεῖπνον was the
main meal of the day and was served in the evening,
whether we today call it "a supper" or "a dinner."
"They made him a supper" means that they prepared
a special feast in Jesus' honor.   The indefinite plural
subject in the verb cannot be restricted to Lazarus,
or to him and his two sisters; other friends joined

with them. Matthew and Mark report that this supper was made in the house of Simon the leper, about whom we lack further information. With this agrees John's statement that Martha was serving, which would be self-evident if the supper were held in her own home; likewise, that Lazarus was one of the guests. It is gratuitous to say that Lazarus is mentioned in order to indicate his complete recovery. He is mentioned as one of the honored guests.

It is fair to conclude that Jesus had healed Simon of his leprosy, and that this was one reason why the supper was made in his house. It is fancy to say that Lazarus was placed on one side of Jesus and Simon on the other. That would be possible if the guests sat at a table in our modern fashion; but these guests reclined upon couches, as the fashion was among the Jews, and consequently the chief place, the upper end of the central couch, was reserved for Jesus, and only one person could be next to him. We have no reason to think that Martha is mentioned as serving (διηκόνει, doing service for the sake of service) because she was the wife of Simon; some think that she was his widow, supposing that, since we hear nothing further about him, he was dead. The fact that Martha alone is mentioned as serving is not stated in order to place her in contrast to Mary, as though Mary was not serving. Mary, as well as others, must have helped, for at least fifteen guests must have been present, all men, of course, since women would not recline in public with men. Martha's serving is noted because of a fine sense of fairness and justice which does not omit Martha in an account where Mary appears so prominently.

3) **Mary, therefore, having taken a pound of perfume of genuine nard, very precious, anointed the feet of Jesus and wiped off his feet with her hair; and the house was filled with the odor of the**

ointment. The connective οὖν has the same force as
in the previous verses. We need not elaborate on the
well-established fact that the act here described and
that recorded in Luke 7:36 differ in time, place, the
owner of the house, the moral character of the woman
anointing the Lord, and in the conversation that took
place. Gregory the Great has the doubtful distinction of identifying Mary of Bethany with Mary Magdalene and with the sinful woman (unnamed) who
anointed Jesus in the Pharisee's house and of giving
this view general currency in the Roman Catholic
Church. The truth, however, was brought out so
forcibly by Luther, Calvin, Calov, and others that this
view never obtained credence among Protestant commentators. The sister of Lazarus is not Mary Magdalene or the other unnamed woman in Luke. In 10:38
this evangelist introduces Mary as a new personage
after the introduction of Mary Magdalene and after
the account of the unnamed woman in the Pharisee's
house. It is unwarranted to assume that, if the same
woman is referred to, Luke would give her three different designations in as many chapters, 7, 8, and 10.
In the accounts of Matthew and of Mark Mary's name
does not occur, although these writers report the word
of Jesus: "Wheresoever this gospel shall be preached
in the whole world, there shall also this, that this
woman hath done, be told for a memorial of her."
Yet in not recording Mary's name the evangelists are
guilty of no omission, for it is her act, not her name,
which is to be praised in all the world. Moreover,
when they wrote, Mary may have still been alive, and
to mention her name might have caused her trouble
and danger.

The quantity of the ointment was ample, "a
pound," λίτραν, twelve ounces according to the weight
of water. The word μύρον is a general term for any
"perfume" or essence with a delightful odor (used

beside ἀρώματα in Luke 23:56). "Nard" is the plant
which furnishes the essence for the perfume, the
finest coming from India. This "nard" is called
πιστική, an adjective that has been much in dispute, but
the meaning of which is now settled; it is derived
from πιστός (πίστις) and means "genuine," "pure," over
against adulterated preparations containing inferior
substances; M.-M., as well as Zahn. Hence not
"liquid" or "drinkable." The word has no connection
with πίνειν, "to drink." The "spikenard" of our versions comes from *Spica Nardus,* the Indian nard
named after its wheatlike tips or spikes; yet πιστικός
does not mean *spicatus,* "spiked." The spikenard
now listed by botanists is a variety of the valerian
family, whose roots furnish a fragrant essence.

All the evangelists remark on the value of the
perfume. Matthew calls the μύρον "exceeding precious," βαρύτιμον; Mark "very costly," πολυτελής; and
John "very precious," πολύτιμος. Judas mentions the
actual value of it. The question is asked as to how
Mary came to have so precious a perfume at hand
on this occasion. The assumption that it remained
over from her former voluptuous life vilifies Mary
by the spurious identification with the harlot mentioned in Luke. The suggestion that the perfume
remained over from the burial of Lazarus is untenable
because of the great value. In lieu of a positive
answer we prefer to think that Mary long in advance
provided this precious essence for an occasion of
this kind, freely spending her money for the honor
of Jesus.

John uses ἀλείφω, the verb for any application of
oil, not χρίω, the word for sacred and ceremonial
anointing. Matthew and Mark record that Mary
anointed the head. John takes for granted that his
readers know these records and supplements them by
stating that Mary anointed the feet. The precious

fluid was abundant; poured out upon the head and flowing upon the neck and the shoulders, enough was left for the feet, in fact, so much that Mary wiped off the feet with her hair. The broken alabaster cruse was thus entirely emptied — all its contents offered to the Master. In the house of the Pharisee the holy feet of Jesus had not been washed as even common politeness on the part of the host required, but at this supper in Bethany the washing certainly had not been omitted. But the devoted heart of Mary is not satisfied with the commoner fluid, she now adds the abundance of this most precious ointment that she was able to find. How many dusty, weary paths those beloved feet had trodden — now they are honored, indeed, as they deserve. The Baptist said that he was unworthy to loose the latchet of the sandals of these feet, and Mary feels the same way. At the feet of Jesus she sat when she listened to the words of life, and these feet had brought the Master of death to recall her brother to life.

It means much that Mary should use her hair to wipe the feet, and John even repeats the word feet, as if he meant to emphasize the humiliation expressed in using the hair of the head upon the feet. But in the case of a Jewish woman this act means more. To unbind and loosen the hair in the presence of outsiders was considered an indecent act. Lightfoot tells of a woman who prided herself on the fact that the beams of her house had never seen her hair. Mary's act is thus one in which she lays her own woman's honor at the feet of Jesus. She takes that honor and makes it a towel for his holy feet. Hers is a different act from that of the woman in the Pharisee's house. If there we may say that the proper place for a sinner's head is at the Savior's feet, here we may add that the proper place for a *disciple's* head is at the **Savior's feet.**

As one who vividly recalls the scene John adds that "the house was filled with the oder of the ointment," another evidence of its supreme quality and at the same time a symbol of the far-reaching influence of Mary's act. "The odor of Mary's ointment has the promise that it shall penetrate and fill the whole world." Nebe. Yet at first it seemed to fail in this respect; to some of those present at the supper it was not at all "a sweet smell, a sacrifice acceptable, well-pleasing to God," Phil. 4:18.

4) **But Judas Iscariot, one of his disciples, who was about to betray him, says, Why was not this ointment sold for three hundred denars and given to poor people?** On "Iscariot" see 6:71. The very name exhales an evil odor, the absolute opposite of that of Mary's ointment. A sad note is sounded in the apposition, "one of his disciples." It seems incredible, impossible — one of the chosen band, favored to see and to hear everything, honored by Jesus with the highest office in the world, who should have been first to applaud, to understand, yea to vie with Mary in doing something equally great and significant for his Master's honor. Beside "one of his disciples" John puts, "who was about to betray him," ὁ μέλλων with the present infinitive in place of the future, R. 1118. This explains everything. The faulty translation, "which *should* betray him," must not lead us to think of a divine compulsion. The traitorous act of Judas was not the result of a divine decree, it was entirely his own act, just as other wicked deeds are the product of men's own hearts. Judas resisted all the grace of God, all the blessed influences and warnings of Jesus, and thus betrayed him. When grace is in vain, only almighty power is left; and this power cannot convert or save, all that it can do is to carry out the purposes of God among the wicked,

so controlling their wickedness that it shall further
God's plans.

John mentions that only Judas objected to Mary's
act, while Matthew says "the disciples" and Mark
"some" had indignation. Nowhere are we told that
all the disciples objected. When John focuses our
attention on Judas he supplements the accounts of the
other evangelists by showing us how the objection
to Mary's deed arose. Judas started the movement
by unhesitatingly pronouncing adverse judgment. His
plea is specious, and some others are carried away
by it, evidently not taking time to think for themselves. It is often thus. As Mary's perfume filled
the house with its odor, so the poison of Judas' words
contaminated at least some hearts. In the basest of
moves a man can find some supporters and abettors,
especially if he is able to hide his motive and his intention under some plausible argument.

5) Judas might have found many things to object to in Mary's deed and Jesus' acceptance of it, for
instance, that it ill became a man of simple manners;
that anointing the feet as well as the head was a
piece of extravagance and effeminacy offensive to
Jewish custom; that such luxury did not agree with
the life of a prophet; that Jesus himself had said
that they that wear soft clothing dwell in kings'
houses, and among them but not for one like Jesus
the use of perfumes might be considered appropriate.
But the point to which Judas directs attention is characteristic of the man. His eye is set on money, and
so he sees the financial side. "Why was not this
perfume sold for three hundred denars?" Incidentally we thus learn the probable price of the perfume,
between \$40 and \$50 ($\delta\eta\nu\acute{a}\rho\iota o\nu$, 16c). The addition:
"and given to poor people" ($\pi\tau\omega\chi o\~\iota s$, poor people in
general) sounds as though Judas is concerned about the
poor, prompted by the noble motive of charity. Yet

the words cover the gravest kind of a charge not
merely against Mary but against Jesus himself.
Judas implies that Jesus is robbing the poor; that
he is lavishing upon himself what should be devoted
to charity; that for his own glorification he allows a
waste that is wrong; that his example is harmful to
others — and that Judas is the man who knows what
is right, proper, charitable, and is not afraid to come
out with it! This is the traitorous touch in the proceeding of Judas. He is a traitor now as he reclines
among the Twelve and partakes of the hospitality of
Jesus' friends. We now see why John in his deeper
view of things brings Judas and his actual words to
our attention.

6) John himself bares the root of Judas' treachery.
**Now he said this, not because he cared for the poor,
but because he was a thief and, having the box, was
carrying what was cast therein.** Urging the needs
of the poor without caring for the poor, speaking the
words of charity without a heart of charity, marks
the hypocrite. In this case hypocrisy is linked with
secret criminality: Judas actually was a thief. When
this stealing was discovered we are not informed, but
John's positive accusation is based on fact.

How Judas managed to steal is also explained:
he was the treasurer of the little band, he carried the
γλωσσόκομον. The term, originally used to designate
a case in which to keep mouthpieces (γλῶσσαι) for
flutes, came to be used for any boxlike receptacle,
here one to hold coins, and was translated "bag" by
the Vulgate, which translation Luther and our versions followed. The dispute as to whether ἐβάσταζεν
means "was taking away" (stealing), or "was carrying," is not decided by pointing out, on the one hand,
that John has already called him a thief, or, on the
other hand, that John has already said that he had
the moneycase. This imperfect verb is to be con-

strued with τὰ βαλλόμενα. Judas was in charge of
the offerings made by friends for the support of Jesus
and his disciples, βάλλειν being the regular verb for
the act of making an offering. To translate, "he was
stealing the offerings," would say entirely too much.
He had charge of them, and thus his little peculations
occurred with regard to *sacred* money, offerings made
to the Lord. This makes his crime the blacker. Incidentally, we see that Jesus and his disciples had a
common purse. What was his was theirs; and Judas,
Jesus' familiar friend, who lifted up his heel against
him, ate his bread.

Why did Jesus, who undoubtedly was aware of the
thieving Judas, not take the treasury from him? This
is only a part of the larger question as to why God
does not by his omniscience and omnipotence interfere
in every case of crime, preventing it from being carried out. Jesus brought all his grace to bear upon
Judas; if that proved ineffective, nothing could change
the heart of the traitor-thief. This answer is truer
than to say that the counsel of God prevented Jesus
from interfering.

7) **Jesus, therefore, said, Let her be, that she
kept it for the day of my entombment.** After the
parenthetical remarks in v. 6 οὖν resumes the course
of events. Mary is silent, Jesus makes her defense.
John restates only two points of this defense; his
readers know what Matthew and Mark have recorded.
The first point is that Mary has anointed him for his
entombment; the second is that the disciples will not
have him always. Both of these briefly stated points
John selects because they speak of Jesus' death, now
so near at hand. What he records on these points
agrees perfectly with the statements of the other
evangelists.

"In the N. T. ἄφες is not yet a mere auxiliary as
is our 'let' and the modern Greek ἄς," R. 931. This

shows that the rendering of the A. V., "Let her alone," is correct; and that of the R. V., "suffer her to keep it," is wrong, for it makes ἄφες a mere auxiliary to τηρήσῃ. This is unlikely also because of the intervening ἵνα; for when ἄφες came to be used as an auxiliary it was directly connected with the main verb, see the examples in R. 931-932. The word has a ring of sharpness, like Matthew's, "Why trouble you the woman?"

Textually the reading ἵνα τηρήσῃ is established in preference to τετήρηκεν without a conjunction. The latter is easier grammatically: "against the day of my burying hath she kept this" (A. V.), namely in advance to anoint me as she has done for my burial. The sense of the reading with ἵνα and the subjunctive is the same. What has prevented some from seeing this is, in the first place, ἵνα, which they regard as final, and, in the second place, the subjunctive, which they regard as future to the moment when Jesus spoke. Now some have come to read this ἵνα as sub-final and the aorist subjunctive as future to the moment when Mary bought the ointment. The aorist of this subjunctive should have been a help for understanding this word of Jesus; if Jesus has in mind a keeping, future to the moment of his speaking, the present subjunctive would have been in place. Zahn translates in this manner: *dass sie es aufbewahre.* This, then, is interpreted out of keeping with the context, as though αὐτό does not refer to the μύρον, *all* of which was used by Mary in her act, but to a supposed portion that is still left; and this portion, Jesus is thought to say, Mary shall be allowed to keep without blame until the coming entombment of Jesus. Yet the objection of Judas was not raised in regard to such a remainder but in regard to the ointment used upon Jesus. One reason for this incorrect grammar and this interpretation is the fact

that commentators regard one evangelist as contradicting another instead of allowing each to help in
understanding the other.   Matthew writes very plainly, "For in that she poured this ointment upon my
body, she did it for my burial"; and Mark, "She
hath anointed my body aforehand for the burying."
Exactly this John means when he says that Jesus
ordered Judas to let Mary alone — on what matter?
"that she kept the ointment for the day of my entombment," i. e., anointing me now ("aforehand") for
that day.   Besides, Jesus was not anointed after he
was removed from the cross; he knew that he would
not be; Mary of Bethany was not on Calvary; and
any keeping of ointment by Mary for that actual day
of entombment would have been in vain.   The only
anointing the body of Jesus received for his entombment it received here at Bethany at the hands of
Mary.   Yet it is improper to call the day of the supper in Bethany the day of the entombment, or to
think that Jesus spoke of it as being such; for Mark
writes, "aforehand for the burial," and Matthew, "to
prepare me for burial."

But did Mary actually think that she was anointing the body of Jesus there at the supper for his
entombment?   Some think of only a providence and
regard Mary's purpose as an unconscious one.   Some
let Jesus "lend" this significance to Mary's act.
Some think of a foreboding, an indistinct premonition.
Only a few state that when Mary bought and had
the ointment ready, she did this consciously for the
very purpose Jesus so clearly states.   Let us remember that what Jesus spoke in Galilee, Matt. 16:21;
what he told his disciples so plainly at the beginning
of his last journey, Matt. 20:17, Mark 10:32, 33,
Luke 18:31-34; and what he told his enemies in Jerusalem, John 7:33; 8:21-23; 10:11 and 17, 18, and
what these enemies well knew, Mary must also have

known. She knew in addition about the threats and
the plots of his enemies with which Jesus, too, had
charged them openly, John 5:18; 7:1 and 19; 8:59;
10:31, etc.; 11:53 and 57. The disciples, it is true
enough, did not realize what was so close at hand.
But why should not at least one heart realize it? The
character of this woman is such that it ought not to
surprise us that, where dull-witted men failed, she
saw that Jesus was, indeed, going straight to his
death — even to crucifixion, as he himself said. Thus
her mind leaped to the conclusion that, when the
tragedy now broke, it would be utterly impossible
to anoint the dead body of Jesus. That is why she
acted now, unhesitatingly embracing the opportunity
which she had hoped would come and for which she
had prepared.

Only if Mary knew that she was anointing the body
of Jesus for its burial, is the tremendous praise
accorded her act by Jesus himself justified: "Verily
I say unto you, wheresoever this gospel shall be
preached in the whole world, that also which this
woman hath done shall be spoken of for a memorial
of her," Matt. 26:13. Nebe is right when he points
out that those who let Jesus "lend" a purpose to
Mary's act that is not in Mary's mind make Jesus
a modern lawyer who invents motives for his client
at which the client himself is then surprised; and
that Jesus acts as such a lawyer in the shadow
of his own death and on the very subject of that
death.

8) Regarding the poor John adds only so much
from the words of Jesus: **For the poor you always
have with you, but me you have not always.** The
verbs are plural, addressed quite properly to all
present. "The poor" has the article of previous
reference, Judas having referred to them. Even today they are with us in spite of all social and economic

reform. Jesus is the last to forget or to neglect the
poor. Mark writes, "And whensoever ye will ye can
do them good" — a strong hint for thieving Judas,
who, by secretly robbing the treasury of Jesus, was
robbing also the poor, to whom Jesus was wont to
give (13:29). Where Jesus is anointed the poor will
never suffer. Mary is a better almoner than any
Judas that ever lived. A mean, low, beggarly spirit
of utilitarianism is offended at every costly gift, every
beautiful· ornament, every display of genius and art,
which honor Jesus and do not rob him to enrich the
poor. While we spurn this, let us not go to the
opposite extreme, of which some are guilty who do
great and notable things ostensibly in honor of Jesus
yet forget the Lazarus at their door.

"Me you have not always" is prophetic of the death
so near at hand. It would have been a shame if he
who was going into death for all of us should not
have been honored by at least one who understood in
a way that was befitting his death. Because of its
very nature this opportunity could come but once.

9) **The great multitude of the Jews, therefore,
learned that he was there, and they came not for
Jesus' sake only but in order to see also Lazarus,
whom he did raise from the dead.** As was the case
in chapter 7, the ὄχλος consists of pilgrims who had
come for the Passover feast. Many of these had come
days before (11:55), and their number grew constantly. The combination ὁ ὄχλος πολύς is unusual in
that the noun and the adjective seem to form "a composite idea," R. 656. The news spread in Jerusalem
and in its environs in the most natural way, for Jesus
and his little band were part of the caravan that
moved from Jericho toward Jerusalem, and while
Jesus halted at Bethany, the rest went on to the city.
This, too, is how the crowds learned where Jesus was:
ὅτι ἐκεῖ ἐστι, the Greek retaining the tense of the direct

discourse, "He is there," i. e., in Bethany. John most likely adds "of the Jews" because presently he intends to tell about certain Greek pilgrims (v. 20). None of the latter went out to Bethany, only crowds of Jewish pilgrims did so. What these Jewish pilgrims did on Sunday is told in v. 12, etc. (ὄχλος πολύς repeated). "Of the Jews" cannot refer to emissaries of the Jewish leaders in Jerusalem, nor to Jews who were residents in the capital.

The account regarding Lazarus had spread, and so crowds flocked out to Bethany all day Saturday to see not only Jesus, who had wrought this astounding miracle, but Lazarus as well, the man who had been dead and buried for four days. No hostile attitude or intent on their part is manifested. The two miles to Bethany were no hindrance as regards a Sabbath day's journey, for hosts of pilgrims always had to camp outside of the city at the time of the great festivals.

10) At once the Jewish leaders heard of these visits of the curious to Bethany and took action. **But the high priests took counsel with each other to kill also Lazarus because on his account many of the Jews were going away and were believing on Jesus.** These were only the high priests, Caiaphas and his Sadducee relatives, who headed the Sanhedrin. The Pharisees in this body were left out, evidently because they were not of a kind to consent to the murder of a perfectly innocent man. These unscrupulous rulers consulted with each other (ἐβουλεύσαντο, reciprocal middle, R. 811) and came to the decision (aorist) to kill also Lazarus (ἵνα non-final, stating the substance of the decision, R. 993-994). The reason (ὅτι) for this decision is astounding. The man himself had done absolutely nothing that was in any way punishable; only others were doing something that was also absolutely non-punishable, coming out to see

him and in consequence believing in Jesus. For this
reason Lazarus was to be killed. The criminality of
the Sadducean rulers was outrageous. The imperfects ὑπῆγον and ἐπίστευον are descriptive of repeated
action, and while the two actions are grammatically
coordinate, the former is merely circumstantial for
the latter.

The Royal Entry, 12-19

John's account of the royal entry is purposely brief,
frankly presupposing that of the other evangelists, yet
it has some distinct features of its own.

12) **On the morrow a great multitude that had
come to the feast, having heard that Jesus was coming to Jerusalem, took the palm branches of the
palm trees and went out to meet him and kept
shouting, Hosanna! Blessed he that comes in the
name of the Lord, even the King of Israel!** "On
the morrow" = on the next day, namely on Sunday,
the day after the supper of Saturday evening. At
once, when Jesus prepared to leave Bethany for Jerusalem, the pilgrim visitors, described in v. 11 as constantly coming out from the city to see Lazarus as
well as Jesus, rushed the news back to the city that
Jesus himself was now coming to Jerusalem. "Jesus
is coming!" was the word passed along. This caused
"a great multitude" of the pilgrim host, "that had
come to the feast" (ὁ ἐλθών), to form a grand procession to meet Jesus on the way and to bring him into
the city. The synoptists speak of two multitudes, and
John makes clear how this is to be understood: one
was with Jesus as he leaves Bethany, the other started
from Jerusalem to meet him on the way.

13) The latter "took the palm branches of the
palm trees." John does not add what they did with
them, for this had already been told. To say that
John means that the people kept them in their hands

while the other evangelists tell us that the people laid them in the road for Jesus to ride over, is to find a contradiction where none exists. Nor do the articles mean that this use of the palm branches was a customary one like the carrying of the "lulab" or festive spray at the Feast of Tabernacles. This is placing too great an emphasis on the articles, which refer only to the branches of the trees that lined the road up the Mount of Olives. Those palms and their branches, well known in those days as gracing that road, have long since disappeared — now all is bare. Since τὰ βαΐα already means "the palm branches," the addition τῶν φοινίκων constitutes a kind of pleonasm. The other evangelists refer only to "trees"; John records that these were palm trees. To get the right impression of the scene we must know how the orientals regarded palm trees: majestic in their height, the queens of all lowland trees, with their proud diadem of great fronds, spreading with their face to the sun, in immortal green, unceasingly replenished with new life from the deep-set roots, in those desert lands and in many an oasis the picture of life in a world of death (Delitzsch on Ps. 92:7). To the oriental the palm tree was the perfect tree, embodying everything a tree should really be; even its life, extending to 200 years, made it a symbol of immortality. We usually regard palm branches as symbols of victory and triumph but the oriental regarded them as symbols of life and salvation.

Luke tells us that the shout of Hosanna was first raised "at the descent of the Mount of Olives," and he adds that "the whole multitude of the disciples began to rejoice" thus. John's imperfect ἐκραύγαζον, "kept shouting," notes only the continuation on into the city, through the streets, to the Temple. Tissot's painting of one of the scenes of the Entry into the Temple shows the boys of the age of twelve and over who had come to the festival mimicking their elders, parading in festival white in front of Jesus, keeping step to their clapping and rhythmic shouts.

The words are taken from Ps. 118:25, 26, to which interpretative additions are made: compare also Luke 19:38. Psalms 113-118 are termed the *Hallel,* and this was sung at the Passover when the festival procession was received by the priests; it was sung also, a part before and a part after the Passover meal (Mark 14:26). The most distinctive part of the chant was "Hosanna," three of the evangelists recording the Hebrew transliteration: *Hosh'ah-na, schaffe Heil,* "grant salvation" ("save now," A. V.) In greeting Jesus the word seems to have been used by the multitude less like a prayer to God and more like a joyful acclamation, a little like our: All hail!

The rest of the words taken from the Psalm: "Blessed he that comes in the name of the Lord" (Jehovah), constitute a welcome. The perfect εὐλογη-μένος, "having been blessed," has its usual present force, "having been and thus now still blessed." And ὁ ἐρχόμενος, here too is a Messianic designation, especially since it is coupled with the phrase, "in the name of Jehovah." The enthusiastic multitude thus acclaims Jesus as blessed by Jehovah, not merely with words of benediction, but with all the gifts and treasures implied in the benedictory words, coming thus to Jerusalem bearing these blessings. For we must remember that John supplies what the other evangelists omit, namely the connection of this acclaim with the great miracles of Jesus, the last of which, the raising of Lazarus, has stirred the hearts of these pilgrims to their very depths. As the One so blessed they greet him with the Messianic title, "the One who Comes" and whose coming is "in the name of the Lord," i. e., in connection with the revelation (ὄνομα in this sense, compare the explanation in 1:12) of Jehovah.

Luke has more of the additions made to the words taken from the Psalm (19:38), yet despite all his brevity John records, "even the King of Israel." Beyond question this means the Messiah-King. It is fruitless to speculate on the meaning attached to these words by the multitude. Whatever of wrong earthly expectation still beclouded the vision of these "disciples" (Luke) and of the multitude generally, a holy enthusiasm had caught their hearts on this Sunday, a wave of real spiritual feeling and joy, the direct product of "all the mighty works they had seen" (Luke), which moved them when thus welcoming Jesus to "praise God" (Luke). This helps us to explain why Jesus accepted this honor and by his very act lent himself to this enthusiasm, riding into the city as the King of Israel that he was.

14) **Now Jesus, having found an ass, sat upon it, as it is written, Fear not, daughter of Zion! Thy King comes, sitting on an ass's colt.** Here is the picture of the King on his royal entry. Since we know from the other records how Jesus "found an ass;" John is very brief and mentions only the fact, although in v. 17 he indicates the aid of others in securing the ass: "they had done these things unto him." Only the essentials are given, first, of the fulfillment; secondly, of the prophecy. The extensive perfect, "as it has been written," includes the present: is still on record.

15) John quotes Zech. 9:9. In the call, "Fear not!" he reproduces only the sense of the original, "Rejoice greatly!" For when fear goes out, joy comes in, i. e., over against God. One may quote the *ipsissima verba,* but an entirely legitimate form of citation is to restate the sense in equivalent terms, especially

such parts of a quotation as are not to be stressed. Here the call to rejoice is entirely minor; the point of the quotation is the statement about the King's coming, riding upon the foal of an ass. This remarkable feature is the one stressed by Zechariah. "Daughter of Zion," to which the prophet adds, "daughter of Jerusalem," is one of the honor names of Israel. "Zion" seems to have been the name of the locality where Jerusalem came to be built and was then used as a designation for the highest eminence in the city. The Temple, however, was not on this high point but on Moriah, which lies lower. Thus "the daughter of Zion" names the people according to the most prominent eminence which distinguishes its capital. By a legitimate transfer this poetic title is now applied to the New Testament Israel, the Christian Church.

By losing the regular verb accent, the circumflex, and carrying the acute, ἰδού becomes an interjection that is equivalent to our "lo!" Here it points dramatically to the figure of the Peace-King, marked as such by coming to his capital, not in the panoply of war, but sitting upon the colt of an ass. There is symbolism in the animal which Jesus rode, a symbolism intended by Zechariah in his prophecy. It has well been observed that the ass is lowly as compared with the horse; it symbolizes *peace*, as the horse does *war*. Thus the ass was chosen to bear the meek and lowly, yet divinely royal Prince of peace in his triumphal entry to his capital. When, however, the colt is called untamed, and the symbolism is carried farther so as to include the universal domination of Jesus over nature as well as over spirit, this goes too far. The colt was gentle enough, but with the clause, "whereon yet man never sat," Luke 19:30, indicates why a colt was chosen instead of an older animal. Jerusalem deserved the fate that her King should come with power to punish her wickedness and unbelief, but this was still the day of grace, and the crowning deeds of grace were yet to be done. So this King came with grace and salvation, not to be feared and dreaded, but to be loved, trusted, and joyfully followed. John emphasizes the *literal* fulfillment of the prophecy. This would not be so striking if Jesus had usually ridden about the country (like the good Samaritan, Luke 10:34), but he always walked until this day when, by his own orders, the beast was found for him to ride on.

16) John makes a confession at this point; compare 2:22; 20:9. **These things his disciples did not realize at the first; but when Jesus was glorified, then they remembered that these things had been written about him, and that they had done these things for him.** "These things," made emphatic by two repetitions, include the entire occurrence as the fulfillment of a specific prophecy. The Twelve are referred to, who, though they knew the Scriptures, never at the time realized that they were helping to fulfill a prophecy plainly recorded in these Scriptures. The fact that Jesus realized this is evidenced, if by nothing else, then by his sending his disciples for the colt. Not until Jesus was glorified (risen from the dead, etc.) did the disciples see the connection between "these things" that had been written by the prophet and "these things" which they themselves on that day had done for Jesus. Even then, we may say, it was only by the promised aid of the Holy Spirit (14:27 and 45) that they remembered and realized, although John does not here hint at this final teaching of Jesus. John has several of these striking references to prophecy, beginning with that of Jesus, 2:19-22; the unconscious prophecy of Caiaphas, 11:50-52, finally 18:31-39; 19:24 and 34-37. On ἐπ᾽ αὐτῷ, "in his case," see R. 605.

17) **The multitude, therefore, that was with him kept bearing witness that he called Lazarus out of the tomb and raised him from the dead. On this account also the multitude met him, because they heard that he had done this sign.** The resumptive οὖν continues the narrative after the explanation in regard to the disciples in v. 16. Verse 9 reports that between Friday and Sunday many went out to Bethany to see both Lazarus and Jesus. Thus on Sunday when Jesus started for Jerusalem, a mass of people were in Bethany and accompanied Jesus when he left for the city. This is ὁ ὄχλος ὁ ὢν μετ᾽ αὐτοῦ, "the multitude that was with him." This multitude naturally "kept testifying" to the miracle regarding Lazarus, "that (ὅτι) he did call Lazarus out of the tomb and did raise him from the dead." Note the double statement, the first half regarding the manner of the miraculous act ("did call," etc.), the second regarding the effect ("did raise," etc.). The doubling also makes the testimony emphatic. On ἐκ νεκρῶν see the explanation of 2:22. While ὅτε has better textual evidence than ὅτι, the present consensus is in favor of the latter. For if we read, "the multitude which was with him *when* he *called*," etc., we should have to go back of v. 9 to the people who actually were present when the miracle was performed, namely residents of Jerusalem (11:31, etc.), of whom John would now say that they kept spreading the report of the miracle. Yet we have already heard (11:46) that some of these told the Pharisees, and that even the Sanhedrin took action in consequence. The whole matter was thus already public from the very start. It would seem strange that John should at this point tell us that this multitude (the original witnesses) were still testifying, ἐμαρτύρει; and ὁ ὢν would have to be read as a kind of imperfect participle, R. 892. It is far more natural that John advances us to the crowds that came out

to verify the story about Lazarus (v. 9), in particular, on this Sunday, to the multitude now in Bethany for this purpose, i. e., "the one being with him" now. Having seen Lazarus with their own eyes, having also inspected the tomb, they now kept testifying to the wondrous deed.

18) In v. 12,13 we noted that a great multitude started out from the city to meet and to greet Jesus when they heard that he was coming from Bethany. John now adds that all these had heard of the sign Jesus had done. "On this account also the multitude met him," etc. This is a different multitude, one that gathered in Jerusalem, that did not go to Bethany but met Jesus on the way ("at the descent of the Mount of Olives," Luke 19:37). "On this account because they heard," etc., means that what stirred them to action was the report spread all over the city during the past days that Jesus "had done this sign." The infinitive in indirect discourse after the verb of hearing is sharper than a participle would be, R. 1103. Since this is indirect discourse, these people heard the report in this form: Jesus "has done this sign" — "he has done it," and it now stands as done; τὸ σημεῖον, "the sign," a deed full of the highest significance, revealing Jesus as the Messiah-King (v. 13). By giving these details John supplements the accounts of the other evangelists and informs us just how the enthusiasm started that produced the royal welcome which Jesus received on his entry into the capital. Note also the tremendous contrast in the effect of this sign on the Sanhedrin (11:47-53, and v. 57) and in that on the pilgrim hosts that filled the city.

19) **The Pharisees, therefore, said to each other, Behold how you profit nothing! See, the world has gone away after him!** This graphically depicts the reaction of the Pharisees. Two parties seem to be represented, the one, more unscrupulous,

siding with the radical Sadducees, the other, more
lenient, hesitating to propose violent measures. The
former address the latter who were in the majority
and had thus far prevented violence. Their words,
full of helpless wrath, taunt the milder party, declaring that all their temporizing has proved abortive and
useless: "you are profiting in no respect," gaining
nothing whatever. Against this negative they place
the positive: "the world" is running after him — passionate hyperbole. This royal entry seemed like a
public challenge of the authority which had issued
orders for Jesus' arrest and had formally resolved
to destroy him. *Inscii prophetant*, writes Bengel.
Unconsciously they utter words such as the prophecy
of Caiaphas, for soon enough thousands turned to
faith, and the church spread over all the world.

The Greek uses the aorist to indicate what has just
happened and is present at the moment. This aorist
seems awkward in English, which, however, is due
only to the English. We must translate with either the
present or the perfect: "the world is going after him,"
or "has gone after him"; read R. 841-843. With
ἀπῆλθεν the Pharisees mean, "away from us," and thus
"behind" or "after him," indicating the gulf between
him and them. This dark background of hate in the
hearts of all the leaders in Jerusalem makes the whole
spectacle on Palm Sunday dramatic in the highest
degree: and this the more when we realize that all
this murderous hate was perfectly known to Jesus,
and that in the very face of it he followed his sure
course.

The Request of the Greeks Reminds Jesus of the End, 20-36

20) This one incident from the days following
the royal entry on Palm Sunday is preserved by John,
not on account of the Greeks, who furnished only the

occasion, but on account of the testimony of Jesus
regarding his death now so close at hand. The Pharisees say, "the world goes after him," and here even
these Greeks want to see Jesus. "Just as the setting
sun sends out its most beautiful rays and lights up
the circle of the earth afar, so the glory of our Lord
Christ, standing at the threshold of death, sends out
its rays, and the desire to see him is roused even in
the hearts of Gentiles coming from afar; in the same
manner at the dawn, in his childhood, the wise men,
as the first-fruits of the Gentiles, were drawn by the
light of the wondrous star from faraway Persia."
Gerhard. Bengel calls their coming "a prelude of
the transition of God's kingdom from the Jews to the
Gentiles."

**Now there were certain Greeks of those ac-
customed to come up to worship at the feast.** These
Ἕλληνες were not Greek Jews or Hellenists but "proselytes of the gate," the φοβούμενοι or σεβόμενοι τὸν Θεόν
of the Acts, former idolaters who had accepted the
essentials of the Jewish religion and some of its
customs and practices without formally being received into the synagogue by circumcision, which
would have made them "proselytes of righteousness."
They resembled the Ethiopian eunuch, the centurion
Cornelius, and others. The present participle expresses customary action: ἐκ τῶν ἀναβαινόντων (ἐκ partitive), "of those accustomed to go up"; many of these
proselytes visited the great Jewish festivals. Their
purpose was "to worship at the feast" like the Jews
whose faith they shared. Whether they also went
up for purposes of business we do not know; John
intimates nothing on that score, rather the contrary. Solomon's prayer at the dedication of the
Temple expressly refers to such "strangers"; read
I Kings 8:41-43.

21) **These, therefore, came to Philip from Bethsaida, of Galilee, and were requesting him, saying, Sir, we want to see Jesus.** John does not state why these Greeks approached a disciple and in particular Philip. It may be that Jesus was in the Court of the Men, where Gentiles were not allowed to enter. Happening upon Philip either passing in or out, they addressed him. John mentions the home town of Philip, which seems to hint at the fact that these Greeks had met him there and thus knew him. They present their request with all due respect, as κύριε shows. "To see Jesus" is modest for meeting Jesus and receiving an opportunity to hear him. If these Greeks desired only to look upon this famous person as men generally are curious to see great people and proud to report that they have seen them, abundant opportunity offered itself daily as Jesus moved about in the Temple courts. These Greeks ask for a personal interview.

22) **Philip comes and tells Andrew; Andrew comes and Philip, and they tell Jesus.** The hesitation of Philip is usually explained in whole or at least in part by calling Philip timid; yet this seems too much like inventing an explanation where none is given in the text. Philip and any other disciple had reason to hesitate. Jesus had instructed them not to go in the way of the Gentiles (Matt. 10:5) ; he had declared concerning himself that he was sent only to the lost sheep of the house of Israel (Matt. 15:24) ; likewise, he had placed the gathering of the other sheep into the future (John 10:10). Yet he had heard the petition of the woman of Canaan, had spoken of many coming from the east and the west and sitting down with the patriarchs in the kingdom of heaven (Matt. 8:11), and had praised the great faith of the centurion at Capernaum (Matt. 8:5-10; Luke 7:2-9). Thus argument might be advanced in either direc-

tion. Moreover, here in the Temple hostile eyes watched every movement of Jesus with the most vicious intent. For him to make advances to these Greek proselytes might involve him in great peril. So Philip consults Andrew, one of the three disciples that formed the inner circle of the Twelve, and together they tell Jesus.

23) We hear nothing further about the Greeks. John is faulted for this and for similar apparent omissions in his narrations, yet the fault lies with those who do not see that John is not telling the story of these Greeks but of Jesus. The important thing for us is to learn what Jesus testified at this moment. For little did Andrew and Philip imagine how this request of a few Gentile proselytes would affect Jesus. Both the omission of John in not telling us whether Jesus allowed these Greeks to confer with him, as well as the words which he spoke when their request was brought to him, have been urged as indicating that Jesus declined their request. Yet it is hard to see how this conclusion can be drawn. It would not be like Jesus. We prefer to think that at an opportune moment Jesus allowed these Greeks to meet him. **And Jesus answers them, The hour has come for the Son of man to be glorified.** The following verses show that the answer to Andrew and Philip was given in the audience of "the multitude." Repeatedly we have heard that "the hour" has not yet come, 7:6 and 30; 8:20, etc. Here Jesus now announces that it "has come," ἐλήλυθε, the extensive perfect, a state that has arrived at completion (R. 992), like a vessel that is finally filled up. The Greeks often use ὥρα for "hour" in the wider sense, as when they speak of "the day and the hour," the specific date and the appropriate time (Matt. 24:36). So here. The actual day of Jesus' death was not yet come, but "the hour" or time for his death had now arrived.

Yet, strange to say, Jesus calls this "the hour for
the Son of man to be glorified." In the one word
δοξασθῇ he sums up everything — the passion as something glorious, the exaltation following, and the
future adoration by the hosts of believers the world
over and in heaven. Jesus was glorified by the
obedience he rendered to the Father even unto the
death of the cross, and in the redemption he thus
achieved for the fallen world; he was glorified when
the Father highly exalted him, giving him a name
above every name and seating him at his right hand;
he was and is glorified in the work of the Holy Spirit
("he shall glorify me," 16:14) as it leads thousands
to the feet of the Savior. Those who do not include
the passion in the glorification should consider carefully 13:31, 32; 17:1. The glory begins with the
passion — Jesus sees how from his passion and his
death a magnificent vista opens, reaching onward
through the ages into all eternity, and it is one shining path of glory. The passive verb ascribes the
glorifying act to the Father. On the Messianic title
"the Son of man," which Jesus here again gives himself, see 1:51.

24) With solemn assurance Jesus depicts the
inwardness of what this great "hour" brings. **Amen,
amen, I say to you** (see 1:51), **Unless a grain of
wheat, having fallen into the earth, dies, itself remains alone; but if it dies it bears much fruit.** The
weight of this utterance is marked by the double seal
of verity and the added seal of authority. To Nicodemus, the Jew, Jesus speaks of the serpent being
lifted up in the wilderness; for these Greeks, to whom
this word will presently be reported, he speaks of the
grain of wheat, a symbol which is clear to Jew and
to Gentile alike. With divine mastery Jesus pictures
the glorification which is about to begin for him. The
image chosen perfectly illustrates both the necessity

of the cross and its resultant glory. The *tertium comparationis* is fruit through dying — the former only through the latter. As in nature, so in Jesus. In every illustration we are confined to the tertium; whoever goes beyond this disturbs the sense. Here the *tertium* has nothing to do with the wheat germ, the sprouting, and the growing unto harvest. It uses only the death of the grain as a necessity for the following fruit.

If a grain of wheat be not put into the soil, it will, indeed, not die, but it will then "itself remain alone" and produce nothing. So will the Son of man remain alone if he does not stoop to death on the cross. But if the grain falls into the earth, dies, and is consumed, it brings much fruit. So the Son of man, God's incarnate Son, by dying will produce millions of children of God, fruit in most glorious abundance. "The death of Christ was the death of the most fertile grain of wheat." Augustine. In the petition of these Greeks Jesus sees the great harvest that will go on and on as the product of the great Grain of Wheat (himself) which fell in the earth. The present tenses in the apodosis are timeless, as often in maxims, R. 1019.

25) Jesus is like the grain of wheat which by dying produces much fruit, i. e., makes many thousands of children of God. Now these are all like Jesus as regards loving their life, they aim to achieve something higher, the ζωὴ αἰώνιος. **He that loves his life loses it; and he that hates his life in this world shall protect it.** By ψυχή the Greeks understood the immaterial part of man in so far as it animates the physical body, while πνεῦμα is this same immaterial part in so far as it is able to receive impression from the Πνεῦμα of God. Thus ψυχή comes to mean "life." On the difference between φιλεῖν, the love of mere affection, over against ἀγαπᾶν, the love of intelligence

and purpose compare 3:16. He who clings to his earthly life with passionate attachment, Jesus says, by that very act of clinging to it with such love loses it. It cannot be held thus and kept indefinitely; for him who is thus attached to his life, that life with all its happiness and its treasures, yea with its very form as counted so dear, slips away and disappears. "If you have loved ill, you have hated; if you have hated well, you have loved." Augustine. The world is full of these blind lovers who love themselves to their undoing. Many will at last hate themselves bitterly for not having hated themselves properly in this life.

The first paradox is followed by a second. The effect of the two is heightened by making the ·second the direct reverse of the first. Not only this, but the positives and the negatives are placed chiastically:
The lover (positive) ——————— loses (negative)
The hater (negative) ——————— shall protect (positive)
This perfection of form makes the double paradox sink into the mind and stay there without effort. Here μισεῖν is used relatively, as in Luke 14:26 and Rom. 9:13, which is indicated also by the modification "in this world"; hence "he that hates his life in this world" = he who is ready to go contrary to his natural inclinations and desires in his life here on earth, to wound, grieve, deny, crucify, mortify self in repentance and in sanctification. He may look as though he is losing his life by getting nothing out of it, yet in reality he is the only one who is taking care of and protecting even his earthly life, for by thus treating his life he will protect it "unto life eternal." The verb φυλάσσω means "to stand guard over" and thus "to protect"; note also αὐτήν, the ψυχή or natural life. The lover of his natural life "is losing it," present tense, which leaves open the hope that he may see

his folly before it is too late and may learn to hate his life as the other one does. Concerning the other one Jesus uses the future, "he shall protect it," which counts on his doing so permanently, so that the heavenly life ever remains his. He shall thus get out of his natural life what God intends him to get (αὐτήν) and at the same time attain "the life eternal" with all its glory in the blessedness of heaven. Here the word used is ζωή, the very principle of life which joins to God, the source of this life, and, passing unharmed through physical death, lives forever with God; see the exposition in 3:15

It is worth while to note that ὁ κόσμος οὗτος is not identical with ὁ αἰὼν οὗτος The latter is the present "world eon or era" as distinguished from the one about to come, ὁ αἰὼν μέλλων, the former being filled and characterized by passing temporalities, the latter being filled and characterized by the eternal treasures promised by Christ. "This world," ὁ κόσμος οὗτος, is the world as a place, *ein dinglicher Organismus* (S. Goebel), and the context must decide whether sinfulness is included (as in 12·31, 16·11) or only remotely implied (as in 9:39, 11·9, 13·1 18:36; I John 4:17). Although in the present passage some stress the sinfulness of "this world," the context does not justify this view Our natural life can be lived only in this orderly cosmos of God's own creation

Although the Christlikeness has been mentioned in v 26 (brought out strongly in Heb 12:1-3), the great difference between the divine Grain of Wheat, dying to give us life and us, "much fruit," must be noted Only Jesus could do and did what he says in 10:18, only Jesus could by his dying produce the church of believing children of God All that we can do — and that only by his grace not of ourselves — is to use our earthly and natural life so as to gain for ourselves the life eternal. He alone is the Savior, we are nothing but the saved. He needed no salvation; we cannot save even our own selves

26) It may sound cryptic to say that by hating one's life in this world one protects it for life eternal. Jesus explains in simple words just what this means. **If me anyone serves, me let him follow. And where I myself am, there also my own slave shall be. If me anyone serves, honor him will the Father.** This is not smooth English but it may serve to indicate the points of emphasis which are quite essential for the sense. Not to love one's life but to hate it in this world in the sense of Jesus, means to serve *him* not self as all worldly men do; ἐμοί, emphatic over against τὴν ψυχὴν αὐτοῦ. "Anyone" is both individual (for this serving is a highly personal matter) and universal (open to any and to all) The two conditions of expectancy (ἐάν with the subjunctive) vividly contemplate such future servants and their service. The present subjunctive speaks of continual service, a life devoted to this service. The verb διακονεῖν signifies voluntary service, service just for the sake of service, which one delights to render. He who would thus serve ME, "ME let him follow," continue to follow! This is a sweet gospel command (10:4). To follow Jesus is to keep close to him, to walk in the path of his choosing (true obedience), to hear his voice and word (not relying on our own wisdom). Service and following always go together; this injunction is thus most natural. Yet it has been said — only too truly — the Son of man has many admirers but few followers. Some even bid others follow but are themselves remiss in following.

"Let him follow me" is really the offer of a high privilege, for not Jesus but the follower derives all the benefit (6:68, 69). And the blessing thus intended is to continue forever: "And where I myself am, there also my own slave shall be." He speaks as though this will be a delightful place indeed, 14:2, 3. To the unbelieving Jews he said the very opposite, "And where I am, you cannot come," 7·34; "Whither I go, you cannot come," 8:21. The fact that Jesus is speaking of a place to which he will presently go and where he will remain permanently, is indicated in the broad character of the promise, which, while it is again worded in the singular ("my own slave") and thus is directly personal, is at the same time universal, including every servant of his He refers to heaven, or, as he stated repeatedly to the Jews (7:33; 8:14), the heavenly presence of his Father. On the future sense of εἰμί see R 869-870· "It is not merely prophecy, but certainty of expectation that is involved." Both ἐγώ and the possessive adjective are strongly emphatic· "where *I myself* go," I, the Lord and divine Master, "there also *my own* slave shall be." The two belong together Yet this is not an association like that of a common master and his servant; for we know that in heaven all such service will be ended. This is the association in which Jesus receives us to himself (14:3), where we share in his glory and honor and sit with him in his throne (Rev. 3:21). Where did earth ever show a master who treated his slaves thus? Think of our poor service here, even though it be διακονία, and this reward that is promised us! The future ἔσται, "shall be," is divine promise.

Nor is this all For Jesus is the Son whom the Father sent on his great mission, the Son who will return in glory to his Father when that mission is carried out Thus all who by this Son's mission are joined to him are brought also to the Father (Heb 2·10, "bringing many sons unto glory"). Therefore the addition· "If me anyone serves, honor him will my Father." The protasis is the same as the preceding one and speaks of our service in this

life; the apodosis is future and speaks of what shall
be in heaven when we are there united with Jesus.
The emphasis is on τιμήσει not on αὐτόν. This is the
climax when the Father shall do no less than *honor*
the servants of his Son. "It was something great
when Joseph was honored by Pharaoh, the King of
Egypt, and Mordicai by Ahasuerus, the Persian
prince; but it is something immensely greater for
the Blessed and Only Potentate, the King of kings
and Lord of lords, to honor the servants of Jesus
Christ." Gerhard. Perish the thought of any merit
on our part! This reward is in accord only with
the infinite greatness and magnanimity of him whose
delight it is to bestow it. If the Father so honors
the servants of his Son, how will he honor and
glorify the Son himself after the service which this
Son rendered!

27) In the request of the Greeks Jesus sees his
own death standing before him. While he calls it a
glorification of the Son of man, in particular as
regards the glorious fruit that will result, nevertheless, this impending death stirs the soul of Jesus to
its very depth. **Now my soul has been troubled.
And what shall I say? Father, deliver me out of
this hour? But no — for this reason I came into
this hour.** Jesus is not addressing the disciples and
the bystanders. This is a monolog, uttered before a
higher presence; yet uttered audibly for those at
hand to hear. They are granted a glimpse into what
transpires in the soul of Jesus. "Now" is defined in
v. 23: "the hour has come." "Now my soul has been
troubled," deeply stirred and agitated, reveals what
Jesus feels in his human soul as the death shadow begins actually to envelop him. The perfect tense is intensive (R. 895), for the agitation that is now upon
Jesus reaches back, although its present intensity
leads him now to reveal it.

Not by any means coldly, indifferently, or without feeling is Jesus going into his death. He was perfectly aware of all that his death entailed. His was not to be a death like that of the Christian for whom the terrors of death have been removed by the cancellation of sin and guilt; nor like the death of the unbeliever who is blind or realizes only in part what awaits him. Jesus was to die with all the world's sin and guilt upon him. The curse and damnation of that guilt was to strike him and to crush out his life. All the dreadfulness of this impending death was fully revealed to him he saw all that was awaiting him. Moreover, he was going into his death voluntarily. No power compelled him save his own will, which was one with that of his Father He was free even now to withdraw from that death. But since the hour has come, the act of sacrifice is about to begin, the frightfulness, the utter horror, the inconceivable dreadfulness of death came over the soul of Jesus. All that was human in him recoiled from the rending ordeal, just as our body, to use a weak comparison, shrinks from some painful contact and quivers when it begins yet submits and endures, no matter what the pain, held to the agony by the power of the will. The sinless, holy Jesus, God's only-begotten Son, was to stoop beneath the damning guilt of the world and by his own death as a man to expiate that guilt. Thus was his soul shaken in this hour.

We must read together as really forming only one question: "And what shall I say? (Shall I say:) Father, deliver me from this hour?" Jesus is speaking to his Father. The thought is: shall this be what he shall say to the Father, that the Father shall save him from this hour? The verb $\epsilon\mathring{\iota}\pi\omega$ is a deliberative aorist subjunctive, the proper form for a question in which one asks himself what he shall do. The aorist imperative $\sigma\tilde{\omega}\sigma o\nu$ is used because the deliverance would

be accomplished by one decisive act. Unfortunately,
both of our versions read the second part of the question as a declaration: Jesus actually asking the
Father to deliver him. The context not only forbids
this sense but actually annuls it. For the Greek ἀλλά
negatives the idea of such a prayer: "But no —
for this very reason I came into this hour." Then
follows the prayer that Jesus does make. R. 1187
tells us that ἀλλά "interrupts the thought," in fact, it
contradicts the very idea of such a prayer. As in
Gethsemane, Jesus merely thinks of the possibilities
obtaining in his case, namely that even now, though
the hour has come, he might ask the Father to deliver
him completely from it. In plain human fashion, true
man that he was, he looked at that possibility, allowed
us to hear his thoughts, and then at once dismissed
them from his mind — he had come to suffer and he
was resolved to suffer. The phrase διὰ τοῦτο has no
grammatical antecedent; it is construed *ad sensum*.
For this very reason, namely to die for the world,
Jesus "came" into this hour, the aorist ἦλθον to indicate
a coming that has just occurred, R. 843. "Into" this
hour is in contrast to the preceding "out of" (ἐκ)
this hour, i. e., the one on which Jesus had just
entered, R. 598. For this hour is the one which is
to crown all his previous life and work.

28) Instead of praying to be delivered, this is
what Jesus prays in this great hour, **Father, glorify
thy name!** The one, and in the highest sense the
only, purpose of Jesus, now as ever, is the Father's
glory and will. Any thought apart from that, or
merely omitting that, Jesus puts away; never for an
instant does it find lodgment in his heart. The aorist
imperative δόξασον is both decisive and complete regarding the act requested. And the ὄνομα is the revelation of the Father, the unveiling of himself in his
will and his purpose. To glorify that "name" is to

make it stand out before men in all its truth, grace, power, and other attributes; for the δόξα of the Father is the sum of the divine attributes or any portion of them, and the act of δοξάζειν their display. The unveiling here referred to is the one that results from the passion and the exaltation of Jesus as our Redeemer. Jesus prays that the Father may help him carry his redemptive work to completion, thereby displaying his truth, love, righteousness, power, etc., to all the universe. So few the words, so immense the sense!

Instantaneously a miraculous response to this prayer came from the Father. **There came, therefore, a voice out of heaven, I both have glorified and will again glorify it.** We recall the voice heard at the time of the Baptism of Jesus and in connection with his Transfiguration. The Father speaks audibly from heaven. He himself supports and strengthens Jesus as he passes into this hour. The English must supply the object with at least an "it" (ὄνομα) The absence of the common circumstantial participle "saying" makes the narrative more dramatic. The Greek may use his aorist ἐδόξασα, whereas we prefer the perfect, "I have glorified," R. 845. The Father did glorify his name in and through Jesus through all his past life and work, for in the entire mission of Jesus as accomplished thus far the grace, power, and blessed purposes of the Father shone out with resplendent clearness. And he will do this also in the hour now begun through the passion and the resurrection of Jesus. Note how the Father combines the past and the future as though the former is to serve as the assurance for the latter

29) **The multitude, therefore, that was standing by and heard it were saying it had thundered; others were saying, An angel has spoken to him.** This multitude is part of the pilgrim host that has come to attend the Passover They heard the sound

from heaven without distinguishing the words. Compare Acts 9:7, where Jesus from his throne of glory speaks to Saul on the road to Damascus, and where likewise only they understand for whom this address is intended, while the rest hear only a sound. The question of faith or of its lack should not be brought in as an explanation for understanding the words or for hearing only a sound — Saul certainly had no faith, yet he understood. The understanding was accomplished in those for whom the word was intended; yet in the case of the rest God wanted the impression of a supernatural manifestation connected with Jesus. The astounding sound coming from heaven was called "thunder" by those who sought a natural explanation. Perhaps the sound resembled thunder to their ears. Others, nearer the truth, connect the sound with Jesus and imagine that an angel from heaven has spoken to him. The thunder hypothesis would be offered by the skeptics of today, who deem any but a natural explanation of supernatural phenomena "superstition." Yet for the clear skies of Palestine thunder is a poor hypothesis, it is rather on the order of the new wine spoken of in Acts 2:13. The two perfect tenses are intensive (R. 908) and alike although the one is used in indirect discourse, "that thunder has occurred," and the other in direct discourse, "An angel has spoken to him." Intensive means that the effect of what has just been heard is present when these explanations are offered.

30) **Jesus answered and said, Not for my sake has this voice come but for your sake.** On ἀπεκρίθη καὶ εἶπεν compare 1:48. The former is used as a middle without a previous question and may meet only a situation or an occurrence, as here, where no dative "to them" follows. This word of Jesus is addressed only to his disciples, who, together with Jesus, had heard and understood the Father's reply. Jesus him-

self needed no audible answer from the Father to any
of his prayers; he knew that the Father always heard
him. This miraculous reply was for the disciples, that
they might hear directly and with their own ears
both that the Father had, indeed, answered Jesus
and what that answer was. It was another attestation
of the Father, of the clearest and the strongest kind,
that Jesus was his well-beloved Son. This explanation
Jesus gave with others standing by, who thus might
also learn what really had taken place.

31) Since the voice from heaven spoke audibly
in order that the disciples might hear, Jesus explains
his own prayer and the Father's answer. **Now there
is a judgment of this world; now the ruler of this
world shall be thrown out.** The two emphatic
"now," refer to the hour already begun, in which the
Father will answer the prayer of Jesus by glorifying
him. This hour is a judgment of this world, κρίσις
without the article. An act of judgment will now
take place upon "this world" (objective genitive),
a κρίσις resulting in a κριμα or verdict. The fact that
this will be adverse is not expressed in κρίσις but follows from the second statement. On "this world"
see v. 25 also 8:23. The cosmos as an ordered complex is referred to, in which men stand at the head
with all else focusing upon them. It may appear
as though by rejecting Jesus this world is pronouncing a verdict upon him, in reality, by doing this very
thing a judgment descends upon the world itself —
a terrible condemnation — it loses its right to exist.
"By killing Jesus the world pronounced its own death
sentence, lost its right to exist," Zahn. The case of
the world is like that of the Jews and their Temple
in 2:19; by destroying him for whom the Temple
stood they destroyed their Temple and themselves.
Not that the world will at once end, but this hour
decides that its enduring character has passed — it

is vain, empty, transient, passeth away (I John 2:17), it is doomed.

The second statement is parallel to the first; each illumines the other. Here is the same emphatic "now" for the hour already begun in which the Father glorifies Jesus. By bringing a judgment on this world this hour throws "the ruler of this world" out of his domain and dominion over the world. By inciting the world to kill Jesus the devil wrecked his own domain. Its right to existence has passed, his own rule and reign meets its doom. He who rules the world by using all the things of nature for his purposes which are hostile to God, inciting men against their God by all that the world contains, he is now himself dethroned, and all that is left to him is the shadow of power.

The future tense, "shall be thrown out," is punctiliar. This is not a gradual pressing back of his control that runs its course through the centuries until the day of judgment but a sudden dethronement in the hour that is now at hand. The devil receives his doom in the death and the resurrection of Jesus. Compare the symbolic description in Rev. 20:1-3, and the exposition in the author's little volume *Saint John*. Bound in the bottomless pit by the great Angel of the Covenant (Jesus), Satan "should deceive the nations no more" for the era of the thousand years, the great New Testament period. Not that the world is now wholly rid of the devil and goes on with him being completely removed. The judgment on his kingdom ("this world") is the judgment on his rule over this kingdom, the decree that throws him out. What remains to him is the hopeless attempt of an already dethroned ruler to maintain himself in a kingdom, the very existence of which is blasted forever.

32) In the hour now at hand the world and its ruler seemed to win, for Jesus was crucified and slain,

his earthly work brought to a tragic end. But the very reverse was the fact. Over against the judgment of this world and the doom of its ruler Jesus sets the triumph of his mission **And I, if I be lifted up from the earth, will draw all unto myself.** This emphatic "I" is placed over against "this world" and "the ruler of this world." Over against their fate as embodied in his glorification, Jesus places the triumph of his mission as summarized in his glorification now to take place in the hour that has come. While the clause, "if I be lifted up," is conditional, it is the condition of certain expectancy, "if I be (or shall be) lifted up," as, indeed, I shall We must read no contingency or doubt into this clause, Jesus vividly imagines the lifting up as being accomplished (aorist). Some texts read ἄν, which is only the abbreviated ἐάν, R. 190, 1018

In contrast with Satan, who shall be thrown ἔξω, Jesus says of himself that he shall be lifted ἐκ τῆς γῆς, the preposition denoting separation, R 597. Both ἔξω and ἐκ refer to "this world." The difference lies in the verbs. Satan is thrown out "outside," Jesus is lifted up "out of" The connection of Satan with this world is shattered, that of Jesus is only modified That is why Jesus with reference to himself here employs ἐκ τῆς γῆς, "out of the earth," which implies "into heaven" and the corresponding higher form of existence, whereas "out of this world" would here be misleading because of the preceding reference to Satan Jesus is speaking of the transfer of his body and human nature to the right hand of God's power The days of his humiliation will cease, the eternity of his glorification will begin While this refers to his human nature, it does not mean that Jesus will no longer be present with his disciples according to his human nature. The entire God-man, divine and human, will be with them to the end of the world, and where two or three are gathered together in his name, he will be in their midst. Yet not as now, walking visibly on earth and in humble form, but with the glory of transcendent power and in the manner of his eternal exaltation. Just as what now is about to occur on Calvary and in Joseph's tomb is the doom of this world and the dethronement of its ruler, so it will for Jesus constitute his enthronement in heaven forever.

Hence the conclusion, "And I . . . will draw all unto myself." This is the same drawing as that mentioned in 6:44 (compare 6:37), there predicated of the Father, here of Jesus; for the *opera ad extra sunt indivisa* and are thus predicated of all the persons, now of one, now of another, and never of one to the exclusion of the others. This is the drawing exerted by grace through the means of grace (Word and Sacrament), alike in effectiveness and seriousness for all men, not in any way limited on God's part. Yet here, as in 6:37; 6:44; 10:16; 11:52, and other connections, Jesus is speaking of this universal and unlimited grace only in so far as it succeeds in actually drawing men from the world to himself. All are alike drawn, but by their perverse obduracy many nullify all the power of grace and harden themselves in unbelief (Matt. 23:37), while others, in equal sin and guilt, are converted by this same power of grace. Why some are thus lost and others won, all being under the same grace, constitutes a mystery insoluble by our minds, about which we know only this, that those who are lost are lost solely by their own guilt, while those who are won are won solely by divine grace.

Jesus is speaking only of the latter when he says, "I will draw all unto me." These πάντες are all "his servants," of whom he says in v. 26 that he wants them to be with him in heaven. They constitute the "much fruit" of v. 24. They form the "one flock" of 10:16, "the children of God" now scattered abroad

(11:52) through all the world in all ages. To the eyes of Jesus, though they are yet unborn, they are all present. Jesus will see to it that all of them shall come to him (6:37), and that not one of them shall be lost (6:39). The volitive future ἑλκύσω is simply futuristic (R. 889) and tells how Jesus will draw them "unto myself" in the glory of heaven. Thus will all the glorious fruit of his redemptive mission be garnered at last.

33) At this point John adds the explanation which helps us to see fully what Jesus had in mind. **Now this he was saying, signifying by what manner of death he would die.** The imperfect ἔλεγε bids us dwell on what Jesus "was saying." The moment we observe that σημαίνων refers to Jesus and not to John we are relieved of the idea that John is giving us *his* interpretation of what Jesus said. It is Jesus who, by using the verb ὑψωθῶ, "signifies" or plainly indicates the manner of his death, namely crucifixion. This, then, is not "a mystical interpretation" by John "after the manner of his time" and "without effect on the historical sense" of what Jesus really said, nor is this an ambiguity involved in the word "be lifted up." Jesus purposely chooses this word as he used it in 3:14, and in 8:28 (where the Jews are designated as those that will lift up Jesus), because it is a pregnant term which is capable of expressing both his return from earth to heaven and the manner of death by which this return would be effected These two are really not two but a unit For not merely by returning to heaven will Jesus become the Savior who draws us to heaven after him, but by returning to heaven through the death on the cross as the sacrifice for our sins. The participle "signifying" thus means "prophesying", wherefore also in 18:32 the fulfillment of this very prophecy is noted. Instead of John's inserting his own thought into what Jesus says,

John is recording just what Jesus himself had in mind and said.

34) **The multitude, therefore, answered him, We for our part did hear out of the law that the Christ remains forever; and how art thou for thy part saying, The Son of man must be lifted up? Who is this Son of man?** The crowd of pilgrims surrounding Jesus and intent on what he says in answer to the request of the Greeks is puzzled. Note the emphatic contrast in ἡμεῖς and σύ: "we" on our part, "thou" on thine. They state what *they* did hear and thus learn "out of the law," the Old Testament Scriptures. It is "that the Christ remains forever," i. e., that, when the Messiah comes, he will establish an earthly kingdom in which he will rule eternally, remaining right here as the King. But Jesus seems to have an entirely different idea. "And how sayest *thou,* The Son of man must be lifted up?" i. e., transferred from earth to heaven. The contrast lies in both the predicates: "remain forever" here — "be lifted up" away from here; and in the subjects: "the Christ," the title common among the Jews, and "the Son of man," this strange title employed by Jesus (v. 23) to designate himself. While Jesus had not used δεῖ, "must" be lifted up, this addition by the spokesman of the multitude is not out of line with Jesus' words. On εἰς τὸν αἰῶνα see 8:35 and 14:16.

The entire difficulty is brought to a point in the question, "Who is this Son of man?" Since τίς here = ποῖος, R. 735, and "the Son of man" may be predicative to οὗτος, we may translate, "What kind is this person — the Son of man?" Can Jesus by this strange title be referring to himself as the Christ (so it would seem) and yet be predicating of himself something that is quite contrary to what these Jews find in the Scriptures? The pilgrims who put this question to Jesus are not hostile to him as were the Sanhedrists. In fact, they are not adverse to accepting Jesus as "the Christ" if he will live up to what *they* expect "the Christ" to be. However, they have no understanding for the Christ who is "the Son of man" about to leave the earth and to ascend to his Father

35) It is useless for Jesus to attempt a direct answer to these people   After all that he has said and done they cling to their self-made opinions   **Jesus, therefore, said unto them, Yet for a little time the light is with you. Walk while you have the light, in order that darkness may not befall you. And he that walks in the darkness does not know where he is going. While you have the light, believe on the light, in order that you may be sons of light.** Jesus "said" this to them, in the strict sense of the word it was not a reply to their specific question. In a way this is a reply   the one they needed not the one for which they asked   How can Jesus say that he must be lifted up, he the Son of man? The answer is: Believe on the light, and you will know — and unless you believe, how can you ever know, remaining as you do in darkness? Faith alone is able to settle all questions, remove all doubts, for faith is like coming out into the light where one can see, while unbelief is like remaining in the darkness, wondering and questioning about things that are in the light and which cannot be understood without going and seeing them in the light.

"Yet for a little time (accusative of extent of time) is the light with you," as Bengel says, is quite the opposite of the conception which these pilgrims have, who think that the Christ will rule as an earthly king forever. Their delusion prevented them not only from understanding what Jesus said about his death but also from perceiving the passing of the day of grace which had come for them in the earthly life and work of Jesus. Jesus is speaking of himself as "the light" (1:9; 8:12; 12:46). Light is associated with truth, the revelation of divine and spiritual reality. Jesus here speaks of himself as the embodiment of saving truth and its revelation to men. This is far more than the expression of moral perfection, serving either as a mirror to reveal the sinfulness of men or as an example that men are to imitate. As the light Jesus is the source of salvation for sinful men; men must receive him as the light in their hearts by faith and thus be changed inwardly to become "sons of light." The phrase ἐν ὑμῖν is substantially the same as μετ' ὑμῶν in 7:33, "in your midst" or "with you." Only a few days and the visible presence of Jesus would be removed. The "little time" may be extended to include the preaching of the apostles on and after the day of Pentecost, but even then the time would be brief.

In 7:33 and 8:21, etc., Jesus sounds a similar warning to the Jewish leaders, foretelling their judgment and damnation. Here, in addressing this crowd of festive pilgrims, his words are milder, full of warning, indeed, but combined with earnest admonition. "Walk while you have the light." The image refers to one who seeks to reach a goal, say a traveler far from home. The imperative is absolute, "Be walking!" do not dally, use the light while the way may be seen. Since a temporal modifier precedes, namely "a little time," we must here and in v. 36 regard ὡς as temporal, "while you have the light," not as qualitative, "as the light requires that you walk." To have the light means to have its radiance shining over us and lighting the way for us.

This call and admonition is re-enforced by the warning, "in order that darkness may not befall you." "Darkness," or "the darkness," as the opposite of Christ, the light, is not merely the absence of light (merely negative) but always like an evil power (positive). Hence καταλαμβάνειν, used with reference to darkness in this sense, means to seize upon you, lay hold on, befall you like a monster that destroys.

Instead of continuing the clause with ἵνα μή, "lest darkness befall you, and you know not where you go," the latter warning is made an independent sentence, "and he that walks in the darkness knows not where he is going." This makes the statement axiomatic, hence the present tenses. This man is lost. It is the tragedy of the darkness. "But who believes that it is such a serious thing of which Christ here speaks? How little is the light esteemed, and people imagine they can get it at any time when they want it, even if now they do not take it. But Christ says: No! if you despise it, the darkness will overtake you." Luther. Too late, too late to reach the goal when the darkness descends. "He that walketh in the darkness," ὁ περιπατῶν ἐν τῇ σκοτίᾳ, a true description of the Wandering Jew, of the orthodox as well as of the Reformed Jew, and of thousands who, like them, have rejected Christ, the light. "Knows not where he is going" (ποῦ used like our "where" for "whither") points out the lost man's subjective condition. He may imagine and talk a great deal; but he does not know. He is like a man in the desert without a path, without a guide, without a goal, without one star of hope above him, yea, without eyes and power to see; I John 2:11, "and knoweth not whither he goeth, because that darkness hath blinded his eyes." Jesus knows whither such men go, 8:21; whither he is going they cannot come, 8:14.

36) The admonition is repeated and thus intesified. The figurative "walk" is explained by the literal "believe." The arrangement is chiastic:

Walk ———— while you have the light!
While you have the light ———— believe!

Man's own activity is not implied in the figurative term "walk" and is not to be ascribed to the literal term "believe." This is contrary to the Scripture doctrine of faith. "I believe that I cannot by my own reason or strength believe in Jesus Christ my Lord, or come to him." Luther. Whenever Jesus or the Scriptures bid us believe, the very words by which they do this contain the power that works faith and actively direct upon us the divine effort to produce faith. This is the case here as Jesus calls on these Jewish pilgrims to believe. The fact that they and others like them may successfully resist this faith-producing power of the light, namely of Jesus and of his Word and Spirit, so that no faith is kindled in their hearts, in no way proves that such power is not present and active.

The ἵνα clause in v. 36 is the opposite of the ἵνα μή clause in v. 35. "In order that you may be sons of light," matches the thought contained in the verb "believe." The implication is that those who are lost in the darkness are the sons of darkness. In each case the light or the darkness is not something external, only surrounding the person, but something internal that forms the very nature of that person. Never is Jesus called "a son of light," always he himself is "the light." The term "sons" denotes derivation. "For ye were sometimes darkness, but now are ye light in the Lord," Eph. 5:8. Even when we are called "the light of the world," Matt. 5:14, this derivation holds good, Luke 16:8; John 8:12; II Cor. 4:6. We may translate γένησθε either "be" or "become" sons of light. The point to hold to is that no gradual process is involved in this aorist, for the moment we believe we are no longer darkness, the first reception of "the light" makes us "sons of light."

The Conclusion of the First Half of John's Gospel. Summary, 37-50

In the first paragraph of this conclusion John himself sums up the results of the public ministry of Jesus. In the second paragraph the attestation made by Jesus throughout his public ministry is summarized in a compact selection from his teachings.

37) These things Jesus said and went away and hid himself from them. The entire paragraph shows that this statement refers not merely to the scene in the Temple just described but to the entire public ministry. "These things Jesus said" summarizes all his past teaching among the Jews. Properly we have ἐλάλησεν, for from now on Jesus remained silent and no more taught in public. He was through teaching publicly. Robinson's *Harmony of the Gospels* fixes this day as the Tuesday after Palm Sunday. "And having withdrawn, he hid himself from them," means, having withdrawn from the Temple and public places, he placed himself where the public could not find him. Not that Jesus went into hiding; he simply retired from further public appearances. He most likely went to quiet Bethany and remained in the circle of his friends in the village until two days later Judas betrayed him.

As the sun sets quietly after a glorious day, taking all its brightness and radiance with it, so Jesus withdrew from his public work. His action was the beginning of judgment upon the unbelieving nation. It was symbolic of his final and eternal separation from these unbelieving Jews.

Yet though he had done so many signs before them, they were not believing in him. This is the echo of 1:11, "His own received him not." Now all has been done, and this is, indeed, the sad, sad outcome. This is not recorded, however, as though Jesus had failed — he cannot fail; nor as though this outcome of his labors were a perplexing, disappointing, unexpected thing — quite the contrary. It was all positively and fully foretold; it was the will of God himself (this will, of course, rightly understood) ; it was all fully taken into account by God from the very beginning. The genitive absolute is concessive: "though," etc., R. 1129. The imperfect ἐπίστευον expresses the course of action on the part of the Jews, the course now in progress. The number of the "signs" is emphasized because their number had a cumulative effect. These "signs" as signs should also have been enough to elicit faith; for each one of them, to say nothing of all of them taken together, indicated and revealed so much. On the term "sign" consult 2:11. These "signs" were placed ἔμπροσθεν αὐτῶν, a veritable *demonstratio ad oculos,* before the very faces of all to see and to take to heart. Although John records only six of these signs in his own Gospel, he counts on his readers knowing those recorded by the other evangelists, to which also he himself refers incidentally in 7:31; 9:16; 11:47.

38) The Jews remained without faith, **in order that the word of Isaiah, the prophet, might be fulfilled, which he spoke,**

Lord, who did believe our report?
And the arm of the Lord, to whom was it revealed?

On the critical question whether Isaiah wrote the second half of the book which bears his name (chapters 40-66) consult *Jesaias II,* by Aug. Pieper, *Einleitung.* The overwhelming evidence for Isaiah's authorship of the entire book cannot be brushed aside by the remark, which begs the question, that "evidently John did not know any better." The two poetic lines quoted from Isa. 53:1, follow the LXX translation, which adds to the Hebrew the word of address,

"Lord." It should be self-evident that John is not putting the prophet's words into the mouth of Jesus; v. 38 and 41 present Isaiah as the speaker.

The great *Ebed Yahweh,* the Servant of Jehovah, the Messiah, is presented in Isa. 52:13-15 as with his deep humiliation and with his lofty exaltation he will affect the Gentiles, who shall see what they have never been told and will consider what they have never heard. Over against these Gentiles, to whom the gospel story of the Messiah comes as something entirely new, Isaiah places Judah, the chosen people, who have for a long time had the fullest information concerning this Servant of Jehovah from Jehovah himself through his prophets. Even in his fifty-third chapter Isaiah pictures at length and in detail the coming Messiah, his passion and his death and his glorious exaltation. But as the prophet looks forward to the day of fulfillment, he exclaims: "Who did believe our report? And the arm of the Lord, to whom was it revealed?" The implied answer is negative, i. e., as far as the mass of the chosen nation is concerned. This prophecy of Isaiah's, John writes, is now fulfilled as Jesus closes his public ministry.

"Our report," ἀκοὴ ἡμῶν, is generally understood to mean: the hearing which we, the chosen people, have had (objective). The sense of the question then is: "Who did believe the message that has come to us all along about the coming Messiah?" The advantage of this interpretation is the fact that the "we," running through v. 1-6, is throughout: we, God's people. Only those who deny that the Servant of Jehovah is the Messiah, and let this Servant signify Israel as a nation, say that "we" still refers to the Gentiles mentioned in 52:15. The other view regards "our report" as meaning: the hearing which we, the prophets of God, have given to the chosen people (subjective). This has "we" in v. 1 denote the prophets and "we" in v. 2-6 the

chosen people together with the prophets. If it is
objected that such a change in subjects is unlikely, the
answer is that throughout this section Isaiah speaks
dramatically and keeps changing the speakers; in
52:13-15, it is the Lord ("my servant"), in 53:1, the
prophets, in 53:2-6, the people, and in 7-9 the Lord.
It seems most natural to take "our report" subjectively; the message which we prophets let the chosen
people hear. In substance little difference is offered
by the other view. But when v. 1-6 are regarded as
the utterance of repentant Israel, confessing that it
once failed to understand and perceive, this should not
be referred to the entire nation, as those do who hold
to a final national conversion of the Jews, but only to
the repentant part of the nation which comes to faith
throughout the centuries.

So Isaiah utters the plaint that the message which
he and the prophets brought to Israel about the coming Messiah was not believed: "Who ἐπίστευσεν (aorist)
actually believed it?" The implication is: hardly anyone, speaking of the nation in general. And this,
John means to say, was actually fulfilled when the
Messiah came, and when his work was about completed. Parallel with "our report," or the prophetic
message from the Lord, is "the arm of the Lord," his
almighty power, evidenced most completely in the
signs (v. 37) wrought by Jesus. The Jews saw these
signs but with their unbelieving eyes refused to see
that Jehovah's arm was revealed in them, that they
were divine works and nothing less. Neither the
divine testimony of the prophets including Jesus himself, nor the divine testimony of the signs wrought
faith in the hearts of the Jews.

This happened, John writes, "in order that the
word of Isaiah, the prophet, might be fulfilled," that
the event might fill up completely the word of prophecy
spoken long before at the order of Jehovah. In other

words, it was God's own intent that the Jews should not
believe.   The case is stated more strongly still.

39)   **On this account they could not believe, that
Isaiah said again:**

> **He has blinded their eyes and did harden their
> heart;**
> **Lest they should see with their eyes and per-
> ceive with their heart**
> **And should turn, and I should heal them.**

The ὅτι clause is appositional to τοῦτο, R. 699: on
this account . . . that (not "for" or "because").
Here John says not only that it was God's intention
that the Jews should not believe in Jesus but that they
could not believe because their unbelief had been foretold.   It was impossible for them to believe because
of the prophecy spoken by Isaiah.

40)   Isaiah 6:9, 10 reads in the Hebrew: "And
he (Jehovah) said, Go and tell this people, Hear ye
indeed, but understand not, and see ye indeed, but
perceive not.   Make the heart of this people fat, and
make their ears heavy, and shut their eyes; lest they
see with their eyes, and hear with their ears, and
understand with their hearts, and convert, and be
healed."   The LXX translates *ad sensum* with two
prophetic future tenses, followed by three aorists
(which may also be considered prophetic).   When
appropriating this prophecy John very properly reproduces neither the imperatives of the Hebrew, which
were addressed to Isaiah, nor the modifications of the
LXX, but uses two past tenses, since the ancient prophecy is now completely fulfilled at the close of Jesus'
ministry.   The perfect, "has blinded," and the aorist,
"did harden," merely view the past actions in two
ways, both of which are pertinent.   The three aorist
subjunctives after ἵνα μή are effective, "lest they
actually see," etc.; and the passive στραφῶσι is reflexive,

"turn themselves," i. e., because of what they see and perceive. The fourth verb is a future indicative, ἰάσομαι, appropriated, it seems, from the LXX and, of course, entirely allowable in the Koine, B.-D. 369, 2, and R. 194. The point John stresses is that God himself blinded and hardened the Jews. When at the end he writes: lest "I should heal them," changing to the first person, we decline to have this mean: "I, Isaiah," by my preaching: but "I, Jehovah," since the Hebrew has the passive: lest "they be healed," in which Jehovah is the agent.

The problem thus presented is how God himself could intend that the Jews should not believe in Jesus, and, apparently still worse, how God himself by blinding and hardening the Jews could make it impossible for them to believe. This should not be evaded, nor should its solution be made easier by in some way modifying either the words of Isaiah or their reproduction by John. We have the identical problem in Matt. 13:14, where Jesus says why he speaks in parables and where he himself quotes the Isaiah prophecy from the LXX; in Acts 28:26, 27, where Paul warns the Jews in Rome; and at full length in Romans chapters 9-11. The question raised is: What caused the unbelief of the Jews? The answer is: God. The question is by no means: In what respect is this unbelief not a reason against but a reason for the Messiahship of Jesus? a question nowhere raised or answered by John. The classic example for the problem here presented is Pharaoh (Exod. 9:16; Rom. 9:17): "In very deed for this cause have I raised thee up, to show in thee my power; and that my name may be declared throughout all the earth." On Pharaoh see *Concordia Triglotta*, 1091, 84-86.

It would be contrary to the entire Scriptures to assume an arbitrary, deterministic will of God, commanding the prophet to declare the unbelief of the

Jews and then, in order to make good the prediction, himself to cause this unbelief in the hearts of the people concerned. The observation is correct that any decree of reprobation is completely shut out by Jesus' own last call to the pilgrim crowd in the Temple, "Believe on the light, that you may be sons of light." "And this call of God, which is made through the preaching of the Word, we should not regard as jugglery (*Spiegelfechten* — literally: fencing before a mirror, sham fencing), but know that thereby God reveals his will, that in those whom he thus calls he will work through the Word, that they may be enlightened, converted, and saved." *Concordia Triglotta*, 1073, 29. The answer to the problem is that in Isaiah's and in John's words we have not the antecedent but the subsequent will of God. This is not a blinding and heardening decreed in advance by an absolute will, forcing damnation upon men; but a judicial and punitive decree upon those whose obduracy God infallibly foresees. They who wilfully and wickedly turn the gospel, which on God's part is meant for them as a savor of life unto life, into a savor of death unto death (II Cor. 2:16), shall, indeed, go to their doom. The announcement of their fate in advance by prophecy is due to the foreknowledge of God, which declares that they who will not believe and be saved shall not believe and find salvation.

41) **These things said Isaiah because he saw his glory and he spoke concerning him.** Some texts have: "when" he saw, etc. "These things" are the ones contained in the two quotations from Isaiah. The prophet uttered them, not as applying only to the nation at his own time, but as applying equally to the Jews of the time of Jesus. Isaiah "saw his glory." "I saw also the Lord sitting upon a throne, high and lifted up, and his train filled

the temple. . . . Mine eyes have seen the King, the Lord of hosts," Isa. 6, 1-5, preceding by a little the last quotation. This is the glory of the exalted Son after his return to the Father, the glory referred to in v. 28. Isaiah beheld it before the Incarnation, John after; Isaiah beheld it in a heavenly vision, John beheld it in the words and the deeds of Jesus, in the person and the character of the God-man on earth: "And the Word was made flesh, and dwelt among us, and we beheld his glory, the glory as of the only-begotten of the Father, full of grace and truth," 1:14. And Isaiah knew that this glorious Son would in the fulness of time appear on earth, to be rejected by the Jews, even as they rejected the Lord in Isaiah's own time (compare Isa. 53). It is thus that the prophet "spoke concerning him," namely Jesus.

42) **Nevertheless, even of the rulers many did believe in him; but because of the Pharisees they were making no confession, in order that they might not be persons banned; for they loved the glory of men rather than the glory of God.** Only once in the New Testament have we the combination ὅμως μέντοι, "nevertheless." It comes as a surprise to read that "many of the rulers" or Sanhedrists actually believed in Jesus (aorist to express the fact as such). Here is strong evidence of the mighty effect of the person and the work of Jesus. Yet this faith was too weak to confess itself: "they were not confessing," the imperfect tense to indicate the course of conduct. Yet, since this is an open tense, it implies nothing as to the eventual outcome, whether in the end after all at least some, like Nicodemus and Joseph of Arimathea, did, or did not confess. These two at least did. The powerful sect of the Pharisees, strongly represented also in the Sanhedrin, and numerous and otherwise dominating, sealed the lips of these believing

rulers. Their weapon was the *cherem* or ban (on which see 9:22), which they had decreed for every confessor of Jesus.

43) How this operated in the hearts of the believing rulers John states with an explanatory γάρ. He uses ἀγαπᾶν in saying that they "loved" the glory of men rather than the glory of God. They have had many followers. Of the two between which they had a choice they gave preference to the former. The two genitives are subjective: the δόξα which men give and that which God gives. Perhaps, in using δόξα instead of "honor" or "praise," John here had in mind the prayer of Jesus and its answer from God in v. 28. It is idle, of course, to speculate hypothetically: What if these rulers had promptly confessed? Would this have blocked the crucifixion of Jesus? Many tragedies are precipitated by the cowardly weakness of those who are silent in the hour in which they should speak.

44) John might have closed the first half of his Gospel with v. 43. He adds another paragraph in which he combines previous utterances of Jesus and fashions them into a brief summary of Jesus' call and testimony to his nation. This constitutes an impressive declaration on the supreme importance of faith and on the fatal error and doom of unbelief. **And Jesus cried and said** — no note of either time or place; no indication of persons addressed, either friends or foes. Verse 36 shuts out the supposition that Jesus spoke what follows when he was in the act of leaving the Temple. "Cried and said" denotes public speaking, which removes the supposition that these words were spoken to the Twelve in explanation of the unbelief of the Jews. Bengel is right in his *Gnomon*: it is the evangelist who here sums up from all the utterances of Jesus the essentials of his testimony to the Jews. This is the call he had

issued to them, this is what he said, and this is
what they definitely refused to believe. The two
aorists are merely historical, stating the past fact
as such.

**He that believes in me does not believe in me but
in him that did send me.   And he that beholds me
beholds him that did send me.**   While these statements are not elsewhere found verbatim, they are
closely akin to 7:16, etc., and 8:42; compare also 14:9.
"He that believes on me" at once strikes the keynote —
everything depends on believing. For this Jesus
lived and labored, taught and wrought. The matter is personal, hence the singular. Believing means
to receive in confidence and trust. We may analyze
faith as knowledge, assent, and confidence (*fiducia*),
but the confidence is the real essential to which
the other two are aids. The present participle is
qualitative with no note of time, save that the
quality is considered as enduring. The object of true
faith is "me" — Jesus in his person, mission, word,
and work, all these combined. He is such as to deserve
and call forth from our hearts the very highest
measure of confidence. The only natural and proper
thing is to respond with such confidence; to refuse it
is unreasonable, wrong, wicked. As in ordinary life,
when a man is revealed to us fully as being good,
true, great, strong, kind, loving, and as extending his
help to us, all that he is calls forth our confidence and
we yield it, yield it because he produces it; so also in
the case of Jesus, but as his person, word, and work
show, on a far higher plane.

He "believes not in me," of course, means: "not in
me alone," as though I stand alone or have come of myself.   Hence the addition: "but in him that did send
me."   Throughout John's Gospel, throughout Jesus'
testimony and his signs we hear this word about "him
that did send me," Jesus' great Sender. Him the

Jews should have known and trusted because of his mighty revelation in the Old Testament. They claimed that they knew him, but when his own Son and Messenger came to them, they did not recognize or trust him. The reason was that they never knew this Sender and would not let Jesus acquaint them with that Sender. But this great Sender is the ultimate basis of our faith in Jesus. Behind Jesus stands God himself; and he who sees that at once sees that Jesus is more than man, is God's own eternal Son in the form of man. Thus he was sent, and this is what believing in him really means — trust in God and in the Son he sent. For this sending is the culmination and complete fulfillment of all God's saving promises. There is no possible higher cause to awaken trust in us miserable sinners, whose only help is in this Sender and in the Son he sent. The aorist πέμψαντα designates the great historic act: "he did send."

45) This second statement emphasizes the first, yet it also deepens the sense. Again we have the qualitative participle, but now it brings out a new shade of thought. "To behold" Jesus is to see and perceive who he really is. It is faith alone that beholds, in fact, beholding *is* faith. No need to add: he "does not behold me" only (as if I could ever be alone by myself, 8:16 and 29). At once Jesus adds, "he beholds him that did send me." These two in whom we trust, one of whom we see, are not far apart, so that from the one we must draw conclusions as to the other, conclusions that are, perhaps, doubtful on this very account. Between the prophets of God and the God who sent them a wide gap appears, which is bridged by the word they brought; between Jesus and his Sender there is no gap — in the one you see the other, for the Son is the express image of the Father, Heb. 1:3. All that the Father thinks is fully revealed in Jesus. More than this, the Father and

the Son are one in essence and so in will and in work. No division and separation is possible between them. To see the Son is thus in full reality to see the Father who did send him, 8:19; 14:9; also 5:19 and 30.

46) **I have come as a light for the world in order that everyone that believes in me may not remain in the darkness,** 8:12; 9:5; 12:35, etc. The perfect "have come" includes, and thus am now here. So he stood before the Jews in all his glorious ministry and now stands before us in the Word. Jesus is, of course, "the Light," besides whom there is none other; he is the Truth itself, the very embodiment of all the saving realities of God for us. But in another sense Jesus is not the only Light that God has sent. In all the prophets of God a bright light shone. In so far as they testified of Jesus he was the Light that shone in and through them, yet in so far as they were bearers of God's light they, too, may be called lights. The phrase εἰς τὸν κόσμον, if construed with the verb, would be rather too emphatic since it precedes the verb. It seems to modify φῶς: "a light for the world," intended for it. The world is assumed to be in total darkness spiritually; it is like chaos before the first day when God called light into existence. This is the darkness of sin and of death. The Light comes to drive away this darkness; this is its great mission and work.

Again we see that the matter is personal because it centers in each individual: "in order that everyone that believes in me," etc. Again faith is the decisive thing, for faith receives the Light and thus escapes the darkness. Yet note the universality in both the term "the world" and in "everyone that believes" (the present participle as in v. 44 and 45). This term "everyone" is like a blank space into which every believer is entitled to write his own name, or — Jesus himself by his Word writes it there for him. The purpose of the coming of the Light is that the believer "may not remain in the darkness." This darkness (note the definite article) is not merely the absence of light but the evil power of ignorance, error, falsehood, and deadly deception. "To remain in the darkness" is to lie helpless under this deadly power. "Not to remain" (note the aorist) is to be definitely delivered from this power. To accomplish this two acts are necessary: Jesus, the Light, must come, and this Light must enter the heart and fill it with faith. Thus the deliverance is effected. In this contrast and opposition of "Light" and "the darkness" lies the most effective appeal. How every soul should delight to escape out of this darkness and to live henceforth in the Light! What a monstrous thing that men, made for the Light, should love the darkness rather than the Light (3:20,21) and deliberately remain in the cold, killing, devil darkness!

47) First faith, then unbelief. **And if anyone shall hear my sayings and shall not guard them, I for my part do not judge him; for I did not come in order to judge the world but in order to save the world.** Compare 3:17 and 8:15. "If anyone shall hear my sayings" implies that Jesus will say or have them said to the man in question. Always he and his Word come to the sinner. In ῥήματα the idea is spoken and audible utterance. Jesus makes his utterances sound in the sinner's ears and consciousness. The plural indicates many such utterances. The underlying thought is that the gospel is to be proclaimed and taught. "And shall not guard them" means disbelief. Instead of valuing the gift and treasure offered him, this man treats it as worthless and throws it aside as something he does not want. To him the gold of Jesus' "sayings" is counterfeit coin. He does not hold tightly to it and see that it

does not slip away from him or is snatched or lured from him. The two aorist subjunctives denote actual hearing and actual refusal to guard. The condition of expectancy (ἐάν with the subjunctive) expects such cases to occur.

"I for my part do not judge him." The emphatic ἐγώ implies that another will attend to this. But Jesus is speaking of himself as at the time being engaged in his mission ("he that did send me," v. 44, 45). So the reason why he on his part is not judging is that he did not come into the world for this purpose. The world did not need judgment (Rom. 5:16), it already had that; it needed saving with all that lies in this mighty concept σώζειν — compare 3:17 — especially the idea of rescue from mortal danger and of being placed in permanent safety. Here again the universal, antecedent, good and gracious will of God for the whole world of men is pointedly stated. The difference between the two tenses is this: not to engage in judging — but to accomplish the saving of the world.

48) But what about such a man and his judgment? **He that rejects me and receives not my sayings has one that judges him. The word that I did utter, that will judge him at the last day.** The double subject: "he that rejects me and receives not my sayings" is an exact definition: Jesus is rejected, cast aside as worthless, when his sayings are not received or appropriated with all that they convey. The two present participles are qualitative; they are like the two used as subjects in v. 44 and 45. This man does not need to attack Jesus or rage against his sayings; simply not to receive them is fatal and insures his judgment. He "has one that judges him," has him now, at this moment sitting on the bench in the great tribunal in his judicial robes with all the court officers in place. In τὸν κρίνοντα we have another

qualitative present participle: "one engaged in judging"; while τὸν πέμψαντα, aorist, in v. 44, 45 makes the
single past act of sending the qualitative designation. See what Jesus here says: whoever hears his
Word has that Word either as his savior or as his
judge. Once you hear that Word, you cannot escape.
Many think they can but they are wholly mistaken.

"The word that I did utter, this shall judge him
at the last day." The WORD is the judge of every disbeliever. Jesus does not say "my sayings" shall be
his judges. He summarizes the ῥήματα with ὁ λόγος.
Though "he did utter" them, and they were thus
"sayings" (the two expressions corresponding to each
other), they are not a mere sound heard, gone, forgotten, like the utterances of men, but a grand unit
of eternal substance and reality. "The Word" as the
majestic expression of the eternal will of Jesus shall
be the disbeliever's judge. This Word which Jesus
spoke the disbeliever heard from the lips and through
the voice of Jesus. It will thus be a mighty familiar
judge whom the disbeliever confronts at the last
day. If there is any surprise, it will be his at meeting
again this Word that he spurned in life. It decides
his fate now ("one that is engaged in judging him"),
although that fate may yet be changed while life lasts;
but when life is done, the final verdict is reached,
which will be proclaimed in public at the last day
before the universe of angels and of men. What a
warning against disbelief! Jesus here combines himself with his sayings or Word. Hence no discrepancy
exists between the statement that Jesus will be the
judge at the last day and this one which says his
Word will be the judge. As the Word now comes
from Jesus' lips, as he is in it and comes to us
through it, so this Word will then come from his lips,
and he will be in it and act through it. In the Word
we deal throughout with Jesus.

49)   **For I on my part made utterance not out
of myself, but the Father that sent me, he himself
has given me direction what I shall say and what
I shall utter.**   Does anyone need to know why the
Word of Jesus is so mighty as to reject all its rejecters
at the last day? Jesus did not think it out and utter
it of himself as his own invention and thus apart from
God, as men do with their wisdom and their notions.
The Word comes from Jesus' Sender whom he now
names: "the Father," the First Person of the Godhead.
"He himself," no less a person, "has given" this Word
to Jesus when he came from heaven on his mission;
and the perfect tense denotes a giving that accompanied
the entire life and work of Jesus. As in all instances
in which Jesus says that something is "given" to him
this giving refers to his human nature. The entire ministry and work of Jesus was thus under the Father's
direction. The Father gave, the Son in human flesh,
in the state of his humiliation, took from the Father
and gave to us. This applies to the miracles as well,
5:19, etc.; 11:41-43. In this sense we must translate
ἐντολήν, "direction" and not "commandment" in the
legal or Mosaic sense but in the gospel sense of good
and gracious behests for our salvation, even as Jesus
now also gives us ἐντολαί, 13:34. For this reason also
the whole work of Jesus is an obedience to the Father,
the Son carrying out the Father's gracious and blessed
will, "a sweet smelling savor unto God," Eph. 5:2.
Thus all that Jesus said and did is the Father's own
Word and will. No wonder such eternal judicial majesty
inheres in the Word.

The two indirect questions: "what I shall say and
what I shall utter," would be questions of deliberation
in direct discourse, hence with the subjunctive, which
the indirect retains, R. 1044. The English is weak in
translating the difference between the two questions.

The first with εἶπω matches ὁ λόγος, the Word as so much substance of thought; the second with λαλήσω matches ῥήματα, the sayings sounded by the lips. So completely is the Word of Jesus that of the Father — both its substance and the very sounds of its utterance go back to him. The two aorists do not refer to "every case," as some explain them, thinking that for every case Jesus received separate instruction. These are constative aorists, summarizing and viewing as a whole all that Jesus spoke and uttered during his mission. This was not doled out to him bit by bit, nor did he have to ask for it bit by bit. It was all one gift and behest.

50) While thus the origin and the full majesty of Jesus' Word is brought out, showing us the terribleness of falling under its judgment, the real purpose of this Word, like that of the entire mission of Jesus, is not condemnation but salvation. **And I know that his direction is life eternal. What, therefore, I myself utter, even as the Father has spoken to me, thus I utter.** This οἶδα, "I know," does not rest on air, is no subjective idea, nor subject to any question whatever. It rests on the reality of the sending. He who was sent and showed by a thousand proofs that he was sent and came from heaven and from the Father who sent him, he could not but "know." Compare on οἶδα 6:64; 7:29; especially 8:14 and 55; 11:42; and other passages in the second half of the Gospel. Jesus knows that the very contents and substance of the ἐντολή or "direction" given him for his mission are altogether "life eternal," the gift of the true life principle itself to us sinners, which unites with God, passes unharmed through death, and lives in heavenly blessedness forever; see 3:14, and the other passages that have ζωὴ αἰώνιος. As the Father's "direction" covers the Word and utterance of Jesus (v. 49), so this Word and utterance is "life eternal." Every

believer receives this "life," every disbeliever casts it away.

Knowing what the Father's will and direction regarding the Word and its utterance is, Jesus finally says, "What, therefore, I myself utter, even as the Father has spoken to me, thus I utter." How could he do otherwise? How could he change, omit, or falsify a single sentence, yea a single syllable? His very mission was to bring life eternal — would he defeat himself? Note the emphasis on ἐγώ corresponding with ὁ πατήρ, likewise the two λαλῶ regarding Jesus, "I am uttering," and εἴρηκε (from λέγειν) regarding the Father: he "has spoken," conveying all the substance ("life eternal") to Jesus when he descended on his mission. The last word, then, of the entire first half of John's Gospel is λαλῶ — the great theme of these twelve chapters of John: Jesus' public testimony. And the last summary of John centers in these three: the Word — faith — life everlasting.

CHAPTER XIII

THE ATTESTATION OF JESUS CHRIST AS THE SON OF GOD IN ITS CONSUMMATION. CHAPTERS 13-21

The attestation of Jesus by means of his word and his work before the Jewish people as such is finished. The hour for his passion and his exaltation has finally come. Yet John treats this portion of the record in a way all his own. With a fulness altogether exceptional and with great detail he shows us what Jesus did and said on the last evening of his earthly life. After that he recounts the tragedy of the death and the triumph of the resurrection.

I

The Attestation in the Discourses of the Last Evening, Chapters 13-17

This is Thursday evening, the 14th of Nisan; on the dating compare 12:1. Yet the evening when the δεῖπνον took place is really the beginning of the Jewish Friday, since the Jews begin the day at sundown. Jesus died on Friday afternoon the 15th of Nisan, and the Sabbath of his rest in the tomb was the 16th of Nisan. Thus at the opening of our chapter we must recall that the Passover lamb had been killed in the afternoon of the 14th, and that after sundown Jesus and his disciples assembled in the tiled upper room, where all had been made ready, to eat the Passover feast.

1.   The Washing of the Disciples' Feet, 13:1-20

1) Verse one constitutes a sort of heading or brief prolog to the entire section chapters 13-17. **Now before the Feast of the Passover, Jesus, knowing that his hour was come to pass out of this world to the Father, having loved his own in the world, he loved them to the end.** The fact that Jesus loved the disciples "to the end" extends beyond the single act of love now to be recorded and includes all that Jesus did for the disciples until the end finally arrived. We need say but little on the construction which makes an extended period of v. 1-4, etc., and connects the opening phrase, "before the Feast of the Passover," with the verb "riseth from the supper" in v. 4. It is already decisive to reply that this would make "he loved them to the end" parenthetical, a thought which no reader would find here. More acute is the debate whether the πρό phrase should be connected with the main verb ἠγάπησεν or with the participle ἀγαπήσας. If the former is done, these two terms for love would have to be taken in different senses: after loving his own before, Jesus now at last before the Passover gave them a signal proof of his love. But if this were the sense, we should expect not "before" but "at" the Passover, and the phrase ought to be placed next to the main verb, and something should be added to show that the main verb differs in meaning from the participle. If the other alternative is chosen, so that we read, "having loved his own before the Feast of the Passover, he loved them to the end," the objection again holds that then the phrase should appear next to the participle. In addition we obtain the strange intimation that as Jesus now approaches the end he might have desisted from the love he had shown his own so fully and so long before. These constructions are here discussed because they have been advocated by notable authorities.

The phrase belongs where John placed it: "before
the Feast of the Passover, when Jesus knew," etc.;
it modifies εἰδώς. However, we ought at once to see
that John does not intend to say that now, just before the Passover meal, Jesus attained the knowledge
that he was about to leave this world; for in the previous narrative Jesus very often deliberately spoke of
his coming end. This πρό phrase reaches back to the
very testimony of the Baptist who called Jesus "the
Lamb of God." The sense hinges on the two participles εἰδώς and ἀγαπήσας. Since such participles do
not themselves indicate the relation they are intended
to express, new alternatives arise. Are they both
causal, or both concessive, or is the first concessive
and the second causal, or vice versa? Both must
express the same relation, otherwise a particle would
be inserted to indicate the difference. Both cannot be causal, because in v. 3 a second εἰδώς follows,
repeating and advancing the thought of the first, and
this second participle is plainly not causal — we cannot translate: *"because* he knows that the Father gave
all things into his hands, ... he arises from the
supper," etc. So we drop the following renderings:
"because he knows before the Passover and *because*
he loved," etc.; *"although* he knows, etc., *yet because*
he loved"; *"because* he knows, *although* he loved," etc.
Both participles are concessive and together with the
third in v. 3 indicate three contrasts.

"Although" Jesus knows already before this last
Passover that he was about to leave this world,
"although" he had loved his own all along (constative
aorist), "although" in these last hours of his earthly
life he might well have turned his thoughts upon himself, his mind was still upon his disciples, "he loved
them to the end" and showed them his love to the
very last. See how he prays for them in chapter 17,

and how even at the time of his arrest he protects them from arrest. It is thus also that "although he knows that the Father had given all things into his hands" (v. 3), he, nevertheless, stoops to wash the disciples' feet. By means of these concessive participles John endeavors to impress upon our minds the contrasts which make the last acts of Jesus stand out with love for the disciples — even in these last hours Jesus forgets himself and devotes all his efforts to them.

The second participle is constative, summarizing all that extends over a period of time. The aorist, "that his hour had come" (we are compelled to use the past perfect in English) indicates what had just happened, R. 843. John has repeatedly mentioned this "hour"; note especially 12:23 and 27, and that ὥρα always resembles καιρός, it is not a part of a day but a special period of time. We must cease regarding ἵνα as final and drop such explanations as "that, of course, the hour can have no purpose, but that God is meant." This conjunction is non-final, here crowding out an infinitive and introducing an appositional clause: the hour "to pass out of this world to the Father." The verb μεταβῇ means "to make a transition." Some still regard "out of this world" as meaning out of "this dark, wicked, hostile world." This connotation is furnished only by the context and not by the expression itself; see the explanation in 12:25. Here "out of this world" simply means: "out of the world to which Jesus was sent to accomplish his mission." So also "to the Father" means: to him who sent him on this mission to report its completion to him. The thought is not that of a sweet exchange: wicked world for holy heaven with the joy thus implied; but that of return after the successful accomplishment of a task with the joy and satisfaction this entails.

This casts its light on "his own in the world." The repetition of the article intends to give this phrase equal emphasis with the noun: they are "his own," truly his own, not like those mentioned in 1:11; and they are "in the world" — their task is not yet finished as that of Jesus is; compare 17:11. To be sure, they have still to contend with sin and temptation, but the thought of Jesus is that he leaves his own behind to work in this world for the spreading of salvation, and that, when the time comes, they as his own servants shall also be with him where he is to share in the Father's honor (12:26). These men Jesus had loved with the mighty love of intelligence and purpose (ἀγαπᾶν, see 3:16) and in this love had showered upon them all his gifts and blessings, making them truly "his own." Yet all this is not enough for Jesus and his loving heart; like a mother who loses herself in her own, so Jesus even in these last moments so freighted with concerns of his own, "loved them to the end," the simple aorist recording only the great fact.

2) **And at supper, the devil having already cast into the heart that he should betray him — Judas, Simon's son, Iscariot, although he knows that the Father did give all things into his hands and that he did come out from God and is about to go back to God, he rises from the supper and lays down his garments and, having taken up a linen cloth, he girded himself.** The array of present tenses and the many details in the narration attract attention and make the scene vivid. The observation that this scene with its minutest features was impressed upon John's memory because he felt so deeply the guilt of all the disciples in bringing it to pass that Jesus, their own Lord and Master, found it necessary to stoop to this lowest service, is surely correct. None of them volunteered for

this work; each declined to stoop beneath the rest. So Jesus himself stepped in and shamed them all.

This "supper" was the Passover meal and not an ordinary supper, eaten on Wednesday evening, the 13th, and not on Thursday evening, the 14th. The very phrase in v. 1, *"before* the feast of the Passover when Jesus knew," etc., makes this supper a *part* of the festival. For if this phrase does not intend to bring us to the Passover supper, it is out of place, and John should have written some indefinite adverb like "already," "this long while." See how this supper is distinguished, not merely by the washing of the disciples' feet but by the farewell discourses. Jesus takes leave of his disciples, Judas goes out to effect the betrayal (v. 30), Jesus proceeds to Gethsemane (18:1, etc.). To say that, if this is the Passover supper, δεῖπνον should have the article is unwarranted, for John does not intend to describe the supper and refers to it only because of what Jesus did and said at this supper. His readers know the accounts of the other evangelists and thus have no trouble with John's brief reference.

It makes little difference whether we read δεῖπνον γινομένου (present tense) or γενομένου (aorist), for in either case the genitive absolute would mean only "at supper," without specifying anything further. In Mark 6:2, for instance, as Zahn points out, the aorist γενομένου σαββάτου means neither "at the beginning of the Sabbath" (Friday evening), nor "the Sabbath being ended," but simply "on a Sabbath." The A. V. is wrong when it translates the aorist "supper being ended"; and the R. V. likewise when it accepts the present participle and translates "during supper," as though this means, "during the progress of the supper." Not the tense of either of these participles determines the point of time regarding the supper.

The decisive circumstance is the fact that with the Jews the washing of the hands (a mere ceremonial act) and of the feet (a custom of propriety and politeness on entering a house, due to the wearing of sandals) always took place before the meal began and never during its progress or at its end. Quietly Jesus and the disciples had come from Bethany, proceeding at once to the upper room which a friend of Jesus had reserved for them. Since this important meal was to be entirely private, no host or no servant was present to do the honors, untie the sandals and wash the feet. Yet the water in a jug, the basin, and the linen apron, intended to serve also as a towel, were in place. After a brief delay the company proceeded to recline upon the couches in the fashion common at that time for dining. No one had said or done anything about the feet. The words in v. 4, "he rises from the supper," read as though Jesus waited until the last moment when Peter and John, who had been ordered to make all things ready and had done so earlier in the day (Mark 14:15, 16; Luke 22:8-13), set the food on the tables. Then at last Jesus proceeded to act. As far as Peter and John are concerned, they probably thought that they had done enough. Certainly, the omission in regard to the feet must have been in the minds of all. Perhaps some expected that Jesus would designate one of their number to play the part of the servant. None of them volunteered.

Washing the feet, of course, had nothing to do with the matter of dining as such; its necessity and its propriety were due to the long walk from Bethany, whether a meal followed or not. It was commanded neither by the law nor by the traditions of the Pharisees; it was only a matter of propriety. As such, however, it was most fitting to be observed by men

who came from a distance to partake together of the
most sacred feast known to their religion.   Whatever
the disciples felt, Jesus would not neglect a custom
that was just now so eminently in place.   Yet not the
mere custom as such prevailed on him to observe it
at this time but the spirit of his disciples who would
not stoop to render each other a service so menial.
This spirit made it quite imperative for Jesus to act.
When it is said that he proceeded only on the spur
of the moment, we observe that this would be wholly
unlike Jesus; his action is thoroughly considered.   The
assumption that some servant of the house had already
attended to the washing before the company reached
the upper room, is contradicted by the provisions for
the washing placed in readiness right in this room.
This assumption also makes the act of Jesus unnecessary, artificial, if not actually theatrical.   Some
would call the act symbolical; but this is contradicted
by Jesus himself in v. 15.   His act was an example;
it was not staged as a symbol, it was performed as
an actual service upon feet that actually needed washing.   Not by turning it into a mere symbol can it be
fitted into the progress of the supper or placed at the
end as being proper there.

In spite of its strong textual attestation the reading: τοῦ διαβόλου ἤδη βεβληκότος εἰς τὴν καρδίαν ἵνα παραδοῖ
αὐτὸν ᾿Ιούδας Σίμωνος ᾿Ισκαριώτης is assailed.   While it is
unusual, this very feature must be regarded as a mark
of genuineness according to the textual canon that
the more unusual and difficult reading is likely the
true one.   The objection that βεβληκότος εἰς τὴν καρδίαν,
without a genitive, must mean that the devil conceived
in his own heart that Judas should betray Jesus is
unsound, because this sense would require the middle
participle, whereas John writes the active participle.
It would also require the absence of the article as the
classic examples with βάλλεσθαι show.   It is thus gra-

tuitous to argue that, since the Scriptures speak of
God's heart, they also speak of the devil's heart. It
is ill-advised to ridicule the reading by stating that it
actually says that the devil had the thought of Judas'
treachery in his hand and threw it into his own (the
devil's) heart. A thought so silly would not appear
in so many, among them the most important, codices.
What heart is referred to by "*the* heart" (or as we may
translate, "*his* heart") the connection makes plain
beyond a doubt.

Those who object to the accepted reading fall
back on the variant which replaces the nominative
Ἰούδας Ἰσκαριώτης with the genitive Ἰούδα Ἰσκαριώτου and
translate as do our versions, "the devil having now (or
already) put into the heart of Judas Iscariot, Simon's
son, to betray him." Thus εἰς τὴν καρδίαν has its
genitive although its position so far removed at the
very end is still unusual. While the substance of the
thought is identical in both readings, the accepted
reading, with the nominative at the end, is decidedly
preferable. John purposely withholds the traitor's
name until the very last. The ἵνα clause, too, contains
no name. So the reader is held in suspense — whose
heart is this? who is this that receives into his heart
to deliver Jesus, i. e., betray him to his enemies? The
final nominative gives the answer: "Judas, Simon's
son, Iscariot." Whether "Iscariot" is also nominative
("the man of Keriot") in apposition with "Judas"
or genitive in apposition with "of Simon"˙ ("son of
Simon, of the man of Keriot") is an entirely minor
point; compare 6:71.

When the devil first injected the thought of the
betrayal into the heart of Judas the perfect participle
does not indicate. It occurred some time before this,
and the perfect tense signifies that the thought continued as thrown into his heart. The non-final ἵνα
clause is the object of the participle: "to deliver him,"

i. e., hand him over, betray him. The form παραδοῖ is
the aorist subjunctive, also written – δῷ and – δώῃ
(Paul's epistles) ; for the form of the optative see
R. 308. The use of βάλλειν for injecting a thought
is usual and does not stress the suddenness. There
is no need to expand this casting as though the devil
knew this man and was rushing him off his feet. The
perfect tense gives us quite a different picture, namely
that Judas harbored the thought for some time, entertained and played with it until he finally acted. If we
may say so, perhaps the decree of the Sanhedrin that
whoever knew where Jesus was should report it
(11:57), was used by Satan for his purpose; this combined with the greed for money of the traitor paved
the way. As early as 12:4 the thought of betrayal
must have occurred to Judas.

Why does John report this about Judas in connection with the washing of the feet? Certainly not because Jesus intended to give him a final warning, for
then the remark would appear in v. 21. Also not because John would say that only the devil could have put
such a thought into Judas' heart, for then the remark
should appear in 6:70, 71, or in 12:4-6. Some think
that John means to say that the time for Jesus to display his love to the disciples was short because Judas
was already betraying him, but Jesus seems in no
hurry whatever, and it has been well said that not
Judas has Jesus in his power, but Jesus has Judas
in his. Others think that John intends to stress the
patience of Jesus with the traitor, or the serene peace
of Jesus and the majesty of his love, although the
traitor is present; but there is nothing in the text that
bears such an intimation. These seem like extraneous
thoughts. The connection seems to be that of contrast: although Judas had already planned the betrayal, Jesus stooped to wash the disciples' feet —
Judas among them. Even the machinations of hell

cannot interfere with the love which Jesus shows to the very last.

3) This contrast is tremendously intensified by the third participial modifier. John sets the action of Jesus into the boldest possible relief: "although he knows that the Father did give all things into his hands," etc. The second εἰδώς should not be separated from the first (in v. 1) on the plea that its object is different — certainly the object would not be the same. This second εἰδώς connects with the first by advancing the object of the first. Jesus knows not merely the arrival of the hour for his transfer out of the world to the Father; we are to think of him as being fully conscious of his power in this hour when the devil, Judas, and his enemies seem to be celebrating the triumph of their power, fully conscious also that he of his own will came from God and now of his own will is in the act of going back to God. This loving Jesus is the almighty Jesus, the sovereign eternal Son who descended from God for his supreme mission and now at its close returns as the Son that he is.

This aorist ἔδωκεν is often misunderstood, likewise its object πάντα. A commentary on the latter is πᾶσα ἐξουσία in Matt. 28:18, where also ἐδόθη is the verb used: "All power (authority) was given to me in heaven and on earth." "All things" is without restriction of any kind, and "into his hands" means for him to do with as he wills, it is like "all power or authority" in Matthew. The aorist is historical: "he gave"; but not in the sense "now already," as if this gift was recently made, or was made as a kind of prolepsis of the coming glorification. Here, in the Matthew passage, and elsewhere, as in 3:35, where the Father gives all things and all power into the hands of Jesus, this invariably refers to the human nature of Jesus (5:27). Omnipotence could be no gift to the divine nature of Jesus. All things were in Jesus' hands when those hands washed the disciples' feet. Yet we see that these hands are still in deepest humiliation — they *have* almighty power but *do not use* this power in majesty. Only exceptionally, in performing the miracles, a limited use of this power was made; compare Luke 22:51, healing the severed ear of Malchus. This aorist ἔδωκεν dates back to the Incarnation when the union of the two natures in Jesus took place. Its date is the same as that of the next aorist ἐξῆλθεν, "he came out from God" entering this world. John emphasizes the consciousness of Jesus that all things were in his hands in contrast with the traitorous action of Judas and all the hellish powers that stood back of this action. John intends to say that, although Jesus knew that all things were in his hands in these hours of hastening toward his death, he did not smite the traitor and the foes in league with this son of perdition but followed his course of love, completed his mission, and of himself laid down his life to take it up again (10:11 and 17, 18).

We must connect and read together the two ὅτι clauses as one object of εἰδώς: "that the Father did give all things into his hands, and that he did come out from God and is about to go back to God." This is the consciousness that animates Jesus as he proceeds to wash the disciples' feet and throughout these important final hours. His whole course from his going out from God until his return lies before him. This is the course of his humiliation during which he possessed power over all things but used that power only as it furthered his mission. In both verbs, ἐξῆλθε and ὑπάγει, we must note the personal, voluntary action. It was his act that "he came," it is his act that "he goes." He himself has spoken thus, 8:14 and 42; compare also 3:13; 6:33, 38, 50, 51, 58; 7:29; 8:23. With this voluntary coming and going we must combine the many statements that the Father "did send" him (ὁ πέμψας με) and must not say that his being sent excludes "his own initiative and independence in thinking and willing." His will and his thinking are one with those of the Father. "He did come out from God" declares his deity, his essential oneness with God. As one who thus came out from God he now goes back to God. The article in πρὸς τὸν Θεόν is resumptive and points to ἀπὸ Θεοῦ: he goes back to this very God. It is not by an act of grace on God's part that Jesus enters heaven; no *assumptio* deifies or glorifies him. "His absolute exaltation above the most elect among the children of men could not be indicated more distinctly." Nebe. Yet he who shares omnipotence with God in essential oneness with him now performs an act in which the very opposite of this divine majesty is brought to view, an act in which divine majesty makes itself the most lowly servant — "who, being in the form of God, counted it not a prize to be on an equality with God, but emptied himself, taking the form of a servant," Phil. 2:6, 7. Here he took water and washed his disciples' dusty feet; presently he poured out his own blood to wash their sinful souls.

4) John puts the action of Jesus before us in all its details. Interspersing the historical present tenses with the aorists adds vividness. Already stretched out on the couch ready for the supper to begin, Jesus "rises from the supper (the article is merely anaphoric) and lays down his garments," τά ἱμάτια, the flowing outer robe and the girdle, "and having taken up an apron," λέντιον, made of linen, "he tied it around him" by means of the attached bands. In other words, Jesus appears clothed quite like the slave or servant to whom the task of washing the feet of guests is assigned. John writes as though the dis-

ciples, lying outstretched, watch this action of Jesus, perceive their Master's intention, and yet — not one of them, not even John himself, jumps up now at least to offer himself for the task.

5) **Thereupon,** grouping these actions separately, **he pours water into the basin,** the one placed there for this purpose, **and began to wash the disciples' feet,** whose sandals had been removed when they entered, **and to wipe them with the apron with which he was bound around.** "He began" by taking them in order as they lay stretched out. He knelt on the floor, set the basin down, and while each disciple made his feet project beyond the edge of the couch, washed them clean with his hands and then dried them with the apron. Still none of them, including John, jumped up to take the menial task from his hands. Whatever their thoughts and their feelings at what they beheld were, no one interfered.

6) **Accordingly he comes to Simon Peter,** who, therefore, was certainly not the first, as some have supposed, although we have no means of knowing how many were washed before Jesus came to him, nor does this make any difference. **He says to him, Lord, thou art going to wash my feet?** The present tense in the question is conative, expressing an action just beginning. The address, "Lord," far higher than "Rabbi," brings out the greatness of Jesus, and the emphatic σύ, "thou," is in contrast with "my feet," μου even being next to σύ. The thought that the Lord, that *he* should be on his knees, washing "my (dirty) feet," is too much for Peter. Those that were washed before him had voiced no protest. Peter's temperament is different, more impetuous than that of most men, by nature he is quicker to speak and to act; his position among the Twelve had developed his natural bent for leadership. This suffices to explain why he makes a protest. Whether the addition

of his old name "Simon" intends to convey the thought that on this occasion he is following his old nature and not the new, is doubtful. His protest lays the emphasis on "thou," and any emphasis on "my" is minor (R. 418), which means that he is not faulting the others whose feet Jesus had already washed — he speaks only for himself.

7) **Jesus answered and said to him,** the two verbs marking the reply as weighty (see 1:48), **What I on my part am doing thou on thine dost not know now, yet thou shalt realize hereafter.** The emphasis is on the two pronouns, which are also placed in contrast: "I on my part . . . thou on thine." Also οἶδας is the ordinary verb for knowing, while γνώσῃ expresses the knowledge of real understanding. Jesus points out to Peter that his protest rests on ignorance, an ignorance which shall be replaced by full understanding in due time. In a way Jesus excuses Peter and thus treats him mildly. By adding the promise that Peter shall later realize what Jesus is really doing in these last hours of his life, he is asking Peter, and making it easy for him, to submit without misgivings or question. The reply of Jesus is full of love and kindliness.

Jesus accepts Peter's emphatic "thou," that *he*, the divine Lord, is washing the feet of his disciples like the veriest servant. But he draws Peter's attention to the plain implication that as the Lord *he* knows what he is doing, which ought to satisfy any proper disciple. The usual interpretation has "what I am doing" refer only to the washing of the feet. But what, then, does Peter as yet not know about this washing? Some say, the lesson Jesus is teaching the disciples by his act. So Jesus would be saying only this, "Just wait a little until I am through, then you shall understand what I am doing"; and presently he again took the couch and explained all. The inadequacy of this view lies in the fact that from the start Peter could see that Jesus was teaching them a very necessary lesson. And yet, even after the lesson is put into words (v. 12, etc.), this lesson alone could not and did not make them understand properly even this one act of Jesus on this night. Others think that the words "what I am doing" refer to a hidden symbolic significance of the washing, that this physical washing symbolizes a spiritual cleansing. They draw this significance from the very conversation of Jesus with Peter. What, then, becomes of the emphatic "now" and "hereafter" in this first reply of Jesus? If Jesus at once explains everything how can he say μετὰ ταῦτα, "after these things," with the plural pronoun in the phrase pointing to a longer interval of time? But the supposed symbolism does not fit, for the washing of only the feet could not and did not symbolize complete spiritual cleansing.

"What I am doing" refers to all that Jesus did this night and should not be restricted as though Jesus says, "What I am *now* doing *to thee* (Peter), or *to you* (Peter and the rest)." The washing of the feet is, of course, included as being of one piece with all that was done this night. Jesus knows well enough that his disciples are in no position to comprehend what he is doing: he does not chide them for that, he excuses them. Only one thing he wants them to know and to know well, that *he himself* knows all about what he is doing — this they are to remember when in due time all is completed. Then at last when all is done, Peter, too, and all the rest will fully understand, knowing then that Jesus knew from the very start. This explains μετὰ ταῦτα, "after these things," i. e., after all of them including the death and the burial of Jesus. The resurrection and the glorification of Jesus will shed a great light on everything. Especially Pentecost will bring the fullest revelation

to them. The infinite love of Jesus actuating him
as he now washes the feet of his disciples and in all
that follows, they could know only after all was done,
including that deepest of all humiliation, the death of
shame upon the cross, followed by the divine exaltation. So Jesus now asks them to wait and to trust him
as their "Lord" in all that he now does.

8) Strange to say, neither the love of the kindly
reply of Jesus checks Peter, nor the promise that in
due time he shall know, implying a request for him
to wait. **Peter says to him, By no means shalt thou
wash my feet ever.** Note the strong volitive aorist
subjunctive with its strongest form of negation οὐ μή
(R. 933), enhanced by the phrase, "for the eon," i. e.,
"ever," or "forever." On εἰς τὸν αἰῶνα see 8:35, also
14:16. In all eternity, never is Jesus to wash Peter's
feet! It almost seems as though the gentleness of
Jesus caused Peter to react with such boldness.
Though he had called Jesus "Lord," he now acts as
though he were lord and Jesus subject to his orders.

**Jesus answered him, If I wash thee not, thou
hast no part with me.** Sometimes this is understood
rather superficially as though Jesus says, "Unless I
wash *thy feet,* thou hast no part with me." If, then,
it seems strange that Jesus makes the salvation of
Peter depend on his washing Peter's feet, the remark
is added that Peter's refusal to have his feet washed
by Jesus is rank disobedience, and persistence in this
disobedience would exclude Peter from salvation.
Whoever, even in a minor matter, refuses Jesus
obedience "forever" certainly cannot enter heaven
with him. Yet the reply of Jesus says nothing about
washing *the feet* of Peter and nothing about disobedience on Peter's part. "If I wash thee not" is
not the same as, "If thou wilt not let me wash thy
feet." Others put this into a stronger form. Peter
will not accept the self-humiliation of Jesus. Yet by

thus contending for the Lord's greatness, which he will not have marred, he is really asserting his own greatness over against Jesus, as one who will not learn humility from the example Jesus is now setting him. Thus by seemingly contending for the greatness of Jesus, Peter is destroying this greatness and is thus separating himself from Jesus. In other words, by his refusal to have Jesus wash his feet, Peter repudiates the Lord as he is and demands a Lord who is otherwise. This has the appearance of a profound interpretation and yet is beside the mark. For the observation is correct: Jesus makes Peter's having part with him depend, not on anything Peter does, but on something Jesus does for Peter: "unless I wash thee."

At this point symbolism is again brought in. This washing of feet is only symbolic, we are told, hence also Jesus is now speaking of washing Peter symbolically. Water is said to be a symbol of sanctification through the Holy Spirit, hence washing symbolizes the cleansing and refreshing of the Spirit. Whoever refuses to receive that has no part with Jesus. Back of this view lies the idea that Baptism is but a symbolic use of water, which is contrary to 3:3 and 5. Moreover, this view is not symbolic but allegorical: physical elements and actions are regarded as pictures of spiritual counterparts, and that without warrant in the words of the text. The symbolism is not present, not even in the form of allegory.

Peter objects to having his dusty feet washed by Jesus, whatever the purpose of this washing may be. What a tiny service this is compared with the vastly greater service, Jesus washing Peter entirely and for a far higher purpose! What makes Peter so blind and foolish to resent the tiny service while accepting the far greater service? The one costs only a few minutes' physical work in washing twelve pairs of dusty feet as required by oriental propriety and politeness; the other costs the entire mission of Jesus including his death and blood, by which alone we are truly washed and cleansed. The one teaches the disciples only a single lesson by means of example (v. 14); the other bestows upon us a part with Jesus in his everlasting kingdom. Or does Peter mean to refuse also this supreme service? Understand the tenses correctly. The present ἔχεις is not futuristic, it is timeless. While it is addressed to Peter, "Unless I wash thee, thou hast," etc., the thought is universal and applies to all men alike, "Unless Jesus washes a person, that person has no part with him." The protasis, ἐάν with the aorist subjunctive, is relative to the apodosis with its present ἔχεις: "unless I first shall wash thee, thou hast," etc. The aorist indicates only that the act of washing is a single act and says nothing whatever about its date. One washing we all need or we shall not have part with Jesus. Like Peter, we may already have it; future believers obtain it when they are brought to faith.

"Unless I wash" is figurative, and certainly the figure is suggested by the act in which Jesus is now engaged. In 4:10, etc., the figure is drinking; in 6:50 it is eating; in both, the water and the bread (life) is the gift of Jesus; and in other connections other figures are used by Jesus. These are figures not symbols. In the present case the figure is quite transparent, for the washing admits us "to have part with Jesus." This expression may mean to share in somebody's fate or possession, or in general to have part in his lot. Here the more general sense is in place. Peter certainly already had a part with Jesus, i. e., was sharing his lot and thus had received this washing (v. 10). That it means an inward cleansing is quite evident from the relation to Jesus which it produces. Thus, since sin and its guilt separate from Jesus, this is a cleansing which removes the sin and the guilt. Those who think this sense too narrow and emphasize sanctification in holy living in place of it are not in harmony with the aorist νίψω nor with v. 10.

9) Frightened at the thought of having no part in Jesus and still failing to understand what Jesus really is doing, Peter, in accord with the precipitation of his nature, not only gives up his opposition, but goes to the other extreme. **Simon Peter says to him, Lord, not only my feet but also my hands and my head,** the other exposed members of his body. In his haste Peter does not distinguish between the washing of which Jesus speaks (spiritual) and the washing in which he is engaged (physical, of the dusty feet). His eagerness for any washing that joins him to Jesus prompts his offer of all the bodily members easily reached for the purpose of being washed.

10) It is easy for the Lord to set him right. **Jesus says to him, He who has been bathed has no need except to wash his feet but is clean altogether; and you are clean, but not all.** Jesus merely extends the figure he used in v. 8 when he said, "unless I wash thee"; he now also adds literal language which places the meaning of the figure beyond doubt. The use of the new verb λούειν is only incidental, for this, too, means only "to wash," and we use the English "bathe" only to indicate the use of a new synonym. The passive is certainly to be understood in the sense of v. 8, with Jesus as the agent who does the washing or bathing. The perfect tense implies present condition: a person once bathed by Jesus remains thus, in other words, "is clean altogether." The extension of the figure lies in the addition: "has no need except to wash his feet." Walking about in sandals, only his feet would become dusty and need ablution. The middle infinitive νίψασθαι, like

ἐβαπτίζοντο in 3:23 and Matt. 3:6, and like other middle forms, really means, in the present connection: "let his feet be washed"; for the oriental custom contemplates a servant as washing the feet of a guest, and in the reality which Jesus has in mind it is again he himself who attends also to this minor service. It would, of course, be out of line to extend this figure still farther and to bring in the need of repeated bathing or washing of the entire body or of the feet as time passes; we must be satisfied with the figure as Jesus employs it and not make inappropriate expansions of our own which would not reflect the reality that Jesus has in mind.

As the body is clean altogether when it is washed and needs only a laving of the feet when we have walked in the dusty road, so we are spiritually clean when Jesus has washed away our sin and guilt; we need only a minor cleansing when we move about in this sinful world with its impure contacts. The question is raised as to the means which Jesus has in mind when he uses this figurative language, first about our general cleansing and then also about the additional cleansing. Some think of Baptism with regard to the former, because the figure is one of washing. In the case of the disciples this would be the sacrament received from the hands of the Baptist. At once a division of opinion arises. Since John tells us only about six of the disciples being baptized by the Baptist, some say that only these six were so baptized and leave open the question whether the other six were baptized, or, if they were baptized, when this occurred and by whom it was performed. Others believe that all twelve disciples had received John's baptism. Since Jesus insisted on John's baptism for himself, it will be impossible to assume that he kept six of his disciples unbaptized. If John himself did not baptize them, then the sacrament must have been administered by their fellow-disciples, 3:22-26; 4:1, 2. This, too, would be John's baptism; see the exposition of 3:22, etc. A graver division of opinion deals with the nature and the effect of this baptism by John and its extension by Jesus. Some deny, and others assert, that it was a true sacrament and bestowed the forgiveness of sins. Those who deny rule out this baptism as mediating the complete cleansing of which Jesus here speaks. On this point compare the findings in 3:5.

Those who deny that John's baptism conferred forgiveness point to 15:3 and make the Word of Jesus the medium for the complete cleansing he has in mind; many of the rest simply add the Word to John's baptism. The objection that the baptism was not administered by Jesus' own hand and hence cannot be referred to when Jesus says, "unless I wash thee," is untenable, since all three Persons of the Godhead operate in and through the Word and the sacrament. Again, when we add the Word to the sacrament, this dare not be done because the latter would be insufficient for this cleansing, a mere preparation for it, the bestowal of only a symbol of cleansing and not of the factual cleansing itself. Jesus names no means on this occasion. The means can be only those which still cleanse the souls of sinners and give them part with Jesus, namely Word and sacrament. Which of the two does the work in any given case when the cleansing first takes place, depends on the case itself. Any future partial cleansing is accomplished by the same means. While baptism is never to be repeated, and while we know of no baptism other than that of John which was administered to any of the Twelve, its cleansing power is not spent in the hour of its application but goes on through life, is present every moment that the child of God grasps its power and blessing anew. This is also true with regard to the absolution in the Word and the seal of the sacred body and the sacred blood in the Holy Supper.

Jesus drops the figure when he adds, "and (or, also) you are clean," using an emphatic ὑμεῖς, "you" who are my true disciples. Yet he is compelled to add, "but not all." The limitation does not lie in the predicate "clean" but in the subject "you." The negative οὐχί "is a bit sharper in tone" than the simple οὐ, R. 1157. Judas is excluded. Not Peter, although his fault in contradicting his Lord was openly apparent at this very moment. This should dispose of the interpretation that the total cleansing of which Jesus speaks includes both the pardon of justification and the holiness of good works. Even the figurative terms which Jesus employed do not permit this mixing of things diverse. The bad works of Peter are like stains upon his feet; his good works are not in the figure, for they are not bestowed upon him by grace but are produced by Peter by means of the grace already in him.

11) "Not all" might include more than one, and just now Peter attracts our adverse attention. To make the meaning of Jesus clear John adds the explanation: **For he knew the man betraying him; on this account he said, Not all are you clean.** Jesus had this knowledge all along (ᾔδει, durative). Also note the present participle, "the man engaged in betraying him," not, "him that should betray him" (our versions). His is not a sin that merely stains the feet but a sin that marks him as being entirely unclean. He is not merely overcome by a fault but has completely lost the faith, is a disciple only in pretense. John repeats the pointed reference of Jesus, for this was a blow at the conscience of Judas, revealing his whole inner condition. With it Jesus conveys the thought to Judas that all his treachery is known; he does this with only two words and in a moment

will do it more completely, in order to frighten Judas
out of his security and to drive him to repentance.
Although Jesus knows that it will all be in vain,
he leaves nothing undone, morally and spiritually,
to deter the traitor, even as he still urges sinners to the last though they harden themselves in
their guilt.

12) With the ominous word "but not all" ringing
in the minds of the disciples, nothing more was said
until all, even Judas, were washed. **When, therefore, he had washed their feet and taken his garments and reclined again, he said to them, Do you
realize what I have done to you?** "Their feet"
and "to you" certainly includes all of them. The
movements of Jesus at the conclusion of his act are
described in graphic detail, just as were those spoken
at the beginning (v. 4, 5). The imprint left on the
evangelist's mind was deep indeed. The aorists in
the temporal clause only mark the acts as past, the
Greek not caring to mark the relative time as the
English does which uses the past perfect, R. 840, etc.
The verb ἀναπίπτω is used like ἀνακλίνομαι literally, "when
he fell back again" upon the couch. The question
Jesus asks is not merely rhetorical to attract the attention of those who do not have the information now
to be imparted to them. The act of Jesus was too
plain for that: he, their Lord, making himself their
servant, whereas they, his servants, had pridefully
avoided the service. They did realize, but Jesus
means that the full import of what they had seen
him do for them is to be brought to their realization.
His action in washing their feet is not a mere rebuke
to their pride, it is an example of true love, the love
that is ready to render the lowliest kind of service
to others. He is not concerned in humbling them but
in making them like himself so that they may be truly
blessed and happy (v. 17). The negative side of

what Jesus had done (the rebuke) needs no statement — this the disciples will feel without further
words; the positive side is the one that needs setting
forth, so that they will actually do what the act of
Jesus has shown them.

13) **You call me The Teacher and The Lord,
and you say well, for I am.** "You" is emphatic,
"you as my disciples" who really know me. Others,
too, addressed Jesus as Rabbi (teacher) and Lord, but
most of these intended these titles only as expressions
of respect. Ὁ διδάσκαλος and Ὁ κύριος are plainly nominatives and not vocatives, R. 1028 and elsewhere. The
matter becomes plain when we note that φωνεῖτέ με
means, "you call me when you speak of me," and not,
"you call me when you address me." In address
they, of course, used vocatives, but when they spoke
to each other about Jesus they said, "The Teacher,"
"The Lord." When Jesus quotes these nominatives
this is far stronger than a quotation of vocatives;
for the nominatives allow the use of the article, giving
these titles a specific and eminent sense: *the* Teacher,
the Lord κατ᾽ ἐξοχήν, who ranks far above the many
others to whom titles of "teacher" and "lord" are also
accorded. In 12:21 the Greeks who wish to see Jesus
address Philip as κύριε, intending only respect. The
disciples think and speak of Jesus with far higher
thought. Jesus commends them for that, for he is,
indeed, all that they thus say and mean. "The
Teacher" refers to the divine words which he utters,
and "The Lord" to the divine power manifested in
him. Nebe is right when he becomes indignant because ὁ διδάσκαλος, for which we generally use "the
Master," has by rationalism been made to mean no
more than an eminent human teacher, one of a class
similar to him. In both titles as used by the disciples
and approved by Jesus lies his deity.

14) Now the deduction: **If I, therefore, washed your feet, I, the Lord and the Teacher, you, too, ought to be washing each others' feet. For an example have I given you, that even as I did do to you, you, too, keep doing.** This is the Lord's own explanation of what he intended with his washing of the disciples' feet. It is to be "an example," ὑπόδειγμα (in the same sense as παράδειγμα), which we are constantly to follow (note the durative present tenses: νίπτειν and ποιῆτε, "be washing" and "keep doing"). It is natural that now in the apposition to the emphatic ἐγώ "the Lord" is placed before "the Teacher," at once bringing out the greatness of Jesus. That, too, is why the apposition is reserved for the very end of the conditional clause and is in a manner made to stand by itself. The example is thus an *argumentum a majori ad minus*.

In the apodosis the emphasis is on "you, too," and the reason for this καὶ ὑμεῖς is self-evident: because they are disciples of this great Lord and this great Teacher, they want to be one with him, learn of him, do his will. "You ought" is like the ἐντολή in v. 34 and in 15:12. The obligation resting upon them is moral and spiritual, naturally growing out of their relation to this Lord and Teacher. This, however, does not imply that an equal obligation rests upon Jesus; it is not "as I ought, so you ought," as I met my obligation, so you should meet yours. The καὶ is to be construed only with ὑμεῖς.

15) This act of Jesus was free and voluntary, chosen by him for the purpose of teaching the disciples. In his love and his wisdom he "has given" (some copies have the aorist "did give") them an example to follow. Just what this example covers is stated in the appositional ἵνα clause, which, of course, is non-final. This shows that "to be washing each others' feet" is figurative and means literally, "that

you keep doing, even as I did do to you," καθώς, not ὅ, "in the same manner," not "the same identical thing." The example of Jesus is to guide them in what they do for each other; it is not for mere mechanical repetition in washing of feet. This answers the question as to whether Jesus intends to institute a symbolical rite or an actual sacrament, which his disciples are to repeat formally by actually washing each others' feet. Such rites belong to the Old Testament only, they have disappeared from the New. The shadows are gone, the substance has come. No sacrament can be intended, for a direct command, *"This* do," is absent, to say nothing of a promise of heavenly grace attached to the act. We should have to have both the specific command and the promise besides the water to constitute a sacrament.

But is the example not at least symbolic? Does it not go beyond the ordinary humble service of love in the common contacts of life and include the symbolic feature that we aid each other in removing fault, sins, and stains of guilt? Though it is emphatically asserted, we are compelled to say that anything of this kind is impossible for disciples and is possible only for Jesus. The appeal to v. 10 overlooks the fact that both the passive ὁ λελουμένος and the middle νίψασθαι think of Jesus as the one who does the bathing and by whom the bathed person lets his feet be washed. No brother can remove a single stain of sin from another brother. The confusion of thought involved in this view of symbolism seems to be due to passages like Gal. 6:1 and the general Christian obligation of rebuke, correction, and admonition. All this, however, hangs together with the same obligation of teaching, exhorting, comforting, etc. In this work one brother applies the Lord's Word to another brother according as there is need. We are only mouthpieces of Jesus; any good done belongs to Jesus and the

Word.   In this work neither Jesus nor we are menial servants of our brethren, rather do we come with divine authority.   Any symbolism pertinent to washing of feet is thus excluded by the nature of what is done.

16)   Jesus has given the disciples an example, and he intends that they should not merely admire but should actually follow it.   He knows what may prevent them from doing so: the feeling that they are just as good as others or even superior to others.   Such comparisons he cuts off completely by his own personal example, which substitutes and calls for quite another and far more pertinent comparison.   By his example Jesus has placed us where we must drop all other comparisons and compare ourselves only with him.   Therefore the solemn declaration with the two "amen" of verity and the assurance of authority, "I say to you" (see 1:51).   **Amen, amen, I say to you, A slave is not greater than his lord, nor one sent than the one that sent him.   If you know these things, blessed are you if you keep doing them.** The statement about the slave and the one sent is, of course, axiomatic.   It is the connection which lends peculiar force to the statement as here made.   If any disciple of Jesus should ever think himself too great to stoop to menial tasks in serving his fellow-disciples, he can do so only by thinking himself greater than Jesus, his Lord, for this Lord had just stooped so low.   And at once another comparison is added, for the Twelve are not to be disciples or believers only but are to hold the highest position and office in the church as the Lord's own representatives, ἀπόστολοι, "men sent," apostles commissioned to found the church and to lead it for all time (by their writings).   This high office does not lift them to a plane where they are too great for the menial service of love, for they can never be greater than Jesus, their Lord, who sent

them. A far higher commission was his, and yet he had washed their feet.

17) It is all so transparent and self-evident and yet it must be made emphatic; for it is one thing to know and quite another to translate that knowledge into action. To procure that action Jesus does not drive with commands but draws with a promise. The first is a condition of reality: "if you know these things," for Jesus rightly assumes that they do know them. The Greek uses ταῦτα, a plural, which conceives the object of the knowledge as composed of parts or items; the English cares nothing for this plural view and says simply "this." Mere knowledge, however, no matter how true and excellent, brings no blessing. The adjective μακάριος is especially significant in this connection, for it denotes the joy and the satisfaction arising from possessing and experiencing the divine favor in the one or the other of its manifestations, C.-K. 711. Whereas he who thinks himself great feels disgraced by a menial task rendered to those beneath him, the true disciple of Jesus regards such a task as a great opportunity and reaps from it the feeling of joy and honor, for the Lord's favor and commendation rest upon him while engaged in such service. In this sense Jesus says, "blessed are you."

But, of course, only "if you keep doing them." Doing is emphatic over against mere knowing. The condition is now one of expectancy, "if you shall be doing them." Jesus expects it of them, yet it is possible that they may disappoint him — will they? the condition asks. The present subjunctive is durative, "keep doing them" always and on every occasion. The very character of the disciples is thus to keep expressing itself.

18) A division is frequently made at this point, so that v. 18-20 is connected with v. 21-30, as dealing with the traitor. But John plainly indicates a divi-

sion at v. 21. **Not of you all am I speaking** is the continuation of v. 17. Jesus harks back to the brief "not all" in v. 10, to which John added his note in v. 11. All that Jesus tells the disciples concerning the example he has given them and the blessedness of following that example applies — sad to say — not to all of them. One of their number has excluded himself. **I for my part know the ones I chose for myself.** The pronoun is emphatic — the treachery of Judas is still hidden from his fellow-disciples but not from the Lord. This evident contrast is quite sufficient. The attempt to add another, namely the counsel and decision of God regarding Judas, is unwarranted; for this is not in contrast with the knowledge of Jesus but in perfect agreement with what Jesus knows. "I for my part know" should not be referred to the past, "I for my part knew," i.e., when I chose and elected you Twelve. Whatever Jesus knew regarding Judas as the future traitor when he chose him as one of the Twelve, is not here indicated. Nor are we entitled to have οἶδα mean, "I know *now*," as though this knowledge has just come to Jesus. How long before this time Jesus knows is left unsaid. We know that his knowledge reaches far back (6:70).

We prefer the reading τίνας, "which ones," "the ones," to οὖς, "whom." The clause is an indirect question not a relative clause. Jesus knows not only "whom" he chose, namely these twelve men and none other; but "the ones" he chose, what kind of men they are, each one of them. For the indirect question, turned into the direct, is, "Who are they?" "Who is this man Simon, this man John, this man Judas?" inquiring not merely about externals but about character and inner type of heart. While Jesus here speaks only of his present knowledge, John has already told us how Jesus knew Simon from the very first (1:42), Nathanael likewise (1:47, etc.), in fact, all men with whom he came in contact (2:24, 25). Undoubtedly he thus knew Judas in the same way, not only when he made him one of the Twelve, but from the very start. But this does not mean that Judas was false when Jesus chose him. Like the others he was a true believer at the time, his defection began later, just when, no one knows. "The one I chose" does not mean that Jesus made a real choice of only eleven; 6:70 is decisive on that point. Therefore also ἐξελεξάμην has nothing to do with predestination, which also is an act that lies far back in eternity. "I chose out for myself" (note the middle voice) means the selection for the apostleship. It should not be reduced to mean only a choice to accompany Jesus as his constant personal following; for these twelve men, who were to be the constant companions of Jesus, were to be trained and qualified as his special witnesses, in order that in due time they might go out as his apostles to evangelize the nations (Matt. 28:19) and to carry the gospel to the ends of the earth (Acts 1:8).

Jesus continues: **but in order that the Scripture might be fulfilled, He that eats the bread with me did lift up his heel against me.** Usually the strong adversative ἀλλά is joined to the preceding sentence, and ἀλλὰ ἵνα is made elliptical as in 9:3 and 15:25. We are asked to read: "I on my part know the ones I chose for myself; but I chose them (or: I chose him; or simply: I chose), in order that the Scripture might be fulfilled," then quoting the Scripture referred to. Yet it ought to be evident that no "him" can be drawn out of τίνας (or its variant οὕς); and because all that follows certainly refers only to Judas, we are barred from supplying, "I chose them," or merely, "I chose," "I made choice" (for the latter would also include all). It is better to drop the idea of an ellipsis, since no one is able properly to fill

the supposed gap. The connection of ἀλλά is with
the negative sentence: "Not of you all am I speaking . . . on the contrary (ἀλλά) . . . he that
eats the bread with me did lift up his heel against
me." Nothing needs to be supplied. In v. 10 Jesus
says, "You are clean, but not all." Now he amplifies
this: "Blessed are you . . . Not of all of you I
am speaking . . . on the contrary . . . (one
of you is excluded) he that eats the bread with me
did lift up his heel against me." The objection that
this makes the ἵνα clause parenthetical and thus robs
it of emphasis, does not hold, for the very position of
this purpose clause insures its emphasis.

The reason why an ellipsis is preferred by some
is the conception that Jesus here states *why* he chose
Judas as he did, namely in order to fulfill the prophecy
of Ps. 41:9. That, too, is why such emphasis is
placed on the purpose clause, "but (I made my choice)
in order that," etc. In other words, Jesus tells his
disciples that he knows all about Judas, and that even
his election to be one of the Twelve was made by
Jesus in order that Judas might betray him. Yet
this is not what Jesus says, even when those who
think so in the proper way combine prediction in
regard to future human actions with fulfillment, not
as deterministically compelling but only as foretelling it with infallible foreknowledge. Jesus says:
ἵνα ἡ γραφὴ πληρωθῇ, meaning that the Scripture in
general must be fulfilled regarding himself not the
Scripture in regard to Judas. He does not place
ἡ γραφή directly before the quotation and does not
say, "the Scripture, saying"; or, "which says."
Jesus takes only one line from the entire Psalm
and even adapts this by substituting for "my bread"
the more general "the bread with me," "in my company," μετ' ἐμοῦ (the better reading). What, therefore, he means to say is that the mistreatment, which

the Scriptures in general describe as coming upon the righteous, has now in a signal manner come also upon him. He selects from the entire body of Scripture a striking parallel to his own case. The treachery which the Psalmist suffered is repeated in Jesus' own case. What at one time happened to David is now again happening to David's greater Son. This is how the Scripture is now once more fulfilling itself. David's case is in so many features typical of Jesus' case. Both nursed a traitor in their bosoms.

Delitzsch translates Ps. 41:9 literally:

> "Even the man of my friendship, in whom I trusted,
> Who ate my bread, lifts high his heel against me."

More literally this is "the man of my peace or well-being," well rendered "mine own familiar friend" (A. V.). His treacherous act is figuratively pictured: "he lifts up (literally: makes great) his heel against me" in order to crush me completely. Compare the description of the same base act in Ps. 55:12-14. These Psalms, Delitzsch writes, show "the most pronounced historically individual physiognomy." David is picturing the traitor Ahitophel. This man, who stood so high in the king's confidence, turned traitor to him, threw in his lot with the rebel Absalom, and evolved a scheme that would indeed have crushed David utterly, II Sam. 16:15-17:4. From Ps. 41 we need only to add that about this time David must have passed through a prolonged illness, enabling Absolom to gain favor with the nation. Ahitophel is the Old Testament prototype of Judas, even to the extent that after his traitorous act he hanged himself, II Sam. 17:23. Those who reject the Davidic authorship of these Psalms and prefer some far later unknown author, leave us without even the shadow of historical background in the hazy land of pure imagination. The poet is supposed to be connected with "the Wisdom teacher," the traitor is some unknown person or merely a creation of poetic fiction. The Psalm itself is charged with voicing "tones of wild fleshly passion" and with offending by appeals to "the poet's own moral excellence," R. Kittel.

Strange as it may seem, the Old Testament contains no direct prophecy concerning Judas. Ahitophel, together with David's references to him in two Psalms, is only a strong type of all traitors and thus a type of Judas. In many ways wickedness — and we may add suffering, joy, rewards, punishments, etc. — repeats itself, often in close parallels. Consider the flood, Sodom, the destruction of Jerusalem, and the final judgment. David, betrayed by Ahitophel, is a type of Jesus, betrayed by Judas. In Matt. 2:18 the calamity and the grief at Rama are repeated in the tragedy at Bethlehem.

19) It is Jesus who in advance reveals the traitorous act of Judas to the disciples. **From now on I state it to you before it occurs, in order that you may believe, when it shall occur, that I am he.** Hitherto Jesus had referred to the traitor in a less open way, "from now on," ἀπ' ἄρτι, this reticence will cease. It must cease. The eleven are not to think, when the tragedy occurs, that Jesus was deceived by Judas, that he was a helpless victim of the traitor and of the Jews. They are not to draw any adverse conclusions from the traitor's seeming success, questioning the deity of Jesus, his divine power and knowledge. Jesus puts the eleven into a position where they can do the reverse. It is Jesus who allows Judas to succeed, who knows his every move, who has power at any moment to frustrate his entire traitorous plan. Jesus is really addressing only the eleven when he

says, "in order that you may believe." Judas must feel this. The very way in which Jesus speaks intends to strike Judas — he is not deceiving his Lord in the least, he îs wholly at the mercy of Jesus. Yet Jesus does not name Judas outright as the traitor, does not charge him with his crime, does not smite him with invective. He speaks with great sadness, as if to touch and to melt the traitor's heart; by using the line from the Psalm he makes the lament of David regarding Ahitophel his own and pictures the utter baseness of Judas — having lifted up his heel against the very King with whom he pretends to eat as a friend, right here at the sacred Passover feast. Jesus would, if possible, melt the traitor's heart ere it is forever too late.

The object of λέγω is the line from the Psalm just quoted. This line is also the subject of τοῦ γενέσθαι and of ὅταν γένηται. These two aorists refer to the actual occurrence of the act that one who eats with Jesus as his friend and disciple lifts his heel to crush him. The aorist ἐπῆρεν in v. 18 refers to the completed act of Ahitophel; "before it occurs" and "when it shall occur" indicate that the corresponding act of Judas is not yet fully completed. We need not translate γένηται "shall have been completed," as though the eleven are to believe only after the traitorous act is a matter of the distant past; their faith ought to begin at once after the act has been done. It is quite immaterial whether we read the aorist πιστεύσητε or the present πιστεύητε (the readings vary), for the sense is practically the same. What the eleven are to believe is expressed by ὅτι ἐγώ εἰμι, "that I am," leaving the predicate to be supplied. Many think that this predicate should be, "that I am the Messiah." Some revert to the Old Testament and make the predicate "the absolute personality on whom all depends," i. e., the person who is really God himself. But in

8:24 and 28, as in other instances where Jesus uses this expression minus the predicate, it is the context alone which fills the gap. Here it must be, "that I am the one who tells you this in advance in order that you may believe." And this is quite enough.

20) The connection at this point is not difficult. Not for one moment are the eleven to think that because Judas has turned traitor their own commission has ceased or is made doubtful. With the most solemn assurance they are to know that their commission as apostles remains in force and that the promise (Matt. 10:40) regarding their reception among men stands as originally given. While Judas eliminates himself, as Jesus knew that he would, Judas is unable to alter the status of the rest in any manner. **Amen, amen, I say to you** (1:51), **He that receives anyone I may send, me he receives; and he who receives me receives him that did send me.** This assurance is intended for the eleven, for they are the ones who are now deeply concerned. To be sure, Jesus here assures also those who may receive his apostles, in fact, the wording points directly to them, although none of these are now present.

The statement is entirely general; it includes every person sent by Jesus and every person receiving one thus sent. It thus extends to all future ages and includes every true witness of Jesus and preacher of the gospel and his reception as such by every true believer. In this respect the present statement reaches farther than Matt. 10:40. The two present participles are qualitative and timeless, merely describing the person as one who receives. Yet we must read these participles together with what belongs to them, "he that receives if I shall send anyone," and "he that receives me," for only thus are the predicates true. The conditional clause of expectancy, ἄν τινα πέμψω, is used in the place of a simple object. Jesus will, indeed, send out the eleven and others, and he uses the same verb to designate his act of sending as he used to express the Father's act of sending him. The great thing in this assurance is the identification of the one thus sent with Jesus himself who sends him and with the great Sender of Jesus. Jesus and his Sender are one with every messenger whom Jesus sends out, so much so that receiving the messenger is equal to receiving Jesus and the Sender of Jesus. Let Judas do what he will, the mighty work of Jesus and his Sender remains unaffected. This wonderful indentification is, of course, mediated by the Word, preached and taught by those whom Jesus sends. The moment this Word is laid aside and something else is put in its place the sending by Jesus ceases, as well as the reception of Jesus and of his Sender. No negative is added because it is obvious that he who does not receive the messenger Jesus sends, by that refusal fails also to receive Jesus, his grace and salvation, and the Father who sent Jesus.

The interpretation which joins v. 20 to v. 13-17 has much against it. Jesus is not speaking of needy persons whom he will send that we may wash their feet, i. e., render them menial service. Jesus never sends needy persons, for we always have them with us, 12:8. With v. 18, etc., the discourse passes on to the new subject, the defection of Judas.

2. The Traitor Exposed, 21-30

21) **Having said these things, Jesus was troubled in the spirit and testified and said, Amen, amen, I say to you that one of you shall betray me.** "Having said these things" undoubtedly marks an interval. The washing of the feet and the discourse connected with it (v. 1-20) occurred before the Passover actually began (see on v. 2). Matt. 26:21:

ἐσθιόντων αὐτῶν, "while engaged in eating," (likewise Mark 14:18) makes certain that the exposure of Judas occurred during the actual eating of the meal. Luke 22:21-23 disregards the exact order of time. When considering the interval marked by John, we must remember that the feast followed a fixed formal order: 1) The first cup with a blessing for the wine and the sacred day. 2) The bitter herbs to recall the bitter life in Egypt. 3) The unleavened bread, the *chasoret,* the roasted lamb, and the meat of the *chagiga* (other sacrificial meat). 4) The housefather dips some of the bitter herbs into the *chasoret* with a benediction for the fruit of the earth, then eats, and the rest follow. 5) The second cup is mixed (wine with water), a son asks, and the father explains the entire feast. 6) The first part of the *hallel* is sung, Ps. 113 and 114, and with a prayer of praise the second cup is drunk. 7) The father washes his hands, takes two cakes of bread, breaks one and lays it on the unbroken one, blesses the bread out of the earth, wraps a broken piece with herbs, dips it in the *chasoret,* eats it and a piece of the *chagiga* and a piece of the lamb. 8) Now all join in eating. 9) The festival meal was concluded when the father ate the last piece of the lamb, which was to be at least the size of an olive, after which no one ate. He washed his hands, and with a benediction the third cup was drunk. 10) The second part of the *hallel,* Ps. 115-118; the fourth cup, and sometimes a fifth; the conclusion of the *hallel,* Ps. 120-137. This is the description of the rabbis.

"While engaged in eating" (Matthew and Mark) thus places the exposure of the traitor at point eight, when the general eating was about concluded. Here we place Matt. 26:21-24; Mark 14:18-21; Luke 22:21-23; John 13:21, 22. Then follows John

13:23-27a; and after a little Matt. 26:25, the traitor's own question, "Rabbi, is it I?" and the answer of Jesus, "Thou hast said," which all heard. Now follows John 13:27b-30 and the departure of Judas. The Passover now reached its last formal stage; but instead of closing in the ordinary manner, the final act at this Passover was the Institution of the Lord's Supper. This also is the answer to the question whether or not Judas received the Lord's Supper.

If Jesus had made the exposure in connection with the washing of the feet, Judas would have been compelled to leave before the Passover began. We see from the accounts of all the evangelists how Jesus prolongs the ordeal of the exposure, increasing the pressure upon Judas' conscience more and more, until Judas at last practically exposes himself. First it is "one of you"; next, after the anxious questions of the eleven, the one dipping into the same dish with Jesus (like Ahitophel); then the word of woe regarding the traitor. All is in vain. John alone adds the incident of the sop by which Judas could see that Jesus pointed him out to John and to Peter. With brazen boldness Judas now challenges Jesus' infallible knowledge, "Certainly it is not I, Rabbi?" addressing him here as in Gethsemane only as "rabbi." Not until this time, when it is impossible to reach the heart fully given over to Satan, is the veil withdrawn, and all the others hear the reply, "Thou thyself didst say it."

Just before the Passover was to be concluded, when at last the sad moment had arrived for exposing Judas, "Jesus was troubled in the spirit," ἐταράχθη, a strong verb and passive because something took severely ahold of Jesus and shook his spirit. His inner disturbance must have appeared in his countenance, his tone of voice, and his entire bearing. The dative τῷ πνεύματι can refer only to the seat of the disturbance; it cannot denote the Holy Spirit as the agent working the disturbance. Augustine simply wonders why he who was so calm and collected when hitherto he referred to the traitor should now all at once be so deeply agitated. What puzzles Augustine others have no difficulty in solving. The entire context points to Judas as the cause of Jesus' severe inward disturbance, for now the sad moment had come to take the final step with regard to this traitor among the Twelve, the tragic moment when he would give himself wholly to Satan and his Satanic work. He who might have been one of those sitting on twelve thrones judging the twelve tribes of Israel (Matt. 19:28) is now about to become tenfold the child of hell and to win a name that is beyond all other names execrable among men to the end of time. The very thing that at one time shook David so deeply in Ps. 41:9 is now to receive its most highly intensified counterpart.

Instead of writing merely "and said," John uses two verbs, both finite, hence both of equal weight, "he testified and said." We are to understand beyond a doubt that the declaration now made by Jesus is more than a surmise on his part, more than a secret report that someone has brought to him. Jesus "testified" as a witness who speaks from direct, first-hand, personal knowledge of the fact. The thing Jesus utters is too tremendous to be uttered in any other way. The gravity of the statement is marked by the preamble, "Amen, amen" (verity), "I say to you" (authority), as explained in 1:51. Brief, but the more terrible because of the brevity, is the announcement itself, "that one of you shall betray me." It is categorical and direct, like a sudden blow in the face, not indefinite as heretofore. The chief point is the verb: it states literally and exactly what this traitor will do. We might prefer to translate "will betray," regarding the future as volitive; for it is the determination of Judas that is had in mind. This statement from the lips of Jesus must have exploded like a bomb in the quiet circle of the disciples. Now in a flash they perceive why Jesus is so agitated. The very thought was a shock full of horror. It is noteworthy that all the evangelists use the identical verb παραδίδωμι to designate the act of Judas, "to betray," literally, "to hand over," but in the sense of "to deliver up" to prison or judgment, M.-M. 483 with illustrations from the papyri. "Will betray me" needs no addition, for it can have only one meaning: into the hands of the Jewish authorities who had plotted for so long to lay violent and murderous hands on Jesus. Even the dullest of the eleven knew what such a betrayal meant. And this act, Jesus says, "one of you" will commit. This one word from his lips, no more — then silence, a silence that grew more tense and stifling with every moment. There was the word in their minds and stared at them. They literally shrank and cowered under its force.

22) Briefly, yet eloquently, John describes the immediate effect. **The disciples were looking at each other, being at a loss concerning which one he was speaking.** The imperfect ἔβλεπον pictures what happened as the tense moments slipped by and at the same time points to what finally occurred. The present participle ἀπορούμενοι indicates action simultaneous with that of the main verb and describes the thoughts of the disciples as they were looking at each other. Note that περὶ τίνος λέγει, an indirect question (not the same as περὶ οὖ), states the question in the mind of each disciple: "Of which one is he speaking?" "Who is it?" John says no more, for he knows that his readers have the accounts of the other evangelists. At first the eleven look at each other, each one, feeling himself guiltless, scrutinizing the

faces of the others in turn in order to detect some
evidence of guilt. They also looked at Judas but
saw nothing telltale there. Then each was seized by
a sudden secret dread of himself. Though none of
the eleven had harbored such a thought, the positive
statement of Jesus made each one shrink with mis-
giving. Before that infallible positiveness the feeling
of innocence wavered. Thus, as two of the evangelists
report, one after the other began to ask, μήτι ἐγώ εἰμι,
Κύριε, "Surely, it is not I, Lord?" Luke 22:23 says
that they began to dispute among themselves who
this one could be. The incident of the sop is reported
by John alone, who, however, omits any reference to
the words about the Son of man going as it is written
of him and about the woe pronounced upon the
traitor (Matt. 26:24; Mark 14:21).

One cannot help but pause here and wonder how
all this affected Judas. His heart must have been
adamant to endure it all and not to break down in
utter repentance and in abject confession.

23) **There was one of his disciples reclining at
table next to the bosom of Jesus, whom Jesus loved.**
While the aorist of εἶναι is not in use, and ἦν often
does duty for it, here, as in many similar instances,
the imperfect seems quite in place. The participle
ἀνακείμενος is merely a predicate. Jesus and John lay
on the same broad couch, stretched out side by side,
each resting on his left side and elbow, and John in
front of Jesus, so that in leaning back to speak to
Jesus John's head would fall upon Jesus' breast, ἐν
τῷ κόλπῳ, "in his bosom," which we venture to render
"next to his bosom." We must know about this position at table in order to understand what follows.

This position at table, which seems to have been
the one regularly accorded to John, is significant as
regards John's personal relation to Jesus. John,
Peter, and James were distinguished by Jesus on

various occasions (at the raising of Jairus' daughter, as witnesses of the Transfiguration, and as the nearest witnesses of the agony in Gethsemane) and thus formed an inner circle among the Twelve. But in this inner circle one stood nearer to Jesus than the other two, and this one was John. No wonder that of the Twelve John alone stood under the cross. Thus John reclined next to Jesus, we must assume, by the arrangement of Jesus himself. The fact has always been noted that John never mentions his own name in the Gospel he composed, nor the name of any of his family, not even that of Mary, Jesus' mother, who, it thus seems, was related to John's mother, Salome. Undoubtedly this is a mark of John's deep humility. Thus, when John records an incident in which he is compelled to refer to himself if he is to record it at all, he uses the description, "whom Jesus loved," with the imperfect ἠγάπα, "was loving" continuously. It is best to assume that neither Jesus nor John himself first used this designation, but that others who saw this close attachment, as here at table and afterward under the cross where Jesus entrusted his own mother to John, so spoke of this beloved disciple.

Jesus loved all his disciples (13:1) with the highest form of love, expressed in ἀγαπᾶν, the love that fully understands and is moved by the highest purpose toward the loved person; compare on the verb 3:16. And yet there are great differences in this ἀγάπη, as when God loves the world, and when Jesus loves his own. God's love understands all about the sin and the guilt of the world and has the wondrous purpose to atone for it all and to save the world; yet as regards "his own" (13:1) who believe in Jesus and are already clean (13:10), this love understands their needs while in the world and has the highest purpose to care for them as his own and to bestow on them his highest blessings. It is the same ἀγάπη, and yet the objects toward which it is directed cause a great difference in its manifestation. So it is with regard to John and the other disciples. Among the Twelve this youngest apostle — about twenty-two years old at this time — understood the mind of his Master best. The hearts of all were near to Jesus, yet John's was nearest. The Lord's Word and spirit penetrated John's soul more completely than the souls of the rest. It is not a matter of the fountain of love in Jesus, which is always full to overflowing, but a matter of the vessel for receiving love on the part of the individual disciple. Some vessels grow larger than others under the training of Jesus and thus are able to contain more. John's greater capacity must have been a joy to Jesus.

"Whom Jesus loved" is used like a fixed designation, for the name "Jesus" occurs immediately before its use here and yet is repeated in the designation; compare 20:2; 21:7 and 20. In 19:26 "Jesus" could not well be added. In 20:2 the verb is changed to ἐφίλει, "for whom Jesus had affection." Probably both verbs were used by those who thus spoke of John, the latter adding to the understanding and the purpose contained in ἀγαπᾶν the tender personal affection. It would be a work of supererogation to prove that "whom Jesus loved" refers to the apostle St. John. All four Gospels make certain that at this Passover only the Twelve are present with Jesus. Among the twelve, three form the inner circle. Among the three Peter is excluded, for he speaks to the unnamed apostle. James is excluded by 19:26 and 21:7 and 20. John alone is left. Much more may be added, but why waste the effort since no critic has ventured to suggest who this apostle could be if he assumed that it was not John? But John's motive for designating himself thus has been assailed. He is charged with trying to make himself the greatest of the Twelve, in

particular with placing himself above Peter. This
charge is unjustifiable. Zahn scores it as an evidence
of "a thoroughly perverted taste," for the humblest
person in the world may say, if it is true, that one
far greater than he has shown him love, even as the
most godly man may praise the love of God for showing him special benefits. Martha and Mary did
not boast regarding Lazarus when they called him,
"he whom thou lovest," 11:3. Only if John had written, "Jesus whom *I* love" (21:15), some critic might
find fault, and then only if he could show that John's
love was less than that of his fellow-apostles.

24) **Simon Peter, therefore, beckons to this one
and says to him, Tell me who it is concerning whom
he is speaking.** The present tenses used here and
in the next two verses make the narration vivid.
Everything shows that John here relates something
in which he had a part. We must discard the *textus
receptus* which reads: "he beckons to him to learn
who it might be," etc. The beckoning shows that
most probably Peter reclined on a couch with only one
other person between him and John. If Peter had
been next to John, he would only have leaned his head
back on John's breast, as John does when he now
speaks to Jesus. If Peter was farther removed from
John, Peter's word to John would have been heard
also by Jesus. Peter's beckoning begs John to lean
forward toward him. When John does this, Peter
whispers to him and asks John to tell of whom Jesus
is speaking. Evidently, Peter assumes that Jesus had
told John, and that thus John already knew. This is
incidental evidence, stronger because it is incidental, of
the intimacy existing between Jesus and John, as this
was recognized and accepted by the other disciples.
The aorist εἰπέ indicates the single act of telling. "Tell,"
of course, means, *"tell* me," not, "tell *me,* or tell *us"*;
and εἰπέ is not the same as ἐρώτα, "ask." Peter, how-

ever, credits John with possessing more knowledge that he has.

25) Himself anxious to know and spurred by Peter's request, John turns to Jesus in all simplicity. Here we have an instance which shows how near the mind of John was to that of Jesus: Jesus is entirely willing to indicate to John who the traitor is. **He thus, having leaned back on the breast of Jesus, says to him, Lord, who is it?** We must note that οὖτως is not the same as οὖν, "then" (A. V.), nor "as he was" (R. V.), with his position being as indicated in v. 23; nor *ohne weitere Umstaende*. The word means "thus," prompted by Peter's whisper. "Having leaned back on the breast of Jesus" is clear from v. 23. It also intimates that the question of John is whispered to Jesus, so that only Peter knew why John leaned back.

It is Peter who takes the initiative, John who plays second to Peter's first. It is Peter, not John, who thinks of thus quickly and quietly getting the coveted information. It is Peter who thinks of utilizing John because of his advantageous position; that thought did not occur to any other disciple. Initiative, natural leadership, masterful efficiency are high talents and therefore prized in the church. And yet the masterful Peter was *not* the disciple "whom Jesus loved" in the way in which he loved John. The mother of Jesus had no leadership worth mentioning in the sacred record; Martha was more of a leader than Mary — and yet the two Marys rank higher in the kingdom than many prominent women with the gift of leadership. Even Paul stands so high, not because he was so masterly, but because of the intimate nearness of his mind and his heart to Jesus.

The title "Lord" is intended in the sense in which the disciples generally used it, which also Jesus commends in v. 13: "Lord" in the supreme sense, namely divine Lord. "Who is it?" merely asks in all simplicity and no more. It assumes that Jesus intends to tell, that he has made his announcement with that intention. It assumes, too, that Jesus will not be offended at the question, though he may give his answer, as he often does, in his own superior way. The question does not mean, "Tell me at least." It does not contemplate securing secret information intended for John alone, for John asks at Peter's instigation, thus it is to be for both of them. Peter, too, is watching to find out who it is.

26) **Jesus, therefore, answers, He it is for whom I shall dip the sop and give it to him. When, therefore, he had dipped the sop he takes and gives it to Judas, the son of Simon Iscariot.** Jesus, we see, has other considerations besides satisfying the desire of John and of Peter at this stage of the exposure. Throughout he is making the strongest effort to show Judas the enormity of his contemplated crime, to break his hard heart in repentance, and thus to save his miserable soul. He has not yet exhausted this effort and therefore refrains from making a public announcement.

The whispered question of John, Jesus thus answers in the same quiet way — a mark of his special love for John. The tenses are dramatic presents. Jesus could have answered John by simply saying, "Judas!" He uses a different way, though one that is just as positive, one that again vividly recalls Ps. 41 and David's experience with the traitor Ahitophel. At the same time, instead of Jesus' branding Judas by name, he lets Judas brand himself by his own act — if he is, indeed, determined to do so. For even this giving of the sop is so designed as to afford Judas an opportunity to decline. The traitor could

not help but observe Peter's whisper to John, followed
by John's whisper to Jesus and the offer of the sop
by Jesus to him — Judas. Since all were keen to
know whom Jesus had in mind, this was decidedly
plain. Why does Judas not now break down inwardly? Why does he not decline the sop, turn and go
out, and, like Peter after his denial, weep bitterly?
For the same reason that when he printed the traitor's
kiss on Jesus' cheek and was met by Jesus' word,
"Fellow, *wherefore* art thou come?" he did not break
even then. The secret of human obduracy, its last and
final cause, is a mystery of the human will, a reason
of unreason, a contradiction of all true reason, a
devilishness which takes hold of a man and in the
very sight of damnation plunges him to his doom.
Three knew with full certainty: Jesus — John —
Judas; the Lord — the disciple beloved — the traitor.
The fourth, Peter, knew by inference.

It was not the question of John that caused Jesus
to select the method of his answer. Note the article in
τὸ ψωμίον, "*the* sop," the one Jesus already held in his
hand. Before John asked, Jesus had already begun
to prepare the sop. And we may fairly conclude that
if John had not asked, Jesus would of his own accord
have spoken some word to John that quietly designated
the traitor. This "sop" is best understood as being
bread not some meat of the lamb. Likewise, "dip"
refers not to the wine which was passed around in a
cup at various times of the feast, even also as we
have no record of dipping anything into the cup.
Jesus dipped the sop into the vessel filled with bitter
herbs or salad, prepared with vinegar and salt as prescribed by the law, or into the dish which the Jews
later added to indicate the fruits of the promised land,
called *chasoret,* prepared with vinegar and water together with figs, nuts, dates, and other fruit, and
forming a thick mass. Perhaps already at this time

only one dish was used; we know that later at least
the bitter herbs and the *chasoret* were combined.
For the head of the Passover company thus to offer
bread to one or to the other at table may or may not
have been a regular custom. Usually the former is
assumed, though without further evidence. We may
just as well assume the latter. At least this is true,
that in the present connection the act of Jesus is
highly significant. He is not content with the fact
that Judas, like the rest, dines at the same table with
him and thus resembles Ahitophel; he makes the
parallel much closer by offering Judas this sop with
his own hand. And Judas actually takes it from
Jesus' hand. We should like to know just where Judas
reclined, whether he took the sop directly from Jesus,
or whether it was passed to him at Jesus' direction; it
is impossible to determine these points.

Both ἐκεῖνος and ἐγώ are emphatic: "*he* for whom
I myself shall dip," etc. The reading with two finite
verbs "shall dip" and "shall give" has the strongest
attestation and lends equal weight to both actions.
We must likewise note the use of two verbs in "he
takes and gives," which makes the action graver and
presents it exactly as John and Peter beheld it. The
eyes of Judas, too, must have been riveted upon the
hand of Jesus, at the same time glancing at his face
and his eyes. What did Judas read in those eyes
and in the extended hand? Could he not behold the
deep pain, the burning love, the mighty warning?
He beheld it all — and was adamant against it all.
"He gives it to Judas" — and Judas takes it. Here
again John writes the traitor's full name: "Judas,
the son of Simon Iscariot." "Iscariot," the man of
Keriot, is to be construed with Simon as in 6:71;
while in 13:2 "Iscariot" is construed with Judas:
John — Judas: in the one we see what the love of

Jesus is able to make of a man; in the other what the power of Satan is able to do to a man.

27) And after the sop, then entered into him Satan. *Post* not *cum*; not with or by means of the morsel but after Judas' deliberate act of taking the morsel. By that act Judas himself opened the door of his heart to Satan, and thus Satan entered in. And this is Satan himself not one of his spirits. In the entire war upon Jesus (beginning with the temptation in the wilderness) the head of the hellish kingdom operates in person. Luke 22:3 reports that Satan entered Judas' heart to betray Jesus. That was the beginning. John states that after the sop Satan entered Judas' heart. That was the conclusion. This, of course, is not a case of bodily possession but one that is far worse; we may call it complete spiritual possession. Just as there are degrees of receiving the Holy Spirit, so there are degrees of letting Satan rule the heart. At first Satan suggested the thought of betrayal to Judas. Judas acts on this. Perhaps he thought that he could keep the matter in hand and could drop the plan if he should after all so desire. But when the sinner yields to the extent of playing with a sin, he often ends by becoming the helpless plaything in the hands of the sin and of Satan who is behind the sin. In the Greek "Satan" is placed emphatically at the end.

The question is asked, "How did Luke and how did John know so positively when Satan made these entrances?" The answer that they saw it in the countenance of Judas is unsatisfactory, for this could not apply to Luke. The other answer, that Luke and John arrived at "a psychological certainty" is too vague and subjective. Both Luke (22:4) and John have the immediate acts of Judas as grounds for their assertions and also the guidance of the Spirit in what they say about Judas.

At this point we insert Matt. 26:25. The traitor's identity, withheld for so long by Jesus and only a moment previously revealed to John and to Peter, is now finally disclosed to all. John's additions to the records of the synoptists are intended to give us a more complete picture of the way in which Jesus revealed the traitor.

Jesus, therefore, says to him, What thou art doing, do more quickly. The present is inchoative: "what thou art occupied with," i. e., "what thou hast begun," R. 880. The aorist imperative is certainly not permissive: "thou mayest do," but peremptory, "do!" or "finish doing!" The adverb τάχιον is comparative and does not mean "quickly" (our versions) but "more quickly," which "may mean more quickly than Judas would have done but for the exposure. Note that this is a conversation, and Judas would understand," R. 664.

Why this peculiar command? It conveys to Judas the thought that Jesus knows not only that he is the traitor but also how far his plan had at that moment advanced. Judas had covenanted to hand Jesus over to the authorities but had not yet fixed the exact time and the place for the delivery. He was now on the alert, looking for the favorable opportunity. The word of Jesus intimates to Judas that he knows just what Judas had begun and what he still had to do. More than this: Judas thought that Jesus was in his hand; Jesus tells him that the reverse is true. It is Jesus who orders Judas about this business, to carry it out when Jesus wants it done and not when Judas may feel like doing it. The situation is like that of the Jews and their plot to destroy Jesus, but *not* at the feast (Matt. 26:5), while Jesus declares that he will be crucified at the feast (Matt. 26:2). When men are determined to do evil, a higher hand controls their deeds for ends that are utterly beyond them. This word of Jesus also dismisses Judas, v. 30.

When Judas leaves the upper room, branded before the eleven as the traitor, he determines to hand Jesus over this very night. This is not obedience to the last word of Jesus, which, of course, Judas fully understood, but obedience to Satan who now completely controlled his heart. We may say that rage filled the traitor's heart when he left the room, blind rage at finding himself exposed. Does Jesus know of the contract with the rulers; does he think, because he knows, that he can frustrate the plot against him? Judas will show him: this very night the deed shall be done! So he obeyed Jesus without wanting to obey him; and so he obeyed Satan because he wanted to obey him. Did Jesus say, "Do it more quickly"? He would surprise him with his quickness.

28) John wrote many years after the event had occurred, and his readers, who know the fact from the accounts of the other evangelists, may think that the eleven, like Judas himself, at the time understood what the order to Judas really meant. A parenthetical statement wards off this misunderstanding and tells us just what the eleven thought when Judas left. **Now this no one knew of those reclining at table for what purpose he said it to him.** "No one" includes also Peter and John; "some" in v. 29 seems not to include John but only a few who ventured to express opinions. The verb means "did not realize." This ignorance need not surprise us. Who of them dreamed that the betrayal might take place in a few hours? If Jesus knew the traitor, would he not, when the betrayal finally took place, nullify the base act? Who of them could at that moment imagine that Jesus actually ordered Judas to proceed forthwith with his deed? In πρός we have aim or end (R. 626), and πρὸς τί means "for what purpose" (R. 739).

29) No one knew, but some guessed. **For some were thinking, since Judas had the box, that Jesus said to him, Buy what things we have need of for the feast, or to give something to the poor.** "For" means that these guesses show that no one knew. And the guess of the critics is no better when they say that what "some" here thought is proof positive that this supper was not the Jewish Passover, did not take place on the evening of the 14th of Nisan (Thursday, counted by the Jews as beginning Friday, the 15th) but on the evening of the 13th, thus placing John in contradiction with the synoptists. They think that "for the feast" means for the Passover meal. They suppose that during the night of the Passover meal nothing could be bought because of the night itself and of the sacredness of the feast. Exactly the reverse is true. On the night following the 13th all activity ceased, and no beggars would be about. But on the night following the 14th and ushering in the 15th there was a great deal of activity. Then everywhere in the city companies of ten to twenty ate the Passover and at the latest hours went home or to their lodgings. The night was treated as though it were daytime. All beggars were about. At midnight the Temple gates were opened, for crowds came thus early to get the sacrifice of *chagiga* (*chag*, "feast"), which was killed on the 15th immediately after the morning sacrifice at nine o'clock. Traders were busy on every hand. "For the feast" means for the entire seven days of the celebration, which required much more than was needed for the Passover meal alone. Nicodemus had no trouble in buying myrrh and aloes (19:39) on Friday, linen was secured, and the women obtained the spices they expected to use on Sunday.

On γλωσσόκομον see 12:6. "Some were thinking" — which afterward proved wrong — that earlier their treasurer Judas had received directions from Jesus as to necessary purchases, and that Jesus was reminding him of these orders. Others thought that the reminder referred to alms for beggars. Note the change from the direct to the indirect discourse with non-final ἵνα introducing an object clause after λέγει (the present retained in the Greek, whereas we change to "said").

30) **After, therefore, receiving the sop, he immediately went out. And it was night.** John recurs to the significant act of taking the sop. That act constitutes the final decision of the traitor. Jesus does not order him to leave, but he feels dismissed and is only too ready to escape from the hated company. "Immediately," εὐθύς, shuts out any delay, however brief. This adverb forbids our placing the Institution of the Lord's Supper prior to the departure of Judas. It is ineffectual to object that Judas could not leave before the formal close of the Passover. Judas left. The Passover was practically ended, and, moreover, this is an exceptional situation in every way.

The simple ending of the narrative: "And it was night," is certainly not merely a statement of time, for we know that this was a "supper" and that its ceremonial features extended it into the night. Nothing of a symbolical or allegorical nature is intended. Yet to have our attention called to the fact that it was night when Judas left Jesus and the disciples, grips us with a frightful, tragic feeling. The child of Satan leaves Jesus and goes out into the night to accomplish a deed fit only for the blackest night.

John does not make even a reference to the Institution of the Lord's Supper, yet most of the interpreters try to find some place in his narrative into which to fit this great act. All that can safely be said is that the Institution cannot be placed prior to v. 30. John omits an account of the Lord's Supper for the simple reason that the four records already in the hands of the church are sufficient; a fifth record was not needed, since John could only repeat what the others had recorded and could not supplement by adding anything new.

3. Jesus Glorified and the New Commandment for the Disciples, 31-35

31) When, therefore, he had gone out, Jesus says, Now the Son of man has been glorified, and God has been glorified in him. And God will glorify him in himself and immediately will he glorify him. The temporal clause, as well as the connective οὖν, connect these words of Jesus most closely with the departure of the traitor on his Satanic errand. The contrast is tremendous: Judas goes out into the night, Jesus sees himself and God glorified by what Judas does. The painful scene with regard to Judas is replaced by a blessed scene in which Jesus shows the eleven all the glory for himself and God and the love that should fill them as it fills him. The words sound as though a great weight has been taken off the heart of Jesus, as though he once more breathes freely again. The aorist ἐξῆλθεν, "did go out" is best translated with the past perfect in English, "had gone out."

Jesus speaks of himself in the third person and uses his Messianic title "the Son of man" (see 1:51), he who is man and yet more than man. This title expresses in one term his being sent by the Father, his Incarnation, and his redemptive work. As this Son of man he now has been and immediately will be glorified. The two aorists ἐδοξάσθη are narrowed down by the adverb "now" and express what has just now occurred, R. 843. The English equivalent is the present perfect, "now has been glorified." In this instance the passives imply no agent, for the context supplies the sense: has been glorified by what has just occurred, namely the action of the traitor going out to bring on the passion of Jesus. The thought is so paradoxical, viewing Judas' act and what it means for Jesus in his redemptive work as a glorification of Jesus, that many seek to modify it. They conceive of glorification and glory as being connected only with the resurrection, ascension, and enthronement of Jesus, and not with his passion. Hence they call these aorists proleptic; R. 847 thinks that they are explained by the two following futures δοξάσει. Against this stands the emphatic νῦν, and it would be strange to repeat one verb four times in two decisively different tenses for one and the same thought, namely coming glory. Others leave the aorists as they stand but have them include the entire past ministry of Jesus. But this again disregards the "now," and the dramatic moment of the departure of Judas, emphasized in the "when" clause, shuts out a reference covering more than three years of work.

It is true enough that God glorified Jesus during his ministry, see, for instance, 1:32-34 and 12:28. But why hesitate to include what Jesus says after Judas leaves, that right now he has been glorified? Jesus' death is now assured, his actual redemptive work is now ushered in, the final decisive act has now begun. Viewing it thus, it is glorious indeed, for his passion and death and long-fixed resolve to endure it all are the most perfect part of his obedience to the Father, which sheds unmeasured honor upon the Son who rendered it, a sweet-smelling savor to God, fairer that any sacrifice or offering ever brought to God. In all heaven and earth there is no act so worthy of praise and honor as this act of Jesus'. Jesus is right, "Now has the Son of man been glorified."

"And God has been glorified in him," ἐν αὐτῷ, in union with Jesus not merely "through him," which would have to be δι' αὐτοῦ. Always the glorification of Jesus is the glorification of God; for he sent this Savior, it was at his bidding that he now faced the cross, it was God's love, truth, and righteousness that Jesus by now entering into his passion made to shine forth for all the world. "God was in Christ, reconciling the world unto himself," and to all eternity men and angels will sing his praise and glorify his name.

32) The note of glory in the passive verbs "has been glorified" is vastly increased by the two active verbs "will glorify," the subject of which is God. Jesus is literally ringing the glory bells as he enters his passion. These futures must be volitive, "will glorify," expressing God's will and determination, and not merely futuristic, "shall glorify," stating only a future fact. "God will glorify him in himself" (God), for, whether we read ἐν αὐτῷ or ἐν ἑαυτῷ, the pronoun refers to God, and the phrase matches the one used in v. 31. As God is glorified in Jesus, so Jesus is glorified in God. This is more than mutual or reciprocal glorification, as when I sing your praise, and you sing mine. These are also not two separate glorifications, although the aorist speaks of the one as having just begun, and the future of the other as just about to begin. The two constitute a unit. When God is glorified "in Jesus," and Jesus is glorified "in God," back of the two phrases lies the unity of the Father and the Son, "thou Father in me, and I in thee," 17:21; also 10:30.

Beyond question, these two (hence emphatic) future tenses refer to the descent into hell, the resurrection, ascension, and heavenly reign, usually summarized as Christ's exaltation. Phil. 2:9-11; John

17:4, 5.   Then the emphatic εὐθύς, over against the
equally emphatic νῦν in v. 31, would mark the close
proximity of the glories, the one shining in the
deepest humiliation of Jesus ("obedient unto death,
even the death of the cross"), the other in his exaltation ("hath highly exalted him"). With this we may
be satisfied — everything is obvious. Yet "immediately" may also be taken to start from the present
hour to which the preceding "now" leads up, so that
God "will glorify" Jesus also in his passion and death,
for these are Jesus' sacrifice to God, God accepts them
as such and thus glorifies Jesus even on the cross
(recall the signs at the time of Jesus' death). In this
connection consider Luke 9:31: while Jesus was gloriously transfigured he spoke with Moses and Elijah
"of the decease which he should accomplish at Jerusalem." In v. 31 the verbs and the subjects are placed
chiastically, laying all the emphasis on the verbs; in
v. 32 the emphasis is on ὁ Θεός and εὐθύς.

33) The glorification of Jesus entails the removal
of his visible presence from the eleven. As he reveals
the glorification to them in the present hour for their
assurance and comfort in view of what has begun, so
he fortifies them by telling of the impending separation. **Little children, yet for a little I am with you.
You shall seek me, and as I said to the Jews, Where
I am going you on your part cannot come, also to
you I say it now.** From what this hour means to
himself and to God Jesus turns to what it means for
the eleven. The diminutive τεκνία occurs only here in
the Gospels. It is a term of the most affectionate
endearment yet connotes the immaturity of those that
are so dear. They are still only "little children," not
yet the men they are to become. A yearning heart
utters the word and adds the thought as to how
short its stay is with them, how soon they will be

left alone, μικρόν, "a little while," actually only a few hours.

Jesus refers to what he told the Jews some months ago (7:34), that he would leave and that they would vainly seek him. What he told the Jews now applies also to the eleven (καθώς . . . καί), namely in two points: vain seeking and inability to go where Jesus will be. Yet mark the significant omission in the reference to the Jews — they would die in their sins (8:21) but not these "little children" of Jesus. They shall only seek him as one whose visible and familiar presence is suddenly gone, seek him with deep longing and great grief, and Jesus implies that the seeking will be vain. The old, familiar association as little children with a father will be ended forever. Since the subjects are so opposite, Jews and these "little children," the kinds of seeking correspond to the subjects. So also with regard to the place where Jesus will soon be in a few hours: "you on your part (emphatic ὑμεῖς) are not able to come" there. For the Jews this meant that because of their unbelief they could never come there; but for the eleven it means only what presently Jesus tells Peter, "Whither I go, thou canst not follow me now; but thou shalt follow afterward," v. 36. There is, therefore, no thought of a contradiction with 12:26; 14:3; 17:24. Moreover, the death of Jesus is one in which he cannot possibly have associates, it will be wholly sacrificial, Isa. 63:3. So while Jesus goes, his little children must remain behind.

34) But when his visible presence is taken from them, they will still have each other, and thus ought to be the more closely attached to each other, loving each other just as Jesus loved them while he was still in their midst. Thus we may connect the new statement. **A new precept I give to you, that you keep loving each other just as I loved you, that you, too,**

keep loving each other. By ἐντολή Jesus means a
precept, a behest, *einen Auftrag*, not a legal command after the order of Moses; see 14:15. It is "new,"
καινή, as regards the old legal requirements, not νέα, as
never having existed before. Many features of this
newness have been pointed out, differentiating the
precept of Jesus from the old law, "Thou shalt love
thy neighbor as thyself," which reaches out to all
men, even to our enemies. But it is best to abide by
the newness which Jesus himself points out: that
you keep loving each other "just as I loved you."
Jesus makes all things new. The newness Jesus
has in mind is not strange and startling to the disciples, it has a familiar and a pleasant mien. Jesus
has brought a new love into the world, a love that
is not only faultless and perfect as love but one that
is intelligently bent on salvation for the one loved.
Only the disciples know from Jesus what this love
is, only they have enjoyed the experience of his love;
hence this precept is for them alone — it would be
useless to give it to the world. So also this love is
to be for "each other" in the circle of the disciples. It
cannot be otherwise, because the tie that binds the disciples of Jesus is a thing apart and cannot include
others. Just as Jesus loves his "little children," and
there is an intimate exchange of love between him and
them, so it is with regard to the exchange of love between these "little children" themselves.

On the verb ἀγαπᾶν see 3:16, and compare 13:1.
As Jesus loves all men, so, of course, should his disciples also. Yet here the circle is narrower, restricted
to the intelligent and purposeful manifestations of love
made possible by the same faith and the same love
in the hearts of those concerned. The two ἵνα clauses
are non-final and in apposition to ἐντολήν, stating what
the order or precept is. The repetition in the second
clause is emphatic: Jesus lingers on the precept

as though he loved to see this love in action. The subjunctives are present to express continuous loving; but with regard to the model set by Jesus the aorist is in place, summing up all the love he has shown them in his contact with them hitherto.

35) **Herein shall all know that you are disciples to me, if you have love among each other.** Once more Jesus dwells on this love and its continuation. Where it exists, it is bound to show itself, and, although it is never ostentatious, those around us will see and thus "know" or realize its presence. It is bound to affect them, if possible also to draw them into this circle of love. Minucius Felix declared with regard to the Christians, "They love each other even without being acquainted with each other." And the scoffer Julian, "Their master has implanted the belief in them that they are all brethren." In his commentary on John's Epistles Jerome tells us that when John was asked by the brethren why he constantly said, "Little children, love one another," he replied, "Because this is the precept of the Lord, and if only this is done it is enough." "Wherever the beginning of the new life from God is found in man, this love in its beginnings is also found. It is not nature which brings this about. Even the very best orthodoxy cannot now take the place of this essential feature (compare I John 3:14). They who are born of God bear a mystery within them, which unites them most intimately in one body, a mystery which no one knows but they themselves. But the power of this mystery appears unto the stranger. It is not a kind of fraternal union, with prideful and hostile exclusion of those who are without. For love widens the heart to love even these with a love that believes all things and hopes all things." Roffhack.

Among the unacceptable interpretations we may note the following: a new commandment inasmuch

as it is one which embraces in a unit all New Testament requirements as distinguished from the many
diverse requirements of the Old Testament; new, because illustrious; the ultimate mandate, i. e., testament; the youngest commandment; one never growing
old, always remaining new; a renewed commandment;
one renewing the old man in us; an unexpected commandment; one containing a new life principle (in itself correct, yet here not stated) ; the new testament
of Christ, i. e., the Lord's Supper.   Over against these
the text is sufficient: "as I did love you," as based on
this love, flowing from it, and thus new, indeed, new as
growing out of faith in Christ.

"If you have love among each other" invites a test,
and ἐάν with the subjunctive expects this test to be
met.   Still false disciples will appear, even the world
will discover that they are false by their lack of love.
The question is not wholly shut out: "Have I this
love which Jesus enjoined upon his disciples the night
in which he was betrayed?"   How many Christians
show malice, spite, hatred, coldness, enmity to each
other?   Where there is no love, there can be no discipleship.   The world also loves its own and has
established many fraternal organizations.   Since they
are not built on the love of Christ by faith, they cannot grow and bring to flower that love which is rooted
in faith and grows in no other soil.   The love of
Christians cannot reach perfection as long as the
flesh dwells in us, but more and more as the flesh is
overcome, this love unfolds until it reaches its full
glory when we attain the glory of Christ above.

4.   Peter Warned, 36-38

36)   Some hold that three warnings were given to
Peter, one recorded by John, one by Luke, and one by
Matthew and Mark.   Others combine all four accounts
and think of only one warning.   The reason for think-

ing of only one warning is theoretical: Peter, once warned, would be silenced, would not disregard that warning, and would thus not again speak and prompt a second warning. Hence the records of both Luke and John are rearranged: Luke 22:39, then v. 31-34; John 18:1, 2, and then 13:36-38 (with nothing said about 14:31, the last sentence). In addition John 13:37 is divided, and between Peter's question and his promise Matt. 26:31 and Mark 14:27, 28 are inserted. This rearrangement is too radical to be justified on theoretical grounds. Not only this, the theoretical ground is untenable; for Peter did not disregard only the first warning (recorded by Luke and by John) but also the second (recorded by Matthew and by Mark), he tried to follow Jesus in spite of all warning he received. In connection with the washing of the feet he yielded; not so now: he refuses to be warned. In the face of this fact we are unable to revise John's record (to say nothing of Luke's) and to transfer 13:36-38 across 14:31 and 18:1, 2 and to place John's record of the warning at this point. Peter received two warnings, the first in the upper room shortly after Judas left, the second on the way to Gethsemane, and he disregarded both of them.

The moment two warnings are noted, another difficulty disappears. In John it is the statement of Jesus, "Where I am going you on your part cannot come" (v. 33), which calls forth two questions on the part of Peter; whereas in Matthew and in Mark it is the statement of Jesus that this night all of the disciples shall be offended in him, which calls forth no questions but the positive assertion that, whatever the rest may do, Peter will not be offended. Mark 14:31 adds that Peter "talked more exceedingly," ἐκπερισσῶς ἐλάλει, on this occasion, and both Matthew and Mark add that (carried away, we may assume, by Peter's vehemence) all the rest spoke as Peter did.

Simon Peter says to him, Lord, where art thou going? The weave of John's record is too close for us to remove this section and to place it elsewhere, for Peter refers directly to v. 33. He, of course, heard what Jesus said about the new precept, but he is not satisfied to give up the presence of his Lord and to pour out his love on his fellow-disciples. Thus also he is not merely asking for more information in regard to the Lord's destination, in order the better to understand the impending separation; he is determined that there shall not be such a separation but that he will cling to Jesus in spite of Jesus' word. This, of course, also shows that Peter has no proper conception of this departure of Jesus. Yet we must not overlook the love that lies back of Peter's question. He wants to know more about where Jesus is going because he is determined to go with him; his love cannot endure the thought of separation; whatever love for others Jesus asks of him, one and one alone is the object of Peter's love. Often enough Jesus had spoken of going to his Father, yet now that the hour for his going has arrived, and now that Peter is determined to go along, he wants to know more, he feels that he has too little information for the great purpose of his accompanying Jesus to the proposed destination.

Jesus understands Peter perfectly and words his answer accordingly. **Jesus answered, Where I am going thou canst not follow me now, yet thou shalt follow me afterward.** On ὅπου in the sense of "whither" see R. 298. No need to answer regarding the destination about which Peter inquires, something more vital prevents his going along. He cannot now follow Jesus. In v. 33 this impossibility is due to the place to which Jesus is going, here it is due to something else. In the debate as to whether the reason is subjective or objective, or possibly both, it is best to discard the subjective idea, namely that Peter is not as yet spiritually strong enough to be crucified with Jesus. For Jesus does not intend to say that, if he had the strength, he might, indeed, now follow him. The reason is objective, Peter's hour for following Jesus is not "now" but will arrive in due time "afterward." Nor does this mean that he shall follow as soon as he acquires the necessary subjective strength; it means that Peter is to serve his Lord in the office of apostleship, and when his work here is done, then in God's good hour he shall, indeed, follow Jesus — follow him by the death of martyrdom by crucifixion. Compare Luke 22:32b. Yes, Peter is to have the greatest possible opportunity for showing his love to his Lord.

37) This should have satisfied Peter, but again (v. 8) his own zeal and determination rise against his Master's word. **Peter says to him, Lord, why cannot I follow thee now? My life for thee will I lay down.** The question is not intended as the expression of a desire that the real reason be stated to him but as an assertion that there is no reason such as Jesus implies: "What in the world is to prevent me from following thee now?" He thinks only of his subjective readiness and declares that this is altogether complete to the point of laying down his life in behalf of Jesus; ὑπέρ is general, implying any reason that might require his death. No doubt, Peter is rash and does not know how weak he is. Worst of all, he is not listening to Jesus' word and pretends to know better. Yet his heart burns with love and devotion to Jesus. "Of such stuff martyrs are made when the fulness of the spirit is added." Hengstenberg. Some texts have the aorist infinitive ἀκολουθῆσαι in both verses (referring to the single act of following); others, the

present ἀκολουθεῖν in Peter's question, "be following thee," i. e., constantly.

38) Now Jesus is compelled to reveal even Peter's subjective weakness. **Jesus answers, Thy life for me wilt thou lay down? Amen, amen, I say to thee (1:51), The cock shall not crow till thou shalt deny me thrice.** Jesus places into striking contrast what Peter promises to do and what he actually will do. He will give his own grand words the lie by doing the exactly opposite of what he says. Instead of laying down his life, he will save it and save it by denying Jesus, not once, not even only twice, but thrice, in three acts, not by implication or silence, but by the loudest declarations with the tongue with which he now speaks in public, before many witnesses. The verb ἀρνέομαι means "to say no" and thus "to disown." Peter will completely disavow Jesus as though he never had the least to do with him.

And this he will do this very night before the day dawns. The reference to the crowing of the cock is not to a casual crowing of some one cock at night. Two crowings were distinguished, one occurring near midnight; the other, just before dawn. They helped to divide the night into the midnight or the silent period, the period before dawn and the period after dawn. Pliny calls the fourth watch *secundum gallicinium*. Mark 14:30, in the second warning to Peter, refers to both crowings: "before the cock crow twice," meaning before the day dawns. John, like Matthew and like Luke, refers only to the one crowing, that preceding the dawn. Yet the reference of Jesus is not merely a designation of time; he refers to the actual crowing which marks the time. The word of Jesus is spoken with a special purpose in mind for Peter. It has in mind more than to foretell how soon he will deny, it intends to aid in bringing Peter to repentance. Peter will actually hear the crowing when it begins; that will bring Jesus' word to his mind, and this together with the look from Jesus' eyes (Luke 22:61) will cause the penitent tears to flow. The effort to discredit the record of the evangelists by asserting that chickens were not kept in Jerusalem, and that thus no cocks crowed within the range of Peter's ears, has been met by ample evidence to the contrary.

Luke, like John, records this first warning to Peter, which took place in the upper room. After Peter's question in v. 37a we may place Luke 22:31, 32. John 37b is parallel with Luke 22:33, likewise John v. 38 with Luke 22:34. Or, we may place after v. 38a what Luke has in v. 31-34, making the last verse parallel with John's v. 38b; compare John Bugenhagen's *The Sufferings and Death of our Lord Jesus Christ*, generally called "The Passion History" and used extensively during Lent.

CHAPTER XIV

5. The Comforting Explanation of Jesus' Departure, 14:1-11

1) The last verse of this chapter shows that the entire chapter was spoken while Jesus and the eleven reclined at table in the upper room. The connection is direct. Jesus spoke of leaving the disciples (13:33) ; he bade them to love each other when he would be gone and to remember how he had loved them while he was with them; then he had to warn Peter who was determined to leave with Jesus — it was all very depressing for these disciples who did not understand the inwardness of it all. This situation Jesus meets with the comforting explanation of his departure.

First the negative command: **Let not your heart be troubled,** stirred up and shaken at the thought of my going away from you. The present imperative with μή forbids what one has begun to do, here, "Stop letting your heart be troubled!" because you have no reason to be troubled. The departure of Jesus, rightly understood, is no cause for distress but the very contrary, though it be a departure. Beside this negative command Jesus places a double positive command: **Believe in God, in addition believe in me.** This is not said with reference to general faith in God and in Jesus but with reference to trust in God and in Jesus as regards the departure of Jesus. God sent Jesus on his mission and desires his return now that his mission is being completed; Jesus came on this mission, is now completing it, and thus returns to God. And this mission, planned and carried out by God and by Jesus, opens heaven for the disciples and for all who believe as they do. In all this the disciples must keep on (the imperatives are durative) trusting God and Jesus. The thought requires that after the negative imperative, "let not your heart be troubled," we read the two verbs that follow as positive imperatives: "believe — believe!" These are followed in v. 2, etc., by what the disciples are to believe. The form πιστεύετε might also be indicative; hence we find four, in fact, five, interpretations: all but the first of which run into difficulties: 1) two imperatives; 2) two indicatives; 3) an imperative and an indicative; 4) the reverse; 5) finally a strange punctuation: "Believe — in God and in me believe," which, however, destroys the beautiful chiasm. By means of the chiasm the two verbs are placed into the two emphatic positions: "Believe . . . believe!" The trouble of the disciples will disappear if now, when all seems so strange and dark to them, they will only believe and trust.

The two "believe" are used in the same sense, demanding the same trust in Jesus as in God. Both are equally trustworthy, and the ground for this is the deity of Jesus, 10:30; 14:9; Matt. 16:16. Elsewhere, too, faith in Jesus is made equal to faith in God, 5:24; 12:44. In the present case the two are considered distinct, and καί adds the one trust to the other. First, the disciples have God with all his promises and his assurances concerning the mission of Jesus; "in addition" (καί) they have Jesus, God's Son, and him in his mission which is now almost accomplished. Either one would be enough, both together are more than enough.

2) The two "believe" do not refer to blind but to intelligent belief. While all true faith of necessity contains an implicit element, one which extends beyond our limited knowledge and the partial experience we may have had in our lives and may yet attain, this always rests on the explicit element, the clear knowledge granted to us and the actual experience we have

in this knowledge and in our spiritual contact with God and with his Son Jesus. Thus the disciples are bidden to keep on believing in view of the departure of Jesus what they have for a long time known from God's revelation and of what Jesus now again assures them: **In the house of my Father are many mansions,** ' μοναί, permanent abiding-places. Ps. 23:6. This figurative language is quite transparent. There is no need to spiritualize the concrete terms which the Scriptures use with reference to heaven, as though they refer to a future condition. Our human minds cannot get beyond conceptions of time and of space, hence the Scriptures always use these with reference to heaven, wisely leaving it to the great future when we shall experience just what eternity and the place (ποῦ) of God's abode is. "My Father's house" lends to the word "Father" and to "our Father, who art in heaven" a richer meaning. He has a house, οἰκία, a home, to which the "household of God" now on earth (Eph. 2:19) and all his children (Gal. 3:26; Rom. 8:14-17) shall be transferred. All the tenderness and the attractiveness, the restfulness and the happiness that lie in the word "home" are thus in the loftiest degree applied to heaven. With only a stroke or two Jesus draws a picture which fills us pilgrims, who are still far from home, with both heavenly homesickness and the sure hope of soon reaching our home.

SUNT, writes Bengel: ARE, in order to bring out the fact that these mansions are realities, are in actual existence. God has provided them, and we may say from all eternity. These mansions are "many," which is stated in reference to Jesus as being only *one* Son; not he alone shall dwell in "the house of his Father" but all the other sons with him, whom he brings unto glory (Heb. 2:10). This statement about the many mansions must thus be read in connection with the mission of Jesus and its accomplishment. It is a covert promise to the disciples that they, too, shall enter those mansions. "Many" thus means far more than that there shall be room for all, or that God's children shall be numerous — thoughts that are rather trivial when the eleven were thinking only of their impending separation from Jesus. The word "many" is misapplied when it is referred to men of all kinds of opinions, convictions, faiths, and the like; for only true believers may enter. Some devout writers use this figurative language of Jesus in their human fancies of what heaven will be like, but it is well to bear in mind that no human thought is able to portray the details, and that the only safe course is to abide by what the Scriptures say.

But if not, I would have told you that I am going to prepare a place for you. The interpretation of this statement should not clash with facts that are assured. One is that Jesus does, indeed, go to prepare a place for the disciples (v. 3); another is that the many mansions do, indeed, exist, just as the entire Old Testament has always said and as Jesus now says, hence Jesus could not now assume their non-existence; and a third is that the abbreviated protasis, because it is so abbreviated, must express past unreality (not present), exactly as does the apodosis. Moving within these fixed bounds, we have this sense: "But if not, i. e., if you had not believed this about the many mansions (as, however, I know that you have), I would have told you (as, however, I have not needed to) that I am going to prepare a place in these mansions not only for others but in particular also for you (ὑμῖν, emphatic)." Then v. 3: "But you have had this faith about the many mansions and about the final part of my mission that I would there prepare a place for you, hence all I now need to do is to assure you that, if I shall thus go and prepare a place for you, which I am, indeed, now on the very point of doing, I most certainly also will add this: I will come again and receive you unto myself."

After saying, not as something new, but as something well-known to the disciples and clear from the Old Testament and from all the teaching of Jesus, that the Father's house has many mansions, i. e., that his love has prepared salvation for so many: Jesus cannot in the next breath add, "If this were (objectively) not so, I would have told you." Our versions and those who so read have a protasis of *present* unreality, whereas εἰ μή is followed by an apodosis of *past* unreality and must thus also be past; "if not" meaning, "if you had not believed." The ὅτι does not mean "for" (our versions and others) or "because," in the sense that, if no mansions existed, Jesus would have said so *because* he is going to prepare a place for the disciples. This would then mean, that with no mansions existing, Jesus would supply the deficiency, i. e., "prepare" or create a place for the disciples. Yet in the next breath Jesus says that since the mansions do exist, he is going "to prepare" a place for the disciples in these mansions. The verb "prepare a place" cannot have two opposite meanings in such close succession, once "to create" a place where none exists and then "to make ready" a place which already exists. Those who see this regard the statement as a question: "If not (if no mansions exist), would I have told you that I go to prepare a place for you?" But where has Jesus hitherto said this to the disciples?

The mansions exist, even as the disciples had all along known and believed. If they had not known and believed, Jesus would have told them about these mansions, told them by saying that he is going to prepare a place for them in these mansions. Jesus says this to the disciples in order to lead them to understand one great comforting reason for his departure, namely that he is going in advance of his disciples to make ready their places in the heavenly mansions so that they may follow him in due time. His departure is not a permanent separation but a necessary step for a

glorious and eternal reunion. Instead of being troubled, the disciples should remember what they have
all along known and believed about the house of the
Father and its many mansions, should connect the
departure of Jesus with their own places in those mansions (he making them ready to receive his own there)
and should thus be comforted and glad.

3) **And if I shall go and prepare for you a
place, I am coming again and will receive you unto
myself, in order that where I myself am also you
on your part may be.** The departure of Jesus
ushers in this glorious and eternal reunion. With this
great promise Jesus plants the comfort of hope in his
disciples. The translation indicates the assured reading of the text.

The condition with ἐάν presents expectancy, but one
coupled with certainty: "If I shall go," etc., as indeed
I shall. The aorists "shall go and prepare" denote
actuality as well as single acts. "Shall go" refers to
the ascension of Jesus. "Shall prepare" or "make
ready" is a heavenly act and, therefore, since no further explanation is added, impossible for us to visualize
in detail. The best explanation is that the presence
of Jesus in his Father's heavenly home makes the mansions ready for our reception; for only through the
presence of our Redeemer in heaven is it possible for
us disciples to enter heaven. Some have pictured the
preparation in a human way: as we prepare a room
for a coming guest, placing in it all that the guest may
like, embellishing and decorating it for his delight.
Perhaps the best analogy is the scene on the Mount of
Transfiguration, where Peter was so anxious to stay
with Jesus, Moses, and Elijah. We shall know all
about this preparation when we are finally received
into the heavenly mansions.

The present tense, ἔρχομαι, especially with πάλιν added
and followed by a future tense, is used in a future
sense, "I am coming again," i. e., "I shall come." Also

the two acts, that of coming again and that of receiving the disciples unto himself occur at the same time. The best commentary on ἔρχομαι is ἐλεύσεται in Acts 1:11; this is the coming of Jesus at the last great day. Those who think of the spiritual coming of Jesus in his Word and sacraments forget that in this sense Jesus never left his disciples. Those who think of the resurrection of Jesus as his return to the disciples have difficulty with the purpose clause, "in order that where I myself am," etc. When this clause is spiritualized in the sense of "the reception into the communion of his heavenly life," whether we are still on earth or already in heaven, the context is ignored with its reference to the heavenly mansions and the preparation of our places there, to say nothing of the resurrection, which then would have to be spiritualized. The promise of Jesus refers to the parousia. The coming again is the counterpart of the going away; visibly Jesus ascends, visibly he returns, Acts 1:9-11. The objection that John does not otherwise mention the parousia follows the mistaken principle that a writer must mention a subject repeatedly, otherwise he cannot be considered as having mentioned it at all. But why rule out "the last day" in 6:39, 40, 44, and 54; and the statements in 5:28, 29?

From other passages we know that the soul shall anticipate the body in its entrance into the heavenly mansions (Lazarus in the parable, the malefactor, Paul in Phil. 1:23); yet Jesus does not "come" for the soul in the sense in which he has promised to come at the last day. The angels, not the Lord, came for Lazarus' soul; dying Stephen beholds Jesus on his heavenly throne, Jesus does not come to him. The interval between our bodily death and the Lord's coming is so brief that he spans it with one word, "I am coming again." "I will receive you unto myself" (volitive not merely futuristic) is made clearer by the purpose clause, "in order that where I myself am also you on your part may be." The reception will be a complete, final, eternal reunion. "Where," ὅπου, reverts to everything said about the "place." The pronouns ἐγώ and καὶ ὑμεῖς are strongly stressed — Jesus and the eleven forever together in heaven. This is what the impending departure of Jesus means: cause for pure joy, the very opposite of distress. In 12:26 the promise is general, to any "servant" of Jesus; here it is made specific, to the eleven alone, and yet, as we read this ὑμεῖς, we see that it applies so decidedly to the eleven because it applies to all true believers.

4) From the glorious day when Jesus will return and receive his own unto himself he again turns, as in v. 1, to the present situation of the disciples whom he is leaving behind. He has told them where he is going and what his departure means for them. He now adds another word of assurance. **And as regards whither I am leaving, you know the way.** Or, according to the other reading, "And whither I am leaving you know, and the way you know." The ὅπου clause is adverbial. Either reading implies that the disciples know both the destination of Jesus and the way to that destination. Yet ὁδός does not refer to the way Jesus is about to take but the way the disciples must take to reach that destination. Whereas Jesus a moment ago used πορεύομαι ("to bring oneself upon the way"), "to travel," he now employs the synonym ὑπάγω (intransitive), "to leave or depart" (slowly or quietly), "to retire." Both verbs refer to the ascension of Jesus to heaven. When Jesus speaks of "the way" by which the disciples are to reach the same heavenly destination, he has in mind neither a miraculous bodily ascension into heaven like his own, nor the reception to himself promised at his return on the last day, but the actual means or medium by which the disciples shall be brought to the Father and to the place of his heavenly presence.

Thus Jesus is right in saying that the disciples already know that way, for they are already moving forward upon it. Jesus has been teaching them this way, leading them forward upon it ever since they joined themselves to him. All they need to do is to continue on this way until Jesus finally comes to take them unto himself forever.

5) **Thomas says to him, Lord, we do not know whither thou art leaving. How do we know the way?** Thomas speaks for all the disciples, taking it for granted that they all feel much as he does. Thomas actually contradicts Jesus, telling him that so little do they know the way that they do not even know the destination for which Jesus is leaving. Yet this is not the ugly contradiction of unbelief but the pessimistic contradiction of discouraged faith when it looks forward and is still unable to see clearly. That, too, is why Jesus does not rebuke Thomas but explains with words so light and clear that we almost feel like thanking Thomas for calling them forth.

In an endeavor to analyze what was in the mind of Thomas we may say that he knew that Jesus was returning to his Father in heaven and that this return involved the death of Jesus, leaving the disciples behind. We recall how in 11:16 he spoke of dying with Jesus. His trouble, however, was not his inability to conceive how a going down into death could be a going up to the Father in heaven. Thomas had no notions of "a realm of the dead" or *Totenreich,* such as some modern interpretation by misunderstanding *sheol* and *hades* attributes to the ancient Jews and tries to incorporate into Christian doctrine. The dark spot in the mind of Thomas was his inability to follow the mission and work of Jesus beyond the boundary of death. For him the mission of Jesus was an earthly kingdom (Acts 1:6) — how, then, could Jesus retire to heaven (ὑπάγω) ; and how could there be a way to this kingdom that would lead via heaven? So Thomas grows down-hearted like one who is lost in the dark; he heaves a great sigh and tells Jesus: You think we know, but really it all seems dark: this your going away and our knowing the road.

6) But the case of Thomas was not nearly as bad as he felt it was. Thomas and the rest knew more than they thought they knew. It was rather their sadness that dimmed their eyes. Jesus had not attributed too much to them; Thomas credited himself and the rest with too little. **Jesus says to Thomas, I myself am the way and the truth and the life. No one comes to the Father except through me.** This he says, not as something new, but as something old, that they all most certainly know. Jesus needs only to restate it for them in all its simplicity; all they need to do is to fix their minds upon these simple facts, then their misgivings will disappear. First, the simple fact about the way; secondly, the equally simple fact about the destination, both that of Jesus and of the disciples, together with this way as the only one to that destination.

Here is another I AM. How simple all this is! "I myself (ἐγώ with strong emphasis) am the way." Because "the way" is figurative, Jesus adds two literal terms, "the truth, the life," to define "the way." He does more, he defines "I am the way" by the δι' ἐμοῦ, "through me," and shows that "way" is to be understood as means: Jesus is the means for reaching the Father. In all simplicity he also combines "the way" as thus made plain with the destination Thomas thought he did not know. This way leads "to the Father," to his heavenly presence, the very place to which Jesus now goes (v. 2). Stated in one proposition, the mission of Jesus is to bring his disciples to the Father above. In simple words Jesus here summarizes all his teaching (doctrine) and all his work.

Koegel preaches: He does not say, "*I show* you the way," like a second Moses; but, "*I am* the way." Nor, "*I have* the truth," like another Elijah; but, "*I am* the truth." Not only, "*I lead* unto life," as one of his apostles; but, "*I am* the life." The emphasis is on ἐγώ, Jesus, the Word become flesh, the Son of the identical essence with the Father and born of the virgin, sent and come on his mission as the one Mediator between God and man, in all that he is and that he does. The moment we discount this Ego and make it less, that moment we also empty the three predicates of their content. Jesus as the way bridges a chasm. If the bridge lacks as little as an inch of reaching across, it plunges down and is not a bridge but a wreck. It may have been intended to be a bridge, but it is a wreck nonetheless. All three predicates have the article: *the* way, *the* truth, *the* life. This means that the subject and the predicates are both identical and interchangeable — a most illuminating and valuable point; see the many examples in R. 768, etc. Jacob saw "the way" in the ladder of his dream. Jesus describes it: "And I, if I be lifted up from the earth, will draw all men unto me," 12:32. Isaiah contrasts it with our own ways: "All we like sheep have gone astray; we have turned every one *to his own way*," 53:6. Only this ONE WAY takes us to the Father. The astounding thing is that this way is a person, this one person. This is not a dead road that one travels with his own strength, but a way such as never existed on earth, that picks us up in its arms and carries us to the destination. The figure falls short of the reality, like so many figures in the Scriptures which are able to picture only one point of the reality. This way, we may venture to say, is like a vast stream which takes our little boat and with its flood-power bears it to the ocean.

Because the way is this one great person, all is clear as to travelling this way. Only in one fashion

can this one person be the way for us to the Father:
by faith in him alone, by entrusting ourselves completely to him, by forsaking all other ways (means)
for reaching God and heaven. *Concordia Triglotta,*
55, 10; 1085, 66.

With καί "the way *and* the truth *and* the life" are
piled on top of each other. The three are, indeed, distinct, each concept having its own content, and yet they
are linked together, each making clearer the other, the
two literal terms especially shedding light on the original figurative term. The two "and" thus do not join
diverse or mutually exclusive terms; all three are also
predicates of the same ἐγώ. The proper order, moreover, is that "the truth" should follow "the way," and
then should come "the life."

"I myself am the truth" and thus "I am the way."
We at once see that this means far more than that
Jesus is truthful, every word of his being the honest
expression of his thought. Nor is he merely of the
truth, illumined and purified by it, his heart being
devoted to truth (18:37 last sentence). If this were
all, Jesus could not be "the way." Jesus is the actual
embodiment of the truth. He is ἡ ἀλήθεια, the very
reality of all God's grace toward us sinners, of all
God's plans of grace and their execution, of all God's
gifts of grace in those plans. The law could be given
by a human mediator like Moses, but the grace and
the truth could not merely be given, they actually came
(ἐγένετο) through the living person of Jesus Christ,
1:17. Moses could give manna, but the actual Bread
of Life descended in the Son Jesus. "The truth" is,
of course, soteriological only. Jesus as "the truth"
or reality in this sense is for our apprehension, to
know and to trust in one inward spiritual act. Every
lie and deception we ought to spurn, but to know and to
receive in fullest confidence the actual reality of God's
blessed grace in Jesus ought to be the delight of our

souls.   For this reality is "the way" (objective) to get
to the Father above, and our faith in this reality is the
manner in which this way carries us (subjective) to
the Father.

Already this is enough, and yet it is not enough.
This way, this reality, is "I myself," Jesus, a person,
this divine Person, and not merely as a divine Being
but in our flesh and together with all his work.   "I
myself am the life," ἡ ζωή.   Not merely ἡ ψυχή, a soul or
breath animating a body, and life in that sense.   There
are many ψυχαί before us but only one ζωή, which word
is never pluralized.   God is himself "life" in his very
existence and nature; but when Jesus, our Mediator,
calls himself "the life," this is soteriological with reference to us.   He is the one and only source of blessed
existence and life for us.   In our sin is death, i. e., the
separation from God.   Left to ourselves, we should
remain in this separation forever, dead beyond hope.
In the person of Jesus God sent us "the life."   Through
himself Jesus abolishes the separation and once more
unites us with God.   This union kindles the ζωή in us,
so that we again have "the life eternal"; see 3:15, 16.
How is this union accomplished?   How does Jesus
become ours, and we his?   The answer is the same:
by faith when he comes to us and kindles confidence
and trust in us.   Then he is in us, and we are in him.
Then God's ζωή again fills us, the blessed life that shall
live with God in heaven forever.   And thus "the way"
to the Father is the reception of Jesus who is "the life."

It is plain: "no one comes to the Father except
through me."   The present tense is timeless and universal.   Here is the destination, once more clearly
stated, "to the Father."   Let Thomas fix his eyes upon
it.   "To the Father," that is the kingdom forever.   To
bring us "to the Father," that is the mission of the
Son, the Messiah, Jesus.   Nothing can be higher,
greater, more blessed.   The three rays, "the way and

the truth and the life," come to a focus in the one phrase, "through me." "Through me," in what I am, offer, give, bestow; "through me," in what I actually make yours. Mediator (διά) = the person as the means.

Take away Jesus, and the way, the truth, and the life are gone; no way, no truth, no life are left. Acts 4:12; John 3:36; Mark 16:16, "He that believeth not shall be damned." All hope of God and heaven outside of Jesus is vanity and worse. "Except through me" is absolute and final.

7) We have two readings, 1) εἰ ἐγνώκατε ἐμέ, καὶ τὸν πατέρα μου γνώσεσθε, 2) εἰ ἐγνώκειτε . . . ἂν ἤδειτε, with some variation in the latter. There is strong textual evidence for both. **If you have known me, also my Father you shall know.** "If you had known me, also my Father you would know." The first reading has a protasis of reality, which admits that the disciples have, indeed, known Jesus, with the perfect tense extending this knowledge to the present. And, surely, it is a fact and cheering for Jesus to state to the eleven in this hour that they have known him. Then Jesus promises that they shall also know the Father. Not that they do not know him at all, but they shall know him as fully as they know Jesus who has been their companion for over three years. This statement of Jesus fits in perfectly with the lament of Thomas, cheering him with a promise, and with the next statement which says when the disciples shall know the Father.

The second reading with its protasis of past unreality denies that the eleven have known Jesus and with its apodosis of present unreality tells them that by not having known Jesus they have failed in knowing the Father. This reading rebukes the eleven and not Thomas alone and does not join well with the next statement, that from now on the eleven know the Father — with not one word about knowing Jesus without whom the Father cannot be known. In 8:19 Jesus rebukes the Jews in this way with only this difference that 8:19 emphasizes the objects "me," "my Father," while here the emphasis would be on the verbs: "if you *had known* . . . you *would know.*" In addition, why the change of verbs, once ἐγνώκειτε and then ἤδειτε? The internal evidence is in favor of the first reading. Even when the protasis of the second is toned down to mean, "if you had *fully* known me," thus charging the eleven with only partial failure to know Jesus, the situation is not improved; for if the eleven know Jesus in part — as they surely did — by that token they would know also the Father in part. Besides, if a qualification is placed in the verb of the protasis, the same would have to be done with the verb of the apodosis.

The disciples have known Jesus — γινώσκειν to designate the knowledge of their experience with Jesus. The acknowledgment means much for the eleven in this depressing hour. The promise that they shall know (the identical verb — surely, no change of verbs is here in place) the Father with equal experience is at once explained. **From now on you do know him and have seen him.** The emphasis is on ἀπ᾽ ἄρτι, which does not mean: since the time when you first believed in me; nor since this moment in view of what I have just told you. "From now on" designates the great new period beginning with the events of this night and extending to all the great experiences about to follow in quick succession: the Father will give his Son into death, will raise him from the dead, will seat him at his right hand (Eph. 1:19-23), will have Jesus send the Spirit (14:26; 15:26; Acts 1:4). What an experience this will be for the eleven! They will know the Father as never before. While "from now on you do know" has the present tense, it naturally refers to the future and might equally (like the previous statement) have the future tense. But the present tense enables Jesus to add the perfect of the next verb (these two tenses matching), "from now on . . . you have seen him." After every one of the impending experiences the disciples will have to say, "We have seen the Father!" namely in every act done in Jesus. What a wealth of comfort for the eleven at this moment!

Most certainly, also in the past the disciples knew and saw the Father in what he had his Son do and say and in what the Father himself did (1:32, etc.; the Transfiguration; 12:28). By it they knew both Jesus and the Father. But now the climax of all this is at hand, the great acts for which Jesus had especially come (12:27). The revelation in these final acts would crown all that had preceded.

8) **Philip says to him, Show us the Father, and we are satisfied,** it suffices for us. Philip does not contradict, he only begs. On the one hand, note the great thing his faith regards Jesus as able to do: actually and visibly to show the Father to the disciples. On the other hand, see how slow Philip is to grasp what Jesus means when he speaks about knowing and seeing the Father. What a mixture! Did Philip think of receiving a theophany such as is mentioned in Exod. 24:9-11; 33:18, etc.? His thought seems to be that if Jesus in now leaving would thus visibly show them the Father, the disciples would be satisfied with this as the crowning revelation until the day when Jesus would return unto them. Such a vision of the Father would show them where Jesus is now going and where they, his disciples, are at last to arrive with Jesus' help. We see what Philip lacks: a comprehension of what the mission of Jesus really is for which the Father sent him.

9) Jesus is deeply pained by what Philip's words reveal. **Jesus says to him, For so long a time am**

I with you, and hast thou not known me, Philip?
The accusative is that of the extent of time; the present
εἰμί expresses past action still in progress, with an
adjunct of time to indicate this, although the English
prefers the perfect "have I been," R. 879.　The "am I"
is thus matched by the following perfect "hast thou not
known me," again using the verb to designate the
knowledge of experience.　Has this long association of
Jesus with his disciples been in vain?　When we think
of the night in which this was said, the poignancy of
the question is increased with its touching vocative at
the end.　Poor, blundering Philip little realized how
he was hurting Jesus.

Philip speaks about the Father, Jesus speaks about
himself.　How this applies the next word shows.
**He that has seen me has seen the Father.　How
dost thou say, Show us the Father?**　12:45.　Philip
wants to see the Father with his physical eyes, little
realizing that such sight would profit him nothing.
Jesus has shown Philip the Father in a far superior
way, so that he could see the Father with his spiritual
eyes and by such sight enter into full communion with
the Father.　Has all this been in vain?　Does Philip
want to repeat the question of the Jews in 8:19,
"Where is thy Father?"　To those unbelieving Jews
Jesus had to reply that if they had known him they
would have known his Father also, but, surely, Philip
believes.　How, then, can he ask such a question?

10)　**Dost thou not believe that I am in the
Father, and the Father is in me?**　10:38.　Yes,
most surely Philip does believe this great fact — he
has seen it with the eyes of faith.　This question will
make him fully conscious of his faith, and he will regret
asking a question that is not in harmony with this
faith.

In order to make this oneness of himself with the
Father altogether clear and to correct any lingering

doubt or misconception in the minds of the eleven, Jesus again points to the constant evidence and manifestation of this oneness which is ever open to the eyes of all who are not determined for ulterior reasons to reject Jesus. **The utterances which I speak to you I utter not from myself; moreover, the Father abiding in me does his works.** Jesus here repeats 7:16; 8:26-28; 12:49, etc.; but now his object is to clarify a faith that at the moment does not see clearly. The very utterances (ῥήματα not λόγοι) by which Jesus expresses his thought (hence λέγω) he utters (hence λαλῶ) not "from himself," as being devised like the utterances of men by their own minds. This negation implies the affirmation: My utterances are derived from the Father; they are really his. This is clear evidence of the oneness of Jesus with the Father. Every time Jesus opens his mouth (λαλῶ, ῥήματα) to say something (λέγω), it is the Father who speaks through his mouth. Not that Jesus is a phonograph or an automaton. Then he and the Father would be anything but one, he would be nothing. This oneness and identity of even the very utterance evidences a oneness of the two persons concerned. For Jesus is not like the prophets who must say, "Thus saith the Lord," showing that God uses them only as instruments and messengers. Quite the opposite. When Jesus opens his lips, he, indeed, speaks (λαλῶ and λέγω), every word and utterance is truly his; but what he says and the words he employs, every word and utterance, are the Father's own thought and speech. The two speak as one because they are one, Jesus in the Father, the Father in Jesus.

Here, too, we see the highest type of true inspiration which is never anything but verbal. The very ῥήματα, the very λαλεῖν, coming from Jesus' lips are the Father's utterances and uttering. Only by giving Jesus and the Father who speaks with Jesus' mind and lips the direct lie can verbal inspiration be abolished.

With a copulative δέ Jesus adds the other evidence, that of his works. Now the statement is positive: "Moreover, the Father abiding in me (μένων, with the thought of never leaving Jesus, ever in him) does his works." We need to hesitate only between the two readings αὐτοῦ and αὐτός, "his works," the Father's, and "the Father himself"; the effect is minor. These works are the miracles especially. Who does them? The Father; but the Father as abiding in Jesus by virtue of the oneness of the Father and the Son. What was said with regard to the utterances is also true with regard to the works. The negative "not from myself" is matched by the positive "abiding in me"; the first person, "I speak" and "I utter," is matched by the third, "the Father does." The sense is: the utterances are "not from myself" but from the Father abiding in me; likewise, the works are done by the Father "abiding in me" not from myself. With the reading αὐτοῦ the Father would do the works of Jesus as *his own* (the Father's); with the reading αὐτός he "himself" would do them just as he speaks the words. The genitive is the best attested reading.

Some are inclined to identify the utterances with the works, regarding every divine utterance as a deed, even also as the miracles are always combined with words. This may pass. In fact, it is a necessary reminder in an age when the utterances of Jesus are so often treated lightly. But in the present connection this identification cannot stand. In 5:19 and 30 works and words are distinct; in 10:25 and 32 Jesus relies on the works as the ultimate evidence; so he also does here.

11) **Go on believing me that I am in the Father, and the Father in me. Yet if not, on account of the very works go on believing me.** The tense of both imperatives is essential to the sense: πιστεύετε, go on with an action already begun, R. 856 (especially regarding this verb). Jesus deals with the eleven as

being believers. The only question is the ground for their believing, believing especially that Jesus is in the Father, and the Father in him, so that whoever hears and sees Jesus' works sees the Father himself in these words and these works. The word and testimony of Jesus should be all-sufficient for their continuance in this faith. "Go on believing me" means believing that I am speaking the truth regarding this oneness of myself with the Father. In 10:38 the order is reversed: the Father in me, and I in him, because there the issue is whether Jesus has come from the Father; here Jesus is named first because in him the disciples are to see the Father. Even points like this are absolutely exact.

But even for the disciples, when their faith must be fortified against misgivings and doubt, Jesus uses the ultimate evidence, the works. These works themselves, αὐτά, *fuer sich*, as such, so exhibit the fact that Jesus is in the Father, and the Father in him, that for the sake of these works taken by themselves the disciples would have to go on believing that what Jesus says about himself and the Father is, indeed, the truth. Recall 7:31 in regard to the effect of the works upon the multitude at the feast; also 11:47.

When Jesus makes this appeal to the works, it must not be urged that they would thus stand alone, hang, as it were, in the air when separated from the utterances of Jesus. For Jesus says: Believe me, i. e., what I say, because of the works as such. Always the works establish the words, and vice versa. Yet always at the ultimate point the works are decisive. With regard to words one may argue, with regard to deeds only one thing is left to be done: to see what they are and to believe, or to shut the eyes (9:39-41) and to disbelieve. See what the deed did for the beggar in 9:31-33.

6. The Condition, Full of Comfort, of Jesus' Disciples after his Departure, 12-31

Jesus goes to the Father and to the Father's house; the disciples shall also be brought thither. They know the place and the way; they have seen the Father. But what in the meantime? Jesus leaves the disciples the most comforting assurances and promises.

12) **Amen, amen, I say to you, He that believes in me, the works that I am doing, he, too, shall do, and greater than these he shall do; because I am going to the Father.** What a mighty assurance, what a magnificent promise and prospect, what abounding comfort! So this is what the departure brings to those left behind! Verity and authority are again combined (see 1:51). In v. 11 πιστεύετέ μοι refers to believing what Jesus says; here ὁ πιστεύων εἰς ἐμέ means believing in the person of Jesus as the way, the truth, and the life (v. 6), one in essence with the Father (v. 10), the Son of God, the Mediator, and the Redeemer. The substantivized present participle characterizes the person as one who continues in this faith. Note the universality of the designation: every such believer. To him this promise is made. The object is placed forward with great emphasis: "the works that I am doing," the very works of which Jesus spoke in v. 10, 11, namely the mighty miracles. The present tense is justified by Luke 22:51. Over against ἐγώ is set κἀκεῖνος, with emphasis again taking up the subject. Did the works which Jesus does astound the disciples — in the days to come they themselves shall do the same works. The future is categorical: ποιήσει — no "if" or "and" about it, and the verb is repeated: "he, too, shall do."

As though this were not enough Jesus adds, "and greater than these he shall do." Can there be greater? Indeed, far greater: convert sinners by God's grace, carry the gospel to the ends of the earth, save souls for life eternal, 4:35-38; 10:16; 12:24 and 32; and the story of the Acts. These are greater because in miracles only omnipotence and goodness are revealed but in saving souls all the grace of God in Christ Jesus. The great works deal with the material, the greater with the spiritual (5:20, 21). For these greater works Jesus leaves the disciples behind.

The reason and ground for this promise is: "because I am going to the Father." Without this exaltation of Jesus no promise of any kind could be made and fulfilled. The present tense is used because the going has virtually begun. He returns to the Father as one having completed his mission, and thus it is possible that, with redemption accomplished, the greater works of the gospel of redemption can begin. This causal clause shuts out the misconception as though these works of the disciples would make them equal to Jesus, one also in essence with the Father. For only through Jesus himself in whom they believe, only through him and his work and exaltation will these disciples, and only as disciples and believers, do what he promises to them. Here, too, is the answer to those who insist that believers today must do miracles such as Jesus and the apostles and others performed in the first church. They do not have in mind all believers but only their special "healers" with their shams and imitations. The miracles of Jesus and those of the apostles were absolutely genuine. And yet these great works were wrought only in support of the greater works until the time when no further supporting works were needed, and when those already wrought and standing as credentials for all time were all the support needed. This is how Jesus, who made his promise, redeemed it, and who is there to demand more?

13) **And whatever you shall ask in my name this I will do, in order that there may be glorified the Father in the Son.** This is not a continuation

of the ὅτι clause in v. 12, "because I am going to the Father, and (because) whatever you," etc. It is unlike John to extend a subordinate clause in such fashion, even attaching two other sub-subordinate clauses. By all tokens this is an independent sentence. Let us note that v. 12 and 13, 14 are parallel, purposely worded thus: first two emphatic ποιήσει (to indicate what the believer shall do), then ποιήσω (to indicate what Jesus shall do). This parallel should not be destroyed by unwarranted subordination.

Furthermore, we should not restrict the indefinite ὅ τι (R. 727) and the constative aorist αἰτήσητε to power and help from Jesus for the performance of miracles and of the greater works. Why this peculiar restriction of an indefinite pronoun when, by promising much more, it surely promises all help needed for these works? Moreover, it is a misconception to look upon the miracles as answers to prayers. In the entire story of Acts no miracle occurs as such an answer. When Peter prayed at Joppa he did not ask for the life of Dorcas; he prayed to know Christ's will in regard to her. All the apostolic miracles are wrought as direct gifts from Christ, on intimation and direction from the Spirit, whereas the miracles of Jesus were wrought on his own initiative and volition in the execution of his mission (very plain, for instance, in Matt. 8:2). All the apostolic miracles are, indeed, wrought "in the name of Jesus"; but this phrase is not used in a prayer to God, asking him for the miracle, but in a command to the person on whom the miracle is wrought. Even the greater works of the apostles and the believers are not to be restricted to answers to prayer. At Pentecost the 3,000 were not converted in response to prayer. Consider Acts 1:8 and Rom. 1:16. While prayer of various kinds is in place in connection with our preaching and our teaching, this our work is done at the behest of Jesus, by the power of his Word, and the results are due to that power alone not to our pleading and prayer.

Thus the first promise with which Jesus leaves his disciples is that they shall do the great and greater works through the power of their exalted Lord. Then follows the second promise: all their prayers shall be answered. Both promises are even doubled. Certainly ὅ τι . . . τοῦτο, "whatever . . . this very thing" is broad. It includes far more than what pertains to our spiritual work among men; it covers every personal need of the disciples, both temporal and spiritual; for instance, daily forgiveness of sin, daily bread — think of the last four petitions of the Lord's Prayer. Yet a natural restriction enters into all these askings: no believer will ask what conflicts with his own faith and status as a believer, or with the purpose and the will of his exalted Lord. He can and will ask nothing "in my name" which is not covered by that name.

This important phrase does not mean: by my authority; in my stead; through my merits; in the element of my life; in my spirit and for my sake; etc. In all the connections in which this important phrase occurs τὸ ὄνομα denotes the revelation by which we know Jesus; see 1:12. This revelation covers his person as well as his work. It is concentrated in his titles, of which we have many, but it takes in all that makes these titles the shining designations that they are. And ἐν has its natural sense of sphere: "in union with," "in connection with." This ἐν draws a circle around the action of asking, the boundary is the ὄνομα. Hence not "on the basis of my name," "through my name," which would change the preposition. To pray in Jesus' name naturally involves faith in the revelation, also that the petition abide in the circle of that revelation. We may or may not use the formula, "in the name of Jesus," only so the heart and the prayer abide in the sacred sphere.

To ask in the name of Jesus implies that the prayer is directed to the Father, yet Jesus promises, "I will do this" that you ask.   This is not an incongruity but a revelation of what it means that Jesus returns to his Father.   His mission continues in his glorious heavenly state.   Thus the answer comes by the act of Jesus. He remains the Mediator, the Father answers through him.   Moreover, these answers are *opera ad externa,* all of which *sunt indivisa aut communa,* attributed to all or to any one of the three Persons.   Jesus says, "I will do" what you ask, preferring this verb to, "I will give or grant," because it matches "shall do" in v. 12, predicated there of believers.   Yet "I will do" is volitive.   Our doing depends on him, hence the believer "shall do" the promised works; Jesus' doing depends on himself and his own will, hence "I will do" what I promise.

He will do what he thus promises, "in order that there may be glorified the Father in the Son."   The English is awkward but it brings out the emphasis which is on the verb.   The divine attributes of love, grace, mercy, power, and wisdom are to be displayed in these answers to prayer, so that we may see and feel them and praise God's name.   Here Jesus again calls himself "the Son."   "In" is not "through," διά, or *per,* although this, too, could be said.   "In" is again "in union with" the Son.   The circle which embraces the Son embraces the glorification of the Father as well. This union rests on the other, of which Philip is reminded in v. 10.   The essential *perichoresis* of the divine persons produces a *perichoresis* of their glory: in every glorious act of one person the other persons are equally glorified.   The disciples will have God's own Son in heaven to care for all their needs while they remain on earth, and all this care of the Son for them will reflect the glory of the Father in the Son. Greater assurance and comfort cannot be imagined by the disciples — and, let us add, by us.

14) This tremendous promise bears repeating, but in the repetition we have important changes. **If you shall ask me anything in my name, I myself will do it.** The textual evidence supports the retention of μέ, as well as of ἐγώ, in place of τοῦτο; with this the inner evidence agrees. The stress is no longer on *what* the disciples shall ask but now on *the person* who answers. To the silent implication that the disciples will direct their petitions to the Father (v. 13) there is now added the explicit statement that they will also direct them to Jesus, "if you shall ask me," etc. The enclitic pronoun has no emphasis and thus no contrast of this "me" with the Father. In v. 13 we have only an implication that it is the Father who is asked, for this is altogether usual; and likewise in v. 14 the enclitic μέ implies that asking Jesus is also usual and in the nature of the case. The objection that, after the Father is indicated as the one to whom the petitions are addressed, Jesus cannot also be so indicated, is pointless, because the very thing Jesus wants to say is that he as well as the Father may be so addressed. If, however, it is assumed that the Scriptures show no warrant for praying to Jesus, this dogmatical assumption, lowering the person of the Son, is more than answered by the Scriptures themselves in Acts 2:21; 7:59, etc.; 9:14 and 21; 22:16; Rom. 10:12, etc.; I Cor. 1:2; II Cor. 12:8; II Tim. 2:22.

When petitions are addressed to Jesus, they still remain "in my name," and this revelation of Jesus naturally includes his true relation to the Father (v. 10). Whichever person we address, the one is always in the other. Now, however, Jesus promises with the fullest emphasis on himself, "I myself (ἐγώ) will do it." In v. 13 ποιήσω does not stress the subject, "I *will do* it." To this Jesus now adds, "*I myself* will do it." Of course, there is no conflict with 15:16, where the Father does the giving. The persons are equal, and their gracious will is one. "I myself" does not mean, "even if the Father would not." This ἐγώ is for the comfort of the eleven as they see Jesus departing from them. When he is gone, they have him in heaven as the one who will himself do for them what they ask whether they address their requests to the Father or to him. Both ὅ τι ἄν (v. 13) and ἐάν (v. 14) expect the disciples to ask, αἰτεῖν, *peto,* the action of a suppliant, a beggar, etc., (never used by Jesus regarding himself toward the Father), as distinguished from ἐρωτᾶν, *rogo* and *interrogo,* the finer term (never used regarding our prayers, always used with reference to Jesus toward the Father), Trench, *New Testament Synonyms,* more correct C.-K. 91.

15) Great are the promises made to the faith of the disciples (greater works, answers to prayer). Yet greater promises are yet to follow (the gift of the Paraclete, the *unio mystica* with the Father and the Son). For the promised works and answers to prayer the main subjective condition is faith; hence v. 12, "he that believes in me," in substance the same as, "if you believe in me." For the promised **Paraclete** and the *unio mystica* the subjective condition must be expanded to include also the fruit of faith which is love to Jesus with the evidence of its actuality; hence now, "if you love me," in substance the same as, "he that loves me." In this advancing love, faith is not left out even in thought, quite the contrary: no love without the presence of faith. He who does not trust cannot possibly love.

If you love me, my precepts will you guard. He is speaking to believers and he expects their love (ἐάν). And this is ἀγαπᾶν, the love of intelligent comprehension and purposeful devotion, not mere φιλεῖν, liking and personal preference. While the condition expects this love, it yet bids the disciples to question themselves whether they have it and show it as they should. The tense is very properly present, "are loving" in constancy.

The existence of love for Jesus is easy to determine, "my precepts will you guard." The entire statement is like ·an axiom; nor is there an exception. The ἐντολαί are not admonitions but *Aufgaben;* and certainly not "commandments" in any Mosaic sense. Luther writes of them, "that you faithfully preach concerning me, have my Word and Sacrament laid upon you, keep love and unity among yourselves for my sake, and suffer with patience whatever on this account comes upon you . . . For I do not mean to be a Moses to drive and to plague you with threats and terrors, but I give you such precepts as you can and will keep without commanding, if you, indeed, love me." Erlangen edition, 49, 131-2. These precepts are the gospel behests of Jesus. The idea of τηρεῖν is watchful care, to cherish and to hold as a treasure, to take all pains not to lose; or to let others violate; see 8:51. Whose heart thus cherishes the precepts will, of course, "keep" or "obey" them, although this is more the resultant effect. We must read the future indicative, not, as some texts do, the aorist imperative. Nor should we narrow the statement to cover only the official work of the apostles. Though addressed to them, it is as broad as v. 13 and includes all believers like v. 12.

16) The thought connection is not that in order to love Jesus and to cherish his precepts the disciples will be endowed with the Paraclete. The very title of the Spirit here used forbids such a connection. Besides, we have the parallel in the second promised gift, the *unio mystica,* where again the thought is not and cannot be that in order to love Jesus and to keep his precepts the Father's love and the indwelling of the Father and the Son will be granted to the disciples (v. 23). Verse 15 describes the disciples as true lovers of Jesus, and v. 16 promises to these his true lovers the two great gifts mentioned. They who dearly love Jesus and who now see him departing are not to be left orphans, shifting for themselves as best they can; they

shall have a substitute for the familiar presence of
Jesus, another Paraclete at their side; in fact, also the
Father and Jesus will come and dwell with them in
invisible presence. That these divine presences will
increase the faith and the love of the eleven is not said;
only this is said, that for them as lovers of Jesus these
presences will surely follow.

**And I myself will request the Father, and
another Paraclete shall he give to you, in order
that he may be with you forever, the Spirit of the
truth, etc.** Jesus himself will have the Paraclete
sent, the disciples need not fear that their need will
be forgotten. Here, to mark the fact that Jesus and the
Father are equals, we have ἐρωτᾶν, "to request"; compare
on the difference from αἰτεῖν in v. 14. The curious question might be asked why, when all three Persons of the
Godhead have the same mind and the same will, the
same love and the same grace for men, the Son should
yet request the Father to send the Spirit; or the Father
should send the Son. Why would not the Son come
of his own accord, the Spirit likewise; or the Father
send the Spirit without request as he sent the Son; or
the Son himself send the Spirit as the Father sent him?
Luther tries to penetrate the council of the Trinity as
regards the Father and the Son by saying that in v.
13, 14 "I will do" refers to the divine nature of Jesus,
while here "I myself will request" refers to his human
nature; "so that ever this article of faith remains
certain and clear, that in this person, Christ, there is
not utter deity nor utter humanity, but both divine and
human nature in one person, undivided," Erlangen
edition, 49, 135. But this by no means solves the mystery. It forms the heavenly background of the entire
plan and the work of salvation. This is nothing less
than the mystery of the Trinity itself, in which we do
not see three Fathers but only one; not three Sons but
only one; not three Spirits but only one. One in
essence, the three are yet diverse. They work to

one end, yet, as in this case, One requests, One gives, One comes. We know certain divine facts, which transcend all human analogies and categories. We can do but one thing: abide by the facts and their blessedness and rest content.

We are not willing to regard "I will request" as implying a condition, "if I request," as R. 1023 thinks we should. "I will request" and "he shall give" are coordinate acts, although the one is the response to the other. The Spirit is a gift from the Father just as is the Son (3:16). We may even say that the Father, too, gives himself to us when he comes and dwells in us (v. 23). The verb δώσει is pure grace.

Jesus calls the Spirit "another Paraclete," implying that he himself was the first Paraclete of the disciples when he walked in their midst. The word is sometimes used in the sense of "advocate" in a court of justice, and John uses the word in this sense in I John 2:1, where he speaks of Jesus as our Advocate with the Father when we sin. Demosthenes uses the word with reference to friends of the accused, who personally urge the judge to decide in his favor. Yet the word was not restricted to courts of law but had a wide range of use. It does not occur frequently in literature, and M.-M., 485, find little enough of it in the papyri. Even Deissmann, *Light from the Ancient East*, 339, etc., finds support only for "advocate." It was used quite freely in ordinary speech, since even the Jews had it in transliteration both in Hebrew and in Aramaic, even as Jesus here employs it in the latter language. In form Παράκλητος is a verbal adjective, one called to another's side to aid him, and the term is derived from the passive perfect παρακεκλῆσθαι, not from the active present παρακαλεῖν, and is thus not the same as ὁ παρακαλῶν, C.-K., 572, etc. References to Philo are beside the mark the moment we note how the word is used in our Gospel. The translation "Comforter"

adopts Luther's *Troester,* which loses the passive sense
and gives only a general idea of what is meant.

The Spirit, as the Paraclete, takes the place of Jesus
at the side of the disciples; he brings all things to their
remembrance which Jesus said to them, 14:26; he
testifies to the disciples concerning Jesus, 15:26; Jesus
sends him to the disciples (16:7), and he shall glorify
Jesus, taking what is his and showing it unto them
(16:14). It is plain that the disciples do not call this
Paraclete to their side, the Father and Jesus call him
to the disciples' side, they give (14:16) and send him
(16:7) to the disciples. The agents in the passive
verbal are the Father and the Son. In these connections the Spirit is shown, not as conducting our case
before God, but as attending to God's case before us.
Thus he is, indeed, "another" Paraclete, one like Jesus
who revealed God to the disciples, who showed them
the Father, and who led them to the Father. With
the departure of Jesus the Spirit will assume this work,
naturally on the basis of what Jesus had already done
and so as to complete it all. Moreover, the Father's
purpose in giving this other Paraclete is that "he may
be with you forever," εἰς τὸν αἰῶνα. In this phrase αἰών
denotes unlimited time and thus eternity, here with εἰς
eternity *a parte post* (from now forward). C.-K., 93.
The stay of Jesus was limited, not so the stay of this
other Paraclete. Compare and correlate in v. 16, 17:
μεθ᾿ ὑμῶν, in your company; παρ᾿ ὑμῖν, within you — the
last being the most intimate. Since the Spirit has been
given and remains forever, it is a misconception to
speak of or to pray for a new Pentecost.

17) **The Spirit of the truth, whom the world
cannot receive; for it does not behold him nor know
him. You know him; for he remains with you
and shall be in you.** The designation "another
Paraclete" does not yet name this Companion who
will always be with the disciples. He is now both
named and characterized, "the Spirit of the truth,"

and the characterization is one that helps to explain
why the world does not receive him, and how the disciples, in contrast with the world, have him in their
hearts. The tenses are present, timeless, because the
statements are doctrinal facts applying to any time.
But the last tense is future, ἔσται, reverting to δώσει in
v. 16, with the coming day of Pentecost in mind. "Of
the truth" is ethically qualitative; the Spirit, the third
Person of the Godhead, belongs to the truth, being
wholly bound up with it. Of course, he has also other
attributes, but this is the one pertinent in the present
connection. Luther's explanation, "a truthful, certain
Spirit, who does not deceive or fail," touches only the
fringe. Luther is thinking of the devil who makes
men certain by his lies which he palms off as truth,
until too late they find they have been deceived. Jesus
himself describes the ἀλήθεια to which the Spirit is
wedded: "Howbeit when he, the Spirit of truth, is
come, he will guide you into all truth: for he shall not
speak of himself (inventions of his own) ; but whatsoever he shall hear (from the Father and the Son),
that shall he speak; and he will show you things to
come. He shall glorify me (who am the Truth, v. 6) ;
for he shall receive of mine, and shall show it unto you.
All things that the Father hath are mine; therefore
said I, that he shall take of mine, and shall show it unto
you," 16:13-15. This "truth" consists in the saving
realities, which the Spirit possesses, bears, and
imparts.

Compare 1:32 on the way in which the Trinity is
known and believed by the Jews on the basis of evidence from the Old Testament, so that Father, Son,
and Spirit are freely mentioned and need no proof or
explanation at any time.

Being what he is, the Spirit of the truth, the
bearer of this specific divine and saving truth, "the
world," also being what it is, namely the opposite of
the disciples and resolved to remain that, cannot receive

the Spirit (λαβεῖν to express the single act indicated).
"Ye are of your father the devil. . . . He abode
not in the truth, because there is no truth in him," 8:44.
Just because Jesus told the Jews the truth, they
believed not, 8:45; if he had told them lies, they would
have delighted to believe him. The Spirit has the
same experience. Jesus is not speaking of the inability
that inheres in all men because of their sinful state;
if he meant this, no man could be saved. He speaks
of the inability of wilful obduracy, which brings about
a state that is still worse, one in which men neither
"behold" nor "know" the Spirit although he is present
with all his grace. They are not even aware (θεωρεῖν)
that it is the Spirit who speaks in the Word and works
in the church. Blinded by the devil's delusion, they
have only false and foolish explanations for the Spirit's
manifestations (Acts 2:13). Naturally they also lack
all experimental knowledge (γινώσκειν) of the Spirit and
his gracious power. In brief, the new Companion of
the disciples will be as foreign to the obdurate world as
Jesus was when he walked with them.

Without an adversative particle but with an
emphatic ὑμεῖς Jesus says of the disciples, "You know
him" with the inner knowledge of experience. For
them this one verb suffices, and there is no need to
speak of their also beholding or of their also receiving
the Spirit. Instead, Jesus points out what causes this
knowledge in the disciples, "because he remains with
you," παρά, at your side, as your Paraclete, "and will
be in you," ἐν, in inner spiritual union with you, in your
very hearts and souls. Beside the present tenses with
their timelessness is set the one final future tense,
which accords with εἰς τὸν αἰῶνα in v. 16. What it means
"to know the Spirit" is thus made perfectly clear. One
who is ever at our side to guide, help, teach, and bless
us with the Word, One who is actually in our very
hearts to mold our minds and our wills with his Word,
him we cannot help but know with deepest intimacy

(γινώσκειν). Every bit of faith, love, obedience, every holy motion, delight in God and his Word, its promises, comfort, etc., is both a mark of the Spirit's presence in us and of our knowledge of who and what he really is.

We must say that the eleven already had the Spirit in their hearts when Jesus spoke these words. "You yourself know him" was true in its present sense. No saving faith was ever wrought even in the Old Testament without the Spirit. Jesus himself had planted the Spirit in the hearts of his disciples; their experience of the Spirit had begun. And yet all their contact with the Spirit had been only through Jesus and through him as being visibly present. This is where the great change would come in the departure of Jesus and in the coming of the Spirit. One Paraclete would take the place of the other. And this not silently and secretly but openly, miraculously, on Pentecost. Compare 7:39. The disciples would have a wondrously new knowledge of the Spirit. The restriction, that all that Jesus here says to the disciples applies to them only in their apostolic office, hence is not applicable to the rank and file of believers, is unwarranted as far as the words themselves go and is certainly contradicted by the number of those who received the Spirit at Pentecost, who were by no means the eleven alone; compare also Acts 10:44.

18) When Jesus is transferred to heaven he will request that the Spirit be sent to the disciples as another Paraclete. But when he now adds: **I will not leave you orphans,** this does not mean that the Spirit's presence as substituting for Jesus will provide them as children with another father; for Jesus at once adds: **I am coming to you.** He will not leave them orphans because after his leaving he himself will come back to them. Only a little while will they be orphaned. What coming does Jesus refer to? The answer is given in the last clause of v. 21 and again in v. 23. The death of Jesus will not be like that

of a father whose little children are then left father-less orphans. The death of Jesus means his return, a return for a higher and a richer union than that before his death and departure. This return is con-nected with the gift of the Spirit. We must not break the thought in passing from v. 17 to 18. Jesus, indeed, does not identify himself with the Spirit so that the Spirit's presence with the disciples is the pres-ence of Jesus; but he does connect his coming with that of the Spirit.

As far as the appearances of Jesus to the disciples after his resurrection are concerned, these have a special import as abounding proofs of his actual resur-rection and of his glorification. As such they are transient, encompassed within forty days. These appearances are not the real fulfillment of "I am coming to you." For then, after all, at the time of the ascension the disciples would have been left orphans save for the foster care of the Spirit. Others identify "I am coming to you" with v. 3, "I am coming again," and make the former, like the latter, refer to the last day. But the connection of the two statements is entirely different. Moreover, then, indeed, the dis-ciples would be left orphans by the departure of Jesus. Nor can we argue that, if Jesus would at once come to the disciples, he would not need to send them the Spirit. For Jesus is so far removed from such thoughts that he now tells the disciples that after his death they will have and will enjoy more than they had before. They will have the Spirit with all that the Spirit is able to do on the strength of the completed redemptive work of Jesus; moreover, they will also have Jesus, not indeed as they had him when he came to work out our redemption, but in a far higher man-ner, using all his divine attributes, in a spiritual pres-ence, like that of the Spirit and combined with him. Matt. 28:20.

19) And this will occur very soon. **Yet a little while and the world no longer beholds me, but you do behold me.** The little while had shrunk to a few hours. The beholding of the world is, of course, only the one of which the world is capable, namely physical sight. Over against the world Jesus places the disciples; "but you do behold me." In the nature of the case and because of the strong contrast this is a different kind of beholding, one accomplished only with spiritual eyes. Jesus is not speaking of his appearances during the forty days. The tenses are present, dating forward from "the little while," but they reach forward indefinitely.

Because I myself live you, too, shall live, ought to be read as an independent sentence and not as the reason why the disciples will still behold Jesus. The causal ὅτι points forward not backward, since the pronouns are so emphatic: ἐγώ, "I myself," paralleled with καὶ ὑμεῖς, "you, too," with all the emphasis resting on these subjects, and with the two verbs also being made parallel. Jesus says that because *he* lives *the disciples, too,* shall live. To be sure, with both Jesus and the disciples living, they will have no difficulty in beholding him. This is the general sense of the statements themselves, the one following the other; and not the force of ὅτι, which belongs only in the second statement. The fact that Jesus and the disciples thus live reaches much farther than their beholding him after his death and his exaltation. This is why Jesus can send them the Paraclete, why he does not leave them orphans, why he comes to them. The καί belongs to ὑμεῖς, "you too," not to the verb, "you shall also live." With Jesus living, it is impossible that his disciples should fall into death.

A glance at C.-K., 470, or any other good dictionary eliminates the notion that ζῆν means "come to life" and not "to live." In fact, when this verb is used regarding the disciples it means "to live in possession of the true ζωή, born in regeneration and connected with God through Christ's redemption." "No wonder that the Scripture should know no higher word than ζωή to set forth either the blessedness of God or the blessedness of the creature in communion with God." Trench, *New Testament Synonyms*, 1, 133. The best commentary on ὅτι ἐγὼ ζῶ is v. 6: ἐγώ εἰμι ἡ ζωή, "I myself am the Life." This clears away the interpretation that Jesus here says, "Because I myself rise from the dead, you, too, shall rise from the dead," I at once, you at the last day; that, likewise, his coming to them (v. 18) and their beholding him (v. 19) means only at the last day when they, too, arise from the dead. What Jesus says is that he lives though he dies; he is the very Life itself, which even swallows up death; and this forms the absolute guarantee (ὅτι) that also the disciples "shall live," shall share in Jesus' ζωή, shall have and continue to have "life eternal" (3:15, 16). Here, too, lies the real explanation for the change in tenses, regarding Jesus the timeless present ζῶ, "I live," while regarding the disciples the future ζήσεσθε, "you shall live." Since Jesus speaks of the time after the "little while," he might have used the future also regarding himself, "I myself shall live." Then, however, the relation between his living and that of the disciples marked by ὅτι would be less clear; for we should think only of his future life. The significant present tense "I live," spoken in the face of death, with its note of timelessness, conveys the thought that no death affects his life, and that thus because of their connection with him the disciples, too, shall continue (future tense) in the spiritual life they have already obtained from him. It should, however, be added that Jesus speaks, not of his life as it inheres in him as the ever-living eternal Logos, irrespective of his incarnation, but of this life of his as made a fountain of life through his incarnation and his redemptive death for all who become his disciples by faith.

20) **In that day you shall know that I myself am in my Father, and you yourselves in me, and I myself in you.** The promises with which Jesus is taking leave of the disciples are carried a step farther. A further great realization awaits them. "In that day" refers to Pentecost. Even if ἡμέρα is taken in the broader sense of season or time, this time starts with Pentecost when the Father "shall give" (v. 16) them the Paraclete, and when Jesus "comes" (v. 18) to the disciples; also v. 3. In that day and from then on they shall know by their own experience (γνώσεσθε) two mighty facts.

The first is "that I myself am in the Father," an abbreviation of v. 10 which adds, "and the Father in me." The abbreviation is natural, since the fuller statement is still in mind, and since the addition now follows, "I in you, and you in me." What Philip and the others are now bidden to believe (v. 10) on the evidence they have thus far had with Jesus in his state of humiliation, on that day they will actually realize when the Spirit descends upon them with miraculous manifestations, coming from the Father and from their exalted Lord. Then they will know in a marvelous new and direct way that he, with whom they had walked in his humiliation, whom they had seen risen in power from the dead, whom they had beheld lifted up in glory on high, is, indeed, true God, one with the Father, or as he states it, "I myself am in the Father." For us who were not present at Pentecost the miraculous manifestations of that day cannot be repeated; we have them only in the apostolic attestation, to which is added the abiding effect of the Spirit in the power and the grace of his Word. In this mediate way we, too, realize that the Son, our Savior Jesus, is "in the Father." For all the love, grace, mercy, light, comfort, joy, hope, and glory, as offered by the Father and the Son, is one. The two are not separate; each is in the other.

This realization is at once combined with another, its product and its proof. "You yourselves in me" through the Spirit poured out in that day, "you yourselves" cleansed, purified, filled with new life and power, joined thus to me with spiritual bonds in the blessed *unio mystica*. All this comes to us by the same Spirit working in us through the Word. Jesus is the circle (ἐν) in which we live, move, and have our being spiritually. Its counterpart is, "and I myself in you," we the circle (ἐν) which Jesus fills, joined inwardly to us in the *unio mystica*, possessing, guiding, governing, blessing us, heart, mind, faculties, members. This is how the exalted Jesus comes to us (v. 18).

Yet the three "in," while each has a double content, differ greatly. The "in" which encircles the Father and the Son tells of the interpenetration of two Persons of the Godhead, each equally filling the circle, in a mystery of being too profound for us even to grasp its fringe. We see only its radiant evidence as revealed in connection with the saving work of the Persons, and all we may do is to bow down in the dust and worship. The other two "in" are due only to divine grace. They encircle unequal persons: "You in me," because drawn into me by my grace; "I in you," because I enter into you by my grace. Again a wondrous interpenetration which only they who are involved know and feel. These "in" mean that we must be taken out of sin and death before we can be in Jesus; and that sin and death must be taken out of us before Jesus can be in us. The divine "in" has no degrees, it is absolute; our two "in" are with gradations, awaiting perfection above.

Those who place the fulfillment of the promises at the end of the world are compelled to do so also with this one; "in that day" is referred to the last day. The objections to this view already stated intensify themselves at this point and do so still more in v. 23.

21) The entire line of promises from v. 15 onward rests on the condition "if you love me." The

Scriptures are quite regular in emphasizing the love
of believers when benefactions are promised to them.
Jesus now recurs to this love, yet not in order to repeat
the condition, but in order to assure the disciples that
they are the ones referred to, and that their love shall
meet with a most wonderful response. **He that has
my precepts and guards them, he it is that loves me.**
This is a pertinent description of the true disciple
whom Jesus acknowledges as such over against the
world or any false disciple. The two participles are
combined under one article: ὁ ἔχων καὶ τηρῶν, for the characterizing actions are always combined. On ἐντολαί and
τηρεῖν see v. 15. The emphatic ἐκεῖνος takes up this subject, but by its emphasis conveys the thought, "he, and
he alone" is the one that loves me. The test is always
obvious and simple: a true disciple, one who really
loves Jesus, always does more than make protestations
or pretenses, he cherishes and guards every precept of
Jesus which he has by holding to it in his heart and
his life against all opposition. Because the predicate
is a participle it requires the article; at the same time
this makes the predicate identical and interchangeable
with the subject, R. 769. As in v. 12, Jesus now again
uses the third person singular with its universal note
— taking in all his believers (v. 12) and all his lovers
(v. 21). In v. 13 and on through v. 19 Jesus used the
second person plural, himself applying everything
directly to the eleven. Now, however, the third person
singular is retained through to v. 24, save for one relative clause in the final verse. The eleven will know
that they are meant.

All the promises hitherto made in this chapter, each
one grand and wonderful in itself, are so many
evidences of something far greater, namely divine love.
And this is subsequent love, which, when antecedent
love has kindled faith and love in us, delights to show
itself to the beloved in most intimate fashion.

And he that loves me with the love just indicated
**shall be loved by my Father, and I will love him
and will manifest myself to him.** The future tenses
refer to the day of Pentecost and thereafter. This
appears especially in the last verb; for the appearances
during the forty days were only preliminary manifestations to be followed by his constant presence, help,
and blessing in the spirit (v. 18). What this love of
the Father means Paul states in Rom. 8:28, and 32.
The fact that his love is stated with a passive verb
while that of Jesus is stated with an active verb is a
mere formal difference.

The verb ἐμφανίζω does not refer to revelations in a
special feeling of the nearness of Jesus, or to a consciousness of spiritual power (perhaps while the physical strength wanes), or to direct inner impressions of
Christ's glory in glimpses of the other world. These
are dangerous ideas, leading to autosuggestion, hallu-
cination, or fanaticism (*Schwærmerei*). Gerhard
points us away from this subjectivism to the objective
Word: "That is a salutary, practical manifestation of
Jesus Christ, when he implants spiritual motions into
the hearts of his believers and lovers: as when they
receive a living, believing impression of the divine love
from the mystery of the incarnation; when they understand the greatness of their sins from the mystery of
the passion, heartily lament them and are assured of
their forgiveness; when they draw an earnest longing
for heaven from the mystery of eternal life, etc. For
thus Christ manifests himself to the soul as the most
gracious Savior, as the most lovely Bridegroom, as
the most faithful Shepherd, as the most mighty King,
as the most wise Teacher, as the most ready Physician;
and by such manifestation faith, love, hope, patience,
and all Christian virtues are produced in the hearts
of the godly and increase from day to day."

22) **Judas (not the Iscariot) says to him, Lord,
what has occurred that only to us thou art about**

to manifest thyself and not to the world? This Judas is usually identified with Thaddeus, also called Lebbeus (Matt. 10:3; Mark 3:18). We may accept it as certain that he was not one of Jesus' brothers, for in 7:5 John writes, "not even his brethren believed on him." Not in order to identify this Judas but to obviate any misunderstanding John adds, "not the Iscariot," the one from Keriot, of whom we have been told that he went out (13:30). No one is to suppose that the traitor had possibly come back, with John now merely noting his renewed presence. Concerning this other Judas (or Jude) the Gospels have preserved only the one little incident now introduced.

Judas notes the marked contrast into which Jesus places the disciples and the world, especially that in the future only the disciples will behold Jesus, that Jesus comes only to them, and will manifest himself only to those that love him. Judas cannot harmonize this marked restriction with the statements of Jesus that he is the Savior of the world, that he has many other sheep not of this fold, that his mission is unto all men. So he asks τί γέγονεν, what has happened to cause this change and restriction? In τί γέγονεν ὅτι we have an extended "why?" R. 739, with ὅτι consecutive, R. 1001. Since ἡμῖν is in contrast with οὐχὶ τῷ κόσμῳ, its force is "only to us"; and μέλλεις with the present infinitive circumscribes the future, "art about to manifest thyself."

23) **Jesus answered and said unto him** (what follows is thus a real answer): **If anyone loves me, my word will be guard; and my Father will love him, and we will come to him and will make abode with him for ourselves. He that does not love me, my words he does not guard. And the word which you hear is not mine but the Father's who did send me.** While Jesus seems simply to go on with his discourse, as if no interruption had occurred, he really answers the point raised by Judas. For the

manifestation which is restricted to the disciples is that intimate personal manifestation which is possible only after Jesus comes to men with his Word. Then some will believe in him, accept, prize, and cherish his Word and thus show that they love him; while others will do the opposite and will remain the world that they are. That clears up the question of Judas.

The first class is again described as in v. 15, but now "my word" is substituted for "my precepts," thus defining what is meant by the latter. Since love is highly personal, Jesus again uses the singular, and the "if" of expectancy (ἐάν) still asks that each of us examine his own heart and life. The promise now added is the same as that in v. 21, but now it is stated in the active, "and my Father will love him" with that subsequent love which answers the love already enkindled in us. Jesus does not need to add that he, too, will love him who shows love by guarding his Word. For this is implied in the extension of the promise, using the plural so as to include both Jesus and the Father, "and we will come to him," etc. This is the same coming as that predicated of Jesus in v. 18. In spite of the clearness of the words the supposition is held that this is the coming at the end of the world. Yet the Scriptures know of no coming of the Father such as this at the end of the world; there will be no joint parousia of the Father and the Son. The promise is that this coming, conditioned by our loving and cherishing Jesus' Word, follows at once upon our love. That this is an invisible spiritual coming, full of additional grace and blessings, is made plain by the addition "and will make abode with him for ourselves" (ποιησόμεθα, reflexive middle). This cannot refer to the last day and to eternity. It is intended as an immediate answer to our present love. Not only will the Father and Jesus come to us, they will do to the full what is always the desire of complete love, namely join themselves permanently to the loved one.

Although the phrase is παρ' αὐτῷ, "at his side," "with him," the sense is quite equal to "in him," as appears from μονήν, "abiding-place," the same term used in v. 2 for our "mansions" or "abiding-places" in the Father's heavenly house. Those who love Jesus will be the "mansions" for the indwelling of the Father and the Son. We may say that this *unio mystica* includes also the Spirit, and in the economy and the cooperation of the three Persons is made possible by the Spirit and mediated by him, since it is his office to implant faith and love in us.

24) The answer to Judas is completed by adding the opposite. They who constitute "the world," to whom Jesus cannot manifest himself as he can to his loving disciples, are all who lack love and its evidence. Again this is personal and individual: "He that does not love me, my words he does not guard." Here Jesus uses the plural, for the one Word is both a grand unit and at the same time composed of parts. Not one of these parts is dear to the worldling. Not one is prized as valuable; all are treated with indifference or with hostility. No need to add that such a loveless person cannot be loved like a disciple and cannot be blessed with the indwelling and the communion of the Father and the Son. His heart, like that of Iscariot, is filled and dominated by another.

The full gravity of this lack of love for Jesus and of this disregard of his Word as evidence of the lack is brought out by once more showing the connection of Jesus and his Word with the Father: "And the Word which you hear is not mine," as if I invented it apart from the Father, "but the Father's who did send me" and who gave me this Word to speak in my saving mission. Compare the same statement in 7:16, where Jesus warns the Jews about treating his teaching with disdain. The Greek is very compact, τοῦ πέμψαντός με πατρός. Jesus returns to the singular, "the Word" and adds, "which you hear," ἀκούετε, a comprehensive pres-

ent tense which views the Word as a great unit, so that,
whenever the disciples hear Jesus speak, they hear this
Word. It is, of course, as much the Word of Jesus as
it is that of the Father. But Jesus is in the flesh and
in the state of humiliation; and when men hear him
speak this Word, they may, in order to escape its truth
and power, attribute it to him alone as the Word of
a mere man. Any such thought is absolutely false.
This is the Word of the great Sender of Jesus. He is
the real author and speaker of his Word.

In saying that it belongs to the Sender of Jesus the
idea is that this Word embodies and presents the entire
saving mission of Jesus. He not only speaks this
Word as a part of his mission (his prophetic office);
this Word reveals and presents to us his mission itself.
In this Word we see the Father, the Son whom he sent,
and the entire mission on which he is sent. To reject
this Word is to reject all three, and these three are
combined when designating the Father as "the Father
who did send me." Thus it is impossible to keep the
Father and yet to discard the Son and his mission.
Refusal to cherish the Word means rejection of the
Father with all the consequences this involves. And
the consequence here stressed is the loss of all the
subsequent love of the Father. He, indeed, would
extend this love with all its benefactions, but they who
belong to the world and attest it by rejecting the Word
of the great Sender of Jesus make any reception of the
Father's love and benefactions on their part utterly
impossible.

Jesus treats only these two cases: the man who
cherishes his Word, and the man who does not. He,
indeed, considers this Word as consisting of parts,
"precepts," "words", but says nothing about the man
who would cherish only certain parts of his teachings
while neglecting or rejecting other parts. We may
say that this man lacks greatly in love, deprives himself of much of God's subsequent love and blessings,

and is in danger of losing the entire Word. For, however many its parts, they ever form one vital unit, and to discard or to antagonize some of its parts weakens and jeopardizes our hold upon the rest. — The entire section, v. 16-24, turns on love, but this follows the section on faith. Faith is always presupposed in love.

25) All that Jesus has thus said is filled with the thought of his impending departure, and now he reaches the point where he begins actually to say farewell. **These things have I spoken to you while remaining with you. And the Paraclete, the Holy Spirit, whom the Father will send in my name, he will teach you everything and will remind you of everything that I myself said to you.** See how this expression, "These things I have spoken to you," carrying the tone of one turning to leave, recurs in 15:11 and 17; and in 16:1, 4, and 25. These chapters read as though Jesus is loth to leave, drawn by tender love to linger as long as possible, pouring out his heart's thoughts during every precious minute still left. The absence of ἐγώ shows that the thought is not: *I* have spoken to you thus far, but now *another* will speak to you. The emphasis is on the participial addition παρ᾽ ὑμῖν μένων. Jesus has thus far spoken to the disciples as one visibly in their presence; hereafter he will speak to them in a different manner, namely by the Spirit. "These things" refers to the discourses of this last evening but as embodying all that Jesus had hitherto conveyed to his disciples.

26) The connective δέ expresses only a slight contrast. "The Paraclete" (v. 16) is now used as an official title like "the Christ" and is at once followed by the actual name of the Person referred to, "the Holy Spirit." Everything points to the personality of this Spirit, although the grammatical gender of τὸ Πνεῦμα happens to be neuter in the Greek; always also τὰ πνεύματα are personal spirit beings. On the personal force of the Greek article see R. 795, and 709 on the demon-

strative masculine ἐκεῖνος. According to v. 16 this spirit is given, but now we learn that he is sent even as the Son was sent; to give is to send him. The adjective ἅγιον is added by a second article thus receiving increased emphasis, R. 418. The Spirit is called "holy," not in comparison with the other two Persons of the Godhead, but because of his divine function and office which is to make holy or sanctify sinners. Jesus names the Paraclete so fully because he wants the eleven to understand how they will be blessed by the presence and the work of this invisible divine Person who will now carry the work of Jesus forward. "In my name" evidently cannot mean "on my authority," but, as in all similar instances, "in connection with me and with my revelation (ὄνομα)." On ὄνομα in these phrases see 1:12 and 14:13. Nor need ἐν be altered into ἐπί "on the basis of," for its native sense is the true one, "in union with" my name (revelation). "He shall send" the Spirit — he did, Acts 2.

"He will teach you everything" has the sense of 16:13, 14, "he shall guide you into all the truth," etc. We see the fulfillment of this promise in the apostolic epistles and in the hearts and the minds of all who, like the 3,000 at Pentecost, "continue steadfastly in the apostles' teaching." This teaching was to a great extent immediate in the case of the apostles; for others it is mediate, the medium being the apostles whose Word forms the foundation of the church, Eph. 2:20. In πάντα is included all that the apostles might need in their work, much also that Jesus could not communicate to them while he was with them.

The second πάντα is narrower, "will remind you of everything that I myself said to you." The fulfillment is exhibited in the marvelous record of the four Gospels, most notably in that of John which contains the extended discourses of Jesus. It is humanly impossible to reproduce with fidelity even human words spoken during a period of over three years, when all the words are understood perfectly at the moment they are heard. It is vastly more impossible to reproduce with exactness the many words of Jesus which the disciples failed to grasp at the time they heard them. The promise of Jesus assures the eleven on this vital point. By means of an immediate illumination the Spirit will enable them to recall every utterance of Jesus in its true meaning. He will remind the disciples and in addition he will teach them what is contained in all of which they are thus reminded. Here is the answer to all the questioning in regard to the four Gospels. This answer covers also the form of these Gospels, the verbal variations in reporting the words of Jesus, the translation of what Jesus said from Aramaic into Greek. The Spirit is back of it all. The final ἐγώ, "what I myself said to you," should not be dropped.

The two πάντα cannot be reduced to one, "he will teach and remind you in regard to everything that I myself said to you." If this were the sense, one πάντα and one ὑμᾶς would suffice. Moreover, the reminding should be first and the teaching second. It is true enough that the words of Jesus are the foundation on which the further teaching of the Spirit rests, but the Spirit's teaching goes beyond that which the disciples had when Jesus left them, 16:12, 13. This further teaching, while predicated of the Spirit, is at the same time the teaching of Jesus who uses the Spirit to convey to the disciples what is his own (16:13).

27) As one who is near the point of leaving Jesus promises the disciples the work of the Spirit which shall be more than a substitute for his familiar presence and teaching. To this he adds his gift of peace. **Peace I leave to you, my own peace I give to you; not as the world gives do I on my part give.** The oriental greeting, "Peace to you!" occurs in the Scriptures as a greeting on arrival (Luke 10:5; 24:36; John 20:19 and 26), as a farewell greeting (Eph. 6:23;

I Pet. 5:14; III John 14), and as a gracious form of dismissal, "Go in peace!" (I Sam. 1:17; 20:42; II Sam. 15:9; Acts 16:36; James 2:16). None of these applies here, nor does Jesus use any of the forms of greeting. And yet these forms must have been in his mind with his departure so near at hand. It is thus that Jesus now speaks of peace. What friends at parting wish each other in their poor human way, that Jesus actually gives and leaves at his parting from the disciples like a sweet, rich treasure for their comfort.

"Peace" is at once defined by "my own peace," one which in a peculiar way belongs to Jesus, which he also can "leave" (like a legacy) and "give" (like a treasure). The very words indicate that this "peace" is objective: the condition and the situation of peace when nothing disturbs our relation to God. This must be distinguished from the subjective feeling of peace. The latter is to flow from the former, yet the feeling may be slight, even altogether absent at times, while the condition itself still obtains. On the other hand, one may feel quite undisturbed, unconscious of any danger while his actual condition should fill him with dismay. "My peace" must mean, "the peace I establish for you." This objective blessed condition Jesus leaves to his disciples, leaves it to them as a precious gift from his own hand. Whether they at once enter into the full consciousness and enjoyment of this peace is a minor matter. The subjective feeling will come in due time where the objective condition prevails.

Thus it is a mistake to think that Jesus leaves his own personal feeling of peace to the disciples. How can they "make his calmness in the presence of danger their own"? The matter is misconceived when we are told that their own faith is not yet strong enough to produce in them a peace of their own and that, therefore, Jesus invites them (he does not use such a verb) for the present to enjoy what they behold in him. Are they then later on when their faith pro-

duces its own peace to discard what Jesus now leaves
and gives to them? The present tenses "I leave," "I
give" are disregarded when others assume that "my
own peace" means "my security in the face of the
deadly attack of the prince of this world," and that
this security is to pass on to the disciples after the
departure of Jesus, so that they, too, will feel perfectly
secure in the dangers that beset them, God being their
protector as he is that of his Son. The peace Jesus
leaves he leaves and gives *now*. The disciples have
already had it (objectively) and even enjoyed it
(subjectively). They are to retain it even though
Jesus now departs. The security and the well-being
intended by this peace relate to far more than to
protection in the hour of danger; they refer to the relation of the disciples to God. "Peace" is a central
concept and should not be reduced by being in some
way turned into mere feeling.

In the addition, "not as the world gives do I on
my part give," the two verbs are without specified
objects. Thus the contrast deals only with the two
modes of giving and not, as is often supposed, with
the two kinds of peace. The world gives only with
empty words which convey no lasting treasures; Jesus
gives with words that actually convey true blessings
whether they are those of peace or of some other
divine grace. This difference in the acts, of course,
includes a difference in the objects. The world has no
true peace, and hence its greetings of peace mean
nothing; Jesus has a true gift of peace for us and thus
is able to bestow it upon us. In abiding by the contrast as drawn by Jesus we lose nothing as regards the
objects; we gain something that reaches beyond the
objects.

**Let not your heart be troubled, neither let it be
afraid,** is not the negative side of the positive gift
of peace as if Jesus said, "Therefore let not your
heart be troubled," etc. As in v. 1, this imperative,

now enhanced by a second verb, ushers in the reason why no troubling fears and no dismay (δειλιᾶν, found only in this passage) should upset the hearts of the disciples. If this injunction against cowardly fear were intended to indicate the proper result of peace in the hearts of the disciples, it would present only one side of the subjective feeling induced by the objective condition of peace, and a side out of line with the great concept of objective peace. Jesus would be made to say, "Because I have made peace between you and God, therefore do not feel afraid when you get into danger!" Yet thus far we have heard of danger only for Jesus not for the disciples. Any fears in their hearts were thus concerned with Jesus and only indirectly with themselves, in so far as his death would leave them alone in the world. The moment we connect this injunction against fear with what follows all is clear: Jesus wants no fear in their hearts when he now goes into his death, he wants the very opposite — joy.

28) Therefore he once more shows them what his death really means, not merely to them, but to himself. The disciples, if they love their Lord at all, ought to be glad that now his mission on earth is done, that he goes back to his Father who is far greater than the human Jesus they have thus far known. **You heard that I myself said to you, I am going away and am coming to you.** The peculiar ἐγώ must not be overlooked. Jesus alone could say a thing like this: in the same breath speak of his leaving and of his coming to the disciples. He repeats what he said before in such a striking way, because this strange combination of the departure and the return to them must be held fast by the disciples. Understanding this double declaration (v. 18, 19), all fear will leave their hearts, in fact, joy will take its place. "Am coming to you," of course, does not refer to the coming at the last day (v. 3) but to the invisible spiritual coming and presence promised in v. 18 and

23. The departure and death of Jesus only ushers in this far higher and more blessed presence of Jesus with his disciples. Jesus, however, has already spoken of the gain this would bring to the disciples (v. 16-23). While they may, indeed, think of themselves they ought also to think of Jesus and of what his departure means for him.

So he continues: **If you loved me** (present unreality, $\epsilon\iota$ with the imperfect) **you would have rejoiced** (past unreality, the aorist with $\ddot{a}\nu$) **that I go to the Father; for the Father is greater than I.** The protasis charges the disciples only with a certain lack of love, namely the lack evidenced by their failure to rejoice at the coming exaltation of Jesus. The disciples did, indeed, love Jesus but not with the clarity and the understanding that would have placed joy instead of fear into their hearts. Their $\dot{a}\gamma\acute{a}\pi\eta$ was not yet fully what the term implies. The mixed condition indicates a shifting of the standpoint (R. 1015). The protasis speaks of a present lack of love, and the apodosis of the past evidence of that lack. But, of course, this present lack of love reaches back to the time when the disciples failed to rejoice; and likewise their past failure to rejoice has not even yet been changed into joy. That ($\ddot{o}\tau\iota$) which from the start should have rejoiced the disciples is the going of Jesus "to the Father" with all that love would see in this elevation for Jesus. Read $\ddot{o}\tau\iota$ $\pi o\rho\epsilon\acute{v}o\mu a\iota$ and not $\ddot{o}\tau\iota$ $\epsilon\ddot{\iota}\pi o\nu$, $\pi o\rho\epsilon\acute{v}o\mu a\iota$ ("because I said, I go unto the Father," A. V.). This $\ddot{o}\tau\iota$ is declarative, it states the object of the joy. It is subjective, stating the object as the disciples should have seen it.

The second $\ddot{o}\tau\iota$ is causal: "for the Father is greater than I." It is objective, Jesus states his relation to the Father. This brief reference, intended only to show the disciples why going to the Father would be an event so happy for Jesus that they should at once have rejoiced when he told them of it, has become the battleground of both exegetes and dogmaticians. Here Jesus is in his humiliation, limited to a narrow range in exercising his divine attributes; but now he goes to the Father, to him who has assumed no limitations of any kind, where, when Jesus arrives there, all limitations will cease also for him. What joy for all who love him! It has well been said and often repeated that the creature that would dare to make a comparison of himself with God by saying, "God is greater than I," would be guilty of blasphemous folly as he who would say, "I am equal to God." When Jesus utters this comparison he does so with the most vivid consciousness of his deity. Merely to note this obvious fact answers the denial of the deity of Jesus.

In 10:29 Jesus calls the Father greater than all hostile powers that may array themselves against him and in that connection makes his own power equal to that of the Father, saying of each (v. 28, 29) that no hostile power shall snatch the sheep out of his hand. When Jesus now says that the Father is greater than he, he does this in connection with his departure by death. This statement of Jesus "can be referred only to the Son of man as he stood in lowliness before the disciples and comforted them in regard to his departure," Philippi, *Glaubenslehre*, 4, 1, 449. Recall 6:62: the Son of man ascends up where he was before, i. e., where he was before as the Son of God. "Greater than I" is usually referred to power. But why this restriction where Jesus makes none? "Greater" means greater in every way. Because we have only the pronoun μοῦ, "than I," which to the disciples meant the Lord as he stood before them in his lowliness, some are not content with this obvious sense, "greater than I as you have seen and now see me," but press this pronoun to mean "the Son." This opens the floodgates of speculation. John's prolog, statements like 5:23; 10:30 are forgotten, and we are offered a variety of views as to how Jesus is in his actual person and being

less than the Father. Some leave us nothing but a
mere man with a high immanence of God; others are
more generous, like Arius and his modern pupils,
Sabellius, all types of subordinationists, the kenoticists,
and a motley array of rationalists. One contends
against the other; we turn away from their conten-
tions. Jesus is here not at all speaking of the inner
Trinitarian relation of the Persons of the Godhead but
only of his person in its present state.

Jesus is going to his greater Father where he will
do all that he promises in this chapter. Hence we
discard the notion that he goes only again to enjoy
the glory and the blessedness of his Father. Likewise,
that he leaves the disciples to the greater protection
of the Father. But we must hold with Luther and
with others that the going of Jesus to his Father means
much also for the disciples, that his own interest in
going involves also theirs, as the entire chapter attests.

29) **And now I have told you before it takes
place, in order that, when it takes place, you may
believe.** "I have told you" means: about my going
away and coming to you. Jesus has an eye to the
future. He says these things now, in advance,
although he knows that the disciples cannot grasp them
at this moment, in order that, when these things take
place, his having told them thus may form the basis
of their faith. Compare the similar statement in
13:19. In both passages the aorist πιστεύσητε denotes
the act of faith that shall then take place. The aorists
γενέσθαι and γένηται designate definite future happenings.

30) **No longer will I speak much with you, for
the world's ruler is coming.** The fact that the time
of parting is quite near is now stated in so many words.
"No longer will I speak much" means that Jesus has
time to say only a few things more. He indicates that
he knows just how much time is left and, of course,
that he will use this most fully. The limit is set by the
coming of "the world's ruler." This time the genitive

is between the article and the noun, making it less emphatic than in 12:31, "the ruler of this world." Here, too, κόσμος is general, the entire world of men and things in which Satan, because of the entrance of sin, is able to exercise his power; not "world" in the sense merely of wicked men. Jesus might have said, Judas and the men sent out by the Sanhedrin are on the way. He says far more, for in what is about to happen the chief agent is Satan who merely uses the miserable tools he has found for his purpose. The present tense ἔρχεται shows that Jesus is aware of every move of his great foe. He thus might nullify or frustrate Satan's plans even now. The disciples are to understand this and are to know that Jesus is freely laying down his life by allowing Satan's plans to proceed, 10:18.

All that now follows is one sentence. **And in me he has nothing; nevertheless, in order that the world may realize that I love the Father, and that just as the Father gave me commission thus I do, arise, let us be going hence.** Satan has nothing in Jesus, and thus his efforts to kill Jesus might properly be resented and nullified. Over against this negative thought ἀλλά sets the strong positive, "nevertheless, to achieve the great purpose (ἵνα) of Jesus and his Father, let us go hence, where Satan can lay hands on me." Those who make, "Arise, let us go hence," an independent statement, secure only a disjointed command, thrust into the discourse without motivation. When this is done, the main verb is supplied: ἀλλὰ ἔρχεται, "but he comes, in order that," etc. Or ποιῶ is regarded as the main verb, as our versions translate. The thought as well as the construction is thus disturbed.

The two thoughts are placed side by side: Satan is coming, and in me he has nothing. The emphasis is on ἐν ἐμοί and on οὐδέν. The Greek doubles and thus strengthens the negation: οὐκ ἔχει οὐδέν. The sense of "nothing" is made plain by the connection with ὁ ἄρχων: nothing that might justify this ruler in coming to strike at Jesus. That is why "in me" is so emphatic. Jesus differs from all other men. No link of any kind exists between him and Satan — only an impassable gulf. That this is due to the absolute sinlessness of Jesus is only part of the truth. The sinlessness is itself due to the deity of Jesus.

31) But if this is the case, why does Jesus yield and submit to Satan on this night? Why does he not rid himself of the devil as he did in Matt. 4:10? The answer is given by ἀλλὰ ἵνα κτλ., by the divine and saving purpose which Jesus and his Father are carrying out: "in order that the world may realize," etc. What Jesus allows to happen this night will be brought to the attention of the whole world of men. He enters his passion and his death with this tremendous consciousness. On γνῷ (or γνοῖ) see R. 308. This strong verb is used because the realization that Jesus has in mind is one that leads to saving faith in what Jesus now does. His act is due to his love for the Father, the love (ἀγαπᾶν) that understands the Father's will and purposes to carry it out. Hence the elucidating addition that just as the Father gave him commission thus he does — also and especially at this decisive moment; καθώς and οὕτως are correlative. On ἐντολή in the sense of "commission" or *Auftrag* see 10:18. All the world is to see this love of Jesus doing just what the Father wills even at the price of Jesus' death. This love and its great saving deed is to win the world to faith. The aorist "gave" refers to the time when Jesus came into the world, and the present "I do" covers all the work of Jesus down to the act now about to take place.

"Nevertheless . . . arise, let us be going hence" ends the Passover feast. No destination is indicated, yet the disciples know that Jesus intends to meet "the world's ruler" and thus once more do the Father's ἐντολή. The asyndeton ἐγείρεσθε ἄγωμεν is idiomatic, as is also the combination of the present imperative with the hortative present subjunctive. The action of arising from the couches on which the company had dined is merely preliminary to the action of leaving the place and going elsewhere. Those who regard "Arise," etc., as a separate sentence incline to the opinion that Jesus left the upper room at this point, spoke the next three chapters somewhere on the way to the Kidron, crossed this at 18:1, and then went on to Gethsemane. When we note that the bidding to arise and to leave is only the conclusion of a longer sentence, that 15:1, etc., indicates no change of place, and that ἐξῆλθεν in 18:1 reads as though Jesus did not leave the upper room until that moment, we are led to conclude that after the company arose from their couches they lingered in the upper room until Jesus finished speaking the next three chapters. This delay consumed only a short time. We cannot think that the next three chapters were spoken while the company was in motion, and John nowhere indicates that they halted at some spot along the way.

CHAPTER XV

7. Abiding in Jesus as Branches in the Vine, Bearing Much Fruit, 15:1-17

1) After rising from the Passover supper, and while still in the upper room (see 14:31), Jesus utters some of the οὐ πολλά (14:30) for which there is still time. He speaks of the disciples as they will fare after his death: first of their connection with him (v. 1-17), then of their position in the hostile world (v. 18, etc.). The rising from the couches caused a slight interruption.

He begins with what Trench, *Parables of our Lord*, has well termed Biblical allegory. Reality and figure are blended together so that interpretation need not be brought in from without. Two kinds of thread are woven together: the silver thread of the imagery, and the golden thread of interpretation. Those who find fault with the tapestry thus woven do not perceive the beauty of the weaving.

It has often been asked how Jesus came to use the imagery of the vine. It is supposition to think of a vine with its tendrils spreading near an open window of the upper room, or that a view through the open window showed the ornamental golden vine at the gate of the Temple, or revealed a distant vineyard with a fire consuming dead branches, or that such a view was afforded when Jesus passed over the brook Kidron — supposing that he spoke this allegory after reaching the brook. Suppositions such as these cannot be supported by pointing out that Jesus does not merely compare himself to a vine, or call himself *the* vine, but implies a contrast with other vines by describing himself as "the *true* vine." For these other natural vines are certainly also true vines, and Jesus might compare himself with them, but he would certainly not contrast himself with natural vines. The adjective "true" deals with a far deeper contrast, one lying not in the mere imagery but in the actual reality. The comparison used by Jesus may have been suggested by the wine, called "the fruit of the vine" in one of the blessings, used at the Passover. The image of the vine was not new or strange, Isaiah (5:1, etc.), the Psalmist (80:8, etc.), and Jeremiah (2:21) having employed it, the two former with great fulness. Thus Jesus comes to use this image in a natural, though not a superficial, way. At once it is made to assume a new depth and richness, it is filled with truth and grace, and because of the truth a touch of judgment is added.

I myself (reality) **am the genuine vine** (figure), **and my Father** (reality) **is the vinedresser** (figure). In this new, great I AM statement the predicate again appears with the Greek article, which makes it identical and interchangeable with the subject (R. 768), a point not to be overlooked. Here, too, the adjective is added with a second article, which gives it great emphasis, "as a sort of climax in apposition" (R. 776). Jesus is not merely like a vine, he is more: the actual original, of which all natural vines, genuine in the domain of nature, are only images. As the real and genuine vine in this supreme sense he exceeds all others who may in some way also be called vines, and he stands forever in contrast with all those who are not real but only spurious and pretending vines. Jesus alone embodies the complete will and purposes of God, which others only foreshadow or reveal in part, and which still others only pretend to reveal. We must distinguish ἀληθινός, *verus*, real, genuine, from ἀληθής, *verax*, true in the sense of truthful. In the present connection the latter would be out of line.

The point of comparison intended by the image of the vine is brought out in the elaboration of the allegory. It centers in the one word "fruit." As the natural vine through its branches and the care they receive brings abundant fruit for the delight of the owner of the vine, so does Jesus in a far higher sense through his disciples for the glory of God. The *tertium comparationis* is, therefore, not that a vine has branches even as Jesus has disciples. This lies in the concept itself: every vine has branches as a matter of course. In v. 2 Jesus introduces the branches without further explanation — the vine and its branches naturally go together. The entire development of the allegory is positive and deals only with the relation of the disciples to Jesus, their remaining in him in order to produce as much fruit as possible, or their separation from him in judgment. The allegory intends to elaborate the thesis expressed in 14:20: "You in me, and I in you." The picture as drawn by Jesus does not concern itself with false Christs who pretend to be vines but are not, nor with the Old Testament Israel in which the true vine, Jesus, was foreshadowed. These contrasts might also have been elaborated, starting from the keyword ἡ ἀληθινή, but Jesus has a different aim. He will dwell in his disciples after he leaves them; they are to understand what this their spiritual relation to him means for all the days to come; they are to bear much spiritual fruit by the power they constantly draw from him, and by their fruit they are to glorify God. What was begun in Israel of old in connection with the promised Messiah is now to be consummated in the new Israel in connection with the Messiah actually come and established in glory forever.

"I myself am the genuine vine" does not yet indicate the point for which the comparison is made.
It still lies veiled in the two emphatic words ἐγώ and
ἡ ἀληθινή. The veil is lifted a little in the next statement: "and my Father is the vinedresser," γεωργός,
one who tills the ground, in this case one who tends
the vine. The point in this figure is at once revealed
in v. 2: this vinedresser busies himself with the
branches. That is really all that lies in γεωργός. The
term itself does not say that this person owns the
vine, that he has planted it, cultivates it, etc. These
are thoughts that we ourselves generally add, drawing
them, not from the imagery, but from the actual relation of the Father to Jesus, our Lord and Savior.
Usually the earthly picture is unable to reflect the
reality in all its fulness. Here the reference to
the vinedresser intends to point only in the direction
of fruit.

2) The work of this particular vinedresser is
described: **Every branch** (figure) **in me** (reality)
not bearing fruit he takes away (figure) ; **and everyone bearing fruit, he cleanses it, in order that it
may be bearing more fruit** (figure). Here the
point of the entire allegory is fully revealed: it is
"fruit," mentioned no less than three times. Here, too,
we see that only such features of the figure are used as
fit the great reality, and other features are purposely
omitted as not applying. Ordinary vines are cultivated and tied to supports; this vine, Jesus, needs
no cultivation. Only the branches need attention.
The objects are placed forward for emphasis,
suspended as it were: "every branch in me not
bearing fruit . . . and everyone bearing fruit";
and then each is picked up with αὐτό. When Jesus
speaks these words, his disciples cluster about him
— he the vine, they the branches. Judas has left

shortly before, the unfruitful branch that had to be removed from the vine.

The branches are at once arranged in two classes: fruitless, fruitful. The vinedresser has a task with regard to each. We need not puzzle about the unfruitful branches being "in me"; for evidently these are disciples whose hearts have lost the faith and the love that once dwelt in them and joined them to Christ, and who thus adhere to Christ only outwardly until even this connection is broken. It is idle to think of branches which are unfruitful from the start because Jesus uses this phrase "in me"; for no man becomes a branch unless fruitfulness is in him from the start. But he may lose his faith, and then he is promptly cast away. How this comes about — who will tell? We, indeed, know the power of the devil, the world, and the flesh, and we see the spiritual wrecks produced by this power. Yet how one who has gained the life in Christ can consent to have it destroyed in his soul remains a mystery of darkness — unnatural, unreasonable, devilish. The fault lies entirely in the branch that dies, not in the vine that once gave that branch life.

The unfruitful branch the vinedresser "takes away," αἴρει he removes it, the tense being a timeless present. The point is regarding fruit alone, which means that we must not think of dead branches in a natural vine — the withering is mentioned in v. 6 when the branch is cut away. It is fruitlessness that seals the fate of the branch. Leaves, shade, beauty, etc., are not the purpose of the branch but only fruit. As a branch is cut from the vine, so the fruitless disciple is severed from Jesus. The Father rejects him. That is enough at this point.

Strange things have been said about the term "fruit," καρπός, making the branches themselves the fruit of the vine, and then reasoning that the fruit of the branches must be similar, namely other branches, souls joined to Christ by us. Such thoughts only confuse and spoil the allegory. No branch ever grafts another branch into the vine. The production of branches is wholly the business of Christ, the vine. The fruit of the branches consists in grapes. What this fruit in reality is, is plainly told in Scripture: "The fruit of the Spirit is love, joy, peace, long-suffering, gentleness, goodness, faith, meekness, temperance," Gal. 5:22, 23; "in all goodness and righteousness and truth," Eph. 5:9; "the peaceable fruit of righteousness," Heb. 12:11. "And this I pray that your love may abound yet more and more in knowledge and in all judgment; that ye may approve things that are excellent; that ye may be sincere and without offense till the day of Christ; being filled with the fruits of righteousness, which are by Jesus Christ, unto the glory and praise of God," Phil. 1:9-11. A branch may have but little of such fruit, but as long as it draws life from the vine, some of the fruit will be found.

The fruitless branches also need the vinedresser's attention. For the unfruitful, αἴρειν, for the fruitful, καθαίρειν, and Bengel notes the *suavis rhythmus*. The two are absolute alternatives: either — or. A taking away occurs in either case, either of the branch itself, or of that which hinders its increase in fruitfulness. Since the fruit consists in all manner of Christian virtues and in the thoughts, words, and deeds in which they manifest themselves, the cleansing will consist in the removal of what remains of our old sinful nature, the flesh with its outgrowths and its manifestations. The Father's work is negative; the positive power for greater fruit rests in Jesus, the vine. Thus the more the flesh is checked, the more the fruits will increase. This is why the Lord and the apostles admonish, reprove, rebuke, and warn us so constantly against the workings of the flesh. Sometimes their words cut deeply, but they must in order that the Spirit may triumph over the flesh and bring forth more fruit meet for repentance. Allied with this cleansing by means of the Word is the tribulation, which also helps to overcome the flesh. II Cor. 4:16; I Pet. 4:1, 2; II Cor. 12:7.

3) This cleansing of the fruitful branches must be distinguished from another cleansing, namely that which first makes us branches. **Already you are clean on account of the word which I have spoken to you** (reality). This is the cleansing of *justification* as distinguished from the other which constantly works upon the branches, namely *sanctification* (in the narrow sense: the production of good works). "Clean" means justified, cleansed by the forgiveness of sins. "Already *you,*" ὑμεῖς (emphatic) implies that many others will follow the eleven. This cleansing is due to "the word which I have spoken to you" as the great means of justification. The entire gospel is referred to, including the Word in the Sacraments. Luther adds the explanatory remark, "when received and embraced by faith." That the Word must be so received in order to cleanse and to justify appears in Acts 15:9, where it is said that God put no difference between Jews and Gentiles, "purifying their hearts by faith"; and in Acts 10:43, "Whosoever believeth in him shall receive remission of sins." In ascribing this cleansing to the Word, Jesus takes all the credit and glory to himself and leaves none to us. The cleansing by the Word through faith (justification) does not exclude the cleansing which follows throughout life in the putting away of all the defilements of the flesh (sanctification). This second cleansing Jesus had just illustrated for the benefit of the disciples by washing their feet: "He

that is washed needeth not save to wash his feet, but is clean every whit," 13:10; I John 1:7; 3:3. By ascribing this second cleansing to the Father, the credit for this is also taken away from us. The Scriptures refer both justification and sanctification to anyone of the three divine Persons; *opera ad extra sunt indivisa aut communa.* Thus sanctification is here predicated of the Father whereas otherwise *per eminentiam* it is ascribed to the Spirit.

4) **Remain in me, and I in you** (reality). **Just as the branch cannot bear fruit of itself unless it remains in the vine** (figure); **thus neither you unless you remain in me** (reality). In the first three verses the great fundamental facts are set before us: the vine, the branches, the vinedresser working for fruit. On these great facts rests the mighty admonition, "Remain in me," etc., fortified by a simple elucidation on how essential this remaining in him is. Μείνατε — count the number of times this word is repeated as if to impress it indelibly upon our hearts. "Remain in me, and I in you" (14:20) implies that the disciples *are* in Jesus, and he in them; also that this vital connection *might* be broken. We must not reduce the greater reality to the lesser figure and thus let ἐν mean: "you attached to me, and I to you." This ἐν contains the *unio mystica*; it is like the constantly used phrase "in Christ," "in the Lord," R. 587. Note the aorist imperative with its peremptory and constative force: "Remain!" once for all.

To remain in Jesus is to believe in him always; and since the chief business of faith is to receive from him, remaining means ever receiving grace for grace, day by day, in ever greater fulness. So the branch remains and receives life from the vine, and so it develops and grows. This remaining and receiving is mediated by the Word and the Sacrament and is impossible without these divine means. This remaining and re-

ceiving will invariably manifest itself in two ways:
it will turn against every influence that would draw
us away from Jesus and would substitute something
in place of him and his Word; likewise, it will constantly respond with good works or fruit (praise,
prayer, and all spiritual activities). "And after God
through the Holy Ghost in Baptism has kindled and
effected a beginning of the true knowledge and faith,
we should pray him without ceasing that through the
same Spirit and his grace, by means of the daily
exercise of reading and practicing God's Word, he
would preserve us in faith and his heavenly gifts,
strengthen us from day to day, and keep us to the
end." *Concordia Triglotta,* 587, 16. "Remain in me!"
is one of the true gospel ἐντολαί (14:15, 21, 23, 24), a
commission to take, to enrich ourselves, to open and
to keep open our hearts, that he may be able to fill
them with his grace, gifts, spirit, and power. He is
the eternal treasure house.

"And I in you" sounds as though he were giving
himself a command to remain in us. But the words
are really a promise that he will remain in us. We
in him, and he in us. These always go together.
Jesus himself is in us when by faith we remain in
him. The very Word and the Sacrament through
which we remain in him convey him to us, to rest in
us and to lodge his gifts in us. The Sacrament in
particular is rightly called "a consolation of all distressed hearts, and a firm bond of union of Christians
with Christ, their Head," *C. Triglotta,* 987, 44. Since
the disciples are already in Jesus, no stress should be
laid on the order, as though we must first be in him,
and then he will be in us. The two are simultaneous. As our hearts expand under his grace, so
he fills them with his grace.

The thought is now elucidated by placing side by
side the illustrative figure and the corresponding

reality. Thus the main point of the allegory is again
brought forward, namely "fruit." The comparison
is worded in negative form because this form is more
suited to bring out the absolute necessity of remaining
in Jesus. We meet this negative again in the last
clause of v. 5 and in the fullest form in v. 6. From
the start it contains a note of warning. In nature
it is absolutely self-evident, a branch bears no fruit
except it remain in the vine. "Of itself" it is fruitless because it would then be dead. So it is with us.
Unless we remain in Jesus we are fruitless, because
we are spiritually dead. Alas, that such branches,
too, are found on the vine! The present tenses μένῃ
and μένητε denote continuous remaining; others prefer
the reading that has the aorist μείνῃ and μείνητε, permanent remaining. "The cause is that they wilfully
turn away again from the holy commandment, grieve
and embitter the Holy Ghost, implicate themselves
again in the filth of the world, and garnish again
the habitation of the heart for the devil. With them
the last state is worse than the first." *C. Triglotta,*
1077, 42.

5) **I on my part** (reality) **am the vine** (figure),
you on yours (reality) **are the branches** (figure).
The first clause is a repetition, emphasizing the fundamental proposition of the allegory. Beside it is now
placed the second clause which reveals our relation
to Jesus, the vine. Ever he is the vine, and this makes
his disciples the branches. To make ourselves something else, to give up this relation of ourselves to Jesus,
is fatal for us. In Luther's words we should then be
nothing but brambles, fit only for the fires of hell.
When Jesus is the vine, and we are the branches, it
follows self-evidently: **He that remains in me,
and I in him** (reality), **he alone bears much fruit**
(figure); **because apart from me you can do nothing**
(reality). From the plural Jesus turns to the singular

since remaining in him is a personal matter; "he that remains," etc.; then, however, he returns to the plural, for regarding all alike it is true that apart from Jesus they can do nothing. "Wherever fruit is borne, which pleases the vinedresser and is sweet to his taste, this hangs upon the branches, but it is the vine which bears both the branches and the fruit, and penetrates them with its sap. All the holy thoughts, words, and works of Christians, which, made sweet by the taste of love, delight God, are altogether fruit of the branches which remain in the vine, with the vine's living sap in them, are altogether gifts received from the abundance of Christ, who is the heart's treasure of love, the mouth's spice of love, the hand's power of love." Besser. The expanded subject is taken up by the demonstrative οὗτος in the sense of "he — he alone."

The point of the allegory is not mere fruit but "more fruit" (v. 2), "much fruit" (v. 3 and 8). For this is no ordinary vine but one with unlimited life and vitality. Thus throughout the assumption is that its branches will bear with the greatest possible abundance. This is the glory of the vine, and no true branch will attempt to make it less. Those who are bearing but little fruit have reason to examine their connection with the vine, whether this is sound and true, lest presently they drop away from the vine.

The reason why he that remains in Jesus bears much fruit is put into negative form: "for apart from me you can do nothing." οὐ . . . οὐδέν, "nothing whatsoever." The positive implication, therefore, is not: "joined to me you can do at least something." We have only two alternatives: much — nothing at all. Joined to Jesus and under the Father's care, so much grace comes to us that the result is always "much fruit"; the alternative is separation from Jesus

and the Father's care, hence no fruit of any kind.
From these alternatives and their causal relation only
one conclusion may be drawn, namely that where in
spite of all the Father's care only little fruit appears,
the connection with Jesus is in jeopardy, the branch
has begun to die.   A strange interpretation is at times
introduced in connection with χωρὶς ἐμοῦ, as though this
applies to actual branches that are still joined to the
vine, such branches trying to produce fruit of themselves without Jesus.   The reality would be disciples
of Jesus trying to serve God by means of their own
powers alone and thus producing nothing.   We may at
once answer that these would cease to be disciples,
except, perhaps, in their own opinion.   "Apart from
me" means just what it says : severed from Jesus, having fallen back into their former state, without saving
faith.   The deduction is wrong that nothing is here
said about the total inability of man, of non-disciples,
to do works acceptable to God.   The very reverse is
said, and that not by way of a deduction but in so
many words.   All who are "apart from Jesus," those
who have never been joined to him, as well as those
who have lost their connection with him, are able "to
do nothing" in the way of acceptable service to God.
They may think that they are doing much, works
which the world lauds and applauds, in the eyes of
Jesus they are doing "nothing."   Read Matt. 7:22, 23.
The world is full of people doing "nothing" in this
sense.   "Therefore let others whittle and trim as they
can until they make a new birth out of works and a
tree out of fruit, they must still prove the truth of this
saying, and out of all of it there shall come nothing."
Luther.   "Man, when brought to the life in Christ, is
not like a clock which, when once wound up, runs
twenty-four hours, but is like a spring of water which
ceases to flow the moment its hidden reservoir beneath
the earth is cut off."   Besser.   Augustine has well

said that Jesus spoke as he did "in order to answer the coming Pelagius."

6) This doing nothing has its dreadful consequences. **If anyone remains not in me** (reality), **he is thrown out as the branch and is withered; and they gather them and throw them into the fire, and they are burned** (figures). Here is the exposition of v. 2, the vinedresser "takes away" the unfruitful branches. "Every branch that does not bear fruit," in v. 2, is now explained by stating the reality: "if anyone remains not in me," μένῃ, present tense, "continues to remain"; some prefer μείνῃ, aorist, "remain permanently." The condition of expectancy (ἐάν with the subjunctive) intimates that some will, indeed, fail to remain in Jesus. Yet Jesus says only, "if anyone remains not in me," and does not add, "and I not in him"; for he never refuses to remain in us if only we remain in him. It is never a question of his willingness but only of ours. He casts no one out, but some cast him off. Jesus does not say, "if a branch bears not fruit"; he at once goes to the inner cause, "if anyone remains not in me," thus, of course, becoming unfruitful.

Now follows the darkest part of the allegory, the fate of the unfruitful branches with the warning this implies for us. First the singular is used in order that every man may smite upon his breast and ask, "Lord, is it I?" Then the plural for, alas, many will meet this fate, and the last part of that fate shall affect them jointly. We note five stages: he is thrown out; is withered; they gather them; they throw them into the fire; they are burned. The first two are aorists, ἐβλήθη and ἐξηράνθη, which Winer and the older grammarians are unable to explain. These aorists have nothing to do with the past; nor do they make the actions so certain, as if they were already done and beyond recall. These aorists are in full harmony with the future idea in the protasis and with the three present tenses following the aorists. R. 836, 847 is sure that they are timeless, not so sure that they are gnomic; B.-D. 333, 1 frankly calls them gnomic, designating acts valid at any time. These infrequent gnomic aorists appear in the New Testament chiefly in comparisons or in connection with them. Here we find them combined with three timeless present tenses, all five expressing actions that invariably follow upon a supposed future case, a man's failure to remain in Jesus.

The unfruitful branch that is taken away by the vinedresser "is thrown out" ὡς τὸ κλῆμα, like the branch cut off from a natural vine. The inner separation is followed by the outer. The unfruitful branch is removed from the midst of the great crowd of fruit-bearing branches. The soul that no longer believes in Jesus betrays its condition by no longer using Word and Sacrament, by no longer enjoying the spiritual fellowship and the worship of the true disciples of the Lord, by no longer cherishing the ἐντολαί of Jesus. Nothing remains but to throw it out. The supposition that this is not done at once, but that time is given for repentance, misconceives the allegory, which states only the results not the steps by which they are reached. The passive "is thrown out" leaves the agent unnamed; he is the vinedresser. The actuality of the divine act is hidden from us, but it usually appears in the outward separation from the church, except in the case of hypocrites who, though outwardly in the church, are no longer of the church.

The passive of ξηραίνω is used in the sense of the middle. The last show of life disappears as when leaf and tendril shrivel up and dry up, all vitality being gone. So King Saul withered, and Judas. God's grace and Word no longer enter the heart; worldly, vain, godless, often vicious and blasphemous thoughts rule the heart. It is terrible to see a poor, stricken

human body wither under the blight of death; it is
unspeakably worse to see a similar process going on in
the soul.

The indefinite plurals: "and they gather them and
throw them into the fire," resemble the German indefinite *man* and may be substitutes for the passives:
"they are gathered and thrown," R. 392, 820. The
preliminary gathering is aptly described by Besser:
thus the company of Korah gathered itself together
against Moses; Herod, Pilate, and the Jews gathered
themselves together against Jesus; the Psalmist (26:5)
sees the evildoers as a "congregation"; who will count
the associations and organizations that are marked by
unbelief, worldliness, Christless worship, worldly
pleasures, and all manner of deception? They seem to
be gathered into bundles even now, in advance, for the
burning. The final gathering is made by the angels
at the time of the judgment, when they will bring in
the sinners of every kind, the traitor Ahitophel with
the traitor Judas and others like them, Jezebel together
with Herodias and others of their kind, the Pharisees
whom Jesus blasted as hypocrites with Ananias and
Sapphira and the rest. Terrible will be these compan-
ionships of the wicked; each shall see his own sin in
the other.

"And they are burned," the final καί piled inexorably
upon the others. The wood of the branches is fit only
for one of two things: to bear fruit, or to burn. We
may regard καίεται as a middle, "they burn." The readings vary between αὐτά and αὐτό, yet "they gather"
matches the former, and the shift from the singular to
the plural occurs throughout allegory. The verb is not
κατακαίεσθαι, "to burn up," and affords no support for
the annihilation of the wicked — the castoff branches
are burning. While the noun "the fire" and the verb
"are burned" belong to the figure, like Matt. 3:10;

5:22; 13:30, these terms are, to say the least, **highly**
suggestive of hell fire, Matt. 7:19; 13:42; 25:41; the
more so since τό πῦρ, "the fire," denotes a fire that is
burning.

7) Again the solemn condition, pounding itself
into our memories and hearts: **If you remain in
me,** μείνητε, aorist, "remain permanently"; but now
the explanation is added: **and my utterances remain in you,** for this is how we remain in Jesus:
by receiving and permanently holding (μείνῃ, aorist)
his utterances, the ῥήματα that come from his lips. He
in us, and we in him, the medium and bond of his
spiritual union being his spoken Word. Compare
14:15 and 21 for the same thought: when we cherish
Jesus' "precepts," his utterances and he himself remain
in us; likewise 14:23, 24, when we cherish his "word"
and "words," he will make his abode with us. The
relation of the two conditional clauses is not that of
cause and effect: "you·in me" (cause), "my utterances
in you" (effect); but of explication, the second elucidating the first.

We have heard that this union of Jesus and the
disciples will make them bring fruit, the supreme
desire of the Father (2), so that he even removes the
branches that refuse to bear fruit. The power to
produce this fruit in us comes entirely from Jesus,
for which reason it is so vital that we remain in him.
In fact, we are to bring much fruit. At this point
we are shown the great aid that is ours for producing much fruit, the aid we possess by being in Jesus,
and he in us. **What you may will, ask for yourselves, and it shall be done for you.** The object is
placed forward in order to make it emphatic. We may
ask anything for which we have the will, θέλητε, present
tense, at any time. We — as remaining in Jesus with
our will; we — with his utterances remaining in us;
we — who will thus seek and will nothing "apart from

Jesus," nothing contrary to him and to his Word. Our will will be to bring much fruit.

The aorist imperative "ask for yourselves" is peremptory. We not merely *may* ask, we *must* ask. This is one of the gospel ἐντολαί or precepts. Of course, the verb is αἰτεῖσθαι, the common word for wanting something, not ἐρωτᾶν, the loftier word (C.-K. 91). The vine orders the branches to ask of it all that it is able to give. And there is no question about the receiving: "it shall be done for you." No limit exists for the vine; the only limit is in our faith, which may not ask though it has the right to ask. Here the verb is impersonal: "it shall take place," γενήσεται; in 14:13, 14 it is personal: "that I will do"; also in 16:23: "the Father will give it to you in my name." These statements elucidate each other.

8) The fact that Jesus is thinking of the chief point of the allegory, namely "much fruit," appears when he continues: **In this is my Father glorified, that you keep bearing much fruit and definitely appear as disciples of mine.** The older interpretations which operate with ἐδοξάσθη as a past tense and with ἵνα as denoting purpose are superseded. This means that ἐν τούτῳ cannot refer back to v. 7: "in this that you obtain what you ask," but is to be construed with ἵνα which is its apposition: "in this that you keep bearing," etc. We are relieved of making ἐδοξάσθη "an aorist of anticipation" and laboring with the stilted thought that thus ensues. This aorist is exactly like the two in v. 6, gnomic, and as such timeless. In English we are compelled to use the present tense to translate it, yet when we do so, we do it without reference to time: "in this is my Father glorified," i. e., at any time when "this" occurs (R. 843, 837) ; we must drop the future notion to which B.-D. 333, 2 still clings, and also the future perfect idea: "shall have been glorified." The grammar of ἵνα is equally simple. It is not a sub-

stitute for ὅτι but, as in so many instances in the Koine, crowds out the infinitive: ἐν τούτῳ . . . ἵνα φέρητε κτλ. = ἐν τῷ φέρειν ὑμᾶς κτλ., "in this . . . that you keep bearing," etc. = "in your bearing," etc. The ἵνα clause is simply appositional, R. 1078, and we decline to follow B.-D. 394 who retains the notion of "will" against that of simple "fact." The Father is glorified, not by his or our *will* to bear fruit, but by the *fact* that we actually bear fruit; and not simply some fruit but "much fruit," as this was explained in connection with v. 5. In this abundance of fruit all that the love, grace, power, etc., of the Father is able to accomplish is fully displayed; thus the glory of his blessed attributes shines forth before the eyes of men and of angels.

The present tense φέρητε makes this durative: "keep on bearing fruit." The reason for the subjunctive is only the construction after ἵνα. Since this clause is appositional and not in any way final, there is no need to find a future force in this subjunctive. The thought is simply this: whenever we go on bearing much fruit, "in this fact" the Father is glorified. The present tense merely pictures the process as an extended one. A second verb is added: καὶ γένησθε ἐμοὶ μαθηταί. The aorist of this clause contrasts with the durative present of the preceding clause: "and definitely appear as dis-ciples of mine," reading ἐμοί, not as a dative: "to me," but as a plural nominative from ἐμός, even as John loves these possessive adjectives. The verb γίνομαι is not to be taken in the sense of "become." We drop the comments which try to explain how the eleven, who already are disciples of Jesus, should yet "become" such disciples. In part this explanation still clings to the idea that ἵνα expresses purpose and futurity. This aorist is exactly like the preceding present save that the latter pictures the bearing of fruit as being extended, while the former pictures the discipleship as definite and fixed (punctiliar). And γίνομαι = to prove oneself, to appear, *sich zeigen, sich beweisen,* especially when it is used, as here, with a predicate. To go on bearing fruit is to prove conclusively that we are disciples. The two facts glorify the Father — do so at any time when these facts exist.

Some texts have the future indicative γενήσεσθε. In the Koine this form may properly follow ἵνα and is often used with a second verb after this conjunction. We may regard it as practically identical with the more usual subjunctive. In the present case this must be done. For the alternative, which would regard this future as a separate sentence: "and so you will prove disciples of mine" (like the R. V.) is not possible since "in this" God is glorified, that we bear much fruit and show ourselves disciples of Jesus. It is best, then, leaving the ἵνα clause as appositional to "in this," to regard this future as equal to a subjunctive. The only question would be whether to make the future punctiliar or durative, for it may be either in this connection. The thought is plain: "much fruit" on our part and established discipleship glorify the Father, who sent Jesus to be our Savior and Lord for this very purpose.

9) The main point in the preceding allegory is the production of "much fruit." That this thought is consistently held to we see in v. 16 where the "fruit" is again emphasized. Essential to this main point is the necessity of remaining in Jesus, which has been repeated from the start ("every branch in me," v. 2) and is thus made prominent. Just what remaining in Jesus means is now fully cleared up. **Just as the Father did love me, I, too, did love you. Remain in my love.** The two aorist indicatives state two past facts, and they are bound together: the one love is exactly like the other. This leads to the conclusion that Jesus here speaks of the Father's love for him as the incarnate Son, not of the ineffable love between the Persons of the Godhead irrespective of the incarnation and the mission of Jesus. This view is estab-

lished by v. 10, Jesus remaining in his Father's love by keeping his Father's precepts. We may thus think of Matt. 3:17, "This is my beloved Son, in whom I am well pleased." The Father loved the incarnate Son for doing his will in the mission of redemption.

This same love filled Jesus and evidenced itself at every turn in his relation to the disciples and in his dealings with them. Looking back to the day when they first met Jesus, they had to say, "He did love us." What makes this love of Jesus for the disciples exactly like the love of the Father for Jesus is by no means the thought that the disciples are on a par with Jesus, but that both kinds of love deal with the mission of Jesus, with its saving purpose. The Father loved him who executes this mission, and Jesus loves those in whom this mission is executed. Thus these two kinds of love are alike.

After laying down these two preliminary facts, their purpose is revealed: "Remain in my love," ἐν τῇ ἀγάπῃ τῇ ἐμῇ, "in this love of mine," so like that of the Father to me. Jesus explains that to remain in him means that we remain in his love. He and his love are one. The aorist imperative means, "remain once for all!" Let its golden circle surround you permanently. Let it ever shine upon you and carry out all its saving purposes for you. On the force of the verb ἀγαπᾶν see 3:16, and on this verb applied to the disciples alone in distinction from the world see 14:23, 24. "In my love" means only Jesus' love for the disciples and cannot be extended to include our love for him, and still less our love for the brethren.

10) The bidding to remain in Jesus' love opens the question as to how the disciples are to do this bidding. In his answer Jesus points to himself and shows how he himself remains in his Father's love. **If you guard my precepts you shall remain in my love, just as I have guarded my Father's precepts and remain in his love.** On guarding the precepts of

Jesus (τηρεῖν and ἐντολαί) see 8:51 and 14:15. There
Jesus presents this guarding of his precepts as the
proof of our love for him; here as the condition for
our remaining in his love to us. The two go together
in a reciprocity of love: one love answering the other.
The great and blessed model for us is Jesus himself.
He has cherished and guarded the precepts (*Auf-
traege*) of his Father. The perfect tense presents all
that he has done in this respect as finished and now
present before his disciples; compare 12:49, 50 and
10:17, 18 on this faithfulness of his carrying out his
Father's will. It includes his act of this night in giving himself into the hands of Satan for his sacrificial
death, 14:31. All that Jesus did for our salvation=
the Father's "precepts" to Jesus; to believe, follow,
love, serve Jesus = his "precepts" to us. Both center
in God's love for us. "I remain in his love," with its
present tense following the perfect "I have guarded,"
declares that now, when all is done, Jesus leaves his
disciples with the Father's love completely enfolding
him. Thus the disciples are to remain in Jesus' love.
Nothing need be added about their remaining also in
the Father's love, for the oneness of the love of the
Father and of Jesus toward them has already been
stated in 14:23.

11) The love of Jesus for the disciples is for them
not merely to have but to enjoy. **These things have
I spoken to you in order that my own joy may be
in you, and that your joy may be made full.** "These
things" is best taken to embrace all that Jesus said
in v. 1-10 about bringing much fruit in accord with
Jesus' "precepts" and the love of the Father and of
Jesus. The purpose of them is the joy of the disciples.
For these "precepts" are not grievous, I John 5:3, like
the burdens of the scribes and of the Pharisees, Matt.
23:4; Luke 11:46. They arouse nothing but joy.
While Jesus does not directly identify the Father's love
for him with his love for the disciples, since the differ-

ence in spite of the close relation is plain, he does
identify his own joy with that of the disciples, for it is
one and the same. This identification precludes the
explanation that Jesus' joy lay in guarding the Father's
precepts and that of the disciples is to lie in guarding
the precepts of Jesus. For these two classes of precepts differ, and thus the joy would likewise differ.
While no object is mentioned as producing the joy, we
at once see that, if the joy of Jesus is to be found also
in the disciples, the object of this joy must be one and
the same. The disciples are to drink from the same
cup of joy from which Jesus drank. What rejoices
him is to rejoice them.

This can be only the blessed state of the disciples,
their union with Jesus ($\mu\acute{\epsilon}\nu\epsilon\iota\nu$, so oft repeated), they in
him, and he in them. To attain this union and its
permanency was the purpose of the Father's precepts
to Jesus and the purpose of Jesus' precepts to the
disciples. The accomplishment of the union with
Jesus is the net result of all these precepts, and in the
union thus accomplished lies the joy of Jesus and of
his disciples. In Jesus this joy is already made full,
for he beholds all that the union of his disciples with
him means both for himself and for them. This is
not as yet the case with the disciples, in fact they
are now troubled (14:1 and 27), and sorrow has filled
their heart (16:6). But the joy of Jesus which is in
them and thus is also their joy is eventually also to be
made full. Note the tenses: first the present subjunctive to indicate the joy now continuing in the disciples;
then the aorist $\pi\lambda\eta\rho\omega\theta\tilde{\eta}$, to designate the final complete
fulness of joy — like a measure at last filled to the
brim. The passive points to Jesus as the agent who
will fill this joy to the full. Compare 17:13. Examples of this great joy are seen in Phil. 2:17, 18; 4:4;
Gal. 5:22; Rom. 14:17.

12) We cannot agree that when Jesus now names
the precept of brotherly love, this one precept con-

stitutes the summary of the plural "precepts" of which he speaks in v. 10 and otherwise. Still less are we able to appreciate the motive back of this summary, namely that the disciples are not to fear the many precepts as though they were like those of the scribes and Pharisees who delighted in multiplying the outward regulations, making as many as possible, and that, therefore, Jesus reduces all his precepts to one only. How does this conception harmonize with 13:34, where the precept of fraternal love is called "a new precept"? We ought to be willing to admit both that Jesus nowhere indicates that brotherly love forms a summary of all his ἐντολαί, and that the nature of this precept is not such as to serve as a summary. What Jesus really does by here introducing this one precept, which he has already laid down as distinctive of our connection with him (13:34), is to offer this one as a sample and illustration of what all his precepts are like. **This is my precept, that you keep loving each other just as I did love you.** *"My* precept" = the one that is mine and as such distinct, and as such both natural and distinctive for all who are mine ("in me"). Note the strong emphasis on the possessive pronoun. The older grammar must be corrected: ἵνα is non-final, it introduces a clause in apposition with αὔτη (feminine because of ἐντολή), one which states the contents of the precept. The sense is not, "that you *should* love," nor is will and intention expressed by ἵνα; it is simply, "to love each other," the verb naturally being a durative present, "keep loving."

This precept, however, includes as its integral part the clause, "just as I did love you." This means with the same kind of ἀγάπη, having the same insight and intelligence, the same motive and purpose. The disciples are not merely to be attached to each other, devoted to each other, helpful to each other. Many

who are not disciples show this kind of love, even calling each other brother.   To love as Jesus loved is to
see what he sees, the soul's needs, the eternal interests;
and since these are fellow-disciples with us, these needs
and these interests in connection with our mutual discipleship, i. e., what our brethren need as brethren in
the bond which binds us most intimately together.
Secondly, besides this insight and understanding our
fraternal ἀγάπη includes that we have the same purpose
and will toward our brethren that Jesus showed toward
us.   He was bent on one thing and one alone toward
his disciples: to keep them in the Father's love which
is life and salvation, to further and advance them in
God's grace, to multiply God's spiritual gifts to them.
This is the love that is "his own," which is different
from the common love of men; and this love is to animate all his disciples in their relation toward each
other.   This, too, makes *his* precept of love "new"
(13:34), although this newness is not emphasized in
the present connection.   We must note the aorist: just
as "I did love" you during all my earthly contact
with you.

13)   Jesus indicates how far this love is able to
go, how great a sacrifice it is able to make.   **Greater
love no one has than this, that one lays down his
life in behalf of his friends.**   This is a general proposition.   The world over it is acknowledged as the
supreme evidence of love that a person voluntarily
gives up his own life for the sake of his friends.
Measured by this common human standard, Jesus is
even now in the act of manifesting this supreme love,
he is laying down his life in behalf of his friends,
the disciples.   And they, not merely witnessing this
act of his but as his friends reaping all the benefit of
this love of his and of this free surrender of his life
for their sakes, are to let the same love fill their hearts
and, when called upon, are to prove their love by

making the same kind of sacrifice for each other. "Herein perceive we the love of God, that he laid down his life for us: and we ought to lay down our lives for the brethren," I John 3:16.

We must resist the tendency to crowd too much into the comparison here made. Jesus, we note, in this connection says nothing about again taking up the life laid down for others. This act places his sacrifice absolutely in a class by itself as we see in 10:17, 18. Here he contents himself with the mention of the sacrifice as such. He does not even mention himself as the one giving this supreme proof of his own love, he allows us to make this application to his love just as we make this application to our own love. This means, furthermore, that in the present connection the redemptive effect of the sacrifice of his own life for us is left out, for none of us, by laying down his life for the sake of the brethren, could possibly duplicate this redemptive effect. Furthermore, Jesus does not intend to say that we must lay down our life for the brethren and that, unless we do, our love will not be like his. For the supreme sacrifice is demanded only in rare instances, such as that of Aquila and Priscilla referred to in Rom. 16:4; and even these two were not required actually to die. What Jesus says is that our love for our brethren must be willing to rise to this height, thus following his own example.

On the expression "to lay down the life" see 10:11 and 17, 18. It is peculiar to John. The tense is properly the aorist, punctiliar because this is a single act. On ὑπέρ see 10:11. In the present connection it is broad: "in behalf of" in any sense of bringing benefit to the brethren. Yet even here this includes the narrower and specific sense, found so plainly in 10:11 and 17, 18, "instead of," with the thought of substitution. It is in vain to deny the thought of substitution in our passage and then to transfer this denial into chapter

10.   After μείζονα we need no ἤ; and ἵνα is so certainly non-final and merely appositional to ταύτης, that the point need not be argued, R. 393, 699, 992, etc.

14) The term "friends" in v. 13 is purposely chosen, for it has two sides: the disciples are friends in relation to each other, and at the same time they are friends of Jesus. **You are my friends if you keep doing what I bid you.**   "Friends," φίλοι, is derived from φιλεῖν, to love with affection, and denotes an affectionate and intimate relation.   The condition on which this relation exists and continues is that the disciples keep doing the Lord's bidding, *was ich euch auftrage;* and ἐάν expects that they will do so.   Note the verb ἐντέλλομαι which is identical with the noun ἐντολή used so often.   Jesus and the disciples are unequal friends.   He condescends greatly when accepting them as friends, they are lifted high by being accepted as his friends.   This relative position is not abolished, hence these lowly friends receive directions and orders from their supreme Friend.   They remain the δοῦλοι they are, "slaves," 13:16; 15:20; yet these "slaves" are treated as "friends" by their divine Lord.

15) How they are, indeed, his friends Jesus at once explains. **No longer am I calling you slaves, because the slave does not know what his lord does; but you I have called friends because all that I heard from my Father I did make known to you.** How long Jesus had been calling his disciples "friends" is not indicated, but note Luke 12:4, where this designation is introduced as a matter of course.   The slave or bondservant simply receives his master's orders and carries them out; his master would not confide his plans and his purposes to him.   Such is the status of the δοῦλος.   That of the disciples has been far different.   It has been that of friends in the fullest sense of the word, for Jesus confided to them all that he had heard from his Father.   This embraces everything pertaining to his mission, that he was to be the light and the

life of the world, to make the blind to see, to satisfy the hungry and the thirsty, to make the dead alive, that he is now giving his life for the world, is now returning to the Father, is coming again spiritually, and is returning at the last day to judge the world and to take his own to himself into the heavenly mansions.

We cannot reduce πάντα to refer only to all things intended for impartation to the disciples, or to all things they now needed for their salvation. He, indeed, says that he has yet many things to say to the disciples (16:12), but these are not new revelations, they are fuller presentations of what he has already said to the disciples (14:26), and thus are delegated to the Paraclete (16:13). Jesus never wanted his disciples to be mere δοῦλοι, blindly obeying orders, but δοῦλοι that were friends, intimately acquainted with all his heart's desires and all his work and mission. He is now parting from them as such friends, still revealing to them his most intimate concerns. The Greek has "I did make known," whereas our idiom would use "I have made known," R. 845.

16) But the term "friends" must be safeguarded. Ordinarily it denotes mutuality and reciprocity. Friends choose each other. This is not the case regarding these friends. **You on your part did not choose me, but I on my part did choose you and did appoint you that you go and bear fruit, and that your fruit remain; that whatever you ask the Father in my name he give you.** By placing the negative and the affirmative side by side Jesus makes the statement strongly emphatic. The negation, "you did not choose me," is proof that the affirmation, "I did choose you," cannot refer to predestination but must refer to the choice of the disciples as the friends whom Jesus selected for himself (middle voice) for the apostleship (6:70; 13:18). Read the sentence aloud with full accent on all the pronouns, which helps to bring out the sense. The action of Jesus was two-

fold: *I* on my part chose *you* and appointed *you*, ἔθηκα, placed you in an important position (no examples of this use are cited in M.-M.).

The two ἵνα clauses are parallel, and both are equal to accusatives; in sense they are like infinitives (R. 992-3). These non-final ἵνα clauses do not express purpose and should not be translated as formerly, "that you *should* go," etc., "that he *may* give," etc. Both simply express the substance of the appointment: for you to go and to bear fruit; for your fruit to remain; for the Father to give you, etc. To "friends" chosen entirely by himself Jesus commits his great work. But he speaks of it not as a task, a burden, or the like, but as an honor, a gift, a blessing. In the doubling "that you go and bear fruit" the first verb is not merely circumstantial but denotes the actual going of the apostolic mission, Matt. 28:19; Acts 1:8. "Bear fruit" reverts only incidentally to the previous allegory and affords no jurisdiction for making ἔθηκα mean, "I planted you," or for bringing in the figure of planting a tree. *"You,"* says Jesus, are to go and to bear fruit, and *"your* fruit" is to remain. The tenses are presents, picturing the actions as they proceed. What a high and glorious position for these friends of Jesus: one graced with abiding fruit! Compare 4:38 and 14:12.

A second ἵνα clause is subjoined, but not as denoting purpose. These apostles are not to bear fruit "in order that the Father may do what they ask"; nor did Jesus make his appointment "in order that" their petitions may be heard. Both thoughts are incongruous and are entertained only because the old idea that ἵνα must be final has not been shaken off. This ἵνα states what Jesus furthermore appointed. He knows that these friends of his, when they are to go to produce fruit of their own accord, may hesitate and fear their inability. Their very appointment takes

care of this; the second ἵνα, like the first, depending
on ἔθηκα. Jesus has appointed that the Father give
them whatever they may ask him. The words are
really a great promise, one that is here connected with
fruit bearing, just as in 14:13 the same promise is
connected with the doing of the greater works. The
same limitation applies also to "whatever you shall
ask," and "in my name" has the same sense, see 14:13.
The aorist subjunctives αἰτήσητε and δῷ refer to any individual case in which the disciples shall ask, and the
Father shall give. In 14:13 it is Jesus who answers
their prayers, here it is the Father. Both persons are
equal; all works are ascribed equally to all three Persons. So also as regards the asking. Here it is the
Father who is asked; in Acts 7:58; I Cor. 1:2; II Cor.
12:8; Rev. 22:20 it is Jesus.

17) **These things I bid you that you keep
loving each other.** This repeats v. 12, only changing the noun ἐντολή, "precept" or "bidding," into the
verb ἐντέλλομαι, "I bid you," "give you precept." This
ἵνα, too, like the one in v. 12 and the two in v. 16, is
non-final for the same reason as the others; it states
what the Lord bids his disciples do. The Greek is able
to use the plural ταῦτα where the appositional clause is
but a single act, "that you keep loving." In such a
neuter plural the Greek seems to view the single act
as composed of detailed parts: "keep loving" now
in one, now in another way, as each circumstance
requires. This explanation would be completely satisfactory if we could point to other examples in which
ἵνα is appositional to ταῦτα, yet these are lacking. For
this reason, and since in the present instance the apposition really cannot be questioned, one may be inclined
to regard ταῦτα as not only covering the ἵνα clause, but
also as referring back and taking in the great motivation for the love of the disciples which Jesus has
introduced since v. 12. They are to love each other as

the chosen friends of Jesus, to whom he has made
his entire mission known, who are going forth to bear
fruit, and whose every prayer in their work the Father
answers. Linked together in this supreme way, how
can the disciples do otherwise than to love each other
with that love of mutual intelligence and purpose
restricted to them in their union with Jesus and with
each other?

8. The Disciples Facing the World, 15:18-16:4

18) The friendship of Jesus means the enmity
of the world. On this subject Jesus informs the disciples most fully in advance. **If the world hates you,
realize that it has hated me in advance of you.**
The protasis is one of reality: the world actually hates
the disciples of Jesus, and they have already experienced this hatred. "Hates you" includes both the
hostile animus of the world toward the disciples and
the hostile manifestations of this animus in word and
in deed. The entire context shows that "the world"
signifies all those opposed to Jesus, who reject him
when he and his saving grace are brought to them.
Both of our English versions translate with the indicative, "you know," but the commentators prefer the
imperative, "know," "realize." The decision must be
made on the basis of the context and the tone of what
Jesus says, and these favor the imperative. Jesus
bids the disciples to keep in mind and to consider how
the world treated him. This will make it seem less
strange to them when they find themselves treated in
the same way. The perfect "has hated me" covers
the entire past hatred Jesus experienced and spreads
it out for the disciples to consider. "Me in advance of
you" both differentiates between Jesus and the disciples and yet implies a connection between them, the
one now set forth.

19) **If you were of the world, the world would love its own; but because you are not of the world, but I on my part did choose you out of the world, therefore the world hates you.** The conditional sentence expresses present unreality, "if you were" — but you are not; "the world would love" — but now it does not. To be "of the world" means to have a nature and a character derived (ἐκ) from the world and thus to be inwardly one with it, i. e., "its own." Naturally the world would "love" its own; and the right word is φιλεῖν, natural affection and passion, and not ἀγαπᾶν, the high, intelligent, purposeful love of an ethical state. The condition is axiomatic and is a major premise.

This is followed by what we may call a minor premise: "but you are not of the world." That, indeed, is the fact, but it needs elucidation. It is by an act of Jesus, reflecting all credit upon him, that the disciples are "not of the world." "I on my part (ἐγώ, emphatic) did choose you for myself (ἐξελεξάμην, middle voice) out of the world." Once the disciples, too, were "of the world," in harmony with its thoughts and its ways. But Jesus separated them from the world. The phrase ἐκ τοῦ κόσμου, used three times, really has the same meaning throughout; the difference lies in the verbs, twice the copula: you were, you are not "from the world," and once a verb, itself compounded with ἐκ: I chose you "from out the world." The context forbids that we think of an act taking place in eternity; this choice occurred when the disciples were drawn to Jesus. Nor must we make the choosing too narrow, for, as John himself shows us in the first chapter, the Baptist had an instrumental part in it. Likewise, since this choice is here conceived as separating the disciples from the world, its object is only discipleship in general and not apostleship in par-

ticular. The world hates all who believe and trust
in Jesus.

Now the syllogistic conclusion: "therefore the
world hates you," διὰ τοῦτο, "for this reason." It is
thus Jesus himself who after a manner has brought
the world's hatred upon the disciples. He himself is
the opposite of the world, and when he joined the
disciples to himself, they as well as he suffered the
world's hate. The world "hates you," μισεῖ, durative,
with a steady, unchanging antipathy. In the case of
the disciples one motive of this hatred is that the world
feels that the disciples originally belonged to it and
have been snatched away from it, have really turned
traitors to the world.

20) The case of the disciples may be stated in
a still clearer and stronger way. **Remember the
word which I said to you, the slave is not greater
than his master. If me they persecuted, you, too,
will they persecute; if my word they guarded, your
word, too, will they guard.** The imperative "remember" is unquestioned, and this helps to make us
certain that we must have the imperative in v. 18.
Verbs of emotion govern the genitive (R. 508), and
among them is "to remember," which accounts also
for οὗ, attracted to the case of its antecedent. Note
the tense: the disciples are always to remember this
word of Jesus. He refers to the word he spoke in
13:16 and in Matt. 10:24, now utilizing it as in the
latter instance. A δοῦλος, one bound as a slave or
bondservant to his κύριος, his master or lord, cannot
possibly be greater than this master. The statement
is again axiomatic. It is negative, thus a litotes, a
stronger way of affirming that a slave is always less,
always lower than his master. The reference to a
δοῦλος matches what Jesus has just said about his
having chosen the disciples. By his choice Jesus
acquired the disciples as his δοῦλοι. A slave is not

allowed to choose his master, the reverse is the case.
Jesus has made these disciples his own.   To be sure,
it is a thousand times better and higher to be slaves
of this glorious Master, who makes his slaves his
confidants and friends, than to remain imaginary
masters of ourselves but in reality slaves of the devil.
But, belonging as we do to Jesus as our Master, this
is certain, we cannot hope to enjoy a better fate than
he has had with regard to the world.

First, the axiomatic general principle, next, two
obvious, undeniable deductions from that principle.
They run in opposite directions, yet each is a complement and a corollary of the other: to persecute — to
cherish.   Both deductions are stated in conditional
form, and both in identical form; yet they are obviously
opposed to each other, the first "if" contemplating what
will be, the second "if" what *will not be.*   The plural
indefinite subjects of the verb forms are drawn from
the collective "the world."   The emphasis is on the
objects: "me . . . you, too," "my word . . .
your word, too"; for this reason the objects are placed
before the verbs.   Since there are no other modifiers
in the clauses, the verbs are put in the last place, thus
also being emphatic, the emphasis being heightened by
the repetition and by the constrasting sense of the two
pairs.   This likewise makes the tenses pointed, two
pasts in contrast with two futures.   Jesus chooses two
activities of the world which apply equally to himself
and to the disciples: persecution and guarding the
Word.   In both Master and disciple fare alike in the
world.

The "if" clauses are clauses of reality and have the
force of questions: Did they persecute Jesus?   did
they keep his Word?   They most certainly did the one
and did not do the other.   Exactly so will they do
with the disciples and with their Word.   And here
we see how the hatred of the world actually shows

itself: by persecution back of which lies hostile unbelief.   The commentators are not agreed in regard to
the second deduction because its implication is the
direct opposite of that involved in the first deduction.
All are satisfied with, "If me they persecuted, you, too,
will they persecute," because this is affirmative: they
did — they will.   But some think it would be ironical
to go on, "if my word they guarded, your word, too,
will they guard," because this sounds negative: they
did not guard — they *will* not guard.   But why should
this be irony?   We have no indication whatever that
Jesus in the first instance means that the majority of
the world did and will persecute and in the second
instance that at least a minority did keep and will keep
the Word.   As Jesus speaks of "the world" it is one;
he does not in either instance indicate a class that will
allow itself to be won from the world.   "The world"
means those permanently opposed to Jesus.   Nor is
he concerned about gradations, some worldlings raging with hostility, some being mildly adverse, some
being merely cold and indifferent.   To be sure, "the
world" shows these gradations, but even those who
politely turn from the Word are "world" and, when
occasion forces the issue upon them, even these will
bear malice toward Jesus and his disciples in no gentle
measure.   The hatred and the opposition are always
in the world and come out as occasion offers.   "My
word" and "your word" are not two different words,
teachings, or doctrines, but identical in substance,
once presented by Jesus in person, then by the disciples as his representatives.

21)   From the manifestations of the world's hatred
Jesus turns to its inner cause, on which especially the
disciples must be clear.   **On the contrary, all these
things will they do to you because of my name, because they do not know him that sent me.**   The
adversative ἀλλά implies a preceding negative and

justifies our explanation: they *did not* keep my Word and *will not* keep your Word, "on the contrary," ἀλλά, etc. They (the world) "will do all these things to you," which Jesus has just briefly summarized, "all" indicating that these hateful things will be many, "because of my name," the emphasis resting on this weighty phrase. Here is the taproot of the world's hatred for the disciples. The case of Jesus and that of the disciples are not mere parallels, even as in the very first place Jesus and the disciples are not mere fellows or associates, both being devoted to the same cause. No; he chose them, not they him; he is the master, they the slaves whom he raised to his side as his friends. Thus all that happens to the disciples is wholly because of Jesus, "because of my name." Here again the significant term ὄνομα denotes the revelation by which Jesus is made known. By his "name" or revelation he comes to men, he and all that he is and has for men. Thus we believe in his name, confess his name, pray in his name, and, as we are now told, suffer because of his name. Always it is his NAME. Of course, we could not suffer because of his name if we were not in vital connection with that name and with the person this name reveals, a connection that is apparent also to the world. The implication is that by word and by deed we confess Jesus' name. This is what the world resents in us. So, not on our own account will the world hate us, but only on account of Jesus. The more it sees of him in us, the more it turns against us. Here we have a hint as to how some disciples manage to evade the hatred of the world: they are not as true to Jesus' name as they should be; they sometimes leave that name at home and fail to confess it before men.

Back of this aversion to Jesus and to all that reveals him to men lies something still deeper. Why will the world persecute the disciples because of his name? Jesus answers, "because they do not know him that sent me." This is not intended to excuse the world but to blame the world in the highest degree, for the next verse brings out the guilt of this ignorance. "They do not know" = they do not as much as know. The world, indeed, talks of God and may even call him Christian names like Father, but theirs is only a figment of the mind, an idol of human invention, constructed according to the ideas of the world; compare 8:19, 38, 42, etc. The true God, who alone exists, who sent his Son to redeem the world, the world does not know; and, holding to its self-made god, the world fights against this true God and his Son and persecutes those who confess this Son and his great Sender. This is the inner reason for the world's hatred, and the disciples of Jesus must understand it fully.

22) What lies in the phrase "because of my name," and what makes the world's lack of knowledge regarding the Sender of Jesus so blameworthy, needs explicit statement. **If I had not come and spoken to them, they would not have sin; but now they have no excuse for their sin.** The conditional sentence has a protasis of past unreality and an apodosis of present unreality. That we must so read it appears from the clause that follows which refers to the present, R. 921, 1013. In the apodosis ἄν is omitted, as is often the case in conditions of unreality; and the form εἴχοσαν is the imperfect with the ending σαν instead of ν. Our versions mistranslate the apodosis by making also it past unreality. "If I had not come and spoken to them" refers to the Messianic coming and teaching of Jesus by which his "name" and revelation was fully made known to the world. "To them" refers to the world as it was at that moment represented in the Jews who rejected Jesus, and thus to any and to all unbelievers who at any time hear the "name" and reve-

lation and turn against it. The coming of Jesus (or of his gospel) to men is always a serious thing; it means either faith or unbelief and, if the latter, unbelief robbed of all excuses.

"They would not have sin" does not mean sin in general but, as the thought indicates, the sin of wilful, obdurate unbelief which rests upon all who definitely spurn Jesus. "But now they have no excuse for their sin" does not imply that otherwise they would have an excuse for their sin of unbelief; for the simple reason that then they would not be in this fixed unbelief at all, they would be only like others who have never as yet heard of Jesus. What Jesus means is that these determined unbelievers have not even as much as an excuse, πρόφασις, *Ausrede*, an "ostensible reason" (M.-M., 555), the figleaf of some pretext behind which to hide. So perfectly has Jesus done his work, so completely did he reveal himself (his name), that no unbeliever is able to find even the shadow of an excuse for rejecting him. On the day of judgment every wicked unbeliever will be like the guest at the king's son's wedding — dumb: "and he was speechless," Matt. 22:12. To all the other sin and guilt for which Jesus offers the richest forgiveness the world only adds this most inexcusable and thus most damnable of all sins for which no forgiveness is possible, namely persistent unbelief. We now also see just what type of ignorance Jesus has in mind in v. 21 in the clause, "because they do not know him that sent me." This is not the vincible ignorance which yields to the light of truth but the invincible ignorance which loves darkness rather than the light, 3:19, 8:45. The world knows the Sender of Jesus because Jesus reveals him; yet the world does not know this Sender because, when he is revealed, the world shuts its eyes against him. For this sin not even a sham excuse can be found.

23) In v. 21 Jesus states two reasons why the world mistreats the disciples: 1) because of my name, 2) because the world does not know my Sender. He now combines these two. The fact that they are really one already lies in the formulation of the second reason, "him that did send me." The "name" reveals that the Father sent Jesus. The world's hatred flows from the combined rejection of Jesus and of the Father. Jesus now lifts this into full clearness. **He that hates me hates also my Father.** He whose characteristic mark is enduring hatred of me (the substantivized present participle) by that very hatred hates also my Father (durative present main verb). These are not two kinds of hatred, they are one. It is impossible to hate Jesus alone. No man is able to separate Jesus and his Father. We know the Father only in Jesus whom he has sent, 1:18; 14:7; and the whole coming of Jesus, his whole work, is to show us the Father, 14:8-11. It is a deep delusion for any man to think that he can love God, honor, and obey God, while he rejects the Son of God and the redemption and atonement which the Son was sent to work out, 8:42, 43.

24) The simple proposition of v. 23 is expanded by introducing the ultimate proof, the works of Jesus. This at the same time amplifies v. 22, which speaks of the words of Jesus. These words alone should have been enough to produce faith; but to cut off the last hope of even specious excuse Jesus now adds the works. **If I had not done the works among them which none other did, they would not have sin; but now they have both seen and have hated both me and my Father.** The entire sentence structure is exactly like that of v. 22, a mixed conditional sentence of unreality (past — present), ἄν omitted, followed by νῦν δέ, "but as it is," R. 1147. Jesus stresses the works he has done as the ultimate convincing proof that

should bar out unbelief; and when they are met with unbelief, this is absolutely inexcusable. He has done this before in 5:36; 10:38; 14:11. The supreme character of these works is stressed: "which none other did," we should say, "has done"; compare 9:32. These works were intended to lift Jesus far above all the prophets the Jews ever had, and they did this. Their Messianic power struck the pilgrims as being beyond question, 7:31. The Jewish leaders dreaded the effect of these works and for this reason especially wanted Jesus out of the way, 11:47, 48. Rationalism, which glibly does away with these miraculous works, had not yet arisen to bring a show of comfort to Jewish unbelief. The miracles of Jesus, once wrought and recorded by inspiration, now stand for all time; their original effect goes on through the ages. "If I had not done the works" puts every unbeliever, be he old or new, fatally in the wrong. What is your answer to "the works"? This decides your fate and mine.

"They would not have sin" (now $\epsilon\tilde{\iota}\chi o\nu$) is to be taken in the same sense as in v. 22, i. e., such sin as they now have, the unbelief that damns. In v. 22 the final adversative statement mentions only the fact that they are now without excuse for their sin. The parallel adversative statement in v. 24 goes deeper and declares how they come to be without excuse: "but now they have both seen and have hated both me and my Father." We have two "both . . . and," and the two objects "me and my Father" belong to both verbs. The perfect tenses of these include the effect as it continues in the present: what they once saw they still see; as they once hated they still hate. This seeing of "both me and the Father" in the revelation made by the miracles of Jesus revealed Jesus as that Father's Son, and the Father as his Father who had sent this Son to do these mighty and gracious works. In v. 21 Jesus says, "they do not know," and here, "they have

seen." Both the negative and the affirmative are true,
but the thought is different. They do not know
although they know; they have seen and yet have not
seen. Real knowing is denied, outward seeing is
affirmed. The two statements are keen complements
of each other.

"They have both seen and have hated" coordinates
two opposite facts and thus brings out the unreason-
ableness which proves the guilt. How could they, how
can they see (both ideas lie in the perfect tense) Jesus
and his Father in the works, and then how could they,
how can they still hate (both ideas again in the perfect tense) the one as well as the other? To do so is
not merely unnatural, it is damnable. The combination of these two actions damns and brands itself.
This hatred of the world directed against both Jesus
and his Father, guilty to the core, self-condemned
from its very start, is the hatred Jesus tells his disciples they will meet in all its viciousness when he is
gone.

25) But let not the disciples imagine that this
hatred is new and without parallel. **Yea, in order
that the word that has been written in their law
may be fulfilled, They did hate me without cause.**
Of course, ἀλλά is elliptical, something must be supplied between it and ἵνα. But we cannot agree with
the idea that in this case ἀλλά is adversative. Our versions, B.-D. 448, 7, and others supply, "but this cometh
to pass" (τοῦτο γέγονεν) ; some prefer, "but they that
hated me," supplying the last preceding verb. Zahn
perceives that what follows ἀλλά is not adversative to
the hatred described in v. 24, yet he finds a strong
adversative in ἀλλά, seeking the adversative idea in
"they have seen." Careful thought leads us to conclude that the adversative idea is incorrect; this ἀλλά,
like the one in 8:26 and in a goodly number of other
places, is copulative and equal to our "yea" or "now";

read R. 1185, etc., and note how simply and perfectly the copulative idea fits the present context, and how it then matters little whether we supply, "yea (this comes to pass) in order that," etc.; or, "yea (they have hated me and the Father) in order that," etc.   In no case could we leap over "they have hated" and supply "they have seen"; such a leap would not merely be impossible, the very sense would forbid our making it. Jesus tells the disciples that this hatred of the world toward him and toward his Father *accords* with what is written in the Scriptures.   The idea is copulative not adversative or contrary to the Scripture word.

Jesus refers to Ps. 35:19, or 69:4 (69:9 is quoted in John 2:19).   But there are two ways — not merely one — in which the fulfillment of Old Testament words took place.   In the one case we have a direct prophecy of a coming event, and the words originally uttered and recorded referred to that future event.   The fulfillment occurred when this predicted event took place. Then we find other statements in the Old Testament which are not intended as direct prophecies of future events but concerning which we are told in the New Testament that these words were fulfilled by happenings that occurred at this time.   The New Testament events are of the same kind as those mentioned in the Old Testament, they are like parallels.   The holy writers, including Jesus, recognize this correspondence and use it with striking effect.   This is the case here. Jesus applies to himself what David uttered concerning himself.   The words that fit David in his suffering fit Jesus even more perfectly.   They would, of course, fit any righteous man suffering wrongfully and might thus be rightly applied to him.   Since Jesus is absolutely righteous, the application to him is the most pertinent and perfect of all.   "Fulfilled" is here to be taken in the sense that once again these words of David are applicable to a case which they fit perfectly.   The divine intention (ἵνα) did not cause the hatred of the Jews against Jesus; this intention was to the effect that all the works of Jesus should be of such a character that those who hated him should have no shadow of an excuse for doing so. Every impartial judge would have to corroborate the words appropriated from David by Jesus: "They did hate me without cause." The LXX translated the Hebrew *chinnam*, Latin *immerito*, "in an unmerited manner," δωρεάν, which means "gratuitously" and may here be rendered "without cause."

This statement (λόγος), Jesus says, "has been written" (perfect tense) and thus stands permanently as so written, "in their law," the term νόμος, as in 8:17, designating the entire Old Testament. Note the pronoun "their" law and in 8:17 "your own" law and the fact that Jesus never says, "our law." His relation to the Old Testament is different from the relation of the Jews to that volume, and Jesus carefully marks that difference. In pointing to "their law" Jesus indicates that the Jews who had this law as theirs, given especially to them for their guidance, should have been warned by this λόγος in their law against this causeless hatred; but they read their own law with blind eyes, and even while they read it repudiated and hated both the Father and the Son of whom this law spoke, to say nothing of giving way to a passion which this their own law brands as utterly godless. Those who hate without a cause carry their verdict in their own sin. And this verdict stands to this day against all who repudiate the Father and the Son now revealed in both Testaments.

26) In v. 18-21 Jesus tells the disciples how the world shall hate them just as it has hated him, and in v. 22-25 he describes fully this hate against him, utterly causeless and damnable as it is. When foretelling this hatred of the world toward the disciples,

something is implied, namely that the disciples will not withdraw from the world but will face the world just as Jesus faced it and will bring the testimony of Jesus to bear upon the world just as Jesus bore his testimony. That is why Jesus now says that the disciples will have the Spirit with them and that he and they will both testify. The hatred of the world against the disciples will go on because they will go on with the testimony of Jesus, now having the Spirit at their side. Nothing is said in this connection about the success of this testimony; how it will win many from the world to faith in Jesus. The fact that the testimony of the Spirit and of the disciples certainly will not be in vain but will bear "much fruit" has already been indicated in v. 1-16; so here this is understood.

But when the Paraclete shall come (the aorist to indicate the single act of Pentecost) **whom I myself will send to you from the Father, the Spirit of the truth who proceeds from the Father, he shall testify concerning me; and you, too, testify because from the beginning you are with me.** On the coming of the Paraclete and on this designation for the Spirit see 14:16. The thing to be noted here is the fact that after saying that the Father shall give the Paraclete at Jesus' request, we are now told that Jesus himself will send the Paraclete. The Father's giving is accomplished by the Son's sending; the Son's sending is accomplished by the Father's giving. We know that the *opera ad extra sunt indivisa,* but why they are stated with reference to the Persons in the peculiar ways found in the Scriptures is a mystery to us; compare the remarks on 14:16. Once more the Paraclete is called "the Spirit of the truth" (see 14:16), here evidently because of his work in the world, testifying to the world concerning Jesus. When Jesus says that he will send this Spirit of the truth, we understand that he is speaking of the mission of the Spirit. Jesus sends him for a mighty work and purpose. The dative ὑμῖν, "to you," is best explained by the Spirit's actual coming, Acts 2:1-4; he came upon the disciples and filled them with his presence.

The added phrase "from the Father" does not indicate a subordination of Jesus to the Father. The same is true in 14:16 with regard to the request of Jesus to the Father. There is an assumption that because he does not act independently of the Father he must be lower and less than the Father. Applying this assumption to the Spirit, he would be still lower and less than the Son, for he, too, does not act independently but comes only at the Son's sending. This stressing of the acts of the Persons in relation to each other in order to make one lower than the other is unwarranted. Against this procedure stands every Scripture passage which places the Persons on an equality. Where equals are a unit in a purpose and a work, the equality remains undisturbed when one of these equals requests another, sends another, allows himself to be sent by another, to perform one or the other great part of that work. All these acts reveal only the perfect harmony of these equals in carrying out their one work, each acting with the other, each with the other's consent. A reconstruction of the Trinity which would make each Person act independently in order to conserve the equality of the three is infeasible. The alternative, either such independence or subordination presupposes a full comprehension of what the Trinity must be when no human mind is capable of comprehending even the little this Trinity has revealed of itself, due to making known to us what God has done and still does for our salvation. As regards the phrase "from the Father," why disregard what Jesus so often repeats, that he is now going *to* the Father and that, therefore, when he sends the Spirit, this will naturally be *from* the Father?

As far as subordination is concerned, the human nature of Jesus always was and always will be subordinate; everything it has even in its exaltation it has as a gift. The incarnation of one of the three Persons in no way affects the relation of the three Persons as such.

Some commentators claim that the second relative clause, "who proceeds from the Father," denotes the procession of the Spirit from the Father *in time,* i. e., his coming for his mission at Pentecost, and has nothing to do with the Spirit's inner-Trinitarian relation to the Father, his proceeding from the Father in eternity. This claim overlooks the climax in the three statements regarding the Spirit: Jesus will send him — he is the Spirit of the truth — he proceeds from the Father. These three, piled the one on the other, reveal the greatness, the absolute competence of the Paraclete who is to stand at the side of the disciples in their battle with a hating world. This claim ignores the separation of the two relative clauses by means of the apposition, "the Spirit of the truth." If the two relative clauses refer to Pentecost, why this separation? Again, why the second clause when Jesus already in the first says what the second would repeat with a tautology, namely that the Spirit sent from the Father comes from the Father? Finally, why the change in tense: "I will send — he proceeds"? It is assuming a good deal to claim that the present tense "receives its modification" from the preceding future tense, in plain language, that "he proceeds" means "he will proceed." Moreover, Jesus himself shuts out such a "modification" by placing the apposition between the relative clauses. "Whom I shall send" refers to Pentecost; "who proceeds from the Father" does *not.*

Quite the contrary. Just as behind the incarnation and the mission of Jesus we have his *eternal* generation by the Father, so here behind the sending and the mission of the Spirit we have the Spirit's *eternal* procession from the Father. The blame cast upon the ancient fathers for here finding the eternal procession of the Spirit from the Father is unjustified. Those fathers were right, and these newer men might well learn from them. "Even as the Lord Jesus is the true revelator of the mysteries of God because as the only-begotten Son he has his sole abiding place in the bosom of the Father (1:18); so the Holy Spirit is the trustworthy witness of the heavenly things because he proceeds from the Father." Besser. As the ray is like the sun, the stream like the source, so the Spirit is of the same essence with the Father because he proceeds from him. The fact that this procession is not from the Father alone but, when fully revealed, also from the Son, we see from Rom. 8:9; Phil. 1:19; II Cor. 3:17; Gal. 4:6; Rev. 22:1; etc., where the Spirit is in various ways called the Spirit of Christ. What the procession of the Spirit really means no man knows. God revealed this much concerning the inner relation of the divine persons because in the work of salvation we must know that each of these persons is wholly divine and yet that each is distinct and in a peculiar relation to the others.

The procession of the Spirit is misconceived when it is made a past act, or when the present tense ἐκπορεύεται is made progressive, "is proceeding" in a continuous progress. These notions carry the idea of time into eternity. But eternity is the very opposite of time, the utter absence of time, it is timelessness. The trouble is that our minds are chained to the idea of time so that our conception of eternity always expresses itself in terms of time, a sort of endless time. Our minds do not actually visualize timelessness. So we must constantly tell ourselves that our limited brain cannot possibly reach to the bottom of this vast ocean deep. Human language had to use the present tense "proceeds," for this was all it could do if it wished to express this divine fact by means of a verb. This tense, however, is what the grammarians properly call a timeless present; it intends to express an act that lies above and beyond all conception of time.

The emphatic ἐκεῖνος (R. 708) takes up the subject with all its modifiers: this Spirit so described, *"he shall testify concerning me."* No limitation as to means or extent is added. The entire revelation of Christ in the world since the day of Pentecost is here summed up in one brief expression. All that the Spirit was to do by means of inspiration, by means of the inspired Word, in and through the apostles, in and through the church, all of it is included. So the work will be carried forward by one who is as great as Jesus himself, one who is at the side of the disciples, working ceaselessly through the ages just as Jesus had worked at the side of his disciples until this hour.

27) Yet Jesus adds, "and you, too, testify," δέ meaning "and" and καί "too" or "also," R. 1185. Some regard μαρτυρεῖτε as an imperative, "and do you, too, bear witness!" Yet an imperative would certainly be strange at this point, especially one with a reason attached which indicates only the qualification necessary for witnessing. The imperative is chosen because a future tense precedes, "the Spirit shall testify," which, it is thought, would not harmonize with a following present indicative. But this view overlooks the present tense in the added ὅτι clause, "because from the beginning you *are* with me." "From the beginning" reaches back to the very start of Jesus' ministry, and the present tense "you are" implies that the disciples are still with Jesus now to witness the last part of his redemptive work. R. 879 thus lists ἐστέ as a progressive present and quotes Moulton to the effect that this tense "gathers up past and present time into one phrase," to which, however, we must add that it

allows this present to continue. In view of this qualification of the disciples Jesus can well use the present
tense, "and you, too, (already) testify" as witnesses
who were always with me and continue with me even
now. The ὅτι clause thus indicates why Jesus says,
"and you, too," "you also on your part." The disciples
are needed to testify of all that they have heard and
seen while they were with Jesus. Their testimony
takes care of the historical realities concerning Jesus,
and most of these they already have.

Some, however, contend that Jesus is thinking of
two kinds of testimony: one by the Spirit, the other
by the disciples. They admit that the Spirit aids the
disciples in giving their testimony and in that way
testifies through them; yet they maintain that there is
a special testimony of the Spirit, namely one that consists in his very presence in the world, in the miracles
which he works, in the powers and the gifts he bestows, in the church which he places into and maintains in a hostile world. The world is nonplussed by
this testimony of the Spirit and by the evidence it
affords of the living presence of Jesus in heaven with
the Father and of the work he still does in the world.
The effort to secure two testimonies makes δέ adversative: "but you also," etc., placing the testimony of the
disciples beside that of the Spirit as being different.
The Spirit, however, is present only in the disciples,
the miracles he wrought were done through these men,
and so it is with all the other testimony that in any
way comes from the Spirit. Down to this day the
Spirit uses the Word which he had the holy writers
record and the church which he has built and maintained. The testimony of the Spirit and of the disciples goes out to the world as one. The disciples are
the Spirit's instruments. He and they are joined
together, and thus the testimony is delivered.

CHAPTER XVI

8. The Disciples facing the World, 15:18-16:4

(Continued)

1) **These things have I spoken to you in order that you may not be entrapped.** Jesus does not say that he has "foretold" these things, he has as yet spoken no special prophecy but has only "told" about the world's hatred, helping the disciples to understand its nature and its guilt and thus fortifying them for the future. And this he has done "in order that you may not be entrapped." The figure in σκανδαλίζω is that of a trap in which a crooked stick (σκάνδαλον) holds the bait and springs the trap when touched. The figure is not that of a stumblingblock over which one trips, although many so translate. The passive may be rendered, "that you may not be caught unawares," i. e., going in for discipleship and then suddenly discovering that it means the vicious hatred of the world, something wholly unexpected. The disciples are fully informed as to what discipleship really means; all of its hard and painful features are fully disclosed — no trap is laid for them.

2) Jesus now names two of the worst forms of persecution which the world's hatred will produce. **They shall make you persons banned from the synagogue; yea, the hour is coming that everyone who kills you shall think he is making an offering of service to God.** On ἀποσυνάγωγος see 9:22, and 12:42. To be excommunicated or banned from the synagogue in a land where all were Jews meant to be treated as religious outcasts and renegades to the

nation. When this was done because of fanatic hatred, it became a vicious infliction, indeed. Here ἀλλά is plainly copulative (R. 1186) as in 15:25: "yea," ushering in something that is still worse; and ἵνα after ὥρα is non-final, simply stating what the contents of that hour will be. R. 998 calls it almost temporal: "the hour when," etc. The aorist participle πᾶς ὁ ἀποκτείνας is punctiliar to express the one act of murder, and with R. 1114 we may call it timeless, referring to any act of such murder, yet it denotes the act as completed. The article substantivizes the participle and characterizes the person thus described: "everyone who kills you." The emphasis is on the predicate so that the fact of the disciples being killed becomes merely incidental, something that occurs as a matter of course. The astounding thing is not that the disciples shall be killed but that their killers shall think that such murder is actually the act of offering service to God, bringing a sacrifice to him, λατρεία, worship by sacrifice. Perversion of worship can go no farther. It seems almost incredible that people who have the Scriptures with their revelation of God can so reverse what these Scriptures teach: murder God's children and think that murder an act of high worship. Yet Jewish fanaticism maintained: *Omnis effundeus sanguinem improborum, aequalis est illi, qui sacrificium facit. Bammidbar Rabba,* fol. 329, 1; and pagan fanaticism followed the same principle.

3) Because this perversion is so monstrous Jesus adds an explanation. **And these things they will do because they did not recognize my Father nor me.** Their failure to obtain the true knowledge of the Father and of his Son Jesus left the Jews with an outrageous conception of God. This is not said to excuse but to reveal their guilt. They had the fullest revelation of God and were not left to think of God according to their own sin-darkened minds. Jesus

does not say, "they did not realize God"; he is not thinking only of the Old Testament revelation — although this reveals enough to make all fanaticism impossible. He says, "They did not realize the Father nor me"; he is thinking of the complete and final revelation of God brought to the Jews by himself. This revealed the Father in all his redemptive and saving love and showed that love engaged in the work of redeeming and saving through his Son Jesus. It revealed Jesus as the Son of the Father, come actually to redeem and to save. "This is life eternal, that they should know thee the only true God, and him whom thou didst send," 17:3. Thus the two are here placed side by side and on the same level: "not the Father nor me." The one is known in the other; to know the one is to know both.

In οὐκ ἔγνωσαν (R. 834) we have the complete past failure from which, Jesus says, will result these future monstrous acts. The English might prefer the perfect, "have not known or realized" (R. 845). The Jews made their own God from the thoughts of their own minds like the pagan world around them, like the world of unbelief today. This fictitious God was one that they thought would delight in the persecution and in the destruction of the followers of Jesus. And so they will offer their God such human sacrifices, a λατρεία that the true God abominates. When the disciples realize this they will not be surprised by what they will be called upon to undergo in the time to come.

4) But these things I have told you in order that, when the hour for them comes, you may remember them, that I myself spoke to you. With ἀλλά Jesus breaks off and returns to the thought of v. 1. All three: ταῦτα and the two αὐτῶν refer to what Jesus has· said in 15:18 — 16:3, in particular, like ταῦτα in v. 1, to the preceding exposition of the hatred of the world. Verse 2 is only an incidental specification, added to the main exposition for the sake of completeness. Once more, then, Jesus speaks of his purpose in making known to his disciples the full inwardness of the world's hatred. It is to fortify the disciples in advance so that, when the time comes, they may remember all that Jesus told them on this subject and may find their faith strengthened by his prophetic revelation and thus joyfully endure what comes to them. Note ἡ ὥρα αὐτῶν, "the hour for them," i. e., the things referred to by ταῦτα in v. 1, and not merely the acts mentioned in v. 2. Also the emphatic ἐγώ, "I myself," who knew everything in advance and who told you when the time arrived, that you might believe with full conviction when the world's hatred shall strike you.

The telling of these things Jesus has put off until this time. Why until this time? **And these things I did not tell you from the beginning because I was with you.** This means that no need existed for telling these things either at the very start or prior to the present hour. Jesus fortifies us when we need to be fortified; he hands us the armor just before the battle begins. "Because I was with you" cannot mean: because I was at hand to protect you; for he will ever be at hand and will ever help and protect his own. "Because I was with you" means visibly with you so that hatred was directed toward him. Hitherto the disciples were considered a negligible quantity; the Jews never troubled about the disciples. All the clashes, all the stones that were ready to be thrown, centered on Jesus and left the disciples out of consideration. They had needed no special protection, because they were never attacked. This situation shall soon change. The disciples will stand alone, without the visible presence of Jesus. They will speak and act as Jesus once did. Then they will feel the brunt of the hatred that Jesus had to feel when he was with them.   This is why Jesus now on taking his leave tells the disciples what he does.

The statement of Jesus that up to this time he had not told the disciples "these things" is challenged. This challenge, however, assumes that "these things" refer to v. 2, excommunication and martyrdom; whereas "these things," from v. 1 onward and down through v. 4, deal with the world's hatred as such and thus refer to 15:18-27.   The moment this is recognized, we see how vain it is to point to Matt. 5:10, etc.; 10:16-28 as proof that Jesus contradicts himself when he now says that he has hitherto not spoken of "these things."   Where has Jesus spoken before of the world's hatred as he does in 15:18-27?   Only the incidental comparison of the slave and his master in 15:20 has been used before in Matt. 10:24.   We remove this challenge without resorting to any of the various explanations that are offered, as that Jesus now mentions only the more terrible persecutions, or has heretofore spoken only in part, or in a more general way without stating the cause, or that the disciples hitherto took no note of what Jesus said, so that to them it was as though he had not spoken at all.   Nor need we think that the synoptists took some of the final statements of Jesus and inserted them into his earlier discourses. But Jesus does not contradict himself, and men might well hesitate before they bring such a charge against him.

9.   The Work of the Paraclete in the World and in the Disciples, 16:5-15

5)   Jesus connects with what he has just said but now passes on to a new subject, the advantage of his leaving and sending the Paraclete who will do what is now described in detail.   **But now I go away to him that did send me; and none of you inquires of**

me, Where art thou going? The connection is adversative: in v. 5, "I was with you," and now, "but I go away," hence δέ. Already in 14:28 Jesus had told the disciples that he was going to his Father. When he now calls the Father "him that did send me," the sense is the same save that now the mission of Jesus is specifically mentioned: Jesus returning to his Sender, having completed his mission and the visible stay on earth which it required. He goes to his Sender in order to make report to him of his successful task. When saying that he is returning to his Sender, Jesus makes a basic statement, one that governs all that follows in this chapter.

The addition: "and none of you inquires of me, Where art thou going?" while it is joined with "and," is adversative, "and yet." Strange to say — and Jesus says it with a touch of gentle reproof and of pain in his own heart — not one of the eleven makes a request of him as to where he is going. "Where," ποῦ, is used, as in common English, for "whither," R. 298. The disciples seem to have no interest in this return of Jesus to his Sender. They make no request (ἐρωτᾶν, the more respectful verb) to learn more about the destination of Jesus and about what it means to him to return to his Sender. Jesus is, indeed, not thinking of what his return means for himself personally, his glorification and the blessedness that awaits him with the Father. He has in mind the significance of his return for the disciples whom he is leaving behind. They are making no request to learn something about that from him. Peter's question in 13:36 was of a different kind; it was only a selfish exclamation which would not hear of Jesus' going away alone. And the assertion of Thomas in 14:5 was nothing but an expression of discouragement and dullness of mind at the thought of Jesus' going away while leaving the disciples to follow later on a way that Thomas felt he did

not know. So here Jesus is leaving, his going to his
Sender means so much to the disciples, and yet none
of them requests one word of this precious information.

6) **On the contrary, because I have told you
these things, sorrow has filled your heart.** Instead
of asking as they should, instead of obtaining comfort and joy for their heart by such asking, they have
done the opposite. Just because Jesus spoke "these
things" about leaving them — ταῦτα here referring to
what Jesus said about going away — sorrow has filled
your heart so completely that no room is found for any
other thought or feeling. The Greek has ἡ λύπη, "the
sorrow," meaning the particular sorrow resulting
from his talk about leaving. This is a discouraging
situation for Jesus who has so much of joy and uplift
to impart in these final moments. Note his complaint
in 14:28. But this, too, Jesus had to bear, that his
own disciples had so little appreciation of what his
leaving them really meant.

7) In spite of this downheartedness and this
grief which dominate the hearts of his disciples so
completely, Jesus persists with his efforts to make
them feel something of the great blessedness that his
going away secures for them. **Nevertheless I tell
you the truth: It is an advantage for you that I
depart; for if I do not depart, the Paraclete will not
come to you; but if I go I will send him to you.**
"Nevertheless," ἀλλά, means: although you are so filled
with sorrow. The strong formula, "I tell you the
truth," ἡ ἀλήθεια, "the fact," intends to drive out some
of this sorrow and to make room for what Jesus wants
to put in its place. Note ἐγώ, "I on my part," whatever you in your sorrow may think. And this is the
truth: "It is an advantage for you that I depart,"
now using ἀπέλθω (aorist, a single act). Non-final
ἵνα introduces the predicate clause after the impersonal

συμφέρει. Jesus uses an understatement when he says that it is expedient or advantageous for him to depart. Often, to say less than one could say penetrates farther than at once to say as much as one might.

With γάρ Jesus at once explains, and for greater effect he employs first a negative and then a positive. If Jesus should not depart but continue his stay indefinitely, as the disciples desire, then the Paraclete will not come to them; then all that his coming means for the crowning of Jesus' work, for the greater blessing of the disciples, for their own great work for which Jesus has trained them so long, cannot possibly follow. Jesus' own work would be abortive, an attempt that crumbled into nothing — just because the disciples want to keep on indefinitely enjoying his visible presence here on earth. Over against this empty negative Jesus sets the rich positive, "but if I go," here using only the terse πορευθῶ, "I will send him to you," compare on this as an act of Jesus the same statement in 14:26. With the coming of the Paraclete the great plan of salvation will be gloriously carried to its consummation to the everlasting joy and glory also of the disciples. On the Paraclete see 14:16, also 15:26, including the question as to why the Spirit cannot come until Jesus departs to his Sender. The thought, of course, is not that, if Jesus does not go to heaven, he would not be there to send the Spirit; but that Jesus must complete his redemptive work by his death, resurrection, and ascension, so that the Spirit may take all his work and by means of the gospel spread its saving power to the ends of the earth; see 7:39.

8) The work of the Paraclete will be twofold. He will direct his activity toward the world (v. 8-11), and toward the disciples (v. 12-15). Yet he will do this work as the Paraclete sent to the disciples by Jesus. He abides permanently in them; and this

means that he works through them upon the world, that they are his instruments. Jesus does not say this in so many words, it is understood. The best commentary on the work of the Paraclete with the world is Peter's sermon on Pentecost. The Paraclete worked through Peter, won 3,000 through his preaching, and convicted the scoffers of their folly. The same working appears in connection with the trials of the apostles before the Sanhedrin. None were brought to faith, but the conviction of all by the Spirit, speaking through the apostles, is evident, Acts 4:8, etc.; 5:29, etc. All this shows that the Spirit will be a true Paraclete for the disciples, one who will aid the disciples mightily in the work Jesus had assigned to them in the world. It is thus that Jesus says: **And when he is come he will convict the world concerning sin and concerning righteousness and concerning judgment.** The aorist participle refers to the Spirit's coming at the time of Pentecost; then this work of his will begin, thereafter to continue for all time. The verb ἐλέγχειν may mean "to convict" so that the conviction is fully admitted by those convicted, or "to convict" so that, whether the conviction is admitted or not, its reality is beyond question. Here the latter sense prevails. For "the world," upon which the Paraclete of the disciples works his conviction, will in part be won by that conviction and in part remain obdurate under that conviction. Yet all who do not bow in repentance will, nevertheless, stand convicted like guilty criminals who may still deny the guilt which has been fully proved against them.

This conviction will deal with three subjects: sin, righteousness, and judgment. Neither in connection with the announcing of these subjects, nor in the following exposition of each of them, are articles added. This, however, does not intend to leave the three subjects indefinite as though anything and everything

concerning sin, etc., is to be treated by the Spirit in
dealing with the world.   The exposition in v. 9-11 is
decidedly specific, dealing only with the essential feature of each subject, the one Jesus has in mind from
the start.   The formal repetition of the preposition περί,
together with καί, is made for rhetorical reasons (R.
566), lifting each noun into due prominence.   Why
the Paraclete selects these three subjects, no others,
and no more than these, will appear in the following.

9)   **Concerning sin, inasmuch as they do not believe in me.**   The particles μέν, δέ, δέ simply place
the three subjects side by side and do not intend to
make the first the chief one and the other two subordinate.   The three ὅτι in v. 9-11 have the same force.
They offer more than an instruction of the world in
regard to what sin, righteousness, and judgment are;
hence we cannot translate "that," or "this that."   They
offer more than a proof to the world that sin, righteousness, and judgment exist; hence we should not
translate "because" (our versions).   What these three
ὅτι introduce convicts the world, lays the finger on the
three points in sin, in righteousness, and in judgment
that strike the conscience of the world either to make
it bow in repentance or to harden it in unbelief.   Hence
we translate "inasmuch as," or use an equivalent like
"seeing that."   It is similar to the conjunctions used
in 2:18; 8:22; 9:17; etc.

The thought is not that the world knows nothing
about sin.   Its daily crime list contradicts that, as well
as its moralists with their repressive and reformatory
measures.   What the world lacks and the Spirit supplies is something that goes far deeper, something that
actually convicts in regard to sin.   This is not the fact
that sin is sin, or that the real essence of sin is unbelief.
The Spirit is not to repeat the work of Moses in preaching the law.   The conviction in regard to sin lies in one
direction: "inasmuch as they do not believe in me."   Yet

note that this is the capital sin. For to believe in Jesus is to be saved from sin, to have sin forgiven; and thus not to believe in Jesus is to remain in sin, to perish forever in sin. The Spirit's work in regard to sin is to confront the world with the terrible fact of its unbelief in Jesus, which means, with the fact that this unbelief leaves it in its damnable sin, doomed and damned forever, in other words, that only he who believes escapes from his sin. This conviction in regard to sin naturally operates in two ways. It will crush some hearts so that they will be frightened at their unbelief and cry out like the 3,000 at Pentecost, "Brethren, what shall we do?" Acts 2:37, and thus be led to repent and to believe. Or it will further harden those who resist this conviction; they will go on, convicted though they are, more obdurate than before, fighting against this conviction until they perish. In this the Spirit will do exactly what Jesus did in 7:33, etc., and again in 8:22-24: "I said, therefore, unto you that ye shall die in your sins; for except ye believe that I am he, ye shall die in your sins."

Some fix their attention on the phrase "concerning sin" and thus fail to see the significance of the word "believe" in the elucidating clause, "inasmuch as they do not believe in me," with its implication that this unbelief leaves them in their sin, and that faith, and faith alone, relieves them of their sin. Thus we get those interpretations which turn only on the word "sin," unbelief as the greatest sin, the real nature of sin, and the like. But the Spirit uses "me," Jesus; believing and not believing in Jesus apply to Jesus, unbelief in him and faith in him to the world's sin — if possible, to save the world from sin, otherwise to brand the world with the conviction of its damning unbelief.

10) This conception of v. 9 helps us in interpreting v. 10, 11. **Concerning righteousness, inasmuch**

as I go away to the Father, and you behold me no more. Here ὅτι has the same force as in v. 9; it lays bare that feature of righteousness which the Spirit brings to the world with convicting power, either to effect repentance and faith or to harden unbelief the more. It is vital to note that all three: sin, righteousness, and judgment are the world's for the obvious reason that the world is to be convicted either in a salutary or in a damning way. Since sin is something negative (ἁμαρτία, missing the mark; ἀνομία, contrary to the law; ἀδικία, ἀσέβεια, all negatives), the elucidating ὅτι clause is also negative: "inasmuch as they do *not* believe in me"; but δικαιοσύνη is a positive concept, and its elucidation is thus properly put into positive form: "inasmuch as I go to the Father," the negative side of this is added only for the sake of emphasis: "and you see me no more." The world is far from freely and frankly admitting its sin. It, indeed, feels and knows its sin, especially the gross forms which are too evident to be denied. But always it seeks to cover up its sin, to excuse it in some way, to make it something less than real sin. The world everlastingly seeks "righteousness" in some form, either making itself the judge of its own case, or, when it thinks of God as the judge, conceiving him as a God who deals gently with sin. Thus men evolve their own schemes for appearing righteous. They may think that their good deeds outweigh or atone for their evil deeds; or they accept religions which teach work-righteousness as the true way to heaven. Always the world seeks to find and to secure righteousness for itself by efforts of its own. Often, in doing so, it makes the way hard for men (Matt. 23:4; Luke 11:46), whereas the divine way to righteousness for the sinner is light and easy (Matt. 11:30). Thus one great feature of the

Spirit's work in the world is to convict the world in regard to righteousness.

"Concerning righteousness, inasmuch as I go away to the Father, and you behold me no more," means that all true righteousness for the world of sinners is connected with Jesus, with his return to the Father from his redemptive mission, with the completion of his earthly work and the withdrawal of his visible presence from his disciples. Righteousness is the state of the sinner whom *God* acquits; all other acquittals by men or by human organizations are useless, they do not stand in the court of heaven. The fact that the term is completely forensic is shown *in extenso* and beyond the shadow of a doubt by C.-K., 311, etc., also that in this soteriological righteousness God alone is the judge. Righteousness comes to the world only by the judicial pronouncement of God which changes our status with God. "I go away to the Father," as well as the negative counterpart, "and you see me no more," refer to the death and to the heavenly exaltation of Jesus. In these, and in these alone, is righteousness for the world. Throughout these final discourses of Jesus he speaks of his death and of his exaltation in this manner. If it be asked why he uses the second person in the last clause, "you behold," and not the third, "the world beholds me no more," the answer is easy. "The world" embraces all men in all ages, also those who never saw or could see Jesus while he was on earth; hence it would be incongruous to speak of the world no longer beholding Jesus.

The Spirit's work is to convict the sinners in this world of the fact that true righteousness is available for them only in him who has passed from the cross to his Father's side, in him who once came from the Father and is now gone from our sight. "Let all the house of Israel (and the whole world as well) know assuredly, that God hath made him both Lord and Christ, this Jesus whom ye crucified," Acts 2:36. "And in none other is there salvation; for neither is there any other name under heaven, that is given among men, wherein ye must be saved," Acts 4:12. After showing at length the death and the resurrection of Jesus in his sermon at Antioch of Pisidia (Acts 13:27-37) Paul adds v. 38, 39: "Be it known unto you therefore, brethren, that through this man is proclaimed unto you *remission of sins*, and by him everyone that believeth *is justified* from all things, from which ye could not be justified by the law of Moses." The verb δικαιωθῆναι, "to be declared righteous," brings about δικαιοσύνη, the "righteousness" of which Jesus speaks. The passages in Acts show how the world is convicted in regard to this righteousness and its connection with the departure and the exaltation of Jesus. It is shown how here alone righteousness for sinners is found. Some accept that righteousness, they believe, are justified, and saved; others rebel under the conviction, but they never escape, having been confronted with the true facts about righteousness.

The divergence among the commentators is due, in the first place, to connecting "righteousness" wrongly with God, with Jesus, or with believers, and not, as it should be, with "the world" which is convicted by the Spirit. Thus we are told that "concerning righteousness" means: God vindicated *his* righteousness as a just God by exalting the Christ whom the world rejected; this is what the Spirit brings home to the world. It is true that this thought appears in the preaching of the apostles when the Spirit through them convicted the world, but only as a subsidiary thought, and only in convicting the world of sin, i. e., of the deadliness of unbelief. One view

makes God's righteousness his retributive justice:
he removes Jesus from the sight of the world. To
arrive at this view the sequence of thought in v. 8-11
is: sin — retribution — judgment; and in the ὅτι
clause the chief point is, "and you behold me no
more," with the explanation that this is equal to
the passive, "I am no longer seen." This view is out
of line. The favorite view is to connect "righteousness" with Jesus. We are pointed to Acts 3:14; 7:52;
22:14; I John 2:1, where Jesus is called "the Just
One." The world crucified him as a sinner, God
exalted and vindicated him as a righteous person.
As true as this is, it again belongs in v. 9, for it
evidences the world's unbelief and contradiction of
God and can be only an auxiliary thought in v. 10.
Augustine, Luther, Calvin, and many others connect
"concerning righteousness" with the disciples and believers in general. This is closest to the truth. Yet
this leaves out the obdurate unbelievers who also are
convicted by the Spirit "concerning righteousness."
We must connect the phrase with "the world." A
part of it is convicted in a salutary manner so as to
receive "righteousness" through the exalted Redeemer; the rest are convicted in a judicial manner
because they spurn the only righteousness that exists
for sinners.

11) **Concerning judgment, inasmuch as the
ruler of this world has been judged.** Here again it
is the world that is convicted "concerning judgment."
As in v. 10 "concerning righteousness" is not to be
connected with Jesus, so here "concerning judgment"
is not to be connected with Satan. As in v. 10 the
world's conscience is to be impressed concerning its
own righteousness by what Jesus does in going to
the Father, so here the world's conscience is to be
impressed concerning its own judgment by what has
already happened to its own ruler. The world is

not yet judged, but it is to be convicted in regard
to judgment. And that feature of the divine judgment will be brought to bear upon the conscience
of the world, which will effect this conviction. The
Spirit will effectively point the world to its own ruler
whose fate is already sealed. "He has been judged,"
and that judgment, once rendered, stands fixed and
irrevocable forever. Jesus speaks of the devil's judgment as having already been effected because his
own death and resurrection, which pronounced the
final judgment on the devil, are already at hand, are
as certain as though they had already been completed.
Even now Satan moves toward his final defeat, 13:2
and 27; 14:30. See also 12:31, and compare Rev.
20:1-3. In the devil's judgment the world may see
something concerning judgment for itself. He is the
world's own ruler, to whose control the children of
this world have submitted. Those who continue in
this submission after the example of Judas in 13:2
and 27, will most certainly share the judgment that
has already come upon the devil. They stand convicted, guilty, and damned forever. Those who accept
the Spirit's conviction when he points them to the
devil's judgment, who let the Spirit turn them from
the devil, escape his judgment. Again, in the one
case the conviction proves salutary, in the other,
judicial.

It confuses the thought of Jesus to bring in the
ideas of defeat and of victory: Jesus, apparently
defeated but really victorious; Satan, apparently victorious but really defeated. The terms here used are
juridical: "judgment — has been judged." The
passive verb implies God as the judge. Both the
noun and the verb, κρίσις and κρίνειν, are neutral and
state nothing in regard to the verdict. This is due to
the fact that the verdict on those who compose the

world may be pronounced either way: acquittal for those saved, condemnation for those lost. Since the verdict on Satan is spoken of as having already been rendered, this, of course, is the verdict of condemnation. He is condemned as "the ruler of this world." The verdict of impeachment has been passed upon him as regards the domain he had hitherto usurped. His throne has toppled over, Rev. 20:1-3. Only as an outcast does he prowl about and work his depredations, James 4:7. Jesus rules; his kingdom spreads far and wide right in the midst of this world; his Spirit is busy gathering in the great harvest. And Jesus tells all this to the disciples in order to fill their hearts with joy now that the Paraclete is so near to his coming for this great work in all the world. Why does sorrow fill their hearts? v. 6.

12) Jesus now turns to the work of the Paraclete in the hearts of the disciples themselves. He thus continues to show them the advantage of his return to the Father, the reason for joy on their part instead of sorrow. First a preamble: **Yet many things have I to say to you, but you cannot bear them now.** While the Greek has the neuter plural πολλά, this may be translated "much" as well as "many things," "much" as "composed of a number of items," or, indicating these items, "many things." "I have" means that these things are on Jesus' heart, and that he would like to speak to the disciples about them. But he takes their condition into consideration, not merely the fact that "now" they are struggling against sorrow, but that "now" they are still at a stage when they are able to carry only a certain load and should not be weighted down with too much. The observation is correct that πολλά refers to no new revelations but to the details of the revelations already made. Jesus had instructed the disciples on all essential and important

points. Yet these were so great that much was yet left to be added in elaborating them. This elaboration the Paraclete would add.

13) **But when he is come, the Spirit of the truth, he shall guide you into all the truth; for he shall not speak from himself, but whatever he shall hear shall he speak, and things to come shall he report to you.** The clause beginning with ὅταν is only a variation from the participle used in v. 8, both pointing to the Spirit's coming at Pentecost. Although the grammatical gender of Πνεῦμα is neuter, we have the masculine ἐκεῖνος immediately before it, because the Spirit is a person. On the apposition "the Spirit of the truth" see 14:17. (16:26). The appropriateness of this designation becomes evident in the description of the Spirit's office: "he shall guide you into all the truth," εἰς τὴν ἀλήθειαν πᾶσαν, or the still better reading ἐν τῇ ἀληθείᾳ πάσῃ, "in all truth." "Into" would mean entrance, while "in" assumes that the entrance has already been made and that all that is needed is to explore what lies within the circle of the truth. Thus "in" would apply specifically to the disciples whom Jesus had already so fully instructed. "All the truth" signifies all the saving realities connected with Jesus and his Father. The term is concrete and decidedly definite. As the Spirit of the truth this guide is absolutely perfect, like Jesus himself who is the Truth. No part of this blessed domain of truth is foreign to this guide, and he will withhold no part from the disciples. From v. 12 we may infer that, when this guide takes charge of the disciples, they will be able to bear all that he has to communicate to them.

With γάρ Jesus adds an exposition. This deals, first of all, with the source of the truth which the Spirit will communicate: "he will not speak from himself," and then with the substance of what he draws from the source he uses: "whatever he shall hear," including also "the things to come." As regards the source the Spirit will be exactly like Jesus, 12:49; 14:10; compare 7:16; 8:28; 14:24. "Not from himself" is, of course, an impossibility for the Spirit as it is for Jesus. It merely wards off a human notion that anything coming from the Spirit could be an invention of his own. A spirit who would speak "from himself" could not be "the Spirit of the truth" but would be the spirit of falsehood, like him who spoke to Eve through the serpent, 8:44.

"Whatever he shall hear" combines the divine source with the divine substance, for from this source only one substance of truth flows forth. "He shall hear" is, as in the case of Jesus, a human term for a divine act, picturing the divine Persons as communicating with each other after the manner of human persons. Being one in essence, each is in the other, and nothing known to the one is ever hidden from the other. This hearing, then, is the inner divine perception, I Cor. 2:11. We see no reason for restricting the hearing of the Spirit to communications from the Father only, excluding those from the Son. For both Jesus (15:26; 16:7) and the Father (14:16) send and give the Spirit. How the hearing from both can be shut out by the verb ἀκούσει (some read ἀκούει) assertion fails to prove. In v. 14 Jesus even says, "he shall take of mine." The revelation given to the disciples is one, to which Luther adds, "that we may have a certain criterion and touchstone by which to judge the false spirits."

From all that the Spirit reveals to the disciples Jesus singles out for special mention τὰ ἐρχόμενα, "the things that are coming." The synoptists report the revelation which Jesus himself made on these things; so here, too, the Spirit will only amplify and deepen. Many think of John's Apocalypse, although the epistles also contain a mass of revelation regarding developments and events, for instance Second Thessalonians 2, and parts of First Corinthians 15.

14) **Me he shall glorify; for he shall take of mine and shall report it to you.** Here we have the one purpose of the Spirit. Note the emphasis on "me." The Spirit's work is to place Jesus before the eyes and into the hearts of men, to make his Person and his work shine before them in all the excellencies of both. It need not be said that this will glorify also the Father and the Spirit. Why the Spirit's work will thus glorify Jesus is explained: "for he shall take of mine and shall report it unto you." "Me" and "of mine" correspond. "Of mine" in this connection (v. 13) must mean "the truth," all the saving realities embodied in Jesus. Taking of these and reporting these to the disciples will certainly be glorifying Jesus before men. By "mine" Jesus means all that is his; the Spirit will take of all this and will convey it unto the disciples. The entire New Testament is the pertinent commentary, the evidence of all that he has conveyed "of mine" to the disciples. We decline to place a limitation here just because the verb ἀναγγελεῖ is repeated from v. 13, where it is used with "the things to come." In our verse the verb has the wider object.

15) **All things whatever the Father has are mine. For this reason I said that he takes of mine and will report it to you.** This is added in order to shut out the possible wrong thought that what Jesus so emphatically calls "mine" and by which the Spirit will glorify "me" could be something belonging to him exclusively apart from the Father. All the things of Jesus are "whatever the Father has." They are identical, they belong to both the Father and to Jesus. Jesus administers them through the Spirit. "Whatever the Spirit shall hear" (v. 13), whatever

he shall take "of mine" (v. 14), and "whatever the Father has" is one substance of truth; the Father has it, the Son owns it, the Spirit takes it. All three combine in making this blessed treasure our own. It is for this reason that Jesus spoke as he did regarding the work of the Spirit in the disciples. When restating what he said Jesus uses the timeless present λαμβάνει, the Spirit "takes," thus speaking more generally than in v. 14 which has the future "shall take."

10. The Little While of Sorrow, 16:16-24

16) The return of Jesus to his Sender brings such an advantage to the disciples (v. 7) in the coming and the work of the Paraclete that joy instead of great sorrow should fill their hearts. Now Jesus adds the further comfort that the separation shall be for "a little while" only. We have the same connection in 14:16, 17, the promise of the Paraclete, and v. 18, 19, the promise of Jesus' coming and of the disciples' beholding him. **A little while, and you no longer behold me; and again a little while, and you shall see me.** The separation is to be short. The first "little while" embraces only a few hours, the afternoon of this very day (Friday); the second "little while" shall be equally short. The change in verbs, first "to behold" and then "to see," is of no special import. However painful a separation may be, if its duration is short, that is great comfort indeed.

17) The disciples, who have listened silently since Judas spoke in 14:22, are now stirred by this promise of "a little while." **Some of his disciples, therefore, said to each other, What is this that he says to us, A little while, and you do not behold me; and again a little while, and you shall see me: and, that I am going to the Father? They were saying, therefore, What is this that he says, The little while?**

We do not know what he utters. Some of the disciples put their heads together and spoke in low tones, not venturing to ask Jesus openly. Here the partitive ἐν is used as a subject, R. 599. They repeat the words of Jesus exactly.   What strikes them is the fact that they are again to see Jesus in "a little while."   Knowing that the little while until his departure is short indeed, the words sound as though the second little while until they shall again see him is likewise short, a matter of hours or, at most, of a very few days. Can Jesus actually mean this?   Then, however, how about what he has said repeatedly, "that he is going to the Father," that this going away is to remove him from their sight (14:12 and 28; 16:10, together with all the statements of what he will do when he has gone to the Father)?   Will he come back from the Father so soon?

18) So they go on asking (ἔλεγον, imperfect) about this strange word τὸ μικρόν, now using the article with it: "the little while."   But they are unable to solve the puzzle: "We do not know what he utters." The little while sounds so hopeful, but the hope cannot rise as it might because of that other word about going to the Father which sounds like a long, indefinite stay.

19) **Jesus knew that they were desiring to inquire of him and said to them, Concerning this are you searching with each other, that I said, A little while, and you do not behold me; and again a little while, and you shall see me?**   Jesus had no difficulty in knowing what passed between the disciples who whispered to each other (3:24, 25; 6:64; 16:30).   The imperfect ἤθελον appears in indirect discourse after the English fashion, whereas the Greek would commonly use the original present tense of the direct discourse; the change to a past tense after a verb in the past tense is occasionally made, R. 1029. Be-

fore the disciples muster up courage to inquire
(ἐρωτᾶν, respectful inquiry), Jesus himself states
their question. Yet he leaves out the part about going to the Father. He does not intend to solve what
seemed like a contradiction or at least a puzzle to
the disciples. This can rest for the time being, for
this will soon become clear in a way far better than
words can now instruct the disciples, depressed as
they are with sorrow. But this about the little while,
with all the sweet comfort it contains, he can make
plain so that they will, indeed, feel relieved.

20) **Amen, amen, I say to you, that you shall
sob and wail, but the world shall rejoice. You shall
be filled with sorrow, but your sorrow shall become
joy.** The special seal of verity (the twofold amen)
and of authority ("I say to you") marks the importance of the statement (see 1:51). And this is
spoken with a clarity that sees the coming hours and
days as though they were already past. In a little
while the disciples shall sob, with loud, unrestrained
weeping, κλαύσετε, yea, they shall wail, utter wailing
cries and moans for the dead, θρηνήσετε. Their beloved Lord and Master will have died a malefactor's
terrible death. The two verbs emphasize the dire
reality in all its poignancy. Note that ὑμεῖς is placed
at the end so as to bring it into sharp contrast with
ὁ κόσμος: "you — the world." "But the world shall
rejoice" states more than a fact, for this fact shall
intensify the sobbing and the wailing of the disciples. Jesus, their beloved Lord, lies dead, a bloody
corpse. The world has wreaked its murderous will
upon him and jubilates in unholy glee. This shall
cut the poor disciples to the heart. Jesus softens
not one word. This is what the first little while
means.

And now the second little while. "You shall be
filled with sorrow," the passive, like the German *sich*

betrueben, but suddenly "your sorrow shall become joy," εἰς χαρὰν γενήσεται, the phrase with εἰς instead of a predicate nominative, R. 458, 595. This does not mean that eventually the sorrow of the disciples shall subside and that in spite of their former grief they shall again become joyful; but that their very grief, i. e., the very thing that plunged them into such excessive grief, shall turn into joy, i. e., into a glorious cause of joy. The identical event shall plunge them into grief and then lift them into joy. A little while, and then the downward plunge; and again a little, and then the upward rise.

21) But can one and the same thing produce such entirely opposite effects with only a brief interval between them? Here is a telling illustration. **The woman, when she gives birth, has sorrow because her hour has come; but when she has given birth to the child she no longer remembers the anguish because of the joy that a man has been born into the world.** Here one and the same event first produces the most painful anguish and then the most abounding joy. The interval between them is short. Moreover, the ensuing joy is so great that the brief anguish is altogether forgotten. Jesus applies his illustration, pointing out the *tertium comparationis,* sorrow made joy. Why, then, should anybody allegorize? In this illustration the death of Jesus is not the birth of a new humanity. The theocracy of the Jews is not the woman, and the glorified Christ or the Christian Church the child. Nor does this illustration picture the parousia, the change from a state of suffering in this world to a state of glory in the world to come. All allegorical vagaries are to be avoided.

The article with γυνή is generic, "the woman" concerned, i. e., any woman when she is giving birth, τίκτῃ, in the act of so doing, present subjunctive. The article with παιδίον is also generic. Hence also the present ἔχει to indicate any such case; R. 865, etc., calls this the specific or aoristic present. The aorist ἦλθεν, "did come," as well as the aorist subjunctive γεννήσῃ and the aorist indicative ἐγεννήθη are idiomatic, using this tense where the English uses the perfect to refer to events that have just now occurred; see R. 844, etc.

22) **You, too, now have sorrow; but I will see you again, and your heart shall rejoice, and your joy no one takes away from you.** This is the simple interpretation of the illustration. The little while of sorrow has begun with the fact that Jesus is saying farewell and will presently be removed by death: "you *now* have sorrow." This is like the woman in travail. "But I will see you again" — the painful little while will soon pass away; "and your heart shall rejoice," etc. — this is like the woman after the birth of the child. Yet we must note that, as in the illustration so in the reality illustrated, it is one and the same thing that by producing great sorrow presently produces the greatest joy: the birth of the child — Jesus' going to the Father. His entering death and dying causes the sorrow; seeing Jesus again brings the joy.

The question is debated as to just what Jesus means in v. 16 by "you shall see me." We have reserved this question until now when Jesus himself furnishes the answer. Nothing decisive is gained by turning back to 14:19: "but you behold me," in conjunction with 16:10: "you shall behold me no more." All preliminary statements are naturally made clearer by the final statement which Jesus now utters. The question is whether "you shall see me" in v. 16 and the following means seeing him at the parousia or seeing him spiritually after Pentecost, or the latter combined with the appearances during the forty days after the resurrection. Those who contend for the parousia must make the second little while cover the entire New Testament era, which is certainly more than a little while. This view also conflicts with Rev. 1:7: "and every eye shall see him, and they which pierced him." This limits the question to the latter alternatives, the seeing after Pentecost and the seeing which began at Easter. Are the appearances during the forty days excluded or are they included? "I will see you again" includes them. The joy of the disciples began when the risen Savior appeared to the disciples on Easter Day. Then the promise was fulfilled, "and your heart shall rejoice" with the addition that no man would ever after take this joy from them. Nor can one say that the final word, "I will see you again," is the equivalent of the earlier word, "you shall see me" (v. 16, etc.), and then to say that the seeing of the disciples did not begin until Pentecost. This might pass if Jesus had not interpreted, "you shall see me" by adding, "I shall see you again." This means mutual seeing. Just as the disciples see Jesus, so he sees them. And they saw each other during the forty days. If only the spiritual sight after Pentecost is referred to, then either Jesus, too, had only such spiritual sight of the disciples and had it only after Pentecost (and who would assert this?) or we must in some way get rid of the plain statement, "I will see you again." We arrive at the same result when we consider the joy. This began at Easter and was not delayed until Pentecost.

23) **And in that day you shall not inquire of me on anything.** Here Jesus uses ἐρωτάω, which takes up the same verb from v. 19. Inquiries for information the disciples will no longer make of Jesus on anything when the promised day fully arrives. Not that they will then inquire of the Father; we have no reason to press ἐμέ to produce such a contrast. Trench interprets correctly: "In that day, he would say, the day of my seeing you again, I will by the Spirit so teach you all things that you shall be no longer perplexed, no longer wishing to ask me questions, which yet you

dare not put." "In that day" refers to no special day but to the time in general when Jesus will again be with his disciples through the Spirit. Hence no argument can be drawn from this phrase against allowing the joy of the disciples to begin with his again seeing them during the forty days.

But while they will know they will still need. And so Jesus once more tells how all their needs will be met. **Amen, amen, I say to you, whatever you shall ask the Father he will give to you in my name.** Compare 14:13, 14; 15:7 and 16; and on "amen," etc., 1:51. Here the verb used is αἰτεῖν, "to ask," "to beg." As regards the knowledge of the truth, neither asking nor inquiring will be necessary for the disciples, for the Spirit of the truth will attend to that of his own accord, 14:26; 16:13, 14. Jesus equipped his apostles completely in this respect, Acts 1:8. They will not inquire as Peter and John did in 13:24, etc.; as Peter alone did in 13:36, etc.; as Thomas did in 14:5, or Philip in 14:8, or Judas in 14:22; or as several would like to have done in 16:17, etc. The one inquiry just before his ascension in Acts 1:6 belongs with the others just listed, for the Spirit had not yet come. But as regards petitions of all kinds in all the exigencies of life, Jesus most definitely invites them.

"Whatever (ἄν τι = ἐάν τι) you shall ask" with its natural restriction is explained in 14:13; also what these petitions cover. We have the same constative aorist αἰτήσητε. That the disciples are to petition Jesus as well as the Father, Jesus himself tells them in 14:14 (see the exposition). So also the fulfillment comes both from Jesus and from the Father, 14:13, 14 (Jesus), 15:16 (the Father). Here it is again the Father's answer to prayer that is promised, yet now Jesus says, "he will give it to you in my name." On ὄνομα see 1:12, and on the phrase 14:13. Here we learn that, even as the petitions are made in Jesus' name, so also the giving of what is asked is done in his name,

i. e., in connection with the revelation of Jesus as this
is embraced by faith.

24) **Up till now you did not ask anything in
my name. Keep asking, and you shall receive in
order that your joy may be fulfilled.** In 14:13, 14
the matter of asking in Jesus' name is stressed as
something that is altogether natural for disciples of
Jesus. So in 15:16 "in my name" again appears as a
matter of course. Now, however, we learn that "in my
name" pertains to the Giver as well as to the petitioner;
as we pray, so the Father (or Jesus, 14:13, 14) gives
"in my name." Hence the disciples must use this
name. They must in all their needs come not merely
with the name "Jesus" on their lips or attached to their
prayers but with the revelation (ὄνομα) of Jesus in
their hearts by faith. Up to this time, Jesus says, the
disciples have not prayed in this manner. Some think
that Jesus points to a shortcoming, a weakness, a fatal
deficiency in the praying of the disciples. If this were
the case, the blame would fall on Jesus himself, since
he delayed until this time to impress upon the disciples
the necessity of using his name in prayer. Until this
time Jesus himself had allowed the disciples to pray as
all true Jews prayed in connection with the name of
God as it was known to them from the old covenant
made with Abraham, Isaac, and Jacob. In their prayers hitherto they used the Old Testament promises and
prayed in connection (ἐν) with them. But now the
fulfillment of these promises had arrived in Jesus; in
a few hours the new covenant would be sealed with the
blood of Jesus. Thus faith had to advance and to
embrace this new covenant, the fulfillment of the old
promises in Jesus. It thus had to use Jesus' name and
revelation when praying. The reason for the advance
to Jesus' name is objective. The Spirit will take "of
mine" and will report this to the disciples (16:14, 15).
Thus subjectively, too, the disciples will now turn to

Jesus' name. Refusal so to do would mean the rejection of the revelation (name) of Jesus.

"Keep asking," the present durative imperative αἰτεῖτε, means: from now on keep asking for all you need "in my name." They had been asking before this, so that it is not necessary to tell them to keep on; but now they must use Jesus' name in all their asking. To say that this imperative is not an injunction but merely a substitute for the future tense, "you will ask," to match the following future, "and you shall receive," is to advance an untenable claim. Jesus tells the disciples to ask; he gives them the gospel precept (ἐντολή) to do so, namely to ask "in my name." This injunction he seals with the promise, "and you shall receive" what you ask in my name. This unqualified promise simply repeats the previous ones given in 14:13, 14; 15:7 and 16. But now this promise is amplified by the divine purpose back of it, "in order that your joy may be fulfilled." This is the joy described in v. 22. The Greek has the periphrastic perfect (R. 3, 75), which R. 907 calls the extensive perfect, here durative-punctiliar, emphasizing the consummation: the joy filling up more and more until it is completely full. The passive implies that he who answers our prayers in Jesus' name will by these answers fill our joy to the full.

With this true picture of what the second little while means before them the disciples could only wish that the hour of joy were already at hand.

11. In Anticipation of the Day of Victory, 16:25-33

25) **In paroimias have I spoken these things to you. The hour is coming when I no longer shall speak to you in paroimias but will report to you with openness concerning the Father.** The note of anticipation runs through this closing section of the

final discourses. Jesus contrasts now and the day
when his victory has been achieved. Only briefly he
touches what lies between these two points (v. 32).
In a manner this section continues the exposition of
the little while when the ordeal will be over. Jesus
would like to speak with complete openness, but this is
impossible before the events take place. Their nature
is such that this cannot be done. An attempt to do so
nonetheless would fail of understanding on the part
of the disciples. The events must first take place.
They will bring their own light. When this is available, it will be easy to speak of them with full openness; and then the disciples will understand in a way
that is impossible at the present moment. On παροιμία
see 10:1. Here the plural is used and this in contrast
with παρρησία, which means "freedom to say anything,"
"utter frankness." Thus paroimias are veiled utterances or forms of speech over against complete plainness and direct language. The term cannot here be
restricted to the figures and illustrations (15:1-8;
16:21) which Jesus used, although these are by no
means excluded. All that Jesus said, even when he
spoke as literally as possible, was veiled, compare v. 28,
which the disciples thought so clear. This explains
ταῦτα which puzzles so many. Yet Jesus himself defines
"these things" in the phrase "concerning the Father,"
and more fully in v. 28. He has in mind all that pertains to the Father, his entire mission, his return to
the Father, all that Jesus and the Father will then do.
This embraces the last discourses and takes in all else
of a similar nature spoken in earlier days.

When Jesus says that "the hour is coming" when
he will be able to lay aside such veiled language and
instead use utter plainness of speech, this hour is identical with "that day" in v. 23 and 26. Often, too, the
word ὥρα is wider than ἡμέρα, meaning "time" over
against "day" (a specific day); here, however, the
terms are quite synonymous. The best commentary

on how Jesus will make report (ἀπαγγελῶ) to the disciples concerning the Father is found in the apostolic
preaching (Acts) and in the letters. Here we see the
"openness" of speech and the full understanding that
could not be effected until the day of Pentecost was
fully come. We need not debate about including or
excluding the forty-day period; for all are agreed that
this was an intermediate period, an advance on the
three years that preceded, aided greatly by the death
and the resurrection as accomplished facts, and yet not
the complete advance to the final openness after the
ascension and the coming of the Spirit. After Pentecost, as v. 23a shows, the disciples will have no questions to ask such as they asked at various times during
the final discourses.

26) **In that day you shall ask in my name,**
bringing your petitions to the Father, as enjoined in
v. 24, "in my name" (see 14:13); **and I do not say
to you that I myself shall make request of the
Father pertaining to you; for the Father himself
has affection for you because you on your part have
had affection for me and have believed that I on
my part came forth from the Father.** Here Jesus
amplifies v. 23, 24. "In that day," after Pentecost,
the petitions directed to the Father by the disciples in
Jesus' name will not need the support and the intercession of Jesus in order to be granted by the Father.
Hence Jesus does not say to them that he will second
their petitions by himself (emphatic ἐγώ) making request of the Father as pertaining to them (περὶ ὑμῶν,
"concerning you" and what you may ask, R. 618).
This will not be needed for the happy reason that is
added. Not that Jesus will not need to intercede for
the disciples with the Father in other respects I John
2:1, 2. When speaking of Jesus and the Father, the
verb ἐρωτᾶν and not αἰτεῖν is in place, since the Father
and Jesus are equals; see on v. 23 and consult C.-K. 91,

27)   The reason why Jesus does not need to second the prayers of the disciples is the Father's own affection for them.   Here Jesus uses φιλεῖν not ἀγαπᾶν for he wishes to express the intimate love of a father to his children; see 3:16.   The Father is so attached to the disciples that his affection constantly goes out to them, φιλεῖ, durative present, ready to supply their every need.   This, of course, is the subsequent love of the Father, bestowed on us after his antecedent love (which is always expressed by ἀγαπᾶν and ἀγάπη) has made us his children.

This appears in the ὅτι clause.   The Father loves the disciples in the way indicated "because you on your part (emphatic ὑμεῖς in distinction from the hostile world) have had affection for me and have believed (two perfect tenses to express actions that still continue) that I on my part (ἐγώ) came forth from God."   Our affection toward Jesus calls forth the Father's affection toward us.   Love is rewarded with love.   All the answers to our prayers prove this reward.   Our relation to Jesus is here first expressed by φιλεῖν and then by πιστεύειν.   Because love always springs from faith, the order: faith — love is in some way found also in this passage which has affection first and faith last.   We are told, the two are here reversed in order to bring the disciples' affection next to the Father's affection — a mere formal reason; or the two are melted together in a hendiadys; or faith is here made a kind of advanced faith because of the object here mentioned with it.   We leave the order as it stands.   As Jesus speaks of the subsequent love of the Father, indicating that he has this in mind by using φιλεῖν, so he speaks of the subsequent love of the disciples, therefore again using φιλεῖν.   After becoming disciples (by first believing), daily contact with Jesus developed close attachment and tender affection for him which nothing ever disturbed.   For this affection the Father in turn has affection.   Following this affection came faith,

also subsequent, as disciples show it after being affec-
tionately attached to Jesus, their daily love for him
stimulating their increased confidence in him.   For
this, too, the Father on his part returns affection.   It
is not a matter of dogmatics but one of ordinary Christian psychology.

Therefore also we do not make the object clause,
"that I on my part (emphatic ἐγώ) came forth from
the Father," denote the advanced content of faith.   A
glance at 1:34 and 1:49 should satisfy on this point.
All true faith has this content from the start; without
it faith would not be faith in the Biblical sense of the
term.   The disciples began with this content; but here
Jesus speaks of the afterdays, of their abiding in this
faith.   The more their affection for Jesus grew
through their intimate contact with him, the more they
believed in his divine origin.   And thus for this enduring affection, which opened their eyes in enduring confidence in his origin, the Father treated them with
affection as being his children.   On παρά with the ablative (genitive), used only regarding persons as here,
see R. 614: "from the side of"; also R. 579. It "implies
the coming of Christ from the Father" (R.) but, as ἐκ
in the compound verb shows, something more, namely
oneness with the Father, the full deity of Jesus.   This
coming forth involves the entire mission on which
Jesus came.   The longer the disciples were with Jesus,
the more they were certain of his divine origin (person) and of his saving mission (work).

28)   Apart from the faith of the disciples Jesus
now states in an objective way the essential facts
concerning himself.   In a brief, clear, and lucid summary he once more places them before his disciples
in order to make them understand what is now about
to take place.   **I came out from the Father and
have come into the world; again I am leaving the
world and am going to the Father.**   These, indeed,
are the four vital points, nor can language word them

more simply.   The first is simply historical, one past
act (as in the last clause of v. 27), hence the aorist
ἐξῆλθον and again ἐξῆλθον.   But now ἐκ τοῦ πατρός, "out
from the Father" (origin, R. 598) defining "from the
side of the Father."   One in essence (ἐκ) yet two in
Person (παρά).   Very God of very God left heaven to
come to us on his mission.   "And have come into the
world," ἐλήλυθα, now a perfect tense to designate the
arrival in the incarnation plus the stay in the world
since that time.   This arrival and this stay cover his
mission in the world.   It is now almost finished.   The
disciples have witnessed it all, and now only the finish
is left.

Now the other side introduced by "again."   "I am
leaving the world," my work is almost done.   "And
am going to the Father" from whom I came forth, who
sent me on my mission, to whom I return at the close of
my mission.   These two are present tenses: Jesus is
now in the act of leaving and of going.   The two are
really one act: by leaving he goes, by going he leaves;
one act but with different relations: ἀπό (in ἀφίημι),
"from the world," and πρός, "to the Father."   Note
well, this is wholly an act of Jesus, done by his will
alone.   No hostile power forces him to leave, the
Father does not call him home.   He has come and has
done what he came to do, and so with the work finished
he now leaves.   By his own will and act he accepted
the mission of his Sender, by his own will and act he
completed that mission, and so by his own will and act
he returns whence he came.   Twice he mentions the
Father — he is the Son; twice he mentions the world —
his mission comprised no less.   As simple as the words
are, so mighty is their import.   They reach from
heaven to earth and back again; they span both God
and the whole world.   So speaks the Son — a divine
and infinite word filled with fathomless love and heavenly farewell.   Only eleven man had their eyes on him
and heard the words come from his lips; but these

words stand forever; millions bow as they read them in the Word of inspiration, and the universe shall know them, for they concern even the angels of God and the devils in hell.

29) Both the clarity and the content of what Jesus has just said prove so effective that voices are raised among the eleven that express the sentiment of all. Hitherto individual disciples felt moved to speak, and in v. 17 some of them whispered to each other; now, however, **his disciples say, Lo, now thou speakest with openness and speakest no paroimia. Now we know that thou knowest all things and dost not have need that one inquire of thee. By this we believe that thou didst come forth from God.** On three things the eleven are unanimous: the way in which Jesus now speaks, the wonder of his knowledge, the support this gives their faith on the vital point regarding Jesus. They feel that already now he is using the openness of speech he has promised for the future day, and that he has left the use of veiled language behind. They are justified in this declaration, taking their present standpoint into consideration. They feel that the language of Jesus could hardly be more lucid and direct. And yet they do not realize the full measure of what Jesus had in mind in v. 25; they could not until they had had actual experience of the way in which Jesus would communicate with them after Pentecost through the Spirit. Jesus does not attempt to correct them; he is content to wait until that day comes, when they will correct themselves.

30) Impressed as the disciples are by the clarity and the directness of Jesus' words, they are equally impressed by the contents of his words. They are again convinced that he knows "all things," namely by the evidence he has just given them, that he has no need, like other men, to wait until someone asks him about a matter, for without their asking him he has completely and in detail answered all the things that

were in their minds and that they had communicated to each other only in whispers. He reads the unspoken thoughts of their minds, the secret communications they have with each other. He who is able to do this, as Jesus has just now done (v. 19, etc.), must know all things. The evidence they adduce includes one more point that is not expressed directly but is implied in their words. Jesus had answered their questioning hearts regarding a matter that still lies in the future, he had elucidated the two "little while" that seemed so puzzling to them. They now knew what the future would bring. Only he who knew all things could give an answer like this in a way like this (unasked).

From this fact the disciples draw the right conclusion in regard to the person of Jesus. They express this conclusion in a formal confession of their faith: "By this we believe that thou didst come forth from God." This is the last confession of faith the disciples made before the death of Jesus. It is couched in the terms used by Jesus himself in v. 28. While it repeats only the first of the four statements used by Jesus, this first statement is of such a nature that of necessity its acceptance involves equal acceptance of the other three. It is impossible to assume that the disciples believe that Jesus came forth from God and yet hesitate about believing that he came into the world and is now leaving the world and going back to the Father. Thus, by using only the first statement, the eleven intend only to abbreviate their form of confession; they confess faith in all that Jesus says in v. 28. They retain ἀπό as at the end of v. 27, "from," but certainly including ἐκ as in v. 28, "out from." "From God" is only a formal variation for "from the Father" used by Jesus. In this solemn hour the disciples confess the deity of Jesus and with this deity the divine, saving mission of Jesus. Through the dimness caused by their sorrow in these moments of farewell the clear ray of this great confession breaks like brilliant sunshine. The clouds of dimness are still about them, but the sun is above them and here it breaks through the clouds. Soon the clouds will again close over them, but this moment of clear shining will not have been in vain.

When R. 589 explains ἐν τούτῳ as denoting the "occasion" he is not making the preposition clear; we abide by its usual force, "in connection with this (what the disciples have just stated) we believe," etc. Nor do we combine ἐν τούτῳ ὅτι as R. 699 does, "by this that thou art come forth from God we believe." The ὅτι clause is the object of πιστεύομεν, "we believe." These disciples had this faith all along; what they now say is that they have received "in this," in the fact that Jesus answered their unspoken question as he did, new and still more evidence for their faith and convictions that he, indeed, came forth from God and that all he says in connection with this is true. The ἵνα in the first sentence is, of course, subfinal, appositional to χρείαν.

31) This confession of the disciples undoubtedly gave Jesus great satisfaction. **Jesus answered them, Now you do believe.** We do not follow our versions and others who translate the verb as a question: "Do you now believe?" How can Jesus here express doubt about their believing? This is settled by the positive declaration of Jesus in 17:8: "They knew of a truth that I came forth from thee, and they believed that thou didst send me." Jesus fully acknowledges the faith of the disciples. While he says only πιστεύετε, we see from 17:8 that he includes the object expressed by the disciples: "you believe that I did come forth from God." Nor does the appended adverb "now" lessen this acceptance, as though Jesus intends to say: "*Now*, indeed, you believe, but will it be shortly?" This *now* points backward not forward. It declares that what Jesus had so long labored for has *now*, indeed,

been attained: the disciples believe, yea, they believe no less than this that Jesus came forth from God with all that this involved.

32) But even as the disciples had said that Jesus knows all things so he now adds the severe trial that already awaits their faith. **Behold, the hour comes, yea, has come, that you shall be scattered, each for himself, and me you shall leave alone; and (yet) I am not alone because the Father is with me.** Both ἴδε (active, v. 29) and ἰδού (middle) are used as interjections. With ὥρα the following ἵνα is non-final and states the contents of the hour. "Behold" points to the astonishing thing that shall happen. The time for this is not only coming but in a manner has already come; for Judas and his band of captors are ready to proceed. What will happen is that the eleven will be scattered in all directions; each will run εἰς τὰ ἴδια, "for himself." Some take this phrase to mean "to his own house" or lodging; but this hardly fits the situation, nor does the phrase always refer to the house or home. Here it evidently means that each will flee to cover where he thinks he can best find it for himself, each will look out for his own interest. The verb is passive, "shall be scattered," namely by a vicious, hostile power. The fraternal fellowship in which the disciples have lived shall suddenly be shattered. We may recall 10:12, the wolf scattering the sheep; also Matt. 26:31; Mark 14:27, the prophecy cited from Zech. 13:7 on the way to Gethsemane. While the passive expresses no guilt on the part of the disciples but only that they shall suffer this scatterment, the addition, "and *me* you shall leave alone" with its emphasis on "me" adds the guilt.

They shall all flee (Matt. 26:56), but not so Jesus. He shall remain behind. They shall flee from him and thus shall leave him alone, *him* whom they have just now so ardently confessed. We must not fail to feel the strong emotion in this word, "*me* you shall leave alone." Where would be their love, their faith, their courage, their gratitude? "Alone," μόνος, Jesus left alone in the hands of his enemies, yea, deliberately remaining alone — what pathos, what divine purpose, 10:17, 18! Jesus does not chide the eleven for what they will do. They will do it, and he will bear it, that is enough. As far as the disciples are concerned Jesus will, indeed, be alone but not as far as his Father is concerned: alone and yet not alone because, although invisibly, the Father of whom he had told the disciples so much would be with him. Where the disciples fail — and Jesus pities them — the Father cannot fail. The emotions that intermingle in these few words of Jesus can be better imagined than described.

33) Why does Jesus say these things to his disciples? **These things I have spoken to you in order that in me you may have peace. In the world you have anguish; but be courageous — I have conquered the world.** "These things" embrace all the final discourses. The reference is general because Jesus is now at the end, and because the purpose now predicated of his speaking these things is also general, attaching to all he has said. This purpose (ἵνα) is "peace" with its manifestation of courage. The full commentary on this εἰρήνη we have given in 14:27. The same "peace" is had in mind here. In the former passage Jesus says that he leaves and gives this peace to the disciples, and thus he marks its objective character: peace as the objective condition and situation when all is well between us and God. Now Jesus indicates that he gives this gift to the disciples, leaving it as his blessed legacy when departing from them. And he does this by means of his Word, "these things I have spoken," etc. By saying all these things to the disciples he places them into a condition that is truly designated as "peace," "my peace," something of which the world has no conception. Of course, this involves

faith in the Word. "In order that you may have peace," ἔχητε, pictures the disciples with peace now and ever as a personal possession. In this safe condition they now are, and in it they are to remain.

Of course, the disciples are also to enjoy this peace. This subjective feeling of peace, resulting from the objective possession of peace, Jesus touches upon negatively in 14:27, when after telling them that he gives them peace he bids them not to be troubled and afraid. He now does the same thing by a positive admonition to be courageous. We are courageous when we are not troubled and afraid. On this night these poor disciples could not rise to the enjoyment of the peace they had. They were filled with sorrow (v. 6) and, worse than this, fear would soon scatter them in Gethsemane. Jesus refers to this when he says, "in the world you have anguish," θλῖψις, the same word used in v. 21, "anxiety," the feeling of trouble and of fear (14:27), which is due to the world's hatred and persecution (15:18, etc.). At times this feeling will prevent the feeling of peace though, of course, without destroying the disciples' condition of peace. Hence Jesus bids them fight against the feeling of depression, "be courageous," untroubled and unafraid (14:27). No matter what the world does to them, they have peace with God through Jesus. Hence they can face the world's hatred with a heart that is cheerful and strong (θαρσεῖν), enjoying their peace in spite of opposition from the world. This the disciples achieved fully after Pentecost, Acts 5:41, "rejoicing that they were counted worthy to suffer shame for his name."

Without a connective Jesus adds the great reason why the disciples should go on with peace and courage filling their hearts: "I have conquered the world," ἐγώ, the divine Lord to whom you belong. "Have conquered" once for all means that despite all its rage the world cannot prevail. Jesus' victory appears in the

fact that the ruler of this world has already been judged, 16:11, and is now to be cast out, 12:31. Jesus' victory is that of the disciples, for they are in him, and he in them, 13:20 (6:56); and so faith in Jesus is victory over the world, I John 5:4, 5. How foolish to be afraid of a crushed and conquered foe!

Serene and majestic is this final word of the last discourses. Jesus has conquered all the powers of evil as they are centered in the hostile world. All his last words pulsate with this victory and triumph. Its fact stands. The disciples believe that fact. All they need is to get the power, courage, and joy of it into their hearts. In trying to achieve this for them Jesus is not working merely for immediate results. He knows all things (v. 30), also the limitations of the present hour for the disciples, which, however, shall soon pass. Then full peace and joy shall fill their hearts when they realize, indeed, that Jesus has conquered the world.

CHAPTER XVII

12. The High-Priestly Prayer, Chapter 17

1) Chytræus calls this chapter the *precatio Summi Sacerdotis*, the High-Priestly Prayer, and Luther says, "that he might entirely carry out his office as our only High Priest." We surely have a prayer here. The counterclaim that this chapter presents only another solemn testimony addressed to the disciples, a final benediction for them, is contradicted at every turn. Jesus utters this prayer aloud for the simple reason that he wants his disciples to hear his communication with the Father. For his own person a silent prayer might have sufficed. To the last his interest includes the disciples. They are to see how he enters his passion as a victor and to hear with their own ears the thoughts that rise to the Father from his heart, thoughts concerning himself (v. 1-5), concerning the disciples at his side (v. 6-19), and concerning all future believers in all the world (v. 20-26). This prayer is to deepen and to intensify all that the last discourses contain. Its power is to work in the hearts of the disciples throughout the coming days. Jesus does not pray with the disciples, does not ask them to lift up their hearts and to join him in prayer as we do at times when saying farewell. This prayer lies on a plane that is so exalted that no disciple can join in its utterance. Jesus prays before his disciples, they can only witness this prayer. Its serenity, its majesty, and its authority befit only the heart and the lips of him who is the Son. Before this prayer all our prayers fade like tapers in the sun.

These things said Jesus and lifted up his eyes to heaven and said, Father, the hour has come. Glorify thy Son in order that the Son may glorify thee. The three introductory verbs are finite and thus equally important, although the variant reading that has the participle, "having lifted up his eyes, said," is also well attested. The statement, "these things said Jesus," intends to mark the division between the discourse and the prayer. Thus also Jesus now lifts his eyes to heaven; but εἰς τὸν οὐρανόν is too slender a thread to bear the conclusion that Jesus is now somewhere in the open and no longer in the upper room; see 14:31. In 11:41, where Jesus is in the open, John writes only ἄνω, "he lifted up his eyes." The attitude of looking up to heaven naturally accompanies prayer, since for us on earth God is always above, not in a physical, but in an ideal or spiritual sense.

The simple address, "Father," repeated in v. 5, 21, and 24, is peculiarly fitting for the Son in the sense in which Jesus differentiates "my Father" from "your Father" in 20:17. He speaks as the Only-begotten who came from his Father on his great mission. In v. 11 Jesus uses "holy Father," and in v. 25 "righteous Father," to accord with the thought of his prayer in these sections, yet these variations, like the unmodified address "Father," still eminently fit the lips of the Son. "The hour has come," with its perfect tense, means that, having come, it is now here. It is the hour for which in a special sense Jesus had come into the world, 12:27; not the hour for his death merely but the time for his death, his resurrection, and his ascension, these taken together.

The time has come for two reciprocal acts: for the Father to glorify the Son that the Son may glorify him. Both the imperative and the subjunctive are aorists. The latter is constative (R. 832), embracing, as it evidently does, the entire activity of Jesus in his heavenly exaltation in making the glory of his Father shine forth in all his wondrous attributes before the eyes and the hearts of men. This aorist also indicates that the Son will actually effect the glorification of the Father. The first aorist δόξασον may refer to the resurrection and the ascension as the acts that glorify Jesus. Yet, "glorify thy Son" may be conceived as a single act, that of investing the human nature of Jesus with the full use of the divine attributes, v. 5. Then the aorist would be effective (R. 834). These observations show that the two acts of glorification are not identical, which appears also from the conjunction ἵνα. The Father is to exalt Jesus by investing his human nature with the unlimited use of the divine attributes in the glory of heaven (Phil. 2:9); and this he is to do in order to effect the purpose (ἵνα) that the Son may make the glorious attributes of the Father shine out in all the world through the work of the Spirit in the gospel and in the church. In the Son's case his own person receives an augmentation of glory apart from any effect upon men, by way of what is done to his human nature. In the Father's case his own person receives no augmentation, and only what he already is from all eternity is revealed to the world which needs this revelation. The Father glorifies the Son in the Son's self; the Son glorifies the Father in the world (see v. 3).

The position of σου before its noun does not make this genitive emphatic: "seeing he is *thy* Son," as some of the older commentators suppose; for these possessives are naturally placed forward in the Greek.

Verse 5 thwarts the efforts of rationalism to reduce the glorification of the Son to the bestowal of moral perfection upon Jesus at his reception into heaven or during his passion. It also refutes the notion that God is to increase the power of attraction which Jesus is to have among men because of his spiritual perfection. These ideas rob Jesus of his deity and leave him no more than a man even though he be made the greatest of men. — To charge orthodoxy with teaching that the glorification of Jesus consists in his enjoyment of divine happiness and glory is to state an unwarranted charge.

Jesus uses the third person, calling himself "thy Son" and "the Son" not merely "me" and "I." By designating himself thus he evidently intends to indicate his eternal relation to the Father (1:1, 2; 1:18). But here we make the observation that Jesus may designate his person in any way, according to either of his two natures or without reference to his natures, so long as he only designates his person, and then may predicate of himself anything that pertains to the one or to the other or even to both natures. Here "Son" names him as God, and yet "glorify" predicates something that is possible only to his human nature. The same manner of expression appears in 1:14; Acts 3:15; I Cor. 2:8; Gal. 4:4; I Tim. 3:16; the reverse, in Acts 17:31; Isa. 9:6; etc.

2) **Even as thou didst give him authority over all flesh that — everything thou didst give him — he give to them life eternal.** We need not say with R. 963 that καθώς is almost causal, "since thou didst give," etc. It expresses correspondence. When God glorifies Jesus in order that Jesus may glorify him, this is in perfect harmony with what God did when he gave Jesus authority over all flesh, etc. What Jesus now requests is in absolute accord with this past act of God. In order to carry to completion what God began in the past he will now certainly glorify Jesus. Jesus and the Father are in absolute harmony on all features of his great mission regarding the world. This harmony Jesus puts into words. For one thing, the disciples are to hear it, and not merely

as a point of instruction, but in a loftier way, namely as a communication between the two divine Persons in this most solemn moment. Our rationalizing minds might ask why this perfect agreement of Jesus with the Father is not enough in itself, why Jesus needed to put it into words. And further, why did Jesus ask the Father to do what in the nature of the case the Father himself intends to do? We may remark that these and similar questions may be asked at every turn where the divine Persons deal with each other. Our answer has already been given in connection with 14:16. Who is able to penetrate into the mystery of the Trinity and to say more?

The Father gave to Jesus "authority over all flesh," ἐξουσίαν πάσης σαρκός, an objective genitive for which we need the preposition in our idiom: "over all flesh," R. 500. John uses "all flesh" only here. The sense is obvious: the entire human race, all mankind as made of flesh and as, therefore, now mortal. The authority over all flesh is the rule and dominion over all men. The aorist ἔδωκας is historical: when the Son came on his mission he received this authority. His mission was to the entire world of men, and hence, when he came on this mission, he received this universal authority. It was the Father's gift to the human nature which his Son assumed in the incarnation. According to his divine nature the Son already possessed this authority and could not be given what he already had by virtue of his deity. But as man he could, indeed, and did, indeed, receive this gift. "He put all things in subjection under his feet, and gave him to be head over all things," Eph. 1:22. During his humiliation Jesus had this authority but did not exercise it save in a very limited degree. The humiliation was a brief, transient period, the prelude to the exaltation or glorification of the human nature when Jesus exercises

to the full also according to his human nature the
authority that came to it as the Father's gift in the
assumption of the divine mission.

The ἵνα clause is subfinal and as such defines the
contents of the "authority" given to Jesus. He has
authority to give life eternal (see 3:15), the life of
eternal salvation, to all whom the Father gives to
him. This does not describe or define all that the
authority covers, it names only the supreme part,
which is here sufficient. In other connections such
as 5:28 and 12:48, we learn that the judgment is
included and that this part of the authority is given
to Jesus as the Son of man, i. e., to him as man: "he
will judge the world in righteousness by *the man*
whom he hath ordained," to whom he gave this
authority, Acts 17:31. "For to quicken, to have all
judgment and all power in heaven and on earth, to
have all things in his hands, to have all things in subjection beneath his feet, to cleanse from sin, etc., are
not created gifts, but divine, infinite properties; and
yet, according to the declarations of Scripture, these
have been given and communicated to the man
Christ, John 5:27; 6:39; Matt. 28:18; Dan. 7:14;
John 3:35; 13:3; Matt. 11:27; Eph. 1:22; Heb. 2:8;
I Cor. 15:27; John 1:3; 14:51." *Concordia Triglotta,* 1033.

In describing the salutary work of the authority
given to Jesus the construction is broken: "everything
thou didst give him" hangs in the air. We might call
it an accusative absolute, or with R. 437, 718 recognize it
as an anacoluthon. This construction is intentionally
employed by John, for it lifts into special prominence
the universality indicated by πᾶν, "everything" which
thou didst give to him, the neuter singular indicating
the entire mass as one great unit; compare the identical expression in 6:37 and 39. The entire mass
(namely of believers), though scattered through all

the world in all ages, the Father gave to Jesus in and by the act by which he gave to Jesus authority over all flesh. To the Father and to Jesus this entire mass is already present and can thus be regarded as a gift. Reading on in 6:40, Jesus defines πᾶν as composed of πᾶς ὁ θεωρῶν τὸν υἱὸν καὶ πιστεύων εἰς αὐτόν, "everyone beholding the Son and believing in him." In 6:44 we further learn that the Father's giving to Jesus involves for those who constitute the gift a gracious and efficacious drawing (ἑλκύειν), bringing them to behold and to believe in the Son.

After naming the mass as a gift Jesus states what his authority is to do with those embraced in this mass: "that he give to them life eternal." Between the plural masculine αὐτοῖς and its antecedent, the neuter singular πᾶν, we have no breach either of number or of gender, R. 400 (mass, a collective), and 411 (the human individuals composing the mass). In the Greek the neuter singular is like an abstract term for the unit idea (note ἕν in v. 21) which is then spread out in its concrete contents by the masculine plural pronoun. They all receive the gift of life eternal. Note how the verb "to give" keeps recurring and how, whether the giving is one to Jesus on the part of the Father, or on the part of Jesus to us, the divine grace to us poor sinners motivates the gift. This grace is intended for all men, and none are excluded by the giving of the Father or that of Jesus. No limitation is made by either Person. Only by excluding themselves do unbelievers bar themselves from the gift to Jesus and from receiving the gift of life. The readings present both δώσει, which is preferable, as a future indicative afer ἵνα (permissible in the Koine), and δώσῃ, apparently an aorist subjunctive from the late aorist ἔδωσα (on which the grammars have much to say).

3) **And this is the eternal life that they know thee as the only real God and him whom thou didst commission, Jesus as Christ.** Jesus is not defining the nature of eternal life but describing in what its reception and its possession consist. He has spoken of giving this life, he now states what receiving and having it mean. The demonstrative αὕτη is feminine because of its antecedent, R. 699. "This is eternal life" is equal to saying, "this is what it means to have the gift of eternal life." Here, as so often in John, ἵνα is non-final, introducing an appositional clause to "this"; hence, "that they know thee," and not "should" or "might know thee" (our versions), R. 992. This knowing is durative (present tense) and might be expressed by the infinitive "to know thee."

Interpreters differ as to whether to read the statement as an apposition: "thee, the only real God," or as a predication: "thee, as the only real God." The main issue, however, is on the second object. Is it apposition, "whom thou didst commission, Jesus Christ (one name); or predicative, "whom thou didst commission, Jesus as Christ"? Grammatically either is possible as all interpreters freely admit. The argument is offered that the predicative reading makes the objects of γινώσκωσι too intellectual, namely two dogmatical propositions: "thou art the only real God" — "Jesus, whom thou didst send, is Christ." If this could be de defended, it would be decisive. But the claim is excessive. "To know thee" and "to know Jesus" with the verb γινώσκειν, which, when the object is a person as here, means, "to have intimate personal experience" and nothing less, already settles the meaning, and then it makes no difference whether the addition to the two personal designations "thee" and "Jesus" is an apposition, a predicative term. or. as it might be, a relative clause or some other modifier. The true heart knowledge lies in the verb as such with its personal objects. Those who oppose the view that these terms are appositions center on the second object and claim that it would be anachronistic to let Jesus call himself "Jesus Christ," for only at a later time does this double name appear. The answer that this later use was inaugurated by Jesus himself just before his death is, of course, only a claim. What is rather decisive against making the terms appositions is the confessional force of the two objects. Jesus, indeed, states the personal relation of the believer to the true God and to Jesus, but he does more: he states the definite personal summary by which faith in the true God and in Jesus is confessed. This confession is, first of all, directed against pagan polytheism: the Father "as the only real God," all pagan gods being fakes, no gods at all. It is also directed against Jewish unbelief, hence, "him whom thou didst commission, Jesus, as Christ." Overagainst the pagan gods it is necessary that the predication have the article: τὸν μόνον ἀληθινὸν Θεόν; since Judaism does not have other Messiahs, who are set overagainst Jesus, the term needs no article. It may, of course, be employed, but in I Cor. 12:3 the confession is, "Jesus is Lord" (not "the Lord") ; also Phil. 2:11; and Acts 2:36, "God made him both Lord and Christ" (no articles). In the Aramaic, in which Jesus spoke, no article was added; compare 4:24. Thus also, as Zahn states, in the present case John reports literally.

The object is necessarily double, for the real God is and can be known in true heart knowledge only by likewise knowing "him whom he did send on his mission (ἀποστέλλειν), namely Jesus" (14:7-11). Already Luther refutes the rationalistic claim that "the only real God" is intended to be in opposition

to Jesus, who thus would not be "real God." By saying that the only real God sent him Jesus "mingles
and weaves himself into the same one divine essence,
power, and might, since he wills to be known with the
Father as he who gives eternal life; which knowledge
pertains to no one save to the real God." The entire
Gospel of John in any number of individual statements bars out the contention of ancient and of
modernistic Arianism and rationalism that Jesus is
devoid of deity and not one in essence with the
Father.

Another claim along this line is that verse 3 is
not a part of the prayer but an insertion by John;
or that this verse proves the entire prayer to be a
fictitious composition by the author of this Gospel. It
is sufficient to point to the second person "thee" and
"thou didst send" as clear evidence that these are true
words of prayer to the Father. Their connection is
equally evident, passing from the divine giving of
eternal life to its reception and its possession. The
holy garment of this prayer is seamless.

4) Verses 1 to 3 request the glorification of Jesus
with a view to what Jesus will do after he is glorified.
This is only the half. Verses 4 and 5 repeat the
request in view of what Jesus has already done. This
is the other half. And the two halves belong together.
When adding the other half Jesus amplifies by describing the glory for which he makes request. He also
now turns from the third person "the Son" to the first
"I" and "me." **I glorified thee on the earth, having
brought to an end the work which thou hast given
to me that I do it. And now glorify thou me,
Father, at thine own side with the glory which I
had at thy side before the world was.** Twice the
pronouns are emphatically brought together: ἐγώ σε,
and then in reversed order με σύ. A similar contrast
appears in "thee on the earth" and "me at thine own

side," namely in heaven. Jesus glorified his Father on earth, revealing the Father with his divine attributes and with his blessed plan and work of salvation for men to see and to worship with adoration. The aorist states the great fact. This, Jesus says, he did by bringing to an end, by completing the work the Father gave him to do. This "work" is the mission of Jesus on earth. While it is entirely for the benefit of men, namely for their redemption, it involved a higher purpose, the glorification of God. The world shines with the radiance of him who sent his Son to redeem us and to draw us to himself. Jesus says that he has brought this work to its completion. Its crowning point is his atoning death. He can speak of this as being already a fact, for at this very moment he is laying down his life in compliance with his Father's behest (10:18). Note how the verb "to give" again appears: "which thou hast given to me," a gift that stands as such (perfect tense). The entire redemptive mission is viewed and is executed by Jesus, not as a burden, but as a loving gift to him on the part of the Father.

5) "And now" after the earthly part of the work has been completed, the heavenly part may begin. This latter is the Father's own will just as was the earthly part now completed. The request of Jesus for the heavenly part is in perfect accord with the Father's own desire. Certainly, Jesus is conscious of having done the Father's work flawlessly and perfectly in every point; he speaks as the Sinless One. But it is idle to bring this in, for the thought of Jesus rises far higher. He is thinking of the glorification of the Father not of the absence of something negative in himself (fault or sin), but of the presence of something ineffably great concerning the Father. Again, since Jesus did this work voluntarily as far as the Father's behest is concerned and vicariously as far

as men are concerned he achieved infinite merit. But
it is idle to bring this into his words and to read a
therefore into his request: "therefore now glorify thou
me." Jesus is not requesting a reward for his work.
His prayer again moves on a far higher plane, the
one already indicated in verses 1 and 2. By being
himself glorified Jesus will glorify the Father among
men in all future ages; by being himself glorified
Jesus will bring to eternal life and glory all whom the
Father has given to him. In this sense we must
understand his request, "glorify thou me," just as we
understand it in v. 1.

Now, however, we have a fuller view of what δόξασόν
με means. First we have the two παρά phrases: "at
thine own side," and "at thy side," both in contrast to "on the earth" and both expressing a relation
possible only to the Persons of the Godhead, the first
phrase speaking of a return to the Father, the second
of the former eternal presence with the Father. Jesus
asks to be in the heavenly glory with the Father as he
was with him before the incarnation. To the verb
"glorify" the cognate noun "glory" is added, "glorify
with the glory." This intensifies the verb; it also
enables Jesus to specify what glory he has in mind:
"the glory which I had at thy side before the world
was." The article with the infinitive is rare in John's
writings (R. 765), only here is it found with the
present infinitive (1074), only here with πρό (891)
and in a temporal sense (978). The reason Jesus does
not say: with the glory which I had with thee "before
thou didst send me into the world," or, "before I
came into the world," is his desire to place beyond
question the nature of the glory he has in mind. It
is the glory of the Godhead, the eternal, divine glory
that extends back into all eternity before the cosmos
or any creature or created glory existed. Yet, to conclude that because this eternal glory is referred to,

the state of humiliation must extend back to the beginning of the cosmos, to the day of its creation, is to draw an unwarranted conclusion.

Kenoticism uses this passage as a *dictum probans*. In a variety of formulations, one contradicting the other, intermingled with subordinationism, or docetism, or even views that approach pantheism, kenoticism empties the Logos of his deity, his divine attributes or glory, makes his immutable being mutable and changes him into a being that only appears as man, or into one that is nothing but man, many even adding human fallibility, mistaken ignorance, and actual faults. We pass by the many vagaries which appear in these views. Some kenoticists find their proof in the personal pronouns. When Jesus says, "glorify *me* with the glory which *I* had," etc., they claim that in the incarnation the Logos emptied himself of his Logos nature, attributes, and glory and now asks that this nature and this glory be returned to him as the Logos. They admit that also his flesh or human nature will thus be glorified, but this is only incidental to the resumption of glory by the Logos. The answer to this contention is obvious. When Jesus says "I" he may add a predicate that belongs either to the divine or to the human nature. It is unwarranted to claim that "I" must always be followed by a divine predication. "I thirst" (19:28); "I wash" (13:8); "I speak, I say" (12:49), and a number of other predications refer to Jesus as man, i. e., to what this divine person does according to his human nature. "They bound him" (18:12); "why smitest thou me?" (18:23); "they crucified him" (19:18), and a number of other statements that have "him" as the object refer to the human nature of the divine person only. On the other hand, "I proceeded forth and came from God," and "he sent me" (8:42), and many similar statements containing "I" and "me" refer to the divine nature of Jesus. Not the pronouns decide but what is predicated of the pronouns. And this is equally true when in place of the pronoun some name of Jesus is used, no matter what the name may be (see on v. 1, last paragraph).

Thus "now glorify thou me" means, "in my human nature"; "with the glory which I had with thee before the world was," means, "with the glory of my divine nature." The Logos did not empty himself of his divine glory when the world began nor at any point in time. In the incarnation he veiled this glory and did not use it according to his human nature during his humiliation because of his work among men. But now that the work is completed he requests to be glorified according to his human nature with the glory that was his before the world began. The immutable Logos cannot empty himself of his glory even in part without ceasing to be the Logos, without going out of existence. The Logos that does what kenoticism claims is a fictitious being, like the God who is not Triune. He exists on paper, in books, not in Jesus as he walked on earth nor in heaven at his Father's side. This answers also the contention that the glory for which Jesus here asks is a different glory from the one John and the disciples beheld, cf. 1:14. John himself tells us that they beheld "his glory, glory as of the Only-begotten from the Father," naming especially two rays of that glory, "grace and truth." The glory of Jesus, the Logos made flesh, is one. During the humiliation it was covered yet shone through the veil of the flesh. The disciples saw it thus and beheld in Jesus the eternal Son. In the exaltation this eternal glory shone forth in unrestrained and unlimited splendor also in the human nature. That this may now become reality Jesus requests in his prayer. During the forty days, in the wondrous appearances of Jesus to the disciples, his

glorified human nature was veiled to such a degree
that the disciples were able to behold their glorified
Lord. Similarly in Acts 7:55 and 9:3, etc.

6)   After praying for himself Jesus now prays
for his disciples, the eleven gathered about him
(v. 6-19). **I did manifest thy name to the men
whom thou didst give me out of the world; thine
they were, and to me thou didst give them, and thy
word they have guarded.** In v. 6-10 we have the
motivation for the prayer for the eleven, and in
v. 11-19 the intercessory petitions coupled with the
necessary details. First of all, then, we are allowed
to see just how Jesus regards his disciples now that
he is on the point of leaving them. He is voicing his
inmost thoughts regarding them. Nor is this a cold,
intellectual estimate of what the disciples are; these
are the utterances of profound love, with every
word telling how Jesus and his great mission are
wrapped up in the disciples, how his great work has
succeeded in them and brought them to the present
hour when in leaving them Jesus can place them
into the Father's care. This intense love wells up
from Jesus' heart in word after word, delighting to
reveal how inexpressibly dear these men are to Jesus.
Not as though the Father himself does not see and
know it all without any telling on Jesus' part, but in
true human fashion laying all his inmost thought and
love for the disciples before the Father's own loving
and responsive heart.

The very first statement thus connects with what
Jesus has already said of his own mission on earth,
how he glorified God and finished the work given him
(v. 4). One great part of this task now lies completed
in the eleven: "I did manifest thy name to the men,"
etc. The aorist records the accomplished fact, and the
verb φανεροῦν is comprehensive, "make visible and
clear," hence more than "to teach," somewhat like "to

reveal" by all that Jesus is, says, and does. Therefore the object, too, is "thy name" and not merely
"thee"; for "the name" or ὄνομα is the revelation by
which God is brought to us that we may apprehend
and receive him into our hearts. Jesus calls the
eleven "the men whom thou didst give me out of the
world." Of course, more than eleven belong to this
class; we think of the 120 in Acts 1:15, and of the
more than 500 in I Cor. 15:6. Here, however, the
eleven are singled out from this class as the ones
especially to be sent out into the world as the apostles
of Jesus (v. 18), for whom he thus prays in a special
way. How the eleven were given to Jesus by the
Father we see in v. 2, compared with 6:37 and 44.
This is the giving due to universal grace as this grace
becomes effective in the individual heart; and all those
thus made a gift to Jesus are already present to the
divine mind. They are given "out of the world," for
originally, by their natural birth, they were part of
the world; compare 15:19. Abbott (R. 598) may
doubt this sense of ἐκ in connections like the present,
yet it is quite assured, and no other sense can be substituted.

When Jesus adds, "thine they were" (σοί not the
dative singular from σύ but the nominative plural of
the possessive adjective σός) he thinks of the eleven,
not as creatures who belonged to God by virtue of
creation, but as former members of the old covenant.
The eleven were believing Israelites; as such at least
six of them (1:35, etc.) had been with the Baptist
and were induced by him to follow Jesus. All the
eleven were given to Jesus as former true members of
the old covenant. What that covenant promised they
had found in Jesus. With a glad heart Jesus adds the
evidence for this, "and thy word they have guarded,"
τηρεῖν, "to watch over," not to lose it from their hearts,
nor to violate it in their lives, not to let anyone else

tamper with it (8:51 and 14:15). "Thy word" is in
substance the same as "thy name"; compare "my
saying" in 8:51; and the equivalents in 14:15, 21,
23, 24; 15:10 and 20. On the perfect forms τετήρηκαν
(instead of – ασι) and ἔγνωκαν in v. 7 see R. 337. The
force of the tense is that of an action reaching a final
and completed state, R. 895.

7) **Now they have realized that all things
whatever thou hast given me are from thee.**   This
shows how much is included in the statement that
the eleven have guarded the Father's Word. The
tense again denotes action that has arrived at a completed state. All their past knowledge and realization culminated in what the eleven now realize; compare their confession in 16:30. The adverb "now"
makes it certain that the two perfect tenses have
their climax in the present moment. "All things
whatever thou hast given me" (δέδωκας, and what
I thus now have) is spoken from the standpoint of
Jesus and the Father, not from that of the eleven,
otherwise the predicate, "are from thee," would be
tautological.   We must not reduce πάντα to refer only
to the teaching of Jesus, nor add only his works. The
term is emphatic and includes everything in and about
Jesus. The eleven believed in Jesus from the start,
but the longer they were in contact with him, the more
they arrived at the realization that everything about
him was from the Father. R. 820 regards παρά as
denoting agency, but this cannot be the case with ἐστίν;
the preposition indicates source and origin: "from,"
yet not ἐκ, "out of."

8) Both the reason for this realization on the
part of the eleven and also the supreme part of what
they thus have realized is now stated. **For the utterances which thou didst give me I have given to
them, and they on their part did receive them and
did realize of a truth that I came forth from thee**

and did believe that thou thyself didst commission me. The ῥήματα are the words as spoken by the lips; λόγοι would point to the thoughts conveyed by words. Even the utterances which the eleven heard from the mouth of Jesus were the Father's gift to the Son. The very language was divine. We realize this today in the Scriptures generally and then in a high degree in the utterances of Jesus, so simple, so brief, and yet so profound and rich, so perfect in every detail. The aorist is constative, all the giving being one comprehensive gift. In the utterances of Jesus the disciples heard the very voice of God (8:43, also v. 26 and 28). The utterances, Jesus says, "I have given to them," namely by speaking them for the disciples to hear. The gift Jesus received he passed on as a gift to the disciples. The perfect is to indicate the course of giving which is now complete (R. 895 β). Jesus is happy to be able to add, "and they on their part (αὐτοί, emphatic) did receive them," namely as given to Jesus by the Father himself. They accepted and appropriated in their hearts the gift so graciously extended to them. *They* did this; many others spurned the gift in unbelief. This is how the disciples realized what Jesus says in v. 7.

And now he names the supreme part of what they realized: "and did realize of a truth that I came forth from thee (8:42; 16:27) and did believe that thou thyself didst commission me" (5:36, 38; 6:29; 7:29; 8:42; 10:36; 11:42; 17:3). Compare the exposition of 8:42. The two verbs "did realize" and "did believe" indicate substantially the same act, for true heart knowledge is faith, and vice versa. So also the two objects go together: proceeding forth from God is the incarnation, and, while it is an act in itself, it goes together with the other act, commissioning Jesus for his great work. All that the Father gave to Jesus (v. 7) centers in this going forth and being

commissioned. Jesus went forth on his own volition
— the verb expresses an activity of Jesus. Jesus
accepted the Father's commission — here the verb
expresses an activity of the Father. Both verbs are
historical aorists, narrating the past facts. The other
two aorists, "did realize" and "did believe," are constative, each summarizing a course of past action.
The entire characterization of the disciples consists of
a description as to how the word of Jesus attained its
great effect in them. They are the ones who in an
eminent sense have received Jesus into their hearts as
who and what he really is.

9) Thus Jesus continues: **I on my part make
request concerning them; not concerning the world
do I make request but only concerning them whom
thou hast given to me because they are thine** (σοί
as in v. 6). **And my things all are thine, and thy
things are mine; and I have been glorified in them.**
The emphatic ἐγώ is in place because of the great personal interest Jesus has in the disciples; this is why
he makes request for them. Jesus uses the superior
word ἐρωτῶ in addressing his Father, speaking as an
equal; not αἰτεῖν which is proper for a subordinate.
Trench, *Synonyms,* though see also C.-K. 91. Jesus
here makes request for the disciples alone and not
for the world, for those whom the Father has given
to him not for the rest. On this so-called *intercessio specialis* see Heb. 7:25; 9:24; I John 2:1;
Rom. 8:34. This special intercession deals with believers only inasmuch as they alone are able to receive the gifts which the Father has for his children.
We must include among the disciples all those who
eventually come to faith (v. 21). It is generally
assumed that Jesus prays also for the entire world
of men in the *intercessio generalis* on the basis of
Isa. 53:12; Luke 23:34, even as we, too, are bidden to

intercede for all men, I Tim. 2:1; Matt. 5:44. Little can be said on this point.

In words of utmost simplicity yet profound beyond human thought Jesus dwells on the relation of the disciples to himself. The Father has given them to him, but this is not a dismissal of the disciples from the Father; the very reason why Jesus prays for them is "because they are thine." As a gift to Jesus they are the Father's; as the Father's they are a gift to Jesus. Strange interaction and interrelation — no one comes to the Father save through Jesus, so that we may say Jesus gives us to him, and yet Jesus considers us as given to himself, and even, when so given, as still being the Father's.

10) The key to this blessed double ownership, to this giving which bestows and still retains, to this receiving which still leaves what it receives, is that "my things all are thine, and thy things are mine." Both σά and ἐμά without the articles are predicates, R. 685, 770. What pertains to the disciples is only part of the blessed mystery; it embraces "my things all," everything that Jesus in any way has as his own. And how much is included we see in the reverse statement, "thy things are mine." While "all" is not again added, it is certainly intended: all that in any way is the Father's is equally the possession of the Son Jesus. Luther's comment is best, exceedingly simple and yet profoundly to the point: "Everyone may say this, that all we have is God's. But this is much greater, that he turns it around and says, all that is thine is mine. This no creature is able to say before God." It shuts out the limitation, as though Jesus here speaks only of what pertains to his work, saying only that he and the Father have a purpose, plan, work, means, and results in mutuality, all this

belonging equally to both. Luther: "Understand
this now not only of what the Father has given him
on earth but also of his divine being with the Father.
The word: all that is thine is mine, leaves nothing
whatever excluded. Are all things his, then the eternal deity is also his; otherwise he could not and
dared not use the word all." Luther has caught the
full force of these neuters. They are not merely a
collection of objects, a mass or sum of earthly things;
these neuters as neuter possessive adjectives are abstract, and the abstract idea is intensified by making
them plural. These neuters differ greatly from the
abstract πᾶν in 6:37 and 39, which, as the context
shows, denotes the great mass of believers. In the
present connection the joint possession of the believers
is explained by the inner relation of the divine Persons
themselves. Hence we have not merely πάντα, "all
things," but τὰ ἐμά and τὰ σά, with πάντα only as a modifier: all that is attributed to thee. Earth is left behind, heaven itself opens. We catch a glimpse of the
oneness of the Father and the Son — two persons, indeed, ("mine," "thine") but in a union exceeding
human powers of comprehension.

In the light of this relation of the Persons "they
are thine" though given to Jesus. In this light we
are to understand the addition, "and I am glorified in
them." Jesus is made great and illustrious in the
hearts of the disciples by their realizing that he came
forth from God and by their believing that he was
commissioned by God. They recognize him for what
he is and trust him accordingly (v. 8b). "I am
glorified" is the passive, but v. 8a shows how this
came about. Jesus does not add that thus the Father
is also glorified in the disciples. This follows of
itself when we reflect on the glorification of Jesus
in the disciples. Here the former fact is enough, for
all that is needed is the motivation for the action of

Jesus that he on his part (ἐγώ, v. 9) intercedes for the disciples with the Father.

11) The profound preparation is ended. We see how infinitely precious the disciples are in the eyes of Jesus as well as in the eyes of the Father. Would that we might always think of ourselves in this exalted light! On the basis of this grander and broader motivation rests the narrower one which now follows, and on both rises the great request which is now expressed. **And I am no longer in the world, and these are in the world, and I come to thee. Holy Father, guard them in thy name, which thou hast given to me, in order that they may be one, even as we.** Jesus leaves the world while the disciples still remain in the world. It is thus that he comes to the Father with his request. Like ἐγὼ ἐρωτῶ in v. 9, Jesus now says ἐγὼ πρός σε ἔρχομαι; compare also v. 13. This cannot mean the coming to heaven; not only is this included already in Jesus no longer being in the world, but ἔρχομαι is nowhere else used in this sense by Jesus. For this he has ὑπάγω, πορεύεσθαι, and ἀπέρχεσθαι. The expression ἔρχεσθαι πρός is used to describe those coming with a request in Mark 1:40; Luke 7:7; 18:3; John 7:37. The marked repetition of "the world" seems to indicate the danger to which the disciples will be exposed when Jesus departs from and leaves them in the world.

So Jesus now voices his request, "Holy Father, guard them," etc. The adjective is emphatic after twice using only "Father." It contrasts with the mention of the world which is unholy, and it harmonizes with the request now made to guard the disciples against all unholiness while they are still in the world. God is holy in that he is absolutely separated from and actively opposed to all sin. Here his holiness is emphasized in so far as by his grace he works to save men from sin, separates them from the world, and keeps them for himself as separate and holy. Thus Jesus asks, "guard them in thy name, which thou hast given me." On τηρεῖν see 8:51 and 14:15: "to watch over." In v. 6 it is used with reference to the disciples, and the object is the Word; now it is used with reference to the Father, and the object is personal, namely the disciples. While the action is according to the objects, the modification "in thy Word which thou hast given me" brings the guarding predicated of the disciples closely together with the guarding attributed to God. In fact, what Jesus requests is that the disciples, who under his care have thus far guarded the Father's Word, may now be in the Father's care, guarded by him and kept in his Word. For ὄνομά σου designates the contents of the Word, the revelation by which we know him whose "name" is thus made ours. Hence Jesus also says that the Father has given him this "name." The implication is that Jesus was to give this "name" (revelation, Word) to the disciples, which he says he did (v. 6). Another implication is that the disciples received this "name" (v. 8) and are now "in" this name, in living connection with what it reveals to them. But, still being in the world which is full of delusion and spurns this name, the disciples need divine care lest they lose their connection with the saving "name." Here it is "thy name," the Father's, elsewhere, as in Acts 4:10-12, it is Jesus' name. The contents of both is the same.

The purpose of thus guarding and keeping the disciples in connection with the blessed name is "that they may be one, even as we." The neuter ἕν signifies "one thing," a unit, one body, over against the world. And ὦσιν with its present tense is durative, "may continue to be" a unit. Yet the imperative τήρησον is an aorist, either ingressive, "take and keep," or effective, "actually keep"; and while it is true that in prayers these aorist imperatives, so constantly employed, denote "instant prayer" (R. 948), they reveal not only the fervor of the petitioner but also his certainty that what he asks will actually be done, thus in the present case that the disciples will go on indefinitely in being one. The model for this one-ness of the disciples is the oneness of the Father and Jesus: "even as we," i. e., are one. The idea in καθώς is analogy not identity. When identity is assumed, the oneness of the Father and the Son is reduced to an ethical oneness of love, of agreement in purpose and action, etc., which oneness can, of course, be repro-duced in the disciples. Such a conception is shut out as being inferior by v. 21-23. Jesus is speaking of the oneness he has mentioned in 10:30 and 14:10, the essential oneness of the Persons of the Trinity. This cannot be duplicated, yet it can be imitated. All believers are one spiritually by their living connec-tion with God. The same living Word and "name," the same faith and life, is in them all. By that they are one, inwardly in the great *Una Sancta,* "the com-munion of saints" (third article of the Apostles' Creed), the church invisible. This is the oneness that is like unto the oneness of the Father and the Son. The latter, indeed, as Bengel puts it, is *ex natura,* the former only *ex gratia.* The former embraces only three Persons, the latter millions.

Yet Jesus does not here pray for this oneness of the disciples, i. e., that it may come to pass. Perhaps this misconception is due to the translation; "may be one" is taken to mean, "may get to be one." But ὦσιν does not have this force. It assumes that the disciples are already one; v. 6-10 shows that beyond question. Since they are already one in the name that the Father gave to Jesus, he requests that the Father guard them "in order that they may go on being one." The verb is not the aorist γένωνται, "become," "get to be one."

This thought pertains only to those who are not yet disciples and applies to them only when they enter discipleship. Even in v. 21 Jesus does not introduce this idea. He prays only for this, that the oneness already established may remain unbroken by the guardian care of the Father. How will it be kept intact? By keeping the disciples "in the name," in the Word, in the utterances of Jesus (ῥήματα, v. 8). How may this oneness be endangered, how may a disciple drop out of it? By any teaching or doctrine contrary to the Word. This cuts into the bond that ties the disciples together and may easily cut it altogether and thus sever some of the disciples from the oneness, dropping them back into the world. The entire prayer has the one great burden that we may be preserved in oneness by complete adherence to the Word.

12) **When I was with them I myself kept guarding them in thy name which thou hast given to me; and I did protect them, and not one of them went to perdition save the son of perdition; in order that the Scripture might be fulfilled.** Until this time Jesus had made himself the guard of the disciples; and he had succeeded in his protection. The imperfect ἐτήρουν tells that the guarding went on from day to day; then comes the aorist ἐφύλαξα and sums up the finished result, stating that Jesus actually did protect the disciples. The verbs are synonymous in the sense "to keep watch over," "to keep an eye upon," the former verb being used in the wider sense; both, too, easily come to the further meaning "to keep," also "to observe." The difference in the present use lies more in the tenses than in the meaning of the verbs. The imperfect shows the daily effort of Jesus, the aorist reports the successful result. It is inexact to make τηρεῖν mean *conservare* and to connect it with something internal, and to make φυλάσσειν mean *custo-*

dire against foes from without. Jesus uses both verbs as applying to "in thy name." The effect of the tenses is completely reversed when we are told that "through φυλάσσειν the τηρεῖν was accomplished"; for it is the imperfect which brings about the aorist.

The accepted reading simply repeats from v. 11, "in thy name which thou hast given to me." This would have the effect of emphasis, although the reason for an emphasis here is not obvious. The other reading, though less well-attested, substitutes οὕς for the attracted relative ᾧ and seems much more to the point. Here we have a case where the internal evidence seems superior to the external (that in the codices). We should then read: "I myself kept guarding them in thy name; whom thou hast given to me I also did protect," etc. This, moreover, is strongly substantiated by 18:9, "whom thou hast given to me, not one of them did I lose." Here the same relative clause with οὕς appears. It is quoted as a former saying of Jesus (namely from our passage), is placed forward in the same way, and only the main clause is changed from a positive statement ("I did protect") to the negative which has the same sense ("I did not lose one of them"). It is almost exactly like the corresponding statement in our passage. On the giving of the disciples to Jesus by the Father see v. 2 and 6:37 and 39.

All whom the Father has given to Jesus he "did protect" so that "not one of them perished," i. e., spiritually; see 3:16 on the word, its true meaning and its perversion. Usually, however, Judas is taken to be "the sad exception" (Bengel) in whom all the guarding and protecting of Jesus failed; and εἰ μή is then translated "except," R. 1188. But this is not correct. Judas is not an exception, he was never given to Jesus by the Father; εἰ μή must be rendered "but" (our versions), or "save," as in Gal. 1:7 and 19; Rom. 14:14. Likewise, we must note the correspondence in terms: "not one of them went to perdition save the son of perdition." This ethical or qualitative genitive marked Judas from the start; and εἰ μή only introduces something that must be added to the previous negation by way of explanation lest a misunderstanding result. Jesus, indeed, labored with Judas as he did with the Jews and persisted in his labors to the last; but as in the case of the Jews Jesus knew that Judas was not his own. Not that Judas never believed — we may be quite sure that he did at first; but even then he was "the son of perditon," a son or product of eternal damnation; compare the similar designations in Matt. 23:15; II Thess. 2:2. For Judas is not given this awful title because he went to perdition and thus *ex eventu* became a son of perdition. The reverse is true: being a son of perdition, he went to perdition, "fell away, that he might go to his own place," Acts 1:25; only for a time was he numbered among the apostles, only for a time had he a portion or lot in this ministry, Acts 1:17.

"In order that the Scripture might be fulfilled" modifies the preceding clause, "save the son of perdition," i. e., that as such he, indeed, did perish. This ἵνα, like all the others referring to the Scripture fulfillment concerning the wicked, is not deterministic; it rests on the infallible foreknowledge of God. God foresaw all that Judas would become and would do in spite of all the grace vouchsafed to him. He beheld Judas dying as the son of perdition, thus to remain the son of perdition forever. Therefore in God's foreknowledge and counsel Judas was the son of perdition from the beginning, and God prefigured Judas by Ahitophel in Ps. 41:9; some add Ps. 55:12-15; Ps. 109:8 (Acts 1:20). Due to the

infallibility of the divine foreknowledge, these predictions in the Old Testament types were bound
to be fulfilled in Judas. See 13:18 on this fulfillment, and 6:64 and 71; 12:4 on the case of Judas
itself.

13) Thus far Jesus had personally watched over
the disciples. **But now I come to thee,** namely with
my request and prayer from now on to place them
into the Father's keeping; compare the same words
in v. 11. "But now" is in contrast with "when I was
with them" in v. 12; now Jesus is on the point of
leaving his disciples. Hitherto he assumed the protection of the disciples, now the Father is to assume
that care. The former type and kind of protection
through the visible presence of one of the divine Persons is to be superseded by another kind through the
invisible agency of another Person. Hence Jesus adds:
and these things I speak, i. e., in audible words for
the disciples to hear, **in order that in the world they
may have my own joy as having been made full in
themselves.** The disciples, who are to remain in the
world for the great mission they are to execute in
the world, are to have in their hearts the very joy
that fills the heart of Jesus; and the measure of this
joy is to be complete, it is to be like a vessel that has
been filled to the brim ($\pi\epsilon\pi\lambda\eta\rho\omega\mu\acute{\epsilon}\nu\eta$) from which they
may draw at any time. On the perfect participle
as here used with $\check{\epsilon}\chi\omega$ see R. 902. In stating this
purpose for speaking his prayer audibly ($\lambda\alpha\lambda\tilde{\omega}$, to
speak instead of being silent) Jesus treats his own
joy as something objective, just as he does in the
case of his own peace in 14:27. Just as Jesus places
his disciples into the condition of peace in order that
from it they may draw the feeling of peace, so he
places them into the condition of joy in order that
they may draw the feeling of joy from it. Having
the true source of joy and this in full measure, the

rejoicing itself will follow; and though the rejoicing should cease at times, it will be sure to return. Compare 16:20-22.

Usually ἐν τῷ κόσμῳ is construed with ταῦτα λαλῶ: "these things I speak in the world." But why so obvious a remark? In 14:25 his speaking while he is yet with the disciples has point, for it contrasts with the coming teaching of the Paraclete. Here, however, no such contrast appears. Even if the previous statement, "but now I come to thee," is thought to mean, "now I return to thee," the very adverb "now" implies, what also the eleven see with their own eyes, that Jesus is still "in the world." The phrase must belong to the ἵνα clause and is placed in front of the conjunction for the sake of emphasis. Already now, in the midst of a hateful world (v. 14), the disciples are to have not only courage and peace but the true source of joy and the happiness it will give them. John often uses this form of emphasis with ἵνα.

Luther has put into simple words the purpose Jesus wanted to attain: "In order that through the Word, caught with the ears and held in the heart, they be comforted, joyfully rely upon it, and be able to say: See, this is what my Lord Christ said, so faithfully and fervently he prayed for me, this have I heard from his mouth, etc. What is needed here is that one hold to the Word with his whole heart and take comfort in that." As the purpose of this audible prayer must be rightly understood, so also the great request it contains. When Jesus protected the disciples hitherto, this was not done apart from or without the Father (10:30; 5:19; etc.); when the Father would now protect them, this would not be done without Jesus (14:18; Matt. 28:20). The *opera ad extra* are always *indivisa*. As far as the intercommunication of the divine Persons and their interaction con-

cerning any part of the work of salvation is concerned, what is revealed to us in great condescension is the actuality of these activities. They are
shown to us in an attractive human way, the object
being faith and joy, not in a transcendent way as
if our minds could penetrate into the mystery of
the Trinity and from the inwardness of that
mystery comprehend all the profound whys and
wherefores.

14) Once more (see v. 6 and 8) Jesus states:
I have given them thy word. This time he uses the
word λόγος, which points especially to the substance;
but he retains the verb "to give," for the Word is
always a pure gift which emanates from grace in the
Giver, and the perfect tense indicates that the gift
is still in the possession of the disciples: he is leaving them with this divine gift in their hearts. But
now the thought advances beyond what this gift has
made of the disciples (v. 6 and 7) to what the world
has done to them as a result: **and the world hated
them** (adding the inward reason) **because they
are not of the world** (15:18, 19), the gift of the
Word having changed the spiritual nature of the
disciples, making them foreigners to the world.
They are like Jesus: **just as I myself am not of the
world.** The aorist is ingressive, "began to hate";
and the two ἐκ have an ethical force: "of the same
nature, kind, and quality as the world," so that the
world, which is very keen in this respect, would
recognize the disciples as its true children. The comparison with Jesus adds the positive idea to the
negative description. "Not of the world" means that
the disciples are like Jesus; they are not of the world
in the same sense as Jesus is not of the world. They,
of course, are such by the gift of the Word, by grace;
he, as the Giver of the Word, by his own divine nature.
Once, by natural birth, they, too, were of the world,

but now, by the new birth through the Word, they have left the world. Through their contact with Jesus this has become so manifest that the world considers them traitors and renegades to itself, hating them accordingly. And this hatred is intensified when the disciples now preach and teach the Word and begin to make still further inroads upon the world. Note how the two thoughts match: "in the world" the disciples are to have joy (v. 13, when the phrase is thus construed) in spite of the fact that the world vents its hatred upon them.

15) Since the disciples have a great work to do in the world, the simple solution of just taking them out of the world and thus beyond the reach of any hatred of the world cannot be applied. **I do not request that thou take them out of the world, on the contrary, that thou guard them from the evil one.** The two ἵνα introduce non-final object clauses in which Jesus states *what* he requests; hence this word is not to be translated, "that (in order that) thou shouldest," etc. These clauses are the equivalents of infinitives, "I do not request for thee to take, etc., but to guard, etc." The first aorist "take," denotes a single act, the second, "guard," is constative to indicate a successful course of action. The phrase ἐκ τοῦ πονηροῦ may be either masculine, "from the evil one," the devil; or neuter, "from the evil" that exists in the world.   It is thus ambiguous. Naturally the commentators are divided regarding its force.   One argument in favor of the neuter force is the fact that Jesus nowhere else in this prayer mentions the devil but refers only to the world. Why he would have to mention the devil at least twice before a single mention could be assured is, of course, not obvious.   Despite repeated mention otherwise the ambiguity of our phrase would remain. Because ἐκ is used with τηρεῖν, and because this combination occurs

only once more, in Rev. 3:10, and there with "hour," some feel certain that the devil cannot be referred to. But ἐκ is suitable in either sense, and no more so with evil than with the author of evil; in I Cor. 9:19 the object is personal: ἐκ πάντων (namely ἀνθρώπων). Nothing is gained by making the noun a neuter; for evil and the evil one are so clearly joined that protection from the former involves protection from the latter. And that is true even in the case of those who prefer to make man his own devil.

If during this last night which Jesus spent on earth we did not have the example of Judas who fell a prey not merely to something evil but to Satan, the evil one (Luke 22:3; John 13:27), so that he himself is called "a devil" (6:70), we might content ourselves with the neuter in our passage. If during this last night Jesus had not repeatedly mentioned the prince of this world (12:31; 14:30; 16:11), connecting him with the world as its ἄρχων or ruler, we might consider the neuter sufficient when now, in the final prayer, "the world" is mentioned so repeatedly. In I John 5:18, where τηρεῖν also occurs, the man born of God guards himself so that "the evil one" (Satan) does not touch him. All the hatred of the world against the disciples is inspired by Satan. The work of the disciples is to war not merely against flesh and blood but against demon spirits with "the evil one" at their head (Eph. 6:13 and 16), and our protection is to be directed against his fiery darts. This is the protection for which Jesus now prays. He does not stop halfway in his request, he includes the devil and thus includes all else.

16) Protection for the disciples is something negative: guarding them against the evil one. Now the positive is to be added. Hence once more (see v. 14): **Not of the world are they just as I myself am not of the world.** On this ground rests the

request for the protection of the disciples, on it rests also the request for their sanctification.

17) **Sanctify them in the truth; thine own word is truth.** The aorist imperative is like the one in v. 11; it is either ingressive, "take and sanctify," or constative, "actually sanctify," embracing all the sanctifying activity of God. The verb ἁγιάζειν means "to set apart for God," thus on the one hand, to separate from all profane connection and, on the other hand, to devote only to him. But in the case of the eleven this setting apart unto God is not the first act of this kind. Jesus has already said, "thine they were," etc., v. 6; "they are thine," v. 9; "I guarded them in thy name," v. 12; "I have given them thy Word," v. 14. Thus also negatively "they are not of the world," v. 16. All that Jesus has done for them in the past by his personal work must be called a sanctifying and setting apart of the disciples unto God. This work might be considered completed if the disciples were now to leave the world in company with Jesus; the final sanctifying would then take place in the moment of their death. But they are to remain in the world, and so they need the sanctifying of the Father in order to keep them as they are, a body wholly separate from the world.

Jesus prays, Sanctify them "in the truth." The reading "in thy truth" lacks support and would also make the emphasis on the following "thine own word" pointless. The ἐν should not be considered equal to διά or ὑπό, "through" or "by" the truth. The thought goes deeper than means or agency. The preposition indicates sphere. Jesus has already placed the disciples into this sphere; they are no strangers to the truth. It now surrounds their souls, lifting them away from the world and upward to God. And this is to continue, to be intensified, perfected in all directions and thus carried forward to its ultimate goal: all in union with the truth. As to the ways and means and the agency Jesus has already said, by "the Spirit of the truth" remaining permanently in the disciples (14:17), teaching them, etc. (14:26), bearing witness to them of Jesus (15:26), and guiding them into all the truth (16:13). As in these previous passages, plus 8:32 and 14:6, so here again ἡ ἀλήθεια with its definite article is concrete and designates that specific divine spiritual and saving reality embodied in Jesus. This reality is neither indefinite nor abstract just as Jesus and all that he is and does are not abstract.

"The truth" names the substance itself in living connection with which the sanctifying work proceeds. This substance, however, is transmitted to us so that we are brought into contact with it and with its sanctifying power by the Word, ὁ λόγος, that which conveys the actual substance and significance of thought. It is thus that, exactly as in 8:32, Jesus connects "the truth" with the Word. In 8:32 he calls it "my own word," while now he calls it "thine own word." The two are, of course, identical (8:26; 14:24; etc.). Yet in this instance Jesus does not identify "the truth" with "thine own word"; he does not say, "thine own word as *the* truth." There is only the slenderest textual evidence for the insertion of the article. If the article were present, the subject and the predicate would be identical and convertible (R. 768) as in many other utterances of Jesus. Then Jesus would say only this, "By the truth I mean thine own Word." Without the article ἀλήθεια expresses quality. By using the noun instead of the adjective ("truth" instead of "true") this quality is most forcefully expressed. Jesus thus says: "Thine own Word is truth, composed wholly of truth, without an admixture of falsehood." By adding this statement without a connective Jesus makes it so much stronger.

You may place it by itself, its weight will be unchanged.

This ἀλήθεια, whether it be used with or without the article, must be properly understood. The thought is not that Jesus would support his request for sanctification by saying that the Father cannot but grant it seeing that his Word is very truth itself. For the hearing of his request Jesus counts on what is in the Father's own heart: "thine they are." The assumption that Jesus must indicate where "the truth" is to be found after mentioning "the truth" misses the point. In the case of Jesus it goes without saying that the saving reality is entirely in the Word. Why else did he give the disciples the ῥήματα that the Father gave him (v. 8), namely the Father's Word? We see the same in v. 6: Jesus manifested the Father's "name" to the disciples; and in v. 11: the Father is to guard them "in thy name." This "name" is the Word as containing the entire revelation of the Father, we may say all "the saving truth" (reality) concerning the Father. *Where* "the truth" is found has thus been settled all along: the Word is filled with it. Of this blessed Word Jesus now predicates that it is verity and truth itself. Those who seek "the truth" that saves and sanctifies by going to the Word will find that Word true on every point and in every respect. The quality of reality marks it throughout. At no point does this true Word leave us in doubt or make us uncertain in regard to "the truth," all the concrete substance of it or any part of that substance.

In "thine own word" the addition of the possessive adjective with a second article lends emphasis: ὁ λόγος ὁ σός not merely ὁ λόγος σου. This is the only Word that is wholly truth. Often only the correspondence between "sanctify them" (make them holy) and the address "holy Father" in v. 11 is noted; but "truth"

also corresponds with holiness. By means of "the
truth" alone and of the Word whose essential quality
is "truth" can the "holy Father sanctify us." Another correspondence appears in the phrases with ἐν
when Jesus at first prays, "guard them *in* thy name,"
and now, "sanctify them *in* the truth." By so sanctifying the Father will guard them. "Thine own word
is truth" certifies the inerrancy and infallibility of the
Word excepting no portion cf it. The holy garment
of the Word is seamless; it has no rents of errors —
or call them mistakes — which hands today must
sew up. "Thine own word" signifies all of it, the
Word of the Old Testament on which Jesus placed his
approval again and again, plus the revelation that
Jesus added in person with the promise of its perfect preservation through the Paraclete (14:26;
16:13).

18) The sanctification which Jesus requests the
Father to bestow upon the disciples in continuance of
the sanctification he himself has already bestowed
upon them has its reason in their mission in the
world. **As thou didst send me into the world, I, too,
did send them into the world.** Both Jesus and the
the disciples were sent on a mission (ἀποστέλλειν, to
commission), both are thus sent into the world. The
difference appears in this that Jesus, who himself was
sent, sends them. Jesus thus carries the Father's
mission to a certain point and then uses the disciples to carry it to completion. A certain part of the
great work is thus graciously transferred to the disciples. The translation "even so" is inexact. The
parallel is not regarding the manner but in regard
to the persons: "*I, too*, sent them." This reveals the
true greatness of Jesus: he sent — the Father sent.
The first sending contemplated the second. In it, as
well as in his own mission, the Son executed the
Father's will. Both sendings are "into the world":

their range is nothing less than universal, far beyond
the narrow limits of Judaism. Often the mission of
the eleven, who alone are here present with Jesus, is
taken in too narrow a sense. Without question the
commission of which Jesus here speaks included their
apostleship; the very word ἀπόστολος is derived from
the verb here used, ἀποστέλλειν. But already as followers of Jesus they are sent into the world; all believers have this general commission. Separated from
the world and dedicated to God as his own peculiar
possession, we are here for the world's sake, in order
to show forth the praises of him who has called us
out of the kingdom of darkness into his marvelous
light, I Pet. 2:9. In v. 21 Jesus states of our oneness that its purpose is "that the world may believe."
Let us keep together what belongs together. On the
basis of the grand mission of the church in the world
rests every special office in the church, beginning
with the highest, the apostolate. The aorist "I sent"
is historical and refers to the first appointment of
the Twelve, who now in due time would receive
the further order to proceed with their work amid
all nations.

19) How the commissioning of the disciples is
connected with their sanctifying is made plain by noting the parallel in Jesus. **And in their behalf I on
my part sanctify myself in order that they may be
also on their part such as have been sanctified in
truth.** The tense is present, "I on my part (ἐγώ)
sanctify myself." This, then, is not the sanctifying
mentioned in 10:36, which preceded and accompanied
his entrance into the world and made him in a supreme
sense the Holy One of Israel. Jesus is speaking of a
sanctifying act in which he is engaged at the present
moment. In our endeavor to understand just what he
means we must hold fast to the fact that the verb
"sanctify" cannot have two different meanings in the

present connection. We cannot admit a play on the word and make, as some desire, the variant sense of "sanctify" the very point of what is said. The two acts are essentially alike although that pertaining to Jesus is active and that pertaining to the disciples passive. "I sanctify myself" does not mean, "I set myself apart as a sacrifice in behalf of them" (ὑπέρ being equivalent to "instead of") ; for the disciples were not to be set apart to become such a sacrifice. The play on the word breaks down when Jesus is thought to sanctify himself as a substitutionary sacrifice for the disciples while the disciples on their part are to be sanctified for an entirely different purpose. The Old Testament references to *kidesh* or *hikdish lajaveh*, sanctifying something as an offering to God (Exod. 13:2; Deut. 15:19; II Sam. 8:11) cannot apply here even as regards the sanctifying of Jesus. The Hebrew always has the dative, and Jesus does not say, "I sanctify myself *to thee*"; in the Hebrew someone else sets the object aside for God, but Jesus sanctifies himself. The parallels fail.

The correspondence is marked: "in their behalf I on my part — they also on their part (or: they also themselves)." Both are equally to be set apart although, of course, the office of the one is infinitely above that of the other: "I in their behalf" — but only "they on their part." Both are sent, both have a mission, both missions are divine, both are holy, and so both need to be set apart, devoted in a holy sense to do their work. Jesus does this of his own accord and power. Some are satisfied with the thought that of his own volition he now prepares himself to die. This would mean a sanctification for the climax of his mission. But the discourses have given us a wider vision: Jesus is going to the Father, he prays to be glorified. By his death he enters on his glorious heavenly mission in which his world-wide work will begin when he will send the Spirit, be with the disciples in a spiritual presence, and finally receive them unto himself. For the entrance upon this heavenly mission Jesus now sanctifies himself by voluntarily entering his sacrificial and atoning death. But for this act of his, for which no one can set him apart, for which he himself must give himself freely, of his own accord, no sanctification and no mission of the disciples could be possible. This is the complete sense of the emphatic phrase "in their behalf."

Hence the purpose clause with ἵνα. The sanctification of Jesus for his heavenly mission is to make possible the sanctification of the disciples. Jesus does not say that in like manner they may be sanctified. That would be impossible, granting even their lesser task. They are only to receive sanctification (ἡγιασμένοι, passive) by a gift from the Father, v. 17. And this gift to them is to proceed from what Jesus now does for them. Yet they, too, (καί) are to be set apart for a mission. Out of the one sanctification the other is to proceed; thus the two are placed side by side. Some again are content to make the sanctification of the disciples signify only their cleansing from sin through the death of Jesus. But it surely includes all that Jesus has said about their reception of the Paraclete and of their mission in the world. This wider view comports with the predicate καὶ αὐτοὶ ἡγιασμένοι. We regard αὐτοί, not as the subject, but as part of the predicate; and the perfect participle, not as part of the subjunctive verb (a periphrastic perfect, R. 907, 360), but as a participial modifier of αὐτοί: "such as also on their part (or: themselves) have been sanctified." The participle thus includes all by which this completed state (durative-punctiliar, R. 907) is reached.

The sanctification of Jesus alone can be ὑπὲρ αὐτῶν; to that of the disciples no such phrase can be attached.

The phrase for them is ἐν ἀληθείᾳ, "in truth." Both grammatically and exegetically there is much discussion as to whether this phrase means only "truly," equivalent to ἀληθῶς, or is in effect the same as ἐν τῇ ἀληθείᾳ in v. 17. We note that if only "truly" is meant, we should expect the adverb, and this the more to avoid confusion because a phrase has just preceded. When the absence of the article is urged over against the previous phrase with the article, we note that in v. 18 ἀλήθεια without the article appears between the two phrases. "Truly" would be out of place after the perfect participle with its perfective sense; for this participle denotes a completed state of sanctification. Can there be two such states, one "truly" and in reality such, and one not "truly" such? On the other hand, the phrase without the article cannot be identical with the phrase containing the article; in other words, the absence of the article is not negligible. We are aided by II John 1 and 4; III John 1, "in truth," compared with III John 4, "in the truth." "In the truth" is specific, the truth the disciples had heard and learned; "in truth" is general, all truth, whatever the Spirit would reveal to the disciples (16:13). Since "in order that they may be also," etc., refers to the future and does this after v. 18 declares that thy Word is "truth" (no article), it seems perfectly in order that Jesus should advance the thought of v. 17 from sanctification "in the truth" (specific, concrete) to sanctification "in truth" (general, in all that bears this quality of being true), v. 18. With both "the truth" and "truth" preceding, each in a decisive sense, it is impossible for us to regard "in truth" as nothing more than an adverb, which is then superfluous.

20) The previous verses still refer directly to the eleven, yet in the nature of the case they must also reach farther. The eleven, sent into the world as

apostles, will not be sent in vain. Whatever opposition they encounter, their work will succeed. Sanctified and enabled by God, they will bring thousands to faith. Hence the prayer expands: **Not concerning these alone, however, do I make request but also concerning those believing in me through their word.** On ἐρωτῶ see v. 9. It is as an equal that Jesus "makes request"; as a designation for our praying this verb is too high. Jesus makes a clear distinction between "these," the eleven, and "those believing in me through their word." While it is distinct, the prayer embraces both as belonging together. For these coming believers will become believers "through their word," that of the eleven. Thus the office of the apostles is connected with the whole church, and all that Jesus has requested for the apostles refers mediately also to the entire church. In the singular "word" all the teaching and the writing of the apostles is summarized as a unit; yet λόγος has the idea of communication. The Word communicated by the apostles is the means for producing faith and making believers — note διά. It is "their" Word, not as though they originated it but only as being the special agents for its dissemination and transmission. In reality it is God's Word (v. 17), and its substance is "truth." Word and faith are correlative; the one intends to produce the other, and the other has no basis but the one. Apart from the Word there is no church, because there is no faith apart from the Word; and the church is constituted out of those and those alone who have faith. The Word is the vital means and the root of faith. At once it appears how dangerous it is to be ignorant of the Word or to alter and to falsify it in any way. Eph. 2:20 shows that Jesus considers the Word as given to the church through the apostles the foundation of the church for all time. Only few men heard

the apostles while they lived; they still speak "through
their Word" in the New Testament and still win ever
new believers. Jesus sees them down through the
ages (1:16) and in this prayer reaches out and presses
them to his heart.

21) And this is what Jesus requests: **that they
all be one even as thou, Father, art in me, and I
in thee, that also they be in us.** Here is a fuller
statement of the request made in v. 11, "that they be
one even as we." This ἵνα clause is non-final, an
object clause, stating *what* Jesus requests; in v. 11
ἵνα denotes purpose. "That they all be one," πάντες
(compare the neuter πᾶν in v. 2) stresses the great
number of believers. The Greek abuts πάντες and ἕν,
making the contrasting terms "all" and "one" stand
out in relief: though so many in number all believers are to be one unit, one body, one spiritual
whole. Of course, the apostles themselves are included as believers. This oneness is in distinction
from the world, in fact, in opposition to the world.
The fact that καθώς expresses analogy and not identity,
and that the oneness is not merely ethical, as is often
thought, has been shown in v. 11. Our mystical oneness as believers is a resemblance to the essential oneness of the divine Persons. What in v. 11 is con-
densed to the two words καθὼς ἡμεῖς is now unfolded:
"even as thou, Father, art in me, and I in thee, that
also they may be in us." Between the Father and the
Son (and we are free to add the Spirit) a wonderful,
incomprehensible interpenetration exists, called the
perichoresis essentialis by the dogmaticians. This is
absolutely the highest type of oneness known. This
and nothing less is to be the model and pattern for
the oneness of believers. The very idea of duplicating
in us the interpenetrating oneness of the divine Persons is so impossible that we decline to consider it.

The only idea possible is a resemblance of the human oneness to the divine. Recall the resemblance (and no more) when man was created in God's image. In Eph. 5:23, etc., the divine oneness of Christ and the church is the model (and no more) for the Christian marital union, something pertaining only to this life. So it is here.

Therefore we do not need to fear connecting the καθώς clause with what precedes. Every reader will do this automatically. We are not compelled to construe the καθώς clause after the second ἵνα: "that they all be one, that, even as thou, Father, art in me, and I in thee, they also be in us." In v. 11 the disciples are to be one "even as we" (Jesus and the Father); in v. 21 all believers are to be one "even as thou art in me, and I in thee," i. e., as we (Jesus and the Father) are one. But now we see how these two are one, namely by the ineffable divine interpenetration. And now Jesus adds the second ἵνα as appositional to the first. It defines how all the believers are to be one, how their oneness is to resemble that of the divine Persons, namely thus: "that also they be in us." All believers being in the Father and the Son, they will certainly be one. This will not be a mere human oneness (national, racial, political, in a society, or the like). It will bear the divine stamp: a. oneness in the true God, in actual spiritual union with him. This is why so high a model and pattern is set for our oneness. Here, too, we see that our oneness is not merely placed beside the oneness of the divine Persons as though all that exists between them is a likeness. The two are vitally connected; this is why they have the resemblance of which Jesus speaks. We believers can be one with each other only by each of us and all of us being one with the Father and Jesus. Union with God and with Christ makes us a unit in ourselves. Jesus here omits the other side, namely that as the believers are in God and his Son, so these are also in us (14:23, add v. 16).

The enclitic pronouns are generally accented after prepositions, as ἐν σοί, R. 234. In the Greek the copula is omitted: "even as thou (art) in me, and I (am) in thee," R. 395. The vocative may be written as the nominative: πατήρ, R. 264, 461, etc.

On the view that Jesus prays for the oneness which already exists among all believers by faith, instead of for the oneness that is to be the result of this faith in perfect adherence to the Word, see v. 11. It is true, indeed, that even the smallest measure of faith joins us to God and to the mystical body of the church. But this is only the beginning. Our apprehension of the Word is to grow, the range and the inner power of our faith in that Word likewise. As this advances and is perfected, our oneness with God and with Christ and our oneness with each other becomes more and more what Jesus wants it to be. This is the burden of Jesus' prayer (v. 17). The mystical side must never blind us to the medium, the Word. We have no Christ and no God without the Word and no oneness among ourselves without the Word. On the other hand, the more we have of the Word in our hearts by faith and thus also ruling us in our lives, the more perfect is our oneness. Being spiritual and mystical, this unity is of necessity invisible and does not consist in any form of outward organization. How far, however, it is from being merely imaginary appears the moment we look at the Word. We are as much one with each other and with God and with Christ as we believe, teach, live, and confess all that is contained in the Word. Every deviation in doctrine, life, and practice from the Word mars and disrupts our oneness and hinders the fulfillment of Jesus' prayer. Those rend the church who deviate from any part of the Word, also those who demand things

other than the Word demands. Those permit Jesus'
prayer to be fulfilled in them who bring every thought
and every act of theirs into subjection to the Word.
"That they be one" means one in the Word; "that also
they be in us" means in us through and by the Word.
Thus Jesus prays.

The third ἵνα introduces a purpose clause, "in order
that the world may believe that thou didst commission me." "This is the fruit which is to follow from
this oneness, namely that Christ's Word is to break
forth more and more and be accepted in the world
as God's Word, in which an almighty, divine, unconquerable power and the treasure of all grace and
blessedness reside." Luther. What stirs the world
is not our faith but our faith arrayed as a unit behind the Word. This oneness of faith voicing the
Word, adhering to it in every part, obeying its every
precept, is bound to act powerfully upon the world.
The greater our oneness in the Word, the greater
our victories in the world. The more schism,
heresy, and ignorance prevail, the less will our
victories be.

Jesus does not intercede for the world as he does
for his own (v. 9). His own are already one by
faith. For them he can ask that by this faith they
be one also in the Word. Yet the world is still the
object of Jesus' love, and his saving efforts extend
to it; this, however, only through the church as the
bearer of his Word. In this way Jesus here prays
for the world. It is to believe "that thou didst commission me," i. e., believe in the entire mission of Jesus
as the Savior, and that means in the gospel. The
purpose is one of pure grace. The idea is not that the
whole world will finally believe, nor that the power
which works faith in men is the oneness of the church.
Many will not believe in spite of the Word and however a united church brings the Word to them. The

power that creates faith lies wholly in the Word. Yet it makes a great difference how the church acts in bringing the Word to men. If the church is only in part a unit on the Word, if great parts of the church repudiate or pervert parts of the Word, the saving impact of the Word on the world is reduced. The channel of the church through which the Word with its power is to flow to the world is more or less blocked, and less of the power of the Word gets through to the world. Let all missionary agencies of the church mark this and second the prayer of Jesus for the complete oneness of the church in the Word!

22) **And the glory which thou hast given me I on my part have given to them in order that they may be one even as we are one, I in them, and thou in me in order that they may have been brought completely unto oneness.** "What glory is this which Christ has and gives?" Luther asks and then misses the answer. It cannot be our oneness for the glory given us is to produce the oneness. It is impossible to dissociate the glory the Father has given to Jesus from the glory mentioned in v. 1 and 5. This is the eternal glory which the Logos had before the world was, the uncreated and essential glory of God, consisting of the sum of the divine attributes. This glory was given to Jesus in his human nature at the incarnation when the Logos assumed that nature. This glory the apostles beheld in Jesus, shining through the veil of his flesh (1:14). In v. 5 Jesus does not ask that this glory be given to him. It had been given to him, i. e., to his human nature; what Jesus asks is that he be glorified with this glory, namely that his human nature should shine and radiate with this glory, exercising all the divine attributes in the exaltation of heaven. The Scriptures know of only one glory not of two or more. "Thou hast given," like the follow-

ing, "I have given," denotes an act in time not one in eternity. The gift of the divine glory could not have been made to the divine nature of the Son, for this nature never was without this glory, in fact, this glory is his divine nature. Only the human nature could receive the divine glory as a gift. The perfect tense "has given" is the proper form: the gift made in the instant of the Incarnation remains as such to this moment and on indefinitely.

This text is variously interpreted. The glory is found in the power to work miracles, or is the glory of office. Such a glory the Father is to have given to Jesus, and then he to the apostles. Yet "to them" means to all believers, the multitude of whom has neither miraculous powers nor offices. Some date the gift back in eternity and have it received by the Logos before the world was. Some add "in idea" to the verb, really making "thou hast given" proleptical; the gift belonged to Jesus, but he has yet to take it for himself. These and similar ideas are then also applied to the next clause.

This divine glory, which Jesus received in his human nature at the time of the incarnation, he says, "I on my part have given to them," namely to all believers, for this part of the prayer deals with all of them. As the gift to Jesus was of necessity made only in a way in which he could receive it, namely by way of his human nature, so again the giving of this gift to the believers was only accomplished in a way in which they could receive it. They received it by the indwelling of Jesus by which they were made partakers of the divine nature, II Pet. 1:4; II Cor. 3:18; Heb. 12:10; I John 3:2: This our glory, received from Jesus, is invisible while we are in what we may call our state of humiliation; the consummation at the time of the Parousia will reveal it in all its excellence, Rev. 3:21. In Rom. 8:30 ἐδόξασε, "them he also did glorify," is an exact parallel to our passage, "the glory I have given to them." This perfect tense is again not proleptical, as R. 898 makes it, a futuristic prophetico-perfect; for Jesus is not speaking prophetically. Nor is this gift one made only "ideally" not yet in reality.

The purpose that Jesus has in making this gift is now added: "in order that they may be one even as we are one." The gift of the divine glory unites us in one body. We, of whom Jesus says in v. 19, "that also they be in us," are by this made one in the divine glory that thus comes to us. When the three καθώς, v. 11, 21, and now 23, are placed side by side, each sheds light on the other. The last adds the predicate which is left out in the other two: "even as we are *one*." In this restatement of the oneness of believers we must not forget the Word. This Word mediates the indwelling of Jesus in us and thus the reception of his glory in us, and thus the oneness that results. When Jesus says, "even as we are one," his human nature must not be left out. This is the nature that received the divine glory, received it for our sakes in order that we might be partakers of it through his indwelling. Through his human nature in which all the Godhead dwells bodily (Col. 2:9) Jesus is our Savior; and all his saving gifts come to us through this nature, here in particular the gift of his glory.

23) "I in them, and thou in me," etc., is not a separate sentence with the verb to be supplied but an apposition to something that precedes. Not to ἡμεῖς (although "I" and "thou" = "we") because the thought prevents this. "I in them, and thou in me" cannot be an apposition to "we are one." Somewhat more likely is the apposition to the preceding ἕν, or to the clause itself: "that they may be one," . . . "I in them," etc., adding this as explaining their

oneness. But why not follow the "we" in "I" and "thou" to its source? This apposition goes beyond the preceding ἵνα clause which is only subordinate; it is to be attached to the main clause with its "thou" and "I": "And the glory which thou hast given me I on my part have given to them, . . . I in them, and thou in me," etc. These two givings need an explanatory apposition, and this apposition does explain them. "I in them" explains how the believers have the glory of Jesus, how it was given them; and "thou in me" explains how the Father gave this glory to Jesus and how he now has it — "thou in me" even in my human nature. Thus v. 22, 23 become a compact whole which the thought most certainly requires. With Jesus dwelling in the believers, his glory is made theirs even as the indwelling of the Father in Jesus makes the Father's glory his.

The three ἵνα clauses in v. 21 correspond in a striking way with the three ἵνα clauses in v. 22, 23. Write each pair together and so study them. Take the second pair, "that they may all be one in us" (v. 21); "that they may have been brought completely into one" (v. 23). *All* are to be *completely* brought to oneness. The verb τελειοῦν means, "to bring to a τέλος or goal," "to make complete"; and εἰς ἕν states the goal. The periphrastic perfect subjunctive, ὦσι τετελειωμένοι, has its usual force: brought to the goal of complete oneness and thus continuing there indefinitely. The passive has Jesus as the agent; it is he who intends (ἵνα) to bring the believers completely into oneness so that in every way they may be one body. Take it all together: just as the fuller reception of the Word completes the oneness of believers more and more by mediating the indwelling of Jesus and the Father in them, so this indwelling in us and the consequent gift of the glory to us constitute our oneness and constitute it as something that has been made complete and now remains thus. The realization of this purpose, the actual complete oneness, is attained in every age in all those believers who unite in accepting the Word as they should. Those who, though they are still believers, in any way deviate from the Word hinder the consummation of the oneness and prevent the fulfillment of Jesus' last prayer as far as they are concerned.

As in v. 21, so now in v. 23 a third ἵνα follows, which deals with the world: **in order that the world may realize that thou didst commission me and didst love them even as thou didst love me.** "May realize" is substantially the same as "may believe" in the parallel clause in v. 21. Both verbs are aorists and signify actual realizing, actual believing. The verb "may realize" is emphatic by position. By beholding the oneness of believers as this manifests itself especially in the united confession and proclamation of the Word (these two by both lip and life), the world is to come to an inner realization of the significance of this oneness. To be sure, a saving realization is referred to, one that induces faith ("may believe," v. 21). Many in the world will not yield to this impression. They will harden themselves when they come in contact with believers and their oneness in Christ and in the Word. Often they will use the divisions caused by faulty believers as an excuse for unbelief. But the unity of true believers in Christ and in the world will always have its salutary, saving effect.

In v. 21 the object of believing is summarized in one statement, "that thou didst commission me." Jesus now repeats this but here amplifies by adding in harmony with the intervening elaboration, "and didst love them (the believers) even as thou didst love me." This double love of the Father shines forth in the great act of the Father in sending Jesus on his great mission. The church proclaims this great act by means of the Word. The whole gospel tells how the Father gave his Son for the salvation of the world (3:16). Here is the ἀγάπη of God for the world, his comprehending and purposeful love, seeing the plight of sinners and purposing to save them (on ἀγαπᾶν see 3:16). This saving love blesses all those who yield to it (the believers) with life everlasting and with all the divine gifts that go with this life. Many of those in the world will be drawn (6:44) by this love. Its sweetness and its gifts will win them. They will desire to share in all this blessedness.

One ὅτι unites the two verbs: "that thou didst send me" and "didst love them," etc. The two are treated as a unit. In the sending of Jesus there is manifested this love of the Father which the believers now enjoy to the full. They constitute the fruit of the sending; upon them the love of the Father can pour itself. What a happy realization when any man who is still in the world begins to see this! And this love of the Father to the believers is after the manner (καθώς) of his love for Jesus. Here again we must not lose sight of the incarnation and think only of the love of the Father to the Son in their relation in the Trinity. We must think of 10:17; Matt. 3:35; 12:18; 17:5, and similar statements, voicing the love of the Father for the incarnate Son in carrying out the commission of the Father. In this love to Jesus the love to us believers is embraced. We may even say how this comes to pass, for this Jesus who so perfectly did the saving will of the Father is now in us, and we in him. By this identification we share with Jesus in the Father's love. Blessed are all those who join us in the reception of this love!

24) We may say that now the epilog or conclusion of the prayer begins. This contains no more

petitions. The epilog rests on all that precedes and crowns the whole. **Father, what thou hast given me, I will that where I myself am also they on their part may be with me; in order that they may behold my own glory which thou hast given me; because thou didst love me before the foundation of the world.** The best reading has the vocative in nominative form, which often occurs. The emphasis is first on the clause, "what thou hast given me," which is, therefore, also placed forward in the form of an absolute nominative which is picked up by the following κἀκεῖνοι; secondly, on the non-final ἵνα clause which states what Jesus wills. The neuter ὅ (inferior reading οὕς) is like the neuters found in 17:2; 6:37 and 39 (R. 653, 713) and views the entire mass of believers as a mass although it is composed of persons. How the giving has been effected is explained in 6:37 and 17:2. The perfect tense "hast given" must be left as it stands: a past act with a continuous present effect. It is neither a prophetic perfect nor in effect a future perfect. All believers in all ages were present to God, and thus he gave them all to Jesus, and they are his even though they are as yet unborn.

Regarding these believers Jesus expresses his will. When the American committee on the R. V. translates θέλω "I desire," it weakens the word. Jesus expresses nothing less than his will. This, however, is not a demand: *sic volo, sic jubeo!* nor as when one makes his last will and testament. Jesus came to execute his Father's will and does not now demand that the Father execute Jesus' will. The position of the word shows that it bears no emphasis. To do so it would have to head the sentence. Nor is there an emphatic ἐγώ, "I on my part," "I myself will." Jesus says, "I will," as expressing the will of the Father in what he wills. He and the Father are in perfect accord. If it be asked, why he then needs to say so to the Father, we might answer that no need compels him but that, as in all other instances, the divine Persons, one in thought, will, and work, freely express this oneness that we may know of it. As far as the Persons themselves are concerned, we may not penetrate into their unity nor ask why they communicate as they do.

What Jesus wills is stated in the object clause, "that where I myself am also they on their part may be with me." Here both ἐγώ and ἐκεῖνοι are emphatic and parallel. It is certain that in giving us to Jesus the Father intended no separation of Jesus from us, or of us from him, but the very contrary. What Jesus wills is plain from what is now about to occur. Death will soon remove his visible presence from the disciples, but this is to be only a temporary separation. All believers are to be "where I am," in heaven, in the glory into which Jesus is returning. The will of Jesus lifts the whole church from earth to heaven, from the lowliness here below to the exaltation above.

Already in μετ' ἐμοῦ, "in my company," lies the thought of participation in the glory of Jesus in heaven. This thought is fully expressed in the purpose clause, "in order that they may behold my own glory which thou hast given me." The stress is on the verb, and θεωρεῖν, "to gaze upon as a spectator," is used with regard to objects that are extraordinary. The believers are to see all the wonders of the glory of Jesus with unspeakable delight. The present tense indicates continuous beholding. The glory the believers are to behold is, of course, the one divine glory of his attributes. We need not here dispute about the *visio Dei*, whether our glorified eyes shall behold God as he is. When Jesus adds, the glory "which thou hast given me" (some read the aorist, "didst give"), he again refers to his human nature. The

glory we shall behold is thus the glory of the Son
ἔνσαρκος shining out from his exalted human nature.
This beholding is the very essence of heavenly blessedness. "With me," "where I myself am," implies our
transfer into heaven and into the heavenly presence
of Jesus and at the same time our own glorification,
I Cor. 15:48; I John 3:2, for only glorified eyes can
behold in blessedness the glory of the exalted Redeemer. On the clause, "which thou hast given me,"
see v. 22; the perfect tense is not prophetic or proleptic.

It is usual to combine: "which thou hast given
me, because thou didst love me before the foundation
of the world." The words then mean just what they
say: in all eternity the Father did love Jesus as he
would eventually walk here on earth in the flesh and
do his good and gracious will. The love which
declared, "This is my beloved Son," goes back to
eternity. And in this eternal love, when Jesus came
to earth, he received in his human nature the glory
of God and after the days of his humiliation were
accomplished, entered his exaltation, and all the glory
shone forth in unrestrained splendor from his human
nature. All these wonders of grace in the Son of
man, wrought in time and culminating in our own
glorification and in our beholding Jesus' glory in
heaven, go back to all eternity and center there in
the love of the Father. The prayer of Jesus reaches
back into all eternity, to the eternal love of God, and
at the same time reaches forward to all eternity and
to the blessedness which shall there be ours. When
the last two clauses are connected in this usual manner, no occasion exists for dating back the act of
giving the glory to Jesus to the time when the Father
did love him, namely in eternity "before the foundation of the world." The attempt to find this meaning
in the words violates the grammar, clashes with the

parallel clause in v. 22, and produces an unacceptable thought.

It seems strange, however, to attach to a mere relative clause like, "which thou hast given me," merely repeated from v. 22, the weighty ὅτι clause, "because thou didst love me before the world began." So grave and great a reason should be attached to a weightier statement. We suggest that in the mind of Jesus the connection was made with the highly unusual verb θέλω, and that Jesus here states why he is able in this final prayer to address the Father with the words, "I will." "I will, . . . because thou didst love me before the foundation of the world." On this eternal love rests the will for what Jesus here states. Read thus, the love in eternity may be left as the love between the Father and the Son ἄσαρκος. Since in any case this love is dated in timeless eternity, it is immaterial whether the tense is the aorist or the perfect.

25) Jesus closes with a word of complete confidence in the righteousness of the Father, yet he leaves unsaid what action he expects from this righteousness. He does not need to say this, for the Father will most assuredly act in righteous accord with what Jesus here lays before him. **Righteous Father, both did the world not know thee, yet I knew thee, and these did know that thou didst commission me.** Jesus simply lays the facts before his righteous Father. This suffices for the three aorist tenses for which the English would probably use perfects (R. 843). "Both — and," καί . . . καί, in this instance as in 6:36 and 15:24, correlate opposites, the world as not knowing, the disciples as knowing. Between these two is placed the clause with δέ, placing Jesus in contrast with the world: "the *world* did not know thee, yet *I* (emphatic ἐγώ) knew thee."

This reference to Jesus is necessary in order to bring out the guilt of the world. It is terse, saying only that Jesus knew the Father but implying that he made his knowledge known, and that thus the world should have known the Father. It did not know him and, of course, made this its lack of knowledge known (8:55). Both are true, the fact that the world did not know the Father, and that "these" did know him. Both facts Jesus places side by side before his righteous Father. Only in regard to "these" he says: they did know "that thou didst commission me," thus establishing the fact that they really knew the Father (compare v. 3, and 14:7 as showing that the Father is known only in Jesus whom he sent).

By "these" Jesus refers to the eleven, but what applies to them applies to all believers alike: they all know what Jesus says. The verb "know" is used in an intensive sense with reference to the knowledge of full realization. By thus correlating the world with the eleven and by Jesus placing himself between the two, the thought is that when the eleven faced the alternative of following the wilful ignorance of the word or the knowledge which Jesus made known, they were drawn to the latter and knew the Father in Jesus. The stress is thus placed on the disciples and on their blessed knowledge. This means that by placing these facts before the Father, Jesus is concerned chiefly about the disciples and about the verdict of the Father in regard to them. What the Father may do regarding the world is a minor matter. In his righteousness he can do only one thing with the disciples who have turned from the world to Jesus, he can only leave them with Jesus that they may be with him forever.

26) What the terse clause, "yet I knew thee," only implies is now brought out, not, however, as

regards the world but as regards the disciples
with whom Jesus is so deeply concerned. **And I
made known to them thy name and will make it
known in order that the love with which thou didst
love me may be in them, and I myself in them.** The
verb γνωρίζω is chosen to match γινώσκω in v. 25; in v. 6
the same thought is expressed with φανεροῦν, "I did
manifest thy name," etc., ὄνομα, here again the revelation which makes the Father known. The two καί
are not correlative, each only adds to what precedes.
To the fact that the disciples did know Jesus as sent
by the Father is added the other that Jesus made the
Father's name known to them, namely effectively;
and to this is added the thought that he will yet make
this name known to them. How the latter will be
done in the future the discourses have fully stated.
The emphasis is on the following purpose clause
as stating the intent of both what Jesus has done
and will yet do. This his intent Jesus places before the Father with the certainty that in his
righteousness he will second it and give it perfect
approval.

This is the great purpose, "in order that the love
with which thou didst love me may be in them," etc.
The Greek has the cognate object of the inner content,
ἥι ἠγάπησας, besides the personal object "me" (R. 478).
This is the love of the Father for Jesus mentioned
in v. 24. Reaching back into eternity, it is now to
fill the disciples. We need not puzzle as to how this
love of the Father will be "in them." It will fill them
as a blessed treasure, a possession of which they can
have constant experience. "In them" is evidently
chosen because of the Father's own indwelling in the
hearts of the disciples (14:23). Hence Jesus adds as
the further purpose, "and I myself in them" (this
indwelling as in v. 23). Only here Jesus presents this
his intent to the Father that he may weigh it in his

righteous dealings with the disciples. Jesus is in indissoluble union with them, and the Father will look upon them and treat them as he does Jesus who is in them.

In these three closing verses Jesus expresses his assurance that the Father will hear him. It is like a grand "Amen, amen, Yea, yea, it shall be so!" The purpose and the object of Jesus and of his work shall be attained.

CHAPTER XVIII

II

The Attestation in the Passion and the Resurrection, Chapters 18-20

Since he was an eyewitness, John selects his material in an entirely free manner in accord with his particular plan and purpose in writing this Gospel. He thus omits a record of the agony in Gethsemane and the traitorous kiss of Judas. He is not writing a complete narrative but presenting those events and those features in these events, which, while they draw a clear and full picture, do so by revealing how here, too, Jesus is attested as the Christ of God.

1. The Arrest, 18:1-11

1) **Having said these things, Jesus went out with his disciples beyond the winter-brook Kedron, where was a garden into which he went, he and his disciples.** After the discourses and the prayer Jesus left the city with his disciples. The fact that Jesus did not leave the upper room until this time appears from our interpretation of 14:31, which see. Ἐξῆλθε means that he left the city, because it is followed by the phrase "beyond the winter-brook Kedron," which lies in the declivity between the walled city and the Mount of Olives toward the east. John alone mentions this crossing of the Kedron. He describes this correctly as a winter-brook which was dry except for a little water in the winter season when the abundant rains furnished a supply. On the form of

the word see R. 275. Zahn, *Evangelium des Johannes,*
615, etc., shows that we should read neither τῶν Κέδρων
nor τοῦ Κέδρου, but τοῦ Κεδρών (used as an indeclinable
word). "Kedron," instead of the masoretic "Kidron,"
is not derived from ἡ κέδρος, the word for "cedar," but
signifies a black, turbid brook. Even when it flowed
with water it was easily forded almost anywhere.
"Beyond the Kedron" is a brief way of saying, "to a
place beyond the Kedron," to which is then added,
"where was a garden." This is Gethsemane. Instead
of giving us the name, which we already know from
the synoptists, John tells us that it was "a garden,"
which is new information. Gethsemane means "oil-
press." This, then, was a "garden" in the sense of
a grove of olive trees which had the equipment for
making olive oil, was fenced with a stone wall, stone
being plentiful. Here Jesus entered, and with a touch
of pathos John adds, "he and his disciples."

2) **Now Judas, too, who was betraying him,
knew the place because Jesus frequently was
gathered there with his disciples.** Only on the first
night after Palm Sunday did Jesus return to Bethany
(Matt. 21:17), the following nights he spent in Gethsemane, sleeping in the open in this retired and sheltered place (Luke 21:37; 22:39, 40). Judas had
spent these nights there with Jesus and thus knew the
place. His plan to capture Jesus was based on this
knowledge. The second past perfect ᾔδει is always
used as an imperfect; and the present participle
ὁ παραδιδούς graphically describes the traitor as now
being engaged in his nefarious work. It goes without saying that Jesus used this garden with the friendly permission of its owner, just as he had the use of
the upper room in the city for the Passover and the
use of the ass for his triumphal entry on Palm Sunday.
Purposely, it seems, Jesus had spent the past three
nights in Gethsemane; he may have used its shelter

also during previous visits to the city. Judas was to
know where Jesus could be found when the hour had
come. We also see how easily Jesus could have frustrated the plans of Judas; all he needed to do was
to avoid Gethsemane and to go to some new place for
the night. By again going to Gethsemane, Jesus, who
knew the plans of Judas, deliberately placed himself
into the hands of his enemies — the hour for this had
now come.

3) John at once proceeds with the account of the
arrest. **Judas, therefore, having received the cohort
and underlings from the high priests and the Pharisees, comes there with torches and lanterns and
weapons.** The entire action is represented as that
of Judas; he received, he comes with lanterns, etc.,
John alone reports the composition of the force sent
out with Judas. In τὴν σπεῖραν the article is significant,
pointing to the cohort of Roman soldiers which garri-
soned the castle Antonia near the Temple, a force of
600 men in all. We need not assume the presence of
the entire cohort with Judas, since the castle would
be all but abandoned. Judas had only a strong detachment under the command of their chief officer, the
chiliarch himself (v. 12). Some assume that Roman
soldiers were ordered out by Pilate himself, but no intimation to this effect appears anywhere in the account.
It is enough to assume that the representatives of the
Sanhedrin importuned the chiliarch who then acted
on his own responsibility. After the demonstration
of the pilgrim crowds on Palm Sunday it was easy
to persuade this officer to act, for the proposed arrest
might easily result in a great demonstration by
the crowds that filled the city for the Passover
feast. He took with him a force sufficient for all
eventualities.

In addition to the soldiers there were the ὑπηρέται
of the Sanhedrin, a force of Temple police, also large

in number.   They would be under the command of the
Temple στρατηγός⁻ or chief officer.   With these were
some of the δοῦλοι or servants of the chief priests (v. 10
and 26), and a crowd of voluntary followers who followed to witness the excitement.   The synoptists mention only "a multitude" and "a great multitude"; it
is John who tells us more.   By the "high priests and
the Pharisees," here combined under one preposition,
we must understand the Sanhedrin as such; its full
authority went with these its "underlings."   The size
of this armed force, sent out to arrest Jesus, has
caused skeptical readers to question the reliability of
the evangelists but certainly without just grounds. The
Sanhedrin had to reckon with all eventualities.   Their
own police force had failed them on a previous occasion (7:45, etc.) and might do so again even if Jesus
were found.   Besides, anything might happen if the
effort to effect the arrest of Jesus should become
known in the city   Hence the Roman legionaries were
deemed necessary, a force sufficient to cope with any
mob.   We may, indeed, wonder that so large a force
was sent out to bring in one lone man who had with
him only eleven unarmed friends, but we must not
forget the thousands of pilgrim visitors filling the
city at this time.   The Sanhedrin was reckoning with
these.

John has the dramatic present tense: Judas "comes
there."   This fits well with the following aorists, yet
it lifts into prominence the arrival of Judas.   At this
moment 14:30 was fulfilled, "The ruler of this world
comes, and has nothing in me."   Judas comes there
"with torches and lanterns and weapons."   Of course,
these are in the hands of the men with him, but John
writes as though they were in the hands of Judas, as
in a sense only too true they were.   That is how
"one of the Twelve" now comes to his heavenly
Master!   The "weapons" of John are "the swords and

clubs" of the synoptists. When they write "swords"
they intimate the presence of the soldiers without
otherwise indicating their presence. Only the Temple
police carried the clubs, their usual weapons. John
alone mentions the torches and the lanterns; φανός is a
torch, and λαμπάς a lantern, frequently mentioned as
being fed with oil. It was the time of the full moon,
and the night was chilly (v. 18), hence cloudless. Why
then these torches, etc.? Evidently these captors expected Jesus to hide at their coming; also, being one
of a number of men, they wanted lights to make sure
of his identity.

4) Jesus was made known to his captors in two
ways: by the kissing of Judas and by his own repeated declaration, "I am he." Which came first?
Opinions are divided. John helps us a little. He
makes no reference to the kiss but he does say in v. 5
that, when Jesus made himself known by his own
declaration, Judas was standing μετ' αὐτῶν, in the
company of the captors. The kiss must have come
first. When Judas stepped back after giving it he
was in the company of the armed crowd; and this
means that he did not step forward into the company
of the eleven who were ranged behind Jesus. Thus,
where he stood was highly significant. It is too difficult to assume that Jesus so positively identifies himself to his captors and that he then allowed Judas
to confirm this identification by the sign he had pre-
arranged, the traitorous kiss. Leading the crowd,
Judas quickly stepped forward the moment Jesus
came through the entrance of the garden and, when
he had given the promised sign to his followers and
had stepped back for them to close in around Jesus,
there took place what John alone describes in v. 4-9.
**Jesus, therefore, knowing all things coming upon
him, went out and says to them, Whom are you
seeking?** With οὖν John connects the coming forth

of Jesus with the arrival of Judas and his large force.
Moreover, John wants us to know that Jesus acted
in full consciousness of all that now awaited him.
In 13:27 he told Judas to do quickly what he was
about to do, speaking of it as though he knew all
about it. So here the entire way to the cross lies
plainly before the eyes of Jesus, and of his own will he
enters upon this way. Knowing "all things" means
just what it says. Why try to discount πάντα by inserting "except the details"? Is it more difficult for him
into whose hand God had given "all things" (13:3)
to know the little things that awaited him than the
greater ones?

Jesus "went out," compared with v. 1 "went into,"
means that he came out through the gateway of the
garden, his disciples closely behind him; and not that
he came out of the house, that some imagine to have
been in the garden (no evangelist says anything regarding a house), nor that he came out of the inner
part of the garden, nor that he came out of the circle
of the eleven. In front of the entrance Judas
embraced and kissed Jesus fervently and repeatedly
(this is the sense of κατεφίλησεν αὐτόν, Matt. 26:49;
Mark 14:45, *abkuessen*), and then Jesus at once faced
the crowd of captors and demanded, "Whom are you
seeking?" Judas was allowed to carry out his pre-
arranged plan regarding the kiss, but immediately
Jesus takes the situation out of Judas' hands into his
own. Not by a secretly arranged sign is Jesus to
be identified to his captors but by an open declaration
of his own. All the impressiveness and the authority
of the personality of Jesus confront the armed multitude that is crowded behind Judas. With the
voice that had constrained the devil himself (Matt.
4:10), the demons of the possessed, and even
death to obey, Jesus demanded, "Whom are you
seeking?"

5) **They answered him, Jesus, the Nazarene. Jesus says to them, I am he.** The answer came from the chiliarch who spoke for all, certainly not in a chorus from the whole force. This answer sounds like the repetition of the exact instructions he had received from the Sanhedrin. We assume that the Roman soldiers had marched in front and now stood with the underlings of the Sanhedrin behind them. Authoritatively challenged, their commander makes reply for all present. Judas had already indicated the person of Jesus as the one to be arrested, and some ask why the answer to Jesus' question was not, "We are seeking *thee!*" We cannot reply by pointing to the uncertain moonlight and to the shadow of trees. Jesus stood forth in the view of all, for he had come to deliver himself into their hands. The torches and the lanterns illumined his figure and his face clearly. His voice and his bearing plainly indicated who he was. The act of Judas was performed in view of all. The chiliarch knew that the man demanding answer was most certainly Jesus. Yet his reply is objective, "Jesus, the Nazarene." Two things help to explain the form: the unexpected challenge in the question of Jesus and the ringing note of authority demanding an answer. "The Nazarene" is added in order to specify, for the name "Jesus" or Joshua was borne also by other persons. These men are seeking the Jesus who hails from Nazareth of Galilee; compare Pilate's superscription on the cross (19:19).

In the briefest and the most direct manner Jesus identifies himself, "I am he," i. e., Jesus, the Nazarene, the man you seek. With this identification of himself Jesus brushes aside the secret and cunning identification Judas had made; it is wholly superfluous and unnecessary. Its implication that except for the cunning of Judas Jesus might yet hide and allow one of his disciples to be captured in his place, is revealed in all its baseness. By instantaneously replying, Ἐγώ εἰμι, Jesus himself by his own volition and act delivers himself into the hands of his captors. The word implies, "I am the man — take me!" In v. 8 we see that it implies even more. Here is fulfilled 10:17, 18: Jesus himself lays down his life, and no man takes it from him. The glory of his sacrifice is the fact that it is absolutely voluntary.

With δέ John adds a parenthetical remark: **Now Judas also, who was betraying him, was standing with them.** Compare the remarks on v. 4. John says so much regarding Judas because all his readers will think of what the synoptists report about the traitor's kiss on which John, however, does not intend to dwell. He is reporting certain important features of the arrest which the synoptists omitted. Yes, here was Judas, standing with the captors of Jesus, his traitorous kissing done. This is why John inserts the statement here. It is difficult to assume that John intends to say that Judas now delivered the kiss; εἰστήκει, the past perfect, always used in the sense of the imperfect, means that Judas continued to stand in the company of the men he had led hither. Between v. 5 and 6 no interval can be assumed; for the moment Jesus pronounced the words, "I am he," the crowd before him stumbled back and fell to the ground, and Judas, who was standing with them, must be included. That, too, is why John inserts this parenthetical remark at this place.

To be sure, it has a tragic tone: Judas standing with them. But this is only an incidental feature and not the chief reason for John's remark. Unlikely is the supposition that John intimates that Judas still had a spark of good in him. No; Satan ruled him completely, Judas stood with those among whom he belonged. That he did this in a bold and brazen way needs no saying although some have thought this to be the object of John's brief statement. Judas is even pictured as leaning against the garden wall or against a tree, one leg leisurely across the other, as much as to say, my part is done, and the rest is the part of the others. But why overdraw the picture? The brazenness of Judas is also only incidental. John brings in the traitor here because he wants his readers to remember what the other evangelists have reported with all sufficiency regarding the traitor's kiss, to which John desires to add nothing more.

6) **When, therefore, he said to them, I am he, they went backward and fell to the ground.** The fact that the remark about Judas is only parenthetical is shown by the way in which John connects the reply of Jesus with its astonishing effect. He even repeats the reply, "I am he." This it was that caused the multitude to go backward and then to fall to the ground. Both verbs have their subjects only in their endings: ἀπῆλθον and ἔπεσον, "they went back, and they fell down," two aorists to denote the two facts. The preposition in the first verb (ἀπό) indicates that they shrank and retreated *from* Jesus who was facing them. This cannot mean that only some of the men stumbled backward and fell. We might imagine it so, but John, who with his own eyes saw what happened, does not say this. He could easily have inserted "some" or another limiting subject; but he writes no subject at all, the verb endings are sufficient. He, indeed, might have added "all," either with or without emphasis; but by leaving out an expressed subject, the verbs carry the emphasis: "they went backward, and they fell to the ground."

All the ancients regard this as a miraculous effect, and to this day many follow them. But others seek to explain what happened as a natural and a psychological effect. They call to mind the miracles of Jesus, the belief of so many Jews in the divinity of Jesus, his grand entry into Jerusalem, and his second cleansing of the Temple. They adduce a few similar instances from ancient history. Then they imagine that only a few men in the front ranks actually fell down. But when all is said that can be said about the unexpectedness of Jesus' demand and answer and about the sudden panic this inspired, it fails to convince, granting even that only some fell prostrate. Men might pause and hesitate in such a situation; a few might take a step or two backward, but that would be all. If in stepping backward any should stumble they would be held up by coming against those standing behind them. Here, however, several hundred men fell down as though struck by the word, "I am he." They were given no time to think — they went backward, they went down completely. Moreover, we are bound to place the Roman cohort, which marched and which stood in military rank and file, at the head of the entire force, directly facing Jesus; for in v. 3 the cohort is named first, and it is hard to imagine the chiliarch with his military detachment in full armor bringing up the rear behind the non-military underlings (ὑπηρέται) who were equipped only with clubs. Army men would today demand the front place. Something more happened than a psychological and a natural effect. Trained soldiers of the Roman type, standing in formation, do not go down so easily, including even their chief commander. Luther is right: "John did not want this to be left unsaid in order that by means of the actual act he might indicate with certainty who this person is: so that no one is to think that this is only a common man but a person who with seven letters: Ἐγώ εἰμι, hurls them all back upon the ground, both the cohort and the servants of the high priest, including also Judas, the traitor. This was a peculiar and divine power which Jesus intended to display, not only in order to frighten the Jews, but also to strengthen the disciples. For from this they could conclude, if the Lord did not voluntarily intend to give himself into death, he would have been well able to protect himself and to hinder his enemies, not needing other people's help though the disciples dared to offer it. Very properly they should have thought: lo, if this man can do this with a single word, which is not even a curse but a friendly answer, it surely must signify something especial that he so willingly yields himself and allows himself to be captured. He could defend himself, yet he does not do so but he suffers. Therefore, the divine power which he so often and now in the garden displays in one word, this power will not be able to allow itself much longer still to be restrained, his foes must go down, but he will rule. This the disciples especially were to conclude from this miraculous act."

7) Jesus pauses and allows the men to rise to their feet. **Once more, therefore, he requested of them, Whom are you seeking? And they said, Jesus, the Nazarene.** This time John uses the dignified verb ἐπερωτάω. His captors had lost their dignity by tumbling over each other, not so Jesus. With the same authority he repeats his question. Nothing is left for them but also to repeat their answer. Luther is one of the very few who pause at this answer: "Here we may learn what an abominable thing an obdurate heart is, in order that we may learn to abide in the fear of God. They feel themselves falling to the ground but they do not recede in their hearts from the intention and evil purpose, thinking that their falling backward must be due to some witchcraft. These are hearts of utter steel and adamant. And the rogue Judas, the evangelist tells us, also stood with them, is so obdurate and hard and falls to the ground with the rest; yet he is not moved that he

should think: Man, quit defying him who hurls us all back with one word. Even if heaven and earth were created anew before the eyes of such people, and the greatest miracles were wrought that could possibly be wrought, it would avail nothing."

8) **Jesus answered, I said to you that I am he; if, therefore, you are seeking me, let these be going their way; in order that the word might be fulfilled which he spoke, Those whom thou hast given me, not one of them did I lose.** Twice Jesus made his captors repeat the instructions that they were to take him. The repetition brings out the point that they had no instructions to take any man besides him. With the same impressive authority Jesus now orders that they abide by their instructions and keep their hands off his disciples. The scene is remarkable indeed! Jesus faces these armed men, a host of them, with their proud commanders, and *he* issues *his* orders to them, "Let these be going their way!" And Jesus is obeyed. We have no reason to assume that any move had as yet been made to take either Jesus or any of his disciples. Luther writes: "Christ can strike down his enemies and defend his disciples with one word and did this when he was weak and willed to suffer; what may and can he do now that he is exalted to the right hand of God? And what will he do at the last day?" We may say that the Sanhedrin had entirely disregarded the disciples. With Jesus out of the way, what could the disciples do? Moreover, it might prove inconvenient to have also the disciples brought in. It was easier to make away with only one man. Yet the zealous agents of the Sanhedrin might easily have gone beyond their instructions and, while they were at it and had the opportunity, might have arrested also the disciples. Nor would the authorities have chided their agents for showing such zeal. It is Jesus who settles the matter that they must

capture him alone. Even when sacrificing himself the Good Shepherd spreads his protection over the sheep. The disciples are left alone.

9) Jesus uttered this command to his captors in order that the word which he spoke in his high-priestly prayer, 17:12, might be fulfilled, namely, that in this extremely critical moment he so guarded his disciples that he lost none of them. We cannot agree that John intends to say only that he (John) noted this fulfillment, at least noted it later on and so placed it into the record. While v. 9 is a statement added by John to draw our attention to the fulfillment, this ἵνα clause expresses the intention which Jesus had when he gave this order to his captors. It was Jesus who saw the danger of his disciples, it was he who had in mind the word he had spoken in his prayer, it was he who now acted so that this word should be fulfilled, it was he who protected his disciples accordingly. To deny this intent on the part of Jesus would compel us to assume that his word spoken in 17:12 was inadvertently fulfilled merely in an accidental way. For us this alternative is impossible.

In 17:12, however, Jesus speaks of his success in keeping the souls of his disciples so that none was lost by falling into unbelief and thus perishing forever as Judas did. Here the success of Jesus consists in keeping his disciples out of the clutches of the men who were arresting Jesus. This seems like a discrepancy to some who, therefore, are inclined to regard v. 9 as an interpolation. Luther has long ago cleared up this verse: "The evangelist here indicates that in this word Christ spoke of becoming lost in a temporal sense, while in 17:12 the text is clear that the Lord speaks of becoming lost in an eternal sense. This, however, is really not a contradiction; for if the disciples had been arrested on this occasion, they

would also have been lost in body and soul eternally."
What Luther means is that by their arrest the disciples would have been plunged into a spiritual test
that was at this time altogether beyond their strength.
We see this in the case of Peter who disregarded the
warnings of Jesus (13:36-38) and ignored the protection Jesus spread over his disciples here at the
time of his arrest. How quickly he succumbed, how
miserably he denied Jesus! But in the end Jesus
saved even him.

10) How Peter nearly brought on the very calamity Jesus was warding off is now added to the record;
but the main point of this addition is the word
addressed to Peter which, like the entire paragraph,
attests that Jesus entered his passion voluntarily
to carry out his Father's will. **Simon Peter, therefore, having a short sword, drew it and struck the
high priest's servant and cut off his right ear. Now
the servant's name was Malchus.** Luke 22:38 tells
us that there were two swords in the hands of the
disciples; μάχαιρα, a Roman short sword. Those who
know Peter will not be surprised to find that he carried one of them. The Lord's word to the captors
declared his readiness to submit to arrest but forbade
the arrest of the disciples. At this point a move must
have been made to act on the word of Jesus, namely
to lay hands on Jesus in order to bind him. From
Matthew's and from Mark's accounts we need not conclude that the arrest had already been effected before
Peter acted. Luke 22:49 tells us that the disciples,
seeing what was coming, asked Jesus whether to smite
with the sword. But Peter asks no question, awaits
no answer. He draws his sword and delivers a blow
which severs the ear of the high priest's servant. All
was done in an instant. It is easy to imagine what a
calamity this blow might have precipitated. Instant-

ly Jesus interferes and wards off the effect of Peter's rashness.

We must reckon with the excitement of the moment. Then the tumbling over of the entire armed force at the one word of Jesus may have made the disciples and Peter feel that, though armed with only two swords, they might rout this entire opposing force. Another such word of Jesus and the disciples would be victors. And had not Peter protested that he was ready to lay down his life for Jesus? and had not the others, stimulated by Peter, done the same? So Peter now redeems his word. Jesus is to see that he meant it. Some refer to the love of the disciples for Jesus, and who would leave this out? But what a poor show of love was this readiness for violence? Had the last discourses of Jesus been spoken in vain? Had none heard Jesus say that he intended to lay down his life and by death go to his Father? And right here at the garden had they not heard Jesus offer himself to his captors, commanding them to let his disciples go their way? Was this not a command also to the disciples, namely that they should go their way while Jesus submitted to arrest? Peter acts as though Jesus really meant none of the things he had said. His love does not listen and obey; it assumes to dictate its own course.

It is John who names Simon Peter as the disciple who cut off the servant's ear; the other evangelists withhold the name. The conjecture may be correct that the earlier evangelists, who wrote while Peter was yet alive and the Sanhedrin was still in power, did not deem it safe to mention his name, and that when John wrote a long time after Peter's death and Jerusalem's destruction, such considerations were no longer necessary. As far as a derogatory effect in the first church is concerned, this can offer no explanation, for Peter's rash blow with the sword is completely outdone by his threefold denial of Jesus. If anything hindered Peter in his work, it would have had to be the latter. Why has τὸν δοῦλον the article? This man was not one of the "underlings" called ὑπηρέται in v. 3; for in v. 18 the two classes of men are distinguished, and in 22 one of the underlings speaks, while in v. 26 it is one of the servants. This δοῦλος belongs to the high priest, while the ὑπηρέται are the police force sent out by the Sanhedrin, v. 3. "The servant" is taken to mean the one especially delegated by the high priest to accompany this expedition. He must have been one especially trusted and prominent in the household of the high priest. That may also explain his position in front of the soldiers and thus close to Jesus, so that Peter found him as his first target. In a parenthetical remark with δέ John tells us his name, and John alone does this. The name itself cannot be so important. Its insertion substantiates what John writes in v. 15, 16 about his acquaintance with the high priest and with his servants, enabling him to get Peter past the doorkeeper of the courtyard. In v. 26 this intimate knowledge again comes out, for John knows that the servant there mentioned is a relative of Malchus'. These and many other touches vouch for the authorship of this entire Gospel; it bears John's signature in a large number of places.

The diminutive ὠτάριον does not mean a part of the ear but the entire ear. The Greeks loved to use diminutive terms to designate the parts of the body. Malchus seems to have dodged Peter's blow, who certainly aimed to strike the head and to kill the man. It was providence that let the blow do no more damage. John does not report the miraculous healing of the ear. Some are inclined to think that it was not sheared off entirely but hung by a portion of the kin.   The verb, however, allows us no such option.

11)   Jesus at once interposes.   First, the order to put up the sword, only in its wording a little different from Matt. 26:52, and certainly a peremptory command: **Sheathe thy sword!** literally, "Throw the sword into the scabbard!"   The word is a strong rebuke to Peter.   Jesus disowns the rash deed of his follower.   Luke reports how Jesus at once repaired the damage (22:51), thus protecting Peter from the dire consequences of his deed.   To wound the special representative of the high priest was no small matter for one who was already in disfavor as a follower of Jesus.

Jesus said more in rebuke of Peter, for his act militated against the gracious plan of God and the will of Jesus.   To this rebuke, as recorded by Matt. 26:52-54, John adds a new and significant statement left unrecorded elsewhere: **The cup which the Father has given me, shall I not drink it?**   Does Peter intend that Jesus shall turn away from that cup, or does he intend to prevent Jesus from drinking it?   With great emphasis the nominative absolute places the object in front and then picks it up as the object with the redundant pronoun αὐτό (R. 683).   John omits mention of the agony in the garden, but this word about the cup given to Jesus by the Father plainly refers to the prayers uttered by Jesus in his agony.   The explanation that the figure of drinking the Father's cup is quite ordinary and hence has no reference to prayers of Jesus is surely insufficient.   Even if the figure were common — which it certainly is not — the connection is too evident.   "This cup" means the contents and thus is only a grammatical figure, naming the vessel instead of what it contains, Krauth, *Conservative Reformation*, 778, etc., quoted in the author's *Eisenach Gospel Selections*, 532.   This

ordinary grammatical form of speech is here used
together with the corresponding verb with regard to
drinking as a metaphor. The experience of the bitter
passion awaiting Jesus is compared with the drinking
of a bitter potion. This is an uncommon metaphor,
although its use by Jesus has made it familiar to us.
The emphasis is on ὁ πατήρ. He places this cup to
Jesus' lips; his will is that Jesus drink this cup. Shall
Jesus, who has come for the very purpose of doing
his Father's will, now evade that will and refuse the
cup? This cup and its drinking on the part of Jesus
are not mere incidental parts of the Father's will but
the supreme part of that will ("obedient unto death,
yea, the death of the cross," Phil. 2:8). Shall Jesus
fail the Father in the essential part of his will? The
entire context reveals that the cup is filled with bitterness, requiring utter self-abnegation to drink it —
"not my will, but thine be done." The implied
bitterness (figure) pictures the coming suffering
and death of Jesus (reality). The aorist subjunctive πίω has the strong negative οὐ μή (R. 929,
etc.; 1174, etc.).

2. The Inquiry before Annas and the Denial of Peter, 18:12-27

12) **So the cohort and the chiliarch and the
underlings of the Jews arrested Jesus and bound
him and led him to Annas for the first; for he was
father-in-law of Caiaphas who was high priest of
that year.** The first three aorists simply report the
facts in a summary way. These three acts are
ascribed to the entire force that had come out to take
Jesus prisoner. Yet the chiliarch or military tribune
(R. V. margin) is mentioned personally in second
place, after the cohort which he commanded. We
shall not be wrong when we assume that the chiliarch
issued the order to several of the Roman soldiers to

place Jesus under arrest and to tie his hands or his arms. The rest of the cohort was commanded to surround Jesus. The underlings of the Jews likewise surrounded Jesus. By "Jews" John refers to the Jewish authorities, the Sanhedrin. Nothing is said about the eleven who fled at this point, Matt. 26:56, nobody paying any attention to them. The three synoptists report that Jesus protested against his arrest, including the manner in which it was made, and revealed what lay back of it in the counsel of God and in the power of darkness.

The procession formed and marched back to the city. Here John amplifies the account of the synoptists. Matthew and Mark omit the judicial inquiry before Annas and thus report that Jesus was brought to Caiaphas and the Sanhedrin, following this with an account of the trial proper. Luke 22:54 reports that Jesus was led to the high priest's house; he omits the trial at night, reporting only the abuse and the mockery that marked its close. From John we learn that the trial during the night was preceded by a judicial examination under Annas. The captors had orders to bring Jesus to Annas who, most likely, lived in the house of his son-in-law Caiaphas. John reports the full details of the abortive preliminary examination before Annas; then, however, he at once takes us to the prætorium of Pilate (v. 28). Yet by saying, "they led him to Annas for the first," πρῶτον, John intimates that presently Jesus was brought before the Sanhedrin itself; this is the sense of the direct statement in v. 24. See B.-D., 55, and R. 254, etc., on the Greek declension of Annas and of Caiaphas.

13) John again gives evidence of his acquaintance with the high priest's family by informing us that Annas was the father-in-law of Caiaphas; and he assigns this relationship as the reason why Jesus was ordered to be brought before Annas for the first. We

may read a bit between the lines. Annas had been
the high priest from the year six to the year fifteen;
a son of Annas was the immediate predecessor of
Caiaphas, and another his successor. During the
years to 66 three additional sons and one grandson
of Annas held that office. We may speak of "the
dynasty of the house of Annas" in the high-priestly
office.   It seems that Annas bore the title of high
priest after he was no longer high priest, and the
same may be true regarding his son. He was most
certainly a man of tremendous influence among the
Sadducees and in the Sanhedrin. He was of one mind
with his son-in-law concerning Jesus, and thus was
designated as the man into whose hands Jesus was
to be delivered if he were captured on this night raid.
Naturally also it took a little time to assemble the
Sanhedrin with its membership of 71 men in the
middle of the night. The moment news of the capture
arrived messengers flew through the dark streets to
gather at least a quorum of the High Court. The
leaders felt that they dared not wait until morning
but must secure action at once. The legal restrictions
forbidding trials at night were summarily set aside,
and the Sanhedrin was summoned. Modern Jews
assail the evidence of the evangelists on this vital
point and declare that this trial by night never took
place; but the evidence of the Gospels cannot be over-
thrown by modern Jewish assertion that this evidence
is false. The leaders who deliberately plotted the
murder of Jesus were not the men who balked at a
technicality of legal procedure when they had their
victim in their grasp.

The reason why Jesus was brought for the first
to Annas is the one assigned by John. This reason
is personal not official. It was not Annas who issued
the order to arrest Jesus. Annas was not the real
high priest with Caiaphas being only his second; nor

did the two in some way divide the office, either by
official or by private arrangement; nor did the office
alternate between them annually. Annas was not the
vicar (*sagan*) of Caiaphas, nor the president (*nasi*)
of the Sanhedrin. No vicar would be mentioned
ahead of his chief as is done in Luke 3:2 and Acts 4:6;
and none but the president of the Sanhedrin would
dare to speak as Caiaphas speaks in 11:49, etc. The
effort to combine into one the examination by Annas
and the trial proper under Caiaphas is fruitless; the
two differ in every point. Transpositions of the text,
especially placing v. 24 before v. 19, are unwarranted.

Once more (see 11:49 and 51) John remarks that
Caiaphas was high priest "of that year," i. e., of that
notable year in which Jesus was done to death. Being
high priest during the years 18-36, his term included
this tragic year.

14) A parenthetical remark is added in order to
indicate how the relationship to Caiaphas made Annas
the man to whom Jesus was sent at first. **Now
Caiaphas was he who gave counsel to the Jews that
it was expedient that one man die instead of the
people.** Annas was the father-in-law of the man
who not only voiced this thought (11:51) but was
now in the act of carrying out that thought. The
two men were of one mind. Thus John furthermore
indicates what treatment Jesus might expect of Annas
during the wait for the convocation of the Sanhedrin.
R. 1058 regards the accusative with the infinitive as
the subject of the impersonal συμφέρει which the Greek
retains in the present tense of the direct discourse. The exposition of this word of Caiaphas is
given in 11:50.

15) For the moment John leaves Jesus and turns
to Peter. **And there followed Jesus Simon Peter
and another disciple. Now that disciple was known
to the high priest and went in with Jesus into the**

court of the high priest. Luther remarks on how elaborately all four evangelists describe Peter's denial, whereas many important events pertaining to Jesus are omitted by one or the other or are briefly treated. Why is so much space devoted to Peter? Luther answers that it is due to the fact that Peter's case illustrates the great fruit of the passion, the forgiveness of sin, which, though it pertains so directly to you and to me, is yet the hardest article to believe. John's account amplifies that of the synoptists quite materially. First we learn that two disciples and not merely one followed Jesus. All fled in Gethsemane when the soldiers closed in on Jesus at the tribune's command. But presently two began to follow at a safe distance (so the synoptists). Love drew them to follow, fear kept them at a distance. We have already seen that John never names himself nor any of the members of his family. While some have thought of this or that person, the consensus of opinion is that this unnamed disciple is John himself. John here relates his part in the story of Peter, not merely in order to add what the other evangelists omit but to make a confession of sin for his own part in it, to tell how he aided and abetted Peter in entering the high priest's court where Peter fell, and how, but for his aid, Peter could not have entered.

John feels compelled to tell how he was able to aid Peter in gaining entrance. John was a person known to the high priest, known to such an extent that even the doorkeepers were quite familiar with him. This is astonishing, but we shall have to stop with the astonishment; for no clue is offered us by which we could safely hazard a guess as to how John could be so well known to the high priest and to his household. Various opinions have been expressed, the best of which is that, perhaps, John was related to the high priest. Yet, γνωστός does not mean a relative. "The high priest," who is twice mentioned in this verse, must be Annas who still retained this title although he now no longer held this office; note the plural in Luke 3:2, and in John 18:35. Caiphas is mentioned only in the parenthetical remark in v. 13. It may be possible that John knew both men, also that both lived in the same palace; for very likely this was a large rectangular structure surrounding an open court with many rooms on the four sides. When the crowd of captors brought Jesus in, John and Peter followed along in the rear, and John passed in with the rest, but Peter held back.

16) **But Peter was standing at the door without. Accordingly the other disciple, who was known to the high priest, went out and spoke to the doormaid and brought Peter in.** Perhaps John saw Peter through the gate; he stepped outside, spoke a few words to the doormaid, secured her permission, and thus enabled Peter to enter — doing his friend an ill-service. The reason why John recounts all these details is because he is taking full blame. Instead of reminding Peter of the warning of Jesus and taking Peter away, John, even John himself, helps to make Peter disregard that warning. Here was direct disobedience. Here was another case of rashness. Here was a useless act. Peter wanted to see the τέλος or outcome, Matt. 26:58, and had not Jesus foretold exactly what that would be? That was not enough for Peter. His disobedient curiosity leads him into a situation so full of danger that he cannot hope to escape unscathed. After bringing Peter in, John, privileged as he was, went into the palace, to the hall where Jesus was before Annas.

17) Mark and Luke first tell about the fire, and then about the denial. John does the opposite. We are at once told what happened, and then the circum-

stances are added. **Says, therefore, the maid, the
doorkeeper, to Peter, Certainly thou, too, art one of
the disciples of this man? He says, I am not.** From
John we learn that the very maid who let Peter in
exposed his identity. But from the synoptists we
gather that she left her post at the door, came over
to Peter, fixed her eyes upon him, and then put her
sudden, startling question. What made her do that?
Was she afraid that she had let the wrong man in,
and did she take this means of making the man
known? If so, then what about John whom she knew
much better? The καί in her question, "thou, too,"
indicates that she knew John as a disciple of Jesus.
She makes no issue of John. Was she merely teasing
Peter, trying to make him uncomfortable when she
saw him hiding his identity? Her words do not sound
like light banter. The most probable guess is that
she wished to make herself important by letting the
men know that she knew something they did not know.
Here they were talking about Jesus and what had
just taken place and yet did not know that right
in their own midst there was one of Jesus' own disciples. No doubt, they all cocked their ears at the
question. Its form with μή expects a positive answer.
Jesus is designated as "this man," a derogatory
appellation.

Peter is compelled to reply, and he denies his discipleship. John reports this first denial in the
simplest way, "I am not!" with which the synoptists
agree although they add other words. Thus Peter
fell. It took only a menial woman to bring the chief
of the Twelve to his fall. Gone were all his high and
heroic protestations to Jesus; gone all the courage
from his heart and from the hand that a short time
ago had snatched out the sword. Here stands the
arrant coward, unable to confess his Lord, cringing
in lying denial. We cannot agree with those who

think that Peter misjudged the situation, that in
reality he was in no danger and might freely have
confessed his discipleship. They paint the situation
accordingly. Strange to say, they make no reference
to John about whom the doormaid hints that he was
also a disciple of Jesus. It seems likely that she concluded from Peter's connection with John, when the
latter spoke to her to allow Peter to enter, that Peter,
too, must be a disciple of Jesus. Yet this would not
prove the absence of danger for Peter even if no danger existed for John because he was known in the
high priest's house.   Peter would most likely have
been arrested, brought before Annas, and held for
a time. We can hardly think that his life was
in danger. What swept Peter off his feet was the
suddenness of his exposure, its publicity before the
crowd about the fire, and the guilty feeling that he
had of his own will and against warning walked into
this trap. He was thrown into a panic. Frightened,
he saw no way out except to lie. The devil still loves
to pounce upon the foolhardy and to sweep off their
feet those who boast of their strength.

18) Now John gives us a glimpse of the situation,
adding these details to the main point of the narrative.
**Now there were standing the servants and the under-
lings, having made a charcoal fire, for it was cold,
and they were warming themselves; and Peter also
was standing with them and warming himself.** Introduced by δέ, this description is like a parenthesis,
which also explains the imperfect tenses. Verse 18
must, therefore, be regarded as describing the situation at the moment when the maid confronted Peter,
not as narrating what occurred after Peter's denial.
The latter would require aorists. Of course, after
the denial Peter lingered awhile. "The servants" or
δοῦλοι are those who belong to the palace, while "the
underlings" or ὑπηρέται belong to the Temple guard

and are under orders of the Sanhedrin. The latter
had helped to bring in Jesus. We hear nothing
further about the Roman cohort and its commander.
These returned to their barracks in Antonia. We cannot imagine that the cohort entered the palace hall
where Jesus was examined; the number of men was
altogether too great for that. Only a few underlings
led Jesus before Annas. An ἀνθρακιά is a heap of charcoal, and "to make" such a heap means to pile it up
and to make it burn.

19) At this point John shifts the scene to the
examination of Jesus within the palace. **The high
priest, accordingly, inquired of Jesus concerning
his disciples and concerning his teaching.** The resumptive οὖν connects with v. 12: Jesus, having been
brought for the first to Annas, is now examined by
Annas and after this is sent to Caiaphas by Annas
(v. 24). "The high priest" who interrogates Jesus is
thus Annas. But this is denied by some. We are
told that Jesus was brought to *the house* of Annas
although John writes, "to Annas." It is said that
the owner of the house need not be the person to make
the examination — though no one makes such a claim
— but the trial judge alone is qualified for that — but
Caiaphas was not "the trial judge" in the true sense
of this term. The case of Jesus did not come before
Caiaphas as the trial judge but before the entire
court of 71 judges serving as one bench. Any one of
this bench might have been delegated to undertake
the preliminary judicial examination. The fact that
Annas was chosen has been explained in v. 13 by the
γάρ. Jesus was not brought to him only "to honor
the old gentleman." Nor did Caiaphas conduct this
examination "chiefly for the information of Annas."
The reverse is true: Annas conducted this examination in order to extract some information for the use
of Caiaphas. The assertion that whenever ἀρχιερεύς

is mentioned in this chapter without further addition (as in v. 15, 19 and 22) it refers to Caiaphas overlooks the point that up to this time Caiaphas has been introduced to us, not as "high priest," but as "he who was high priest of that year" (11:49-51; 18:13). This enables John to designate Annas as "the high priest" without causing a misunderstanding. See also the comment on v. 24.

Preliminary hearings or preliminary judicial investigations have always been a part of recognized legal procedure with prisoners after arrest and before regular trial. We see that in the present case Jesus gives answer to the probing question put to him by Annas in the capacity of examining judge. By answering, Jesus recognizes the authority of Annas. If he had refused to answer he would have denied that authority. John states only the substance of the question which Annas put to Jesus. It covered two closely related points: "concerning his disciples and concerning his teaching" or doctrine. Note that John employs two prepositions. Jesus has been gathering adherents or disciples, meaning not merely the Twelve but all those who accepted what he taught. What is this peculiar doctrine that Jesus is promulgating? Luther pictures the proud ecclesiastic in all his haughty arrogance, acting as though he did not know what Jesus taught, as though he had not deemed it worth while hitherto to acquaint himself with the teaching of this inferior man. Of course, Annas takes for granted that the doctrine of Jesus for which he gathered adherents is heretical and contrary to the teaching of the Old Testament, the accepted standard of Judaism. The question is thus full of hostile intent. Its one purpose is to find something in whatever Jesus may say about his doctrine that may be used for condemning him to death.

20) **Jesus answered him, I on my part have spoken publicly to the world. I on my part did always teach in synagogue and in the Temple, where all the Jews come together, and in secret did I speak nothing? Why dost thou question me? Question those who have heard what I said to them. Behold, these know what I on my part said.** There is no reason to bring in the spiritual condition of Annas in explaining why Jesus gave answer to his question or why he answered as he did. The reason for both the fact and the form of Jesus' answer is that Jesus recognized the judicial authority of Annas. Though Annas may abuse his authority and prostrate it to unrighteous ends, Jesus submits to the proper legal authority and gives an answer. But the course which Annas pursues is wrong. Therefore Jesus points this out and indicates what the right course should be. Jesus answers only in regard to his doctrine. This, however, does not mean that he ignores the question regarding his disciples. For only if the doctrine of Jesus is false would it be wrong for him to win disciples, whether many or few. Thus in answering the main point the minor point is also covered.

With three emphatic ἐγώ Jesus states what he on his part has done. Others may spread their doctrine secretly, Jesus has promulgated his only in the most public way. Annas and all those present know this beyond question. The perfect "I have spoken" covers the entire period from the day on which Jesus began to speak until the day when he ceased teaching. All this speaking was παρρησίᾳ, "in a public way," a dative of manner. It was so public that it was addressed "to the world." Jesus does not say merely παντὶ τῷ λαῷ, "to all the people," i. e., to all the multitude who heard him or to all the chosen nation; but τῷ κόσμῳ, "to the world." Nebe well says that Jesus used

Palestine as his pulpit from which to preach to the whole world. What if only a limited number had heard him hitherto, the teaching of Jesus is addressed to a vastly greater audience which shall yet hear what he has spoken. "To the world" is prophetic fact.

This first statement is broad, the second is specific, hence the two constative aorists ἐδίδαξα and ἐλάλησα. Whatever others may do, "I on my part," Jesus says, taught publicly "in synagogue" (no article), using synagogues as my forum with their public audiences, "and in the Temple, where all the Jews come together" at the time of the great Jewish festivals. There are many synagogues, hence no Greek article, but only one Temple, hence the article. These two emphatic positives are re-enforced by an equally emphatic negative, "and in secret did I speak nothing," never opened my mouth even to speak, to say nothing of teaching. Jesus had no esoteric doctrine. He did not present one kind of doctrine in public for the crowd and another doctrine behind locked doors for the initiate. Reference has been made to Matt. 10:27 and Mark 10:10, but what Jesus there says he himself declares shall be shouted from the housetops. Jesus simply states the facts regarding the utter publicity of his teaching. Did Annas not know that? Is it not ridiculous for him to ask about something that has been published so openly before the entire nation for over three years? Others may conspire in secret like the Sanhedrin, not so Jesus; others may have secret teachings which they communicate behind locked and guarded doors under seal of oaths, not so Jesus.

21) Hence the pertinent question, *"Why* dost thou question me?" The emphasis is not on the pronoun "me" but on the reason and the intent of Annas. Jesus lays his finger on the evil motive of Annas. He touches the old sinner's callous con-

science. Annas is not seeking to know what Jesus actually taught, he is seeking to lay hold of something that Jesus may now say in order to misuse this against him. Jesus lets Annas feel that he sees through the farce he is putting on in this pretended judicial examination. The evil questioner is himself questioned, and he has no answer except one which would incriminate himself. And this question is followed by a direction. Does this judge not know the right course? "Question those who have heard what I said to them. Behold, these know what I on my part said." These thousands of hearers are the ones who should be called in to testify, provided Annas in truth desires to know what Jesus taught. These are the witnesses by whom to prove that Jesus taught something false and wrong if, indeed, such a charge is to be made. Does Annas fear to lose the case against Jesus by calling in such true witnesses? Does he probe Jesus alone because the verdict of his condemnation is already signed and sealed?

Despite all his shrewdness and cunning Annas has messed up the proceedings. His proposed judicial investigation is mired beyond hope. Annas is at the end of his resources. The tables are turned. He sits there nonplused, unable to proceed.

22) One of his henchmen comes to the rescue. **And when he had said these things, one of the underlings standing by gave Jesus a blow, saying, Thus dost thou answer the high priest?** The nature of the case decides whether the action of an aorist participle precedes that of an aorist main verb or occurs at the same time. Here αὐτοῦ εἰπόντος precedes while εἰπών accompanies. One of the ὑπηρέται, not a δοῦλος, strikes Jesus, evidently one of the police force of the Sanhedrin sent out to capture Jesus and now standing as a guard beside the bound prisoner. He was quick to see the discomfiture of Annas, caught the oppor-

tunity to curry favor with a superior by giving the
situation a quick new turn, and hit Jesus a violent
blow in the face. Some have thought that ῥάπισμα
means a blow with a rod, because of its derivation,
but the word was used for "a blow on the cheek with
the open hand," M.-M., 563, thus distinguished from
κολαφίζειν, to strike with the fist. The blow with the
hand was considered especially shameful. Compare
Isa. 50:6, 7; Micah 5:1. It was an outrage to strike
a prisoner in the presence of the judge while the
former was making his defense. This underling
dared to strike Jesus only because he knew with certainty that his action would please Annas, especially at
the moment when Annas was cornered and knew no
way out. He receives no rebuke of any kind. By his
silence Annas seconds the blow.

The man tries to justify his blow by exclaiming
with a show of indignation, "Thus dost thou answer
the high priest?" but he carefully refrains from intimating what is wrong in either the substance or
the form of Jesus' answer. Both the blow and the
word accompanying it are basely hypocritical. The
hands of Jesus are bound so that he cannot raise
them to ward off the blow. He receives its full impact
— an advance indication of the treatment to follow. Here one man vents his viciousness upon Jesus;
what will happen when many not only unite but vie
with each other?

**23)   Jesus answered him, If I spoke in an evil
way, testify concerning the evil; but if in a good
way, why dost thou bruise me?** Jesus answers the
ruffian's attack with perfect calm and exposes its
baseness just as he had exposed the farce of
Annas' judicial examination. Both κακῶς and κακόν
are opposites. If Jesus had spoken evil in any manner, the one thing for the man to do was to testify
and to specify the evil so that the judge might hear

and decide. The condition of reality assumes for the moment that something wrong was contained in Jesus' reply. On the other hand, if Jesus had spoken properly, and this he most assuredly had, why had the man struck Jesus? Here again Jesus lays bare the ugly motive prompting the man's vicious blow. Jesus uses the strong verb δέρειν, "to flay," indicating the violence of the blow he had received. It produced a contusion of the skin. This reply of Jesus helps to interpret Matt. 5:39, the word of Jesus concerning our turning the other cheek. Luther writes: "You are to understand that a great difference exists between these two: holding out the other cheek and rebuking with words the one who strikes us. Christ is to suffer, and yet the word is placed into his mouth that he is to speak and to reprove what is wrong. Therefore I am to distinguish between *the mouth* and *the hand*. The mouth I am not to yield to condone the wrong; but the hand I am to hold still and not to avenge myself. We are not only to allow ourselves to be struck on the cheek, but are to allow ourselves to be burned for the sake of the truth. But that I should say to the judge, 'Dear judge, you are certainly doing right to burn me,' this would be to betray and to deny Christ as well as that for which I die. . . . For why should I bid knaves and ruffians do injustice? Why should I say to the thief, 'Sir, come and steal my coat'? Christ does not ask this, but Christ says, 'Whoever shall smite thee on thy right cheek, turn to him the other also.' This means to say, 'if one wills to smite thee, do not resist, do not take revenge, do not repay evil with evil.' "

24) This ended the proceedings before Annas. **Annas, therefore, sent him still bound to Caiaphas, the high priest.** No reason exists for reading this statement in any other way than as reporting the

final action of Annas in disposing of the prisoner sent to him for preliminary examination. The examination had been abortive; it yielded nothing that could be used at the impending trial. Annas had left Jesus bound as he was — this is the sense of the perfect participle; and now he orders the guard of underlings to lead Jesus to Caiaphas. This means to Caiaphas, who as the real high priest presided over the Sanhedrin. Jesus is thus led away to his first trial before this supreme court of the Jews. But we are not ready to let πρὸς Καϊάφαν mean, "to *the house* of Caiaphas," just as πρὸς Ἄνναν in v. 12 does not mean, "to *the house* of Annas." The fact that the preliminary examination took place in the palace of Annas we see, not from this phrase "to Annas," but from other remarks in the narrative ("the court of the high priest," etc.). Jesus was not brought to Caiaphas as he had been brought to Annas. With Caiaphas was the Sanhedrin (Matt. 26:57). This high court had its own hall of assembly and its court facilities. It is gratuitous to assume that this court of seventy-one judges (even though there were some absentees) met *in the house* of Caiaphas. Jesus was conducted into the hall of the Sanhedrin itself.

Those who take "high priest" in v. 15, 19, and 22 to refer to Caiaphas are forced into an impossible situation. Then Caiaphas conducted the preliminary examination; then it was his own palace in which he conducted it (v. 15); then Annas was only present at this hearing — yet Jesus was led *"to Annas* for the first," and, strange to say, *Annas* with Caiaphas present, sends Jesus to Caiaphas! The two high priests follow, and the place to which they go is only the palace of Caiaphas. Some make this only another part of the palace of Annas. The procession is thought to cross only the inner open court to the rooms in which Caiaphas lived. These are patent

impossibilities. Recognizing this and using a few
inferior texts, some resort to the means of putting
v. 24 after v. 14. A few, however, think they have
found a better way. They permit v. 24 to remain
where it is but they regard the aorist ἀπέστειλεν as a
pluperfect: "Annas *had sent* him to Caiaphas." They
make this a parenthetical statement, saying that
Annas did nothing at all with Jesus who had been
sent to him, that Annas only sent Jesus on to
Caiaphas for the preliminary examination. Even
R. 841 thinks this possible because John uses οὖν. The
reverse is true. The οὖν denies a parenthesis; οὖν
means "accordingly," when the abortive effort of
Annas was concluded he sent Jesus to Caiaphas. A
parenthetical remark, bringing in a point that pertains to the entire preceding narrative, would have
to be introduced by δέ, which John always uses for
such belated remarks. And even δέ would leave us
in doubt, for it would have to be followed by the past
perfect to make the statement parenthetical. Followed as it is by an aorist, the natural sense of δέ
would be continuative, "and Annas did send," namely
when his investigation had been concluded.

From Annas Jesus is sent to the Sanhedrin under
Caiaphas (v. 24). Now in v. 28 John reports that
from Caiaphas Jesus was brought to the prætorium of
Pilate. This means that John omits the entire trial
of Jesus before the Sanhedrin, both the trial in the
night and the confirmation of the sentence at a second
session in the early morning. John, then, has nothing
to add to the accounts of the synoptists on these proceedings of the Sanhedrin. John intends to contribute
only the account of the action before Annas, which
the synoptists omit. John helps us to piece the story
together with greater certainty. We see that Matt.
26:57 follows the action before Annas; we also see
that Luke 22:54 is identical with John 18:13, and that

Luke 22:63-65 happened at the close of the trial at
night and is all that Luke records of this trial. Not
satisfied with this course of events, a variety of other
combinations is offered. John 18:19-24 is placed
into the session of the Sanhedrin, and the "high
priest" in John's narrative becomes Caiaphas. Perhaps the Sanhedrin held only one session. The
evangelists are made to contradict each other, and we
are given a choice between three clashing versions,
that of Matthew and Mark, that of John, with a third
by Luke that is midway between the other two. The
net result is that the credibility of our witnesses is
destroyed — they are either ignorant on vital points,
or perhaps worse. We must pick and choose among
their testimony, being always certain that some of it is
false. Any choice that we make is subjective, it is
like the findings of a puzzled jury confronted with
conflicting testimony. We refuse to be drawn into
the maze which special pleaders have thus created.
The testimony of the evangelists is reliable throughout. Each agrees with the other. None tells the complete story, but what each reports joins harmoniously
with what the others report.

25) The synoptists tell the story of Peter's denials
in one consecutive narrative. Yet Luke 22:59 reports
that the third denial followed the other two after what
happened to Jesus during this hour (v. 19-24).
**Now Simon Peter was standing and warming him-
self. They said, therefore, to him, Certainly, thou,
too, art one of the disciples? He denied and said,
I am not!** John reports only the first (v. 17, etc.)
and the third denial (v. 25-27). After the first denial
Peter tried to leave the courtyard and went into the
πυλών (Matt. 26:71), the long covered entry that led
from the courtyard through the building to the street.
Here two maids and a man again charged Peter with
being a disciple, and the cock crowed, but Peter failed

to hear or to note this. Driven back out of the entry
passage, Peter returned to the court. For something
like an hour (Luke 22:59) Peter had respite. The
supposition that he talked loudly and freely in order
to pass himself off as belonging to the crowd has
no support and is unlikely. Loud talking would have
precipitated the third inquiry as to his identity and
would not have given him an hour's rest. Peter himself brought on the second denial by going into the
entry in order to leave. What brought on the third
the writers do not indicate.

John's account parallels Matt. 26:73-75; Mark
14:70b-72; Luke 22:59-62. It was at the first denial
that Peter sat (Luke 22:55); John alone tells us that
he stood by the fire warming himself at the third
denial. The sitting and the standing are no discrepancy whatever. This time a concerted effort is
made. From Matthew we gather that several of the
men talked together about Peter and then came and
confronted him. From Luke we learn that one of
these spoke for the rest and made a confident assertion. Mark and John refer only to bystanders, John
writing only, "they said to him." We see that John
intends to be quite brief. Hence he also records only
the confident question that, surely, Peter is a disciple
and makes no reference to Peter's Galilean dialect.
Likewise he summarizes when he writes that Peter
denied the allegation and said, "I am not." He says
nothing about Peter's oaths and cursing, as do
Matthew and Mark. This answers the assumption
that John's Gospel intends to blacken Peter as much
as possible; the contrary is true, John is very gentle
with Peter.

26) Now, however, John adds a detail omitted by
the synoptists: **Says one of the servants of the high
priest, being a kinsman of him whose ear Peter cut
off, Did not I myself see thee in the garden with**

**him? Again, therefore, Peter denied, and imme-
diately a cock crowed.** Because we know that Peter
made three denials, some have thought that John, too,
records all three. They find the second in v. 25, and
the third in v. 26. But these two verses belong together and report the third denial. Without a connective λέγει continues the story of v. 25. Peter's
denial is itself denied by the kinsman of Malchus who
is rather certain that he himself (emphatic ἐγώ) saw
Peter in Gethsemane. We know that Peter was hard
beset. This time a number of men confronted him;
this time they adduce evidence that Peter is lying.
Matthew and Mark refer to Peter's Galilean dialect.
John informs us that the evidence was not only circumstantial but actually direct. The net was drawn
tight about Peter. It is this evidence that makes him
resort to oaths and self-cursings. Peter feels that he
must rend that net, no matter what the cost. Besides,
having twice denied, he feels that it would be fatal,
indeed, now to admit. One lie compels others until
the liar is submerged.

John's knowledge is detailed and exact. He knows
that the man whose ear Peter cut off is the servant
of the high priest Annas, and that his name is Malchus (see v. 10). He even knows that this other man
is a relative of Malchus and was present in Gethsemane. John probably also knew this man's name.
While he does not say that this man saw Peter slash
at Malchus, the implication in the relative clause is
that he did see the act. What John reports thus
attests itself. Yet this kinsman of Malchus is not
absolutely sure, and that is why Peter dares to go on
with his denial. While οὐκ implies a positive answer
in the questioner's mind, the answer of the person
questioned may be either positive or negative. The
phrase ἐν τῷ κήπῳ has been stressed over against ἐξῆλθε

in v. 4, and the latter is then read in a modified way, namely that Jesus did not come through the garden gate but "came out" from the interior of the garden close to its entrance. But in many instances ἐν means "at" and this suffices here.

27) Peter clings to his denial. John says no more. At that moment a cock raised his voice. The prophecy of Jesus was fulfilled. The crowing was timed with the denial by the gracious power of providence. John says no more. We know the rest from the other records. On the crowing of cocks at night see 13:38. It must have been approaching three o'clock. John helps us to understand how Peter at this time could receive the Savior's look of pity out in the courtyard of Annas. Jesus was being led from the palace of Annas through the courtyard, out the way in which he had been brought in, through the entry passage through which Peter tried to escape about an hour before. As Jesus passed through, surrounded by a heavy guard, his eyes sought those of Peter and found them. In the palace everything was over. Nobody concerned himself about the wretched liar and perjurer who went out unobserved and was no sooner out than he broke into repentant sobs.

John purposely divides the story of Peter, placing the examination by Annas between the two parts. This means that after Jesus entered the palace Peter was caught in his first two denials, and just before Jesus came out again Peter was caught in the third. Yet some find contradictions in the accounts of the evangelists. They read v. 24 as though Jesus had already been led away to Caiaphas when Peter was assailed a third time. So, they say, John makes it impossible for Jesus to have looked upon Peter. We have given our answer to such claims.

3. The Trial Before Pilate, 18:28-40

28) Matt. 26:59-68; Mark 14:55-65 report the trial before the Sanhedrin; Luke 22:66-71 report the session in the early morning. Trials at night were illegal; and the death sentence could not be pronounced on the day of the trial, at least one day had to intervene. In the case of Jesus both of these legal provisions were violated. A semblance of legality was secured by holding a second session of the Sanhedrin in the morning. This was not an adjourned session, nor was its object only to decide on how to carry out the death sentence upon Jesus; it was a formal second session, conserving the point of having two sessions in capital cases, and in this second session Jesus was made to repeat his alleged blasphemy, thereby sealing his fate in a kind of legal manner. We hear of no discussion concerning the execution of the death sentence. It seems that the Sanhedrin accepted the legal plan of obtaining the Roman governor's confirmation of the Jewish verdict.

Accordingly they brought Jesus from Caiaphas to the Prætorium, and it was early. The sessions of the Sanhedrin were most likely held in the regular hall of assembly. For forty years prior to the destruction of Jerusalem the Sanhedrin no longer met in the hall situated in the Temple area; though just where they met no one states. Matt. 26:3 reports a meeting held in the αὐλή or hall of Caiaphas. It is not likely that the trial of Jesus was held in this hall of the high priest's palace. John does not write "to Pilate" but here designates the place to which Jesus was taken, namely the Prætorium, because in the next statement he must tell us that the Jews dared not enter this building. The Prætorium is the seat of the prætor or commander of the soldiery, who was Pilate, the governor. This must have been the castle Antonia and not Herod's palace, since Herod himself occupied that at this very time. While Josephus (*Wars,* 2, 14, 8) reports that Florus, the governor, set up his judgment seat before Herod's palace, this does not apply to Pilate. What John tells us is that Jesus was transferred from the court of the Sanhedrin to that of Pilate.

John thus frankly omits mention of the two sessions of the Sanhedrin, although he indicates that they were held. For one thing, he is satisfied to make no additions to the accounts which the synoptists present on these two sessions; on the other hand, he is able to amplify materially the rather brief statements of the synoptists on the trial before Pilate. Thus the section in v. 28-32 is entirely new except the statement that Jesus was conducted to Pilate. Perhaps, too, as some think, John deemed the trial before the Gentile judge more important for attesting the character and the divinity of Jesus for his many Gentile readers than the trial before the Sanhedrin. The remark that it was "early," πρωΐα (supply ὥρα), indicates that as soon as the daylight session of the Sanhedrin has confirmed the death sentence upon Jesus, the Sanhedrin took Jesus to Pilate in order at once to secure its execution. Roman courts were open from dawn to sunset, hence no special credit is due to Pilate for being ready to act at this early hour of the morning, between six and seven o'clock.

And they on their part did not go into the Prætorium in order that they might not be defiled but might eat the Passover. A great procession arrives at the Prætorium: Jesus guarded by a heavy contingent of "the underlings" or police force of the Sanhedrin, all the high dignitaries of the Sanhedrin probably with some of their personal servants, most of the other Sanhedrists, and a crowd of common people who had discovered the extraordinary proceedings

that were in progress. The heavy police force and
the presence of the high priests and the Sanhedrists
is to prevent a rescue of Jesus by his numerous friends
among the Passover pilgrims, and at the same time
to impress the governor with the gravity of the case
against Jesus with a view to gain his prompt assent
to the verdict of the Sanhedrin. The Jews are using
all their resources to gain their end. It is unwarranted
to think that only representatives of the Sanhedrin or
a small delegation went with Jesus. Having arrived
at the Prætorium, a halt is made outside, and the
Roman guard at the entrance is sent to call the governor. The emphatic αὐτοί merely draws attention to
the Sanhedrists. No contrast with Jesus is indicated as though Jesus was turned over to the Roman
guard and marched into the Prætorium. It is only
supposition when Pilate is thought to have lent the
cohort for the arrest of Jesus, so that he thus knows
all about the case of Jesus and is ready and waiting
to receive Jesus at this early hour. If this were
true, Pilate would have kept Jesus in his own hands
and would never have turned him over to the Sanhedrin for trial. No; Pilate has not been apprised
of the case. No guard has orders to accept a prisoner from the Sanhedrin. With their prisoner in
their own midst, these Jews halt and wait for Pilate
to come out.

They fear to become defiled by entering a Gentile
abode, especially also because on this day such defilement would debar them from eating the Passover.
The Old Testament ceremonial regulations contained
no item to this effect, only the rabbis extended the
law of defilement to include entrance into Gentile
habitations. These rabbinical prohibitions were general and not restricted merely to the Passover week
and not based on the presence of leaven in Gentile
houses. Here we see men openly bent on no less a

crime than judicial murder yet stickling about a human tradition devoid of divine sanction. They swallow camels but strain at gnats. The aorists μιανθῶσιν and φάγωσι convey the idea of actual defilement and of actual eating.

Since the Quartodeciman controversy near the end of the second century debate has been carried on concerning John's expression "to eat the Passover." The opponents of the Quartodecimans, whom many still follow, are positive that here "the Passover" means the Passover lamb; hence that John here corrects the synoptists. Whereas the synoptists place the eating of the lamb on Thursday evening, thus making Thursday the 14th of Nisan, John, they say, places the eating of the lamb on Friday evening and makes Friday the 14th of Nisan. We have already shown in 12:1 and in 13:1, that John agrees perfectly with the synoptists. In the present connection it is impossible to make the eating of the Passover mean the eating of the Paschal lamb. For the defilement which these Jews feared would not have debarred them from eating the Paschal lamb if this lamb was to be eaten on Friday evening. Defilement of this type lasted only until sundown and could then be removed by a bath. The Paschal lamb was not eaten until some time after sundown. Already this settles the contention of the opponents of the Quartodecimans and that of the moderns who have John contradict the synoptists. It settles the case so completely that only unsupported denial has been offered and an attempt to make an exception of the defilement on this festal day. But Num. 19:22, coupled with the apocryphal Judith 12:7-9 as an illustration, makes denial fruitless.

"To eat the Passover" may, of course, mean to eat the Paschal lamb, when the connection so requires; but it may also mean to eat of the other sacrificial feasts, the so-called *Chagigah*, during the seven days

of the celebration. The *Chagigah* on the 15th of Nisan
(Friday) was especially attractive. Whereas the eating of the lamb on Thursday evening was a sad and
a solemn celebration, the *Chagigah* of sacrificial meats
on Friday was regarded as a feast of great joy. This,
however, was eaten during the afternoon before sundown. It was this happy feast the Jewish leaders and
their followers did not care to miss because of defilement by entering the Prætorium. The other New
Testament references to the eating of the Passover
are wholly indecisive, and to stress them, as is done,
is useless, because they refer to the Paschal lamb and
occur in no connections such as our present passage.
Yet πάσχα itself is used in the wide sense to designate
the entire week of the festival, as in 2:23; 18:39; etc.
Zahn is right: "To stake everything upon one little
subordinate clause, . . . and to leave out of consideration everything that is said elsewhere in the
book, and the clear relation of the whole narrative to
the older accounts, is not exegetical accuracy, but
violates the laws of historical interpretation," *Introduction to the New Testament*, III, 283 (also his
elaborate notes). Again he remarks that it is quite
incredible to believe that with an entirely incidental
expression, not at all connected with the Passover as
such or with the actions of Jesus but solely with the
scruples of the Jews, John should wish to overthrow
a view of his readers which he has left entirely undisturbed throughout all of his preceding chapters. As
decisive for the wider use of the expression "to eat the
Passover" compare in the Old Testament Deut. 16:2,
etc.; II Chron. 35:6, etc.

29) **Pilate, accordingly, went out to them outside and says, What accusation are you bringing
against this man?** It was not graciousness on
Pilate's part or consideration for the religious scruples
of the Jews that made him come, not merely to the

entrance of the Prætorium, but altogether "outside." The Roman court proceedings were conducted in the most public manner, even on the street or in a market place as occasion arose. So here, in front of the Prætorium, Pilate now opens court. He takes his seat in the judge's chair on the rostrum and begins in the regular manner of a Roman trial. The Roman method was not inquisitorial but dealt with straightforward accusations. Pilate assumes that the Sanhedrists have come with one or more charges against Jesus; he takes them to be the accusers. Hence his demand to hear the accusation. Jesus, too, faces Pilate. "Against this man" means that Pilate pointed to Jesus as the one whom the Jews evidently intended to accuse. The Romans dealt with the accusers and the accused face to face. Jesus had not been turned over to the Roman soldiers and been led inside. Pilate has often been praised for being ready so early, for coming outside, etc. These were matters of course with the Romans. So in demanding the accusation Pilate proceeded as a Roman judge should.

30) But this is the last thing the Sanhedrists desire. They want no retrial of Jesus under a Roman judge; they want Pilate to accept their verdict and on the strength of this verdict to order the execution of Jesus. **They answered and said to him, If this were not an evildoer, we would not have delivered him up to thee.** The readings vary but have the same meaning: κακοποιός, κακὸν ποιήσας, "one who did evil," and κακὸν ποιών, "one who does evil." The protasis is one of present unreality, and the apodosis one of past unreality. Both are negative in form but strongly positive in substance: Since there is no question about his being an evildoer, we have delivered him up to thee. The demonstration the Sanhedrists were putting on certainly looked as though Jesus must be a terrible criminal. And yet, if his criminal-

ity was so enormous and so unquestionable, why all
this demonstration, the appearance of the high priest
in persona accompanied by all these other dignitaries?
Why not state the charge and the evidence if everything is so terrible and also so assured and let Pilate
see for himself? With their negative conditional sentence the Sanhedrists do not state what they want
Pilate to do in the case. This they leave entirely to
inference. Pilate is to sign the Jewish verdict and
to make it his own by ordering the execution of Jesus
forthwith. They are the judges, Pilate is to be the
executioner. By their numbers and their great show
of certainty the Sanhedrists hope to crowd Pilate into
assent.

Their statement implies that the Sanhedrin has
tried Jesus and has in due legal form condemned him
as a criminal so dangerous that they are now delivering him up to Pilate for immediate execution. To
Pilate's ear the term "evildoer" could mean only one
thing, namely that Jesus was a great criminal against
the Roman law. This is what the Sanhedrists intend
Pilate to understand. But this charge against Jesus
and this report of the trial to which the Sanhedrin had
subjected him are a barefaced lie. No criminality
against Roman law had been even as much as intimated against Jesus at his trial. The death sentence
had been pronounced upon him for calling himself the
Son of God in the presence of the Sanhedrin, this
self-designation being construed by his judges as
an utterance of blasphemy. They had not even attempted to prove that Jesus was *not* the Son of God.
They dared not reveal the facts to Pilate, for he would
at once have turned them away from his tribunal.
The Romans would never entertain a religious charge
that lay outside of Roman law and pertained only to
the religious notions of a subject nation. That is why
these Sanhedrists come to Pilate with a bold lie. Yet

they flatter Pilate. They come to him as recognizing his authority, for are they not delivering Jesus up to him? Can Pilate ask more of them? These Sanhedrists, however, safeguard themselves in the event that after all Pilate should investigate the case or should insist on something like a trial by himself. By calling Jesus an "evildoer" they make it possible to bring any number of charges against Jesus that would condemn him under Roman law. If they must they will yet prove Jesus guilty under this alien law.

31) Cunning as was the reply of the Jews, Pilate is not deceived. He refuses to play the role of a mere executioner for the verdict of the Sanhedrin. His pride and the sense of official dignity, not merely as a Roman judge, but as the governor and the representative of the emperor, assert themselves. **Pilate, therefore, said to them, Take him yourselves and judge him according to your law.** The answer of Pilate is more to the point than is sometimes recognized. The Sanhedrists have, indeed, appeared before the tribunal in full force, from which fact he could, and no doubt did, conclude that the Sanhedrin had already tried Jesus. But their spokesmen had as yet failed to inform Pilate of this important fact. Like other vital points, Pilate is to take also this for granted. He is aware of the omission and therefore acts as though he thinks the Sanhedrists have not yet tried Jesus in their own court. This explains the neutral verb κρίνειν, "to judge," "to try a case," which cannot be considered as κατακρίνειν, "to condemn," "to render the verdict, guilty."

When Pilate came out and took the seat of the judge he assumed that the Sanhedrists had come as the accusers with Jesus as the accused, and according to Roman procedure he had at once demanded to hear the accusation, holding himself ready to begin the trial in due form. Now, however, Pilate learns that this is not at all the intention of the Sanhedrists. They are not here to have the governor try this "evildoer." They say that they are delivering him up to Pilate but they fail to say why. This omission also has not escaped Pilate. To be sure, he sees what the Sanhedrists want, but he is certainly right not to accept mere intimations. Pilate, therefore, declines to receive the man delivered up to him in such a manner. He is ready to act as a Roman judge, namely to hear and to try the case. If this is not what the Jews want, Pilate very properly turns the case back to the Sanhedrists. Let them try the man according to their own law. We find no irony nor mockery in Pilate's reply. His reference to the law of the Jews is also in order. They are free to try all manner of cases according to their own law, and as yet Pilate has not been informed by them that this case exceeds the jurisdiction of their law. In other words, the Jews are not frank, hence Pilate keeps to his legal position as governor and judge and just to what these Sanhedrists actually say and no more.

The Jews said to him, For us it is not lawful to put anyone to death. Even now the Jews do not supply the omissions we have noted. Even now Pilate is left to draw certain necessary inferences. All that they say is that the Roman power has deprived them of the right to execute criminals. The *jus vitae et necis* is reserved for the Roman governor. All that the Jews could inflict was expulsion from the synagogue and scourging with rods up to a certain number of blows. It was bitter enough for the Sanhedrists to admit what they do under the compulsion of the present circumstances. But now at last they reveal, although still indirectly, what their purpose is in coming to Pilate. Jesus is to be put to death according to the findings of their supreme court, and their court is without legal power to execute anyone. Pilate alone has this power. The fact that Jesus has already been tried by the Jews is only intimated, and the order that they try him is thus represented as being pointless. They are concerned only about the execution of Jesus, and Pilate is to infer that they are delivering Jesus up to him only for the purpose of being executed. This reply of the Jews indicates that they did not understand Pilate's word to grant them permission to try Jesus and, if he is found guilty of death, to execute him. They dared not even to misunderstand Pilate's word to this effect.

32) John adds that the Jews said what they did **in order that the word of Jesus might be fulfilled which he spoke signifying the manner of death he was about to die.** The word to which John refers he himself at the time marked for us as bearing this sense, namely 12:32, 33. Hence we need not fall back on passages in the synoptists which expressly mention crucifixion. John has the singular "the word," and the participle σημαίνων, "signify," and thus is not quoting. See the exposition of 12:33. Like the death itself so also the manner and the form of the death of Jesus were under God's control. Jesus was not to suffer death by stoning, crushing, and mutilating his holy head, the death penalty customary among the Jews (Stephen), but by crucifixion, the form of execution used by the Romans for slaves, traitors, and the worst types of criminals. Human prognostication would have surmised that the Jewish rejection of Jesus would result in the Jewish mode of execution; divine prophecy foresaw the reality and foretold that. Thus the Sanhedrists came to say just what Jesus had indicated long before this time. But more must be said. God himself so shaped the course of events that finally, when the Jews had Jesus in their power, they could bring him to death only in this one way. When they sought to stone him they always failed in the attempt,

and, if they contemplated secret assassination, they failed also in this. Providence left only one avenue open when the hour arrived and God was ready to let Jesus lay down his life. The Jews themselves would not have chosen this avenue; they chose it, nevertheless, because they found none other open for their purpose, and because they were determined not to swerve from that purpose.

33) The altercation between Pilate and the Sanhedrists, which led up to the presentation of actual charges against Jesus, is recorded only by John. The Jews were compelled to make charges. Luke 23:2 records them: "We found this fellow perverting the nation, forbidding to give tribute to Caesar, saying that he himself is Christ, a King." It is thus that John proceeds: **Accordingly, Pilate entered again into the Prætorium and called Jesus and said to him, Thou, art thou the king of the Jews?** This implies that Pilate takes up the case and proceeds with an actual trial. And this in turn means that, just as Luke 23:2 reports, the Sanhedrists yielded and presented specific charges: 1) that by his activity Jesus had perverted the Jewish nation; 2) that he had forbidden to pay the taxes levied on the Jews by Caesar; 3) that he was proclaiming himself as the King of the Jewish nation. We are astounded to hear these indictments and that the Sanhedrists declare that they "have found" these charges to be facts, i. e., that at their own trial the Sanhedrists had proved these charges against Jesus. Every word is an absolute lie. These charges are the inventions of the moment, so formulated in order to force a hearing from the Roman governor. Only too well the Sanhedrists know that he would most certainly refuse to entertain such a charge as the one on which they had based their verdict, namely that Jesus said that he was the Son of God. Pagan Rome let the religion of its conquered nations

alone. Yet we need not at all be astounded at these Jews — men who plot murder will not scruple about employing lying witnesses at their own trial and lies of their own at the trial under another judge. Those who seek a criminal end are ready to use the necessary criminal means. Such was the moral state of the Jewish leadership.

Pilate accepts these charges as, indeed, he must. He takes the most direct means for investigating them. He re-enters the Prætorium, orders Jesus inside, and questions him. Until this time Jesus stood where the Jewish police force had halted with him. We have no reason to understand ἐφώνησε to mean that Pilate called Jesus as one who was already inside the building. Not until Pilate had accepted the charges against the prisoner would he accept the prisoner himself. We may set it down as certain that the officers of the Jews did not lead Jesus into the building. Pilate's soldiers took him from their hands. Jesus passed over to the jurisdiction of Pilate and the Romans. The supposition that Pilate questioned Jesus in total privacy is without evidence. The Roman manner of conducting trials avoided secrecy. Those who cared to hear were free to hear. Pilate might have questioned Jesus from his judgment seat outside of the Prætorium, but this would have left the prisoner in the hands of the Jewish police force. Therefore Pilate goes inside and by this move has the prisoner turned over to him. The Sanhedrists might come along to hear for themselves if they desired to hear what defense Jesus would make. The proposition with which they had come to Pilate was not of such a kind as to make him accomodate himself to their unpleasant scruples about defilement any more than was absolutely necessary.

Of the charges preferred against Jesus Pilate selects the main one. He rightly judges that with this one the other two will stand or fall. The Jews charge

that Jesus claims to be Christ, "a king." Cunningly
they add the latter term, for Pilate's mind must understand this in a political sense, as a reference to a king
claiming secular power, and thus wanting to be the
head of a Jewish rebellion against the authority of
the Roman emperor. This is the very kingship Jesus
had repudiated (6:15). When at the time of his
entry into Jerusalem he allowed himself to be
acclaimed "the King of Israel" (12:13), the entire
proceeding was without the least political tinge. The
Sanhedrists put into Jesus' own mouth the words "that
he himself is Christ, a King," and that they have
established this as a fact at their trial (Luke 23:2).
They make it appear that they are wonderfully loyal
to Caesar, quick to render a verdict of death against
this Jewish king, only asking of Pilate that he carry
out this verdict. Yet we cannot say that Pilate is
impressed. He has never before known these Jews to
be so loyal; quite the contrary, they submit to Caesar's
taxation only because of Caesar's power. As the
governor of the Jews, Pilate has kept a watchful eye
on every movement in the land under his jurisdiction.
He has never heard of earthly royal pretensions on
the part of Jesus. No reports have come to him that
this man was gathering a force to oust the Romans.
What he knew about Jesus — and he must have known
something (Matt. 27:19) — was of an entirely different nature. Yet the accusation of the Sanhedrists
is positive; they have even heard Jesus say that he is
a king. Thus Pilate is compelled to find out the truth
in this charge.

It is thus that Pilate asks, "Thou, art thou the king
of the Jews?" We see the thought of Pilate and note
that he understands the term "king" in a common political sense. He could take the word in no other sense,
for the Jews themselves, whose direct charge he is investigating, expect their Messiah to be a grand earthly

king. The notion of a spiritual King, the opposite of a secular king, is foreign to their minds. They should have expected such a King, but they certainly did not; and certainly Pilate could have no conception of this kind. The emphasis is on συ: "Thou, art thou," etc.? Pilate's question is tinged strongly with incredulity. He cannot bring himself to think that this man, humbly clad as he is, arrested alone without adherents or followers, can be making pretensions to earthly royal power. Has the question also a touch of mockery? It seems so. Pilate despised the people over whom he ruled. The personal dignity of Jesus does not seem to have registered with Pilate thus early. Pilate's opinion of the Jews at first included also this Jew Jesus. "The King of the Jews" — did this Jew think himself to be the Jewish king? Grand king he would be if he did! Pilate's mind had quite a different picture of what earthly kings looked like.

The attempt is made to regard John's account of the trial before Pilate as complete in itself, although throughout his Gospel we see that John presupposes our knowledge of the records of the synoptists. If nothing intervenes between v. 31, 32 and v. 33, the question must be answered as to how Pilate comes to examine Jesus and then how he comes to ask Jesus about his being the king of the Jews. Both points are answered perfectly if we read John in connection with Luke 23:2. Both points are left to our imagination if we fail to do this. Some think that Pilate ordered out the cohort to help arrest Jesus and that thus he knew that Jesus was charged with pretending to be a king. If this were the case, the cohort would have been ordered to bring Jesus to Pilate and not to Annas. A man like Pilate would not turn a reputed Jewish king over to Jews. Some think that Pilate did this nevertheless and therefore arose early, anticipating that the Sanhedrin would bring Jesus to him. Then why does Pilate at first refuse to try Jesus? If he knows the charge against Jesus, why does he demand to hear the charge? Not until we read v. 33 do we see that Pilate has the charge, and, of course, then he takes the case. The weak feature of these explanations is the fact that the Jews plotted to kill Jesus on any pretext they might find. They tried false witnesses and failed. Not until then did they prefer the charge of blasphemy when Jesus declared himself to be the Son of God. They tried to crowd Pilate into ordering Jesus' death forthwith and here again they failed. Not until they were compelled to meet Pilate's demand for charges did the Jews invent their charges, including Jesus' kingship. And it is thus that Pilate proceeds to try Jesus and asks the question John reports.

34) **Jesus answered, Dost thou say this of thyself, .or did others say it to thee concerning me?** The synoptists, who also report Pilate's question, follow it with only the final answer of Jesus, which John mentions in v. 37. The fact that this final answer was preceded by additional dialog we learn only from John. By answering as he does Jesus acknowledges Pilate's authority in general and his right to question him in particular. Here, too, he renders unto Caesar what is Caesar's, thereby also rendering unto God what is God's. Pilate probably expected Jesus to say, "I am not!" The synoptists report that Jesus said, "Thou sayest it!" meaning, "I am, indeed, a King!" But we at once see that neither of these two answers is really in place. Jesus is witnessing a good confession before Pilate, I Tim. 6:13. He is not merely dodging the charge of the Jews in order to escape; nor is he admitting the charge, which, as it was made by the Jews, is false. From John we learn that Jesus, like a true witness (8:14) though testifying concern-

ing himself, put Pilate off with no half-truth and left his judge under no misunderstanding. The lying Jews have no scruples in leaving Pilate under the impression that Jesus claims to be a secular king. In this sense Pilate, too, asks this question, and in this sense Jesus might simply deny the allegation. But this would be only half of the truth, and all half-truths are virtual lies, because those who have no more think that they have the whole truth. In a very real sense Jesus is indeed a king. On the other hand, were Jesus simply to reply to Pilate that he is a king, he would leave Pilate under the impression that Jesus admits the lying allegation of the Jews concerning his secular kingship. The synoptists, who abbreviate the answer of Jesus, at once report that Pilate pronounces the charge of the Jews false, and thus they reveal that Pilate had learned the full truth concerning Jesus' kingship. John informs us how Pilate obtained the whole truth.

Before replying Jesus asks a question. This is not done because Jesus does not know whether Pilate is asking his question ἀφ' ἑαυτοῦ, "from himself," or only on the allegation of ἄλλοι; but because Jesus deems it necessary for Pilate himself to realize clearly that his reference to "the king of the Jews" only echoes the charge of the Jews. Jesus, Pilate is to understand, will shape his reply on the original question accordingly. By asking his question Jesus allows Pilate himself to say what otherwise Jesus would have to state; and it is better for Pilate to assert emphatically that he has in mind only the charge of the Jews than for Jesus to point this out to Pilate. For with their "Christ, *a* king," the Jews had in mind a false Christ who was trying to be a common earthly king (like Herod of Galilee) ; yet Pilate said "*the* King of the Jews," which, rightly understood, means, "the true Messianic and eternal king promised to the Jews."

If Pilate had anything like this in mind he would be inserting into his question something "from himself," something beyond what "others" such as the Jews had told him. Pilate does not intend this, and Jesus makes him say it. For this is the King who Jesus is, and this is what Jesus will make clear to Pilate in a moment.

The question of Jesus is misunderstood when it is regarded as a demand to know who his accusers are, Jesus here using his legal right to make that demand. Such a demand would be an empty gesture. Jesus knows who is accusing him, has heard the accusation with his own ears, and is not trifling with Pilate by asking him a vacuous question. Also the question with its alternatives "of thyself . . . or others" is not a demand to have the accusers named. A common misconception understands "from thyself" to mean, "Hast thou a personal interest in asking about my kingship?" with the alternative, "Or dost thou ask only as a judge?" Preachers often regard the counterquestion of Jesus in this way and then attach their homiletical applications to this sense. They overlook the fact that it is entirely too early in the contact of Jesus with Pilate for him to try to touch the soul of his judge. Jesus does this presently, he is not hasty in a matter so vital, by his haste defeating his own end. A third misunderstanding takes "from thyself" to mean: as a Roman would understand the word "a king," and takes "others" to mean: as the Jews would understand "Christ, a king." The Roman would think of a secular king, and the Jews of a theocratic king. But the Jews intend that Pilate should think only of a secular king, and that they themselves are not thinking of a theocratic, divine king. What Jesus actually does by his question is that he makes Pilate say that he is asking his question only in the sense intended by the Jews and is adding nothing beyond that sense, nothing emanating "from himself."

35) This appears from Pilate's reply. **Pilate answered, Am I a Jew? Thine own nation and the high priests did deliver thee up to me. What didst thou do?** The first question with its negative interrogative word μήτι is like an exclamation, "Thou certainly dost not suppose that *I* am a Jew!" The emphasis is on ἐγώ spoken with full Roman pride and with scorn for the predicate "a Jew." Pilate implies that nobody but a Jew would dream of charging Jesus with wanting to be a king. As little as one would charge Pilate, the haughty Roman governor, with being a Jew, real or pretended, so little, Pilate says, would he, the Roman, think of charging Jesus, this lone captive Jew, with being the Jewish king, real or pretended. The quick reply of Pilate voices disdainful pride. We are not ready to add that he felt insulted by the question of Jesus. While that question surprised him, he did not resent it or rebuke Jesus.

A Roman like Pilate would not "from himself" investigate any kingship that anyone might attribute to Jesus. The only reason why Pilate makes this investigation is because the own nation of Jesus, together with their chief leaders, the high priests, have with this strange charge delivered Jesus up to Pilate. Pilate uses ἔθνος, "nation" in the secular sense, referring to the entire crowd of Jews assembled before the Prætorium, which became greater every moment. He specifies especially "the high priests," the entire connection of Caiaphas and Annas, the heads of this "nation," who ruled it with their limited authority. This plural "high priests" is important for determining that "the high priest" mentioned in v. 15 and the following is Annas. Pilate knew of more than one man who bore the title "high priest." The aorist παρέδωκαν is frequently used to indicate an action that has just occurred, whereas we prefer the perfect. Pilate bothers with the present business only because this action of the Jews compels him to do so. And this action, it seems to him, could have been precipitated only by something that Jesus has done. Hence the question, "What didst thou do?" another aorist where the perfect is customary with us.

36) Jesus has cleared the mind of Pilate for understanding the answer he now gives to Pilate's original question. **Jesus answered, The kingship that is mine is not of this world. If the kingship that is mine were of this world, my own underlings would fight that I be not delivered up to the Jews; but now the kingship that is mine is not from hence.** The answer is full and complete on the negative side; this negative provokes Pilate to ask for the positive, which he then receives with equal completeness. To Pilate anything like a kingship of Jesus seems incredible; Jesus speaks of his kingship as something that is self-evident. The term βασιλεία may refer to either "kingdom," the territory or the subjects ruled by a king. Here the issue is not as to any subjects or any domain that accept Jesus as king, but as to Jesus' own person, who and what he really is. Moreover, Jesus is the opposite of all earthly kings. They are actual kings because their subjects make them kings; in and of themselves they are not at all kings. Jesus is king with a kingship that is independent of any subjects, with a kingship that inevitably creates its subjects. In this sense Jesus says three times in succession ἡ βασιλεία ἡ ἐμή, with emphasis on the possessive adjective: "the kingship that is mine," over against the kingship that belongs to all other kings. The kingship of Jesus is in a class by itself, in its very nature is infinitely superior to that of all merely

secular kings. The repetitions of this designation
compel Pilate to pay attention to the claim of Jesus.

The origin of Jesus' kingship explains its unique
character: it is "not of this world." Take the whole
wide world as it is. It has produced many earthly
kings and rulers. They all sprang out of (ἐκ) this
world and were kings that corresponded to such an
origin. This king Jesus came out of heaven as the
Son of God and thus holds a kingship of an entirely
different type. It is foolish to place him in the category of secular kings or to rank his kingship with
theirs. Pilate was right when, on taking Jesus over
from the Jews for trial, he saw nothing resembling
earthly kingship in Jesus. He was wrong in concluding that therefore Jesus had no kingship and was
in no sense a king.

The plainest kind of proof lies at hand to establish
the fact that the kingship inhering in Jesus is not of
this world, is not one that clashes with the imperial
secular authority of Caesar or of any earthly ruler.
If the kingship of Jesus were of this world like that
of earthly rulers, Jesus would have what they have,
namely ὑπηρέται of his own, a host of men who would
uphold him as king, who would fight with earthly
weapons to prevent his dethronement by delivery into
hostile Jewish hands. The conditional sentence is
one of present unreality, εἰ with the imperfect plus
the imperfect with ἄν, R. 1015. Pilate sees that Jesus
was delivered up to the Jews who in turn delivered
him up to Pilate. Where are the underlings of Jesus
that rallied around him, who fought or are now fighting in his behalf? Has Pilate heard of a fighting
force that was gathered by Jesus? Have the Jews
dared to charge that he assembled such a force? The
proof is utterly plain: Jesus is not a king of this
kind. The ἵνα clause is subfinal, introducing the pur-

port or object rather than the purpose, R. 993. With a logical (not temporal) νῦν Jesus states the evident conclusion: "but now the kingship that is mine is not from hence."

By declining to interpret ἡ βασιλεία as "the kingdom," we are relieved of trying to explain what Pilate could have understood by this kingdom that is "not of this world." In the positive part of Jesus' answer (v. 37), which merely presents the other side, we see that Jesus does not speak of his kingdom, namely his subjects, but of himself as king, describing just what his kingship is. As regards the ὑπηρέται, some have thought that Jesus refers to the angels, the twelve legions that would come at his command; but this is untenable, for if Jesus were a mere earthly king, how could he have an army of heavenly warriors at his command? What Jesus says is that earthly kings have earthly defenders, as Caesar has his Prætorian guards in Rome, as the Sanhedrin has its police force, as even Pilate has his soldier cohort. Nor can Jesus have in mind disciples, either the eleven or his adherents in general. These men were attached to him spiritually as their spiritual king. In the conditional sentence Jesus speaks only of what would be the case if he were a common earthly king. He is speaking hypothet'cally: if he were an earthly king (but he is not) he would have earthly defenders (but he has none whatever). When the disciples and Peter tried to assume that role, they were promptly squelched.

37) **Pilate, therefore, said to him, So, then, thou art a king?** With οὖν John indicates that Pilate's question results from Jesus' reply. On οὐκοῦν, *igitur*, without negative force (hence not *non igitur*, or in questions *nonne igitur*) see R. 1165, 1175; it is found only here in the New Testament. The question shows that Pilate understands what Jesus has said

and also that he is satisfied that the Jewish charge of
pretending to earthly or political kingship is false.
Yet Jesus frankly and even emphatically claims a
certain kind of kingship, one that is entirely new to
this Roman pagan. Pilate is well satisfied regarding
the negative feature of this kingship, with the fact
that it is "not of this world." But what, then, is
this kingship if it is "not of this world"? Pilate asks
for a positive explanation which Jesus also proceeds
to furnish. The question of Pilate contains a note
of surprise. So after all there is something in the
Jewish charge which denominates this prisoner as "a
king." He sees through the Jewish falsification which
seeks to make Jesus a secular king. But this leaves
him curious to know what kind of a king he really
is, or rather what this peculiar claim of Jesus to kingship signifies. The question has a touch of incredulity, for a kingship "not of this world" is a total
novelty to Pilate. Some would add a tinge of mockery;
but this is unwarranted, for σύ is now put at the
end of the question, and while it is still emphatic, it
is not like the σύ in the first question. Pilate, moreover, drops the specific designation "the king of the
Jews" and uses only the general term "a king," i. e.,
some kind of a king, wondering what this may be.

**Jesus answered: Thou sayest that I am a king.
I for my part have been born to this end and have
come into the world to this end that I testify to the
truth. Everyone who is of the truth hears my voice.**
Jesus affirms that he is, indeed, a king. Pilate has
understood correctly. We must translate ὅτι, "that,"
introducing *what* Pilate says, not "because," for *the
reason* that Jesus is a king does not move Pilate to
ask what he does. Jesus repeats Pilate's statement
about his being a king in order to emphasize that fact,
just as he thrice spoke of his kingship. The statement has no ἐγώ at the end, needing no such emphasis,

as also the best texts show. The form of affirmation
here used, "Thou sayest," etc., is idiomatic (Matt.
27:11; Mark 15:2; Luke 23:3; Matt. 26:64). The
synoptists also report this answer of Jesus as they do
the reply to the original question of Pilate in v. 33.
They omit what John tells us intervened.

Jesus now states fully and clearly just what kind
of a king he is. The pronoun ἐγώ is full of majesty;
"I for my part" in contrast with all others who ever
have been termed kings. He uses two verbs: "have
been born," "have come into the world." These perfects have the usual meaning: having been born and
having come, Jesus is now here. Jesus was born a
king, he has not usurped his kingship, he is most
legitimately the king that he is. He speaks of his
incarnation. But he must say more. Also many
earthly kings are born to the throne, inheriting their
earthly kingship in a legitimate earthly way by right
of succession. By being born Jesus "has come into
the world." This is not a mere synonym for having
been born, nor a figurative expression for assuming
his office. "I have come into the world" is never used
by Jesus in such a sense. Nor is the sense merely
that the world is the place or the theater into which
Jesus has come to exercise his kingship. "I have
come" goes back of "I have been born"; it declares
the pre-existence of Jesus. From another world he
came into this world, from heaven to this earth
(16:28). He might have said, "I was sent"; but this
would imply a Sender, namely the Father. The Jews
would understand that since they had the revelation
of the Father and the promise of the Father to send
them his Son. Pilate is a pagan who knows nothing
about these promises. Then, too, kings are not sent,
for they are themselves supreme unless, like Herod,
they be only inferior kings, subject to an emperor.
So Jesus says, "I have come" by will and act of my

own as behooves a supreme king, to say nothing of
a king who is the very Son of God. Yet we must
hold to the strong reference to the human nature
of Jesus in his kingship. He has come and has
entered this world by having been born a man. He
is the king for us, not merely according to his divine
nature, but according to both natures, which are joined
in his person. By his birth he made himself the
king. "King" is always used in a soteriological
sense.

The phrase εἰς τοῦτο, "to this end," is repeated and
thus made emphatic. The appositional ἵνα clause states
what this end or object is: "that I testify to the
truth"; this clause is not final, "that I should testify,"
etc. While abstract nouns like ἀλήθεια may or may not
have the article in the Greek, we should lose the meaning of Jesus if we here referred τῇ ἀληθείᾳ to truth in
general. Jesus has not come to make known to us
any and every truth or reality; he has not come
only in a general way to declare true things. His
work is to bring to us that specific truth which he
saw and heard with his Father, the truth we need
for our salvation, 14:6; 17:17. It is summarized in
3:16, and in 17:3. When Jesus says that he testifies
of this truth, this testifying is one that accords with
his person as coming from heaven to earth. His is
the original and thus fundamental divine testimony
(1:18). Also others testify, but their testimony rests
on that of Jesus. The aorist subjunctive denotes testifying that is fully accomplished; his testimony has
left nothing to be added later.

The combination of "a king" and the work of testifying has caused some to think that Jesus here turns
from his royal work to his prophetic work, or that he
combines the prophet and the teacher with the king.
Then efforts are made to justify Jesus for doing this.
But Jesus keeps to his kingship. As the king of sal-

vation he rules by means of his Word, and his Word is truth (17:17). His Word imparts knowledge, but his Word is always power, and that makes it tally with kingship; see the power of this Word in 5:21-29; Rom. 1:16; etc. Even the judgment is exercised through the Word, 12:48. A strange king, indeed, in the eyes of a man like Pilate — covered with the majesty, the power, the triumphant glory of the truth! The Jews, indeed, had lied in making Pilate think that Jesus pretended to be a common king. That he was not. But what was he? Jesus opened an entirely new world to Pilate. Would Pilate be drawn into that wondrous world?

Jesus lays hold of Pilate's heart. The hour of grace has come for Pilate, the blessed hour when the King of grace draws his heart, yet a fatal hour if that King's grace is spurned. Jesus uses the third person, "Everyone who is of the truth." This is perfect psychology. When unbelievers are to be won, an address in the second person often calls forth resentment. But who can resent a statement in the third person which simply holds up to the heart the picture of blessedness revealed in the believer? Some regard "everyone who is of the truth" as a description of a special class of men: those who by nature are better than others, who by a better use of their own natural and unregenerate powers have a love, desire, or affinity for truth, i. e., truth in general. These are often termed "truth-seekers." The supposition is that when the King of the Truth comes to them, they quickly accept him while the other great class, not caring for the truth, turns from him. Our own daily experience contradicts this supposition. The malefactor on Calvary, the publicans, the harlots, and the sinners were no "truth-seekers" but the very opposite; and yet Jesus won them. "The truth" is not shaped and fashioned by God to grip only a certain class of

men but is designed for all men alike. All men are
totally depraved (Eph. 2:12), all are equally lost, all
need the same quickening, for all are alike spiritually
dead (Eph. 2:1-9). These "truth-seekers" are as
hard to win as the open and gross sinners against the
moral law. Not *before* the saving truth reaches a
man can it be seen whether he is "of the truth" but
only *after* the truth has come to him. And "to be
of the truth" means to believe the truth Jesus has
brought to him. Nor is ἐκ partitive in this connection; while it differentiates between those who are
of the truth and those who are not of the truth, ἐκ
denotes origin and thus only does it differentiate.
To be "of the truth" refers to the same divine saving truth of which Jesus says that he has come
to bring it with his testimony; we even again have
the article.

Just as ὤν is timeless in this general proposition,
so is the present ἀκούει, "he hears my voice" (10:16).
Thus to hear is to believe; and thus to hear and to
believe is to be of the truth. Jesus says, "he hears
my voice." Not only does his voice sound forth nothing but "the truth," his voice is characteristic of his
person. No one else has a voice like that of Jesus.
When his voice sounds, we know that it is he and thus
rush to his side. From the voices of all others the
sheep flee (10:5). Compare 6:68, 69, and 8:43-45;
also 3:6 as explaining 3:20, 21 and 8:47.

38) Pilate sensed what Jesus was attempting to
do for his heart. **Pilate says to him, What is truth?**
He says nothing further about Jesus' kingship, nor
does he dwell on other points of Jesus' reply. He
centers on the essential point "truth." If, however,
Pilate had asked in reply, "What is *the* truth?" he
would have asked Jesus to tell him what he meant by
the specific truth of which he was speaking. Pilate
is not seeking to learn about this truth, nor, in fact,

about any religious truth whatever, and thus he omits
the article.   Note that τί is the predicate (R. 411) and
asks about the essence of the ⸳concept "truth" (R.
736).   But the tone is that of an indifferent worldling
who by his question intends to say that anything in
the nature of religious truth is a useless speculation.
Some think that Pilate pitied Jesus because he endangered his life for the sake of such a hopeless thing as
trying to propound anything like religious truth.
Others think that Pilate's question was a sneer.   He
may have shrugged his shoulders as he arose to leave.
He does not sneer, his word is not one of contempt,
for the sequel shows too plainly that Pilate was deeply
impressed by Jesus.   His word is simply that of the
practical pagan skeptic.   The educated Roman world
had many men of this type.   They had no faith in
their own gods although they continued the usual
idolatrous rites.   They were inwardly indifferent, cold,
and haughty and adjusted themselves to an immoral
world with an eye only to what they might selfishly
squeeze out of such opportunities as it offered.   The
educated Pilate clan is still very numerous.   When
the divine truth and its heavenly King face them, they
see nothing that they desire.   Pilate, however, is not
one of the worst type.   While he thrusts Jesus from
his heart he does not fight him and his truth as so
many of these worldly skeptics do.

**And having said this, he again went out to the
Jews and says to them, For my part I find no indictment in his case.**   Pilate awaits no answer on
the part of Jesus regarding the truth he mentions in
his question.   He has heard enough to convince him
that the Jewish charge against Jesus is baseless.   So
he breaks off the conversation abruptly and proceeds
with the business in hand.   He goes out to confront
the Jews.   Some think that he left Jesus inside and
had him brought out later; but it was the Roman

custom to confront the prisoner with his accusers.
Jesus was led out behind Pilate. Resuming the seat
of judgment outside, Pilate delivers his judicial finding. He acquits Jesus. The emphatic ἐγώ is in contrast with the Jews, and αἰτία is like our "indictment,"
charging that a crime has been committed. See also
19:4. The phrase ἐν αὐτῷ = in his case, R. 587, 6.
But this is all that Pilate does. He stops short and
does not order the release of Jesus, giving him the
necessary protection; he does not order the crowd
of Jews to leave the premises and, if necessary, drive
them away by ordering out the cohort. Here is the
first fatal flaw in the action of Pilate.

Thus far John has supplemented the synoptists,
but now he lets us follow their accounts, touching only
briefly the incident with regard to Barabbas. At
this point, then, we must insert the renewal of the
Jewish accusations with excessive vehemence. Jesus,
even on Pilate's appeal to him, remains silent to the
astonishment of Pilate. Hearing of Galilee, he sends
Jesus to Herod who returns him without furnishing
Pilate any relief. Summing up his own and Herod's
finding, Pilate offers to chastise Jesus and to let him
go, Luke 23:13-16.

39) At this point Mark 15:6-8 helps us. New
crowds augmented those already congregated before
the Prætorium. Among them must have been many
friends of Jesus, and these reminded Pilate of the
annual custom of releasing a Jewish prisoner at the
time of the Passover festival. This reminder made
Pilate drop his proposal to scourge Jesus and thus to
let him go. He saw an opportunity to effect the release of Jesus by way of this old custom. Here we
insert what John now adds: **But you have a custom
that I release one to you at the Passover. Are you
willing, therefore, that I release to you the King of
the Jews?** Mark 15:8 shows that the multitude

reminded Pilate of this custom, and, therefore, those are in error who think that Pilate bethought himself of this custom. Pilate had always followed it; in the spurious passage, Luke 23:17, it is called a necessity although it is John who informs us that it was followed only at the time of the Passover feast. How far back this custom dates, and how it originated, is not known. Perhaps it dates back as far as the era of the Maccabees. The release of a condemned prisoner was probably intended to symbolize the release of ancient Israel from its Egyptian bondage.

We have no reason to assume that the usual procedure was not followed in the present instance. The governor would nominate two candidates for release, and the people would choose one of the two. This Pilate now does, naming as the two candidates Barabbas and Jesus, Matt. 27:17. But in this case Pilate does more than simply to submit the choice to the Jews; he indicates the choice he desires the Jews to make, as we see from both Mark 15:9, and from John. After nominating the two candidates, Pilate asks whether the Jews are willing that he release their king to them. On the paratactic use of βούλεσθε ἀπολύσω (most probably an aorist subjunctive) without a connective see R. 980, 935. All the evangelists name Barabbas, which is a patronymic: "Son of Abba," and "Abba" is most probably the honorable title of the father, a scribe or a rabbi, who was called "Abba" or "Father." This ignoble son of a worthy father is selected by Pilate as the extreme opposite of Jesus in order that the Jews may surely choose Jesus for release. The reading "Jesus Barabbas" must be rejected together with the assumption that Pilate thought of Barabbas because he, too, had the name Jesus, and that thus one Jesus was pitted

against another Jesus. We likewise decline the play
on "Barabbas," "Son of the Father," and on the
designation of Jesus as the Son of the Father, since
the Scriptures in no way indicate that such a contrast is intended. Barabbas is merely named as other
persons are named for us in the sacred record.

Pilate did Jesus the gravest injustice by nominating him along with Barabbas. Only convicted and
condemned criminals were thus nominated, and Pilate
himself had twice declared that he was able to find
no indictment against Jesus. How, then, could he
make such a nomination? The injustice began when
Pilate after his first examination of Jesus (v. 38b)
failed to release him as being guiltless. The injustice
grew with every act that followed. Pilate was no
longer functioning as a judge, dispensing justice, but
as a weakling who finds himself cornered and caught
and is ready to employ any and every means to
escape. By nominating Jesus as one of the pair
he would be willing to release Pilate calls Jesus "the
king of the Jews" just as he did in questioning Jesus
(v. 33). Why does he use this title when he himself had learned from Jesus that Jesus was in no
sense what Pilate and the Jews understood this to
mean? When answering this question we must not
overlook the mocking acclaim of the Roman soldiers
in 19:3, Pilate's mocking repetition of it in 19:14, 15,
and the superscription Pilate placed on the cross,
19:19. Pilate uses this title to mock and to insult
the Jews, especially the high priests and the Sanhedrists. The mockery is the more bitter and cuts to
the quick because the Jews would love to be under
a king of their own in complete independence of
Rome; because Pilate knew that the Jewish leaders
were envious and jealous of Jesus (Matt. 27:18;
Mark 15:10), fearing to lose their prestige when so

many of the people flocked to Jesus (11:48a) ; and because Jesus, standing bound and helpless between Roman guards, seemed a pitiful figure to be called a king. The keenness of the mockery lies also in the fact that Pilate's offer sounds as though by granting the Jews the opportunity to have their king released, he is doing them a wonderful favor. He practically says, "Do you not want your own king?"

But is Pilate not defeating his own end? He wants to release Jesus, he puts up the worst kind of a criminal as the alternate choice for release, he is sure that, restricted to the choice between these two, Jesus will be chosen. Why, then, does Pilate dose his offer with insult and mockery? Because Pilate is not only a weakling but also a fool. Throughout the means he uses to secure his end, though they seem shrewd and wise to him, only convince the Jews that presently Pilate will surrender to their will. Despising the Jews to begin with, he despises them to the utmost because of their undertaking to rid themselves of Jesus by making the governor their tool. His vast pride, lacking the necessary courage to assert itself against the humiliation put upon it by these Jews, boils with inner resentment and anger. He is unable to check his tongue. He strikes back if only with a word; and the blow, wholly ineffectual, only marks him as what he is. Because of his past crimes and misdeeds, subject to denunciation before Caesar by these Jews, he now feels powerless and vents his helpless spite. Blind to all but the one effect of his word, namely to insult the Jewish leaders, he lets his tongue speak the words, "the king of the Jews." And yet he thinks that Barabbas cannot possibly be chosen, at least not by the Jewish populace, so many of whom are certainly friendly to Jesus. Yes, he will give them Jesus, he will defeat these Jewish leaders, he will make them take Jesus off his hands as what they themselves called him, "a king" — "the king of the Jews"!

40) The choice was the prerogative of the people as such, not of the high priests or of the Sanhedrin in its official capacity. Hence a delay ensued which enabled the crowd to become united on the choice. Here we may insert the disquieting message sent by Pilate's wife, Matt. 27:19. Quick action follows on the part of the Jewish leaders. They and their minions circulate through the crowd, throwing all their weight and their influence into the demand that Barabbas be chosen. Matt. 27:20. When presently Pilate demands what the choice is, **they, therefore, shouted again, saying, Not this one but Barabbas!** Both Luke and John use strong verbs; a roar of voices unanimously calls for Barabbas. From Luke we learn that not even a small minority pleaded for Jesus or dissented from the choice of Barabbas. "Again" refers to the previous shouting which demanded that Pilate release a prisoner. This adverb plainly shows that John has in mind Mark 15:8, and that he is making only the briefest reference to the present episode of Barabbas. Because of the imperative idea in the shout we have μή as the negative, R. 1172, 1173. Jesus is not as much as named. This Jewish crowd will not as much as sully its lips with the use of his name.

We may marvel at the fact that the entire crowd so readily did the bidding of the Sanhedrists. They were ruled by fear (7:13; 9:22; with which combine 19:38; 20:19). Fear sealed the lips of any who shrank from outright obedience. Perhaps the derogatory τοῦτον only echoes the designation the Sanhedrists applied to Jesus when belaboring the crowd to choose Barabbas. Pilate is dumbfounded. This was the last thing he expected. He commits the further folly of arguing with the crowd, helplessly asking what he shall do with Jesus. He only provokes the crowd to cry, "Crucify, crucify him!" and to keep this up until he entirely capitulates. Luther, "But they would rather have begged for the devil to go free." "But ye denied the Holy One and the Just, and desired a murderer to be granted unto you; and killed the Prince of Life, whom God hath raised from the dead," Acts 3:14, 15. Pilate releases Barabbas, he has no alternative; Jesus is still left on his hands. The situation is really more desperate than ever for Pilate.

In a parenthetical remark, indicated as such by δέ, John adds: **Now Barabbas was a robber.** We feel the tragic note. Such a man the Jewish nation, represented by its leaders and a concourse of the ordinary people, chose in place of Jesus! Yet, whom they chose, his they were. By this choice they murdered Jesus and made themselves true moral brothers of the murderer Barabbas. John's word is an understatement, for Barabbas was worse than a robber, namely a murderer, Mark 15:7, and an exceptional one at that, Matt. 27:16.

CHAPTER XIX

4. The Final Attempt to Release Jesus, 19:1-16

1) Each of the synoptists mentions in one breath the release of Barabbas and the sentencing of Jesus to the cross. Matthew and Mark insert the scourging by means of ony one word, the participle φραγελλώσας. This compactness of narration leads some to think that Pilate ordered the three acts simultaneously: the release, the crucifixion, and the scourging. They substantiate this view by a mass of evidence which shows that scourging always preceded crucifixion. Yet the point to be established is the opposite: in the case of Jesus we must be shown that crucifixion always followed scourging. This, of course, none attempt to show. It is John who clears up this matter, as he does so many others. He records the events in detail. From him we learn that Jesus was not scourged in order to be crucified but in order to escape crucifixion.

After briefly telling us that Pilate's attempt to save Jesus through Barabbas saved only Barabbas through Jesus, John tells us, not that Pilate ordered Jesus to be crucified, but to be scourged. From Luke 23:16 we learn that before the attempt to save Jesus through Barabbas failed, Pilate had offered to scourge Jesus and then to let him go free. After this failure Pilate, without agreement with the Jews and solely on his own initiative, orders the scourging of which he had already thought. He even lets his soldiers stage a mockery of this King of the Jews. Why this strange procedure? In order to satisfy the Jews so that they may turn away from the wretched figure, a man who

is too helpless and too ridiculous to give another
thought to.   But this time Pilate's effort to save Jesus
more than fails.   At sight of Jesus, scourged and
dressed as a mock king, the Jews find the word that
forces Pilate to complete surrender (v. 12).   Thus
at last Pilate is driven to order the crucifixion (v. 16).
And John solemnly notes both the place where the
order was given and the hour when the fatal word
was spoken.

Barabbas was released.   **Then Pilate, therefore,
took Jesus and scourged him.**   By means of οὖν, as
well as by means of τότε John connects the scourging
of Jesus with the release of Barabbas; we now see
why John had to make at least brief mention of Barabbas.   We cannot suppose that already now the order
for the crucifixion was issued.   That would have been
the main order, if this procedure had been usual, and
John could not have taken it for granted as merely
accompanying the scourging.   He might have
recorded the order to crucify, taking for granted that
this included scourging; he could not do the reverse.
Not until the object of the scourging and the mockery
failed did Pilate consent to crucify Jesus.

Whereas Matthew and Mark devote only one word
to the scourging, John writes a complete sentence
although it is necessarily brief.   He adds a circumstantial verb, "took," thereby lending more weight to
the main verb "scourged," which it also most certainly
deserves.   Both verbs are causative, R. 801: "had him
taken and had him scourged," Pilate issuing the order.
The two synoptists use φραγελλοῦν, the Latin *flagellare*;
John has the original Greek term μαστιγοῦν.   Stripped
of clothes, the body was bent forward across a low
pillar, the back stretched and exposed to the blows.
To hold the body in position the victim's hands must
have been tied to rings in the floor or at the base of
the pillar in front and the feet to rings behind.   We

cannot agree that the hands were tied behind the man's back, for this would place them across the small of the back where some of the blows were to fall and would shield the ribs where the whipends were to lacerate the flesh. The Romans did not use rods, as the Jews did, each rod making only one stripe, cutting only the back; they used short-handled whips, each provided with several leather lashes, ugly acorn-shaped pieces of lead or lumps of bone being fastened to the end of each short lash. The strokes were laid on with full force, and when the executioners tired, the officers shouted: *Adde virgas!* (Livy 26, 16), or: *Firme!* (Suetonius, Caligula 26), demanding more force. The effect was horrible. The skin and the flesh of the back were gashed to the very bone, and where the armed ends of the lashes struck, deep, bloody holes were torn. When Jesus, the son of Ananus, who cried woe over Jerusalem, was scourged by the procurator Albinus, "he was whipped until his bones were laid bare," Josephus, *Wars*, 6, 6, 3. In Smyrna just before Polycarp's martyrdom a number of other martyrs were scourged until, as Eusebius 4, 15 reports, the deepest veins and the arteries were exposed, and even the inner organs of the body were seen.

None of the evangelists gives a description of the scourging of Jesus. We do not know how many blows he received. In trying to visualize this ordeal we are left to such outside data as we are able to secure, and then we know that the details we imagine are only probability and no more. One detail seems certain, namely that the scourging took place outside of the Prætorium before the eyes of Pilate and in full view of the Jews; for in reporting the mockery that followed both Matthew and Mark state that for this ordeal Jesus was taken into the Prætorium, Mark specifying the αὐλή or courtyard which was roomy

enough to accomodate the entire cohort. To the
scourging must be attributed the fact that Jesus died
after being only six hours on the cross; also his breaking down under the weight of the cross on the way to
Calvary.

2) Matthew and Mark narrate the mockery as
a separate event; by the way in which he combines
the scourging and the mockery John informs us that
these two acts go together, the one not merely following the other, but the two constituting a whole. No
sooner has the scourging been completed when the
mockery begins.   This answers the question as to
how an act such as this mockery of Jesus came to
be staged. The attempt is not made to show that it
was a proceeding that was customary in the case of
men who were scourged, for it certainly was not. It
is so exceptional in every way that no counterpart
for it has ever been found. Those who think that
Jesus was scourged as one who was already condemned to the cross suppose that the mockery was
undertaken merely to fill in the time until the cross
and the other paraphernalia for the execution had
been made ready. But even then, why was the time
filled in with such an exceptional proceeding? If
Jesus was scourged merely in preparation for crucifixion, this mockery is inexplicable. Those who note
that Jesus had not as yet been condemned to the cross,
make the mockery an inspiration of the soldiers who
guarded Jesus. We are told that Pilate left them to
their own devices, allowed events to take their own
course, paid no attention to the commotion going on
inside of the Prætorium. These are unsatisfactory
explanations. When Matthew and Mark report that
the soldiers took Jesus into the courtyard of the Prætorium, this can mean only that they did so on an
order from Pilate. In his presence they could not
move the prisoner about as they might please. In

v. 4 we see that Pilate himself was in the Prætorium during the mockery, for it is he who comes out with Jesus after the mockery, with Jesus dressed as a mock king. All this has but one solution: Jesus was scourged and mocked on Pilate's order. His plan was to show these Jews what this man really was about whom they were making such a violent demonstration: "king," indeed, "the king of the Jews," a joke of a king! let them see for themselves! Crucify him? act as though this dreamer about the truth amounted to anything? The very idea was ridiculous.

And the soldiers, having plaited a crown out of thorny twigs, set it on his head and threw around him a purple cloak. They dress Jesus as a king. John mentions the crown first which was roughly plaited or twisted together of thorn-bearing twigs, a kind of circlet to go around the head. Many guesses have been offered as to the nature of the shrub from which the ἄκανθαι were cut, but the real name for it is not definitely known. On some coins emperors are represented with a laurel wreath encircling the head, and kings have always been distinguished by wearing crowns. So a crown is improvised for Jesus. How the soldiers hit upon the idea of a crown of thorny twigs, and where they found the plant from which they cut them, who will say? The presence of the plant, perhaps twining upon the wall of the courtyard, may have caught the eye of one of the men and suggested to him a chaplet, one wound of these ugly thorny twigs instead of noble laurel. Two purposes were thereby served: to make this king ridiculous and to do this with cruelty by forcing the crown with its lacerating thorns onto his head. The soldiers certainly considered their procedure as a perfect joke. Everybody would recognize the circlet as a crown, and what a bloody crown it was! Little trickles of blood disfigured the victim's face, not with the artistic elegance of so many of our painters, but with the stark hideousness of cruel reality.

Secondly John mentions the purple ἱμάτιον which Matthew calls a scarlet χλαμύς. The former color is lighter than the latter, but the ancients often failed to make a distinction between them, and this *sagum paludamentum*, or soldier's cloak, was old and worn, a cast-off mantle, its color darkened with age. This figured as the royal robe, for at least the color resembled the purple of kings. John abbreviates and thus does not mention the scepter. As to Jesus' own clothes, we take it that they were left where they had been thrown outside of the Prætorium; for Matthew tells us that he was stripped when the soldiers dressed him up as a king, and we cannot think that after the scourging outside they dressed him there only again to strip him in the courtyard. After Pilate led Jesus out and then finally sent him to the cross, his own clothes were restored to him.

3) Dressed for the part, the mockery begins. **And they kept coming to him and kept saying, Hail, King of the Jews! and kept giving him blows.** The entire cohort had been called into the courtyard for the mockery. The imperfect tenses are descriptive of the scene as it progressed; ἐδίδοσαν, where it is found instead of ἐδίδουν, is also imperfect, R. 1214. The soldiers stage a mock royal reception. "They kept coming to him" means that they filed past Jesus. John omits the genuflection and worshipful bowing. Each man greets Jesus with, "Hail, King of the Jews!" This greeting, using Pilate's own word (18:33), which, therefore, had not been spoken in complete privacy, is the key to the entire mockery. Jesus is formally acclaimed king of the Jews. We shall see (v. 19) that to the last Pilate adheres to this designation although Jesus had told him the kind

of king he is.   Weak Pilate cannot let go of the verbal
insult to the Jews he despises.   This persistence on
his part helps to convince us that the mockery of the
soldiers is due to some order which he gave in connection with the command to scourge Jesus.   The
greeting χαῖρε, "be glad," "be happy," coupled, as here,
with a vocative, is like our, "Hail!"   A nominative
with the article is frequently used as a vocative, R. 769.
Of the further abuse, the spitting, the smiting with
the rod, etc., John mentions only the fact that each
man as he came to Jesus gave him an ugly blow
with the hand; ῥαπίσματα is the same word used in
18:22, which see.   The marvel is that Jesus did
not collapse under this mass of horrible abuse.   How
long did it last?

4)   The other two evangelists who record this
mockery tell us only that finally, again dressed in his
own clothes, Jesus was led away to be executed.   John
brings the full details.   **And Pilate went out again
outside and says to them, Behold, I am bringing
him out to you in order that you may realize that
I find no indictment in his case.   Jesus, therefore,
came out outside, wearing the thorny crown and
the purple cloak.   And he said to them, Behold,
the man!**   Pilate had had Jesus scourged and
mocked in order to effect his release; and only when
this final effort failed, was the order to crucify
issued.   John alone narrates this final effort of
Pilate's, materially augmenting the reports of the
synoptists.

Since Pilate went out again he must previously
have gone in.   This cannot have occurred, as some
think, after releasing Barabbas, 18:40.   It was Pilate
who ordered Jesus scourged (v. 1).   We have seen
that the scourging took place outside in the presence
of Pilate and of the Jews.   Not until after the scourging was Jesus taken inside on Pilate's own order.

Then Pilate went in. He went in to witness the mockery of Jesus. When enough had been done to suit his purpose, he called a halt and ordered Jesus to be brought out again, Pilate himself preceding Jesus as they went out. The proposed alternative is unacceptable: that Pilate withdrew to some room in the Prætorium because he was disgusted and in a huff; that the horseplay of the soldiers with Jesus was their idea which Pilate merely suffered to be carried out, in his room listening to the gales of laughter in the open courtyard; that not until now he conceived the thought of making one more effort to free Jesus. The unlikeliness of all this is increased when we are told to add that Jesus had already been remanded to the cross and was scourged only for this reason; that of their own accord the soldiers mocked Jesus as a man who had lost all legal rights, the mockery only filling in the time until the paraphernalia for the execution had been assembled; that in remanding Jesus to the cross Pilate had neglected to pronounce the formal verdict and, bethinking himself of this, utilized the neglect for making another effort at release, that, when this effort failed, the formal sentencing took place in v. 16.

Pilate strides out first and, before Jesus is led out, announces to the Jews what he is now doing and to what intent he is doing this. Pilate is presenting a significant spectacle to the Jews, "Behold, I am bringing him out to you!" The Jews had certainly often seen Jesus; Pilate means that they will now see him as they had never seen him before. This means also that Pilate had seen how Jesus looked during the mockery — it was the way he wanted him to look. The soldiers had not on their own account taken liberties with Jesus, so that now, when Pilate ordered him brought out again, they would hastily remove the royal trappings and lead him out naked as

they had brought him in; for his own clothes lay outside where he had been scourged. The soldiers had
merely done Pilate's will in making Jesus a mock king,
a figure of utter wretchedness and shame.

This figure Pilate puts on display in order to convince the Jews that he finds absolutely no indictment
against Jesus. He uses the same legal formula as
in 18:38; in fact, he repeats it a third time in v. 6.
It is the verdict of the examining judge, much like
that of our grand juries, when the evidence offered
fails to support the crime charged: "No indictment!"
We must note, however, that οὐδεμίαν αἰτίαν refers only
to the crime charged, the one for which the Jews
demanded the death penalty for Jesus. Hence Pilate
also says, "not a single αἰτία," not a single count on
which to draw an indictment such as the Jews demand.
The aorist γνῶτε means that the Jews are actually to
realize what Pilate tells them in his verdict. His purpose is to convince these persistent accusers. This
is a proceeding that is wholly unjudicial, and it is
that for any examining judge, not to say for Pilate,
the great Roman procurator himself. Since when
must the judge obtain the consent of the accuser to
the verdict he has found? Since when does a judge
treat his own finding and verdict as non-final until the
accuser gives it his approval? Since when has the
accuser the power to make the judge alter his verdict
if that verdict does not satisfy the accuser? If Pilate
haggles about his own verdict and fails to see what
this implies on his part the Jews see it only too
clearly and use the advantage Pilate grants them to the
fullest extent. Pilate defeats himself before his effort
gets under way.

5) Immediately after this announcement on the
part of Pilate Jesus came out. Soldiers guarded him
and marched him to a place beside the governor. All
eyes were riveted upon the spectacle, men in the rear

crowding up to get a look. John describes the figure but, after the manner of all evangelists, with utmost restraint: "wearing the thorny crown and the purple cloak." They all saw what Pilate intended them to see. John has φορῶν, bearing or wearing continuously, and thus this is stronger than φέρων. The moment grows tenser as the spectacle is taken in. At its climax Pilate, turning his eyes from Jesus to the Jews, utters what sounds like an involuntary exclamation, "Behold, the man!" That word has gone on, ringing down the centuries: *Ecce homo!* It has well been said that each of us puts into that word exactly what he really thinks of Jesus. But we must think only of Pilate and of the Jews, what he meant, and what they understand. "Behold," ἴδε, or as some write ἰδού, merely exclaims; for ὁ ἄνθρωπος is vocative, the article with the nominative indicating this, as in v. 3, R. 769.

All honor to the many commentators who read pity into Pilate's proceeding and give him credit for assuming that the hearts of the Jews will be moved just as his own heart is. Luther may speak for them all: "Pilate is a heathen and a regular bloodhound. For the heathen who knew nothing of God dealt with men as we do with swine. Nevertheless, this heathen and bloodhound is moved." Some would add a touch of mockery and contempt to Pilate's word of pity. The greatest support for this view would be Pilate's conviction of the innocence of Jesus, but few base Pilate's pity on this ground. What overthrows this conception, however it may be varied, is the fact that it was no one but Pilate himself who deliberately made Jesus this object of pity. Pilate had had Jesus scourged; Pilate had had Jesus mocked. Even if we should say, as some do, that Pilate only permitted the mockery, his case is not thereby altered. One word on the part of Pilate would have prevented the latter

outrage. This supposed pity on Pilate's part comes
entirely too late. No man with a heart that pities
allows a fellow-creature to be converted into a sad
and pitiful object and then starts to pity that object
and calls upon others to do the same. Bloodhounds, as
Luther terms them, are beyond the noble feeling of
pity. To put pity into Pilate's word is to substitute
our own feeling for his.

Pilate, indeed, regards Jesus as innocent. But it
is less his sense of justice as a judge that prompts his
motive in the case of Jesus or at any time, than his
pride which refuses to be bowed into the dust before
these despicable Jews. He, the great Roman procurator, will not let these Jews dictate his verdict.
The fact that justice is on his side in the present
case helps to stiffen his pride, but justice is only an
adjunct. Since he has twice failed to win out with
his pride he once more tries to win. He uses desperate
means. If pride had not clouded his good judgment,
he should have seen in advance that these last desperate
means would also prove futile. In order to save his
pride against the Jews Pilate gives Jesus over to the
scourge and the mockery. These are only means to
gain his end, the triumph of his will over that of
the Jews. *They* want Jesus crucified for claiming
to be a king. Well, Pilate shows them in a *demonstratio ad oculos* that as the Roman governor *he*
cannot entertain this charge. "Look!" he cries dramatically; "take in the man!" "King?" — why a
ridiculous king! "King, dangerous to Caesar, calling
for the procurator's power to destroy him?" — why,
he is absolutely powerless, abjectly helpless! Look
and see for yourselves! This is the sense of Pilate's
act and his word. Who could think of insisting that
the procurator should crucify a man such as this?
Yet, invincible as the case thus put by Pilate seems
at first glance, it shows a fatal psychological flaw when

it is carefully examined.   By making the charge
against Jesus appear ridiculous and pointless Pilate
made also the Jews appear as men foolish enough to
press such a charge with all the power at their command.   This was bound to react in a way to defeat
Pilate, the more so since the Jews saw that he lacked
the courage to force the issue against them.

**6)   When, therefore, the high priest and the
underlings saw him they shouted, Crucify, crucify!**
Whereas John otherwise writes "the Jews," he now
writes "the high priests and the underlings," the
police force of the Sanhedrin.   The moment these
leaders take in the situation that Pilate had created,
before a voice could be raised in favor of Jesus among
the crowd of common people before the Prætorium,
these leaders with their immediate subordinates again
raise the shout to crucify.   When Barabbas was put
beside Jesus, the leaders had time to belabor the
crowd; Pilate's new move leaves them no time.   So
they do not argue with Pilate.   They simply leap in
with frantic yells, "Crucify!"   They intend to sweep
the crowd along to join in the cry, at least to drown
out any voice that might be raised in behalf of Jesus.
What the common crowd did is left unsaid.   We read
of no one who dared to contradict.   The issue is
squarely drawn.   Let Pilate demonstrate all he pleases
that the Jewish charge is baseless and even ridiculous,
the leaders insist on their will nonetheless.   Pilate
dare not triumph.   They cry him down.   They will
force him to yield to their will.   If he will use unjudicial means, so will they.   They yell for what they
want.   This judge shall not judge — they never
intended that he should — he shall simply do what
they demand.   It has been well said that a wild beast
cannot be placated by showing it blood; to do so only
enrages it the more.   Too late Pilate sees that his calculation has again miscarried; his dramatic presenta-

tion of Jesus has only inflamed the temper of the **Jews**
still more.

Finally the yelling subsides. **Pilate says to
them, Take him yourselves and crucify him; for
I on my part do not find an indictment in his case.**
The governor keeps his dignity, he does not shout in
return. He meets the frantic outbursts of the Jewish
leaders with biting scorn. Very well, if they are so
determined to have Jesus crucified, let them take him
themselves and crucify him! This is not consent on
Pilate's part, turning Jesus over to the Jews for the
purpose of crucifixion. The Jewish mode of execution
was not by crucifixion but by stoning; and Pilate says,
"Crucify him." Note also the emphatic ὑμεῖς, "you
yourselves," over against which Pilate then sets his
emphatic ἐγώ. Pilate taunts the Jews. They have lost
the right to put a criminal to death; the governor
alone can send a man to death. By his ironical order
to go ahead and to do the crucifying themselves Pilate
strikes back viciously at these Jews who try him so
sorely, pressing their advantage to the limit. The
Jews understand perfectly what Pilate means; they
make no move to take Jesus and to crucify him, for
once using the Roman way of execution.

Pilate's vicious thrust is only a sign of his weakness. To jab the beast only makes it snarl the more.
In the midst of the yelling Pilate should have raised
his hand to the commander of the cohort in an order
to clear the place before the Prætorium. With drawn
swords the cohort should have charged the mob, and
all would have been over. Pilate's past crimes had
made him a coward. He was afraid of the Jews
whom he taunted. Proudly enough he asserts for
the third time that he for his part has no indictment
(see v. 4) against Jesus. In the strong ἐγώ there speaks
the consciousness of the Roman governor who alone
has the power of life and death. Alas, it did not

speak loud enough! Note the variation in the negation: in v. 4 "no indictment," now, however, I "do
not find." Pilate means that it is his finding alone
not that of the Jews which decides on crucifixion.
We must read γάρ, not as illative, but as merely explanatory, R. 1190.

Too much is made of Pilate's conscience, of how
hard it was for him to act against his conscience in
condemning an innocent man to death. He did hold
out for a long time, and at the end he washed his hands
of the guilt and tried to shift it to the Jews (Matt.
27:24). But this is all that his conscience accomplished. In estimating the part Pilate's conscience
played we must note his past record of cruel and con-
scienceless acts. The innocence of Jesus did not deter
Pilate from scourging this innocent prisoner and then
submitting this innocent man, thus scourged, to the
most brutal mockery. The washing of his hands was
a theatrical act like his display of the mock king
not a genuine act of conscience, not real dread of the
judicial murder to which he at last gave consent.
Whatever conscience functioned in Pilate was pitifully
weak. His scorn of the Jews, his Roman pride as
governor, challenged by the brazen demand of these
same Jews and scorning to bow before them, actuated
him much more than the voice of his conscience.

7) **The Jews answered him, We on our part
have a law, and according to that law he ought
to die; because he made himself God's Son.** The
emphatic and contrasting ὑμεῖς and ἐγώ in Pilate's
taunt produce an equally emphatic ἡμεῖς in the reply
of the Jews. For the third time they hear Pilate's
verdict: the indictment they want not found! All
their violent accusations, centering in the alleged
kingship of Jesus and thus intended to appeal to
Pilate on the score of the Roman law, he answers
again and again, "*I*, according to *my* law, find no

charge!" This drives the Jews to assert the authority
of *their* law to which Pilate had made slighting
reference when they first came to him (18:31). *"We
have a law,"* they tell him, *"we Jews* over against
you Romans." With νόμον, though it is without the
article, they refer to the *Torah* or Old Testament which
is often called " the Law" for short. And when they
say, "we have," they mean more than that they as
Jews are bound by this their law; when the Romans
conquered the Jews, they followed their usual policy
and left the law of this nation in force; gave it the
sanction of the Roman authority except on one point
— capital punishment was placed in the hands of the
Roman governor.

It is thus that the Jews inform Pilate that what
they so insistently demand of him is "according to
that law," the article being used in a specific sense.
According to their law Jesus "ought to die," he has
committed a capital offense, he has been tried under
their law, to which as a Jew he is subject, and the verdict of death has been pronounced against him. What
is demanded and must be demanded of Pilate is that
he seal that verdict by ordering the execution. Thus
they set their ἡμεῖς against his ἐγώ. Not, however, that
they would permit Pilate to retry Jesus under their
law, or even let him review the case, for which they
would consider him incompetent, being a Roman. The
specific paragraph of their law under which Jesus is
guilty of death is undoubtedly in their minds, Lev.
24:16, the law against blasphemy.

Provoked by Pilate's insistence on *his* finding and
in order to pit *their* finding against his they blurt out
the actual αἰτία on which they have found a verdict
against Jesus: "he ought to die because he made himself God's Son." They say "to die" without naming
the mode of execution since this is different for Jews
and for Romans. Until this moment the Jews have

kept hidden from Pilate the real crime on which they sentenced Jesus. This was a crime that was strictly religious, which they knew Pilate would disregard as being no crime at all. They instead trumped up everything possible in the way of crime that they imagined would impress Pilate but now saw that they had not at all impressed him. So at last the truth comes out. It was false that Jesus had gone about in the land proclaiming himself a secular king; what he had done was to declare himself "God's son." Here we meet a most remarkable fact. Divine providence so controlled and so guided everything at the Jewish and now also at the Gentile trial of Jesus that he was condemned to death, not on some false, trumped-up charge, but on the true fact, on the actual reality, on his divine Sonship, which was turned into a charge. The Jews say, "he made himself" God's Son; but he was God's Son, the Only-begotten from the Father, and had manifested and proved his divine Sonship to the Jews in countless ways. The Jews condemned God's Son because he was God's Son.

Here John shows that, although he omits the Jewish trial from his record, all its details are known to him, and his very omission only corroborates the records of the synoptists. In the trial before Pilate the humanity of Jesus is made prominent in the fullest possible manner. It is John alone who reports Pilate's exclamation, "Behold, the man!" The synoptists bring out the divine Sonship in the Jewish trial; John only adds that also in the trial before Pilate this Sonship was attested, and that not by Jesus but by the Jews themselves. All who today deny that Sonship either in an outright manner or by manipulating or reducing the concept, range themselves alongside of the Jews and consent to their verdict that Jesus was not in reality what under oath he declared himself to be, "the Christ, the Son of God," Matt. 26:63.

8) **When, therefore, Pilate heard this word he was the more afraid.** Here we learn that in the complex of motives actuating Pilate there was a degree of fear, inspired by Jesus himself, his entire personality, his words to Pilate, his bearing throughout the agony heaped upon him. The warning sent him by his wife (Matt. 27:19) fostered that mysterious fear. And now came "this word," and not from Jesus but from the Jews themselves that this strange man whom Pilate had dressed up as a mock king made himself "God's Son." Actual fear gripped Pilate. The indefinite feeling that he had all along now received definite support. Turning, his eyes searched the face and the figure at his side, and the thought shot through his mind: What if "this word" of the Jews were true? Like a flash it shot through Pilate's mind that "this word" might, indeed, be the key to everything. Too late the Jews see that their ardor in pitting their law against Pilate's law had made them reveal too much. They had made a false move — they had stiffened Pilate's reluctance.

As a pagan of the Roman world Pilate took "God's Son" in a pagan sense, namely that in Jesus one of the gods or of the demigods had appeared among men. The mythologies of the pagan faith contained stories enough of this type. We see their effects cropping out in Acts 14:11, etc., and in 28:6. Skeptic though Pilate was, laughing at the old mythological stories with the rest of the educated and sophisticated Roman world, like all men of this type his skepticism was no armor against secret superstition. This thin armor was now pierced. Pilate had had Jesus scourged and mocked — what vengeance of the gods would strike him if it were true that this man was in reality a god?

9) **And he went into the Prætorium again and says to Jesus, Whence art thou?** Jesus, however,

gave him no answer. Once more, now under the spur of superstitious fear, Pilate orders that Jesus be conducted into the Prætorium for questioning, away from the presence of the Jews. Uneasiness because of their palpable mistake must have filled them as they waited and talked with each other outside. This second private examination is like the first (18:33, etc.), not completely private between Pilate and Jesus alone, but with at least the soldier guards present. All Pilate's fears are concentrated in the one question, "Whence art thou?" "Whence" is to reveal who Jesus really is. For if he is a god in human form, his origin must be supermundane. But we must add as explaining this question the former word of Jesus himself that his kingship is "not of this world." That answer of Jesus helps to prompt the question "whence" against "who."

Jesus returns no answer. Calmly his eyes look into those of Pilate, but his lips remain sealed. This is the only silence of Jesus during his trials which John reports. Each of these silences has its own reason. What is the reason here? Is it that Pilate's question is not that of a judge but a personal question coming from Pilate's own frightened heart? How could Jesus stand on a technical distinction like that? In the other silences we see that Jesus seals his lips even when his judges demand an answer as judges. Moreover, as we know Jesus, the very fact that a question comes from the heart would induce him the more to answer that heart. Did Jesus fear that by telling Pilate whence he really was he would so frighten Pilate that he would never order his crucifixion? Was it that Pilate's fear should not block the will of God that Jesus should be crucified? Such hypothetical constructions are precarious. How do we know that Pilate's fears would have been increased to that point? Had Jesus not already told Pilate of his heavenly origin? Yet Pilate had given him over to the scourge and the mockery. But the objectionable feature of this solution is the fact that the silence of Jesus is thought to contribute to Pilate's sin of sending Jesus to the cross. We should have Jesus himself justifying the means by the end. No consideration such as this keeps the lips of Jesus closed.

Refuge is sought in the intellectual or in the ethical disability of Pilate. He would not understand if Jesus did tell him what he asked. Or he would not have the moral courage to act on what Jesus would tell him even if he should understand. We deny the first statement. Jesus is always able to make men understand what he wants them to understand. The blindest and most obdurate Jews were made to understand. Jesus has already made Pilate understand (18:36, 37). This answers also the second statement. The power that works obedience to the truth lies not in men but in the truth they are made to hear. But whether they allow that power to work obedience in them or not, the truth with its power is brought to them nevertheless. Nor is Pilate treated as an exception. By not accepting these solutions of the silence of Jesus the true solution has already been touched. Luther has it: "The cause is this: he had already given Pilate answer which was abundant enough, 18:37; but Pilate replied mockingly, 'What is truth?' The silence of Jesus means that his former answer stands, 'My kingship is not of this world, etc. I am a king. To this end have I been born, and to this end have I come into the world, that I testify to the truth,'" etc. We must add that when Jesus gave this answer to Pilate, the circumstances were far more favorable for Pilate's acceptance than they are now. Pilate had made no wrong move, had not yet sent Jesus to Herod to shift responsibility, had not yet paired Barabbas with Jesus, had not yet scourged and mocked Jesus to make his kingship seem ridiculous and harmless. These acts had been Pilate's reply to the mighty and clear testimony regarding who Jesus was and whence he had come. Why repeat that testimony? Silence now was also an answer, and it spoke louder and more effectively than words.

10) **Pilate, therefore, says to him, To me thou dost not speak? Dost thou not know that I have power to release thee and have power to crucify thee?** Here Pilate reveals himself more fully than at any other point. Here Pilate justifies the previous silence of Jesus. His was no anxious heart, fearful lest he offend one of the several gods, ready now at least to yield to the truth at which he had scoffed at the start. His first question is not one of surprise, for the emphatic ἐμοί reveals that he is angered that Jesus dares to treat *him* and *his* question with silence: *"To me* thou offerest silence?" This the second question corroborates in which he boasts with all his pride as Roman procurator over against this Jew Jesus what tremendous authority and power (ἐξουσία) he wields. He alone has this power. He is the man before whom to stoop, to whom humbly to appeal. Note how he repeats, "I have power." Is not Jesus aware of the greatness of the man before whom he stands? The supreme motive which actuated Pilate here bursts into view: his overweening pride which considers the silence of Jesus a covert insult. He is so filled with pride that his tongue overdoes the good thing. He talks as though he could bestow life or death at will with the turn of the hand, exactly as he pleases. He really does himself injustice — he is not a man who is as bad as that.

Pilate is pitiful, thinking himself so great and mighty and yet being swayed like an unstable reed. Caiaphas has been compared to a rock, unyielding, unscrupulous, unhesitating, having a will that conquers all the rest; Pilate to a reed, his head very high but swung by every wind. Euthymius is right, "Now he is frightened, now he frightens." First "God's Son" unnerves -him, next he thunders as though he were a god, and Jesus, God's Son, a beggar. Extremes meet. Why objection should be raised against mentioning the power to release in the first place with the power to crucify in the second, is hard to see; yet some prefer a transposition against the strongest textual authority. To say that the course of the trial suggests the reverse order fails to see the situation as it was. In Pilate's mind release was uppermost not crucifixion, and it is Pilate who speaks. Moreover, there is a climax when release is placed first and crucifixion second. Release is often conceived as a covert promise to Jesus seeking to attract him, and crucifixion as a threat seeking to cow him. It is nearer to the thought of Pilate to conceive the two alternatives, life on the one hand and death on the other, as the great extent of his power to which this Jew Jesus is wholly subject. Pilate tells Jesus that he has Jesus entirely in his hand.

11) With this the answer of Jesus accords, which refers to neither promise nor threat but only to Pilate's power. **Jesus answered him: Thou hast no power at all over me except it had been given thee from above. For this reason he that did deliver me up to thee has greater sin.** Silent before, Jesus now answers. For silence would mean that Jesus knows that Pilate has the power over him which he proudly claims. Jesus pricks that proud assertion with the direct contradiction, "Thou hast no power over me at all." Pilate dilates on his power: "power to release and power to crucify"; Jesus combines the two: "power over me." Because Jesus uses ἐξουσία only once, some think that in his reply Jesus thinks only of Pilate's power to crucify and not also of his power to

release.   Hence they translate κατά, "against me."   But
why should Jesus deny to Pilate only the one power —
does he admit the other?   The root meaning of κατά
is "down," which becomes "against" only in certain
contexts (R. 606, etc.) ; here the preposition means
"over me," as from a superior down upon an inferior,
and thus includes both functions, release and condemnation.   The assured reading is ἔχεις, "thou hast,"
and not εἶχες with ἄν omitted, "thou wouldest have."
The denial is direct not merely conditional; and
οὐδεμίαν, "not a single," refers to power in either direction.   It may offend this proud procurator to
have his boast denied; but his dream that he has
the double power he thinks he has must be shattered by this lowly prisoner who ever testifies to the
truth (18:37).

Yet in a certain sense he has power: it has been
given to him from above.   Jesus is not thinking of
Caesar as having invested Pilate with power but of
God whose providence had allowed a man of Pilate's
stamp to be placed in the procurator's office at this
time.   For Pilate's boast was not that he was
sovereign, independent of Caesar.   It is unusual to
attach a conditional clause of past unreality to a
simple declarative sentence of present time, but the
sense is perfectly plain.   With the neuter ἦν δεδομένον
the subject cannot be the feminine ἐξουσία but must
be the infinitive ἐξουσίαν ἔχειν; "to have power" had
been given to Pilate.   This is far better than to make
the subject the last infinitive which Pilate used: "to
crucify me," again omitting the other infinitive: "to
release me."   The purpose of Jesus in answering
Pilate thus is not to impress upon this pagan governor
the right conception of his exalted governmental office,
that he should think of it as held under God with constant responsibility to God.   Pilate was not the man
to be receptive to such teaching, nor is the present

acute situation such that a moral reminder of this kind would be in place. The interest of Jesus is to testify to Pilate and to those present that no human power whatever, whether that of Pilate or of any other ruler, is able to pass on whether God's Son shall live or shall die. Jesus alone has the ἐξουσία to lay down his life if he so wills, or to refuse to lay it down (10:18). The fact that he is in his present position, suffering these agonies, and on his way to death, is due to his own volition. Pilate is to know that it is not he who holds Jesus in his hand; a higher hand holds Pilate.

It was God's punitive justice which had to remove the scepter from Israel and make Israel subject to Rome, thus transferring the power of life and death from the Jews to the Romans. This usually seems simpler to us than the next step, that at this very time God's providence should place men like Caiaphas and Pilate in control of the government; yet it is all of a piece with the other. The world produced such men, it would have them as its rulers, one as unscrupulous and as hard as Caiaphas; and one as unscrupulous and as weak as Pilate. God took them in their wickedness and used them for his good and gracious ends. It was he who placed his Son into their hands, and his Son of his own will yielded himself to his Father's gracious will. The one, Caiaphas, with his relentless hardness would force the other, Pilate, with his haughty weakness to kill Jesus, who would thus die, not by stoning, but by crucifixion. As in the ancient case of Pharaoh and his abusing of Israel, God and his Son did not use their almighty power to nullify the wickedness of these men, but they did warn these men with the full power of grace against the dreadful acts to which their wickedness was driving them. Thus their full responsibility remained upon them when in spite of all moral deterrents they let their wickedness fill the measure of their guilt by actually carrying out their desperate deeds. What is true of these wicked men is endlessly repeated in all others who make themselves the devil's tools. The problem is the same in each case, even as the solution is the same.

So also the guilt is proportionate, that of Pilate is less than that of Caiaphas though in itself it is great enough: "He that did deliver me up to thee has greater sin." The thought is concentrated, for it is not the mere formal act of bringing Jesus before Pilate's tribunal that constitutes the greater sin but this act with all that goes with it, the relentless will of Caiaphas to crucify Jesus. Between the two men the guilt of Pilate is less. We see no gain in making the singular "he that did deliver me up" one of category, hence applying not to Caiaphas alone but also to all who were associated with him in his deed. Even then Caiaphas remains the moving spirit in whose guilt all the rest only shared. "He that did deliver me up to thee" cannot refer to Judas, for he had nothing to do with Pilate, he betrayed but did not deliver up Jesus. This word of Jesus' must have struck home more deeply in Pilate's mind than even the outright denial of Pilate's ἐξουσία. He was told that even if he crucified Jesus he would not have the chief guilt; for he was not the prime actor in this drama, his pose to that effect was hollow, another wicked man outranked him. Even at this critical stage when the question had turned to one about the judges instead of one about the prisoner, Jesus compels Pilate to see the truth. Jesus' word, however, has a deeper object. It reminds Pilate that he and his power are on trial before the divine tribunal itself, the judge whom none can deceive. More than that. Jesus here pronounces the divine verdict upon all his wicked judges. Pilate, the judge, is now judged by a greater judge.   Another than Pilate has "greater sin," and that means that Pilate's sin is next in greatness.   Here stands Jesus, the King indeed, travestied in most cruel fashion by this governor, and from his royal lips Pilate hears his sentence.   Jesus strikes home in the callous conscience of Pilate.   It is the last warning to Pilate.   Yet Jesus speaks as though Pilate had already remanded him to the cross.   This King's knowledge is infallible.   The verdict pronounced by Jesus is the last word Pilate heard from those holy lips.

12)   **As a result of this Pilate was seeking to release him.**   John has used ἐκ τούτου only here and in 6:66 (which see).   In neither instance is the phrase temporal: "from thence," "from that moment," because no antecedent of time can be supplied for the demonstrative pronoun.   The phrase means that as a result of what Jesus said to Pilate the latter tried to release him.   The imperfect ἐζήτει already indicates that Pilate's effort failed.   John writes only "he was seeking" and adds no μᾶλλον, as might be expected, since Pilate had sought to free Jesus before this: "he was seeking the more."   Why is such a reference to Pilate's previous efforts absent?   In order to convey the thought that now at last Pilate made the real effort, one that was so strong that his previous efforts do not count in comparison.   We, therefore, decline to make ἐζήτει a conative imperfect (R. 885): "he began to seek"; it is simply durative and marks the tenacity of Pilate's effort.   The impression Jesus had made upon Pilate's conscience was so powerful that this was the result.   Pilate was determined to free Jesus, do what the Jews might.

John is all too brief and compels us to read between the lines.   **But the Jews were shouting, saying: If thou releasest this one thout art not a friend of Caesar.   Everyone who makes himself a**

king speaks against Caesar. So Pilate, though not
Jesus (v. 13), is again outside of the Prætorium con-
fronting the Jews. The Jews yell in frantic rage.
Pilate must have addressed them. What did he say?
Undoubtedly much more than he had said at any time
hitherto. So far he had declared only his inability
to find an indictment against Jesus. He had stopped
short with that. From the answering yells of the
Jews we gather that now at last Pilate declared the
release of Jesus exactly as John informs us Pilate was
determined to do. Whether the altercation between
Pilate and the Jews included more exchanges of words
we are unable to say. It matters little. Whether at
once or after a little, the Jews now find the word that
brings Pilate to his knees. If he releases τοῦτον, "this
fellow," he is not a friend of Caesar. Again it is
Pilate who is put on trial and this time before a
judge whom he dreads more than any god, namely
Caesar. Diabolic cunning drove home this deadly
thrust. The title φίλος τοῦ Καίσαρος was in a formal
way granted to Roman courtiers and officials who distinguished themselves in loyal service to the emperor,
and these constituted a kind of *cohors amicorum*
for the throne. Yet we have no information that
Pilate had received this distinction from the emperor.
The term is used by the Jews more like a litotes:
"not a friend of Caesar" in the sense "in reality an
enemy of Caesar." Cunningly this is put in the negative form, "not a friend," not loyal, not true to
Caesar. This negative leaves open a wide range of
possible charges against Pilate. Its very indefiniteness was intended to frighten cowardly Pilate. All
his past misdeeds could be brought against him in
addition to his present act of releasing an alleged pre-
tender to the Jewish throne. Pilate and the Jews
were fully aware of the suspiciousness of the emperor

who never hesitated to sacrifice an official concerning whose loyalty he had the least doubt.

Pilate is not left in doubt as to his own danger: "Everyone who makes himself a king speaks against Caesar." The proposition is put forth as self-evident. The fact that Jesus had never made himself a secular king and had never even by one word proclaimed himself such a king, goes for naught. The lie of this intimation is as rank as all the other lies of the Jews and as flagrant as their attempt to suborn perjured witnesses against Jesus at their own trial. The Jews count on their own insistence, false though it is, that Jesus claims to be a king. Any man who in any way can be charged with calling himself a king thereby "speaks against Caesar." We need not take ἀντιλέγει in the sense of "opposes," which would involve overt acts; the very proclamation of kingship is overt act enough. Pilate is crushed. The very thought that Caesar may get to hear what these Jews now shout into his ears completely unmans him. He sees ruin opening at his feet like a gulf — his position, his liberty, his very life are at stake. He faces the alternative: either he sacrifices Jesus or he sacrifices himself. Here, writes Luther, is "a picture of all the saints who are holy before the world and have not God's Word, faith, and Christ." Resolve they ever so earnestly to do right, down they go before the devil's onslaught!

What a frightful snarl of lies and hypocrisy! Jesus, who bids the Jews give to Caesar what is Caesar's, is made an enemy of Caesar's by those who know the contrary and is allowed to stand as such an enemy by the judge who also knows the contrary. Pilate, loyal enough to Caesar, is made to face the charge of disloyalty by the Jews who, disloyal to the core, play the role of loyalty; and this while both

Pilate and the Jews know that he is loyal and that they are traitorously disloyal. The scene was a devil's masterpiece in lying.

13) **Pilate, therefore, having heard these words, brought Jesus out and sat down on the tribunal in a place called The Pavement, but in Hebrew, Gabbatha.** Pilate had left Jesus inside the Prætorium when he had gone out to announce the release. This is noteworthy, for this act shows that Jesus was to be kept under the protection of the governor in the Prætorium. When Pilate now heard "these words" of the Jews, and his courage gave way utterly, he ordered Jesus to be brought out once more and sat down on the $\beta\tilde{\eta}\mu\alpha$, a movable platform with several steps, on which was placed the judge's chair (or several chairs if more than one judge held court, or if notable persons were invited to sit with the judge). The plural "these words" is in place because of the two statements of the Jews referred to. Pilate now ascends the "tribunal" to pronounce sentence on Jesus. John is quite circumstantial in relating this climax of the trial. When he says that the governor now ascended and took his seat, we must not suppose that he had not done this at other moments during the trial; for he certainly was seated as the judge in 18:29-31, and again in 18:38-40. These, however, were only incidents in the trial, hence Pilate's seating himself is not mentioned in particular. Now the fateful moment had come, and now we must know that Pilate is seated for the final judicial act.

John mentions even the place: "in a place called The Pavement," $\Lambda\iota\theta\acute{o}\sigma\tau\rho\omega\tau o\nu$, the Greek name, the neuter adjective made a proper noun: a mosaic pavement of stone. John adds also the Hebrew, i. e., Aramaic name of which, however, the Greek was not a translation: "Gabbatha," a word of uncertain derivation, usually taken to mean a raised place.

14) **Now it was the Passover Preparation; the hour was about the sixth.** The first statement should cause no trouble whatever. Luke 23:53 writes, "it was the day of the preparation, and the Sabbath drew on"; compare Matt. 27:62. Mark 15:42 has, "the preparation, that is, the day before the Sabbath," προσάββατον, "the pro-Sabbath." And John himself repeats παρασκευή, "the Preparation," in v. 31 and 42. All this means that the day of the condemnation and the crucifixion of Jesus is Friday. Because it preceded the Sabbath it was called "the Preparation" in the sense that this was its regular and common name. When John uses the exceptional combination παρασκευὴ τοῦ πάσχα, "Preparation of the Passover," he simply has in mind the Friday of the Passover festival, the one that occurs during the festival week. The Sabbath of this great week was considered especially holy, and preparation was made accordingly. The παρασκευή refers to all the cooking and the other work that had to be done before the Sabbath set in and in preparation for the Sabbath. R. 501 lists τοῦ πάσχα among the genitives of "looser relation," which are objective, and writes regarding our passage that John's expression "probably already means the day 'before' the Sabbath (Friday)."

Yet some regard "Preparation of the Passover" as referring to the day on which the preparation was made *for* the Passover feast proper, for the eating of the lamb. They hold that this Passover meal had not yet been eaten when Jesus was condemned to the cross, that it was to take place after sunset of this Friday when the Sabbath began. The fact that this makes John clash with the synoptists seems rather welcome, and no attempt is made to find an agreement. Jesus, then, never celebrated this last Passover; the scene in the upper room was an ordinary meal. All that the synoptists record about Jesus' eating the Passover on Thursday evening must be set aside as a mistake. We need not follow the argument in detail. The data cited from the four evangelists are decisive. Equally decisive is the fact that παρασκευή is never used in the sense of "the preparation" or of "the day of preparation" for a festival but only in the sense of the preparation for the Sabbath. The law provided complete rest from work only on the Sabbath (Exod. 16:5) ; all preparation of food had to be made on the day before; but the law provided nothing of the kind for the great festival days, for on these days (save as one might occur on a Sabbath) food could be cooked as on any other day. The attempt to show that the festival days also had a παρασκευή has failed completely.

John was especially concerned to fix the day of the week on which Jesus died. When he wrote his Gospel, the entire congregational life was determined by the day on which Jesus died and thus also the day on which he arose. The former was a Friday, the latter a Sunday. The church had selected Sunday for its weekly day of worship because this day brought to mind the Lord's resurrection. The church, therefore, always celebrated its Easter on a Sunday, irrespective of the calendar date of the month, and thus emancipated itself from the Jewish Passover date. John, therefore, also in his Gospel, lends full support to the synoptists and to the Sunday and the Easter observance of the church. He, too, fixes these days: Friday and Sunday.

He also fixes the hour as about the sixth. He writes so many details that we conclude that he must have been present. On the whole subject of the "hour" in John see the comment on 1:39, also on 4:6 and 52. According to Mark 15:25 Jesus was crucified at the third hour, our 9 A. M. With this Matthew and Luke agree who speak of Jesus as having hung upon the cross for some time when the miraculous darkness set in at noon. All the synoptists, as no one disputes, reckon the hours in the Jewish fashion, namely twelve for the period of daylight, starting with the dawn and ending with sunset. If John reckons in the same way, he would say that Pilate did not sentence Jesus until about noon. Besides this ordinary way of reckoning the hours, which was generally used also by the Romans, the legal way of reckoning had twelve hours from midnight until noon, and another twelve from noon until midnight, just as we do now. If John reckons in this fashion he would say that Pilate sentenced Jesus at 6 A. M. Neither of these alternatives can possibly be correct. Both conflict hopelessly not only with the hours mentioned in the synoptists but equally with the whole course of events as recorded by all four of the evangelists. It is impossible to concentrate all that preceded the sentencing by Pilate into the time before 6 A. M., and again impossible to find time for what happened after the sentencing if this is placed at noon.

To attack the reading ἕκτη, "sixth," seems hopeless in the face of the textual evidence; for only a few texts have the reading τρίτη, "third," (9 A. M.). To assert that John corrects the synoptists and to place the sentencing at noon is an unwarranted solution, in fact, no solution at all. Attempts to make much of ὡς as used by both John and Mark, even when "about" is stretched to the utmost, from 6 A. M. upward and from 9 A. M. downward, prove insufficient. We must add the difficulties regarding the way of reckoning the hours in the other passages in John's Gospel. No solution has as yet been found. As to the facts, these are certain: Jesus was crucified at 9 A. M., and therefore was sentenced before 8:30 A. M.

Pilate seats himself to pronounce judgment against Jesus but inwardly he rages because he has been forced to yield to these despicable, lying Jews. **And he says to the Jews, Behold, your king!** All the scorn and the sarcasm of which he is capable is put into the exclamation. If he must yield he will sting and lash them while he is yielding. "King, king," they have shouted to the last — well, let them look, this is *their* king. Did they expect the coveted verdict from Pilate's lips? An insult is hurled into their faces. Here the character of the man comes out. He is too weak for courageous mastery, he is strong in vicious verbal thrusts. Those who think that Pilate still had in mind to force Jesus' release overlook the fact that he took the judge's seat in order to remand Jesus to the cross. It is thus beside the mark to call Pilate's exlamation unwise and to point out that bitterness only produces bitterness. Pilate deliberately keeps the Jews in suspense the while he seeks the satisfaction of little souls by enraging his opponents with insults.

15)   He gets what he wants: still more frantic outcries. **They, therefore, shouted, Away, away with him, crucify him!** Note ἐκεῖνοι, which points emphatically to the antecedent, "the Jews." As Jews Pilate insulted them by pointing to Jesus as *their* king, and as Jews, John wants us to understand, they repudiate this their king. The three aorist imperatives are highly peremptory, each is shouted out by itself, hence there are no connectives. These, too, are words, but words backed by an implacable will. They are the more frantic because Pilate still holds out, and the Jews are not yet certain that his will is broken.

The chance is good, and Pilate gives them another vicious thrust. He will sentence Jesus but he will take his time in doing so, aggravating the Jews to the utmost. **Pilate says to them, Your king shall I crucify?** This feigned tone of surprise cuts to the quick. What, do they mean to say that they want their own king, their supreme hope, to be crucified by a Roman like a slave. Pilate is speaking from the Jewish standpoint not from his own. All the hopes of the Jews for breaking the Roman yoke centered in the rise of a Jewish Messianic King. Here he is, Pilate says, and now you want the Roman power to give him this worst death of shame? Pilate acts as though he cannot believe his ears. He intimates that they should beg for Jesus' release in order to rally against Rome beneath his banner. He is staging a farce in order to get what revenge he can.

The high priests answered, We have no king except Caesar. Driven to the limit, this fatal word escapes the high priests. John writes, "the high priests," whereas before he writes, "the Jews." This cannot mean that the few persons who bore this title made this declaration while the rest of the Sanhedrists refused to do so, and while the populace dissented. They were all of one mind, no dissent arose at any time. Where the leaders went all the rest followed. Some followed because of fear, but whatever their low motives, they followed. John names "the high priests" in order to inform us that this declaration came, not from irresponsible persons in the crowd, but from the very heads of the Jewish nation, from the most responsible of all, the most highly representative, whose very position entitled them to speak for all.

These heads of the nation are not content to disown Jesus alone. They do not cry, "This is not our king!" They disown any and every king of their own and pledge themselves only and wholly to the pagan Caesar. These high priests, to whom the highest spiritual hopes of Israel were committed, here reveal themselves as traitors to those hopes and to

the nation that should cherish them. They stand as
apostates to the entire Old Testament faith. Only
pagan Caesar is the king they acknowledge. They lie
worse than pagans, for they hate Caesar. They
demonstrate that they deserve no other king. Their
word was another thrust at Pilate on the subject of
loyalty to Caesar, a thrust to drive him to crucify this
man whom they lyingly charged with making himself
a secular king. John does not say so, but here again
we have a word like that of the high priest Caiaphas
in 11:50, a word of unconscious prophecy. Since the
day of Christ's death the Jews have never had any
king of their own but only Gentile rulers. Scattered
all over the world, divine judgment has followed them
like a shadow. Repudiating their one divine King,
they remain kingless forever. As a nation they are
cast off without hope of return. Only a remnant shall
be saved and only by repudiating Judaism and by
amalgamating with the Christian Church. The high
priests spoke as true representatives of the Jewish
nation; their nation has stood with them to the
present day.

16) **Then, therefore, he delivered him up to
them that he be crucified.** Pilate's own words are
not recorded, the fact as such suffices for John. Yet
he states the substance of Pilate's verdict. It must
have been given in briefest form and without specifying any crime. After three times saying in so many
words that he finds no indictment against Jesus, Pilate
cannot now allow an indictment and base his verdict
on that. God saw to it that his Son was sent to the
cross not merely in innocence but even without a false
charge against him. He delivered him up "to them"
means "to the high priests," yet, as the sequel shows,
not that they and their police force should execute
Jesus by crucifixion but that they should have their
will. Pilate's soldiers were to crucify Jesus for the

Jews. The Jews went with the detachment of soldiers and saw the sentence carried out.

Pilate washed his hands in water but he could not remove the stain of guilt. His name is covered with infamy to this day. In the year 36 he was deposed, sent to Rome to face charges, and then seems to have been banished and to have committed suicide. Matthew and Mark report that immediately after the sentence the soldiers took off the purple cloak Jesus had worn until now and put on him his own clothes. Nothing is said about the crown of thorns. Some say that it too, after having served its purpose, was removed. But had it completely served its purpose? The superscription on the cross calls Jesus a king in three languages. To leave the crown on Jesus' head would differentiate Jesus as a king from the malefactors at his right and his left. Pilate wanted Jesus marked as a king to the last. The crown of thorns is so exceptional in every way that, when the two evangelists mention the removal of the purple cloak, two or three words more would have sufficed to note that also the crown was removed if, indeed, it too was taken off. The crown remained on Jesus' head.

5. "Crucified, Dead, and Buried," 19:17-42

17) **They, therefore, took Jesus over,** παρέλαβον, namely, the Jews from Pilate's hand. No change of subject is indicated, not even in v. 18, "they crucified him." John wants us to see that these are Jewish acts, although they are carried out by the Roman soldiers under Pilate's command.

From the events that follow John makes his own selection, adding materially to what the synoptists report. Each section is full of detail, and each is distinct in itself.

And bearing the cross for himself he went out to the place called that of the Skull, which is called in Hebrew Golgotha. Immediately after the sentence had been pronounced Jesus was led to the place of execution. The law did not require a delay. In the provinces of the empire no such law existed. The imperial laws on this point applied only to Roman citizens. The general practice compelled the condemned man to carry his own cross to the place of execution, and no exception was made in the case of Jesus. John omits a statement regarding the transfer of the cross to Simon of Cyrene. To attack his Gospel on that account, or to deny the synoptic report on the ground of John's silence is unwarranted. Executions took place outside of the city, and this was true in the case of the Jews (Num. 15:35; Acts 7:58; Heb. 13:12) as well as in the case of the Romans. Generally, the prisoners were led through the most populous streets, and the place of execution was near a highway where many people would congregate. The traditional *via dolorosa*, which is now shown in Jerusalem as the street over which Jesus passed, is of late construction: the city was completely destroyed several times. Pilate could not delay the execution because of the nature of the Jewish charge, and the Jews wanted it rushed to completion because of their hate and also because of the nature of the day.

Much has been written on the shape of the cross; see Nebe, *Leidensgeschichte*, II, 169, etc. It was neither an ⨯ nor a ⊤, but an upright post with a crossbeam a little beneath the top †. The two beams were fastened together at the start. All the evidence shows that Jesus was burdened with the entire cross and not merely with the upper crosspiece or *patibulum*. Jesus' own act in literally bearing the cross on which he died lends powerful effect to his word about our taking up the cross to bear it after

him, Matt. 10:38; 16:24. The place of execution
bore the name Κρανίον in the Greek and "Golgotha"
in the Aramaic, both of which signify "Cranium,"
hence "Skull," or, latinized, "Calvary," undoubtedly
because the hill had the shape of a cranium, the top
of a skull. The site has long been in dispute. It is
only too certain that the site now shown in Jerusalem
in the Church of the Holy Sepulcher is spurious.
Far more acceptable is the skull-like hill, now a
Mohammedan cemetery, which rises above the recently discovered "Garden Tomb," the rock-hewn
sepulcher which bears so many marks of being the
actual tomb in which the body of Jesus rested. The
author was deeply impressed with these sites, the
cranial elevation and the secluded garden with its
tomb corresponding in such detail to the Gospel
accounts.

18) John records the actual crucifixion only with
a subordinate clause: **where they crucified him and
with him other two, on this side and on that, and in
the middle Jesus.** Among the astounding things in
the Scriptures are these records of the supreme events
in all history — one word for the scourging, one word
for the crucifixion, one word for the resurrection.
Events so tremendous, words so brief and so restrained! Who guided the mind and the heart of
these writers to write in this astonishing manner?
Here is one of the plain marks of the divine inspiration in the product itself. "They crucified him,"
ἐσταύρωσαν, that is all! The Jews did this by means
of the soldiers' hands. They were the real agents
who had only forced Pilate to do their will. From
the great mass of evidence that has been collected
we gather that, first of all, the cross itself was erected.
Only in very exceptional cases was the cross high.
That on which Jesus was suspended elevated his feet
not more than three feet from the ground, for the

short stalk of hyssop was sufficient to reach his mouth. A block or heavy peg was fastened to the beam, and on this the victim sat straddle. The victim either climbed up himself, assisted, perhaps, by the executioners, or he was raised up to the seat, and then his body, legs, and arms were tied with ropes, and the great nails (of which the ancient writers speak especially) were driven through the hands and the feet. A hundred years ago everybody was certain that the feet of Jesus were not nailed to the cross. Exhaustive research has convinced everybody who has seen the evidence that the feet were also nailed, and not with only one nail through both feet. The central seat or peg kept the body from sagging to one side after the ropes were removed. No mention is made of a loin cloth. The agony of crucifixion needs no description; we refer only to the hot sun, the raging thirst, the slowness of death, which at times did not set in until three or four days had passed. It was a great relief for the malefactor to learn that he was to die that very day.

How the two malefactors came to be crucified with Jesus is not known. Their crucifixion fulfilled Isa. 53:12. Only Pilate himself could have issued the order. Perhaps Barabbas would have been one of the two if the Jews had not effected his release. The very release of this man may have put the thought into Pilate's mind of sending two others like him to death together with Jesus. Pilate's intent is evident: further insult to the Jews who demanded that their king be crucified. The fact that this insult reacted also upon Jesus made no difference to Pilate who had made a spectacle of Jesus by having him scourged and mocked and exhibited to the Jews. The fact that Jesus was placed between the two criminals was hardly due to an order from Pilate; more likely it was the

thought of the Jewish leaders themselves who directed
the crucifixion in person, possibly only the thought of
the soldiers.   Already the fact that these three were
crucified together means that they were to be considered as being of a kind.   The Jews had asked that
Jesus die a base criminal's death; Pilate grants them
their wish, sending two actual criminals to die with
Jesus.

19)   **Now Pilate wrote also a title and placed
it on the cross.   And there had been written, Jesus
of Nazareth, the King of the Jews.**   John amplifies
the record of the synoptists on the subject of the
superscription.   Pilate, we learn from John, wrote
that title, placed it on the cross, and refused to alter
it at the bidding of the Jews.   Pilate insists on having
Jesus crucified as the King of the Jews.   On this John
brings the full details.   The two aorists ἔγραψε and
ἔθηκεν merely state the historical facts that Pilate did
this, of course, not with his own hand but by means
of his orders.   These aorists are not past perfects
and do not allow us to conclude that the inscription
had been attached to the cross already at the Prætorium;   the placing occurred on Golgotha.   Inscriptions stating why a man was crucified were common.   These were also carried and displayed on the
way out to the place of execution although they were
not hung from the culprit's neck, for which latter
claim no evidence has been found.   We read nothing
about inscriptions for the two malefactors.   The mind
of Pilate seems to have been taken up chiefly with
Jesus.   Not until Jesus was crucified did the soldiers
put the inscription in place, and not until that time did
the Jews read the words it contained.   It is possible
that the inscription was an afterthought of Pilate's,
and that he sent it to the centurion by means of a
messenger after Jesus already hung upon the cross;

it seems more probable that it was at once delivered to the centurion, not for display on the way out, but to be affixed after the execution had begun.

The past perfect "there had been written" merely refers back to the aorist "he wrote." When the inscription was affixed, all were able to see what "had been written." The legend was, "Jesus of Nazareth, the King of the Jews." Since the writing was drawn up in three languages, the slight variations in the reports of the evangelists are easily explained. John alone has ὁ Ναζωραῖος, so that we may conclude that this word appeared only in one of the languages. It is impossible to determine just which language each evangelist has in mind. The same is true regarding the order of the languages.

20) **This title, therefore, many of the Jews read, for the place was near to the city, where Jesus was crucified; and it had been written in Hebrew, in Latin, in Greek,** in the Aramaic vernacular, in the Latin of the Roman government, showing that the inscription was official, coming from Pilate himself, and in the Greek as the great world language of the time, thus offering the greatest possible publicity. John mentions "in Hebrew" first, not in order to indicate the prominence of this language but because he is emphasizing the fact that the Jews read the inscription, the very people whom the high priests least of all desired to read it. Crowds of Jews read it, for the place was not only near the city, but the city itself overflowed with Passover pilgrims. We need not hesitate about construing together "near to the city" instead of "the place of the city," for Golgotha was outside of the city. The city was surrounded by massive walls, marking its limits most decidedly; Jerusalem did not spread out and straggle as our American cities and towns do.

21) **The high priests of the Jews were therefore saying to Pilate: Write not, The King of the Jews, but that he said, King am I of the Jews.** We are right, then, in concluding that the high priests did not see the superscription until it was affixed to the cross. If they had seen it before that they certainly would have made an attempt to secure a change. What enraged the high priests was the publicity of the inscription among the Jewish crowds. It is John who calls it a τίτλος or "title," and, in fact, it merely gave Jesus a title. That is the remarkable thing about Pilate's superscription: it names no crime whatever, it only records a most significant title. In three languages and thus to all the world it shouts out the great title of Jesus. No implication of secular kingship appears in Pilate's title. That is completely shut out by "of Nazareth," which John would not have us overlook and on which we may well compare 1:46. The old Jewish kings did not claim origin from Nazareth. Pilate is having his last revenge on "the high priests of the Jews." Only here does John call them thus; and though it has been denied, John certainly has in mind the contrast: "the king *of the Jews*" and " the high priests *of the Jews.*" To the very last these high priests have hurled at Pilate the charge, "King, king!" which he knew was false and which he knew they knew was false. They had forced Pilate to crucify Jesus as a king. Very well then, they should have him on the cross but only as a king, *their* King! Let all the world read, "The King of the Jews"! By simply giving Jesus this title without an added allegation Pilate proclaims the innocence of Jesus, of which he was completely certain. Jesus had told Pilate what kind of kingship he held; and now that all was over, that statement was prominent in Pilate's mind together with the other about Jesus being God's Son, and Pilate sets it down that Jesus is King of the Jews.

Forthwith the high priests hurry from Golgotha to the Prætorium to have this title changed. Whether they succeeded only in sending in word to Pilate, or whether he actually came out to them, is left to surmise. Cunningly they ask for only a slight change, that the article be dropped, and the εἰμί be inserted, thus making the title read, "King am I of the Jews." Instead of a title they want an assertion; instead of a title given by Pilate they want an assertion coming from Jesus. This sounds as though the high priests knew all that passed between Jesus and Pilate when the governor questioned Jesus within the Prætorium. They must have had someone there who reported to them. This, too, answers the question as to how John knew so exactly what was said. He encountered no difficulty whatever.

22) **Pilate answered, What I have written I have written.** John does not say that he answered "them." He may never have come out of the Prætorium but may only have sent his answer to them. The high priests reckoned without their host when they thought that Pilate would again yield to their will. Sore at his defeat, he was immovable. The Jews find him a changed man. Curt, decisive is his answer, no discussion, no parleying whatever. The two perfects are interesting, one being punctiliar-durative, the other durative-punctiliar, R. 895; he wrote, and what he wrote remained written, and what thus remained stands as final. Formally Pilate was correct. The sentence, already executed, could not be legally altered even by a word. The men who commit great crimes often stickle for exact legal rights in minor matters. More than this, the very presence and the indignation of the high priests were exceedingly sweet to Pilate — his taunt had gone home. It showed that the drop of gall which he had cast into their cup of joy in obtaining Jesus' death thoroughly spoiled all its sweetness.

They had made him miserable enough, let them now be miserable in turn. And back of all this clash of human passions was the serene hand of God. Jesus was, indeed, the true spiritual King of the Jews. What was written was written.

23) As John recounts the full details concerning the superscription on the cross, so he does also with regard to the division of Jesus' clothes. But the main point of this episode is the remarkable fulfillment of prophecy. John alone adds this detail, for in Matt. 27:35 the fulfillment is interpolated from John, as all the older codices show. **The soldiers, therefore, when they crucified Jesus, took his clothes, and made four parts, to each soldier a part, and the tunic. Now the tunic was seamless, woven from the top throughout.** With the resumptive οὖν and the temporal clause John takes us back to v. 18. After the execution the executioners divide the spoils. Incidentally we learn that four soldiers were detailed to crucify Jesus. Nothing is said about the soldiers and the division of the clothes of the two malefactors. We conclude that for the crucifixion of each of the malefactors two other quaternions had been given orders. Soldiers were constantly used for this purpose as various old records show, and not only in times of war but also in times of peace. A quaternion was the regular detail of soldiers (Acts 12:4). This need not imply that only twelve soldiers were ordered out on the present occasion; a detachment of some size must have been sent by Pilate because of the great crowd present at the Prætorium and sure to be present on Golgotha.

What is meant by τὰ ἱμάτια αὐτοῦ, "his garments"? And how were the four parts made, with the tunic as a fifth? Our question is easily answered. The synoptists say that the clothes were divided, which fact John explains by saying that the soldiers made four parts of them, to each man a part; then the synoptists say that lots were cast for the clothes. This shuts out the supposition that Jesus wore only two garments, an outer robe, the ἱμάτιον, and a tunic next to the body, the χιτών; and that the four parts were made by slashing the outer robe into four pieces. R. 408 also leans toward this view when he suggests that the plural ἱμάτια may be used only in the sense of the singular ἱμάτιον. Why cast lots when the four pieces were of equal value? Moreover, the loose outer robe could not be worn without a girdle; and Jesus could not have carried his cross unless his robe was bound tightly at the waist by a girdle, for he would have tripped after taking the first steps. Did Jesus go barefooted? To say that his sandals were cast aside as worthless, or that he had none, is without the least warrant. Had Jesus no turban or headcloth? He must have had; a headcovering had to be worn in that climate because of the sun. We still see it today, with the loose folds protecting the neck, throat, and shoulders. Those who think that the thorny crown was removed at the Prætorium when the procession started for Golgotha, have no reason to assume that Jesus had no headcovering. We think the crown was left on Jesus' head — who cared to remove it for him? — and it still left him marked as the king designed by Pilate's inscription. The headcloth was thrown onto the thorn-crowned head and still belonged to Jesus until one of the soldiers secured it on Golgotha. Robe, girdle, sandals, headcovering, four unequal parts, one for each soldier, but to be divided by casting lots.

John alone mentions the χιτών or tunic, for this helped to fulfill the ancient prophecy in the most striking way, and Matthew, who records so many fulfilled prophecies, had left out this one. "And the tunic," as John writes, puts this into a class by itself. A parenthetical δέ explains: this garment was seam-

less, woven from the top on through, all as one piece.
A tunic woven in such an exceptional way would be
made of the best material and thus be quite valuable;
no cheap goods would be worked into such a garment.
Those who think the outer robe was cut into pieces to
make sufficient parts must tell us why the tunic was
not considered as one of the four parts, thus cutting
the robe into only enough pieces to make up four, one
for each soldier.   The likelihood points to five pieces
of wearing apparel, among which the tunic stood
out as being exceptional and especially valuable.   The
denial that a seamless garment could be produced at
this time is untenable, for Josephus, *Ant.* 3. 7, 2 and 4
tells us that the high priest wore such a garment.
Other authorities substantiate this statement.   The
probability is that the ordinary priests also wore
seamless tunics (Winer, also Nebe).   A seamless
tunic, however, possessed no sacerdotal character.
Hence we cannot follow those who regard it as fitting
that our High Priest Jesus wore a seamless tunic.
Jesus never resembled the clerics — among them we
found the Jewish rabbis in Jerusalem — who advertise
their office by their daily dress.

24)   **They said, therefore, to each other, Let
us not cut it but let us draw lots for it, whose it
shall be; that the Scripture might be fulfilled, which
says:**

> **They apportioned my garments among them-
> selves,
> And for my vestment they cast lot.**

The soldiers, therefore, did these things.   Those who
think that the outer robe was cut into pieces seem to
draw this idea from the remark of the soldiers not
to cut up the seamless tunic.   But John makes no mention of the outer robe; besides mentioning the tunic
he speaks only of "the garments," τὰ ἱμάτια.   Nor do

the soldiers say, "Let us not cut *this*," as though they had already cut something else; for αὐτόν is without emphasis. They had already made four parts exclusive of the tunic. Its exceptional nature made them withhold the tunic and decide about that separately. And their decision lies between two alternatives: letting each man again have a part, or allowing one man to have the entire garment. They decide quite sensibly on the latter, for to cut up the tunic would give nothing worth-while to any man. The subjunctives are volitive R. 943. How these men cast or drew lots is not indicated. A common way was to place lots in a helmet and to shake them until one flew out; another way was to reach in and to draw a lot. If the former procedure was followed, one man would be designated, and the first lot that flew out would be his, the lot being marked with a certain portion of the four that had been made, and in the case of the tunic, three lots were blank, and one lot was marked to win.

All this was a common proceeding to the casual observer. The clothes of the crucified belonged to the executioners as a perquisite. The crucified man was treated as one who was dead. The soldiers were great gamblers. For them to gamble for the clothes of Jesus was nothing exceptional. The soldiers who crucified the malefactors probably did the same. John himself was near enough to see and to hear what transpired. The astonishing thing is that the action of these soldiers with regard to the clothes of Jesus fulfilled to the very letter the prophecy of Ps. 22:18, which John quotes from the LXX, a correct rendering of the Hebrew. This fact, indeed, deserves record in the Gospels. The Davidic authorship of Ps. 22 has been violently assailed, and in place of it we are offered a variety of conjectures, the one intent of which is to place the date of the Psalm as far away as possible from David's time. Yet the competent commentator on the Psalms, Rudolf Kittel, while not explicitly admitting David's authorship, prefers to pass by this question in silence. Delitzsch has answered the radical critics quite thoroughly: "Already one consideration nullifies all these notions. No man in pre-Christian times, also no prophet, could combine with the prospect of his deliverance the prospect of the conversion of the Gentiles and the salvation of men through the gospel of this deliverance — no man except the theocratic king faithful in his calling, who, since II Sam. 7, dared to apply to himself what the patriarchal promise of the seed of Abraham declares, that they who bless him shall be blessed, and they who curse him shall be stricken with a curse; and who had to appear to himself not only with a sacred but with a central worldwide significance." With this view all other evidence of the Davidic authorship agrees. "We do not doubt the truth of the heading 'by David.'"

The interpretation is another matter. See the author's *Eisenach Old Testament Selections*, 428, etc., which shows that this is not a typical Psalm but one that is entirely prophetic. David is not describing his own sufferings in such a manner that these picture Christ's sufferings. "As Isaiah in chapter 53 simply prophesied, so David does here. Isaiah wrote poetry, too, only he wrote description; David's poem is drama. Isaiah's verses picture the Redeemer in his suffering and in his glorification; David's verses let us hear the Redeemer himself speak in his agony and in his triumph. There are similar dramatizations in the writings of the prophets. Here the entire poem is of that character. And that, let us frankly confess, is about as far as we dare to go; what lies beyond is behind the veil of the Spirit of revelation and inspiration."

The two lines quoted by John refer to the same
act, the portioning out of the clothes of Jesus by lot.
In the parallelism of Hebrew verse the second line
repeats the thought of the first, but such synonymous
lines always add new features.   It is, therefore, unwarranted to identify b*e*gadim and l*e*bush, "garments"
and "vesture," as though both referred to clothes.
This "vesture" is *one* garment, the tunic Jesus wore.
The Psalm does not say how the other ἱμάτια or "clothes"
were divided; we may infer that this was also done
by casting lots.   But the Psalm pointedly says that
for the single tunic a lot was cast, using the singular
κλῆρος, one lot, so that one man obtained this special
garment.   The prophecy, so unobtrusive in this
detail, was fulfilled to the letter before the very eyes
of John.   He adds, "The soldiers therefore did these
things."   John's mind lingers on them and on their
action and bids us do the same: common, coarse,
ignorant pagan soldiers, gambling again, as so often,
but doing precisely what divine foreknowledge and
prophecy had recorded hundreds of years ago.

25)   The entire incident next recorded has been
preserved by John alone, who also is concerned about
it in the most intimate way. Jesus spoke seven
words from the cross, and in the first four he
attends to his earthly obligations, in the last three
to his affairs with God. The words addressed to
Mary and to John Jerome aptly calls the *testamentum
domesticum* by which Jesus set his earthly house in
order, while in the Lord's Supper, his *testamentum
publicum,* he made his great bequest to all his followers.
**Now there were standing beside the cross of Jesus
his mother and his mother's sister Mary, the wife of
Clopas, and Mary Magdalene.** No contrast is intended by δέ but merely continuation. When John
tells us that these women stood "beside the cross,"
we recall that the other evangelists also mention these

women but say that they stood "afar off." The two statements are not identical; yet they in no way conflict. For no one would suppose that this little group of women with the disciple John stood close by his side during the entire time that Jesus hung upon the cross. Only by waiting for an opportune moment could they have moved up so close; perhaps this occurred when the scoffing high priests and the others had withdrawn. After Jesus had spoken to them, after, as it were, he had bidden them farewell, and the strange darkness fell over the land, the soldiers, becoming alarmed, cleared the space about the cross, and John with the women and the other friends of Jesus (Luke 23:49) could stand only "afar off," watching for the end. This final watching "afar off" the other evangelists note in their records.

How many women does John mention? One answer is three, another answer is four. Those who say that there were three point to the two *καί*, which add to the mother of Jesus two other women; if three others were intended another *καί* would have been added. Exegetically this is convincing over against the proposition that there were four women, grouped in two pairs, one unnamed pair being connected with *καί*, and another named pair also being connected with *καί*. The trouble with this view is that any reader, when more designations are added after the first *καί*, looks for the next *καί*, and the idea that pairs are intended to be mentioned does not enter his mind unless something appears that indicates that pairs are being spoken about, which the mere absence of a *καί* between the pairs fails to do. To say that, if only three women are referred to, John should have written, "and Mary, the sister of his mother, of Clopas," placing her name "Mary" first, is extreme, for this leaves the final genitive "of Clopas" in an ambiguous position. We are able to find only three

women mentioned in John's words. Mark 15:40 and
Matt. 27:56 name the second Mary as the mother of
James and Joses; this agrees with John who adds the
information that she was the Virgin's sister, and that
her husband's name was Clopas.

Matthew and Mark, for some reason that we do
not know, omit mention of the mother of Jesus. She
is not mentioned even in connection with the burial
of Jesus. But these two evangelists tell us that John's
mother Salome was present. Those who find four
women take Salome to be "the sister of his mother,"
whom John is said to designate only in this way. This
close relationship, however, is nowhere indicated in
the Gospels. With the mention of only three women
John would omit his mother, which accords even more
with his constant practice of effacing himself and his
relatives as much as possible from his record. He
would not mention himself in this narrative if he
were not compelled to do so on account of the part
he has in it. He either had to omit the incident
altogether or had to indicate his own presence, and we
are glad that he chose the latter course.

John writes only "his mother" and does not add
the name "Mary" as one might well expect; he did
the same in 2:1, etc., and in 6:42. This omission
seems significant as in a silent way indicating some
relationship between the family of John and that of
Jesus. Many think that Mary and Salome were
sisters, but no further evidence to this effect is at
hand. "His mother" is properly placed first in this
incident because it deals with her. The second woman
is Mary's sister, also called Mary, but she is distinguished from her as the wife of Clopas. One cannot make ἡ ἀδελφή mean sister-in-law, although this
is suggested in order to escape the strange fact of
having two sisters with the same name. Yet the
two women may not have had the same father and

mother, both being brought into the family from former marriages. Besides, many ancient texts have "Miriam" as the name for the mother of Jesus, and "Maria" as the name for her "sister." Speaking in general, the Greek genitive "of Clopas" may mean according to the connection "wife," "mother," or "daughter" of Clopas; here the latter two are excluded (R. 767). We know the names of her children (Matt. 27:56), and a woman of her age would not be designated by a reference to her father. The Greek genitive is constantly used where "wife" is the meaning. Eusebius reports from Hegesippus that Clopas was a brother of Joseph, the husband of the Virgin. A marginal note in one of the Syriac versions states in so many words that these two brothers married two sisters. We may shake our heads at this, but two brothers have not infrequently married two sisters. Clopas is identical with the Alpheus of the synoptists, for they make him the father of the same sons. A reason is demanded as to why this second Mary is designated so fully when she seems to have had no special prominence. But that is the very reason, and also because we have several Marys. Thus each needs clear identification. Matthew and Mark identify her by reference to her children, John by reference to her husband. John also indicates the reason for her presence when he says that she was "the sister of his mother." In this desperate hour this Mary stood by her suffering sister.

Matthew and Mark, who omit mention of the mother of Jesus, consider Mary Magdalene the leader of the women, much as Peter appears as the leader among the men, and therefore place her first among the women that stood "afar off." John properly places Jesus' mother first, and her sister next, and Mary Magdalene last. Other women, such as his own mother, he could pass over in silence, but hardly

Mary Magdalene, of whom he will also soon tell us how Jesus appeared to her after his resurrection. She has often been identified with the prostitute in the Pharisee Simon's house, Luke 7:37, etc., but contrary to all evidence. Asylums for fallen girls have been called "Magdalene Homes," but such naming casts a disgrace on this woman, which fact one can only deplore. The distinctive term "Magdalene" is usually derived from her original home, the town Magdala on the Sea of Galilee, Matt. 15:39; no other explanation has been found. We need not puzzle about the incompleteness of John's short list, for we repeatedly meet this phenomenon in the Gospel narratives. John permits only the narrative itself to indicate his own presence. From Luke 22:49 we learn that "all his acquaintance, and the women that followed him from Galilee, stood afar off, beholding these things." We are unable to say who they were. There must have been a few men among the number, one being John, but no one else of the Twelve was present. We have no hint that they drew close to the cross when John and Jesus' mother and a few other women made the venture.

Stricken and crushed with terrible grief, these few loving hearts, made bold in their timidity by their bleeding love, huddle beside the cross. Those painters err who make the cross high. The Savior's feet were easily embraced, being less than three feet from the ground. Jesus did not need to raise his voice in speaking to his mother and to John. The little group at the cross could hear him perfectly while those farther away did not need to understand.

26) **Jesus, therefore, when he saw his mother and the disciple standing by whom he loved, says to his mother, Woman, behold thy son! Then he says to the disciple, Behold, thy mother!** Jesus is fully conscious in spite of all that his body and his soul

had endured. He forgets, he omits nothing. It was, of course, God's own providence that provided this opportunity for Jesus to attend to this last filial duty and thus to fulfill to the uttermost the Fourth Commandment. As God shaped all things even in the midst of his enemies, so he also arranged this, that the mother of Jesus and a few others with John could come close to the cross at this important moment. He who is here bearing the sins of the whole world amid the most unspeakable personal suffering is, nevertheless, fully aware of what God is now providing for him. Amid severe suffering another person might have his whole mind turned in on himself; not so Jesus. Another, enduring great agony, might overlook an opportunity such as God presented to Jesus and too late think of how he might have used it; not so Jesus. Not with a desire for pity because of his own suffering does this son turn to his mother but in filial, sonlike care for her in her lonely state and suffering. Even now as he dies she is in his heart. Nothing more tender and touching is found in the Gospel story than this love of Jesus for his mother. Usually mother love is rated as the purest and strongest type of human love. The love of Jesus for his mother exceeds even all mother love. It is not true that John's Gospel describes Jesus only as the Son of God; it is full of the humanity of Jesus as well, a humanity that draws our hearts with its truth and its tenderness.

The present tense λέγει, used for greater vividness, is in effect an aorist and thus is to be construed with the aorist participle ἰδών, "having seen." Of course, Jesus saw the entire little group before him. When John writes that Jesus saw "his mother and the disciple standing by, whom he loved," we are to note, not only that Jesus sáw these two in particular but that his mind at once turned to what he wanted these

two to do. Note well: "his mother . . . the disciple whom he loved," the two who in human relationship were nearest to his heart. A holy, human
tenderness lies in these two names: she who once
bore him under her heart and ever bore him in love
within her heart — he whose head had lain next to
his heart and on his loving breast. On John's way
of designating himself, "the disciple whom Jesus
loved," see 13:23.

The perfect participle παρεστῶτα, "standing by," is
always used with a present meaning. This does not
mean merely that John stood beside the cross. Why
should that be said only with regard to John and not
equally with regard to Jesus' mother? Was not, in
fact, the entire little group standing by the cross?
and has this not already been stated in v. 25? "His
mother, and the disciple standing by" means that John
was standing by Jesus' mother. This is an intimate
touch in the narrative. Not beside any of the other
grief-stricken women was this beloved disciple standing but beside his beloved Master's mother. Why
beside her? Surely, not merely by accident as though
the persons in the group just happened to have placed
themselves thus. We have every reason to think that
Mary's sister helped to support her in this terrible
moment; and that the participle, which is used only
with regard to John, tells us that he, the only man in
the group, likewise supported the stricken mother in
her overwhelming grief.

The suffering of John was like that of Mary. These
two belonged together because in the death of Jesus
these two were losing something more than the rest.
Mary was losing her son, John the Master who loved
him beyond the rest. Neither Mary nor John would
ever have Jesus again as they once had had him in
tender, familiar, loving intercourse. Never would
Mary again embrace her son and lay her head upon

his breast; never would John again recline beside him on the same couch at table and be able to lay his head on Jesus' breast. Yes, John supported Mary, but as one who himself needed support just as she did. These two belonged together. In love nearest to Jesus, now that he dies, both are joined before him. And Jesus saw it, and his heart understood.

Alas, what has Roman Catholicism made of this scene! Some of it is like blasphemy of Christ in the very hour of his atoning death. Catholic books are full of this derogation of Christ and the exaltation of Mary. We are told that with her passion Mary comes to the aid of her son on the cross. Alone he could not have accomplished the task; he could never have borne the sins of the world and made atonement for them by himself. "The Mother of God" had to cooperate with the Son of God. This summarizes the Catholic teaching. It invents two mediators where God had only one. It robs Christ in order to deify and to glorify Mary. In doing this blasphemous thing it destroys the real atonement and invents another which does not atone. Simply to state these facts is to abhor them. There is *one* Mediator between God and man, the man Christ Jesus, I Tim. 2:5, 6.

No interval or hesitation ensue. The eyes of Jesus and of his mother meet, and these words come from her son's lips, "Woman, behold, thy son!" Wonderful brevity yet full sufficiency. In Jesus' death Mary loses an earthly son and gains another. In the highest filial love Jesus provides for the last days of his mother. He commits his mother to the care of one whom Jesus so loved that he could entrust to him this dearest charge.

That word "woman" has disturbed many. They hurry to assure us that the word means nothing dis-

respectful on Jesus' part, which, of course, is altogether true.   Yet when all has been said on this point,
"woman" is not identical with the inexpressibly tender
title "mother."   And Jesus does *not* here, even as he
did not in Cana, say "mother."   The marked difference remains and is fully intended by Jesus.   The
reason for his saying "woman" and not "mother" is
certainly not that he wished to avoid paining his
mother by using the tender name.   Nor is it that he
wished to avoid making known the presence of his
mother to the soldier guards; for they certainly
guessed that his words applied only to the woman
who was his mother.   The reason lies deeper.   Ever
since Jesus took up his work of redemption a new
relation to his mother took precedence over the old
relation of mere mother and son.   Jesus was still
Mary's son, but now she was to see in him also and
above all her Lord and Savior.   Once she had him
merely as her son to direct and to command him as
a mother, to obey her mother wishes, dependent on
her parental position.   This yielded to a far higher,
holier, and more blessed relation when that son of hers
began his mediatorial work to win eternal salvation
for her as well as for us all.   It was then that Jesus
said to her γύναι instead of μῆτερ.   Now on Calvary
he is completing that heavenly work.   And in that
work, not as a mere human son providing for his
mother, but as God's Son, her Lord and her Redeemer,
fulfilling for her and for us all the Fourth Commandment, he is making this last filial provision.   That is
why he again says "woman" and not "mother."   And
she who had all along understood understands now.
We hear no outcry from her, no heart-rending call,
"O my son, my son!"   II Sam. 18:33.   She is silent
in her grief — the true mother of this divine Son.

"Behold, thy son!" has been misunderstood to
mean, "Behold, *me*, thy son!"   Mary has enough to

bear; Jesus is not harrowing her feelings with such a word. This interpretation mars the entire act, for it makes the word of Jesus to John rather senseless. Nor do we have the accusative, "behold thy son," for *ὁ υἱός* is nominative. While *ἴδε* would be an imperative, *ἰδέ* or *ἰδού* is an interjection. The entire weight falls on "thy son" in the sense, "this is now thy son." Jesus leaves John as a substitute son to care for Mary. This is his last filial gift to his mother. John was even now doing a son's part for Mary; he is to go on doing that as long as Mary may need a son's care.

What has Roman Catholicism made of this word of the dying Savior? Like Pius IX., Jesus, too, we are told, by this word of his makes Mary the patroness of all Christians who are here represented by the disciple John. It was not Mary who needed John, but John and with him and in him all other Christians who needed Mary. One of these Mary worshippers writes that "in the person of John Mary receives all Christians as her children. And this capacity of Mary entitles us to the right and the trust, that we place all our interest in her hands." What a reversal of the facts! Had Jesus been dependent on Mary, and not she on him? Had she during his ministry provided for him, and not he for her? And since when is all Christendom represented in John? No; Jesus is not adding to the burdens of Mary, least of all a world-burden no human being can possibly bear. He is not deifying this "woman," nor making her do what he alone can do and does for us all. He is comforting his mother, unburdening her, providing for her the support she needs. This sacred word of Jesus cannot be wrested to convey self-conceived ideas. Its sense is crystal clear, and no man shall ever change it.

The word to John is the exact counterpart of the one to Mary; it conveys nothing new. Yet that is why it has been asked, why Jesus added this word. Was not the word to Mary enough? Did not John as well as Mary understand what the will of Jesus was? Would not John without the second word have obeyed the first word with alacrity? Already by his first word Jesus made John his adopted brother, his substitute, his administrator. Yet Jesus had good reason for adding his second word to John. Jesus is making his personal will and testament. Despite all its brevity that will and testament should mention each person to whom a bequest is made. Jesus is not merely by indirection or by an inference asking John to take charge of his mother. Jesus does not treat his beloved disciple in such a way. Therefore he speaks to John just as he has spoken to his mother. All are to know that it is John and John alone to whom this bequest of his mother is made.

Why did Jesus select John? Why could some of Mary's other relatives not have taken charge of her? This was altogether a matter for Jesus to decide, not for us to decide for him. These are highly personal matters, and Jesus made the best possible provision for his mother. John was nearest to Jesus' heart, and so the trust was laid upon him. But how about John's own mother and John's duty toward her? Those who raise this question can scarcely mean that Jesus had overlooked this point and that, while he acted filially toward his own mother, he was inducing John to act unfilially toward his mother. To think this would be to charge a fault against Jesus in this most sacred hour. No; love is not halved by thus adding objects of love. No child loves either parent less for being blessed with two.

27) Willingly John accepts his great Master's last will and testament. **And from that hour the dis-**

ciple took her to his own home. In the Greek the word
ὥρα does not always mean "hour," a period of sixty
minutes. In Matt. 24:36, "of that day and hour
knoweth no man," day is the date, and hour is time in
general. John intends to say that from that time
onward he took care of Mary. So we need not assume
that John at once took Mary away from Golgotha, as
some think, in order to spare her, so that she might
not witness the last agony and the actual death. **Mary
was not that kind of a mother.** As the Lord's hand-
maiden she was strong in spirit to bear whatever load
he laid upon her. By remaining she surely was much
as other mothers are.

What must we understand by εἰς τὰ ἴδια? Evidently
in domum suam, "to his own home," R. 691. It is
reported that John had a house at the foot of Zion hill
in Jerusalem, and that Mary lived there for eleven
years, and that only after her death did John go to
preach in the whole world. But another tradition tells
us that Mary died and was buried in Ephesus where
John afterward labored. Of course, for John to have
property of his own in Jerusalem would not conflict
with the practice of the first congregation in sharing
earthly possessions when this was needed. But all
the property of the Zebedee family seems to have been
located in Galilee. It is simplest and best to assume
that John took Mary to the home where he, his mother,
and his brother lived in Jerusalem, whether he owned
the home or not. When John left the city he took the
mother of Jesus with him. How long she lived and
where she died, no one knows. John perfectly fulfilled
the personal trust laid upon him by Jesus.

28) John now tells his readers exactly how Jesus
died. **After this Jesus, knowing that all things
have already been finished, in order that the Scripture might be accomplished, says, I thirst.** Matthew and Mark tell us that Jesus was given a drink,

but John alone informs us that Jesus asked for a drink and thust received it; he also relates why he asked, namely in order to die with a victorious shout. The sketch of the two synoptists is thus made a complete picture by John.

The phrase "after this" intends only to mark the fact that an interval occurred between what John has just narrated and what he now narrates. It is exactly like other phrases of this kind, all indicating the expiration of an interval. We thus decline to make the phrase mean, that after Jesus provided for Mary he knew that he had done everything to fulfill the Scripture prophecies concerning what he was to do. Providing for Mary was not the last work Jesus had to do to fulfill the Scriptures. More than three hours had passed since the word to Mary and to John had been spoken, during which time the hardest part of Jesus' task was accomplished. After this is over, Jesus asks for a drink. It is now that he knows that all is done, for εἰδώς is used as a present participle and thus is to be construed with the present λέγει.

What is it that Jesus now knows? This, that all things have now been finished or brought to a close in order that the Scriptures might be accomplished or brought to their goal. The keystone had been placed into the arch; that was the last act, and that act completed everything. This last act consisted of the bitter agony during the three hours of darkness when Jesus, covered with our guilt, experienced that even God turned his face from him. When that was over, the final act was finished, and by that final act all was accomplished that the Scripture had foretold concerning the earthly work of Jesus. Nothing more was needed, and thus nothing more had been foretold. Now Jesus could lie down to rest in death. We must see the difference between the synonymous verbs τελέω and τελειόω. The former means to bring to a τέλος, to a close; to finish by adding the last stroke with nothing more to be added. The latter means to bring to a goal, to reach successfully the mark that was set. The former refers only to the last thing; the latter to everything including the last, as constituting a successful accomplishment, a long, great work completely done. The R. V. marks the difference well: "to finish," "to accomplish." The A. V. is too inexact in translating, "that the Scripture might be *fulfilled*." The expression: ἵνα πληρωθῇ, is the common one, used again and again when some special prophecy is fulfilled. "In order that the Scripture might be accomplished" is used only here and means something far grander, namely that the entire Scriptures in all that they present concerning the earthly work of Jesus have now been turned into actuality, the work mapped out by Scripture is now a work actually accomplished. Nor can we say, as some do, that at least one more thing must be added, namely the actual death of Jesus; for death is now here, it is included in the finish and in the accomplishment — Jesus is even now dying. John tells us that Jesus knows that he is at the point of death, and describes this last act. Death does not imply only the instant when body and soul are sundered, it includes the whole act of sundering, most certainly those last moments when the dying man feels his soul slipping out of its mortal tenement. This wrong idea lies back of R. 898 who regards τετέλεσται as a futuristic present perfect equal to a future perfect, "shall have been finished." Here this is the perfect of a completed state (R. 895), exactly as in v. 30.

We cannot divide the sentence so as to read: that Jesus knows that all things have been finished, and then he says, "I thirst" in order that the Scriptures might be accomplished. This would be a contradiction — the last thing has been done, and yet one more needs to be done, one more prophecy needs to be fulfilled. And why say regarding this last prophecy that by it the Scripture is "accomplished"? The word would be out of place; it is entirely too vast. This also makes the ἵνα clause, placed as it is before λέγει, decidedly emphatic. Why such an emphasis? The defenders of this construction have no answer. And how is this prophecy fulfilled (we shall not say "accomplished") by Jesus' saying, "I thirst"? Psalm 22:15 calls for no cry from Jesus' lips. The fact that Jesus suffered dire thirst for many hours we know apart from his last cry, for nothing had passed his lips since the late evening before. Psalm 69:21 is out of the question, for it speaks of gall and vinegar, and Jesus received sour wine and no gall. This passage refers to the stupefying drink offered to Jesus when he was to be nailed to the cross; it was not intended to quench thirst but to help to dull the pain when the nails were driven through the hands and the feet. Men who were to be crucified were generally doped in this way in order to quiet their struggles during the ordeal. Every prophecy which can be referred to thirst has already been fulfilled by the fact of Jesus' thirsting, and yet the construction here called for places the fulfillment in the word of Jesus, "I thirst." This is so evident that some make this prophecy, which they say still requires fulfillment, the actual death of Jesus. This violates the words of John, for he wrote that Jesus said, "I thirst," not that he said, "I die."

Jesus says, "I thirst." Thirst was one of the excruciating agonies of the crucified. Jesus must have thirsted long before Golgotha was reached, and this cry of his body for moisture to slake its burning must have become terribly intensified after he hung upon the cross. Silently he had endured these pangs until now. Why had he not asked for drink ere this? And why does he ask now? In order to fulfill the prophecy, we are told. Yet no such prophecy exists. Others offer strange suggestions. The word "I thirst" is made allegorical: the physical thirst becomes a thirst of the soul of Jesus for the souls of men. Our reaction to this view is that in this solemn moment all allegorical fancies are absolutely out of place. Next is the symbolical interpretation. The vinegar offered to Jesus is made symbolic of the world's treatment of Jesus. Thus ungratefully, with nothing but miserable vinegar (some add the gall mentioned in the Psalm), were his burning lips moistened when in dying he asked for drink! No such symbolical meaning lies in the word "I thirst." If at this moment Jesus had desired to show the ungratefulness of the world toward him why should he have left out the gratitude of all his true followers and given us no final symbol of that? Symbolism is as much out of place as allegory.

Nor did Jesus wish to hasten his end by drinking vinegar. On the other hand, he was not asking for vinegar to lengthen his life. A few drops of this liquid upon scalded lips and a burning throat cannot possibly produce either of these effects. Some are greatly surprised that at this supreme moment Jesus should have indicated a physical desire — he who had set all such desires aside this long while! It is this surprise which leads to the so-called deeper interpretations. Those are right who agree that "I thirst" voices a purely physical desire. It is, indeed, true that now all is finished, the work is done, the battle over, the victory won. Think of some great general who never thought of hunger or of thirst during the long battle hours, but who, when at last the victory is won, again feels the natural cravings. But even this interpretation comes short. It is true that

Jesus feels himself sinking into unconsciousness and
therefore wishes to have his lips wetted. But he
desires far more than merely to die in full consciousness up to the last moment. "I thirst" is a request.
Jesus actually asks for drink. He wanted the vinegar. He is rallying his last strength. He does not
cry aloud, "I thirst"; he *says* this with what strength
he has. He wants his lips and his throat moistened
in order that he may do just what the synoptists report
that he does, namely utter a loud shout and thus die.
Even the centurion was astonished at this mode of
death. This clears up the synoptists who omit to state
how Jesus came to be offered that drink — he himself
had asked for it. John also makes plain that this
request and the actual death were separated by only
a few moments. Two more words followed, loud and
strong, and Jesus was dead.

29) **A vessel was lying there full of vinegar.**
Having, therefore, placed a sponge full of vinegar
around a hyssop, they brought it to his mouth. The
request of Jesus is fulfilled; he receives the drink
for which he asks. The Jews (οἱ λοιποί, Matt. 27:49)
try to stop the soldier who hurries to serve Jesus, but
he answers them almost with their own words
(Mark 15:36) and refuses to be stopped. We need
not trouble ourselves about the strange ideas which
some have attached to the presence of the vinegar,
the sponge, and the hyssop on Golgotha. They were
there for just what was now done with them. In their
raging thirst, men who were crucified cried for drink,
and the executioners used a sponge of vinegar on a
short rod to give them enough to moisten their lips.
The fact that this might prolong their lives need not
trouble us, for crucifixion was intended to be a long,
drawn-out torture. The ὄξος is the cheapest kind of
sour wine, commonly served to soldiers; and it was
entirely serviceable for the purpose here indicated, for

it does allay thirst. We need not doubt that Jesus knew that this sour wine was there and there for this purpose, and so made his want known. We have no reason whatever for special reflections in regard to the "vinegar."

Matthew and Mark report that one man gave Jesus the drink, while John uses the plural endings in the participle and in the main verb. Naturally one man performed the act; that others repeated it is unlikely and even unnecessary. This man must have been one of the four soldiers, for the vinegar, etc., belonged to them. John's plural is explained when we note that this soldier acted with the centurion's consent, who may even have bidden one of his men to act. The indefinite plural thus conveys the idea that the drink came from the soldiers; it was not merely the deed of one who was more tenderhearted than the rest. What the two synoptists call a reed John calls a hyssop, indicating, as in so many other instances, his presence as an eyewitness. This plant has stems about 18 inches in length, which proves the claim that the cross held the victim's body only as high as this stalk indicates. Symbolical ideas have been connected with this word "hyssop"; no symbolism is indicated but only the exactness of one who saw with his own eyes.

30) **When, therefore, Jesus took the vinegar he said, It is finished! and, having bowed his head, he gave up the spirit.** Jesus received the sour wine, which fact shows that "I thirst" was intended as a request. Then, without a pause he said, "It is finished!" From Matthew and from Mark we learn that Jesus cried with a loud voice. To aid him in this he had asked for the wine. These two evangelists record no words, but Luke reports that Jesus cried aloud, "Father, into thy hands I commend my spirit!" and, having said this, died. We need not

question that Luke records the last word uttered by Jesus. From John we learn that Jesus uttered another word just before the last one. He thus again adds to the older records. While John does not repeat what Luke reports, John's statement that Jesus gave up the spirit in a manner implies the last word as recorded by Luke, for Jesus gave up his spirit into his Father's hands even as his last word declared. It is natural, too, that one should commend his spirit to the hands of God only after he could truly say that his entire task had been finished. Thus the Son went home to the Father after doing that Father's will. No wonder his voice rose to its loudest pitch.

"It is finished!" Τετέλεσται, exactly as in v. 28, the perfect of a completed state, denotes an action brought to its termination, it is like a line that ends in a point ——————• Jesus speaks this word to his Father. He makes his report to the Father who sent him. Uttered with a loud voice, it is also intended for all men to hear. Recorded now in Scripture, it still rings out to all the world. Since the whole passion and death of Jesus were intended for us, why set up the contention that this conclusion is intended only for him and not also for us? The verb has no subject. What is it that is here brought to an end? Some think that Jesus has in mind his suffering, which, of course, in a way is true and quite obvious. But this cry cannot mean that Jesus is thinking only of himself and is glad that his pain now ceases. Some think of the ancient prophecies and their fulfillment, which, of course, in a way is also true (v. 28). This is better than the previous view, yet it still is indefinite, and other prophecies are still unfulfilled, namely the resurrection and the exaltation. Many are satisfied to say that the work or task of Jesus is concluded, or even that no further duty holds Jesus to life; this is equally indefinite. A word so important

cannot be explained by so general an interpretation.
The death of Jesus finishes his redemptive work, the
work of reconciliation and atonement. This specific
work is now brought to a close. The Lamb of God
has made his great sacrifice for the world. It is this
that is now done. Our great Substitute has paid the
great price of ransom, paid it to the uttermost farth-
ing. "It is finished" indeed! Others will yet preach
and teach, and Jesus will work through them; as
the King on David's throne his regal work will continue forever; but the redemptive shedding of his blood,
done once for all, is finished and stands as finished forever. Heb. 7:27; 9:12 and 26; Rom. 6:10.

John is satisfied with Luke's record of the final
word of Jesus and so now adds nothing more than
a record of the death itself: "and he bowed his head."
Until the last moment Jesus held his head erect; now
the muscles relax, the head drops forward upon the
chest. Some advance the symbolic fancy that the head
of Jesus inclined toward the side on which the penitent
malefactor hung; but this is fancy and nothing more.
The dropping forward of the head indicates death.
We have no right to assume an interval, a slow,
painful struggle, a gradual lessening of the breathing;
the spirit fled the instant the head dropped forward.

Luke has the single word ἐξέπνευσεν, for which John
writes παρέδωκε τὸ πνεῦμα, the exact counterpart of our
English translation, "he gave up his spirit" and a
reminder of the final word of Jesus with which he
commends his spirit into his Father's hands. All of
the evangelists use choice expressions for stating
the death of Jesus; none is content to say only that
"he died." They also refer to the spirit or πνεῦμα,
none only to the ψυχή, although dying can also be
expressed by using the latter. Jesus is true man and
thus had what is called ψυχή and πνεῦμα. These two
are the immaterial part of our being. This part may

be called by either term when nothing further is intended. But quite a difference may be made when ψυχή is used to designate our immaterial part in so far as it animates our material body and receives impressions from this body, while πνεῦμα is then reserved to indicate this same immaterial part in so far as it is open to a higher world and able to receive impressions from the Spirit of God. This distinction in the Greek terms is largely lost in the English where "soul" and "spirit" are more nearly alike. We at once see this when we note that the Greek derives its adjective ψυχικός from ψυχή, which adjective we are constrained to translate "carnal," for "soul" furnishes us no adjective to express the thought that our immaterial part is moved by the low influences of the body.

Man's personality resides in this immaterial part; his ἐγώ is in the soul or spirit. In Jesus this personality or ἐγώ was the Logos. The death of Jesus dare not be regarded as a separation of the Logos from the human nature of Jesus or from any part of that nature. The union of the Logos with the human nature, once entered into, remains absolutely intact and undisturbed ever after. That union was not made with only one part of the human nature, with only the human soul or spirit; it was a most wonderful and complete union with the entire human nature. In the death of Jesus his human soul or spirit was separated from his body just as this separation takes place in our death. The death of Jesus took place entirely in his human nature and in no way affected the union of the Logos with his human nature. In the sinless person of Jesus the spirit ruled absolutely; thus it is eminently fitting that John and the synoptists use Jesus' own words when they say that in dying he gave up his "spirit."

Certain older medical authorities have held the view that the death of Jesus was induced by a rupture of the walls of his heart, so that we might satisfy our sentimental feelings by saying that Jesus died of "a broken heart." Our latest and best authorities inform us that this is quite impossible. A lesion such as that could result only from a degeneration of the heart, and this occurs only in older persons where disease has left its effects. This covers also the tentative suggestion that perhaps some artery burst and caused death. Again John 10:17, 18 has been used to maintain the view that Jesus died, not from physical causes, but by a mere volition of his will. It requires but little reflection to see the untenableness of this conclusion. That passage deals with the entire action of Jesus in giving himself into death for us. This volition of his is apparent all along when he announces his passion and when he finally enters that passion and endures all its agonies. The death of Jesus is due to the physical effects of his suffering and his crucifixion. This alone is the cause assigned by the Scriptures. When the spirit left the body, Jesus died. Yet we must always conceive his actual death as one full of peace and joy. With the hard and bitter work done, Jesus goes to the Father. Like a tired child he lays his head to rest in his Father's arms.

The spirit of Jesus did not enter *Sheol* or hades, an intermediate place between heaven and hell, the fabled place of the dead, and remain there until the resurrection. This notion is comparable to the idea of certain older theologians that the soul of Jesus went down into hell and there suffered the tortures of the damned. Jesus himself tells us that his spirit went into his Father's hands, and this is heaven. John 17:5 calls it the glory which the Son had from eternity. The paradise into which the penitent malefactor's soul passed to be with Jesus is heaven, the eternal abode of God and his blessed angels and saints.

31) **The Jews, therefore, since it was Preparation Day, in order that the bodies might not remain on the cross on the Sabbath, for great was the day of that Sabbath, requested Pilate that their legs might be broken, and that they might be removed.** Again John contributes an episode that is in no way touched upon by the synoptists and one that is noteworthy in every way. "The Jews" are, of course, the Sanhedrists, probably a delegation of them. The natural way in which to read οὖν is to have it introduce an inference from what precedes: Jesus having died, the Jews take steps to have all the bodies removed from the crosses before sundown. The view that the Jews had left Golgotha some time before Jesus died, and that they thus hoped to have the legs of Jesus, too, broken, but that John tells us that they were frustrated in this by the sudden nature of Jesus' death, is incompatible with οὖν. So also is the view that the request of the Jews was made when the procession first started for Golgotha from the Prætorium. Jesus died about three o'clock. The Jews had gained their great end. And now they think of the approaching Sabbath. They do not want the bodies to remain upon the crosses on the Sabbath day, namely the dead body of Jesus and the still living bodies of the malefactors, no matter when death should come to these. Ordinarily the Romans left the bodies of criminals on the cross until they rotted, although under Tiberius, the present emperor, the relatives might obtain them for burial. The Jews were actuated by their law, Deut. 21:22, etc., which directed that such bodies should be taken down on the day of execution because they were accursed and were not to defile the land. This referred to men who were hung and thus were already dead. But the

Jews would certainly apply this law also to men who had been crucified in the Roman fashion; and here was one who was already dead, and two others, both accursed although not as yet dead.

In the present instance, however, the Jews had a still more potent reason. This was Friday, hence "Preparation Day," i. e., the day before the Sabbath, called παρασκευή because everything had to be prepared in advance before the Sabbath began in the evening when no more work like buying, cooking food, cleaning, etc., could be performed. This was one consideration. It was augmented by another, namely that the approaching Sabbath was a day that was "great" beyond an ordinary Sabbath. This was the Sabbath of the Passover week, which was thereby lifted into a sacredness that was above all other Sabbath days. On the question as to whether this great Sabbath was the first day of the Passover, the day on which the Passover lamb was eaten, see the discussion on 18:28, "might eat the Passover." Thus once more the Jews find themselves compelled to make a request (ἠρώτησαν, with all due respect) of Pilate.

Non-final ἵνα states what they ask: "that their legs might be broken, and that they might be removed." The breaking of the legs is the so-called *crurifragium*, a cruel hastening of death, by its very brutality in no way lessening the original punishment. The form κατεαγῶσιν, although it is a subjunctive (second passive from κατάγνυμι) has an augment, R. 1212, also 365. The breaking of the legs might not at once induce death, but the Jews, no doubt, hoped that the sight of the suspended bodies would at least not meet the eyes of beholders when the Sabbath dawned. From Mark 15:43, etc., we gather that the Jews had not informed Pilate of the early death of Jesus. This implies that Pilate thought that he was ordering the breaking of Jesus' legs.

32) **The soldiers, therefore, came and broke
the legs of the first and of the other who was crucified with him. But having come upon Jesus, when
they saw that he was dead already, they did not
break his legs; on the contrary, one of the soldiers
with a spear pierced his side, and immediately there
came out blood and water.** In this most remarkable manner the body of Jesus is preserved from
mutilation. Pilate seems to have issued the order
without hesitation. His messenger informs the centurion, and the soldiers do their awful work. John
saw it performed, first on the one, then on the other
malefactor. "They came" is only circumstantial, as
an eyewitness would tell the details: "they came" cannot mean that new men had been sent by Pilate,
who carried clubs for this work. For "the soldiers"
are the ones we have met throughout the preceding
narrative. John tells the facts as he saw them. Why,
since Jesus' cross stood between those of the malefactors, did the soldiers pass by his cross and go from
the one malefactor to the other? Why do they leave
Jesus as the last one? Already this is strange. These
soldiers do not seem to be so eager to carry out their
orders upon this strange man on the central cross.
Various surmises are offered. We think that the centurion directed the soldiers; he was deeply impressed
(Luke 23:47), and under his direction Jesus was to
be last.

33) John describes how they now came "upon
Jesus," (ἐπί), paused, examined him, and "saw that
he was dead already," the perfect participle modifying
αὐτόν after a verb of seeing: "him having died,"
R. 1041, etc.; ὡς is almost causal, "since," R. 963. A
brief consultation ensued. Usually subalterns use no
discretion of their own. Orders are orders, and thus,
whether he were dead or alive, the blows would have
crushed the legs of Jesus, too. But matters did not

proceed so in this case.   We cannot think, as has been suggested, that the soldiers desisted because the work was hard and they wished to spare themselves.   These men were not tired even if they had crushed the legs of the malefactors completely.   The centurion must have stayed their hands.   And so the legs of Jesus were not broken.   God watched over his Son.   At this point he called a halt.

34)   Remarkable as already this is, the next act is still more remarkable, and the two combined, transpiring before the very eyes of John, are overwhelming in their significance.   Without orders from Pilate, on their own volition, the soldiers pierce the side of Jesus instead of breaking his legs.   An act as unusual as this must have been performed by one of the four soldiers who crucified Jesus upon the order of the centurion.   A spear was used because this was the more suitable weapon for such a thrust. The verb νύσσειν is strong; Homer often uses it to indicate stabbing to death.   While John does not say which side was pierced, we cannot but think that it was the left side, and that not merely because of the position of the soldier handling the lance but because of the intention to pierce the heart.   For most certainly the thrust was made, not in order to see whether there was still life in the body, but in order to place death beyond the least possible doubt.   The supposition that also the malefactors were pierced through the heart, on the assumption that crushing their legs with clubs would not promptly kill them, must be rejected.   John relates all the details, that first one malefactor and then the other had his legs crushed; in their case this was all.   There is a strong impression that Jesus was treated in a way that was altogether exceptional, both in escaping the crushing and in receiving the spear thrust.   Here something occurred that no man could have anticipated or

even thought possible. John, however, saw it with his own eyes.

"Immediately there came out blood and water." The history of the exegesis of this brief statement would fill many pages. Blood and water afford an opportunity for bringing in symbolism of one kind or the other, and the opportunity has been used to the full. Medical authority also steps in with its declaration that blood and water could not flow forth from a wound such as this after death had set in. This makes many certain that John intends to report a sign or miracle. Then comes the debate about whether blood and water came out together at the same time, or first blood and then water, and whether this was real water or a colorless fluid, and whether it gushed out in a stream or was small in quantity. A study of the text reveals that as far as John in concerned he treats as significant the fulfillment of two prophecies, the one that no bone of the body of Jesus was broken, the other that Jesus was pierced — and that is all. Say what we will regarding the blood and the water, John mentions only this effect of the spear thrust. What *he* thought this phenomenon implied or proved he does not say. We have no right to shift the emphasis of his account to the blood and the water, he does not place it there. This is certain, the spear thrust, followed by the issue of blood and water, establishes also in John's mind the fact of Jesus' death. By this thrust all doubt is removed that Jesus was merely unconscious, that life could still remain in his body, and that he did not actually and truly arise from the dead on Sunday morning. Jesus was dead beyond question. The reason for John's emphasis on this fact is found in the heretical teaching against which already 1:14 is directed, the Docetic notion that Jesus had not become flesh, that, therefore, he had not already died and had not actually arisen from the dead. The form of this teaching as represented by Cerinthus, as well as the Judaistic form reported by Ignatius, or any other such form of doctrine, is here squarely denied by reporting the actual facts, which settle the matter that Jesus was dead beyond all question. As far as present medical conclusions are concerned, these are quite useless regarding the point of the water and the blood. We know from Acts 2:27 that no form of corruption touched the body of the God-man. The ordinary processes of decay never appeared in that holy body. Deductions drawn from observations of our dead bodies cannot be applied to the fluids of the dead body of him who knew no sin.

35) **And he that has seen has borne testimony; and genuine is his testimony. And that one knows that he says things true, in order that you, too, may believe.** So weighty is what John reports that he, too, now does something entirely exceptional. No evangelist, and not even John in the rest of his Gospel, breaks the narrative to address his readers personally and to assure them in regard to his testimony. Yet John now does this. It ought to go without saying that he refers to himself when he writes, "he that has seen." John loves these perfects which carry the past acts down to their present effects. This perfect means that what John once saw is still, as it were, vividly before his eyes although many years have passed. With this perfect the next accords: "he has borne testimony," namely right here in this record, and this testimony, once borne, now stands indefinitely and speaks on and on. We know that John never mentions himself or any member of his family or wider relationship by name. He always uses the third person and even this only when literally compelled to do so. Yet critics have used the present passage in their efforts to deny John's authorship

of this Gospel.   Here the supposed writer forgets himself in an impersonation of John and speaks of John
without detecting that his impersonation is thus betrayed.   Those who will may believe in such a forger.
We cannot, of course, share their views.

"Genuine is his testimony," ἀληθινή, the adjective
being emphatic.   His testimony is competent, based
on personal vision, not on what others have seen and
told him.   Any court would accept his testimony.

The battle about the next statement will, no doubt,
continue indefinitely: "and that one knows that he
says things true," ἀληθῆ, things really so, not mere
imaginings or falsifications.   Who is referred to by
ἐκεῖνος?   Is it John himself or a second witness corroborating John?   The word itself can be understood
in either way.   Sometimes it implies a contrast with
another, yet often it does not.   A case in point for
the latter is 9:37; R. 707 presents his personal opinion
as far as the language is concerned.   B.-D. 291, 6
falls back on textual criticism, as though this makes
it uncertain whether John wrote v. 35; but the textual
evidence is solid for the genuineness of v. 35, the only
variant reading of the verse amounts to nothing.
This means that no one has really been able to glean
anything decisive from the words as they stand.   We
must fall back on other considerations.   John has
made the matter one of testimony and has shown that
his testimony is competent.   If by ἐκεῖνος he refers
to himself, he would appeal for the truth of his testimony only to his own consciousness that he is indeed
stating the truth.   But this would add nothing whatever to his testimony, for who would think of charging him with something that he feels is not true, or
that, to say the least, is doubtful to his own mind?
He has shown us that in the case of Jesus himself,
when it comes to testimony, Jesus offered more than
his own word although he knew his own testimony

to be true. Jesus appeals to the corroborating testimony of the Baptist (5:32, etc.), of his works (5:36; 14:10), and of his Father in the Scriptures (5:37, etc., 8:18). Can John do less when he appears as a witness? Can he exempt himself from this essential requirement in regard to testimony, that whatever he testifies must be corroborated and supported by another witness in order to evoke credence?

It is thus that ἐκεῖνος comes to refer to a second witness, who indeed knows that what John has here testified is true and a statement of the facts. John might have in mind the thought that this other is God himself, and an appeal to him would be proper; for John at once quotes two Scripture passages which might be regarded as God's corroborating testimony. Yet thus far in the narrative God has not been mentioned in any way while, on the other hand, Jesus has appeared as the supreme person. In addition, ἐκεῖνος is repeatedly used by John without an antecedent as an emphatic designation for Jesus: "HE" (I John 2:6; 3:3, 5, 7, 16; 4:17), much as others used the word during the lifetime of Jesus (17:11; 9:28; 19:21). So it is Jesus to whom John appeals as corroborating his witness as being true. Even in III John 12 Demetrius has testimony from more than one source; and when John there says "we, too, testify," he even adds to this, "thou knowest that our testimony is true."

The purpose clause, "in order that you, too, may believe," is best construed with the verb "says"; the verb "has borne testimony" is too far away. The aorist subjunctive πιστεύσητε (not the present, which some texts have) implies definite and final believing. The present πιστεύητε would speak of only continued believing which goes on without disturbance. John is writing to those who already believe; he addresses them personally, "you, too." They are to believe just as John himself does. The verb, however, has no object but is used in a broad way regarding faith in general and is not restricted to the exceptional facts John has just stated. His genuine and truthful testimony regarding the death of Jesus and regarding what occurred with his body has as its purpose the enduring faith of the entire church. As John writes he thinks of himself as being present in the congregation of believers who hear these words read, and thus the personal note creeps in. He does the same in 20:31, where his purpose is more fully stated: "in order that you may believe that Jesus is the Christ, the Son of God," etc.

36) **For these things occurred in order that the Scripture might be fulfilled, A bone of him shall not be shattered. And again another Scripture says, They shall look on him whom they did pierce through.** So many hinge the solemn assurance of v. 35 on the blood and the water as though this is the thing John wants us to believe above all else. Yet beyond the mere mention of blood and water John has nothing further to say about blood and water. "These things," he tells us, refer to the literal fulfillment of two Scripture passages, one regarding the fact that not a bone of Jesus' body should be shattered, the other regarding the piercing of his body. John employs the regular formula for introducing Scripture quotations: "in order that the Scripture might be fulfilled." This remarkable fulfillment of Scripture is to lend abiding support to our faith.

"A bone of him shall not be shattered," Exod. 12:46; also Num. 9:12. In the case of the typical paschal lamb no bone was to be broken. It was not to be treated as an ordinary animal that was slaughtered for ordinary food and thus cut up and portioned out. No part of it was to be carried from one house to another, nor was any portion that might be left over to be eaten later like other meat; it was to be burnt before morning. All these directions, in particular the one to leave the lamb entire and thus to roast it on a spit, not to cut, boil, or prepare it in ways that required sundering, disjoining, or breaking the bones, lifted the paschal lamb above all other sacrifices, and this was done in order that it might in a special manner serve as a type of Jesus. How strikingly the antitype matched the type appears at the critical moment when all ordinary expectations would lead us tc expect the legs of Jesus to be broken — but they were left unbroken. John places the type and the antitype side by side in order that, seeing what he saw, we, too, may believe.

In the face of 1:29, and I Cor. 5:7 it is in vain to reject the references to Exodus and to Numbers and to point to Ps. 34:20, or even to add the passage from the Psalm. The Psalm refers to the godly man who is still in this life not to Jesus who has already been slain by violence. The Psalm also lacks the words ὀστοῦν and αὐτοῦ. And no reason can be assigned why the Mosaic references are not the correct ones.

37) The second prophecy, Zech. 12:10, John translates from the Hebrew, discarding the inexact LXX which has "pierced through" mean only mistreat or insult. The Hebrew *daqar* means to stab to death. In the words of the prophet it is Yahweh himself who is pierced, and the piercing is mortal, for those who pierced Yahweh shall mourn as one mourns for an only son, and that his firstborn. Jesus, as Jahweh or God's Son, was thus pierced, actually pierced through the heart with a spear. While this gashing with a spear did not in itself cause Jesus' death, he being already dead, it was certainly part of the death tragedy, an absolutely deadly wound. The prophet does not mention the weapon, but this does not entitle us to call the wound made by the weapon

only an individualizing feature; on the contrary, this
mortal wound was the exact and specific fulfillment of
the prophecy. Those who had only the prophecy
might wonder how Yahweh could be stabbed to death;
they might, following their reason alone, consider
this only an extravagant figure of speech for most
painfully hurting the feelings of Yahweh. This seems
to be the thought of the LXX when they translated
the Hebrew verb κατορχεῖσθαι, "to insult." But the
moment the fulfillment appears beside the prophecy,
all is clear: the incarnate Son of God was pierced
to death at the instance of the Jews themselves. The
Roman hand that wielded the spear is really the hand
of the Jews who brought Jesus to the cross and wanted
his body taken down from the cross that very day.
Even then every ordinary expectation would have been
that Jesus would suffer on the cross for at least a
couple of days, or that he would have been killed like
the malefactors by the shattering of his legs and his
thighs. Instead of that he dies after only six hours,
no bone is broken, and a spear pierces his side!

John's interest is centered on the piercing of Jesus'
side, and this as a support for our faith. He is here
not concerned with the other verb, "they shall look,"
and with the fulfillment which this shall attain. Generally, however, this point is also discussed. Seeing
they have pierced Yahweh, Zechariah says, the nation
in all its parts shall mourn with the most bitter
mourning as at the death of one's firstborn. When
shall this be, and what is the nature of this mourning?
The fulfillment appears in Matt. 24:30 and in Rev. 1:7.
The mourning which the prophet describes is hopeless — with the death of an only son, the firstborn,
all is lost. This the Jews shall realize too late, namely when the Son returns to judgment. "They shall
look on him whom they pierced through" means that
they shall do this too late. Many, however, hold the

view that this look and its resultant mourning signify repentance. They see the fulfillment beginning already in Luke 23:48, in the 3,000 believers at Pentecost, and in all the further conversions of Jews on through the centuries. Millennialists, of course, add the final conversion of the Jews as a nation when the expected millennium arrives. Often this repentant mourning is combined with the mourning of unbelief at the time of the final judgment. The author formerly presented this view in *The New Gospel Selections*, 473. Some even refer to the blood and the water as streams of grace. The Scriptures, however, do not thus combine two opposite types of mourning, one progressing through the ages, the other confined to the judgment. Matt. 24:30 and Rev. 1:7 seem to be quite decisive. As far as repentance is concerned, Zechariah 13:8, 9 restricts this to a remnant of the Jews. In 13:1 he reveals the "fountain" of grace that shall be opened for repentance. And this deliverance of the remnant is not in any sense described as a mourning.

38) John now proceeds to narrate the burial of Jesus, which the synoptists had also done quite fully. But John adds the part which Nicodemus played, and he explains how the body came to be placed into Joseph's tomb, this being quite near to Golgotha. **Now after these things Joseph of Arimathæa, being a disciple of Jesus, yet having kept himself hidden on account of the fear of the Jews, requested Pilate that he might take away the body of Jesus; and Pilate gave permission.** Joseph was rich (Matt. 27:57), a noble, godly man (Mark 15:43; Luke 23:50), a Sanhedrist, opposed to the action of the body to which he belonged (Luke 23:51). He is named according to his home town in order to distinguish him from other Josephs: "of Arimathæa," which is Rama. The section in which it is located was originally a part of Samaria but was transferred to Judea,

which explains Luke's: "a city of the Jews." Like Matthew, John describes this man as "a disciple of Jesus," yet as one who up to this moment had hidden his discipleship, κεκρυμμένος, "having kept himself hidden" as to his inner conviction. And this "on account of the fear of the Jews," the fear which they inspired (7:13; 9:22; 20:19) with their hostility to Jesus and their threat of expulsion from the synagogue of any who confessed Jesus.

This man now does an astounding thing: he suddenly casts his fear and cowardice to the winds, boldly goes in to Pilate, and asks to be permitted to take and to bury the body of Jesus. And this bold and courageous confession of his is now made after Jesus has died on the cross of shame! When all the eleven but John had fled, when all who had believed and confessed were giving up their faith (Luke 24:21), this man's faith rises out of its secrecy with full power and heroism! Jesus dies, but the malefactor believes and confesses, the very centurion under the cross does the same, and this rich, high, noble Sanhedrist joins them. His action is his confession, speaking more loudly than words. Joseph thus becomes God's instrument in preserving the body of his Son from being cast into a felon's grave, in giving it fitting burial, and in thus preparing for the resurrection of that body. "With the rich in his death," Isa. 53:9, is now being fulfilled.

The Jews had already secured an order from Pilate regarding the removal of the bodies from Golgotha. But this pertained to the coming Sabbath. The order had reached the centurion who also had begun its execution. When Matthew and Luke tell us that Joseph went to Pilate (προσελθών), he must have gone from Golgotha. We may take it that the Jews went to Pilate when Jesus dropped his head forward and died; and that Joseph hurried to Pilate after the soldiers had broken the legs of the malefactors and plunged the spear into Jesus' side. Some think that a delay ensued at this point because the soldiers would wait until the two malefactors actually died, since they could not be taken down before that time. Yet Jesus was dead, and one may suppose that the soldiers would begin with him, take his body down and carry it to the pit to be put out of sight. So we assume as being most likely that Joseph spoke to the centurion of his intention to secure the body of Jesus for burial, and thus the soldiers waited in regard to Jesus until Joseph returned. The soldiers had time enough. A man of such prominence as Joseph would easily gain their consent. We even know what the centurion thought of Jesus (Luke 23:47) ; he would be only too glad to accede to Joseph's request. The selfish motive that the soldiers would be relieved of removing Jesus' body may be left out of consideration.

Joseph actually enters the Prætorium and makes his request of Pilate. It is usually assumed that by this act, which was so different from that of the high priests who feared the ceremonial pollution of entering a Gentile abode, Joseph broke completely with his Jewish religion, but this deduction is too strong. The Jews avoided this pollution only in order to be able to eat the *Chagiga* on Friday afternoon; see 18:28. Joseph intended to bury Jesus, would thus not eat this sacrificial meal this afternoon, and would be made unclean by helping to handle the dead body of Jesus, if, indeed, his request should be granted. Pilate was ready enough to grant Joseph's request. It was no exceptional favor, for the Romans quite generally allowed the relatives and the friends of men who had been executed to bury their bodies if they so desired. But Pilate was surprised to hear from Joseph that Jesus was already dead. He had not heard it from the high priests who also would not have told him.

Pilate makes certain of the fact (Mark 15:44) and then gives the body of Jesus to Joseph. The ἵνα clause is non-final and simply states what Joseph requested. When Mark writes (15:43) that Joseph "dared" (τολμήσας) to go in to Pilate, he refers, not to the pollution this entailed, nor to any danger from Pilate, but to the hatred this act of one of their number would arouse among the Sanhedrists. But God sustained Joseph and did not let his courage fail.

From the Prætorium Joseph does not at once hurry out to Golgotha. Mark tells us that he bought linen for the body and so came again to Golgotha. This was easy to do, for he may not even have had to go out of his way to make the purchase, readily finding a shop where linen strips for burial purposes were always on sale. Let us note that Joseph bought only the linen. **Accordingly he came and took away his body.** This means that on Joseph's return to Golgotha it was he who took charge of affairs. This is most likely the reason why all the synoptists report at length who Joseph was and what he did and omit mention of Nicodemus. He must have been a masterful person. Joseph was not alone. The synoptists speak of the women, and Matthew and Mark name some of them. Enough friendly hands were present to take the body down. How this was done we have no means of knowing. It was done as gently as possible. Perhaps the cross was raised from its socket in the rocky soil, gently lowered to the ground, and then the body removed from the cross. Did the soldiers help? Some think they did. The centurion was certainly ready to assist. Perhaps the cross was left in place while the body was removed. Then means must have been at hand to reach the crosspiece, and tools, with which to draw the nails that held the hands. We are left to surmise.

39) **And there came also Nicodemus, he who at the first came to him at night, bringing a mixture of myrrh and aloes, about a hundred pounds.** The sequence in the narrative would indicate that Nicodemus arrived on the scene when the body had already been removed from the cross. John 3 has already introduced Nicodemus, and 7:50 has again done so. As in 7:50, so now again Nicodemus is identified as the man who at the first came to Jesus at night. Here is a duplicate to Joseph, another Sanhedrist, made bold by the death of Jesus to show his true color at last. Now when all seems forever lost he, too, reveals himself. He came with a supply of myrrh and aloes. We cannot think that he turned up entirely unexpectedly with just these burial requirements. The picture so often drawn of him and of Joseph, the two now meeting with mutual surprise on Golgotha, each now discovering the other's secret, cannot be correct. Joseph bought only the linen, Nicodemus brought only the spices. This indicates a mutual understanding: the two had arranged what each should bring, otherwise either or both would have provided all that was to be used. The linen would have been considered insufficient without the spices, and the spices would have been useless without the linen. The mutual surprise must be dated earlier. Nicodemus was present on Golgotha hours before this; he left with Joseph after Jesus had died, each with the understanding as to what he was to buy.

Myrrh was used in liquid as well as in powdered form. Mary has the liquid (see 12:3), Nicodemus the powder. It was made of the aromatic gum resin, exuding from the gray odorous bark of the *Balsamodendron myrrha*; it was also used extensively by the Egyptians for burial purposes. Mixed with the myrrh was aloe, the Hebrew *ahalim,* a powdered wood, most highly prized for the delightful odor which it releases when the wood decays. The most valuable variety of aloe is grown in India. The astounding thing is the quantity of this mixture brought by Nicodemus, about a hundred pounds. Judas should have been there to estimate the price. It has been well said that Jesus received a royal burial. How did Nicodemus carry such a load that distance, he being an old man? But we have so many questions to which answers are denied. Perhaps the merchant who sold that expensive quantity of spices to Nicodemus sent bearers to deliver the load to Golgotha.

40) **They, therefore, took the body of Jesus and bound it with linen bands, together with the spices, as the custom is for the Jews to bury.** Compare the remarks on Lazarus, 11:44. It was impossible to wash and to anoint the body under the circumstances on Golgotha. Perhaps some of the sour wine of the soldiers was secured for removing the blood and for cleansing the wounds. At Bethany Mary had anointed Jesus beforehand for his burial (Mark 14:8), having grasped the fact that his enemies would slay him, and that then anointing would be impossible. With the body itself prepared as well as this could be done, the friends of Jesus — John now uses plural verbs — now wrap it with the ὀθόνια, the bands of fine linen brought by Joseph. As the bands of linen were passed around the limbs and around the body again and again, the powdered mixture of myrrh and aloes was strewn in with generous hand. Some think that a portion remained to be strewn in the tomb where the body was laid, but no one can possibly know. For the sake of his Gentile readers John adds the remark that the method pursued was that customary to the Jews.

41) **Now in the place where he was crucified there was a garden, and in the garden a new tomb,**

**in which no one was yet laid.   There, then, because
of the Preparation of the Jews, since the tomb was
nearby, they laid Jesus.**   The body was ready for
burial, but where should it be laid?   Close to Golgotha,
in a garden — as John alone reports — in a quiet,
secluded place, a tomb was waiting, than which none
better could have been found.   It was entirely new, so
new that no dead body had ever occupied it.   Matthew
informs us that this tomb belonged to Joseph.   He
must have constructed it for his own family.   Eagerly
he now offers it for the body of Jesus.   John does not
say that the tomb belonged to Joseph; what he
emphasizes is its nearness to Golgotha.   The friends
of Jesus were pressed for time; the burial had to be
completed before sundown; the body could not be taken
a great distance.   So this tomb was chosen.   The fact
that John omits mention of the ownership and remarks
only on the nearness of the tomb, has been termed a
contradiction with Matthew who does the reverse.
We are told that if Joseph owned the tomb, it would
have been improper for John to omit a statement of
this fact.   So Matthew must be wrong.   Some other
friend of Jesus owned this tomb in the garden; who
this may have been we are left to guess.   But are
we to imagine that these friends of Jesus simply appropriated a tomb without the owner's consent, friend
of Jesus though he might be?   John evidently intends
to supplement the record of Matthew by telling us
that Joseph's tomb was chosen for Jesus, not because
it was Joseph's, but because it was nearby.   Here was
consent, availability, and much besides, leaving no
question of choice.

    A new tomb, "in which no one was laid" ($\dot{\epsilon}\tau\dot{\epsilon}\theta\eta$;
some read $\tau\epsilon\theta\epsilon\iota\mu\dot{\epsilon}\nu o\varsigma$), where no decay or odor of death
has yet entered — this was a fitting place for the body
of Jesus which no corruption or decomposition dared
to touch.   Here his holy body could have sweet rest,

all its dreadful, painful work done. In a garden
man lost life, in a garden life would be restored to
man, life and immortality. Jesus borrows a tomb.
Sinful men construct tombs or graves for themselves;
they must have them for their bodies. Jesus was not
intended for a tomb. He needs one only on our
account, and only until the third day. Luther writes:
"As he has no grave, for the reason that he will
not remain in death and the grave; so we, too,
are to be raised up from the grave at the last day
through his resurrection and are to live with him
in eternity."

42) "The Preparation of the Jews" signifies Friday; compare v. 31, and v. 14. The μνημεῖον (Mark:
μνῆμα), sepulcher or tomb, is often misconceived. The
recently discovered "Garden Tomb," now to be seen
just outside of the walls of the present Jerusalem in
a secluded spot below a skull-shaped hill, corresponds
in every detail to the data furnished by the Gospels.
It is as an ample chamber, hewn out of the solid cliff
of rock, the face of which is smooth and perpendicular.
The floor is not sunken, does not need to be. It is a
rich man's tomb, for the door admits one to an ante-
chamber, and the main part has only three places for
bodies, on the floor, along the three sides, the fourth
side fronting the vestibule. Ample space was used;
the owner could afford to have all this space hewn
out. The tomb is new. Only one place for a body is
finished, the one toward the cliff itself. This is a boxlike place, and on its floor the stone is hewn out a
little lower, thus outlining the form of the body, head
and all. This is finished and might receive a body
today. Strange to say, the other two places for
bodies are not yet completely hewn out. The tomb
is so new that it is not yet finished. If, indeed,
this is Joseph's tomb, he never used it after he gave
it for the burial of the body of Jesus. At the foot-

end of the boxlike finished place and likewise at the headend where the next boxlike place is situated opposite the vestibule, the stone is left thick enough to afford a seat, so that an angel could sit, "one at the head, and the other at the feet, where the body of Jesus had lain" (20:12), and the latter would even be "sitting on the right side" (Mark 16:5) as one enters the vestibule. These heavier rock sections across the footend and on the left of the headend are still intact, while the thinner wall between them, shutting in the body, is broken down. One feels compelled to say: if this is not the actual tomb in which Jesus was laid, it duplicates it in every respect. So many fake sites are shown in the Holy Land that to view a site like this leaves an unforgettable impression.

CHAPTER XX

6. The Linen Wrappings — Empty! 20:1-10

Those who deny the bodily resurrection of Jesus have arrayed against them not only the four evangelists but the entire New Testament, plus the prophecies of the Old. They are answered in the most decisive way by Paul, first, on the fact of the resurrection, in I Cor. 15:3-11, and, secondly, on the significance of a denial of the resurrection, in v. 12-19. If Christ is not risen from the dead, we have no Christianity, no Christian faith and hope, and no Christian Church in any sense of the word; for then we have no Christ, no Redeemer, no Savior, and no Lord.

John, of course, assumes that his readers know the accounts of the synoptists. What he himself adds is almost throughout new material, hence of supreme value on that account. He writes with exceptional detail and great vividness; R. 868 draws special attention to the tenses employed in the entire twentieth chapter. As regards alleged disagreements between John and the synoptists, these can be satisfactorily explained. Careful reading removes most of them. The few difficulties that remain are due to our ignorance of the full details of the story; and this, in turn, is due to the plain fact that each of the evangelists presents only a part of the story, so that we must piece their testimony together. In doing this we may at times be puzzled, and even make mistakes, but the truth of all that is offered us by the evangelists remains beyond question. Some may deny the latter, yet doubt and denial alter no facts. It is easier to believe every word of the Gospels than to believe the statements of the critics who find contradictions and discrepancies.

1) **Now on the first day of the week Mary Magdalene goes early, it still being dark, to the tomb and sees that the stone has been taken away from the tomb.** A continuative δέ simply proceeds with the narrative. The Jews had no names for the weekdays and therefore designated them with reference to the Sabbath, thus τῇ μιᾷ (ἡμέρᾳ) τῶν σαββάτων would be "on the first (day) with reference to the Sabbath," i. e., the first that follows the Sabbath. The plural σάββατα, however, may mean either the Sabbath day, designated by a plural like the festivals in order to include all that belongs to the festive celebration; or an entire week, a length of time bounded by two Sabbaths. Thus we may here translate, "on the first day of the week." Since John wrote for Greek readers, the latter translation seems preferable. Luke has "very early in the morning," Mark, "at the rising of the sun"; while John writes, "early, it still being dark," literally, "darkness still being" (a genitive absolute). All three are correct. The women left home early while it was yet dark and arrived at the tomb at dawn. Here some find the first contradiction. We are told that Matthew writes ὀψὲ σαββάτων, "late on the Sabbath" (R. V.), "in the end of the Sabbath" (A. V.), and the Moffatt commentary, "at the close of the Sabbath." This would be late on Saturday before sunset. But only in classical Greek does ὀψέ mean "late"; in the Koine it means "long after," *erst nach* (Zahn); Mark, "when the Sabbath was passed." Matthew himself at once adds: "as it began to dawn toward the first day of the week." Are we to think that Matthew contradicts himself, first

writing "late on Saturday" and then "at the dawn of Sunday"?

John intends to tell us only what one of the women did, namely how Mary Magdalene summoned him and Peter; so he writes only about her. It has often been pointed out that John himself indicates that Mary Magdalene was not alone, for in v. 2 he reports her as using the plural: *"we* do not know." The effort to nullify this plural by pointing to v. 13 where she says, *"I* do not know," is unavailing. To John and to Peter, who knew that a number of women had gone out to the tomb, Mary Magdalene just after leaving the other women properly says, "we do not know"; while afterward, when speaking to the angel, she says just as properly, *"I* do not know." The assumption that John either did not know the facts as already recorded by the synoptists, or intended to contradict their reports, is unwarranted. On Mary Magdalene compare 19:25. We decline to think that she preceded the other women; they must have gone together. The scene is not hard to imagine. On the way out the women bethink themselves of the stone which closed the opening of the tomb. Will they be able to roll it away? Then they come within sight of the tomb, and to their consternation see that the stone has already been removed, the door is exposed. They all leap to the natural conclusion that the tomb has been rifled by the enemies of Jesus, the Jews. This conclusion is the more natural when one has seen the Garden Tomb, which we have described in 19:41. The door of this tomb was closed by a great circular slab of stone, rolled into a groove in front of the door, fitting tightly against the face of the cliff into which the tomb had been hewn. Like a wheel this slab could be rolled to the left in its groove, thus exposing the door. The groove slanted so that its lowest point was in front of the opening of the tomb.

Now what the women saw was not that this circular slab had been wheeled to the left in its groove but had been thrown out of its groove, away from the opening, and was lying flat on the ground. The evidence of violence was beyond question.

John writes "the stone," as though his readers know all about it from Matthew and from Mark; we may note that Luke 24:2 does the same. Note the participial construction τὸν λίθον ἠρμένον, "the stone having been taken away," after βλέπει. The article speaks of the stone as of the one which the readers know. Matthew tells us that an angel descended from heaven and rolled the stone away and then sat upon it. Moffatt labors under a misconception when he calls it "a great boulder," as do others who think of a rectangular slab of stone set into the opening or door. Matthew brings us nearest to the resurrection of Jesus. We may combine as follows. While the women are on the way, the dead body in the tomb comes to life (this is the so-called *vivificatio* or quickening, I Pet. 3:18) and moves out of the closed tomb through the rock. Because of its very nature this act was witnessed by no one. The soldiers guarding the tomb saw and knew nothing of it. The tomb was now empty. In the next instant an earthquake shook the ground, an angel flashed from the sky, perhaps touched the stone, making it fly from its place, the soldiers lay like dead, recovered, and fled. The stone, lying flat on the ground, revealed that the tomb was empty; the angel sat upon it, waiting for the women. Before they arrived he entered the tomb. We have no means of tracing the movements of the second angel, v. 12.

2) She runs, therefore, and comes to Simon Peter and to the other disciple, for whom Jesus had affection, and says to them, They took away the Lord out of the tomb, and we do not know where

they put him. What Mary Magdalene saw all the
rest saw too and with the same dismay. Frightened
exclamations must have been exchanged, perhaps in
the same words that come to Mary Magdalene's lips
when she found Peter and John. The women were
convinced that the body of Jesus had been stolen by
the Jews. Now Mary Magdalene turns and runs for
help. She may have shouted, "I am going for help!"
Perhaps she was the youngest and fleetest in the group.
No reason appeared why all should run back for help.
Some at least felt that they should investigate and
see just what had been done in the tomb. Mary
Magdalene's quick thought and her instantly acting
on that thought prevented any one of the other
women from joining her in running back. At
least no one did. Some have said that fear numbs
the limbs, but sometimes exactly the reverse is true —
fear is the most potent power to incite speed.

Mary Magdalene finds Peter and John. The repetition of πρός has led to the supposition that she did
not find the two together but hurried from one to the
other. That this deduction is not necessary is shown
by R. 566, since in later Greek especially the preposition is frequently repeated where more than one noun
is used. The most that we may conclude is that Mary
looked first at one and then at the other when she
exclaimed about the removal of the body. Her excited
eyes wanted to see that her words had the proper
effect. How did it happen that Peter and John were
together? We are reminded of 18:15, 16, and can say
no more. Where were these two? Where the rest of
the eleven? Who can tell? Only these two were
here — that is all. If Mary Magdalene knew where
the others were, she knew, too, where to find these
two and felt that she could count on them, and so she
hastened to where they were. John again hides his
identity but this time he designates himself as "the

other disciple, for whom Jesus had affection," using
φιλεῖν and not, as heretofore, ἀγαπᾶν. This may suggest
that a difference is here intended. In 21:15-17 John
brings out the difference in the strongest way. Always
ἀγαπᾶν is the love of full understanding and of purpose
combined with that understanding, while φιλεῖν is the
love of personal affection, liking, and preference. The
verbs are used with fine tact in 11:3 and 5. The
former is by far the higher type of love. When the
two are used in relation to each other, then, according
to the situation, this relation becomes important. In
chapter 11 the sisters appeal only to the affection of
Jesus, while Jesus himself deals with Lazarus according to the highest kind of love. In chapter 21 Jesus
questions Peter first as to Peter's higher love, and
when Peter, who once boasted of his love as being
greater than that of the other disciples, now in his
deep humility ventures to assert only his affection for
Jesus (φιλῶ), Jesus raises a question regarding even
that love. But with regard to John the opposite is
true. First he tells us that Jesus embraced him
with ἀγάπη, and now he adds that Jesus felt also
φιλία for him. Over and above the love of intelligence and purpose Jesus had also the love of affection for John.

Mary Magdalene exclaims: "They took away the
Lord out of the tomb, and we do not know where
they put him." She certainly said more than this.
Questions must have been thrown at her, and she
promptly answered them. But the gist of all that
passed lies in the word John placed into his record.
He preserves even the excitement with which Mary
Magdalene spoke — how she at first said nothing
about the stone, about whom she suspected of removing the body, or about any other details. Only two
frightful facts: the body gone, and no one knows
where it is. The two aorists state only the facts as

facts, whereas for acts that have just recently happened the English prefers the perfect, R. 845. "They
took away" indicates no subject. R. 1202 lets this
mean: "people took away"; but this can scarcely be
correct. Mary Magdalene means that the Jews did
this. Who but they would rifle the grave? Not satisfied to kill Jesus, their hate for him has now desecrated even his dead body. They will not let him lie
in this fine tomb of Joseph's, they have made away
with his body in some hideous way. She calls Jesus
τὸν Κύριον, "the Lord," the title Peter used in 6:68,
which in chapters 11, 13, and 14, constantly comes
so naturally to the lips of Jesus' followers. Although
Mary Magdalene thinks he is dead and all his work
for nought, she cannot do otherwise than still call him
"the Lord." It is a little touch, yet how genuine!
The supposition that the indefinite "they" might indicate that some of the disciples or the friends of Jesus
are the people Mary has in mind, does not agree with
the entire situation. It is incredible that the women
would not have known about this act; incredible that
Mary would not have asked, "Where have you put
him?" or, "Do you know where they put him?" Every
feature in John's description would be out of line.

"We do not know," etc., means, "we women who
went out to anoint his body." The significant plural
has been explained in v. 1. It most perfectly links
up John's account with that of the synoptists. By
using this plural Mary Magdalene is not assuming
something, namely that the other women think as she
does. She does not say "we" when she really had a
right to say only "I." Who can prove that no interchange of opinion took place among the women before Mary Magdalene left? They were all of one
mind: the Jews had snatched the body away, and the
women feared the worst. Mary Magdalene's word to

Peter and to John is a request for help.   Their action
is the proof.

3)   **Peter, therefore, went out, and the other
disciple, and they were coming to the tomb.   And
the two were running together, and the other disciple did run ahead, faster than Peter, and came as
the first to the tomb.**   At this point we must bring in
Matt. 28:1-10; Mark 16:1-8; and Luke 24:1-12.   Two
ways are open.   Either Peter and John did not at
once start after hearing Mary Magdalene's report, so
that on their way back the other women came to
them with the report of the angel's message and of
the appearance of Jesus; or Peter and John did start
at once, met the other women on the way, heard their
astounding report, and then ran to the tomb.   The latter is preferable and seems to harmonize best with
the action as described by John.   The aorist "went
out" states that the two started.   Then John turns
painter and with an imperfect, "they were coming
to the tomb," shows us the two disciples on their
way still some distance from the tomb.

4)   We see the two on their way but not as yet
running.   First only ἤρχοντο as if Mary Magdalene had
indeed stirred them to action but had not excited
them.   Now follows another imperfect, "and the two
were running together."   Why did they break into a
run, a regular race, in which John left the older Peter
behind?   Why this sudden excitement, in which John
paid no attention to Peter but ran with all the speed
he had and left Peter behind?   We take it that the
two disciples had met the women and had heard from
them what they had to tell.   What they heard seemed
indeed "like idle talk" (ὡσεὶ λῆρος, Luke 24:11) also to
all the rest who presently heard it, but it did excite
these two.   Now they could not get to the tomb rapidly
enough; they started to run, first side by side with

incredulous but excited exclamations, then John forging ahead. Luke 24:12 is summary, as the aorists ἀναστὰς ἔδραμε plainly show, which report only the fact and nothing more. It is John who helps to fill in the connection and the details. While Luke mentions only Peter in v. 12, in v. 24 we see that Peter was not alone: "certain of them (τινές) that were with us went to the tomb," namely Peter and John, as John informs us.

So these two were the first to hear what the other women had to say. This removes an old difficulty that is otherwise encountered, namely how Peter and John reached the tomb without encountering the women who were returning from the tomb. The old solution that several roads led to the tomb, and that thus no meeting took place, is not necessary. The two parties met on the way. We also see what caused the sudden running of Peter and of John. All we need as an explanation for John's outrunning Peter is his youth. Some think of his greater love, others of Peter's feeling of guilt, and Gregory the Great even allegorizes. One adequate explanation settles the question; additions then become superfluous.

5) **Having glanced in, he sees the linen bands lying, yet he did not go in.** Our versions translate παρακύπτειν, "to stoop and look in," the A. V. emphasizing the stooping; this, it seems, was done because the translators imagined the entrance to be low. Some have thought of a low passageway. The entrance required no stooping; in fact, stooping would prevent the vision of the linen bands, lying flat on the floor of the casket-like place hewn out for the body. John had to look down into the place, over the top edge of the thin rock wall that formed one side of the receptacle for the body. The verb means to peep, to glance to the side, or just to look. John again has the vivid aoristic present "he sees." What he sees is remark-

able indeed: the linen bands (11:40) lying wholly
undisturbed in their proper place with the body of
Jesus gone out of them. Commentators ask why John
did not go in. Such haste to reach the place, and now
this reluctance about going in! First such an alarm-
ing report and then such an incredible report, both
completely upsetting the mind; yet John ventures only
as far as the door! It will not do to say that John
saw enough with that first glance, for presently he
follows Peter in and looks more closely. The usual
explanation is best, namely the psychological difference between John's personality and that of Peter.
Impetuous Peter strides right in; the deep, tender soul
of John at first only glances in and then, struck by
what it sees, pauses at the inexplicable sight. Fears
of ceremonial pollution are far from his mind. Natural dread of entering the place of the dead, even
such dread intensified by the thought that this is his
beloved Master's tomb, is an insufficient explanation.
It is what John sees from the entrance that rivets
his feet.

6) **Simon Peter, therefore, also comes, following him, and went into the tomb and beholds the
linen bands lying, and the cloth, which was upon his
head, not lying together with the linen bands but
apart, having been folded up, in a place by itself.**
Those who think of Peter's feeling of guilt as slow-
ing up his speed in running to the tomb must make
him forget this when he now arrives at the tomb, for
he steps right in. The same sight greets his eyes:
τὸ ὀθόνια κείμενα, which John repeats, reversing participle
and noun. This is the astounding phenomenon: "the
linen bands lying." Nothing whatever had been done
with them, they were merely lying. We are not to
imagine that they had been unwound from the body
as was done with the grave bands of Lazarus when
he came to life. Neither had they been cut or stripped

off in some other way. They lay just as they had been wound about the limbs and the body, only the body was no longer in them, and thus the wrappings lay flat. All the aromatic spices were exactly as they had been strewn between the layers of linen, and these layers, one wound over the other, were numerous, so that all those spices could be held between them.

For his own glance from the door John writes βλέπει, "he sees"; for Peter standing inside close beside the casket-like place in which the linen bands lay John writes θεωρεῖ, "he beholds," "he views." Peter stood there, looking and looking at those bands.

No human being wrapped round and round with bands like this could possibly slip out of them without greatly disturbing them. They would have to be unwound, or cut through, or cut and stripped off. They would thus, if removed, lie strewn around in disorder or heaped in a pile, or folded up in some way. If the body had been desecrated in the tomb by hostile hands, this kind of evidence would appear. But hostile hands would have carried off the body as it was, wrappings and all, to get it away as soon as possible and to abuse it later and elsewhere. But here the linen bands were. Both their presence and their undisturbed condition spoke volumes. Here, indeed, was a sign to behold. It corroborated what the women had told Peter and John on the way out to the tomb: Jesus was risen from the dead!

7) A second sign lay beside the first. The σουδάριον, which had been on the head of Jesus, bound around it to envelop the head, lay in a place apart from the wrappings, neatly folded up, or we may say, rolled up. It had not been snatched off and thrown aside. The perfect participle is passive: somebody had carefully folded this cloth and had laid it there in the most orderly way, that it should serve as a second

witness to testify to the resurrection of Jesus. The
Greek term is the Latin *sudarium,* taken over also into
the Aramaic, the German *Schweisstuch,* literally
"sweat-cloth." "Napkin" was a good translation in
the time of Shakespeare and the A. V. but will not
do now even if modern translators use it for lack of
something better; "handkerchief" is likewise inappropriate. It is well that John describes it: "which was
upon the head." The difference between the way in
which the linen bands were simply "lying" and the
way in which the headcloth was folded up and laid
"apart in a place by itself" is too marked, too intentional, to warrant the conclusion that the bands were
also folded up after having been stripped off (Nebe).
The very opposite is indicated. If both the headcloth
and the bands had been folded up, neither would indicate the miracle of the resurrection. Then Peter and
John could conclude only that friendly human hands
had for some strange reason unclothed the dead body
and taken it away. What these disciples saw was
vastly more.

One may ask why Jesus had not left the cloth as
he did the bands, simply passing out of it and leaving
its fastenings undisturbed; for that, too, would have
been an eloquent sign. One answer is that then both
the cloth and the bands would have uttered the same
testimony; then Jesus would have left but one witness. He left two (Matt. 18:16). Folding up the
cloth and placing it apart from the bands indicates an
ordering hand. We may think of an angel. The preposition εἰς is static, R. 593: "in one place" (not "into"), and χωρίς appears as an adverb only here in the
New Testament, R. 648.

8) **Then, therefore, went in the other disciple
also, who came as the first to the tomb, and he saw
and believed.** Strange exegesis when Catholic
writers here find the primacy of the pope: John

would not step into the tomb ahead of Peter, John thus bows to the supremacy of Peter. Strange in another direction is the opinion that what John believed was Mary Magdalene's word that enemies had dragged the body away. Even Luther makes this mistake. No, when John saw what Peter saw, John "came to believe," ἐπίστευσε, ingressive aorist. Luke 24:12 informs us regarding Peter: "he went home, wondering at what has occurred," θαυμάζων τὸ γεγονός. Peter only wondered and wondered, trying to figure out what had occurred. He got no farther. Where was his papal primacy? But John believed.

Yet he writes this word with no joy at all; he writes it with bowed head as a confession. John has to say, "he *saw* and believed," he could not say simply, "he believed." In v. 29 Jesus says to Thomas: "Because thou hast *seen* me, thou hast believed. Blessed they that have *not seen*, and have believed." Recall also 4:48, "Except you see signs and wonders, you in no wise believe." John says nothing about Peter (Luke has said enough); all he does is to confess that he was really no better than Thomas — both had to see before they believed. Yes, John "believed." And in this context the word must mean that he believed in the resurrection of Jesus. The effort to make it mean only that John believed in Jesus in a general way would say nothing. "He saw and believed" means that he believed in consequence of what he saw. The evidence before his eyes he read aright. And yet how weak this faith was! John never opened his mouth even to Peter, and he said nothing to anyone after he reached home. None of the eleven believed the testimony of the women and that of Mary Magdalene (v. 18). Even now John failed to speak and to confess. He had only littleness of faith; his faith could not rise above his doubts; he was only one step removed from unbelief. Those who repre-

sent the disciples as a credulous lot sadly misrepresent
them. They were the reverse. They finally believed
only after they could not do otherwise. Let us not
blame them overmuch; for their holding out so long
against believing is added proof to us that the proofs
of the resurrection of Jesus are convincing beyond the
shadow of a doubt. He who will not believe today
establishes his own guilt. The kind of proof he
demands he shall, indeed, receive at last when it is
too late, when he, too, shall *see* and shall mourn with
eternal grief, Rev. 1:7.

9) John explains how it came about that he
had to see before he believed: **For not yet knew
they the Scriptures that he must rise from the dead.**
This was the trouble, they followed their own thoughts
even when Jesus spoke so plainly to them. Take
Luke 18:31-34, where Jesus foretold his passion and
his resurrection in the plainest terms, stating that "all
things that are written by the prophets concerning the
Son of man shall be accomplished"; and yet "they
understood none of these things," etc. With deep
regret John again brings out this blindness. Since
Jesus himself presented his resurrection as the fulfillment of Scripture, John here goes back to the
Scripture and does not refer to what Jesus himself
had said about his resurrection. Here we learn the
minor value of signs: they are only steppingstones
to faith. The real basis of faith is "the Scripture,"
the revealed and inspired Word of God. On this
basis faith is to rest. John is here not minimizing
the words of Jesus as compared with the Old Testament Scripture. What he does imply is that as yet,
not understanding the Scripture, the disciples, of
course, also failed to understand the words of Jesus.
With the divine promise still dark in their minds, the
words of Jesus regarding the fulfillment were necessarily also dark. What hid the one from them hid

also the other. The past perfect ᾔδεισαν is always used as an imperfect: "they were not yet in possession of knowledge." Luke 24:44-47 shows most decisively how the risen Savior himself grounded the faith of the disciples on the Scriptures. Even the appearances of Jesus to the disciples are to convince them, not by their mere reality alone, but as the fulfillment of the Scriptures. In this Jesus is consistent to the last.

The Scripture to which John here refers is Ps. 16:10, used as proof for the resurrection of Jesus in Acts 2:24, etc., and 13:35, etc. To this prophecy we must add Ps. 2:7 on the basis of Acts 13:33. Likewise Ps. 110:1 and 4, used in Heb. 6:20. But we cannot stop with these merely on the ground that they are used for establishing the resurrection in the New Testament record. From Luke 24:44 we see that Jesus went much farther; he had used "the law of Moses" (the Pentateuch), the prophets, and the Psalms, hence all manner of passages. And these he had expounded in the same illuminating manner concerning his own resurrection as he expounded Exod. 3:6 and 16 to the Sadducees in Matt. 22:29, etc., concerning the general resurrection. Of them Jesus said just what John says of himself and of Peter: "Ye do err, *not knowing* the Scriptures."

It is well enough to say that δεῖ, "must," predicates "moral necessity." What God promises he is morally bound to fulfill. But in Matt. 22:29 Jesus adds concerning the general resurrection "the power of God." In I Cor. 6:14 this power is back of both our resurrection and that of Jesus. In Rom. 1:4; Eph. 1:19, 20; Phil. 3:10 this power is further emphasized. Beside the moral necessity we place the power of God and the necessity of God's own will which carries his purpose into effect so that no question about it can possibly arise. The phrase ἐκ νεκρῶν is explained in 2:22. One more thing deserves notice. John indicates that, apart even from the Scriptures, the evidence left in the tomb by Jesus was so great and convincing that already this wrought faith in him, albeit only a certain degree of faith. When he now would know the Scriptures, this faith would become mighty indeed.

10) **The disciples went away again to their own home.** They did not touch the linen. When their hungry eyes could look no longer, they turned back. Nor does πάλιν mean that they had been here before and now went back a second time. The phrase πρὸς ἑαυτούς, like the singular in Luke 24:12, means "to their own home." It is frequently used in this sense. What did Peter and John say when they got back? Luke 24:24 tells us: that they found what the women had reported, that "him they saw not." That was all. No word of faith even from John.

7. Jesus Appears to Mary Magdalene, 11-18

11) John's purpose is to tell us about the appearance of Jesus to Mary Magdalene, which the synoptists omit save for the short account in Mark 16:9-13. When Mark states that Jesus appeared "first" (πρῶτον) to Mary Magdalene, this may mean "first," not in an absolute sense, but with reference to the two other appearances mentioned by Mark. **Now Mary was standing at the tomb outside sobbing. As, therefore, she was sobbing she glanced into the tomb and beholds two angels in white sitting, one at the head, and one at the feet, where the body of Jesus had lain.** After summoning Peter and John, Mary Magdalene followed them out to the tomb. They had left by the time she arrived at the tomb. Naturally she could not go as fast as they did. One thing seems quite certain: Mary did not meet the other

women on the way. The evidence is that she knows nothing about the angel in the tomb, does not recognize the two angels as such when presently she glances into the tomb. Her whole action betrays that she had not heard from the other women that Jesus had appeared to them alive. We have assumed that Peter and John did meet the women but would not believe what they reported. Could not the same assumption be made regarding Mary? Evidently not; her action at the tomb is so different from that of Peter and of John. We are compelled to say that Mary had *not* met the other women. How did it happen that she failed to meet them?

Had she failed to meet also Peter and John? This is the general assumption. The explanation offered is that several paths led to the tomb. It is used, too, by all those who assume that Peter and John did not meet the other women on the way. Two paths out to the tomb would be enough. The women took the one back to the city, Peter and John and after them Mary, the other in hurrying out to the tomb. Or, if Peter and John met the women, Mary took the other path and did not meet them. On returning, Peter and John took one path while Mary was going out by the other. All this seems well enough. One thing makes us hesitate as to Peter and John and the women: why the two men all at once started to race as they did? Their meeting the women would explain this action. So we have ventured to assume that they met. Now as to a possible meeting of Mary with the returning Peter and John. We note a change of thought in her. When she summons Peter and John, all her fear is that the enemies of Jesus have snatched away his body. But now, again arrived at the tomb, her thought is that some friendly person (perhaps the gardener upon Joseph's order) has removed the body, shall we say to a place deemed safer? Her sorrow is only that she does not know where the body is. She does not look for the men she so frantically summoned. She only stands and sobs. This change in Mary gives us pause. She is no longer looking for help; she is asking of supposed friends where she might find the body. She has dropped the idea of enemies; for, of course, these would not let her know even where the body is, to say nothing of letting her go to the body. All this makes the impression that Mary had met Peter and John, had been assured by them that no enemies had had a hand in what had happened as she first thought, but, of course, had also been told that they saw nothing of the body. This agrees perfectly with Luke 24:24: "certain of them which were with us (Peter and John) went to the sepulcher, and found it even so as the women had said (when they met them in going out), but him they saw not." This is exactly what Mary seems to know as she weeps before the tomb. Neither Peter nor John, plus the other men, believed the women's "idle talk" about having seen Jesus and hence said nothing of this "talk" to Mary; and John's faith was locked in silence all day long until the evening (Luke 24:34).

Thus we now have Mary, her frightened excitement gone, quietly standing in front of the tomb. The mystery of the disappearance of the body is unsolved. She seems to know that Peter and John could do nothing. They left the tomb, she cannot do so. She cannot leave the beloved place. Her helpless love breaks out in sobs, for κλαίειν means loud, unrestrained weeping. It was a woman's way to give her tears full course.

With the imperfect ὡς οὖν ἔκλαιε John describes Mary standing there sobbing. The aorist παρέκυψεν notes the mere fact that she glanced into the tomb (see v. 5 on the meaning of the verb).

12)   But the vivid aoristic present θεωρεῖ tells how her eyes, blurred with tears, rest upon the two angels in the tomb.   Though clad in white, ἐν λευκοῖς (supply ἱματίοις, R. 653), and thus conspicuous in the shadowed tomb, Mary, though she sees them, really does not see them.   She is neither startled nor does she address them.   Only one explanation has been found for this apparent riddle.   Mary has so completely given her heart to one thought and to the deep grief it brought that all other impressions fail to register in her mind. "No man is so bravehearted but what he would be terrified if unexpectedly he should behold an angel; and she even a woman.   Yet she moves about so that she neither sees nor hears nor inquires about anything; so completely her heart is elsewhere." Luther.

The white color is symbolical of the purity and the holiness of heaven.   The angels are seated as though waiting for Mary.   If they were standing, this would imply that they were about to act or about to leave. Quietly, peacefully they sit.   For, indeed, this tomb was both a holy and a blessed place.   Though it is the house of death, no death had been here, no odor of death clung here.   Those linen bands spoke of death but of death destroyed and overcome, and thus of life and immortality brought to light.   This house, intended for death, was the very portal of heaven. Angels, indeed, belonged in this tomb.   Little had Joseph thought what kind of a tomb he had the workmen hew out for him.   It is John who tells us that two angels were present.   The linen bands and the headcloth were two earthly witnesses, and these angels two heavenly witnesses to attest the Lord's resurrection to men.   Heaven and earth unite in the tomb of Jesus.

The synoptists mention only one angel.   Those who will may register another discrepancy.   One angel spoke for the two, and thus the synoptists mention one, namely the speaker. It is, of course, possible that the other women saw only one angel; but we prefer to think that from the moment of the earthquake onward two were present. Why did Peter and John not see them? The answer is not that the angels stepped into another passage in the tomb and hid themselves. The heavenly messengers make themselves visible to those who are to see them. The deeper question is not asked, why Peter and John were not to see and to hear the angels, why only the women and Mary. God arranged the whole matter of the revelation of his Son's resurrection. We have no more to say. "One at the head, and one at the feet" has well been compared with the position of the cherubim at either end of the mercy seat or lid on the ark of the covenant in the Holy of Holies in Solomon's Temple. While ἔκειτο is imperfect in form, it is used as a past perfect: "had lain," R. 906.

13) **And they say to her, Woman, why art thou sobbing? She says to them, They took away my Lord, and I do not know where they put him.** If the angels had not accosted Mary, she probably would have paid no further attention to them, such was her state of mind. John uses the plural ἐκεῖνοι as though both angels spoke, although we may well suppose that one spoke for both. The address, "woman," recalls the way in which Jesus addressed his mother in 2:4; 19:26. The question as to why she is sobbing intends to call her to herself, to give her pause. It breathes friendly sympathy, and it intimates that no cause for her sobbing really exists. Indeed, why does she weep? — when we should all have had cause to weep to all eternity if what she wept for had been given her, the dead body of her Lord! Why does she weep? — when the empty tomb, the shining angels, the way

in which the linen lay, which fact so impressed Peter and John, are trying their best to call to her mind her own Lord's words that on the third day he would rise again! But we are often like her, grieving where no real cause for grief exists if only we would heed God and his Word which opens to us such fulness of joy. O these blinding tears that dim both eyes and hearts!

In John's report of Mary's answer ὅτι seems to be only recitative and not a part of her answer. It is her conduct in general which lends to her answer the meaning that she now no longer thinks of the Jews as the ones who have removed the body of her Lord but of friends of Jesus, whoever they may be. Except for the intimate "*my* Lord" and the singular "*I* do not know," Mary's word is the same as that addressed in v. 2 to Peter and to John. This makes many think that the sense is the same; it has also been thought that the present singular "I know" makes the plural "we know" in v. 2 equivalent to the singular. But the situations are entirely different. "The Lord" is enough in v. 2; now to these persons sitting in the tomb, not known to Mary, she says, "my Lord." Her grief is due to the fact that she does not know where the body of Jesus now is. Dead though Jesus is, he is still *her* Lord; dead though his body is, her love so fervently desires its presence. It is the last link binding her heart to him — and now this, too, is broken. In the second aorist ἔθηκαν the κ of the singular is also used for the plural.

14) **Having said these things, she turned herself back and beholds Jesus standing and was not aware that it was Jesus.** What caused Mary to turn around? And what made her fail to recognize Jesus when she actually beheld him (θεωρεῖ, the same verb as in v. 12)? The text offers no answer, and for this reason we might pass these questions by. But we are

not ready to have them ruled out as improper questions, improper because Jesus' body is now in a glorified state and is recognized or not recognized as he alone wills. This idea is imported from Luke 24:16. What happened there cannot be applied to all the other appearances of Jesus. In the present instance we should have to include the angels. Mary "beholds" them but does not recognize them as angels, exactly as she "beholds" Jesus and does not recognize him. Was she *not* to recognize them? We refuse to believe that Jesus did not will the recognition, i. e., that here the cause lay in him. It surely lay in Mary alone.

What made Mary suddenly turn around when facing the angels in the tomb cannot have been the noise of Jesus' approach. This assumes that he had walked as ordinary men walk to the place where Mary stood. But in his new state he suddenly appeared here at the tomb. Besser's suggestion is far more appropriate: the action of the angels made Mary turn about. At the sight of Jesus they arose and bowed in adoration, and thus Mary recognized the presence of another. But just as the white garments of the angels failed to register in her mind, so also this action of the angels, and so also the appearance of Jesus himself. The thought that Jesus had arisen from the dead was far from her mind. In her paroxism of grief one thought, and one alone, filled her soul: the dead body of her Lord is gone. This breaks her heart and closes her heart against what is before her eyes. Mary's blindness is subjective. May we add anything of an objective nature? We agree with those who do. Jesus had changed. It was the same Jesus who stood before Mary in the very body she had seen laid in the grave, yet now he was in a new state. What his form and his features were like, who will say? In the case of Lazarus it was different, for he returned to his former mode of existence; Jesus appeared in a new mode. He was in a supernatural state. The eyes that beheld him as he now appeared did not see an appearance that was a mere duplicate of that of the days when he walked familiarly with his disciples. We cannot describe the change, but we also cannot deny the change. In comparing the accounts of the different appearances we may even say that they were not always the same. Mary held only one image of Jesus in her mind, that of the former days; the image now presenting itself to her eyes was different. This change helped to prevent her instant recognition of Jesus. The supposition that "the evangelist probably supposed it still to be dark" rests on the denial of the Johannine authorship of the fourth Gospel and puts the supposed writer in conflict with the plain facts.

15) For a few moments this continues. **Jesus says to her, Woman, why art thou sobbing? Whom art thou seeking?** The first question shows the perfect accord of Jesus with his angels. From two sides comes this identical question, aiming at the same effect in Mary. Yet Jesus again asks after Mary has given an answer to the angels. That means that her answer is not complete enough, she has not caught all that the question implies. In order to help her Jesus adds the second question, "Whom art thou seeking?" Now Mary has already said that she is seeking "my Lord," but what she had in mind was "the dead body of my Lord." This second question of Jesus with its interrogative pronoun "whom" implies a living person as the one sought. Jesus does not ask "what" art thou seeking. He intends to correct Mary's reply to the angels. She would be right in seeking one living; she is wrong in continuing to seek one still dead. More than this. The person speaking to Mary would intimate to her that he could help her find the living

but could not help her find the dead. *"Whom* art thou seeking?" Behold, I am here, not the dead body of thy Lord but thy living Lord himself!

It is impossible to think that the question of the angels and those of Jesus are not intended in their evident sense, namely to open the eyes of Mary to what is actually before them. These questions are in open conflict with the idea that Jesus is still keeping Mary's eyes veiled, or is still on his part withholding from her the revelation of his identity. These questions intend to open Mary's eyes. She is to stop sobbing, to see the proof of Jesus' resurrection, to see Jesus himself, risen from the dead and living forever.

But as in so many instances (take as an example Philip in 14:8, etc.) the intent of Jesus is not at once attained. Not that his effort is therefore wasted and lost; its fruit is only delayed. And all these efforts of his reveal only his kindly, patient love, and that to more than the person who may be directly concerned. **She, thinking that he is the gardener, says to him, O sir, if thou didst carry him away, tell me where thou didst put him, and I will remove him.** The maze in which Mary moves has not yet cleared away. Nothing but the dead body of Jesus is in her mind. From that she cannot break away. Yet one change in her thought strikes us: she now thinks that a friendly hand has carried the body away, for Joseph's gardener would be a friend, and Mary appeals to him as such. Matt. 27:57 calls Joseph "a rich man." His new spacious tomb attests his wealth. He owned the spacious grove or "garden" in which the tomb was situated, and this would be in charge of a keeper. We should not think of a common laborer, tilling vegetables and flowers. This was not a garden such as that. An ordinary laborer could not presume to remove a body from the tomb, nor would his master assign such a task to such a man. This "gardener" had the entire place in his charge and would have his dwelling in one part of it, say near the entrance.

Very unworthy ideas have been connected with this "gardener." One is that Jesus first appeared as a common laborer and then suddenly changed. Another is that he had to look around for clothes to cover himself and found a shed with a laborer's dirty clothes and put these on for lack of something better. He has even been dressed only in a loincloth, and this is supposed to be the way in which fieldhands were usually covered. One can only be surprised at meeting such ideas. It has been well said that the question where Jesus obtained his clothes for his different appearances during the forty days is as foolish as the one where the angels obtained their white garments. Jesus here appeared to Mary as he appeared to the women on the way from the tomb and as he appeared to the other disciples at various times. Mary would not address this supposed keeper of the garden with the honorable title κύριε if he had been dressed in common, soiled clothes. Besides, this was Sunday of the great Passover week when little labor was done, and when people dressed for the celebration.

When Mary speaks of Jesus as "my Lord" she uses Κύριος as we do when we capitalize the title, as we do with "God." When she addresses the supposed keeper of the garden as κύριος she uses the term in the current way, like our "sir" in respectful address. It is all very well to say that she does this because she is making a request, the fulfillment of which is in the nature of a favor. Yet should we not say more? Even though Mary fails to recognize Jesus, her eyes see a person of dignity, one whom Mary or any stranger would involuntarily address in a respectful manner. The verb βαστάζω means to pick up and carry to some place, while αἴρω means to lift and thus to remove. It seems too much like pressing the singulars to have them mean that the keeper of the garden lone-handedly carried away the body, and that Mary, equally lone-handedly would remove the body. Luther does this with the latter verb, exclaiming: "A woman undertakes to carry a dead body!" Why press these singulars? Mary means that by the keeper's directions the body was taken elsewhere for good reasons of his own, and that she will direct its removal to a place which she and her friends will select. No one asks what place she had in mind when she spoke. It is not necessary. The moment she knows where the body now rests *she* (ἐγώ, emphatic) will take the necessary steps to have it removed to a place which she and her friends deem proper.

16) Now follows what has aptly been called the greatest recognition scene in all literature, and it is painted with only two words. **Jesus says to her, Mary! She, having leaned forward, says to him in Hebrew, Rabbuni! which is to say, Teacher.** No disguise in the appearance or in the tone of voice is dropped — Jesus is no actor. Only the one word Μαριάμ! This is the probable form on excellent textual authority. Like a flash it went through Mary's mind; she recognized Jesus on the instant. Who does not know the effect of suddenly calling a person's name when that person thinks himself entirely among strangers? It was not merely the fact that Jesus and the angels had first said "woman," as though addressing a stranger, and that now Jesus showed that he knew her name. Then Mary's response would not have come so instantaneously. It is as though Jesus struck a bell, and the peal rings out at the very stroke.

John writes λέγει, as he does regularly, which means that Jesus did not use a loud tone of voice as if to startle Mary out of her wrong thoughts. Yet now, when her own name is pronounced, she instantly recognizes that the voice is that of Jesus. "The sheep hear his voice, and he calleth his own sheep by name, . . . for they know his voice," 10:3, 4. It was the voice that Mary thought had been stilled in death forever. Here it spoke again with all that intimate quality that distinguished it from all other human voices. One word, yet so full of meaning. It was addressed to Mary in her deep grief and instantly turned that grief into joy. It found her with her faith crushed and left her with faith instantly revived. In that one word and its tone was all the love, the sympathy, and the helpfulness of Jesus, and coupled with that an impressive seriousness, a deep gravity, an arresting grip: "Miriam!"

In v. 14 ἐστράφη εἰς τὰ ὀπίσω means that Mary turned completely around so that she faced Jesus. When in v. 16 John now writes στραφεῖσα, some think that the expression in v. 14 implies that Mary made only a half-turn; yet this is certainly incorrect, εἰς τὰ ὀπίσω is too decisive. Nor would a half-turn agree with θεωρεῖ. Others suppose that after her request to the supposed keeper of the garden Mary again turned partly away from him. But this is surely wrong, for she would certainly look at this "gardener," expecting his reply. Mary was facing Jesus when he spoke her name, and στραφεῖσα means that she leaned forward and so uttered her reply. The participle is used as in Luke 9:55; 10:23, where Jesus, too, leans toward his disciples, whom he already faces, and does not turn in order to face them. That also explains the aorist tense. That word "Mary!" struck her, her eyes opened wide, she bent forward, and then came the response from her lips, "Rabbuni!" John retains the original Aramaic and then, as in previous instances, translates the term, "Teacher." This, however, does not convey the full meaning, which one of the Latin codices preserves in *magister et domine,* two others using *domine* alone. "Rabbuni" is far more choice than "Rabbi," which is quite common and was frequently used by the disciples. In the latter the possessive suffix "i" has lost its meaning; it simply meant "teacher" and no longer "my teacher." In "Rabbuni" this was less the case. Zahn gives "Rabbun" as an equivalent of *'Adon,* which is thus used extensively in Jewish literature for God in connections like "Lord of the world" or "of the worlds." If Jesus had revealed himself by a work, Mary would probably have exclaimed, Κύριε, "Lord." Compare 13:13.

Two things are worthy of note. First, that Jesus, who hitherto has used chiefly his Word in working upon the hearts of his disciples, now that he has entered his state of exaltation still uses the Word. He is still the Master-Teacher. We are not to expect a new medium for the building of his kingdom. "Not by the splendor of his divine majesty, not by the outward manifestation of his supermundane glory will he hurl to death the children of men." Nebe. He retains the Word. Mary's response, "Rabbuni," uttered involuntarily, is exactly true. Secondly, Jesus still seeks the individual soul. "If it is the glory of the great God who made heaven and earth that he telleth the number of the stars, and called them all by their names (Ps. 147:4), that he bringeth out their host by number, and calleth them all by names (Isa. 40:26; see *Eisenach O. T. Selections,* 517), it is likewise the glory of the Son of God that he is the Shepherd who calleth his sheep by name and leads them out, that he turns his eyes upon each individual and takes him to his heart." Nebe.

17)   From what Jesus now says we see that Mary, when she bent forward at the call of her name, sank to the ground and clasped tightly the limbs of Jesus. **Jesus says to her, Stop clinging to me; for not yet have I ascended to the Father. But be going to my brethren and tell them, I am ascending to my Father and your Father, and my God and your God.** The first word Jesus here utters has been variously understood. It surely does not mean, "Do not worship me now!" for Jesus accepts the worship of others. Nor, "Hold me not fast, because I must go to the Father," for he intends to delay for yet forty days. Nor, "because thou must hasten to my brethren," which ignores the reason Jesus himself assigns. Nor, "Touch me only with the hands of faith," which cannot be based on 14:28 and 16:22 as possibly being misunderstood by the disciples, this misunderstanding being conveyed also to Mary. Jesus' word contains no contrast such as physical grasping and spiritual grasping. The verb is not $\theta\iota\gamma\gamma\acute{a}\nu\epsilon\iota\nu$, to touch lightly, or $\psi\eta\lambda\alpha\phi\tilde{a}\nu$, to feel over, but $\ddot{a}\pi\tau\epsilon\sigma\theta\alpha\iota$, to cling to, to grasp tightly. As Mary recognizes Jesus, the first impulse of her heart is to seize hold of him whom she had lost and feared not to find again. Here he is, not dead, but marvelously alive again! All her loss is turned into sudden possession. She clasps him as her own, never, never to lose him again. The old days that were before the tragedy on Golgotha have now returned, and she intends that they shall now stay, stay forever.

Kindly, firmly Jesus must say, "Stop clinging to me; for not yet have I ascended to the Father." In prohibitions the present imperative forbids an act that has already begun, hence $\mu\grave{\eta}$ $\ddot{a}\pi\tau o\nu$ means, "stop clinging." Why shall she stop? The reason is really twofold. First, Jesus has not yet ascended, is thus still remaining where his disciples can see him. Mary is not to fear that in a moment she will again lose Jesus. Secondly, she must know that Jesus has not come back into his former life to go on with that as heretofore. He will ascend to the Father; he is now in a new state, the consummation of which will follow presently. No; she will not lose him after all. He will be nearer than ever to her then, seated at God's right hand and thus forever with all those who are his (Matt. 28:20). And this blessed news is not for Mary alone but for all the disciples, who certainly cannot receive it too soon.

Hence the command, "But be going to my brethren and tell them," first the durative present imperative for an action that naturally takes time, "be going," then an aorist for the short delivery of the brief message. Here Jesus calls the disciples "my brethren." Hitherto he had called them "friends" (15:14, 15); a new, higher, a permanent relation now begins. The disciples are to know that, although Jesus has risen and is glorified and duly worshipped by them, he acknowledges them as no less than his "brethren." "If now Christ is our brother, I would like to know what we still lack? Brethren in the flesh have common possessions, have together one father, one inheritance, otherwise they would not be brethren; so we have common possessions with Christ and have together one Father and one inheritance, which does not grow less when divided, but whoever has one part of the spiritual inheritance has it all." Luther. The emphasis is on what thus becomes ours, not, as some have thought, on our work for our Brother. Zinzendorf made the mistake of turning the word of Jesus around, calling him "Brother Jesus" in familiar fashion; the church had tact enough not to follow Zinzendorf in this.

In his message to the disciples Jesus himself makes the marked differences, "my Father and your Father,

my God and your God." Never does he combine himself with the disciples and say, "our Father," "our
God." "It is one thing when he says *my*, it is another
when Jesus says *your*; by nature *mine*, by grace *yours*.
My God, under whom I also am as man, *your* God,
between whom and you I am the Mediator." Augustine. "He is the Father's natural Son, born from all
eternity, and not an adopted son (*Kuehrsohn*), and
this superiority he has over all others." Luther. "O
blessed relationship between us and Christ, our most
wealthy brother, who owns heaven by a double right:
once it is his from eternity, and again he has
obtained it in time; the former is for his own enjoyment eternally, the latter he presents to his brethren."
Bernhard.

To Mary Jesus gives a higher message than he
gave to the women whom he met on their return from
the tomb. They were to announce the meeting of
Jesus with the disciples in Galilee, she is to tell of
the Father, the glorified Master ascending on high,
and of all the disciples lifted to his side as brethren.
"I am ascending" is the present tense to indicate an
act that is near and as certain as though occurring
even now. See this tense in 8:14 and 21; 13:33
and 36; 14:4 and 28; 16:5, 10, 16, 17. This tense is
frequently used in predictions; it is not merely prophecy but also certainty, R. 870. Jesus speaks of the
ascension as his own act, for his human nature now
exercises all the divine attributes in which it shared
since the incarnation. What a majestic word, "I
am ascending"! What shall we say to the modern
critics who misapply this prophetic present tense in
order to place the ascension between v. 18 and 19, and
thus produce what they call "post-ascension" appearances of Jesus? Thus are manufactured grave conflicts with what these critics call "primitive tradition."

18) How Jesus ended the interview with Mary we are not told. **Comes Mary Magdalene, announcing to the disciples, I have seen the Lord! and that he said these things to her.** The two present tenses paint a vivid picture. This is a changed Mary. The fear, the grief, the tears all gone—radiant with superlative joy she sails, like a vessel laden with precious freight, into the place where the disciples are gathered. Just who was there we are not told. Exultantly she exclaims, "I have seen the Lord!" not dead but living, risen. Then she reports her message. She does not expand on the beautiful emotions, the wonderful feelings she has had but soberly, earnestly reports every word Jesus said to her, especially his message to his brethren, every syllable a treasure, a priceless, heavenly possession. Did the eleven believe? They did not, save for what we know of John (v. 8). The recitative ὅτι is made to do double duty, introducing also the last object clause.

8. Jesus Appears to the Disciples, 19-23

19) Now the situation is the following. Ten of the eleven were together with a number of other disciples. The women who had met the angels and then had seen and heard Jesus early in the morning had brought this news. Peter and John had seen the strange sight in the tomb. Mary Magdalene had seen the angels and Jesus himself and had brought the message from him. What thus occurred in the morning of this wonderful day did not produce faith among the disciples (Luke 24:11 and v. 22, etc.), save the littleness of faith in John's silent heart (v. 8). Then came the appearance of Jesus to Peter (Luke 24:34; I Cor. 15:5), of which we know the fact and the effect but no details, not even the hour or the place. Finally came the report of the two disciples who had gone to Emmaus, Luke 24:35; when these two re-

turned, joyful faith had already spread among all those gathered together. While the two from Emmaus are still speaking (Luke 24:36), Jesus appears to the entire company. Luke 24:36-48 and John 20:19-23 deal with the same event.

It, therefore, being evening, on that day, the first one of the week, and the doors having been locked where the disciples were on account of the fear of the Jews, came Jesus and stood in their midst and says to them, Peace to you! John states the time very fully. From Luke we see that it was late in the evening. "On that day" evidently means "on that most notable day." John regards the evening as belonging to Sunday. The Jews regarded the evening as the beginning of a new day (Monday), and yet the evening was frequently connected also with the daytime just passed, this the more for Gentile readers whom John had in mind when he wrote in Ephesus at the close of the first century. "On that day" would be enough, yet John adds, "the first one of the week" (on which compare v. 1). Perhaps John is so specific because the church had selected Sunday as its regular day of worship. But, even apart from this consideration, the specification of the day is of importance. The connective οὖν joins the new paragraph to the one that precedes and shuts out the critical contention that the ascension of Jesus took place, according to the assumed author of this Gospel (never the apostle John, of course), on this Sunday. Where the considerable company of the disciples was gathered we do not know. From Mark we conclude that they had dined together, the meal being finished.

The doors had been locked, and a week later we again find them locked (v. 26) "on account of the fear of the Jews" (7:13; 9:22; 19:38), i. e., the well-known fear inspired by the hostile Jews who had murdered Jesus and had threatened to expel from the synagogue all who confessed Jesus as the Messiah. The plural "doors" does not occur often; we may think of the outer door to the building itself and of the inner door to the room in which the company had gathered. Having these doors locked was a measure of precaution; but here it is mentioned with reference to the appearance of Jesus. In Luke 24:36 only one verb is used (ἔστη); John is more circumstantial, ἦλθε καὶ ἔστη, "came and stood," marking the arrival as well as the standing. Among the strange ideas connected with these words are these: Jesus climbed up a ladder and through a window; or descended from the roof down a stairway; or sneaked into the house before the doors were locked; or slipped in when the two from Emmaus were let in; or was allowed to come in through the connivance of the doorkeeper. All these agree in denying a miracle. Others make the doors open up of themselves to let Jesus walk in; or they leave them locked while Jesus walks through them as though they were not there; or they have him walk right through the walls of the house and of the room. This is a miracle indeed but conceived in the crudest fashion. Acts 12:10 is useless in this connection, for the body of Peter was not in the same state as that of the risen Savior.

In his risen and glorified state time, space, the rock of the tomb, the walls and the doors of buildings no longer hamper the body of Jesus. He appears where he desires to appear, and his visible presence disappears when he desires to have it so. This is wholly supernatural, wholly incomprehensible to our minds. Nor may we ask or seek to comprehend where Jesus stayed during the intervals between his appearances during the forty days. When our bodies shall eventually enter the heavenly mode of existence, we may know something of these supreme mysteries, but we doubt if even then we shall really comprehend the profundities of the divine omnipresence of which the human nature of Jesus partakes and which he exercised since his vivification in the tomb as in these wondrous appearances. "He came and stood in their midst" is all that human thought and language can say. He did not walk through anything. The disciples did not see him take so many steps from the door or the wall to their midst. He was there, and that was all. The phrase εἰς τὸ μέσον is idiomatic, and the preposition implies no motion, for εἰς is static like ἐν.

The disciples believed that Jesus had risen from the dead, Luke 24:34. But when the living Lord now suddenly stood in the room before their very eyes, the effect was terrifying to them, Luke 24:37, 38, and Jesus is compelled to allay their troubled fears, v. 39-43. The disciples only slowly recognized the powers of the resurrection of Jesus. They were like so many today who seek to apply to the body of the risen Lord some of the notions they associate with bodies in the natural state and with conceptions of spirit beings. These notions still produce all manner of unbelief as regards the bodily resurrection of Jesus. Because the mind is too small and puny to take in the infinitely great it resorts to denial of what lies beyond and above its grasp. Yet even finite nature is full of mysteries too great, too intricate, too profound for the mind ever to grasp and to penetrate; shall we, therefore, come with denials?

The first word is one of greeting, "Peace to you!" But this common form of greeting, meaning only a kindly human wish when spoken by ordinary lips, means infinitely more when spoken by the lips of Jesus. As the person, so the word. When Jesus says "peace" he actually gives what the word says. It is not a lovely-looking package that is empty inside but

one that is filled with a heavenly reality far more
beautiful than the covering in which it is wrapped.
See the full details on this "peace" in 14:27.

20) The peace Jesus gave to the eleven the night
in which he was betrayed was genuine indeed. He
now renews the gift and reveals its genuineness before the eyes of the entire company of disciples.
**And having said this, he showed his hands and his
side to them. The disciples, therefore, were glad
because they saw the Lord.** When John connects
the showing of the hands and of the side with the
greeting of peace, he is not in conflict with Luke 24:37,
etc., where the hands, etc., are shown after the greeting of peace in order to convince the disciples that
they were not beholding a phantom or spirit. Both
purposes in showing the hands, etc., go together. First,
as Luke tells us, the disciples had to be convinced of
the identity of Jesus, which the wounds established;
secondly, of the reality of his body, which was proved
when they handled his body and when he ate before
them. But John points out how these actions (which
he abbreviates to the showing of the hands and the
side) cast their light upon the greeting of peace.
Here Jesus shows the disciples the very price at which
he bought their peace, his pierced hands, his riven
side, the evidence of his death by crucifixion. Luke
mentions the feet, John alone the side. Jesus shows
these parts of his body, not because they are naturally the exposed parts, for as such they are seen by
the disciples without being shown. He shows them,
as v. 27 also indicates, because they have the wounds
made by the nails and the spear. These holy wounds
proclaim that God is at peace with us. They are the
seals which attest this objective peace. The peace
thus pronounced upon the disciples by Jesus is an absolution. They had fled when Jesus was betrayed, they

had given up their faith, but, "Peace to you!" extended
by these pierced hands and this pierced heart, takes
all their guilt away.

Some seem to be afraid that the body of Jesus permanently retained the gaping wounds made at his crucifixion, and so they assure us that these wounds were
not permanent; others turn them into stigmata, marks
indicating where the wounds had been. It is best not
to pronounce on matters unknown to us. If Jesus
wished to retain his wounds he certainly could do so,
and they certainly would always appear as the
evidence in his very body of his glorious work of
redemption. But the idea is farfetched that Jesus
speaks only of his flesh and his bones (Luke 24:39)
not of his blood, because the circulation of the blood
could less easily be felt, and because what was in his
veins might be something else than blood.

The disciples were glad because they saw the Lord
(14:28; 16:22). The participle ἰδόντες is causal,
R. 1128, not temporal. "The Lord" is significant in
this statement of cause, for it indicates what they
saw in the risen Jesus: their heavenly, divine Lord.
Not that all doubt was so quickly overcome and at
once completely eradicated. Jesus appeared again and
again, intensifying faith and joy, until nothing could
ever disturb the solid certainty.

21) **Jesus, therefore, said to them again, Peace
to you! As the Father has commissioned me, I, too,
am sending you.** These and the following words of
Jesus, while they are distinct from those reported at
greater length by Luke, harmonize with them most
perfectly. Compare with this first word that of
Luke 24:48. "Peace to you!" is only in form a repetition of the first greeting. It cannot be regarded as
a farewell greeting, for then it would be placed at the
end of v. 23. This second gift and assurance of peace
forms the basis of the commission now bestowed, the

fundamentum missionis ministrorum evangelii. This peace is not merely to fortify the hearts of the disciples amid all the enmity and hatred of the world; they are to be possessors of the Lord's peace because as his witnesses and messengers they are to dispense this very gift of peace in a peaceless world. The sum of the gospel is "peace" (Eph. 2:17), and it is called "the gospel of peace" (Eph. 6:15), in fact, Jesus himself is "our peace," and all who preach must bring the word sent by God, "preaching peace by Jesus Christ" (Acts 10:36). Those who are to bring peace must have peace.

The first gift of peace does not include all the disciples present, and the second gift only the apostles in the company, though including the absent Thomas. This is an incorrect view of the office established by Jesus. The commission to bring the gospel of peace and salvation to the world belongs to the entire church (Eph. 4:11; I Cor. 12:1-31; Matt. 28:18-20). With this great commission Jesus gave the office of the ministry to the church as his own arrangement for the continuous public work of the gospel administration. Jesus himself selected and appointed the apostles, because their work was unique in that the apostolic Word was to form the foundation of the church for all time (Eph. 2:20). All other preachers the church herself was to select and call. Thus Jesus works in the world through the church as a whole with its public work committed to the Christian ministry by Jesus through the church.

In this sense Jesus says, "As the Father has commissioned me, I, too, am sending you." It will not do to refer "you" only to the eleven; it necessarily includes all the believers present. In the words following the gift of the Spirit is intended for all (*vide* Pentecost), and the power to remit and to retain sins belongs to the church. The part the eleven were to

have in all this, and after them the called ministry
of the church, causes no difficulty. This special part
Jesus had already begun to arrange as far as the
apostles were concerned and would further arrange
when the time came through the apostles under the
guidance of the Spirit. Even the regular membership
of the church would be equipped with different gifts,
each member taking his place and doing his part. As
the Father sent Jesus, so Jesus now sends all his believers, i. e., his church not merely the eleven. In
this sending each member has his place, and Jesus
himself marked that of the eleven. It is essential
to note the emphasis on the two subjects, which are,
therefore, placed side by side: καθὼς . . . ὁ πατήρ,
κἀγώ, "just as the Father . . . I, too." The redemptive mission of Jesus is now finished; this is the
sense of the extensive perfect "has sent me," denoting
an act now complete (R. 895). Now begins the gospel,
the evangelizing mission on the part of all of the
disciples of Jesus. The present tense, "I am sending,"
does not mean that now this work is at once to begin;
as so often, the present denotes an act in progress.
So Jesus was sent when he came into the world, but
his main work began when he was thirty years old.
In a few days the actual evangelizing work of the
church and the part the eleven had in it would begin.
As to the eleven, they had known for a long time that
this would be their work (4:38; 13:16; 15:16; 17:18).
Yet Jesus now rightly tells his disciples of this their
sending. Heretofore his own work was not finished,
and his death made it appear as though all had been in
vain; now risen from the dead and glorified, he tells
the disciples that their work will, indeed, go on.
While Jesus uses two verbs, ἀπέσταλκε and πέμπω, the
sense is quite the same, although the latter seems to
be more general. In the fulness of his divine author-

ity and power Jesus says, "And I on my part send you."

22) **And having said this, he breathed on them and says to them, Receive the Holy Spirit.** As in v. 20, the participial phrase, "having said this," connects the new act with the preceding word. He who sends enables those whom he sends; and the enabling is the gift of the Holy Spirit. The dative αὐτοῖς is to be construed with both verbs and includes all those present at this time. The idea that the gift of the Spirit is necessary only for those called to a special office in the church, or only for the apostles, is a decided mistake. Why is it necessary to make a miraculous act of this breathing upon by saying that the breath of an ordinary person, blown out, would reach only one individual in line with that breath, while the breath of Jesus reached all the disciples present in the room? The breath of Jesus was, indeed, no mere symbol of the Spirit, nor was the act of breathing a mere symbolical act that only represented bestowal. While both the Hebrew *ruach* and the Greek *pneuma* mean "breath," and to expel the breath thus naturally symbolizes the Spirit even as the water in Baptism is a symbol of cleansing, and the bread and the wine in the Lord's Supper are symbols of heavenly food, yet in both of these sacraments, in this act of breathing by Jesus, whatever may be considered a symbol becomes at the same time an actual means of bestowal. The chosen means accords with the purpose for which it is used, with the gift it imparts. It is this accord and fitness which makes it seem like a symbol; but therefore to reduce it to a symbol is to cling to the shell of appearance and to overlook the blessed reality which is the essential. Both the preceding word, "I myself also send you," and the following word, "receive," shut out the use of a symbol and demand

that for the sending and for the receiving an actual
means be employed.   And this need not be a breath of
such astounding volume as to be felt by the faces of
those present.   Physical size and volume is not needed
for the bestowal of divine gifts.   The breathing of
Jesus indicates that the Spirit comes from him.   The
Spirit who is "breath" comes by the breath of Jesus.
It is the source that is essential and the means
employed by that source.

The aorist λάβετε is decidedly punctiliar and denotes
reception then and there and not a process of reception that is to go on and on.   This imperative imparts
a gift, namely by placing the gift into the hearts of
the recipients.   This, of course, is not the first reception of the Spirit on the part of these disciples; all
of them were disciples, i. e., believers, in whom the
Spirit had wrought faith.   So this new bestowal of
the Spirit was the reception of a welcome gift.   It
is a misconception to think that the bestowal was
dependent   on   *"an   act"*   of   faith   on   the   part   of
each disciple.   The bestowal itself wrought the reception.   The   verbal   form   λάβετε   must   not   be
pressed in a wrong way.   The eye receives the sun's
ray in an effortless way when that ray falls into
the eye; the ear receives the sound without an act
of its own when the sound reaches the ear.   So these
hearts received the Spirit when Jesus now gave them
the Spirit.

It ought to be settled, already linguistically, that,
whether we have Πνεῦμα and Πνεῦμα ἅγιον with or without the article, the sense is absolutely the same just
as this is the case with Θεός and Κύριος.   In the present
instance the article is absent just as it is in 1:33;
7:39; Acts 1:2 and 5, and in many other instances.
It is wasted effort to seek a special meaning for Πνεῦμα
ἅγιον because here the article is absent; no such meaning exists.   Those who think of something halfway

between the Word of Jesus, on the one hand, and the
Third Person of the Godhead, on the other hand, pursue a chimera, one to which they themselves are unable to give a name. But if Jesus here actually
bestows the Holy Spirit on his disciples, does this
not clash with Pentecost? The modern critics still
expect us to accept the old hypothesis of Bauer that
John "telescopes" the resurrection, ascension, and
Pentecost, i. e., that he runs them together, the resurrection in v. 1-18, the ascension (assumed, of course,)
between v. 18, 19, and Pentecost in v. 19-23. Thus
Jesus ascended to heaven on Easter Sunday and on
Easter Sunday evening gave the Pentecostal Spirit.

No difficulty exists between the present gift of the
Spirit and that given fifty days later on Pentecost.
We do not need Bengel's solution that Jesus here
gives only the *arrha* or earnest of the Spirit. This
idea rests on the old misinterpretation of 3:34, coupled
at times with a wrong view of 7:39; see the exposition of these passages. If this earnest is something
other than the Spirit himself, how can Jesus say,
"Receive the Spirit"? If this earnest is only a part
of the Spirit, "a measure," as some say, is, then, the
Spirit cut into sections, or is he divided like liquid?
And even then, why does Jesus say, "Receive the
Spirit"? Let us understand once for all that any and
every reception of the Spirit means that the Spirit
himself, the entire and undivided Third Person of the
Trinity, is received. We can no more split up the
Spirit than we can split up the Father or the Son.
Throughout the Old Testament the Spirit was thus
received. In II Sam. 23:2 David speaks "by the
Spirit," not by an earnest or by a measure of the
Spirit. In the Old Testament every believer and not
only the inspired prophets had the actual and undivided Spirit in his heart. All the differences that
appear in the Scriptures regarding the Spirit are due,

first, to the economy of the kingdom of God and, secondly, to the spiritual condition of individuals. At each stage of the kingdom the Spirit wrought according to that stage; Abraham cannot be exchanged with David or with Isaiah, nor the Baptist with St. John or with St. Paul. The work outlined in 14:26 had to wait until the proper time came. Nor are the Spirit's instruments, the individuals, in the different stages of the kingdom alike. I Cor. 12:12, etc., certainly makes this plain.

So it is this Easter evening when Jesus gives the Spirit to these disciples of his. They all received the Spirit for him to work in them personally, for him to implant in them the revelation Jesus here communicated to them and reported in Luke 24:44-48. This was still a preliminary stage, not yet the final one of Pentecost, the climax of all the stages that preceded. Not yet could the disciples "receive power" in the sense of Acts 1:8. That would come at Pentecost and after (Acts 10:44, etc.; 15:8, 9). Hence also the differences in the bestowal of the Spirit. On this evening Jesus breathed upon the disciples and spoke as Luke and John record; at Pentecost the signs and the mode of bestowal were of a grander type. Yet the differences appear even at Pentecost, for 120 were present, yet not all preached as Peter did, and not all healed as Peter and John did (Acts 3:7). Nor need the fact disturb us that those who already have the Spirit are said to receive him anew. Once he comes with one gift and one purpose, then he comes with other gifts and a greater purpose. On Easter evening he came to implant what Jesus revealed in Luke 24:44, etc., but at Pentecost he came to send the gospel into all the world in all the languages of men. On Easter evening none were added to the kingdom, on Pentecost 3,000 souls were ushered into it.

23)   The gift of the Spirit as here made by Jesus
is to enable the disciples to exercise the right, authority, and power with which he now clothes them in their
sending.   **If of any you dismiss the sins, they are
dismissed; if of any you hold the sins, they have
been held.**   Both conditional clauses are clauses of
expectancy.   The functions here described go naturally with the sending or commission bestowed upon
the disciples by Jesus and with the endowment of the
Spirit which he has added.   In fact, these two functions form the two supreme acts for which the disciples are sent and equipped.   Through the disciples
as his church on earth Jesus wants the remission of
sins dispensed to sinners, excluding only those who
refuse remission.   The contention that this word of
Jesus' appears as a novelty in John's Gospel, that up
to this point we have heard nothing about the remission and the retention of sins, is untenable.   All that
is new is the use of the verbs "to dismiss" and "to
hold."   We have read much about "having life
eternal" and "not having life" or "perishing" from
3:15 onward, and no man has life without being rid
of his sins.   The same is true in 1:12, regarding the
"power to become the sons of God."   Compare 5:24,
and in particular 8:21 and 24, "dying in your sins,"
and 9:41, "your sin remains."   In fact, the entire
gospel is full of the fundamental truth of divine grace
and forgiveness and of the reception of this grace
by faith.   All this is now concentrated and brought
to a focus in two weighty statements by which Jesus
bestows upon his disciples the great power he has so
far exercised himself.   They are now to act in his
stead, and he will act through them.

The verbs are highly significant: ἀφιέναι τὰς ἁμαρτίας =
to dismiss, to send away the sins, from which we have
ἄφεσις, the sending away of sins.   The sins are removed
from the sinner, and this completely, as far as the

east is from the west (Ps. 103:12), into the depths of
the sea (Mic. 7:19), blotting out the transgressions
so that the Lord himself will not remember them
(Isa. 43:25). The English words "to forgive" and
"forgiveness" are too indefinite and must be vitalized
from the Greek. The opposite is κρατεῖν, "to hold
fast with strength," "to retain." The sins are held
fast upon the sinner, fixed upon him so that he cannot escape from them now or ever. Judgment finds
him thus, and he is doomed. The moment a sin is committed that sin with all its guilt adheres to the sinner, and no human effort can possibly free him. He
may think he has freed himself in some way, but he
is mistaken; he is held. Only one person is able to
remove that sin, so remove it as though it had never
existed (I John 1:7).

While the readings vary somewhat, we may take
it that the present ἀφίενται and the perfect κεκράτηνται
are correct. The two functions are not identical. In
both of the cases the sins have been committed, and
the respective sinners appear with their sins and their
guilt. In the one case this wonderful thing is done:
the disciples remove the sins as though they had never
been committed: "they are dismissed," namely by the
disciples' act of dismissal. Jesus says so. Hence this
act counts for him. "This is as valid and certain,
also in heaven, as if Christ, our dear Lord, had dealt
with us himself." Luther. In the other case the sins
are held by the disciples. This is no mere litotes,
meaning only that the sins are not dismissed. The
act is positive, the sins are held fast and fixed upon
the sinner. He may do what he will, they are upon
him, and he must face Christ with them. But now
Jesus uses the perfect tense, "they have been held."
This means: from the start, from the moment of their
commission onward. Jesus has already held them,
the disciples join Jesus in this, add their verdict to

his, and so for all time to come (this is the force of
the intensive perfect, R. 894, etc.,) they continue to be
held. Luther's word applies also here.

Jesus here bestows on his disciples what has aptly
been called "the Power of the Keys," Matt. 16:19;
18:17-20. It is true, God alone can forgive sins,
Mark 2:7. Nor has God (Christ) abrogated this
power of his or turned it over to the disciples (the
church). It is still Jesus who dismisses and who
holds sins, yet by his act which empowers the disciples he makes them his agents — he acts through
them. They are thus also by their very commission
bound to dismiss and to hold sins only in accord with
the will of Jesus. They can dismiss, yea, must dismiss, the sins of all those who repent and believe; they
cannot and dare not do otherwise. To attempt to
do so is to forfeit their commission and their power.
They can, yea, must hold the sins of all the impenitent
and unbelieving; they cannot dismiss them unless
they would lose their authorization. All this does not
mean that Jesus enables the church to look into men's
hearts with direct and infallible vision and thus to
expose also all hypocrites. The disciples deal with
the confession of sinners, their confession of lip and
life, and pronounce accordingly. This they do, and
every sinner they deal with is to know that they do
this in conjunction with Jesus, hence always conditional on his infallible finding. The effort has frequently been made to reduce the authorization Jesus
here gives to a mere general announcement that Jesus
forgives the penitent and holds the guilt of the impenitent, much like the general gospel proclamation.
But this view alters the words, "you dismiss," "you
hold." It also alters the two τινῶν, "of any," "of any,"
which indicate two distinct classes. This view also
misconceives the function of the disciples (church),
which is to do more than to preach, teach, and make

known the contents of the gospel in the world of men; they are also personally and directly to deal with individual souls. Compare I Cor. 5:3-5 and 12; James 5:15 and 20; I John 5:16.

In this entire section (v. 19-23) Jesus deals with all the disciples present (Luke 24:33) not with the ten only. This makes it impossible to restrict the power bestowed in v. 21-23 to the apostles and the ministry. It is Luther who brought back to the consciousness of the church the divine right bestowed upon all her members by Jesus. "This power now is here given to all Christians, i. e., to him who is a Christian. But who is a Christian? He who believes has the Holy Spirit. Therefore every Christian has the power, which the pope, bishops, etc., have in this case, to retain or to remit sins. Do I hear, then, that I may hear confession, baptize, preach, give the Sacrament? No! St. Paul says, 'Let everything be done decently and in order,' I Cor. 14:40. We, indeed, all have this power; but no one is to make bold to exercise it publicly except he be chosen thereto by the congregation. Privately, however, he may well use it. As when my neighbor comes and says, 'Friend, I am distressed in my conscience, say an absolution to me'; then I may freely do this, preach the gospel to him and tell him how he is to appropriate the works of Christ and is firmly to believe Christ's righteousness is his, and his sins are Christ's. This is the greatest service I may render to my neigbor! Who can fully set forth what an unspeakable, mighty, and blessed consolation this is, that with one word one man may unlock heaven and lock hell for another!"

9. Doubting Thomas Convinced, 24-29

24) **But Thomas, one of the Twelve, called Didymus, was not with them when Jesus came.** The

reason why the appearance here recorded is not listed by Paul in I Cor. 15:4, etc., is evidently because the appearance on Easter evening and this appearance eight days later are counted as one. This second appearance occurs entirely on account of Thomas as the narrative shows. The work Jesus began on Easter evening he now completes. In v. 19 John wrote "the disciples," and Luke 24:33 mentions the fact that others besides the eleven were present. Now we learn of one notable absentee — Thomas. When John adds "one of the Twelve," this recalls 6:71 and the way in which each of the synoptists refers to Judas as "one of the Twelve." Thomas should by no means have been absent when not only all the rest of the eleven were together but also other disciples with them. "One of the Twelve" is hint enough why Thomas was absent; it was because of his obstinate refusal to believe. After this is fixed, it makes little difference how we imagine his absence, whether we think that he stayed away altogether, or that he was present, became disgusted with the talk about the resurrection, and then left. He succeeded in one thing only: in keeping himself wretchedly miserable in his unbelief for another entire week. To think that "one of the Twelve" could do such a thing as this!

Because John here· adds the Greek name of Thomas: "Didymus," which like "Thomas" means "Twin," some suppose that John intends to mark the character of this disciple as a man divided, as one who always doubts. But what about 21:2 — is he here too to be branded as a doubter? And what about 14:5 where John writes only "Thomas"? See 11:16. "One of the Twelve" suggests the blame resting on Thomas, no more is needed. Thomas was known by two names, one Hebrew, the other Greek, the latter probably being in later times used quite generally amid Gentile surroundings; hence also John alone has preserved this second name, writing, as he did, at a late date.

25) **The other disciples, therefore, were saying to him, We have seen the Lord. But he said to them, Unless I see in his hands the mark of the nails, and thrust my finger into the place of the nails, and thrust my hand into his side, I shall in no wise believe.** "The other disciples" are not merely the ten associates of Thomas but together with these the rest who had seen Jesus. The imperfect ἔλεγον means that they kept laboring to convince Thomas. They were thus beginning to act as Jesus' witnesses, beginning the work of evangelizing and making the start in the right place, with the unbeliever in their midst. They had caught something of the mind of Jesus. But all their solicitous efforts proved in vain. John evidently summarizes when he writes, "We have seen the Lord." Thomas was made to listen to the entire story with all its details, that of the women and of Mary Magdalene, that of Peter and of John who had seen the tomb, that of Peter in particular (Luke 24:34; I Cor. 15:5), that of the two Emmaus disciples, and that of the entire company behind the locked doors. The sum and substance of it all was: "We have seen the Lord," now using this title "Lord" in an eminent sense. The perfect is used and not the mere aorist, because more is to be conveyed than the mere fact, namely the fact plus its present and continuing effect. "We have seen," and the sight remains with us in all its blessed significance.

Unbelief always was and always will be unreasonable. This is glaringly plain in the case of Thomas. For him all this unanimous testimony of all these people, whose character for veracity he knew so well, amounts to nothing. The fact that all of them, like himself, had never dreamed of Jesus' resurrection, had thought it impossible, and had then been convinced from this unbelief by overwhelming evidence, affects Thomas in an opposite way: he determines to set himself against them all. The more they speak to him and the more they present the facts, the more stubborn Thomas becomes. He has been called "doubting Thomas," but he does not doubt, he is openly unbelieving. He challenges the evidence the others present. They have only seen — seeing does not count. If he is to believe he demands two lines of evidence, seeing plus feeling with his own finger and his own hand. And even the feeling must be twofold, that of the holes in Jesus' hands and that of the gash in his side. Thomas demands what he deems a real test. What the other disciples claim to have is not nearly enough for him. Here the silliness of unbelief comes to view. If sight can be deceived, sight which takes in so much, what assurance has Thomas that feeling, which takes in far less, will not also be deceived?

The disciples *had seen* Jesus, but think of the wonder of that sight! Recall Luke 24:30, 31 and 35; John 19:19, the locked doors; v. 20, his hands and his side; Luke 24:39, "handle me and see"; v. 41-43, he ate fish and honeycomb. This was seeing indeed. Some had held his feet in worship (Matt. 28:9); Mary Magdalene had clung to him (John 20:17); they all had also heard him speak. Here is the pride, haughtiness, and arrogance of unbelief: it sets up a criterion of its own. It will have what *it* demands. The unbeliever makes himself a superior person, looking down on believers as credulous fools who cannot be trusted. The wisdom of the unbeliever exceeds that of all other men. Thomas is surely typical of the entire class. But all this action of unbelief reveals that, while it pretends to obey reason and genuine intelligence alone, it does nothing of the kind. It is actuated by an unreasoning and unreasonable will, a secret, stubborn determination, unacknowledged by the unbeliever himself, not to believe (7:17).

John first writes τὸν τύπον τῶν ἥλων, "the marks of the nails," i. e., the great holes made by them; secondly, τὸν τόπον τῶν ἥλων, "the place of the holes" (this is the correct reading), i. e., the place they occupied. Thomas does not mention the holes in the feet. He is generous; he will be satisfied with the hands. Those are hasty who conclude that the feet of Jesus were only bound with ropes and not fastened to the cross. The aorist subjunctives ἴδω and βάλω designate single acts. But Thomas will investigate the gash in Jesus' side. Though ordinarily the garment would cover the side, Thomas will demand that Jesus do what the disciples claim he did: show his side (v. 20) and then he will make sure, not by gently touching the mortal gash with his finger, but by running his hand into the opening. Generally unbelief does not care how gross and coarse its talk is. One of its characteristics is that it loves to shock believers. Here again Thomas acts true to type. This is the way in which he would treat "the Lord." With the subjunctive or a future indicative οὐ μή is the strongest form of negative: "in no way," or, "not at all."

26) The week went on, and nothing happened — no new appearances of Jesus, no change for the better in Thomas. **And after eight days his disciples were again inside and Thomas with them. Comes Jesus, the doors having been locked, and stood in their midst and said, Peace to you.** Since in all such counts the final day is included, the time is again Sunday. Why Jesus waited an entire week has often been asked, but the answers given do not satisfy. Was it to punish Thomas by the delay; or was it to let the continued testimony of the disciples have its full effect on Thomas; or was it to test the faith of

the disciples by the persistent unbelief of Thomas?
All we can say is that the Lord chooses his own time
and generally does not let us know the reason for
his choice. The impression made by John's narrative
is that the present meeting of the disciples is the
exact counterpart of the meeting on Easter evening,
save that now Thomas is present and that Jesus deals
with him. The disciples are again inside a building
with the doors locked, just as a week ago. No need
to repeat that it was evening, or that the locking was
done for fear of the Jews. Some are opposed to the
latter idea and maintain that now the fear of the
Jews had left them, and that the disciples had locked
themselves in only for the sake of privacy. But the
parallel with v. 19 is too evident. The courage of the
disciples did not grow so rapidly.

It is saying too much to have this assembly of the
disciples actually expecting another appearance of
Jesus, and actually expecting one because it was again
Sunday evening. This exaltation of Sunday is placed
far too early. All we can safely say is that the resurrection of Jesus had the effect of reuniting the disciples after his crucifixion had scattered them. The
bond of their living Lord drew them together once
more. We are not averse to thinking that they had
been together already on the previous day. Whether
this was the first time Thomas was again in their
midst we are not told. Generally the question is not
even asked as to how he came to be in his place on
this evening. A few imagine that he had begun to
weaken in his unbelief, but no hint of this kind comes
from John but rather the contrary. For Jesus does
not ask Thomas: "Dost thou still want to thrust
thy finger into the marks of the nails in my hands,
and thrust thy hand into my side?" What Jesus bids
Thomas do is exactly what he had insisted on at the
beginning. Yet somehow Thomas is present. We are

left to think that the old association drew him back into the circle. Where else should he go? The others surely invited him to be with them. Whether they hoped that Jesus would do something in his case is problematical. They may have remembered 17:12 as an assurance that Thomas would not be lost in spite of his present unbelief; but again they had not shown themselves good at remembering more important words of Jesus, so we can venture nothing certain regarding this word.

It has been positively asserted that at the close of the Passover week, thus on the preceding Friday, the disciples left Jerusalem for Galilee; and the reason assigned is that they had nothing more to hold them in Jerusalem, and that they had been told to meet Jesus in Galilee (Matt. 26:32; 28:7 and 10; Mark 14:28; 16:7). We are told that we must imagine that the disciples were in some town in Galilee. But John says nothing about Galilee until 21:1; πάλιν ἦσαν ἔσω, "again were they inside," reads exactly as though they were again in the same house and in the same room where they had been the week before. As far as making the start for Galilee is concerned, the safest view is that the disciples awaited specific directions from the Lord. That they waited in Jerusalem as long as they did merely on account of Thomas and his unbelief is altogether too doubtful. We take it that in all things they again felt themselves under the guidance of their Lord.

From the way in which the genitive absolute, "the doors having been locked" (the same outer and inner doors as in v. 19), is placed, we see that the mention of this fact, while it does not exclude the fear of the Jews as the reason for the locking, is intended to inform us that the situation is an exact duplicate of the one sketched in v. 19, and that Jesus appears once more exactly as he did a week ago, suddenly standing in the midst of his disciples. This, too, is duplicated, that he again greets them all with, "Peace to you!" on which see v. 19. But now he at once turns to Thomas, for this appearance is for his sake. That, however, gives a special meaning to the greeting as far as Thomas is concerned. Jesus has not come to upbraid him. It breathes forgiveness for this disciple's sin. The divine love of Jesus reaches out to gather Thomas, too, into the peace of the safety and the assurance which the other disciples already had. The tremendous impression already made upon Thomas by this miraculous appearance of his glorified Lord is deepened with blessed significance by this greeting of love from Jesus' lips.

27) **Thereupon he says to Thomas, Bring thy finger here and see my hands; and bring thy hand and thrust it into my side: and be not unbelieving but believing.** It is Thomas for whose sake Jesus has come; yet what transpires between Jesus and Thomas is for all to hear and to see. The three statements of Jesus correspond exactly to the three that Thomas had made in v. 25, in part even verbally. Jesus speaks to Thomas as though he himself had heard every word Thomas had uttered when making his demands. This alone must have overwhelmed Thomas and must have struck deeply into his conscience. Think what his divine Lord does: he meets the outrageous demands of this disciple, meets them to the letter. He lets this disciple set up the demands, and he, his Lord, accedes to them. We may well marvel at such astounding condescension. Yet the reason for this action of Jesus' is fully warranted. He is offering to all these disciples πολλὰ τεκμήρια, "many infallible proofs" (M.-M., 628, call this a strong word, equal to "demonstrative evidence") of his resurrection, Acts 1:3, by no means for their personal faith only, which might have been won with far less, but as the

foundation for the faith of the church of all future ages. They were made "witnesses" of his resurrection (Acts 2:32; 3:15) in the fullest possible sense of the word, "witnesses" whose testimony was to stand as being unassailable in all future ages. We may blame Thomas personally as much as we will. Jesus knew that Thomas would have many successors in all ages. Hence, if Thomas, "one of the Twelve," had been left with any justification, however flimsy, even for any degree of doubt as regards the resurrection of Jesus, the effect would have been bad for all time to come. By thus dealing as he does with Thomas, meeting him on Thomas' own ground, he is dealing with all doubt and disbelief in his resurrection in all time to come, closing the mouth of every disbeliever in all future time. We thus really have reason to thank this disbelieving disciple for what the Lord did with his disbelief, converting it into the completest faith.

The two present imperatives φέρε are perfectly in place, "be bringing," for they are preliminary and thus circumstantial to the essential actions for which the peremptory aorists are used, ἴδε and βάλε. Then follows the durative present γίνου, "be," or "show yourself to be," namely as the result of these aorists. Jesus must have extended his hands to Thomas, then also exposing and turning toward him his side. Jesus mentions seeing only once, just as Thomas had done, but in the second place, whereas Thomas has it in the first place. Thomas would verify what his eyes tell him by the thrust of his finger; Jesus bids him at once to apply his finger and thus to see. If the chief proof is to be the thrust of the finger, Thomas is at once to apply his finger. We cannot translate γίνου "become," as some do; for Thomas is not to grow into a believer by a gradual process. If becoming is the sense, it would have to be a becoming forthwith, and the imperative would have to be the aorist. Here, as so often in its use with adjectives and nouns, this present imperative means simply, "be" or "show thyself, prove thyself." Thomas is from now on to show himself as not being unbelieving but as believing. Only if we had the negative alone would the translation be in place, "stop showing thyself unbelieving"; the addition, "but believing," shuts this out. The two adjectives ἄπιστος and πιστός are direct opposites; Jesus uses them because Thomas had said, οὐ μὴ πιστεύσω. This word of Jesus' is simply an admonition not a rebuke. By placing the negative and the positive together, "do not show thyself unbelieving but believing," the admonition is made emphatic.

28) **Thomas answered and said to him, My Lord and my God!** A division of views meets us at this point. Some feel certain that Thomas simply sank to his knees and uttered the exclamation which John reports. The appearance of Jesus, together with the omniscience he displayed regarding the demands Thomas had made, conquered him completely. Those who think thus say that they cannot imagine that Thomas placed his finger and his hand into the wounds of Jesus as Jesus had ordered him to do. If he did so, they feel certain that John would have told us so, in fact, he should have told us. They also point to the text, according to which the answer of Thomas seems at once to follow. Others, however, hold the opposite view. The decision of the former is greatly facilitated when the view of the latter is conceived to be that Thomas is made to feel the hands and the side of Jesus in order to carry out his demands and thus actually to satisfy himself that this was Jesus as the other disciples had said. This, indeed, is unthinkable. If the decision were between this view and its opposite, that Thomas did no such thing, we could not do otherwise than to accept the latter.

But the situation does not turn on such an alternative. The decisive factor is the command of Jesus. It is couched in two peremptory imperatives. It is not Thomas who deliberately does what he said he would have to do before he believed; it is Jesus who now demands that he do this very thing. Those aorist imperatives compel Thomas to do what he now would gladly not do. These two imperatives tell us that Thomas did what he was thus commanded to do. John does not need to add another word. By compelling Thomas to use his finger and his hand as bidden Jesus is not punishing him. Far from it. A week ago he had commanded the other disciples in the same way: "Handle me and see; for a spirit hath not flesh and bones, as ye see me have," Luke 24:39. That the disciples had, indeed, handled Jesus as these two aorist imperatives in Luke plainly imply is evidenced by I John 1:1, "and our hands have handled of the Word of life." That which Jesus considered vital for the other disciples in order to make them "witnesses" in the fullest sense he certainly would not now allow Thomas to fail to do. He was now made a witness to the same extent as the others. Jesus looked far ahead in this insistence with regard to Thomas. For Thomas himself all future doubt and unbelief was made impossible. The thought was never to enter his mind that after all he had not handled Jesus as he had intended to do, and that possibly after all he had been tricked by a spirit. And for the future of the church Thomas, like the rest, was to be able to testify in words like those of John, "and our hands have handled" this risen Lord. We know regarding John that faith had entered his heart, though silently, on Easter morning (v. 8), and yet John had handled and felt the flesh and the bones of Jesus. How could Jesus possibly have allowed Thomas, "one of the Twelve" (v. 24), to do less?

On the force of "answered and said" compare 1:48. Because the older rationalists reduce the reply of Thomas to an ordinary exclamation of astonishment as when one cries out involuntarily, "My God!" we need not disturb ourselves about the grammar by stressing the nominative forms as shutting out this notion. It is already shut out by the preamble that Thomas "answered and *said to him*." Ὁ Κύριός μου καὶ ὁ Θεός μου, although they are nominative in form, are vocatives in force, being addressed to Jesus as exclamations, with nothing whatever to supply. We may indeed say that the exclamation has the sense, "Thou art my Lord and my God," but not that we must supply "thou art." Compare the interesting discussioon between Robertson, Winer, and Abbott in R. 466. The different views regarding the grammar are generally due to the reluctance of admitting that Thomas here unequivocally acknowledges Jesus as ὁ Θεός. R. 462 must stand: Thomas "gave Christ full acceptance of his deity and of the fact of his resurrection." What this involves as coming from a man who had been reared a Jew with the Jewish conception of God is self-evident. We may compare Nathanael's confession in 1:49. He said "the Son of God," and Thomas "my God," but both are to be understood in the same sense. On the knowledge of the Trinity as derived from the Old Testament by the Jews compare the discussion in 1:32 and 49. The two articles and the two possessives "my" make each of the two designations stand out independently. It is often said that the second forms a climax to the first, i. e., that "my God" expresses more than "my Lord." We fear that this view results from stressing the Greek, in which the title κύριος is often used with reference to men (see v. 15, the gardener), so that the question always arises as to how much this title is intended to convey. Thomas, however, in reality spoke Aramaic, and even

if he had used Greek, to him "my Lord" here includes
deity as fully as does "my God." The duplication is
not intended to add to a lesser term one that is greater
but to express the one conviction of Thomas in the most
emphatic way. The two possessives "my" flow in
almost automatically as the natural expressions of
faith. Thus in v. 13 Mary still said, "my Lord."

29) Indeed, Thomas thus obeyed the Lord's admonition, "Show thyself as believing!" Whether Thomas
sank to his knees or prostrated himself on the ground
before Jesus, we do not know; many think he did the
latter. **Jesus says to him, Because thou hast seen
me thou hast believed. Blessed they who did not see
and did believe.** Jesus accepts the exclamation with
which Thomas acknowledges him as his Lord and his
God. Too much stress cannot be laid on this simple
fact. In the face of 2:24, 25 a view such as that
Thomas has in mind one thing, while the acceptance
of Jesus has another in mind, is unwarranted. He
who knew the very words of Thomas uttered in v. 25
knew the very thought of Thomas when he cried, "My
Lord and my God!" Jesus in no way modifies this
exclamation; he corrects it neither downward as though
Thomas says or means too much, nor upward as though
Thomas says or means too little.

It has long been understood that John's Gospel
closes just as it began by proclaiming the deity of Jesus.
"And the Word was God," 1:1, has its counterpart in
the confession of Thomas, "My God!" and in the concluding word of John in v. 31. It was granted to
Thomas to make the final grand confession recorded by
John. This disciple's character, especially also the
psychology back of his sudden turn from the most bold
and pronounced unbelief to the most decisive faith, will
always remain highly interesting. He illustrates the
fact that at times extremes do certainly meet. The

brazen front of much unbelief is hollow after all, and when it caves in it caves in completely.

Jesus accepts the faith and the confession of Thomas for he himself says, "thou hast believed." But he accepts this faith only as what it is: "because thou hast seen thou hast believed." The perfects are extensive, the culmination point having just been reached, R. 95. Jesus does not praise the faith of Thomas as he does the faith mentioned in Matt. 15:28, or in Matt. 8:10. He does not answer Thomas as he does Peter in Matt. 16:17. We may note the parallel to Nathanael in 1:50, who also came to faith as the result of a wondrous revelation of Jesus: "Because I said unto thee I saw thee underneath the fig tree thou believest." As little as we had reason to make this a question directed to Nathanael, so little have we reason to assume that a question was directed to Thomas. The perfect tenses shut this out even more than the present used with reference to Nathanael. Jesus simply acknowledges the fact that Thomas has come to faith. But the acknowledgment in the case of Nathanael is coupled with a wonderful promise to Nathanael, not so the acknowledgment in the case of Thomas. Here the promise is to others, to those who shall believe without first seeing. This difference is due to the difference between the two men. Nathanael's was his first meeting with Jesus at the very beginning of his ministry, while Thomas had followed Jesus for three years to the very end of his ministry. Is Jesus, then, reproaching Thomas when he here acknowledges his faith? Does he intend to say, "Without seeing thou shouldest have believed"? We shall hesitate to assume such blame when we note that the faith of all the disciples present was the outcome of sight, even that of John (v. 8). We shall again hesitate when we realize that Jesus himself intended to furnish the fullest sight to these disciples in order to equip them as his witnesses to the church

of all future ages.   The fault of Thomas was not the
fact that his faith sprang from sight, but that he
spurned the sight of others and demanded even more
than sight for himself, something that set him apart
from and above all the others.   Here lay his fault, and
Jesus, having pardoned him, makes no reference to the
fault.

The first word, "Because thou hast seen thou hast
believed," is only the preamble to the vital statement
that follows.   It was necessary for Jesus to grant sight
to these disciples of his during these forty days after
his resurrection.   In the same way it had been necessary for him to perform many miracles during his
entire ministry.   This necessity would continue for
the work of the apostles and for the early days of the
existence of the church.   Sight had its necessary place
in the economy of grace which wrought out our salvation and founded the church.   But the disciples were
not to think that in all future ages Jesus would use
sight in this way.   Even in their own future work
sight will play only a minor part.   So after the preamble Jesus adds the main statement, "Blessed they
who did not see and did believe," καί, as so often in the
sense, "and yet did believe."   The two aorist participles are by no means to be understood in the sense of
future perfects: "shall not have seen and yet shall have
believed."   They are timeless, R. 859.   Whoever at
any time, past, present, or future, believes without seeing is pronounced "blessed" in the soteriological sense.

The sight granted to the disciples then has a special
significance and purpose.   A certain blessedness, indeed, accompanies also this, Matt. 13:16, namely as
restricted to this significance and purpose.   But where
this no longer applies, I Pet. 1:8 is the normal way:
"Whom having not seen, ye love; in whom, though now
ye see him not, yet believing, ye rejoice with joy
unspeakable and full of glory."   II Cor. 5:7; Heb.

11:1 and 27. S. Goebel has collated the following passages on sight and faith, using only John's Gospel:
1:50; 2:23; 4:45, 48, 50; 6:36; 10:37, etc.; 11:40, 45;
14:11; 15:24; 20:8.

10. The Conclusion, 30, 31

These two verses constitute the formal conclusion
of the Gospel as planned and composed by John. "No
other historical writing in the New Testament, and
few historical writings of antiquity, have such a clear
conclusion as has the Fourth Gospel in 20:31, etc."
Zahn. This verdict needs no support. The only question worth answering is why John closes the body of
his Gospel with the account concerning Thomas, or, in
other words, why he did not add a few more sections,
possibly on the appearance to the five hundred (I Cor.
15:6), baptism, and the ascension of Jesus. This question has already been answered repeatedly whenever
occasion offered to compare John's selection of incidents with that of the synoptists. He selects what
most adequately unfolds his subject: the Attestation of
Jesus as the Son of God. This subject he himself
indicates in v. 31. It is not a question as to what John
might have added under this subject; for all along we
see that his aim is not to multiply but to select. His
last selection thus is the Thomas incident which culminates in the attestation voiced by this disciple, an
attestation which surely forms a climax in every way
— such unbelief turned into the confession, "My Lord
and my God!" The entire Gospel is misapprehended
when its objective nature is made subjective as though
John had intended to trace "the development of the
faith of the disciples and of his own." What he actually traces is the Person of the Son of God in the Attestation of his Ministry and his Passion and his
Resurrection. That Attestation is now before us.

30) The concluding words are brief. **Many
and other signs, therefore, Jesus did in the presence
of his disciples, which have not been written in this
book; these, however, have been written in order
that you may believe that Jesus is the Christ, the
Son of God, and that by believing you may have
life in his name.** It would be misleading to regard
σημεῖα as in any sense being in contrast with "the words"
of Jesus. The ἔργα are at times contrasted with the
oral testimony, as in 10:37, 38, but even then the oral
testimony is attested by the works. The ethical term
"signs" always points to what lies back of these signs,
what these signs manifest and display to men's minds
and hearts. The very term thus involves the words of
the teaching of Jesus. It is John's Gospel in particular
which connects the signs with the discourses of Jesus.
Even when no sign is immediately connected with a
discourse, the signs (or works) yet form the basis and
the background without which the discourses would
hang in the air. "Signs," of course, embraces all the
miracles but extends beyond them to every significant
action which revealed Jesus. Jesus did these signs
"in the presence of his disciples"; the preposition
ἐνώπιον is weighty, just as ἔμπροσθεν is in 12:37. John
has in mind: in their very presence so that the disciples
were able to see them in the most perfect manner.
They were his constant companions so that even when
their presence is not specifically mentioned in cases
like 5:1, etc., where no action on their part required
mention, they were undoubtedly present. In 12:37
the reference is to the Jews in general, but the same
persons (Jews) did not see all the signs, for at times
one set of Jews saw one sign, and at another time
another group saw another sign. In the case of the
disciples this was different, for Jesus had selected the
disciples as his chosen witnesses, and his purpose was
to have them see his signs so fully as to be able to

function as his witnesses indeed (I John 1:1). Besides the Twelve two other men were thus qualified, Acts 1:20-23. In their case the purpose of Jesus was personal faith, which, however, was attained in only a few (12:37); in the case of the chosen disciples the purpose extended farther: they were, indeed, also to be believers but in addition the Lord's selected and qualified witnesses for all future time.

Already these considerations show that John is here speaking of his entire Gospel and that he has in mind not only the last chapter in which he recounts four incidents taken from the resurrection history. We may add that the contrast John uses between the signs he wrote in this book and the many other signs not written by him cannot be crowded into just this one chapter. The sense of John's statement cannot be: I have recorded only four resurrection signs, but Jesus offered many more during the forty days. The number of the appearances was quite limited (I Cor. 15:5, etc.), and in the main they were similar: Jesus presenting himself alive. The term σημεῖα, too, is hardly the one to use if only the appearances are referred to. It fits admirably if John is speaking of his entire Gospel. Furthermore, the phrase "in this book" certainly has in mind the entire "book" not merely its small closing section. When John writes "in *this* book" he intimates that his readers know of other books, those of the other evangelists, in which quite a number of these "many and other signs" are recorded, so that it was not necessary for John to duplicate those well-known records.

31) Verse 30 is only a preliminary statement. John tells his readers that he has made a selection of material in composing his Gospel. Naturally the main statement now follows, namely one which tells us what guided him in his selection. It was no abstract, theoretical, pedagogical, or even doctrinal principle but the supreme practical principle: "in order that you may

believe," etc. John's intention was to write an εὐαγγέλιον, "a Gospel," setting forth the realities concerning
Jesus so that they may produce faith in those who are
not believers and may confirm faith in those who believe. The majority of the texts has the aorist πιστεύσητε, others have the present. John is writing for
readers who already believe; hence this aorist is not
ingressive, "come to believe," but perfective, "may
believe definitely, finally, completely." The second ἵνα
clause has the durative presents πιστεύοντες ἔχητε. John's
purpose in writing what he does is ἵνα πιστεύσητε, "that
you may be believing," i. e., now and ever.

In 19:35 the verb has no object and thus signifies
faith as such. Here in the conclusion John adds the
object, but it is of such a nature that it again indicates
the entire Christian faith and not merely faith in certain important facts such as the actuality of the appearances. When John thus addresses his readers in the
second person in a book which otherwise presents
objective material he indicates his own inner attitude
toward his readers. Throughout the book he feels as
though he himself were present in the congregation
where his lines are read, as though he himself were
speaking personally to his readers. This is the more
significant when we recall that he constantly keeps his
own person as well as all his relatives in the background, not once directly naming them. This humility
on his part, however, is not intended to make him
anything less than a personal witness. That he speaks
as such we are now most certain.

His readers are to believe "that Jesus is the Christ,
the Son of God." "Jesus" is the historical person
who moves through John's sacred pages. On ὁ Χριστός
see 4:25. This designates the office of Jesus into
which the anointing with the Spirit inducted him. We
are to believe that Jesus is the Messiah promised in the
Old Testament, "the Savior of the world," as the

Samaritans put it in 4:42. The apposition, "the Son of God," reveals his deity and his connection with the Father. John's conclusion tallies with his Prolog (1:1-18). In "Jesus" we have the full humanity of the Messiah, and in "the Son of God" his deity, the two joined in the personal union of the incarnation (1:14). It is not true that John's Gospel displays only "the God" Jesus; as in the other Gospels "the man" Christ Jesus is also made to stand before us. If the image of his deity is fully revealed to us, which we most gratefully acknowledge, we are compelled to add that no other Gospel exceeds John's in presenting with such clearness and often with the deepest tenderness the image of his perfect humanity. But the words here used, "that Jesus is the Christ, the Son of God," constitute not only the full sum and substance of the faith of all believers But at the same time the perfect and the most adequate confession of that faith. So adequate is this faith and this confession that it covers all that John has recorded. In so doing it certifies to us its oneness and its identity with the faith and the confession of the other evangelists and of the other New Testament writers. And thus we see that, while John chose only certain parts of the entire gospel story for record "in this book," he did so, not as discounting the other parts, large portions of which the synoptists placed into their records, but as uniting his record with theirs in supporting the faith "that Jesus is the Christ, the Son of God." This, too, is why he weaves his record together with theirs in so many places, counting on it that his readers know their records, and adding to their records new features as well as entire new sections.

The proximate purpose is the faith of John's readers, the ultimate purpose is: "and that by believing you may have life in his name." Compare 1:12, and on the terms "believe" and "having life" 3:15, 16.

Faith and faith alone has life. The present subjunctive is the proper term, for the believer has this life at once, the instant he believes, and possesses this life with all that it contains as long as he believes. "In his name" makes the pronoun αὐτοῦ the final word. Here, as so often before (see 1:12), ὄνομα is the revelation which brings Jesus to us as the Christ, the Son of God, so that we may know and embrace him by faith. The ὄνομα is the one and only means. The preposition should be left in its native sense: "in union, in vital connection with, his Name." The entire Gospel of John, yea, the entire gospel as such, is nothing other than "His NAME."

CHAPTER XXI

The Supplement, Chapter 21

It is quite impossible to regard the last two verses of chapter 20 as anything but the formal and proper conclusion of John's Gospel. The impression made on us is that, when John penned or dictated these final verses, he intended to add nothing further. We must even say more: he left his Gospel together with its conclusion as it was. He did not cancel the conclusion, insert new sections, and then rewrite the conclusion. In an operation such as that he most certainly would not have used the incidents found in chapter 21. For these incidents stand apart, are in a class by themselves, and thus are not in a direct line with those found in chapter 20. They deal with the apostles personally; therefore also Paul does not list the appearance to the seven disciples at the Sea of Tiberias in his record in I Cor. 15:4. Often this vital point, the type and the contents of chapter 21, is overlooked. We should not say simply that here we have another "sign," another appearance of the risen Lord. This is too superficial to be connected with an apostle like John. He could utilize material such as that found in chapter 21 only as he did, namely as a supplement to his Gospel proper. The term "appendix" is not adequate, "supplement" or *Nachtrag* is far better.

No copies of the Fourth Gospel have ever been found from which chapter 21 is omitted, and no trace of such copies has ever been discovered. This means that the Gospel contained 21 chapters from the date of its publication onward. For if any copies that contained only 20 chapters had ever been made, no power on earth

could have prevented their spread, or could have oblit-
erated all trace of such abbreviated copies. And this,
in turn, means that chapter 21 was added to John's
Gospel almost immediately, thus, to say the least, under
John's own eyes and supervision. It is John who
stands back of the entire 21 chapters.

But did John himself write or dictate chapter 21?
This question, naturally, is meaningless for those who
reject the Johannine authorship of this entire Gospel;
doing that, they would not consider as much as the possibility that John wrote chapter 21. This question has
meaning only for those who see and know that John
wrote the twenty chapters preceding. Let us at once
say that the so-called linguistic evidence, the fund of
words and the general style, is in favor of John as being
the writer also of chapter 21. But the assertion is still
made in certain quarters, that the language of chapter
21 differs in a marked way from that used in the body
of the Gospel. The persistence of this assertion is not
due to the evidence at hand. Aside from the type and
the style of the language used, three indications in the
chapter itself necessitate the conclusion that John himself is not the author of this chapter. He could not
himself have written the last two verses. On this point
sound scholarship is in general agreement. But this
might leave the rest of the chapter to John's pen. Yet
would John, who never mentions any member of his
family by name in the long course of twenty chapters,
break this rule and after all now mention his father's
name in 21:2? We cannot think that he would. We
see how John, when he is compelled to refer to himself,
does this in a veiled, reticent way in 13:23; 19:26;
20:2: "the disciple whom Jesus loved." After doing
this in such a marked way in the course of twenty
chapters, is it likely that finally in 21:20 he would
expand this reference by adding the long relative
clause, "who also leaned on his breast," etc? Is it

likely that John's own pen would have made this addition when the simple designation already used three different times and thus made familiar to his readers, would suffice also in 21:20? This long addition betrays another hand.

But while the writing by another hand is thus admitted, this hand wrote the narrative as John himself had told it again and again, for the language is John's own, and the chapter was added under John's supervision. Of course, only one man penned the chapter, but v. 24 proves the presence of other authoritative persons (οἴδαμεν, "we know"). It is a safe conclusion that these men were the presbyters of the Ephesian church. They had often heard John relate the contents of chapter 21, and after John's Gospel had been completed by him and had been read to them, they induced John to have this supplement added. Chapter 21 is thus an addition, not by one hand, but by the will and wish of the entire presbytery. John consented. God used these presbyters for preserving to the church this additional precious revelation. In this connection we may recall how much of the inspired writing was occasioned; and we may include even the twenty chapters by John's own hand or dictation. The reproduction of John's oral narration by the Ephesian presbytery, one of whom did the writing, John himself accepting the result, removes all difficulties as to the inspiration of chapter 21. The view which allows about ten years before the adding of the supplement to the Gospel proper appears arbitrary. It is highly probable that the addition was made without delay. Copies of the work would be made almost at once, and all of them had 21 chapters.

1) **After these things Jesus manifested himself to the disciples at the Sea of Tiberias. Now he manifested himself in this manner.** The connection "after these things," those narrated in 20:26-29, is

in John's usual style. The fact that more is to be added, namely, still later events, although 20:30, 31 has already brought the conclusion, indicates quite sufficiently that what now follows is a supplement. It presents another manifestation of Jesus to the disciples. The verb "to manifest" occurs six times in the preceding chapters, in 7:4 with the reflexive as here, and appears seventeen times in John's writings. Like Paul in I Cor. 15:4, etc., John distinguishes between the appearances of Jesus and regards those to the disciples as a class separate from those to the women. The locality is mentioned: "at the Sea of Tiberias," John's way of naming the sea or lake (6:1) from the pagan city situated on its shores, the only town of all the towns that once graced its shores that has survived. So the disciples had gone to Galilee, which indicates that John knew about the directions they had received to this effect (Mark 14:28; Matt. 28:7 and 10). The fact that John now mentions the change of locality indicates that the appearance to Thomas occurred in Jerusalem. Just when the disciples removed to Galilee is nowhere indicated. From I Cor. 15:6 we conclude that the meeting of Jesus with the five hundred was the chief object of the directions given by Jesus before his death and repeated by him and by the angels after his resurrection. This, however, would not preclude the more incidental appearance here at the seaside.

To say that the addition, "Now he manifested himself in this manner," is unusual for John, is to mistake the situation. This circumstantial addition agrees with the supplementary character of the narrative now introduced, and the "manifestation" thus introduced is itself quite elaborate (v. 2-23), warranting an additional introductory word.

2) **There were together Simon Peter, and Thomas called Didymus, and Nathanael from Cana of Galilee, and those of Zebedee, and two others of**

his disciples. We may ask why five of these seven are identified and two are left unidentified. The real interest of the narrative centers in Peter and John, so that one might expect these two alone to be identified with the additional remark that some others, or five others, were also present. The idea that the five who are named were apostles, and the other two disciples in the wider sense, seems unwarranted. Another answer is that the five have been named in the body of the Gospel and thus have already been introduced to the readers, while the other two have not been thus previously named. The fact that Thomas is mentioned is significant after 20:24, etc. This time we find him where he belongs. Again his Hebrew name is translated into Greek, "Didymus," which is "Twin." Since Thomas is entirely silent in this narrative, this Greek version of his name cannot intend to remind us of any duality in his nature (compare 11:16; 20:24). On Nathanael see 1:46; incidentally we here learn that he was from Cana, which recalls 2:1, etc.

"Those of Zebedee," namely his sons John and James, by actually naming John's father violates the unwritten canon John has obeyed throughout his Gospel not to name himself or any of his relatives (1:35-41; 13:23; 18:15, etc.; 19:25-27 and 35; 20:2-10), extending this anonymity even to the mother of Jesus, so as to make us think that she, too, is one of John's relatives. Here "Zebedee" is suddenly named outright. It is so unlike John to do this that we cannot pass by this naming of his father as being without significance. We can only say that others are here writing not John in his own person. The canon John set up for himself is not foisted upon others by him; they are free to insert his father's name here, he himself would not have done so.

3) **Simon Peter says to them, I go a-fishing. They say to him, We, too, are going with you. They**

**went forth and entered a boat, and in that night
they caught nothing.** The story is told in detail,
which, instead of being unlike John, is much like him.
All is vivid, the persons constituting the party, their
words, and their actions. Since John had often told
these incidents, his presbyters now record them. Peter's word, "I go a-fishing," is one of familiar discourse.
The indicative he uses, as well as that found in the
response made by the others, denotes only definite assertion, R. 923. He declares what he will do in such a
way as to invite the others to join him. On the infinitive with ὑπάγω see R. 353, 990, 1062. The preposition
σύν indicates that the others intend to help him. It was
evening, the best time for fishing being the night.
"The boat" is definite, the one owned by Peter and his
brother. Having originally been fishermen, it was
natural that these men, or most of them, should go back
to their old occupation. All we know is that they did
so this night. The assumption that they plied their
old trade regularly is hastily drawn. The critics
assume this and declare that what is here related is
inconsistent with the commission given in 20:21, etc.,
and thus they place John's narrative prior to the resurrection and make it a version of Luke 5:1, etc. This
type of criticism needs no refutation. It is entirely
like Peter to make the proposition to do a bit of work;
he likes activity. Besides, a good catch of fish will not
come amiss while they wait for the further directions
of their Lord.

But strange to say, though they labored all night
long at their task, they caught nothing. This recalls
Luke 5:5. But an effort to combine the two accounts
into one occurrence goes awry the moment the totally
different details are noted.

4) **Now early morning being already at hand,
Jesus stood on the beach; however, the disciples
were not aware that it was Jesus.** The fact that

John here writes πρωΐα (ὥρα) is due to the genitive absolute and is not an indication of a vocabulary differing
from that of John, such as that in 20:1 where he has
the adverb πρωΐ. The preposition εἰς is static, R. 593.
John told only the fact that the disciples were not
aware that the figure standing on the beach was (the
Greek retains "is") Jesus. Did the morning haze on
the water render sight indistinct? Did Jesus will not
to be recognized at once? Or was his appearance quite
different from the previous appearances? All three
explanations have been offered.

5) **Jesus, therefore, says to them, Lads, you
havn't anything to eat, have you? They answered
him, No.** "Therefore" refers to the action of standing on the beach, so that Jesus could well call out to
those in the boat. On the address παιδία in the sense
of "lads" (not "children"), used even with reference to
soldiers in the papyri, see M.-M. 474. The προσφάγιον is
Zukost, anything eaten with (πρός) bread, and refers
almost exclusively to "fish," M.-M. 551. The question
introduced by μή implies that a negative answer is in
the mind of the speaker. Jesus, of course, knew that
the disciples had caught nothing. He does not ask for
this information but wants to have the disciples themselves state that they have nothing in order that he
himself may direct them what to do.

6) **But he said to them, Throw the net on the
right side of the boat and you shall find. They,
therefore, threw it and were no longer strong
enough to draw it for the multitude of the fish.** The
disciples were aware only of the presence of a strange
man on the beach and this man's apparent good will.
That he seemed willing to buy fish is not indicated;
then his question would have been introduced by οὐ,
implying an affirmative answer. The remarkable thing
is that, when this stranger ordered the disciples to
throw their net on the other side of the boat, they at

once did so. Professional fishermen do not let a stranger, who may know nothing at all about their work, direct their work in this peremptory manner; nor would they accept a stranger's promise of success on rendering him such blind obedience. It is fantastic to say, "Perhaps Jesus had seen a school of fish on that side of the boat." The two sides of the boat are only a few feet apart; those in a boat are able to see what is in the water on both sides, not so a man on the shore more than 300 feet away. Yet these men obey the orders of Jesus with strange promptness. Something compellingly authoritative seems to make obedience to Jesus altogether natural. Something masterfully assuring seems to put the promise of Jesus ("you shall find") altogether beyond question. The plural τὰ δεξιὰ μέρη is idomatic for our singular, "the right parts," for "the right side," R. 408. Nothing occult or superstitious can possibly lurk in this mention of the right side by Jesus as though the disciples are to think of this as the lucky side. They had fished all night, now on this, now on that side of their boat.

The miracle was instantaneous. The net was so heavy with fish that the disciples could not haul it up into the boat. Here ἀπό indicates cause, R. 580. The imperfect ἴσχυον pictures the disciples exerting all their strength. Jesus had filled their net, as he had once before done in Luke 5:6, 7, only the details are entirely different.

7) That disciple, therefore, whom Jesus loved says to Peter, It is the Lord. Here John's regular manner of designating himself reappears unchanged. It is John who recognizes Jesus more quickly than the rest. This astounding catch of fish reveals to him the presence of the Lord. His first thought is to tell Peter. So sadly has John's Gospel been misunderstood that John (or denying his authorship, the imagined author) has been charged with elevating himself above Peter in this Gospel, whereas the truth is constantly brought out that John and Peter are the closest friends. See 1:41; in 13:24 Peter and John act together; in 18:15, etc., John takes the blame for bringing Peter in; in 20:2 Peter and John are together; in 21:20, etc., Peter is concerned about John; in Acts 3:1, etc., Peter and John heal the lame man, and in 8:14 these two inspect the work in Samaria.

Simon Peter, therefore, having heard that it is the Lord, girdled his blouse around him, for he was naked, and threw himself into the sea. By means of the mass of fish Jesus had made his presence known, and Peter abandons everything, boat as well as fish, and runs straight to Jesus. Here is the same old impetuosity of the man. John remains in the boat with the rest. Only an eyewitness could mention the detail about the blouse. The disciples had worked "naked," which, however, does not mean stripped of all clothing, as some suppose. For γυμνός is also used when those parts of the body that are usually covered with clothing are exposed. The disciples had on common working blouses, which reached almost to the knees, had short sleeves, and were left to hang loose. This ἐπενδύτης Peter fastened around his waist with a girdle (R. 810) before he jumped into the water. Comparing 13:4 where Jesus first "took" the linen apron and then tied it around him, we note that here Peter does not "take" the blouse but only draws a girdle around it, evidently because he already has the blouse on. The deduction is therefore out of place that Peter first dressed before he came to the Lord, and that this was due to his reverence for the Lord. When anyone leaped into the water, any garment he wore would become wet and would cling tightly to the body. What John intends to narrate is the haste of Peter. In a second or two he is through, simply fastening his *Arbeitskittel* with a girdle to hold it properly in place. Not that he expects

the other disciples to do the same and thus to abandon
the boat and the rich catch of fish the Lord had granted
to them.   He acts only on his own impulse, leaving
the others to act on theirs.   We shall always meet such
differences, for the Lord's disciples are really complements to each other.

8)   **But the other disciples came by means of
the little boat, for they were not far from the land,
but about two hundred forearm lengths, dragging
the net of fish.**   The dative τῷ πλοιαρίω may be instrumental, "by means of the boat" (R. 533), and thus in
contrast to Peter, or, as R. 521 prefers, the locative,
"in the boat."   The change from πλοῖον, "boat," to the
diminutive πλοιάριον, "little boat," matches the same
change in 6:17-20 and 22.   We have no reason to think
of two boats, one full-sized and one a "punt"; for the
disciples would then be in the punt, and no one in the
big boat.   With γάρ the explanation of the eyewitness
is added that the distance to the shore was not far, only
about 200 πήχεις, (πῆχυς, the "length of a forearm," 1½
feet), thus 300 feet.   We have ὡς ἀπό exactly as in
11:18.   Even with Peter in the boat these seven men
did not have the strength to haul up the net.   With
Peter removed, they were still less able to do so.   They
thus simply dragged the net to shore.   The weight
indicated hints at the size of the fish.   So richly laden
the disciples come to the shore.   Nothing is said about
what Peter said and did after he reached the shore
ahead of the boat.   In the "net of the fish" the genitive
is that of the contents, R. 499.

9)   The astounding manifestations of this early
morning hour are by no means ended with the catch
of fish.   **When, therefore, they went up on the land
they see a charcoal fire laid, and a fish laid thereon
and bread.**   The surprise of the disciples is marked
by the present tense, "they see," namely here on the

shore an ἀνθρακιὰ κειμένη, a charcoal fire that has been
laid, the coals glowing! And on these coals a fish has
been laid, lying there roasting! And bread is there,
too, ἄρτος, a cake of bread to go with the ὀψάριον, the
same word as that used in 6:9 and 11 (which see,
Zukost, regularly used regarding fish)! Everything is
ready for a meal! How did all this get here? We pass
by the answers that Jesus had carried everything to
this place, that he had employed some stranger to do
so, or that Peter had hurried to bring the materials to
shore, had lit the charcoal, etc. The fire, the fish, and
the bread are here through the miraculous power of
Jesus. Those who seek to combine Luke 5 with this
section of John's Gospel are here completely upset. In
v. 13 the article τὸ ὀψάριον settles the question as to
whether the roasting fish was one fish or several,
enough for seven men. The debate on this point overlooks the singular ἄρτον. If several cakes of bread were
in the mind of the writer, the Greek certainly would
have used ἄρτοι. Just as one fish would ordinarily not
suffice for seven persons, so also one cake of bread as
baked in those days would not satisfy so many. When
fire, fish, and bread are provided miraculously, why
insist on quantities? Did Jesus not feed the 5,000 with
only five cakes of bread and two small fishes? First
Jesus blesses his disciples with a rich catch of fish after
a night of labor, then he has everything ready to
refresh them with food, tired and hungry as they now
were.

10) But before the meal begins, the catch of fish,
still in the net and in the water, must be safely brought
to land. In Luke 5 the great catch is left behind by
the disciples, who are asked to follow Jesus, but left
in other hands, not to be wasted and lost; here the
situation is different, the seven disciples are to take
proper care of their catch. **Jesus says to them,
Bring part of the fish which you just caught.** This

command is misread when it is thought to mean: Bring a few more fish to roast, enough for all of you. Verse 11 shows that the disciples did nothing of the kind. The partitive ἀπό (R. 519), "part of the fish," means that only the large fish are to be retained by the disciples, all the smaller ones are to be emptied out of the net back into the lake. So the command really means: Before you eat with me, go and take care of the fish you want to keep; finish your catch and then dine. The aorist ἐπιάσατε indicates an act that has just happened, where we usually write the perfect, R. 843, 845.

11) **Simon Peter, accordingly, went aboard and drew the net to the land, full of great fishes, a hundred and fifty-three; and, though being so many, the net was not torn.** What Peter does is what the Lord wanted done. The top of the net had been made fast to the boat, the prow of which rested on the beach. It was no great labor for one man to unfasten the net and to bring its top to the hands waiting at the water's edge. Then the fish were sorted out of the net, all the sizeable ones thrown into the boat, all the small fry dumped back into the lake. John remembers the exact number, 153 fish in all. He does more. Such a load of fish, yielding so many big ones, would be likely to tear the net and let some of the catch escape. This happened in the incident recorded in Luke 5:6, but not here. It is fanciful to imagine that only these 153 big fish entered the net, and still worse to seek some kind of symbolism or mysticism in the number 153, or some mysterious way in which the number 153 is attained. John's narrative is exact, that is all; he remembers the very number of the fish. The wonder of it all has never faded from his mind. Those who say, "undoubtedly symbolic," need to furnish the proof. The notion that the ancients counted 153 varieties of fish, an idea derived by Jerome from Oppian (end of the second century), cannot be verified and would amount

to nothing if it could be. Pliny might be consulted on a point like this, but he knows of 174 kinds.

12) With the fish properly put away, the disciples may rest and eat. **Jesus says to them, Come break-fast! And no one of the disciples had boldness to investigate regarding him, Who art thou? since they knew that it was the Lord.** The asyndeton: Δεῦτε ἀριστήσατε is a common idiom, R. 949. The entire appearance of Jesus on this occasion is remarkable in that no word is uttered regarding himself and none regarding the relation of the disciples to him. From beginning to end everything is action, and every word spoken by Jesus pertains only to the action, omitting to add even the slightest reason for, or explanation of, the action. The disciples longed for more, especially for some word from Jesus that it was indeed he. But none of them ventured to make investigation. The verb ἐξετάσαι does not mean "to inquire"; it is much stronger than ἐρωτᾶν. It means "to make investigation," to ask or to say something that might lead Jesus to say that it was he indeed. "Who art thou?" is not a direct question put to Jesus but the thought or main point in a possible investigation. The imperfect ἐτόλμα does not mean that the disciples feared to investigate, but that something held them back. They did not feel bold and free to speak as under other circumstances in their former familiar intercourse they would have done without hesitation.

The reason for this reverent timidity is given: "since they knew that it was the Lord." The participle is causal (R. 1128), its case agreeing with οὐδείς, its number with μαθητῶν (R. 437, etc.). But we must note ὁ Κύριος, "the Lord," no longer merely, "Jesus"; compare v. 7. They knew the Lord's presence through the miracles here wrought so wondrously. This statement about the way in which the disciples here feel in the presence of Jesus leads many to think that on this occasion the appearance of Jesus differed to a marked degree from his previous appearances. In fact, we are unable to say whether even any two appearances during the forty days were similar. Perhaps all were different, although who would venture to say in just what manner? It is quite possible that after the disciples truly believed in his resurrection Jesus manifested more and more of his glory to them in his subsequent appearances. Ever more fully he revealed himself as "the Lord." Yet the idea that Jesus passed through a glorifying process during the forty days, gradually growing more divine and heavenly in his human nature until he ascended bodily to heaven; or that his human nature was gradually absorbed into the divine nature and finally was lost in divinity altogether, is speculation only.

13) **Jesus comes and takes the bread and gives to them, and the fish in like manner.** The disciples also come; but the narrative shows that their eyes were looking only at him, watching his actions. Not a word is spoken, the Lord's actions speak for him. He does not need to bless the food as he did in 6:11, when he was still in his state of humiliation; he has himself, as the divine Lord, provided this food, and that is its blessing. No longer does he need to look to heaven and pray his Father to bless the food he dispenses; his own presence and his hands, his own divine touch constitute the blessing. Some think that the blessing was spoken by Jesus in the usual way, and that John makes no mention of that fact because he takes it for granted. But when John writes, "Jesus comes, takes, gives," etc., we cannot think that he would have omitted the one verb or participle necessary to indicate the blessing, if the Lord had indeed spoken the blessing. While some are sure that a blessing was spoken, they yet think that when Jesus said, "come" (δεῦτε), the disciples did not come but held back.

So they think that Jesus comes to them (ἔρχεται) and brings them the bread and the fish. Would they put him to this trouble? Would they not sit on the ground, as Orientals still do, in a close circle about the fire and the food, and thus let Jesus serve them?

Jesus first takes the bread and gives this to the disciples. He breaks pieces from the one cake. It multiplies under his hands, so that these hungry men receive all that they need. He does the same with the roasted fish, and it, too, proves to be enough for all of them. The miracle of 6:10, etc., is repeated, but now with a new significance, one pertaining to the apostles and future ministers of the Lord alone. Did also Jesus eat? He did, we are told, because in v. 5 he asked whether the disciples had anything to eat. Yet why should he ask on his own account, why could not this question have been asked on the disciples' account? The question is certainly properly understood when it is taken in the sense, "Have you anything yourselves so that *you* can eat?" Moreover, the Lord himself provides the food for the disciples to eat, which shuts out the very idea introduced in v. 5 for support of the conclusion that Jesus, too, ate. Acts 10:41 is adduced as proof that Jesus ate. Aside from Luke 24:42, 43 no eating of Jesus is reported in any of the appearances, and drinking is never mentioned anywhere. When the eating and the drinking to which Peter refers took place no one is able to say. Here, indeed, in this one appearance it might have occurred. The reason for hesitation in assuming that it did lies in the character of all that is here done by Jesus — it is all symbolical. If the eating and the drinking on the part of Jesus himself could be fitted into the symbolism here presented, we should be ready to say that it took place. The text itself leaves out such action on the part of Jesus.

The critics have their own version of this incident. Luke 5:1, etc., and John 21:1-14 are one and the same event. Then Matt. 4:18-20 and Mark 1:16-20 are also brought into the combination, with Luke 24:36-43 as "a counterpart." Finally, this is made "a eucharistic meal." Why this term "eucharistic"? Is it to lead us to think of the actual Eucharist, the Lord's Supper, so as to combine the Sacrament with this meal (bread and fish) beside the lake? But criticism should be soundly and sanely historical; in this case it proves altogether unhistorical.

14) **For this, the third time already, was Jesus manifested to the disciples after having risen from the dead.** It is characteristic of John thus to round out and to mark off a narrative by a final statement, separating it from anything that follows. In this case the separate statement proves to be rather important. It shuts out the view of some that v. 1-14 furnish only the general setting for what they consider the main account, the Lord's dealing with Peter and his prophecies concerning Peter and John. Quite the contrary. John would have us understand that the draught of fishes and the meal beside the lake constitute an independent piece full of a meaning and import of its own.

John records this as the third appearance "to the disciples," i. e., to the men who belonged to the Twelve. We see that he classifies the various appearances. He leaves in what we may call the minor class the appearance to the women, to Mary Magdalene, to Peter (Luke 24:34; I Cor. 15:5), and to the two disciples at Emmaus. The major class are the appearances in 20:19, etc., and in 20:26, etc. Paul classifies somewhat differently in I Cor. 15:5, etc. We need not be disturbed about ἤδη, which simply means that these three main appearances followed each other at only short intervals. It surely does not mean to deny other appearances. The participle ἐγερθείς, without the article, denotes the time: "after having arisen," and is not a predicate: "as the one who was risen." The passive is used as the middle. On the phrase ἐκ νεκρῶν see 2:22.

The symbolical character of the entire action connected with this appearance, like that of Luke 5:1-11, has been so generally recognized that we need note only the fact. When Jesus first called the two pairs of brothers to be "fishers of men" he taught them by means of a miracle that their success was absolutely sure if they would obey his command and rely only upon his Word, no matter what their own skill and reason might advise, or how foolish they might appear to the multitude. All night long, fishing in the best places, with their own best skill, they had caught nothing. But, as Peter put it, "casting the net at thy word," now at the worst time in the middle of the day, in the worst place out in the deep of the lake, under the worst circumstances with a critical crowd looking on from the shore, their net had been filled miraculously by the Lord even to breaking, and they had to call for help to bring in the catch. Thus were they to become fishers of men. This symbolical miracle is now repeated after the commission is renewed in 20:21-23, also including Thomas (v. 26, etc.). Again, not all of the apostles are present, although the symbol is intended for all. The place of Judas is as yet vacant. Yet seven are assembled. No real symbolism has been found in either this number or in the number of the great fish caught. The scene is all action with only enough words to insure the action. Again, a night of fruitless labor — human effort alone is nothing. Again the Lord's Word, and the net is filled. Only on the other side of the boat, which the experience of fishermen and all human wisdom would say amounts to nothing, and yet the net is filled. The Lord's Word and his promise filled it, these and nothing else. The entire account of the apostolic labor in the Acts is the commentary of reality on the symbol granted in advance in the miracle. What the Lord revealed in the day of his humiliation he now corroborates in the day of his glorification. The net may be strained to the breaking point, or may be too heavy with fish to be hauled into the boat, the apostles shall not lose anything of their marvelous success. But now the symbol advances beyond that of Luke 5; Matt. 4:18-20; Mark 1:16-20. There the chosen disciples left their catch to other hands; for as the Lord's fishermen he would provide for all their needs (Luke 22:35). This assurance is now repeated. Beside the lake the Lord has his table ready. They are to eat nothing taken from their own catch, they are to be fed with the bread and the fish provided in advance by the Lord. Let the apostles see and learn again, more graphically than before, that the Lord himself will feed and care for them as his own chosen and called servants. Their one thought is to be to do his will and his work according to his Word; all bodily and temporal cares belong in the Lord's hands. Some bring into the symbolism of the meal beside the lake the heavenly refreshment which the Lord has in store for his servants, but the passages adduced (Matt. 8:11; Luke 12:37; 13:29, 30; 14:15) include more than the apostles and their called successors and take in all believers. It is enough to abide by the assured symbolism and not to force it to include more.

We now see why this narrative was not placed into the body of his Gospel by John. The purpose of the Gospel proper is to bring about faith in Jesus as the Messiah and the Son of God. The purpose of the appearance of Jesus to the seven beside the lake is far narrower, namely to establish them in the specific apostolic work to which they were called. John consented to place this narrative into a supplement, and this, indeed, is its fitting place.

15) The risen Lord had appeared to Peter alone on Easter Sunday, Luke 24:34; I Cor. 15:5. What passed between them was never recorded, but we shall not go amiss when we say that this appearance involved Peter's personal absolution from the sin of his three-fold denial. For already when the angel sent the first message by the women he said, "Tell his disciples *and Peter,*" Mark 16:7. Peter was present when Jesus appeared behind the locked doors and gave the disciples the commission, "So I, too, send you." Peter was thus absolved and reinstated into his office and was again established among the believers, including the eleven. His case, however, was so grave that Jesus proceeded to do more. Here at the lakeside he takes Peter in hand in order to eradicate from his heart the last trace of false self-confidence, and at the same time in order to cut off any possible foolish criticism on the part of any members in the church, he formally and publicly reinstates Peter into his office. Two striking circumstances deserve attention, the draught of fishes and the fire of coals. The former recalls Peter's first instatement as a fisher of men, Luke 5:10; the latter the fire of coals beside which Peter forfeited his apostleship. That occurred in the middle of the night, the fire now glows in the early morning. Then he stood and sat among the enemies of Jesus, now he is with Jesus and with six of his fellow-apostles.

When, therefore, they had breakfasted, Jesus says to Simon Peter, Simon of John, dost thou love me more than these? He says to him, Yea, Lord; thou dost know that I have affection for thee. To all that had preceded with regard to Peter is added this breakfast which Jesus had prepared beside the lake for the seven disciples. Jesus had broken the bread for Peter as he had done for the rest. He treats Peter as one who belongs to the rest. But that is the very reason for what Jesus now does with Peter. John always calls him "Simon Peter" (1:42), only once using the latter alone. But Jesus here addresses him, "Simon, son of John," and does not add, "Peter," the name he himself had bestowed on this Simon. Some see no significance in this form of address, but there is a significance. Others err in another direction, taking it that on the part of Jesus the entire past discipleship of Peter was regarded as though it had never existed, but this is rather radical. Jesus uses the old name of this apostle, borne by him before he joined Jesus, in order to remind him of his natural descent and of all that had clung to him in the way of weakness because of this descent. Impetuous and rash by nature, he had spoken and promised grandly and then, when the test came, a test he had foolishly, wilfully brought upon himself, he had fallen miserably, had thrice denied his Lord. He had shown himself only as Simon, son of John; he had been nothing of a Peter. To say that "Simon of John" marks the solemnity of the present occasion and to refer to Matt. 16:17, shows that both solemn occasions are not understood beyond the mere solemnity.

Jesus asks, Ἀγαπᾷς με; and Peter answers, φιλῶ σε. To this day, despite the information long available regarding these two words, some reverse the meaning of these two verbs and let ἀγαπᾶν refer to the lower form of love (the English "like") and φιλεῖν to the higher form. And they confuse the true ideas, for they think of ἀγαπᾶν only as love for a benefactor and of φιλεῖν as love for the person himself. Older commentators think that the two verbs show no difference. An appeal to the Aramaic is beside the mark. While Jesus here spoke this language, the narrative is recorded in Greek. The Aramaic may or may not have two verbs that are the exact counterpart of these used in the Greek; every language has means at hand besides bare verbs for indicating desired differences of thought,

such as are most decidedly indicated in this entire section (v. 15-17). The verb ἀγαπᾶν is the love of intelligence, reason, and comprehension, coupled with corresponding purpose; in this its content it vastly outranks
the other type of love. And φιλεῖν expresses the love of
mere personal affection or liking, including even the
passions where the context requires, and no intelligence
or high purpose is involved; this content places the
verb on a low level. It could never be said of God
that he φιλεῖ the sinful world; as far as φιλεῖν is concerned, he could only abominate the foul world. Jesus
never asked us to love our enemies in the sense of φιλεῖν;
he never himself loved his enemies in this way. But
ἀγαπᾶν — yes, with this love God did love the world, and
we can love our enemies, comprehending all that is
wrong with them and reaching out with the mighty
purpose of removing that wrong, sanctifying the world,
converting our enemies. Compare 3:16, and every
other passage in which either of the verbs is used in
this Gospel. Only in a few cases, where either type of
love would apply, either verb might be used; but even
then the great distinction would remain — the two are
never equal.

"More than these" so evidently refers to Peter's
boasting in Matt. 26:33; Mark 14:29, that we must
read πλέον τούτων as a masculine: "more than these other
disciples." The alternative which would regard this
word as a neuter: "more than these things," i. e., boat,
net, and shall we add fish, is without motivation and
makes the whole scene quite insipid. Why ask only
Peter whether he preferred Jesus to his old profession
when all seven had been fishing? The trouble with
Peter was not that he had fished but that he had thrice
denied the Lord for whom he had claimed love and loyalty greater and more enduring than that of the other
disciples. Here is the sore spot on which Jesus now

lays his finger in order to heal it completely from the inside out.

The direct, personal, intimate question thus addressed to Peter marks a change from the attitude of Jesus displayed in v. 1-14. There the actions speak their symbolical language, here the words of a true pastor and a loving Lord are used.

Peter had learned much since his fall. The loud protestations of that former hour have vanished, a deep humility bows Peter's soul. He does not now venture to make comparisons, and by dropping all comparison with others silently takes back the proud comparison he once made. He does not even venture to assert a love for Jesus such as ἀγαπᾶν indicates. Even now, with bowed head, he himself realizes that his love has been anything but the high love of the true understanding of his Lord and of the sincere purpose of living up to that understanding. So often he has misunderstood, so often Jesus had to correct his wrong impulses. No; he dared not claim real ἀγάπη. So he answers, φιλῶ σε, "I have affection for thee." And even this he cannot say on the evidence of his past record. If that were examined, it would show even lack of affection; for no φιλία, love of ordinary attachment, could possibly be discovered in the three denials, and only a perverted φιλία in his disobedient following of Jesus into the high priest's courtyard. Therefore Peter says, "Yea, thou knowest that I have affection for thee." Compare 2:25. From all his past acts and the sad record he had made Peter turns to the Lord's omniscience. By so doing he truly honors Jesus and places all his trust in his Lord. "Thou knowest," thy divine knowledge of what is in my heart is infinitely more certain than any examination I could make of my heart. By saying this Peter hopes that Jesus will, indeed, find at least a measure of φιλία in his inmost soul. Remember this scene when reading Acts 1:24, "who knowest the hearts

of all men." Peter makes full confession in his answer
to Jesus, and confession is good for the soul.

The Lord accepts his confession and profession.
He pronounces the absolution of Peter, an absolution
so complete as to be crowned with a formal and an
authoritative reinstatement into his apostolic office:
Pasture my lambs! This brief command recalls all
the tender imagery of 10:1-18, also Acts 20:27 and
Isa. 40:11. Those who erase the distinction between
ἀγαπᾶν and φιλεῖν do the same with "my lambs" and "my
sheep" and with the verbs βόσκειν and ποιμαίνειν Jesus
mentions the lambs first, but certainly not because they
are less valuable or require less care; rather the reverse
is true. Think of Matt. 18:1-14 and 19:14; Mark
10:13, etc., voicing the special love of Jesus for children. Jesus here places his most loved possessions
into Peter's care. The spiritual feeding and nourishment of children is here made the first part of the great
apostolic office. Too often the called shepherds of the
flock have forgotten what Jesus here does with Peter.
They have counted the little ones as of little value,
often neglecting them altogether, devoting themselves
to shining in the world. Yet "feed my lambs" stands
in the sacred record as their first essential work. Nor
may pastors ever transfer this work to others as though
it constituted only a minor appendix to their office. The
love of true understanding will follow the example of
Paul in Eph. 5:1, etc., of Luther who wrote the two
precious catechisms, and of all genuine pastors, who
knowing the mind of Christ and making his purpose
their own, have made the spiritual care of the lambs
their most delightful work. This work is never fea-
tured on the front pages of the world's dailies, but the
Lord here features it on the front page of Peter's
commission.

The durative imperative βόσκε means, "be feeding,"
"keep feeding," i. e., providing with forage, with pas-

ture, i. e., with the spiritual nourishment aptly called "the milk of the Word," I Pet. 2:2; "teaching them to observe all things whatsoever I have said unto you," Matt. 28:20; I John 2:12, 13. "To feed means to teach the church the faith with living voice, or to govern by the gospel." Luther. "Do not, my brother, exchange the shepherd staff of the gospel for the driver's stick of the law." Koegel. The care of the lambs has been called "the sunny province" of the pastor's calling. It requires at least the φιλεῖν of Peter, and ἀγαπᾶν would be much better. To feed is, of course, not intended as the opposite of "to shepherd," to tend and to lead, but only lifts out of the pastoral work that part which is especially vital for children. To lead children is easy enough, for they follow easily and trustworthily; their feeding is the real task, for they must grow and become strong and mature.

16) **He says to him again a second time, Simon of John, dost thou love me? He says to him, Yea, Lord, thou knowest that I have affection for thee.** The pleonasm "again a second time" marks the repetition of the question of Jesus as being something unusual. Yet a significant change distinguishes this question from the one that precedes. When in the first question Jesus asked, "more than these," Peter could not but see a reference to his boasting prior to his threefold denial. So now, when in the second question Jesus omits the comparison of Peter with the other disciples, Peter must have been quick to note the omission. Perhaps a flash of gratitude accompanied the perception. Some stop with that idea. But we must note another point, that this second question probes far more deeply than the first. The Lord's three questions to Peter are by no means just repetitions with unessential variations. The question whether Peter loves Jesus more than do the other disciples leaves it unquestioned that Peter loves Jesus at least as much as the

others and reminds him not to put himself above the others. But now this second question asks whether Peter at all loves Jesus. His threefold denial had made it questionable whether Peter had any love left for Jesus, namely love in the higher sense (ἀγαπᾶν). If the first question was justified, then certainly this second one was also in order. Peter thus merely repeats his former answer; for already in that first answer, dropping all invidious comparisons such as he had once made so rashly, he had assured the Lord that he loved him.

Again Jesus accepts Peter's answer, and the acceptance is again a public absolution and a public reinstatement into office. **He says to him, Shepherd my sheep.** The reading is πρόβατα, the ordinary word for "sheep," with somewhat less textual evidence for the variant προβάτια. With the general term "sheep" the general verb ποίμαινε, "be shepherding," be doing the work of a ποιμήν or shepherd, would correspond exactly. "My sheep" are here the entire flock and thus include any lambs, though without mentioning them in particular. Thus also ποιμαίνειν includes βόσκειν, though again without dwelling on the latter in particular. Why erase these distinctive meanings as some do? Why generalize, where the Lord particularizes? Of course, the Lord might call his entire flock "my lambs," τὰ ἀρνία μου, or again the entire flock τὰ πρόβατά μου, "my sheep," or still a third time his entire flock, "my young sheep," "my dear sheep," τὰ προβάτιά μου (v. 17). And again, when he first says "my lambs" and then finally "my young sheep" he certainly does not intend to transfer to Peter's care one section after another of his flock, for "my sheep" in v. 16 embraces all of them. But these observations are untenable. For to picture the whole flock as "my lambs" is impossible without thinking of actual lambs, which is equally true of "my young or dear sheep." And for Jesus in the present connection to mention any part of his flock means, not a divided section as though the lambs were sundered and separated, but this part in its natural connection with the entire flock. The same applies to the change in the verbs employed.

When it is said that no reason appears in Peter's answer to Jesus for distinctions in the commissioning commands of Jesus, since each time Peter asserts only his affection for Jesus, this remark would lead us to look at Peter, whereas we really ought to look at Jesus. It is Jesus who is conducting matters and thus it is he who spreads out his commission in three separate commands. *He* is the one who thus would impress Peter with the greatness of the commission he is entrusting to Peter's love. It is as though "the Shepherd and Bishop of our souls" comes to Peter, leading his entire flock. First he says: "Look at these lambs in the flock; I am placing them into thy care. They especially need feeding; do thou feed them aright!" Then he points to the whole flock, as if to say: "Look at this entire flock; I am placing the whole of it into thy care. It needs all that shepherding implies; be thou its true shepherd!" And even this is not enough for the heart of Jesus. A third time (v. 17) he bids Peter look at the flock, now to impress most deeply upon him what lies in the possessive "my" which is used thrice. For now Jesus calls the flock τὰ προβάτιά μου, using the tender, loving diminutive "my dear sheep," i. e., my little precious ones, for whom my heart goes out, who so much need care. "I place them into thy hands; feed them all as I bade thee to feed my lambs!" Thus all the affection Peter has for Jesus is to flow out toward the flock which is so precious to Jesus. As he feeds and shepherds this flock, so will he prove his affection for his Lord. What is so near and dear to the heart of Jesus will be equally near and dear to Peter's heart.

17) **He says to him the third time, Simon of
John, hast thou affection for me? Peter was
grieved because he said to him this third time,
Hast thou affection for me? And he said to him,
Lord, all things thou dost know; thou dost realize
that I do have affection for thee.** Twice we are
here told that it was "the third time" that Jesus asked
Peter. The hint in the first question, "more than
these," connecting this catechism with Peter's denial,
is here clinched. Three times Peter denied Jesus; it
is proper that now in this public absolution and reinstatement he should confess him and own his love for
him three times in succession. This is the true implication in the repeated adverbial accusative "the third
time." A wrong turn is given the word when Peter is
thought to grieve because Jesus asked him about his
love for the third time. If this were correct, his grieving should have begun when he was asked the second
question. We may well say that, when the first question intimated to Peter that Jesus was referring to his
denials, Peter found it quite in order that Jesus should
now ask of him three successive confessions of love.
The wrong kind of emphasis is placed on "the third
time" by those who fail to see the force of the third
question because they confuse ἀγαπᾶν and φιλεῖν. What
went to Peter's heart was this verb φιλεῖν in the final
question, "Hast thou affection for me?" When Jesus
twice asked about the higher love, once as to its degree
compared with others, and then about its very presence,
Peter with all due humility ventured to assert only the
lower form of love. But now in this third question
Jesus probed even for this lower love, of which Peter
felt so sure that for its presence in his heart he could
appeal to the omniscience of Jesus. This grieved him
so deeply.

But he could not be spared this pain. In his denials
even all common affection and regard for Jesus had

been thrown to the winds. He claimed that he did not even know the man, etc. Peter must drink the cup of full and complete confession. The verb ἐλυπήθη means to be grieved, wounded, made sorrowful; the word should not be translated, "he was vexed," or, "he was annoyed." Jesus does not vex or annoy; like a good physician, he may hurt, but he does this only in order to heal. So we should not read impatience with Jesus or even resentment into Peter's reply. His reply is the same as that given to the other questions, it is only made stronger by stating more fully what the other replies contain: "Lord, all things thou dost know (Ps. 7:10); thou dost realize that I have affection for thee." Even his hurt does not lead him to claim more than the lower form of love. His humility stands the test of this third question. Even his hurt does not mislead him now at least to stand on his own assurance. He survives also this part of the test and clings to the Lord as the one who truly knows. And this reliance on the Lord he bases on the actual omniscience of Jesus: "all things thou dost know." And then he adds a new verb in what may be called a deduction, "thou dost realize" with full, direct, and penetrating insight into my soul "that I do have affection for thee." The answer shows not the slightest annoyance with Jesus. Like the other answers, it states quite plainly that Peter feels that the reason for these questions is not that Jesus doubts his love and is seeking to allay such doubts. Jesus knows. When Peter says this he shows that he, too, realizes what Jesus really intends, namely by this questioning before others in a public way to place him where Jesus wanted him to be.

As before, so again Jesus, who knows all things, accepts Peter's answer. **Jesus says to him, Pasture my dear little sheep.** Here the weight of textual authority is in favor of the diminutive προβάτια with its connotation of tender affection. Since this diminutive appears in the last question it cannot refer merely to "young sheep," half-grown, between lambs and old, mature sheep. It must refer to the entire flock as indicated in v. 16. If the diminutive could be textually assured for the second question, and πρόβατα, "sheep," for the third, we could make three classes: lambs, young sheep, mature sheep. But a study of the textual evidence shuts this out. That προβάτια is genuine in one of the questions is certain. It was easy to carry πρόβατα from v. 16 into v. 17 and make both read alike; likewise some copyists carried προβάτια from v. 17 into v. 16. Hence the confusion in the readings. We have followed the better authorities in both verses.

Some of the interpretations of the Lord's dealings with Peter are fanciful. Cases of triple repetitions such as Matt. 26:36-46; Acts 10:9-16; and II Cor. 12:8, 9, are not analogous, for these are only repetitions, but the three questions directed to Peter contain a marked advance and thus attain a climax. Some explain the three questions as a repetition for the sake of emphasis, but incorrectly, for in order to secure emphasis only one repetition is made. Rome uses this incident with regard to Peter to bolster up its false doctrine. It sees in the lambs the laity and in the sheep the clergy, and both are put under Peter. "As to that which is said John 21:15, etc., 'Feed my sheep,' and, 'Lovest thou me more than these?' it does not as yet follow that a peculiar superiority was given Peter. He bids him 'feed,' i. e., teach the Word, or rule the church with the Word, which Peter has in common with the other apostles." *Concordia Triglotta*, 513. The dealings of Jesus with Peter are no special exaltation of Peter but a serious reminder of his grave defection. The Lord nowhere places Peter above the other apostles. Just as the other apostles had no apostolic successors, so Peter has none. When John wrote his Gospel, Peter had been dead for about 35 years, and

John knows of no successor to Peter. Could John, himself an apostle, have been placed under a papal successor of Peter? We know, too, that Paul, the apostle to the Gentiles, surpassed Peter, yea, all the Twelve together, in the fruitfulness of his work (I Cor. 15:10), especially also in the writings which form the New Testament, the foundation of the church for all time.

18) The next great word connects directly with the commission to feed the Lord's dear sheep: **Amen, amen, I say to thee, when thou wast younger thou wast accustomed to gird thyself and thou wast accustomed to walk where thou wouldst; but when thou shalt be old thou shalt stretch out thy hands, and another shall gird thee and shall carry thee where thou art not willing.** And John informs us: **Now this he said, signifying with what kind of death he would glorify God.** After accepting Peter's love and publicly reinstating him as an apostle, the Lord predicts what kind of death shall crown his career. We recall 13:36, "but thou shalt follow me afterward." Once Peter rashly disregarded the word of Jesus that he could not then follow Jesus, and that rash disobedience had ended in denial. But already then Jesus told Peter that Peter should follow him, namely into death, "afterward." And now, when Peter is again fully restored to his former place, the Lord amplifies the word spoken before Peter's denial, the word about dying for his Lord. It is unwarranted to assume that Jesus is now still testing Peter and as much as asking whether he will furnish the highest proof of love. Nor are these words only an admonition to patience and resignation. No, as John states, these words are direct prophecy. Peter is to know the kind of death he is to die and, knowing this in advance, he will not only go forward joyfully to meet it but will also while his life lasts devote himself most zealously to

the flock entrusted to him. Paul was also told in advance "how great things he must suffer for my name's sake," Acts 9:16.

On the double "amen" (assurance of verity) and on the added, "I say to thee" (assurance of authority), see 1:51. Two contrasting pictures are placed side by side: first, young Peter, girding up his long outer garment himself, doing this whenever he is so minded, and then going wherever he may want to go; secondly, old Peter, now stretching forth his hands to let another person gird him and to bring him where Peter has no wish to go. The thought expressed in these images is quite transparent. The three imperfect tenses in the first picture denote customary actions, R. 971; on ἐζώννυες see R. 314. In the second picture the aorist γηράσῃς indicates a definite point, and the future tenses describe what shall then happen. In οὐ θέλεις the negative is emphatic, R. 969. These two pictures are not trivial: younger Peter going where he pleases, old Peter dependent on others and often taken where he does not please. Note the stretching out of the hands, the singular ἄλλος (not a plural), and the final clause, "where thou art not willing." Jesus describes Peter's active life, feeding and tending the flock during the 35 years of his apostolic ministry; then he pictures his death by martyrdom. Both pictures are drawn in figurative language, and the figure is not that of a shepherd or of a fisherman but of a man at one time free to do as he wills, then at last being forced by the will of another.

Peter was no longer young in age, but here the Lord intimates to him that he shall have a goodly period of active life as an apostle. He was executed in the year 64. John's interpretation of the words of Jesus is historical not ethical. Those who are inclined toward the latter attempt what is unwarranted. Long before his death Peter was thoroughly humble, resigned to the Lord's directions, no longer self-willed. To postpone this ethical development until his old age is to slander the great apostle. Nor can the words, "where thou art not willing" be pressed to mean that in his old age Peter would not be willing to go where the Lord desired to lead him, for the contrary is true during his entire ministry. This ἄλλος, "other man," who finally girds Peter and "will bring" him where he, the other, desires, is Peter's executioner. Peter yields to him. The final girding, done for Peter by this other man, is figurative. Peter holds up his hands in order to have a rope tied around his body. Not his hands or his feet are tied in order to render him helpless, but a rope is tied around his waist as was customary in the case of criminals who were led to execution. Some see in the stretching forth of the hands a picture of crucifixion, a nailing of the outstretched hands to the cross. But that places the crucifixion ahead of the leading to the cross. The text fails to describe the actual mode of Peter's death; it says only so much, that an executioner would lead Peter to a martyr's death. With that we should be content. Eusebius, Book 3, Chapter 1, reports: "At last Peter came to Rome, where he was crucified head downward; for so he himself had desired to suffer"; and in Book 2, Chapter 25, he names the authorities for the fact that Peter was crucified by Nero. This apostle, as far as we know, was the only one to die by crucifixion.

19) Peter's martyrdom "should glorify God" (the Greek retains the future tense "shall glorify," whereas the English calls for "should") by showing the work of the Lord brought to such perfection in Peter that he gave his life for the faith. "As in the case of the feeding of the sheep, so with regard to his suffering in death this favored apostle would follow in the Master's steps and glorify God." Koegel. In the early church the expression "to glorify God" came to have this spe-

cial significance: "to endure martyrdom." "Is it something strange that the servant should die for his good Lord when the Lord died for his evil servants?" Ambrosius. "Not at the end of every Christian's course stands the martyr's cross; but no Christian can finish his course without being led from Peter's youth to Peter's age and being exercised in cross-bearing. . . . According to the judgment of men will power is man's glory, but Christians are manly and strong and grow into a perfect man and unto the measure of the stature of the fulness of Christ (Eph. 4:13) when they rest resignedly in the will of the Lord, whose hand performs miracles with a broken staff and a bruised vine-branch." Besser.

And having said this, he says to him, Follow me! We do not read, "He accordingly says to him," which would merely connect this command with the preceding prophecy. The participle, "having said this," marks the prophecy as having been concluded. Very likely a pause occurred, and then Jesus said, "Follow (really, be following) me!" The command thus stands by itself, and its sense must be according. Since Jesus is no longer in the days of his flesh he cannot intend to say that Peter is to follow Jesus as a disciple follows his master. Peter has his commission and his reinstatement into office; besides this he has the prophecy that after a life of shepherding the flock he will glorify God with his death by martyrdom. It is thus that Jesus now bids Peter to follow him — in the course thus mapped out, to the final goal thus set for him. From beginning to end it is a following of Jesus.

Does this bidding link up with 13:36, "but thou shalt follow me hereafter"? It surely does. For the very first question directed to Peter already carries with it the reference to this passage. While 13:36 tells Peter that he cannot now follow Jesus *into death* but shall follow him thus afterward, this reference to a following in death is now included in the command, "Follow me!" But the present command includes also the long, faithful apostolate. The latter cannot be excluded, so that a following only in death is referred to; for the preceding catechism and commissioning and the long activity before the martyrdom are too pronounced to be left out.

20) **Peter, having turned, sees the disciple whom Jesus loved following, who also leaned back at the supper on his breast and said, Lord, who is it that betrayeth thee?** All the commentators wrestle with this situation, especially with the participle ἀκολουθοῦντα. One thing is acknowledged by all, that this means that John walked behind Jesus and Peter; for "sees him following" cannot possibly be understood ethically. Then, however, it is simplest and therefore best to think that when Jesus said to Peter, "Follow me!" he turned and walked away from the rest with Peter. Having gone a few steps, Peter looked around and saw that his dearest friend John was also starting to follow. It is idle to ask where Jesus was going when he started to walk away and flippantly to inquire whether he was going for a walk. For the answer is that Jesus walked away and then suddenly disappeared. This walking away with Peter walking along may certainly also be considered as a symbolical action, symbolizing the ethical following implied in the command to Peter. In a chapter filled with symbolical actions this final symbol appears perfectly appropriate. But the opinion is unwarranted that Jesus had taken Peter apart from the rest of the disciples already in v. 15, had questioned him privately, and had told him of his coming martyrdom by himself alone. No; all that Jesus said to Peter including, "follow me," was said beside the fire of coals in the presence of the other six disciples.

What induced John to follow when Jesus turned to go with Peter is easy to understand. We know how his heart was drawn to Jesus, and how Jesus had granted him the closest intimacy. He and Peter were also companions of the closest kind (1:41; 13:24; 18:15; 20:2; 21:7; Acts 3:1; 8:14). We have no intimation that Jesus was saying anything more to Peter, or intended to do so. Hence we must not say that John came after them in order to hear what Jesus might say. If anything of a deeper nature may be assumed, it is that when John heard Jesus bid Peter to follow him, John caught the implication of this symbolical act, and his great love to Jesus and to Peter aroused him to indicate that he likewise desired to follow in the life course and to the death goal set for Peter by Jesus. Might it not be possible that Peter and John could go through life together as Jesus had once sent his messengers out two by two, and that John might even be joined with Peter in final martyrdom? And do not Acts 3:1 and 8:14 show that at first these two did work in closest companionship?

That John is here once more designated as "the disciple whom Jesus loved" is perfectly in order, since this is John's way of naming himself. It is with this designation of himself that he himself would have recorded this narrative. As it is, this way of naming him proves beyond question that this entire narration, a closely knit unit from v. 1-23, comes most directly from John. But now there follows a relative clause which still further identifies John, regarding which the judgment is certainly correct that John himself would never have used it, certainly not at this late point and in addition to the fixed formula thus far used regarding himself. That brief formula would surely have sufficed here if John had penned this chapter. Others are writing here, and this elaborate relative clause betrays their hand. They speak of themselves in v. 24. If we ask why they thus go beyond John's reticence and brevity and recall the details of 13:23 so fully we must admit that the narrative itself would be quite complete without this addition. The clause only repeats the evidence of the love of Jesus for John as it came to view at that last supper. For the aorist ἀνέπεσε, as well as the article in ἐν τῷ δείπνῳ, prevent us from assuming that John always reclined next to Jesus when dining. How often this occurred no one knows. The addition reflects the minds of the presbyters at whose instance this chapter was added to John's Gospel. For them the expression "whom Jesus loved" always recalled the scene in the upper room when John leaned back on Jesus' breast. It is thus that they insert the additional clause. Of course, it fits well into the narrative, helping to explain John's following Jesus and Peter at this moment. But this alone is insufficient explanation for its presence even when Peter's concern for John is strongly stressed. We must add the feeling and the thought of the writers.

21) **When Peter, therefore, saw him he says to Jesus, Lord, and what of him?** The nominative absolute οὗτος is followed by the interrogative word τί, and nothing needs to be supplied; δέ, however, intends to place John beside Peter, the latter having received his prophecy from Jesus, the former still being without one. And this is the meaning of Peter's question as to what the Lord may have in store for Peter's beloved friend and companion John. The question emanates from Peter's love for John. It intimates that, having received from Jesus the glorious promises of apostolic service crowned with martyrdom, Peter inquires whether a like glorious prospect awaits his beloved companion John. He sees John, too, starting to follow, i. e., to join him in this significant following. That puts the question on Peter's lips; shall they be joined thus in life and in death? Ye need not assume that

John's following indicated that he himself would like
to ask such a question, for instance, ἐγὼ δὲ τί; and that
Peter's promptness in asking only anticipates John.
John would be content without asking.

But strange to say, Peter's question has been given
the very opposite sense. Peter is supposed to be jealous of John, Peter having drawn the harder lot. He
asks Jesus whether John is to be left off so easy. This
is untenable. Peter has not so soon forgotten the
pointed reminder "more than these" given in v. 15.
Peter is not the base fellow this envy and jealousy make
of him. A conception of this kind cancels all that we
know about the special friendship existing between
these two. It likewise overlooks the fact that from
Peter's first boasting onward, and certainly from v. 19
onward, "by what kind of death he shall glorify God,"
martyrdom was considered the highest possible honor
and distinction any believer might achieve (Matt.
5:12), the only way by which to join the company of
the old martyr prophets. So Peter's question is the
very reverse of envy, for its sense is this: "Shall my
beloved John have less than is promised to me?"

22) **Jesus says to him, In case I will that he
on his part remain until I come, what is that to thee?
Do thou on thy part keep following me!** The answer Peter receives is wholly indefinite. The Lord
uses this word to withhold from Peter what Peter
would really like to know. This was gentle treatment
which we should not try to turn into harshness. The
force of this reply is not, "This is none of thy business!" but a kindly intimation to leave John's future
in the hands of his Lord, whose will in regard to him
will be revealed in due time. For the emphasis on
αὐτόν, placed before θέλω and not after it, and the corresponding emphasis on σύ, are plain. Let Peter leave
"*him*" to the Lord's will; let Peter's care be for himself ("*thou* on thy part") to follow his Lord. The

Lord will see what is best for John. He does not say
whether he has decided what John's lot shall be; ἐὰν
θέλω only supposes something that he might will if he
should be so minded.

It is the strangeness of the supposition thus introduced that has caused so many different interpretations. "Remain until I come" should be understood as
it stands: "remain alive until the end of the world, until
the Lord returns on judgment day."   The next verse
shows that the brethren living in John's own day so
understood these words.   In this they were right; but
they failed to note that Jesus had spoken conditionally,
"Suppose I will."   They changed the conditional utterance into a categorical statement, or took it that back
of the conditional utterance lay the secret decision not
to let John die.   As far as the Lord's coming at the last
day is concerned, when Jesus spoke, no man knew
when this would occur.   All they knew was what the
church of all later ages knew: it might occur at any
time.   We, who live now, indeed know that the Lord
has delayed his coming these many years and may delay
still many more.   But we must guard ourselves against
reading this knowledge of ours into the minds of the
first disciples.   When Jesus said in effect, "what if I
should decide to let John live until I return," they could
certainly not say that this would be impossible.

We thus discard the idea that "until I come" could
mean, "come to John in the hour of his death," or "in
his quiet, natural death."   Nor can the Lord's "coming" here refer to the destruction of Jerusalem, his
coming in the visions of Patmos (in Revelation), his
coming in the conflict with Rome under Domitian, or
any combinations of these preliminary and figurative
comings.   The Lord impresses Peter with his sover-
eignty and his power.   He could let John live as long
as he might decide was best for his kingdom even as
he decides when he himself shall come again.   In the

days of his humiliation he did not know the time of his second coming (Mark 13:32), but this does not apply to his state of glorification. Because we now know that almost 2,000 years have elapsed, let us not curtail the Lord's power as though he could not have preserved John alive until now. The first church misunderstood the Lord's word in one direction; let us not misunderstand it in another. Our misunderstanding would be even worse.

23) **There went out, therefore, this saying among the brethren, that that disciple does not die. But Jesus did not say to him that he does not die; on the contrary, In case I will that he on his part remain until I come, what is that to thee?** The conditional word with which Jesus placed John's career and his end into his own sovereign power was made unconditional; ἐὰν θέλω was made, at least by intimation, a direct θέλω. This was expressed in the saying that went the rounds, "That disciple does not die," the futuristic present expressing the strongest certainty, R. 870. But the two statements, that of Jesus and that of this report among the brethren in Ephesus and in Asia Minor, are not identical in meaning. Jesus did *not* say, "John shall not die." What he did say is therefore repeated with all exactness. However, it is only repeated, and no interpretation of any kind is added. That means that only the wrong ideas of the brethren are here contradicted. That means, furthermore, that even John had no interpretation. His case was similar to that of Peter. Only when Peter was actually crucified in the year 64 was the prophecy spoken by Jesus concerning his martyrdom (v. 18) fully and positively understood. So in the case of John — the event would finally make clear just what the Lord's will concerning him was. The statement here made, therefore, means only one thing: it calls upon all to wait until such time as the Lord

himself will make plain what his will concerning John is. In Peter's case Jesus pronounced an actual prophecy; in John's he declined to utter a prophecy and left John's career wholly in the secrecy of his will.

Verse 23 is of decisive importance for the genuineness and the authorship of the Fourth Gospel. The report, "This disciple does not die," was spread among the brethren when chapter 21 was being written. But this report could not stand a single day beyond the date of John's death. The moment John died, the words of Jesus concerning John would either have to be abandoned as containing a prophecy about John, or some other meaning than this that John is not to die would have to be connected with Jesus' words. After John had died nobody could say, "He dies not." After John had died, nobody could write that brethren are reporting, "He dies not," unless he should add, "But he died, nevertheless." This proves most completely that when v. 23 was written, John was alive, and that John, as well as the writers of this chapter, were waiting to see what the Lord's will concerning him would be. If John was alive when chapter 21 was written, he certainly was equally alive when the preceding twenty chapters were written. And thus once more in the most decisive way the Gospel itself settles the questions regarding its genuineness and its authorship. In the caustic language of Th. Zahn: "It ought to penetrate finally that a man of sound sense could write thus only as long as John was still alive. The manipulations of the critics, who absolutely have to have John dead before this Gospel was written — the longer dead, the better — may becloud the facts and may deceive many but they leave the facts unchanged as they are."

The attack generally follows two lines. Attention is called to the legend, existing in various forms, that in spite of John's natural death and burial he was supposed to be alive in his grave, the earth moving to his breathing, or that his body had been translated to a higher world and there lived on; and we are to believe that v. 21-23 were written to contradict this legend. But Zahn points out that this hypothesis necessitates the ridiculous conclusion that John 21 could not have been written until the third or the middle of the fourth century. For none of the writers intervening, not even the phantastic composer of the *Acta* of John in 160-170, or the bishops of Asia, in whose name Polycrates of Ephesus wrote to Rome in 190, or any others beyond Eusebius, who speak of John's great age, death, and grave, know about this legend. If this late legend began in small circles far earlier and needed contradiction, the one way was to examine the grave, and the one way *not* to contradict this incipient legend was to write as the authors of v. 23 did, leaving the word of Jesus altogether devoid of explanation. The second hypothesis is that John 21 attempts to shield Jesus against the charge of having prophesied falsely since John had actually died. The answer to this is almost too simple. If after John's death either brethren in the faith or outside scoffers still supposed that Jesus had intended to say that John was not to die, simply to repeat the word Jesus had spoken would only have continued to expose Jesus to the charge of having prophesied falsely. To meet such a charge, made after John's death, would have called for an interpretation of the words of Jesus which showed that he never intended to say or said what the charge alleges. But not only is this alleged charge an invention pure and simple, its alleged refutation is no refutation but, if anything, the contrary. Still other hypothetical constructions are offered to make it plausible that John was dead and buried when chapter 21 was written, but when men are determined to have hypotheses, no matter how untenable, rather than facts, nothing more needs to be said.

24) The closing words are attached to the preceding narrative in such a simple and natural way that one must conclude: both come from the same pen. **This is the disciple that is testifying concerning these things and did write these things; and we know that his testimony is true.** Two facts present themselves: that John was alive when this conclusion was written; and that a number of other important persons in Ephesus attest John's writing and authorship and thus reveal that through them this supplement was written and added to the Gospel. Verse 23 deals with John; and now with οὗτος he is indicated as the subject of two actions: ὁ μαρτυρῶν, καὶ γράψας. Both the tenses and the order of these participles are important. The first is present: "he that is testifying concerning these things"; then the second: "and did write these things." Some texts have a second article: ὁ γράψας. If it is genuine, it makes the two actions, already strongly differentiated by the tenses and by the order of the participles, stand out still more as being distinct. It will not do to say that "this disciple," although dead this long while, still goes on testifying concerning these things by the written record he has left of them. If this were the intention, the order of the participles would have to be reversed: "who did write these things and (thus) is continuing to testify concerning these things." Or if the order is left as it is, instead of μαρτυρῶν we should have to have the aorist μαρτυρήσας, "who did testify," or the perfect μεμαρτυρηκώς, "who has testified," i. e., when he was alive in our midst. As the participles stand they say one thing: John is still alive and still testifying by means of his oral statements, and, besides this, in the recent past he has made a written record of these same statements. No manipu-

lation, exegetical or otherwise, will ever upset the two
facts here stated.

Those who deny John's authorship generally ignore
the order of the participles. Only when this is done,
are they able to say, "His 'witness' may continue after
death just as does that of Moses and the prophets
(5:39)." But καὶ γράψας remains, which would say that
John "did write" this Gospel whether he be dead or
alive when v. 24 was penned. To ignore this participle
will not do. As an aorist it states a historical fact. It
is removed, however, by raising a cloud of uncertainty;
it is called "a kind of afterthought." Attention is
drawn away from this aorist by asserting that "most
prominence at all events is given to his having borne
witness" (note that the tense of μαρτυρῶν is changed).
Finally, since the participle still stands where it is, its
plain, honest testimony is annulled by the claim: the
writer of v. 24 "is not quite so sure that he (John) is
the actual author of the Gospel." Need we say that
manipulations like this would destroy any testimony?
It is neither a critical nor a historical canon that, when
a writer uses two verb forms connected with "and,"
he is not sure of the fact expressed by the second of
these verb forms. This sample of the critical method
is taken from a commentary on John's Gospel published in 1929.

"Concerning these things" and the simple accusative "these things," of course, apply to chapter 21.
But whoever would apply "these things" only to the
last chapter is left with the question: "How about the
other twenty chapters? Are they, too, John's testimony, John's writing?" The question answers itself:
"They most assuredly are!" In fact, it is far more
important to know the origin of the body of the Gospel
than to know that of the supplement. The two, however, cannot be disjoined. The very way in which 21:1
begins shows this, and its contents do likewise. If

"these things" apply only to 21:1-23, some plain intimation in v. 24 would have to reveal that this is intended; and then we should be left with the question,
whence come all the contents of the other chapters?
In this connection note what follows in v. 25.

"We know that his testimony is true," i. e., ἀληθής,
placed forward for emphasis: that his testimony
reports the facts as they actually occurred. This
plural "we know" cannot be reduced to a singular. It
is no mere editorial or majestic plural, for John never
uses such a plural. He could not do so here by way of
exception, for no writer could call himself "this disciple" and then in the same breath add "we know,"
meaning "I know." Even those who think that John
himself penned or dictated 21:1-23 admit that others
are responsible for v. 24, 25. Who these persons are
will never be known; their names can never be recovered. All that we can say is that they must have been
the presbyters of Ephesus, the prominent leaders of
the churches associated with John. "We know" is
weighty, and by writing this down through the hand
of one of their number they fully realize what weight
this their attestation will have for all the other churches
to whom this new Gospel record is brought. They
know on the basis of direct and certain evidence. John
has been in their midst for many years, they know his
entire history. Their knowledge reaches back to other
apostles, with whose testimony they could and did compare that of John. These apostles need not have been
in Ephesus itself, for the presbyters could have known
and conferred with them elsewhere. Finally, they had
the other evangelists. Thus the weight of "we know"
is ample. The testimony of the presbyters is not
added to John's Gospel as though without such certi-
fication the veracity of John's Gospel would be subject
to doubt. The synoptists had written long ago, and
their records had been published far and wide. Now,

after so long an interval, this fourth Gospel goes out to the churches from Ephesus not from Palestine. The farther this last Gospel penetrated, the more the question of its origin would be raised. Witness the criticism to which the Fourth Gospel is still subjected! We at once see the value of this attestation at its close. While John is his own witness, and his testimony speaks for itself (just as does that of Jesus, 8:14), the added word of the Ephesian presbytery, in whose very midst this apostle lived, labored, and wrote his Gospel, carries its own additional assurance to the churches. It is like the testimony of the earliest fathers, every scrap of which is carefully treasured to this day; but this attestation directly appended to the Gospel itself by a representative body of men and not merely by one individual exceeds in weight and in value all subsequent testimony by important church authorities.

25) **Now there are also many other things which Jesus did, the which, if they should be written one by one, even the world itself, I suppose, will not hold the written books.** From John as one authority the presbyters in Ephesus learned about the many things that Jesus did and that were not recorded. John himself refers to them in 20:30. But note the simplicity of John's statement compared with the rather strong hyperbole of the scribe who writes for the presbyters. It has been said truly that John would not write in this fashion. It is uncalled for, however, to press the hyperbole as though it were intended to be understood literally; and equally uncalled for to change the meaning of the words in order to eliminate the hyperbole. For χωρήσειν means exactly what it says: "the world itself will not contain, will not hold" all the books that would result; and not the *men* in the world "will not hold *in their minds*" all the books. The hyperbole expresses the writer's feelings and nothing more.

The verb ἐποίησεν is used in a broad sense and intends to cover the entire ministry of Jesus with all that it contained; καθ' ἕν is distributive: "one by one." The singular οἶμαι is no more than a casual adverb, and thus it in no way interferes with οἴδαμεν in v. 24. This plural, as well as both final verses, make it impossible to attribute οἶμαι to John himself as R. 406 does. The future infinitive χωρήσειν is in indirect discourse and replaces the future indicative, R. 1030 and 1040. "The written books" is in contrast with the one already written by John, to which the penman of the presbyters is now adding the last word. This contrast establishes the fact that "these things" in v. 24 refer to John's entire Gospel and not merely to 21:1-23. The reader, then, must content himsef with what John's Gospel and its supplement present. Much more might have been introduced into either or into both. In fact, entire new books in goodly number might have been written. We here have a hint as to how the supplement came to be added. The presbyters had heard its contents from John as they had heard him relate many other things that are not included in the synoptists. While they saw that this appearance beside the lake did not fit into the Gospel proper as this was planned and completed by John, since this appearance dealt only with two of the apostles personally and thus with the holy office established by Jesus, as presbyters and incumbents of the pastoral office they saw the great value of this account for the ministry and the church of all future time. John consented to their just desire. He allowed them to add this supplement, reproducing his own narration in a way which he approved, together with a final word of attestation and conclusion. The Ephesian presbyters have earned the gratitude of the church of all ages for having John close his Gospel with a chapter that is so precious to us all.

Soli Deo Gloria